FORT PIERCE · FORT VANCOUVER · FORT WALTON · FORT WAYNE · FORT WORTH · FOSTORIA · FOX CITIES · FREMONT

GAINESVILLE · GALVESTON BAY · GLOUCESTER · GRAND RAPIDS · GRAND TRAVERSE BAY · GREAT NECK · GREAT SOUTH BAY · GREEN BAY

GREENVILLE · GREENWICH · GREENWICH BAY · GROSSE ILE · GROSSE POINTE · HAMBURG · HAMPTON ROADS · HAGERSTOWN

HARTFORD · HAWCREEK · HELIX · HEMPSTEAD BAY · HOLLYWOOD · HOMESTEAD · HONOLULU · HOOSIER

HOPATCONG · HOUSATONIC RIVER · HOUSTON · HUNTINGTON BEACH · HUNTSVILLE · ILLIANA · INDIAN RIVER · ITHACA

JACKSONVILLE · JOHNSON CITY · JONES BEACH · KALAMAZOO · KANSAS CITY · KENNEBEC RIVER · KENOSHA · KENTUCKY LAKE

KEY WEST · KINGSPORT · KINSTON · KNOXVILLE · LACKAWANNA · LAKE CANDLEWOOD · LAKE CHARLES · LAKE GEORGE

LAKELAND · LAKE LANIER · LANSING · LIMA · LITTLE NECK BAY · LOCKPORT · LONG BAY · LONG BEACH

LONG SAULT · LOS ANGELES · LOUISVILLE · LYNCHBURG · LYNWOOD · MADISON · MAIN LINE · MANCHESTER

MANHASSET BAY · MANSFIELD · MARATHON · MARBLEHEAD · MARIN · MARION · MATTAPOISETT · MERIDEN

MERRIMAC RIVER · MIAMI · MIAMI BEACH · MICHIGAN CITY · MIDDLETOWN · MID-HUDSON · MILE HIGH · MILES RIVER

MILFORD · MILWAUKEE · MINNETONKA · MISSION BAY · MISSISSIPPI COAST · MOBILE · MOHAWK-HUDSON · MORGANTOWN

MORICHES BAY · MT. CLEMENS · MUSCOGEE · MUSKEGON · NANSEMOND RIVER · NAPLES · NARRAGANSETT BAY · NEPTUNE

# PILOTING,
## SEAMANSHIP AND
## SMALL BOAT HANDLING

# CHAPMAN

# PILOTING,

## SEAMANSHIP AND
## SMALL BOAT HANDLING

# CHAPMAN

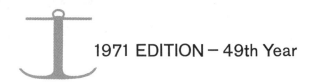

1971 EDITION – 49th Year

# CHARLES F. CHAPMAN

*With Revisions By* ELBERT S. MALONEY,
WILLIAM KOELBEL, JOHN WILDE, H. D. DA BOLL,
*and* GARDNER EMMONS

# About the Author

CHARLES FREDERIC CHAPMAN completed more than 56 years of distinguished service to Motor Boating magazine and the boating public before he retired in January, 1969. For 48 of those years he was both editor and publisher of Motor Boating and a Vice President of Hearst Magazines, the parent organization.

Born in Norwich, Conn., in 1881, Chap was graduated from Norwich Academy in 1900, and went on to earn a degree in Mechanical Engineering at Cornell University where he majored in mechanical and marine engineering, and naval architecture.

Always active in boat racing, Chap served as Chairman of the American Power Boat Association's Racing Commission, sanctioning body for all motor boat races, and as the Association's Secretary—a post he held for 25 years. He was the first to be elected to the Honor Squadron of APBA.

Chap was also a leader in organization of the U. S. Power Squadrons in 1914, and holds USPS Certificate #A 1. He conducted the first national tests for USPS members, designed the USPS ensign, and served as Treasurer, Chairman of the Committee on Rules, and as Vice-Commander before his two terms as Chief Commander in 1946-47. Most recently he has been Chairman of the Flag and Etiquette Committee, and a Member of the Governing Board.

And in 1955, the Ole Evinrude Boating Foundation, in recognition of "long contributions to recreational boating," awarded Chap a silver bowl with a citation which read:

"No other man deserves so much from so many of us in the World of Boating."

## MOTOR BOATING BOOK DIVISION

Publisher — JOHN R. WHITING

Executive Editor — THOMAS R. BOTTOMLEY

Layout & Production — MERRILL A. LAUCK

Type Composition — BORO TYPOGRAPHERS, Inc.

Printed in the United States of America by
AMERICAN BOOK-STRATFORD PRESS, Inc., New York

# CONTENTS

COMPLETE INDEX
ON PAGE 623

# Foreword

Going to sea requires a crew—and so does going to press with a new edition of *Piloting, Seamanship and Small Boat Handling*. In recent years the watch officer was Bill Koelbel, who moved in 1965 from the associate editorship of *Motor Boating* to an even tougher post: the total reconstruction of this book. Chapter by chapter it went on, with improved illustrations on the one hand, more refined technical facts on the other. New parts were added as new phases of boating—such as electronics—came to the fore.

With Bill Koelbel's retirement in 1969, Tom Bottomley took over that watch officer's post on "the blue book." This new edition shows the results. Eight new chapters—the most new material since the first edition in 1922—have been added, and all the remaining chapters have been reworked as necessary to keep them up-to-date. Some of the new chapters show revisions in government equipment requirements, some present instructional material in a new way, and some are entirely new in subject matter. For the first time there are chapters covering activities of two organizations most important to boatmen: the United States Power Squadrons, and the United States Coast Guard and its Auxiliary. The old glossary, which featured many words applicable only to square-riggers, has been replaced by a new nautical terminology chapter, which covers the language needed and used by today's boatmen. New material on Rules of the Road helps clarify requirements for navigation lights and day shapes for all types of vessels, and the conditions governing right-of-way in meeting, crossing, and overtaking situations. Another new chapter provides a modern guide to boat management.

*Piloting, Seamanship and Small Boat Handling* has maintained leadership in its field because Chapman made it a point for the magazine and the book to keep up with all the latest developments in boating, from design trends to federal legislation. Our readers help in this by comments, suggestions, and even temporarily baffling questions.

—John R. Whiting
Publisher, Motor Boating
June 1, 1970

# Preface to the 1971 Edition

THIS, THE 49TH EDITION of *Piloting, Seamanship and Small Boat Handling,* has been widely acclaimed as the acknowledged authority on subjects of vital interest to all who love boats—those who own, handle or cruise as guests aboard them—whether driven by wind or by motor. Its unique reputation as the "bible of boating" has been earned only through dedicated year-by-year editing for technical accuracy, enlargement of the scope of its content to embrace newest developments in the field (while retaining other worthwhile features which have been completely updated), and adoption of a totally new format, organized for clarity and legibility.

Because of the continuing nature of revisions required to keep it up-to-date, a piloting text, unlike a novel, can never be said to be quite "finished." Any reader or student, however, familiar with the radical transformation that has taken place in *Chapman's,* especially in several recent editions, will appreciate that the 1971 edition is almost a *new* book.

It is certainly a far cry, indeed, from the first (1922) edition of only 120 pages. In recent years it has grown, annually, to its present size of more than 670 pages, including the lettered color plates. During these years, *Piloting, Seamanship and Small Boat Handling,* the "blue book," has been the text used in free instruction courses given by the U. S. Power Squadrons and the USCG Auxiliary. It has also been used extensively in courses given by branches of the Navy, Coast Guard, and Army, as well as many nautical schools and colleges.

Acknowledgement is due several contributing editors who have prepared new chapters for recent editions. All have made significant contributions to the educational work of the U. S. Power Squadrons. In the 1966-67 edition, new material included Marlinespike Seamanship by H. D. DaBoll, Weather by Gardner Emmons, the Mariner's Compass by John Wilde, and Electronic Equipment by Elbert S. Maloney. Included in that edition was a revised chapter on Flag Etiquette by the author. In the 1969-70 edition, William Koelbel's Anchoring chapter was fully up-dated and put in the new format.

Special recognition must be given the outstanding work of Mr. Maloney who, in 1966-67, prepared a complete four-chapter section on charts and piloting, followed in 1968-69 by Seamanship, Aids to Navigation, Government Publications, and Signalling. The 1969-70 edition included his new chapters on Safety, Customs and Etiquette, and Clothing and Uniforms. For this 1971 edition, he has prepared new chapters on Nautical Terminology, Government Regulations, Equipment Requirements, Rules of the Road, and Boat Management, as well as on history and operations of the U. S. Power Squadrons and the U. S. Coast Guard and its Auxiliary.

Recent editions also included many additional features. Among the 24 pages devoted to color plates, the newly authorized U. S. Coast Guard Auxiliary Insignia are fully illustrated. The Signalling chapter has been revised to reflect late changes in the International Code, and the Marlinspike Seamanship chapter now includes use and splicing of double-braided line. New color plates in this 1971 edition include U. S. Power Squadrons Flags and Insignia.

Originality is not claimed for all the contents of this book, representing as it does a compilation of data from many sources. The publishers are indebted to many members of the armed forces and the U. S. Power Squadrons for their invaluable suggestions. The unqualified co-operation of the U. S. Coast Guard, the U. S. Coast and Geodetic Survey, Army Engineers, and the U. S. Lake Survey, the author gratefully acknowledges. The U. S. Navy and its Oceanographic Office have been particularly helpful. To all who have contributed so generously toward the success of *Piloting, Seamanship and Small Boat Handling* has achieved, the author expresses his sincere thanks and appreciation.

At no time has the author ever claimed that seamanship or navigation can be mastered from the printed page alone. But the experienced boatman will surely acknowledge that a careful study of the principles of good small-boat seamanship, as presented in the following pages, will be generously repaid. By application of these principles in practice, he will reap a three-fold reward: increasing his own enjoyment of boating, he will make a major contribution to the cause of safety afloat, and be welcomed, in due course, to the ranks of "seasoned skippers."

*C. F. Chapman*

June, 1970

## USPS

# REFERENCES FOR
# INSTRUCTION
# COURSES

## USCG
## AUXILIARY

# REFERENCES FOR
# STUDY COURSE

# CHAPTER 1

Photo by Peter Smyth

# NAUTICAL TERMS

FIG. 101   Both of the above watercraft are "boats"—the term encompasses a wide variety of sizes. They are also both "vessels" in the language of the law.

The Language of Boats and Boating—it's different from that of the land and landsmen, having developed over centuries of use by men who go down to the sea in ships, yet flavored by terms invented in our generation. When you speak of the "stern" of a boat you are using a word that goes back centuries through several languages; yet when you say that in the stern is an "inboard-outboard" engine, you are using a perfectly correct term that has been in existence only a relatively few years.

No, a boatman doesn't have to be excessively "salty" in his speech, nor should he be, but there are strong reasons for knowing and using the right terms for objects and activities and the like around boats. It shows a degree of interest and knowledge, a desire to call things by their right names. In times of emergency, many seconds of valuable time may be saved when correct, precise terms are used for needed tools or actions. In correspondence and other written material, the right word often shortens long explanations and eliminates doubt or confusion.

So learn and use the proper nautical terms for the parts of your boat, her equipment, and activities aboard her—to

do so will mark you as one who is truly interested in his boating and who cares enough to learn about it. But above all, form the habit of *thinking directly* in nautical terms, not in "shore" terms with subsequent mental translation— use the proper words consistently and you will soon find them coming naturally.

## BASIC BOATING TERMS

The terms to be discussed in this chapter are not all-inclusive for the field of boating. No two "experts" would agree on what constituted a "complete" list, and any such list would far exceed the available space. What follows is intended as a basic nautical vocabulary, to prepare you for the various boating topics presented in detail in succeeding chapters. Many terms will be repeated and covered more fully later in the book, and more specialized words and phrases will be introduced at that time. Terms in this chapter will be described in simple, brief remarks rather than comprehensively defined as in dictionaries. Glossaries are available for those who need or desire exhaustive definitions.

**FIG. 102  A motorsailer combines features of the motorboat and powered sailboat. This design includes many of the advantages of each type and is excellent for certain applications, but also suffers from the deficiencies of any compromise.**

## General Terms

What is a *boat?* The term has no really precise definition. It is a water-borne vehicle smaller than a *ship,* which is usually thought of as being used for ocean travel. Indeed, one definition of a boat is a small craft carried aboard a ship, such as a lifeboat. Many consider a boat as a craft not over 65 feet in length—this being the maximum length of vessels subject to certain federal boating laws. The term *small craft* is often used interchangeably with boat.

*Vessel* is a broad term for water-borne vehicles and is used *without* reference to size, particularly in laws and regulations relating to all water traffic. A *yacht* is a vessel used for recreation and pleasure, as opposed to work or business. Usually it is not used for boats under approximately 40 feet in length, but there are no established limits in this respect. The term is also applied to government craft used by officials and dignitaries, such as a presidential yacht or a state governor's yacht.

Although more and more people are coming to refer to boats with the neuter pronoun "it," the traditional "she" remains fully correct in speaking or writing about any size of vessel.

## Categories of boats

Boats may be subdivided into *powerboats (motorboats),* *sailboats,* and *rowboats* as determined by their basic means of propulsion. Remember, however, that sailboats may have *auxiliary engines* in which case they are often called *auxiliaries;* they are considered legally to be motorboats when propelled either by engine alone or by the engine and the sails. A *motor sailer* is a subcategory in which sails can still be used but their area has been reduced and the engine power has been increased. Like most compromises, motor sailers are somewhat less efficient under sail than sailboats and slower under power than motorboats—they

do, however, have desirable features taken from both major categories. There are no precise rules to differentiate between auxiliary-powered sailboats and motor sailers. Some pure motorboats used offshore will have a *steadying sail;* this is not for propulsion but rather for an easier ride in rough seas. See fig. 913.

The term "cruiser" indicates a type of boat with at least minimum accommodations and facilities for overnight trips. The type of propulsion may be added so as to form the terms *outboard cruiser* and *inboard cruiser.* The term is also applied to many sailboats to distinguish them from others designed primarily for racing. Other types of boats include *runabouts* for day fishing or recreational outings on the water and *utility boats* for general service applications.

A *dinghy* is a small open boat carried on or towed by a larger boat or yacht; it may be propelled by oars, sails, or a low-power outboard motor. The slangy contraction, "dink" is often used. *Prams* are small craft with square bows which serve as dinghies and are frequently used for youth program instruction and competitions. *Tenders* include dinghies and larger boats employed to carry persons and supplies to and from large yachts or ships.

*Houseboats* include both cruising yachts whose superstructure is larger and more designed for living aboard, and many smaller vessels that appear to have evolved from land trailers and mobile homes. Houseboats offer more living space than cruisers, but generally at some sacrifice of seaworthiness and rough water cruising ability.

*Hydrofoil boats* have structures called *foils* extending below the normal hull that are scientifically designed to give lift, like the wings of an airplane, when moving through the water at high speeds. These submerged foils

**FIG. 103  The very large cruising houseboats have largely disappeared from today's boating scene, but they have been more than replaced by the modern high-speed design in the 30 to 50 foot size. These are excellent for all but the most exposed boating waters.**

FIG. 104 Hydrofoil craft "fly" on subsurface structures contoured much like the wings of an airplane. The foils may be of the "surface piercing" type, as above, or of the "fully submerged" style.

permit the boat to "fly" just above the water surface with little drag and at much increased cruising speeds.

### Boatmen and yachtsmen

The owner-operators of recreational small craft can be referred to as *yachtsmen* or *boatmen,* the usage often depending on the size of the craft involved, but again without any clear line of demarkation in boat length. The term *boater* is often heard, but it is generally less acceptable than the two just mentioned—perhaps because a "boater" is also an old-fashioned straw hat with a flat top and a broad brim! The term "rag men" and "stink potter" are applied in many areas to the skippers of sailboats and motorboats respectively—sometimes good-naturedly, and sometimes not. A *Corinthian* is any non-professional in the field of boating.

### Directions Aboard a Boat

The front end of a boat is of course its *bow;* the other end is its *stern. Port* and *starboard* (pronounced starb'd) are lateral terms—port designating the left side and starboard the right when on the vessel and facing the bow, or, to express it differently, when facing *forward.* Turning

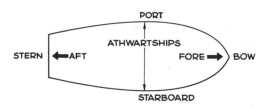

FIG. 105 The basic directions on a boat. Port and Starboard may be kept straight in one's mind by remembering that port is the shorter word and that "left" is shorter than "right."

FIG. 106 The basic hull structural parts of a boat are its keel and frames. Planks close in the sides and bottom on the above type craft and the deck closes over the top. Other types of construction may not employ planking.

around and facing the stern, one is looking *aft.*

The bow is the *fore* part of a boat; the stern is the *after* part. When one point on a boat is aft of another it is said to be *abaft* it; when nearer the bow, it is *forward* of the other. When an object lies on a line or in a plane parallel to the centerline of the vessel it is referred to as lying *fore-and-aft,* as distinguished from *athwartships,* which means right angles to the centerline.

The term *amidships* has a double meaning. In one sense, it refers to an object or area midway between the boat's sides. On the other hand, it can relate to something midway between the bow and the stern. *Inboard* and *outboard,* as directional terms, draw a distinction between objects near or toward amidships and those away from the centerline or beyond the sides.

To express the idea of upward or overhead, one says *aloft. Below* means the opposite direction. Note, though, that *abovedeck* means on deck, and not actually above it as does "aloft." We should not say that a person is in or on a boat—rather he is *aboard,* or *on board.*

### Terms Relating to the Boat

The basic part of a boat is its *hull,* usually consisting of a major central structural member, the *keel,* with *frames* (also called *ribs*) set into it at right angles; this skeleton is covered with a skin—*planks* in the case of a planked wooden boat; *plates* for a metal boat—to make a watertight vessel that provides buoyancy to float the weight of the craft and its load. Boats may be of the *open* type or the hull may be covered over with a *deck;* some boats are partially open, partially decked. As boats get above the smallest sizes, they may have a *superstructure* above the main deck level, variously referred to as a *deckhouse* or *cabin* (cabins also extend below the level of the deck). Small, relatively open boats may have only a *shelter cabin,* or *cuddy,* forward.

The hulls of boats made of metal—usually aluminum or steel—or of fiberglass-reinforced plastics, will differ in some respects from wooden boats, but the basic components of keel, frames, and covering normally will be retained in at least modified form.

### Terms denoting shape

*Sheer* is the term used to designate the curve or sweep of the deck of a vessel as viewed from the side. The side

FIG. 107 Flare is the outward curvature of the sides near the bow. It is characteristic of modern designs, providing more usable forward deck area and making for a "drier" boat by turning aside spray. Tumblehome is the inward curving of topsides near the stern.

FIG. 108 Different bottom designs are used for various types of boats. A flat-bottom craft is inexpensive to build; a vee-bottom is used on fast craft. The "cathederal" hull is used on many small craft for speed and stability.

skin of a boat between the waterline and deck is called the *topsides*. If these are drawn in toward the centerline away from a perpendicular as they go upward, as they often do near the stern of a boat, they are said to *tumble home*. Forward, they are more likely to incline outward to make the bow more buoyant and to keep the deck drier by throwing spray aside; this is *flare*.

The bottom of a boat may be one of three basic shapes—*flat*, *round*, or *vee*—or it may be a combination of two shapes, one forward gradually changing to the other toward the stern. There are also more complex modern shapes such as *cathedral-hull*, *deep-vee*, *multi-step*, and others.

A *displacement* hull is one that achieves its buoyancy or flotation capability by displacing a volume of water equal in weight to the hull and its load, whether under way or at rest. A *planing hull*, on the other hand, is one that achieves the major part of its load-carrying ability by the dynamic action of its underside with the surface of the water over which it is rapidly traveling; at rest, a planing

FIG. 109 A planing hull at high speeds rides more "on" the water than "in" it. Hydrodynamic forces support the craft rather than displacement. Friction is reduced and higher speeds are achieved with the same horsepower.

hull reverts to displacement buoyancy. A *semi-planing* (or *semi-displacement*) *hull* is one that gets a portion of its weight-carrying capability from dynamic action, but which does not travel at a fast enough speed for full planing action. It is often a hull that is round-bottomed forward gradually flattening out toward the stern to provide a planing surface.

Two main types of *multi-hull* craft are the *catamaran* with two hulls of equal size held apart by rigid structural members, and the *trimaran* with a principal central hull flanked on either side by smaller outboard hulls.

## Bows and sterns

The *stem* is the near-vertical major structural member at a vessel's bow. A stem is common to all boats with the conventional type of bow, whereas the square-nosed *pram* or *punt* type has a bow resembling its square stern. The stem of a boat is *plumb* if it is perpendicular to the waterline or *raked* if inclined at an angle for better appearance. The term *overhang* describes the projection of the upper part of the bow or stern beyond a perpendicular from the waterline. *Eye bolts* or *ring bolts* are frequently fitted through the stems of small boats for towing or for pulling aboard trailers.

Flat planking across the stern is called the *transom*. If, however, the stern is pointed, resembling a conventional bow, there is no transom and the boat is called a *double-ender*. The *quarter* of a boat is the after portion of her sides particularly the furthermost aft portion where the sides meet the transom.

## Terms relating to the keel

The keel is the major longitudinal member of a hull. When another timber is fastened along the top of the keel to strengthen it, or as a necessary part of the construction, this is the *keelson*, sometimes *apron*. On some boats an extra piece is fastened externally to the bottom of the keel to protect it. This is termed a *false keel* or *worm shoe*. A metal fitting extending back from the under side of the keel to provide additional protection for the boat is called a *skeg*.

The *rudder* of a craft is the flat surface at or near the stern that is pivoted about a vertical or near-vertical axis so as to turn to either side and thus change the direction of movement of the vessel through the water. The upward extension of the rudder through which force is applied to turn the rudder is the *rudderpost* (or *rudderstock*). A *stuffing box* keeps the hull watertight where the rudderpost enters.

## Planking terms

Each continuous line of planking along the hull from bow to stern is called a *strake*. The lowest strake, next to the keel, is termed the *garboard strake*. The *gunwale* (pronounced gun'l) is the upper part of the *sheer strake*, the

Fig. 110. Multihull sailing craft have become very popular. The catamaran, above, is seen in all sizes from small day sailers to large ocean racers. Trimarans, left, are generally found in sizes from 30 feet upward.

FIG. 113 Reinforcing pieces are often used where two structural members meet. This "transom knee" strengthens the stern and adds rigidity to the craft.

FIG. 111 The stem of a boat is the major structural member at the bow of a planked design or the reinforced area of a fiberglass hull where the forward ends of the sides come together.

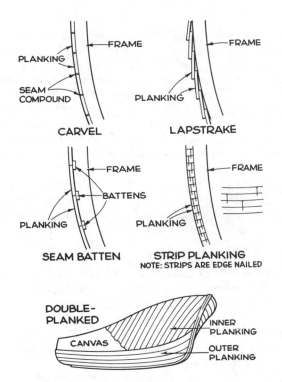

FIG. 112 Despite the increase in popularity of fiberglass and other modern boat construction materials, many craft are still made of wood using one of the traditional planking methods.

top plank of the topsides. If less-than-full-length planks are used in any one strake, the ends of each are *butted* and joined on *butt blocks* on the inside of the hull.

When the topsides are carried substantially above the level of the deck, they are called *bulwarks,* and at the top of the bulwarks is the *rail.* More common than bulwarks are *toe rails,* narrow strips placed on top of the gunwale to finish it off and provide some safety for personnel on deck. *Lifelines* are used on larger craft at the edges of the side decks to aid in preventing people from falling overboard. These lines usually consist of wire, often plastic-covered, supported above the deck on *stanchions.* If made of solid material—wood or metal—they are called *liferails.* Boats may also have waist-high *bow rails* of solid tubing for the same safety purpose. A *pulpit* is an extension, usually a heavy plank with rails extending up from it, beyond the bow of a sport-fishing boat used for spearing or harpooning large game fish. Bow rail installations on sailboats are also often called pulpits, whether they extend forward of the stem or not.

The planking of a boat is termed *carvel*—and the boat is said to be *carvel-built*—if the edges of the planks meet flush, resulting in a smooth surface. The *seams,* joints between adjacent strakes, are usually *caulked* to make the hull watertight. *Batten-seam* construction uses strips of wood, *battens,* on the inside of the hull behind each seam. These are fastened to the planks on either side of the seam with nails or screws and eliminate the need for caulking.

*Strip planking,* a variant of carvel, uses a greater number of "planks" which are much smaller, being roughly square in cross-section. Each of these is *edge-nailed* (and often glued as well) to the strip below it in addition to being fastened to the frames. This type of hull is quite strong but relatively more costly. Construction is *clinker,* or *lapstrake,* if each successive strake away from the gunwale laps over the one below it as the clapboards of a house are sometimes lapped. The overlapping edges are often fastened with rivets.

Some hulls are *double-planked,* in which case there is commonly an inner *skin,* or layer, of planking laid diagonally to the keel and an outer skin laid fore and aft, with waterproof glue, or fabric and glue, between the layers. In other boats, the two skins are both run *diagonally* at an angle of 45° from the keel to the gunwale, planks of the two layers being at right angles to each other. Due to the strength of double-planked hulls, some frames may be omitted.

## Floors and ceilings

These are two terms that have different meanings afloat than ashore. *Floors,* nautically speaking, are not laid as in a house to be walked upon. In a boat they are important transverse structural members, tying together the keel and the lower ends of the frames. *Ceiling* is not overhead, as ashore; it is light planking or plywood sheeting on the inside of the frames.

## Reinforcing pieces

Various kinds of *knees* are used throughout the hull to connect members joined at an angle to each other. These may be of metal, but often a natural growth of wood is selected in which the grain runs in the desired direction for maximum strength.

## Deck openings

Deck openings are commonly referred to as *hatches* (sometimes hatchways). *Companion ladders* or steps lead below from the deck; these are also termed *companion-ways.*

*Cockpits* are open wells in the deck of a boat outside of deckhouses and cabins. *Coamings* are vertical pieces around the edges of cockpit, hatches, etc., to prevent water on deck from running below.

*Scuppers* are holes permitting water to drain overboard from decks and cockpits. A cockpit is said to be *self-bailing* when it has scuppers to drain it.

## Interior terms

Vertical partitions, corresponding to walls in a house, are called *bulkheads. Watertight bulkheads* are solid or are equipped with doors that can be secured so tightly as to be leak-proof. The interior areas divided off by bulkheads are termed *compartments*—such as an engine compartment —or *cabins*—such as the main cabin, aft cabin, etc. Some areas are named by their use; the "kitchen" aboard a boat is its *galley*. The toilet area is the *head* (the same name is also given to the toilet itself).

*Overhead* is the nautical term for what would be the ceiling of a room in a house; the nautical use of the term *ceiling* has been explained above.

The *forepeak* of a boat is the compartment furthest forward in the bow, usually used for the storage of line and/or chain, sometimes for sails. The *forecastle* (pronounced fo'c's'l), if any small craft can be said to have one, is the cabin furthest forward. The term is generally used today to mean the crew's quarters forward.

## Cabin styles

A *trunk cabin* is one that extends above the main deck level, but less than the full width of the boat so that walkways—side decks—are left on either side; such a boat is re-

TRUNK CABIN          RAISED DECK CABIN

**FIG. 114** The cabins of some motorboats and sailing craft are of the "raised deck" type extending the full width of the hull. Other boats have "trunk cabins" with a smaller superstructure set above the level of the deck.

ferred to as a *trunk cabin cruiser*. Conversely, a *raised deck cruiser* is one in which the cabin is formed by extending the topsides above the normal deck level—it extends for the full width of the hull, thus eliminating side decks. A *sedan cruiser* has the main cabin on the same level as an aft cockpit and opening out into it. A *sport fisherman* is a motorboat, usually fast, with special equipment for offshore trolling for large game fish.

The *bridge* of a vessel is the location from which it is steered and its speed controlled. On small craft, the term *control station* is perhaps more appropriate; *helm* is often used aboard sailboats. Many modern motorboats have a *flying bridge*, an added set of controls above the level of the normal control station for better visibility and more fresh air. Flying bridges are usually open, but may have a removable cloth top for shade.

## Portholes and portlights

On a boat, a *port* (or *porthole*) is an opening in the hull to admit light and air. The glass used in it to keep the hull weathertight is termed a *portlight* if it can be opened, a *deadlight* if it cannot.

## The dimensions of a vessel

The length of a boat is often given in two forms. *Overall length* (l.o.a.) is measured from the fore part of the stem to the after part of the stern. The *waterline* of a boat is the

**FIG. 115** The principal external dimensions of a boat are shown above. Don't confuse "draft" with "depth" — an internal measurement used in connection with the documentation of vessels.

plane where the surface of the water touches the hull when she is loaded normally; *length on the waterline* (l.w.l.) is measured along this plane. The greatest width of a vessel is her *beam;* boats of greater than normal beam are described as *beamy.* A vessel's *draft* is the depth of water required to float her. Draft should not be confused with the term *depth,* which is used in connection with larger vessels and documented boats and is measured inside the hull from the underside of the deck to the top of the keel.

The height of a boat's topsides from the waterline to the deck is called her *freeboard. Headroom* is the vertical distance between the deck and the cabin or canopy top, or other overhead structure.

## Other terms aboard a boat

The lower interior areas of the hull of a vessel are called her *bilge* (or *bilges*). It is here that water that leaks in, or is blown aboard as spray, collects as *bilge water,* to be later pumped overboard by a *bilge pump.*

When something is put away in its proper place on a vessel, it is *stowed.* The opposite of stowing, to *break out,* is to take a needed article from its locker or other secure place. To *unship* an item of equipment is to remove it from its normal working location or position.

*Berths* and *bunks* are seagoing names for beds aboard a boat. Closets are termed *lockers,* and a *hanging locker* is one tall enough for full-length garments. Chests and boxes may also be called lockers. A *rope* or *chain locker* is often found in the bow of a boat for stowing the anchor line or chain. *Lazarettes* are compartments in the stern of a vessel used for general storage.

*Helm* is a term relating to the steering mechanism of a craft. An individual is *at the helm* when he is the controls of the boat; he is then the *helmsman.*

### Terms Used in Boating Activities

In addition to the numerous terms for the boat itself, there are many others to be learned in connection with boating in general and the use of craft of all sizes. The list of these is virtually endless, and those that follow are only the more basic and often-used ones.

## Docks, piers, and harbors

There is a difference between a strict definition and popular usage for the term "dock." Most properly speaking, a *dock* is the *water* area in which a boat lies when she is *made fast* to shore installations (and "made fast" is the proper term rather than "tied up"). A *drydock* is one that can be shut off from the surrounding water and pumped out in order to make repairs on the vessel's bottom. *To dock* a vessel is to bring her to the shore installation and make her fast.

FIG. 116(a)   A wharf is a facility along and parallel to a shore to which vessels may be made fast for loading, fueling, etc.

FIG. 116(b)   Right, piers extend outward from the shoreline and craft may be made fast alongside the main structure or in slips separated by catwalks.

FIG. 117(a)   Marine railways are widely used for hauling out craft of all sizes. A cradle is pulled down into water deep enough for the boat to be floated onto it. She is then blocked in place and the cradle is slowly pulled up rails until it is clear of the water.

FIG. 117(b)   Craft up to 60 feet or more in length are now being taken out of the water by travelling lifts that straddle a wet slip. Broad slings are lowered, passed under the hull, and then raised. When the boat is high enough, the lift moves back on shore under tow or its own power.

In boating, however, the term "dock" is usually applied to structures bordering the water area in which boats lie. A *wharf* is properly a structure generally parallel to the shore, while a *pier* projects out from the shoreline. *Piles* are substantial stakes driven into the bottom to which craft may be made fast; a *dolphin* is a group of piles driven close together and bound with wire cables into a single structure. (The name dolphin is also given to the species of sea mammal often called porpoises, and quite separately to a species of ocean game fish.) Piles are often used to form *slips* out from a pier or wharf in which boats can be *berthed*; short *catwalks* (or *finger piers*) may extend out between the slips for easier access to the boats. A boat is made fast *to* a pile, *in* a slip, and *alongside* a pier or wharf.

A *harbor* is an anchorage which affords reasonably good protection for a vessel, with shelter from wind and sea. Strictly speaking, it applies to the water area only. *Port* is a more comprehensive term, including not only the harbor but, collectively, all the facilities for freight, passengers, and services as well, such as wharves, piers, warehouses, etc. A *yacht basin* or *marina* is a protected facility primarily for recreational small craft.

*Jetties* are dikes or embankments connected to the shore; when these are used to protect a harbor, and have no connection to the land, they are generally referred to

as *breakwaters*. *Groins* are jetty-like dikes built out at roughly a 90° angle from the shore to prevent erosion of the beach.

Boats are *hauled out* of the water on inclined planes at the water's edge called *ways* (also *marine ways* or *marine railways*). The framework which supports a boat as she is hauled out is termed a *cradle*. Small and medium sized boats are also lifted bodily out of the water and set on shore for storage or work with *slings*, which are lowered, passed under the hull, and raised by *cranes* or *traveling lifts*.

### Ropes and lines

Generally speaking, the word *rope* is used but little aboard a boat; the correct general term is *line*. "Rope" may be bought ashore at the store, but when it comes aboard and is put to use it becomes "line." *Marlinespike seamanship* is the term applied to that portion of the art related to the use of line and the making of *knots*, *bends*, *hitches*, and *splices*. Chapter 11 is devoted to this important subject.

Lines used to make a boat fast to a shore structure are usually called docking lines. *Bow lines* and *stern lines* lead forward and aft from these respective parts of the craft. *Spring lines* lead from the bow aft or from the stern forward to prevent the boat from moving ahead or astern. See fig. 841.

A *painter* is a line at the bow of a small boat, such as a dinghy, for towing or making fast. The line by which a boat is made fast to a mooring buoy is called a *pennant* (sometimes *pendant*).

*Heave* is a nautical term for throw or pull. One *heaves in* on a line when he pulls in the slack and *takes a strain* on it. When a line is let out, one *pays* it out; to lessen the strain on a line or let it out slightly or slowly, one *eases* it. A line is *snubbed* when its outward run is checked; it is *cast off* when it is let go. (A boat is cast off when all lines have been taken off the pier or other object to which it has been made fast.)

The *bitter end* of a line is the extreme end, the end made fast when all line has been paid out. The middle part of a line not including either end is the *bight,* particularly when formed into a loop. If a strain is put on a line heavy enough to break it, it *parts*.

*Heaving lines* are light lines, usually with a knot or weight at one end which makes it easier to throw them far and accurately. The knot that encloses a weight at the end of a heaving line is called a *monkey's fist. Belay* has two meanings—a line is belayed when it is made fast without knotting to a *cleat* or *belaying pin; belay* as a command signifies "stop" or "cease."

Ends of lines are *whipped* or *seized* when twine or thread is wrapped around them to prevent strands from untwisting or *unlaying*. Ragged ends of lines are said to be *fagged. Hawsers* are very heavy lines, in common use on tugboats and larger vessels but rarely found on boats.

*Tackle* is a broad, general term applied to equipment and *gear* used aboard a boat. It has a specific use, however, to mean a combination of line and *blocks* (pulleys)

FIG. 118 A set of blocks and some line can be used to increase lifting or pulling power. The set shown here has a theoretical "mechanical advantage" of 3 — actually less due to friction in the blocks.

used to increase a pulling or hoisting force. The wheels or rollers of the blocks are the *sheaves* (pronounced shivs). When a line is passed through a block or hole it is *reeved;* to *render* is to ensure that the line will pass freely through the block or hole.

Lines have *standing parts* and *hauling parts*. The standing part is the fixed part, the one which is made fast; the hauling part is the one that is taken in or let out as the tackle is used. Lines are *foul* when tangled, *clear* when in order to run freely.

## Anchors and moorings

An *anchor* is a specially shaped metal device designed to dig efficiently into the bottom under a body of water and hold a vessel in place despite winds and currents.

FIG. 119 There are many types of anchors used on boats. The old-fashioned, or yachtsman's type, left, and the modern patent (Danforth), right, are only two; many others are illustrated in Chapter 6.

*Ground tackle* is a general term embracing anchors, lines, and other gear used in anchoring. On boats, the anchor line may be referred to as a *rode. A mooring* is a semi-permanent anchorage installation, consisting of a heavy anchor (usually of the *mushroom* type), chain, a mooring buoy, and pennant of nylon or manila. See fig. 652.

The anchor carried on a boat for most normal uses is its *working anchor*. A heavier model carried for emergencies is termed a *storm anchor,* and a smaller, lighter anchor for brief daytime stops when the craft will not be left unattended is popularly called a *lunch hook*.

Anchors come in many styles—*kedge, stockless, grapnel,* and modern *light-weight* types such as the *Danforth, Northill,* and *plow*. More on this subject will be found in Chapter 6.

The term *kedge* is also applied to an anchor of any type that is used for getting a boat off when it has run aground. The kedge is carried out by a dinghy or other means and set so that a pull on the line will help get the boat off or at least keep it from being driven harder aground; this process is called *kedging*.

When a boat is anchored, the ratio of the length of line

FIG. 120 A boat must always be anchored with adequate "scope." This is the ratio of the length of the anchor line in use to the distance from the bow chocks to the bottom of the water (not just the depth of the water!). See also fig. 631.

in use to the distance to the bottom of the water as measured from the deck is termed *scope*. An *anchorage* is an area specifically designated by governmental authorities in which vessels may anchor; special regulations may prevail in these areas.

## Motions of a boat

A vessel *grounds* when she touches bottom, and if stuck there she is *aground*. When a boat moves through the water, she is said to be *underway* (or *under weigh*). According to government laws and regulations, a vessel is underway at any time that she is not aground, at anchor, or made fast to the shore. The direction in which she is moving may be made more specific by stating that she makes *headway* (moving forward), *sternway* (backwards), or *leeway* (to one side or the other, as when pushed by a beam wind). A boat is said to be *underway with no way on* when she is free of the bottom or shore but is making no motion through the water *(adrift)*. A vessel has *steerageway* if she is making enough speed through the water for her rudder to be effective. A vessel's anchor is said to be *aweigh* when it has broken out of the bottom and has been lifted clear.

FIG. 121 Nearly all boats leave an area of disturbed water—wake—behind them as they move forward through the water. Each skipper must be careful that the waves caused by this motion do not disturb or damage others.

The disturbed water that a boat leaves astern as a result of her motion is her *wake*. *Wash* is the flow of water that results from the action of her propeller or propellers. Both of these effects are commonly lumped together as "wake."

Sidewise rotational motion in rough water is called *roll*; vertical motion as the bow rises and falls is termed *pitching*. A craft *yaws* when she runs off her course to either side as she might if she didn't steer properly. If she yaws too widely and is thrown broadside into the *trough* of the sea (between the crests and parallel to them), she *broaches to,* a dangerous situation that should be carefully avoided. In very rough seas a small boat can be thrown end-over-end; this is *pitchpoling.*

A boat may *capsize* without *foundering*—in the first instance she turns over, in the latter she fills with water and sinks. If a boat fills with water from over the side, she *swamps*. Before his vessel is reduced to such straits, the wise skipper *heaves to,* reducing headway and generally lying with the bow slightly off from meeting the waves head on. He may put out a *sea anchor (drogue)* that will hold the bow at the most favorable angle; a sea anchor does not go to the bottom, it merely serves as a drag.

## Trim

*Trim* relates to the way a boat floats in the water. When she floats properly as designed, she is on an *even keel;* but if she inclines to port or starboard, she *lists. Heel* conveys the same idea as list, a sideward inclination from the vertical. If a vessel is too heavily loaded forward, she *trims by the head;* if her draft is excessive aft, she *trims by the stern.*

## Directions from the boat

*Dead ahead* refers to any point which the vessel is approaching directly on a straight course. *Dead astern* is, of course, the opposite direction. To convey the idea of opposite, or at right angles, we say *abreast*. An object that is at right angles (90°) to the centerline (keel) of a craft is *abeam,* or *broad on the beam*. If the boat passes near to it, it is said to be *close aboard*. (Vessels are *abreast* of one another when they are side-by-side.)

If we look ahead from abeam to a direction that is midway between abeam and dead ahead, this is *broad on the bow,* port or starboard as the case may be. Going in the other direction, an object seen midway between abeam and dead astern is *broad on the (port* or *starboard) quarter.*

To express the direction of another vessel or object relative to our boat, we say that it *bears* so-and-so, using the phraseology above. For intermediate directions through a circle centered on the observer's boat, the *point* system can be used, with 32 points making a complete circle. Each direction in the point system is named. A ship or other object seen from your craft might be said to bear *two points abaft the port beam, one point on the starboard bow, etc.* See fig. 123. Half-points and quarter-points exist

FIG. 122 The three basic motions of a boat are roll, pitch, and yaw. At sea, these are often combined with uncomfortable results!

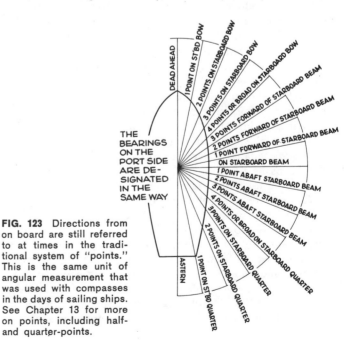

FIG. 123 Directions from on board are still referred to at times in the traditional system of "points." This is the same unit of angular measurement that was used with compasses in the days of sailing ships. See Chapter 13 for more on points, including half- and quarter-points.

but are rarely used. The direction of a remote object is its *bearing*.

*Windward* (pronounced wind'ard) means toward the direction from which the wind is blowing. A boat goes to windward, but in speaking of the side of a vessel and the parts on that side on which the wind is blowing, it is better to refer to the *weather* side.

Opposite to windward is *leeward* (pronounced *loo*ard), the direction away from the wind, toward which it is blowing. The *lee* side is, therefore, away from the wind, and a boat makes *leeway* when blown sideways off her course.

## Terms Relating to Equipment

*Chocks* are deck fittings, usually of metal, with inward curving arms through which lines such as mooring or anchor lines are passed so as to lead them in the proper direction both on board and off the boat; they should be smooth so as to prevent excess wearing of the line. *Cleats* are fittings of metal or wood with outward curving arms or horns on which lines can be made fast *(belayed)*.

FIG. 124 Cleats, bitts, and chocks are found on both motorboats and sailboats. Their shape and size may vary with the craft that they are on, but all are basic forms of deck hardware.

While cleats are generally satisfactory for most purposes on a boat, wooden or metal *bitts* are often preferred where heavy strains are to be taken. These are stout vertical posts, either single or double. They may take the form of a fitting bolted securely (never screwed) to the deck, but more often, as in the case of a wooden *samson post,* passing through the deck and *stepped* at the keel or otherwise strongly fastened. Sometimes a round metal pin is fitted horizontally through the head of a post or bitt to aid in belaying the line; this is a *norman pin*.

*Towing bitts* are also called *towing posts*. Towing bitts on a towboat are located well forward of the stern, as near amidships as possible, to permit the stern to swing to either side for better steering and maneuvering.

*Fenders* are relatively soft objects of rubber or plastic (older models were canvas cases filled with cork) used between boats and piles, pier sides, seawalls, etc. to protect the topsides from scarring and to cushion any shock of the craft striking the fixed object. Fenders, sometimes referred to in a landlubberly fashion as "bumpers," are also used between boats when they are tied, or *rafted,* together. *Fender boards* are short lengths of stout planking, often with cushion material or metal rubbing strips on one side.

FIG. 125 For protection against rough piers or other boats, a skipper will often need to hang fenders (don't call them "bumpers") over the side. Modern ones are made of rubber or plastic. Where necessary, fenders may be hung horizontally, or two of them may be used vertically behind a fenderboard; see fig. 855.

They may be used with two fenders hung vertically, or occasionally by themselves, to provide a wider bearing surface against a single pile.

*Life preservers* provide additional buoyancy to keep a person afloat when he is in the water. They take the form of cushions, belts, vests, jackets, and ring buoys. Life preservers must be of a Coast Guard-approved type to meet the legal requirement as set forth in Chapter 2.

A *boathook* is a short shaft of wood or metal with a fitting at one end shaped to aid in extending one's effective reach from the side of a boat, such as when putting a line over a pile or picking up an object dropped overboard. It can also be used for pushing or fending off.

A *boarding ladder* is a set of steps temporarily fitted over the side of a boat to assist persons coming aboard from a low pier or float. A *swimming ladder* is much the same except that it extends down into the water. A *swimming platform* is a narrow wooden shelf attached to a boat's transom just above the waterline.

*Grab rails* are hand-hold fittings mounted on cabin tops or sides for personal safety when moving around the boat, both on deck and below. Whenever these or other fittings such as cleats and chocks are installed, *bedding compound* should be smeared on the surface of the fitting that will be in contact with the hull, deck, etc., to seal out moisture.

Magnetic *compasses* are mounted near the control station in boxes or other protective casings known as *binna-*

FIG. 126 A boarding ladder can either be hung over the gunwales of a small boat or fitted into brackets on the topsides of a larger craft to make easier boarding from a low float or dinghy. A longer ladder reaching down into the water is used for swimming.

**FIG. 127** The principal parts and dimensions of a flag are shown above. For flags the usual ratio between the fly and the hoist is 3:2. This may vary in the case of some pennants.

cles. Compasses are swung in *gimbals,* pivoted rings that permit the compass *bowl* and *card* to remain relatively level regardless of the boat's motion. To enable the helmsman to steer a compass course, a *lubber's line* is marked on the inside of the compass bowl to indicate direction of the vessel's bow. Much more on compasses will be found in Chapters 13 and 14.

A *lead* (pronounced led) *line* is a length of light rope with a weight (the lead) at one end and markers at accurately measured intervals from that end. It is used for determining the depth of water alongside a vessel. A *depth sounder* is an electronic device for determining depths; often such devices are referred to as "fathometers"—this is incorrect as that term is the trademark of one particular manufacturer of electronic depth sounders. Boats used frequently in shallow waters may be equipped with a long slender *sounding pole* with depth in feet and fractions marked off from its lower end.

A *barometer* is often carried aboard a boat; it measures and indicates (in some cases, records) atmospheric pressure. Knowledge of the amount and direction of change in atmospheric pressure is useful in predicting changes in the weather.

*Binoculars* are hand-held optical devices that aid in detecting and identifying distant objects. Separate sets of lenses and prisms enable the user to see with both eyes at the same time.

A *winch* is a mechanical device, either hand or power operated, for exerting an increased pull on a line or chain, such as an anchor line.

## Flags

Strictly speaking, a vessel's *colors* are the flag or flags that she flies to indicate her nationality, but the term is often expanded to include all flags flown. An *ensign* is a flag to denote the nationality of a vessel or her owner, or on a boat to denote the membership of her owner in an organization (other than a yacht club).

The *hoist* of a flag is its inner vertical side; also its vertical dimension. The *fly* is its length from the hoist out to the free end. The *union* is the upper portion near the hoist —in the U.S. national flag, the blue area with the white stars. The *union jack* is a flag consisting solely of the union of the national flag.

A *burgee* is a triangular, rectangular, or swallow-tailed flag usually denoting yacht club or similar unit membership. A *pennant* is a flag, most often triangular in shape, used for general designating or decorative purposes. See Chapter 22 for additional information on flags and how they should be flown.

### Terms of Distance and Speed

On salt water, distances are measured in *nautical miles,* a unit about 1/7th longer than the land or *statute* mile with

which we all are more familiar. The international nautical mile is slightly more than 6076 feet, whereas, of course, the statute mile used on shore and fresh water bodies is 5280 feet.

Where nautical miles are used for distance, the unit of speed is the *knot,* one nautical mile per hour. Note carefully that the "per hour" is included in the definition—to say "knots per hour" is incorrect. *Miles per hour* is the correct term for most inland fresh water bodies, as it is on shore. A *speed curve* is a plot of speed through the water versus engine speed in revolutions per minute (RPM), expressed on a graph.

In modern practice with small craft, depths are usually measured in feet, but offshore the unit *fathom* may be used—it is equal to six feet.

**FIG. 128** Patent logs indicate distance traveled through the water by the turning of a rotor at the end of a line trailed astern. Other designs use a small impeller mounted on a strut a few inches below the hull; speed and distance are indicated mechanically or electrically.

### Miscellaneous Terms

When any part of the vessel's gear or equipment breaks or gives way, it *carries away;* an object goes *by the board* when it goes *overboard.* If a boat is *stove* (planking broken in from outside), the craft *springs a leak* or *makes water.* When water is dipped out of a small boat the process is called *bailing.*

The term *clear* has many meanings. Before leaving for a foreign port, a ship must clear through Customs authorities. She clears the land when she leaves it, clears a shoal when she passes it by safely. The bilges are cleared of water when they are pumped out. Tangled *(foul)* lines are cleared by straightening them out and getting them ready for use.

A boat *stands by* when she remains with another craft to give her assistance if necessary. When used as an order, stand by means to be prepared to carry out an instruction. *Aye,* or *aye aye,* is a properly nautical (if somewhat military) way of acknowledging an order or instruction, indicating that it has been heard and understood, and will be obeyed.

Entries are made in a *log* (book) to record all events occurring aboard; more on this in Chapter 30. A *patent log* is a device to record distance traveled. One *raises* a light or landmark when it first becomes visible; he makes a *landfall* when the shore is first sighted on coming in from sea. *Passage* is generally construed to mean a run from one port to another; *voyage* includes both the outward and homeward passages. *Watches* are periods of duty, usually four hours long, aboard a vessel; *dog watches* are shorter, two-hour periods between 4:00 and 8:00 pm (1600 and

2000 in the 24-hour system of time, see page 374). A period of duty at the helm is a *trick*.

## Tides and currents

The word *tide* is almost certainly one of the most misused of nautical terms, so much so that its misapplication has come to be widely accepted even though incorrect. Properly speaking, it means only the rise and fall, the vertical movement, of bodies of water as a result of the interacting gravitational pulls of the moon and sun. Commonly, but wrongly, "tide" is also used to refer to the inflow and outflow of water as a result of changes in tidal level. *Current* is the proper term for a horizontal flow of water, *tidal current* for flows resulting from tidal influences. It is proper to say a two-knot current, but not a two-knot tide.

The incoming tidal current running toward the shore, or upstream in a river, is the *flood*; the retreating, or downstream, current is the *ebb*. The *range* of the tide (difference between the height of *high water* and *low water* (or *high tide* and *low tide*) is not always the same as the days go by. *Spring tides* occur when the moon is new or full and have a greater range than those at other times. *Neap* tides are those occurring at quarter moons; and these have a less than average range.

## Water movements and conditions

Various terms are used to describe specific water movements or conditions of the surface. A broad term, *waves*, is frequently used for disturbed conditions on a body of water; these actually represent vertical movement of water particles regardless of their apparent forward motion. *Sea* is a general term often used to describe waves and water action on the surface, but properly it should be applied only to waves produced by wind. *Rips* are short, steep waves caused by the meeting of currents. The confused water action found at places where tidal currents meet is also called a *chop*, but this term is more often applied to

**FIG. 129** The horizontal motion of water is current, not tide, although they are termed tidal currents if they result from tidal influences. Such currents "flood" (flow in from sea) and "ebb" (flow out). Tides, vertical changes in water level, do not "come in" and "go out"; they "rise" and "fall."

**FIG. 130** Waves result from local wind action on the water surface. Large deep-water swells may come from great distances away; they crest over and become breakers as they move into shallower water near shore.

U.S. Coast Guard Photo

small, closely spaced waves resulting from wind action on inland bodies of water.

*Swells (ground swells)* are long heavy undulations of the surface resulting from distubances some distance away on oceans and sea. *Surf* is produced when waves leave deep water forming *breakers* on the shore as they *crest* and curl over. A *following sea* is one that comes up from astern, running in the same direction as the boat is going. A *head sea* is just the opposite; one where the progress of the waves is against that of the craft which must meet them head on. *Beam seas* come from either side. *Cross* or *confused seas* are irregular ones with components from two or more directions.

## Powerboat Terms

A number of basic boating terms are applicable specifically to boats equipped with some form of engine, whether *inboard* (mounted within the hull) or *outboard* (mounted on the transom and detachable).

### Propulsion

Thrust for the movement of the boat through the water is achieved by the rotation of a *propeller* (or *screw*) which draws in water from ahead and pushes it out astern. Boats with two engines and propellers are referred to as *twin-screw* craft. An often-used slang term for a propeller is *wheel*. A very few boats achieve their thrust from the reaction of a *water jet*.

A more recent development is the *inboard-outboard* (or *I-O*, or *stern-drive*, or *outdrive*). Here the motor is of the inboard type mounted within the hull at the stern with an external driving unit closely resembling the *lower unit* of an outboard motor, even to the extent of being capable of being tilted up. Power is applied to the propeller through two right-angle sets of gears resulting in another name sometimes used, *Z-drive*.

### Engine mountings

An inboard engine is mounted on *engine beds*, stout structural members running fore-and-aft across the floor timbers. On single-screw boats, the *deadwood* is a heavy fore-and-aft timber that lies above the keel and may extend beyond it. (On sailboats the deadwood may be beneath the keel timbers of the hull.) *Shaft logs* are timbers through which the *propeller shaft* passes; a *stuffing box* prevents water from entering at this point. The *propeller post*, if one is used, stands vertically behind the deadwood and is joined to it and to the keel. On many boats, the propeller shaft is supported externally under the hull by one or more *struts*.

In some designs of boats, the engine is turned about so that the shaft leads forward to a gear box which reverses its direction to come out under the hull in a normal manner; this *V-drive* permits a compact engine-in-the-stern arrangement.

### Reverse and reduction gears

*Reverse gears* change the direction of rotation of the propeller to give a thrust in the opposite direction for stopping the craft or giving it sternway. *Reduction gears* are often combined with the reversing function so that the propeller, turning at a slower rate than the engine, will have increased efficiency.

**FIG. 131** Some small craft are "jet propelled." The engine drives a multistage pump and the reaction from the high-speed stream of water coming out of the stern provides the forward propulsion. Such systems are excellent for very shallow water but are less efficient overall than conventional drives.

**FIG. 133** On displacement-type hulls of heavy construction, the propeller shaft normally runs through a "deadwood" above the keel. On higher-speed hulls, struts extend downward from the bottom of the craft to support the exposed shaft. Long shafts on larger craft may have two or more struts.

**FIG. 132** Inboard-outboard drives combine the advantages of using conventional inboard engines with the flexibility of outside drive units much like an outboard motor. Steering is accomplished without rudders by pivoting the drive units; these can also be tilted up for service.

The gears of outdrive and V-drive units include the reversing capability and a reduction ratio if required.

## Engine accessories

A complete engine normally includes a *fuel pump* to feed fuel under pressure (to the *carburetor* if gasoline is used), an *oil pump* to supply lubricating oil where needed within the engine, and one or more *water pumps* for circulating cooling water. An engine is *raw water cooled* if water for cooling is drawn in through a hull fitting, circulated in the engine, and then discharged overboard. A *closed cooling system* uses a separate quantity of fresh water to circulate solely within the engine; heat picked up by this water is transferred to raw cooling water in a *heat exchanger,* or is dissipated to the water in which the boat is floating by means of a *keel cooler.*

*Engine instruments* usually include gauges for indicating oil pressure, cooling water temperature, and battery charging or discharging (ammeter). Speedometers and odometers (distance traveled indicators) are not normally used on powerboats although they do exist; instead a *tachometer* indicates the speed of the engine in revolutions per minute (RPM) and may indicate the total revolutions or operating hours as a guide for the performance of routine maintenance. Gasoline engines are fitted with *flame arresters,* screen-like metal fittings over the air intakes of carburetors so that any flame from a backfire will not come out dangerously into the *engine compartment.*

On many small outboard motors a *shear pin* is part of the propeller assembly. This small pin of relatively soft metal breaks apart—shears—when the propeller strikes a hard underwater object, thus saving the motor from more serious damage; the pin is easily replaced.

## Sailboat Terms

Although some powerboat terms will also be applicable to many sailboats (especially those with auxiliary engines), "ragmen" really have a language of their own. All boatmen, including powerboat skippers, should have a working knowledge of the basic terminology of sailing and sailboats.

### Basic sailboat components

The principal components of a sailboat are its *hull, spars,* and *sails.* The hull is essentially as decribed before in this chapter with certain modifications and additions resulting from the use of the wind as a means of propulsion. A portion of the wind forced on the sails drives the boat forward, but another portion tends to make it move sideways. To counteract this, the exterior keel is much enlarged in area, or the craft is fitted with a *centerboard,* a relatively thin plate that can be put down vertically through the keel for greater lateral area, but which can be raised when it is desired to lessen the boat's draft. To permit this raising and lowering action, the centerboard is normally pivoted on a pin near the lower forward corner.

To maintain the watertight integrity of the hull, the centerboard is housed in a *centerboard trunk* which extends internally to above the waterline. On some very small sailboats, a *daggerboard* is forced down vertically in lieu of a pivoted centerboard.

### Ballast

The sideward thrust of the wind, besides making leeway, also causes a sailboat to heel to leeward. To lessen such heeling and to increase stability, many larger sailing craft carry *ballast,* additional weight either *external* in the form of a heavy mass (usually lead), on the bottom of the keel, or *internal* ballast within the hull. In smaller sailboats, the crew shifts its weight about within the craft (or just over the side) as a form of readily movable internal ballast.

### Spars

The term *spars* is used broadly to cover masts, booms, gaffs, etc. *Masts* are, of course, the principal vertical spars from which sails are *set.* They are *stepped* when put in position and are *raked* if the mast is inclined aft at an angle rather than being exactly vertical.

# Nautical Terms / CHAPTER 1

The horizontal spar along the lower edge of a fore-and-aft sail is a *boom*. A four-sided fore-and-aft sail has an additional spar along its upper edge; this is a *gaff*.

## Rigging

All of the various lines about a vessel that secure the sails, masts, and other spars are collectively referred to as *rigging*. Lines or wires bracing the mast and certain other fixed spars comprise the *standing* rigging; those used for hoisting and adjusting the sails make up the *running* rigging.

The standing rigging—usually wire—from the mast to the sides of the boat are called *shrouds*. Those commonly used to support the mast in a fore-and-aft plane are *stays*—*forestays* run to the bow and *backstays,* if used, support the mast from aft.

The slack is usually taken out of a stay or shrouds by the use of a *turnbuckle,* a metal sleeve threaded right-handed in one end and left-handed in the other so that when turned in one direction eyebolts in both ends are drawn in so as to shorten the fitting; turning the sleeve in the other direction increases its overall length and provides slack.

## Sails

*Canvas* is a general term for a boat's sails, although most modern sails are made of lighter synthetic materials. Sails *draw* when they fill with wind and provide power to drive the craft through the water. One *makes sail* when the sails are hoisted; he *shortens* sail when the area of sails in use is reduced. A sail is *reefed* by partly lowering it and securing it so that it continues to draw, but with reduced area and power. The sail is *dowsed* (or *doused)* when it is lowered quickly, *furled* when it is folded and

**FIG. 136** Square-rigged vessels no longer sail in great numbers as they did before the days of steam, but some are still seen as training ships or cruise vessels. There are many types of rigs for these ships.

rolled and then secured to a boom or yard. One *looses sail* when *unfurling* it.

Most recreational sailing craft are now fitted with triangular-shaped sails and are said to be *Marconi rigged* (or *jib-headed*). If a four-sided sail with gaff is used, the boat is described as *gaff-rigged.*

A *suit of sails* is a complete set for any particular boat.

## Sailing rigs

*Rig* is the general term applied to the arrangement of a vessel's masts and sails. The principal sail of a boat is its *mainsail*. If the boat has only this one sail, it is a *catboat,* and may be either Marconi- or gaff-rigged.

A sail forward of the mast, or ahead of the most forward mast if there are more than one, is a *headsail;* a single headsail is usually termed a *jib*. A boat having a single mast, with a mainsail and a jib, is a *sloop*. On some sloops additional headsails are set from a *bowsprit,* a spar projecting forward over the craft's bow. A sloop without a bowsprit,

**FIG. 134** The principal components of a basic small sailboat are identified above. Every boatman, even those only active with motorboats, should be familiar with these terms.

**FIG. 135** The various rigs of modern sailing craft are shown above. Careful attention is sometimes necessary to differentiate between sloops and cutters; yawls and ketches are more easily distinguished from one another.

**FIG. 137** A sailboat normally changes direction by bringing her bow through the wind—this is "tacking." If the wind passes astern, she "jibes," a maneuver that can be dangerous if not carefully controlled.

**FIG. 138** (a) A sailing craft pointing as close to △ the wind as possible is "beating."

(b) As the wind moves more aft, she is "reaching." ▽

(c) With the wind astern or nearly so, she is "running." ▷

on which the jib is set from a stay to the stem, is sometimes called a *knockabout,* but this term has fallen into relative disuse.

A modern *cutter* is a variation of the sloop rig in which the mast is stepped further aft, resulting in a larger area for headsails. A cutter normally sets two headsails, a *forestaysail* and a jib ahead of it.

*Yawls* have two masts, the after one of which is much smaller and is stepped abaft the rudder post. A *ketch* likewise has two masts with the after one smaller, but here the difference in height is not so marked and the after mast is stepped forward of the rudder post. The taller mast is the *mainmast;* the shorter after mast of both rigs is the *mizzenmast,* and the sail is the *mizzen* (may be either jib-headed or with a gaff).

*Schooners* are *fore-and-aft rigged* (as distinguished from square-rigged) and have two or more masts. Unlike yawls and ketches, the after mast of a two-masted schooner is taller than the forward one (in rare designs, the two masts may be the same height). Thus the after mast becomes the mainmast and the other the *foremast.* Additional names are used if there are more than two masts.

## Square-rigged vessels

Vessels on which the principal sails are set generally athwartships are referred to as *square-rigged.* These four-sided sails are hung from horizontal spars known as *yards.* Headsails are carried as on other rigs, forward of the foremost mast. Staysails may be used, and the aftermost mast of square-rigged vessels normally carry a fore-and-aft sail.

## Sailing terms

As sailboats cannot sail directly into the wind, the wind is almost always coming over one side or the other. If the wind is coming over the starboard side, the boat is said to be on a *starboard tack;* the *port tack* is, of course, just the opposite. A boat *tacks* when she *comes up* (heads) into the wind and changes the side over which it blows. In tacking, a boat *goes (comes) about.* Changing tacks with the wind passing astern rather than ahead of the boat is called *jibing* (pronounced with a long *i* as in ice), or *wearing*

15

*ship;* jibes (also spelled gibes or gybes) sometimes occur accidentally when sailing downwind (the wind nearly dead astern) and can be dangerous.

After the sails have been *hoisted* by their *halyards,* they are trimmed with their *sheets (jibsheets, mainsheets,* etc.), lines used to control their lateral position and movement. To *harden* is to haul in and tighten up on the sheet attached to a jib, mainsail, etc. Sheets are *eased* when they are let out. Headsails normally have two sheets so that they can be trimmed on either tack; other sails have only one sheet.

Although a detailed discussion of sailing techniques is beyond the scope of this chapter, all boatmen should know that a sailboat is *close hauled (full and by)* when she is sailing with the wind as far ahead as possible, about 45° off the bow in most boats (this is also termed sailing *on the wind,* to *windward,* or *beating).* As the boat is steered further away from the wind, it *bears off* and is *reaching,* with *close* reaching, *beam* reaching, and *broad* reaching occurring successively as the wind moves aft. With the wind astern, the sailboat is *running* (or sailing *downwind, off the wind, free,* or *scudding).*

## Miscellaneous Basic Terms

There are many other basic boating terms that do not fit neatly into one of the above categories. Among these are words and phrases relating to the operation of the vessel, navigation, etc.

### Navigation and piloting

*Navigation* is the art and science of safely directing the movements of a vessel from one point to another. The basic boatman is primarily interested in one of its subdivisions, *piloting,* which is navigation using visible references, the depth of the water, etc. Other forms of navigation include *celestial,* taking *sights* by *sextant* on the sun, moon, planets, and stars, used for long offshore passages; and *electronic,* which may be used in varying degrees by inshore and offshore boatmen.

### Courses

A *course* is the direction of movement prescribed for a vessel from one place to another. A *true course* is one taken from the chart with reference to true (geographic) north—it is the angle between the boat's keel and the geographic meridian when she is on course. The *magnetic course* is the angle between her keel and the magnetic meridan passing through that position; it is almost always different from the true course. A *compass course* is the course indicated by the vessel's compass—it is the angle between the vessel's keel and the direction indicated by the north point on the compass card when she is on course. The *heading* is the direction a vessel's bow points at any given time.

### Bearings

A *bearing* is the direction of a terrestial object from the observer and may be stated in terms of true, magnetic, or compass values. A *relative bearing* is the direction of a terrestial object from the observer measured from the vessel's heading clockwise from 000° to 360°.

### Variation and deviation

*Variation* is the angular difference between true north and the direction of magnetic north at a given point on earth. It is the direction indicated by a magnetic compass that is unaffected by local influences. Variation is "easterly" if the north mark of a compass card points to the east of true north, "westerly" if the opposite.

*Deviation* is the error in a magnetic compass caused by local magnetic influences on the boat. It is easterly or westerly as the compass points east or west of magnetic north. *Compass error* is the algebraic sum of variation and deviation.

### Plotting and charting

In navigation, one *plots* various data on a *chart* (never map), takes *bearings* to determine his *position (fix),* and takes a *departure* to establish an exact point from which to commence his *dead reckoning* (a plot of courses steered and distances travelled through the water). *To chart,* a verb, is to record information, usually additional information, on an existing chart of the area.

Much more on the above terms will be found in Chapters 13, 14, 17, 19, and 21.

### Aids to navigation

Various governmental authorities establish and maintain *aids to navigation,* artificial objects to supplement natural landmarks. These may be used to indicate both safe and unsafe waters; the boatman must know the meanings and use of each.

*Buoys* are floating aids to navigation of characteristic shapes and colors. They may be lighted or unlighted; they may or may not have audible signals such as bells, gongs,

**FIG. 139 Navigation includes all methods of safely directing the movements of a vessel from one point to another. The techniques range from simple buoy-to-buoy coastal piloting to celestial navigation on the high seas using a mariner's sextant.**

**FIG. 140** Relative bearings are measured as angles from dead ahead clockwise around the starboard side, past the stern, and back up the port side to the bow. Directions are always described in three-digit groups using zeros as necessary, i.e., 050°, not 50°

**RELATIVE BEARINGS**

## Other terms

*Lubberly* is used to describe the doing of any task aboard a boat or ship in an ignorant or sloppy manner.

In nautical terminology, *hard* means fully or completely as in turning a steering wheel *hard aport* (fully to the left) or *hard over* (in either direction).

A *beach* is the land immediately in from the water's edge. In tidal regions, it includes the area between the high- and low-water lines. To go *to the beach* is a nautical expression meaning to go ashore, even if not to an actual beach.

A *bar* is a build-up, usually of sand, that reduces the depth of water; it may or may not be partially exposed above the surface of the water and it usually has an elongated shape. Bars frequently form across the openings (*mouths*) of rivers, creeks, harbors, etc. Larger, broader areas of shallow water are often termed *flats*.

# Advanced Boating Terminology

Once a boatman has mastered the basic "language" of this field of interest, he is ready to go further into the subject, learning terms perhaps not necessary to everyday operation of his boat, but rather words and phrases that will expand and broaden his knowledge. The terms discussed here will by no means exhaust the possibilities, but they will add to the skipper's understanding of his craft and its use.

These additional terms occur in many areas of boating; they are, however, perhaps most noticeable in those relating to boat construction and sailing—these fields of interest have extensive vocabularies all their own.

### Additional Boat Construction Terms

Vessels, including boats, are normally designed by a *naval architect.* In so doing, he prepares detailed *plans* and *specifications,* including the *lines* (shape) of her hull. *Clean* is a term applied, not to a boat's condition, but rather to her lines. If the lines are *fine,* so that she slips easily through the water, the lines are said to be clean.

A *marine surveyor* is a highly qualified expert who makes detailed inspections—the *survey*—of boats and ships to determine the condition of their hull, equipment, machinery, etc.

## Hull shape terms

In addition to being used for the lower interior portions of a vessel, the term *bilge* is also applied to the area of the hull of a round-bottom craft where the bottom gradually becomes the topsides; a somewhat longer but perhaps more descriptive term for this is *turn of the bilge.* If the boat is flat or vee-bottomed, the bottom and the topsides meet at a well-defined angle rather than a gradual curve—this is the *chine* of the boat. The smaller the angle of intersection of these planes, the *harder* the chine. *Soft* chine craft have a lesser angle; this term is sometimes applied to round-bottom boats, but this is not correct. Some modern boats are designed with *multiple chines (longitudinal steps)* for a softer ride at high speeds in rough water.

Larger round-bottom vessels may be built with *bilge keels,* secondary keels at the turn of the bilge to reduce their tendence to roll in beam seas.

**FIG. 141** A skipper makes a plot on his chart to record his position at various times and his craft's movements, past and projected, through the water. This is important should an emergency arise as he must be able to quickly and accurately determine his location.

whistles, etc.

*Daybeacons* (not "markers") are fixed aids normally consisting of a distinctive sign, the *daymark,* mounted on a pile or group of piles driven into the bottom. Daymarks will have a characteristic shape and color or colors.

*Lights* (not "flashers") are aids consisting of a light source mounted on a fixed object (as distinguished from lighted buoys). Each light will have a characteristic color and on-off pattern; most light structures will also have a daymark for daytime identification. The term "light" covers all such aids from the relatively weak minor light on a single pile to the largest seacoast lighthouses.

Detailed information on aids to navigation will be found in Chapters 15 and 16.

**FIG. 142** Aids to navigation are among a boatman's best friends. Unlighted buoys and daybeacons are the most numerous types of aids; these and many others are described and discussed in Chapters 15 and 16.

FIG. 143 The shape of a vessel's hull, particularly the underwater portions, is shown by her "lines" in several views. These are the basic determinations of a naval architect when he designs a boat.

The significance of the term *deadrise* can be appreciated by visualizing a transverse section across a hull. If the bottom were flat, extending horizontally from the keel, there would be no deadrise. In a round- or vee-bottom boat, where the bottom rises at an angle to a horizontal line outward from the keel, the amount of such rise is the deadrise, expressed in inches per foot or as an angle.

With normal sheer, the bow of a boat, as viewed from the side, rises and the stern is at least level with amidships. *Reverse sheer,* however, has the deck sloping downward at the bow, or stern, or both.

*Flam* is that part of the flare of the topsides just below the deck. If it curves outward sharply, it will both increase deck width and reduce the amount of bow spray that blows aboard. The *cutwater* is, naturally enough, the forward edge of the stem, particularly near the waterline. *Stem bands* of metal are frequently fitted over the stem for protection from debris in the water, ice, pier edges, etc. The *forefoot* of a boat is where the stem joins the keel.

If the boat has an *overhanging* stern, this part of the hull is the *counter.* Her lines aft to her stern are her *run;* lines forward to the stem are her *entrance* (or *entry*). The descriptions "fine" and "clean" are often applied to the entrance and run. The term *bluff* is applied to bows that are broader and blunter than normal.

FIG. 144 Some modern high-speed deep-vee hulls are designed with multiple chines or longitudinal steps for better rough-water performance. The skipper shown above, though, is driving his boat too hard for existing conditions, despite its special design!

FIG. 145 Much expert carpentry work goes into a planked wooden boat to provide a strong, watertight hull.

## Planking details

On a planked wooden hull, the sheer (or uppermost) strake is sometimes thicker than other lines of planking. When a second plank, next below the sheer strake, is also thicker than the others it is called a *binding strake. Bilge strakes* are those fitted at the turn of the bilge and these, too, may be heavier than others in the topsides.

A heavier strake in the topsides extending beyond the exposed face of the planking is termed a *rubbing strake* and is intended to protect the topsides from the roughness of piles, pier faces, etc. A strip of wood for the same purpose added externally to the planking is generally called a *rubrail* or *guard.* Both of these may be faced with metal strips for their own better protection.

Many hulls are fitted with a *spray rail* external to the planking just above the waterline. Such a rail usually extends about halfway aft from the stem and deflects downward any spray from the bow wave.

Frame members such as the keel and stem are *rabbeted* to receive the ends and edges of the planks. This *rabbet* is merely a longitudinal recess cut into the wood in the proper size to take the plank. Plank ends at the stem and stern are the *hood ends.*

The term *fastening* is applied to the screws or specially-designed nails which hold the planks to the frames. It may also be applied to screws, bolts, and similar items used to hold down equipment, cleats, chocks, etc. *Through fastenings* are bolts that go all the way through the hull or other base timbers and are secured with a washer and nut on the inside; a *backing block* is generally advisable to spread the stress for additional strength.

*Waterways* are gutters along the edge of a boat's deck to aid in draining off water through the *scuppers.* (This same term is also applied to water areas suitable for navigation, particularly improved channels in rivers, lakes, etc.)

*Wedges* are sometimes placed on the underside of a boat's hull at the transom to provide additional "lift" to the stern, preventing *squat* and so improving running trim. Wedges provide a fixed action; more sophisticated electrical-mechanical-hydraulic devices can be built-in or installed to provide adjustable amounts of wedge action.

## Bulwarks and taffrails

When the topsides are carried above the level of the deck, this portion is called *bulwarks* and the top of the bulwarks is the *rail.* The *taffrail* is the rail at the stern, farthest aft. A *taffrail log* is a type of patent log that is

FIG. 146 Adjustable electro-mechanical or hydraulic "trim tabs" are a modern replacement for the wedges often added at the stern of a boat to reduce "squat." These can markedly change the riding angle of many hulls, increasing both speed and fuel economy.

that it can be pulled back and forth a short distance to clean them out.

Some boats are severely damaged by "dry rot," a fungus attack on wooden areas. The name is incorrect, as moisture is essential for the growth and spread of the fungus. The wood is greatly weakened by the action of the fungus. Prevention of standing water in corners and pockets, and adequate ventilation, are the best defenses against dry rot; chemical treatments can be used to attack existing rot infestations.

A *collision bulkhead* is sometimes found in larger craft; it is a solid one near the bow intended to preserve flotation in case of a bow-on accident.

## Stringers, beams, and carlines

*Stringers* are longitudinal members fastened inside the hull for additional structural strength. If they run along the turn of the bilge (the turn of the hull below the waterline) they are termed *bilge stringers*. Stringers fastened inside the gunwale are referred to as *clamps*.

*Deck beams* are the athwartships members that support the deck. Their outer ends usually rest on the clamps, although a horizontal *shelf* may be used above the clamp in which case the beams rest upon this on either side.

A *carline* (also spelled *carlin* or *carling*) is a short timber running fore-and-aft between deck beams. These will be found, for example, at the port and starboard sides of any opening in the deck.

Open boats often have a *finishing piece* which runs along the gunwale, lying on the top of the *clamp* or *inwale* and covering the top edge of the planking and the heads of the frames. This is *capping*. In many boats, however, capping is omitted so that there is nothing to catch dirt and water when the boat is heeled over on its side to be emptied, instead of being bailed out. Such a boat would be said to have *open gunwales*.

## Interior details

For strengthening the hull, there are *bosom* knees, and *carling* knees, *dagger* knees and *hanging* knees, *lodging* knees, *panting* knees, *thwart* knees, and many others. The name of each is derived from its location in the boat. They are strength members used wherever two structural members meet at an angle and reinforcing is required. For example, *quarter* knees are used at each side of the transom.

A *breasthook* is a triangular reinforcing member, usually of wood but sometimes of metal, placed horizontally behind the stem of a boat to strengthen her bow.

On a boat whose stern extends beyond the end of her keel, the *horn timber* is the backbone structual member to which the after frames are fastened. One-piece timbers running the full length of the keel are often not available. In such cases, shorter pieces are bevelled and bolted together in a joint called a *scarph* (scarf); similar joints may be used elsewhere, such as in the stem. A *stopwater* is a dowel (round rod or pin) of soft wood driven into a hole drilled through the joint line of a scarph; it swells when wet and prevents water from entering.

*Sister frames* are additional frames added at a later date next to original frames that may have cracked or split. Such a frame is not fastened to the broken frame but to the planking.

*Limber holes* are passages cut into the lower edges of floors and frames next to the keel to allow bilge water to flow to the lowest point of the hull from whence it can be pumped out. These limber holes must be kept clean so that drainage to the lowest point can occur; on some larger vessels a *limber chain* is run through these holes so

## Deck terms

The sheer plank has been defined as the topmost strake of the topsides, where the sides join the deck. The *plank sheer,* on the other hand, means the outermost plank of the deck. Sometimes called a *covering board,* it covers the tops of frames and the upper edge of the sheer strake on a decked boat, just as capping does in an open boat. Covering boards are usually wider than any of the other deck planks. The center plank of a deck is the *king plank*. If a deck is arched to aid in the draining off of water, it is said to be *cambered*. Similarly, camber occurs on the tops of cabins, deckhouses, etc.

The deck over the forward part of a vessel, or the forward part of the total deck area, is termed a *foredeck*. Similarly, the *afterdeck* is located in the after part of the vessel. The deck of a cockpit or interior cabin is often called a *sole*.

## Other construction terms

*Composite construction* is the use of two or more materials in the hull of a vessel. Often this consists of wood planking over iron or steel frames.

*Sea cocks* are valves installed just inside *through-hull fittings* and ahead of the piping or hose running from the fittings. They are important safety devices. See fig. 1010.

The *boot top* is that portion of the exterior hull at the

FIG. 147 Limber holes are notches cut into frames or floor timbers where they join the keel so that bilge water can run to the lowest point to be pumped out. These must be periodically checked to make sure that they are free of any obstructions.

waterline. It is usually finished with special paint—*boot-topping*—of a color to contrast with the *anti-fouling paint* of the bottom and the paint of the topsides.

Areas that are varnished to a high gloss are termed *brightwork*. (In naval usage, this term may be applied to polished brass.) A *tack rag* is a slightly sticky cloth that is wiped over surfaces that are to be varnished just before the brush is applied in order to remove all dust and grit.

When the rudder of a boat is exactly centered, one spoke of the steering wheel should be vertical; this is the *king spoke* and is usually marked with special carving or wrapping so that it can be recognized by feel alone.

**FIG. 148** A balanced rudder has a portion of its blade surface—much less than half—forward of the axis of rotation. This design considerably reduces the force required to turn the rudder against the pressure of the passing flow of water.

A boat's rudder is said to be *balanced* when a portion of its blade area extends forward of the axis of rotation. Such a rudder is easier to turn than one that is not so designed.

Many motorboats will have a small *signal mast* from which flags can be flown—see Chapter 22. These flags are hoisted on signal halyards. When partially hoisted they are said to be *at the dip;* when fully hoisted, they are termed *two-blocked.*

## Sailboat and Sailing Terms

An *offshore* wind blows from the land; an *onshore* wind, towards it. A *weather shore* is one from which wind is blowing toward a vessel. A *lee shore* is a good one to *give a wide berth* (keep well clear of). Many use this term in the opposite, erroneous, sense, thinking that there is protection under the lee shore. But since this is the shore on the lee side of the vessel, it is the one onto which the wind is blowing, and thus it is a dangerous one. When a sailboat is caught on a lee shore and has to work her way clear, she is *clawing* off. To be *under the lee* of an island is to be on the sheltered side, the safe side in stormy weather.

Wind *veers* when it shifts by changing its direction clockwise as would be seen looking down from above the earth. It *backs* when it shifts in a counter-clockwise direc-

tion, such as going from southerly to more easterly.

On a sailboat, wind changing from abeam to further forward *hauls;* moving from abeam aft toward the stern, it *veers.*

## Measurement and classes

*One-design* class sailboats are virtually identical craft built and equipped to the same set of plans for racing. *Measurement-rule* boats are not identical, but the total effect of design variations theoretically cancel out differences in performance so that they can compete without handicaps. Other racing sailboats are individually *measured* and *rated* to determine the *time allowance* (handicap) to be used in any given competition.

## Details of sails

The forward edge of a triangular (Marconi or Bermudan) sail is its *luff;* its after edge is its *leech* (also spelled leach); and the lower edge is the *foot.* The foot is normally attached to a boom, but if it is not, or is attached only at the ends, the sail is said to be *loose-footed.*

The upper corner of such a sail is the *head;* the lower forward corner, as where the boom and the mast meet, is the *tack;* and the after lower corner, at the outer end of the boom if there is one, is the *clew.* The same terms apply to the sides and corners of all triangular fore-and-aft sails.

For four-sided (gaff-rig) sails, the term "head" is applied to the upper edge, with the upper forward corner, where the gaff and the mast meet, being the *throat;* the upper after corner, at the outer, higher end of the gaff, is the *peak.*

A *bolt rope* is often sewed into the edges of a sail to strengthen it. *Tabling* is the reinforced part of a sail to which the bolt rope is sewed. The leech of a fore-and-aft sail is usually cut with an outward curve called the *roach* of the sail. To support the roach and preserve its shape by flattening the leech, *battens* (thin flat strips of wood or plastic) are inserted in *batten pockets* in the sail along its after edge. This flattening results in a more efficient sail. A few designs use *full battens* extending across the sail from luff to leech.

Most sails are *bent* (attached or fastened) to the mast by the use of *slides* attached to the luff which ride on or in a track attached to the mast. A similar arrangement holds

**FIG. 149** The marconi style of sail is by far the most popular design for sailboats today. The major parts are labeled in the above sketch. Such sails may be made of cotton canvas or of dacron and other synthetic materials.

**FIG. 150** Gaff-rig sails are still seen but not so often as formerly. They are usually found on larger or older sailing craft. Note that the term "head" here applies to a side of the sail rather than to a corner as on the marconi rig.

Fig. 151(a). This ketch is flying a mizzen staysail between her masts in addition to mainsail, spinnaker, and fore staysail.

Fig. 151(b). Right: A spinnaker is a foresail of very light material that is full in shape, nearly spherical. It is set in light or moderate breezes that come from well astern; usually in lieu of a regular jib.

FIG. 152 The masts of some sailing craft are mounted in "tabernacles" located above the deck. These permit the mast to be easily lowered rather than unstepped for inland cruising or shipment.

the foot of the sail to the boom. Headsails are fastened to the *jibstay* (or to the *forestay*) with *snaps*.

On some small sailboats the sail is held to the mast by sliding the bolt rope of the luff up an internal groove in the mast. If gaff-rigged, *hoops* encircling the mast are used to hold the luff in place with respect to the mast.

Jibs are headsails set forward of the foremost mast, but they often *overlap* and extend aft of this mast. Large overlapping jibs are called *Genoas*, in slang terms, "gennies," and *reaching jibs* or *reachers*. In coming about, care must be taken that the clew of an overlapping jib gets around the mast without fouling so that the new tack can be assumed smoothly. Smaller, non-overlapping jibs lack the "power" of larger jibs, but these can be self-trimming when tacking; to make them so, a light spar, called a *club*, not a boom, may be attached to the foot of such a jib.

*Spinnakers* are large, three-sided sails of very light material set from booms called *spinnaker poles* on the opposite side of the main or fore boom when running before a *fair wind*.

*Staysails* are triangular jib-like sails set from the stays which support the masts, including the stays between the masts of yawls, ketches, and other multi-masted sailing craft.

*Plain sails* are the ordinary working sails, not including the lighter jibs and staysails. *Storm canvas*, on the other hand, includes jibs, staysails, and *trysails* of extra heavy material for use in strong winds.

## Masts and booms

The foot of a mast, its lower end, is called the *heel;* it fits into a *step* in the keel. Masts are often secured in place where they pass through the deck or cabin top with *mast wedges* which bear against the *mast partners* (or *mast bench),* the heavier framing around the opening, the *mast hole,* through which the mast passes. In some sailing craft, the mast ends in a *tabernacle,* a pair of side-by-side vertical

timbers, or equivalent metal fitting, on the deck or cabin top, this fitting often has a pin so that the mast is in effect hinged and can easily be lowered for passing under bridges, trailering, etc.

The topmost end of a mast is the *masthead,* often capped with a *truck,* a flat circular piece of wood. Hence the expression "from truck to keel" as including everything in a ship from top to bottom. At the masthead there will normally be a *masthead fitting,* a metal fixture for the attachment of shrouds and stays; it may also include one or more sheaves for halyards.

A *jury mast* is any spar rigged temporarily as a mast in the event that the mast itself has carried away. If such an accident occurs, the vessel is said to have been *dismasted.* A *jury rig* is any device or arrangement fashioned from available materials in an emergency as a substitute for regular gear that has broken.

The *jaws* of a gaff are the extensions of the forward end that partially encircle the mast.

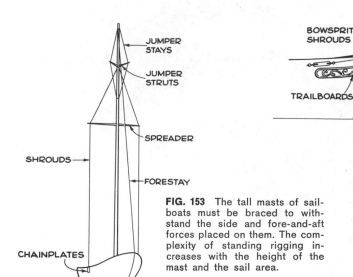

**FIG. 153** The tall masts of sailboats must be braced to withstand the side and fore-and-aft forces placed on them. The complexity of standing rigging increases with the height of the mast and the sail area.

**FIG. 154** Larger sailboats usually have a bowsprit to extend further forward the lower end of the forestay. The bowsprit in turn needs its stays and shrouds for bracing. Trailboards are merely decorative.

**FIG. 155** (a) Sail area must be reduced by "reefing" when the wind blows too hard for safety. The sail is lowered slightly and the reef points are tied around the foot of the sail, never around the boom. Many larger sails have two or more rows of reef points.

(b) Many modern jibs are reefed by rolling them up windowshade-fashion around their luff. Mainsails are roller-reefed around the boom.

## Standing and running rigging

Horizontal spars fitted on a mast to spread the shrouds for more effective bracing are called *spreaders*. *Tangs* are metal plates attached to a mast where standing rigging is to be made fast; they distribute the strain over a wider area of the mast. The lower ends of shrouds are attached to *chainplates*, metal fittings in the form of straps that extend downward on the topsides across several strakes to distribute the load.

*Jumper stays* are short stays on the forward side of a mast that come down from the masthead and back into the upper part of the mast rather than extending down to the deck. The *jumper strut* holds these stays out from the mast so that bracing action is achieved.

A *topping lift* is a portion of the running rigging used to support or hoist the outer end of a boom. A *peak halyard* is used on a gaff-rigged sailboat to hoist the peak end of the gaff and the head of the sail. A separate *throat halyard* is used to hoist the throat end of the gaff.

A *clew outhaul* is a short length of line attached to the clew of the sail which is led outward to the end of the boom, around the sheave, and back to a cleat or small winch; it is used to stretch the foot of the sail.

A *boom vang* (or *boom jack*) is a line or tackle used to hold a boom down in a more effective position when reaching or running before the wind.

*Lazy jacks* are light lines run down from the masthead to the boom on either side of a sail. Their purpose is to contain the sail when it is lowered, keeping it from spilling onto the deck or over the side, and thus making it easier to furl.

## Pin rails and fife rails

*Belaying pins* are short bars or pins, usually of wood, about which the lines of a sailboat's running rigging may be made fast. The same line is always *belayed* to the same pin for quick and easy identification at night or in an emergency. Belaying pins are mounted in *pin rails,* racks at a boat's side, usually at the shrouds, and in *fife rails* around the lower part of a mast at a handy height above deck level.

Cleats are more often used for securing sheets and halyards of modern sailing boats, but pin rails and fife rails will be found on larger and more tradition-minded vessels.

## Bowsprits and boomkins

While a mast is stayed in a vertical position, bowsprits are *guyed* horizontally (or at a slight angle) by *bowsprit shrouds* at the sides and in a vertical plane by a *bobstay*—often chain—from below. A short, downward spreader to the bobstay is a *dolphin-striker.*

A bowsprit projects forward from the stem, and on quite large sailing vessels a *jib-boom* may be rigged out beyond the bowsprit. A jib-boom is thus a fixed spar and not like the other "booms" (remember, too, a spar along the foot of a jib is not a boom either, but a "club").

Short spars sometimes project aft from the stern, particularly on yawls, where the mizzen boom overhangs the stern considerably; these are *boomkins.*

*Trailboards* are added pieces of wood on either side of the bow of a sailboat, often elaborately carved and painted or gilded. They sometimes lead forward to a *figurehead.*

## Reefing

To permit reefing a sail when the wind increases beyond a safe strength, there are usually strips of additional material, *reef bands,* sewed to the sail parallel to the foot. Short lengths of line, *reef points,* are attached at intervals along these bands; these are tied around the foot of the sail—never around the boom—to reduce the sail area.

A *reef cringle* is an eye in the leech or luff of a fore-and-aft sail in line with the reef points. *Reef earings (or pendants)* are short pieces of line spliced into the cringles to permit the latter to be secured to the boom when the sail is reefed.

Many modern sailing rigs use *roller reefing* in which the *gooseneck* fitting where the boom attaches to the mast is designed with a swivel to permit the boom to be rotated and thus roll up the foot of the sail like a window shade as the halyard is slacked off. In a few smaller rigs, the mainsail is reefed by winding it around the mast.

Jibs are sometimes roller furled around the stay upon which they are set; a single jib can have its effective area varied so widely that it will eliminate the need for carrying and setting various sizes of jibs for many different wind conditions.

## Construction details

A metal rod called a *horse* (or *deck horse* or *boom horse)* is sometimes bolted to the deck and on it the ring of a *sheet block* can travel from side to side as the boom swings over on a change of tack. This is the *traveller.* A more modern rig uses a section of metal track instead of a horse; the sheet block is attached to a *slide* or *car* that rides the track. On small boats, a wire bridle often takes the place of the metal rod type of horse or track. Often, but inaccurately, the deck fitting or wire bridle is itself called the "traveller."

FIG. 156 Many sailboats are fitted with a traveller across the deck near the stern. With this device, the trim of the mainsail on each tack can be more closely controlled. Stops may be used to limit the movement to either side of the lower block on the mainsheet.

A *tiller* is a horizontal arm extending forward from the top of the rudder or rudderstock and which is moved from side to side for steering. It is much used on sailboats as it is said to provide a better "feel" of the boat's performance than a wheel, and is also cheaper.

On small sailing craft, the rudder is often detachable from the transom or stern post. Ordinarily, the rudder is fitted with downward pointing hooks or pins, called *pintles,* which fit into metal eyes, *gudgeons,* on the hull of the boat.

A *fin keel* is one in the form of a relatively thin plate extending below the hull to give a sailboat greater *lateral resistance;* it may have a concentrated weight of metal on its lower edge for increased stability effectiveness, this is a *bulb keel.*

A *boom crutch* is an upright strut temporarily put in place to support a boom when the sails have been lowered.

Small, shallow-draft sailboats, such as sailing canoes, are sometimes equipped with *leeboards* in lieu of a center-board or daggerboard. These are a pair of flat surfaces extended over each side of the boat, normally pivoted at the top for easy lowering and raising. Only the leeward board is lowered when underway. They are also used on certain types of foreign sailing craft of considerable size.

## Sailing terms

A sailboat *carries weather helm* if she has a tendency to *head up* into the wind and the tiller must be kept to windward to hold her on course. Lee helm is the opposite with a tendency to *fall off* the wind and a need to hold the tiller to leeward. A boat with *balanced helm* shows neither of these tendencies.

Generally speaking, it is well for a sailboat to carry a small amount of weather helm. Then if the tiller is accidentally let go, the boat will *round up* into the wind, a relatively safe action, instead of falling off into what might become a dangerous jibe. Too much weather helm, however, is undesirable as the constant rudder angle creates drag and slows the boat down. The angle of rake of the mast and the trim of the boat, determined by the distribution of the weight of the crew and ballast, have much to do with what helm and how much of it the boat will carry.

A *stiff* vessel returns quickly to her normal upright position from a rolled or heeled position. If she rolls in a seaway without quick action or sudden movements, her roll is *easy.* When a boat's center of gravity is too high and stability is low, she is *tender; crank* conveys the same idea.

A skipper *fetches* a given objective if he is sailing a course to windward and reaches the mark without tacking. When working to windward, each *leg* or tack may be called a *board,* and, depending upon the length of each leg, there may be *long boards* and *short boards.*

If a sailboat attempts to come about and the bow does not fall off on the other tack, she is *caught in* (or *misses) stays,* or is said to be *in irons.* A sailboat is *pinched* when she is steered so close to the wind that the *sails shiver.* A vessel is said to *luff* when she is brought up into the wind so as to spill some of it out of the sails, thus relieving the pressure and *easing* her.

Sailing before the wind, sails are sometimes set on opposite sides of the boat; this is called *wing and wing.* A light

FIG. 157 Daysailers often have easily detachable rudders. Pintles on the rudder fit into brackets — "gudgeons" — on the transom. The boat may be more easily beached or trailered with the rudder removed.

START  OBJECTIVE

LONG AND SHORT TACKS  WIND

FIG. 158 When a sailboat's objective is more nearly upwind than the craft can sail, a series of tacks, or boards, must be used. These will be a combination of long and short legs if the objective is not directly upwind.

LATEEN SAIL  SPRIT SAIL  GUNTER RIG

LUG SAIL

FIG. 159 Minor sailing rigs are often encountered on some types of small catamarans and sailing boards. They are rarely used on conventional sailboats.

HANDLE OR GRIP   OAR   TIP
BUTTON   LEATHER   LOOM   NECK OR THROAT   BLADE

FIG. 160 Engines do fail and gas tanks do run dry! Every boatman should know at least the fundamentals of oars and rowing. Small outboards should be equipped with oars or paddles as determined by their design.

FIG. 161 Canoes are light, easily propelled craft for protected inland waters. Paddles are sometimes double-ended for convenience in solo operation.

*whisker pole* may be used to wing out the jib so that it will draw more effectively.

One boat *blankets* another when, being just to windward, she takes the wind out of the other's sails. She *outfoots* another craft by sailing faster, *outpoints* her by sailing closer to the wind.

## Minor sailing rigs

A *lateen* rig consists of a single mast and a triangular sail whose forward edge is sharply raked aft at an angle of roughly 45°. This edge is attached to a light spar, or yard, which in turn is attached to the mast, the near mid-point of the yard to the near top of the mast. A boom is used which extends forward of the mast to the lower end of the yard. This rig is widely used for small catamarans and, in modified form, for *sailboards,* small sailing craft whose hulls resemble surfboards.

A *sprit* rig is used on some dinghies and other small craft. In this type of rig the upper aft corner (peak) of the four-sided fore-and-aft sail is held aloft by a light spar known as a *sprit* inserted in an eye in the sail called a grommet. The *sprit* at its lower end is supported by a *snorter* or *becket* consisting of a light line about the mast with an eye in the lower end to take the sprit. Although the sail is four-sided, no gaff at the head or boom at the foot is required, although a boom is sometimes used with its forward end held in a becket as the sprit above it.

*Lug* rigs are of various types and their use is also confined to small craft. The *standing lug* has a yard which crosses the mast obliquely while the tack of the four-sided sail (forward lower corner) is made fast to the mast. In a *dipping lug* the tack is made fast to the stem, ahead of the mast, so that the yard must be *dipped* around the mast when tacking.

A *gunter* (or *sliding gunter*) rig uses a triangular sail whose luff is attached to a spar which is hoisted much like a gaff except that it is hoisted to a fully vertical position where it becomes an extension of the short mast. A jib may also be used.

## Rowboats and Rowing

Although this book is primarily for the skippers of motorboats and sailing craft, the well-informed boatman knows the essential facts about boats propelled by musclepower. Dinghies are often rowed, and light motorboats are at times rowed or paddled to safety when the engine fails. The technique of paddling and rowing is an art unto itself and is best learned by practice under proper instruction, but the terms involved can be made familiar here.

## Rowboats and oars

*Rowboat* is the term generally applied to a light craft propelled by one or more persons using *oars*. These are long slender wooden shafts shaped into a round *handle* (or *grip*) at one end and a flat *blade* at the other; between these ends the shaft of the oar is termed the *loom*.

The transverse seats in rowing craft are called *thwarts*. The ends of thwarts land on *risers* (or *risings*) which are fore-and-aft pieces or stringers fastened to the inside of the frames. To support the thwart, a vertical piece is often fitted amidships, called a *thwart stanchion*. *Stretchers* (also called *foot boards,* although this creates confusion with an alternate term for bottom boards) are sometimes fitted athwartships against which the *oarsman* can brace his feet.

The terms *rowlock* and *oarlock* are synonymous. These are the fittings in the gunwale which hold the oars when rowing. There are many styles of rowlocks; some open, others closed; some mounted permanently, others removable; some attached to the oars. In place of rowlocks, wooden *thole pins* are sometimes driven into holes or sockets.

Where the loom of the oar bears against the rowlock, it is often protected from excess wear by a *leather* (which may be of leather or rubber). On the side of the leather toward the handle, there may be a *button,* a ring around the oar to keep it from slipping outward through the rowlock. Where the loom becomes the blade is the *neck* (or *throat*) of the oar. The *tip* of the blade, its outer end, may be metal sheathed for protection from wear, but this is not common on oars used with light rowboats.

A man who is *sculling* would stand in the stern and propel the boat by working a single oar back and forth, using either one or two hands.

## Canoes and paddles

*Canoe* is the term applied to very lightly built open craft of narrow beam and shallow draft that are *paddled* rather than rowed; they are normally double-ended. A *paddle* is much like an oar except that it is shorter. The various parts of a paddle are named the same as for an oar. The grip is shaped differently as the paddle is used vertically rather than horizontally; the blade will normally be somewhat wider for its length in comparison with an oar.

Some paddles are *double-ended* (double-bladed) so that they may be more conveniently dipped alternately on either side of the canoe, an advantage when one person is propelling the boat rather than two.

## Documentation and Tonnage

Large ships and many commercial vessels are *documented* by the United States government (and foreign vessels by their governments). This procedure can also be used for medium and large size recreational craft. Such documentation is in lieu of *registration (numbering)* with state authorities. Before documentation can be considered, however, a discussion of "tonnage" is in order. The procedures and effects of documentation are covered in Chapter 2.

### Admeasurement and tonnage

The *tonnage* of ships and boats is determined in several different ways; it may be a measurement of either (1) weight, or (2) size without regard to weight. Persons unfamiliar with the term as it is used in connection with vessels are likely, in error, to think only of the common ton which is a measure of weight—either 2000 pounds in a short ton or 2240 pounds in a long ton. This is a part, but only a part, of the situation when ships are considered.

The determination of the "tonnage" of a vessel is called *measurement* or *admeasurement,* the latter term being found mainly in legal documents. (This measurement should not be confused with the measurement of racing sailboats for rating purposes, a quite different process.)

### Gross and net tonnage

The documentation law repeatedly refers to vessels of a certain tonnage, as for example when it states that a yacht of 5 net tons or over may be documented. *Net tons* are derived from gross tonnage which is a measurement of volume rather than weight.

FIG. 162 **Large vessels are measured in various kinds of tonnage —gross and net, displacement and register. See text for differences and how each is measured.**

*Gross tonnage* is the total enclosed space or internal capacity of a vessel, calculated in terms of "tons" of 100 cubic feet each. This was agreed upon many years ago as the average space or volume required by a ton (by weight) of general merchandise. Gross tonnage includes all spaces below the upper deck as well as permanently closed-in spaces on that deck.

*Net* (or *registered*) tonnage is a measurement of the earning power of a vessel when carrying cargo. Thus to arrive at a net tonnage figure it is necessary to deduct from the gross the volume of such spaces as would have no earning capacity or room for cargo. For example, on a ship there would be deducted the volume of the fuel compartments, engine room, crew's quarters, bridge, etc. In the case of recreational boats and yachts, deductions would mainly be for engine compartments and control stations. Many charges against vessels, such as canal tolls, harbor dues, etc., are based on net tonnage.

### Displacement and deadweight tonnage

Although not closely related to documentation or boats, a yachtsman should have some knowledge of several other forms of "tonnage" used in connection with ships.

*Displacement tonnage* is the actual weight, in tons of 2240 pounds, which a vessel displaces when floating at any given draft, such as "light" or "loaded." The displacement is calculated by figuring the volume of the vessel under the water in cubic feet and dividing by 35, as 35 cubic feet of sea water weighs one long ton.

*Deadweight tonnage* is the carrying capacity of a vessel figured by weight in terms of tons of 2240 pounds. If her displacement were calculated when the vessel was "light" (with fuel and supplies but no cargo) and again when she was loaded (with the same fuel and supplies aboard), the difference would express the deadweight tonnage.

## Miscellaneous Terms

The meaning of the word *lay* depends on its usage. One *lays aft* when he goes to the stern of the vessel. The lines of a boat are *laid down* before she is built. A boat is *laid up* when she is decommissioned for the winter in northern climates. A sailboat *lays her course* when she can make her objective without tacking. When an oarsman stops rowing, he *lays on his oars.* Referring to rope, *lay* is the direction of the twist (right or left hand) and its tightness (hard or soft).

When a vessel is hauled out of the water she is *shored up* with supports to hold her upright. If she is not supported properly, so that she is held amidships while the bow and stern settle, the boat will assume a shape that is described as *hogged.* Contrarywise, if the amidships portion of the keel is not adequately supported and droops, she is said to be *sagged.*

A vessel is said to *hail* from her home port; one *hails* another vessel at sea to get her attention, *speaks* to her when communicating with her.

The direction in which a current flows is its *set* and its velocity is its *drift.* (The amount of leeway that a vessel makes is also its drift.) *Slack* is the period of time between flood and ebb currents when there is no flow in either direction. *Stand* is the period when there is no rise or fall in the tidal level; slack and stand usually do not occur simultaneously at any given place.

FIG. 163 The lines of any craft should be protected from chafing and wear wherever they come in contact with abrasive surfaces, other lines, etc. Modern devices such as shown above may be slipped over the line, or in an emergency the line may be wrapped with old rags.

FIG. 164 A shackle permits the attachment of a line or chain to an anchor or any sort of ring. The pin of the shackle should be secured with safety wire to prevent its accidental loosening. The thimble in the eye splice prevents excessive wear on the line at a point of high stress.

A line *chafes* when it rubs on a rough surface and wears excessively. To prevent this, *chafing gear* is used; the line may be encased with plastic or rubber tubing. *Baggy-wrinkle* consists of short lengths of old line matted together and placed on shrouds, spreaders, etc. to protect sails from chafing and wearing.

A *shackle* is a roughly U-shaped metal fitting with a pin that can be inserted through a hole in one arm of the U and screwed or pinned in the other arm to close the link. Some special-purpose shackles close with a hinged *snap* or have a *swivel* built in. A *thimble* is a round or heart-shaped metal fitting with a deep outer groove around which line or wire can be eye-spliced. It protects the line from wearing on a shackle where it is joined to a chain, fastened to a deck fitting, etc.

A *fid* is a smooth, tapered pin, usually of wood, used to open up the strands of a rope for splicing.

A *waterlight* is an electric light, often automatically operated, that is attached to a life ring with a short length of line. It is intended for use in man-overboard accidents at night.

The term "charter" has usage both as a verb and a noun. *To charter* a craft is to lease her from the owner for a temporary period of time. She may be chartered on a *bare boat* basis, without crew, or as a *time charter* with crew. The contract covering the use of the boat is termed the *charter*.

Ships and large vessels may have compartments below deck used solely for carrying cargo, these are *holds*. The hatch giving access through the deck to such a hold is covered over with canvas and *battened down* with wooden strips around the edges *(battens)* to secure it against storms and water across the deck. The same term is used for the general securing of a boat against adverse weather conditions.

Another vessel is said to be seen *hull down* when she is at such a distance that her superstructure and/or masts are visible but the hull is not seen due to the curvature of the earth.

*Flotsam* is material floating on the surface of the water after a vessel has broken up and sunk. Larger pieces may be dangerous to the hull or shaft and propeller of small craft. *Jetsam* consists of items of equipment or cargo that have been deliberately *jettisoned* (thrown overboard) to lighten a vessel endangered by heavy seas.

A *bollard* is a heavy single or double post set into the edge of a wharf or pier to which the lines of a ship may be made fast.

FIG. 165 Ocean cruising, and particularly ocean racing, sailboats usually are fitted with a horseshoe type of life preserver mounted aft near the helmsman's position so that it can be quickly thrown to a man overboard. For nighttime use, an automatic waterlight is attached to the life preserver.

FIG. 166 Bollards are massive metal fittings placed along wharves and piers to which the heavy lines of large vessels are made fast.

*Cavitation* occurs when a high-speed propeller loses its "bite" on the water, creating a partial vacuum, loss of thrust, and excessive shaft speed; continued cavitation can result in blade wear. On outboard motors where the propeller is relatively near the surface of the water and aft of the transom, there may be a *cavitation plate* mounted above the propeller to deflect downward the water discharge from the blades—a more correct term might be "anti-cavitation plate" but this is not used.

If the galley stove is of the type that requires its own vent above deck, the pipe for this is sometimes referred to as a *Charlie Noble*.

A boat is *ship-shape* when everything is in good order;

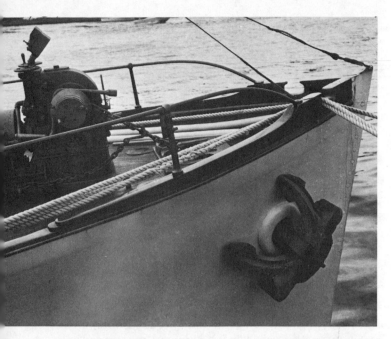

**FIG. 167** The anchors for large yachts and ships become too heavy to be hoisted on deck. They are drawn up into hawse pipes with power-operated winches.

*well-found* when it is well equipped. *Bristol*-fashion is a term used to describe an especially well-cared-for vessel. One *swabs* (or *swabs down*) the deck when he washes it down with a mop, called a *swab* in nautical language.

A task aboard a boat—such as lowering the dinghy—is done *handsomely* when it is done slowly and carefully. To do something *smartly* is to do it in a quick and lively manner.

The term *gangway* is applied both to the area of a ship's side where people *come aboard (board)* and *disembark*, and to the temporary ramp or platform used between the vessel and the wharf or pier. In the latter case, the terms *gangplank* and *brow* are also used.

A *windlass* is a particular form of winch with its *drum* on which the line is wrapped turning on a horizontal axis. If the drum's axis is vertical, the device may be called a *capstan*.

When an anchor line or chain is brought through the topsides rather than over the rail, it enters through a *hawse hole* and runs upward through a *hawse pipe*. An *anchor chock* is a fitting for holding an anchor securely on a deck.

Small boats, such as dinghies and runabouts, are hoisted aboard larger craft by *davits*, mechanical arms extending over the side or stern, or which can be swung over the side, plus the necessary lines and blocks.

When subjected to heavy strains in working her way through high seas, a vessel is said to *labor*. If she takes the large waves easily, she is said to be *sea kindly*. A boat that takes head seas heavily and comes down hard on successive waves is said to *pound*; this is more likely to occur with a hard-chined hull. If she takes little spray aboard when running into a choppy sea, she is termed *dry*.

To *flemish down* a line is to secure it on deck in a tight, flat coil roughly resembling a mat. When a line is laid down in loose, looping figure-eights it is said to be *faked* (or *flaked*) *down*; each loop is a *fake*, see pages 227-228.

To *put* is to take action, as to *put about, put into port,* etc.

A boat is said to be *off-soundings* when she is so far out from the shore *(offshore)* that depths *(soundings)* cannot be conveniently measured nor are used in navigation; this is commonly taken as the 100-fathom line. Contrary-wise, a boat is *on-soundings* when she is within this line.

*Admiralty law* is the body of law pertaining to ships and to navigation and commerce on the seas.

## Pollution Control Systems

Boatmen on almost all waters have been faced with a rising tide of water pollution control laws. State and local regulations have varied widely as to the restrictions imposed and the type of device, if any, that will be accepted. A federal law has been enacted but is not yet effective. The designs of *marine sanitation devices* that will be "certified" under this Act have not been announced, but will undoubtedly be drawn from those described below.

The *macerator-chlorinator* device takes the discharge of a marine toilet, grinds up all solids to very fine particles, and treats the resultant waste with a disinfectant to reduce the bacteria to a safe count. This chemical is usually a chlorine compound which may be introduced either as a liquid (such as the household bleach, sodium hypochlorate, bought as "Clorox" or the equivalent), or in tablet form. The mixture of waste and treatment chemical is retained in a small tank until the next time the "head" is used, at which time it is pumped overboard and a fresh batch is taken in from the toilet. These units may be added to an existing toilet, or may be installed as a complete, self-contained device.

*Holding tanks* are simply what their name says, additional tanks installed on a boat to take the waste fluids

**FIG. 168** Dinghies and small speedboats may be hoisted to the upper decks of large yachts with hand or power operated davits. On smaller yachts, dinghies are often carried on stern davits.

**FIG. 169 Marine sanitation devices are coming into widespread use aboard all types of boats large enough to have one or more installed toilets. A number of different designs are available, but not all are acceptable on specific bodies of water.**

and solids from the toilet and retain them temporarily. Some models provide the option of overboard discharge—for use when in waters where this is permitted—as well as pumping-out to a shore facility, but many states withhold approval of a system that would allow overboard discharge. Tanks are available in various sizes such as 10 and 20 gallons which will permit a few days' use of the head (with restraint!) before pump-out is necessary. A chemical is usually added to the tank for partial disinfecting action and to deodorize the contents. A vent over the side is required.

*Self-contained toilets* are closely related to holding tanks. These devices are "charged" with a few gallons of water and special chemicals. The internal mechanism re-circulates this treated water plus the wastes that are added each time the head is used. The toilet can be used a number of times over a period of several days before pump-out is required. This is the type of facility used on modern airliners.

*Incinerators* dry liquid wastes pumped into them from marine toilets and reduce the resultant solids to ash. This final product is of low volume and need be removed only at infrequent intervals, roughly monthly. Heat is obtained from either bottled LP gas or electricity.

## But Don't Overdo It!

There is literally no end to the list of boating terms that could be included here, but practical limitations of space must prevail. What has been covered in this chapter will serve as a framework for the remainder of the book. As the boatman gains experience in this form of recreation, his vocabulary will broaden proportionately and naturally.

It is to be hoped, however, that his enthusiasm for boating will not cause him to toss indiscriminate Avasts, Ahoys, and Belays into every conceivable nook and corner of his conversation. The natural, proper use of correct terms is much to be desired; strained efforts to effect a salty lingo are conspicuously inappropriate.

# CHAPTER 2

# BOATING LAWS and REGULATIONS

**FIG. 201   All boating, commercial and recreational, is subject to certain laws and regulations for the safety of the craft involved and all on board. Federal rules are often supplemented by state and local requirements and restrictions.**

Although boating is certainly not an inherently unsafe form of recreation, there are dangers and hazards for ignorant and careless individuals. To protect such persons, and "innocent bystanders," too, there has arisen a body of federal, state, and local laws and regulations. The basic intent of such restrictions is the safety of persons and property; to a much lesser degree do such factors enter as registration and taxation.

Boating laws and regulations can be roughly divided into two major categories. The first subdivision includes those that relate to the craft and its equipment; the second group covers the operator of the boat and his use of it. Formerly, the first category was greatly predominant, but in recent years regulations regarding boat operation have expanded rapidly.

## Comparison of boating and motor vehicle laws

A quick comparison may be made between recreational boating and the field of ownership and operation of automobiles, an activity so much a part of our everyday lives. Here the trend has been rather in the reverse direction. Some years ago motor vehicle laws focused almost entirely on operational matters such as driving and parking, with a minimum of attention to details of equipment. In more recent times we have seen a considerable push

toward legislated standards for safety equipment and design features. The obvious comparisons can be drawn in such areas as the requirements for headlights and turn signals on cars with the need for navigation lights on boats; and the necessity for both types of vehicles to observe rules as to relative right-of-way in congested areas. The principal point of difference at the present time is the lack of any requirement for an operator license or permit for the noncommercial skipper; the duration of this difference is a matter of some doubt. Some states are now requiring operator licenses on wholly inland bodies of water, but as yet there is no overall federal requirement.

In both boating and automobile operation the goals are essentially the same—the prevention of accidents insofar as possible, and the minimization of death and injury in those that regrettably do occur. Restrictive laws and regulations are irksome to all of us, but they should be known, understood, and accepted as proper guidance for our self-protection and the protection of others' lives and property.

## Registration and numbering

A third category of boating laws and regulations includes those relating to registration and assignment of identification numbers to craft. This may perhaps be considered a minor category as compared with rules for safety

FIG. 202 Water traffic must be subject to "Rules of the Road" which prescribe relative right-of-way between boats encountering each other. They are especially important in congested waters.

as they can be navigated continuously from the sea, often a considerable distance for such great waterways as the Mississippi, Missouri, Ohio, and Tennessee Rivers.

A second type of body of water subject to federal jurisdiction is any that overlaps or separates two or more states, even though not connected with the ocean. Inland rivers and lakes often fall into this category which is based on the fact that one can travel by water from one state to another; this is "interstate commerce" and subject to regulation by the U.S. Congress. A typical example is Lake Mead that borders both Nevada and Arizona. A third qualification places waters under federal jurisdiction if they can be used for travel to or from a foreign nation.

equipment and boat operation, but still these must be known and obeyed.

Again a close comparison can be drawn with motor vehicles, although in the case of boats it is probable that regulation is rather more related to taxation and revenue-raising than it is to identification—not many watercraft get "tickets" for overtime parking. The regulations relating to numbering must be followed by boatmen even though they have little to do with his safety or that of others.

## FEDERAL VS. STATE JURISDICTION

This book will concentrate on federal laws and regulations relating to boating rather than state and local ordinances, rules, etc., due to the obviously wider applicability of the former. State and municipal regulations will be touched upon later in this chapter, but only in broad terms because of the wide variations between different jurisdictions. Each conscientious boatman must individually familiarize himself with the local requirements and restrictions for the waters that he uses.

### Limits of federal jurisdiction

"Navigable waters of the United States"—where federal law prevails—are defined in broad terms by law and are specifically delineated by Coast Guard regulations. These include waters off the beaches along the coast and all bodies of water open to the sea or connected to the open sea by navigable rivers and channels. Typical of this category are all harbors and bays as well as major rivers as far

FIG. 204 The construction of dams, and locks for the passage of vessels around them, have extended far inland the limits of navigable waters subject to Federal jurisdiction. These limits are set forth in official publications.

The construction of a dam does not change the navigable status of a river. In fact, the building of a dam and lock system may serve to extend the river's navigability. The Coast Guard makes determinations of the bodies of water that do or do not fall under federal jurisdiction; such rulings are subject to challenge in Federal courts. The determinations will be found in Part 2 of Title 33, Code of Federal Regulations; changes are published in the daily Federal Register.

An understanding of federal jurisdiction over navigable waters is essential for all boatmen, especially those far from the coasts of our nation. Federal jurisdiction means the

FIG. 203 Boats entering inland waters through an inlet from the open ocean will pass from one set of Rules of the Road to another. Skippers must know both sets of rules and be alert for the change.

applicability of federal laws and regulations, aids to navigation by the Coast Guard, and charting by the Coast & Geodetic Survey or Army Corps of Engineers. It does *not* deprive state and local authorities of their rights to regulate certain aspects of the use of the waters that are *not in conflict* with an applicable federal law or regulation; local rules might relate to speed limits, restrictions on water skiing, etc. Many state boating laws also require safety equipment on boats in excess of that called for by Acts of Congress and Coast Guard Regulations.

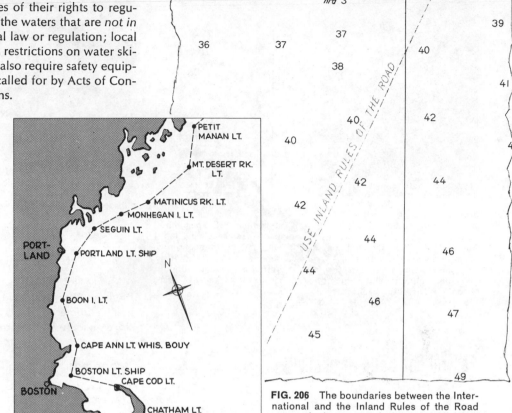

**FIG. 205** At the entrances to major rivers, harbors, bays, etc., and along some, but not all, stretches of shoreline, there have been established boundaries to mark the transition from International to Inland Rules of the Road. These boundaries are defined in terms of geographic features and aids to navigation.

**FIG. 206** The boundaries between the International and the Inland Rules of the Road are marked on coastal charts by a broken magenta line appropriately labeled.

## "INLAND" WATERS DEFINED

Within the areas subject to the jurisdiction of the federal government there is a sub-category known as "inland waters." By an Act of Congress of 1895, with subsequent amendments, authority was established for the prescribing of boundary lines dividing the "high seas" from rivers, bays, sounds, harbors, etc. These boundaries are of primary importance in connection with the Rules of the Road as will be discussed in Chapters 4 and 5.

Federal waters inshore of these boundary lines are subject to the Inland Rules of the Road and the Inland Pilot Rules, except for certain interior areas where other laws and regulations known as the Great Lakes Rules and the Western Rivers Rules are in effect. Offshore of the boundary lines, the International Rules of the Road (the full name of which is the International Regulations for the Prevention of Collision at Sea) are effective. It should be noted that the International Rules have been adopted by the United States and are legally applicable to all vessels in U.S. national waters *within* the three-mile limit of national sovereignty, as well as to U.S. vessels on the high seas.

### Delineation of boundary lines

The International-Inland boundary lines are drawn at all major entrances to harbors, rivers, bays, etc., roughly paral-

lel with the general trend of the shoreline. The lines are established with respect to aids to navigation—lighthouses, lightships, buoys—for ease of identification; see fig. 205. Boatmen in waters where such boundaries exist should be familiar with them. Boundary lines are printed in various government publications—such as the Rules of the Road, International-Inland, CG-169; see fig. 1708—and are printed on applicable charts, fig. 206. As a result of their being defined in terms of such objects as buoys, boundary lines between the Inland and International Rules are subject to change as these aids to navigation may be relocated or changed. Such modifications to the boundaries are published in the daily Federal Register available at many libraries.

Formal boundary lines are established only at major harbor and other entrances, or where there are a series of offshore islands such as along the Maine coast and the Florida Keys; this procedure is not applied to the islands off the southern California coast. At other buoyed entrances from seaward for which official boundary lines have not been established, the waters inshore of a line approximately parallel with the general trend of the shore, drawn through the outermost buoy or other aid to navigation, are considered "inland" waters. Along relatively open straight stretches of the coast, the International Rules are applicable right up to the shore except for minor coves and other indentations.

31

# Boating Laws & Regulations / CHAPTER 2

FIG. 209 Boats are divided into "classes" by the Motorboat Act of 1940. Shown above is a Class 1 craft. Smaller boats, those under 16 feet in length, are Class A; those 26 feet or more in length are in Classes 2 and 3, with 40 feet length being the dividing line.

FIG. 207 Coast Guard Publication CG-258 contains the full text of regulations implementing the Motorboat Act of 1940. The language may be somewhat legalistic and complex, but it is the official word. Changes are published in the Federal Register between editions of the basic pamphlet.

FIG. 208 This small and convenient USCG pamphlet summarizes in simple language the basic federal requirements for recreational craft. It is available without charge from most Coast Guard offices.

## Federal Laws and Regulations

Recreational boating—and commercial boating and shipping, too—is subject to "laws" and "regulations." The former consist of Acts of Congress and provide basic policies and rules upon which more specific and detailed regulations may be promulgated. Regulations have the advantage of greater flexibility, being more easily created, modified, or revoked than laws which are subject to the full legislative process for any changes.

### Coast Guard regulations

Most federal boating regulations are issued by the United States Coast Guard under authority given by Congress to the "Secretary of the Department in which the Coast Guard is operating." This rather cumbersome wording is necessary as federal laws make possible the transfer of this armed service from its normal peacetime Department (now Transportation, but formerly Treasury until 1967) to its wartime Department (Navy). The authority given by Congress to the Departmental Secretary is, in most instances, routinely delegated to the Commandant of the Coast Guard.

Coast Guard regulations cover a wide variety of matters including boat equipment and operation, lights for special-purpose vessels, aids to navigation, inland water boundary lines as mentioned above, and many other topics.

### Other regulatory agencies

Boatmen on some waters will also be affected by regulations issued by other federal agencies such as the Corps of Engineers, U.S. Army; and the National Park Service. The operation of radio and radar transmitters on boats on all waters is subject to the rules and regulations of the Federal Communications Commission as explained in Chapter 25.

## MOTORBOAT ACT OF 1940

The Motorboat Act of 25 April 1940 (MBA) is currently the basic law applicable to recreational small craft and to many commercial craft. It has been amended several times since enactment, but not in any major aspect. The full text of the Act will be found on pages 612 and 613.

### Scope and applicability

As used in the MBA, the term "motorboat" includes every vessel propelled by machinery that is 65 feet in length or less, except tugboats and towboats propelled by steam. Note that other types of steam-propelled craft within the length limitation *are* considered to be motorboats. The term includes all boats permanently or *temporarily* equipped with a detachable motor. (Vessels *more than 65 feet* in length, propelled by machinery other than steam, are termed "motor vessels" by the Coast Guard; these are not considered in this chapter.)

A sailboat without mechanical power does not come within the definition of a motorboat as quoted above, but is subject to some of the provisions of the Motorboat Act such as Section 13 relating to negligent or reckless operation. A vessel with *no* means of propulsion is termed a "barge" in Coast Guard regulations.

The Motorboat Act is applicable on the navigable waters of the United States, its Territories, and the District of Columbia, including Puerto Rico, the Virgin Islands, and Guam.

It is important to note that the Motorboat Act *also* applies to every motorboat owned in a State (including the other areas mentioned above) *and used on the high seas,* this including waters offshore and beyond the normal three-mile limit of jurisdictional authority.

### Classes of motorboats

For the purpose of applying graduated requirements for equipment as the size of the craft increases, the MBA divides all motorboats into four "classes" based on length. This is "overall length" as measured in a straight line parallel to the keel from the foremost part of the craft to the aftermost part, excluding sheer and excluding bowsprits, boomkins, rudders aft of the transom, outboard motor brackets, and generally similar fittings.

**Class A**—Motorboats less than 16 feet in length
**Class 1**—16 feet and over, but less than 26 feet in length
**Class 2**—26 feet and over, but less than 40 feet in length
**Class 3**—40 feet and over, but not more than 65 feet

## Required equipment

The Motorboat Act contains many provisions for required equipment including life preservers, fire extinguishers, whistles, bells, and other items. Because of the importance of these items, they are covered separately in Chapter 3, which is devoted entirely to equipment. The MBA also prescribes navigation lights for motorboats, but as these are also included in the Rules of the Road, they are considered separately in Chapter 4, Navigation Lights and Day Shapes.

## Civil penalties

If any motorboat or other vessel subject to the Motorboat Act is operated or navigated in violation of the Act or any regulation issued under its authority, the owner or operator—either one or both—may be subjected to a penalty of $100 in addition to any other penalty prescribed by law.

For boats carrying passengers for hire, the above penalty is doubled for violations relating to life preservers, fire extinguishers, or licensed operators.

These are "civil penalties" that may be imposed administratively at an appropriate level of Coast Guard authority *without* formal arrest and conviction in Federal court. Their existence makes possible the imposition of penalties for minor violations without the lengthy, complex, and expensive proceedings of a criminal trial. Proper safeguards have been established for appeals to higher authority and for mitigation or remission of the fine.

For any such civil penalty, the motorboat or vessel itself is liable and may be proceeded against in Federal District Court wherever the motorboat or vessel may be found.

## Negligent Operation

The Motorboat Act of 1940 as amended in 1958 clearly states that "no person shall operate any motorboat or any vessel in a reckless or negligent manner so as to endanger the life, limb, or property of any person." The term "operate" means to navigate or otherwise use the boat, and

FIG. 211 Boating accidents must be reported if they involve more than specified levels of damage or personal injury. This is true whether one or more craft are concerned. In many areas, reports are made to state authorities rather than the Coast Guard.

"any person" includes the operator himself so that danger to another person is not necessary for the use of the boat to fall within the scope of reckless or negligent operation.

## Penalties

In addition to being liable for civil penalties as previously discussed, the Motorboat Act provides that any person who operates a motorboat in the manner defined above as reckless or negligent is guilty of a misdemeanor and may be taken into any court of competent jurisdiction for trial. Upon conviction, the penalty may be a fine not exceeding $2,000, imprisonment for not more than one year, or both, at the discretion of the court.

## Boating Accidents

Sometimes, despite the best of care, boating accidents of one kind or another do occur. They may involve only a single craft, or two or more vessels may be concerned. In any case, there are obligations imposed on the skippers at the scene and afterwards.

## Duties in case of accident

In the case of collision, accident, or other casualty involving a motorboat or other vessel subject to the MBA, it is the duty of the operator, if and so far as he can do so without serious danger to his own vessel or persons aboard, to render such assistance as may be necessary and practicable to other persons affected by the incident in order to save them from danger as a result thereof. The operator must also give his name and address, and the identification of his vessel, to any person injured and to the owner of any property damaged.

The duties prescribed above for the operator of a vessel are applicable whether or not the incident was the result of apparent negligence. They are also in addition to any other duties provided by law.

FIG. 210 Sailboats without any mechanical power need not meet the equipment requirements of the Motorboat Act, but are subject to its prohibitions on reckless or negligent operation and the penalties of the Act for such violations.

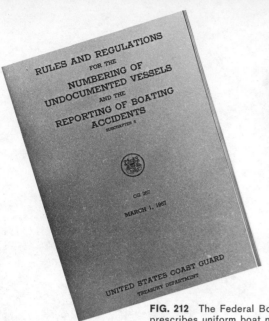

FIG. 212 The Federal Boating Act of 1958 prescribes uniform boat numbering and accident reporting systems for state use. The Act and its implementing regulations are in the free Coast Guard pamphlet CG-267.

U.S. Coast Guard Photo

FIG. 213 In addition to their frequent rescue missions, Coast Guard patrol craft have enforcement powers for the Motorboat Act and other federal boating regulations. They are always clearly marked, fly the Coast Guard Ensign, and are manned by uniformed personnel.

## Accident reporting

In the case of collision, accident, or other casualty involving a motorboat or other vessel subject to the MBA, the operator of the craft must make a report under certain circumstances. A report is required if the incident results in death, or injury causing any person to remain incapacitated for a period in excess of 72 hours, or actual physical damage to property (including vessels) in excess of $100.

Whenever death results from a boating accident, a written report must be submitted within 48 hours. For all other reportable boating accidents, a written report must be submitted within five days after occurrence of the incident.

Most state boating laws require that reports of boating accidents be made to a designated state office or official. If, however, there is no state provision for reporting such incidents, a report must be made to the Coast Guard Officer in Charge, Marine Inspection, nearest to the place where the accident occurred.

The Coast Guard regulations on boating accidents reporting (see page 620) enumerate the information that must be furnished. The Boating Accident Report Form—CG-3865—may be used in reports to the Coast Guard. States normally use this form or one of their own patterned after it.

## Enforcement Authority

Any officer of the United States authorized to enforce the navigation laws of the U.S. has the power and authority to swear out process warrants and to arrest and take into custody, with or without process, any person who violates the provisions of law and regulations relating to reckless or negligent operation. Legal safeguards are provided for the protection of individuals accused of such offenses.

Federal boating regulations in general are enforced by the Coast Guard. USCG boarding vessels are identified by the Coast Guard ensign (see page Z) and uniformed personnel. A vessel underway upon being hailed by a Coast Guard vessel or patrol boat is required to stop immediately and lay to, or to maneuver in such a way as to permit the boarding officer to come aboard. Failure to

stop to permit boarding may subject the operator to a penalty of $100 in addition to any other penalties for other violations.

Many state and local governmental units have navigational ordinances and regulations backed up with patrol boats. Skippers should be alert for posted signs or regulatory buoys indicating speed limits, "no wake," etc., and should stop immediately upon being hailed by any official craft.

Many law-enforcement vessels—Coast Guard and state or local—are now equipped with a characteristic blue revolving light like those seen on police cars in many areas; see page 64(n) and Fig. 430.

## FEDERAL BOATING ACT OF 1958

The preamble of the Federal Boating Act of 1958 (FBA) includes the phrase "to promote boating safety," but its major provisions relate to the establishment of the current system of boat registration and numbering. It also contains provisions making changes in the Motorboat Act of 1940 (these have been included in the preceding section) and establishing a system of boating accident reporting and statistics.

The full text of the Act, as amended, will be found on pages 614 and 615. As usual with such laws, authority is granted to the Secretary of the Department in which the

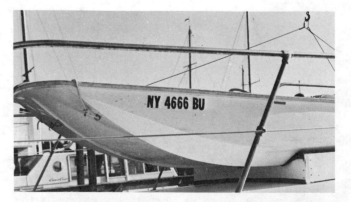

FIG. 214 Although the Federal Boating Act of 1958 only requires the registration of boats with motors of 10 or more horsepower, many states have extended the requirement to lesser limits or to all watercraft. For example, New York requires numbers on this dinghy carried aboard a yacht regardless of the size of motor attached.

Coast Guard is operating to issue detailed regulations to implement and enforce the Act, with such authority typically being delegated by the Secretary to the Commandant of the Coast Guard. Regulations derived from the FBA will be found on pages 617 to 618.

## Statement of Congressional policy

An important aspect of the Federal Boating Act is its explicit statement that it is the policy of Congress to encourage uniformity of boating laws, rules, and regulations among the several States and the Federal Government to the fullest extent practicable, subject to reasonable exceptions arising out of local conditions. It is also stated in the Act that it is Congressional policy to encourage the highest degree of reciprocity among the several jurisdictions. Agreements are authorized between the Federal Government and other jurisdictions for the fullest possible cooperation in the enforcement of both State and Federal laws, rules, and regulations relating to recreational boating.

## Registration and Numbering

The Federal Boating Act establishes a system of boat registration and numbering that is uniform throughout the United States and its Territories although the actual process of issuing certificates and number assignments may be done individually by the States. As of late 1969, all but three states had elected to assume this function within their jurisdiction; in the states of Alaska, New Hampshire, Washington, and in the District of Columbia and Guam, the registration process is carried out by the Coast Guard.

The FBA establishes broad standards for the numbering of vessels and provides for the issuance of more detailed and specific regulations by the Secretary of the Department in which the Coast Guard is·operating. The individual States prepare their boat registration laws and regulations in accordance with the Federal standards and then submit them to the Secretary for approval. The Act provides for the withdrawal of approval if the State does not administer its system in accordance with the Federal requirements. In the rather unlikely event of this occurring, the Coast Guard would take over the numbering function.

Several states have attempted to withhold certificates of boat numbers until proof was presented of payment of property or other taxes or of compliance with anti-pollution requirements. The Coast Guard has rules that such actions are *not* permissible as the Federal Boating Act of 1958 permits states to register craft solely for identification and safety purposes. Warnings have been issued that the Coast Guard might revoke the approval of a state's numbering program if it persisted in its efforts to attach unrelated and illegal conditions to the award of numbering certificates.

## Boats subject to the FBA

All watercraft, other than seaplanes on the water, which use the waters of the United States, the Commonwealth of Puerto Rico, the Virgin Islands, Guam and the District of Columbia are subject to the Federal Boating Act, with certain specified exceptions discussed in the subsection below.

Also subject to the Act are vessels used on the high seas but owned in a State or other jurisdiction named above.

FIG. 215 A boat must be registered in, and receive its numbers from, "the state of principal use" even though this is not the owner's state of residence nor where the boat is stored on a trailer and out of the water for more days than it is used in the water.

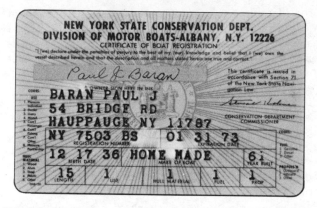

FIG. 216 The assignment of identification numbers issued by the Coast Guard is made on a "Certificate of Number" which must be on board whenever the craft is in use. State numbering authorities issue a generally similar registration card.

## Limitations on applicability

The numbering provisions of the FBA, and the state systems established under its authority, do not apply to vessels which are "documented" (see pages 41-44).

Also excluded under the basic provisions of the Federal Act are boats propelled by machinery of 10 horsepower or less. (A number of states, however, have required the numbering of all craft or those of lesser horsepower; this is permissible as it includes all boats subject to the federal requirements.) The "machinery" mentioned above need not be the principal source of propulsion.

"Horsepower" is that normally rated by the manufacturer at maximum RPM as taken from the engine's nameplate or instruction book; it is the total of all engines if there are more than one. In any dispute over horsepower, the responsibility lies with the owner to prove his claimed value of actual horsepower.

Other exceptions include foreign vessels; those owned by the United States, states, and municipalities; ship's lifeboats; and other craft specifically exempted by the Secretary. Dinghies, tenders, etc., carried aboard a vessel for other than lifesaving purposes are *not* excluded. By regulation, undocumented boats used exclusively for racing and those operated under valid temporary certificates are exempted from the general provisions of numbering.

## "State of principal use"

It is important to note that the FBA makes it mandatory for the owner of a boat subject to the Act to secure a number "in the State in which it is principally used." This has been interpreted literally—where the boat is most used on the water, not the state of residence of the owner nor the state in which the boat might set on land on a trailer for a far greater proportion of the time. In this application, "used" is interpreted as meaning the time that the vessel is "on" the navigable waters of the United States whether in motion, at anchor, or moored.

When a vessel is used principally on the high seas, it should be numbered in the State in which it is usually docked, moored, housed, or garaged.

## Certificate of number

The identification number issued for a vessel is shown on a *Certificate of Number*. This Certificate must be on board whenever the vessel is in operation. The FBA specifies that the Certificate of Number must be of "pocket size."

A Certificate of Number *issued by the Coast Guard* is valid for three years from the date of the owner's birthday next occurring after the date that the Certificate is issued, unless sooner surrendered or cancelled. Certificates issued by States may be valid for a period not exceeding three years; many states are issuing registrations for lesser periods. All certificates may, of course, be renewed at or prior to their expiration date.

## Numbering systems

The specific details of the numbering of boats under the Federal Boating Act of 1958 are covered in regulations issued by the Commandant of the Coast Guard.

The number pattern is divided into two parts. The first part consists of a two-letter symbol identifying the state of principal use. This is followed by a second part consisting of a combination of numerals and letters for individual vessel identification. The list of state designators appears on page 620.

It should be noted that the set of two-letter abbreviations adopted by the Post Office Department for use with its automated Zip-coded addressing system is *not* consistent with the state designators for boat numbers. For example, Mississippi is "MS" to post offices, but these letters on a boat mean Massachusetts (which is "MA" to Mr. Zip!). Likewise, a Mississippi boat is marked "MI" but these mean Michigan to a mailman. An entirely unnecessary source of confusion from two Federal agencies!

The individual vessel's identification consists of not more than four arabic numerals and two capital letters, *or* not more than three such numerals and three such letters. The group of digits appearing between the two sets of letters in the total number *must be separated* from those letters by hyphens or spaces. The hyphen or blank space must be equal to the width of any letter other than "I" or any numeral except "1." (This matter of spacing is by far the most commonly observed violation of boating regulations;

**MI 2345 AB**

OR

**MI-2345-AB**

CORRECT

**MI2345AB**

INCORRECT

**FIG. 217** Undoubtedly the most widespread violation of boating regulations is the faulty application of numbers. There must be either a space or a hyphen (dash) before and after the block of numerals to set them off from the letters that precede and follow them. In some areas, as much as a majority of boats will be seen with the letters and numerals run together.

*ME 456 R*

AND

*ME 456 R*

INCORRECT

**ME 456 R**

CORRECT

**FIG. 218** The regulations that implement the Federal Boating Act of 1958 specify "block letters in good proportion." This phrase has been officially interpreted to mean vertical characters of plain style— script, slanting, or other "fancy" style characters are not acceptable.

the required space is all-too-often omitted; see fig. 217.)

Since the letters "I," "O" and "Q" may be mistaken for the arabic numerals one and zero, these three letters are not used as part of individual boat identifications. The regulations also prohibit use of two or three letter combinations that form "objectionable" words.

The Coast Guard regulations (46 CFR 171.05-1) specify that the state identification letters shall be "followed by a combination of numerals and letters" for individual vessel identification. It is interesting to note that despite this clearly-stated requirement at least one state—Massachusetts—issues some boat numbers without letters following the numerals.

## Size and style of numbers

The FBA regulations require that boat numbers provide good legibility and contain certain specifications as to their style and size. The letters and numerals must be in "block characters of good proportion not less than three inches in height." The characters must be of vertical style; not slanting, not script. It is preferred that they be plain, without border, trim, outlining or shading. If any border, trim, etc. is used, it is *not* counted in determining the three-inch height minimum. The letters and numerals must be of *one* color only, exclusive of any border, trim, etc.

## Contrast

Numbers must provide good contrast with their background—black on white or white on black best meets this requirement.

A backing or mounting plate may be used. If so, it must be of sufficient size to provide good contrast, and thus good legibility, for the numbers without regard to the hull. By itself, the use of a border, trim, etc., around a letter will not meet the contrast requirements.

## Display of numbers

The identification number must be painted on, or attached to, either side of the forward half of the vessel, and

FIG. 219  A common misconception is that the numbers must be on the "bow" of a boat. The legal requirement is that they must be on the "forward half of the vessel" and actually they should be sufficiently aft from the stem to ensure ease of readability despite any pronounced flare of the forward hull.

FIG. 221  When a boat is taken from one state to another, Federal law requires that the new state of use grant at least 90 days recognition to the existing registration and numbers. This is of great value to skippers who may trailer their craft to distant vacation areas.

no other number may be displayed there. In most cases the numbers are quite near the bow, but since they have only to be displayed on the "forward half" of the boat, it is frequently desirable in the case of boats with considerable flare to their bows to place the numbers well aft from the stem so that they will be on a more nearly vertical surface and so will be more easily seen and read.

Numbers are placed on a boat so as to read normally from left to right on both sides of the bow. They may be on the hull, or on a permanent superstructure.

Identification numbers must be maintained properly to ensure legibility at all times.

Names or insignia may be displayed on the bow of a boat, but only in such a manner that they will not detract from the legibility of the official numbers.

## Special numbers

The Coast Guard regulations relating to the numbering of boats make special provisions for "livery" (rental) boats, and for manufacturers' and dealers' boats; see page 620.

Manufacturer or dealer numbers may be printed on or attached to removable signs which are temporarily attached to the boat being demonstrated, transported, or tested.

## Application for numbers

The addresses of State and other authorities to whom application for a Certificate of Number must be made are listed on page 616.

The same numbers are assigned by a regular renewal Certificate. If not renewed within one year after expiration, the number will be voided and a new number assigned.

FIG. 220  In all but a very few jurisdictions, application must be made to state authorities for boat registration and assignment of numbers. The appropriate state agencies and their addresses are listed on page 621.

Upon sale or transfer of ownership, where the vessel continues with the same state of principal use, the old number stays with the craft and is assigned to the new owner.

Numbers may not be transferred from one boat to another, except for special dealers' and manufacturers' numbers issued for demonstrating, transporting, or testing boats.

## Fees

For Certificates of Number issued by the Coast Guard the fee is $6 for original numbering and for each renewal. For the reissue of a lost or destroyed Certificate the fee is $1.

Under the FBA, the States set their own fees to be charged for the registration and numbering of boats. The fees vary widely from state to state—in some jurisdictions, these merely cover the cost of administering the numbering program; in others, they are used as sources of revenue for the state.

## Reciprocity

The Federal Boating Act provides that each state shall recognize the validity of a Certificate of Number issued by another state under the provisions of the Act, or a number issued by the Coast Guard, for a period of at least 90 days. This is of considerable advantage to boatmen who may cruise or trail their craft to other state waters for vacation periods.

After the expiration of the established reciprocity period, the boat must, of course, be re-numbered in the new state of principal use.

## Notification of changes

Coast Guard regulations require, with respect to numbers issued by them, that whenever a vessel is lost, destroyed, abandoned, or transferred to another person, the Certificate of Number must be surrendered to the issuing office within 15 days.

If the Certificate is lost or destroyed, notice of this must be given to the issuing authority.

Changes of address must also be reported. If the state of principal use is changed, the owner must make application for a number in the new state within 90 days, surrendering the old certificate at that time. A change of motor only is not required to be reported.

State regulations may differ slightly from the above, but are generally similar. A boat owner should have a copy or digest of the boating laws and regulations of the state in which his craft is registered.

37

## Penalties

A civil penalty of $50 may be imposed on the owner of a boat for the violation of the numbering provisions of the Federal Boating Act of 1958 or the regulations authorized by it. The same penalty may be imposed on the operator of a craft not properly registered or numbered for each violation of the Act or its regulations.

## Accident Statistics

The Federal Boating Act of 1958 provides that as part of an approved state registering and numbering program there must be a requirement for reports to be made of all accidents comparable to those requiring reports to the Coast Guard. The Act also provides for the compilation of statistics and the forwarding of such data to the Secretary of the Department in which the Coast Guard is operating.

### National statistics

The Coast Guard, in turn, is charged with the responsibility of combining state reports with its own to form national statistics as to the number of registered motorboats by class; accidents by type, cause, surrounding circumstances, etc.; and other related data. Reports are compiled on the basis of calendar years.

### Privacy of information

Information as to the identity and ownership of vessels numbered by the Coast Guard will be made available to Federal and local officials as needed in any enforcement or assistance program.

In general, files relating to the numbering of boats under the provisions of the FBA are considered "public records," and as such, information from them may be released to anyone subject only to reasonable restrictions necessary to carry on the functions of the records office.

On the other hand, individual "Boating Accident Reports" or extracts therefrom are *not* releasable. These reports are intended to furnish the information necessary for the Coast Guard to make findings as to the cause of accidents and recommendations for their prevention, and to compile appropriate statistics. Their privacy permits the filing of full and accurate reports without the possibility of their contents being used against the individual in civil suits.

## Operators' "Safety Certificates"

A little-noticed provision of the FBA is the optional authority for states to require the operator of a vessel that comes within the scope of the marking provisions of the Act to "hold a valid safety certificate to be issued under such terms and conditions as may be provided by State law."

There are no Coast Guard regulations in furtherance of this provision of the FBA [Section 3 (c) (ii) ], and little use has been made of it except in the case of young persons.

## RULES OF THE ROAD

The "Rules of the Road" are sets of statutory requirements enacted by Congress to promote safety of navigation. The rules consist of requirements for navigation lights and day shapes, steering and sailing rules, sound

**FIG. 222** Boating accident reports must contain all information required by regulations. The use of an official form will aid in ensuring completeness. States will either use the Coast Guard form shown above or one much like it.

signals for both good and restricted visibility situations, rules for conduct in restricted visibility, and distress signals.

There are different sets of Rules for various bodies and areas of waters.

## International Rules

The International Regulations for the Prevention of Collisions at Sea—generally referred to as the International Rules of the Road—have been adopted at international conferences and amended at various times. They have been made effective for U.S. waters and U.S. vessels by Act of Congress.

The International Rules are effective outside the boundary lines described on page 31. Boatman who go offshore along the coast must be familiar with their provisions.

## Rules for U.S. waters

There are currently three sets of Rules of the Road for U.S. inland waters. The "Inland Rules" are applicable inside of the boundary lines mentioned above, *except* where the "Great Lakes Rules" or the "Western Rules" are in effect.

The **Great Lakes Rules** are applicable on the Great Lakes and their connecting and tributary waters as far east as Montreal for all U.S. vessels, and for all vessels, including foreign ones, while within the portions of these waters that are under U.S. jurisdiction. This phraseology is required by the fact that a considerable portion of the Great Lakes and St. Lawrence River are Canadian waters.

The **Western Rivers Rules** are applicable on the Mississippi River from its source to the Huey P. Long Bridge (at New Orleans) and all of the tributaries emptying into the Mississippi, and their tributaries. These Rules are also in effect on that part of the Atchafalaya River above its junction with the Plaquemine-Morgan alternate waterway, and on the Red River of the North.

It should be noted carefully that the "Western Rivers" Rules do *not* apply to rivers on the West Coast of the United States—such rivers as the Sacramento or the Columbia; the Inland Rules are in effect for all rivers emptying into the Pacific Ocean.

**FIG. 223** The Western Rivers Rules of the Road apply to specific inland waters of the United States. They are not applicable to rivers on the West Coast, such as the Sacramento and Columbia, that empty into the Pacific Ocean.

### Provisions of the Rules

The four sets of Rules of the Road are of such importance and contain such extensive information that two chapters in this book are devoted to them and their implementing regulations.

Matters relating to navigation lights and day shapes are covered in Chapter 4 for all sets of Rules. Chapter 5 covers other topics of the Rules such as the steering and sailing rules, whistle signals, etc.

### Official publications

The Coast Guard publishes three pamphlets covering the Rules of the Road. CG-169 includes both the International Rules and the Inland Rules; see fig. 1708. CG-172 contains the Great Lakes Rules, and CG-184 covers the Western Rivers Rules.

Copies of these publications are not required to be on board motorboats, but they are desirable documents to have at hand. They are available, without charge, from Coast Guard District offices or from Headquarters in Washington, see page 609.

### Additional regulations

Each of the three sets of U.S. Rules of the Road contains authority for the issuance of additional rules and regulations by the Secretary of the Department in which the Coast Guard is operating. These are termed "Pilot Rules" and are covered later in this chapter.

### Penalties against persons

The Inland, Great Lakes, and Western Rivers Rules contain essentially the same language as to penalties for their violation, or violation of regulations issued under the authority of the Rules. There are minor differences in wording but the maximum penalties are the same.

A licensed or unlicensed master, mate, pilot, or engineer of any vessel subject to the Rules who is in violation is liable to a penalty not to exceed $500. In addition, the Inland and Western Rivers Rules specify that such person shall also be liable for all damages sustained by any passenger in his person or baggage as a result of such violation. (It is provided that these penalties against the individual do not relieve the vessel, its owner, or corporation from any liability as a result of the violation.)

### Penalties against vessels

Penalties may also be assessed against any *vessel* subject to the Rules that may be navigated in violation of them. The penalty is fixed at $500, and the Inland and Western Rivers Rules provide that one-half of this sum may be paid to "the informer." Under all sets of these Rules the vessel may be seized and proceeded against in the Federal courts for the collection of the penalty.

### Penalty for failure to give aid

As noted before, the master or person in charge of a vessel in collision has duties to the other vessel and her crew and passengers (see page 33 ). A specific penalty is provided for failure, without reasonable cause, to meet these responsibilities. Such a person may be found guilty of a misdemeanor and subjected to a fine of $1000, or imprisonment for not more than two years, or both. The vessel may be proceeded against in Federal court with the penalty assessed being divided equally between the informer and the United States.

### International Rules

The statutory enactment of the International Rules of the Road as U.S. law does not prescribe any specific penalties for violation of the Rules. Individuals and vessels, would, of course, be liable for civil suits for damages as a result of violations of these Rules.

## Federal Boating Regulations _____

It is not feasible to attempt to include in this chapter a complete set of federal boating regulations—and probably no two authorities would agree as to what constituted a "complete" set—but major items of regulatory matter will be discussed or referenced. If needed, additional information can usually be obtained from Coast Guard District offices or Headquarters in Washington.

Regulations implementing the Motorboat Act of 1940 and the Federal Boating Act of 1958 have been discussed earlier in this chapter in connection with consideration of the basic Acts.

### PILOT RULES

The implementing regulations issued under the authority of each of the three sets of U.S. Rules of the Road are termed **"Pilot Rules."** (There are no parallel regulations for the International Rules of the Road.) There are thus three sets of Pilot Rules varying in considerable detail for the different waters for which each are effective.

Most of the contents of the Pilot Rules have to do with the same topics as the basic Rules of the Road: navigation lights, steering and sailing rules, whistle signals, etc. These regulatory provisions are covered with the basic Rules in Chapters 4 and 5.

### Duplication of the Rules of the Road,

As a result of certain old administrative requirements, each of the sets of Pilot Rules contain a number of provisions that are directly duplicatory of some provisions of the applicable Rules of the Road. This duplication has no

RULES OF THE ROAD

GREAT LAKES

UNITED STATES COAST GUARD
TREASURY DEPARTMENT

U.S. GOVERNMENT PRINTING OFFICE
WASHINGTON : 1966

FIG. 224 The Rules of the Road, and related information, for the various areas of United States waters are published in a series of small Coast Guard pamphlets which may be obtained without charge from major USCG offices. They make excellent reference reading for any skipper.

significance and can be ignored. Other provisions of the Pilot Rules—the majority of them—are, of course, not duplicatory and must be understood.

## Use of searchlights

The Inland Pilot Rules and those for the Great Lakes contain a specific regulation prohibiting the flashing of a searchlight or other blinding light onto the bridge or into

FIG. 225 All sets of Pilot Rules contain specific prohibitions against the use of a searchlight in such a way as to flash its rays onto the bridge or into the pilothouse of any vessel underway.

the pilothouse of another vessel while underway. Violation may lead to the suspension or revocation of the offending person's license or certificate.

## Penalties

The penalties for violation of the Pilot Rules are the same as for offenses against the basic Rules of the Road; see page 39.

### BILGE VENTILATION REGULATIONS

Of particular interest to the owners of motorboats using *gasoline* as a fuel are the Coast Guard regulations relating to the ventilation of engine and fuel tank compartments. The regulations are discussed and illustrated on pages 604-607.

### REGATTAS AND MARINE PARADES

The Coast Guard has established a set of regulations covering the holding of regattas and marine parades. In some areas, the authority to regulate such events has been passed on to State authorities, but under the same general provisions regarding application to hold the event, special local regulations, patrolling, etc.

The text of these regulations will be found in each of the pamphlets covering the Rules of the Road; CG-169, CG-172, and CG-184.

### DEPARTMENT OF THE ARMY REGULATIONS

As a result of the provisions of several Acts of Congress, it has been necessary for the Army Corps of Engineers to

issue "navigation regulations" for certain waters. To a very great extent, these are duplicatory of the Pilot Rules. Skippers should be aware of their existence, but they need not be given the detailed study that the Great Lakes and Western Rivers Pilot Rules should receive from those who travel on these waters.

### PARK REGULATIONS

The use of boats on many natural lakes and man-made reservoirs are subject to regulations issued by the National Park Service of the Department of the Interior. Other such bodies of water are controlled by state or local authorities. These rules and restrictions will vary from one body of water to another and each area must be individually checked to ensure that laws are not inadvertently violated.

# State Boating Laws and Regulations

Most state laws and regulations relating to boats go well beyond the provisions of the Motorboat Act of 1940 and the Federal Boating Act of 1958. Typically, registration and numbering are required of boats below the 10 horsepower Federal minimum; boats are required to carry additional safety equipment such as an oar or paddle, and an anchor; riding on decks or gunwales is prohibited, etc. In addition, there are usually laws and regulations relating to boat trailers and their use.

The old saying that "Ignorance of the law is no excuse" is quite applicable to skippers of recreational boats. Each should know the requirements and restrictions of his state, and should take steps as appropriate to expand his knowledge if he plans to cruise in other states. He should particularly be alert to varying state laws about boat trailering on highways.

Information on applicable state laws and regulations may be obtained from each state, usually from the same office that handles registration and numbering; see page 621. The Outboard Boating Club of America publishes four regional handbooks that are thorough compilations of laws and regulations relating to boats of all sizes, trailers, boating activities, and taxation. These are up-dated when necessary by supplements. These may be ordered from OBC at 333 N. Michigan Avenue, Chicago, Ill. 60601.

FIG. 226 To ensure safety of life and property, the Coast Guard has a set of regulations covering regattas and marine parades. Advance application must be made and approval secured. In some areas, this control has been given to state agencies.

FIG. 227 State boating laws and regulations vary widely. The Outboard Boating Club has prepared sectional compilations of these requirements and restrictions, with supplements published as required by changes.

# Miscellaneous Regulatory Matters _____

Boatmen will have need of knowledge of other regulatory matters in varying degrees as determined by the size of their craft, their cruising area, etc. Skippers should be alert to changes in these factors which may require additional knowledge in matters previously of no interest to them.

## DOCUMENTATION

Not all boats are numbered—many are "documented." This is a process whereby official papers on the craft are issued by the Coast Guard in much the same manner as for large ships. (Formerly this was done by the Bureau of Customs of the Treasury Department, but the function was transferred to the Coast Guard in 1966.) The *numbering*

requirements of the Federal Boating Act do not apply to documented vessels; other provisions of this Act, however, *are* applicable.

Documentation of a craft used solely for non-commercial recreational purposes is *optional,* and certain requirements must be met. The vessel must be owned by a citizen of the United States (or a corporation 51% or more owned by U.S. citizens) and it must be of a specified minimum size, 5 net tons as explained below. The captain of a documented vessel, if other than the owner, must be a U.S. citizen.

## Tonnage

Before a vessel can be documented it must be *measured* for its tonnage. ("Admeasured" is the more formal term, but it means the same and is gradually being dropped in favor of the simpler language.) The details of gross and net tonnage are explained on page 25.

## Types of Documents

The documents that are issued to vessels are of five forms—register, enrollment and license, license, yacht enrollment and license, and yacht license. Only the latter two are of interest to the owners of noncommercial craft, but all should be generally understood.

### Yacht documents

A **yacht enrollment and license** may be issued to a vessel used *exclusively for pleasure* of 20 net tons or more. A **yacht license** may be issued to such a vessel of 5 net tons or over but less than 20 net tons.

### Other types of documents

An **enrollment and license** may be issued to a vessel of 20 net tons or more and, if the vessel meets certain qualifications, may authorize it to engage in the coasting trade, the mackerel fishery, the cod fishery, the whale fishery, or

---

A TRUE COPY OF THE LATEST CONSOLIDATED CERTIFICATE OF ENROLLMENT AND YACHT LICENSE

The United States of America

OFFICIAL NO.

Certificate No.

Measured at , 19
Rebuilt at , 19
Remeasured at , 19    Horsepower

## CONSOLIDATED CERTIFICATE OF ENROLLMENT AND YACHT LICENSE†
### LICENSE OF YACHT UNDER TWENTY TONS‡

In conformity to Title L, "Regulation of Vessels in Domestic Commerce," and Chapter Two, Title XLVII, "Regulation of Commerce and Navigation," of the Revised Statutes of the United States, and to "An act to amend Sections 4214 and 4218 of the Revised Statutes Relating to Yachts," approved August 29, 1912

having taken and subscribed the oath        required by law, and having sworn        that

citizen    of the United States and the sole owner    of the vessel called the
of
and that the said vessel was built in the year 1    at        of
as appears by
and                                    having certified that
the said vessel is a                                ; that she has
deck        mast    a        stem, and a        stern; that her
register length is    feet, her register breadth    feet, her register depth    feet,
her height    feet; that she measures as follows:

| | TONS | 100ths |
|---|---|---|
| Capacity under tonnage deck | | |
| Capacity between decks above tonnage deck | | |
| Capacity of enclosures on the upper deck, viz: Forecastle ; bridge ; poop ; break | | |

To have and to hold the said vessel and appurtenances thereunto belonging unto the said buyer(s)    executors, administrators, successors, and assigns, to the sole and only proper use, benefit, and behoof of the said buyer(s)    executors, administrators, successors, and assigns forever; And the said seller(s) ha    promised, covenanted, and agreed, and by these presents do    promise, covenant, and agree, for    executors, administrators, successors, and assigns, to and with said buyer(s)    executors, administrators, successors, and assigns, to warrant and defend the said vessel and all other before-mentioned appurtenances against all and every person whomsoever

FIG. 228 Craft over a specified minimum size may be "documented" in much the same way as are large ships. This action, in lieu of state or Coast Guard registration and numbering, has both advantages and disadvantages.

the coasting trade and mackerel fishery. A vessel authorized to engage in the "mackerel fishery" may be used in the taking of fish of any description.

If a vessel is to be used for towing, dredging, freight or passenger carrying, or a combination of any of these functions, its document must so state.

Special enrollments and licenses are issued on the frontiers, authorizing vessels to engage in the foreign and coasting trades. Vessels of 5 net tons or more may be granted an enrollment and license for navigating the waters of the northern, northeastern, or northwestern frontiers.

A **license** may be issued to a vessel of 5 net tons or over but of less than 20 net tons and, if the vessel meets certain qualifications, may authorize the vessel to engage in any one of the employments for which an enrollment and license may be issued as discussed above.

A vessel under a **register** which is not limited by a prohibitive endorsement on its face may engage in any trade, including the foreign trade, the coastwise trade, and the American fisheries. Registered vessels, however, may be required upon arrival in a port of the United States to pay certain pilotage fees and other charges from which other documented vessels are generally exempted.

## Temporary and permanent documents

Marine documents are also described as "permanent"—issued to vessels at their home ports, or "temporary"—granted to vessels at ports other than their home port.

## Advantages of Yacht Documentation

Important privileges extended by documentation of vessels as yachts include (1) legal authority to fly the yacht ensign, which authority is not formally granted to other boats; and (2) the privilege of recording bills of sale, mortgages, and other instruments of title for the vessel with federal officials at her home port, giving constructive legal notice to all persons of the effect of such instruments and permitting the attainment of a preferred status for mortgages so recorded. This gives additional security to the purchaser or mortgagee and facilitates financing and transfer of title for such vessels.

The former advantages of documented yachts over registered (numbered) non-commercial motorboats when returning to the U.S. from a foreign port have now been eliminated in the general simplification of procedures that has occurred in recent years; see pages 48-49.

## Obtaining Documentation

A procedure has been established under which the owner of a boat used *exclusively for pleasure* may file an "Application for Simplified Admeasurement" with the Officer in Charge, Marine Inspection in his local Coast Guard District.

In brief, the simplified measurement method uses the numerical product of three dimensions—the overall length (L), overall breadth (B), and depth (D)—note that this is "depth," an internal dimension, and not the boat's "draft." The **gross tonnage** of a vessel designed for sailing is assumed to be $1/2(LBD/100)$; for vessels not designed for sailing it is calculated to be $2/3(LBD/100)$.

The gross tonnage of a catamaran or a trimaran is determined by adding the gross tonnages of each hull as calculated above.

Where the volume of the deckhouse is disproportionate to the volume of the hull—as in some designs of houseboats—the volume of the deckhouse, calculated by appropriate geometric formulas and expressed in tons of 100 cubic feet each, is added to the gross tonnage of the hull as calculated with L, B, and D.

The **net tonnage** of a sailing vessel is recorded as 9/10 of the gross tonnage; for a non-sailing vessel, the multiplying factor is 8/10. If there is no propelling machinery in the hull, the net tonnage will be the same as the gross tonnage.

Application for simplified admeasurement is by letter; there is no standard form of application unless one has been prepared by the local Officer in Charge, Marine Inspection. The owner may take his own length, breadth, and depth measurements and complete the transaction by mail, quickly and without cost.

Considerable information on documentation can be obtained from the Coast Guard pamphlet "Yacht Admeasurement and Documentation"—CG-177, available without charge from Coast Guard offices.

## Formal measurement

The owner of a boat may elect to have formal measurement rather than use the simplified method; this is *required* if the vessel is to be used *commercially*.

If an owner is contemplating formal admeasurement, it is suggested that he first make an estimate of the tonnage by using the simplified method. If the resulting net tonnage is less than 5 tons, it is not likely that the vessel will be 5 net tons or more when formally measured.

An application for formal measurement should be prepared in writing and submitted to the Officer in Charge,

**FIG. 229** Much useful information on documentation requirements and procedures can be obtained from this free Coast Guard pamphlet. A copy should be obtained and studied before any decision is made regarding the possible documentation of a boat.

COAST GUARD

# Yacht Admeasurement and Documentation

Are you the citizen owner of a yacht or boat of 5 net tons or more, used for recreation only? If so, you may elect to have it documented as a yacht by the U.S. COAST GUARD.

- Generally Speaking
- Optional Simplified Measurement Method for Pleasure Vessels
- Definitions
- Gross Tonnage
- Net Tonnage
- Notes
- Application for Simplified Measurement
- Formal Measurement
- How to Get Your Document
- Establishing Title
- Renewal of Your Document
- One Thing More
- Fees
- Further Information

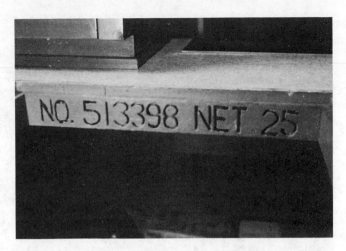

**FIG. 230** A documented vessel, including a boat, must have its "official number" and "net tonnage" deeply carved or permanently marked on her "main beam." Special provisions have been made for fiberglass boats.

Marine Inspection, for the area in which the vessel is located. The information that must be submitted is listed in CG-177.

Under formal measurement procedures, a definite date and place should be agreed upon between the measuring officer and the owner, or his agent, so that the vessel may be physically measured and examined by the measuring officer.

## Application for document

The measuring officer who calculates the tonnages by the simplified method, or who visits the vessel for formal measurement, will provide the necessary forms which must be filled out to receive the document. Further assistance may be obtained by writing, calling, or visiting the nearest Documentation Office, U.S. Coast Guard.

## Establishing title

A vessel may be documented only in the name of the holder of legal title. It is necessary therefore for the owner

**FIG. 231** A craft documented for pleasure only—no commercial use—must have her name and hailing port marked "on some conspicuous place on the hull." This is normally done on the stern, but such is not mandatory. Detailed specifications must be met regarding the lettering.

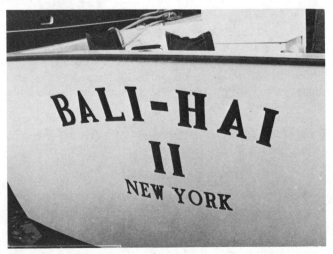

to present adequate title papers with his application.

If the vessel was built for the present owner and has never been owned by anyone else, that person should have the builder furnish a "Builder's Certificate" on Form 1261 to establish title.

If there were previous owners, the proper documents are the Builder's Certificate and bills of sale in recordable form from each of the previous owners, preferably on Form 1346, available without charge from the Documentation Office. If these steps are impracticable, consult the Officer in Charge, Marine Inspection, for alternative procedures.

## Fees

No charge is made for the documentation of a yacht or for renewing a yacht license. There is no charge for measuring and certifying the tonnages of a vessel, except that if the physical presence of a measuring officer is required outside certain local limits, a charge is made to cover his salary, travel, and subsistence expenses. If a vessel is to be measured on a Saturday or Sunday, substantial charges for overtime may be involved; it is suggested that a convenient weekday be proposed in the application to avoid such charges.

A small charge is made for recording each bill of sale or other recordable title instrument; the average cost of recording a bill of sale is approximately $2.

## Markings of a Documented Boat

The owner or master of a vessel to be documented must file a certification with the Coast Guard Documentation Officer that the boat is properly *marked*. He must arrange for an official inspection of the marking if this is requested by the Coast Guard.

## Official number and net tonnage

Every documented vessel, as a prerequisite to documentation, must have its official number and net tonnage carved or permanently marked on the *main beam* of the vessel.

The main beam is the beam at the forward end of the largest hatch on the weather deck and is usually located forward of amidships. If the vessel has no hatch on the weather deck, the main beam is any structural member integral to the hull.

The *official number* must be preceded by the abbreviation "NO." and the net tonnage must be preceded by the word "NET"; see fig. 230.

In a wooden vessel, the legend must be carved or cut on the main beam in arabic or block type letters three inches high, or as high as the width of the main beam will permit. In a vessel built of metal, the legend must be outlined by punch marks and painted over with oil paint using a color that contrasts with the background.

On fiberglass boats, the legend can be carved into a plastic sheet or plate in much the same manner as a wooden beam, and this plate then fastened with epoxy to the hull, usually in the bow. The plate will normally be six inches high by as long as required to carry the prescribed information.

## Name and hailing port

All documented yachts are required to have their name and hailing port marked on *some conspicuous place* on their hull; this is usually done on the stern. The letters must be Roman type and not less than four inches in height. They may be painted, gilded, cut, or cast letters, and must be in a color that provides adequate contrast with the background surface.

The hailing port may be the port where the vessel is permanently documented, or the place in the same district where the vessel was built or where one or more of the owners reside.

Documented commercial vessels must have the name and hailing port marked in full on the stern, plus the name in full marked on both bows.

Special provisions are made for vessels with square bows and for double-enders.

### Block letters required

For documented vessels, whether used for pleasure only or commercially, *the use of script or italic lettering is not acceptable.* It is *not* permissible to place the name or hailing port, on a board and attach the board to the hull, or to use cut or carved letters joined in one continuous piece. (For boats that are numbered rather than documented, there is no requirement that a name be shown nor specifications as to how one may or must be displayed.)

### Use of Documented Boats

If a vessel is given a document as a yacht, that paper will authorize its use for *pleasure only.* A yacht document does *not* permit the transporting of merchandise or the carrying of passengers for hire, such as the taking out of fishing parties for a fee charged directly or indirectly. Any violation of this limitation may result in the imposition of severe penalties against the craft and its owner. See also section below on "Commercial Operation."

The documentation of a vessel as a yacht *does not exempt* it from any applicable State or Federal taxes. Further, the fact that a boat is federally documented will not excuse the owner from complying with safety and equipment regulations of the state or states in which it is operated.

Vessels that are documented are not required nor permitted to have a number issued under the Federal Boating Act.

### Renewal of Documents

A yacht license or enrollment and license must be renewed each year; this is probably the only disadvantage to documentation. The owner will ordinarily be notified by mail and will be sent the required renewal form and instructions several weeks in advance of the expiration date. Failure to receive this notice, however, will not affect the requirement for renewal.

### For vessels under simplified measurement

At the discretion of the Officer in Charge, Marine Inspection, concerned, a document issued under the simplified measurement procedures *may* not be renewed, or another document issued, until the Coast Guard has verified the overall dimensions given in the application for such measurement.

Any correction of the stated overall dimensions of a vessel as a result of the above verification is deemed to be a change in the description of the vessel and the outstanding document will no longer be in force.

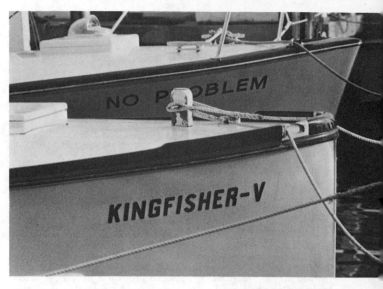

FIG. 232 A craft documented for any commercial use must be marked with her name and hailing port on the stern, and additionally must have her name on both sides of the vessel's bow. The style, size, and colors of the lettering are specified by regulation.

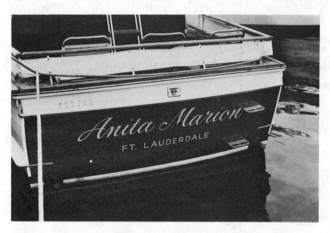

FIG. 233 The name in script-style letters on the stern of this boat is legal as she is numbered rather than documented. Such style of lettering is not acceptable on any documented boat or ship.

## COMMERCIAL OPERATION

The Federal Government does not require that the owner of a motorboat or yacht of any size whatever have any knowledge of his boat or navigation or the handling of his vessel. Neither does the Government require that a *motorboat* or motor yacht under 300 gross tons not engaged in trade or carrying passengers for hire should have on board a licensed officer.

No licensed officers are required on *motor vessels documented as yachts* except on those of 200 gross tons and over when navigating the high seas.

### Carrying Passengers For Hire

Persons wishing to operate a motorboat carrying passengers for hire must have a license. There are two categories of licensing as determined by the number of persons carried—six passengers and less, or more than six. Neither of these should be confused with the licenses required to be held by pilots and engineers on vessels of more than 15 gross tons or 65 feet length engaged in trade. Motorboats under 65 feet in length carrying freight for hire are not required to have licensed pilots and engineers.

## Definition of "passenger"

Of particular interest to boatmen who use their craft exclusively for recreation is the definition, in the regulations, of a passenger. "A passenger is every person other than the master and the members of the crew or other persons employed or engaged in any capacity on board a vessel in the business of that vessel." (There are, however, certain exceptions. For example, aboard vessels on international voyages, children under one year of age; the owner or his representative; employees of the owner or charterer; and persons aboard tugs and towboats not over 50 gross tons who have not contributed for their carriage.)

The most important exception, insofar as the boatman is concerned, is the following—"any guest on board a vessel which is exclusively being used for pleasure purposes who has not contributed *any* consideration, *directly or indirectly,* for his carriage." (Emphasis added).

## When is a boat carrying passengers for hire?

It is of considerable importance that a skipper have some understanding of circumstances that might be considered by the authorities as "carrying passengers for hire." Some situations are obvious—such as taking persons on a fishing trip for a specified amount of money for each individual or for the group as a whole—but other cases are more borderline and must be examined carefully.

It has been held that the following situations *do not* put the vessel and operator into the carrying-passengers-for-hire category.

1. When the boat owner invites guests aboard and one or more of them brings a gift of food or drink to be used on the trip.

2. Where the cruise guest takes the skipper ashore for dinner and entertainment.

3. Where during a cruise one of the guests aboard offers to buy a tankful of fuel or some like event.

4. When the owner is a businessman who takes associates or customers aboard for the purpose of creating good-will and negotiating business matters not related to the trip.

On the other hand, if there is a *prearranged plan* or *agreement in advance* that the guests are to pay their proportionate share, or any specific amount, of the expenses of the cruise, this *is* a case of carrying passengers for hire. The operator of the craft would have to be properly licensed and the vessel would have to be equipped in accordance with the requirements for those carrying passengers for hire.

A way of "getting around" such a situation was brought forth in an opinion expressed by the Coast Guard in 1953 and still effective. "It is possible, of course, for the owner of any vessel to operate it on a share-the-expense basis if all guests are willing to enter into a written agreement that the voyage will be a joint venture and that all parties to the contract will share all liabilities as well as benefits. In this situation, the owner would not be considered as transporting passengers for hire. Expenses could then be shared.

In case of a casualty, all parties to the contract would be jointly responsible in case of suit."

If a boat is chartered with the crew furnished by the owner, it has been held that the craft is then carrying passengers for hire and must be in charge of a licensed operator.

### Licenses for Six or Less Passengers

Motorboats, and other vessels of 15 gross tons or less propelled by machinery other than steam, while carrying passengers for hire, must be operated by a person licensed under the Motorboat Act of 1940, with certain minor exceptions.

### Application for licenses

Licenses are issued by Officers in Charge, Marine Inspection, U.S. Coast Guard. These officers are located in many major port cities on the coasts and Great Lakes.

An applicant must submit a sworn application to one of these officers who will examine him concerning his character and fitness to hold such a license. The Officer in Charge, or his representative, investigates the proofs submitted concerning the applicant's character and ability, and determines whether his "capacity, knowledge, experience, character, and habits of life" qualify him for licensing as a Motorboat Operator.

The applicant must submit documentary evidence of at least one year's experience in operating motorboats.

**FIG. 234  A craft carrying passengers for hire must be operated by a person possessing a valid Coast Guard license for the number of passengers on board and the waters navigated.**

**FIG. 235** The circumstances which distinguish between a "guest" on board and a "passenger for hire" are quite complex, but have been established with reasonable clarity. All boat operators should study the situation with some care to avoid law violations.

## Examination

An oral examination is given which is based on subjects which any person operating a motorboat carrying passengers should know before being entrusted with its operation and navigation.

Questions deal generally with regulations governing motorboats, Rules of the Road and Pilot Rules for local waters, fire protection, lifesaving equipment, safe operation of gasoline engines, methods of operating and navigating boats carrying passengers for hire, and elementary first-aid.

As the Rules of the Road and Pilot Rules differ in various parts of the country, the holder of a license has the duty to familiarize himself with the prevalent rules if he should shift his operations to other waters.

Licenses to operate motorboats carrying passengers for hire are not issued to persons under 18 years of age. The applicant must be able to read and write.

## Physical fitness required

Applicants must be physically fit or a license will not be granted. Normally, they must be examined by a U.S. Public Health Service surgeon or a reputable physician. Bad hearing or eye-sight, color blindness, use of narcotics, insanity, or presence of certain diseases are grounds for rejection of the applicant.

## License issuance and renewal

Licenses are issued and signed by Officers in Charge, Marine Inspection; see fig. 236. Every license for certificate

**FIG. 236** A "Motorboat Operator License" is one issued by the Coast Guard for carrying **six or less** passengers for hire. There are no restrictions on the size of the craft nor on the waters navigated.

**FIG. 237** To legally carry more than six passengers for hire, a skipper must have either an "Operator" or an "Ocean Operator" license. These are issued in terms of the gross tonnage of vessels that may be operated and with specific limitations as to the waters on which it is valid.

of lost license, see below) must be signed by the person to whom it is issued, who also places his thumbprint on the back. It is valid for five years, after which it can be renewed. There is no charge.

To renew the license, the individual must present it to an Officer in Charge, Marine Inspection, together with a certificate of color vision, within one year after its expiration date. If more than a year has elapsed since the license expired, the person must take another examination. In most situations, a brief test on the Rules of the Road will be a part of the renewal process. Except under extraordinary circumstances, renewal cannot be made more than 90 days before the expiration date.

## Lost licenses

In the case of loss of license, except where it has been revoked or suspended, a certificate can be obtained from an Officer in Charge, Marine Inspection, on presentation of satisfactory evidence of the loss. This certificate is then as valid as the license for the unexpired term.

## Suspension or revocation

If any operator is found guilty of incompetence, misbehavior, negligence, endangering life, or willfully violating any safety law or regulation, his license may be suspended or revoked. If revoked or suspended, the license must be surrendered to the official before whom the hearing was held. If an appeal is made, the license must still be surrendered but a certificate will be issued covering the period during which the appeal is pending.

### Licenses for More Than Six Passengers

Rules and regulations for small passenger vessels are prescribed in an Act of 10 May 1956, frequently called the "Ray Act." Under this Act, a "passenger-carrying vessel" means any vessel which carries *more than six passengers* and which falls into one of the below categories.

1. Propelled in whole or in part by steam or by any form of mechanical or electrical power and is of 15 gross tons or less.

2. Propelled in whole or in part by steam or any form of mechanical or electrical power and is of more than 15 but less than 100 gross tons and is not more than 65 feet in length.

3. Propelled by sail and is of 700 gross tons or less.

A few exceptions are made, including: foreign vessels, vessels operating on non-navigable waters of the U.S., vessels laid up and out of commission, public vessels, and lifeboats.

## Operator licenses

A person holding only a license under the Motorboat Act, as described above, is *not* authorized to operate passenger-carrying vessels under the Ray Act. A separate license issued under the terms of this Act is required and its scope varies according to the waters navigated. For off-shore waters, an "Ocean Operator's License" is issued. Within the coastline and on the Great Lakes, it is an "Operator's License"; see fig. 237. In both cases specific geographic limits are normally prescribed. Licenses are issued for a specified maximum gross tonnage, in multiples of 10, and are valid for five years.

Application is made to the nearest Officer in Charge, Marine Inspection. Physical fitness must be established and a written examination must be passed. Proof of appropriate experience is required.

### Vessel Inspection

Vessels subject to the Ray Act must be inspected by an Officer in Charge, Marine Inspection, from whom applications for inspection may be obtained. These are among the vessels generally referred to in Coast Guard regulations and publications as "inspected vessels"; ordinary motorboats are categorized as "uninspected vessels."

Certificates of inspection are valid for three years. They describe the area in which the vessel may be operated, the maximum number of passengers that can be carried, the minimum crew required, minimum lifesaving and firefighting equipment to be carried, etc.

**FIG. 238** A boat returning to the United States from foreign waters must report to the proper authorities at the first port touched. In some areas, a single Federal agency has been assigned to handle all forms and reports for all authorities concerned.

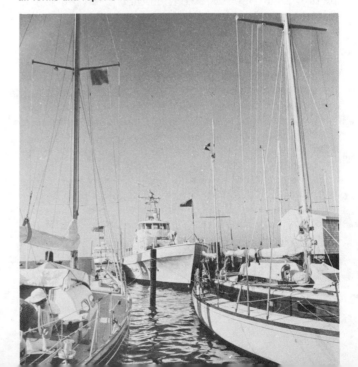

## INTERNATIONAL VOYAGES

When an American boat crosses the national boundaries of the United States to visit a foreign port, or a foreign yacht visits an American port, certain customs, immigration, and other regulations must be obeyed. As a result of various provisions and exemptions applying to yachts, not engaged in trade, the procedure has been so simplified that there is nothing in these legal requirements to deter a recreational craft from enjoying a cruise outside the limits of U.S. waters. Severe penalties, however, are provided for failure to observe the applicable regulations.

### Clearing and Entering

The terms "clearing" and "entering" are commonly used in connection with a vessel's voyage between ports of two nations. **Clearing** involves the obtaining of permission to sail by presenting the ship's papers to a customs official. **Entering** relates to arrival, when the owner or master "enters" his vessel by having his ship's papers accepted by customs authorities. Thus a U.S. vessel might be required to clear from an American port and enter on arrival at a foreign port. Then for the return passage, the vessel would clear from the foreign port and enter upon reaching an American harbor.

Foreign vessels are not only subject to the requirements of entry and clearing on foreign voyages, but must also enter and clear when proceeding between U.S. ports.

If desired, *bills of health* may be secured free of charge before leaving for a foreign port. This is not compulsory, but may make entry into the foreign port quicker and easier; the procedure is used chiefly by vessels going to tropical countries where epidemics are prevalent.

### Report on arrival

There are four separate legal aspects to entering this country from a foreign nation, each involving its own government agency and officials. These are (1) **Customs,** relating to the bringing in of dutiable merchandise; (2) **Immigration,** relating to the eligibility for entry of persons; (3) **Public Health Service,** for the prevention of importation of human diseases; and (4) **Animal and Plant Quarantine,** for the prevention of entry of contaminated plants, fruits, and vegetables, or infected animals.

On arrival at a foreign port, the owner or captain of a yacht (any size) should report to the authorities mentioned above, or to such of them as exist for this port. When reporting, the crew and guests must remain aboard the boat until permission has been granted to land. Any additional or local regulations to be complied with, including details in connection with clearing from that port, will be supplied by the authorities.

Every vessel, whether documented or not, arriving in the United States from a foreign port or place must come into a *port of entry* and, within 24 hours, must report to the customhouse at that port. The crew and guests must remain aboard (one person may get off for the sole purpose of telephoning or otherwise notifying the authorities of the vessel's arrival), and no baggage or merchandise should be removed until the customs, immigration, and other officials have given their approval.

**FIG. 239** Cruising with pets may introduce new problems into international voyages. Be sure to check the laws and regulations of all countries to be visited before departing from the United States. Investigate, too, any problems that may arise on your return to the U.S. from foreign shores with animals aboard.

All boats, regardless of size, must report to the immigration authorities on return to a United States port. Any alien passengers aboard must be reported and a heavy penalty may be imposed for failure to detain passengers and crew if ordered to do so by the authorities. A report giving names, nationalities, and other information concerning any paid crew aboard must be made on a crew manifest.

In many U.S. ports a "one-stop" service has been established whereby for the simple situations of a noncommercial craft from nearby foreign waters a single government official from one of the agencies will represent all of the authorities and bring all necessary forms to be filled in by the skipper.

### Exemptions for non-commercial craft

Neither a licensed yacht nor an undocumented American pleasure vessel (not engaged in trade nor in any way violating the customs or navigation laws of the U.S.) is required to clear upon departure from the United States for a foreign port or place. Similarly a licensed yacht of any size or an undocumented American pleasure vessel (not engaged in trade nor in any way violating the customs or navigation laws of the U.S., and not having visited any other vessel "hovering" off the coast) is exempted from *formal* entry. These craft, however, *must* make a report to the proper authorities to cover such matters as the importation of items purchased while outside the United States.

### At the Canadian border

U.S. yachts going into Canada may secure *cruising permits* with the right of free entry and clearance from 1 May to 1 October. These are issued without charge by the Canadian customs authorities at the Canadian port where the yacht first reports and must be surrenderd when leaving the country. Provided that the boat does not leave Canadian waters, she is then free to visit other Canadian ports until the permit is surrendered, though reports must be made at any port called where a custom officer is located.

Canadian boatmen with craft of less than 5 tons can enter the border waters of the United States for a day's outing without applying for admission at a U.S. port of entry. The Canadian Border Landing Card doesn't require advance application and is good for repeated 24-hour visits throughout the navigation season. It is good only for border waters; if the Canadian boatman wants to go farther into the U.S., he must apply at a port of entry and submit to inspection.

### Arrival from coastwise cruises

There is a little-known law on the books that requires foreign vessels and documented vessels of the United States (but not numbered boats) navigating the "high seas" on coastwise cruises to give 24 hour's notice of their time of arrival to the Captain of the Port at their next intended port of call.

Bodies of water like Long Island Sound and Chesapeake Bay are excluded from the Act's definition of "high seas" but waters of the open sea below the low-water mark—as, for example, offshore along the Florida coast—are included.

This is basically a safety and security measure to control the entrance of commercial vessels into U.S. ports. For a time, the law was occasionally invoked against documented yachts, but now, however, these are specifically exempted in an amendment which excludes, among several types of vessels, "United States yachts, arriving at a U.S. port or place from a port or place outside the United States, or destined from one port or place in the United States to another port or place in the U.S."

### Miscellaneous Provisions

Foreign yachts meeting certain requirements may receive from customs authorities in the United States a *cruising license* granting them special treatment while in United States waters.

### Yacht "commission"

A documented yacht, belonging to a regularly organized and incorporated yacht club, may be issued a *commission* to sail for pleasure on a foreign voyage. Application for this document may be made to any Collector of Customs in the United States. The commission serves mainly as an identification of the vessel and her owner. It must be surrendered upon return from the foreign country.

### Additional information

A boatman who *leaves* this country with foreign-made articles—such as cameras made in Japan or Germany—will find their reintroduction into the United States facilitated if these are registered with the U.S. Customs officials

*prior to departure.* Take such articles to a customs office at a port, airport, etc., and get a Form 4457 filled out and signed. Show this upon reporting in on your return and there will be no question of duty on such articles.

For further detailed information with regard to customs requirements, the boat owner should consult the nearest customs office. Likewise, for information regarding immigration, public health, etc., he should contact any convenient office of the applicable government agency. Information on the legal aspects of visiting a specific foreign country can best be obtained from that nation's consular offices in various major cities of the U.S. or its embassy in Washington, D.C.

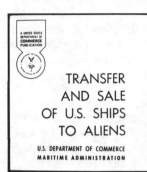

**FIG. 240** There are legal restrictions on the sale of American vessels to foreigners. Some blanket exceptions have been made for smaller numbered, but **not** documented, boats. An owner should carefully check the laws and regulations before completing such a transaction.

### SALE OF CRAFT TO FOREIGNERS

A quite complex set of laws and regulations govern the sale of either documented or undocumented vessels to aliens. Some provisions are applicable at all times; others are in effect only in times of war or National Emergency (this latter condition exists *now* and has since 16 December 1950). The Maritime Administration of the Department of Commerce is the federal agency charged with the enforcement of these rules.

The war or National Emergency provisions extend to vessels of *any* size, including pleasure craft, motorboats, and yachts. Certain blanket approvals of transfer of title have been made for smaller *undocumented* craft, but these contain exceptions, and in any case do not apply to documented boats. A Maritime Administration pamphlet "Transfer and Sale of U.S. Ships to Aliens" is available without charge and contains the applicable laws and regulations. The general complexity of sales to foreigners, however, makes advisable the obtaining of expert advice before any such transactions are completed.

# Federal Water Pollution Law

The "Water Quality Improvement Act of 1970" was passed in April of that year. This new law served to amend and extend the existing "Federal Water Pollution Control Act" passed several years earlier.

The 1970 federal law touches upon many aspects of pollution; of most interest to boatmen is the new Section 13 added to the older act, entitled "Control of Sewage from Vessels."

### BASIC PROVISIONS

The newly-added section relates to all watercraft, large and small, commercial and recreational. The law does, however, permit enforcing authorities to distinguish among

classes, types, and sizes of vessels (a boat is a vessel), as well as between new and existing vessels. There are provisions for waivers for groups of vessels, and for individual cases, where warranted.

### Performance standards

The general approach of this federal legislation is the establishment of "standards of performance" for marine sanitation devices. These include all equipment on a vessel to "receive, retain, treat, or discharge sewage, and any process to treat such sewage." The term "sewage" is defined to mean human body wastes and the waste from toilets and other receptacles intended to receive or retain human body wastes." (continued)

Standards are to be developed in coordination by the Secretary of the Interior and the Secretary of the department in which the Coast Guard is operating. Other federal departments, the states, and various interested parties will be consulted before the standards are promulgated.

The law states that performance standards must be consistent with maritime safety standards and marine laws and regulations. It specifically notes that in the development of standards consideration must be given to "the economic costs involved" and "the available limits of technology."

### Regulations

The Secretary of the department in which the Coast Guard is operating is charged with the issuance of regulations governing the design, construction, installation, and use of marine sanitation devices on vessels.

### Effective date

The law does not specify a deadline for the promulgation of the performance standards. It does, however, state that the initial standards and regulations will become effective for *new* vessels *two* years after promulgation, and for *existing* vessels *five* years after promulgation.

### Application of the Law

The Secretary of the department in which the Coast Guard is operating will establish testing procedures for marine sanitation devices. If these meet applicable performance standards, they will be "certified." Once these procedures are established, manufacturers must not import, sell, or deliver such units unless each is substantially the same as a device that has been certified.

### Use and sale of vessels

After the *effective* date of the standards and regulations —not the date of promulgation, but two to five years later— the Act states that it shall be unlawful for any vessel subject to these standards and regulations to operate on the navigable waters of the United States if such vessel is not equipped with an operable marine sanitation device of a certified design. The law does *not* apply to craft *without* an *installed* toilet.

The Act also states that after this effective date it will be unlawful to manufacture or distribute for sale, or sell or offer for sale, any vessel subject to the standards and regulations unless it has a marine sanitation device of certified type.

### Enforcement

The regulations relating to Section 13 will be enforced by the Coast Guard and may be enforced by other federal agencies and state officers by agreement with the Secretary of the department in which the Coast Guard is operating.

The law specifically authorizes Coast Guard and other enforcement personnel to board and inspect any vessel upon the navigable waters of the United States to check compliance with the provisions of this section.

### Penalties

The penalty for operation of a boat without an operable marine sanitation device of "certified" type is a civil penalty of not more than $2,000 for each violation. Note that this is an administrative type of penalty and one that does not require trial and conviction in court. No penalty will be assessed until the alleged violator has been given an opportunity for a hearing.

The penalty rises to $5,000 per violation for manufacturers and dealers in such devices and vessels.

### PREEMPTION

A most important aspect of this federal anti-pollution law is "preemption." The Act provides that after the *effective* date of the initial standards and regulations "no state or political subdivision thereof shall adopt or enforce any statute or regulation with respect to the design, manufacture, installation, or use of any marine sanitation device on any vessel subject to the provisions of this Section."

There is a clause, however, that allows a total prohibition of the discharge of sewage, treated or not, into specific bodies of water when requested by a state and found necessary by the Secretary of the Interior to meet water quality standards.

### THE EFFECT OF FEDERAL LAW

The federal law of 1970 is wisely written in broad terms of performance standards which are to be prescribed by regulations. Thus changes can be made to take advantage of advances in technology without the necessity for further Congressional action. The Act also omits any direct mention of specific devices and treatment processes, again leaving these to implementing regulations, and changes with the passage of time.

The federal law, *when it becomes effective,* will supersede state and local laws and so permit the cruising or trailering boatman to comply with *one single set of requirements* in most situations. There will remain, however, some possible problems on smaller inland bodies of water not subject to federal jurisdiction, and in those other areas where special provisions have been allowed by the federal authorities.

---

At the time of preparation of this chapter, legislation was pending in the Congress which would replace the present Inland, Great Lakes, and Western Rivers Rules with a single set to be called the "U.S. Nautical Rules." Passage of this Act is probable, but the date is uncertain. In any event, such new Rules would not be effective for a period of time—probably one year—after passage, and during that time this chapter, as well as Chapters 4 and 5 and any others affected, would be revised.

Also pending in Congress is a new "Federal Boat Safety Act" which would replace portions of the Motorboat Act of 1940 and essentially all of the Federal Boating Act of 1958. This bill, H.R. 15041 in the 91st Congress, is broad in scope and provides for details of required equipment to be spelled out in implementing regulations and "safety standards." Such regulations would not be effective for at least six months following their publication, and this would be some time after the enactment of the new law, particularly as they will go into areas not previously regulated by the Coast Guard, such as navigation equipment and ground tackle. During this time before the effective date of the new requirements, this chapter will be revised in accordance with the FBSA regulations.

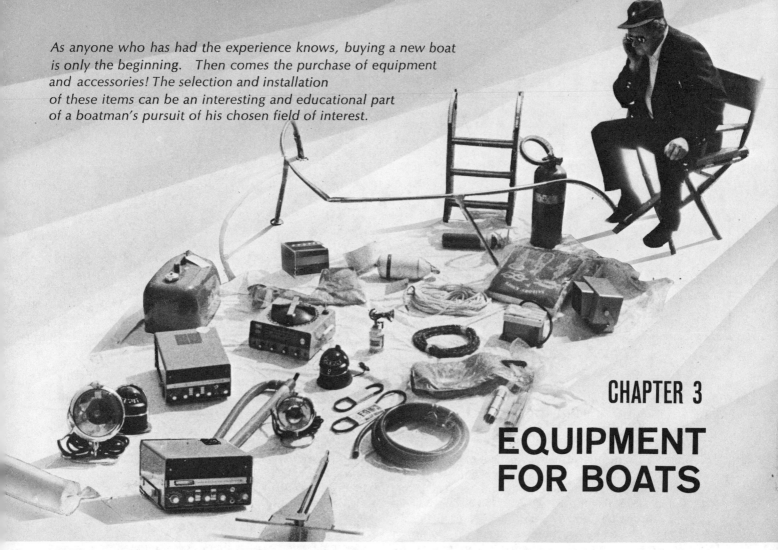

As anyone who has had the experience knows, buying a new boat is only the beginning. Then comes the purchase of equipment and accessories! The selection and installation of these items can be an interesting and educational part of a boatman's pursuit of his chosen field of interest.

# CHAPTER 3

# EQUIPMENT FOR BOATS

FIG. 301 Many items of equipment are required for any boat. Some are needed to meet legal requirements, others for safety in basic operations, and still others for the general comfort and convenience of the crew and guests.

## Categories of equipment

Equipment for a boat can be conveniently divided into three categories for separate consideration. These major groupings are—

1. **Equipment required by law—federal, state, or local.** This list is rather surprisingly limited. It has little flexibility; items are strictly specified and usually must be of an "approved" type.

2. **Additional equipment for safety and basic operations.** This list is less limited and greater flexibility is possible in the selection of individual items.

3. **Equipment for convenience and comfort.** Here the skipper can turn loose his imagination and be limited only by his financial resources.

## Factors affecting selection

In all of the above categories, the items and quantities will vary with the size of the craft involved and the use that is made of her. The legally required items will be determined in most cases by the "class" of the boat as set by Section 2 of the Motorboat Act of 1940; see page 33. The equipment in the other categories will be governed by size generally, the waters boated upon, and the type of boating activities, together with other factors such as the amount of electrical power available on board, cost, etc.

## Legally Required Equipment

The basic source of requirements for equipment on boats is the Motorboat Act of 1940 (MBA). The type of craft subject to the Act is discussed in Chapter 2, see page 32. Boats without mechanical power of any sort, including detachable motors, are not subject to the equipment provisions of this law. Vessels over 65 feet in length are, in most cases, governed by other laws and regulations.

### Federal equipment regulations

The basic statutory requirements for equipment in the MBA have been spelled out in greater detail in regulations issued by the Commandant of the Coast Guard. These are a part of the Code of Federal Regulations, Title 46, Part 25. They also appear in a small pamphlet "Rules and Regulations for Uninspected Vessels"—Publication CG-258—which is available without charge from Coast Guard District offices or from Headquarters, U.S. Coast Guard, Washington, D.C. 20591.

### Craft to be considered

The consideration of this chapter will be focused on non-commercial operation of motorboats not more than 65 feet in length except where specifically noted other-

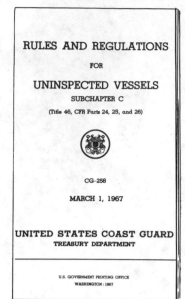

RULES AND REGULATIONS

FOR

UNINSPECTED VESSELS

SUBCHAPTER C

(Title 46, CFR Parts 24, 25, and 26)

CG-258

MARCH 1, 1967

UNITED STATES COAST GUARD
TREASURY DEPARTMENT

U.S. GOVERNMENT PRINTING OFFICE
WASHINGTON : 1967

**FIG. 302** The federal regulations regarding equipment on the various classes of boats will be found in a free Coast Guard pamphlet CG-258, "Rules and Regulations for Uninspected Vessels."

**FIG. 303** Power-driven craft more than 65 feet in length are not subject to the provisions of the Motorboat Act of 1940 (except as regards reckless and negligent operation). In Coast Guard terms, these are "motor vessels" and are subject to a separate set of regulations.

wise. Sailing craft with any sort of mechanical propulsion are "motorboats" in this consideration.

### State Equipment Requirements

Almost all states have their own boating laws which, in addition to covering the registration and numbering of watercraft, contain requirements for equipment and regulations governing the use of boats. On waters of "concurrent jurisdiction" where federal laws are applicable, states may also make and enforce rules that are not in conflict with the federal requirements and restrictions. State regulations are thus based on the federal rules, but generally go beyond them in details and requirements for additional items.

It is beyond the limitations of this book to consider in detail the requirements of each set of state boating laws and regulations. Every skipper should, however, obtain a copy of these for all such states whose waters he uses, and be guided by them. He should be alert, too, for any special local requirements.

### Required Equipment as a Minimum

**Skippers should regard the legal requirements as a minimum.** If a particular boat is required to have two fire ex-

tinguishers, for example, its owner should carefully consider if this number will give adequate protection for *his* craft. Two may satisfy the authorities, but a third might be desirable, even necessary, to ensure that one is available at each location on board where it might be needed in a hurry. Two bilge vents may satisfy the regulations, but four would certainly give greater safety. Think "safety," not just compliance with the minimum in order to be "legal"!

### Non-approved items as excess

Some boatmen carry items of equipment no longer approved—older, superceded types, or items never approved, as "excess" equipment in addition to the legal minimum, or more, of approved items. This is not prohibited by regulations, but such action may give a false sense of protection and security. The danger of reaching for one of these sub-standard items in an emergency, rather than the proper item, must be recognized and positively guarded against. Some obsolete items of safety equipment, such as certain types of vaporizing-liquid fire extinguishers, see below, are actually hazardous on a boat and should not be on board even as "excess" equipment.

### LIFESAVING EQUIPMENT

The Motorboat Act requires that any motorboat subject to any of its provisions must carry one life preserver, life belt, ring buoy, or other authorized device for each person on board, and that these must be readily accessible. [Section 6] The term "persons on board" is construed to also include any person in tow, such as a waterskier; the

**FIG. 304** Any craft 65 feet or less in length that is propelled by machinery is a "motorboat" under Coast Guard regulations. The additional propulsion gained by having sails hoisted does not change this auxiliary's status as a motorboat.

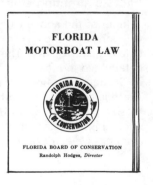

**FIG. 305** The skipper of any craft must also know state and local laws that relate to his boating. These may differ in some details from Coast Guard regulations. Florida's Motorboat Law, for example, does not stop at 65 feet in length, and "FL" numbers may be seen on vessels quite large enough to be termed "ships."

FLORIDA
MOTORBOAT LAW

FLORIDA BOARD OF CONSERVATION
Randolph Hodges, *Director*

52

FIG. 306a Coast Guard regulations specify a minimum number of safety devices and features for each size class of boat. Having more than the minimum requirements, bilge vents in this instance, is desirable for greater safety.

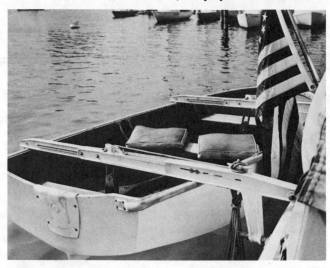

FIG. 306b This Class 3 boat carries several buoyant cushions for use as lifesaving equipment in the dinghy. Such cushions, however, are not acceptable toward meeting the requirements for lifesaving equipment on the Class 3 boat.

term "life belt" appears in the Act, but there is no longer any approved device by such name. Section 6 further provides for more stringent requirements to be placed on boats and vessels carrying passengers for hire; this is done in regulations issued by the Commandant of the Coast Guard.

### Types of Lifesaving Equipment

Coast Guard regulations recognize a number of different types of lifesaving equipment and contain specifications that must be met or exceeded if each is to be approved. Lists, and changes thereto, are published of the approved products of various manufacturers. Each such item must be marked with its approval number and all other information, such as limitations on its use, required by the specifications.

**Life preservers**—Probably the safest and best lifesaving device is a *life preserver*. These are made in two basic styles—jacket and bib, see figs. 308 and 309. The flotation

FIG. 307 When determining the number of lifesaving devices required to be on a motorboat underway, any water skiers being towed by the craft must be included in the count of "persons on board."

material of the jacket type will be pads of kapok or fibrous glass material; these are inserted in a cloth cover fitted with the necessary straps and ties. Kapok or fibrous glass *must* be encased in sealed plastic film covers; older life preservers without plastic inner containers are no longer acceptable. Old style cork and balsa wood life preservers manufactured as approved items before 1 July 1965 may still be accepted as initial or replacement equipment if they are in good and serviceable condition.

Life preservers of the "bib" type may be of cloth containing unicellular plastic foam sections of specified shape, or they may be of uncovered plastic foam material with a vinyl dip coating. The bib type must have a slit all the way down the front and have adjustable body straps.

Life preservers come in two sizes—*adult*, for persons 90 pounds or more in weight, and *child*, for individuals weighing less than 90 pounds—and are so marked in large letters. The adult size may be used for children, but the child size is not acceptable for adult use.

A basic feature of life preserver design, either bib or jacket type, is the requirement that it shall support the wearer in the water in an upright or slightly backward position, providing support for his head so that his *face* is held above water even though he becomes exhausted or unconscious. A life preserver must be capable of turning the wearer to this position regardless of his initial position on entering the water.

Approved life preservers will also be marked with the type, manufacturer's name and address, and USCG approval number, plus a date and place of individual inspection together with the inspector's initials. All USCG-approved life preservers are now required to be international orange in color.

*Life preservers* are distinguishable from other lifesaving gear by the words "Approved for Use on All Vessels and Motorboats" which appear near the other markings. (Life preservers manufactured before 1 July 1966 may not have this marking.)

**Life rings**—*Ring life buoys* may be made of cork, balsa wood, or unicellular plastic foam. The ring is surrounded

**FIG. 308** The most desirable type of lifesaving equipment for a boat is the "life preserver." It is produced in two styles, one of which is the "jacket" type shown above. Such devices are individually inspected at the factory by a representative of the Coast Guard.

**FIG. 309** The "bib" style of life preserver of approved design is acceptable on all classes of motorboats used for any purpose. Certain older models without the slit down the front may no longer be counted toward the legal requirements.

**FIG. 310** Ring life buoys which bear a USCG approval number and inspector's markings are acceptable on any motorboat. Approval is given only to ring buoys of 20, 24, and 30 inch diameter; rings of smaller size are not acceptable as a part of the legal minimum number of lifesaving devices.

by a light grabline fastened at four points and used to obtain a better grasp of it; see fig. 310.

Standard sizes are 20, 24, and 30 inches in diameter. Life rings of smaller diameter are often seen decorating the sides of boats, usually marked with the craft's name. These may possibly be of some value if thrown to a person in the water, but a ring smaller than 20" will *not* be of an approved type and *cannot be counted* toward the legal minimum requirements on boats of any class.

Balsa wood or cork rings will be covered with cloth and marked generally as noted above for life preservers. These ring buoys may be either international orange or natural gray in color for use in U.S. waters, but must be orange on a vessel on an international voyage.

Rings of plastic foam with special surface treatment will carry a small metal plate with approval information including the inspector's initials. Ring buoys of this style may be either international orange or white in color; as above, orange is required for buoys on vessels on an international voyage.

**Buoyant vests**—Approved buoyant vests are of various designs and may be of any color. They use the same flotation materials as life preservers and have the same requirement for plastic inner cases, but vests are smaller and *provide less buoyancy*, hence somewhat less safety for a person in the water. Their design must be such as to float the wearer in the same safe position as required for life preservers.

Buoyant vests are made in three sizes—one for adults and two for children, medium and small; weight ranges for children's sizes are marked on each vest. The adult size may be counted for children, but not vice versa.

Buoyant vests are marked with the model number, manufacturer's name and address, approval number, and other information. These water safety items are approved by lot and are *not* individually inspected and marked. They also carry the notation that they are approved for use *only* on boats of Classes A, 1, and 2 not carrying passengers for hire.

**Buoyant cushions**—Probably the most widely used item of lifesaving equipment on small boats is the *buoyant cushion*—and from a safety viewpoint, it is probably the least desirable type! Although adequate flotation support is provided, actually more than by a buoyant vest, the design of cushions does *not* provide safety for an exhausted or unconscious person.

This device consists of kapok, fibrous glass material, or unicellular plastic foam in a cover of fabric or coated cloth fitted with grab straps. Kapok or fibrous glass material pads must be encased in sealed plastic film covers.

Buoyant cushions are approved in various shapes and sizes, and may be of any color. Approval is indicated on a label on one side carrying generally the same information as for buoyant vests. Cushions are approved by lot number and are not individually inspected. All cushions manufactured since 1961 will carry the warning, "Do not wear on back."

**Special purpose devices**—This category covers many different designs as determined by their application—waterskiing, hunting, racing, etc. Included are both devices to be worn and those to be grasped. These are acceptable on boats of Classes A, 1, and 2 not carrying passengers for hire.

The design of *special purpose water safety buoyant devices* is examined and approved by recognized laboratories, such as the Yacht Safety Bureau, see page 193, and this approval is accepted by the Coast Guard. These devices are labeled with information as to the use for which intended, the size or weight category of the user, instructions as necessary for use and maintenance, and an approval number. Devices to be grasped rather than worn will also be marked "Warning: Do not Wear on Back."

**Work vests**—Buoyant *work vests* are items of safety equipment for crew members and workmen when working over or near water under favorable conditions and under supervision. They carry a USCG approval number, 160.053, but are *not* acceptable as lifesaving devices on any boat or vessel; they may be carried only as *excess* equipment.

**Other devices**—Rafts and wood floats are subject to Coast Guard inspection and approval, but are *not* applicable toward the requirements for lifesaving equipment on recreational motorboats.

## Requirements by Boat Classes

Motorboats of Classes A, 1, and 2, *not carrying passengers for hire,* must carry for each person on board or in tow an approved life preserver, ring life buoy, buoyant vest, buoyant cushion, or special purpose water safety buoyant device.

### Larger recreational motorboats

Motorboats of class 3, *not carrying passengers for hire,* are more limited in the types of lifesaving equipment that are acceptable. Such craft must have for each person on board or in tow an approved life preserver or ring life buoy. Note that such items as buoyant vest and cushions or special purpose devices are not acceptable on boats 40 to 65 feet in length; special purpose devices may be carried as excess equipment on such craft.

### General requirements

The Coast Guard regulations repeat the statutory requirement that the lifesaving equipment on any vessel must be so placed as to be "readily accessible."

The regulations also require that all lifesaving equipment be "in good and serviceable condition"; if not, such items are not counted toward the minimum number required to be on board.

## General Considerations

Lifesaving equipment is rarely needed on a boat—perhaps never—but when it must be used, it is of paramount importance. For this reason, every boat owner should carefully consider equipping his craft with the very best possible. The skippers of recreational boats of Classes A, 1, and 2 will find the small additional cost of life preservers over that of buoyant vests or cushions to be a sound investment

**FIG. 311** Buoyant vests are smaller and less expensive devices than life preservers, and provide less buoyancy. They are acceptable only on boats of Classes A, 1, and 2 not carrying passengers for hire. They may be of any color.

**FIG. 312** Buoyant cushions are widely used in smaller craft. They provide adequate flotation to a person in the water, but have a serious safety deficiency in that they do **not** keep an exhausted or unconscious person in a safe position as do life preservers and buoyant vests.

**FIG. 314** This buoyant cushion is not in "good and serviceable condition" as required by Coast Guard regulations. It will not be counted toward the legal minimum requirements. Items such as this generally cannot be repaired and must be replaced.

**FIG. 313** Special purpose water safety buoyant devices are produced in a wide variety of designs, including sport vests, water skiing vests, hunters' jackets, and others. Check carefully for a USCG approval number before purchasing any such device for use on a boat.

**FIG. 315** In northern areas, survival times "over the side" are severely reduced by the cold temperatures of the water. Life rafts, preferably with a canopy, furnish protection that life preservers cannot provide from the elements.

**FIG. 316** Hand-portable fire extinguishers using a dry powdered chemical as the extinguishing agent are widely used on boats. Such units must have a pressure indicator to show their readiness for use. (Certain exceptions permit the continued use of some older models without pressure gauges.) Peter Smyth Photo

**FIG. 317** Larger craft powered by inboard engines, particularly those using gasoline as a fuel, are often fitted with a built-in CO-2 fire extinguishing system. This is actuated automatically by temperature-rise detectors or it may be operated manually.

**FIG. 318** Small outboard craft (not carrying passengers for hire) may or may not be required to have a fire extinguisher. Any one or more of the above construction features, see text for identification, will require one B-I fire extinguisher on board.

**FIG. 319** The construction features identified above, see text for explanation of numbers, do **not,** in themselves, require that a fire extinguisher be carried—but one is still desirable for safety.

in safety, see page 202. Boatmen who fish or cruise in colder northern waters should study the purchase of a life raft to supplement other lifesaving gear and increase the chances of survival offshore. A raft with a canopy provides the best protection to its occupants.

## FIRE EXTINGUISHERS

All hand-portable fire extinguishers and semiportable and fixed fire extinguishing systems must be of a type that has been approved by the Coast Guard. Such approvals are published in the pamphlet "Equipment Lists"—CG-190—with changes in the daily Federal Register.

All fire extinguishers and extinguishing systems approved for use on boats will have a metallic nameplate attached with information as to the manufacturer, type, and capacity. For those manufactured between 1962 and 1965, the nameplate must contain the wording "Marine Type USCG Type _____ Size _____"; those made since 1965 must have the above label plus "Approval No. 162.068/_____." (See below for information on "type" and "size").

### Kinds of extinguishers

Fire extinguishers for boats are described in terms of their contents, the actual extinguishing agent.

**Dry Chemical**—This type of extinguisher is widely used because of its convenience and relative low cost. These have an advantage over other types in that they may be quickly "recharged" by screwing another cylinder onto the discharge nozzle and valve assembly. Spare cylinders may be carried on board for increased safety.

The cylinder contains a dry chemical in powdered form together with a propellant gas under pressure. Coast Guard regulations now require that such extinguishers be equipped with a gauge or indicator to show that normal gas pressure exists within the extinguisher. (Some older models do not have indicators and must be checked by very careful weighing. Such extinguishers must have been manufactured before 1 June 1965 to be acceptable, but may continue to be carried if they are in good and serviceable condition.)

**Carbon dioxide**—Some boats carry portable carbon dioxide ($CO_2$) extinguishers; such units are advantageous as they are the only type to leave no messy residue to clean up after use, and they cannot cause harm to the interior of engines as other types may do. This type must be used where a fixed system is installed in an engine compartment. Such a system may be operated either manually or automatically by heat-sensitive detectors in the space to be protected.

Carbon dioxide extinguishers consist of a cylinder containing this gas under high pressure, a valve, and a properly designed discharge nozzle at the end of a short hose. The state of charge of a $CO_2$ extinguisher can only be checked by weighing the cylinder and comparing this figure with the one stamped on or near the valve. All such extinguishers should be checked at least annually; this is a service best done by a qualified technician. The *total* weight of the extinguisher must not be down by more than 10% of the *net* weight of its contents; if the weight loss is greater than this amount, the cylinder must be recharged. The lead seals on the valve triggering mechanisms must be unbroken. See page 210 for other maintenance of $CO_2$ extinguishers.

**Foam**—Fire extinguishers using chemical foam are legally acceptable on boats, but this type is rarely used as they leave a residue that is difficult to clean up after use and may require a partial engine disassembly.

Foam extinguishers are not pressurized before use and do not require tests for leakage. Such units contain water and must be protected from freezing. Foam extinguishers should be discharged and recharged annually.

**Non-acceptable types**—Vaporizing-liquid extinguishers, such as those containing carbontetrachloride and chloro-bromomethane, are effective in fighting fires but produce highly toxic gases. They are *not* approved for use on motorboats and should NOT be carried as excess equipment because of their danger to the health or even life of a user in a confined space.

## Classification of extinguishers

Fires are classified in three categories, A, B, and C, according to the general type of material being burned; see page 178. Fire extinguishers are similarly classified as to "type" and in addition are placed in size groups, I (the smallest) through V.*

The primary fire hazard on boats results from flammable liquids and so type "B" extinguishers are specified. (Some "B" extinguishers have adequate or limited effectiveness on other classes of fires; some should *not* be used on other types of fires, such as foam extinguishers on class "C" electrical fires.) Only the two smaller sizes, I and II, are hand portable, size III is a semi-portable fire extinguishing system, and sizes IV and V are too large for consideration here.

The type and size classifications for various extinguishing agents are shown in Table 3-1 at the end of this chapter.

## Requirements on Boats

Fire extinguisher requirements are prescribed in terms of the four "classes" of boats as established in the Motorboat Act of 1940.

**Class A and 1** boats must have at least one type B-I hand portable fire extinguisher, except that boats of these classes propelled by outboard motors, not carrying passengers for hire *and* of such open construction that there can be no entrapment of explosive or flammable gases or vapors, need not carry an extinguisher.

A fire extinguisher is required on outboard boats under 26 feet in length if *one or more* of the following conditions exist, see fig. 318.

1. Closed compartment under thwarts or seats in which portable fuel tanks may be stored.

2. Double bottoms *not* sealed to the hull, or which are not *completely* filled with flotation material.

3. Closed living spaces.

4. Closed storage compartments in which combustible or flammable materials are stowed.

5. Permanently installed fuel tanks. (Tanks which exceed 7 gallons are not normally classed as portable tanks and render the boat liable for meeting the standards of permanently installed tanks unless the craft is of fully open construction with a tight cockpit floor and no bilge or similar area accessible to spills or susceptible to the accumulation of explosive vapors.)

The following conditions do *not*, of·themselves, require that fire extinguishers be carried, see fig. 319.

1. Bait wells.
2. Glove compartments.
3. Buoyant flotation material.
4. Open slatted flooring.
5. Ice chests.

**Class 2** boats must carry at least *two B-I* approved hand

portable fire extinguishers, *or* at least *one B-II* unit.

**Class 3** craft must carry at least *three B-I* approved hand extinguishers, *or* at least *one B-II* unit *plus one B-I* unit.

**Boats with fixed extinguisher systems** in the engine compartment may have the above minimum requirement for their size reduced by one B-I unit. The fixed system must meet Coast Guard specifications.

**Exemptions**—Motorboats propelled by outboard motors, while engaged in a previously arranged and announced race (and such boats designed solely for racing, while engaged in operations incidental to preparing for racing) are exempted by Section 9 of the MBA from any requirements to carry fire extinguishers.

### Keeping Safe

Don't merely purchase and mount fire extinguishers, and then forget all about them. All types require some maintenance and checking; see page 210 for guidance in keeping up the level of fire protection you gain when first installing new extinguishers.

All members of your regular "crew," and to a lesser extent any guests that may be aboard, should know both the location and operation of all fire extinguishers.

### BACKFIRE FLAME CONTROL

Every inboard gasoline engine installed in a motorboat must be equipped with an acceptable means of backfire flame control (with certain quite limited exceptions to be discussed below). Such a device is commonly called a

FIG. 320 With certain quite minor and technical exceptions, a gasoline engine used on a boat must be equipped with a "flame arrestor." This metal grid over the air intake to the carburetor prevents the exit of backfire flames into the engine compartment.

"flame arrestor" and must meet specific Coast Guard specifications to be approved. Accepted models will be listed by manufacturer's number in equipment lists or will have an approval number marked on the grid housing.

In use, flame arrestors must be secured to the air intake of the carburetor with an air-tight connection, have clean elements, and have no separation of the grids that would permit flames to pass through.

### Exceptions

There are four categories of engine installations that are not required to have an approved flame arrestor, but these will actually include very few craft. The exempted situations are (1) Engines installed prior to 25 April 1940. (2) Installations made prior to 19 November 1952 which meet

*These USCG classifications B-I, B-II, etc., are not to be confused with Underwriters Laboratories classification 1-B, 2-B, 10-B, etc., which may also appear on extinguishers. The UL classification provides a better guide to extinguisher capacity, but they have not been written into USCG regulations as yet.

the lesser requirements then in effect and which are still in a good and serviceable condition. (3) Engines of a design inherently free from any backfire flames; each design must be tested and specifically approved by the Coast Guard. (4) Installations such that any backfire flames would be vented outside the vessel in such a manner as to not be dangerous to the craft; no formal inspection and specific approval is required.

## VENTILATION REQUIREMENTS

All motorboats, except open boats, which use fuel having a flashpoint of 110°F. or less—gasoline but not diesel—must have at least two ventilation ducts for every engine and fuel tank compartment. These ducts must be fitted with cowls or the equivalent for the efficient removal of explosive or flammable vapors. (Power exhaust blowers are desirable but are not legally required.)

Additional information on bilge ventilation will be found on pages 607 to 610.

## OTHER REQUIRED EQUIPMENT

Additional items of equipment required by the Motorboat Act and Coast Guard regulations include whistles and bells. As with other equipment, the requirements are graduated with the size of the craft when used on inland waters.

### Whistle

Motorboats operating on waters governed by the Inland, Great Lakes, and Western Rivers Rules of the Road must be equipped with an "efficient" whistle or other sound producing mechanical device (horn) as follows:

Class A — None required.
Class 1 — Mouth, hand, or power operated; capable of producing a blast audible at a distance of at least one-half mile.*
Class 2 — Hand or power operated; capable of producing a blast audible at a distance of at least one mile.*
Class 3 — Power operated; capable of producing a blast audible at a distance of at least one mile.*
    *All blasts to be of at least two seconds duration.

The term "efficient" is nowhere defined in the laws or regulations. It has generally been held by enforcement authorities and the courts that the device must be suitable for the boat or vessel on which it is used—a horn (or bell) suitable for a small motorboat would not be suitable, and

**FIG. 322** If a bell is normally carried inside the bridge, cockpit, or cabin, there should be a second bracket for it mounted well out in the clear, usually forward. A bell is rung at anchor in fog for safety, not merely for compliance with the Rules of the Road!

thus not "efficient," for a large yacht, a ship, or a noisy tugboat.

### Bell

Motorboats operated on waters subject to the above Rules of the Road must carry an "efficient" fog bell if they are 26 or more feet in length (boats of Classes 2 and 3).

### Exceptions

Motorboats engaged in a race which has been previously arranged or announced, or engaged in operations incidental to preparing for such a race, need not carry a whistle or a bell.

### May be needed although not required

Despite their not being required by the Motorboat Act to carry a whistle or bell, smaller boats of Class A or 1 are *not exempt* from sounding the whistle and fog signals required by the Rules of the Road; see Chapter 5.

### Requirements of the International Rules

Motorboats of any size operated on waters governed by the International Rules of the Road, see page 38, must be provided with the whistle, bell, and fog horn required by those Rules. No range of audibility is specified, only that the device be "efficient."

**FIG. 321** All motorboats 16 feet or more in length must be equipped with a "whistle" or horn. The type of device—mouth, hand, or power operated—and its audibility range varies with the size classification of the boat. All must be capable of producing blasts of at least two seconds' duration. Shown are a whistle, hand operated horn, and electric horn.

FIG. 323 Navigation lights are part of the equipment requirements of the Motorboat Act and its implementing regulations. These are covered in Chapter 4 together with the lights for all type of vessels.

FIG. 324 Some boats use liquified petroleum (LP) gas for cooking, and possibly for heating. Such installations are acceptable on recreational craft (strict safety precautions in installation and use must be observed), but these are prohibited on boats carrying passengers for hire.

## NAVIGATION LIGHTS AND DAY SHAPES

The requirements for navigation lights for vessels subject to the Motorboat Act of 1940 appear in Section 3 of that Act. Essentially the same requirements, however, also appear in the Inland and other U.S. Rules of the Road, and so lights for boats are considered in Chapter 4 together with the navigation lights and day shapes of larger vessels.

Motorboats are permitted to carry the lights prescribed for them by the International Rules of the Road while operating in inland waters, but *not* vice versa. The International lights for small craft will also be found in Chapter 4.

## EQUIPMENT FOR COMMERCIAL OPERATION

Boats used in commercial fishing and the carrying of passengers for hire are subject to more stringent equipment requirements.

### Commercial fishing motorboats

Commercial fishing motorboats of Classes A, 1, and 2 are allowed to carry wood floats (made to Coast Guard specifications), but not special purpose water safety buoyant devices.

Commercial fishing motorboats of Class 3 are allowed the use of wood floats in addition to the acceptable life preservers and ring life buoys permitted on recreational motorboats of this size.

### Carrying Passengers for Hire

Motorboats of any class (and also motor vessels and barges) carrying passengers for hire must be equipped with an adult type life preserver for each person carried. In addition, unless the service is such that children are never carried, there must be on board approved life preservers suitable for children in a quantity at least equal to 10% of the number of adult type life preservers carried. Motorboats, but not motor vessels or barges, *may* carry special purpose water safety buoyant devices of an approved type as *excess* equipment.

### Use of LP gas fuel

Vessels carrying passengers for hire are prohibited from using liquidified petroleum gases and certain other flammable liquids for cooking, heating, or lighting purposes.

### More than six passengers

Motorboats carrying more than six passengers for hire are subject to a separate Act and set of Coast Guard regulations. These craft must be "inspected" and the certificate resulting from such action will specify minimum equipment such as lifesaving gear and fire extinguishers; see page 57.

FIG. 325 A sailboat without installed mechanical power and with no detachable motor mounted is not subject to the equipment requirements of the Motorboat Act of 1940, but must have certain items on board to comply with the Rules of the Road. They may also be subject to requirements of state laws.

FIG. 326 Every skipper must understand that merely meeting Coast Guard requirements for equipment will not ensure the safety of his boat. Additional items are needed on board, some of which may be required by state laws.

# Equipment for Boats / CHAPTER 3

**FIG. 327** The Courtesy Motorboat Examination program of the Coast Guard Auxiliary lists equipment requirements over and above the legal minimums. These requirements are an excellent guide to all boat owners in equipping their craft for full safety.

**FIG. 329** It is desirable on all but the smallest boats to carry two or more anchors. These may be of different types, or of the same type but of different sizes, to meet varying situations.

**FIG. 328** Distress flares for night use **and** smoke signals for day use should be aboard all craft to aid in obtaining assistance in an emergency. Other devices, such as signalling mirrors and orange flags, are also available and should be considered.

**FIG. 330** Small electric bilge pumps are found on most boats, but these should be backed-up with a hand-operated pump for emergency use. Larger craft may also be fitted with a high-capacity pump belt-driven from a main engine.

## EQUIPMENT FOR SAILBOATS

Sailboats completely without mechanical power, either installed or detachable, are *not* subject to the equipment requirements of the Motorboat Act. There are no federal requirements for fire extinguishers or lifesaving devices on sailing craft not carrying passengers for hire. They must, however, carry lights, fog horns, and bells to meet the requirements of the applicable set of Rules of the Road. They may also be liable for compliance with any applicable state requirements.

## SUMMARY

The federal equipment requirements for non-commercial motorboats are summarized, by class of boat, in Table 3-2 at the end of this chapter. To these must be added any applicable state requirements.

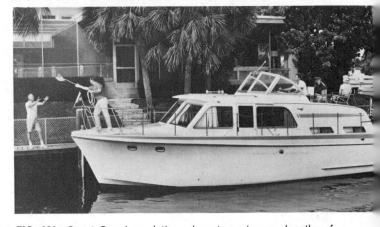

**FIG. 331** Coast Guard regulations do not require any lengths of line aboard a boat for use in docking, anchoring, etc., but these are essential for the operation of any craft. The number and length will vary with the size and use of the boat. Some state laws require an anchor and line of appropriate size and length.

## Additional Equipment for Safety

In view of the existence of two major federal laws and many implementing regulations, a newcomer to boating might be excused for thinking that he would be fully set to go if he ordered his new craft with "all equipment required by regulations." Actually, such is far from the real situation if one considers only the existing federal requirements. The problem may be ameliorated somewhat if state requirements are added in, but their lack of uniformity clouds the picture.

No quarrel can be made with the statutory and regulatory federal requirements; the sole problem is that they stop too soon. Even the smallest rowboat requires at least one length of line with which to make fast to a pier, or mooring, or anchor; and a 40-footer will need some six to eight dock and anchor lines—yet none are required by Coast Guard regulations. Only the most foolhardy and ignorant venture far from shore without some sort of distress signalling equipment—but again none are required by federal law or regulation.

These are but two of the more obvious examples of additional equipment required for safe operations—with the emphasis on both operations and safety. This section will consider the above items and others, but can establish no firm, fixed list for all skippers. Each boat owner must carefully examine his own needs and equip his craft accordingly.

## Possible liability

Another factor that cannot be ignored in considering what equipment is truly needed is the possibility of liability in case of an accident. It is a mistake to think that the boating equipment specified by the government is the only equipment that you are *legally* bound to have aboard. The boatman must consider as well the far-reaching rules of negligence, as developed over the years in court cases. Technically, negligence is the unintentional breach of a legal duty to exercise a reasonable standard of care, thereby causing damage to someone. More simply stated, it is the failure to conduct oneself as a *reasonable* man would have under the circumstances. If, for example, our reasonable man would have carried charts, you may be liable to an injured party for an accident arising out of not having them available. If he would have had an anchor, compass, flares, lines, tools and spare parts, etc., you may be held liable for not having them when needed. It is no defense to argue that no regulations require you to carry them on board.

## Sources of information

The U.S. Coast Guard Auxiliary has a program of voluntary Courtesy Motorboat Examination; see pages 191-192. The requirements and recommendations of this program make an excellent source of items and actions so desirable as to almost be categorized as "essential."

### ITEMS REQUIRED FOR USCGAUX DECAL

For a boat to receive the Auxiliary's Courtesy Motorboat Examination (CME) decal, it must, of course, first meet all of the legal requirements of the Motorboat Act of 1940 and related Coast Guard regulations. Further, some of the legal requirements are "beefed up" and made more stringent; additional items and conditions are imposed.

## Lifesaving equipment

An approved lifesaving device of the appropriate type is required for *each berth* on the boat; this may be a greater number than the legal requirement of one for each person on board at the time of a check. In addition, a boat with no bunks, or with only one, must still have a minimum of two lifesaving devices aboard.

## Fire extinguishers

The Auxiliary standards for fire extinguishers on smaller boats are likewise more demanding than the law or regulations. Although a boat under 26 feet in length that is of "open construction," or one which has a built-in fire extinguisher system, need not carry an additional hand portable extinguisher to meet the legal minimum, it must have one for award of a CME decal.

**Additional fire extinguishers**—The prudent skipper considers whether he will be adequately safe with only the minimum required number of fire extinguishers. An im-

**FIG. 332** Despite the convenience and widespread use of modern electronic depth sounders, an old-fashioned hand-held lead line is often handy to have aboard, such as for checking depths all around the sides of a craft that has gone aground.

portant safety factor is the ready availability of an extinguisher close at hand when a fire emergency suddenly bursts forth. An extinguisher should be considered for *each* of the following locations: (1) the helm, where there is always someone when underway; (2) the engine compartment; (3) the galley; and (4) adjacent to the skipper's bunk, for quick reach at night. On smaller craft, the legally required minimum, or even the USCGAux requirements, may not be enough to provide one at all desirable locations.

## Navigation lights

The law does not require that a boat operated only in the daylight have navigation lights, but these must be fitted and in good working order to meet the Auxiliary's standards.

## Distress signals

At least one distress flare must be on a boat for it to pass the CME check, and preferably there should be several. Other emergency signalling equipment that is desirable includes smoke signals (better for day use than flares), dye marker (to aid aerial searches), a signalling mirror, and an orange flag or the new "Canadian" signal described on page 38.

## Anchor and line

An anchor of suitable type and weight together with line of appropriate size and length is required for the CME decal. This is a valuable safety item should the engine fail and the craft be in danger of drifting or being blown into hazardous waters.

## Smaller craft requirements

All Class A boats must have an oar or paddle, a manual pump or bailer, and a whistle meeting the legal requirements for Class 1 boats.

## Installation standards

In addition to requiring the above items of equipment, the CGAux program has established standards for the installation of fuel systems, electrical systems, and galley stoves. Information on gasoline fuel systems and electrical systems will be found in pages 196-201.

# Equipment for Boats / CHAPTER 3

FIG. 333 As determined by their normal use and area of operations, all craft should carry an emergency supply of drinking water, and possibly some emergency food supplies. These should be checked periodically and replaced if they show signs of deterioration.

FIG. 334 The set of tools and spare parts carried on board must be individually tailored to the craft, her equipment, her use, and the capabilities of her crew. An item for all boats is a spare bulb of each type used in the navigation lights.

The Auxiliary requires that a galley stove be of a marine type and be installed so as to present no hazard to the craft and its occupants. Any common fuel is acceptable except gasoline and derivatives or distillates of naphtha and benzene. LP gas stoves or heaters which use an integral fuel container or one which fastens directly to the appliance are not acceptable for award of the decal.

### Equipment Recommended by the USCGAux

The CME checklist also contains a number of items recommended for the proper operation of a craft or for its safety, items beyond those required for award of the decal. The actual selections of items from this list will vary with the size and use of the particular boat involved.

This list of generally recommended items includes many that are *required for "Facilities,"* the boats of members of the Auxiliary that have been brought to higher standards for use in their programs of search and rescue, regatta patrolling, etc.

### Anchors

The carrying of a second anchor is recommended in addition to the one required to pass the CME check. This additional anchor may be a lighter one for non-emergency daytime use. Chapter 6 of this book in general, and page 99 in particular, provide guidance as to the selection of the proper size of anchor in several varying styles.

It is recommended that a length of chain be used between the anchor and the nylon line. Shackles used on either end of this chain should have their pins secured with safety wire.

### Bilge pumps

One or more mechanical or electrical bilge pumps are recommended for all boats, and these should, of course, always be in good working order. Facilities of Class 2 or 3 should have at least two such pumps, and their bilges must be clean and free of any oil or grease; wood chips or other debris that could clog pumps and limber holes must be removed.

### Lines

Every boat should have mooring (dock) lines suitable in length and size to that particular craft. These should be of

FIG. 335 Windshield wipers, manually or electrically operated, are essential for the good vision of the helmsman despite rain or spray. When spray, especially that from salt water, is intermittent, fresh water washers on the windshield help in keeping it clean.

several different lengths for convenience in use. No generalization can be made as to the lengths, but the diameter should roughly correspond to that of storm or working anchor rodes.

A heaving line of light construction is desirable if the craft is large enough to require the use of heavy mooring lines. The use of polypropylene line, or other material that is brightly colored and will float, is recommended for this purpose.

### Life rings

A ring life buoy with a length of light line attached is recommended for rendering assistance to swimmers or accident victims in the water. This can also be used to float a heavier line across to a stranded boat. If of an approved type, this ring buoy can count as one of the lifesaving devices required to be on board. A water light (a device which automatically lights up in contact with the water) enhances the use of a ring buoy at night.

### Operational equipment

Recommended operational equipment includes fenders in appropriate sizes and numbers for the craft involved. Not only will these be used in normal berthing, they are also necessary if two craft must make fast to each other while underway or at anchor. A boathook will be found very useful for fending off, placing lines over piles, picking up pennants of mooring buoys, recovering articles dropped over the side, and many other uses.

A searchlight—installed on larger craft, hand-held on smaller boats—serves both as a routine aid in night piloting and as an emergency signalling device. A multicell flashlight or electric lantern can serve these functions, but not so well as a searchlight.

Navigation publications and charts should be carried aboard boats in accordance with their use; see Chapters 17 and 18 for further details. Compasses are discussed in detail in Chapters 13 and 14; here we need merely to note that one is desirable on almost any boat for emergency if not regular use. Piloting and plotting instruments are covered in Chapter 19.

A hand-held lead line is a useful back-up to the more complicated electronic depth sounder; one is particularly handy when one must probe around a stranded boat in search of deeper water.

An emergency supply of drinking water—and perhaps food, too—should be carried on all craft. It may never be used, but when needed it can literally be a "lifesaver." Supplies of this nature should be periodically freshened or replaced to ensure acceptable quality when needed. Distilled water should be carried for periodic replenishment of any storage batteries on board; this can, of course, serve as an emergency source of drinking water.

A first aid kit is an essential item of safety equipment; see pages 211 to 213. The kit should be accompanied with a manual or separate book of instructions.

The list of tools and spare parts to be carried aboard must be developed by each skipper individually for his craft. The items will be governed by the type of boat, its normal use, and the capabilities of the crew to use them. An item required on USCGAux Facilities is one or more spare bulbs for the navigation lights. Items for all craft include simple tools, plugs, cloth, screws, nails, wire, tape, and other objects for the execution of emergency repairs at sea. Mechanical and electrical spares will be highly individualized by the particular boat and skipper.

## Further Operational and Safety Items

A sea anchor or drogue, see pages 165-166, is an essential item of safety equipment for boats operating in many areas, but one is not legally required. As noted above, life rafts, preferably with a canopy, are much needed safety items in many waters.

Electric windshield wipers are excellent items of equipment when running into rainy or rough weather; safety is

FIG. 337 The conscientious skipper does his part in keeping our waters clean. Pollution control equipment of several basic types is rapidly becoming standard equipment on new boats. The variations in state and local laws do, however, confuse the situation at present.

often much improved by their availability and use. The installation of washers that squirt fresh water on windshields will help greatly when spray, particularly of salt water, is intermittently received over the bow.

Many electronic items that will add to operational safety are described in Chapter 25. These include radiotelephones, electronic depth sounders, radio direction finders (RDFs), and fuel vapor detectors for engine rooms and bilges of gasoline-powered craft. Alarm systems are available to alert the skipper of dangerous conditions of engine overheating, low oil pressure, or high water in the bilge. Electric bilge exhaust blowers will add to the safety of the required ventilation systems for all engine and fuel tank compartments. All of these are in the "desirable," or even "necessary," category. Less vital items are discussed in the next major subdivision of this chapter.

Pollution control equipment is rapidly moving from the operationally desirable to the necessary category. All skippers should be looking forward to their needs and problems in this area.

Cleaning gear may not be "glamorous," but it is certainly operational. Specific lists will vary from boat to boat, but all may be expected to contain a swab (mop), bucket, sponges, chamois, metal polish and rags, and similar items.

## Sailboats

Sailboats without mechanical power, either installed or detachable, do not come within the equipment requirements of the Motorboat Act, nor are they checked as a part of the Courtesy Motorboat Examination program. Such craft over 16 feet in length are, however, eligible to become Auxiliary Facilities and must meet certain prescribed standards. These requirements can serve as a guide to all owners of sailing craft as to desirable safety equipment above the legal requirements.

Sailing Facilities under 26 feet in length are required to have one B-I hand fire extinguisher and larger craft must have on board two such units. These sailboats must meet the CME standard of one approved lifesaving device on board for each berth, with a minimum of two such devices. Further, such craft must meet all standards for motorboats other than those relating to propulsion machinery, fuel systems, and ventilation of related compartments. This would leave in the requirements such items as an anchor with line, distress flare, galley stove installation and general electrical system—all matters appropriate to the safe operation of any sailboat.

FIG. 336 Electric-motor-driven blowers for bilge vents are not required by regulations but are actually essential for safety, especially when starting up engines with no wind across the deck to provide natural ventilation.

FIG. 338 An automatic steering mechanism — often called an "autopilot" — offers much convenience on long open-water passages. Provided that a proper lookout is maintained, use of such a device increases safety through the elimination of fatigue.

FIG. 340 An anchor windlass on the foredeck can supply mechanical power for breaking the anchor out of the bottom and raising it to the surface. These are most useful if the anchor is drawn up into a hawsehole rather than being lifted onto the deck.

## Equipment for Convenience and Comfort

Many, but certainly not all, of the items of *equipment for convenience and comfort* fall into the electronic or electrical categories. These items are covered more fully in Chapter 25 and include navigational aids such as automatic radio direction finders, radar, and sophisticated positioning equipment including loran, decca, and others. Speedometers and logs will provide speed and distance information that will assist in piloting. An automatic steering mechanism—the so-called "autopilot"—adds greatly to the convenience of cruising. Loudhailers and intercom systems increase the convenience of operating or living aboard larger boats. Twin engine craft will benefit from engine synchronization indicators, and even more from equipment that will automatically do the function of matching engine speeds.

Electrical equipment items include pressure fresh water systems, water heaters, electrical refrigeration, showers with drain pumps, plus heating and/or air conditioning equipment.

All of these demand increased electrical power from the boat's system, either AC or DC. Auxiliary generating plants will permit the use of "shore-type" heavy-drain equipment when underway or at anchor. Inverters are very useful items to permit the operation of moderate-drain AC equipment without the noise of running a gasoline or diesel engine driven generator. Marine converters will supply the needed DC power without operation of the main engine if AC power is available; these will keep the boat's storage batteries at full charge when in port.

Outside the electrical-electronic field, equipment items for convenience and comfort are numerous and varied. Many skippers will want to have a boarding/swimming ladder for ease in going over the side and returning. A platform across the stern of larger boats is a great convenience for swimming or using a dinghy. The dinghy itself, perhaps with sails or a small outboard motor, may well be classed as an item of convenience equipment.

FIG. 339 A platform across the stern of a motorboat is a convenience item in connection with either swimming or the use of a dinghy. Some installations are fixed in place; others fold up against the transom when not in use.

Fresh water making equipment—stills to convert salt water to potable water—will often add immeasurably to a boat's cruising endurance. Stabilizers are now available for medium and larger motor yachts to eliminate much of the rolling from offshore cruising.

An anchor windlass on the foredeck will remove a major part of the physical labor involved in "getting the hook up" —it may even put this chore back into the category of duties of the "first mate."

Weather instruments — barometer, thermometer, and anemometer, and perhaps a hygrometer for measuring the relative humidity—will add to the interest of boating. With study and practice, they can add to the safety, too, of a craft and its crew. A recording barograph will provide interesting permanent records of atmospheric, and thus weather, changes.

The spare parts inventory of a boat can be expanded beyond the limits of necessity into the area of convenience. Carrying spare propellors, and even shafts, can often greatly reduce delays at a strange port away from home if these major components should become damaged. These may be beyond the capability of the crew to install, but their ready availability can often reduce repair times from days to hours.

Diving gear, either of the simple mask and snorkle style or the more complex SCUBA type, can make boating in many areas more interesting and can at times be of real value in making underwater inspections and repairs. "Wet suits" may be required for colder water areas.

### Boating Insurance

Insurance coverage is not something ordinarily thought of as boating "equipment," but to a prudent skipper it is as much a part of the outfitting of his craft as the compass or anchor.

Various coverages of marine insurance include those against loss of or damage to the boat itself, its hull, machinery, sails, and equipment; protection against liability for damages to the persons or property of others; and medical payments to cover the care and treatment of the owner or guests resulting from accidents on board. Other coverages can include boat trailers and the land transportation of the craft itself.

It is beyond the scope of this book to go into details of marine insurance, but the boat owner is reminded that an insurance policy can be one of his most valuable items of "equipment." Consult a reputable insurance agent for specific information on coverages applicable to your craft and her use—better yet, talk with two or three agents for proposals on coverages and quotations of rates.

At the time of preparation of this chapter, there was pending in Congress a bill known as the Federal Boat Safety Act. This legislation would largely repeal the provisions of the Motorboat Act of 1940 as they relate to required equipment on **recreational** motorboats. There would be substituted a set of more flexible regulations covering equipment in even wider scope than the present law. All boats, sail and power, used non-commercially or carrying no more than six passengers for hire would be included.

Regulations would extend to ground tackle, electrical systems, navigational equipment, and other items in addition to lights, whistles, bells, etc., now covered. In addition, "minimum safety standards" would be issued for boats and associated equipment, placing on manufacturers and dealers a measure of responsibility for the initial safety qualities of craft placed in use. To prevent variations from state to state, the Federal Government would preempt regulation of such matters.

Other sections of the proposed Act would replace the Federal Boating Act of 1958 with essentially the same system of boat numbering and accident reporting. Federal financial assistance would be made available to the States for boating safety programs. A National Boating Safety Advisory Council would be established with representatives from federal, state, and local governments; boat and associated equipment manufacturers; boating organizations; and the general public.

Congressional Committee hearings are likely in early 1970 for this bill, H.R. 15041. Progress toward final enactment into law cannot be predicted, and some changes in its provisions are possible before passage. New regulations resulting from the Act would not be effective for at least six months, and probably much longer, after enactment. During such time, the contents of this chapter will be appropriately revised.

### TABLE 3-1

| Hand Portable types | Foam (minimum gallons) | Carbon Dioxide (minimum pounds) | Dry Chemical (minimum pounds) | Carbon Tetrachloride (See note) |
|---|---|---|---|---|
| B–I | 1¼ | 4 | 2 | Approval discontinued. |
| B–II | 2½ | 15 | 10 | |

### TABLE 3-2

#### Minimum Required Equipment

| EQUIPMENT | CLASS A (Less than 16 feet) | CLASS 1 (16 feet to less than 26 feet) | CLASS 2 (26 feet to less than 40 feet) | CLASS 3 (40 feet to not more than 65 feet) |
|---|---|---|---|---|
| BACK-FIRE FLAME ARRESTER | One approved device on each carburetor of all gasoline engines installed after April 25, 1940, except outboard motors. | | | |
| VENTILATION | At least two ventilator ducts fitted with cowls or their equivalent for the purpose of properly and efficiently ventilating the bilges of every engine and fuel-tank compartment of boats constructed or decked over after April 25, 1940, using gasoline or other fuel of a flashpoint less than 110°F. | | | |
| BELL | None.* | None.* | One, which when struck, produces a clear, bell-like tone of full round characteristics. | |
| LIFESAVING DEVICES | One approved life preserver, buoyant vest, ring buoy, special purpose water safety buoyant device, or buoyant cushion for each person on board or being towed on water skis, etc. | | | One approved life preserver or ring buoy for each person on board. |
| WHISTLE | None.* | One hand, mouth, or power operated, audible at least ½ mile. | One hand or power operated, audible at least 1 mile. | One power operated, audible at least 1 mile. |
| FIRE EXTINGUISHER— PORTABLE | | | | |
| When NO fixed fire extinguishing system is installed in machinery space(s). | At least One B–I type approved hand portable fire extinguisher. (Not required on outboard motorboat less than 26 feet in length and not carrying passengers for hire if the construction of such motorboats will not permit the entrapment of explosive or flammable gases or vapors.) | | At least Two B–I type approved hand portable fire extinguishers; OR At least One B–II type approved hand portable fire extinguisher. | At least Three B–I type approved hand portable fire extinguishers; OR At least One B–I type *Plus* One B–II type approved hand portable fire extinguisher. |
| When fixed fire extinguishing system is installed in machinery space(s). | None. | None. | At least One B–I type approved hand portable fire extinguisher. | At least Two B–I type approved hand portable fire extinguishers; OR At least One B–II type approved hand portable fire extinguisher. |
| | Note: Dry Chemical and Carbon Dioxide ($CO_2$) are the most widely used types, in that order. The others, while acceptable, are seldom seen on boats. | | | |
| | Fire extinguishers manufactured after 1 January 1965 will be marked, "Marine Type USCG Type —— Size —— Approval No. 162.028/EX . . ."** | | | |

*NOTE.—Not required by the Motorboat Act of 1940; however, the "Rules of the Road" require these vessels to sound proper signals.
**NOTE.—Toxic vaporizing-liquid type fire extinguishers, such as those containing carbon tetrachloride or chlorobromomethane, are not accepted as required approved extinguishers on uninspected vessels (private pleasure craft).

# CHAPTER 4

# RULES OF THE ROAD / Lights and Day Shapes

FIG. 401 The navigation lights shown by a vessel at night identify her as a water craft and give some indication of her type, size, and relative heading. (left) Lights are also used at night to indicate the status of a vessel. The single white light shown above signifies to another vessel that the boat is at anchor. This is often called a "riding light" to distinguish it from a "running light."

Nautical Rules of the Road are somewhat broader than their land counterparts. On the water, such sets of rules include not only the expected "keep to the right" and the "vessel to your right has the right-of-way" provisions, but they also cover many other matters related to safety of operations, principally through the avoidance of collisions.

Although requirements for navigation lights are included in the Motorboat Act of 1940 for craft subject to its scope, the various Rules of the Road prescribe lights for *all* vessels and thus those for boats will be considered together with lights for larger ships.

## WHY NAVIGATION LIGHTS AND DAY SHAPES

On a vessel, *navigation lights* are lights shown of specified color (white, red, green, amber, blue), arc and range of visibility, and location as required by law and regulations. Their basic purpose is the prevention of collision by providing identificaton of a vessel and some information regarding her activities. Lights will indicate the relative heading of one vessel as seen from another, and may give some clue as to her size, special characteristics, and/or current operations. Most important is the information as to her relative orientation with respect to your vessel; a fact that must be known to determine who has the right-of-way.

Navigation lights are sometimes referred to as *running lights* (those shown under way) and *riding lights* (those

shown while at anchor or moored), but this terminology is unofficial and does not appear in the Rules of the Road.

*Day shapes* are objects of specified shape, size, color, and placement on a vessel as required by law and regulations. They serve some of the same purposes by day that navigation lights do by night. In normal visibility situations, the relative aspect and motions of two vessels can be determined by observation and no day shapes are required. They are, however, used to indicate special situations, such as being anchored or engaged in fishing, and some conditions not detectable by eye, such as a sailboat with her sails up but engine also in use—as will be noted in Chapter 5, such a craft is regarded as a power-driven vessel and is not entitled to any of the right-of-way privileges of sailing craft merely because her sails are up.

## SEQUENCE OF CONSIDERATION

As noted in Chapter 2, there are *three separate sets* of Rules of the Road currently in effect on U.S. waters, the Inland, Great Lakes, and Western Rivers Rules. For the sake of simplicity, these sets of Rules will be collectively referred to in this book as the "U.S. Rules," although this is not an official designation. Further, the boatman is faced with the applicability of the International Rules of the Road along the seacoasts outside of the boundary lines specified in page 31.

Because of their applicability to a greater number of

boatmen, the Inland Rules will be the primary consideration of this chapter. The Great Lakes and Western Rivers Rules will be discussed in terms of their differences with the basic provisions of the Inland Rules. This will in turn be followed by an explanation of the provisions of the International Rules of the Road regarding navigation lights and day shapes; this will be of particular interest to boatmen whose activities take them offshore along the coasts. The chapter is concluded with a review of the status of pending legislation that would extensively change the requirements for navigation lights and day shapes on the inland waters of the United States.

Regulations issued by state or local authorities on the topics of this chapter are too detailed and varying for consideration. Each skipper should check for those that will affect his boating.

The various sets of Rules of the Road also cover matters other than navigation lights and day shapes—such as right-of-way, whistle signals, fog signals, distress signals, etc.; these are the topics of Chapter 5.

### Numbered "Rules"

All of the sets of Rules of the Road, except the Inland Rules, consist of various sections which are numbered as Rule 1, Rule 2, etc. (The Inland Rules consist of a series of numbered "Articles" which are essentially the same as "Rules.") This chapter will deal only with those Rules relating to navigation lights and day shapes.

While there is some parallelism in the contents and numbering of Rules and Articles in the various sets, this, unfortunately, is not complete and cannot be relied upon when going from one set to another. There is some hope for greater uniformity in the future, though, see page for pending changes in the U.S. Rules.

### Indication of references

Numbers and letters shown in brackets are references to the applicable Article or Rule.

### DEFINITION OF TERMS

The verbatim U.S. Rules make considerable use of the term "steam vessel," but specifically state that the term includes any vessel propelled by machinery; this would, of course, include motorboats and auxiliary-engine driven sailboats. For the sake of clarity, in this chapter and Chapter 5, the phrase "power-driven vessel" will be used; this is the same, more inclusive phraseology that is used in the International Rules.

**Sailing vessel**—Every vessel which is under sail and is *not* being propelled by machinery is a *sailing vessel* for the purposes of the Rules of the Road.

**Power-driven** *(steam) vessel*—A vessel propelled by machinery, *whether or not she is also under sail,* is a *power-driven (steam) vessel*.

**Underway**—A vessel is *underway* when she is not at anchor, made fast to the shore, or aground.

**Visible**—Where the Rules require a navigation light to be visible for a stated distance, this visibility is understood to be on a "dark night with a clear atmosphere."

### Arcs of visibility—"points"

With the exception of the International Rules, the arc of visibility of navigation lights is specified in terms of "points"—in the International Rules, both points and degrees are used. These "points" are the same units of angular measurements as used for compasses and bearings—see page 9, and pages 270 to 271. One point is equal to $11\frac{1}{4}°$. See fig. 123.

Lights are generally 10-point ($112\frac{1}{2}°$), 12-point ($135°$), 20-point ($225°$), or 32-point ($360°$ or all around the horizon). Lights *should not,* of course, show through any wider arc than that prescribed by the Rules. It must, however, be recognized that in most practical cases, especially on quite small craft, the arcs will not exactly conform to the requirements and combination red-and-green bow lights in particular may show over somewhat wider arcs than 10 points for each color.

## The Inland Rules

The **Inland Rules of the Road** are applicable to all U.S. waters inside boundary lines established to limit the application of the International Rules of the Road—see page —*except* for waters specifically excluded and placed under the Great Lakes and Western Rivers Rules.

The Inland Rules consist of introductory material and 31 "Articles" numbered 1 through 32, less #4, containing the actual requirements, restrictions, etc. Not all Articles are applicable to the topics of this chapter; certain ones are covered in Chapter 5. With changes over the years, some sub-sections have been deleted without re-numbering the Rules as a whole; for example, there is no Article

**FIG. 402 During the day, when lights would be ineffective, "day shapes" are used to indicate the special status of vessels. Other information provided at night by lights—type, size, and relative heading—can be determined in daylight by direct observation.**

FIG. 403 The U.S. Inland Rules of the Road are written in terms of requirements for "steam vessels," but this is defined as including all vessels propelled by machinery of any type.

| 10-POINT | 12-POINT | 20-POINT | 32-POINT |

FIG. 404 The arc of visibility of navigation lights are specified in the Inland Rules in terms of "points." Each of these units of angular measurement equals 11¼°. A complete circle consists of 32 points.

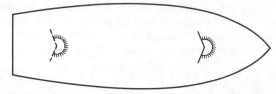

FIG. 405 Under the Inland Rules, all power-driven vessels carry a white forward light in the forepart of the vessel. This is a 20-point light, visible on ships for at least five miles and on motorboats for at least two miles. A sea-going vessel may also carry a similar light aft and higher.

15(b) although there is a 15(a), (c), etc., and there is now no Article 4 in the Inland Rules.

## NAVIGATION LIGHTS

Navigation lights will be discussed for various categories and sizes of vessels in the sub-sections below; they are also summarized in Tables 4-3 and 4-4 in this chapter.

### When lights are shown

Vessels are required to show the proper navigation lights from *sunset to sunrise* in all weathers, good and bad. During these times, no other lights which might be mistaken for navigation lights may be displayed. [Article 1]

Although not specifically provided for in the Inland Rules, nor prohibited by them, the prudent skipper does not hesitate to turn on his navigation lights during the day between sunrise and sunset under conditions of reduced visibility.

### Lights for Power-driven Vessels Underway

Lights for power-driven vessels underway will be first considered from the viewpoint of "vessels," all waterborne vehicles other than sailing vessels and seaplanes on the water. Special provisions for "motorboats" will be considered separately.

### Forward lights

A power-driven vessel, when underway, must carry in the forward part of the vessel (on or in front of the foremast if there is one), a white light showing over an unbroken arc of 20 points, from dead ahead to 2 points abaft the beam on either side. This white forward light must be visible at a distance of at least five miles. [Article 2(a)]

A *sea-going* power-driven vessel—one which goes into waters subject to the International Rules—may, while in waters of the Inland Rules, carry a second white light similar to the one described above. These two lights must be placed in line over the keel so that the after light will be at least 15 feet higher than the forward light, and their horizontal spacing must be greater than their difference in height above the hull. [2(e)]

Power-driven vessels, *except* sea-going vessels and ferryboats, *must* carry a central range of two white lights with the after light at least 15 feet higher than the forward

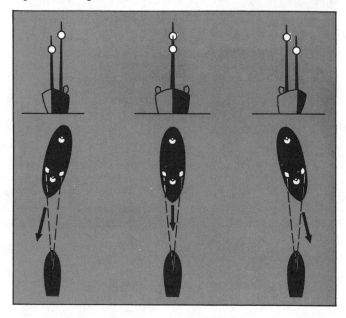

FIG. 406 The two white lights forming a central range on a vessel are an excellent indicator of her relative heading as seen from another vessel. These lights will normally be seen well before the colored side lights.

light. The forward light must meet the 20-point arc of visibility requirements of the light of Article 2(a); the after range light must be a 32-point light showing all around the horizon. This Article, 2(f), does not include a requirement as to the distance to which the after light must be seen.

**Value of range lights.** Range lights are a valuable aid in determining the relative heading of another vessel when she is first sighted at night. These white lights are both brighter and higher than the side lights, and consequently they normally will be seen well before the colored light or lights can be detected and read for their meaning.

The relative location of the two range lights will be the key. Should they be seen one directly over the other, the other vessel is headed *directly toward* the observer and danger of collision exists. Should the lower forward range light be seen to the right or left of the higher light, the other vessel is on an oblique course and the angle can be roughly gauged by the horizontal separation between the lights. See fig. 406.

FIG. 407 Any vessel or craft not showing a white light visible from astern must, under the Inland Rules, carry a separate white 12-point light visible for two miles or more. This light must be at the stern and should be on the same level as the sidelights.

If the lower light is to the left of the upper one, the red port light of the other vessel should be visible or become visible later. This has particular significance as it means that the other vessel is in the observer's "danger zone" and has the right-of-way; see page 73.

Any change in the horizontal separation of the other vessel's range lights, together with any change in the relative bearing of the other ship or craft will provide information as to the degree of danger of collision that exists. The relative speeds of the two vessels and any change of distance separating them, as each of these can be roughly judged at night, must be taken into consideration.

## Stern light

A vessel, when underway, *if not carrying one or more lights visible from aft,* such as the after range light of Article 2(f), must carry at her stern a white light showing over an arc of 12 points, six points on either side of dead astern, and visible for at least two miles. This stern light is to be mounted on the same level as the side lights, or as nearly so as practicable. [10(a)]

## Side lights

Power-driven vessels, when underway, will show a green light on the starboard (right) side and a red light on the port (left) side. These lights must show through an unbroken arc of 10 points from dead ahead to two points abaft the respective beam. Note that the sum of the arcs of the side lights is the same as the arc of the white forward light. The red and green lights must be visible for at least two miles. [2(b) and (c)]

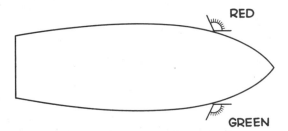

FIG. 408 In addition to white navigation lights, vessels show colored "sidelights"—red to port (left) and green to starboard (right). These lights show through an arc of 10 points each, from dead ahead to two points abaft the respective beam.

These side lights are required to be fitted with *inboard screens* projecting a minimum of three feet forward of the light. These screens are installed so as to prevent the side lights from being seen across the vessel's bow. [2(d)] On boats, the hull is frequently used to screen the side lights from being seen across the bow.

FIG. 409 Sailing vessels, with no mechanical propulsion being used, show the colored sidelights but not the white forward light. Since no other light would show aft, they also carry the 12-point white stern light (on small craft in bad weather, a white lantern or flashlight to be shown when needed).

### Lights for Sailing Vessels Underway

A sailing vessel underway—and remember that if any propelling machinery is in use, she is *not* a "sailing vessel" —will carry the same side lights and stern light of power-driven vessels, but will *not* carry the white forward light or lights of such vessels. [5]

### Lights for Small Craft

The requirements for lights on vessels subject to the Motorboat Act of 1940 are generally similar to the above, but with modifications as might be expected for smaller craft.

### Boats of Classes A and 1

Motorboats of Classes A and 1, those under 26 feet in length, see page 33, carry one white light which must be visible all around the horizon to a distance of not less than two miles. It is to be located aft and is normally on the centerline, but if necessary because of the construction of the boat, it may be located off the centerline. This

*text continued on page 64(h)*

FIG. 410 Boats less than 26 feet in length, meet the requirements of the Motorboat Act of 1940 by showing a white 32-point light located aft and as near the centerline as practicable. They also show a combination red-green light forward over 10-point arcs to either side.

## LIGHTS FOR VARIOUS TYPES OF VESSELS—INLAND RULES
### TABLE 4-3

Note: Vessels lighted according to the International Rules are not required to change their lights when navigating waters subject to other Rules of the Road.

| | | Bow (Foremast or Forward) | Side | Range | Remarks or Additional Lights |
|---|---|---|---|---|---|
| 1 | MOTOR BOATS Class A—under 16' Class 1—16' to less than 26' | None | Combination red and green each color showing 10 pts.* | White 32 pt.[1] Visible 2 mi. | [1]Placed higher than combination *Visible 1 mi. |
| 2 | Class 2— 26' to less than 40' | White—20 pts. | Red—10 pt. Green—10 pt. Screened so as not to show across bow. Visible 1 mi. | White—32 pt. Visible 2 mi. Placed higher than bow light. | |
| 3 | Class 3— 40' to 65' | Visible 2 mi. | | | |
| 4 | Motorboats and auxiliaries driven by *sail only*, as in illustration 4, show the colored lights appropriate to their class, and fixed white 12 pt. stern light showing aft, visible 2 miles, carried as nearly as possible at the level of the side lights. Motorboats and auxiliaries, under *motor and sail*, are lighted as motorboats of their respective classes. In bad weather, small boats may, if necessary, show an electric torch or lighted lantern to overtaking vessels. Small sailing vessels under way in bad weather, if they cannot keep their side lights fixed, may keep side lights at hand ready to show in time to avert collision. Note:—Under Motor Boat Act, motorboats of any class, may, optionally, carry lights prescribed by International Rules while operating on other than the high seas; on the high seas they must carry such lights. | | | |
| 5 | Sailing vessel or vessel in tow (except barges, canal boats, scows, etc. | None | Red—10 pt. Green—10 pt. | None | *12 pt. white showing aft, visible 2 mi., at level of side lights (See comments in item above regarding bad weather) |
| 6 | Steam or motor vessels over 65' in length (except those vessels falling in classifications noted below) | White 20 pt. Vis. 5 mi. | Red—10 pt. Green—10 pt. Vis. 2 mi. 36 in. screen | White 32 pt.[2] | [2]At least 15 feet higher than foremast light (On *sea-going* vessel, horizontal spacing must be at least as great as vertical separation) |
| 7 | Double-ended[3] ferry boat | White 32 pt.[4] Vis. 2 mi. | Red—10 pt. Green—10 pt. Vis. 2 mi. Three-foot screens | White—32 pt.[4] | [3]If not of double-ended type, carries same lights as inland steamer [4]On both ends at same height. Special light amidships may designate line |
| 8 | Steam pilot vessel on station[5] on pilotage duty and underway[6] | None | Red—10 pt. Green—10 pt. Three-foot screens[6] | None | White 32 pt. at masthead 8' above red 32 pt., each vis. 2 mi. Shows flares at intervals of not more than 15 min. [5]If not on station, carries same lights as other steam vessels [6]On station at anchor, side lights are extinguished |
| 9 | Fishing vessel underway engaged in commercial fishing[7] | None | None | None | Red 32 pt. 6' to 12' above white 32 pt. not more than 10' apart horizontally. White vis. 3 mi. red 2 mi. [7]If underway, but not fishing carries usual lights of her class except vessel under 10 gross tons may show combination red and green lantern to other vessels, in lieu of fixed side lights |
| 10 | Inland[10] tug without tow[8] | White 20 pt. Vis. 2 mi. if not over 56'; vis. 5 mi. over 65' | Red—10 pt. Green—10 pt. Three-foot screens | White 32 pt.[9] | [8]Lighted same as ordinary inland steam vessel [9]At least 15' higher than foremast light [10]For lights of ocean-going tug on inland waters, see International Rules, Table 4-5 |
| 11 | Inland tug with tow alongside or pushed ahead | Two white 20 pt. vertically arranged, at least 3' apart *or* lights mentioned in fourth column. Vis. same as item 10, above | Red—10 pt. Green—10 pt. If side light is obstructed by vessel towed, light is transferred to outside of tow. | Two white 32 pt. vertically arranged, at least 3' apart *or* foremast lights mentioned in second column | With 20-pt. towing lights forward, may carry 32-pt. white range light aft. May carry small white light aft for tow to steer by, not visible forward of beam. With 32-pt. towing light aft, may carry 20-pt white light forward. When pushing tow ahead and using 20 pt. white towing lights forward, carries two amber 12 pt. lights aft vertically arranged |
| 12 | Inland[10] tug with tow astern | Three white 20 pt. vertically arranged, at least 3' apart *or* lights mentioned in fourth column. Vis. same as item 10, above | Red—10 pt. Green—10 pt. | Three white 32 pt. vertically arranged, at least 3' apart *or* foremast lights mentioned in second column | |
| 13 | Rowboat (under oars or sail) | None | None | None | White light shown on approach of another vessel |
| 14 | Vessels working on a wreck | White 32 pt. (each outside vessel) at least 6' above decks | None | White 32 pt. stern light (each outside vessel) at least 6' above decks | Two red 32 pt. in verticle line, 3' to 6' apart, at least 15' above decks |

## LIGHTS FOR VARIOUS TYPES OF VESSELS—INLAND RULES
### TABLE 4-3 (Continued)

| | | Bow (Foremast or Forward) | Side | Range | Remarks or Additional Lights |
|---|---|---|---|---|---|
| 15 | Dredge (held in position by moorings or spuds) | None | None | None | White 32 pt. each corner at least 6' above deck. Two red 32 pt. in verticle line 3' to 6' apart, at least 15' above deck. Scows moored alongside show white 32 pt. on each outboard corner, at least 6' above deck |
| 16 | Dredge (self-propelling suction type, underway, with suction on bottom) | White 20 pt. Vis. 2 mi. if not over 65'; vis. 5 mi. over 65' | Red—10 pt. Green—10 pt. | White 32 pt. | Two red 20 pt. under the white 20 pt. foremast light, 3' to 6' apart. Upper red light 4' to 6' below white light. At stern two red 4 pt. showing aft, in verticle line 4' to 6' apart |
| 17 | Vessel towing wreck | Carries lights same as described for inland tug with tow astern (see No. 12) except that in lieu of the regular 3 white towing lights she shows 4 lights vertically arranged, 3' to 6' apart, upper and lower white, two middle lights red, 20-point if carried on the foremast, 32-point if carried aft | | | |
| 18 | Naval and other U.S. | 12 | 12 | 12Both the Inland and International Rules provide, in Article 13, that these rules shall not interfere with special rules made by the Government of any nation with respect to additional station and signal lights for two or more ships of war or for vessels sailing under convoy, or with exhibition of recognition signals adopted by ship owners, properly authorized by their respective Governments | |
| 19 | At anchor—vessel under 150' in length | One white 32 pt. forward, vis. 2 mi. where best seen | None | None | In specially designated anchorage areas, vessels under 65' need no anchor light. |
| 20 | at anchor—vessel 150' in length or over | One white 32 pt. forward at least 20' above hull. Vis. 2 mi. | None | None | One white 32 pt. aft. at least 15' lower than forward light. Vis. 2 mi. |

## LIGHTS FOR BARGES, CANAL BOATS AND SCOWS IN TOW ON INLAND WATERS
### TABLE 4-4

Except Great Lakes, east to Montreal—Red River of the North—Mississippi River and tributaries above Huey P. Long Bridge—that part of the Atchafalaya River above its junction with the Plaquemine-Morgan City alternate waterway—Gulf Intracoastal Waterway and certain connecting waters, from the Rio Grande to Cape Sable—Hudson River (Troy to Sandy Hook)—East River and Long Island Sound—Narragansett Bay—Lake Champlain—and other tributaries.

| | | Bow | Side | Stern | Remarks or Additional Lights |
|---|---|---|---|---|---|
| 21 | One barge or canal boat towed astern of tug | None | Green—10 pt. Red—10 pt. Vis. 2 mi. | Two white 32 pt. athwartship horizontal. At least 5' apart and at least 4' above deckhouse | None |
| 22 | More than one barge or canal boat towed astern in tandem | None | Green—10 pt. Red—10 pt. Vis. 2 mi. | 13One white—12 pt. Vis. 2 mi. | 13Except last vessel of tow which carries instead two 32 pt. white athwartship horizontal at least 5' apart and at least 4' above deckhouse |
| 23 | More than one barge or canal boat towed astern abreast (one tier)14 | None | Green—10 pt. Red—10 pt. Vis. 2 mi. (carried at outer sides of bows of outside boats) | 14One white—32 pt. on each outside boat | 14If more than one tier, white stern lights are placed on outside boats of last tier only |
| 24 | Barges, canal boats or scows towed alongside of tug | None | Colored side lights carried on outer side of outside barge if side lights of towing vessel are obstructed by barge | None | None |
| 25 | Scows towed singly or tandem | White 32 pt.15 Vis. 5 mi. | None | White 32 pt.15 Vis. 5 mi. | 15Lights to be carried at least 8' above surface of water. |
| 26 | Scows massed in tiers, two or more abreast, astern | White 32 pt. on outer side of all outside scows. Vis. 5 mi.15 | None | White 32 pt. on outer side of outside scows last tier only. Vis. 5 mi.15 | 15Lights to be carried at least 8' above surface of water. |

NOTE:—When barges, canal boats or scows are *pushed ahead* of the tug, head boat carries red 10-pt. and green 10-pt. side lights on outer bows, or if more than one abreast, they are shown from outer bow of outside boats.

12 and 22

10 PT. LT.
20 PT. LT.
32 PT. LT.

11 and 24

19

20

12 and 23

12 and 25

C

## LIGHTS FOR VARIOUS TYPES OF VESSELS—INTERNATIONAL RULES
### TABLE 4-5

| | | Bow (Foremast or Forward) | Side | Range | Remarks or Additional Lights |
|---|---|---|---|---|---|
| 27 | Power-driven vessels less than 65 feet in length[17]<br>NOTE—Small power-driven boats may carry white light forward at height less than 9 feet but it must be carried not less than 3 feet above the side lights or combination red and green light. | White—20 pt. at least 9' above gunwale. Vis. 3 mi. | Red—10 pt. Green—10 pt. Vis. 1 mi. or combination red and green, each color showing 10 pts. At least 3' below foremast light | None | 12-pt. white showing aft.<br>[17]Instead of the lights called for here these vessels may optionally carry those lights intended for larger power-driven vessels (see item 31) |
| 28 | Vessels under oars or sails under 40 feet | None | Combination red and green, each color showing 10 pts. shown to approaching vessels | None | |
| 29 | Rowboats, under oars or sails | None | None | None | Show electric torch or lighted lantern to prevent collision |
| 30 | Sailing vessel or vessel in tow | None | Red—10 pt. Green—10 pt. Vis. 2 mi. 36 in. screens | None | 12 pt. white light showing aft. Vis. 2 mi. Sailboats may optionally carry on top of foremast two 20 pt. lights, upper red, lower green, visible 2 mi., sufficiently separated for distinction |
| 31 | Power-driven vessels generally (ocean liners, sea-going yachts, etc.) | White 20 pt. 20' to 40' above hull. Vis. 5 mi.<br><br>Both (see "range") 20-pt. white lights must be in line with, and over, the keel | Red—10 pt. Green—10 pt. Vis. 2 mi. Three-foot inboard screens | White 20 pt. at least 15' higher than foremast light vis. 5 mi. Optional on vessels under 150 feet. Horizontal distance between white lights at least 3 times the vertical distance | White 12 pt. showing astern. Vis. 2 miles. Carried at, or near, level of side lights |
| 32 | Pilot vessels (power-driven | On station, under way, carry white 32-pt. masthead light not less than 20 ft. above the hull, and 8 feet below it a red 32-pt. light, both vis. 3 mi. | Normal red and green side lights only when underway | Normal stern light when underway | Show flare or intermittent 32-pt. white light at intervals of not more than 10 minutes. Normal anchor lights if at anchor |
| 33 | Vessels engaged in trolling | [18] | [18] | [18] | [18]Show only lights appropriate for power-driven or sailing vessel |
| 34 | Vessels engaged in fishing but not trolling or trawling | None[19] | When making way through the water same side lights as under items 27, 28, or 31 above | Two vertical 32-pt. lights, upper red, lower white, 4' to 12' apart. Boats under 40' may show the white 3' under red and not less than 9' above gunwale; larger craft must show it at height above side lights of at least twice distance between vertical lights[19] | 12-pt. white stern light. If outlying gear extends more than 500', another 32-pt. white light 6' to 20' away from vertical lights toward outlying gear and neither higher than white light nor lower than side lights<br>[19]When not actually engaged in fishing, show normal lights of vessel their size |
| 35 | Vessels engaged in trawling | None[19] | Same as item 34 | Same as item 34 except that upper of two vertical lights is green[19] | Same as item 34 |
| 36 | Vessels at anchor | 32-pt. white light at or near bow, vis. 2 mi. On ships 150 feet or more, at least 20' above hull, vis. 3 mi. | None | None | At or near stern of vessels 150' or more, a 32-pt. white light at least 15' lower than forward one and vis. for 3 mi. After light is optional for vessels under 150' in length |
| 37 | Vessel aground | Same as in item 36 | None | None | Same as in item 36 plus two red vertical 32 pt., at least 6' apart. Vis. 2 mi. |
| 38 | Vessel not under control | None | None, unless under way with way on, when side and stern lights are carried | None | Two red 32 pt. in vertical line at least 6' apart. Vis. 2 mi. |
| 39 | Cable-laying vessel | Three 32-pt in vertical line at least 6' apart. Upper and lower red; middle white. Vis. 2 mi. | None, unless under way with way on, when side and stern lights are carried | None | Same rules apply to vessels laying or picking up a navigation mark, or engaged in surveying or underwater operations |
| 40 | Power-driven vessel with one vessel in tow, or more, if tow is 600' or less in length from stern of tug | Two white 20 pt. in verticle line not less than 6' apart. Lower light must be not less than 14' above the hull. | Red—10 pt. Green—10 pt. Vis. 2 mi. three-foot screens | White 20 pt. (optional if tug is less than 150' in length) | Must show either the fixed white 12-pt. stern light, or small white light aft for tow to steer by, not visible forward of beam |
| 41 | Power-driven vessel with tow over 66' in length | Three white 20 pt. in vertical line at least 6' apart. Lower light may be not less than 14' above hull | Red—10 pt. Green—10 pt. Vis. 2 mi. three-foot screens | White 20 pt. (optional if tug is less than 150' in length) | Must show either the fixed white 12-pt. stern light, or small white light aft for tow to steer by, not visible forward of beam |

*continued from page 64 (e)*

permissive variation takes into account the small craft with an outboard motor mounted on the center of the transom; there, the light would be mounted to either side of the motor well or bracket.

Boats of this size must also carry a combined red and green light in the fore part of the craft with each light covering its normal 10-point sector to a distance of at least one mile.

### Boats of Classes 2 and 3

Boats of from 26 to 65 feet length, Classes 2 and 3, must, under the requirements of the Motorboat Act of 1940, carry a white 20-point forward light as near the stem as possible, a white 32-point light aft, and separate 10-point red and green side lights. The stern light must be on the centerline and higher than the forward white light. The white lights are required to be visible for two miles and the colored lights for one mile. Inboard screens or other shielding (hull or superstructure) must be used to prevent side lights from being seen on the wrong side across the bow. [Section 3, MBA]

### Sailboats

"Motorboats when propelled by sail alone" are sailboats insofar as the Inland Rules are concerned. Those of Classes A and 1 show only the combination red and green light, *not* the all-around white light aft. Such craft of Classes 2 and 3 show only the screened separate side lights and *neither* of the white lights. There is conflict between the Inland Rules which require a stern light and the Motorboat Act which requires only the availability of a lantern or flashlight. In the interest of safety, a motorboat of any class under sail alone should carry the 12-point stern light of Article 10 for otherwise she would have no light regularly visible from astern.

FIG. 411 Under the Motorboat Act, powered craft 26 feet and more in length carry separate sidelights and a 20-point white bow light in addition to the all-around light aft. The white lights must be visible for at least two miles, and the colored lights to a distance of not less than one mile.

### "Bad weather"

The Inland Rules permit certain variations "if it is not possible on account of bad weather or other sufficient cause" for normal stern and side lights to be mounted in accordance with the requirements of the Rules.

When the regular stern light of Article 10(a) cannot be mounted, the operator of the vessel must have a lantern or flashlight readily available in order to show a white light in time to prevent a collision with an overtaking vessel. [10(b)]

If bad weather prevents vessels of less than 10 gross tons from showing the prescribed colored side lights, such lights may instead be kept close at hand, lighted, and ready for use upon the approach of another vessel. When

FIG. 412 A motorsailer—a boat designed for primary propulsion by either sails or machinery—shows the lights of a motorboat when underway at night under power, whether or not her sails are hoisted.

When propelled by sails alone, (right) no machinery in use, this same motorsailer shows the lights of a sailboat at night—colored sidelights and white stern light; no white lights visible from ahead.

Rosenfeld Photo

FIG. 413 Quite small craft, propelled by oars or sails, need not carry regular navigation lights, but instead must have a lantern or flashlight showing a white light and this must be exhibited in sufficient time to prevent collision at night.

FIG. 414 A motorboat on inland waters has the option of displaying either the lights of the Motorboat Act of 1940 or those prescribed by the International Rules of the Road for craft of her size.

this occurs, the red and green lights must be shown on the appropriate sides and over the normal arcs of visibility soon enough to prevent an accident. Care must be taken that the red and green lights are not accidentally reversed, and to help prevent this, the outsides of the lanterns must be painted with the color of the light. The requirement for adequate inboard screens remains in effect. [6]

## Miscellaneous small craft

Rowing boats, whether propelled by oars or sails, do not carry any regular navigation lights, but instead must have a white light to be shown in ample time to prevent collision with another craft. [7]

Rafts or other watercraft not specifically provided for in the Rules, operated by hand power, horse power, or the current of the river, will carry one or more white lights as prescribed by the Commandant of the Coast Guard. [9(d)] These lights are spelled out in detail in the Pilot Rules.

FIG. 415 Navigation lights of the Fresnel lens type are generally considered "old-fashioned" and seldom appear on new boats. They are, however, considerably more efficient than the plain lens type and permit the use of smaller bulbs.

## Option for International Rules

Boats subject to the Motorboat Act of 1940 have the *option* of carrying lights complying with the requirements of the International Rules of the Road for craft of their size in lieu of the normal lights required by the MBA, even when in "inland waters." See pages 64(t) to 64(u) for the applicable provisions of the International Rules.

This option is of value to the owners of boats that may be operated outside the Inland Rules boundary lines at night as it eliminates any need for making a change in lights when going from one body of water to the other. The navigation lights of the International Rules are permitted on inland waters, *but not vice versa*. A boat lighted for the Inland Rules may be in violation when proceeding seaward of the boundary lines.

## Candlepower requirements

Although the statutory requirements remain in terms of being seen for so-many miles on a clear, dark night, the Coast Guard has, by regulation, established a more scientific criteria for the power of lights. Data have been worked up translating miles range to candlepower *immediately outside the light*; see Table 4-1. These values must not be confused with the candlepower rating of the bulb used, an entirely different matter. See page 66.

These light intensity standards are applicable as of 1

January 1973. New navigation lights and replacements of existing lights made on and after this date must be of an approved type.

## Recommended bulb sizes

To be even more practical, the Coast Guard has prepared a list of bulb types, by manufacturers' standard numbers, that will provide a light intensity adequate to meet the requirements of the paragraph above. Using the recommended standard bulb, a skipper need not concern himself about having light intensity measurements made, or with getting a mile or two away from his boat on a clear, dark night.

The recommended bulb types are listed in Table 4-2 for two kinds of installations, with and without Fresnel lenses. These lenses, more common to older and larger navigation lights, are composed of sets of prisms and lens rings which concentrate the light from the bulb source into beams in the desired direction. Navigation lights with Fresnel lenses may be equipped with bulbs of much lesser intensity than lights with plain lenses; for example, a No. 90 bulb rated at 6 candlepower rather than a No. 1142 bulb of 21 candlepower.

It should be noted that because of the low transmission factor (2%) for light through a green lens, there currently is no adequate standard bulb to recommend for a plain-type lens starboard side light. The strongest for each voltage—#1130 for 6 volts, #1142 for 12 volts, or #1230 for 32 volt circuits—should be used, if it will physically fit; its inadequacy, however, should be recognized.

FIG. 416a The Inland Rules require a single white all-around light in the forward part of vessels at anchor that are under 150 feet in length. This light need not be shown on craft 65 or less feet in length if in a designated "special anchorage area."

FIG. 416b Larger vessels—150 feet or more in length—must show a second white light aft in addition to the basic anchor light shown forward. The forward light must be at least 20 feet above the hull with the after light at least 15 feet lower.

FIG. 417 A tug towing a barge alongside or pushing one ahead in waters of the Inland Rules displays special towing lights which indicate her status. See text for permissive, but not mandatory, range lights. *The two amber stern lights are used only when pushing ahead, not for towing alongside, and only when the towing lights are carried forward.

FIG. 418 A different set of towing lights is prescribed for a tug towing a barge or string of barges astern on a hawser. Boatmen should know all towing lights so as to recognize the situation when underway at night.

FIG. 419 A towed vessel—not a barge—shows lights prescribed by the Inland Rules of the Road. Lights for towed barges are regulated by the Inland Pilot Rules and vary for different bodies of water.

## Lights for Vessels at Anchor

Under the Inland Rules, vessels less than 150 feet in length at anchor display a single white light in the forward part of the vessel where it can best be seen all around the horizon. This light must be visible for at least two miles. [11(a)]

If the anchored vessel is 150 feet or more in length, she must show a white 32-point light in the forward part of the vessel at least 20 feet above the hull, *and* a second white all-around light at or near the stern at least 15 feet lower than the forward light. Both of these lights must be visible for a distance of not less than two miles. [11(b)]

## Special anchorage areas

There are, however, locations on the inland waters designated as "special anchorage areas" where anchor lights need not be shown by vessels 65 feet or less in length. In these special areas, barges and similar craft 150 feet and more in length may display only the one anchor light of Article 11(a) rather than the two required by 11(b) of the Inland Rules. If two or more barges or similar craft are tied together and anchored as a unit in such areas, the anchor light need be shown only by the vessel having its anchor down. [11(c)]

These special anchorage areas are frequently found off yacht clubs and similar facilities. For the boatman, they offer the possibility of legally leaving his craft unattended at a mooring for extended times without having an anchor light burning continuously or turning one on each sunset.

## Lights for Towing

Vessels which are either towing another or are being towed have, because of this condition, much less maneuverability than vessels proceeding singly. To indicate this situation at night, special navigation lights are prescribed for vessels towing or being towed.

## Towing alongside or pushing ahead

A power-driven vessel when towing another alongside or pushing another ahead carries, in addition to her normal side lights, *two* white lights, one over the other and not less than three feet apart. These lights must be shown, but may be carried at *either* the position of the white forward light of Article 2(a) *or* the after range light of Article 2(f). In each case, they have the same arc of visibility and distance seen requirements as the 2(a) or 2(f) lights and one of the towing lights replaces such light so that there are only two lights at that location. [3(a)]

## Towing astern

If the towed vessel is astern of the towing vessel, regardless of distance, there will be *three* white lights vertically as described above for either variation, with the third light three feet above or below the others. (Note that in this case the "not less than" phraseology is not used and the separation is specific.) [3(a)]

## Range lights when towing

The Inland Rules are simply not clear as to the whole picture of white lights carried by towing vessels. If Article 3 is read as the sole requirement for white lights, it would then result that a towing vessel *would not* show a central range of lights. If, on the other hand, Article 3 is read in conjunction with Article 2, then range lights *would* be shown.

It has generally been held that the showing of range

Red 32 Points

White 32 Points

**FIG. 420** Fishing vessels—those trawling, dredging, or fishing with any sort of drag nets or lines—show special red-over-white all-around lights at night to indicate their occupation and limited maneuverability. When not fishing, they show normal navigation lights.

ably in different geographic areas. The prudent skipper knows well those of his home waters, and he checks the applicable regulations before venturing into new areas.

### Lights for Fishing Vessels

All vessels when trawling, dredging, or fishing with any kind of drag nets or lines must show from some part of the vessel where they can best be seen a red light above a white light with a vertical separation of not less than 6 nor more than 12 feet. If these lights are separated horizontally, this distance must not be more than 10 feet. These are 32-point all-around lights, the white must be visible for at least three miles and the red light for not less than two miles. [9(c)] The phrase "Red over white, inland fishing at night" will aid in remembering this combination of special lights, but note it is for Inland waters only.

Fishing vessels of 10 gross tons or more, when underway and *not* fishing, will carry the same lights as other vessels underway. [9(b)] Such vessels under 10 gross tons *may* substitute for fixed side lights a portable lantern with red and green glasses to be shown upon the approach of another craft. [9(a)]

### Lights for Pilot Vessels

Pilot vessels, when on station and engaged in pilotage duty, do not show normal lights for vessels of their size, but rather they display a white all-around light at the masthead and will also show a "flare-up" light at intervals of 15 minutes or less. On the near approach of or to other vessels, the pilot vessel must have her side lights ready and flash or show them at short intervals to indicate the direction in which she is headed.

A pilot vessel of such smaller size as needing to go alongside another vessel to put the pilot aboard may "show" the required white light rather than having it fixed at the masthead, and may show a portable lantern with red and green glasses in lieu of the regular side lights.

A power-driven pilot vessel engaged in pilotage duty and on station, but *not* at anchor, displays the all-around and flare-up white lights of such a vessel as described above, and in addition will show normal side lights plus a red light mounted eight feet below the white light and visible out to two miles or more all around the horizon. If anchored, she omits the colored side lights but shows the others. This combination of lights has led to the memory-aiding phrase—"White over red, pilot ahead," which is suitable for both Inland and International waters.

A pilot vessel when not engaged in pilotage duty on her station will carry the usual lights of a vessel of her size and type. [8]

lights by towing vessels is *permissible, but not mandatory.* In view of the safety value of range lights—they usually provide another vessel with relative heading information before the colored side lights can be seen—it would appear the wiser procedure to show a white 32-point light higher aft if the two or three "towing" lights are carried as 20-point lights forward *or* show a single 20-point white light forward if the towing lights are 32-point lights located aft. In both cases, a range is established and no confusion is likely to result, despite the vagueness of the rules.

### Amber lights

If the white towing lights are carried in the forward location in lieu of the light of Article 2(a), a vessel pushing another ahead *must* carry at or near her stern *two amber* 12-point lights vertically one above the other and spaced not less than three feet apart. Each of these lights must show six points to either side of dead astern for a distance of not less than two miles. [3(b)]

Such a vessel *may* carry the after range light of Article 2(f), but if she does, then the amber lights must be shown in a vertical line with and at least three feet lower than this after range light.

### Steering light

A vessel towing one or more other vessels astern and carrying the three white towing lights in the forward location *may* carry, in lieu of the normal stern light of Article 10, a small white light abaft the funnel for the towed vessel to steer by; but this "steering light" must not show forward of the beam. [3(b)] This Rule assumes that the tug is *not* carrying the optional and recommended 32-point after range light—such light, if carried eliminates the need for either the regular stern light or a steering light.

### Lights for towed vessels

Any vessel being towed by a power-driven vessel, except a barge, scow, etc., will carry her normal side lights but will *not* show the white forward or range lights of Article 2. She will, however, display the Article 10(a) white stern light. [5]

### Lights for towed barges

Navigation lights for barges, scows, and the like are covered by regulations in the Pilot Rules. Lights for such towed craft are, in many cases, quite complex.

These rules for lights on towed craft may vary consider-

**FIG. 421** A motorsailer underway with sails up and engine not in use may hoist a day shape of one black ball to indicate that she is then a "sailing vessel" and entitled to the right-of-way privileges of such a craft over a power-driven vessel.

FIG. 422 A ship anchored or moored in a channel or fairway is required by the Pilot Rules for Inland Waters to hoist a day shape of one black ball not less than two feet in diameter. This is not required for craft 65 feet or less in length.

FIG. 423a A barge towed astern is lighted in accordance with one of several sets of requirements as determined by the waters being traversed. See the various applicable sections of the Inland Pilot Rules.

FIG. 423b A group of barges towed astern is fitted with navigation lights as prescribed by the section of the Inland Pilot Rules applicable to the waters traveled. Any one of several sections may be applicable.

FIG. 424a A barge being pushed ahead will carry sidelights on each outside corner of the bow; these must be fitted with suitable inboard screens. If there are several barges being pushed as a unit, the sidelights will be on the outside bow of the outside leading barges of the group.

FIG. 424b If the height of the tow alongside is such as to obscure the tug's sidelight, then such colored light must be shown from the barge. On some waters, a scow towed alongside must have white lights at each outer corner.

## Special Purpose Lights

Article 12 of the Inland Rules authorizes any vessel to additionally show a "flare-up" light, or make any detonating signal that cannot be mistaken for a distress signal, if this is necessary in order to attract attention.

## Naval lights and recognition signals

The Inland Rules contain a section that allows the use of additional special lights on vessels sailing in convoy. It also allows the use of recognition signals adopted by shipowners and authorized by the government if such have been duly registered and published. [13]

## DAY SHAPES OF THE INLAND RULES

The Inland Rules prescribe only one day shape; many others, however, will be found in the Pilot Rules for Inland Waters to be discussed later in this chapter.

## Power-driven vessel under sail only

Article 14 provides that a power-driven vessel proceeding under sail only—meaning a power-driven type of vessel not then using her machinery—"but having her funnel up" *may* carry in the daytime, where it can best be seen, one black ball or shape two feet in diameter. This rather

archaic language can be interpreted in more modern terms as meaning a vessel which gives the outward appearance of being power-driven but at the moment is not so propelled. The carrying of this optional day signal is advantageous to such a vessel as it identifies her as a sailing vessel under the Rules and aids her in claiming her proper right-of-way over power-driven vessels.

## EXEMPTIONS FOR GOVERNMENT VESSELS

Any requirements regarding lights—their number, placement, or arc of visibility—shall not apply to those displayed on vessels of the Navy or Coast Guard if the Secretary of the Department concerned certifies that this is not possible due to the special construction of these vessels—for example, submarines and aircraft carriers. In such cases, however, their lights must comply as closely as the Secretary finds to be feasible.

Details of the non-complying lights for each vessel or class of vessel are published in Notices to Mariners and other official documents.

## PILOT RULES FOR INLAND WATERS

The **Pilot Rules for Inland Waters** are issued under authority contained in the preamble to the Inland Rules and are applicable to the same waters.

These Pilot Rules for Inland Waters are a part of the Code of Federal Regulations, Title 33, Part 80. For boatmen however, they are more conveniently found in Coast Guard publication CG-169, pages 43-66.

Lights and day shapes prescribed by the Inland Pilot

**FIG. 425** At night, a moored dredge shows two red lights arranged vertically to indicate her status, plus a white light at each corner to mark her outer limits. Anchor marker buoys are fitted with a red light, and scows alongside show a white light at each outside corner. All lights are 32-point and must be visible for two miles. Day shapes for the dredge are shown in the inset, upper right.

Rules will be considered concurrently where both are applicable for a type of vessel or situation. In most instances, the reason for such lights and day shapes is to provide for early recognition of the limited maneuverability of the particular vessel displaying them.

Numbers in brackets are references to the applicable sections of the Pilot Rules.

### Day shape for vessels anchored or moored

Vessels *over 65 feet in length,* when anchored or moored in a channel or fairway, must display during the day a black ball not less than two feet in diameter. This is shown in the fore part of the vessel where it can best be seen by other vessels. [80.25]

### Lights for barges and related craft

The navigation lights for barges and similar towed craft are relatively complicated, and are made all the more so by the fact that the requirements differ on various bodies of water.

On much of the waters subject to the Inland Pilot Rules, side lights are carried on barges towed astern or on the outer sides of the outer barges if two or more are abreast. A barge towed astern, or the last barge if a string is towed astern, carries *two* white all-around stern lights not less than five feet apart *horizontally,* and not less than four feet above the deckhouse. Barges in a string, other than the last one, carry a normal single 12-point white stern light. If more than one abreast, each barge carries a single white light at its stern. Normal arcs of visibility are prescribed for side lights and a two-mile range of visibility is required for both white and colored lights.

Barges and similar craft towed alongside are fitted with an outboard side light if their height is sufficient to obscure the corresponding side light of the towing vessel. Barges, scows, etc., pushed ahead are lighted with side lights on the outboard bows of the leading barge, or on the outboard bows of the outboard leading barges if there are two or more abreast. [80.16]

Somewhat different sets of requirements prevail on inland waters along the Gulf Coast, on the Hudson River and Lake Champlain, and on Long Island Sound and cer-tain adjacent waters. These modified requirements will be found in the Pilot Rules for Inland Waters and should be studied by boatmen whose activities will bring them into these areas. [80.16a and 80.17]

The Pilot Rules recognize that barges and related craft being towed by power-driven vessels may pass from waters where one set of lights is used into an area where the requirements are different. Such transients are not obliged to change their lights from those specified at the place where the trip begins or ends. If, however, such barges are used for local purposes in other than their home waters, then their lights must be changed to comply with local rules. [80.16b]

Under an "Interpretative Ruling" of the Inland Pilot Rules, a barge which travels on waters subject to the International Rules *and* on those of the Inland Rules may, for the duration of such a voyage, display the navigation lights and shapes required by International Rule 5; see pages 64(v), 64(y). [86.05-10]

### Moored dredges

By day, dredges which are held in place by moorings or spuds (pile-like metal tubes that are forced into the bottom under the water) are identified by two red balls not less than two feet in diameter carried in line vertically between three and six feet apart. These must not be less than 15 feet above the deckhouse and where they can best be seen from all directions.

At night, such dredges show a white light at each corner of the deck plus two vertically spaced red lights where they can best be seen from all directions. These red lights must be not less than three feet nor more than six feet apart and must be at least 15 feet above the deck. [80.20]

The two paragraphs immediately above well illustrate the complexity of the rules and regulations relating to navigation lights, and the care that must be taken to read and study them carefully. Note that the red lights shown at night must be a minimum of 15 feet above the "deck," but that the day shapes must be displayed the same distance above the "deckhouse." These are two quite different levels aboard a dredge. The use of two different reference points adds considerably to the complexity of the requirements of a single section of the Inland Pilot Rules.

Where scows are made fast alongside a dredge, a white light must be shown from each outboard corner of them not less than six feet above the deck.

Pipelines attached to dredges, and either floating or supported by trestles, must display a line of *amber* lights between 8 and 12 feet above the water approximately equally spaced horizontally and sufficient in number to mark the length and course of the pipeline. The interval between lights where the pipeline crosses navigable channels must not be more than 30 feet. The shore or discharge end of the line is marked by two red lights in a vertical line three feet apart with the lower one at least eight feet above the water. If the pipeline is to be opened at night for the passage of vessels, a similar vertical pair of red lights will mark each side of the opening. [80.23]

These white and red lights must each be visible for a distance of at least two miles.

### Vessels working on submarine construction

Vessels which are moored or anchored and are engaged in laying cables or pipes, dike construction, excavation, or

FIG. 426 A pipeline extending from a dredge must be properly lighted at night to prevent its being a hazard to the safe navigation of vessels. The pipeline must be lighted along its length and have special lights at the discharge end or any point of opening for the passage of vessels.

similar submarine construction work will display by day two balls not less than two feet in diameter. These balls will be hoisted one over the other with three to six feet separation. The upper one will be painted with alternate black and white vertical stripes; the lower one will be solid red. They must be shown not less than 15 feet above the deck and where they can best be seen from all directions.

Note the use of height above "deck" here as distinguished from height above "deckhouse" for dayshapes in the preceding subsection.

This type of working vessel will display at night three red lights in a vertical line with three to six foot separations and the lowest light not less than 15 feet above the deck. These lights are to be located where they can best be seen from any direction to a distance of not less than two miles.

If there is a "stringout" of such vessels, the three red lights are carried on the channelward end of the series. If the stringout crosses a navigable channel and will be opened at night for the passage of vessels, two sets of such red lights will be displayed, one at either side of the opening, in lieu of a single display at the channelward end of the stringout. The series of vessels must also be marked by a row of amber lights not less than four feet above the deck (above the deckhouse if there is one) in a position where they can best be seen from all directions at a distance of two miles or more. The spacing between such amber lights must not exceed 50 feet. [80.22]

### Day shapes for fishing vessels

The Inland Pilot Rules require that all vessels or boats fishing with nets, lines, or trawls, when underway in the daytime, display a basket where it can best be seen as an indication of their activity to an approaching vessel. If such fishing vessels or boats have their gear out while at anchor, they must, on the approach of other vessels, show the same signal in the direction from their anchor back toward the nets or gear. [80.32a]

### Coast Guard vessels at aids to navigation

A vessel of the Coast Guard while handling or servicing an aid to navigation during the daytime will display two orange and white vertically striped balls not less than two feet in diameter. These will be hoisted in a vertical line

FIG. 427 Vessels that have restricted maneuverability because they are working on submarine cables or pipelines, or other forms of sub-surface construction work, must show special lights or day shapes as appropriate to indicate their status.

FIG. 428 The Inland Pilot Rules require that day shapes be shown by fishing vessels much the same as special lights are required at night by the Inland Rules of the Road. Such craft hoist a basket as their distinctive day signal.

separated not less than three nor more than six feet.

By night, Coast Guard vessels engaged in such work will show two red lights arranged and separated as above, from a location on board where they can best be seen. [80.33a]

### Distinctive light for law-enforcement craft

The Pilot Rules for Inland Waters authorize a distinctive light for law-enforcement vessels which may be shown by day or night whenever such vessel is engaged in direct law enforcement and identification of its status is desirable or where necessary for safety reasons. This light is in addition to normal navigation lights.

This light is authorized for law-enforcement vessels of the United States, or its political subdivisions, including municipalities, having administrative control over navigable waters as authorized by a controlling Federal or

FIG. 429 Coast Guard buoy tenders and other vessels working at aids to navigation show a special day signal of two orange-and-white vertically-striped balls. The night signal is two red lights, one over the other.

FIG. 430 (Below) A distinctive light is authorized for law-enforcement craft and may be used by day or night in addition to normal navigation lights. It is a blue revolving beam of low intensity mounted on the forward part of the craft.

when the pilot is in total darkness except for the lowest possible of illumination for the compass or other essential instruments; this illumination should be dim red in color.

### Other special lights and day shapes

The Pilot Rules for Inland Waters also contain provisions for lights and day shapes for other special vessels and situations which are less likely to be encountered by the average boatman. These are listed below with the applicable section number from the Code of Federal Regulations, Title 33, Part 80; they are also included in publication CG-169.

> Ferryboats—80.15
> Dredges underway and engaged in dredging operations—80.21
> Vessels made fast alongside a wreck or moored over a wreck—80.19
> Vessels engaged in hydrographic surveying—80.33
> Vessels towing a submerged or partially submerged object not carrying lights—80.18
> Rafts and other miscellaneous craft—80.32

These sections of the Inland Pilot Rules may be consulted for information on these lights as required by the individual boatman's circumstances.

State governmental agency.

The distinctive light is a *blue* revolving horizontal beam of low intensity light. It may actually rotate, or may appear to do so because of a revolving reflector behind a steady light which results in a pulsating or periodic peak intensity effect.

The blue light will be located at any effective point on the forward exterior of the craft. A shield or other device, fixed or movable, to restrict the arc of visibility of this light may be used if desired. [80.45]

### Warning signal for dangerous cargo

A vessel made fast to a dock, when loading or unloading dangerous cargo such as explosives or flammable liquids or gasses, must display a red flag by day—this is usually the "B" flag of the International Code of Signals—or a red light at night. There are no specifications in the Pilot Rules as to the height or placement of this red flag or light although it may be assumed that each should be visible from all directions.

A vessel engaged in such operations while at anchor must fly a similar flag in the daytime, but there is no requirement, or authorization, for a red light at night. [80.38]

### No unauthorized lights

The Pilot Rules contain a prohibition against the display of *any* light not required by law which would in any way interfere with the prescribed lights. [80.36]

At night, good practice dictates that no lights other than the legally required navigation lights be shown anywhere on the decks of a vessel. Not only are extraneous lights disconcerting to the pilots of other vessels, but the direct or reflected rays of lights on his own craft will interfere with the night vision of the skipper. Vision at night is best

FIG. 431 When necessary to pass under a bridge, a vessel may lower any navigation light or day shape. After passing under the bridge, the light or shape must be promptly restored to its required height or position.

### Modifications while passing under bridges

Any vessel, when passing under a bridge, may lower any light or day shape if required to do so by the available vertical clearance. When clear of the bridge, such lowered lights or day shapes must be immediately raised to the positions or heights required by law or regulations. [80.40]

### PENALTIES

The penalties for violation of the Inland Rules or Pilot Rules for Inland Waters are described in Chapter 2; see page 39.

For certain specified violations, the penalty is prescribed as the possible suspension or revocation of a master's or pilot's license.

## Great Lakes Rules

The **Great Lakes Rules of the Road** are derived from an Act of Congress of 8 February 1895 with subsequent amendments. From this Act, authority is granted to the Secretary of the Department in which the Coast Guard is operating, and on to the Commandant of the Coast Guard, for the issuance of regulations which become the **Pilot Rules for the Great Lakes;** these will be covered later in this chapter.

These Rules apply on waters that may be generally described as the Great Lakes and their tributaries and connecting waterways—exact limits are set forth in Chapter 2.

The format of the Great Lakes Rules is generally the same as for the Inland Rules except that the term for major subdivisions is "Rule" rather than "Article." Also, as noted before in this chapter, there is little parallelism in the numbering of rules relating to the same general subject matter although in some places identical, or nearly

FIG. 432 The Great Lakes Rules of the Road allow a double after range light. The horizontal separation of the two lights must not be greater than 30 inches, and one or the other, or both, of the lights must be visible from all directions.

identical, language is used.

The Great Lakes Rules will be considered here in terms of their differences from the Inland Rules discussed in detail above. Identical requirements, even though appearing in differently numbered rules, will *not* be repeated.

### Lights for Power-driven Vessels Underway

The white navigation lights required by the Great Lakes Rules (GLR) are generally the same as those of the Inland Rules (IR). The GLR do, however, require that the forward white light be at a greater height above the water than the colored side lights. [3(a)]

### Range lights

On the Great Lakes, a power-driven vessel *over 100 feet in length* must carry a central range of white lights. The after light is visible all around the horizon to a distance of three miles; it must be at least 15 feet higher and 50 feet further aft than the forward light (which must be visible for five miles. [3(e)]

FIG. 433 On the Great Lakes a sailing vessel regularly shows only her red and green sidelights at night, but will, on the approach of a power-driven vessel, show a "lighted torch" in that direction.

In lieu of such a single second light aft, there may be carried *two* white lights placed not more than 30 inches apart horizontally and arranged so that one or the other, or both, will be visible from all directions. (The logical placement of such lights would be on either side of a mast or stack.) [3(e)]

Vessels *100 feet or less in length* must carry a bright white all-around light aft higher than the forward light, but with no specified difference in height or horizontal separation, and with no specified minimum distance of visibility. [3(f)]

### Lights for Towing

A Great Lakes power-driven vessel having a tow other than a raft must carry the basic forward 20-point white light plus a second white light of the same characteristics not less than six feet above or below the basic light. The towing vessel must also carry a small bright light abaft the funnel or aftermast for the towed craft to steer by; this "steering light" must not be visible forward of the beam. The towing vessel carries the usual side lights, but does *not* show the after range light of Rule 3(e) or 3(f). [4]

### Towing a raft

The lights of Rule 4 above do not apply if the tow is a raft. In this case, there are two white *all-around* lights arranged *horizontally* athwartships not less than eight feet apart. Each light must be visible for at least five miles. These lights are to be mounted in the fore part of the ship (on or in front of the foremast if there is one) at a height above the hull of at least 20 feet, except that if the beam of the vessel exceeds 20 feet, then the height must equal the beam up to a maximum height of 40 feet. Such a vessel carries normal side lights and the steering light aft. [5]

### Towed vessel

A vessel in tow carries normal side lights and must also show a small bright light aft, but such light must not be visible forward of the beam. Rule 6 does not, however, define or specify any details of "small" or "bright." Neither does the Rule state a color for this light, but it is set as white in the Pilot Rules for "canal boats" being towed.

### Lights for Other Vessels

A sailing vessel underway carries *only* the usual red and green side lights. She will, however, upon the approach of any power-driven vessel show a "lighted torch" in the direction of approach of the other vessel. [6 and 12]

## Open boats

On the Great Lakes, "open boats" are not required to carry the side lights specified for vessels; but if they do not, then they must carry a lantern with a green glass on one side and a red glass on the other which shall be exhibited in sufficient time to prevent collision.

Open boats, when at anchor or stationary in the water, must show a bright white light. They may also use a flare-up light if this is considered expedient. [11]

## Miscellaneous craft

Tugs under 100 feet in length in harbor service, fishing boats, canal boats, rafts, and other miscellaneous craft are lighted in accordance with regulations issued by the Commandant of the Coast Guard. [7 and 10]

### Anchor Lights

The Great Lakes Rules require that the anchor light of a vessel under 150 feet in length be at a height not exceeding 20 feet above the hull and be visible for one mile. (The Inland Rules do not specify a height and require two miles range.) [9]

For larger vessels, those 150 feet and more in length,

**FIG. 434** The Great Lakes anchor lights for vessels 150 feet or more in length are quite complex. A pair of white lights is shown forward with another pair aft and lower. In addition, white lights must be shown at 100-foot intervals along both sides.

**FIG. 435** A vessel is "not under command" when it is underway but incapable of maneuvering, such as might result from a steering system failure or breakdown in propulsion machinery. Such a ship shows two red lights at night in lieu of the white forward lights. Sidelights are shown only if she is making way through the water.

the anchor lights of the GLR are *very* different from those of the IR. For such ships, there must be *two pairs* of lights plus additional lights along the deck. In the fore part of the ship, there will be two white lights at the same height of not less than 20 feet nor more than 40 feet above the hull. These lights must be not less than 10 feet apart on an athwartships line, and arranged so that one or the other, or both, is visible all around the horizon to a distance of at least one mile. At or near the stern, there must be another pair of white lights similarly arranged but not less than 15 feet lower than the forward pair. In addition to these four anchor lights, there shall be at least one white light shown for every 100 feet along the deck measured from the forward pair of lights; these lights must be at least two feet above the deck and insofar as intervening structures permit, they should be visible from any angle of approach. No range of visibility is specified for these deck lights. [9]

### Lights for Special Situations

The Great Lakes Rules prescribe lights for vessels of *over 65 feet length* in two special situations. There are no similar lights in the Inland Rules.

## Vessels not under command

A vessel "not under command"—a better phrase might be "not under control"—is one such as might have suffered a breakdown of propulsion machinery or a steering failure. At night, such a vessel must show two red lights one over the other in lieu of the basic white forward light of Rule 3(a). These are 32-point lights separated by at least three feet vertically, shown where they can best be seen and visible for not less than two miles.

Such a vessel will show her usual colored side lights if she is making way through the water, but will not show side lights if no way is being made. [30(b)]

## Vessels aground

A vessel of over 65 feet in length, when aground at night, will show the two red "not under command" lights of the above paragraph *plus* the appropriate white anchor lights of the GLR for a vessel of her size. No other navigation lights will be shown. [30(c)]

### Inland Rules Lights Not Used

The Great Lakes Rules do *not* contain any provisions for lights comparable to the distinctive lights for pushing ahead or towing alongside as distinguished from towing

**FIG. 436** By day, a vessel not under command indicates her situation by hoisting two black ball shapes similar to the one used when at anchor. A vessel aground hoists three such shapes. Craft 65 feet or less in length need not show these day shapes of the Great Lakes Rules.

astern; amber lights for towing vessels; special lights for fishing or pilot vessels; 12-point stern lights; and signal lights to attract attention.

## Day Shapes

The Great Lakes Rules prescribe day shapes for three situations, all for vessels *over 65 feet in length*. An additional day shape appears in the Pilot Rules for the Great Lakes.

**FIG. 437a** On waters subject to the Great Lakes Pilot Rules, small harbor tugs of under 100 net tons show sidelights plus a 20-point white "headlight" (usually located on top of the pilothouse). An additional white forward light is shown when actually towing.

**FIG. 437b** Barges ("canal boats") pushed ahead on the Great Lakes carry the usual colored sidelights with inboard screens on the leading outer bows, and may show a 20-point amber light visible for three miles on the centerline forward on the barges.

## Vessels anchored

When at anchor between sunrise and sunset, one black ball not less than two feet in diameter must be displayed in the forward part of the vessel where it can best be seen. The GLR omit the "or moored" language of the Inland Pilot Rules and do *not* limit the application of this requirement to vessels anchored "in a fairway or channel." [30(a)]

## Vessels not under command

When not under command during the day, a vessel hoists two black balls in a line vertically similar to the anchor ball described above; the separation between the shapes must be three feet or more. [30(b)]

## Vessels aground

The day signal for vessels *over 65 feet in length* when aground is three "anchor" balls hoisted vertically and separated by not less than three feet. [30(c)]

### PILOT RULES FOR THE GREAT LAKES

As in the case of the Inland Rules, the Great Lakes Rules authorize the issuance of Coast Guard regulations which are known as the *Pilot Rules for the Great Lakes*. These are a part of the Code of Federal Regulations, Title 33, Part 90, but are most conveniently found in Coast Guard publication CG-172.

## Small harbor tugs

Tugs under 100 net tons used primarily for harbor towing carry the normal side lights and a white 20-point forward light ("headlight") on the top of the pilothouse (at the foremast head if there is one).

When towing, other than towing a raft, such a tug will show an additional white light of the same characteristics as the headlight not less than three feet above or below the headlight.

When towing a raft, the two headlights will be all-around lights carried on a horizontal line not less than four feet apart.

All of these headlights must be visible to a distance of at least three miles. [90.16]

## Other lights

The Pilot Rules for the Great Lakes also prescribe lights for miscellaneous craft and situations as follows—numbers refer to sections of Title 33 of the Code of Federal Regulations; these will also be found in CG-172.

    Ferryboats—90.18
    Canal boats towed astern—90.19
    Canal boats pushed ahead—90.19a
    Craft propelled by handpower, horsepower
      or by current—90.20
    Rafts—90.21
    Boats navigated only on the River St.
      Lawrence—90.17

The term "canal boat" as used in the above sections of the Great Lakes Pilot Rules also includes barges, scows, and "other craft of nondescript type not otherwise provided for by statute or regulations."

**FIG. 438** On the waters governed by the Western Rivers Rules, a "river-type" power-driven vessel—one with two stacks in line athwartships—may carry red and green lights that show forward, abeam, and aft on their respective sides. These are in lieu of normal 10-point sidelights.

**FIG. 439** The after range light is mandatory in the International Rules of the Road for vessels 150 feet or more in length, and it is optional for smaller vessels. Note that it is a 20-point light, not 32-point as in Inland Article 2(f). The required 12-point white stern light is not visible in these views.

### Applicability of Certain Inland Pilot Rules

The Great Lakes Pilot Rules prescribe the same lights and day shapes for Coast Guard vessels working at aids to navigation as the Inland Pilot Rules, and the same lights and warning flags for vessels handling dangerous cargo. They authorize the same distinctive blue light for law-enforcement craft, and they contain the same prohibition on the carrying of unauthorized lights that would interfere with the detection and understanding of required lights.

### PENALTIES

The penalties for individuals and vessels violating the Great Lakes Rules of the Road or the Pilot Rules for the Great Lakes are discussed on page 39. They are close to, but not exactly the same as those provided for the Inland Rules.

### ARMY REGULATIONS FOR THE GREAT LAKES

There exists in Title 33 of the Code of Federal Regulations a set of regulations issued by the Corps of Engineers, Department of the Army. These appear as Part 201, General Regulations. Such regulations are necessary to meet statutory requirements placed on the Army Engineers by Acts of Congress as discussed in Chapter 2.

The requirements of these Army regulations relating to lights and day shapes do not conflict with the Great Lakes Rules of the Road or Pilot Rules. They duplicate some of the requirements and add details, mainly relating to floating plant (dredges, etc.) working in channels.

## Western River Rules ⎯⎯⎯⎯⎯⎯⎯

The **Western Rivers Rules of the Road** consist of numbered "Rules" like the Great Lakes Rules, but again the numbering is not parallel in most cases although often the provisions are essentially the same.

An unusual provision of the WRR, not found in any of the other sets of Rules, pertains to special lights for "river steamers"—vessels with two stacks on a line athwartships, typical of the old-time stern-wheelers. Such vessels *may* carry, *in lieu of* normal side and range lights, a red light on the outboard side of the port stack and a green light similarly on the starboard stack. These lights show *forward, aft, and abeam* on their respective sides. [6]

Because of their lesser applicability to boatmen as compared with other sets of U.S. Rules of the Road, the Western Rivers Rules and their associated Pilot Rules will not be considered in detail in this chapter. The skipper concerned with these waters—principally the Mississippi River and its tributaries, see page 38 for exact limits—should obtain a copy of Coast Guard pamphlet CG-184 and study it carefully.

The Army Engineer navigation regulations applicable on the Great Lakes also apply on the Western Rivers. (In fact, they also apply on limited portions of waters of the Inland Rules, all rivers emptying into the Gulf of Mexico and their tributaries.) These regulations appear in full in CG-184 which should be consulted if there is need for knowledge of their detailed provisions.

## International Rules of the Road ⎯⎯⎯⎯

Careful study of the U.S. Inland Rules of the Road provides an excellent basis for an understanding of the "International Regulations for the Prevention of Collisions at Sea"—the full and formal name for what is generally referred to as the **International Rules of the Road.**

These regulations—created by international conferences and made applicable to U.S. waters and U.S. vessels by Act of Congress and Presidential proclamation—consist of a series of numbered "Rules" plus an "Annex." Certain of these Rules relate to lights and day shapes, and will be discussed in this chapter. Other Rules and the Annex are covered in Chapter 5.

The consideration of the International Rules in this chapter will be focused on their differences and variations from the basic U.S. Inland Rules. Where no difference is pointed out, the provisions of a Rule of the International Rules of the Road (IntRR) are the same as those of the Inland Rules (IR) although not necessarily the Article with the corresponding number.

### Applicability

The International Rules, as established under U.S. authority, are applicable to two situations:

1. To *all* vessels in waters within United States sovereignty outside the prescribed boundary lines at entrances to bays, rivers, harbors, etc.; see page

2. To all U.S. vessels *on the high seas* not subject to another nation's geographic jurisdiction.

### Additional definitions

International Rule 1(c) formally defines a number of terms used in the Rules in addition to those in the Inland Rules. (The IR definitions, page 64(c), are applicable except that the IntRR uses "power-driven vessel" instead of "steam vessel" for the same meaning.)

**Vessel**—The word "vessel" includes every description of watercraft, other than a seaplane on the water, used or capable of being used as a means of transportation on water. This definition obviously includes a boat of any size or means of propulsion.

**Seaplane**—The word "seaplane" includes a flying boat and any other aircraft designed to maneuver on the water.

**Height above deck** — The term "height above deck" means height above the uppermost continuous deck.

**Length and breadth**—The length and breadth of a vessel shall be her length overall and her largest breadth. (Length and span of a seaplane are also defined in the IntRR.)

**Fishing** — The term "engaged in fishing" means fishing with nets, lines, or trawls, but does *not* include fishing with trolling lines.

### NAVIGATION LIGHTS

In general, the requirements of the International Rules regarding navigation lights are for brighter lights placed at greater heights or with greater separation. These factors stem from the larger size of vessels normally affected by the IntRR and the need for detection and comprehension at greater distances.

The IntRR specifically authorize the showing of navigation lights between sunrise and sunset in conditions of restricted visibility and in all other circumstances where they are deemed necessary. This is, of course, in addition to the requirement that they must be shown from sunset to sunrise. [1(b)]

## Lights for Power-driven Vessels Underway

As before, lights for vessels in general will be considered first, followed by exceptions and variations for small craft.

**POWER-DRIVEN VESSELS LESS THAN 65'— OPTION 1**

A twelve-point white light visible for at least two miles

A 20-point white light visible for at least three miles and mounted not less than 9' above the gunwale

Green starboard and red port ten-point side-lights visible for at least one mile from dead ahead to two points abaft the beam

**ANY VESSEL UNDER SAIL—**

Optional—two 20-point lights sufficiently separated as to be clearly distinguished and visible for at least two miles, the upper light to be red and the lower light to be green

A twelve-point white light visible for at least two miles

Green starboard and red port ten-point side-lights visible for at least two miles from dead ahead to two points abaft the beam

**POWER-DRIVEN VESSELS LESS THAN 65'— OPTION 2**

A twelve-point white light visible for at least two miles

A 20-point white light visible for at least three miles and mounted not less than 9' above the gunwale

A 20-point combination red-and-green light visible for at least one mile from dead ahead to two points abaft the beam and mounted not less than 3' below the 20-point white light

**POWER-DRIVEN VESSELS LESS THAN 40'— OPTION 1**

A twelve-point white light visible for at least two miles

A 20-point white light visible for at least three miles and permitted to be mounted less than 9' above the gunwale but not less than 3' above the sidelights

Green starboard and red port ten-point side-lights visible for at least one mile from dead ahead to two points abaft the beam

**ANY SAILING CRAFT LESS THAN 40'**

Optional—two 20-point lights sufficiently separated as to be clearly distinguished and visible for at least two miles, the upper light to be red and the lower to be green

A twelve-point white light visible for at least two miles

A combination red-and-green lantern (points not specified; probably 20-point intended) placed where it can best be seen and visible for at least one mile—the green light shall not show to port and the red light shall not show to starboard

**POWER-DRIVEN VESSELS LESS THAN 40'— OPTION 2**

A twelve-point white light visible for at least two miles

A 20-point white light visible for at least three miles and permitted to be mounted less than 9' above the gunwale but not less than 3' above the combination light

A 20-point combination red-and-green bow light visible for at least one mile from dead ahead to two points abaft the beam

**FIG. 440** Rule 7 of the International Rules of the Road provides for lesser light requirements for craft less than 65 feet in length. Two options are available for power-driven boats and two size groups are established. These lights must be shown by craft on offshore waters beyond established boundary lines. They are acceptable on inland waters in lieu of the lights of the Motorboat Act and various U.S. Rules of the Road.

## Forward lights

The International Rules require a central range of two white lights (except on small craft). The basic forward 20-point white light must have the same characteristics as for the Inland Rules. [2(a)(i)]

The after light of the two must be higher by at least 15 feet with both lights in line over the keel. The IntRR require that the horizontal distance between these two white lights be at least three times their vertical separation. The lower of the lights, the forward one, must be at least 20 feet above the hull; if, however, the breadth of the vessel is greater than 20 feet, then it must be above the hull by a distance equal to that breadth, but need not be more than 40 feet above for wider vessels. In all instances these white forward lights must be so placed as to be above and clear of all other lights and obstructing superstructures. [2(a)(iii)]

It should be noted that the International Rules do *not* allow the alternative of a 32-point after range light as in the Inland Rules, but rather require a 20-point after light for vessels 150 or more feet in length, and permit one for smaller vessels. A separate 12-point stern light is required; see below.

## Stern light

International Rule 10(a) does *not* contain the Inland Rules requirement that the stern light be carried as nearly as practicable on the same level as the side lights. The IntRR are silent as to the height of the 12-point white stern light visible for at least two miles.

## Side lights

The requirements for and specifications of side lights and inboard screens under the International Rules are the same as for the Inland Rules with one exception. Rule 6(a) allowing side lights to be kept ready rather than fixed in position in bad weather does *not* contain the Article 6 size limitation to "vessels of less than ten gross tons," and so would be applicable to all size vessels.

### Lights for Sailing Vessels Underway

International Rule 5(a) spells out the requirement for sailing vessels underway to carry the normal stern light of Rule 10, which requirement exists in the Inland Rules but is not so explicitly stated.

## Additional optional light

International Rule 5(b) has no counterpart in the Inland Rules. It describes *optional* additional forward lights for sailboats to be carried at the top of the foremast. These are a red upper light and a green lower light sufficiently separated so as to be clearly distinguished. They are 20-point lights and must be visible for at least two miles.

### Basic Lights for Small Craft

Power-driven vessels of less than 65 feet in length, vessels under oars or sails under 40 feet in length, and rowing boats may carry *either* the forward and side lights specified in the basic rules for "vessels," *or* alternatively may follow the special provisions of Rule 7 which allow for several options.

## Power-driven craft under 65 feet

Power-driven vessels of less than 65 feet length may carry in the forepart of the craft where it can best be seen a 20-point, 3-mile, white light not less than 9 feet above the gunwale. They must also show normal red and green side lights visible for one mile *or* a combination red-and-green light carried not less than three feet below the white forward light. [7(a)] (The regular stern light requirement of Rule 10(a) must also be met.)

## Power-driven craft under 40 feet

If the power-driven craft is less than 40 feet in length, she may carry the white forward light at a height of less than nine feet above the gunwale, but such light must be not less than three feet above the separate side lights or the combination red-and-green light. [7(c)]

## Sailing craft under 40 feet

Vessels of less than 40 feet in length, under sails or oars, may carry, in lieu of fixed side lights, a lantern showing a green light on one side and a red light on the other, of such intensity as to be visible for at least one mile and so fixed that the colors show only on the proper sides. Where this light is not fixed in place, it must be kept ready for immediate use and exhibited in sufficient time to prevent collision. [7(d)]

## Smaller craft

Small rowing boats, whether under oars or sail, are required only to have an electric torch (flashlight) or a lighted lantern showing a white light which will be exhibited in time to prevent a collision. [7(f)]

The term "small" is not precisely defined in the Rule, but it apparently would apply to dinghies and the like.

In "a small vessel"—again not precisely defined as to size—if it is not possible to carry a fixed stern light by reason of bad weather or other sufficient cause, then an electric torch or lighted lantern may be kept at hand and shown to an overtaking vessel in sufficient time to prevent a collision. [10(b)]

### Lights for Vessels at Anchor

The International Rules of the Road require the same anchor lights as the Inland Rules but further allow the second light, mandatory for vessels 150 feet or more in length, to be shown by smaller vessels (this option is not available under the IR). International Rule 11 does *not*, however, contain any provisions for "special anchorage areas" where the requirements for lights and shapes are lessened. This is to be expected as the open waters of the International Rules provide relatively less sheltered locations for anchorages.

**FIG. 441** Vessels 150 feet or more in length at anchor in waters subject to the International Rules must show two anchor lights at night similar to the Inland Rules. Here, however, the second light may also be shown by smaller vessels.

## Lights for Towing

The requirements of the International Rules for lights on towing vessels are quite different from the corresponding Inland Rules provisions, being rather briefer and simpler.

Basically, International Rule 3 does *not* provide lights to distinguish between towing astern and towing alongside or pushing ahead as does Inland Article 3. Rather, the differences in IntRR lights serve to distinguish between tows that are more or less than a certain overall length behind the towing vessel. The IntRR require two towing lights for tows measuring 600 feet or less from the stern of the towing vessel to the stern of the last vessel towed. Three lights are prescribed for tows exceeding 600 feet.

### Light characteristics

These towing lights are white, show through an arc of 20 points to a distance of five miles, and one of them replaces the basic forward light of Rule 2(a)(i). The vertical separation between the lights must be at least six feet, and if there are three lights the two separations must be the same; the lowest light must be at a height of not less than 14 feet above the hull. [3(a)]

The towing vessel must also show her normal side lights and *either* the usual stern light or a small white light abaft the funnel for the towed vessel to steer by, but such light, if used, must not show forward of the beam. [3(b)] The after 20-point range light is *not* carried.

### Lights for towed vessels

Vessels being towed carry the side lights of Rule 2, but not the forward white lights of that Rule. They also show the normal stern light of Rule 10, except that vessels other than the last one in a string of two or more may substitute a small "steering light" for the stern light. [5(a)]

A vessel being pushed ahead—a rather uncommon procedure on the more open waters of the International Rules—will carry red and green lights at her forward end that meet the usual requirements of Rule 2 for arc of visibility, range, and side screens. A group of vessels being pushed ahead will be lighted as if they were a single large vessel. [5(c)]

### Small craft

Power-driven craft less than 65 feet in length, when towing or pushing ahead another vessel, will carry two white lights in a vertical line one over the other and not less than four feet apart. These are 20-point lights visible to a distance of at least three miles. One of these two lights replaces the basic white forward light of Rule 7(a); in a vessel with a single mast, these lights may be carried on the mast. Such craft will show their usual separate side lights or combined red-and-green light, plus a stern light or a steering light. [7(b)]

Vessels less than 65 feet in length, when towed or pushed ahead, may carry either the separate side lights or the combined red-and-green light for craft of their size. If, however, a group of small craft being pushed exceeds 65 feet in length, these provisions of Rule 7(e) do not apply and the regular lights of Rule 5(c) must be exhibited.

If such craft are being towed astern, they also carry the usual stern light of Rule 10(a), except that if more than

**FIG. 442a** The towing lights of the International Rules distinguish between tows longer than 600 feet and those of shorter overall length from the stern of the towing vessel. Towing alongside or pushing ahead is seldom done on these waters.

**FIG. 442b** Tows longer than 600 feet are identified by the three white towing lights of the tug. The after 20-point light shown above is optional rather than required as this tug is less than 150 feet in length.

**FIG. 443** Vessels towed on waters of the International Rules will carry normal side lights but not white forward (range) lights. At their stern, they will show the usual 12-point stern light except that all but the last vessel in a string of several may substitute a small white "steering" light.

one are being towed, all but the last one may substitute a steering light.

## Lights for Special Purpose Vessels

Specific lights or combinations of lights are prescribed for various categories of vessels so that they may be more easily and quickly identified as such at night.

### Power-driven pilot vessels

Under the International Rules the white masthead light of a power-driven pilot vessel underway and engaged in her duties must be at least 20 feet above the hull and visible for three miles or more (no height or range for this light is specified in the Inland Rules). An all-around red light visible to the same distance is carried eight feet below the white light. If, however, the pilot vessel is less than 65 feet in length, she may show the white masthead light at a lower height but not less than nine feet above the gunwale with the red light four feet lower. As in the Inland Rules, a "flare-up" light or lights must be shown, but the maximum interval is specified as 10 minutes rather than 15. The IntRR permit the use of an intermittent white all-around light in lieu of the flare-up lights. [8(a)]

FIG. 444 A power-driven pilot vessel shows white over red all-around lights, and when underway, normal side and stern lights. Flare-up lights are shown at intervals of not more than 10 minutes. When not underway, stern and side lights are extinguished and an anchor light, below red light on illustration at left, is shown if appropriate.

FIG. 445 The fishing lights of the International Rules are of two types. Vessels trawling show a green-over-white combination; vessels other than trawlers show red over white lights. When making way through the water, side lights are shown. When gear extends more than 500 feet into the seaway, a white light must be shown to that side.

FIG. 446 Vessels of limited maneuverability show a red-white-red combination of three all-around lights in a vertical line in lieu of the normal white forward lights. Normal side and stern lights are shown.

Such vessels also carry the normal side and stern lights for their size.

## Sailing pilot vessels

Sailing pilot vessels are specifically provided for in the International Rules. Such a vessel shows a white all-around three-mile light at the masthead (no minimum height above the hull specified) plus normal side and stern lights. She does *not* show the red light beneath the white masthead light as provided for power-driven pilot vessels, but she does show the flare-up lights (the substitution of an intermittent white light for the flare-up lights is not mentioned for sailing pilot vessels). [8(b)]

## Pilot vessels generally

All pilot vessels engaged in pilotage duties but not underway will carry the white-over-red (power-driven) or white only (sail) all-around lights and show flare-up lights as appropriate; if at anchor, they will also exhibit the normal anchor lights. [8(c)] They will not show colored side lights in these situations.

Pilot vessels *not* engaged in pilotage duty show only the usual lights for craft of their size. [8(d)]

## Fishing vessels

International Rule 9 regarding lights for fishing vessels is rather different from Inland Article 9. Separate sets of lights are provided for trawling and for other forms of fishing.

**Trawling**—Vessels engaged in trawling—the dragging of a dredge net or other apparatus through the water—must carry two lights in a vertical line with not less than 4 nor more than 12 feet separation between them and the lower light must be above the level of the side lights a distance not less than twice the amount of separation. The upper light is to be green and the lower will be white; both are 32-point lights.

Such vessels *may* also carry a white 20-point light, but if so, it must be carried lower than and abaft the all-around green and white lights. [9(c)]

**Fishing other than trawling**—Vessels engaged in fishing other than in trawling, carry a pair of lights as above except that the upper light is red rather than green. If such a vessel is less than 40 feet in length, the upper red light may be carried at any height not less than nine feet above the gunwale with the white light not less than three feet below it. [9(d)]

If such vessels have outlying gear extending more than 500 feet into the seaway, they must carry an additional all-around white light at a horizontal distance of from 6 to 20 feet away from the vertical lights in the direction of the outlying gear. This additional white light must not be higher than the white lower light of the vertical pair, nor lower than the side lights. [9(f)]

**All fishing vessels**—All lights referred to above must be visible for at least two miles. [9(b)]

Fishing vessels, when making way through the water, must also show the appropriate side lights or combined red-and-green light, plus the usual stern light. When *not* making way through the water, they will show neither the side lights nor the stern light. [9(e)]

In addition to the lights of this section, a vessel engaged in fishing of any sort may, if necessary to attract the attention of an approaching vessel, show a flare-up light or direct the beam of her searchlight in the direction of a danger threatening the other vessel. [9(g)]

Fishing vessels may use working lights on deck, but their skippers must take into account that especially bright or insufficiently screened working lights may impair the visibility and distinctive appearance of the mandatory lights of the Rules.

Fishing vessels when not engaged in fishing will show the normal lights for similar vessels of their size. [9(a)]

## Lights for vessels not under command

A vessel not under command will show, *in lieu of* the normal white forward (or range) lights, two red lights, in a vertical line one above the other and separated not less than six feet. These are 32-point lights that must be visible for at least two miles. [4(a)]

Vessels less than 65 feet in length, when not under command at night, are *not* required to show these two red lights. [7(g)]

## Lights for vessels aground

A vessel aground at night will show the same lights as for one of her size anchored, see page 64(u), plus the two lights of Rule 4(a) above for a vessel not under command and unable to get out of the way.

Vessels less than 65 feet in length are not required to show the two red lights when aground at night. [7(g)]

## Lights for vessels with limited maneuverability

A vessel engaged in laying or picking up a submarine cable or navigation mark, or a vessel engaged in surveying or underwater operations, or a vessel engaged in replenishment at sea, or in the launching and recovery of aircraft, when from the nature of her activities she is unable to get out of the way of approaching vessels, will show, *in lieu of* the forward white lights, three lights in a vertical line, red—white—red. The spacing of these lights must be equal and not less than six feet. All lights are 32-point and must be visible for at least two miles. [4(c)]

A vessel engaged in minesweeping operations will carry at the fore truck a green light and at the end of the fore yard on the side or sides on which danger exists another green light or lights. These lights are carried *in addition to* the normal white forward lights. Such green lights are 32-point and must be visible for at least two miles. [4(d)] The showing of these lights indicates that it is dangerous for other vessels to approach closer than 1000 yards astern or 500 yards on the side on which danger is indicated.

**General**—The vessels referred to in this and the preceding subsection, when making way through the water, will show normal side and stern lights, but when not making way through the water, they will not show either. [4(e)]

The lights described in Rules 4(a), 4(c), and 4(d) above are to be understood by other vessels as signals that the vessels showing them is not under command and therefore cannot get out of the way. They are *not* to be taken as signals of vessels in distress and requiring assistance. [4(f) and (g)]

### General Provisions

Rule 13(a) generally follows the provisions of Article 13 of the Inland Rules regarding the operation of special rules by governmental authority. The IntRR adds the category of "fishing vessels fishing as a fleet" to those for which special lights may be authorized.

### Naval vessels

International Rule 13(b) provides the authority for variation of the regulations regarding lights where required by the special construction characteristics of naval or military vessels.

### Signals to attract attention

International Rule 12 closely parallels Inland Article 12 in allowing the use of a flare-up light (or detonating or other efficient sound signal) if needed in order to attract attention. The IntRR wording is slightly different, but the effect is the same.

### Lights for Seaplanes

The International Rules include requirements for navigation lights on seaplanes while on the water. The Inland

FIG. 447 Naval minesweepers show special lights and day shapes to indicate the hazardous nature of their operations. Ships and boats should keep well clear of all vessels displaying green lights at night and black balls by day at the fore truck and end or ends of the fore yardarms.

FIG. 448 Submarines show normal navigation lights but with vertical and horizontal placement and separations modified as made necessary by their special design. A special amber quick flashing (rotating) light serves to distinguish submarines from other craft.

Rules do not touch on this subject, leaving it to the regulations of the Federal Aviation Agency.

Because of their rather limited applicability and interest to boatmen, portions of rules relating to such lights have been omitted. If needed, full details can be found in the International Rules in CG-169.

### Submarine Special Lights

The normal navigation lights of submarines have been found to be easily mistaken for those of small craft whereas actually submarines are large, deep-draft vessels with limited maneuverability when they are on the surface. In accordance with International Rule 13(a) and Inland Article 13, the display of a special distinctive light by U.S. naval submarines in international and inland waters of the U.S. has been authorized. This light is in addition to all other lights prescribed by law or regulation.

The distinctive light for submarines is an amber rotating light producing 90 flashes per minute all around the horizon to a distance of at least three miles. The light will be located not less than two feet nor more than six feet above the masthead navigation light.

## DAY SHAPES OF THE INTERNATIONAL RULES

In the interests of collision prevention and greater overall safety on the water, the International Rules prescribe a number of day shapes for certain situations and categories of vessels.

## Vessels at anchor

International Rule 11(c) requires that "every vessel" at anchor between sunrise and sunset must carry, in the forepart of the vessel where it can best be seen, one black ball not less than two feet in diameter.

This requirement is modified, however, by Rule 7(g) which allows a smaller "anchor ball" on vessels less than 65 feet in length.

## Vessels under sail and power

A vessel proceeding under sail, when *also* being propelled by machinery in the daytime, *must* carry forward where it can best be seen, a black conical shape, point downwards. The base of this shape must be not less than two feet in diameter. There is *no exception* for smaller craft. [14]

International Rule 14 should not be confused with Inland Article 14 for they cover different situations regarding a vessel which is power-driven in appearance but which has sails up. The Inland Article prescribes an optional signal that will assist a vessel with sail propulsion only in getting the right of way to which she is entitled. On the other hand, International Rule 14 sets a mandatory signal to indicate that the vessel, although having sails set, has mechanical propulsion also and this is *not* entitled to the right-of-way privileges of a sailing craft. For this reason, the day shapes of the two rules are different.

## Vessels towing and being towed

Between sunrise and sunset, a power-driven vessel having to tow astern the length of which exceeds 600 feet must carry where it can best be seen a black diamond shape at least two feet in diameter. [3(c)]

In such cases, the vessel being towed must carry a similar shape where it can best be seen. [5(d)]

## Vessels engaged in fishing

Vessels engaged in fishing by day must indicate their occupation by displaying where it can best be seen a black shape consisting of two cones point to point one over the other, each cone being not less than two feet in diameter.

If the vessel is less than 65 feet in length, a basket *may* be substituted for the two-cone shape.

If their outlying gear extends more than 500 feet into the seaway, vessels engaged in fishing must additionally show one conical shape, point up, in the direction of the outlying gear. [9(h)]

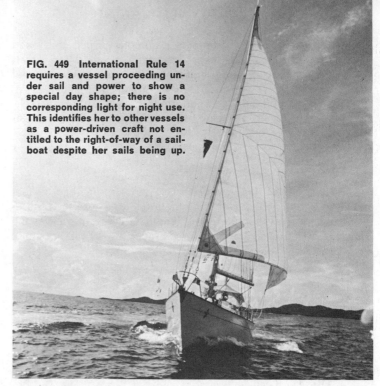

FIG. 449 International Rule 14 requires a vessel proceeding under sail and power to show a special day shape; there is no corresponding light for night use. This identifies her to other vessels as a power-driven craft not entitled to the right-of-way of a sailboat despite her sails being up.

Photo by Gary Miller

## Vessels aground

A vessel aground by day must hoist three black balls, each not less than two feet in diameter, in a vertical line with not less than six feet separation. [11(e)] This signal is *not* required of vessels less than 65 feet in length. [7(g)]

## Vessels not under command

A vessel not under command, see page 64(w), must hoist by day two black balls, each not less than two feet in diameter, in a vertical line with not less than six feet separation. [4(a)] This signal is *not* required of craft less than 65 feet in length. [7(g)]

## Vessels with limited maneuverability

A vessel engaged in laying or picking up a submarine cable or navigation mark, and certain similarly restricting tasks, see page 64(x), displays by day three shapes in a vertical line not less than six feet apart. The upper and lower shapes must be globular and red in color, the middle one must be diamond in shape and white in color; all must be not less than two feet in diameter, except that they may be smaller if the vessel is of less than 65 feet in length. [4(c) and 7(g)] Such vessels if at anchor also hoist the usual anchor ball day shape.

A vessel engaged in minesweeping by day displays black balls in locations where green lights would be shown at night, page 64(x). [4(d)]

The shapes prescribed in the preceding two paragraphs are to be understood by other vessels that the vessel displaying them is not under command and therefore cannot get out of the way. They are *not* to be taken as signals of vessels in distress and requiring assistance. [4(f) and (g)]

### Day Shapes for Small Craft

As noted in the various sections above, International Rule 7(g) relaxes the requirements for day shapes for craft

FIG. 450 By day, a vessel aground in waters of the International Rules hoists three black balls not less than two feet in diameter. A vessel "not under command" displays two such shapes. Neither of these requirements are applicable to craft less than 65 feet in length.

less than 65 feet in length. In summary, such craft need not show the day shapes generally required for vessels aground or not under command, and may display smaller shapes for vessels at anchor or involved in activities restricting their ability to get out of the way of other vessels, such as laying or picking up submarine cables or navigation marks, etc.

## Size limitations

It might be noted that the Inland Rules (and the Motorboat Act of 1940) refer to craft "not more than 65 feet in length, whereas the International Rules use the phraseology "less than 65 feet in length." Where this leaves the owner of a craft measuring exactly 65'–0" is not quite certain!

**FIG. 451** Deep-draft vessels operating in narrow channels may carry a special signal. Small craft may not demand a normal right-of-way over such larger vessels with limited maneuverability.

## Additional Signals for Deep-draft Ships In Narrow Channels

Although not strictly a part of the International Rules of the Road, an agreement has been reached by maritime nations regarding an additional signal—lights or day shape —that *may* be carried by deep-draft ships when operating in narrow channels. In view of the provisions of Rules 20 and 25 (see Chapter 5, pages 73 and 75 ) that small craft may not demand a normal right-of-way over such larger vessels with limited maneuverability, these lights and day shapes should be known by all boatmen.

It is officially *recommended,* but not required, that deep-draft ships operating in narrow channels carry at night, in addition to all normal navigation lights, three red lights in a vertical line one over the other so that the upper and lower lights are the same distance and not less than six feet above and below the middle light. Such lights must be carried where they can best be seen and must be visible all around the horizon to a distance of at least two miles. By day, such a vessel *may* carry, where it can best be seen, a black cylinder not less than two feet in diameter and 3½ feet in height.

## PENALTIES

As noted in Chapter 2, the International Rules prescribe no specific penalties for violation of their provisions, including, of course, the requirements for various navigation lights and day shapes.

| Distance of visibility, in nautical miles | Candlepower |
|---|---|
| 1 | 1.0 |
| 2 | 5.5 |
| 3 | 17.6 |
| 5 | 100.0 |

**TABLE 4-1** To translate the visibility requirements of navigation lights from the rather inexact terms of "seen for so-many miles on a clear dark night" into more precise terms, the Coast Guard has established a set of intensity standards for the brightness of each type of light. These are in terms of candlepower measured outside the lens and must not be confused with candlepower ratings of the bulbs used. See p. 64i for effective date of these standards which will supplement, but not replace, the basic requirements of the Rules of the Road and Motorboat Act.

| Distance of visibility, in nautical miles | Color | Lamp number for certain voltage systems— | | | | | |
|---|---|---|---|---|---|---|---|
| | | With fresnel lens | | | Without fresnel lens | | |
| | | 6 | 12 | 32 | 6 | 12 | 32 |
| 1 | Red | 82 | 90 | 1 226 | 1 130 | 1 142 | 1 230 |
| 1 | Green | 88 | 94 | 1 228 | | | |
| 2 | White | 64 | 68 | 1 224 | 82 | 90 | 1 226 |
| 3 | White | 82 | 90 | 1 226 | 1 130 | 1 142 | 1 230 |

**TABLE 4-2** To assist vessel owners in meeting the light intensity standards of Table 4-1, the Coast Guard has prepared and published a list of recommended lamp numbers for use with lights using either plain or Fresnel lenses. Although only recommendations rather than requirements, this table should be a useful guide to every boat owner. See p. 64i for the significance of the lack of any recommendation regarding a lamp for use with a plain green lens.

Legislation was introduced in the 90th Congress (1968) to replace the existing Inland, Great Lakes, and Western Rivers Rules with a single new set for all inland waters to be known as the "U.S. Nautical Rules." The requirements for lights and day shapes would be extensively changed and brought more nearly into conformity with the International Rules, still taking into consideration the nature of inland waters and vessels. It may be noted, however, that boatmen would be relatively less affected than the operators of large ships— all lights prescribed or permitted by the Motorboat Act of 1940 would continue to be allowed under the U.S. Nautical Rules.

The bill was introduced late in the session and no action was taken before adjournment. It was reintroduced in the 91st Congress in January 1969 as H.R. 214. As of March 1970 it was still awaiting the start of committee hearings.

The eventual passage of the U.S. Nautical Rules can be expected, but no date can be forecast. In any event, however, its effective date would probably be one year after enactment and during this time the contents of this chapter will be revised to reflect the requirements of the new Rules for lights and day shapes.

# CHAPTER 5

# RULES OF THE ROAD

**M**OST OF US have had the experience, when walking down a street, of meeting another pedestrian, giving way to the right and having him turn to our right, then turning to the left and having him dodge to the same side, and finally bumping into him. To pedestrians on a sidewalk, such actions and subsequent collision are merely comical; between vessels on the water, it is very serious. Yet the skippers of ships and boats are human and might do the very same thing if there were not rules to guide them.

In the case of pedestrians on sidewalks, and even cars and trucks on highways, it is a fairly simple matter to keep clear of approaching danger. Both individuals and vehicles follow well-defined paths or lanes, and by keeping to their right, the danger of collision is nearly eliminated.

On the water, however, it is often a far different matter. Except in a limited number of areas, there are no narrow paths or channels to follow. Boats generally have a wide and open expanse of water on which to navigate, with their courses constantly crossing the tracks of other craft and vessels that may be in the vicinity. Thus the caution that must be observed on the water, even though the total traffic is much less than on land, is just as important as on sidewalks, streets, and highways.

## RULES AND REGULATIONS

With the objective of preventing collisions, very carefully considered rules have been laid down so that the duty of the skipper of any vessel at the time of an encounter with another vessel is quite definitely prescribed. These rules are of three general classes. First, there are the International Rules of the Road, adopted at conventions of maritime nations and subsequently enacted into United States law. Secondly, there are the three sets of U.S. Rules —Inland, Great Lakes, and Western Rivers—enacted by Congress as laws of this country. These rules will be referred to *collectively* in this book as the "U.S. Rules," but this is *not* an official designation. On the third level are regulations issued by the various departments and agencies of the federal government. Most of these are promulgated by "the Secretary of the Department in which the Coast Guard is operating" (see page 32) or by the Commandant of the Coast Guard under authority delegated by the Secretary; these are termed "Pilot Rules." State and local authorities may also issue regulations covering the topics of this chapter, but these are too varying to be considered in this book. In general, these conform to the Coast Guard rules and go further with certain minor details. Skippers should inform themselves of such regulations for the waters that they use.

### Numbered "Rules"

The International Rules and two of the three sets of U.S. Rules—Great Lakes and Western Rivers—contain various sections which are designated as numbered "Rules." These concern the relative right-of-way between two vessels encountering each other, whistle signals, fog signals, distress signals, the general conduct of vessels in reduced visibility situations, etc. The provisions of the U.S. Inland Rules are in numbered "Articles," but these are in effect rules and are often so referred to in everyday speech.

These "rules of the nautical road" for both inland and offshore waters also prescribe navigation lights to be carried at night and certain shapes to be displayed by vessels during daylight; these are covered in Chapter 4.

### "Privileged" and "Burdened" Vessels

In any consideration of the right-of-way aspects of a set of rules, two terms that almost invariably will enter the discussion are "burdened" and "privileged" with respect to the status of the vessels involved.

The "privileged" vessel is the one that has the right-of-way, the right to proceed unhindered by the other.

**FIG. 501** Many boating areas are relatively open expanses of water without specific channels. Craft may approach from one or more directions, often several at the same time. Knowledge of the right-of-way rules and whistle signals is important to every skipper.

The "burdened" vessel is the one that does **not** have the right-of-way, the one that must take any necessary action to keep out of the way of the privileged vessel.

## Sequence of Consideration

As in the preceding chapter, the rules will first be considered in terms of the provisions of the U.S. Inland Rules (IR) as these cover the activities of a greater percentage of recreational boatmen than any of the others. Then the Great Lakes Rules (GLR) and the Western Rivers Rules (WRR) will be relatively briefly reviewed in terms of their differences and variations from the Inland Rules. This will in turn be followed by an explanation of the International Rules of the Road (IntRR) covering the topics of this chapter, again primarily in terms of how the IntRR differ from the IR. Because of their importance, distress signals will be discussed in a separate section at the end of this chapter.

### Indication of references

Numbers and letters shown in brackets are references to the applicable Article or Rule, or portion thereof; or to the Section or Paragraph of the Pilot Rules.

## U.S. Inland Rules

The **Inland Rules** consist of introductory material and 31 numbered "Articles" containing the actual requirements, restrictions, etc. Not all of the Articles are applicable to the topics of this chapter; certain ones are covered in Chapter 4 as noted above.

With changes over the years, some subsections have been deleted without a renumbering of the Rules as a whole. Article 18 has subsections designated as "Rules I, III, V, VIII, and IX," but not the intervening numbers. There is no Article 4 in the Inland Rules.

### AREA OF APPLICABILITY

The Inland Rules apply to all federal navigable waters of the United States (see page 31) inside of boundary lines established at the mouths of rivers, bays, harbors, etc., to limit the applicability of the International Rules, *except* for waters specifically excluded and placed under the Great Lakes or Western Rivers Rules. These boundary lines are described in Coast Guard publications and are printed on charts; see fig. 206.

As noted in Chapter 2, the boundaries between waters of the International Rules and those of the Inland Rules should not be confused with territorial limits of national authority. The *IntRR* apply outside these boundary lines over wide expanses of ocean waters that are *within* the three-mile limit of U.S. sovereignty.

### Where not applicable

There are portions of the "inland waters" of the United States where the Inland Rules do not apply. One such area may be broadly defined as the Great Lakes and their tributaries and connecting waterways. The other waters consist of the Mississippi River above New Orleans, its tributaries and their tributaries, and certain other specified rivers. Information on the specific limits of the Great Lakes and Western Rivers Rules will be found in Chapter 2, page 38.

### DEFINITION OF TERMS

The definitions of the Inland Rules that were discussed in Chapter 4, page 64(c), are also equally applicable in this chapter. Additional definitions are as follows:

**Prolonged blast**—A *prolonged blast* in the whistle signals is formally defined to mean a blast of from four to six seconds duration.

**Short blast**—The Inland Rules make frequent use of the term "short and distinct blast," or merely "short blast," but no definition or specification is provided in the Rules. It should be noted, however, that the regulations known as the Pilot Rules for Inland Waters specify that "a short blast means a blast of about one second duration."

**Long blast**—The Inland Rules and related Pilot Rules require a signal for each of two situations which is termed "one long blast." Nowhere, however, does either of these sets of rules define a "long" blast. By general acceptance, this has come to mean a blast of approximately 8 to 10 seconds in duration, sufficient to distinguish it from a "pro-

**FIG. 502** Coast Guard pamphlet CG-169 shows the International and Inland Rules of the Road in parallel column format with material covering the same situation side-by-side. International "Rules" and Inland "Articles" are numbered, but not always the same for similar situations.

| POWER-DRIVEN VESSELS MEETING END ON | (e) A vessel which has the wind aft shall keep out of the way of the other vessel. |
|---|---|
| | RULES AND WHISTLE SIGNALS FOR VESSELS MEETING, NEARING BENDS, LEAVING BERTHS AND OVERTAKING |
| RULE 18   (a) When two power-driven vessels are meeting end on, or nearly end on, so as to involve risk of collision, each shall alter her course to starboard, so that each may pass on the port side of the other. This Rule only applies to cases where vessels are meeting end on, or nearly end on, in such a manner as to involve risk of collision, and does not apply to two vessels which must, if both keep on their respective course, pass clear of each other. The only cases to which it does apply are when each of two vessels is end on, or nearly end on, to the other; in other words, to cases in which, by day, each vessel sees the masts of the other in a line, or nearly in a | ART. 18. RULE I. *When steam vessels are approaching each other head and head, that is, end on, or nearly so, it shall be the duty of each to pass on the port side of the other; and either vessel shall give, as a signal of her intention, one short and distinct blast of her whistle, which the other vessel shall answer promptly by a similar blast of her whistle, and thereupon such vessels shall pass on the port side of each other. But if the courses of such vessels are so far on the starboard of each other as not to be considered as meeting head and head, either vessel shall immediately give two short and distinct blasts of her whistle, which the other vessel shall answer* |

FIG. 503 The Inland Rules of the Road are not applicable on all "inland" waters. Specific areas are subject to the Great Lakes Rules or the Western Rivers Rules. Boundaries for all sets of rules are given in free Coast Guard publications.

longed" blast but not so long as to be unreasonable or objectionable. (This duration is supported by the Great Lakes Rules which describe the signal for a similar situation as being a blast of "at least 8 second's duration.") Remember—"long" is longer than "prolonged" insofar as the Inland Rules are concerned.

### "Steam" vessels

As in Chapter 4, the more modern and more inclusive term "power-driven vessel" will be used rather than the verbatim phraseology of the Inland Rules, "steam vessel"—the meaning is the same.

## STEERING AND SAILING RULES

The basic purpose of any set of rules of the nautical road is the prevention of collisions. A major subdivision known as the "Steering and Sailing Rules" is particularly aimed at that goal. There is a saying attributed to the ancient Greek historian Thucyides in the 5th century B.C. that is just as true in modern times—"A collision at sea can ruin your entire day!"

Technically, the right-of-way rules do not come into effect in a situation between two vessels until the possibility of a collision exists—they are not applicable otherwise. If, however, a collision does result, the rules must have been applicable—a "risk of collision" obviously existed before the event itself occurred. Although not a "rule," a basic principle of collision prevention is that, where the depth of the water permits, two vessels should not get so close to each other that risk of a collision need materially

FIG. 504 Believe it or not—this is a "steam vessel" insofar as the Inland Rules of the Road are concerned! The rather dated term is applicable to all power-driven craft. Note that this sailboat, although powered, does not have numbers on her bow as she is being propelled by an outboard motor of less than 10 HP.

arise. A collision between two vessels is almost an impossibility provided that *each skipper fully and properly* obeys the applicable rules of the nautical road.

### Early and decisive action necessary

In interpreting and applying the rules of the road, any action that is taken should be positive and in ample time. For example, a change of course to clear another vessel should be of sufficient magnitude that the action will be noticed and understood by the other skipper. Your judgment—your "seaman's eye"—may tell you that only a slight change will be sufficient, but such might well go undetected, leaving the other skipper in doubt as to your assessment and reaction to the situation. Make your actions both timely and boldly!

### Determining risk of collision

An excellent method of determining whether your craft is on a collision course with another is to watch the relative bearing of the other vessel. If this bearing does not change appreciably, either forward or astern, a risk of collision exists, the rules of the road apply, and appropriate action should be taken. More on this subject will be found on pages 449 and 450.

Boatmen are cautioned, however, against presuming the absence of any risk when there is an appreciable change in bearing. The courts have held (112 F. 161) that such a presumption might, under some circumstances, be unwarranted. Each situation must be considered on its own merits.

### Whistle Signals

One- and two-blast whistle signals to be used between power-driven vessels encountering each other on the water will be discussed with the consideration of the relative right-of-way and necessary actions to be taken by the vessels. Under the Inland Rules, these signals are to be used *only* when the vessels are within sight of each other and the position and course of the other can be determined in daytime by an actual sighting of the vessel, or at night by seeing her navigation lights. These signals must never be used in fog, mist, falling snow, or heavy rain storms when the vessels are not visible to each other; only fog signals may be used at such a time. [Article 18, Rule IX] The Pilot Rules for Inland Waters require an exchange of such signals at all times when the vessels, visible to each other, will pass within one-half mile or less. [Section 80.3]

### Danger signal

If in any situation where two power-driven vessels are approaching each other, either one fails to understand the course or intentions of the other, the vessel so in doubt should sound the **danger signal**—four or more short blasts rapidly following one another. [18-III]

This is also used by a skipper as a signal that he considers the actions of the other vessel as dangerous to *either* vessel—such as a *negative* reply to a proposal to pass in a certain manner. *The giving of such a danger signal does not relieve a vessel of her obligations or responsibilities under any rule.*

### Whistle signals by boats

Although the Pilot Rules specify that whistle signals "shall be given on an efficient whistle or siren sounded by

FIG. 505 All changes of course in the presence of a ship or another boat should be so pronounced and definite that they will be noticed and properly evaluated by the other skipper. Slight changes may be technically enough, but may fail to make intentions clear.

FIG. 506 When you are possibly on a collision course with another vessel, keep a close check on her relative bearing. To be safe, there should be a distinct change in either direction; this will indicate that she will pass either ahead or astern of you. A constant or slowly changing bearing indicates probably danger.

steam or by some substitute for steam," it is recognized that this cannot be accomplished literally on all small craft. The Motorboat Act of 1940 requires such craft to carry "an efficient whistle or other sound producing mechanical appliance." Thus boats will normally make their "whistle signals" by sounding their horn. The implementing regulations for the Motorboat Act prescribe graduated requirements for the horns of various classes of motorboats; see Chapter 3, page 58.

The Rules require an "efficient" whistle or horn without in any way defining or describing this term (which is similarly used in connection with fog horns and bells). In general, enforcement authorities and courts have held that the item must be suitable to the size and nature of the vessel on which it is used. For example, a whistle or bell that would be suitable—"efficient"—on a motorboat would not so qualify on a large ship or a noisy tugboat.

FIG. 507 Whistle signals are prescribed for various encounters between vessels under the Inland Rules of the Road. These are used only when the vessels are within sight of each other and the position and course can be determined.

FIG. 508 In a confused situation—here caused by a boat backing into a dangerous encounter—it is important that the Inland Rules "danger signal" of four or more blasts be sounded promptly by a skipper uncertain of the other's intentions.

## Rules for Power-driven Vessels

The rules of the road recognize *three* types of encounters between two approaching vessels—*meeting, crossing,* and *overtaking*. These may be collectively referred to as "passing situations"; see fig. 510. The rules governing the relative right-of-way, whistle signals to be given, and actions to be taken with regard to course and speed changes are given below for power-driven vessels. Remember that a boat being propelled by both machinery and sails is treated as a power-driven vessel.

### Meeting situation

When two power-driven vessels are approaching one another head on, or nearly head on, this is a *meeting situation*. In this situation, it is the duty of each to pass on the port side of the other. [Article 18, Rule 1] *Neither vessel has the right of way over the other* and both must alter course to starboard if necessary to provide sufficient clearance for safe passage. This is exactly the same, it will be noted, as for two cars meeting on a narrow road.

For the rule of the meeting situation to be applicable, *both* of two requirements must be met. First, the vessels

must be meeting in such a manner as to involve risk of collision. Secondly, each must be end on, or nearly end on, to the other. In other words, each vessel, by day, must see the masts of the other in a line, or nearly in a line, with her own; by night, each must see *both* sidelights of the other (the range lights may be seen one directly above the other before the side lights can be seen).

FIG. 509 A small hand-held horn powered by compressed gas in a cylinder meets the Rules of the Road requirements for an "efficient whistle" for small and medium size craft. Its audibility range should be checked against the requirements of the regulations that implement the Motorboat Act of 1940.

**FIG. 510** The Inland Rules of the Road—and others, too—recognize three types of "passing" situations—meeting, crossing, and overtaking. Specific procedures are established to govern the actions and signals of both vessels in such encounters.

**FIG. 512** Only if their courses are sufficiently well clear of each other's will a starboard-to-starboard meeting situation be legal without a change of course. The signal is two blasts, answered with the same; either vessel may signal first.

**FIG. 511** In a nearly head-on meeting situation, both vessels must give way to starboard and sound one blast; neither has the right-of-way. If their projected courses are such that they will pass clear of each other, port-to-port, then neither must change course, but either signals one blast and the other answers similarly.

Rule I of Article 18 does *not* apply to two vessels which will, if both keep on their respective courses without change of heading or speed, pass clear of each other. It also does *not* apply to situations by day in which a vessel sees another ahead crossing her own course; nor by night to cases where the red light of one vessel is opposed to the red light of the other, or where the green light of one vessel is opposed to the green light of the other. It does *not* apply to situations where a red light without a green light, or a green light without a red light, is seen ahead; nor to where both the red and green lights of another vessel are seen anywhere but ahead.

Article 18, Rule I also recognizes the meeting situation in which the courses of the two vessels are in opposite directions but are so far to starboard of each other as to not be considered meeting "head to head." In such circumstances, each vessel may continue on to pass on the starboard side of the other after exchanging the proper whistle signals as described below.

**Signals**—This rule also requires that in a normal meeting situation *either* vessel must give, as a signal of her intention to pass port-to-port, one short and distinct blast of her whistle. This signal must be answered by the other vessel with a similar one-blast signal, *or* with the danger signal if she considers such passing dangerous or is in doubt as to the situation. There is no rule as to which vessel should signal first—both craft are on an equal basis and either can make the first signal to the other.

If it is the second situation with vessels well clear to starboard of each other, the whistle signal to be given and answered is two short and distinct blasts.

Note that a vessel must **never** answer a one-blast signal with two blasts, or a two-blast signal with one blast. This is known as "cross signals" and is strictly prohibited. [Pilot Rules, Section 80.2]

When in a meeting situation one vessel sounds the danger signal, *both* vessels must *immediately* reduce their forward speed to bare steerageway. Neither vessel should attempt to proceed or pass until agreement is reached through the exchange of the same whistle signal, either one blast or two.

## Crossing situations

When two vessels are *not* meeting head on, or nearly so, *and* each has the other forward of a direction two points ($22\frac{1}{2}°$) abaft the beam, there exists a *crossing situation*.

When two power-driven vessels are crossing, so as to involve risk of collision, the vessel that has the other on her own starboard side must keep out of the way of the other. [19] See fig. 514.

This rule leads to the definition of a craft's "danger zone." This is the arc from nearly ahead to two points abaft the starboard beam; fig. 515. If you see another vessel within this danger zone, she has the right-of-way in a crossing situation—she is the privileged vessel, yours is the burdened vessel.

The Pilot Rules require that the vessel that has the other in her danger zone must keep out of the way of the other by directing her course to starboard so as to not cross ahead but rather to cross the other vessel's stern. She must slacken her speed, or stop or reverse, if necessary. The privileged vessel, on the other hand, must hold her course and speed. [80.7]

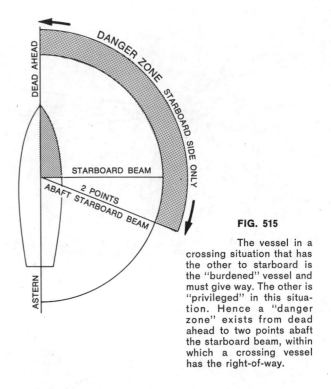

**FIG. 513** It is strictly forbidden to answer a one blast signal with two blasts—or a two-blast signal with one. If a signal cannot be properly and safely answered with the same, the skipper must sound the danger signal, and take immediate action to stop or reduce his speed to mere steerageway.

**FIG. 515**

The vessel in a crossing situation that has the other to starboard is the "burdened" vessel and must give way. The other is "privileged" in this situation. Hence a "danger zone" exists from dead ahead to two points abaft the starboard beam, within which a crossing vessel has the right-of-way.

**FIG. 514** Vessels are "crossing" if they are not meeting head on, or nearly so, and each has the other on a relative bearing forward of two points abaft either beam, port or starboard. The Rules of the Road determine relative right-of-way if there is risk of collision.

**Signals**—Whistle signals are *not required* by the Inland Rules in a crossing situation, but the Pilot Rules *permit* the privileged vessel to sound a one-short-blast signal as an indication that she will hold her course and speed. [80.03(a)(3)] Although not specifically covered in the Pilot Rules, it would be normal for the burdened vessel to acknowledge with the same signal.

If from any cause the situation is such that either vessel cannot take the prescribed action or comply with the other vessel's signals, this condition must be made apparent to the other vessel at once by sounding the danger signal of four or more short, rapid blasts. When this happens, both vessels must immediately be stopped, and backed if necessary, until signals for passing with safety have been made and understood.

Note that this rule is applicable only if there is risk of collision. If the situation is such that the vessels will pass free and clear of each other, there is *no* privileged or burdened vessel, and whistle signals are not appropriate. In case of doubt, however, the safer procedure is to assume that the rules *do* apply and exchange signals to be sure that the intentions of each are known to each other.

## Overtaking situation

If one vessel is coming up on another, she being astern of a direction two points abaft the beam of the other vessel and making greater speed so as to close the distance between them, the first vessel is said to be *overtaking* the latter vessel; fig. 517. At night, this situation would exist when the vessel astern could not see either of the navigation side lights of the vessel ahead. By day, the overtaking vessel cannot always know with certainty whether she is forward or abaft the direction two points abaft the other vessel's beam—if in doubt, she should assume that she is an overtaking vessel. [24]

Notwithstanding *any* other provision in the Rules of Road, *every* vessel overtaking another must keep out of the way of the overtaken vessel. The overtaking vessel is burdened; the overtaken vessel is privileged. [24]

The Rules are very specific that once a vessel is in an overtaking status, she remains as such for the remainder of the encounter—no subsequent alteration of the bearing between the two vessels will serve to make the overtaking vessel a crossing vessel within the meaning of the rules, or relieve her of her duty of keeping clear of the overtaken vessel until she is finally past and clear. In other words, should the overtaking vessel come upon the starboard side of the overtaken vessel, and so into the latter's normal danger zone, she does *not* by this movement become the privileged vessel with the right-of-way over the overtaken craft. [24]

**Signals**—If the overtaking vessel desires to pass on the port side of the vessel ahead—as would be normal if the slower vessel were keeping to the right of a channel, see fig. 519a, she must sound a two-short-blast signal. If the privileged vessel agrees with such a passing, she should immediately sound the same signal of two blasts. The faster vessel then directs her course to port and passes as proposed and agreed.

Should the vessel astern desire to pass on the other's starboard side—not normal, but legal, see fig. 519b, she sounds a one-short-blast signal which is returned in kind by the privileged vessel if she consents.

If in either of the above situations, the vessel ahead

FIG. 516 The overtaking boat is here coming up on the larger craft's starboard quarter. This is the less-than-usual overtaking situation, but it is not illegal. The larger craft is privileged and holds her course and speed.

FIG. 517 Although the smaller craft has moved up into the overtaken vessel's "danger zone," the relative right-of-way has not changed and she is still burdened and must make any necessary course and/or speed changes to pass safely.

does *not* consider that the passing can take place safely as proposed by the burdened vessel, she must *immediately* sound the danger signal of four or more short, rapid blasts. (The danger signal would likewise be applicable if the overtaking craft attempted an unsafe passing without first giving a whistle signal of her intentions.)

An overtaking vessel that receives a danger signal in reply to her stated intention to pass should immediately cease all actions related to passing and reduce speed so as to not close further on the overtaken vessel; fig. 519c. No attempt should be made to pass until the proper signals have been given and answered. [18-VIII] Although not provided for in the Rules, it is reasonable for a privileged vessel to give the danger signal, pause, and then give the other passing signal to the burdened vessel—in effect saying, "The side that you proposed is unsafe, but the other is ok." This initiation of the proposal and agreement for passing by the privileged vessel is not normal, but often it is logical considering that the leading vessel has better observation of the conditions ahead.

As in the meeting situation, "cross signals"—answering one blast with two, or two blasts with one—are *prohibited.* Answer a signal **only** with the same signal as given by the other vessel, or with the danger signal.

Although the slower vessel ahead is privileged, she must in no case attempt to cross the bow or crowd upon the course of the passing vessel. [18-VIII]

## Meeting in restricted waters

Every power-driven vessel when proceeding along the course of a narrow channel shall, when it is safe and practicable, keep to the side of the fairway or midchannel that lies on the starboard side of such vessel. [25] This is merely the same general provision as used on streets and highways —keep to the right of center. Although the Rules are silent as to which side an overtaking vessel should pass the slower craft, it is a logical extension of the above rule that the faster craft moves to the left with a two-blast signal and passes as two automobiles might do on a road.

In narrow channels, a power-driven vessel of less than 65 feet length must not hamper the safe passage of a vessel which can navigate only inside that channel. The size or nature of this latter vessel is not relevant if she meets the requirement of having to stay within the channel. [25]

## Rounding bends in a channel

A special "alarm" or "bend" signal is provided in the Rules for a situation in which a power-driven vessel approaches a bend in a channel where another vessel approaching from the opposite direction on the other side of the bend cannot be seen for a distance of a half-mile because of the height of the banks or other cause. In this case, when within a half-mile of the bend, a vessel must sound one "long" blast (generally taken as 8 to 10 second's duration) of her whistle. This signal will be answered with a similar long blast by any vessel within hearing around the bend. If such an answer is received, normal whistle signals must be exchanged *when* the vessels come within sight of one another. If no reply to her alarm signal is heard, the vessel may consider the channel ahead to be clear and govern herself accordingly. [18-V, and 80.5(a) and 86.10-1] Normal good judgment, however, dictates special alertness and moderate speed at blind bends.

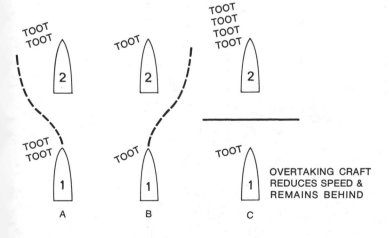

FIG. 518 a, b, c The overtaking craft signals first as indicated by the numbers above. The overtaken (privileged) vessel replies with the same signal (and the passing occurs normally) or with the danger signal (and the overtaking craft must not attempt to pass until the proper signals have later been exchanged).

73

**FIG. 519** Vessels, including boats, approaching a bend in a river, where a craft approaching from the other direction could not be seen at a distance of a half-mile, must sound a special signal of one "long" blast. This is generally considered to mean one of 8 to 10 seconds duration.

In a winding channel, a vessel may *first* sight the other at an oblique angle rather than "head on, or nearly head on". Nevertheless, the situation is to be regarded as a *meeting* situation as such will be the case when the actual passing occurs. Each should keep to her own right side of the channel and neither has the right-of-way over the other.

## Leaving a berth

Whenever a power-driven vessel is moved from a berth or dock, she shall give a signal of one long blast (approximately 8 to 10 second's duration) on her whistle. Immediately *after* clearing the berth so as to be fully in sight, she is then governed by the applicable steering and sailing rules. [18-V and 80.5(b)]

Note that although it is not explicitly so stated in the Rules of the Road or the Pilot Rules, it may be inferred that a craft just emerging from a slip or berth does *not* have the right-of-way over another vessel passing in the channel or nearby open water even though she is in the other's danger zone. Her privileged status in a crossing situation is *not* established until she is "fully in sight."

**FIG. 520  A boat leaving its slip in a marina, or exiting from between parallel piers, should sound a long blast of 8 to 10 seconds duration. She does not have right-of-way until out in the clear.**

## Ferry boats

Although there are no express provisions in the Inland Rules of the Road and related Pilot Rules that give any special privileges to ferry boats, the courts have repeatedly ruled that ferries are entitled to a reasonable degree of freedom of entrance to and exit from their slips. The same is true in regard to other craft using slips and piers. Boats should avoid passing unnecessarily close to piers, wharves, etc., where they may be caught unawares by the unanticipated movements of other craft.

## Sailing Vessels

The provisions of Inland Article 17 are applicable only to situations involving two sailing vessels—*neither* may be under power or a combination of sail and power.

When two sailing vessels are approaching one another, so as to involve risk of collision, one of them must keep out of the way of the other in accordance with the following conditions.

(a) A vessel that is running free must keep out of the way of a vessel that is closehauled.

(b) A vessel that is closehauled on the port tack must keep out of the way of a vessel that is closehauled on the starboard tack.

(c) When both vessels are running free with the wind on different sides, the vessel that has the wind on the port side must keep out of the way of the other.

(d) When both are running free with the wind on the same side, the vessel that is to windward must keep out of the way of the vessel that is to leeward.

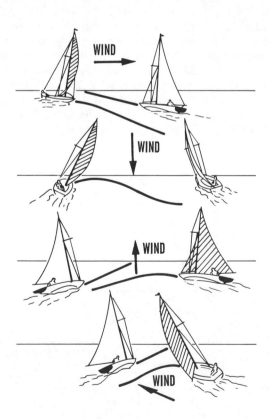

**FIG. 521**  The Inland Rules contain right-of-way statements for five situations between two sailing vessels. These rules are not the same as those of the International Rules and the differences must be kept in mind. Burdened sailboats are shown with shaded sails.

**FIG. 522 a** In any encounter between a sailing vessel and a power-driven vessel, the former has the right-of-way unless she should be overtaking the other. Whistle signals are not sounded by a motor-boat in such a situation as the sailboat is not equipped to reply.

**FIG. 522 b** The right-of-way of a sailboat over a power-driven vessel does **not** prevail if the latter cannot safely navigate outside the limits of the channel she is using.

(e) A vessel that has the wind aft must keep out of the way of the other vessel.

It should be noted that the right-of-way rules between two sailing vessels under the Inland Rules currently *differ* in wording and effect from the International Rules and from the right-of-way rules commonly used in yacht racing. This difference is expected to disappear when the pending action on new U.S. rules takes effect; see page

**Signals**—Sound signals are *not* used in passing situations between two sailing vessels.

## Encounters Between Sailing and Power Vessels

In general, a sailing vessel has the right-of-way over a vessel propelled by machinery or by sail and machinery concurrently. The power-driven vessel must keep out of the way of the sailing vessel. [20] There are, however, some exceptions and they should be thoroughly understood.

Should a sailing vessel overtake a power-driven vessel —not likely, but possible—the overtaking situation rule prevails and the sailing vessel is the burdened one regardless of the means of propulsion.

Likewise, a sailing vessel is not the privileged vessel in an encounter with certain vessels engaged in fishing.

### Further limitation

The normal privileged status of a sailing vessel over a power-driven vessel does *not* give her the right in a narrow channel to hamper the latter vessel if such can navigate safely only within the limits of the channel. [20]

### No whistle signals

Power-driven vessels do *not* give whistle signals when encountering sailing vessels as the latter are not equipped to reply, and an unanswered signal would create a situation of doubt.

**FIG. 523** Fishing vessels are accorded certain special privileges over other vessels when they are engaged in their work. These privileges are not, however, unlimited; see Inland Article 26. Yachts should stay well clear of fishing craft at work.

## Right-of-Way of Fishing Vessels

Inland Article 26 accords special right-of-way status, within limitations, to vessels engaged in fishing.

Sailing vessels underway must keep out of the way of sailing vessels or boats fishing with nets, lines, or trawls. Although not explicitly stated in the Inland Rules (as it is in the IntRR), power-driven vessels likewise should also keep clear of fishing vessels.

This rule does *not* give any vessel or boat engaged in fishing the right of obstructing a fairway used by vessels other than fishing vessels or boats.

## General Right-of-Way Rules

There are a number of Inland Rules of the Road that relate generally to all vessels regardless of their means of propulsion.

### Privileged vessel's duty

Where the Rules of the Road require that one vessel is to keep out of the way, the other—the privileged vessel—*must* maintain her course and speed. [21]

Although the matter is not very clearly covered in the Inland Rules, it should be obvious that if such action by the privileged vessel brings her into a situation where collision cannot be avoided by the actions of the burdened vessel, then she, too, must take such measures as will best avert an accident. When such a situation becomes apparent (and this is usually a very difficult decision), the privileged vessel is to take whatever action she deems necessary to avoid or minimize disaster. The courts have consistently held that *any* action (except *no* action) is proper in such circumstances.

FIG. 524  In any encounter between two vessels where one has the right-of-way over the other, both have responsibilities. Not only must the burdened vessel give way; the privileged vessel has the duty of maintaining her course and speed.

FIG. 525  The "General Prudential Rule" requires that due regard be given to any special circumstances that may render a departure from the Rules necessary to avoid immediate danger. A typical example occurs when more than two craft are involved in an encounter and strict compliance cannot be had for all pairs of vessels.

## Burdened vessel's duty

Every vessel that is directed by the Rules of the Road to keep out of the way of another is a burdened vessel and must, if the circumstances of the situation permit, avoid crossing ahead of the other—the privileged vessel. [22]

Every power-driven vessel that is burdened must, on approaching the privileged vessel, slacken her speed if necessary, or stop or reverse. [23]

## GENERAL PRUDENTIAL RULE

Article 27 is often termed the "general prudential rule" and is of great importance because of its wide applicability.

In obeying and construing the Rules of the Road, due regard must be given to all dangers of navigation and collision, and to any special circumstance that may render a *departure* from the Rules necessary to avoid immediate danger.

### Interpretation of "immediate danger"

Courts have placed considerable emphasis on the words "immediate danger" of Article 27 in rendering their decisions. The basic principle is that the Rules must *not* be abandoned whenever perceptible risk of collision exists, but *only* when *imperatively* required by special circumstances in order to avoid such danger.

## SOUND SIGNALS FOR VESSELS WITHIN SIGHT

In the Inland Rules, sound signals, given on the horn in the case of most motorboats, are used for the purpose of indicating the intention of the skipper of a craft, his agreement to a proposed action, or to warn others of a situation considered dangerous.

Although sailing vessels *never* give whistle signals, if such a craft is equipped with an auxiliary engine, then she must have a horn for use when under sail and power or power alone.

### Passing signals

Whistle signals for power-driven vessels encountering one another have been discussed above in connection with the passing situations, pages 69 to 74.

The danger signal of four or more short, rapid blasts was discussed on page 69.

### Backing signal

The Inland Rules contain provision for a "backing signal." When vessels are within sight of one another, a power-driven vessel underway whose engines are going at full speed astern must indicate this fact by sounding three short blasts on her whistle. [28]

FIG. 526  The Inland Rules call for a three-blast signal when a vessel's engines are going at "full speed astern." In normal practice, it is used whenever engines are in reverse or the vessel is beginning to make sternway.

Note that the Rules *require* this signal only when the engines are going at *full speed* astern—in actual practice, a three-blast signal is sounded by vessels whose engines are going astern at any speed, or who are making sternway, in the presence of other vessels. Note also that this signal may be made to sailing vessels as it does not require a reply.

### "Alarm" or "bend" signal

As noted on prior pages of this chapter, the Rules provide for an "alarm signal" of one long blast (generally taken as from 8 to 10 seconds duration, although no length is officially specified), for vessels approaching a blind bend in a channel. This same signal is used by a vessel about to be moved from a berth or slip.

### Caution in use of whistle signals

Whistle signals should be used with caution in conditions of heavy traffic on the water. Such a circumstance might exist when three or more vessels were in the vicinity

FIG. 527 Signals for the opening of a drawbridge vary somewhat with different geographic areas, but the one most often used is three blasts. This is also used for canal locks on many waterways. There are also signals of reply from the bridge or lock. See appropriate Coast Pilot or equivalent publication for details.

and there existed a combination of meeting, crossing, and/or overtaking situations, there being no way to direct a whistle signal to one vessel exclusively. In such cases, the omission of whistle signals might well be a safer course of action than indiscriminate "tooting."

## Signals for drawbridges and canal locks

The whistle signals for opening drawbridges are not a part of the Rules of the Road, but should be known by boatmen. Such signals vary somewhat with different localities; a three-short-blast signal is common in many areas. The bridge tender will sometimes reply with a three-blast signal if he is going to open without delay, or with four blasts (two blasts in some areas) if not able to open immediately.

A skipper should always consult the applicable volume of the Coast Pilot, or corresponding publication for other waters, for the specific signals for bridges, and for canal locks which usually follow similar procedures.

## No whistle salutes

Yachts and boats should never exchange salutes or greetings by means of whistle blasts. Commercial craft sometimes do this, but it is not authorized by the Rules. By Coast Guard regulation, the "unnecessary sounding of the whistle is prohibited within any harbor limits of the United States."

## SOUND SIGNALS IN REDUCED VISIBILITY

Article 15 of the Inland Rules prescribes sound signals to be given by different types of vessels in various circumstances when visibility conditions are reduced from "normal." These are often termed "fog signals," but they are equaly applicable in cases of mist, falling snow, heavy rainstorms, or any other condition similarly restricting visibility. They are equally applicable by day or night.

Courts have held that fog signals should be sounded when visibility is reduced to the distance at which side lights are required to be seen, one mile in the case of waters subject to the Inland Rules.

These sound signals serve two purposes. Basically, they alert other vessels to the presence in the vicinity of the vessel sounding the signal and a rough indication of her position. Secondly, they may provide an indication of her

activities (which tack a sailboat is on) or limitations on her maneuverability (towing, at anchor, etc.).

## Equipment

The Inland Rules require that a power-driven vessel be provided with an efficient whistle or siren sounded by steam or by some substitute for steam, so placed that the sound will not be intercepted by any obstruction.

Article 15 also requires that such vessels be equipped with an efficient fog horn and with an efficient bell. Sailing vessels of 20 or more gross tons must have an efficient fog horn and bell.

FIG. 528 Coast Guard motorboat regulations do not require a bell on craft under 26 feet in length. The Rules of the Road, however, make no exception for such boats from the requirement for sounding a bell when certain conditions prevail.

FIG. 529 On waters governed by the Inland Rules of the Road, a power-driven vessel underway in reduced visibility sounds one prolonged blast—four to six seconds duration—at intervals of not more than one minute.

Although the Inland Rules state "all vessels" and contain no clear exception for small craft, the implementing regulations of the Motorboat Act of 1940 prescribe lesser requirements for vessels 65 feet or less in length; see page 58. This, however, does *not* excuse them from compliance with the requirement for giving the specified signals should they become involved in a reduced visibility situation where they are applicable. For example, a 24-foot Class 1 motorboat is not required by the Motorboat Act to be equipped with a bell—yet if this "power-driven vessel" were to be anchored in a fog, she is *not* excused from the need for ringing a bell. Boats must be equipped for situations in which they may find themselves even though this requires items on board over and above the minimum requirements of the MBAct.

## How sounded

All signals prescribed by Article 15 for vessels underway

in reduced visibility shall be given—

By power-driven vessels, on the whistle;

By sailing vessels, on the fog horn.

It is interesting to note that although the Inland Rules require a power-driven vessel to be equipped with a whistle or siren *and* a fog horn, the same Article states that fog signals are to be made on the whistle or siren—no mention whatever is made of any use of the fog horn for such vessels!

Motorboats sound their fog signals on their whistle or horn.

### Power-driven Vessels Underway

On waters subject to the Inland Rules, a power-driven vessel underway in conditions of reduced visibility, day or night, sounds one prolonged (four to six seconds) blast of her whistle at intervals of not more than *one* minute. [15(a)] It has been held by court rulings that a vessel approaching an area of reduced visibility, such as a well-defined fog bank, should start her signals before she herself actually enters the area.

### Sailing Vessels Underway

A sailing vessel, when underway in restricted visibility of any kind, is required by Article 15(c) to sound the following signals at intervals of not more than one minute (the length of the blasts is not stated as prolonged or any other specific duration)—

When on a starboard tack, one blast;

When on a port tack, two blasts;

When with the wind abaft the beam, three blasts.

### Vessels Towing and Being Towed

A power-driven vessel, when towing another in fog, gives a special signal *in lieu of* the usual one prolonged blast to indicate her more limited maneuverability. She sounds one prolonged blast followed by two short blasts; the same one-minute maximum interval is observed. [15(e)]

A towed vessel *may* give this signal, but no other.

Other vessels of limited maneuverability, such as fishing vessels with their nets out have no special signal in the waters of the Inland Rules and can only indicate whether they are underway or at anchor. If concern arises over the apparent too-close approach of another vessel, the danger signal may be sounded, see below.

### Miscellaneous Vessels

All rafts and other types of craft not otherwise provided for in Article 15, navigating by hand power, horse power, or by the current of the river, when in conditions of reduced visibility must sound one blast (duration not specified) on a fog horn, or an equivalent signal, at intervals of not more than one minute. [15(f)]

### Vessels at Anchor

A vessel at anchor in fog or other condition reducing normal visibility, whether by day or night, must ring a bell rapidly for about five seconds at intervals of not more than one minute.

The same signal is used by vessels made fast to a mooring buoy. Vessels made fast to a pier or wharf do not sound fog signals unless they project out into a channel or fairway and so constitute a hazard to others.

This requirement for ringing a bell is waived for vessels

FIG. 530 Sailing vessels underway in conditions of restricted visibility sound one of three different signals on their fog horn to indicate their point of sailing. These are sounded at least once each minute.

FIG. 531 A tug towing another vessel in fog, heavy rain, snow, etc., sounds a special signal of one prolonged blast followed by two short blasts. The towed vessel **may** give this same signal, but no other.

FIG. 532 A vessel at anchor in fog or other conditions reducing visibility must ring her bell rapidly for about five seconds at intervals of not more than one minute. A craft of 65 feet or less length anchored or moored in a "special anchorage area" is not required to sound this signal.

FIG. 533 The Inland Rules have no specific signal for vessels aground in conditions of reduced visibility, but it is logical for them to sound the danger signal of four or more blasts rather than ringing the bell. This will warn other vessels not only of her presence, but also of the hazard.

FIG. 534 A boat underway in reduced visibility must not only sound the proper fog signals but also must go no faster than a "moderate" speed. This is not defined in the Rules of the Road but numerous court interpretations exist.

not more than 65 feet in length, and barges, scows, and similar craft, if located in a "special anchorage area" as discussed in Chapter 4, page 64(j). [15(d)]

### Fog Signals in General

Although not specifically covered in Article 15 of the Inland Rules, several aspects of fog signals have arisen from court interpretations and rulings, and from general experience.

### Danger signal

It is reasonable for a vessel to sound the danger signal of four or more short blasts in rapid succession if the skipper considers that another vessel is approaching with risk of collision; this can be done underway or at anchor. Other "steering signals" are *not* given in reduced visibility situations until each vessel has actually sighted the other.

### Vessel aground

A vessel *aground* should sound the *danger signal* as a warning to other vessels that the shoal water may be dangerous to them, information that the normal signal of an anchored vessel would not convey.

### Not too often!

The Inland Rules prescribe an interval of "not more than one minute" between the successive soundings of fog signals. This is a rather brief time and should not be further reduced by skippers concerned over the risk of collision. The interval between signals—used for listening for other vessels' blasts—is equally as valuable for safety as the actual blowing of one's own whistle or horn. The timing, if not done by automatic means, should be measured to reasonable accuracy by a second hand on a clock or watch.

## CONDUCT IN RESTRICTED VISIBILITY

In addition to providing for sound signals, the Inland Rules set forth restrictions on the navigation of vessels when visibility is reduced for any reason. The basic rule for the operation of vessels in fog, mist, falling snow, heavy rainstorms, or other conditions similarly restricting visibility is quite brief and logical. It is required that all vessels in such conditions go at a "moderate" speed having careful regard for the existing circumstances. [16]

It is, of course, impossible to define "moderate" in terms of knots or miles per hour—this is a judgment that must be left for each situation to the individual skipper concerned, who must be prepared to defend it should he be in a collision. A general interpretation is that a vessel should be going no faster than a speed which would permit her to be brought to a complete stop in *one-half* of the range of existing visibility—the theory being that thus both of two vessels on a collision course could stop short of each other if action were initiated as soon as one became visible to the other.

It should be carefully noted that courts have held that the only "moderate" speed in some dense fog situations was *zero*, meaning that the vessel should not have gotten underway, or should have stopped and anchored or laid to.

### On hearing another vessel

A power-driven vessel hearing—apparently forward of her beam—the fog signal of another vessel the position of

FIG. 535 A good listening as well as visual lookout is essential in reduced visibility situations. On power-driven boats, this normally means sending a man to the bow, farther away from the noise of the craft's own engines. Kodachrome by Bill Koelbel

which has not been ascertained, must, so far as the circumstances of the case permit, stop her engines and then navigate with caution until danger of collision is over. [16] The phrase "so far as the circumstances of the case permit" allow for situations where power must be kept on for safe control, such as in swift currents, but should not be abused to the extent of continuing ahead.

Radar is an aid in determining position of other vessels in conditions of limited visibility, but it is not a justification for immoderate speed. The possession of information obtained from radar does not relieve any vessel of the obligation of conforming strictly with the Rules and in particular with the obligations of Article 15, Sound Signals in Restricted Visibility, and Article 16, Conduct in Restricted Visibility.

## THE RULE OF GOOD SEAMANSHIP

Article 29 is the broad, summing-up "rule of good seamanship." It provides that nothing in the Rules shall exonerate any vessel, or the owner, master, or crew thereof, from the consequences of any neglect to carry lights or signals, or any neglect to keep a proper lookout, or the neglect of any precaution which may be required by the ordinary practice of seamen, or by the special circumstances of the case.

### Lookouts

The need for a proper lookout is often taken rather too lightly by the skippers of boats and yachts, and this is a *serious* mistake. Under normal circumstances, the helmsman will satisfy the need, but he must be qualified, alert, and have no other responsibilities. The use of an automatic steering mechanism (so-called "autopilot"), see page 512, is *no* justification for the absence of a human helmsman at the controls observing *all around* the horizon and ready to immediately take over if needed. The use of radar at night or in fog is *no* justification for the absence of an additional person as a lookout, stationed outside the bridge, usually forward, where he can *hear* as well as see. The noise level at the control station of most motorboats renders the helmsman totally ineffective as a listening watch.

### Supplementary Signals

Every vessel may, if necessary in order to attract attention, in addition to the lights which she is by the Rules required to carry, show a flare-up light or use any detonating signal that cannot be mistaken for a distress signal. [12]

## PILOT RULES FOR INLAND WATERS

As noted in Chapters 2 and 4, the statutory Inland Rules of the Road provide authority for the issuance of regulations which are known as **Pilot Rules.** This material sometimes repeats what is in the basic Rules of the Road, but also additionally expands and implements them.

Many of the provisions of the Inland Pilot Rules covering topics of this chapter have been discussed above in connection with the applicable basic Article.

### Passing Coast Guard vessels

Paragraph 80.33(b) requires that all vessels passing a Coast Guard vessel servicing an aid to navigation must reduce speed sufficiently to ensure the safety of both vessels. If passing within 200 feet of the Coast Guard vessel—which will be displaying two orange-and-white vertically-striped balls by day or two red lights by night in a vertical line—the other vessel's speed must not exceed five miles per hour.

### Unnecessary whistling prohibited

Section 80.35 of the Pilot Rules prohibits any unnecessary sounding of the whistle "within any harbor limits of the United States." Any licensed officer who authorizes or permits a violation of this regulation may face hearings which could result in the suspension or revocation of his license.

### Distress signal

The Inland Pilot Rules, Section 80.37, authorize a daytime distress signal which is covered with the other distress signals on pages 87 to 88.

### Copy required on board

Paragraph 80.13(b) requires that all vessels and craft *over 65 feet* in length must, where practicable, carry on

FIG. 536 Pilot Rules are Coast Guard regulations that implement and supplement the statutory Rules of the Road. They exist for all sets of U.S. Rules, but there are none for the International Rules.

board a copy of the current edition of CG-169 and have it available for ready reference.

Motorboats subject to the 1940 Act are specifically exempted, but this does not excuse a boat operator from knowing its contents. The conscientious skipper keeps a copy of this Coast Guard pamphlet on board whether required or not; it is a handy publication to have and occasionally review.

## PENALTIES

The penalties for violation of the Inland Rules or Pilot Rules for Inland Waters are described in Chapter 2; see page 39.

For certain specified violations, the penalty is prescribed as the possible suspension or revocation of a master's or pilot's license.

# Great Lakes Rules

The **Great Lakes Rules of the Road** are derived from an act of Congress of 8 February 1895 with subsequent amendments. These Rules apply on waters than can be broadly described as the Great Lakes, their tributaries, and connecting waterways. Exact limits are set forth in Chapter 2 on page 38.

The format of the Great Lakes Rules is generally the same as for the Inland Rules discussed above, except that the term for each major provision is "Rule" rather than "Article." Also as noted before in this chapter, there is little parallelism in the numbering of rules relating to the same general subject matter although in some places identical, or nearly identical, language is used.

The Great Lakes Rules will be considered here in terms of their differences from the Inland Rules discussed in detail above. Identical requirements, even though appearing in differently numbered rules, will not be repeated.

## STEERING AND SAILING RULES

The Steering and Sailing Rules for the Great Lakes are roughly the same as those of the Inland Rules. Rule 16 relating to right-of-way of sailing vessels is identical with Article 17 except that subsection (e) of that Article, which states that a vessel with the wind aft must keep out of the way of the other vessel, is omitted.

### Power-driven Vessels

The right-of-way and maneuvering rules for the meeting, crossing, and overtaking situations are generally similar to the provisions of the Inland Rules as discussed above, but they contain nothing on the whistle signals to be given; these are contained in separate Rules, see below.

The Great Lakes Rules of the Road do *not* specifically recognize the alternative situation of Inland Article 18, Rule I, where meeting vessels are sufficiently to starboard of each other so as to make a port-to-port passing unnecessary, but this is contained in the Pilot Rules. [90.5]

Likewise, the situation of a vessel approaching a blind bend or curve in a channel is covered (in a manner generally similar to the Inland Rules) by the Great Lakes Pilot Rules rather than the basic Rules of the Road. The duration of the long blast here is specified as "at least 8 seconds." [90.6]

The requirement for a similar long blast on the whistle by a vessel leaving a dock also appears in the Great Lakes Pilot Rules [90.7] rather than in the basic Rules of the Road.

### Whistle Signals

Great Lakes Rule 23 prescribes whistle signals for course changes authorized or required by any of the other Rules. These signals are given **in all weathers** whether or not the vessels are within sight of each other; note carefully the difference from the Inland Rules.

One blast means "I am directing my course to starboard."

Two blasts mean, "I am directing my course to port."

Every power-driven vessel receiving a signal as above from another vessel must promptly respond with the same signal or the danger signal as described below.

This Rule specifically states, however, that the giving or answering of any whistle signal does not change the responsibilities and obligations of the vessels involved.

On the Great Lakes, there is **no** three-blast "backing" signal—actually this signal is used in reduced visibility situations as the basic underway vessel signal, see below.

### Danger signal

The danger signal on the Great Lakes is described in Rule 26 as consisting of "several short and rapid blasts," but the Pilot Rules are more specific in requiring "not less than **five** blasts. If the vessels have approached within one-half mile of each other at the time of sounding the danger signal, *both* must be immediately slowed to bare steerageway, and if necessary, stopped and reversed, until the proper signals have been given and answered or the vessels have passed. [90.2]

### Crossed signals prohibited

The Great Lakes Pilot Rules also specifically forbid "cross signals"—answering one blast with two, or vice versa. If a pilot considers it injudicious to reply with the

**FIG. 537** The danger signal for waters subject to the Great Lakes Pilot Rules consists of **five** or more short and rapid blasts of the whistle or horn. It is used to indicate dissent to another vessel's signalled intentions as well as for danger.

**FIG. 538** The Great Lakes Rules of the Road give the right-of-way to vessels traveling with a current over those making their way upstream. This is based on the relative controllability of the craft involved; it is a courteous action on waters of the Inland Rules although not legally required.

same signal sounded by the other vessel, he must sound the danger signal in lieu of a "cross" signal. [90.3]

### Restricted Waters

In all channels less than 500 feet in width, no power-driven vessel shall overtake and pass another going in the same direction unless the privileged vessel consents to being passed. This restriction does not apply to passing a disabled vessel. [Rule 25]

When two power-driven vessels going in opposite directions meet in such a channel, both vessels must slow down to a "moderate" speed as determined by the circumstances. [25]

In all "narrow" channels (no width specified) a power-driven vessel less than 65 feet in length must not hamper the safe passage of a vessel (no size specified) that can navigate only inside the channel. [25] A similar restriction applies to sailboats. [19]

### Rivers and channels with currents

In all narrow channels where there is current, and on five specified rivers, a power-driven vessel going *with* the current ("descending") has the right-of-way when meeting another such vessel proceeding against the current ("ascending"), and she must initiate the exchange of whistle signals before the separation of the vessels is reduced to a half-mile. [24]

### FOG SIGNALS

The Great Lakes Rules' requirements for fog signals for power-driven vessels differ *considerably* from the provisions of the Inland Rules. A skipper going from waters governed by one set of rules to those of the other set should carefully prepare himself with knowledge of the new signals.

The fog signals for sailing vessels under the two sets of rules are in effect identical. The only difference is that the GLR specify that the wind must be forward of the beam for the one- and two-blast signals, whereas the IR merely imply such a condition. The GLR also specify that the sailing vessel is "not in tow." [14(d)]

### Equipment

On the Great Lakes, a power-driven vessel must be provided with an efficient whistle sounded by steam or by some substitute for steam *and* this whistle must be placed forward of the funnel not less than eight feet from the deck. It must be of such character as to be heard "in ordinary weather" at a distance of at least two miles. The vessel must also be equipped with an efficient bell. (There is no mention of fog horn as required by the Inland Rules.) [14]

For craft subject to its provisions, however, the implementing regulations of the Motorboat Act of 1940 prescribe lesser requirements than the preceding paragraph, see page 58.

A sailing vessel must be equipped with an efficient fog horn and an efficient bell. [14]

### When required

Fog signals are sounded on the Great Lakes either by day or night whenever there is "thick weather" resulting from fog, mist, falling snow, heavy rainstorms, or other cause.

#### Power-driven Vessels Underway

A power-driven vessel, other than one with a raft in tow, must sound *three distinct* blasts of her whistle at intervals of not more than one minute; the duration of the blasts is not specified. [14(a)] (Note carefully the difference between the basic fog signal of the GLR and the IR.)

#### Vessels Towing and Towed

A power-driven vessel towing other than a raft sounds the basic three-blast signal.

A power-driven vessel with a raft in tow will sound a unique fog signal at the same interval—a screeching or "Modoc" whistle for from three to five seconds.

A vessel *being towed* by another *must* sound a bell signal of four strokes in two groups of two strokes each. This is to be sounded at intervals of one minute. [14(b)] Note that here the interval is specific, rather than maximum—the usual "not more than one minute" of other sections of Great Lakes Rule 15 is not used; note also that the fog signal of a towed vessel is mandatory on these waters, rather than optional as in the Inland Rules. The GLR require that the bell be "good and efficient and properly placed."

#### Vessels Anchored or Aground

A vessel at anchor or one aground in or near a channel or fairway must sound *two separate signals*. At intervals of not more than *two* minutes, she must ring her bell rapidly for from three to five seconds. *Additionally*, at intervals of not more than *three* minutes, she must sound on her whistle or horn a signal of one short, two long, and one short blasts in quick succession. [14(e)] (This requirement might possibly have been made more complicated, but just how is not readily apparent!)

#### Special Provisions

Vessels of less than 10 tons registered tonnage, *not* power-driven, need not give the above fog signals, but if they do not, then they must make some other efficient sound signal at intervals of not more than *one* minute. [14(f)]

Fishing boats, produce boats, rafts, and other watercraft navigated by hand power or by the current of the river, or anchored or moored in or near a channel or fair-

**FIG. 539.** The Great Lakes fog signal—sounded in any kind of "thick weather"—is three distinct blasts of the whistle at intervals of not more than one minute. Note carefully the difference between this signal and the corresponding one of the Inland Rules.

way and not in any port, and not covered by any of the preceding rules, will sound a fog horn or equivalent signal at intervals of not less than *one* minute. [14(g)]

## CONDUCT IN RESTRICTED VISIBILITY

The Great Lakes Rules differ slightly from the Inland Rules in the action to be taken by a vessel in conditions of reduced visibility, called "thick weather" on these waters.

Rule 15, in addition to requiring moderate speed as in the Inland Rules, also requires a power-driven vessel, hearing another, apparently not more than four points from dead ahead, to at once reduce speed to bare steerageway and navigate with caution until the vessels have passed each other. This zone of 45° on either side of the bow contrasts with the zone of 90° to either side specified by Inland Article 16.

## RULE OF PRECAUTIONS

The Great Lakes "Rule of Precautions," Rule 28, is the same as the Rule of Good Seamanship of the Inland Rules; see page 79.

### Supplementary signals

There are no provisions in the GLR comparable to Inland Article 12 which authorizes a flare-up light or detonating signal if necessary to attract attention.

## PILOT RULES FOR THE GREAT LAKES

The regulations authorized by the Act of Congress which established the Great Lakes Rules of the Road are known as the **Pilot Rules for the Great Lakes.** These will be found in Title 33 of the Code of Federal Regulations, Chapter I, Subchapter E, Part 90. They are more readily available to boatmen in the free Coast Guard pamphlet CG-172 which also contains Part 92 of this CFR title, "Anchorage and Navigation Regulations; St. Mary's River, Michigan."

**Fig. 540.** If in or near a channel or fairway, a vessel anchored or aground in fog on the Great Lakes must sound two separate signals —one at two-minute intervals and the other at three-minute intervals. See text for the characteristics of each signal.

Portions of the Pilot Rules are duplicatory of the provisions of the basic Great Lakes Rules and will not be repeated here. Other portions of the Pilot Rules have been discussed above in connection with the specific requirements of the Rules of the Road.

## Boundaries with the Western Rivers Rules

Two demarcation lines are established to separate waters subject to the Great Lakes Rules from those of the Western Rivers Rules.

These are the Thomas J. O'Brien Lock and Controlling Works on the Calumet River and the Ashland Avenue Bridge over the Chicago River. [90.03]

## Posting of Pilot Rules

Paragraph 90.15(b) requires that vessels must keep the Pilot Rules posted in *two* conspicuous places, one of which shall be the pilothouse. (This requirement for the posting of a copy of the "Pilot Rules" rather than the "Great Lakes Rules of the Road" is one reason that some of the GLR provisions are repeated in the Pilot Rules.) The posting can consist of a placard containing the Pilot Rules or a copy of the CG-172 pamphlet secured in plain sight.

Motorboats, as defined in the Motorboat Act of 1940, are exempted from the requirement above for posting copies of the Pilot Rules or for carrying them on board. This exemption from the legal requirement, however, should not serve to keep a boat skipper in these waters from having a copy of the latest edition of CG-172 on board—he is still responsible for knowing its contents.

## Other provisions

Many provisions of the Pilot Rules for the Great Lakes are similar to those for the Inland Waters, such as rules prohibiting any unnecessary sounding of a vessel's whistle.

Other provisions are unique to the Great Lakes Pilot Rules, such as the inclusion of a set of signals between the master or pilot and the engineer for controlling the direction and speed of the vessel's engine. [90.15(a)] These Pilot Rules also contain many more distress signals than the single one listed in the Inland Pilot Rules. [90.15(a)] See pages 87 to 88.

**FIG. 541** Department of the Army Navigation Regulations require that craft passing within 200 feet of "floating plant"—moored dredges and the like—must reduce their speed to not more than five miles per hour.

## ARMY ENGINEER NAVIGATION REGULATIONS

To comply with the requirements of the River and Harbor Acts of 8 August 1917, the U.S. Army Corps of Engineers has issued navigation regulations which appear in Title 33 of the Code of Federal Regulations in Chapter II as Part 201. These are included in CG-172.

These regulations, in part, relate to navigation and whistle signals of vessels passing "floating plant"—dredges, pile drivers, and the like—working in navigable channels. The provisions do not conflict with nor contradict the Rules of the Road, but do add some specifics such as a speed limit of five miles per hour when passing within 200 feet of floating plant and the stopping of propulsion machinery when passing over the lines of a plant. [201.11]

The locations of anchors used to hold a floating plant in position must be marked with barrels or other suitable buoys. [201.13] Light-draft vessels must keep outside of such markers wherever possible. [201.12], and all vessels must avoid running over these buoys, or any buoys, stakes, and marks placed for the guidance of floating plant operations. [201.16]

Further details of these regulations will be found in CG-172 or in the applicable volume of the Code of Federal Regulations.

# Western Rivers Rules

The **Western Rivers Rules of the Road** consist of numbered "Rules" like the Great Lakes Rules, but again the numbering is, in most cases, not parallel between the two sets of rules although the provisions are essentially the same.

Major differences include a different "bend" signal, several important variations in fog signals, and the requirement that a privileged vessel hold only her course (rather than course and speed). The **Pilot Rules for Western Rivers** contain a section covering the right-of-way between two vessels meeting at the junction of two rivers.

Because of their lesser applicability to the majority of boatmen, in comparison with the Inland and Great Lakes Rules, the Western Rivers Rules of the Road and their associated Pilot Rules will not be considered in detail in this chapter. The skipper concerned with these waters—principally the Mississippi River and its tributaries, but also including two other rivers—see page 38 for exact limits—should obtain a copy of Coast Guard pamphlet CG-184 and study it carefully.

The Army Engineer navigation regulations applicable on the Great Lakes and connecting waters also apply on the waters of the Western Rivers Rules. These regulations appear in full in CG-184 and do not conflict with or contradict the Rules of the Road or Pilot Rules; they do, however, contain some additional requirements and restrictions at noted above for the waters of the Great Lakes.

## International Rules of the Road

An individual who has carefully studied the provisions of the U.S. Inland Rules will have few problems when faced with the "International Regulations for the Prevention of Collisions at Sea"—the full and formal name for what is generally referred to as the **International Rules of the Road.**

These regulations—created by international conferences and made applicable to U.S. waters and vessels by Act of Congress and Presidential proclamation—consist of a series of "Rules" numbered from 1 to 31 without omission of any numbers, plus an "Annex." Those Rules relating to the topics of this chapter, and the Annex, will be discussed below primarily in terms of their differences and variations from the U.S. Inland Rules. Where no difference is pointed out, the provisions of a Rule of the International Rules of the Road (IntRR) are the same as those of the Inland Rules (IR), although not necessarily of the Article with the corresponding number.

Rules of the IntRR dealing with navigation lights and day shapes are discussed in Chapter 4.

### Applicability

The International Rules of the Road, as established under U.S. authority, are applicable to two situations:

1. To **all** vessels in waters of the United States sovereignty outside the prescribed boundary lines at entrance to bays, rivers harbors, etc.; see page 31.

2. To *all U.S.* vessels *on the high seas* not subject to another nation's geographical jurisdiction.

### DEFINITION OF TERMS

International Rule 1(c) includes definitions of two terms related to the topics of this chapter which were not formally defined in the U.S. Inland Rules.

Many of the Chapter 4 basic definitions of the Inland Rules [page 64(c)] and the International Rules [page 64(s)] are also applicable to this chapter.

### Additional definitions

**In sight**—Vessels are deemed to be within sight of one another when one can be visually observed from the other.

**Whistle**—the word "whistle" means any appliance capable of producing the prescribed short and prolonged blasts. (These blasts are also specifically defined in Rule 1(c) in the same terms as in the Inland Rules of the Road or Pilot Rules.)

### STEERING AND SAILING RULES

The "Preliminary Statement" to the Steering and Sailing Rules of the International Rules includes a directive that is not a part of the Inland Rules, but which is an excellent one that should be known and heeded on all waters.

"In construing and obeying these Rules, any action taken should be positive, in ample time, and with due regard to the observance of good seamanship."

The Preliminary Statement also contains a caution regarding the limitations of seaplanes in the act of landing or taking off, or operating under adverse weather conditions. This, too, is applicable to all waters by reason of logic if not law.

International Rules 17 through 24 relating to right-of-

FIG. 542 The International Rules of the Road not only affect all vessels in U.S. off-shore waters, but they also apply to all U.S. vessels anywhere on the high seas—the ocean waters not subject to the jurisdiction of any nation.

way between vessels are specifically limited to vessels "in sight of one another." This limitation does not appear in the Inland Rules, except indirectly in Article 18.

### Passing Situations

International Rules 18, 19, and 24 direct the same actions for power-driven vessels in meeting, crossing, and overtaking situations as the Inland Rules, but **without** the whistle signals of intent and agreement as to the side to be passed on.

### Sailing vessels

International Rule 17 covering the right-of-way between two sailing vessels encountering each other is phrased quite differently from the provisions of the Inland Rules.

When each has the wind on a different side, the vessel which has the wind on the port side must keep out of the way of the other.

When both have the wind on the same side, the vessel which is to windward must keep out of the way of the vessel that is to leeward.

For the purpose of Rule 17, the windward side is considered to be the side opposite to that on which the mainsail is carried (or in the case of a square-rigged vessel, the side opposite to that on which the largest fore-and-aft sail is carried).

### Sound Signals for Vessels Within Sight

The one- and two-blast sound signals of good visibility situations in the International Rules are indications of *taking action to alter course* rather than the U.S. Rules signals of intent and agreement. The International Rules signals are frequently termed "rudder signals"; they do not involve a reply and the IntRR do not speak of an "exchange" of whistle signals.

FIG. 543 The whistle signals of the International Rules of the Road indicate changes of course (rudder signals) rather than intentions to pass under certain conditions. In this well-clear, port-to-port meeting, no signals would be exchanged.

Rule 28 of the IntRR states that one short blast means "I am altering my course to starboard" and two short blasts mean "I am altering my course to port." The three-short-blast signal has the meaning "My engines are going astern"—the same generally as the Inland Rules, but without including the words "full speed."

## Signal of doubt (Danger signal)

Whenever a power-driven vessel that is required to hold her course and speed in a situation with another is in sight of that other vessel and is in doubt as to whether sufficient action is being taken to avoid a collision, she *may* indicate such *doubt* by sounding *at least five* short and rapid blasts on her whistle. The giving of this signal does not relieve a vessel of her obligations under the Rule of Good Seamanship, the General Prudential Rule, or any other of the rules of the road, including her duty to sound other whistle signals as indicative of her intentions to alter course. [28(b)]

Note that the International Rule signal is *limited* to a *privileged* vessel, and thus to those situations wherein there is relative right-of-way—crossing and overtaking. Its use is optional, as contrasted with some situations under the Inland Rules where the danger signal must be sounded.

## Whistle light

Any International whistle signal *may* be further indicated by a visual signal consisting of a white light visible all around the horizon to a distance of at least five miles. This light, if used, must be so installed that it operates simultaneously and in conjunction with the sound signal mechanism; it must light and remain lighted for the same period as the sound signal. [28(c)]

This is essentially the same visual signal as required by the Western Rivers Pilot Rules for many types of vessels, except for color and required distance of visibility.

FIG. 545 a, b Under the International Rules a power-driven vessel starting a change of course within sight of another vessel must sound a whistle signal. This is not returned by the other vessel, and thus there is no "exchange" of signals.

FIG. 546 In waters subject to the International Rules of the Road, the danger signal may only be given by a privileged vessel in doubt as to whether the action being taken by the burdened vessel is sufficient to avert collision.

FIG. 547 Any whistle signal authorized by the International Rules may be visually indicated by a light synchronized with the sound-producing apparatus. This is to be an all-around white light visible to at least five miles.

## Sound Signals in Reduced Visibility

The principal difference here between the requirements of the IntRR and those of the IR is that power-driven vessels need sound their fog signal only at intervals of *two* minutes or less, rather than one minute. [15(c)(i)]

An additional signal is prescribed for power-driven vessels underway but stopped and making no way through the water—as might be the case in fog so dense as to make any speed at all greater than "moderate," often in water too deep to anchor. This is a two-prolonged-blast signal with about one second's spacing between blasts; it is repeated at the normal interval of not more than two minutes. [15(c)(ii)]

## Sailing vessels

The International Rules prescribe the same fog signal for sailing vessels as do the Inland Rules, including the *one* minute interval.

## Vessels of limited maneuverability

In situations of reduced visibility, a vessel towing another, or a vessel engaged in laying or picking up a submarine cable or navigation mark, or a vessel underway

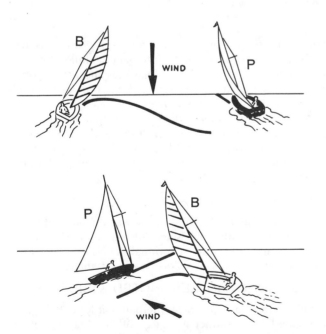

FIG. 544 a, b International Rules 17 covers the relative right-of-way between two sailboats encountering each other an off-shore waters. The language of this Rule varies considerably from Inland Article 17.

that is not under command or is unable to maneuver as required by the rules of the road, *must* sound a special signal *in lieu of* the normal fog signals of power-driven and sailing vessels. This consists of three blasts in succession—one prolonged, and two short—sounded at intervals of not more than *one* minute. [15(c)(v)] For vessels engaged in towing, this is the same signal as prescribed in the Inland Rules; the other classes of vessels covered by this rule are not mentioned in the Inland fog signals.

### Vessels being towed

If manned, a vessel being towed (or the last vessel if several are being towed in a string) must sound a fog signal of four blasts—one prolonged and three short blasts—at intervals of not more than *one* minute. When practicable, this signal should be sounded immediately after the signal of the towing vessel. [15(c)(vi)] This signal differs from that of the Inland Rules and is mandatory rather than optional.

### Vessels at anchor

The IntRR prescribe the usual fog signal for a vessel at anchor, the ringing of a bell for about five seconds at intervals of not more than one minute, and provide an *additional* signal for vessels over 350 feet in length. In such vessels, the regular bell must be rung in the fore part of the ship *and* in the after part at the same interval there must be sounded for about five seconds a gong or other instrument the tone and sounding of which cannot be confused with that of the bell.

Further, *any* vessel at anchor in waters of the International Rules, regardless of size, *may* sound a three-blast signal—one short, one prolonged, one short—to give warning of her position and status to an approaching vessel that might collide with her. [15(c)(iv)]

### Vessels aground

A vessel which is aground in International Rules' waters in reduced visibility must give the normal bell signal of a vessel at anchor (and the gong signal if required by her size), and *additionally* sound three separate and distinct strokes of the bell *before and after* the rapid ringing of the bell. [15(c)(vii)] There is no parallel signal in the Inland Rules; as noted above, such vessels there should sound the danger signal on their whistle in lieu of ringing a bell.

### Fishing vessels

A vessel "engaged in fishing" [see definition on page 64(s)] *when underway or at anchor* must sound the signal described above for vessels of limited maneuverability—one prolonged blast followed by two short ones. A vessel fishing with trolling lines and underway sounds only the normal signal of a sailing vessel underway or a power-driven vessel underway or underway with no way on. [15(c)(viii)]

### Exceptions

A vessel of less than 40 feet in length or a rowing boat is not obliged to give the signals of the above subsections of Rule 15(c), but if she does not, she must make some other efficient sound signal at intervals of not more than *one* minute. [15(c)(ix)]

A major difference between the IntRR and the IR for

**FIG. 548** In waters of the International Rules, the one prolonged blast—four to six seconds—signal for vessels making way through the water when visibility is reduced need be sounded only once every **two** minutes. If the vessel is "underway with no way on," the signal is two prolonged blasts.

**FIG. 549** A vessel towed astern in waters of the International Rules (the last vessel if more than one is being towed in tandem) must, if manned, sound a signal of one prolonged blast followed by three short blasts; this should be sounded immediately following the tug's fog signal.

**FIG. 550** The International Rules prescribe the same fog bell signal for smaller vessels as in the Inland Rules, but require an additional —gong—signal for vessels over 350 feet in length. Further, **any** vessel at anchor in these waters **may** sound a one short—one prolonged —one short whistle signal also.

sound signals in conditions of reduced visibility is that there are no exceptions in the International Rules for "special anchorage areas." This is logical as the usually open waters of these Rules are less likely to provide safe anchorages for small craft and barges.

A further, but minor, difference is that International Rule 15(a) requires that power-driven and sailing vessels over 40 feet in length must have an efficient fog horn "to be sounded by mechanical means"; this language does not appear in the Inland Rules.

### Pilot vessels

When engaged in her duties, a power-driven pilot vessel *may* sound an "identity" signal of four short blasts. This would be in addition to the normal signals of a vessel underway, underway with no way on, or at anchor.

## CONDUCT IN RESTRICTED VISIBILITY

Subsections (a) and (b) of International Rule 16 regarding speed and conduct in fog or other situations of reduced visibility are essentially the same as Inland Article 16, but the IntRR contains a subsection (c) with an *additional requirement*.

**FIG. 551** A vessel aground in waters of the International Rules sounds the normal bell signal (and gong signal if large enough to require it) and additionally makes three separate and distinct strokes on the bell before and after the rapid ringing.

A power-driven vessel which detects the presence of another vessel forward of her beam before hearing her fog signal or sighting her visually—this would normally mean detection by radar—may take early and substantial action to avoid a close-quarters situation, but if this cannot be avoided, she *must,* insofar as the circumstances of the situation permit, stop her engines in proper time to avoid collision and then navigate with caution until danger of collision is over.

The "may take early and substantial action" in the above paragraph is the way that the International Rule is formally worded—for all practical purposes, however, considering the Rule of Good Seamanship, it ought to be "should take early action," or even "must."

## GENERAL RIGHT-OF-WAY RULES

With respect to the "duty" of the privileged vessel, International Rule 21 contains the same language as Inland Article 21 regarding her requirement to keep her course and speed, but the IntRR go on to state that when, for any cause, the privileged vessel finds herself so close that collision cannot be avoided by the actions of the burdened vessel alone, she, too, must take such action as will best aid in the prevention of a collision. This is only logical, but does not so clearly appear in the Inland Rules.

### Burdened vessel's duty

International Rule 22 contains the same requirement as Inland Article 22 for the burdened vessel to keep out of the way and avoid crossing ahead, but also specifically states that she must, so far as possible, take positive early action to comply with her obligation.

Rule 23 regarding the slackening of speed, or stopping or reversing, is identical with Article 23.

### RADAR ANNEX

The International Rules contain an "Annex" which has no counterpart in the Inland Rules. This annex is entitled "Recommendations on the Use of Radar Information as an Aid to Avoiding Collisions at Sea."

Skippers of boats equipped with radar should be thoroughly familiar with the contents of this Annex—it is mandatory on waters subject to the International Rules, and it makes good sense on all waters.

# Distress Signals

Because of their great importance, the accepted forms of distress signals have been written into the various Rules of the Road or related Pilot Rules.

Some signals are the same, or nearly so, in all sets of Rules; others appear in only one or two sets. Table 5-1 lists the various *officially recognized* signals for each set of Rules of the Road or Pilot Rules, but in a true emergency a skipper can use *any* means within his capabilities to summon help.

### Additional distress signals

The Coast Guard also recognizes two additional distress signals that are particularly well-suited to the needs of small craft. One is an excellent signal, developed in Canada, that any boat owner can make (it is also available for purchase in many stores). This signal consists simply of a 45" x 72" rectangular piece of fluorescent orange-red cloth on which are marked a black 18" square and a black 18" circle separated by an 18" space, symmetrically arranged with a 9" space at each end. It is based on the International Rule signal of "a square flag having above or below it a ball . . . " This piece of cloth could be displayed vertically to other vessels or horizontally across the boat cabin top as a signal to aircraft.

Also recognized is a simple orange-red flag of any size, waved from side to side.

### Use of inverted ensign

Most American boatmen would recognize the flying of an *inverted* U.S. national or yacht ensign as a signal of distress. It should be carefully noted, however, that such a signal has **no** official sanction. This stems from the fact that the national flags of many maritime nations have no "top" or "bottom" and would appear exactly the same if turned upside down!

### Radio alarm signals

The radiotelephone is, of course, a major means of announcing a distress situation and requesting help; see pages 496 to 498. Vessels in distress may use the radiotelephone alarm signal to secure attention to distress calls and messages. This consists of two different tones transmitted alternately and rapidly for from 30 seconds to one minute. It is very distinctive and effective.

There is also a radiotelegraph alarm signal, but this is of little interest to boatmen.

### Submarine distress signals

Distress signals used by submarines of the U.S. Navy are not included in the U.S. or International Rules, but these should be known by the skippers of all craft plying offshore waters.

U.S. submarines are equipped with signal ejectors which may be used to launch identification signals, including emergency signals. Two general types of signals are used: smoke floats, and flares or stars. The smoke floats, which burn on the surface, produce a dense colored smoke for a period of 15 to 45 seconds. The flares or stars are propelled to a height of 300 to 400 feet from which they descend by small parachute, burning for about 25 seconds.

The color of the smoke or flare/star has the following meaning:

**Green or black**—Used for training exercises only to indicate that a torpedo has been fired or the firing of a torpedo has been simulated.

**Yellow**—Indicates that the submarine is about to come to periscope depth from below periscope depth. Surface ships and craft should clear the area; do *not* stop propellers.

**Red**—Indicates an emergency condition within the submarine, and that it will surface immediately, if possible. Surface ships and craft should clear the area and stand by to give assistance after the submarine has surfaced. In case of repeated red signals, or if the submarine fails to surface within a reasonable time, she may be assumed to be disabled. Mariners should determine the location, buoy it, look for the submarine's marker buoy, and advise U.S. Naval or Coast Guard authorities immediately.

Legislation is pending in the Congress which would replace the existing Inland, Great Lakes, and Western Rivers Rules of the Road with a single set for all inland waters to be known as the "U.S. Nautical Rules." The provisions regarding right-of-way, whistle signals, and fog signals would be extensively changed and brought more nearly into conformity with the International Rules, still taking into consideration the nature of inland waters and vessels. Distress signals for all inland U.S. waters would be the same as those of the International Rules with one additional signal authorized.

The bill was originally introduced late in the 90th Congress and no action was taken before adjournment. It was re-introduced in the 91st Congress as H.R. 214. As of March 1970, it was still awaiting the start of committee hearings.

The eventual passage of the U.S. Nautical Rules can be expected, but no date can be forecast. In any event, however, its effective date would probably be one year after enactment, and during this time the contents of this chapter will be revised to reflect the new right-of-way rules, and whistle, fog, and distress signals.

## Know the Rules

It cannot be emphasized too strongly that (1) a skipper of any boat must know the rules of the road relating to his craft and waters; and (2) it is too late to start learning them when he gets into a tight situation! Rules must be studied carefully and thoroughly, and they should be periodically reviewed as a refresher.

**FIG. 552** The various Rules of the Road and Pilot Rules each list a set of distress signals; no two sets are the same, however. The square flag and round shape, and the code flags "NC" are from the International Rules but do not appear in the Inland Rules of the Road or Pilot Rules.

| Table 5–1 DISTRESS SIGNALS | | | | |
|---|---|---|---|---|
| | Rules of the Road or Pilot Rules | | | |
| Distress Signal | Inland | Great Lakes | Western Rivers | International |
| Continuous sounding with any fog-signal apparatus | D/N | D/N | D/N | X |
| Firing of a gun or other explosive signal | D/N | D/N(2) | D/N(2) | X(2) |
| Flames on the vessel (as from a burning tar or oil barrel, etc.) | N | N | N | X |
| A signal consisting of a square flag having either above or below it a ball or some object resembling a ball | | D | D | X |
| Slowly and repeatedly raising and lowering arms outstretched to each side | D | D | D | X |
| Rockets or shells, throwing stars of any color or description, fired one at a time at short intervals | | N | D/N | X |
| The International Code signal of distress indicated by NC | | | D | X |
| The signal SOS sent in the Morse Code (. . . — — — . . .) sent by any means | | | | X |
| The spoken word "Mayday" by radiotelephone | | | | X |
| A rocket parachute flare or a hand flare showing a red light | | | | X |
| A smoke signal giving off a volume of orange colored smoke | | | | X |

The above signals can be used singly or in any combination.

Notes 1—D = Day use; N = Night use; D/N = Day or night use; X—IntRR do not specify in terms of day or night use.
2—fired at intervals of about one minutes

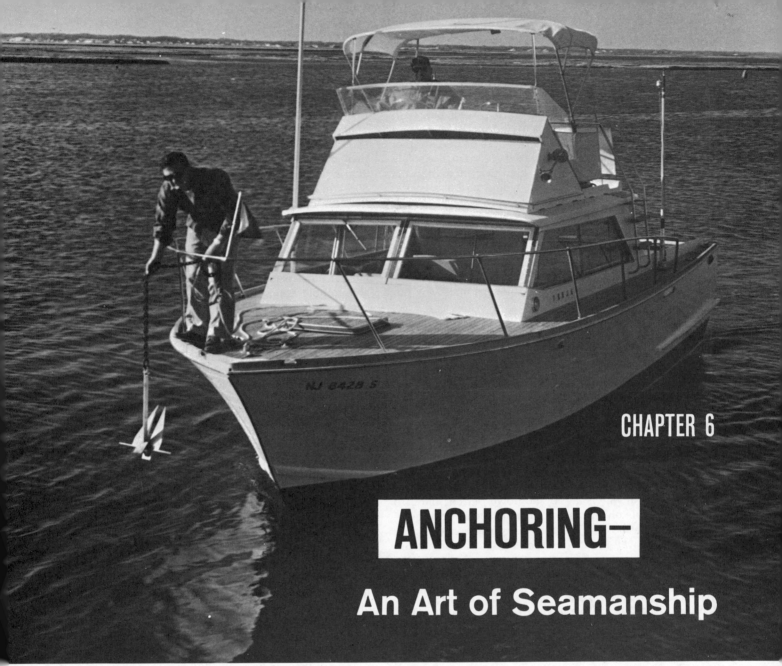

# ANCHORING—

## An Art of Seamanship

Photograph by Peter Smyth

**CHAPTER 6**

**O**f all the skills involved in seamanship, the art of anchoring is one the boatman must master if he is to cruise with an easy mind. Perhaps he is just getting by with inadequate gear, despite bad practices acquired in home waters. Sooner or later, carelessness and ignorance will lead to difficulty—probably inconvenience, possibly danger.

The essence of successful anchoring is to "stay put," without dragging, whenever the anchor is let go. Corollary to this is the need to respect the rights of nearby boats which could be fouled or damaged by your dragging.

Though the art may not be learned from the printed page alone, this chapter should help the tyro to get off to a good start, the seasoned boatman to round out and update his technique.

In quiet anchorages, in familiar surroundings, *ground tackle* (the gear we use) and the methods used are seldom put to test. Cruising into strange waters, find inadequate shelter in an exposed anchorage during a hard blow, and the elements will surely take the measure of both tackle and technique. The ultimate test, of course, would come in deep water on a lee shore with nothing between you and breakers on the beach except dependable gear. Ask yourself *now,* in a situation like that, would I hold . . . or hope?

The problem, then, breaks down into two principal parts—(1) the equipment we should carry, and (2) knowledge of how to use it. It is in this sequence that we treat the subject here, however anxious the reader may be to plunge headlong into the "how" aspect before he is quite familiar with the "what."

# Anchoring / CHAPTER 6

## Conditions vary

In approaching the subject, it is imperative to have a sense of perspective, impossible to achieve if one is so wedded to the lore of one locality (no matter how good or effective) as to be blinded to practices proved in other areas. Lay down universal rules based on experience solely with one type of anchor in one kind of bottom, and the gale that would test your "rules" would be but a breeze compared to the storm of controversy you might raise in other knowledgeable quarters.

When we realize that the gear we see aboard that visiting boat from a distant port may have been dictated by proved and practical experience foreign to our own, we will have gone a long way toward broadening that perspective we need . . . and, who knows, perhaps improving our own anchoring skill as well.

## Some of the variables

The man who has cruised in many areas, over many years, knows he can list nine or ten important variables. To cite a few: the size and type of boat; whether she is of light or heavy draft; the size and design of anchor; the nature of the bottom in which the anchor is bedded; the protection afforded by the anchorage; and the amount of sea running.

To say that any one kind of ground tackle would be ideal under all conceivable conditions for all boats of a given length is to discount the combined knowledge of the saltiest boatmen in waters all up and down our coastline. To rule out completely the value of certain specialized equipment is to overlook the fact that many a seasoned skipper has his own well-founded preferences . . . or prejudices.

**FIG. 601  A century ago, wooden stock anchors were still in use. This one snagged the net of a dragger in the late 1940's, off Chatham, Cape Cod, offshore of Pollock Rip Lightship. It's likely that it was lost by a four- or five-masted coastal cargo schooner.** (From Kodachrome by Wm. H. Koelbel)

## Evolution of the modern anchor

It is beyond the scope of this chapter to delve deeply into the history of anchors, interesting though that may be. Touching on it briefly, however, we get an insight into the evolution from ancient to modern design, and what lies behind the quest for an anchor that will *bury*, not drag. At this point it will be helpful to refer to the sketches, fig. 602, and labeled diagram, fig. 604, which, later, will clarify the meaning of terms used to describe the anchor's parts.

Going back to primitive times, the earliest "anchor" of which we have record was a simple stone used with a crude rope. Though it may have served under ideal conditions to prevent the drift of an ancient watercraft, dragging at times was inevitable, when sheer weight was unable to hold against the pull of wind and current.

Obviously what was needed was a device to engage the bottom, giving rise to the addition of simple wooden (and later, iron) hooks, forerunner of the arms and flukes found in later developments. To this day, survivors of this early anchor concept may be found Down East in Nova Scotia, where fishermen still fashion by hand their "killicks" of wood, stone and manila. Colloquially, we drop a "hook" when we lower an anchor.

Modifications of the hooking type of anchor evolved and, roughly 4,000 years ago, the Chinese added a stock at the crown end of the shank, perpendicular to the plane of the hooking arms, to put them in position to get a bite in the bottom. Junks still use this type today. In an ancient Greek design (about 750 B.C.) the stock had moved to the ring end of the shank.

In due course, in an effort to increase holding power, broad triangular flukes were added to the arms, giving rise to the old-fashioned kedge, fig. 603, often with a wooden stock, fig. 601, at the ring end of the shank, as used on naval vessels well into the 19th century. In 1821 the first of a series of stockless (patent) Navy anchors was invented Elimination of the stock permitted the shank to be drawn up into the hawsepipe of a vessel, flukes lying flat against the topsides.

Toward the middle of the 19th century, the mushroom anchor appeared, its design restricting its principal value to use in permanent moorings. Though their holding power is low, very small craft often use them for brief stops in light weather.

The principle of placing the stock at the crown end was brought to a relatively high state of development in the Northill design, where short, broad, thin flukes provided better penetration, and a folding stock improved stowage characteristics.

In 1933, a radical innovation in design was introduced in England—the plow, a stockless type in which conventional flukes were replaced by a casting resembling a plow, pivoted at its point of attachment to the shank.

Supplanting mass and weight with scientific design, R. S. Danforth in 1939 developed what has been referred to by the U.S. Navy as the *lightweight-type* anchor in which broad pivoted flukes, stabilized by a stock, not only penetrate the bottom but bury completely until firm holding ground is reached. It is this feature, primarily, which distinguishes the *burying* anchor from a type that is prone to drag.

So much for history.

FIG. 602 How several anchor types differ. Principal parts of each are shown. All have shanks; not all have stocks.

# Ground Tackle

## Some terms and definitions

To prevent possibility of confusion in the use of terms, refer again to the labeled illustration of the parts of an anchor, fig. 604, and the more general definitions in Table 6-1. A popular version of the kedge was chosen to illustrate the parts, because it is a type frequently visualized as a conventional anchor. Subsequently we shall see how the proportioning and placement of parts have varied with the introduction of later designs. Many otherwise well-informed boatmen have often spoken of the shank and

stock as though the terms were interchangeable. In fact, however, most anchors (with few exceptions) have shanks, but some are stockless.

To illustrate graphically the basic fundamentals in anchoring, one authority sketches, in fig. 605, what has been referred to as *the anchoring system*. Though *scope* has been defined in Table 6-1 as a relation between length of rode and depth of water, there are other vital considerations in determining the length of rode to be paid out—the height of bow, range of tide, etc. This will be dealt with more fully later, as scope is one of the most important of all factors in determining holding power.

Finally, to forestall argument as to the validity of the term *rode*, it should be noted that the word has, on rare occasions, been challenged. Without going to its defense here, we can say that our best boating authorities have long accepted its usage in nautical jargon, and it is unlikely that it will ever be lost to the language.

## TYPES OF ANCHORS IN USE

### Lightweight type (LWT)

Scan a marine hardware catalog and, without experience, you may be confused by the diversity of designs offered today. What you should be buying, essentially, is holding power; sheer weight is no index of that. On the contrary, scientific design is the key to efficiency and a lightweight type, *if properly manufactured*, unquestionably stands at the top of the list today on a holding power-to-weight basis.

The lightweight type was originated just prior to World War II by R. S. Danforth. Its efficiency in war service was so high that it made possible the retraction of amphibious craft in assaults on enemy-held beachheads. Its versatility in sand and mud bottoms quickly won widespread popularity among yachtsmen as models were developed specifically for convenience aboard pleasure craft. Generally, with a little caution, the lightweight anchor can even be hooked in rocky bottoms.

In the Danforth anchor, flukes are long and sharp, designed so that heavy strains bury the anchor completely. Tests have proved that it tends to work down through soft bottoms to firmer holding ground below, burying part of

---

## TABLE 6-1. SOME BASIC DEFINITIONS

**Anchor**—A device designed to engage the bottom of a waterway and through its resistance to drag maintain a vessel within a given radius.

**Anchor Chocks**—Fittings on the deck of a vessel used to stow an anchor when it is not in use.

**Anchor Rode**—The line connecting an anchor with a vessel.

**Bow Chocks**—Fittings, usually on the rail of a vessel near its stem, having jaws that serve as fairleads for anchor rodes and other lines.

**Ground Tackle**—A general term for the anchor, anchor rodes, fittings, etc., used for securing a vessel at anchor.

**Hawsepipe**—A cylindrical or elliptical pipe or casting in a vessel's hull through which the anchor rode runs.

**Horizontal Load**—The horizontal force placed on an anchoring device by the vessel to which it is connected.

**Mooring Bitt**—A post or cleat through or on the deck of a vessel used to secure an anchor rode or other line to the vessel.

**\*Scope**—The relation between the length of an anchor rode and the depth of the water in which a vessel is anchored.

**Vertical Load**—The lifting force placed on the bow of a vessel by its anchor rode.

*Definitions adopted by the American Boat and Yacht Council in drafting a code of recommended practices and standards covering ground tackle.   \*See caption fig. 605.*

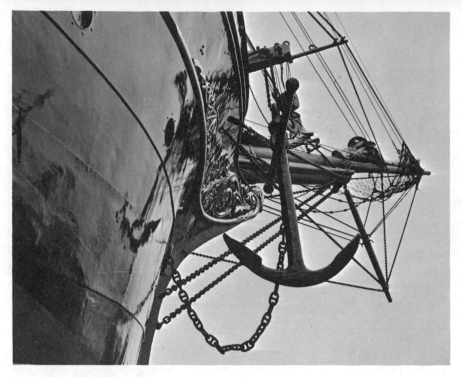

FIG. 603 Old-fashioned kedges survived into the 20th century. This one, with iron stock, aboard the Joseph Conrad, is shown *catted* (hoisted up to the cathead).

the rode as well, fig. 609(b).

In place of a stock through the head, the lightweight type has a round rod at the crown end to prevent the anchor from rolling or rotating. This placement of the stock does not interfere with its being drawn into the hawse-pipes of larger craft for stowage. (Many yachtsmen slip protective rubber tips over the stock ends.)

The lightweight-type Danforth is made in two models, the Hi-Tensile and Standard, fig. 606. They bear a close family resemblance but differences in materials and manufacture permit the Hi-Tensile to achieve maximum holding power on a given weight. In selecting any anchor, remember that all manufacturers have their individual concepts of design and "look-alikes" do not necessarily hold alike.

While not put forth as a size recommendation for boats in general, one impressive evidence of holding power is the experience of a 40-foot auxiliary cruising sloop which held in all bottoms, including soft mud six feet deep in 25-mile winds, with a 5-pound Danforth!

The success of the lightweight type anchor manufactured by Danforth has prompted other manufacturers to offer their own versions, varying in efficiency with details of design and construction, as in fluke angle and welding practices. Finishes vary, too; some are rubber-covered or enamelled instead of hot-dip galvanized. Some are good; others cannot compare with the efficiency of the original.

### The plow

The plow anchor is unique in design, resembling none of the other types. It originated in England as a result of a challenge to Professor G. I. Taylor of Cambridge University from a cruising companion to invent an anchor of greater holding power on lower weight. He called it the CQR (secure). It found wide acceptance because of its demonstrated efficiency in a variety of bottoms. Opinions vary as to its effectiveness in heavy weed, which is not surprising in that certain weed growths resist penetration by any anchor. Some European versions of the plow failed to equal the efficiency of the original. The Plowright, fig. 608, is an improved model recently developed and manufactured in this country.

When a plow is lowered, the anchor first lies on its side

on the bottom. See fig. 609(a). Then when a pull is put on the rode, it rights itself, driving the point of the plow in, and finally burying the plow completely. The Plowright is claimed to hold up to 300 times its weight, depending naturally on the kind of bottom. CQR suggested catalog weights vary from 10 pounds for a 20-footer to 75 pounds for 75—125-footers.

Because of the pivoting feature of the shank, the tendency of the plow is to remain buried when the angle of pull is changed by wind or current. There is no projecting fluke to foul the rode and it breaks out easily when the pull is vertical, in position to bring the anchor up on deck.

### Kedges

In discussing kedges it is important to make a sharp distinction between the more massive ancient types and later versions which have been designed for yacht use. In glossaries, "kedge anchors" as a rule are light anchors (of any design) carried out from a vessel aground to free her by winching in on the rode. Here, however, we refer to the kedge as an anchor with the more conventional type of

FIG. 604 Wilcox Crittenden's Yachtsman anchor, with parts labeled. The stock can be folded to lie along the shank.

FIG. 605 The anchoring system includes not only the anchor but rode L, the length of which is referred to in terms of scope. In practice, however scope may be defined, the boatman must make due allowance for height (H) of his bow chocks above water, and any increase a rising tide may add to depth (D).

FIG. 606 Two models of Danforth lightweight anchor — (a) the Standard and (b) Hi-Tensile. Both are burying types, with high holding power.

FIG. 607 Newest Danforth is the Utility model shown (a) with stock folded and (b) with stock set up in position ready for use.

arms, flukes and stocks as distinguished from newer lightweight types.

The earliest kedges, aside from their mass, were characterized by roughly triangular flukes and relatively dull bills. See fig. 610. The shoulders on the flukes, being nearly square with the arm, invited fouling of the rode as a vessel swung at her anchorage with shifts in wind and current. The dull bills made it difficult to bite in hard bottoms. Other kedges, like sand and trawl anchors, designed for use primarily on hard bottoms, had very small flukes and sharp bills. Both of these types left much to be desired for general yacht use, though often right for special purposes.

### Yachtsman and Herreshoff anchors

Types of anchor which evolved from earlier kedges include the Yachtsman, fig. 604, and Herreshoff, fig. 611(b), designs. Though varying in details of construction, the principle used in both was a redistribution of the weight, a different proportioning of the length of stock to the chord measured from bill to bill, and a drastic change in the shape and size of fluke relative to the arm.

A major distinguishing feature of these modified kedges is the diamond-shaped fluke, embodied in the design to reduce risk of fouling, on the theory that the rode would slip off an exposed fluke where no squared shoulder was presented. At the same time, sharpening of the bill permitted better penetration in hard bottoms.

Neither of these kedges is claimed to be a "burying" type, as the shank lies on the bottom and one fluke remains exposed. On the other hand, its "hook" design recommends it, probably above all other types, on rocky bottoms where one fluke can find a crevice, and retrieval, with proper precautions, is not too difficult. (More about this later.)

### The Northill

The concept of light weight was first brought to kedge design with the introduction of the Northhill, fig. 612. Originally made in stainless steel, the current model is fabricated of rugged malleable iron, hot-dip galvanized for resistance to corrosion.

The Northill is also unique, resembling the kedge only to the extent that it is a "hooking" type. Here, however, for the first time in our modern anchors, the stock has moved to the other end of the shank, square with the arms, but movable to fold against the shank for better stowage.

93

Patterned after a principle utilized on wooden anchors in Malaysia through thousands of years, the Northill stock adds to the anchor's holding power when the fluke is buried. Arms are at right angles to the shank, and the broad reinforced flukes with sharp bills are set at a carefully computed angle to assure a quick bite. See fig. 613. Narrow fluke arms allow the anchor to penetrate well.

The Northill has demonstrated its efficiency in sand and mud, and has performed well even in heavy kelp and on rocky bottoms.

## Other types

All the anchors discussed thus far have been of the so-called *stock-type*, though the stock, as we have seen, may be placed at either the ring or crown end of the shank. Although some stock anchors are made with a fast stock, for pleasure boat use they are more likely to have a loose stock which can be folded for better stowage. Frequently, a key is required to pin the stock of a kedge in its open position when set up ready for use, the key in turn being lashed in its slot to hold it in place.

Some anchors, however, are *stockless*. Frequently these are cataloged as Navy-type anchors. Inexperienced boatmen, seeing them on large vessels, sometimes jump to the conclusion that they are consequently the best for all vessels, including boats. Nothing could be further from the truth. Ships use them because stockless anchors can be hauled up with power into hawsepipes. On pleasure boats, the ratio of weight to holding power is so great that, if it is heavy enough to hold, it is a back-breaker; if weight is held within reason, holding power is far below the limits of safety. The Sea-Claw is an improved version of the Navy anchor, with a different proportioning of its parts, and round stock at the crown. See fig. 614.

When we speak of *folding anchors*, we think not so much in terms of a Yachtsman's kedge with movable stock as a highly specialized design in which, at some sacrifice of holding power, all parts fold against the shank into the smallest possible space for most convenient stowage. In one stockless type, the Norwegian SAV (imported by Canor Plarex) there are two pairs of flukes at right angles to each other, almost in the manner of a grapnel. In rocky bottoms, they hook readily and may be rigged to pull out easily, crown first. See fig. 646.

*Grapnels,* though used more extensively by some commercial fishermen than many boatmen realize, are not recommended for general anchoring service aboard pleasure boats. These are also stockless models with, as a rule, five curved sharp-billed claw-like prongs symmetrically arranged around the crown end of the shank. Eyes may be cast in both ends of the shank—at the head in lieu of a ring for attachment of a rode (if used as an anchor) and at the

FIG. 608 Woolsey's Plowright anchor has plow-shaped flukes, causing the anchor to bury deep. The shank is pivoted.

FIG. 609 How burying anchors work when an anchoring strain is put on the rode. In (a) below, a plow lands on the bottom on its side (1) gets a quick bite (2) and rights itself (3), digging deep. In (b) a lightweight anchor lands with flukes flat (1), penetrating (2) as the strain comes on the rode, and (3) burying in the holding position.

FIG. 610 Early kedges used aboard yachts had dull bills and shoulders on flukes that often fouled the rode when the boat swung in a complete circle at an anchorage.

**(a)** **(b)**

FIG. 611 (a) Flukes of this sand anchor are relatively small, the bills sharp, to penetrate hard bottoms. In soft bottoms holding power is low. (b) The Herreshoff version of the kedge. Note difference in fluke area.

FIG. 612
The Northill Utility anchor combines the hooking action of a kedge with relatively high holding power.

crown end for a buoyed trip line. By dragging a small grapnel back and forth, a boatman may *grapple* for a piece of equipment lost on the bottom. See fig. 615.

Discussion of *mushroom* anchors, fig. 652, will be reserved till later as, properly, their principal use is in conjunction with permanent moorings, at anchorages. Modified versions of the mushroom are manufactured for small craft like canoes and rowboats, but their efficiency as "anchors" is at the lowest end of the scale.

All the anchors under discussion in this chapter are devices designed to keep a boat from drifting, by engagement with the bottom. *Sea anchors* do not fall in this category. These are intended to float at or just below the surface, serving merely as a drag to hold a boat's bow (or stern) up toward the seas to prevent her from lying in the trough. Sea anchors are rarely used aboard pleasure boats, and then only in the heaviest weather offshore, where there is room to drift to leeward. See chapter 9, Seamanship (pages 165-166) for a discussion of sea anchors and their use. *Drogues,* like the highly effective Fenger-type, are devices made up with planks, chain, weights and rode, to serve the purpose of a conventional sea anchor which, in some cases, they are reported to have bettered in efficiency.

## THE RODE

All of the gear, taken collectively, that lies between a boat and her anchor is called the *rode*—whether it be synthetic fiber (like nylon), vegetable fiber (like manila), chain, wire, or a combination of fiber and chain. When his rode is nylon or manila, a knowledgeable boatman will not refer to his anchor "rope," as rope in a coil becomes "line" when cut for specific uses. Thus, with fiber rodes, it is quite appropriate to refer to the "anchor line."

### Nylon

Since the introduction of synthetics, a quiet revolution has been taking place in the choice of material for anchor rodes. Good quality manila was once the accepted type of line. Synthetics, however, have brought new properties that make them even better adapted to the boatman's use.

FIG. 613 Pitch of the flukes of a Northill causes it to penetrate and dig in quickly. Here the anchor is already turning to its ultimate horizontal position. The stock is at the crown end.

Because other synthetics, such as dacron, polypropylene, polyethylene, etc., have little elasticity, they are not recommended for anchoring and towing. Nylon, on the other hand, has high elasticity and is the outstanding choice today.

Any differential in cost between nylon and manila is more than made up by differences in strength and longer life, both on the side of nylon. (See Table 11-1, breaking strengths, page 216.) Several times the strength of manila, nylon can be used in smaller diameters, light and easy to handle. See fig. 616. Though it can be damaged by rust from iron fittings or rusty chain, it is highly resistant to the rot, decay and mildew that attack vegetable fibers.

For anchoring purposes, nylon's greatest asset is its elasticity, stretching a third or more under load. Its working elasticity of 15 to 25% is several times greater than that of manila. When a boat surges at anchor in steep seas, there is a heavy shock load on fittings and ground tackle unless provision is made to absorb it gradually. Nylon's elasticity does exactly that.

Some boatmen unwittingly lose part or most of the advantage inherent in nylon by buying too strong a line. Within the limits of safe working loads, the smaller the diameter the better the elasticity for given conditions. A

FIG. 614
The Sea-Claw is an improved version of the Navy type, with parts proportioned differently, and stock added.

FIG. 618 On this large yacht, *wildcats* in the winch engage the links of the all-chain rodes. Chain, leading down to the anchors through hawsepipes, is shown here *stoppered*, held by split-hook *devil's claws*.

FIG. 615 A grapnel, shown here as it might be used in grappling to recover a mooring chain.

FIG. 616 Nylon (a) and manila (b). Nylon's great elasticity makes it popular for anchor rodes. A 3/8-inch diameter nylon line (breaking strength 3650 lbs.) will replace 9/16-inch manila (3450 lbs.).
(Gordon S. Smith photo)

BRAIDED INNER ROPE

BRAIDED OUTER ROPE

FIG. 617 Because of its construction, braided synthetic line has no tendency to twist. Braided nylon, for anchor rodes, retains high elasticity; braided polyester, with little stretch, is better for sheets and halyards.

FIG. 617 (a) Braided line coils best when faked (or flaked) down in a figure 8.

practical limit is reached when small diameters (though rated high enough for breaking strength) are not convenient to handle. Some of the most experienced boatmen use nylon as light as ³/₈-inch diameter on the working anchors of their 30- to 40-foot cruisers.

## Braided synthetic line

Most of the nylon currently in use today for anchor rodes is the type that is laid up by twisting three strands, in the same manner as manila. Synthetics, however, may also be laid up by braiding. For anchoring, mooring and towing, a braided outer cover of nylon surrounds a braided inner synthetic core. See fig. 617. The result is a line of exceptional stability with no inherent tendency to twist because of the nature of its lay. Consequently, it can be fed down into rope lockers without fear of kinking.

When braided nylon is handled on deck, it is advisable to fake it down in figure-8 pattern, rather than the conventional clockwise coil used with twisted fibers to prevent kinking. Because of the relatively smoother surface of braid, with more fibers exposed, chafe is less of a problem than it is with the twisted three-strand lay. Braided nylon retains a high degree of elasticity (14% at working loads, as against 25% for twisted nylon).

For sheets and halyards, where it is preferable to eliminate the stretch, an outer cover of polyester is used. Double-braided nylon is becoming increasingly popular for mooring pennants.

Double-braided synthetic rope is a quality product, its smooth, soft handling characteristics recommending it highly as a "yacht" line. Obviously it requires a special splicing technique, covered in detail in Samson Cordage Works' Splicing Manual.

## Manila

Most of the arguments that could once have been advanced for the selection of manila have quite generally been settled with the increasing trend toward nylon. It is a fact that manila is still in common use on many lighter anchors and in some areas it survives among boatmen of

FIG. 619 Manila line, badly chafed on a rough coral bottom. A fathom of chain, shackled between the anchor and fiber rode, would have prevented this.

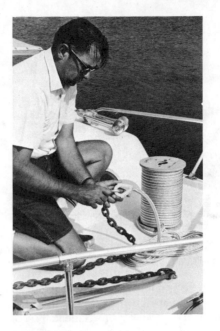

FIG. 620 A thimble, shackle and eye splice are commonly used to secure fiber rodes to the anchor ring. Lashings hold the key when inserted into the stock as the anchor is set up.

the old school who are not yet ready to give up the line they've grown up with. They find it easy to handle, light in weight (for required strength), comparatively inexpensive, and capable of enough stretch to absorb some shock load. Above all, it holds knots and splices better than the more slippery synthetics. Even at that, the experience of some of the hardest working commercial craft, like the charter fishermen who anchor day in and day out in open water in all weathers, is hard to deny. They've turned to nylon.

## Chain

Nylon in diameters up to 1 inch is used on boats up to 50 or 60 feet in length—even larger, under normal conditions. Any fiber line, however, more than 1½ inches in diameter, is hard to handle, so chain is often chosen for larger craft. BBB chain is recommended (its size designated by the diameter of material in the links). To handle it, the boat should be equipped with a winch having a *wildcat* to fit the chain. See fig. 618.

From this it should not be inferred that chain is not also in use on smaller craft. On boats that cruise extensively and have occasion to anchor on sharp rock or coral, chain is often preferred—in cases, regarded as indispensable, as it stands chafing where fiber won't. Some boatmen with wide cruising experience have used four or five fathoms of chain shackled between the anchor and fiber line. Others prefer chain throughout.

In the larger diameters, the weight of chain tends to produce a sag in the rode which cushions shock loads due to surging. Once the sag is out, it is quite generally agreed that the shock on both boat and anchor is greater than with nylon or even manila. Too much emphasis should not be placed on the cushioning effect of a chain's sag, in small sizes. One test made in a moderate wind with generous scope of 10-to-1 revealed not a single link of chain resting on the bottom. On the other hand, in larger sizes, exhaustive tests on a 104-footer with ½-inch and ⅝-inch chain showed the weight of chain to be beneficial, reducing the maximum load on the anchor to as little as 5% of that recorded in a similar test with wire rope. Wire cable has

been used on some larger craft; though strong, it has no elasticity.

## Nylon-and-chain

Today the concensus appears to be that for most average conditions, the ideal rode consists of a combination of nylon and short length (a fathom, more or less) of chain between the nylon and anchor. The only exception to this is in the very softest bottoms where one authority claims that the lightweight anchor bites best without chain.

The effect of chain in a combination rode is to lower the angle of pull, because chain tends to lie on the bottom. Of equal, perhaps greater, significance is the fact that modern lightweight anchors often bury completely, taking part of the rode with them. Chain stands the chafe, fig. 619, and sand has less chance to penetrate strands of the fiber line higher up. Sand doesn't stick to the chain, and mud is easily washed off. Without chain, nylon gets very dirty in mud.

Chain used in this manner may vary roughly from ¼-inch diameter for 20-footers up to ⁷⁄₁₆-inch for 50-footers. It should be galvanized, of course, to protect against rust. Neoprene-coated chain is an added refinement, as it will not mar the boat.

## SECURING THE RODE

### To the ring

Various methods are used in securing the rode to the anchor ring. With fiber line, the preferred practice is to work an eye splice around a thimble and use a galvanized shackle to join the thimble and ring. See fig. 620. Using manila, the common galvanized wire-rope thimble is satisfactory; with nylon more care must be taken to keep the thimble in the eye. A tight, snug splice will help and seizings around the line and the legs of the thimble, near the V, will keep the thimble in the eye splice when the line comes under loads that stretch the eye. A better thimble, fig. 621, is available in bronze alloy or plastic for use with synthetic rope. This is designed to hold and protect the line.

FIG. 621 Improved types of Newco thimble in plastic or bronze alloy for use with synthetic rope prevent line from jumping out of the thimble when an eye splice stretches under load.

| TABLE 6-2 ANCHOR WEIGHT* (pounds) | | | |
|---|---|---|---|
| BOAT LENGTH (Maximum) | Lunch hook | Working anchor | Storm anchor |
| 20' | 4 (10) | 5 (20) | 12 (40) |
| 30' | 5 (15) | 12 (30) | 18 (60) |
| 40' | 12 (20) | 18 (40) | 28 (80) |

*Bold-face figures based on modern lightweight burial-type anchors of efficient design. Figures in parentheses show how weights would be increased, using a formula of 1/2, 1 lb. and 2 lbs. per foot for certain kedges.

FIG. 622 Some boatmen prefer to make the rode fast to the anchor ring with an anchor bend. For added security, the free end may be seized to the rode. Line illustrated is braided nylon.

With this kind of rig, it is a good idea to put a bit of silicone spray, Lubriplate or graphite grease on threads of the shackle pin. This will keep the threads from seizing. Wire the pin to prevent its working out accidentally. For convenience, and to prevent loss of the pin, many prefer to bend a piece of marline to the eye of the pin, so that it can be lashed to a link of the chain. Watch for corrosion if different metals are used in thimbles, shackles and rings. Also beware of rust stains on nylon; cut out and resplice on new thimbles if the line is rust-stained.

With a thimble and shackle, a ready means is provided of backing up your line with a length of chain, if desired, shackling the chain in turn to the anchor ring. Shackles should be large enough so as not to bind the fiber against the ring and cause chafing.

When an anchor has an eye cast into the head of the shank, but no ring, it is generally convenient to use a shackle in the eye, even if the rode is to be bent to the anchor without an intermediate length of chain.

## Anchor bends and bowlines

Some boatmen would rather bend their line directly to the ring using an anchor bend, fig. 622, seizing the free end to the rode. In the Chesapeake, and elsewhere, they use a bowline with an extra round turn around the ring, fig. 623, pointing out that this makes it easy to turn the line end-for-end occasionally or to remove the line from the anchor for easy handling when stowing.

Turning a line end-for-end greatly extends its useful life, as the lower end which has chafed on the bottom becomes the inboard end. Shackles and eye splices may be used at both ends of the rode, or may be added as necessary when the rode is turned.

Another convenient rig on small craft is merely to work a big eye splice in the end of the line, pass it through the ring, over the anchor while the stock (on stock types) is folded along the shank and then tighten the eye by hauling it up on itself at the ring.

Even where the regular working anchor is kept made-up with a combination of line and chain, it is well to know how to bend a line directly to the anchor. Often this is the handiest way to drop a light "lunch hook" for a brief stop, or to make up a second anchor when a bridle or stern anchor is needed.

Shackles, fig. 624, must be used to secure chain cables to the anchor, stout swivels, fig. 625, being an added re-

finement on combination rodes. As swivels are a weak point, they must be large. On an all-chain rode, they are a *must*. Swivels, however, should *not* be used with twisted soft-laid synthetic lines; a hockle, fig. 626, may be the result. Double-braided synthetic lines will not hockle, even though subjected to very heavy strains.

## At the bitter end

To guard against loss in case the anchor goes by the board accidentally, the bitter (inboard) end of an anchor cable should preferably be made fast to some part of the boat. Sometimes this is accomplished by leading the line below, perhaps through a deck pipe, and securing to a Samson post or other strong timber. On sailboats, it may be secured to a mast. On small boats where the entire length of rode is carried on deck, it is usually feasible to have an eye splice in the bitter end to fit the post. Run this down close to the deck and use a clove hitch above the eye splice to adjust the scope.

## HOW MANY—AND HOW HEAVY?

The number of anchors to be carried aboard will be conditioned upon several things—the size of boat, whether she is used only in sheltered waters or cruises extensively offshore and, to some extent, the type of anchor.

Though some small boats, like runabouts and utilities, are occasionally found with only a single anchor, this can by no stretch of the imagination be considered adequate. Even discounting the possibility of fouling one anchor so badly that it cannot be retrieved, there are many occasions when it is desirable to lie to two. Again, one anchor heavy enough for extreme conditions could be a nuisance in ordinary weather.

Many boats carry two anchors, proportioning the weight in the ratio of about 40 percent in one, 60 percent in the other. For cruising boats, three are undoubtedly better. This allows for two to be carried on deck—a light *lunch hook* for brief stops while some one is aboard, and a *working anchor* for ordinary service, including anchorages at night in harbor. The third might well be a big spare *storm anchor*, carried below, selected with an eye to its holding no matter what else lets go, even under extreme conditions of wind and weather. Break this out when you find it necessary to anchor overnight in an exposed anchorage, and you will sleep better. On long cruises, some experienced yachtsmen carry four.

## Anchor size and holding power

Down through the years there have been repeated attempts to reduce anchor weights to a simple formula or table based on boat length or tonnage. Recommendations varied widely, up to as high as 3 or 4 pounds per foot for the heavy spare on cruising boats, assuming this would be a kedge type.

With the introduction of new anchors of lightweight design, it becomes obvious that the older figures no longer apply. Recognizing further that inefficient copies of a well

(Gordon S. Smith photo)

FIG. 623 The anchor bowline, an alternate method of bending the rode to the anchor ring. Note the extra round turn around the ring.

### TABLE 6-3   SUGGESTED RODE AND ANCHOR SIZES*

#### For Storm Anchor (Winds up to 60 knots)

| L.O.A. | BEAM SAIL | BEAM POWER | RODE NYLON | RODE CHAIN | ANCHOR NORTHILL | ANCHOR STANDARD | ANCHOR HI-TENSILE |
|---|---|---|---|---|---|---|---|
| 10' | 4' | 4' | 100'-¼" | 3'-³⁄₁₆" | 12 lb. (6-R) | 8-S | 5-H |
| 15' | 5' | 5' | 125'-¼" | 3'-³⁄₁₆" | 12 lb. (6-R) | 8-S | 5-H |
| 20' | 6' | 7' | 150'-⅜" | 4'-¼" | 27 lb. (12-R) | 13-S | 12-H |
| 25' | 6' | 8' | 200'-⅜" | 4'-¼" | 27 lb. (12-R) | 22-S | 12-H |
| 30' | 7' | 10' | 250'-⁷⁄₁₆" | 5'-⁵⁄₁₆" | 46 lb. (20-R) | 22-S | 20-H |
| 35' | 8' | 12' | 300'-½" | 6'-⅜" | 46 lb. (20-R) | 40-S | 35-H |
| 40' | 10' | 14' | 400'-⅝" | 8'-⁷⁄₁₆" | 80 lb. (30-R) | 65-S | 60-H |
| 50' | 12' | 16' | 500'-⅝" | 8'-⁷⁄₁₆" | 105 lb. (50-R) | 130-S | 60-H |
| 60' | 14' | 19' | 500'-¾" | 8'-½" | 105 lb. (50-R) | 180-S | 90-H |

#### For Working Anchor (Winds up to 30 knots)

| L.O.A. | BEAM SAIL | BEAM POWER | RODE NYLON | RODE CHAIN | ANCHOR NORTHILL | ANCHOR STANDARD | ANCHOR HI-TENSILE |
|---|---|---|---|---|---|---|---|
| 10' | 4' | 4' | 80'-¼" | 3'-³⁄₁₆" | 6 lb. (3-R) | 4-S | 5-H |
| 15' | 5' | 5' | 100'-¼" | 3'-³⁄₁₆" | 6 lb. (3-R) | 8-S | 5-H |
| 20' | 6' | 7' | 120'-¼" | 3'-³⁄₁₆" | 12 lb. (6-R) | 8-S | 5-H |
| 25' | 6' | 8' | 150'-⅜" | 3'-³⁄₁₆" | 12 lb. (6-R) | 8-S | 5-H |
| 30' | 7' | 10' | 180'-⅜" | 4'-¼" | 27 lb. (12-R) | 13-S | 12-H |
| 35' | 8' | 12' | 200'-⅜" | 4'-¼" | 27 lb. (12-R) | 22-S | 12-H |
| 40' | 10' | 14' | 250'-⁷⁄₁₆" | 5'-⁵⁄₁₆" | 46 lb. (20-R) | 22-S | 20-H |
| 50' | 12' | 16' | 300'-½" | 6'-⅜" | 46 lb. (20-R) | 40-S | 35-H |
| 60' | 14' | 19' | 300'-½" | 6'-⅜" | 80 lb. (30-R) | 65-S | 35-H |

#### For Lunch Hook

| L.O.A. | BEAM SAIL | BEAM POWER | RODE NYLON | RODE CHAIN | ANCHOR NORTHILL | ANCHOR STANDARD | ANCHOR HI-TENSILE |
|---|---|---|---|---|---|---|---|
| 10' | 4' | 4' | 70'-¼" | 3'-³⁄₁₆" | 6 lb. (3-R) | 2½-S | 5-H |
| 15' | 5' | 5' | 80'-¼" | 3'-³⁄₁₆" | 6 lb. (3-R) | 2½-S | 5-H |
| 20' | 6' | 7' | 90'-¼" | 3'-³⁄₁₆" | 6 lb. (3-R) | 2½-S | 5-H |
| 25' | 6' | 8' | 100'-¼" | 3'-³⁄₁₆" | 6 lb. (3-R) | 4-S | 5-H |
| 30' | 7' | 10' | 125'-¼" | 3'-³⁄₁₆" | 6 lb. (3-R) | 4-S | 5-H |
| 35' | 8' | 12' | 150'-¼" | 3'-³⁄₁₆" | 12 lb. (6-R) | 4-S | 5-H |
| 40' | 10' | 14' | 175'-⅜" | 4'-¼" | 12 lb. (6-R) | 8-S | 5-H |
| 50' | 12' | 16' | 200'-⅜" | 4'-¼" | 12 lb. (6-R) | 8-S | 12-H |
| 60' | 14' | 19' | 200'-⅜" | 4'-¼" | 27 lb. (12-R) | 13-S | 12-H |

*Suggested sizes assume fair holding ground, scope of at least 7-to-1 and moderate shelter from heavy seas.

PLOW ANCHORS—Woolsey, manufacturer of the Plowright anchor, makes the following recommendations for winds up to 30 knots: for *working anchors*, 10'-21', 6 lbs.—22'-32', 12 lbs.—32'-36', 18 lbs.—36'-39', 22 lbs.—39'-44', 35 lbs. For *lunch hooks*, they advise stepping down one size. For *storm anchors*, up one size.

KEDGES—Holding powers vary widely with the type. Best to consult manufacturer for individual recommendations.

FIG. 624 A shackle is used at the anchor to secure a short piece of chain in a nylon-chain rode.

FIG. 625 Swivels are required on all-chain rodes to prevent snarls.

designed anchor may vary tremendously in holding power, it is equally evident that a hard-and-fast table of anchor weights could easily be an over-simplification. With this caution, Table 6-2 is offered, merely as a point of departure, to be modified as necessary in individual cases. This same caution applies to Table 6-3, giving suggested rode and anchor sizes for boats from 10 to 60 feet in length.

### Horizontal loads as criteria for anchor sizes

In a recent project to establish an advisory code of safety standards for all kinds of small craft up to 65 feet in length, the equipment division of the American Boat and Yacht Council took a different tack in recommending practices and standards for ground tackle. They have set up a Table (6-4) specifying, for boats of 10 to 60 feet in length, typical minimum *horizontal loads* (in pounds) which an anchor should be able to hold, assuming freedom to swing and moderate shelter from seas proportionate to hull size. This, too, is broken down into three sizes of anchor—lunch hooks, working anchors, and storm anchors. Armed with these figures, you can consult the recommendations of the manufacturer of the particular anchor you prefer.

### STOWAGE

The boatman's seamanship is often measurable by the amount of common sense and foresight he displays in every-day boating practice. It shows up, for example, in the attention he gives to stowage of his ground tackle. Exactly how he goes about it depends to some extent on the kind of boating he does, the size of his boat, and the way it is equipped. In any case, unless his deck is uncluttered, with gear ready for immediate use, yet secured so that it cannot shift, he will never rate high as a seaman.

Ordinarily a cruising boat will carry one, sometimes two, anchors on deck, made up ready for use. On some small boats, where it is not feasible to leave anchors on deck at all times, or in cases where lines are stowed below at the home anchorage, one anchor and line at least should be prepared and made ready before getting under way from the dock or mooring. Engines have been known to fail and, when they do, it's likely to be at an embarrassing moment, with wind or current setting you down on a shoal or reef. Then it's too late to think about breaking out gear that should have been ready at hand.

An anchor lying loose on deck is a potential hazard. If the boat happens to roll deep in a seaway or be caught by the heavy wash of a passing boat, it may slide across the deck, leaving in its wake scars on woodwork and damage

| TABLE 6-4 TYPICAL HORIZONTAL LOADS (pounds) | | | |
|---|---|---|---|
| Length over all | Lunch hook | Working anchor | Storm anchor |
| 10' | 40 | 160 | 320 |
| 15' | 60 | 250 | 500 |
| 20' | 90 | 360 | 720 |
| 25' | 125 | 490 | 980 |
| 30' | 175 | 700 | 1,400 |
| 35' | 225 | 900 | 1,800 |
| 40' | 300 | 1,200 | 2,400 |
| 50' | 400 | 1,600 | 3,200 |
| 60' | 500 | 2,000 | 4,000 |

to equipment, conceivably going over the side, and taking line with it, at the risk of fouling a propeller. To forestall this, every anchor on deck should be stowed in chocks. See fig. 627. These are available at marine supply stores to fit standard anchors. Lashings hold them down to prevent their jumping out of the chocks. Hardwood blocks, prop-

FIG. 627 Anchors stowed on deck should be lashed down in chocks.

FIG. 628 A short "pulpit" on this motor sailer provides for the housing of a plow anchor.

FIG. 626 To avoid a hockle, swivels should not be used with twisted soft-laid synthetic lines.

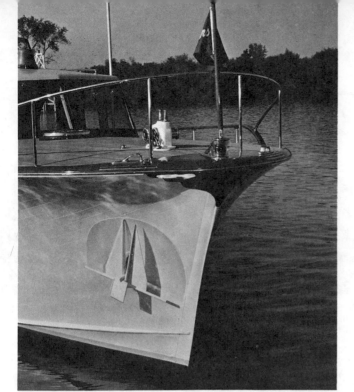

**FIG. 629 Hawsepipes are commonly seen on large vessels, and may also be used on some yachts. The planking is protected by a circular pad.**

erly notched, have often been used in lieu of metal chock fittings. Rubber caps should be fitted over the round stock ends of lightweight type anchors.

As an alternate to chocking on deck, anchors carried aboard auxiliaries may be lashed to shrouds, off the deck, where there is no risk of their getting underfoot, and less risk of their fouling running rigging. In one Dutch yacht, a foreign-built lightweight type anchor is carried in hooks provided in the bow rail. Some cruisers and motor sailers equipped with bowsprits or pulpits have a roller at the outboard end so that a plow can be carried in this outboard position as a regular working anchor. See fig. 628. There are devices that combine the anchor with a kind of well fixture to be let in flush with the deck. In considering such equipment, be sure the anchor weight and design are such as to meet the boat's requirements as to holding power. On some yachts provision is made to haul the anchor into a hawsepipe fitted into the topsides forward. See fig. 629.

### Stowing the storm anchor

As the big spare storm anchor is used only on rare occasions, it is customary to carry it in some convenient location below. Frequently this will be a lazarette or in stowage space below a cockpit deck, accessible through a hatch. Chocks here should be arranged to carry the weight on floors or frames, never on the planking. If the big anchor gets adrift, it could easily loosen a bottom plank and start a leak.

The big risk in stowing a spare anchor away in some out-of-the-way corner is the possibility that other gear may be allowed to accumulate over and around it. Guard against that. Its sole value may some day depend upon your being able to get that big hook over quickly, bent to a long and strong spare rode that must be equally accessible.

Lunch hooks are small and seldom needed in a hurry, so there's justification for stowing them in some convenient

locker. Keep them away from the compass, however, as they can be a potent cause of deviation. That goes for all anchors and any ferrous metal that might inadvertently be left too close to the compass.

### Rope and chain lockers

Though small craft frequently carry their lines coiled on a forward deck or in an open cockpit, many cruising boats are built with rope lockers in the forepeak. Nylon dries quickly and can be fed down into lockers almost as soon as it comes aboard. Manila, on the other hand, must be thoroughly dried on deck before stowing below. Gratings are sometimes provided as an aid to drying lines on deck before stowage. Lockers must be well ventilated and arranged to assure good air circulation at all times. See fig. 630. Dark, wet lockers are an invitation to dry rot. A hatch over the rope locker will permit exposure to sun and air.

The rode should always be ready to run without fouling. Line is often passed below through a deck pipe, slotted so that it can be capped even when the line is in use. Slots must face aft to prevent water on deck from finding its way below. Caps are usually connected with a length of chain, preferably of brass, as galvanized chains may rust out too quickly. Some cast mooring bitts are also made with an opening on the after face, through which line can be passed below.

Chain won't soak up moisture like manila and is easy to stow in lockers. Where weight of chain in the bow of a small offshore cruising boat is objectionable, this can be overcome by splitting a long cable into two or three shorter lengths, stowed where convenient and shackled together as necessary. The chain portion of a combination nylon-and-chain rode is ordinarily shackled in place for regular use, but small-diameter nylon, if left on deck, should preferably be shaded from the sun to protect surface fibers from damage by ultraviolet rays.

### SCOPE

Later, in a discussion of anchoring techniques, we will go into the matter of holding power but at this point it seems appropriate to cover, in advance, the subject of *scope*. See fig. 631. Once an anchor of suitable design and size has

**FIG. 630 Lightweight anchors chocked on deck, their round stock-ends fitted with rubber tips. A grating provides ventilation to the forepeak. Inboard ends of the nylon dock lines are *flemished* in spiral mats.**

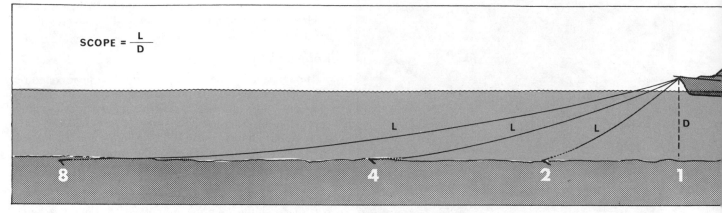

SCOPE = $\frac{L}{D}$

**FIG. 631** Scope is the ratio of length of rode (L) to depth of water (D), plus allowance for height of bow above water. At (1) length of rode equals the depth. At (2) rode length is twice the depth, at (4) four times the depth. Note how the angle between rode and bottom decreases. At (8) the scope is 8:1 and the short length of chain at the anchor lies flat on the bottom.

been chosen to provide adequate holding power, scope is the factor that will determine whether you will, in fact, hold or drag. Too short a scope can destroy the efficiency of the best anchor.

Although definitions may be found that would refer to scope as "the length of cable from hawespipe to anchor," and others that roughly call it the ratio between length of rode paid out (between boat and anchor) and depth of water, two important factors are frequently overlooked: the height of bow chocks above water and the range of tide.

Let's assume we anchor in 10 feet of water with 60 feet of rode paid out. Theoretically, one might suppose this is a reasonable scope of 6:1. Our bow chock, however, is 5 feet above the surface. Immediately the ratio is cut to 4:1 (60:15). Six hours later the tide has risen another 5 feet. So now we have an actual scope of 3:1 (60:20), exactly half of the original theoretical ratio.

What is a proper scope? Under favorable conditions, 5:1 might be considered a *minimum*; under average conditions, 7 or 8:1 is regarded as satisfactory. Government tests have indicated that proper scope ratios will range between 5:1 and 10:1, the latter for heavy weather. Even in a very hard blow, in an exposed anchorage, the chances are that you will never need a scope of more than 15:1 with an anchor of suitable holding power. Boatmen who carry more than one kind of anchor have found that effective scope required under a given set of conditions may vary with the type.

In our hypothetical example above, the length of rode paid out should have been 140 (7:1) to 160 (8:1) feet; 100 feet (5:1) might be regarded as a minimum.

To provide maximum efficiency, all anchors require a low angle of pull—preferably less than 8 degrees from the horizontal. With short scope, holding power is reduced because the angle of pull is too high, tending to break the anchor out. As the pull is brought down more nearly parallel with the bottom, flukes dig in deeper with heavier strains on the line. Surging, as a boat pitches in a sea, throws a great load on the anchor, particularly on short scope. With long scope, the angle of pull is not only better, but the elasticity of a long nylon line cushions the shock loads materially.

**FIG. 632** A plastic marker used to indicate the scope of anchor line paid (or veered) out.

## Marking a rode for scope

Granting that we know how much scope is required, how do we know when we have paid out enough? Estimates are risky. Plastic cable markers, fig. 632, may be bought in sets to mark 30, 50, 70, 100, 125 and 150 feet. These are attached simply by inserting them under a strand of the line. In daylight, when the figures are legible, these are fine. Some saltier yachtsmen, harking back to traditional methods of marking lead lines, have improvised markings using strips of leather, white cotton and red flannel rags, and pieces of marline with knots in them. These can be identified by touch in the dark.

For all practical purposes, five or six marks at intervals of 20 feet (say 60-140 feet) should be adequate. One practical method would be to paint wide and narrow bands of a red vinyl liquid called Whip-End Dip at significant points, calling wide bands 50 feet, narrow ones 10. On chain rodes, as a measure of scope, some boatmen have painted links white at intervals.

One method that has proved successful on a 150-foot line with an additional 8 feet of chain is to whip the line at 50 and 100 feet from the chain with red sail twine. This gives an exact measure of 58 and 108 feet; other lengths can easily be estimated with sufficient accuracy.

# Anchoring Techniques

## HOW TO ANCHOR

Thus far we have discussed only equipment, or ground tackle. Let's consider now the technique—the art of anchoring. As a matter of fact, good equipment is more than half the battle; anyone can easily learn to use his gear correctly.

If, on the other hand, your anchors are of doubtful holding power, and your lines too short, then you can never escape the uneasy feeling associated with wondering whether, some day, you'll find yourself dragging on a lee shore. No part of your boat's equipment is more important, so don't stint here.

Before you can think about *how* to anchor, you must decide *where* you'll anchor, and here, as in all other phases of seamanship, a little foresight pays off handsomely.

### Selecting an anchorage

There will be times, of course, when you will stop briefly in open water, coming to anchor for lunch, a swim, to fish, or perhaps to watch a regatta—but, in the main, the real problem of finding an anchorage comes down to choice of some spot where there's good holding bottom, protection from the wind, and water of suitable depth. Such an anchorage is the kind you'd look for in which to spend the night, free from anxiety about the weather.

### Use the chart

The chart is the best guide in selecting such a spot. Sometimes you will be able to find a harbor protected on all sides, regardless of wind shifts. If not, the next best choice would be a cove, offering protection at least from the direction of the wind, or the quarter from which it is expected. As a last resort, anchorage may be found under a windward bank or shore—that is, where the wind blows from the bank toward the boat. In this case, watch for wind shifts, which could leave you in a dangerous berth on a lee shore.

Anchorages are sometimes designated on charts by means of an anchor symbol. Areas delineated on the chart by solid magenta lines, marked perhaps by white buoys, are often shown as special anchorage areas, where lights are not required on vessels less than 65 feet in length. See fig. 633. Never anchor in cable areas or channels, both indicated by broken parallel lines.

Shallow depths are preferred for an anchorage, because a given amount of scope will then provide better holding and reduce the diameter of the circle through which the boat will swing. Consideration, however, must be given to the range of tide, so that a falling level does not leave you aground, impaled perhaps on the exposed fluke of your own anchor, or bottled up behind a shoal with not enough water to get out at low tide.

### Characteristics of the bottom

Character of the bottom is of prime importance. While the type and design of anchor fluke has a direct bearing on its ability to penetrate, as already noted, it may be stated broadly that mixtures of mud and clay, or sandy mud, make excellent holding bottom for most anchors; firm sand is

FIG. 633 In special anchorage areas shown on the chart, lights are not required on boats less than 65 feet in length.

| Bottom characteristics: | | | | |
|---|---|---|---|---|
| Cl. clay | M. mud | Oys oyster | stk. sticky | gn. green |
| Co. coral | Rk. rock | hrd. hard | bk. black | gy. gray |
| G. gravel | S. sand | rky. rocky | br. brown | wh. white |
| Grs. grass | Sh. shells | sft. soft | bu. blue | yl. yellow |

FIG. 634 Abbreviations of some bottom characteristics as shown on charts.

FIG. 635 How ranges may be used to select an anchorage by lining up visible charted objects. At the intersection of one range through the tank and flagpole, and another through two towers, the boat has 14 feet of water (at low tide) in hard bottom, clear of rocks, with room to swing outside of shoal water.

good *if* your anchor will bite deep into it; loose sand is bad. Soft mud should be avoided if possible; rocks prevent an anchor from getting a bite except when a fluke is lodged in a crevice; grassy bottoms, while they provide good holding for the anchor that can get through to firm bottom, often prevent a fluke from taking hold.

Sometimes bottoms which ordinarily provide reasonably good holding will be covered with a thick cabbage-like

FIG. 636    In this crowded anchorage, there's risk that the swinging circles of boats may overlap.

growth that positively destroys the holding power of any anchor. Even if you happen to carry one of the fisherman's sand-anchor types, with its thin spidery arm and small flukes, expect it to pick up half a bushel of this growth. All you can do is clean it off and try elsewhere.

Characteristics of the bottom are always shown on charts. By making a few casts with the hand lead, a check can be had on the depth, and if the lead is armed with a bit of hard grease or tallow, samples of the bottom will be brought up as a further check. Abbreviations for some bottom characteristics are shown in fig. 634.

## Approaching the anchorage

Having selected a suitable spot, try to run in *slowly* on some range ashore, selected from marks identified on the chart, crossing ranges, fig. 635, or referring your position to visible buoys and landmarks to aid you in locating the spot. Later these aids will also be helpful in determining whether you are holding or dragging, especially if the marks are visible at night and it comes on to blow after dark.

If there are rocks, shoals, reefs or other boats to consider, give them all as wide a berth as possible, keeping in mind a possible swing of 360 degrees about the anchor with wind shifts or current changes.

Remember, too, that large yachts nearby may swing to a much longer scope than you allow—and, conversely, that you may swing much further than a smaller boat nearby lying on short scope. See fig. 636. Such conditions bring about an overlapping of the swinging circles.

The risk of fouling a neighboring craft is aggravated when, in a current, the deep-draft vessel holds her position while a light-draft boat swings to a shift of wind not strong enough to influence the other. Keel sailboats may lie one way in a light current, power boats another.

The boat that has already established her location in an anchorage has a prior claim to the spot and can't be expected to move if you later find yourself in an embarrassing position. Consequently, allow room enough so that you

can pay out more scope if necessary in case of a blow, without being forced to change your anchorage, perhaps at night.

The way other boats lie, together with the set of nearby buoys, will help to determine how you should round up to the chosen spot. Estimate the relative effects of wind and current on your own boat and come up, *slowly*, against the stronger of these forces—in other words, heading as you expect to lie after dropping back on the anchor. Running through the anchorage, take care that your way is reduced to a point where your wake cannot disturb other boats.

FIG. 637    With its stock set up, this anchor can be let go quickly by casting off the lashing. Chain leads outboard through a hawsepipe up to the ring. Davit tackle can be hooked into the ring of the balancing band on the shank. On the port side of the winch a gipsy is provided for use with fiber rode.

## Letting the anchor go

These preliminaries disposed of, you are ready to let the anchor go. Unless you are forced to work single-handed, one man should be stationed on the forward deck. Enough line should be hauled out of the locker and coiled down so as to run freely without kinking or fouling. If previously detached, the line must be shackled to the ring, stock set up (if of the stock type) and keyed. See fig. 637. Many an anchor has been lost for failure to attach the rode properly. Rodes, too, have gone with the anchor when not secured at the bitter end. Lightweight anchors are always ready for use and do not have to be set up, but always check to see that the shackle is properly fastened.

Despite the fact that in certain localities some experienced boatmen have adopted the practice of letting go while the boat has headway, depending on way to snub the anchor and give it a bite, the amateur motor boatman would do well to make it a standing rule *never* to let go while his boat has any way on.

In a motorboat, or auxiliary under power, the bow should be brought *slowly* up to the spot where the anchor is to lie, and headway checked with the reverse gear if necessary. Then, just as the boat begins to gather sternway slowly in reverse, the anchor is lowered easily over the side till it hits bottom, crown first.

Never stand in the coils of line on deck and don't attempt to "heave" the anchor by casting it as far as possible from the side of the boat. Occasionally, with judgment, a light anchor in a small boat can be carefully thrown a short distance—taking care that it lands in its holding position—but the best all-around rule is to *lower* it as described. That way, the possibility of fouling is minimized.

## Setting the anchor

With the anchor on bottom and the boat reversing slowly, line should be paid (sometimes spoken of as *veered*) out as the boat takes it, preferably with a turn of line around the bitt. When a scope of about 7 or 8 times the depth has been paid out, *snub* the line by holding and the anchor will probably get a quick sure bite into the bottom, after which the line can be shortened if the anchorage is so crowded that such a scope would be excessive. Snubbing too soon may cause the anchor to drag.

In setting lightweight burial-type anchors, a little more care is required, particularly in soft mud bottoms where the anchor shank and chain can sink through the mud and cause the anchor to skid. This skidding can be readily avoided by lifting the chain and shank out of the mud with a short two-to-one scope, starting the plow or flukes to dig in, then backing down to lay out full scope.

Regardless of the type of anchor, after full scope has been paid out, a back-down load in excess of any anticipated loads should be applied. This is particularly important if the boat is to be left unattended.

Sometimes the anchor may be shod with a clod of mud adhering to flukes, in which case it is best to lift it, wash it off and try again.

When you must work single-handed, you can get your ground tackle ready to let go, long before you arrive at the anchorage, bring the boat up to the chosen spot, and then lower the anchor as the boat settles back with wind and current, paying out line as she takes it.

## Making fast

After the anchor has gotten a good bite, with proper scope paid out, the line can be made fast and the motor shut off.

On small boats equipped with a Samson post, the best and easiest way to secure is with a clove hitch, similar to that usually thrown when making fast to a pile. The principal objection to the clove hitch on a small post is that it will sometimes jam pretty tight, especially when wet, if the strain is heavy.

On winches, three or four round turns can be taken on the gipsy, belaying the end on a cleat or on the winch itself with a clove hitch. Where a stout cleat is used to make fast, take a round turn around the base of the cleat, one turn over each horn crossing diagonally over the center of the cleat, and finish with another round turn around the base. Some boatmen prefer to finish with a half-hitch on one horn. Clove hitches have also been used on cleats in cases where the proportion of rode diameter to clearance under the horns has been such as to obviate risk of jamming. On small metal cleats it could be risky.

The fundamental idea in making fast is to secure in such a manner that the line can neither slip nor jam. If the strain comes on top of a series of turns on a cleat, fig. 638(a), then it will be practically impossible to free if you want to change the scope, without first taking the strain off it by using power.

If it becomes necessary to shorten scope, clear the bitt

FIG. 638 The wrong way (a) to cleat a line. With a strain (arrow) on the half hitch, it could be difficult to clear the line from the cleat. At (b) a round turn is first taken on the base of the cleat, the strain properly taken in the direction of the arrow. A turn over each horn and a half hitch on one will finish the job.

(Gordon S. Smith photos)

first of old turns or hitches. Don't throw new ones over the old.

A trick worth using when the sea is so rough that it is difficult to go forward on deck—especially if you are single-handed—is to set up the anchor in the aft cockpit, lead the line forward on deck through a closed chock, and back aft to the cockpit. If there are stanchions for life lines, the lead of the rode from chock to anchor must obviously be outside any such obstructions. When you're ready to let go it can be dropped on the weather side from the cockpit, and the line secured on a bitt or cleat aft.

## Anchoring without power

When anchoring under sail you don't have the same maneuverability that power supplies and, of course, there is no positive way to dig your anchor in. Here it is best to approach your anchorage with wind abeam so that you can spill most of the wind out of your sails, thereby slowing the boat down. If necessary trim your sail in to gain more headway as needed. Approach the anchorage with all sails down except the mainsail and with enough headway to keep the boat under control. Just before you are ready to let the anchor go, you should have steerageway, but no more. Let your sheet run and, with tiller hard-alee, shoot your bow directly into the wind and drop the mainsail. As your boat loses headway her bow will fall off and the boat will begin to drift to leeward; now lower your anchor.

Pay out scope as the boat drifts back and, occasionally, give a few jerks on the line. This usually helps to set the anchor. Hand-test the line by pulling it. You will be holding when the boat is drawn toward the anchor. Then pay out the usual scope of 7 or 8:1.

## Hand signals

Anchoring, like docking, is one of the situations where it's a great help to have another hand aboard. The problem is communication between the anchor man on deck and the skipper at the wheel. With engine and exhaust noise, it's usually difficult for the skipper to hear, even though the man on deck can. Wind often aggravates the problem. If the skipper is handling the boat from a flying

bridge, he can usually hear better and, from his higher position, can see the trend of the anchor line.

In any case, it helps to have a pre-arranged set of hand signals. There is no need for standardization on this, as long as the helmsman clearly understands the crew's instructions. Keep the signals as simple as possible. Motion of the hands, calling for the helmsman to come ahead a little, or back down, can take the most obvious form. Pointing ahead or aft accomplishes the same purpose. A simple vertical wave of the hand may be used to signal "stop."

## WHEN THE ANCHOR DRAGS

Let's assume now that you have anchored with a scope of 8:1, have inspected the rode, and taken bearings, if possible, as a check on your position. Though the wind has picked up, you turn in, only to be awakened at midnight by the boat's roll. Before you reach the deck you know what has happened—the anchor's dragging and the bow no longer heads up into the wind.

This calls for instant action—not panic. A quick check on bearings confirms what the roll indicated. You're dragging, with the wind abeam. Sizing the situation up swiftly, you note that danger is not imminent; there is still plenty of room to leeward and no boats down-wind to be fouled. Otherwise you would have to get under way, immediately.

The first step in trying to get the anchor to hold is to pay out more scope. Don't just throw over several more fathoms of line; pay it out, with an occasional sharp pull to try to give it a new bite. If you're dragging badly and can't handle the rode with your hands, take a turn around the bitt and snub the line from time to time. If this doesn't work, start the engine and hold the bow up into the wind

**FIG. 639 Two schools of thought on the use of sentinels (kellets). In (a) below, the traditional use of a weight (about 25 pounds) or light anchor sent down the rode by means of a shackle over the rode, with light line to control the scope between sentinel and boat. In (b) below, a buoy rather than a weight has been proposed as a superior method, utilizing the principle commonly found in permanent mooring systems.**

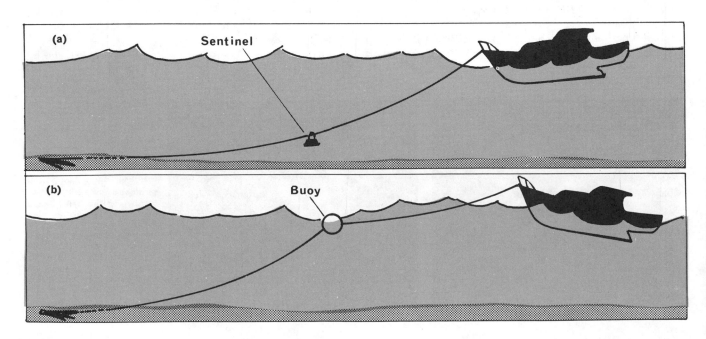

with just enough power to take the strain off the rode. This gives the anchor a chance to lie on the bottom and perhaps get a new bite as you ease the throttle and let the boat drift back slowly. If you haven't held when the scope is 10:1, get the anchor back aboard and try again with your larger storm anchor.

## Sentinel—or buoy?

Suppose, now, that we have no spare storm anchor to fall back on. Can anything be done to increase our holding power? Here we enter an area of controversy with weight of experience on two opposing sides. We'll present both views.

For generations, seasoned cruising boatmen have known of the device known as a *sentinel,* or kellet. See fig. 639(a). Many have reported using it successfully; few have challenged its effectiveness. In principle, the sentinel is nothing more than a weight sent more than half-way down the rode to lower the angle of pull on the anchor and put a sag in the rode that must be straightened out before a load is thrown on the anchor. Working only with what came readily to hand in such a case, boatmen have shackled or snapped their light anchor to the main anchor rode, and sent it down the main rode with a line attached to the ring of the lunch hook, to be stopped at a suitable distance. A pig of ballast or other weight would do as well, provided it could be readily attached.

The other school of thought claims that when this principle is used with short scope in order to limit swinging room, it has proved inadvisable and dangerous, on the theory that, under storm conditions, a resonant condition

FIG. 640 A plastic foam buoy. Note how the strain is transmitted by solid rod through the buoy.

may be encountered which could quickly snap the line. Their alternative would be to use a buoy, fig. 639(b) rather than a weight, claiming that, properly used, the buoy can carry most of the vertical load in an anchoring or mooring system, limiting the basic load on the boat to the horizontal force required to maintain the boat's position. The argument is advanced that the buoy permits the boat's bow to ride up easily over wave crests, rather than being pulled down into them, with excessive loads on both rode and anchor.

## What to watch

From these opposing views, certain conclusions may be drawn. To be most effective, a buoy, if used, should preferably be of the type found in a permanent mooring system, fig. 640, where its efficiency is undoubted. Its connection into the system should be as positive as it would be in a

mooring buoy, all strain being carried directly by the rode—in short, no "weak link" here! Provision should be made for carrying it as part of the "emergency" equipment, rather than trusting to a makeshift device improvised under stress of weather.

On the other side of the picture, if the sentinel is to be used, it should be done *with ample scope,* and every precaution taken to avoid a chafing condition on the main rode.

In support of advocates of the sentinel, we cite the scientific test made under controlled conditions aboard a 104-footer in which a *30-pound* weight, suspended from ⅝-inch wire cable used as the main rode, cut the maximum anchor load practically in half. Obviously, wire rope is less suited to the average pleasure boat than it was to this test boat, it has no stretch and stands chafe of the sentinel's shackle, but figures on reduction of the load are irrefutable.

## An alternate system

We offer a compromise. Carry a boat-length of substantial chain and a 25-pound pig of lead with a ring bolt cast in it. Stow them away somewhere in lieu of ballast. When the chips are down, with breakers to leeward, shackle the chain to your biggest and best anchor, and the chain in turn to your best and longest nylon rode, with the ring of the pig lead shackled in where chain and nylon join. It cannot be anything but an improvement over the same long scope of nylon without benefit of the extra scope of chain and added weight. This would seem to eliminate the twin problems of chafe (at the sentinel) and any tendency to hold the boat's bow down in the surge of pitching seas.

## GETTING UNDER WAY

When you are ready to *weigh anchor* and get under way, run up to the anchor slowly under power, so that the line can be taken in easily without hauling the boat up to it. Ordinarily the anchor will break out readily when the line stands vertically.

As the line comes in, it can be whipped up and down to free it of any grass or weed it may have picked up. This clears the line before it comes on deck. If the anchor is not too heavy, mud can be washed off by swinging it back and forth near the surface as it leaves the water. With care, the line can be snubbed around a bitt and the anchor allowed to wash off as the boat gathers way, preferably astern. Two things must be watched: don't allow the flukes to hit the topsides, and be careful that water flowing past the anchor doesn't get too good a hold and take it out of your hands.

Manila, if used, must be coiled loosely on deck and allowed to dry thoroughly before stowing below. When the anchor is on deck, the stock (if there is one) can be folded and the anchor lashed down securely in its chocks.

On larger craft, equipped with a davit, the anchor is brought up with the winch to a point where a light tackle can be hooked into a ring in the balancing band on the anchor's shank. With the anchor suspended over the side, mud can be washed off with a hose.

In all this anchor handling, try to avoid letting the anchor hit the hull at any time as planking is soft and will get badly gouged and dented. Fiberglass finishes and metal hulls can also be marred. Guests often are eager to "help" by getting the anchor up, but unless they have had some experience, it's better to handle this part of the job your-

**FIG. 641**  In rocky bottoms when an anchor fouls, the first attempt to clear it should be made by reversing the original angle of pull (a), with moderate scope, so as to draw it out as shown in (b).

self. Handle and stow lines carefully. If a bight or end of line slips over the side it is almost certain to run back under the bottom and get hopelessly fouled in the propeller.

In a boat under sail alone, have your mainsail up before you break the anchor loose. The same procedure is used as stated above but there is no motor to help. However, it is possible to use your sails to assist.

## Clearing a fouled anchor

If an anchor refuses to break out when you haul vertically on the line, snub it around the bitt and go ahead with the engine a few feet. If it doesn't respond to this treatment, it's an indication that the anchor may have fouled under some obstruction. To clear it, try making fast to the bitt and running slowly in a wide circle on a taut line. Changing the angle of pull may free it, or a turn of line may foul an exposed fluke (if it's a kedge) and draw it out.

Sometimes a length of chain can be run down the anchor line, rigged so that another boat can use her power to haul in a direction opposite to that in which the anchor line tends, thus changing the angle of pull 180 degrees. With kedges, if one fluke is exposed, a chain handled between two dinghies can occasionally be worked down the rode to catch the upper arm and draw the anchor out, crown first.

If the anchor is not fouled in something immovable, it may be broken out by making the line fast at low water and allowing a rising tide to exert a steady strain. Or, if there is a considerable ground swell, the line may be snubbed when the bow pitches low in a trough. There's some risk of parting the line this way, in case the fluke is fouled worse than you think.

In rocky bottoms, the first thing to try is reversing the direction of pull, opposite to that in which the anchor was originally set, using a moderate amount of scope. See fig. 641.

There is a type of anchor in which the ring is free to slide the full length of the shank. Properly rigged, it is claimed to be virtually snag-proof. More about this later.

If you have been anchored for a day or two in a brisk wind, the anchor may be dug in deep. Don't wait till you're ready to sail; 20 minutes before departure shorten the scope—*but keep a sharp watch.* Motion of the boat will tend to break the anchor out and save a lot of work.

## HOLDING POWER

Before getting into some of the special techniques of anchor use, some understanding of holding power is in order. We have already seen how important anchor design and scope are in determining relative holding power, assuming of course that we are comparing anchors of equal weight. To understand just how critical design can be, remember that a change of as little as 1 degree in fluke angle may cause as much as a 50 percent reduction in efficiency. Lacking equipment to make individual scientific tests, one can readily appreciate how essential it is to rely on the reputability of the manufacturer.

### Some factors involved

Tests have shown that the normal strain on an anchor due to wind and current in average weather is comparatively small. Current is a relatively small factor as compared with the pressure exerted by wind on exposed surfaces. Surge when a boat pitches in a seaway may throw a tremendous strain on the boat and all her ground tackle. Weight of the boat is also significant.

In calculating holding power required under average conditions, manufacturers have taken into account all of these factors, including such boat dimensions as length, beam, hull depth, draft, displacement, and height of superstructure. One has tabulated it as a percentage of gross

**TABLE 6-5  HORIZONTAL HOLDING POWER DANFORTH ANCHORS (pounds)**

| Hi-Tensile | Soft Mud | Hard Sand | Standard | Soft Mud | Hard Sand |
|---|---|---|---|---|---|
| 5-H | 400 | 2,700 | 2½-S | 140 | 800 |
| 12-H | 900 | 6,000 | 4-S | 230 | 1,600 |
| 18-H | 1,250 | 8,750 | 8-S | 480 | 3,200 |
| 28-H | 1,600 | 11,000 | 13-S | 720 | 4,900 |
| 60-H | 2,400 | 17,000 | 22-S | 1,200 | 8,000 |
| 90-H | 2,900 | 20,000 | 40-S | 1,500 | 10,000 |
| 200-H | 5,000 | 35,000 | 65-S | 2,300 | 15,000 |
| 500-H | 7,500 | 50,000 | 85-S | 2,700 | 19,000 |
| 3000-H | 21,000 | 140,000 | 130-S | 3,100 | 21,000 |

weight—for centerboard sailboats 5%; small motorboats 6%; larger cruisers 7%; keel-type sailboats 10%. As wind pressure varies as the square of the velocity, the same manufacturer has suggested another formula for extreme conditions where a boat is anchored in a gale. For sailboats, the formula says that pull (in pounds) $= AV^2/186$, for motorboats $AV^2/220$. (V is wind velocity in miles per hour, A a factor derived by multiplying height, from waterline to deckhouse top, by overall beam.) An added safety factor of one-third should be allowed.

## Varies with bottom

In preparing tables of holding power for specific anchor sizes, the manufacturer must give proper consideration to the kind of bottom in which his tests are run. Table 6-5 illustrates how wide the discrepancy can be between results in soft mud and hard sand. The figures also bring into sharp focus the variation in holding power between different models of equal weight offered by the same manufacturer.

## One test the boatman can make

A simple test that any boatman can make has been suggested by the owner of a 40-foot auxiliary sloop. He found that a well-powered boat can use her engine to throw a load on an anchor greater than she will normally register when riding to that anchor.

The pull of an engine can be approximated by multiplying the horsepower by 20, a value that works out about right for a fairly heavy-duty propeller. With a high-speed propeller of small diameter, the pull is reduced somewhat.

**(a)**

**(b)**

FIG. 642 **Using two anchors out ahead, it is better to have the rodes form an angle as at (a), instead of in line as at (b).**

The anchor to be tested is let go astern and scope of 7 or 8:1 paid out before making fast. Then the engine is speeded up till the anchor drags. Sufficient speed is maintained to drag the anchor at one or two knots, meanwhile noting the engine rpm. Testing other anchors the same way provides a basis for comparison in the varying rates of rpm required to move each.

Actual test readings of the load can be made by using spring scales in the line, rigged if necessary to permit a small scale to register heavy loads. If a lever-operated winch is available, the scale can be attached at the end of the lever. The scale's reading is then multiplied by the ratio of the radius of the lever arm to the radius of the drum on which the chain or rope is carried.

The originator of this idea determined that his 40-footer, powered with a 52 hp engine driving a 20-by-12 propeller through 2:1 reduction, under full power pulled about 1,000 pounds. Under normal conditions of anchoring, he found that the boat would rarely surge to a value higher than 400 pounds, especially if generous scope were paid out.

When making a comparison of holding powers it is interesting to note that holding power is proportional to the area of buried fluke multiplied by the distance it is buried in the bottom. Consequently, for given areas of fluke, the design which permits deepest penetration is the most effective.

## USING TWO ANCHORS

Two anchors are sometimes laid for increased holding power in a blow. If your working anchor drags, you can run out your spare storm anchor, without picking up the working anchor. The important thing to remember is to lay them out at an angle, not in line, to reduce the risk of having one that drags cut a trough in the bottom for the other to follow. See fig. 642.

## To stop yawing

Deep-draft sailboats lie well head to the wind but motorboats often "tack" back and forth at anchor. Skiffs, with high freeboard and little draft forward, are among the worst offenders in this respect.

You can stop this yawing by laying two anchors, lines leading out from either bow, making an angle of about 45 degrees between them. To do this, get one anchor down first and have a man tend the line carefully as you maneuver the bow off to one side before letting the other go. Then you can settle back on both lines, adjusting scope as

FIG. 643 **Two anchors set as shown not only limit swing but provide security against an anchor failure to reset itself after a wind or tide shift. (Sketch not to scale.)**

( l. and 2. are equal )

109

necessary. *Fouling the wheel in slack line under the boat in maneuvers like this is disastrous.*

With good handling, it is possible to get two anchors down single-handed. The easiest way is to settle back on one anchor, making fast when the proper scope has been paid out. Then go ahead easily with the propeller, rudder over enough to hold the line out taut so you can keep an eye on it at all times. When the line stands out abeam, stop your headway, go forward and let the other anchor go, then drop back and adjust the lines to equal scope.

If a dinghy is available, the second anchor can be carried out in it, lines being adjusted as required after both anchors are set.

## To guard against wind or current shifts

When anchoring overnight, or if the boat is to be left unattended, a wise precaution is to lay two anchors, made fast forward but set as shown in figure 643. It provides an extra measure of security against the risk of having a single anchor break out with a 180-degree wind shift and failure to reset itself again. See fig. 644.

If the two-anchor technique is used in a crowded anchorage to limit swinging radius, remember that other nearby boats may lie to one anchor only, so risk of having the swinging circles overlap is increased. Use of three anchors cuts the swinging circle to a minimum.

When setting a second anchor for use as described above, set the up-wind anchor in the conventional way and then back down till double the normal scope is out. After the down-wind anchor is set, adjust the scope at the bow chocks till both are equal. In ranging ahead, with a rode tending aft, take every precaution to prevent its fouling in the propeller.

## Stern anchors

In some anchorages, boats lie to anchors bow and stern. The easiest way to get these down is to let the bow anchor go first, and then drop back with wind or current on an extra long scope (15-18 times the depth), drop the stern anchor, and then adjust the scope on both as necessary, taking in line forward. In tidal waters make allowance for increasing depth as the tide rises. The value of this arrangement is pretty well restricted to areas where permanent moorings are set explicitly for this purpose, as in narrow streams, or on occasions where there is no risk of getting a strong wind or current abeam. Under such conditions, the strain on ground tackle could be tremendous.

Sometimes a stern anchor will be useful if you seek shelter under a windward bank. The stern anchor can be let go aft, carefully estimating the distance off as it is dropped, and scope paid out as the boat is run up toward the bank or beach. A second anchor can then be bedded securely in the bank, or a line taken to a dock or tree ashore.

The stern anchor will keep the stern off and prevent the boat from ranging ahead. But, again, *watch that stern line, while the propeller is turning!*

## At docks

A berth on the weather side of a dock is a bad one, as considerable damage can be done to a boat pounding heavily against piles, even with fenders out. Anchors can help to ease the situation in a case where such a berth is unavoidable. Keeping well up to windward, angling into

**FIG. 644 When a boat swings with wind or current about an anchor, fouling a line around an exposed arm, holding power is destroyed.**

**FIG. 645 A buoyed trip line to the crown will permit an anchor fouled in rocky bottom to be hauled up fluke first.**

the wind as much as is practicable, have a man let one anchor go on a long scope off the quarter (the port quarter, if you'll lie starboard side to the dock). As he pays out scope, run ahead and get another off the port bow, judging positions of both so you can drop down to leeward toward the dock on equal scope, with lines tending off at a 45-degree angle. Properly executed, this maneuver will prevent you from hitting the dock, and the lines you then carry ashore will be needed only to prevent the boat from moving ahead or astern.

## RAFTING

At rendezvous several boats frequently lie to a single anchor. As many as ten boats have been observed rafted together, too many for safety even in a quiet cove. After one boat is anchored, the second pulls alongside with plenty of fenders out on both. Stay six to ten feet away from the anchored boat and heave bow and stern lines. If this can't be done, run up to the anchored boat's bow at an angle of about 45° and pass a bow line first, then your stern line. Make sure you have no headway when lines are passed. As soon as the bow line is aboard the anchored boat, stop your engine so that there will be no chance of going ahead, breaking the anchor out.

Allow your boat to drift astern until transoms align. Then let the bow swing off and pull the sterns in close so it will be easier to step from one boat to another. To keep the transoms in line and fenders in position a spring line

**FIG. 646** Scowing an anchor. The rode to this Norwegian SAV folding anchor is attached to the crown and led back along the shank, to be lashed at the ring. When it fails to release at (1), an upward strain (2) parts the lashing and the anchor is drawn out as shown at (3).

must be run from the stern of the second boat forward to the anchored boat.

If a third boat ties up, the anchored boat should be in the middle; if more tie up always alternate them, port and starboard of the anchored boat. Each succeeding boat should use the same technique, always with a spring from the stern of the outboard boat forward to the one next inboard. Keels of all boats in the group should be nearly parallel. Naturally boats should raft only when there is little wind and a relatively smooth surface. When four or more are tied together, it is a good precaution for the outboard boats to carry anchors out at a 45° angle. When it's time to turn in for the night, every boat should have its own separate anchorage.

## OTHER TECHNIQUES

### On rocky bottoms

Earlier we spoke of certain steps that could be taken to clear a fouled anchor. Hazardous at best, rocky bottoms should preferably be avoided, regardless of the type of anchor used. Before leaving a boat unattended, a load should be applied to the anchor, after setting, well in excess of any expected load.

If you normally anchor in rocky bottoms or suspect that the bottom is foul in the area where you must anchor, it is better to forestall trouble. One time-tested device is the *buoyed trip line*. See fig. 645. Make a light line fast to the crown (in some anchors an eye is provided). This trip line should be long enough to reach the surface (with allowance for a rising tide) where it is buoyed with any convenient float—a block of wood, ring buoy or plastic disposable bottle. If the anchor doesn't *trip* readily at the first pull on the rode, haul in the trip line and the anchor will be withdrawn, crown first.

An alternate scheme is to *scow* the anchor, fig. 646, by bending the rode to the crown, leading it back along the shank, and stopping it to the ring with a light lashing of marline. With sufficient scope, the strain is on the crown and not on the lashing. When hove up short, the strain is on the lashing. When this parts, the anchor comes up crown first.

There are anchors (the Sure-Ring, fig. 647, is typical) that have a slotted shank in which the ring can travel freely from end to end. If the anchor should snag, the theory is that when the boat is brought back over the anchor, the sliding ring can slip down the shank so the anchor will be drawn out backwards. The Sure-Ring has an added refinement—a unique ring design that permits the rode to be

bent to an eye in the shank for overnight or unattended anchoring. In the Benson anchor the shank is formed of round rod, along which the ring slides when the anchor is to be backed out.

### Kedging off a bar

The term *kedging* is often, and properly, applied to the use of a light anchor (not necessarily kedge-type) carried out to deep water in a dinghy to haul a stranded boat off a shoal. If you ever have to resort to this, coil the line down carefully in the dinghy, so that it pays out freely from the stern as you row. The dink might well become unmanageable in a wind or strong current if an attempt is made to pay the line out from the deck of the stranded boat.

### Anchoring at night

Anchoring at night, you must display a white 32-point light, visible at least 2 miles, rigged forward where it can be best seen. Vessels over 150 feet in length show a white light forward at least 20 feet above the hull, and another aft at least 15 feet lower than the forward light. Vessels over 65 feet at anchor display a black ball as a day mark.

**FIG. 647** In the Danforth Sure-Ring anchor, a ring slides in a slot down the shank so the anchor can be drawn out backwards if it snags. For overnight use, the line can be shackled through the eye in the shank.

In certain specially designated anchorage areas, fig. 633, no lights need be displayed at night on vessels less than 65 feet in length.

When anchoring overnight, if you have no ranges to check your position (or if those you have are unlighted) you can rig a *drift lead* (the lead line will do). Lower it to the bottom, leave some slack for swinging, and make fast. If it comes taut, you've dragged. Don't forget to pick it up before getting under way.

FIG. 648 Salisbury plastic Chafe-Gard protects mooring lines from abrasion at the bobstay of this auxiliary.

FIG. 649 Chafe-Gard is lashed by thongs to the rode to hold it in place to protect against chafe at the chock.

## SOME CAUTIONS

### Guard against chafe

Every possible precaution must be taken to avoid chafe on fiber lines. Wherever the line comes in contact with chocks or rails and rubs back and forth under continuous strain, outer fibers may be worn to such an extent as to seriously weaken the line. Mooring pennants, fig. 648, are particularly susceptible to this.

When lying at anchor, you can *freshen the nip* by paying out a little more scope from time to time, or parcel the line at the point of chafe with strips of canvas wrapped around it. Modern chafing gear is available in the form of plastic or rubber sleeves, fig. 649, which can be snapped over the line, centered in a chock and seized with thongs to prevent shifting. Chafing gear also comes in the form of a white waterproof tape, to be applied around the line at bitts, chocks and other points of contact.

The increasing use of relatively light anchor rodes of small diameter (frequently $3/8$ inch) points up the necessity of preventing chafe. The chafe that a $3/4$-inch line could tolerate might render a $3/8$-inch line unsafe.

### Chocks, bitts, cleats and other fittings

Chafe is aggravated wherever a fitting has a rough surface to accelerate abrasion of the fiber. Even small nicks and scratches in a chock can damage a line by cutting fibers progressively, one at a time. Serious weakening of a line develops when it is forced to pass around any fitting with relatively sharp corners, such as a square bitt with only a minimum chamfering of the edges, especially when the bitts are too small for the job they have to do. Theoretically the ideal bitt is round, of generous diameter. The best chocks are those of special design with the largest possible radius at the arc where the line passes over it.

Mooring bitts especially must be fastened securely. The best bitt is the old-fashioned wooden bitt, fig. 650, long enough to have its heel fastened deep in the boat's frame. If a cast fitting must be used on deck, it should be through-bolted, the deck below reinforced with husky partners. Bitts have been torn completely off the decks of boats anchored in open water with chain rode.

All fittings playing a part in the use, handling or stowage of ground tackle should be designed and installed not with

FIG. 650 The drum of an electric windlass and, behind it, a substantial well-rounded wooden Samson post. The horizontal Norman pin keeps line from slipping off the top. At lower left, a deck pipe through which the rode is passed below.

Ultraviolet Ray Exposed

FIG. 651 Small-diameter nylon line must be protected from damage by exposure to ultraviolet rays of the sun.

an eye to just getting by in fair weather, but proof against failure in the worst blow the vessel will ever encounter.

### Damage from ultraviolet rays

The outer layers of all types of rope are subject to some degree of damage from ultraviolet rays of the sun. See figure 651. With nylon line of relatively large diameter (upwards of $3/4$ inch) damage from this cause is probably negligible. As the diameter decreases, the problem becomes proportionally more serious. In $3/8$-inch nylon it is an important factor to be reckoned with. Every possible precaution should be taken to shield such lines from unnecessary exposure to direct sunlight. Often the rode can be fed down into a locker. If it must be carried on deck, it pays to shade it.

## CARE AND INSPECTION

### Anchors and chain

Galvanized anchors are usually coated by the hot-dip process which leaves a tough protective finish, normally requiring no care except ordinary washing off of mud that may be picked up in use. Occasionally, they are freshened up in appearance by a coat of aluminum paint.

On soft bottoms chain may come up fouled with mud

FIG. 653 This mushroom anchor has a heavy bulb cast into the shank at the shackle end.

FIG. 652 A small permanent mooring system consisting of mushroom anchor, chain, buoy and pennant, with necessary swivels, shackles, thimble and eye splices. Rigged as shown, no strain is carried by the buoy.

because its weight has caused it to lie on the bottom, where even a light strain would keep all but a few feet of fiber line from touching bottom. Obviously, the chain needs thorough cleaning and on some larger yachts a hose is carried on deck for the purpose.

## Fiber Lines

Fiber lines should be kept free from sand and grit; manila must be dried before stowing. A low-pressure hose can be used to wash off grit or you can slosh the line overboard, tied in a loose coil. Throwing a strain on a kinked fiber or wire line can be fatal. To a lesser degree, short bends are injurious.

Good practice dictates the need for one long spare rode in good condition. Too often this is an "old but new" unused manila line, which has rotted in its locker. This might fail in the emergency for which it is broken out.

Lengths of line in regular use may be turned end-for-end periodically, as most of the chafe and wear come on the anchor end. On small boats it is often feasible to standardize on one size of line for all uses. A new one can be laid by in the spring as a spare and the old spare is then put into regular service.

Nylon should be unreeled from the coil like wire, not up through the coil like manila. Neither should it be towed like manila when new to take out the kinks. When splicing, tape and fuse the ends with a hot knife or flame. Strands should be kept twisted, and an extra tuck taken, the ends to be left a little longer, when trimming, until the splice is well set under strain. Use synthetic rope thimbles or splice thimbles in tightly to prevent them from dropping out when the nylon stretches. On deep-sea tugs the "legs" of thimbles are seized to the line. All whipping and seizings should be made tightly so they cannot slip.

## Periodic inspection

Periodic inspection of all lines, particularly anchor lines, pays big dividends. Look for and appraise the effect of abrasion, cuts, rust on nylon, broken or frayed yarns, variations in strand size or shape, burns, rot and/or acid stains, and fiber "life." Rotten manila fibers have little or

FIG. 654 Diagram of mooring practice recommended by the Lake Michigan Yachting Association and approved by the U.S. Coast Guard. A weight added at the shackle between lengths of heavy and light chain would increase holding power.

no strength when broken individually. Nylon line may fuzz on the surface although the yarns are not broken. This seems to act as a cushion, reducing further outside abrasion.

Consider the remaining cross-sectional area as compared to new rope. Untwist and examine the inside of strands. They should be clean and bright as in new rope. If powder or broken fibers appear, the line has been overloaded or subject to excessive bending. Nylon may be fused or melted, either inside or out, from overloads.

Most old-timers in yachting know cordage. If you are in doubt, replace your line or get an expert's opinion. For a more detailed discussion of marlinespike seamanship, see Chapter 11.

# Permanent Moorings

*Permanent moorings,* as distinguished from ordinary ground tackle in daily use, consist of the gear used when boats are to be left unattended for long periods, at yacht club anchorages, for example. See fig. 652. The traditional system has often consisted of a mushroom anchor, chain from the anchor to a buoy and a pennant of stainless steel or nylon from the buoy to a light pick-up float at the pennant's end.

Mushroom anchors, especially the type with a heavy bulb cast in the shank, fig. 653, have been able through suction to develop great holding power under ideal conditions if they are allowed time enough to bury deep in bottoms that will permit such burying. Unfortunately ideal bottom conditions are not always present.

Complicating the problem is the fact that anchorages are becoming increasingly crowded so that adequate scope cannot be allowed each boat because of overlapping swinging circles. Add to this the threat of abnormally high hurricane tides, reducing scope to a ratio allowing no safety factor and you have the explanation for devastation wrought by several hurricanes along the Atlantic Coast, beginning in 1938.

## Systems used by typical yacht clubs

The problem faced by the Manhasset Bay Yacht Club at Port Washington, N. Y., is typical of that existing in numerous anchorages. Here about 200 boats are moored in a limited space. If it were possible to permit each boat to use a length of chain equal to 5 to 7 times the depth of water (maximum 30 feet), safety would be assured, but this would require a swinging radius of several hundred feet for each boat, which is not possible. After exhaustive study, they prepared a set of recommended standards, given in Table 6-6.

**FIG. 655 A modern permanent mooring system scientifically designed as a vast improvement over single-mushroom systems. Three lightweight anchors are bridled 120 degrees apart. From the intersection a relatively short rode limits swing.**

A similar system was adopted by the Lake Michigan Yachting Association, their standards approved by the U.S. Coast Guard. See figure 654.

Guest moorings are often available at yacht clubs. The launch man will know which of those not in use for the night will be heavy enough to hold your boat. As a rule, it's easier and safer to pick up such a mooring. In some places, a charge may be made.

## A multiple anchor system

One hurricane that ravaged the North Atlantic Coast swept through an anchorage in the New York area and tore almost every boat from her moorings. Only two survived. What these two had in common was an "unconventional" mooring system—multiple (3) anchors bridled to a common center, with chain and pennant leading from that point to the boat. The principle is diagrammed in fig. 655.

---

**TABLE 6-6-**      **SUGGESTIONS FOR PERMANENT YACHT MOORINGS**
**For Wind Velocities Up to 75 M.P.H.**

| Boat Length Overall | Mushroom Anchor (Min. Wt.) | Heavy Chain | | Light Chain | | Pennant | | | | Total Scope (Chocks to Mushroom) |
|---|---|---|---|---|---|---|---|---|---|---|
| | | Length | Diameter | Length | Diameter | Length (Minim.) | Manila | Nylon | Stainless Steel | |
| **—FOR MOTOR BOATS—** | | | | | | | | | | |
| 25 | 225 | 30 | 7/8 | 20 | 3/8 | 20 | 1 | 7/8 | 9/32 | 70 |
| 35 | 300 | 35 | 1 | 20 | 7/16 | 20 | 1-1/4 | 1 | 11/32 | 75 |
| 45 | 400 | 40 | 1 | 20 | 1/2 | 20 | 1-1/2 | 1-1/4 | 3/8 | 80 |
| 55 | 500 | 50 | 1 | 20 | 9/16 | 20 | 2 | 1-1/2 | 7/16 | 90 |
| **—FOR RACING TYPE SAILBOATS—** | | | | | | | | | | |
| 25 | 125 | 30 | 5/8 | 20 | 5/16 | 20 | 1 | 7/8 | 9/32 | 70 |
| 35 | 200 | 30 | 3/4 | 20 | 3/8 | 20 | 1-1/4 | 1 | 11/32 | 70 |
| 45 | 325 | 35 | 1 | 20 | 7/16 | 20 | 1-1/2 | 1-1/4 | 3/8 | 75 |
| 55 | 450 | 45 | 1 | 20 | 9/16 | 20 | 2 | 1-1/2 | 7/16 | 85 |
| **—FOR CRUISING TYPE SAILBOATS—** | | | | | | | | | | |
| 25 | 175 | 30 | 3/4 | 20 | 5/16 | 20 | 1 | 7/8 | 9/32 | 70 |
| 35 | 250 | 30 | 1 | 20 | 3/8 | 20 | 1-1/4 | 1 | 11/32 | 70 |
| 45 | 400 | 40 | 1 | 20 | 7/16 | 20 | 1-1/2 | 1-1/4 | 3/8 | 80 |
| 55 | 550 | 55 | 1 | 20 | 9/16 | 20 | 2 | 1-1/2 | 7/16 | 95 |

NOTE:—Heavy chain to be shackled to mushroom anchor, light chain shackled to end of heavy chain.
With stainless steel pennants, use special bow chocks and mooring bitts to eliminate sharp bends.

| LENGTH O.A. | BEAM | | PENNANT NYLON | *RODE (COMBINATION) | | RODE CHAIN⊕ ONLY | ANCHOR | | DANFORTH | |
|---|---|---|---|---|---|---|---|---|---|---|
| | SAIL | POWER | | NYLON | CHAIN | | †MUSHROOM | NORTHILL | STANDARD | HI-TENSILE |
| 10' | 4' | 4' | 4'-⅜" | ⅜" | 5'-¼" | ¼" | 250 lb. | 12 lb. (6-R) | 8-S | 5-H |
| 15' | 5' | 5' | 6'-⅜" | ⅜" | 6'-⁵⁄₁₆" | ⁵⁄₁₆" | 400 lb. | 27 lb. (12-R) | 13-S | 12-S |
| 20' | 6' | 7' | 8'-⅜" | ⅜" | 6'-⁵⁄₁₆" | ⁵⁄₁₆" | 550 lb. | 27 lb. (12-R) | 22-S | 12-H |
| 25' | 6' | 8' | 10'-⅞" | ⁷⁄₁₆" | 8'-⅜" | ⅜" | 750 lb. | 46 lb. (20-R) | 40-S | 20-H |
| 30' | 7' | 10' | 12'-⁷⁄₁₆" | ⁷⁄₁₆" | 8'-⅜" | ⅜" | 1050 lb. | 80 lb. (30-R) | 65-S | 35-H |
| 35' | 8' | 12' | 14'-½" | ½" | 10'-⁷⁄₁₆" | ⁷⁄₁₆" | 1350 lb. | 105 lb. (50-R) | 85-S | 60-H |
| 40' | 10' | 14' | 16'-½" | ½" | 10'-⁷⁄₁₆" | ⁷⁄₁₆" | 1800 lb. | 105 lb. (50-R) | 130-S | 60-H |
| 50' | 12' | 16' | 18'-¾" | ¾" | 12'-½" | ½" | 2400 lb. | — | 180-S | 90-H |
| 60' | 14' | 19' | 20'-1" | 1" | 14'-⅝" | ⅝" | 3000 lb. | — | 300-S | 90-H |

**TABLE 6-7 SUGGESTED ANCHOR SYSTEMS FOR PERMANENT MOORINGS — (Winds up to 75 knots)**

NOTE: *Total scope with combination rode to be a minimum of 7:1. ⊕Scope with chain only to be a minimum of 5:1. Buoy with each system to have lifting power (in pounds) of 1½ times the submerged weight of total rode. †Suggestions offered (by Danforth) in table above may sound excessive to those accustomed to lighter tackle. Experience, however, under storm conditions has proved the wisdom of providing for loads of unexpected severity. Sizes suggested assume fair holding ground, scopes as recommended, and moderate shelter from heavy seas.

A casual inspection of figure 655 reveals the obvious advantages of the system. Regardless of how the wind shifts, the boat swings through a small circle, despite the advantage of a relatively long total scope from boat to anchor. The short rode up from the three-way bridle minimizes any "tacking" tendency. Always there will be one or two anchors to windward, the strain tending in the same direction. Using modern lightweight anchors instead of mushrooms, the greater the load the deeper they bury. Mushrooms often need a relatively long period to bed in securely, but lightweight anchors will dig in almost immediately. Using a safety factor of 1.5, each anchor in the 3-anchor system should have a holding power equal to the design holding power of the moorings.

A scientific 3-anchor system of this kind overcomes all of the weaknesses inherent in poor systems using inadequate scope and concrete blocks, railroad car wheels and old engines, all categorized as "dragging" types of "anchor."

## Mooring buoys

To comply with new uniform state waterway regulations (applicable on waters under state control), mooring buoys should be white with a horizontal blue band. Buoys used in any mooring system should be of a type that transmits strain directly through chain or rod. See fig. 640. Buoys perform a useful function in removing much of the vertical load, the pennant is under a more nearly horizontal load, and the boat's bow is freer to lift to heavy seas.

Pennants of stainless steel have often been preferred because failures frequently were traceable to chafing of fiber pennants. When fiber is used for the pennant, it should be carefully protected with chafing gear, especially if there is a bobstay against which it can saw. See figure 648.

**FIG. 656 The Rubbermaid snubber, bent into a mooring line with clove hitches as shown, leaving a loop of slack, absorbs heavy shock loads on line and fittings. Tensile strength is 2000 pounds.**

### Annual inspection necessary

Because ordinary moorings often depend for holding power on a period of time to silt in, annual inspection of chain, links, shackles and pins should be made early in the season—never disturbed just about the time storm warnings are issued. On the other hand, it is also wise to give the pennant from buoy to boat a double-check in midseason, just before the August-September months when hurricanes most often strike.

Table 6-7 includes figures suggested for Danforth and Northill anchors when used in place of mushroom anchors in a permanent mooring system.

# CHAPTER 7

# THE SKIPPER

## His Duties and Responsibilities

The yachtsman is properly interested in the pleasure and comradeship that he obtains with his boat; the rigorous routine of a battleship has little, if any, place on the bridge of a 40-foot cruiser. However, we amateurs can learn from Navy practices. As many of these practices have as their sole purpose insurance of the safety of the ship and her personnel, it is especially appropriate for us to know something of them and apply to our own cruising those that will contribute to our own safety. *The first responsibility of a skipper is the safety of his ship and his people.*

### LEADERSHIP AND DISCIPLINE

Suppose we think first about leadership and discipline. These are subjects that are rarely considered by the yachtsman but in them we find much that can be of value in that sudden emergency for which all of us who cruise must always be prepared.

Discipline; shades of a hickory stick. But, discipline is not subservience, discipline is self-control. It means prompt and cheerful obedience to necessary laws and regulations, laws and regulations designed for the sole purpose of our safety. It also means a square deal to our shipmates; the skipper who expects discipline of his crew must likewise discipline himself. A well-disciplined boat is a secure and safe boat.

Discipline does not mean a long string of commands with a crew constantly scurrying about the deck. Gold braid is not necessary to discipline. Discipline does not mean that all the joy is gone out of the job. There can be discipline on board the smallest yacht without there being any apparent show of it. Real discipline is a function of leadership and leadership can be exercised in dungarees on board a 20-foot sailboat; it is a characteristic that all of us should cultivate and practice.

Leadership is based on three things: (1) each man must know himself, his abilities and his limitations; (2) he must know his job, know it so well that he doesn't have to think about the details of doing it; (3) he must know his men and his boat and what he can reasonably expect of them in an emergency.

### Authority and obligations

From the lowest third class Petty Officer to the Admiral of the Fleet, every man of the Navy charged with authority has two functions to perform: (1) his function as a military leader; (2) his function as a specialist in some technical phase of his profession. It is relatively easy for any of us to become technically skilled in shaping a course, making

FIG. 701 The primary responsibility of every skipper is the safety of his boat and crew.

a mooring, even swabbing a deck. All of these have to do with our technical ability and are equally applicable in the Navy and in amateur cruising.

But there usually comes a time, and it is always an emergency when seconds count, when there are too many jobs for even the most skillful of us to handle them all. This is the time when our capacity for leadership will bring us to port or put us aground. In one way, leadership on a motor cruiser is even more important than it is on an aircraft carrier; our friends on board may not be skilled in the operation of a boat. We have to make up for their lack of technical ability.

Let's look at it another way. There is an old saying that you get more out of a job when you have to work at it; the average guest on board should more quickly feel at home and should have pleasanter memories of his cruise if he has some of the boat's work to perform, if he must coordinate his efforts with those of his shipmates. As skippers, we all welcome the guest who is eager to turn to and do his share.

### Assignment of tasks

A good skipper will privately catalog in his own mind the abilities of his guests and think ahead to the tasks that he will request them to do should an emergency arise. See fig. 702. He may and should go one step further; without making it obvious, he should see to it that all on board are given various jobs to do not only so that he can find the best spot for each but also so that they are able to do more than one thing. *Our first obligation is the safety of our boat and her people.*

One good U. S. Power Squadron skipper makes it a practice to have "informal formal" watches, which amount to Navy watch, quarter, and station bills. From the stories told of cruises in his schooner, everyone on board has a bang-up good time, as well as a safe cruise. This man is a real leader and he doesn't hesitate to work at it.

Let's not try to define leadership; there have been as many definitions of this word as there have been writers. Any intelligent man thoroughly understands the meaning and significance of the term. Taking honesty and integrity for granted, it is the first characteristic that a man should develop. Out of leadership comes confidence, pride, emulation on the part of our associates; out of it will come the pleasant cruise that all of us want.

## FORESIGHT

Next to leadership comes forehandedness or foresightedness. A first class skipper doesn't wait for an emergency to arise; he has long before formulated several solutions to any emergency with which he may be faced. Commander Frost, one of the foremost destroyer captains in the Navy, put it something like this: "The most expert captain is the first to admit how often he has been fooled by some trick of wind or current. Dangerous situations develop with startling suddenness so even when things look easiest, watch out. Have an answer to every threat and a trick to take you out of every danger." An officer must always look ahead, a minute, an hour or a day as the circumstances of his situation dictate. And, whether we like it or not, a yacht skipper is an officer, good or bad.

## VIGILANCE

Next in importance to forehandedness is vigilance. In no position more than that of the skipper is "eternal vigilance the price of safety." He must see intelligently all that comes within his vision, outside and inside the ship. And his vigilance must extend beyond this to the faculty of foreseeing situations as well as seeing them. The rule of the airlines that a pilot must be able to get into alternate fields as well as the airport of his destination holds meaning for the boat skipper too.

## COMMON SENSE

One more check point; it is common sense. The successful skipper has a sense of proportion and of the fitness of things; let us adjust ourselves to our situation. For example, it is obviously ridiculous to dress in white flannels and blue coat when kedging off, although we might do so when the ladies are on board of a quiet Sunday afternoon. Yet we all probably can recall cases where, through a failure to exercise common sense, we did things as silly as that suggested above. The old adage "use your head" applies equally well on shipboard.

One more quotation from Commander Frost. He has defined the art of handling a ship: "Systematic application of knowledge and skill, acquired by study, observation and experience, in effecting the safe, smart, effective and economical operation of your ship." Think it over.

## COURTESY

There is a courtesy extended by large ships that is worthy of attention: dipping the ensign when passing a ship of the Navy. Pleasure craft frequently do not do this but it is a mark of respect that is highly desirable for all to show. As your bridge draws abeam the bridge of the Naval vessel, dip the ensign and immediately hoist it two-blocks. All persons on board except the helmsman should face the warship and stand at attention. Any in uniform should salute.

## DUTIES AND RESPONSIBILITIES

We come now to the duties and responsibilities of a skipper, of those activities with which you must be familiar while on the bridge.

Approximately in the order of their importance, the responsibilities of the skipper or of the man having the watch are as follows:

- Safe navigation of his boat.
- Safe and efficient handling of the boat in company with or in the presence of other boats. See fig. 703.
- Safety of personnel and matériel on board.
- Rendering assistance to all in danger or distress.
- Smart handling and smart appearance of the boat.
- Comfort and contentment on board.
- A good log.

These are some of the instructions that the U. S. Navy gives to watch officers, men who are charged with the

**FIG. 702  The good skipper will catalog in his mind the abilities of guests and crew, assigning tasks accordingly.**

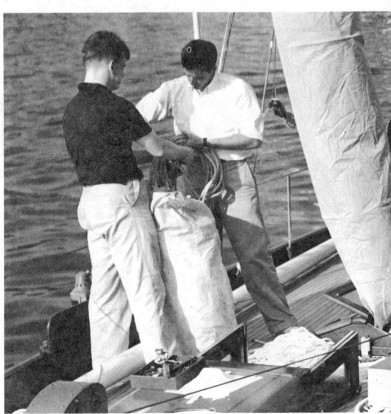

responsibility for the ship. They form a pattern that all of us, whatever the size of our craft, can follow with benefit. They presuppose that a man know himself, his job, his crew, and his ship. Let's see what they mean in terms of actual practice.

## Check of equipment

Before a boat can be gotten under way, it is important that a check-up be made to determine if she is ready to sail. Not alone should the equipment required by law be on board and in proper condition for use but all navigational and other equipment should be at hand. See fig. 704. Water and gasoline tanks should be sounded, the ground tackle inspected, stores checked, and all those other little odd jobs that can be done at the mooring, but not at sea in an emergency, completed. These things sound elementary and worthy of little consideration but all of us can recall results that might have been different had the proper attention been given in advance to such minor details.

The Navy provides each ship with a check list that the officer must use before he takes charge or gets the ship under way. The yachtsman could profitably make up his own check list and either actually or mentally go over it as he steps from the dock to the deck. The whole subject of safety is so important that every yachtsman should consider himself disqualified until he so thoroughly knows the requirements that he executes them as second nature.

## Physical condition of the skipper

Another point in the safe navigation of a ship has to do with the physical condition of the skipper. The constant vigil which is necessary requires the complete possession of all faculties as well as a sense of physical well-being. No man should expose his boat or his people to danger, except in an extreme emergency, unless he is in good physical and mental condition.

## Avoidance of risk

The good skipper will not permit any of his personnel to take needless risks. If a dangerous job that may result in a man's being swept overboard has to be done, he will insist that that man wear a life jacket. This may not be customary in yachting circles but that omission does not justify contempt for danger. In this connection, the state of the weather should be carefully observed and every effort made before getting under way to ascertain what the weather will be for the period of the cruise. A little foresight in this regard may save a ship or a life.

In conclusion, for those of us who wish to cruise tomorrow as well as today, let us think first of the things that spell safety; then the fun will take care of itself.

## IMPORTANT THINGS TO DO

Here is a short check list of things to do:

• Frequently check and plot the boat's position when in sight of land or aids to navigation; be certain of the identification of the objects used to fix position.

• Take soundings and heed their warning.

• Note the effect on the boat of wind and current, especially in close waters or when maneuvering with other boats.

• Do not follow other boats blindly; steer a safe course and do not assume that the other fellow is on a safe course.

• When in doubt as to position, slow down promptly; do not wait until the last minute.

• Remember that the other fellow may not see us and always be alert immediately to take such steps as will prevent a collision.

FIG. 703   One of the major responsibilities of a skipper is the safe and efficient handling of his boat in the presence of other craft.

## Maintenance of a lookout

A small cruiser cannot readily utilize the lookout routine of the large vessel but the implication of vigilance and caution of that routine should be acknowledged. We should make it a matter of pride that we, as skippers, will observe any danger before any other person on board sights it; this is definitely our responsibility.

---

**Regarding Refuse**  The admonition (see item below) against throwing refuse overboard is more than a matter of etiquette alone—it is based on law. Complaints received by both the Coast Guard and Army Engineers concerning refuse in coastal waters have fostered an official appeal by both agencies to the public. While asking each citizen to do his part voluntarily the appeal pointed out that "throwing, discharging, or depositing either from or out of any floating craft or from the shore refuse matter of any kind into any navigable waters of the U.S. or into any tributary of any navigable waters from which the same shall float or be carried into such navigable water is a violation of federal law (33 USC 407)." And for any who might take the warning lightly the appeal adds that such violation is punishable by a fine not exceeding $2500, not less than $500 or by imprisonment for not more than one year nor less than 30 days, or by both fine and imprisonment.

Official U.S. Coast Guard photo.

FIG. 704  **The skipper must take full responsibility for seeing that all essential equipment, including that required by law, is aboard (and in proper condition for use) before casting off.**

---

YACHT_____

# Glad To Have You On Board

*The Skipper and Mate welcome you on board. We look forward to your company during our cruise and ask*

*Please*

DO make yourself at home. The mate will show you your locker. There is no lock on the refrigerator and the berths are said to be comfortable. Decks are usually swabbed down at 0900.

DO be informal. Old clothes are fit companions for swabbing decks, weighing anchor, and securing from chow.

DO ask us all the questions you wish—while we are not handling the boat. If you have a yen for rope-work or other ship's business, let us know. Too, you may find a helpful magazine or book on board.

DO locate your life-belt and learn how to use it. We will show you how to toss a life-ring, if you do not know. Not looking for trouble, but we want to be ready for it.

DO the same for the fire extinguishers. In case of fire, the Skipper will tell you what to do—and not to do.

DO report any danger or unusual occurrence to the Skipper at once: what it is, where it is, what it is doing.

DO go swimming at every opportunity. Swim upstream, keeping an eye on your shipmates and on the boat.

DO fish too, if you wish. But watch out for fouling the propeller and mooring lines, watch out for that fish-hook.

DO conserve fresh water. Use all that you need but remember, the supply is limited.

DO likewise conserve electricity. Lights out on the bridge when under way at night.

DO learn to work the "head." The Skipper or Mate will gladly show you.

DO stand clear of dock lines and anchor rode, of all boat controls.

DO remember that sound carries far over the water especially late at night.

*Please*

DO NOT smoke or strike a match or cigarette lighter or touch off the galley stove while fueling or starting the engines.

DO NOT take chances on deck, especially if the sea kicks up. Remember, rubber-soled shoes often slip on a wet deck.

DO NOT fall overboard or cause another to do so, while under way or at anchor.

DO NOT use any equipment with which you are not familiar. See the Skipper or Mate.

DO NOT jump from deck to dock without watching your footing. Landing on a rope-end usually results in a sprained ankle.

DO NOT jump into the dinghy; it isn't built to "take it."

DO NOT let go the dinghy painter until you are ready to clear.

DO NOT jump over the side while wearing a life-belt; your chin may be the worse for wear.

DO NOT throw refuse overboard without instructions from the Mate. Puncture cans at both ends; fill bottles with sea water and jettison only in deep water.

DO NOT use the "head" for cigarettes, matches, chewing gum or bulky articles; plumbers are scarce afloat.

DO NOT wear hard-soled or high-heeled shoes on deck; a good varnish job is too hard to come by.

DO NOT use the Skipper's binoculars or chart without permission; he may need them in a hurry.

DO NOT intrude on the privacy of others.

Morning colors at 0800—Evening colors at sunset—Recognition Signal—COOPERATION

_____Mate          _____SKIPPER

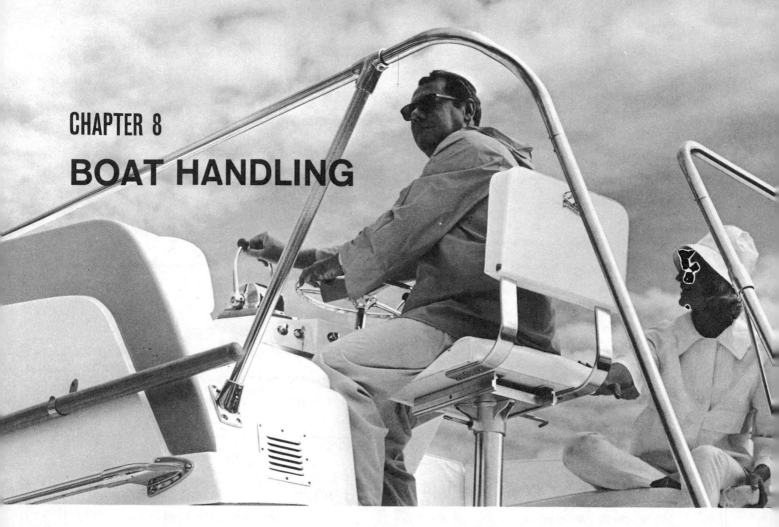

# CHAPTER 8
# BOAT HANDLING

*"The art of handling a vessel may be defined as the systematic application of knowledge and skill—acquired by study, observation and experience—in effecting its safe, smart, effective and economical operation."*—COMDR. H. H. FROST, USN

Without a doubt some of the finest exhibitions of skill in the art of handling motor boats are often given by men who may never have read a printed page on the subject of seamanship. Their facility at the helm of a motor boat is their sheepskin from the sea's school of experience — in which the curriculum, admittedly, may be tough.

Witness, for example, the consummate skill some commercial fisherman might display in maneuvering his skiff into a tight berth under adverse weather conditions, finally to bring her up against the wharf in a landing that wouldn't crack an egg. Such proficiency, developed over long years of meeting every conceivable kind of situation, eventually manifests itself almost as an instinct, prompting the boatman to react right whether he has time to think the problem out in advance or not.

Sometimes the old-timer's methods might appear, to a novice, to verge on carelessness, but that's probably be-cause the old salt in a practical way understands exactly what the minimum requirements are for the safety of his craft and therefore doesn't waste any time on non-essentials. Consequently if he uses three lines where the text book says six, don't jump to the conclusion that he wouldn't know how to use more if they were needed.

So, in approaching a study of the principles of boat handling, it's helpful to keep in mind that the goal is not so much to be able to repeat verbatim definitions or the prescribed answers to a set of questions for the sake of passing a quiz as it is to understand the "why" of some of the curious capers your boat may cut when you're out there handling her. If she stubbornly refuses to make a turn under a given set of conditions, or persistently backs one way when you want her to go the other, you will be less likely to make the same mistake twice when you understand the reasons behind her behavior.

## First Principles

The paragraphs above lead up to a very fundamental thought. Learn all you possibly can about the principles according to which average boats respond under normal conditions; supplement this with all the experience you can get aboard your own boat and other types as well, and then learn to act so that controlling elements aid you rather than oppose you.

Some of the ideas to be developed later may seem applicable only to larger vessels, but remember that some day you may be at the wheel of a craft double the size of your own familiar 30-footer. Then the significance of these points will be more apparent.

No two boats will behave in identical manner in every situation, so great is their individuality. This applies even to "standardized" craft which to outward appearances may be alike as two peas in a pod. Exactly how the boat will perform depends on many things—among them the design; the form and shape of the hull's underbody; the construction; the shape, position and area of the rudder; the trim; speed; the weight; load; strength and direction of wind and current; and the nature of the sea, if any.

## EFFECT OF WIND AND CURRENT

Wind and current are particularly important factors in analyzing a boat's behavior as they may cause her to respond precisely opposite to what you would expect without these factors to reckon with. As a case in point, many motor boats have a tendency to back into the wind despite anything that can be done with the helm.

Given two boats of roughly the same size, one of which (A) has considerable draft forward but little aft, and another (B), with relatively greater draft aft but more superstructure forward—you will find radical differences in their handling qualities. What governs is the relative area presented above water to the wind as compared with the areas exposed to the water, both fore and aft.

The former (A), with wind abeam, might hold her course reasonably well when the bow of the latter (B) would persistently pay off, requiring considerable rudder angle to hold her up. On the other hand, with wind and sea aft, B might go along about her business with little attention to the helm while A insisted on "rooting" at the bow and yawing off her course despite the best efforts of the helmsman.

As a general rule, the boat with low freeboard and superstructure but relatively deep draft tending toward the sailboat type, fig. 801, will be less affected by wind and more by current than the light draft motor boat, fig. 802, with high freeboard and deckhouses. The latter floats relatively high in the water and has little below the waterline to hold her against wind pressures acting on areas exposed above water to drive her to leeward.

**FIG. 801** Section of a deep-draft sailboat with relatively low freeboard, as compared with a typical motorboat.

**FIG. 802** In this motorboat the draft is small compared to the height of superstructure exposed to windage.

In the type of motorboat where the greatest draft and least freeboard are aft, the greatest exposure to windage is presented by the relatively higher bow and cabin forward. Obviously her bow will be affected by wind pressures more than the stern. With wind abeam, the tendency would be for her bow to be driven to leeward more than the stern. To offset that, she would need a certain amount of rudder angle to hold her on her course and compensate for leeway.

For the same reason if she is drifting in a smooth sea with engine stopped, wind pressure on her bow will make the bow pay off so that the wind finally is brought abaft the beam. The action might also be compared to that of a sailboat in which a flattened jib, but no other canvas, is set.

But, just as an illustration to show how boat behavior may vary, suppose it is raining and cockpit curtains are buttoned down on that same cruiser. Here a new factor is introduced and the windage aft is increased to such an extent that it may more than offset the effect of the windage forward. Under such conditions she might be very hard to handle in close quarters because of the great amount of total windage compared to her draft.

Although flying bridges, fig. 803, on modern cruisers tend to add to the windage, they have an undeniable ad-

**FIG. 803** A modern cruiser being brought up to a finger pier. The flying bridge and twin screws are a great advantage in handling, from the standpoint of visibility and control. Crew tends bow line.

vantage in better visibility when maneuvering, and running at night or in strange waters.

Some boats require humoring under certain conditions. For example, because of a combination of excessive superstructure forward and little draft at the bow, it may be practically impossible to turn a boat in close quarters by the conventional technique.

## HELMSMAN MUST DEVELOP JUDGMENT

From these and many other variations in boat behavior it begins to be evident that the boatman must develop judgment, based on understanding of the individual boat he is handling and the forces acting upon her. Combina-

FIG. 804 Approaching a bridge. At this point the helmsman waits for the span to open. When about to enter the opened span, he will square away parallel with the center line.

tions of conditions are infinite, so he must be able to appraise the situation and act promptly, with decision.

A good helmsman will be prudent and try to foresee possibilities, having a solution in mind for the problem before it presents itself. On that basis, it's likely that he'll never meet an "emergency." To cite a simple example, if you're running down a narrow channel with a strong wind abeam, and you have a choice as to which side to take, the windward side is the better bet. If the engine should stop, you'll probably then have a chance to get an anchor down before going aground on the leeward side.

By the same token, you wouldn't skirt the windward side of a shoal too closely. To leeward, in case of engine failure, you would drift clear, but to windward you'd be driven down on the shoal. A strong current might have the same effect, and would have to be taken into account.

As another example of how the helmsman should try always to be prepared for possibilities, suppose you are approaching a bridge, fig. 804, having a narrow draw opening with a strong wind or current setting you down rapidly on it. If you were to approach the opening at an angle,

and power or steering gear failed, you'd be in a jam. On the other hand, if you are prepared and straighten out your course while still some distance off so you will be shooting down the center of the opening in alignment with it, the chances of doing any damage are practically nil because her straight course will tend to carry her through in the clear in any case.

In developing your boat sense, draw from as many sources as possible. Observe the way experienced yachtsmen, fishermen and Coast Guardsmen handle their boats, making due allowance for differences in your own boat when you try similar maneuvers.

## TERMINOLOGY OF BOAT HANDLING

Before getting too deep into discussion of actual problems of maneuvering it is necessary in advance to get some of the correct terminology fixed in mind.

The *port* side of a boat is the *left* side facing forward; the *starboard* is the *right* side. This is easy to visualize while the boat has headway but when the boat is reversing the operator may face aft and get all mixed up when the terms right, left, starboard and port are used.

Therefore, bear in mind that the port side is the port side *no matter which way the boat is going*. When we speak of the boat's going to port it means that her bow turns to port when she has headway and her stern to port when she has sternway. Figure 805 makes this clear. At A the boat has headway and her bow is turning to port. At B she is going astern and her stern is going to port.

The old terms of port helm and starboard helm have now given way to new terms which prevent misunderstanding. In Figure 805 the boat has *left rudder* in both cases and with headway, as at A, her bow goes to port. *Right rudder,* which is not illustrated, is just the opposite. The rudder is then on the starboard side of the boat's centerline and her bow goes to starboard when the boat has headway.

A *balanced rudder,* fig. 806, is one in which the area of the blade surface is distributed so that part of it lies ahead of the rudder stock. An unbalanced rudder would have the stock attached at the edge of the blade.

While the proportion of this balanced area may be only

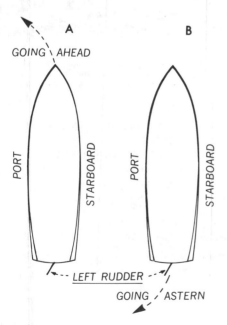

FIG. 805 With left rudder in a boat going ahead (A) the stern is thrown to starboard, bow to port. Going astern, left rudder throws stern to port.

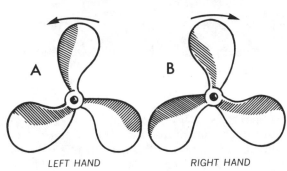

FIG. 806 A balanced rudder, in which part of the blade area (shaded section) projects ahead of the rudder stock.

FIG. 807 Left-hand and right-hand propellers. This is how they turn when you stand astern of them, looking forward at the aft side of the blades.

LEFT HAND          RIGHT HAND

20 per cent of the total rudder area, it exerts considerable effect in taking strain off the steering gear and making steering easier, though it may slow the boat on a turn more than the unbalanced type.

## RIGHT- AND LEFT-HAND PROPELLERS

Propellers are right-handed or left-handed, depending on the direction of their rotation. It is vital that the difference be understood because this has a great bearing on how a boat maneuvers, especially when reversing. To determine the hand, stand outside the boat, astern of the propeller, and look forward at the driving face of the blades, fig. 807. *If the top of the propeller turns clockwise when driving the boat ahead, it is right-handed; if counterclockwise, left-handed.* A is left-handed; B, right-handed.

Most propellers on marine engines in single-screw installations are right-handed although some are left-handed. In any maneuvering problems which follow, the assumption is that the propeller on a single-screw boat under dis-

cussion is right-handed unless specifically noted to the contrary.

In twin-screw installations the ideal arrangement is to have the *tops of the blades turn outward* for better maneuvering qualities. In fig. 807 the port engine swings a left-hand wheel, the starboard engine a right-hand wheel.

Don't be confused by the term right- and left-hand as applied to the engines that are driving the propellers. If you stand inside the boat, facing aft toward the engine, fig. 808, and the flywheel turns *counter-clockwise* (as in most marine engines) it is a *left-handed engine* and requires a *right-hand propeller.* A right-hand engine takes a left-hand wheel.

FIG. 809 The discharge screw current from a propeller is given a spiral twist by the propeller blades, as this view of an outboard lower unit shows. A left-handed inboard engine, driving a right-hand propeller, would create an opposite (clockwise) spiral.

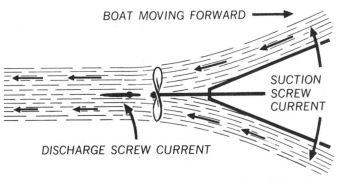

FIG. 810 The screw current which drives a boat through the water. Here the boat has headway. Suction current is shown leading into the propeller, the discharge current driven out astern.

FIG. 808 Direction of rotation is marked on this marine engine flywheel housing. This is a left-hand engine, as shown by the counterclockwise direction of the arrow. It takes a right-hand propeller.

FIG. 811 The lower unit of an outboard motor which, unlike the inboard engine, pivots to provide steering control.

FIG. 812 The inboard-outboard, like the inboard boat, has an inboard engine. Unlike the inboard, it has an outboard drive unit which pivots like the outboard. This boat has twin engines.

## HOW THE PROPELLER ACTS

Motor boats are driven through the water by the action of their propellers which act almost like a pump, drawing in a stream of water from forward (when going ahead) and throwing it out astern. This stream moving astern reacts on the water around it to provide the power for propulsion. Sometimes an analogy is drawn between propeller action and a screw thread working in a nut, but this fails to give a correct picture of what really is happening at the propeller.

Actually all of the water drawn into the propeller does not flow from directly ahead like a thin column of water but for our purposes here it can be considered as coming in generally parallel to the propeller shaft. The propeller ejects it and as it does so imparts a twist or spiral motion to the water, fig. 809, its direction of rotation dependent on the way the propeller turns. This flow of water set up by the propeller is called *screw current*.

### Suction and discharge screw currents

Regardless of whether the propeller is going ahead or reversing that part of the current which flows into the propeller is called the *suction screw current*. The part ejected from the propeller is the *discharge current*, fig. 810. The latter is not only spiral in motion but is also a more compact stream than the suction current and exerts a greater pressure than the suction current.

By locating the rudder behind the propeller in this discharge current a greater steering effect is possible than if it were to be placed elsewhere, to be acted upon only by water moving naturally past the hull. For that reason a twin-screw cruiser is likely to have twin rudders, one behind each propeller, thus keeping their blades at all times more directly in the propeller's discharge current. Exactly what the effect of each part of the screw current on the boat's behavior will be depends upon what part of the boat it is acting upon.

In boats driven by outboard motors, steering action results from rotation of the lower unit, fig. 811, around a vertical axis, so that the propeller's discharge current acts at an angle to the boat's keel. (See Chapter 29, Outboard

Seamanship.) A similar action results from control of the outboard drive units of inboard-outboard boats, fig. 812, even though the motor itself is permanently mounted inboard. As will be pointed out later, the inboard boat gets its steering effect from the action of the propeller's discharge current on a movable rudder.

There is also a *wake current*. This is a body of water carried along by a vessel with her as she moves through the water due to friction on her hull. This has its maximum effect near the surface, is practically of no consequence at the keel.

### Unequal blade thrust

Finally, there is another factor of some moment that needs to be understood in analyzing a boat's reaction to propeller rotation. While this has been sometimes referred to as sidewise blade pressure, it is more properly an unequal thrust exerted by the ascending and descending blades of the propeller, fig. 813.

Here we are looking at the starboard side of a propeller shaft, inclined, as most shafts are, at a considerable angle to the water's surface and to the flow of water past the propeller blades. The actual pitch of the blades as manufactured, of course, is the same, but the water flows diagonally across the plane in which the blades revolve.

*Relative direction of water flow*

*Projected pitch of ascending blade (port side)*

*Projected pitch of descending blade (st'b'd. side)*

FIG. 813 With rudder amidships, bow of boat with right-hand propeller may swing to port. Angularity of the propeller shaft has the effect of increasing the pitch of the descending blade relative to that of the ascending blade, so greater thrust is exerted on starboard side.

Figure 813 shows clearly how the effect of this is to increase the pitch of the descending starboard blade as compared with the ascending port blade, when considered relative to the direction of water flow past the propeller.

The importance of this factor is reduced as the shaft angle is decreased, and naval architects, taking cognizance of this, sometimes take pains to have the engine installed as low as possible to keep the propeller shaft nearly parallel to the water's surface and the flow of water past the blades. This naturally contributes to propeller efficiency, and is a worth-while factor to be considered wherever consistent with other requirements of the design. Limitations in some designs, however, make it necessary for the engine and shaft to be installed at a considerable angle.

## Effect of unequal blade thrust

The relatively greater pitch of the blade on the starboard side has the effect of creating a stronger thrust on this side with the result that the bow of the boat tends to turn to port. Putting it another way, insofar as this single factor is concerned, there is a natural tendency for the stern of a single-screw boat with right-hand propeller to go to starboard when the propeller is going ahead, and for the stern to go to port when it is reversing.

Again, when such a boat has headway, the bow apparently wants to turn to port if the rudder is held amidships, so a certain amount of right rudder may be necessary to maintain a straight course. To correct it, shafts are sometimes splayed to port, fig. 814, or a small trimming tab may be attached at the after edge of the rudder blade, on the side toward which the boat tends to pull.

The effect is a great variable, so small in some cases as to be negligible; quite pronounced in others.

### HOW INDIVIDUAL BOATS DIFFER

We have seen how the helmsman has many things to consider when handling boats, due partly to individual characteristics which cause them to respond differently under identical conditions of wind, weather and current.

We have dealt too with the effect which draft and freeboard have on a boat's behavior, showing how high freeboard creates windage which acts to drive a boat to leeward whereas deep draft gives her a grip on the water with which to oppose that tendency.

The general principle is easily observed in the case of a deep keel sailboat, where deep draft acts to hold her on her course, and minimum freeboard is designed into her to reduce the windage factor.

Not only the draft, but the trim, has a bearing on a boat's handling qualities. Later we will see how the effect of rudder action in steering is to cause a boat to pivot about a point near the bow. But if she trims by the stern, that is,

FIG. 814 Ordinarily engines are installed on the center line, but unequal blade thrust tends to make stern go to starboard, bow to port (assuming a right-hand propeller). Sometimes shaft is splayed to one side of the center line as illustrated to offset that tendency.

FIG. 815 Boats under sail only have no propeller discharge current to increase the rudder's effect in steering. Their maneuverability is limited, and there are many tight places into which a motor boat could be worked where the sailboat (without power) could not.

deeper than normal aft, the tendency is for that pivoting point to move aft.

## The tendency to stray off course

Different boats require varying degrees of rudder angle to compensate for any tendency to fall off from a straight course. Depending on differences in construction, arrangement of rudder blade, and the hand of the propeller, the bow may tend to fall off to port or starboard. These are all factors that the helmsman should understand before attempting maneuvers with a boat.

Using a concrete example to make the significance of the last point more clear, a certain group of boats of almost identical design were found to have a strong tendency to pull off course to port. In some of these, the condition was corrected by the simple expedient of lowering the rudder blade, without changing its size or shape but merely by lengthening the stock an inch or two.

Before correcting that condition, these boats would make a quick and easy turn to port but would be obstinate in turning to starboard. As a matter of fact, unless steering controls were rigged with worm and gear to hold the wheel against pressure on the rudder, the boat would immediately swing into a short circle to port the instant the wheel was left unattended. While this is an exaggerated condition, far from normal, it does illustrate the handling characteristics the helmsman must pay attention to, especially in an unfamiliar boat.

Then again, the state of the sea will have an effect on a boat's performance. A heavy, deep-draft boat or one which is heavily loaded will carry her way through the water longer than a light one when the propeller is disengaged by throwing the reverse gear level into neutral. This is likely to be even more marked in a seaway, the light displacement boat losing her way against the sea much sooner than a heavier craft would.

## HOW THE RUDDER ACTS

Although there are some boats, like fast hydroplanes, which have bow rudders, the conventional arrangement for steering on most inboard boats is by means of a vertical rudder blade at the stern pivoted in hangers or on its stock so that movement of the steering wheel or tiller throws it to port or starboard of the boat's centerline.

In a sailboat, or auxiliary, fig. 815, when the engine is not driving a propeller, when the boat has headway water flows past the hull and if the rudder is moved to one side of the keel a resistance on that side is created together with a current at an angle to the keel. The combined effect is to throw the stern to port with right rudder, to starboard with left rudder.

But note that *any control from the rudder is dependent on the boat's motion through the water.* Even if she is drifting, with motion relative to the bottom, but none so far as the surrounding water is concerned, her rudder has no effect. Only when the water flows past the rudder and strikes it at an angle does the boat respond. The faster she is moving, the stronger the rudder effect. It makes no difference how her headway has been produced—she may even be in tow—there is control as long as there is motion relative to the water.

### Propeller current's action on rudder

In a motor boat the situation is different from that encountered in a sailboat. Here the rudder blade is almost invariably directly in the discharge current of the propeller which is pumping a strong stream of water astern. Moving the rudder to one side of the keel deflects the stream to that side. The reaction which pushes the stern in the opposite direction is much stronger than it would be in the absence of that powerful jet.

At very slow propeller speeds the boat's headway may not be sufficient to give good control over the boat if other forces are acting upon her at the time. For example, with a strong wind on the port beam, even with rudder hard over to port, it may not be possible to make a turn into the

**FIG. 816** With right rudder, as boat moves from A to B to C, stern is driven against piles, with risk of damage. Rudder should be amidships till boat is clear.

**FIG. 817** When a boat's rudder is put over to make a turn, her stern is kicked away from the direction in which the rudder moves. Then, after sliding obliquely along the course (as shown from A to B) she settles into a turning circle in which the bow describes a smaller circle (solid line) than the stern (dotted line).

wind until the propeller is speeded up enough to exert a more powerful thrust against the offset rudder blade.

Here is a fundamental principle to remember in handling motor boats. In close quarters a motor boat can often be turned in a couple of boat lengths by judicious use of the power. If, for example, the rudder is set hard to starboard (that is, right rudder) while the boat has no headway and the throttle is suddenly opened, the stern can be kicked around to port before the boat has a chance to gather headway. The exact technique of turning in limited space will be described in detail further along.

## KEEP STERN FREE TO MANEUVER

As soon as the boatman understands the underlying difference between the steering of a boat and a car, he will always be conscious of the need to keep the stern free to maneuver in close quarters. Furthermore, when he lies alongside a dock, a float or another boat, and wants to pull away, he will never, automobile-fashion, throw the wheel over until the stern is clear.

To set the rudder to starboard, for example, while lying port side to a dock and then attempt to pull away by going ahead, fig. 816, would only throw the port quarter against the dock piles and pin it there, to slam successively into one pile after the other as the boat moves ahead, with the

**FIG. 818** A dramatic comparison of the turning circles of two boats at high speed. At "a" (left) the outdrive unit permits a tight turn in less than two boat lengths. At "b" (right) the inboard's propeller is fixed, and she responds only to rudder angle for steering.

**FIG. 819** On inland waterways, boats may get into shoal water. This reduces the speed and also affects their handling qualities, response to the rudder being sluggish.

likelihood of doing damage.

Steering gears on motor boats are almost invariably rigged today so that they turn with the rudder, that is, turning the top of the wheel to port throws the rudder to port. Consequently, with the usual rig, the boat having headway, putting the wheel over to port gives her left rudder which kicks the stern to starboard so that the bow, in effect, moves to port. Conversely, turning the wheel to starboard gives her right rudder, throwing the stern to port so that the boat turns to starboard.

## TURNING CIRCLES

When the boat has headway and the rudder is put over to make a turn (to starboard, let us say), the stern is first kicked to port and the boat then tends to slide off oblique- ly, "crab-wise." Due to its momentum through the water it will carry some distance along the original course before settling into a turn, in which the bow describes a smaller circle than the stern, fig. 817. The pivoting point about which she turns may be between one-fourth and one-third of the boat's length from the bow, varying with different boats and changing for any given boat with the trim.

The distance a vessel moves in the direction of her orig- inal course, after the helm has been put over, is called the *advance*.

While there is always a loss of speed in making a turn, the size of a boat's turning circle will vary but little with changes in speed, assuming a given rudder angle. Whether

she makes it at slow speed or at wide open throttle, the actual diameter of the turn is about the same.

There is, however, a great difference in the size of turn- ing circles for single-screw inboards as compared with out- boards or inboard-outboards because, as has been noted, the shaft and propeller of the inboard are fixed on the center line and cannot be rotated. This is dramatically illus- trated in fig. 818. The twin-screw inboard, on the other hand, provides excellent maneuverability, as will be seen later.

Stops are invariably put on a rudder to limit its maxi- mum angle. Beyond that point an increase of rudder angle would result, not in a smaller turning circle, but a larger one. That's why Naval vessels usually have a maximum rudder angle of 35 degrees.

When the boat has sternway (reversing) the rudder nor- mally would be turned to port (left rudder) to turn the stern of the boat to port, while right rudder should nor- mally tend to turn the stern to starboard in backing. How- ever, the subject cannot be dismissed as easily as that and we shall see later how, under certain circumstances, the effect of the reversing propeller may more than offset the steering effect of the rudder.

Just as the speed of a boat is cut down in shallow water, fig. 819, so the depth has an effect on a boat's steering. Even though the keel may not actually be touching the bottom, it will be noticed that the boat's response to rud- der action in shallow water is almost always sluggish.

## Response of Boat to Propeller and Rudder

Let us consider now a number of typical situations to see how the average inboard motor boat will respond to propeller and rudder action *(assuming a single-screw boat with right-hand propeller)*.

### NO WAY ON, PROPELLER TURNING AHEAD

Picture her first without any way on, engine idling and rudder amidships. Being dead in the water there is no wake current to act on the propeller blades. Now the clutch is engaged and the propeller starts to turn ahead.

Until she gathers headway, the unequal blade thrust (refer back to fig. 813) tends to throw her stern to starboard. As she gets headway, wake current enters the picture, increas- ing pressure against the upper blades (remember wake current is strongest at the surface, has little effect at the bottom of the keel) and this tends to offset the effect of unequal blade thrust.

What happens under identical conditions, except that the rudder is hard over at the time the propeller is en- gaged? In this case the propeller's discharge current strikes the rudder and exerts its normal effect of kicking the stern to port with right rudder, or stern to starboard with left rudder. With right rudder the kick to port would be much stronger than the effect of unequal blade thrust.

## WITH HEADWAY, PROPELLER GOING AHEAD

After the boat has gathered normal headway, with rudder amidships, the average boat tends to hold her course in a straight line fairly well. From a purely theoretical standpoint, the unequal blade thrust, with a right-hand wheel, should tend to move the stern to starboard, and bow to port. In most cases, however, this is a relatively unimportant consideration.

It is only in a comparatively few cases that the unequal thrust of the propeller blades has a pronounced effect.

Now, the boat having headway, assume the rudder is put to starboard. The water flowing past the hull hits the rudder on its starboard side, forcing the stern to port. The propeller's discharge current intensifies this effect by acting on the same side and the boat's bow turns to starboard, the same side on which the rudder is set. With rudder to port the action would naturally be just the opposite.

## WITH HEADWAY, PROPELLER REVERSING

A boat has no brakes as does a car, so she depends on reversing the propeller to bring her to a stop. Assuming that the boat has headway, rudder amidships, and the propeller is reversed, the effect is to throw the stern to port as the boat loses headway. The rudder has no steering effect in this case, and unequal blade thrust of the propeller (which, remember, is reversing) tends to throw the stern to port. At the same time the propeller blades on the starboard side are throwing their discharge current in a powerful column forward against the starboard side of the keel and bottom of the boat, with nothing on the port side

to offset this pressure. The stern, of necessity, is thrown to port.

This principle explains why a boatman will bring his boat up to a landing port side to the dock, if he has a choice. The stern then is thrown in toward the dock by the reversing propeller instead of away from it.

### With rudder to port

Going back now to the case where the boat has headway and the propeller is reversed—this time with rudder over to port, let us say. Here the situation is more complicated. As before, we have the unequal blade thrust and propeller discharge current both driving the stern to port.

In addition there are two opposing factors. If the boat has much way on (ahead) her left rudder tends to throw the stern to starboard. However, her propeller suction current is being drawn in from astern in such a manner that it strikes the back of the rudder blade, tending to drive the stern to port.

Which combination of factors will be strongest depends on the amount of headway the boat has, fig. 820. If she has been running at some speed, the steering effect of left rudder will probably be the dominant factor and her stern would be thrown to starboard at first. As this steering effect weakens with reduced headway, the propeller slowing her down, then the effect of the suction current is added to help the tendency of the stern to port until eventually, with all headway killed, even the steering tendency to starboard is lost and all factors combine to throw the stern to port.

## NO WAY ON, PROPELLER REVERSING

Now if the boat is lying dead in the water with no headway, rudder amidships, and the propeller is reversed, we again have that strong tendency of the stern to port as the

FIG. 820 Factors governing a boat's response to propeller and rudder depend, in part, on the amount of headway she has. Here, in close quarters, the helmsman slows down and keeps his boat under control. Effect of wind must be considered.

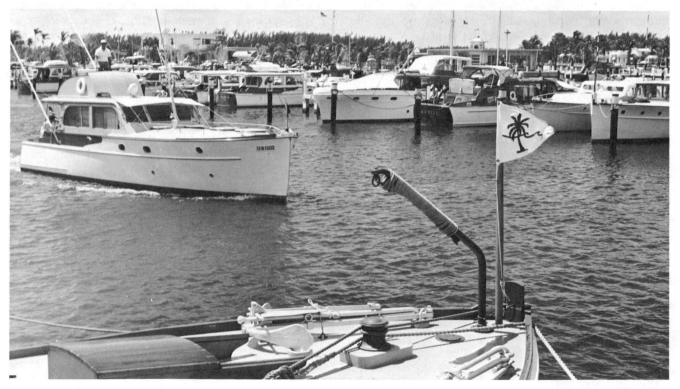

discharge current strikes the starboard side of the hull. You see, in each of the cases where the discharge current of the reversing propeller is a factor, the strong current on the starboard side is directed generally toward the boat's bow but upward and inward in a spiral movement. The descending blade on the port side, on the other hand, tends to throw its stream downward at such an angle that its force is largely spent below the keel. Therefore, the two forces are never of equal effect.

Until the boat gathers sternway from her backing propeller it would not matter if the rudder were over to port or starboard. The discharge current against the starboard side is still the strong controlling factor and the stern is thrown to port. (Come back to this later when we discuss the matter of turning in a limited space.)

## WITH STERNWAY, PROPELLER REVERSING

Now visualize the boat gathering sternway as the propeller continues to reverse. Here arises one of the seemingly mystifying conditions that baffle many a helmsman during his first trick at the wheel. The novice assumes that if he wants to back in a straight line his rudder must be amidships, just as it must be when he goes ahead on a straight course. Under certain conditions his boat may even respond to *right* rudder as he reverses by going to *port,* which is exactly what he doesn't expect, and if he is learning by trial-and-error he comes to the conclusion that it depends on the boat's fancy, while rudder position has nothing to do with control.

Let's analyze the situation, however, to see if he's right and whether there is anything that can be done about it. Fortunately, there is.

### Backing with left rudder

At the outset we can rule out any effect of wake current as that force now is spent at the bow. Considering first the most obvious case, let's assume we have left rudder. Here there are four factors all working together to throw the stern to port. Unequal blade thrust is pushing the stern to port; the discharge current of the propeller is adding its powerful effect; and now we add the steering effect of the rudder acting on the aft side of the rudder blade, against which the suction current of the propeller is also working.

Remember this condition well for it is the answer to why *practically every single-screw vessel with right-hand propeller naturally backs to port* easily when she may be obstinate about going to starboard when reversing, fig. 821.

### Backing with rudder amidships

Now, while backing to port, let's bring the rudder amidships and see what happens. Here we have eliminated the effects of suction current and steering from the rudder, leaving unequal blade thrust and the discharge current to continue forcing the stern to port.

### Backing with right rudder

Assuming further that we have not yet gathered much sternway, let's put the rudder to starboard and see if we can't possibly make the boat back to starboard as you might expect she should with right rudder. The forces of unequal blade thrust and discharge current still tend to drive her stern to port, but the suction current of the pro-

Boat Backing, Propeller Reversing, Left Rudder — Boat's stern goes rapidly to port

Boat Backing, Propeller Reversing, Rudder Amidships — Boat's stern still goes to port

Boat Backing, Propeller Reversing, Right Rudder — Boat's stern may still go to port though with sufficient sternway and Full right rudder, she should back to starboard

**FIG. 821 Three different situations where a boat is backing, her propeller reversing, with rudder set in various positions. Some boats back to port no matter how the rudder is set, but usually with right rudder and good sternway, they can be turned to starboard, though the turn to port is much better.**

peller wants to offset this. The effect of the discharge current is stronger than the suction so the tendency is still to port. Now, with sternway, the steering effect of right rudder is to starboard, but as yet we haven't way enough to make this offset the stronger factors.

## STEERING WHILE BACKING

Just about the time we are about to give it up on the assumption that she can't be made to back to starboard, we try opening the throttle to gain more sternway. This finally has the desired effect and with full right rudder we find that the steering effect at considerable backing speed is enough (probably) to turn her stern to starboard against all the opposing forces. How well she will back to starboard—in fact, whether she will or not—depends on the design.

All of this means that if the boat will back to starboard with full right rudder, she may also be made to go in a straight line—but not with rudder amidships. There's no use trying. She will need a certain amount of right rudder depending both on her design and the speed. Some boats, while their backing to port is always much better than to starboard, can be controlled with a reasonable degree of precision by one who understands the particular boat he is handling.

In cases, boats may even be steered backwards out of crooked slips or channels—not, however, without a lot of backing and filling if there is much wind to complicate the situation. Generally the trick is to keep the boat under control, making the turns no greater than necessary so as to prevent the boat from swinging too much as a result of momentum and making it correspondingly difficult to get her straightened out again.

In maneuvers of this kind it is best to set the rudder first and then get added maneuvering power by speeding up the propeller in the desired direction, instead of trying to swing the rudder after the propeller is turning fast either ahead or astern.

## WITH STERNWAY, PROPELLER TURNING AHEAD

There is one other situation to be considered, where we wish to kill our sternway by engaging the propeller to turn ahead. Regardless of rudder position, unequal blade thrust with the propeller going ahead now tends to throw the stern to starboard while the suction current is of no consequence. Unequal blade thrust may or may not be offset by the steering effect and the discharge current.

With rudder amidships, there is no steering effect and the discharge current does not enter our calculations. Therefore the stern will go to starboard. Now if you throw the rudder to port the discharge current of the propeller hits the rudder and drives the stern to starboard—even though the normal steering effect of left rudder would be to send the stern to port, with sternway. The powerful discharge current from the propeller going ahead is the determining factor.

If the rudder is put to starboard, the steering effect works with the unequal blade thrust tending to move the stern to starboard but the discharge current strikes the starboard side of the rudder and acts to kick the stern to port. Application of enough power so that the force of the discharge current outweighs the other factors will result in the stern's going to port.

## PROPELLER ACTION GOVERNS

From this analysis it will be seen that in a single-screw inboard boat one must constantly keep in mind what the propeller is doing in order to know how to use the rudder to best advantage. What the propeller is doing is even more important than whether the boat at the time may have headway or sternway.

To cite an example to make this clear, let's suppose you are backing in a direction that brings your port quarter up toward a dock. The tendency if you were to try to steer away from it would be to use right rudder. But the efficacy of that would be doubtful, because of the boat's inclination to back to port.

Therefore, we plan to kick the stern away by going ahead with the propeller so we set the rudder to port (left rudder, *toward* the dock), throw the reverse gear lever into the forward position and go ahead strong with the engine. The discharge current checks the sternway and, striking the rudder, throws the stern to starboard, clear of the dock.

It takes a lot of experience with any given boat to learn all her whims and traits—to know her strong points and use them wisely to overcome the weak ones. But boats, like individuals, do respond to understanding treatment.

# Practice at the helm

Proficiency in motor boat handling is a matter of 10 percent principles, 90 percent application of these principles in practice. Therefore, the sooner we get afloat and start experimenting, the better. We've absorbed enough of the theory to have a broad idea of what to expect in practice; the next step is to get at the helm of a boat and actually learn by doing.

## POINTS TO REMEMBER

Here are a few basic ideas to keep in mind, summarized from what has gone before.

• Remember that *the boat is always under better control with headway* than when she has sternway, because of the effect of the propeller's discharge current on the rudder when steering.

• Until the boat has gathered headway the stern has a tendency to swing (to starboard, with right-hand propeller) even with rudder amidships, as the propeller starts to turn ahead. *With good headway, rudder angle is the principal factor affecting control.*

• *Backing, there is a strong tendency to go to port* regardless of rudder angle, except (ordinarily) with full right rudder and considerable sternway. To back in a straight line you need a certain amount of right rudder varying, probably, with the speed.

• *With no way on there is no rudder control,* yet the stern can be kicked rapidly to port or starboard by putting the rudder over and applying plenty of power before the boat has a chance to gather way.

• *With left-hand propeller, the boat's reaction will be contrary to that outlined for the right-hand propeller.*

## THE FIRST TIME OUT

The first step in applying these principles will be to take the boat out in open water—preferably on a day when there is little wind and no current. These factors should be ruled out at first and studied separately later, after the boat's normal reactions are fully understood.

With unlimited room to maneuver and no traffic to worry about, try putting the boat through all the maneuvers already discussed. Practice with every combination of

FIG. 822 In channels like this, speed must be held down to avoid damage to other craft and discomfort to their passengers. A boat is liable for damage caused by her wake.

conditions—with headway, sternway, and no way on; with right-rudder, left rudder and rudder amidships; with propeller turning in the direction of the boat's way, and also those cases where the propeller is turning opposite to the direction of the boat's way.

In each of these maneuvers note whether the rudder or propeller has the greater effect; note, too, how changing the speed alters the boat's response. Put the rudder hard over each way and see what happens when considerable power is applied before the boat has any way on.

Practice turns to determine the size of the boat's turning circle and the space required to bring the boat to a full stop with varying amounts of way, up to full speed.

## GAINING EXPERIENCE

Later, when these fundamentals are mastered, go out again and observe how wind and current and sea alter the situation. Note how she tends to back into the wind until good steerageway is reached. How, if she is lying in the trough in a seaway, she tends to stay there with rudder amidships, because wave action is stronger than her natural tendency in smooth water to back to port.

Watch too how her stern starts to settle, and the bow comes up, when you get into shoal water. If there's just enough water to permit her to run without grounding, a wave will pile up on her quarter, steepest on the shallower side, as the natural formation of the wake is disturbed.

You should, of course, pick your maneuvering grounds from the chart to avoid danger of grounding, but if you see the first wave of your wake stretching away on the quarter in a sharp inverted V, tending to break at the top, beware of shoal water on that side.

## GETTING UNDER WAY

Whenever you are about to get under way, assuming that you are starting a cold motor, don't spend too much time at the dock or mooring "warming up." There are a few things to check before getting under way and by the time these have been taken care of you will be ready to cast off and let the warming up of the motor be accomplished under load, at about half speed. Long periods of idling are bad for the clutch and the motor will warm up better and quicker with the propeller engaged.

Before casting off, check the oil pressure and see that the cooling water is circulating. In most all marine installations sea water is circulated through the engine water jackets. Leaving the jackets, part or all of this water goes into the exhaust to be discharged overboard. Until this water flows from the exhaust pipe it is unsafe to get under way.

If the water doesn't circulate, investigate at once as overheating can cause much damage, especially if the cold water is suddenly picked up and pumped into the hot cylinder block. Cracking of the casting might result.

Never race the motor as it idles, especially when cold. If the propeller is the right size and the throttle stop properly set, the motor should be able to take the propeller when the clutch is engaged at idling speeds. Boats don't require transmissions with a change of speeds as in cars, because the propeller slip automatically takes care of picking up the load gradually as the clutch is engaged.

After the clutch is in, the throttle (which almost invariably is hand-operated) can be opened gradually. Roughly speaking, normal cruising should be done at about two-thirds or three-quarters throttle. The extra few hundred revolutions available at wide open throttle seldom yield an increase in speed proportionate to the extra power required and the corresponding increase in fuel consumption. In congested waterways speed should be moderate, taking care that no damage is done by the wake, fig. 822.

One caution to observe when first learning to maneuver the boat is to avoid operating at too high a speed. Later, after you have become more familiar with the boat and its response to wheel and throttle, you will be able to use more power in certain situations—to accomplish a quick turn, for example—without getting into a jam.

## CHECKING HEADWAY

Before attempting the maneuver of picking up a mooring you will want to experiment with the technique of checking the boat's headway while she is out in open water. Having no brakes, you must reverse the propeller to bring the boat to a stop. In by-gone days when many boats had no reverse gears the engine itself had to be stopped, permitting the boat to coast up to a landing, and it was often quite a trick to estimate exactly when the ignition should be cut. Reverse gears make the problem relatively simple.

Your experiments will show how effective the propeller is in killing the boat's headway. Generally speaking the larger diameter propellers, acting on a large volume of water, will exert the greatest effect. Small propellers, poorly matched to heavy hulls, may churn up much water before they are able to overcome the boat's momentum.

Many fast boats can be stopped in an incredibly short distance. When their throttles are closed, the boat changes her trim suddenly and headway is quickly lost, even before the propellers are reversed.

Whenever it is necessary to go from forward into reverse or vice versa, close the throttle to slow the engine down while going through neutral. If you make a practice of cracking the reverse gear from full ahead to full astern, look out for trouble. This is hard on the gear even if it doesn't fail—which it might do just when you're counting on it most.

FIG. 823A

Boat starts turn at left side of channel (1) allowing room for stern to swing to port. Headway is checked at (2) by reversing propeller.

FIG. 823B

Rudder is kept to starboard (right rudder) throughout the maneuver. Unequal blade thrust and propeller discharge current force stern to port as boat backs from (2) to (3), propeller reversing.

FIG. 823C

Going ahead again, sternway is checked at (3) and propeller turning ahead kicks stern to port as shown at (4) before the boat has had a chance to gather headway.

FIG. 823D

Reversing once more, headway is checked at (4) and boat backs to (5). If necessary, alternate going ahead and backing can be repeated. Space available for the turn governs this. Turning in two boat lengths is easy.

FIG. 823

At (5) boat is in a position to go ahead with right rudder, bringing it amidships at (6), where she i ready to proceed, having re versed her course 180° fro her original position at (1

## TURNING IN CLOSE QUARTERS

Turning a boat in a waterway not much wider than the boat's length often seems a bugbear to the novice but, once he has mastered the technique, it's no more difficult than turning a car on a narrow road.

Take a look at fig. 823. The situation sketched might apply in many cases. Perhaps you've run to the head of a dead-end canal and must turn around. Or possibly the waterway is a narrow channel, flanked by shoals. In the former case you must allow room so the swinging stern doesn't hit the canal bulkhead; in the latter, a similar allowance must be made to avoid throwing the stern up on shoal water.

Referring to fig. 823A, we start at (1), on the left side of the channel, running at slow speed. Putting the rudder hard over to starboard, the boat swings toward position (2), her headway being checked by reversing. *Always* execute this maneuver (if the propeller is right-handed) by going ahead to starboard, backing to port, to take advantage of the boat's natural tendency, as explained before.

Now (see 823B) *leave the wheel hard over to starboard* (right rudder). Normally you would expect to use left rudder in backing from (2) to (3), but this is unnecessary as the boat has no chance to gather sternway. As the reversing propeller stops the boat at (2), open the throttle for an instant and the stern will be kicked around to port to position (3).

Any attempt to shift from right rudder while going ahead to left rudder while going astern only results in extra gymnastics at the wheel at a time when you want your hands free for the throttle and reverse gear lever.

Throttling while we engage the clutch to go ahead, the sternway is checked at (3). Opening the throttle again, just for an instant, keeps the stern swinging to port toward position (4)—see fig. 823C. Now the operation described in 823B is repeated, backing from position (4) to (5) as shown in 823D.

If this happens to be a bulkheaded slip you are maneuvering in, allow plenty of room so that the port quarter is not thrown against the head of the slip as you go ahead

again at (5)—see 823E. The stern will continue to swing to port as the boat straightens away toward (6). At this point the rudder can be brought amidships, the boat having executed a 180-degree turn.

### Backing around a turn

Fig. 824 illustrates the successive steps required to work out another practical problem in boat handling. Suppose (see 824A) you are in a narrow slip or canal at position (1) and want to back around a sharp turn, to starboard.

Reversing with full right rudder, you will not be able to turn short enough to steer around the 90-degree angle. Most likely you will back to a position about as indicated at (2), gaining a little to starboard. Now (see 824B) by going ahead with left rudder the stern is kicked over to starboard, placing the boat at (3).

Reversing once more, with full right rudder, the boat backs to (4), necessitating our going ahead once more with left rudder. This puts the boat at (5) (824D) in a position to back down on the new course.

Note that if she is expected to back down in a straight line from (5) she will need right rudder, though not necessarily hard over.

### Backing to port from a slip

Fig. 825 illustrates a variation of the maneuver just described. Suppose the boat is lying in a slip, at A, and wishes to back out into the channel, space being limited. Fig. 824 showed how it would be necessary to work her around if the turn were to starboard. In fig. 825 her problem would be exactly the same if she had to back around in the direction of C.

However, if there is a choice, and she can back out to port, the probability is that with left rudder she will work around from A to B without any special maneuvering. To do it, her initial position in the slip must be about as shown at A with some clearance on her port side, but considerably more on the starboard side.

Clearance on the port side is needed because in reversing her stern immediately starts to move to port. More clearance on the starboard side is necessary because the

**FIG. 824A**

To back around to starboard, where space is limited, as in a slip, boat starts at (1) with right rudder, and backs to (2). She cannot turn short to starboard.

**FIG. 824B**

At (2) rudder is shifted to port and, with full left rudder, stern is kicked around to starboard by going ahead strong for a few revolutions of the propeller.

**FIG. 824C**

From position (3) boat can be backed down to (4) by reversing with full right rudder. Boat may back nearly in a straight line or gain a little to starboard.

**FIG. 824D**

At (4) wheel is swung hard over again, to give left rudder, while propeller, turning ahead, moves boat to (5). Backing down from (5) she will need right rudder to hold a straight course.

**FIG. 825**

Boat should make a short turn to port from A to B, when reversing with left rudder, but watch points X and Y.

bow will swing over toward point (x) as she backs.

In fact, points (x) and (y) are the ones to watch in executing this maneuver. If the boat shouldn't turn as short as expected, and doesn't swing directly from A to B, but takes a position as shown by the dotted lines at A', the starboard bow is in danger of touching at (x) and the starboard quarter at (y). This could be corrected at A' by going ahead with the propeller a few revolutions, using right rudder, to kick the stern over to port. This must be done carefully as there is no latitude here for much headway.

Having straightened her up, you could then back with left rudder to B and finally square away with rudder amidships to proceed toward C.

## LEAVING A MOORING

For permanent berths, boats lie either at docks or moorings. Most yacht clubs have anchorages for members' boats, using mushroom anchors and mooring buoys to which the boat is secured by a pennant or mooring line over the forward bitt.

Getting away from the mooring when you are about to start a cruise is among the simplest of maneuvers, yet there is a right and a wrong way to go about it. The principal hazard in doing it wrong is the possibility of getting either the mooring line or dinghy painter fouled in the propeller. Handling of the boat is dictated by whatever is necessary to accomplish this with a minimum of fuss.

As soon as the motor is running, shorten up the dinghy painter so that the reversing propeller cannot pull any slack down into it, to be hopelessly fouled around the shaft and wheel. See that any boarding ladders, fenders or boat booms are aboard and send a man forward to let the mooring line go. The pennant usually has a small block of wood or metal buoy to float the end, making it easy to pick up again on return to the mooring.

In a river or stream where there is a current, the boat will lie head to that current (unless the wind is stronger). But in a bay on a calm day there may be neither wind nor current to move the boat even when the mooring line is let go. To go ahead under such conditions would almost certainly result in fouling the propeller.

To avoid this, back away a few boat lengths, far enough so you can keep the buoy in sight and allow sufficient room to clear it when you go ahead, with particular regard for any swinging of the stern. Whether you back away straight or turn as you reverse depends largely on the position of neighboring boats in the anchorage.

Until you are clear of the anchorage, run well throttled so as not to create a nuisance with your wake. Then, as you open up to cruising speed, the dinghy can be dropped back near the crest of the second wave astern. If she is astern of that crest, she will tow too hard, running "uphill" with bow too high. Shorten the painter from this point until the pull on it lessens as she flattens out to a better trim, but don't have her run "down-hill" either, if there is any tendency for her to yaw off the course. Exactly how you trim the dinghy by the length of the painter will depend largely on boat speed and sea conditions, fig. 826.

### When there is wind or current

When your mooring is in a stream or if a tidal current flows past it, the boat will be set back when the mooring line has been let go. This usually simplifies the problem of getting away; reversing may not be necessary.

In a wind (assuming the current is not stronger) the boat will be lying head to the wind. As she drops back from the mooring, whether or not the reverse gear is used, the bow will pay off to one side and shape the boat up to get away without additional maneuvering.

All boats with considerable freeboard have a strong tendency to "tack" back and forth as they lie at anchor in a wind, and the same is true to an extent at permanent moorings unless the gear is so heavy as to retard this action.

If the bow is "tacking" this way and you want to shape the boat up to leave the buoy on one side or the other, wait till the boat reaches the limit of her swing in the right direction and then let the pennant go. The bow will pay off rapidly as she catches the wind on that side.

Sometimes, if the boat isn't too big or the wind too strong, you can help to cast the bow in the right direction by holding the pennant to one side so that the wind will catch that side and cause her to pay off toward the other.

## PICKING UP A MOORING

Returning to the anchorage when the cruise is finished, approach your mooring at slow speed, noting carefully how other boats are lying at their buoys. They are heading into the wind or current (whichever is stronger) and your course in approaching the buoy should be roughly parallel to the way they line up-wind or against the current. Shorten the dinghy painter as necessary.

Now slip the clutch into neutral when you estimate that you have just way enough to carry you up to the buoy. A man should be stationed on the bow with a boathook to pick up the pennant float when it comes within reach. If you see that you are about to overshoot the mark, reverse enough to check the headway as the bow comes up to the buoy. If you fall short, a few extra kicks ahead with the propeller should suffice.

FIG. 826 Length of the dinghy painter will determine how well she tows.

Don't expect the man forward to do the work that the engine should accomplish in holding the boat in position until the signal is given that the pennant eye has been secured on the bitt. Watch especially that the boat doesn't tend to drop astern while the man forward tries to hang on with the boathook. Also try to avoid having the buoy chafe unnecessarily against the hull.

When running through an anchorage keep an eye peeled for other moorings so as not to foul or cut them. If yours is the only mooring in the anchorage, you will have to gauge the effect of wind and current on your own boat as best you can so as to approach up-wind or against the current or directly against any combination of these factors. Don't try to execute this maneuver with wind abeam or astern. When the pennant is secure forward, and only then, the motor can be stopped.

# Landing at a Dock

The knowledge you have already acquired in turning a boat where space for maneuvering is limited will stand you in good stead when you tackle the next problem of bringing her in neatly to a dock or float.

The factors involved here are, in part, the same as in coming to a mooring, with certain modifications. For example, when you pick up a mooring you have wind and current to consider, generally determining the angle of your approach. Wind and current must also be reckoned with at docks, but there are many occasions when the angle of approach to a dock is not a matter of choice.

With no wind or current to complicate the situation, landing, with a right-handed propeller, can be accomplished most effectively by bringing the boat in port side to the dock. Our previous analysis of propeller action when reversing makes the reason for this clear.

### Keep boat under control

Don't come in with a grand flourish at high speed but throttle down gradually to keep the boat under control, fig. 827. When you see that you have way enough to reach the dock, slip the clutch into neutral and use the reverse gear as and when necessary to check headway as the boat goes into her berth.

If your speed has been properly estimated you will be several boat lengths from the dock when the clutch is thrown into neutral. Coming in at too high a speed you will be forced to go into neutral a long way from the dock (losing maneuverability with the propeller disengaged) or face the alternative of trusting the reverse gear to check excessive headway.

This is a good time to exercise judgment, keeping the way necessary for good maneuverability, yet using no more

FIG. 827 This boat, properly, is being maneuvered near her berth at slow speed.

FIG. 828 When landing port side to a dock, approach at an angle of 10 to 20 degrees as shown. Discharge current of the reversing propeller (if R.H.) will set the stern to port, as at (2), even though rudder is amidships.

than required. Remember that just because a destroyer does her maneuvering at 15 knots it doesn't follow that it would be good seamanship to do the same with a little cruiser where 15 knots represents her maximum speed.

As the reversing propeller throws its discharge current against the starboard side aft, the stern is carried to port. For this reason it is customary to approach, not exactly parallel with the dock, but at a slight angle—say 10 to 20 degrees. Then as she comes up to the dock her stern will be brought alongside, fig. 828, with the boat parallel to the dock, properly berthed.

In docking, lines should be kept ready to run fore and aft and fenders placed if necessary to keep the boat from chafing against unprotected piles.

## WIND OR CURRENT PARALLEL TO DOCK

When the dock happens to be on the shore of a river or bank of a tidal stream so that the current flows parallel to it, it is best to govern the direction of approach by the current flow, even though this puts the starboard side toward the dock. Heading into the current will enable you to keep the propeller turning over slowly—right up to the moment of reaching the dock, if the current is strong enough.

The same is true if wind is the force you are opposing. If your course puts the wind over the stern you will have to make a wide swing, starting far enough from the dock to permit you to round up to leeward of it, coming in against the wind. To miscalculate here by not allowing room enough for the turn would be embarrassing, as you head for the bank with wind or current sweeping you downstream. Hence the importance of preliminary practice in open water, noting the size of turning circles under various conditions, before attempting the actual docking maneuvers.

In starting a turn like this, even at some distance from the dock, it will be necessary to throttle down long before the dock comes abeam. Otherwise the wash the boat throws may carry along and leave you wallowing in your own wake just when you're trying to come alongside.

In coming up against wind or current, you use that force to check your headway, instead of the reverse. Therefore, allowance usually need not be made for the effect of a reversing propeller.

## LANDINGS DOWN-WIND OR WITH CURRENT

Avoid, if you can, the landing in which wind or current is setting you down towards the dock in the direction of

your course. In cases of this kind you are dependent on your reverse gear and even though they are practically 100 percent dependable an error in judgment or minor motor ailment would put you on the spot.

However, you will meet such situations, where space does not permit a turn before docking. For example, suppose you are coming in to a canal lock with a strong wind astern. Hold the speed down to a minimum consistent with adequate control and by all means take the port side of the lock, unless there is no choice.

Plan to get a line out from the stern or port quarter as soon as headway is checked. If necessary, the boat would lie well enough temporarily to this line alone, whereas to get a bow line fast first and then miss making the stern line fast would be to risk being turned end-for-end by the wind. This has happened repeatedly to inexperienced boatmen on their first cruise through canals, to the embarrassment of other boats already berthed along the lock walls.

### Handling the lines

If you have a couple of hands aboard, assign one to the bow and one to the stern to handle lines, with instructions not to make fast until headway is checked. The seriousness of checking the boat's way by means of a snubbed bow line instead of reversing the propeller is only too obvious. If single-handed, you will have to work smartly, with a stern line fast to the after bitt coiled ready to carry ashore, and a bow line, preferably run in advance along the deck back to the cockpit. Such lines of course would have to be led outboard of all stanchions, to be clear when taken ashore.

The problem is no different if you are making your landing with a fair current. In either case you must be ready with the reverse on the approach, using it as strongly as necessary to hold the boat against its momentum and the push of wind or current. The propeller ordinarily should be turning over slowly in reverse for the last boat length or two of headway, the throttle being opened gradually and as needed to kill all headway at the right instant.

## WHEN BOATS LIE AHEAD AND ASTERN

Let's vary the problem by assuming that boats are already lying at the dock, leaving you little more than a boat length to squeeze into your berth. The technique is decidedly not the one you are accustomed to in parking a car at a curb.

Referring to fig. 829, boats A and B are already in their berths astern and ahead, respectively, of the berth we, in

FIG. 829 Landing at a dock between boats (A) and (B), C approaches at an angle. At (C-2), a spring line is run aft to dock from forward bitt. Going ahead with propeller and right rudder, boat swings into berth at (C-3).

boat C, want to slip into. The position of boat A necessitates our going in at a greater angle than if the dock were clear, and there is no room to go either ahead or astern once we have nosed up to position C-2.

Consequently a man is stationed forward to take a line (in this case technically called an after bow spring) leading aft from the forward bitt to a pile or bollard on the dock. He takes a turn around the pile and holds fast while we go ahead with the propeller, setting the rudder to starboard. The spring prevents the boat from going ahead and the stern is thrown in toward the dock until she assumes her final position against the dock, as at C-3.

As the boat swings in, the spring must be slacked off a little and often a fender or two will be necessary at the point of contact.

## USING WIND OR CURRENT

In a case such as that covered by fig. 829, with conditions the same except for a wind from the south (assume boats A and B are headed east) we could have used the wind to advantage in bringing the boat in.

Under such conditions the boat could be brought up parallel to her final position at C-3, allowing the wind to set her in to her berth at the dock. The bow, probably, would come in faster than the stern, but this would not matter.

During this maneuver, the engine would be idling and, if there were any tendency for the boat to go ahead or astern, it could be offset by a turn or two of the propeller as needed, to maintain her position midway between A and B.

### Balancing current against propeller action

A variation of this problem is sketched in fig. 830, where a current is flowing east. Here the boat is brought up to a position C-1 parallel to her berth at C-2. The propeller will have to be turning over very slowly in reverse (perhaps at the engine's idling speed) to hold her at C-1 against the current.

Now if the rudder is turned slightly to port the boat will tend to move bodily in toward the dock, though the stern is likely to come in first. An after quarter spring should be

FIG. 830 The boat can be worked into her berth, using the current, by setting the rudder to port and using just enough power to offset drift of the current. In this case, propeller must be reversed to hold her against the current.

run first, to hold the boat against the current as the propeller stops turning.

Only enough rudder and power should be used to work the boat slowly sidewise. Too much power will put her out of control and too much rudder may cause her stern to go to port too fast, permitting the current to act on the boat's starboard side.

FIG. 831 A berth at the leeward side of a dock, using a stern anchor.

Under identical conditions, except for a current setting west instead of east, the propeller would be allowed to turn slowly ahead, just enough to hold the boat against the current. Then, with rudder slightly to port, the boat would edge off sidewise to port, the bow coming in slightly ahead of the stern. The forward bow spring would be the first of the mooring lines to make fast in this case.

## LANDING ON THE LEEWARD SIDE

Sometimes you will run into situations where a pier juts out into the water, with wind blowing at right angles to it, giving you a choice of sides on which to land. If there is much wind and sea, the windward side can be uncomfortable as the boat will pound against the piles.

The rougher it is, the more important it becomes to take the leeward side. The wind will then hold her clear, at the length of her mooring lines. If there is much wind you will have to work smartly when bringing the boat up to such a berth and it will help to have men ready at both bow and stern to run the mooring lines.

### Bow line first

The bow line of course must be run first and made fast. The stern line may present more of a problem since the boat has had to approach at an angle to allow for the wind's tendency to blow the bow off. The stern line can be heaved ashore by the man aft to the other on the dock, after the latter has made his bow line fast. The bow line, if necessary, can be used as a spring to bring the stern in by going ahead with rudder to starboard, on the principle sketched in fig. 829.

This maneuver, single-handed, would be difficult. It could be accomplished by getting a bow line off to use as a spring, working the stern up to the dock with the power, and lashing the wheel (unless you have a worm-and-gear steerer) to keep the rudder to starboard while you get a stern line fast.

Often it is a question of just how smartly the boatman works as to how much maneuvering he must go through. If he knows his boat and his crew know their job, he probably will get his lines ashore fast enough so that the spring line may not be needed to get the stern in.

## STERN ANCHOR TO LEEWARD

Fig. 831 illustrates a method by which boats often line up at a dock beam to beam. Each has a secure berth on the leeward side of the dock and a maximum number of

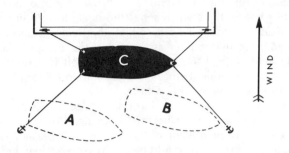

**FIG. 832** Laying anchors to windward from the bow and quarter to keep a boat from pounding on the windward side of a dock.

boats are accommodated for a given amount of dock space. The principal objection is the difficulty of stepping ashore from the bow.

The arrangement shown makes a snug berth even in a hard blow but a shift of wind might necessitate a shift of berth if the wind came abeam, throwing a heavy strain on the stern line and anchor.

The principle of getting into a berth like this is obvious from the sketch. Simply run up against the wind or current, propeller turning over just fast enough to give steerageway, and have a man let the anchor go over the stern, paying out line until the bow is close enough to get a line on the dock. The stern line is available as a check though the helmsman should make it his business to bring the bow up as required without over-shooting his mark and hitting the dock.

After passengers have been discharged the bow line can be slacked and the stern anchor line shortened, though this means that one person must be aboard. If all are to go ashore, adjust the stern line so that it just checks the boat from touching the dock. Then if there is room, carry the bow line off at an angle to another pile. This increases the clearance at the bow, and the wind or current acting on one side will help to hold her clear.

The sketch is not to scale. Often the scope of the anchor line astern will need to be much greater than that indicated to provide holding power in a given depth. Seven times the depth of water is a rough-and-ready rule to determine the scope of anchor lines though this is qualified by dozens of factors.

## USING ANCHORS TO WINDWARD

If you see that a berth on the windward side of a dock is inevitable and there is reason to believe that the hull will suffer even with fenders strategically placed, plan in advance to get anchors out to windward. This trick is not used nearly as often as it should be, especially if the boat is to occupy such a berth for a considerable time.

You will need a man on the bow and another on the stern to handle anchor lines, though in a pinch the helmsman can handle the stern line if he takes every precaution to keep slack lines from fouling the propeller. Referring to fig. 832, the stern anchor is let go from the quarter when the boat is at A, moving slowly ahead, to be checked at B, when the man forward lets his anchor go. If someone is tending the line aft, the helmsman can back a little as necessary to place the boat as the wind carries her down to her berth at C.

### Tend lines carefully

On the other hand, if the helmsman must leave his wheel and tend the stern line, then the boat can be jockeyed into position merely by adjusting the length of the various lines. This probably will necessitate hauling in some of the stern line while the bow line is slacked away. Throughout, the lines should be carefully tended. Dock lines can be run from the port bow and quarter.

Note that at A and B the boat is not parallel to the dock, but has been headed up somewhat into the wind. As she drifts in, after the engine is put in neutral at B, the bow will come in faster than the stern.

This plan should be used with a full understanding of the great strain the anchor lines are carrying with the wind hitting the boat abeam, especially if there is some sea running as well. The stronger the wind and the rougher the sea, the longer the scope required if the anchors are to hold without dragging.

If you plan to land on the windward side of the dock without using anchors to hold her off, make due allowance for leeway on the approach and keep the bow somewhat up to windward if possible, checking headway while abreast of the berth you will occupy. Then have fenders handy as she drifts in.

## WHEN CURRENT SETS TOWARD DOCK

Let's suppose now a situation in which the boat must find a berth off a dock in such a position that the current will be flowing from the boat toward the dock, fig. 833.

In this hypothetical case it may be assumed that the outside of the dock, which ordinarily would be the natural choice for landing, must be kept clear for ferries, perhaps, or other boats, while the lower side of the dock is also restricted for some reason. The only remaining berth is above it, at A in the illustration.

This situation should be sized up to determine exactly where the anchor is to be let go, with certainty that you will have sufficient scope. If your anchor drags here, you will be in a bad spot as the current will set the boat down on the dock. Therefore make sure that the anchor really gets a bite.

The spot where the anchor is to be let go may be approached from any direction as long as the boat is rounded up into the current. The procedure, if we wish to land bow to the dock with a stern anchor out, has already been outlined in fig. 831. This, however, is not feasible above the dock because of the difficulty of backing away into the current when leaving.

**FIG. 833** A situation where an anchor is let go and the boat drops back with the current to berth stern to dock.

## Tending scope of anchor line

After the anchor has been let go, the boat can be dropped back toward her berth at A, simply by paying out more scope on the anchor line. The current will do the work though the engine could be used to help control the

**FIG. 834** Making a landing with starboard side of the boat toward the dock. Approaching slowly at (A), nearly parallel with the dock, rudder is shifted to full left at (B), swinging stern to starboard. At this point, give the boat a kick ahead with the propeller (if necessary) to swing the stern. Then reverse to check headway.

**FIG. 835** A forward bow spring restrains this boat from moving astern. Clearance at her stern may be limited.

boat's position if wind tended to throw her out of line.

Just before the stern reaches the dock, a stern line can be made fast to a pile, after which the boat's position can be adjusted by the lines as desired. If the anchor is holding securely (and the berth should be left if it isn't) the stern can be brought close enough to the dock for passengers to step comfortably ashore.

The boat should not be left unattended in this position as she may safely be if berthed as in fig. 831. In fig. 833, where a convenient wing of the dock is available alongside the boat, a breast line could be run as shown. Then, before leaving the boat, the anchor line could be shortened to give ample clearance at the stern. Slacking the stern line would permit stepping ashore at B, after which the stern line could be adjusted from the dock.

The breast line is left slack but is available to haul the boat back in to B when boarding again after slacking the stern line. If the breast line is made fast too far aft it would be difficult to haul the stern in because of the "tacking" action of the boat in the current. Made fast forward of amidships, the boat will come in readily.

## LANDING STARBOARD SIDE TO DOCK

Though a dock on the port side is preferable, as already explained, a good landing at a dock on the starboard side can be made, if care is exercised.

Referring to fig. 834, the boat is approaching the dock at (A), nearly parallel to it, engine idling or turning over just enough to insure control.

Just before it is necessary to reverse to check the headway, the rudder is shifted to full left (at B) to swing the stern in toward the dock. If she does not respond, give the propeller a kick ahead while the rudder is full left. This definitely kicks the stern in and, as she swings, the reverse can be used to kill the headway.

# The Use of Springs and Mooring Lines

Lines play an important part in the handling of vessels at a dock. Obviously, the larger the craft the more lines are likely to be called into play. It would be absurd for the motor boatmen to burden his 30-footer with a spider-web of breasts, springs and other lines that would be appropriate only on a large vessel.

## TERMINOLOGY

Nevertheless, it is well to be familiar with correct terms and the functions of lines that may be used. They may come in handy some time—though not necessarily all at once.

Motor boatmen often speak loosely of bow and stern lines—and little else—depending on whether the line is made fast forward or aft and regardless of the direction in which it leads or the purpose it serves. To be strictly correct, according to nautical terminology, there is *only one bow line*. This is made fast to the forward bitt and run along the dock as far as practicable to prevent the boat from moving astern.

Conversely, a *stern line*, properly, leads from the after bitt to a distant pile or bollard on the dock astern of the boat, to check her from going ahead. The special virtue of

such lines as applied to small boats is the fact that, with but little slack, they may allow for considerable rise and fall of the tide.

*Breast lines,* on the other hand, lead athwartships nearly at right angles to the vessel and to the dock, to keep her from moving sidewise away from her berth. Large craft may use bow, waist or quarter breasts, depending on whether they are made fast forward, amidships or aft.

Naturally breasts on large vessels are more important than on small craft. If a vessel has a 100-foot beam, her bow is 50 feet from the dock and the bow breast must be somewhat longer than that. On a small boat with 10-foot beam, the bow is only 5 feet from the dock, and other lines may serve to keep her from moving away from the dock.

Another point to remember is the fact that a majority of small pleasure boats have only two bitts or cleats—one forward and one aft—to make fast to and no other cleats amidships or elsewhere, to which waist lines can be made fast.

As we shall see later, a small boat might be adequately moored with springs alone, using no breasts. Sometimes boatmen attempt to make fast to a dock with bow and stern breasts only and get into trouble because slack must

FIG. 836  Boat sprung in to dock by going ahead on after quarter spring.

FIG. 837  Bow swung sharply in toward dock by going ahead on after bow spring.

FIG. 838  Stern swings in when backing on forward quarter spring.

FIG. 839  Reversing on forward bow spring, the boat comes in nearly parallel to the dock.

be left in the line to allow for tide. If adjusted right for low water, they may be entirely too slack at high water and the boat gets a chance to catch in some stringer or projection of the dock when her bow or stern swings in.

## KINDS OF SPRINGS

Springs are not as long as bow and stern lines, but they lead forward and aft to check motion astern and ahead, respectively. There may be four springs—the *forward bow spring*, the *after bow spring*, the *forward quarter spring*, and the *after quarter spring*. Bow springs are made fast to the vessel at the bow, quarter springs at the quarter.

Forward springs lead forward from the vessel to the dock, so the forward bow spring, fig. 835, and forward quarter spring check motion astern. After springs lead aft from the vessel to the dock. Thus the after bow and quarter springs check motion ahead.

To keep this clear in mind, remember that the terms *forward* and *after* applied to such lines relate to the *direction* in which the line runs *from* the vessel, not to where it is made fast, the latter being indicated by the terms *bow, waist* and *quarter.*

We have already seen, fig. 829, how, by means of an after bow spring, the stern can be brought in to a dock by going ahead with rudder set away from the dock. In this case the boat lay obliquely to the face of the dock, with bow against it.

Now if the boat lay parallel to the dock but some distance off, she could be breasted in bodily by hauling in on bow and stern breasts, but with a vessel of any size this might require considerable effort.

### Effect of after springs

If it were possible to secure an after spring at the boat's center of gravity, she could be sprung in bodily to the dock and her parallel alignment (or any other position) could be held by means of the rudder as the propeller goes ahead, because the stern would be free to swing as the discharge current acts on the rudder.

Actually this is not feasible as we probably have only the bow and stern (or quarter) bits to make fast to, while

the center of gravity may be nearly amidships. Now if we rig an after quarter spring, and go ahead with rudder amidships, the combination of forces is such that the boat will be sprung in nearly parallel to the dock. Her stern will come in till the quarter touches the dock, while the bow may stand off somewhat, fig. 836.

If the rudder were put to port at position (1) in fig. 836, in the expectation that the bow would thus be thrown to port, it would be seen that the effect is negligible, as the stern is prevented from being kicked to starboard by the taut spring. Putting the rudder to starboard would throw the stern in to port fast, however.

Turning to fig. 837, let's rig the after spring from the bow and see what happens.

With rudder amidships, going ahead on this bow spring will cause the bow to be swung abruptly in toward the dock, as the bitt describes an arc of a circle, the length of the spring its radius. With left rudder, the bow turns in even faster as the stern is thrown to starboard further away from the dock. With right rudder some of the bow's sharp turn inward to port toward the dock is offset but probably not enough to bring the boat in parallel—unless the spring is made fast further aft.

## REVERSING ON A SPRING

The action is just the opposite if we reverse on a spring. Turning to fig. 838, note how the stern is swung sharply in toward the dock by the action of the forward quarter spring when reversing. Compare this action with that illustrated in fig. 837, picturing the boat turned end for end.

Now note what happens, as in fig. 839, when backing on a forward bow spring. The turning effect of the spring on the boat is not important here, and she springs in nearly parallel to the dock in an action which might be compared with that in fig. 836—once again considering the boat turned end for end.

## ALLOW FOR TIDAL RANGE

Boatmen located on fresh water streams and lakes have no tidal problem confronting them when securing to a dock with mooring lines, but failure to take this action into account in tidal waters can part lines, and even sink the boat.

Springs provide an effective method of leaving a boat free to rise and fall, while preventing her from going ahead or astern or twisting in such a way as to get caught on dock projections.

The longer a mooring line can be, the more of a rise and fall of tide it can take care of with a minimum of slack,

FIG. 840 How long spring lines act with great changes in tidal level. If water level drops 11' from E to D, a 30' spring line (A to B) would cause the boat to move about 2' astern of the position shown. Using a 32' spring (AC), cleat C is at F at the higher level. Principle is a right triangle ($32^2 = 30^2 + 11^2$) approximately. Advantage of long springs is obvious.

FIG. 841 Usual method of mooring a small vessel to a dock with springs. Lines required are (1) bow line, (2) stern line, (3) after bow spring, and (4) forward quarter spring.

FIG. 842 When a vessel is large enough to justify the use of breasts in addition to springs, her mooring lines may be used as shown—(1) bow line, (2) forward bow spring, (3) forward (bow) breast, (4) after bow spring, (5) forward quarter spring, (6) after (quarter) breast, (7) after quarter spring, (8) stern line. Don't burden a small boat with them all. Aboard ships, mooring lines are numbered from the bow aft, depending on where they are secured aboard ship.

FIG. 843 Use of mooring lines at a dock. Note eye splice of after bow spring (A) run up through eye (B) of forward quarter spring. Either can be cleared without removing the other.

fig. 840. Yet every line must be allowed slack enough so that all do not come taut together at either extreme stage of the tide.

Manila lines are left slack, too, to allow for shrinkage when wet or, if "made up" wet, must be checked when dry for excessive stretch. When nylon is used, generally the lines are "made up" taut, as they don't change much with the weather and will stretch to take up changes in wind strength. This point must be carefully observed in narrow slips or close quarters. Better tight than so loose the boat will move too far.

As a general rule, where space permits, a bow line should be run well ahead of the boat to the dock, and a stern line well aft. If these two lines are run off at an angle of about 45 degrees to the centerline of the boat, they will often prove sufficient for small pleasure boats, breasts being entirely unnecessary and the springs (one or two) resorted to only if the necessary slack of bow and stern lines allows the boat to move about too much at her berth.

## MOORING A YACHT

What might be considered a typical satisfactory arrangement of mooring lines on the average cruiser or yacht— even up to 80-footers—is illustrated in fig. 841. Only three cleats, piles or bollards are required on the dock to make fast to, the middle one of which comes about amidships. Both the after bow spring and the forward quarter spring can be run to this, while bow and stern lines run forward and aft, respectively, to the two other points on the dock.

Breast lines here would be superfluous, serving no useful purpose, and therefore should be omitted. In the service, 110-foot sub-chasers have found this arrangement adequate and there is no point in burdening smaller craft with more, except under unusual conditions. Some yachtsmen prefer to run the stern line to the outboard bitt.

Fig. 842 illustrates eight mooring lines that could be used on a large vessel.

If two lines are used anywhere with the idea of getting double the strength of one, they must be of equal length when strain is put upon them. Otherwise one carries the load first and parts, and then the other follows suit.

A boat moored as shown in fig. 841 will lie comfortably at her berth, regardless of changes in tide level, shifts of wind or current, or the wash of passing boats. This last factor can be a serious matter if lines are laid in such a manner that the boat is free to surge fore and aft because of too much slack.

### Two lines on one bollard

Frequently, mooring lines may have an eye splice of suitable size in the end which goes ashore, to be dropped over the pile or bollard. Fig. 841 shows both the after bow spring and the forward quarter spring secured to a single bollard about amidships. If these are dropped one over the other, the upper one must first be cleared in order to get the lower one free.

Inasmuch as one or the other of these springs may be needed to get clear of the dock, depending on wind and current conditions at the time, it is well to rig these so that either can be freed without disturbing the other.

Assuming that the eye splice of the forward quarter spring has been placed on the pile first, take the splice of the after bow spring and run it up from below through the eye of the quarter spring and then drop it down over the pile, fig. 843.

This way either line can be cleared without disturbing the other, though it may be necessary to use a little power to ease the strain on one if its eye happens to nip the other line between itself and the pile.

If a boat has much freeboard, the tide is high, and dock piles are relatively short, so that a mooring line leads down at a fairly sharp angle from deck to dock, there may be some risk of its slipping up over the top of the pile. An extra round turn of the eye splice taken over the pile will prevent this, fig. 844.

## HEAVING LINES

Part of the essence of good seamanship lies in knowing when a certain method of procedure is applicable to the size of vessel one is handling. Use of big ship technique on small motor boats is amusing to a seasoned boatman. Application of motor boat principles aboard a big vessel may be distressing to a ship captain.

So it is with heaving lines. When a pleasure boat is brought up smartly to a dock, there is rarely any need for springs or heaving lines, though a spring is often helpful in getting clear when leaving.

On small boats the mooring lines are properly kept neatly coiled until needed and then broken out of the locker for use in docking just before required. Manila lines of even 50- and 60-foot yachts are relatively light—say between 1-inch and 1½-inch diameter—and can be handled easily as the boat is brought alongside. Or, if nylon is used, ⅝" or ¾" diameter is an easy size to handle. A diameter of ½" or ⅝" is good for 30- to 40-foot yachts. Sending out any unnecessary springs or sending lines out too soon is not in order.

### Messengers and monkey's fists

The lines of a big vessel are heavy hawsers, hard to handle, and impossible to heave. Therefore they make use of heaving lines, which are light lines weighted at the end by a "monkey's fist" (an intricate woven knot which encloses the weight). This heaving line is bent to the hawser near the eye splice—not in the loop where it might be jammed when a strain is thrown on the hawser—and the line is sent from ship to dock, dock to ship, or ship to ship as soon as possible as a messenger, fig. 845.

FIG. 844 An extra round turn in the eye splice of a mooring line should be taken around a pile if the lead is high from dock to deck. This prevents it from slipping up.

On small boats this is more of a principle to remember for possible use than a precept to practice in ordinary run-of-the-mill docking maneuvers. Generally your crew can step ashore with necessary lines and there is no need for getting lines out at some distance from the dock, as in ship-docking procedure.

Even if necessary to heave your regular mooring lines on a small boat, they will carry some distance if properly coiled, half held loosely in the left hand and the remaining half heaved by the right, fig. 846, all uncoiling naturally in the air, without fouling up into a knot and falling short. If necessary, a weight can be added at times to carry a line but this is seldom used.

If, in passing a line for towing purposes, for example, you had to send a heavier line a long distance, then break out the heaving line principle and use it to good advantage.

## TURNING AT A DOCK

Turning a boat at a dock—called *winding ship* in the case of a large vessel—is easy if wind or current is used as an aid, or if the engine is used in the absence of these factors.

Fig. 847 illustrates a boat lying, at position (1), with her stern toward the current and the problem is to turn her to head into the current. The first step is to let all lines go except the after bow spring.

Normally the effect of the current will then be sufficient to throw her bow in toward the dock and her stern out into the stream toward the position sketched at (2). If any factor, such as a beam wind, tends to keep her stern pinned against the dock, the stern can be kicked out by going ahead easily with right rudder. A fender should be kept handy as a protection to the starboard bow.

FIG. 845 A monkey's fist carries this light heaving line to a lightship from a Coast Guard cutter. The end will be bent to a heavier line or hawser.

FIG. 846 Mooring lines on pleasure boats are usually light enough to heave, if held properly coiled.

141

Some steps should be taken to prevent the bow from catching on the dock as she swings, thus exerting a great leverage on the spring. A small boat may roll the fender a little and the boat can be eased off by hand, but in larger craft it is customary to reverse the engine just enough to keep the bow clear, as shown at (3).

As she swings in with the current, the fender should be made ready near the port bow as shown at (4). At this point she may tend to lie in this position, depending on just how much strain there is on the bow spring. If she does not come alongside readily, perhaps helping her by going ahead a little with right rudder, a forward quarter spring can be rigged. Then, by taking a strain on the quarter spring, and easing the bow spring, she will set in to her new berth.

Larger vessels executing this maneuver would get a forward bow spring out on the port bow when the ship reaches position (3), rigging it not from the extreme bow but a point further aft. Going ahead easily with right rudder on this spring alone (the first one having been cast off), the ship could be kept under control and eased in nicely.

In turning a boat this way it is always easier and better to make the turn with the bow to the dock rather than the stern. The procedure would be the same as outlined in a case where wind is blowing in the direction in which the current sets in the illustration.

## Turning with power

Considering a problem similar to that sketched in fig. 847, except that we assume there is neither wind nor current to assist in turning, the power of the engine can be used to swing her.

Going ahead on an after bow spring with right rudder (starboard side being toward the dock as in the figure) would throw the stern out away from the dock, a fender being used as in the previous illustration to protect the bow. In this case the stem is allowed to nose up against the dock, using another fender if necessary to cushion it.

FIG. 847 Turning a boat at a dock, using the current and springs.

As the boat swings toward a position at right angles to the dock, the spring will have to be eased. With the bow against the dock, engine going ahead slowly, and rudder amidships, the boat can be held in this position while the bow spring is cast off from the dock and re-rigged as an after bow spring on the port side. With right rudder again, the stern will continue to swing all the way around, fenders being shifted once more to protect the port bow.

[CAUTION: If nylon springs and lines are used, remember that they stretch and can store energy enough to snap the boat back when power is removed. If nylon is stretched to the breaking point, it can snap back with lethal effect.]

This principle has many applications and will be found useful in dozens of situations when the theory is understood. In a berth only inches wider than the overall length of the boat, without room to go ahead and astern, she can be turned end for end with no line-hauling or manual effort of any kind.

If there happens to be wind or current holding her against the dock, the first half of this maneuver may be used to get the stern out into the stream, preliminary to backing away when ready to get clear of the dock.

# Getting Clear of a Dock

When the master of a ship takes his vessel out of her berth at a dock, he speaks of "undocking," a term the appropriateness of which may be questioned when speaking of small pleasure boats. To some boatmen, "undocking" a 20-footer sounds affected.

As a matter of strict terminology, in fact (especially where ships are concerned) purists never refer to a "dock" when, technically, they mean "pier" or "wharf." The reader may decide as to whether he wants to refer to his "2-by-4" structure as a "wharf."

Elsewhere we have discussed the technique of backing a boat out of her slip, turning either to port or starboard, preparatory to getting under way. A variation of this is illustrated in fig. 848, where the boat is pictured lying in a slip at right angles to the outer side of a dock.

## BACKING AROUND

The problem may be to back her around so as to have her lying along the outside of the dock, or the principle might be used as a method of backing clear of the slip, preliminary to getting under way, especially if there is little

FIG. 848 Use of a forward quarter spring when backing a boat out around the end of a dock. When spring is taut, boat reverses with full right rudder.

room for maneuvering. The idea in this case is to use a forward quarter spring.

At (A) in the illustration, the boat is shown lying starboard side to the dock. The first step is to make the spring ready from a point near the corner of the dock to the after bitt, either amidships if there is only one, or the bitt on the starboard quarter, if there are two.

With the spring ready, but left slack and tended, the bow line is cast off, or slacked away and tended by a man on the dock and the boat is backed easily with full right rudder. At (B), a strain is taken on the spring to prevent her from backing further and this causes her to pivot as the stern is pulled around to starboard, as at (C). As she continues to back toward (D), the boat assumes a position parallel to the outer face of the dock.

At (D), the spring can be cast off the bollard and carried further up the dock to be made fast elsewhere as a stern line, if the boat is to remain in this new berth. The bow line in turn can be used to control the bow and prevent the boat's swinging too far; then made fast as necessary, perhaps to the bollard formerly used to secure the spring.

This method is especially useful when there is a breeze off the dock that would tend to blow her away if maneuvering without lines. No manpower is required and it can be accomplished leisurely in a seamanlike manner.

## GETTING UNDER WAY

In the event that the maneuver is used preparatory to getting under way, the bow line is not required. When the boat has pivoted far enough, with starboard quarter near the corner of the dock, the engine can be idled while the spring is cast off the bollard and brought aboard. Getting under way from such a position, the rudder must be set amidships till the quarter clears the dock, then full left rudder turns her bow out into the stream.

Spring lines used this way should have a loop of convenient size in the end, formed either by an eye splice or a bow line so as to slip quickly and easily off the pile, bollard or cleat, yet stand the strain of holding the boat against application of power, without slipping. The eye splice is best; the bowline is quickly turned into the end of a line having no splice.

*WIND*

**FIG. 849** Making a brief stop on the leeward side of a dock, boat can be held in position by going ahead on an after bow spring with rudder hard over (in this case, to port).

In this or any other maneuver involving the application of engine power against the spring, it is obvious that strain must be taken up slowly, easily. A sudden surge of power puts a shock load on deck fittings that they were never designed to carry—may even tear cleats right out by the roots, so to speak. If the fastenings hold, the line may part —perhaps with a dangerous snap, as the parted ends lash out.

Once the strain has been taken up easily, proper deck

fittings and good line of adequate size will stand the application of plenty of power, in those cases where the power is really needed. Bear this principle in mind when you are preparing to tow or in passing a line to a stranded boat with a view toward hauling her off.

## HOLDING WITH ONE SPRING

While we are talking of springs there is another trick worth remembering that deserves to be used more often, fig. 849.

In the illustration we assume that you have run up along the leeward side of a dock, to remain there for a short time while you pick up guests or perhaps put some one ashore. Instead of getting lines out to make fast fore and aft as you would for a longer stop, or expect the crew to hold the boat against the wind's pressure, try using one line as an after bow spring, as illustrated.

After coming alongside, rig the line and go ahead easily till it takes a strain; then go ahead, with left rudder, with power enough to hold the stern up against the dock. This is a maneuver that you can accomplish single-handed without too much difficulty, by having your spring fast to the forward bitt as you come in, with the end ready to pass ashore for someone on the dock to drop over a pile.

### Doubling the spring

Single-handed, you might prefer to use the spring double, with the bight of line around the pile and both ends of the line fast to your bitt. Then, when your guests are all aboard, you can slip the engine into neutral, cast off one end and haul the spring back aboard without leaving the deck. This would be helpful if the wind were of some force, the bollard well back from the dock edge, and no one ashore to assist. This way there would be no risk of the boat's being blown off as you step ashore to cast off the line.

In any case, when the line has been cast off forward, the wind will cause the boat to drift clear of the dock, the bow ordinarily paying off faster than the stern. Whether you go ahead or reverse to get under way will be dependent on the proximity of other docks and boats, etc., and whether your course is to be up- or down-stream. The same maneuver would be applicable if current were setting in the direction that the wind is blowing in the illustration.

## FROM A WINDWARD BERTH

When either wind or current tends to set the boat off the dock as shown in fig. 849 there is little difficulty in getting clear when you are ready to get under way. In fig. 850, however, we have assumed a situation in which the wind (or current) tends to hold the boat in her berth against the windward side of the dock. This is a bad berth if there is wind enough to raise much of a sea.

If the principle of the spring is not used in a case like this there may be a great deal of effort expended with boat hooks and manpower doing a lubberly job, with the possibility, even, of damage to the boat. Correct use of an after bow spring is the seamanlike solution.

Referring to fig. 850 (A), all mooring lines have been cast off except the after bow spring. If the boat has been lying to bow and stern lines only, the stern line can be cast off and the bow line transferred to a position on the

FIG. 850 How an after bow spring is used to leave the windward side of a dock. Boat goes ahead on the spring with rudder set toward dock, then backs away into the wind.

FIG. 851 Rigging an after bow spring.

dock as shown in fig. 851 to convert it into a spring.

Going ahead easily on the spring with right rudder tends to nose the bow in and throw the stern up into the wind away from the dock. If it does not respond with the rudder hard over, open the throttle to provide the kick necessary to work the stern around against wind pressure. Depending on the nature of the dock and type of boat, you may need a fender or two at the critical spots between dock and boat.

## Ease the spring

At (B), fig. 850, it is evident that the continued turning of the stern would throw a great strain on the spring. Therefore, it is generally necessary to ease the spring, yet keep the stem from slipping along the dock. One of the best ways to accomplish this is to have the spring made fast on the bitt by means of several round turns and a half hitch. With the half hitch cast off, the turns can be allowed to slip a little to ease the spring as necessary.

Here, again, remember the stretch of nylon with the possible reversal of direction when power is removed. In addition, if sufficient load is placed on a nylon line wound around a cleat or bitt the first turn or two may seize and grab the cleat so the line cannot be eased or slipped if there is a strain or load on the line. It may "jump" loose when turns are removed, causing a rapid and sudden change in control of the vessel by the line.

At (C), the boat has turned far enough so that the stem is not likely to slip, though the boat could be allowed to turn further till her stern was squarely into the wind. At this point the spring and fender can be gotten aboard and the boat backed away with rudder amidships.

## When single-handed

This is another of those maneuvers that can be accomplished single-handed with little effort if done in a seamanlike manner. If single-handed, the rudder must be set amidships when the stern has worked up into the wind, giving the helmsman a chance to go forward and cast off

the spring. Furthermore, it will not be easy for him to go forward and ease his spring, but this can sometimes be done by momentarily going into neutral, which allows the spring to pull the stem toward the bollard. This, however, may not be expedient with much wind, requiring the help of a man forward to handle it properly.

When the boat lies with head to the dock and rudder amidships, there may be a natural tendency for her to work her stern around to starboard, because of the effect of unequal blade thrust (with a right-handed wheel). This usually is of little consequence as it takes but a moment to get forward and cast off.

With a worm-and-gear type steerer, which holds its position against pressure on the rudder, or any other type of control that will maintain rudder angle without a hand on the wheel, it can be set in a case like this for just enough right rudder to compensate for the effect of unequal blade thrust.

## WITH WIND OR CURRENT ASTERN

The procedure just outlined can be used in getting away from a dock if the wind or current comes from astern—which is along the lines of the technique described in connection with fig. 847 for turning a boat at a dock.

Instead of merely casting off all lines and going ahead in such a situation, it is better to get the maneuverable stern out away from the dock, shaping the boat up to go astern first, before going ahead on the course. The reason, obviously, is that this technique gets the boat away from the dock where there is no risk of scraping her topsides as you pull away—especially if the rudder is not exactly amidships.

Turning again to fig. 850, but assuming the wind is east or that the current sets westward (top of diagram being north) the after bow spring allows her stern to go out into the stream, to be kicked out if necessary by power, going ahead with right rudder. Often in such a case the stern swings out without aid from the power.

When the boat has swung anywhere from 45 to 90 de-

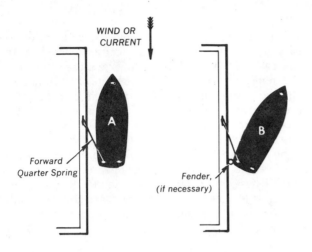

WIND OR
CURRENT

A

B

Forward
Quarter Spring

Fender,
(if necessary)

FIG. 852 When wind or current is ahead, backing on a forward quarter spring turns the stern in and bow out, shaping the boat up to get clear by going ahead.

grees, depending on circumstances of the particular case, the spring is cast off and the boat reverses far enough to clear the dock nicely when you go ahead with left rudder.

## WIND OR CURRENT AHEAD

Now, referring to fig. 852, let's consider the boat as lying with her bow toward the north. There is a wind from the north or a current which sets south so that its effect is in a line parallel to the dock and opposite to the direction in which the boat is heading.

If, in attempting to get clear of this berth, all lines were cast off immediately, the boat might drift bodily back along the dock or, if power were applied ahead, the helmsman would have to exercise care that the boat was kept exactly parallel in order to pull away without damage.

Again, it is more seamanlike to use a spring (unless the boat is so small that a person stepping aboard at the bow can merely push her bow out enough). This time we need a forward quarter spring on the port side. It is likely that this is already in use as one of the dock mooring lines, so all other lines can be cast off.

If the bow does not swing out at once with the effect of wind or current, backing easily on the spring will pull the stern in toward the dock, probably necessitating use of a fender on the port quarter to protect the hull.

In maneuvers where the bow swings in toward the dock, the fender is not always important if the bow has a good metal rub strip and the topsides are well flared. On the

other hand, in cases like the one under discussion, the stern comes in against the dock and a fender is usually in order, especially if the topsides tumble home. Good stout metal-shod rubrails are a fine thing on any boat that has occasion to maneuver much around docks.

In fig. 852, when the bow has swung out as sketched at (B), the boat has been shaped up to pull directly away by casting off the spring and going ahead with rudder amidships.

## MAKE USE OF FENDERS

We have noted from time to time in the foregoing illustrations the necessity of protecting the hull with fenders in maneuvering around rough dock piles, or in lying alongside other craft, fig. 853. Articles on equipment have repeatedly pointed out the desirability of carrying plenty of good fenders, but often the equipment actually provided falls far short of being adequate.

The standard types of yacht fenders are satisfactory if large enough and provided in sufficient number. When a boat lies at a dock with no motion, except the rise and fall of tide and the flow of current, even the lightest of guardrails may be alright. But you can't count on these ideal conditions to prevail at all times.

The combination of topsides that are heavily flared forward, tumble home aft, high superstructure that reaches out practically to the deck edge, and comparatively light guard moldings, possibly of wood not even metal-shod with half-oval, all make for potential damage when the boat starts to roll and pound against piles, either as a result of the swell created by passing craft or wave action from the wind or a ground swell.

The ordinary fenders (not "bumpers") for pleasure boats are of several types of construction—canvas covers filled with ground cork for small craft; woven manila or cotton covers, also cork-filled; and all manila rope, braided so that no central core or filler is required. Newer types, fig. 854, include those of synthetic or rubber construction containing air or minute gas-filled cells; others have canvas covers enclosing sponge rubber, shredded rubber or cork and rubber. Kapok is also used as a filling.

The smallest of these fenders sometimes have a grommet, eye or rope ring at one end only, to take the pennant by which it is suspended from fender hooks on the boat. Better practice is to have an eye at each end so that the fender can be rigged horizontally as well as vertically, sometimes by hanging it over the pile, instead of from the

FIG. 853 Rafted boats properly protected by substantial fenders.

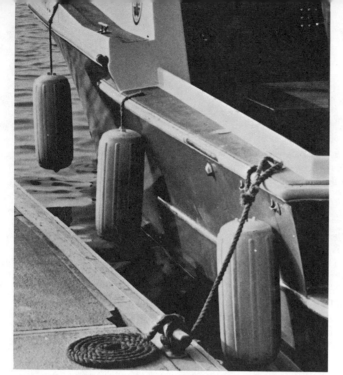

FIG. 854 Light-weight pneumatic fenders which can be inflated to various pressures for the service required. Lines may be run through them lengthwise to hang them horizontally.

boat where it moves as the boat moves. Some modern fenders have a longitudinal hole through which a line can be run, especially convenient when the fender is used horizontally.

Half a dozen substantial fenders are not too many to carry and if the boat is equipped with few, or no, hooks, go over it with a critical eye to see that stout fender hooks are placed where needed.

### Sideboards or fenderboards

The solution to many problems of protecting the hull has been found in the use of sideboards or fenderboards,

carried aboard in addition to a full complement of good heavy fenders. Yachtsmen have carried such boards in some cases but, due to lack of stowage space or other considerations, they have not always been of suitable size.

If fenders are hung vertically from the boat's side, they give protection in cases where there is a horizontal stringpiece to bear against as the boat moves fore and aft. If there are vertical piles to lie against, vertical fenders cannot be expected to stay exactly in place. Movement of the boat fore and aft shifts them between the piles and their value is destroyed. Hanging the fender horizontally by both ends is only a slight improvement and then only if hung on the pile where it is independent of the boat's movement fore and aft. As a matter of fact, even this

FIG. 855 A side board or plank used in conjunction with ordinary fenders proves invaluable in cases where adequate protection to the hull cannot be provided by fenders alone. The rubber cushion-board illustrated is encased in a thick cover of tough white Nordel rubber with two rubber cushions to absorb the shock of impact.

doesn't provide well for rise and fall of the tide.

The applicability of sideboards and fenders to boats lying side by side is easily seen. If each craft suspends several fenders over the side with a horizontal sideboard to bear directly against the board of the other, each is as comfortable as though moored to a dock and there is no possibility of damage even to high rolling superstructures because the hulls are held well apart.

The method of rigging sideboards is illustrated in fig. 855.

## Maneuvering at Slips in Tight Quarters

Some berths provide for piles to tie to, lying off a dock so that boats lie beam to beam, each occupying its own individual slip. In one variation of this, catwalks are provided between the various boats to allow more convenient access to each.

### A BERTH BETWEEN PILES

Figure 856 illustrates a problem where a boat must be backed into such a berth in a basin. Complicating the situation is a bulkhead along the east (leeward) and south sides, which prevents approach from any direction except west, down-wind.

If the space between piles and the south bulkhead is sufficient to allow the boat to make a turn, going ahead with right rudder, as in 2-3-4-5, she may round up this way, until, as in (5), she has headed partly into the wind.

If space, turning power, or wind prevent her from getting around any further than the position sketched at (4), her position is awkward as the wind will tend to blow her bow down to leeward faster than the stern so that her angle of approach will not conform with the path sketched

at 6-7-8. In that case, she would have to work out another technique.

Assuming that she can round up under power to position (5) with right rudder, she has been placed so that she can back along the line 6-7-8 without shifting her rudder. Remembering that the stern normally tends to port, and that with full right rudder she might back practically in a straight line, it can be seen how her position at (5) allows

FIG. 856 Backing into a berth in a basin between piles, where space allows a turn ahead under power to maneuver the bow partly up into the wind.

**FIG. 857** A variation of the situation sketched in Fig. 856. Here springs are used on the piles, on the assumption that the boat has insufficient room to maneuver to get into position (5), figure 856.

WIND

**FIG. 858** In this case, arrangement of bulkheads in the basin permits approach against the wind, varying the technique employed to back into the slip.

WIND or CURRENT

**FIG. 859** How to get clear of a pile when pinned against it by wind or current.

for the wind to blow the bow down to leeward.

At (7) her bow should still be somewhat up into the wind, and her starboard quarter close to the pile (F). Having her head up into the wind more than is shown at (7) is alright as a kick ahead with left rudder will straighten her out to exactly the right angle. If that kick throws her stern too close to the pile (F), idling a moment allows the wind to carry her down into position.

As she passes pile (F), a line should be passed to it—or picked up if one is attached to the pile—and made fast forward when a man at the stern has been able to get another line on cleat (I). Lines to cleats (G) and (H) can be run at leisure.

Before the line to (G) is fast, backing easily draws the stern close enough for a man to step ashore from the stern. Adjusting and securing the line at (G) after all are ashore prevents the boat from going too far astern.

## Using springs to the piles

With a good breeze, it might be impossible to get the bow around as shown at (5). In that case there is an alternative, using springs. You might approach close to the line of piles A B C D with the intent of bringing her up alongside piles (C) and (D), heading east, as at position (1), fig. 857. Now run an after bow spring, doubled, from the bitt around pile (D) and back to the bitt. Going ahead easily with left rudder will cause the stern to swing around to the south as at (2). Engine idling, she will swing completely around and if the spring is slacked a little she will lie starboard side against piles (E) and (F), as at (3). It may be necessary to back a little between positions (2) and (3).

Next rig a forward quarter spring on the starboard side to pile (F) and cast off the bow line to (D). The reason why this was doubled is now evident, as you can get the line back aboard by casting off the second hitch.

Reversing on the quarter spring throws her bow to the south and her stern in toward her berth as at (4). This spring can be carried forward by a crewman walking along the starboard side to the bow, where it becomes the forward bow spring to (F) when secured to the forward bitt.

## Approaching up-wind

In fig. 856 and 857, if this were not a closed basin, so that approach could be made against the wind, heading west, it would be comparatively easy to swing up into a position approximately as shown at (7) in fig. 856, heading perhaps more closely into the wind—say a 45-degree angle

from the line of piles—with starboard quarter close to pile (F). This would have been accomplished by turning with left rudder as the berth came abeam.

Fig. 858 illustrates such a case. At (2) left rudder, while the boat is still moving ahead, throws the stern in toward the slip and pile (F) as at (3). Backing with right rudder brings her down to position (4), the bow sagging off to leeward somewhat, while the rudder is set to port and the propeller given a strong kick ahead. This throws the stern up to windward as at (5), shaping the boat up to back in with right rudder.

Between positions (4) and (6) it may be necessary to go ahead and back several times but in any case the combination of the engine kicking the stern to windward while the wind blows the bow to leeward can be used effectively to work her in neatly.

Another alternative, at (3), would be to pass a line around the pile (F) and hold on while the wind blew the bow to leeward just enough to shape the boat up, as at (5), to back in. A little reversing between positions (3) and (5) might be indicated. At (5), of course, the line from the starboard quarter is cast off and carried forward to become the forward bow spring on the starboard side, secured to pile (F) for mooring.

## Getting clear of a pile

In your maneuvering around piles, as outlined in foregoing illustrations, there is a possibility that you may sometime be caught in a position where the wind or current or both will act to pin the boat against the pile and hold her there so that she is temporarily unmaneuverable.

The solution to this predicament is to rig a forward spring from the pile to a bitt aft, preferably on the side of the boat away from the pile, as shown in fig. 859. Then, by reversing with left rudder, the boat can be wound around the pile and her bow brought into the wind or against the current as in position (2), properly shaped up to draw clear by going ahead with the power as the spring is cast off the pile.

In getting clear from this point, it may be necessary to use a little left rudder to keep the stern clear of the pile, but not enough to throw her stern so far over that the starboard quarter is in danger of hitting the other pile.

As a matter of fact, at position (2) the wind may catch the bow on the port side, easing the boat away from the pile, so that you will be in a position to pull directly away with rudder amidships—always alert, however, to throw the stern one way or the other if needed by proper use of the rudder.

## MAKING A TIGHT TURN

Earlier in this chapter when we were discussing the general principles of a boat's response to rudder action, we observed that speed has little effect on the size of the turning circle. The general rule is that the rudder angle will control the diameter of the turning circle; the faster the speed, the shorter the time in which the turn is completed.

While this is theoretically true, there are situations where a burst of speed for a short period may help the boat to turn within the limits of a channel or stream where she couldn't turn at low engine speeds.

Consider the following case in point. In fig. 860, we have a boat bound south in a narrow canal or stream with a strong northerly wind, her dock being on the west side. The south end of the illustration may represent the dead end of a canal or the stream may continue further. This is irrelevant except that if the stream widens further on it would be wise to go on down-stream and take advantage of the greater width for turning, then come back upstream against the wind to dock.

Preferably, if there is room, the helmsman should wait till he is beyond the dock before he starts his turn as this would allow more room for straightening out at the dock. Referring to the illustration, he has slowed down, the boat is under control and he gauges his distance from the east bank so that there is just sufficient room for the stern to swing to port with right rudder at (B) without hitting the bank.

From experience in this maneuver he knows that in the absence of wind he can round up nicely through track A-B-C-D-E-F with full right rudder at low speed. Now if he tries the same thing at low engine speed with the northerly wind, instead of moving from (C) to (D), the wind catches him abeam and tends to hold the bow down to leeward as at (D').

### Using power at slow speed

At (D') he would be in a bad way, forced to reverse to avoid hitting the west bank and fortunate if he could back

FIG. 861 A boatman's skill is often quickly revealed by the way he handles his lines.

out quickly enough to prevent his bow from being driven down by the wind on the south bank, if this is a dead end.

Therefore at (B), if the boat is moving slowly, a sudden burst of power at the propeller acting on the full right rudder will bring her around quickly. At (D) the helmsman must be ready to close his throttle in order to prevent the boat from gathering so much way that landing at the dock is difficult.

This is not a maneuver to be guessed at, but if you have occasion to make the same one repeatedly in bringing her in to her usual berth, you will soon get to know whether the strength of the wind will allow you to use these tactics or whether you must resort to some other procedure such as landing down-wind and allowing her to turn at the dock on a spring.

## PLAN MANEUVERS IN ADVANCE

In previous pages we have outlined most of the basic ideas or principles by means of which the average single-screw motor boat can be handled when maneuvering around docks and moorings. Obviously the number of possible situations, considering the differences in boats, and the strength, direction, and effect of wind and current is almost infinite. Usually, however, the application of one of the principles we have mentioned, modified perhaps to suit conditions, will permit a seamanlike handling of the problem.

Understanding these principles as a background, you will be less likely to work in opposition to the forces of the elements and will use the control you have over the boat with propeller, rudder, and lines to best advantage. The seamanlike solution usually requires the least manpower and is accomplished with a minimum of confusion, fuss, shouting of orders, and other unnecessary hindrances to an orderly accomplishment of the task.

Even though you know the principles you are to use in executing a maneuver, you will find that it pays to think

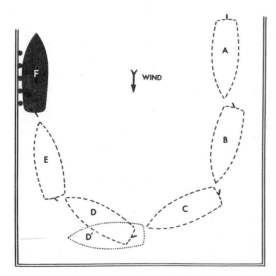

FIG. 860 Turning downwind in close quarters with wind astern. As boat approaches slowly at (B), a sudden short burst of power will turn her, when she may not be able to get around at slow speed.

out in advance the steps you will take, and their succession. With a plan of action clearly worked out, you can take each step slowly and easily, and have time to keep the boat under perfect control. This does not conflict in any way with the truth that there will be occasions that call for bold, swift, and decisive action. Rather, under such circumstances, the need for calm ordered judgment is accentuated.

The lubberly handling of a situation may eventually achieve the end that is sought, but often at the expense of strained lines, fittings, and equipment, not to mention the nerves, muscles, and temper of both skipper and crew.

## Common sense in executing the plan

If your planned line of action requires amendment or even complete abandonment because of unforeseen conditions, don't hesitate to act accordingly. If, for example, your plan for a clean approach to a dock has been upset by a freak current you couldn't calculate, back off and square away for another attempt. That in itself is good seamanship and good judgment regardless of how others may judge your apparent "miss" on the first try.

Common sense, if you act with deliberation, will enable you to work out a solution for any combination of conditions. Sometimes, understanding the idiosyncrasies of your own boat, you may put it through evolutions never mentioned in the books but if it achieves your end better than conventional practice, it's still good seamanship.

When you are at the helm and you have men on deck handling lines, fig. 861, issue the necessary orders to each so that all action is coordinated and under your control, instead of having two or three acting independently to cross purposes. This is especially imperative when your crew is not familiar with boats or your method of handling one.

## ORDERS TO THE CREW

On larger vessels here are some of the orders used in connection with the handling of lines at a dock. You can be the judge as to whether you consider them appropriate on your own boat, having due regard for its size and the number of men in the crew. The giving of such orders presupposes that crewmen will understand what they mean.

When docking, the order "Stand by to dock" puts the crew in readiness, each standing by his respective line, seeing that it is properly coiled ready to heave. If no men are available on the dock to receive lines, others aboard stand ready to step ashore to receive the lines.

At the command "Heave——(bow line, stern line, or whatever line is named)" deck men heave the line named to the dock.

"Take in slack on——" requires deckmen to take a turn on the cleat or bitt and pull in slack.

"Take a strain on——" means that deckmen are to pull lines named up tight, taking an extra turn if necessary on the cleat or bitt, but allowing it to slip.

"Ease off on——" means that the line should be allowed to slip off more freely.

"Hold (or snub)——" means to check the line temporarily.

"Secure lines" means to make fast permanently, adjusting to proper length and rigging chafing gear if necessary.

In each case the blanks above imply that a line or lines will be named to complete the order.

On leaving a dock, the order "Stand by the lines" prepares men on the dock to stand by bollards ready to cast off lines and men on deck to take them in when ready. This is followed by the order, "Cast off the lines" at which dock men clear the lines from the bollards and toss them to deck men, keeping them clear of the water, if possible.

## Easy does it

As previously explained, the procedure is so simplified on a small boat that docking may involve only the stepping ashore of one man each at bow and stern with their respective lines, others to be passed as and if required after these are secured.

One mistake that crewmen often make in helping to handle lines on a small boat is that, in their eagerness to assist, they insist on snubbing them immediately when as a matter of fact the skipper wants them merely to be tended and left slack so that his boat is free to be maneuvered further with the power. A case in point is where the boat is coming in to a landing at a dock and the bow man snubs his line instead of allowing the boat to ease up and draw alongside as the skipper intended.

One caution that cannot be emphasized too strongly is that, in handling lines, whether they are mooring lines, anchor lines, or any other kind, they must not be allowed to get over the side in such a way that they will be sucked down into the propeller and wrapped around the shaft and wheel.

## RESUME OF FACTORS AFFECTING CONTROL OF SINGLE-SCREW BOAT

To sum up all the effects which the skipper of a single-screw (R. H.) boat must have in mind as he maneuvers his craft, the following will provide a condensed summary.

I—ENGINE
   (1) *Going ahead*—No effect (or slight tendency of bow to port).
   (2) *Going astern*—Stern goes to port, bow to starboard.

II—RUDDER
   (1) *With headway*
      (a) Left rudder turns stern to starboard, bow to port.
      (b) Right rudder turns stern to port, bow to starboard.
   (2) *With sternway*
      (a) Left rudder turns stern rapidly to port, bow to starboard.
      (b) Right rudder usually turns stern to starboard, bow to port, if sternway is sufficient. With little sternway, boat may back in a straight line, or stern may even go to port.

III—CURRENT
   (1) Sets boat bodily in direction of its flow.
   (2) Other factors interacting (boat held, for example, by waist breast), current normally acts with greater effect on the stern because of deeper draft here.

IV—WIND
   (1) Usually affects bow more than stern, throwing it to leeward.
   (2) Engine backing, boat backs into wind.

V—TWO OR MORE FACTORS COMBINED
   (1) Helmsman must determine relative effects of each on basis of his experience with the boat.

149

## Handling Twin-Screw Boats

It is important to note that practically everything that has been said thus far in regard to the handling of an inboard boat has presupposed a single-screw craft with right-hand propeller, a category which includes a majority of pleasure boats.

Twin screws, however, are increasingly popular, partly because of their superior maneuverability. In the twin-screw boat, the propellers are usually arranged so that the tops of the blades turn outward, so that the starboard wheel is right-hand, the port wheel is left-hand. The effect of this is to give a maximum of maneuverability.

Going ahead with the starboard wheel for a turn to port, the offset of the propeller from the center line is adding its effect by throwing the stern to starboard. Similarly, offset of the port wheel going ahead helps the steering effect when the port propeller is turning ahead for a turn to starboard.

When reversing, the starboard wheel throws its discharge current against the starboard side of the hull to help the turn of the stern to port. Likewise, the port pro-

FIG. 863  Twin-screws give control independent of rudder position. Helmsman here is backing on his port engine, throwing his stern to starboard. Photo, courtesy of Vermont Development Department.

FIG. 862  For maximum maneuverability, twin rudders are placed behind propellers of twin-screw boats, in the discharge currents.

peller reversing throws its stream against the port side of the hull to help the swing of the stern to starboard.

The important factors in turning and steering are thus combined by the outward-turning wheels. The steering effect is exerted in the same direction as the turning moment caused by the off-center location of the propellers.

### THE ADVANTAGE OF TWIN RUDDERS

While some boats are rigged with a single rudder between the propellers in the midships line, this arrangement is more common in larger vessels. The trend today in pleasure boats is to use twin rudders, one each directly behind the propellers in the discharge currents, fig. 862. This, too, improves maneuverability by rudder.

It is readily seen that the location of two propellers, one each on the port and starboard sides at some distance from the center line of the keel, gives the operator of such a boat the means of throwing one side or the other ahead or astern, independent of rudder control, fig. 863. In fact, much of the boat's maneuvering at low speed is done without touching the steering wheel  as the two throttles

are the principal key to flexibility of control.

If there is only one rudder, a little thought will show that its chief influence in slow-speed maneuvering is felt only when it is placed astern of a propeller going ahead. Its effect behind a propeller reversing is negligible.

Visualize, for example, such a boat making a short turn bow to starboard, by going ahead on the port propeller, and astern on the starboard wheel. If the single rudder is put to starboard (right rudder) nothing is accomplished due to lack of headway. See (A), fig. 864. The rudder is set obliquely behind the reversing starboard wheel and there is no blade behind the port wheel to increase its turning effect. The port engine going ahead is trying to turn the bow to starboard yet it can act on the rudder blade only when the rudder is set for a turn to port, as in (B), fig. 864.

Putting it another way, with a single rudder (neglecting for a moment the action of the starboard propeller) if the port propeller is turned ahead to swing the bow to starboard, turning the rudder to starboard throws it away from and out of the port propeller's discharge current. If the rudder is set to port to get into that current, its steering effect would be to kick the stern to starboard and thus offset the tendency of the port propeller to swing the bow to starboard.

At reasonable speeds, the twin-screw boat can be handled by, and is responsive to, its rudder whether the blade area is all in a single midships rudder or divided between two. Maneuvering in tight corners, the rudder can be set amidships and forgotten while the reverse gear controls are handled to throw the propellers ahead or astern and the throttles are used to control the relative amount of power applied on each.

### TURNING IN A BOAT LENGTH

To make a tight turn, a single-screw boat must make a little headway and sternway as the stern is kicked around. Furthermore, it involves going ahead and astern with the propeller, even though the rudder is set to starboard (right rudder) throughout. The throttle, too, must be tended to

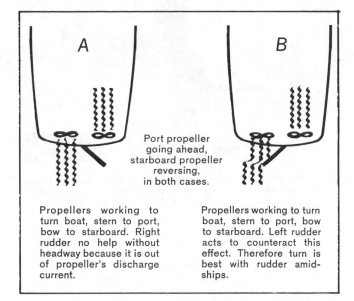

FIG. 864 Why twin-screw boat with one rudder is maneuvered at low speed with propellers, rudder being kept amidships.

Inside fig 864:

A

B

Port propeller going ahead, starboard propeller reversing, in both cases.

Propellers working to turn boat, stern to port, bow to starboard. Right rudder no help without headway because it is out of propeller's discharge current.

Propellers working to turn boat, stern to port, bow to starboard. Left rudder acts to counteract this effect. Therefore turn is best with rudder amidships.

makes some sternway as the reversing starboard wheel pulls her around, stern to port.

## ONE PROPELLER GOING AHEAD OR BACKING

Again, there is the alternative of casting the stern one way or the other by going ahead or backing on one propeller only without turning the other propeller at all. Some headway or sternway in these cases accompanies the turn.

Referring to (A), fig. 867, a kick ahead on the port propeller throws the stern to port, bow to starboard, as in a single-screw boat with right rudder. If there are twin rudders, right rudder helps this kick. A kick ahead with the starboard wheel throws the stern to starboard, bow to port, as shown at (B). Reversing the port wheel only, pulls the stern around to starboard and vice versa. See sketches (C) and (D).

When reversing with one propeller, the other being stopped, unequal blade thrust, discharge screw current and the offset of the working propeller from the center line all combine to throw the stern in a direction away from the reversing propeller.

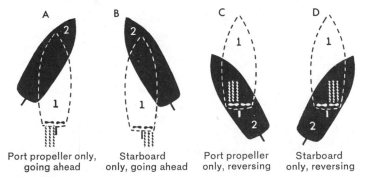

FIG. 865 In tight quarters, the twin-screw boat can turn in her own length. Here she backs on the port engine. Under perfect control, she could be made to complete a 180° turn, with starboard engine going ahead. With starboard engine idling, her reversing port engine would probably bring her up to the bulkhead, stern toward the transom of the docked cruiser. (Photo courtesy Palm Beach Isles Sales Corp.)

apply sudden bursts of power without allowing the boat to gather way.

In contrast to this, the twin-screw boat can be made to turn in a circle the diameter of which is only a little greater than her length, fig. 865. The turn to port is accomplished as readily as a turn to starboard since such effects as unequal blade thrust on two propellers rotating in opposite directions offset each other.

Turning bow to starboard, the rudder can be set amidships, while the port engine goes ahead and the starboard engine reverses, fig. 866. The engines will probably be turning at nearly, not exactly, the same speed. The boat drives forward more easily than it goes astern and the propeller at a given r.p.m. has more propelling power ahead than astern. Therefore the r.p.m. on the reversing starboard wheel may be somewhat higher than that on the port propeller, to prevent her from making some headway as she pivots.

By setting the throttle for the reversing starboard engine this can be left alone and the port throttle is adjusted till the size of the turning circle is established. A rate of r.p.m. can be found where she is actually turning in her own length. If the port engine is then speeded up a little, the circle is larger and she makes some headway. If the port engine is slowed down, the circle is also larger but she

FIG. 866 Turning twin-screw boat, bow to starboard, stern to port, in her own length. Rudder amidships, port propeller going ahead, starboard propeller reversing (probably at somewhat higher r.p.m. than port propeller). Changing r.p.m. can give her headway or sternway as she turns.

| Port propeller only, going ahead | Starboard only, going ahead | Port propeller only, reversing | Starboard only, reversing |

FIG. 867 What happens in a twin-screw boat when one propeller is thrown ahead or astern.

## USING SPRINGS WITH TWIN SCREWS

When a twin-screw vessel is lying at a dock and a spring is used to throw the bow or stern out as an aid to getting clear, one engine may be used. For example, with an after bow spring, going ahead on the outside engine only, throws the stern out away from the dock. Or propellers can be turned in opposite directions.

Sometimes a twin-screw vessel is gotten clear of a dock by rigging a forward bow spring and reversing the propeller on the dock side to throw the propeller discharge current on that side forward between the boat and dock as a "cushion." Naturally this is most effective if the dock under water is solidly bulkheaded rather than built on open piling. The discharge current from the inside wheel forces the boat away from the dock and the line is then cast off. Further reversing on the propeller nearest the dock while the other propeller turns ahead, as necessary, shapes the boat up to get the stern clear. The speed of the two motors will vary with conditions of wind and current and the rudder is left amidships till the boat is clear and ready to pull away.

## DOCKING A TWIN-SCREW BOAT

Landing at a dock, a twin-screw vessel will approach at slow speed at an angle of 10 to 20 degrees, as is the case with a single-screw boat. When she has just way enough to carry her in nicely, the rudder is swung over to the side away from the dock to bring the stern in as the engines are thrown into neutral. To check headway as she comes up parallel to the dock, the outboard engine is reversed.

Landing either port or starboard side to the dock is accomplished with equal ease because of the starboard propeller turning counter-clockwise as it reverses in a port-side landing, or the port propeller turning clockwise in reverse on a landing starboard side to the dock.

## STEERING WITH THE THROTTLES

In maintaining a straight course with a twin-screw vessel, the speed of the motors can be adjusted so that the leeward engine compensates for the effect of leeway. That is, the leeward engine can be turned a little faster to hold the bow up into the wind.

If she happens to sustain some damage to her steering gear, whether it be the rudder(s) or any part of the gear inboard, she can still make port by steering with the throttles. One motor can be allowed to turn at a constant speed—the starboard one, let us say. Then opening the throttle of the port motor will speed up the port propeller and cause a turn to starboard. Closing the throttle of the port motor slows down the port propeller and allows the starboard wheel to push ahead, causing a turn to port. And we have also shown that she is at no great disadvantage when she finally maneuvers into her berth after getting into port as the throttle and reverse gears are adequate for complete control here too.

## RESPONSE TO RUDDER WHILE BACKING

A twin-screw vessel starting from a position dead in the water, with both propellers backing at the same speed, is at a great advantage over the single-screw vessel as she can be made to take any desired course by steering with her

FIG. 868 Maneuvering his twin-screw boat, the helmsman can leave his rudders amidships, may even set his throttles, and handle the boat with a touch of one or both of his reverse gear controls.

rudders whereas the single-screw vessel, it will be remembered, is obstinate about backing her stern to starboard. In the twin-screw vessel opposite rotation of the propellers means that the forces which normally throw the single-screw vessel off course are balanced out.

In addition to use of the rudders, the twin-screw vessel offers the possibility of using her throttles to speed up one motor or the other as an aid to steering while maintaining her sternway or she can even stop one propeller or go ahead on it for maximum control in reverse, fig. 868.

While the twin-screw vessel backs as readily to starboard as to port, she is still subject to the effect of wind, waves, and current though the helmsman is in a better position to exercise control over them as we have seen in the case of leeway, offset by different engine speeds instead of holding the rudder offset from the midships line.

## OTHER TWIN-SCREW MANEUVERS

If one propeller is stopped while the boat has headway, the bow necessarily turns in the direction of the propeller that is dead. Consequently, if one engine of a twin-screw power plant fails, and the boat is brought in on the other, a certain amount of rudder angle on the side of the operating propeller is necessary in order to maintain a straight course, or some kind of drag must be towed on the side of the working propeller.

A basic principle in the maneuvering of a twin-screw vessel is to use the rudder primarily in relation to the direction of the vessel's movement through the water (that is, whether she had headway or sternway). Elsewhere, it will be recalled, the principle as given for the single-screw vessel was that the rudder should be considered in relation to the direction in which the propeller happens to be turning, regardless of whether the vessel has headway or sternway.

When a twin-screw vessel has headway, both propellers turning ahead, and a quick turn to starboard is desired, the starboard engine is reversed with right rudder. The fact that the vessel has headway in this instance means that the right rudder adds its steering effect to shorten the turn.

With sternway, both propellers reversing, if a quick turn to port is wanted, the port engine is thrown ahead, with left rudder. Again, due to the vessel's sternway, the rudder's effect is added to that of the propellers in causing a short turn to port.

If a twin-screw vessel has considerable headway and her engines are reversed with rudder hard over, the stern will normally swing away from the rudder (to port with right rudder and vice versa) until the headway is overcome by the reversing engines. After she has gathered sternway, her stern tends to work toward the side on which her rudder is set. Then the vessel's stern in the illustration just cited would eventually move to starboard with right rudder, after her headway had changed to sternway.

## HANDLING A LARGE YACHT

As a rule, most of our average sized pleasure boats are handled by their owners; the larger yachts are frequently in charge of professional skippers. It's of interest, nevertheless, to note an instruction technique regarded as applicable to craft in the 100-foot category when leaving and returning to a berth alongside other vessels.

In fig. 869 this vessel is the middle one of three tied abreast lying port side to a dock headed toward the beach. Let's call the boats A, B, and C. Our boat is B, the middle one; A is at the dock; C is the outside boat.

The engines are warmed up preliminary to getting under way and when they are ready lines are cleared as follows: First, C's bow breast is cast off from B's bow and run to A, forward of B's stem, with some slack to allow B to maneuver a little.

C now casts off all lines except the bow breast which has been transferred to A and gets a heaving line ready for use after B has pulled out.

B then casts off all lines securing her to A except an after bow spring which is slacked a little to allow B, going ahead, to get the bulge of her bow past that of A's bow and thus permit B to pivot better.

B now goes ahead 1/3 on the outside (starboard) engine and back 1/3 on the inside (port) engine. Two men are standing by with fenders. As B moves slowly ahead a few feet, the spring line takes the strain and the stern works out, to starboard.

### Backing clear

C is being swung along with B but no lines secure the two vessels and there is nothing to prevent B from drawing clear as she backs both engines 1/3 after having swung her stern far enough around to starboard.

With B clear, C heaves to A the line she has already prepared. At this point she can either run a stern breast to A and heave in on it or else rig an after bow spring to draw alongside A by using power. In the latter case, she will

**FIG. 869** Large twin-screw vessel leaving berth between two others in a slip. At (1) stern has been sprung out by going ahead on bow spring to (A), starboard engine going ahead, port engine reversing. At (2) spring having been cast off, she has backed clear with both engines reversing. At (3) sternway is checked and stern kicked around to (4) by going ahead on the starboard engine. At (5) she is straightened out and, after headway is gained, responds to her rudder which has been left amidships during the maneuver.

go ahead on the inside (port) engine and reverse the outside (starboard) engine. If the bow breast to A tends to check the swing of C's bow, it must be slacked. Back alongside A, C rigs all mooring lines to A as she was formerly secured to B.

B, in the meantime, has backed out into the slip and backs the port engine 2/3 while the starboard engine continues to back at 1/3. The effect of this will be to give her better clearance from the dock and swing her while backing.

### Checking sternway and turning

The boat draws well clear of the dock under this maneuver but presently gathers too much sternway so that the starboard engine is thrown ahead 2/3 which checks the sternway and causes her to turn more rapidly, throwing the bow around to port.

When finally straightened out in the slip, both engines are run at 1/3 ahead to gather steerage-way. Then both are stopped (idled in neutral in the case of a boat with reverse gears) while steering with the rudder and a long blast is blown on the whistle as a warning prior to leaving the slip.

Moving out of the slip, the current catches the port bow and tends to set the vessel back toward the dock so she is given a short kick ahead on the starboard engine to offset it. Clear of the dock, she goes ahead 2/3 on both engines.

### Returning to her berth

The same craft is now ready to return to her berth alongside another vessel. Keeping well out in the stream till the slip is almost abeam, she turns and passes into the slip about midway between the piers, favoring one side a little to allow for current. No abrupt changes of course will be needed.

Engines are stopped (or, with reverse gears, idling in neutral) passing the pier heads while the vessel is steered to a point just ahead of the other vessel's pilot house. The angle of approach to the other vessel should be small. If it appears that the angle is too wide the helm should be used decisively to place her in position in plenty of time to straighten out.

With reduced speed, the helmsman handles the wheel smartly, using considerably more helm to achieve a given response than he would need if the vessel had good headway. What he does is to get the bow to swing, then shifts the rudder smartly for a moment, then shifts back to the midships position.

Engines are kept stopped (or idling, as the case may be) as she comes in at a moderate angle, her bow about six feet from that of the other vessel. A bow spring is passed, slack taken up and secured. Now the outside (starboard in this case) engine is backed 1/3 while the inside (port) engine goes ahead 1/3. This is just a momentary kick to be repeated if necessary.

The effect of the reversing outside engine is to kill the headway and swing the stern to port toward the other vessel, assisted by the kick ahead on the inside engine. The last of the headway, acting on the spring, also contributes to the same effect. No heaving lines have been used during this maneuver and, under ideal conditions, only the outside engine will be called on for a short kick astern while the inside engine may not be needed at all.

# The Fine Art of DOCKING

*How large vessels are handled—as adapted to small-boat practice*

EVERY DAY, in hundreds of ports the world over, vessels are brought to dock, undocked, and moored. All manner of vessels, from 25,000-ton super-tankers to tiny harbor tugs, are handled expertly—even casually—by men to whom the sea is a profession. From all this, and often from bitter experience and mishap, comes a wealth of knowledge on ship handling which could well be adapted to use by the skipper of a small boat.

The purpose of this article is to bring out several of these ship-handling "kinks" which are particularly adaptable to small-boat maneuvering. They will ease the day-to-day docking of these craft—but, more important, aid during those times when foul weather and adverse seas make docking, more than ever, a matter of judgment and practical skill.

These are by no means *the* ways to dock a boat. But perhaps among them you will find one or two methods which will treat you well, or will be of particular use to your type of boat or waters.

To handle a boat, or a ship, you must first *know* it. Know *what it will do, how fast it will do it,* and *in what space.* No article or text can give you this knowledge—it can come only from actual experience and practice. But attention can be drawn to certain basics which will enable you to get much more from experience. Some of the more important of these. . . .

A. *The propeller controls the direction of a boat when docking, almost as much as the rudder.*

A vessel with a propeller that turns in a clockwise direction when viewed from astern with the engine turning ahead (called a right-handed vessel) is the most common. This vessel's bow will usually swing to port slowly when going ahead, even with the rudder amidships, *but* the stern will swing rather sharply to port when the vessel is going astern, often regardless of where the rudder is. For left-handed vessels the effects are reversed.

B. *This "turning effect" of the propeller is much more pronounced when going astern.*

Since much of a rudder's effect comes from the wash of the propeller rushing past it, if the engine is reversed this wash will be directed in a direction *away* from the rudder and much of the effect of the helm is lost. The propeller takes over in a pronounced fashion.

C. *Brief spurts of engine power may be*

FIG. 870-a  In this case, the slip is on the starboard side of a canal. The helmsman turns to port to place his boat in position to back into the berth.

## A Typical Docking Maneuver with a Modern Twin-Screw Cruiser

FIG. 870-b  Here he goes ahead easily with the starboard engine, his port engine backing. He turns without making headway and watches clearance at the stern.

*used to turn the bow or stern of the vessel as desired, without getting the boat under way.*

With the rudder to starboard, a brief spurt of the engine (throttle is opened momentarily) will swing the bow to starboard *but*, if the engine is cut off before the vessel gathers way, most of the power of the engine will have gone into turning the vessel rather than getting it moving through the water. The heavier the boat, the more this is so. Don't be afraid to gun your engine briefly to gain maneuverability. A boat's pretty heavy and won't shoot ahead the moment power is applied.

*D. The wind, tide, and current can often be as much help in docking as the engines and helm.*

Nature will often dock your boat for you, if given half a chance. Why waste gas and temper fighting her. A good policy many times is "Ride with the current."

Now to the actual processes of docking. These are presented in outline form to make it easier to grasp details without wading through a lot of text. The word "wind" will be used to cover whichever factor has the most effect on the vessel at the moment, whether it is actually the wind, or whether it may be tide or current. In calm or still water almost any of the methods outlined will work equally well. Boats are shown port side to the docks; for the reverse condition, simply reverse the rudder orders, but maintain the same engine speeds and directions.

## LEAVING A DOCK

### Alongside Dock; Wind Ahead (Fig. 1)

1. Single up to one stern line. No power, no rudder.
2. Let the wind swing the bow out, perhaps helping with boathook or with brief *spurts* ahead against a rudder hard right. (But watch port quarter.)
3. When the bow has swung out 15 or 20 degrees, hard left rudder and spurts ahead to swing stern out clear of the dock. (This is rarely done by small-boat handlers; consequently the stern scrapes along the dock as they pull away. There is no reason for this when a little power and a bit of rudder will get you away without a scratch.)
4. Let go the line when the boat is a few feet off the dock and go ahead slow, steering her *gradually* away from the dock with slight rudder. (Too much rudder will swing the stern right back against the dock and you'll end up no better off than if you had left it there to begin with.)

### Wind Off the Dock (Fig. 2)

1. Single up to one stern line and let the wind swing the bow out. Ease off on the stern line and the stern will go out as well. You're now clear of the dock, both bow and stern, without a scratch or a touch of the throttle.
2. Let go the line. Slow ahead and steer her away *easily*.

### Wind Astern (Fig. 3)

1. Single up to a bow line (spring).
2. Let the wind swing the stern out from the dock or use the engine in spurts against a hard left rudder.
3. Engine astern to back off slowly— cast off line and use rudder to back her off properly.
4. When well clear of dock, engine ahead and easy right rudder to steer her away.

### Wind On the Dock (Fig. 4)

1. Single up to one bow line (spring) led well aft onto the dock. Spurts ahead

*(continued)*

**FIG. 870-c** Now the transom is centered at the entrance to the slip and the boat is making neither headway nor sternway. Crewman stands ready in the cockpit.

**FIG. 870-d** With his boat aligned as carefully as wind and current permit, the helmsman starts to back easily. With rudders amidships, he tends the throttles.

> *If a skipper knows his boat, uses common sense, and plans his maneuvers carefully, he will soon acquire a reputation as a skillful boatman.*

against a rudder hard left to swing the stern out.

2. Half to full astern (depending on wind) to back her away from the dock. The stern will swing slowly to port of its own accord. Help it to do so with rudder if desired. When boat is roughly parallel to the dock let go line. . . .

3. Slight right rudder and full ahead. Or (Fig. 5).

**(Fig. 5)**

1. Single up to one stern line (spring) led well up onto dock.

2. Half to full astern to swing bow out. *No* rudder.

3. Rudder half left and engine slow ahead to swing stern out. When away a bit, let go line and steer her off carefully. Power used here will depend, again, on the force of the wind.

## LEAVING A SLIP (Fig. 6)

This method will work on both a walled slip or with a boat moored bow or stern to a dock between two stakes or piles.

1. Single-up to one stern line of a length sufficient to reach from the stern chock forward about ²/₃ the length of the vessel. Make the outboard end of this fast to the outer end of the slip.

2. Slow astern till the line is taut, then hard left rudder and the boat will swing her stern to port easily and under *full control*. The line acts as a pivot. This method is especially useful in restricted waters where there is little room to "pull out" from the slip. I know of no method that will get a boat out of a slip in less space or with better control.

3. Cast off when out far enough and slow ahead·giving a *slight* kick of left rudder to swing the stern out clear of the end of the slip or the dock.

This maneuver will do equally well for almost all conditions of wind and sea. More or less power or rudder may be needed but the steps are exactly the same.

This "controlled backing" method keeps you, the slip and your neighbor free from scrapes and gouges, fits of temper . . . and repair bills.

## DOCKING

### Alongside; Wind Ahead, or Off the Dock (Fig. 7)

1. Approach slowly at an angle of about 30 to 40 degrees to the dock.

2. Engine astern to stop her about 1 foot off the dock—bow line ashore.

3. Right rudder and spurts ahead to bring the stern in or allow the wind to drift her in.

4. Tie up.

### Wind Astern (Fig. 8)

1. Approach *closely* to dock, about 10 to 15 degrees.

2. When near to dock, one or two feet, right rudder and spurts ahead to *start* stern swinging in. As soon as the stern begins to swing in (Boat about parallel to dock). . . .

3. Astern to stop her. This action will keep the stern swinging in toward the dock. (Only practice will tell just where to shift

---

# A Typical Docking Maneuver (continued)

FIG. 870-e  With barely enough clearance on both sides, the helmsman is alert to keep his alignment parallel with the dock, the boat centered as closely as possible.

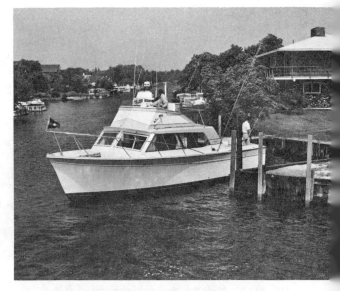

FIG. 870-f  As he backs gently into his berth, the helmsman keeps a sharp eye on his starboard quarter, prepared to kick the stern a little to port if necessary.

from ahead to astern.)

4. Bow should now point about 5 to 10 degrees *outward* from the dock. Stern line onto dock. Let her bow now drift into the dock after stopping engine or help it in with spurts ahead against hard left rudder.

5. Tie up.

### Wind On the Dock (Fig. 9)

1. Approach the dock at a *steep* angle (60 to 80 degrees) to allow you to use the engine as a brake on the boat's headway. This is vital in any heavy wind.

2. Astern to stop bow about a foot or two off the dock. Ease her with a boathook if possible. Bow line ashore.

3. Let the wind swing the stern in—braking its speed with the rudder hard right and the engine astern. (This will also help to keep the bow from being forced into the dock.)

4. Tie up.

I've had this method succeed where winds were of sufficient force to send other boats crashing into docks in a shower of paint chips and splinters.

### ENTERING A SLIP

**Wind Anywhere but Astern (Fig. 10)**

1. Approach slowly and roughly parallel to end of slip till you are able to pass a line to the cleat or pile nearest your approach.

2. Astern to slow the approach and *stop* her just *short* of the far piling, with the line taut.

3. Rudder hard left and gun ahead on engines to swing her into the slip using the line and the pile as a pivot.

5. Ease her into the slip and tie up.

### Wind Astern (Fig. 11)

1. Approach as previously described but use enough power astern to stop her positively. Pass a stern line and

2. a bow line, hauling both taut.

3. Using engine, wind and rudder, ease her around and into the slip.

4. Tie up.

This is one of the best methods to use in

any reasonably fresh wind as the control you have over the boat is positive and there is little chance that she can get out of control.

### TO SUM UP . . .

- Try to visualize just what conditions will be at the dock *before* you get there.
- Use fenders generously and pad your slip or dock well.
- Keep your engine in good shape and your control cables taut.
- Keep your mooring lines healthy and use chafing gear whenever possible.
- Favor a bight of line around a pile as the last line to let go (as it is an easy matter, when casting off, to let go the end on the vessel.)
- Watch lines to see that they don't foul your propeller.
- Remember that a boat will pivot about a point about 1/3 of her length aft from the bow and will not "follow the front wheels" as does a car. When the bow goes to starboard *the stern will also swing out to port* so that, when turning, a boat cuts a considerably wider path than its beam. It goes around a turn "crab-fashion."

Try the maneuvers (in easy weather first) and see how they treat you. I believe you'll find them kind to your boat, safe under most conditions, and easy to learn and use.

Pacemaker photographs pages 148-151 by Rosenfeld

**FIG. 870-g** As the boat eases astern, the helmsman keeps his eye on the transom, using his controls to turn his propellers ahead just enough to check the sternway.

**FIG. 870-h** Settled in her berth, the crewman makes fast with docklines, giving attention first to the spring that will prevent the boat's ranging too far astern.

Every good boatman aspires to be known, ultimately, as a good seaman. Perhaps it would be difficult to make a nice distinction between the two. Their skills merge, and overlap. Yet, one may handle his boat effectively in ordinary maneuvers in day-to-day sailing, but lack the inborn instinct of a "good seaman" when faced by a critical situation at sea. The subtle qualities of a seaman can be conveyed neither by word of mouth nor by printed page alone. Instruction can, however, go a long way toward teaching principles based on experience, which the seasoned skipper applies in practice. It is on this premise that the Seamanship chapter which follows has been prepared. Its text is completely new, generous use has been made of illustrations, and both are combined in the new format to which all revised material in recent editions conforms. Its subject matter has been keyed closely to requirements of instruction courses given by the United States Power Squadrons. Studied in conjunction with related chapters which form an integral part of the subject, we believe it constitutes the best and most practical seamanship text ever presented.

# SEAMANSHIP

Photograph by Pacific Studio

# CHAPTER 9 SEAMANSHIP

The term "seamanship" is a broad one. It encompasses many topics and probably would be defined differently by various persons qualified in the subject. In its broadest scope, *seamanship* for the recreational craft skipper may be considered to cover such areas as knowledge of his craft, its construction and maintenance, its handling under favorable and adverse weather conditions, and the actions to be taken in emergencies. It also covers such subjects as nautical terms and language, and the use of lines, knots, and splices.

Several topics that fall under the general heading of "seamanship" are of such major importance that they are presented as separate chapters. Typical of these are boat handling, anchoring, and marlinespike seamanship. Other subject areas, highly specialized, are also covered separately—seamanship in breaking inlets and outboard seamanship. This chapter will include topics that are not considered elsewhere and thus complete the coverage of this broad but most essential subject area, seamanship.

## THE CREW

Recreational boating is usually a family affair—indeed, one of its most pleasing aspects is that essentially the whole family can share in the activities.

One aspect of boating that should not be overlooked is the *training* of the crew. No boat of any appreciable size should depart its slip or mooring for an afternoon's run or a cruise measured in days without an adequately trained crew, especially an alternate for the skipper. The first mate, usually the skipper's wife, should be fully competent to take the helm under all normal conditions of wind and

FIG. 901 In a family crew, the "First Mate"—the Skipper's wife—should be qualified to take the helm and make simple maneuvers, such as coming alongside a pier or anchoring. (Gordon Manning photo)

waves, and hopefully to do so under adverse weather conditions. The mate should be capable of bringing the boat alongside a pier or of anchoring it. A sudden incapacitating illness (heart attack, stroke, etc.) or accident such as a broken arm or leg or blow on the head, may thrust heavy responsibilities upon the mate completely without warning. If that person has been trained ahead of time, the emergency will be significantly less drastic and much more easily handled.

### Training the crew

A training program need not be either onerous or unpleasant. It should be planned and carried out on a formal basis so that the skipper can be *sure* that everyone knows what he has to know. The secret to a successful family crew training program is to make it *fun,* and not let it take the pleasure out of pleasure boating. This is not an impossible task; it is not even a difficult one.

With just a little imagination a man-overboard drill can be made into a game without losing one bit of its effectiveness. With patience and adequate opportunities for practice, the mate and older children can be developed into skillful helmsmen. Every member of the crew should know where the fire extinguishers are located *and should have had actual experience in using them.* It is well worth the small price of recharging one or two extinguishers to have had the experience of having put out a fire with one. (By the way, skipper, have *you* ever actually put out a fire with an extinguisher of the type now on your boat?) This practice should not, of course, be carried out on the boat, but it is easily done ashore.

The mate, at least, and preferably several others of the crew, should know how to place the radio set in operation,

how to change channels, which channel is to be used for emergencies, and what to say. All persons aboard, crew or guests, should know where the life preservers are stowed *and how they should properly be worn.*

### Instruction plus practice

A proper training program consists of two parts—instruction and practice. The skipper first learns for himself what should be done and how, and then passes this information on to his crew. For routine matters such as boat handling, ample opportunity should be given each crew member to acquire proficiency—it may be quicker and easier on the nerves for the skipper always to bring the boat alongside a pier, but he must have the patience to let others learn how by doing. For emergency procedures, there should be both planned and snap, unannounced drills.

All aboard, *including the skipper,* can be trained to do the right thing instinctively, quickly and unquestioningly should a real emergency ever occur. Not only can they be trained, they must be—this is part of "seamanship" for the crew.

## Boat Handling Under Adverse Conditions

Perhaps the greatest test of a skipper's seamanship abilities comes in his handling of his boat under adverse conditions of wind and waves.

The size of his craft will have little bearing on its seaworthiness. This is fixed more by design and construction. The average power cruiser or sailboat is fully seaworthy enough for all of the conditions that she is likely to encounter in the use for which she is intended. Note carefully that qualifying phrase—"for which she is intended." Don't venture into water areas or weather conditions beyond those for which your boat was obviously designed. It is only good common sense that a craft designed for lake and river use should not be expected to be suitable in all weather offshore.

FIG. 902 Boating is usually a family affair and all members of the "crew" should be given informal training in their duties. Guests should be given a few of the essential "do's" and "don'ts" soon after coming aboard.

FIG. 903 "Rough" seas is a relative term. This ocean-racing sailboat can weather almost any condition of wind and waves if her skipper and crew are good seamen.　　(Rosenfeld photo)

It is a fact, however, that just what a boat will do is governed to a great extent by the skill of the man at the helm. Thus a good seaman will bring a poor craft through a blow that a novice might not be able to weather in a larger, more seaworthy craft.

## "Rough" weather

Rough weather is purely a relative term and what seems a terrible storm to the fair-weather man may be nothing more than a good breeze to the man who has known the sea in all its tantrums.

On large, shallow bodies of water, such as Long Island's Great South Bay, Delaware Bay and River, or Lake Erie, even a moderate wind will cause a steep, uncomfortable sea with crumbling crests because the depth of water is not great enough to permit waves to assume their natural form. Offshore, or in a deeper inland body of water, the same wind force might result in a moderate sea, but the slow, rolling swells would be no menace to a small craft.

## Use good judgment—don't panic

Sane small craft skippers don't ask for trouble afloat. Nobody wants to grip the spokes of a wheel when seas are breaking green over the bow or coming over the transom— at least nobody in his right mind. Unfortunately, however, at some time during your cruising career, you may be caught by an unexpected line squall, or obliged to thread your way through an inlet while breakers crash on the bar. *If you apply the fundamentals of good rough weather seamanship, you'll moor at your home berth and have a whopping good yarn to tell.* The casualties stem from those who panic—from boatmen who lose their heads when the going gets rough.

## Know your boat

Boat handling under adverse conditions is a quite flexible and individual matter, since no two boats are exactly alike in the same sea conditions. When the going begins to get heavy, each different hull design reacts differently— and even individual boats of the same class will behave differently because of such factors as the way they are loaded and trimmed.

Each skipper must learn his own boat to determine the precise application of general principles to be covered in the following sections. Reading this book and taking courses are important first steps, but they won't be enough when the chips are down. You can pick up the basics of good seamanship by absorbing factual data and principles, but you'll have to pick up the remainder—the elusive quality that makes the "real" skipper—by applying your book and classroom learning on the spot when the wind blows.

## Preparations for rough weather

In anticipation of high winds and rough seas, there are certain precautions and preparations that a prudent skipper takes. No single list will fit all boats or all weather conditions, but among the actions that should be considered are these:

1. Secure all hatches; close all ports and windows.
2. Pump the bilges dry and repeat this action as often as required. ("Free" water in bilges adversely affects the

FIG. 904 Each skipper must learn the individual traits of his own boat—how she handles under good and adverse conditions, and what weather she can safely take. Study seamanship, but learn by doing. (Loyd Sandgren photo)

craft's stability.)

3. Secure all loose gear; put away small items and lash down the larger ones.
4. Break out life preservers and have all on board wear them if the situation worsens; don't wait too long.
5. Break out emergency gear that might be needed, such as hand pumps or bailers, sea anchor, etc.
6. Get a good check of your position if possible and update the plot on your chart.
7. Prepare plans for altering course to a protected harbor or sheltered waters if necessary.
8. Reassure your crew and guests; instruct them in what to do and not to do; give them something to do if possible to take their minds off the situation.

## HEAD SEAS

Little difficulty should be experienced by the average well-designed power cruiser when running generally into head seas. Spray will be thrown, and in some hull designs there may be a tendency to pound against the waves. If the seas get too steep-sided, or if pounding is encountered, it will be necessary to slow down. This will give the bow a chance to rise in meeting each wave rather than being driven hard into it.

### Match speed to sea conditions

Should the conditions get really bad, and there be any danger of "starting" leaks in the planking or tearing loose heavy objects in the bilge, slow down until you're making bare headway, holding your bow at an angle of about forty-five degrees to the swells. The more headway is reduced in meeting heavy seas, the less will be the strain on the hull.

### Avoid propeller "racing"

You must reduce speed to avoid damage to either the hull or powerplant for your propeller will "race" as the seas lift the screw clear of the water. It sounds dangerous—and it may be. First, there's a rapidly increasing crescendo of sound as the engine winds up. Then an excessive vibration as the screw bites the water again. Don't panic—simply slow down and change your course till these effects are minimized. Keep headway so that you can maneuver her readily.

### Adjust trim

It is possible to swamp your boat if you drive her ahead too fast or if she is poorly trimmed. In a head sea, a vessel with too much weight forward will plunge rather than rise. Under the same conditions, too much weight aft will cause her to fall off. You must give the bow time to rise as she meets the swells instead of driving straight into them. The ideal speed will vary with different boats and power plants —experiment with your craft and discover her best riding speed before you have to utilize the knowledge under storm conditions.

Change the weight aboard if necessary. On outboards, you can shift your tanks and other heavy gear. In any boat, you can direct your passengers and crew to remain where you place them. Under dire emergency situations, you can tow a pail or other form of sea anchor behind you, helping to steer a straight course, slowing your speed forward while enabling you to keep the throttle open wide enough to maneuver. Be careful, however, that you don't foul the line in your propeller.

### Meet each wave as it comes

You will be able to make reasonable progress by carefully nursing the wheel—spotting the steep-sided combers coming in and varying your course, slowing or even stopping momentarily for the really big ones. If the man at the wheel is able to see clearly so he can act before dangerous conditions develop, you should be able to weather moderate gales with little discomfort. *Make sure the most experienced seaman aboard acts as helmsman!*

**FIG. 905** Close-hauled, with lee rail awash, this yawl is being driven hard. Wind pressure on sails keeps her from rolling as a motor boat would in a beam sea. (Rosenfeld photo)

## IN THE TROUGH

If the course to be made good is such that it will require you to run broadside to the swells, bouncing from crest to trough and back up again, you will be rolling heavily, perhaps dangerously. It would probably be wise to resort to what might be called a series of "tacks" much like a sailboat.

### Tacking across the troughs

Change course and take the wind and waves at roughly a 45° angle, first broad on your bow and then broad on your quarter. This results in a zig-zag course that makes good the desired objective, while the boat is in the trough for only brief intervals while turning. With the wind broad on the bow, the behavior should be satisfactory; on the quarter, the motion will be less comfortable but at least it it will be better than running in the trough. Make each tack as long as possible for the waters that you are in so as to minimize the number of times that you must pass through the trough when changing tacks.

If you want to turn sharply, allow your powerboat to lose headway for a few seconds, throw the wheel hard over, then suddenly apply power. She will wheel quickly as a powerful stream of water strikes the rudder, kicking you to port or starboard, *without making any considerable headway.* You won't be broadside for more than a minimum length of time. This is the same technique as used in docking in close quarters with adverse current or wind conditions; it is particularly effective with single-screw powerboats.

## RUNNING BEFORE THE SEA

Your course may be such that the swells are coming from directly behind you. Running directly before the sea is well enough if the stern of your craft can be kept reasonably up to the seas without being thrown around off course. This is known as *yawing.* But when the seas get too heavy, the boat tends to rush down a slope from crest to trough, and, stern high, the propeller comes out of the water and races. The rudder, also partly out of water, loses its grip, and the sea may take charge of the stern. At this stage, the boat may yaw so badly as to *broach,* to be thrown broadside into the trough out of effective control. This must be avoided through every possible action. Unfortunately, modern cruiser design emphasizes beam at the stern so as to provide a large, comfortable cockpit or afterdeck—this added width at the transom increases the tendency to yaw and possibly broach.

### Reducing yawing

Slowing down so as to let the swells pass under the boat usually will reduce the tendency to yaw, or at least will reduce the extent of yawing and so lessen the chances of broaching. While seldom necessary, consideration can be given to towing a heavy line or small sea anchor astern to help check the boat's speed and keep her running straight.

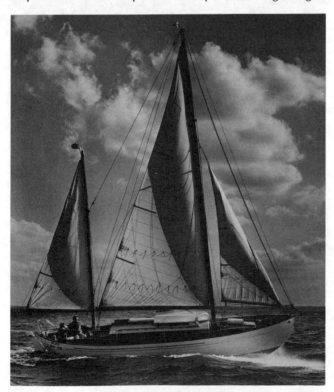

**FIG. 906 Sharp lines at the stern of this double-ender make for easier handling in a following sea. Motorboats with wide transoms are much more difficult to keep from yawing as heavy seas pass under the stern.** (Rosenfeld photo)

Obviously the line must be carefully handled and not allowed to foul the propeller. Do not tow soft-laid nylon lines which may unlay—even though seized—and cause hockles (strand kinks).

Cutting down the engine speed will reduce the strain imposed on the motor by alternate laboring with stern deep down before an overtaking sea and racing as the head goes down and the propeller comes out at the crest.

### Pitchpoling

The ordinary swell off shore is seldom troublesome on this point of running, but the steep wind sea of the lakes and shallow bays makes steering difficult and reduced speed imperative. Excessive speed down a steep slope may cause a boat to *pitchpole,* that is, drive her head under in the trough, tripping the bow, while the succeeding crest catches the stern and throws her end over end. When the going is bad enough to result in risk of this, it helps to keep the stern down and the bow light and buoyant, by shifting weight if necessary.

Shifting any considerable amount of weight aft will reduce a boat's tendency to yaw but too much might cause her to be "pooped" by a following sea breaking into the cockpit. *Do everything in moderation rather than in excess.* Find out if she acts more stable, adjusting her trim bit by bit rather than doing it all at once. Too much speed forward with the incorrect weight distribution might cause a small boat to pitchpole.

### Tacking before the seas

Previously, a form of tacking was suggested for avoiding the necessity of running dead into heavy seas or with them directly abeam. This same technique of alternately heading to either side of the base course can also be used when it is desired to avoid large swells directly astern.

Try a zig-zag track so that the swells are off your quarter, minimizing their effects—experiment with slightly different headings to determine the angle at which the waves will have the least tendency to cause your boat to yaw off course. Be careful at all times to keep your craft under control and prevent an unexpected broach.

## RUNNING AN INLET

When offshore swells run into shallower water along the beach, they build up a steeper ground swell because of resistance created by the bottom. Natural inlets on sandy beaches, unprotected by breakwaters, usually build up a bar across the mouth. When the ground swell reaches the bar, its form changes rapidly, and a short steep-sided wave is produced which may break where the water is shallowest.

This fact should be taken into consideration when approaching from offshore. A few miles off, the sea may be relatively smooth while the inlet from seaward may not look as bad as it actually is. The breakers may extend clear across the mouth, even in a buoyed channel.

The shoals shift so fast with the moving sand that it is not always feasible to keep buoys in the best water. Local boatmen often leave the buoyed channel and are guided by appearance of the sea, picking the best depth by the smoothest surface and absence of breakers. A stranger is handicapped in such a situation because he may not have knowledge of uncharted obstructions and so may not care to risk leaving the buoyed channel. In a case of this kind,

FIG. 907 Boats that must cross a bar with breaking waves must avoid "pitchpoling"—being thrown end over end if caught driving hard down the face of a steep sea, burying the bow. This double-ended fisherman just misses being caught on the forward face of a breaker. This is no place for pleasure boats.

he should have a local pilot if possible. Otherwise it will sometimes be well to anchor off, if necessary, until you can follow a local boat in.

If it becomes necessary to pick a way through without local help, there are several suggestions which may help to make things more comfortable. Don't run directly in but wait outside the bar until you have had a chance to watch the action of waves as they pile up at the most critical spot in the channel, which will be the shallowest. Usually they will come along in groups of three, sometimes more, but always three at least. The last sea will be bigger than the rest and by careful observation it can be picked out of the successive groups.

When you are ready to enter, stand off until a big one has broken or spent its force on the bar and then run through behind it. Ebb tide builds up a worse sea on the bars than the flood, due to the rush of water out against and under the incoming ground swell. If the sea looks too bad on the ebb, it may be better to keep off a few hours until the flood has had a chance to begin.

This section has concentrated on entering inlets rather than departing through them. This latter action is less hazardous as the boat is on the safe side of the dangerous area and usually has the option of staying there. If the skipper does decide to go out, dangerous areas are more easily spotted from the inside, and a boat heading into surf is more easily controlled than one running with the swells. On the other hand, the skipper of a boat outside an inlet may have little option as to whether or not he can remain in the open sea indefinitely; he may have to enter and can only attempt to do it in the safest possible manner.

For additional information on safely entering a breaking inlet, see Chapter 27.

## HEAVING TO

When conditions get so bad offshore that a boat cannot make headway and begins to take too much punishment, it is time to *heave to,* a maneuver that varies in its execution with the type of craft under consideration. Motor boats, both single and twin screw, will usually be most comfortable if brought around head to the seas, or a few points off, using just enough power to make bare steerageway without trying to make any considerable progress through the water. In fact, the boat is likely to be making some sternway or leeway even though kept nearly bow on to the waves.

Sailing craft, when heaving to, will shorten sail, carrying just enough canvas, principally aft, to keep the vessel's head to the sea or nearly so where she can ride comfortably without making progress ahead.

The object always is to lay the craft in such a position that she will take the seas most comfortably, in a manner that is easiest on both the hull and the crew. For some vessels, this may mean allowing her to drift naturally, perhaps with the seas on the quarter, but this is not normal for small craft. For short periods, when the fuel supply permits, the average motorboat will be most comfortable when the propeller is allowed to turn over slowly, giving steerageway enough to keep her head in the desired relationship to the swells as determined by the period of the waves and the natural motion of the boat.

## THE SEA ANCHOR

In extreme cases, a *sea anchor* is occasionally used. Normally, this will consist of a canvas cone-shaped bag having an iron hoop to keep it open at the mouth. To this hoop, a bridle and a heavy line is attached which is paid out from the bow and made fast to the forward bit. A trip line is

FIG. 908 A sea anchor. Tow line is made fast to the ring at left; trip line is bent to the ring at apex of the cone. This end is often open, to allow water to flow through. Oil is allowed to drip slowly from the bag.

attached to a ring at the end of the cone. This is used to spill the bag and make it easier to haul the anchor back aboard. In use, the theory of the anchor is not to go to the bottom and hold, but merely to present a drag or resistance which will keep the boat's head up within a few points of the wind as she drifts off to leeward. A sea anchor, sometimes called a *drogue*, will usually float a short distance beneath the water's surface.

There are also available on the market, sea anchors made up of a series of plastic floats of a more modern design. These fold compactly for storage and are said to be more effective in holding a boat's head to the sea.

Whatever style of sea anchor is carried on your boat, make sure that it is of sufficient size to be effective. A small one may be easier to stow, but there's no point to having it if it won't do the job.

### Improvised sea anchors

In the absence of a regular sea anchor, any form of drag rigged from spars, planks and canvas or other material at hand that will float just below the surface and effectively keep the boat from lying in the trough, would be worth trying. If it could be launched successfully and swamped, with a stout line securely attached, a dinghy could be tried in lieu of the sea anchor, but such procedure is easier to talk about than to accomplish when conditions are bad enough to justify the attempt.

### Use of oil with sea anchors

Sea anchors are sometimes equipped with an *oil can* which permits oil to ooze out slowly and form a slick on the surface, thus preventing seas from breaking. The oil might be distributed from a bag punctured with a few holes and stuffed with oakum or waste saturated with oil. (See also the following section on the use of oil.)

Make sure this equipment—sea anchors, trip lines, oil bag lines, lead lines, etc.—is in good condition and not rotten from long disuse or old age. Cotton and manila emergency equipment should be discarded in favor of synthetics.

### Sea anchors and lee shores

Sea anchors can be used only if there is sufficient sea room as there is naturally a steady drift to leeward. When a vessel is driven down onto a lee shore and is forced to use her regular ground tackle to ride out a gale, it is imperative that a constant watch be maintained to guard against dragging. Merely having a heavy anchor down doesn't guarantee safety. If ranges are taken on landmarks ashore, dragging can be detected. Engines may have to be

used to ease the strain on the anchor during the worst of the blow and a long scope of cable will give the anchor its best chance to hold.

## THE USE OF OIL ON ROUGH WATER

Many years of experience at sea have established the value of using oil for the purpose of modifying the effect of breaking seas. Oil is easily dispensed and quickly dispersed; the effect of even small amounts is significant.

The following summary of information on the use of oil on rough waters can guide the small craft skipper should he ever be in a situation requiring its use.

1. On free waves, *i.e.*, waves in deep water, the effect is greatest.

2. In a surf, or waves breaking on a bar, where a mass of liquid is in actual motion in shallow water, the effect of the oil is uncertain, as nothing can prevent the larger waves from breaking under such circumstances, but even here it is of some value.

3. The heaviest and thickest oils are most effectual. Kerosene is of little use; crude petroleum is serviceable when nothing else is obtainable; but all animal and vegetable oils, and waste oil from the engines, will have a useful effect.

4. A small quantity of oil suffices, if applied in such a manner as to spread to windward.

5. In cold water, the oil, being thickened by the lower temperature and not being able to spread freely, will have its effect much reduced. This will vary with the type of oil used.

6. For a boat at sea, the best method of application appears to be to hang over the side, in such a manner as to be in the water, small canvas bags, capable of holding from 1 to 2 gallons of oil, the bags being pricked with a sail needle to facilitate leakage of the oil.

The position of these bags should vary with the circumstances. Running before the wind, they should be hung on either bow and allowed to tow in the water.

With the wind on the quarter, the effect seems to be

FIG. 909 The skipper of this sailboat is a good seaman. Note lifelines around the decks for safety. Note, too, the absence of any clutter of lines or gear on deck.

less than in any other position, as the oil goes astern while the waves come up on the quarter.

Lying-to, the weather bow, and another position farther aft, seem the best places from which to hang the bags, using sufficient line to permit them to draw to windward while the vessel drifts.

7. Crossing a bar with a flood tide, to pour oil overboard and allow it to float in ahead of the boat, which would follow with a bag towing astern, would appear to be the best plan. As noted before, however, under these circumstances, the effectiveness of oil can not always be depended upon.

On a bar, with the tidal current ebbing, it is probably useless to try to use oil for the purpose of entering.

8. For approaching a stranded boat, it is recommended that oil be poured overboard to windward of her before going alongside or close. The effect in this case will greatly depend upon the set of any current and depth of water.

9. For a boat riding in rough water from a sea anchor, it is recommended that the oil bag be fastened to an endless line rove through a block on the sea anchor. By this means, the oil can be diffused well ahead of the boat and the bag can be readily hauled on board for refilling whenever necessary.

10. The general principle involved is to get the oil slick to spread to windward if possible and around the boat in such a way that she stays in the slick. If the oil goes off to leeward or astern, it is of no use.

## SEAMANSHIP IN "THICK" WEATHER

Another form of "adverse condition" that will require special skills in seamanship is "thick" weather—conditions of reduced visibility. The cause for this lessoned range of vision may be fog, heavy rain or snow, haze, etc. Of all these, fog is probably the most often encountered and most severe. The general rules and procedures to be considered here are, however, applicable whatever the situation.

### Avoiding collisions

Seamanship in fog is primarily a matter of safety, avoiding collisions. Piloting and position determination, the legal requirements for sounding fog signals, and the meterological aspects of fog are all covered elsewhere in this book. Here we will consider only the aspects of boat handling and safety.

The primary needs of safety in fog or other conditions of reduced visibility are to *see and be seen—to hear and be heard*. The wise skipper takes every possible action to see or otherwise detect other craft and hazards, and simultaneously takes all steps to ensure that the presence of his boat will be most surely and easily detected by others.

### Reduce speed

The detection by sight or sound must be made early enough to allow proper corrective action. All of the Rules of the Road—International, Inland, and others—require a reduction in speed for all vessels in circumstances of low visibility. Specifically, the Rules require that all vessels "go at a moderate speed, having careful regard to the existing circumstances and conditions." Admiralty court decisions over the years have generally established "moderate speed" as that at which the vessel can come to a complete stop in one-half the existing range of visibility. This, obvi-

ously, is subject to varying interpretation rather than precise definition, but it should always be conservatively considered from the viewpoint of safety.

The preferred situation is to be able to stop short in time, rather than having to resort to violent evasive maneuvers to dodge the hazard. The Rules also require that a power-driven vessel hearing the fog signal of another vessel forward of the beam, and not knowing the position of the other vessel, shall insofar as circumstances permit, stop her engines and then navigate with caution until the danger of collision is past.

### Lookouts

Equally important with a reduction in speed is the posting of *lookouts*. This, too, is a requirement of the Rules of the Road, but it is also simple common sense. Many, if not most, modern motor and sail boats are designed in a manner such that the helmsman is *not* so located as to be an effective lookout, and thus one or two additional persons are required for this function in thick weather.

### Look . . . and listen

Despite the "look" in "lookout," such a person is as much for *listening* as he is for seeing. A person assigned as a lookout should have this duty as his sole responsibility while on watch. A skipper should certainly post a lookout as far forward as possible when in fog, and, if his helmsman is at inside controls, another lookout for the aft sector is desirable. Lookouts should be relieved as often as nec-

**FIG. 910  The primary needs of safety in fog are to see and be seen—to hear and be heard.**  (Bob Ruskauff photo)

essary to ensure their alertness. If the crew is small, an exchange of bow and stern duties will provide some change in position and relief from monotony. If there are enough persons on board a larger craft, a double lookout forward is not wasted manpower. Care should be taken that they do not distract each other from their duties.

A bow lookout should keep alert for other vessels, sound signals from aids to navigation, and hazards in general. In the latter category are rocks and piles, breakers, and buoys—in thick weather, aids to navigation without audible signals can indeed become hazards. A lookout aft should be primarily alert for overtaking vessels, but he may also hear fog signals missed by the man on the bow.

The transmission of sound in fog is uncertain and tricky. It may seem to come from directions other than that toward the true source, and it may not be heard at all at ranges which would be expected as normal. See the discussion of fog signals in Chapter 16.

### Stop your engine

When underway in fog in a powerboat, consideration should be given to slowing the engines to idle, or shutting them off entirely, at intervals in order to aid in hearing the fog signals of other vessels and aids to navigation. This is not a legal requirement of the Rules of the Road, but it is an excellent, practical action to take.

During these periods, silence should be maintained on the boat so that even the faintest signal will be heard. These periods of listening should be at least one minute in length in inland waters and two minutes on the high seas to conform with the legally required maximum intervals between the sounding of fog signals. Don't forget to continue to sound your own signal during the listening period —you may get an answer from close-by!

When proceeding in fog at a moderate speed, any time your lookout indicates that he has heard something, immediately cut your engines to idle, or stop them altogether, in order that the lookout may have the most favorable conditions for verifying and identifying what he believes he has heard.

### Radar and radar reflectors

Radar comes into its greatest value in thick weather conditions. If you are so equipped, be sure to turn it on and use it; but not at the expense of posting a proper lookout.

Even if you do not have a radar set, you should have a passive radar reflector (see page 509); then is the time to open it and hoist it as high as possible.

### Cruising with other boats

If you are cruising with other boats and fog closes in, you may be able to take advantage of a procedure used by wartime convoys. Tie onto the end of a long, light line some object that will float and make a wake as it moves through the water. A life ring, or a glass or plastic bottle with a built-in handle, will do quite well. This object is towed astern with the boats traveling in column, one object behind each craft except the last.

When the object is kept in sight by the bow lookout on the next boat in column, he knows just where the boat ahead of him is located even though he cannot see her and perhaps cannot even hear her fog signal.

### Anchoring and laying-to

If the weather, depth of water, and other conditions are favorable, consideration should be given to anchoring rather than proceeding through conditions of low visibility; but do not anchor in a heavily-traveled channel or traffic lane.

If you cannot anchor, then perhaps laying-to—underway with no way on—may be safer than proceeding at even a much reduced speed. Added quiet will provide increased safety.

Remember that different fog signals are required when you are underway, with or without way on, and when you are at anchor. By all means, sound the proper fog signal and keep your lookouts posted to *look* and *listen* for other craft and hazards.

## Helmsmanship

One of the characteristics of a good seaman is the ability to steer well. This is called *helmsmanship*. Here is another quality that cannot be learned entirely from the book, or in a classroom, but there are basic principles that can and should be studied. Knowledge of these, coupled with experience, can make a skipper a better man at the helm than one who has not taken the time and trouble to develop his ability.

### Boat's individuality

When considering the general principles of helmsmanship, it must always be borne in mind that these are truly "general" principles. Boats are nearly as individualistic as people, and nowhere is this more noticeable than in their steering characteristics.

Deep-draft and shallow-draft vessels will handle differently. Boats that steer by changing their thrust direction— outboards and inboard-outboards—will respond entirely different than boats steered by rudders. Heavy, displacement hulls will react to helm changes quite unlike light, planing hulls.

FIG. 911 Handling characteristics of various boats are nearly as different as personalities of people. Not all boats will turn as sharply as this fast runabout. A good helmsman knows well the response to the helm of his own craft.

The secret of good helmsmanship is to "know the boat." If you are the skipper of your own craft, this will come relatively quickly as you gain experience with her. If you are invited to take the wheel or tiller of a friend's boat, take it easy at first with helm changes, and make a deliberate effort to get the "feel" of the craft's response.

## Steering by compass

At sea and in many larger inland bodies of water, steering is often done by compass. The helmsman must keep the lubberline of the compass (also referred to as the lubber's line; see Chapter 13) on that mark of the card that indicates the course to be steered. If the course to be steered is 100 degrees, and the lubberline is at 95 degrees, the helmsman must *swing the boat's head,* with right rudder, 5 degrees to the right, so that the lubberline is brought around to 100. **Remember, the card stands still while the lubberline swings around it.** Any attempt to bring the desired course on the card up to the lubberline will produce exactly the *wrong* result.

FIG. 912 **Steering by compass is a skill that must be acquired by practice. The compass card remains in essentially the same position with relation to the earth and the boat is moved about it.**

As a vessel swings with a change in course, there is a tendency for the inexperienced helmsman to allow her to swing too far, due to the momentum of the turn and the lag between turning of the wheel and the craft's response to rudder action. That's why it is necessary to "meet her" so that the vessel comes up to, and steadies on, the new course without over-swinging. This often requires, partic-

ularly in larger and heavier cruisers, that the helmsman return the rudder to the neutral, amidships position noticeably before the craft reaches the intended new heading. It may even be necessary to use a slight amount of opposite rudder to check the boat's swinging motion.

A crooked course, yawing from side to side, brands the inexperienced helmsman. A straight course is the goal to shoot at; this can be achieved, after the boat has steadied, by only slight movements of the wheel. It calls for anticipation of the vessel's swing and correction with a little rudder instead of letting her get well off the course before the rudder is applied. A zig-zag course is an inefficient course. The mileage is longer and any offset of the rudder from the center-line tends to retard the craft's progress.

A good helmsman will not only use small amounts of rudder, but he will also turn the wheel slowly and deliberately. The actual manner of steering is again a characteristic of each individual boat and can only be learned by experience with that particular craft.

In piloting small craft, it is often better to pick out a distant landmark, if there is one, or a star at night, to steer by. This helps to maintain a straight course as the compass is smaller and less steady than aboard a larger vessel. The helmsman can then drop his eye periodically to the compass to check his course. Avoid steering on a particular cloud formation as these move with the wind and change shape. In some situations, a boat may be steered for a short time with reference to reflections on the water from the sun or moon, but always remember that these are moving rather than fixed reference points.

## EFFECT OF WIND AND SEA

A beam wind will have considerable effect on the steering as the bow, with its relatively greater proportion of freeboard to draft, tends to be driven off more than the stern, and the rudder angle must be sufficient to compensate for this. In a heavy sea, the direction from which the seas are coming will have an effect on the steering. A head sea will be less troublesome than a following sea.

Driving into a head sea, a boat will probably be slowed down to prevent unnecessary pounding, and the swing of the bow will have to be corrected with *slight* rudder changes. In a following sea, the tendency for the stern to be thrown around by overtaking waves (yawing) must be anticipated and checked as much as possible. When the stern is tossed high before an overtaking sea, if it tends to be thrown to starboard, the helmsman must meet her by applying right rudder; a considerable amount of rudder may be required.

Broaching should be avoided at all costs. Ordinarily, if the seas are not too bad, it is possible in handling a small boat to watch astern for the big seas that might cause the boat to yaw excessively. Then by speeding up the engine, with rudder set against the direction of the yaw, the corrective effect of the rudder will be enough to straighten her out and keep the stern up to the sea. As the wave passes the bow, the throttle can be closed again to its previous setting and the rudder brought back to amidships.

## SHALLOW WATER

Small craft in heavy following seas such as are built up on inlet bars and in big shallow bodies of water sometimes tend to broach despite anything that can be done by the

FIG. 913  A small steadying sail may be used to advantage to damp the rolling action of a motor cruiser in a beam sea. (F. Raymond Photo)

helmsman. Rudder hard over one way, the boat may run in the opposite direction. When conditions are as serious as that, a drag astern, consisting of a small sea anchor or length of heavy line has been recommended as an aid in keeping the stern up to the sea. The great risk in speeding up too much when the boat has acquired considerable momentum down the descending side of a wave is that of pitchpoling. If she is allowed to trip by running the bow under in the trough between steep seas, the next sea astern may throw her end over end.

Shallow water, besides tending to create a more bothersome steep-sided sea when the wind blows hard, also has a decided effect on the speed and steering of a vessel. A suction is created, the stern settles, and speed is decreased because of the change in the vessel's trim. Propeller and rudder action are both sluggish, so that response to the wheel is not as good as it will be in deep water.

In a small motor boat with exhaust at the stern near the waterline, warning of shallow water is often had before actual grounding, as the exhaust starts to bury under water and a difference in its sound is detected. This happens without any change in the throttle setting.

### BEAM SEAS

All craft have what is known as a "natural" period of oscillation, or rolling period, which is the time required by a vessel to roll from one side to the other. If this period happens to coincide with the period of the waves in which she is running, as in a beam sea, the synchronism should be broken by a change of course (and speed, if necessary), to avoid excessive rolling. It is seldom necessary, in such a case, to meet the seas squarely bow-on.

Slight changes of course often damp the rolling enough to make the vessel comfortable. If the craft is disabled, with power not available, then the only way to prevent heavy rolling is to get out a sea anchor or drogue to hold the bow up to the sea, used perhaps in conjunction with storm oil if the waves are breaking.

Occasions may arise, as in preparing to heave to, when a vessel that has been running before a following sea must be brought around head to sea. This calls for skill and judgment and a knowledge of the steering qualities of the particular craft involved. By watching carefully the procession of waves as they pass, taking into consideration their height and the distance between them and space required for the turn, it will usually be possible to avoid having her caught broadside to a dangerous swell.

Invariably a boat is under better control when her engine is going ahead rather than in reverse. The propeller, in the first instance, is throwing a stream of water past the rudder blade. In general, if left to her own devices, with engines stopped, the bow of the average boat will fall off until the wind comes somewhat abaft the beam, because of the relative height of bow and superstructure forward as compared with that aft where the draft is normally greater.

## Stranding, Assisting, and Towing

It is an unwritten law of the sea that one should never pass an opportunity to render assistance to any vessel in need of aid. Of course this is one of the primary functions of the Coast Guard, but there are plenty of occasions when a little timely help on the part of a fellow boatman may save hours of labor later after the tide has fallen or wind and sea have had a chance to make up.

As often as not, assistance is likely to take the form of a tow line passed to another skipper to get him out of a position of temporary embarrassment or perhaps to get him to a Coast Guard station or back to port in case of failure of any of his gear.

Or perhaps the situation will be the other way around. If you do a normal amount of boating, and poke your bow into a number of strange places, the chances are that some day *you* may go aground. It is equally possible that some day a balky motor may force you to ask a tow from a passing boat, or you may be on the passing boat from which a tow is requested.

In either case, you should know what to do, and why. Let us consider the problem and possible solutions from each of two points of view—being in need of help yourself, and being the boat that assists another.

## STRANDING

Simple stranding, running aground, is more often an inconvenience than a danger and, with a little "know how" and some fast work, the period of stranding may be but a matter of minutes.

If it should happen in that before-mentioned strange harbor, the very fact that it is strange presupposes that you have been feeling your way along and so, probably, have just touched bottom lightly, in which case you should be off again with a minimum of difficulty, *provided* that your immediate actions do not tend to put you aground more firmly.

### Right and wrong actions

One's first instinctive act on going aground is to throw one's engines into reverse and gun them to the limit in an effort to pull off; this may be the one thing that you should *not* do.

If in tidal waters, the first thing to consider is, of course, the stage of the tide.

If the tide is rising, and the sea quiet enough so that the hull is not pounding, time is working for you, and whatever you do to assist yourself and the boat will be much more effective after a little time has passed. If, on the other hand, you grounded on a falling tide, you will have to work quickly and do exactly the right things or you will be fast for several hours or more.

About the only thing you know offhand is the shape of the hull, its point of greatest draft, and consequently the part most apt to be touching, but bottom contours may be such that this premise will not be true. If, however, the hull shows any tendency to swing, due to the action of wind or waves, the point about which it pivots is most apt to be the part grounded.

### Cautions in getting off

The type of bottom requires immediate consideration. If it is sandy, and you reverse hard, you will be apt to wash a quantity of sand from astern and throw it directly under the keel, with the obvious result of bedding the boat more firmly to the bottom. Always exercise discretion in reversing while aground due to the risk of pumping sand or mud into the engine. If the bottom is rocky and you insist on trying to reverse off, you may drag the hull and do more damage than with the original grounding. Also, if grounded forward, the well known tendency of

the stern to swing to port, when reversing with a single-screw boat having a right-hand wheel, may swing the hull broadside onto exposed pinnacles or to a greater contact with a soft bottom.

### How to use a kedge

The one *right* thing to do immediately after grounding is to take out an anchor and set it firmly; this is called a *kedge;* the act of using it is *kedging.*

Unless the boat has really been driven on, the service anchor should be heavy enough. Put the anchor *and* the line in the dinghy, make the bitter end fast to the stern bitts or to something solid and row out as far as possible, letting the line run from the stern of the dinghy as it uncoils. Taken out this way, the oarsman's task will be much easier than if he tries to drag the line from the large boat through the water.

FIG. 914 The most important thing to do after going aground is to get out a *kedge*—an anchor to keep you from being driven further aground and possibly a means of pulling yourself free as waves or the wake from another boat lifts your craft.

If you do not carry a dinghy, it is often possible to swim out with an anchor provided that the sea and weather conditions do not make it hazardous to go into the water. Life preservers or buoyant cushions—one or two of either—can be used to support the anchor out to where you wish to set it. Be sure to wear a life jacket or buoyant vest yourself so as to save your energy for the work to be done.

If there is *no* other way to get a kedge anchor out, you may consider throwing it out as far as possible. Although this is, of course, contrary to the basic principle that an anchor is never thrown over the side, the importance of getting a kedge set is sufficient to warrant the use of this technique under the circumstances. It may be necessary to pull in the anchor and throw again one or more times to get it set firmly.

When setting out the kedge, consider again the sideways turning effect of a reversing single screw and, unless the boat has twin screws, set the kedge at a compensating angle from the stern. If the propeller is right hand, as those of most boats are, set the anchor slightly to starboard of the stern. This will give two desirable effects. When pulling together with kedge line and reverse the boat will have practically a straight pull on it, and when used alternately, first pulling on the line and then giving a short surge with the reverse, the action may give a sort of wiggling action to the stern and the keel, which will be a real help in starting the boat moving.

### Getting added pulling power

If you can find a couple of double-sheave blocks (pulleys) and a length of suitable line on board, make up a handy-billy or fall and fasten it to the kedge line. Then you can really pull! Such a handy-billy should be a part of the boat's regular equipment, anyhow.

Whatever else you may do, during the entire period of grounding, persist in keeping that kedge-line as taut as the combined strength of those on board can make it. You may be agreeably surprised by having the boat yield suddenly to that continued pull, especially if a passing boat throws a wake to help lift the keel off the bottom.

Two kedges set out at an acute angle from either side of the stern and pulled upon alternately may give that desired stern wiggle that will help you work clear.

## Working off

If the bottom is sandy, that same pull, with the propeller going *ahead* may result in washing some sand *away* from under the keel, with the desired result. If the kedge line is kept taut, you may try it with a clear mind. At least you will not do any harm.

Move your crew and passengers quickly from side to side to roll the boat and make the keel work in the bottom. If you have spars, swing the booms outboard and put men on them to heave the boat down, thus raising the keel line. Shift ballast or heavy objects from over the portion grounded to lighten that section and if you can, remove some internal weight by loading it into the dinghy or by taking it ashore if that is possible.

## When to stay aground

All of the above is predicated on the assumption that the boat is grounded, but not holed or strained open. If either of these last has happened, you may be far better off where she lies than you would be if she were in deep water again. If she is badly stove, you may want to take an anchor ashore, to hold her on or pull her further up until temporary repairs can be made. Perhaps, as the tide falls, the damaged portion may be exposed far enough to allow some outside patching; always presupposing that you have something aboard to patch with! A piece of canvas, cushions, bedding, these are all illustrative of items that can be used in an emergency as temporary hull patches.

## What to do while waiting

While waiting for the tide to rise, or for the Coast Guard to come, you do not need to sit idle. Take soundings all around the position where the boat lies aground. It is possible that a swing of the stern to starboard or port may do more for you than any amount of straight backward pulling; soundings will reveal any additional depth that may exist to either side to help you out.

If there is another boat present, she may be able to help you even if she is not suitable for pulling. Have the other skipper run his craft back and forth at a speed that will make as much wake as possible. The rise and fall of his wash may lift your boat just enough to permit you to back clear.

Even though the hull is unharmed, and you are left with a falling tide to sit it out for a few hours, you may as well be philosophical and get over the side and make good use of those hours. Undoubtedly you would prefer to do it under happier circumstances, but this may be your chance to get a good check on the condition of the bottom, or do any one of a number of little jobs that you could not do otherwise, short of a haulout.

FIG. 915 If you go aground on a falling tide, you may find yourself "high and dry." If so, try to brace the boat so that she will stay upright; she will refloat easier if you do. While you are out of water, make an inspection of the bottom. (Photo by Charles True)

If she is going to be left high and dry, keep an eye on her layover condition. If there is anything to get a line to, even another kedge, you can make her lie over on whichever side you choose, as she loses buoyancy. If she is deep and narrow she may need some assistance in standing up again, particularly if she lies over in soft mud. Both the suction of the mud and her own deadweight will work against her in that case.

## ASSISTING

If, rather than being stranded, you are in a position to render assistance to another skipper who has been so unlucky as to go aground, it is just as important that you know what to do, and what not to do, in the circumstances.

It is of *primary* importance to see that the assisting boat does not join the other craft in its trouble! Consider the probable draft of the stranded vessel in comparison with the draft of your boat. Consider also the size and weight of the boat that is aground in comparison with the power of your engines—don't tackle an impossible job; there are other ways of rendering assistance.

## Getting a line over

It may seem easiest to bring a line in to a stranded boat by coming in under engine power, bow on, passing the line and then backing out again, but the maneuver should not be attempted unless one is sure that there will be water enough under the assisting boat, and also, unless the boat backs well, without too much stern crabbing due to the action of the reversed screw. Wind and current direction will greatly affect the success of this maneuver. If all conditions are adverse and tend to swing the boat broadside to the shallows as she backs, it will be best to try to pass the line in some other manner.

Perhaps the assisting boat may back in, with wind or current compensating for the reversed screw, thus keeping her straight and leaving the bow headed out with consequent better maneuverability. In any case, after the line is once passed and made fast, the assisting boat should do the actual pulling with engines going ahead, to get full power into the pull.

If conditions are such that a close approach is unwise, it will be far better for the second boat to drop anchor, or even two anchors, well off the stranded boat and then send the line over in a dinghy, or else buoy the line and attempt to float it in to the grounded boat.

## Making the pull

If wind or current or both are broadside to the direction of the pull, the assisting boat would best stay anchored even while pulling. Otherwise, as soon as she takes the strain (particularly if the line is fast to her stern) she will have lost her own maneuverability, and will gradually make leeway, which could eventually put her aground broadside.

If the pulling must be done with the assisting boat under way, the line should be made fast well forward of the stern so that while hauling, she can angle into the wind and current and still hold her own position.

Tremendous strains can be set up, particularly on the stranded boat, by this sort of action, even to the point of carrying away whatever the tow-line is made fast to. Ordi-

nary recreational craft are *not* designed as tug boats! It is probable that the cleats or bitts available for making the line fast are not strong enough for such pulling, and even more likely that they are not located advantageously for such work.

It is far better to run a bridle around the whole hull and pull against this bridle rather than to risk starting some part of the stern by such straining. The assisting boat should also be bridled if there is any doubt of her ability to withstand such concentrated strains.

When operating in limited areas, the stranded craft should have a kedge out for control when she comes off. She should also have another anchor ready to be put over the side if necessary; this may be required to keep her from going back aground if she is without power.

Through all of this maneuvering, it is imperative to see that all lines are kept clear so as not to foul the propeller and that no sudden surge is put on a slack line.

FIG. 917 Most small craft must make the pull with the line made fast near the stern. This restricts maneuverability and, for safe control, a bow anchor should be put out. Slack of the anchor line should be taken up as the stranded boat comes free to prevent the pulling boat from being carried around into shoal water.

FIG. 918 To aid in maneuverability if a bow anchor cannot be set, the tow line may be made fast to a cleat forward of the stern on the up-wind or up-current side. This cleat *must* be capable of taking heavy strain.

FIG. 919 Tremendous strains are set up when trying to free a stranded boat. Most bits and cleats on recreational small craft cannot take such a load. It is safer to put a bridle around the superstructure of both boats. Pad pressure points to protect against chafing and scarring.

FIG. 916 If a line is to be sent to another boat, you can heave a light line which can then be used to pull the heavier towing line across. A weighted end on the light line will make it easier to throw—this can be a "monkey's fist," as shown.

## TOWING

Somewhere in the course of your boating experience you are likely to run up against a situation where you wish to take another vessel in tow. In good weather with no sea running, the problem is comparatively easy, involving little more than the maneuvering of your boat into position in line with, and ahead of, the other boat and the passing of a tow line.

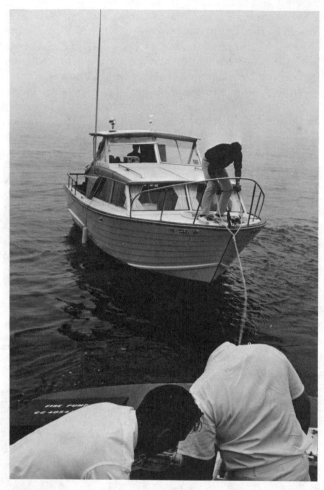

FIG. 920  It is generally desirable to pass a line from the assisting boat to the one being aided. If the weather is rougher than as shown here, or for any reason the other boat cannot be approached, the rescuing boat can float a line over, using a life ring or buoyant cushion.

Generally speaking, it is best for the towing boat to pass her tow-line to the other craft. It may be desirable to emulate large-ship practice and first send over a light line, using that to haul over the actual towing line. Plastic water ski tow lines that float are excellent for use as this initial ("messenger") line to the other boat.

When approaching a boat, dead in the water, with the intention of passing a line, if there is any kind of sea running, do not be dramatic and try to run in too close. Just buoy a long line with several life preservers, tow it astern and take a turn about the stern of the disabled one, but don't foul their propeller in so doing. The occupants will be able to pick it up with a boathook from the cockpit with far less fuss than by any heave-and-catch method.

The forward bitts are usually rugged and so the towed one may make the line fast at that point; then, with someone at the wheel to assist by steering, there is little more

to do than to have an anchor ready to drop if, for any reason, the tow-line parts or is cast loose.

### Handling the towing boat

The tow boat, however, requires some real handling!

The worst possible place to make the tow-line fast is to the stern of the lead boat, because the pull of the tow prevents the stern from swinging properly in response to rudder action and thus interferes with the boat's maneuvering ability. The tow-line should be made fast as far forward as practicable, as in tug and tow boat practice. If no suitable place is provided, it is best to make a bridle from the forward bitts, running around the superstructure to a point in the forward part of the cockpit. Such a bridle will have to be wrapped with chafing gear wherever it bears on the superstructure or any corners, and even then, some chafing of the finish is almost bound to occur.

### Towing lines

Manila makes a good tow line; nylon is even better because of the spring in it. The "poly" ropes have an added advantage in their floatability. Size and strength must be considered, whatever the choice.

Anything that tends to produce a spring to ease heavy shocks when towing in heavy weather is helpful. It is on this principle that long heavy tow lines are used for easy towing. The sag in the tow line is desirable and can be increased if necessary by bending an anchor to the middle of the line. This will relieve excessive strains on the towing hawser. In rough weather a long tow line should be used, even if the tow is light.

### Cautions in towing

The tow-line should be made fast so that it can be cast loose if necessary or, failing that, have a knife or hatchet ready to cut it. This line is a potential danger to anyone near if it should break and come whipping forward. Nylon, when it breaks or lets go, acts like a huge rubber band and there have been some bad accidents. In one case a cleat pulled loose from the deck and came through the air like a projectile. Never stand near or in line with a highly strained line and keep a wary eye out at all times.

If for any reason you have to approach a burning vessel, be sure to approach it in such a manner that the flames are blowing away from you. If there are reasons it must be towed (for instance, to prevent it from endangering other boats or property) your light anchor with its length of chain thrown into the cockpit or through a window could act as a good grappling hook.

Never at any time in the process of towing have people on deck to fend off with hands or feet as even the smallest boats coming together under these condition can cause broken bones or severed fingers. Also never allow anybody to be caught between two large vessels where they will be exposed to this danger. The risk here could be the loss of a whole limb.

Never allow anyone to hold a towing line while towing another vessel regardless of size. Badly torn tendons and muscles could make them cripples for life, or they could be dragged overboard.

### Starting the tow

Start off easy! Don't try to dig up the whole ocean with

your screw, and merely end up with a lot of cavitation and vibration without getting anywhere in particular. A steady pull at a reasonable speed will get you there just as fast and with far less strain on boats, lines, and crews.

## Towing principles

When towing, boats should be kept "in step," as it were, by adjusting the length of tow line so that the lead boat and her tow are both on the crest or in the trough of seas at the same time. Under certain conditions, with a confused sea, this may be largely a theoretical consideration, but the general principle is to prevent, if possible, a situation where the tow is shouldering up against the back of one sea, presenting a maximum of resistance, while the towing boat is trying to run down the forward slope of another sea. Then when this condition is reversed, the tow alternately runs ahead and surges back on the tow line with a heavy strain. If there is any degree of uniformity to the waves, the strain on the hawser will be minimized by adjusting it to the proper length.

As the tow gets into protected, quiet waters, shorten up on the line to allow better handling in close quarters. Swing as wide as possible around buoys, channel turns, etc., so that the tow will have room to follow.

A small boat in tow should preferably be trimmed a little by the stern because trimming by the head causes her to yaw. In a seaway this condition is aggravated and it becomes increasingly important to keep the bow relatively light.

In smooth water motor boats may at times borrow an idea from tugs which often, in harbor or sheltered waters, take their tow alongside for better maneuverability. If the tow is a big one the tug will make fast on the other craft's quarter.

It is easy for a larger boat to tow a smaller vessel too fast, causing it to yaw and capsize. Always tow at a moderate speed and make full allowance for adverse conditions of wind and waves.

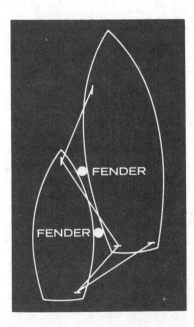

FIG. 921  How springs are used when a boat takes a larger vessel in tow alongside. Fenders are rigged at points of contact, springs made up with no slack. When the towing boat puts her rudder to port or starboard for a turn, both boats respond as a unit.

FIG. 922  A boatman should always be ready to render assistance. In some cases, the best that can be done is to call for assistance and stand by. The Coast Guard 40-footer shown is well equipped to pull a stranded boat free and take her in tow; her crew, too, is better trained and more experienced.  (U.S. Coast Guard photo)

## When not to tow

Towing can be a dangerous undertaking, as well as an expensive one, if not properly done. If you are not equipped to do a proper towing job, stand by the disabled vessel. It may, however, be feasible to put a line across and assist by holding the other craft's bow into the sea at a comfortable angle while waiting for a more suitable towing vessel.

Call the Coast Guard or other salvage agency and turn the job over to them when they arrive. Don't try to be a hero, as you are more than likely not experienced or trained for this type of work. No boat is worth a life.

# Emergency Procedures

The average boatman is a relatively typical person in that he tends to believe that emergencies and accidents happen to "the other guy," and not to him. The seasoned skipper—the good seaman—reasons otherwise. It is not likely to happen to him, but it *could,* and so he prepares himself just in case it does. He also prepares his crew, and, to a lesser extent, the guests aboard his boat.

The best seaman is the one who is prepared for any emergency, before the need arises to meet it.

## Value of planning

An emergency is, by definition, not a planned event, but actions to cope with foreseeable ones can be preplanned and rehearsed. Any emergency will be much less severe and much more easily countered if there is a routine to be executed almost instantly when needed.

It must be recognized, of course, that the actual circumstances will surely vary somewhat from those used for planning and practice, but nevertheless a basic approach and assignment of duties will be of immense help in coping with the unexpected. There is nothing more valuable than fast and correct action when something goes wrong.

## Need for drills and practice

The best plans are of little value if they have not been tried out and evaluated to the best extent practicable short of having a full occurrence of the emergency.

When the plans have been tried out and modified as needed, the next step is to have periodic drills. This should not be done so much as to become boring or irksome, but there are reasonable minimums that should be met. Every boating family should run through its emergency procedures at the beginning of each boating season, and once again on a staggered schedule later in the season. As mentioned earlier in this chapter, every effort should be made to make the drills enjoyable without reducing their business-like nature.

## Guests aboard

Crew training extends, of course, to preparation for emergencies. But do not overlook any guests whom you may have aboard; on most boats, they are at least "temporary crew." You may not be able to train them in drills, but as a minimum they should be shown the location of life preservers and instructed, if necessary, in their use. Do this in a casual, relaxed manner so that they are informed but not alarmed.

If the guests are going to be aboard for an extended cruise, their indoctrination can be correspondingly extended to such items as the location and operation of fire extinguishers, bilge pumps, etc. Use your good judgment as to how far this should be carried with various individuals.

## Types of emergencies

The preceding major section of this chapter dealt with what is probably the most common of boating accidents, running aground. Here we will consider emergencies that are more serious, but fortunately much less likely to happen—man overboard, fire, sudden leaking, and abandoning ship.

## MAN OVERBOARD

At the cry "Man Overboard" fast—*immediate*—action is of the utmost importance; every second counts, particularly at night, in heavy weather, or in cold water. The actions of the helmsman and other crew members should be automatic and without many shouted orders.

It is helpful to the following action if the cry of "Man Overboard" is supplemented by an indication of which side he went over—Port or Starboard, or even Left or Right. This focuses attention of those who did not see the accident and guides their actions.

## Immediate actions

It is customary for the person at the helm to cut the throttle immediately, put the engines in neutral, and swing the stern to the side away from the person in the water. In actual practice, this is of questionable value—a 30-foot boat doing 12 knots moves one boat length in 1½ seconds. Thus even if the person fell off the bow, the stern would be past him before effective action at the controls could be taken. If the victim should fall overboard from

the cockpit, you will be well beyond him almost instantly —don't waste time with throttles or gear shifts, go on immediately with the next steps of the rescue.

## Post a lookout

It is imperative that the person in the water be kept in sight at all times, or at least the spot where he was last seen. Heave over some buoyant object *at once*. Preferably, this will be a standard life ring or a buoyant cushion, but throw something over *immediately*. This will serve to mark the spot and perhaps provide assistance to the person overboard. Designate a specific crewman to do *nothing*

FIG. 923 The "Sav-a-Life" plastic ball can be thrown farther and more accurately than a standard life ring or cushion. When it hits the water, it automatically opens and inflates into a buoyant ring that will support a person in the water. Although not an accepted substitute for legally-required life preservers, it can be helpful in man-overboard emergencies.

but watch the person or his last known location. If more than one crew member is available, assign two to this as their *sole* duty. If it is night-time, have a member of the crew man the searchlight and keep it on the person in the water while the boat maneuvers to pick him up.

## Throw over a life preserver

Throw overboard a life ring or buoyant cushion even though the person in the water is known to be a strong swimmer. Throw as closely as possible to the person without directly hitting him. He may have had the breath knocked out of him when he hit the water, he may be burdened with clothing and shoes, he may even panic despite his swimming ability—for all these reasons, he should have added buoyancy as soon as possible. A water-activated light attached to a life ring is the most effective nighttime device for man-overboard emergencies.

## No "heroes"

Don't let a would-be "hero" jump over the side immediately to rescue the victim—then you would only have two persons rather than one to fish out of the water. The only exception to this would be in the case of a small child or an elderly or handicapped adult. If this must be done, be sure that the rescuer takes with him a life ring or cushion; never let a person enter the water without some added buoyancy.

## Maneuvering to return

Whether you turn to port or starboard had best be decided by experiment in advance. Ordinarily a boat with a right-handed propeller turns quickest to port, but practical experience shows that some boats behave otherwise. By this maneuver you should be able to get back to the scene, with boat under perfect control, in less than a minute. You might find that reversing and backing will be more effective for your boat, but the odds are against it. At any rate make a few tests. Throw a paper or cardboard box overboard and experiment in recovering it until you know precisely what to do if the need should ever arise.

If your craft is a sailboat, the maneuvers necessary to return to the location of the accident and recover the victim will vary widely with your point of sailing at the time and the direction of the wind. In some situations, the boat should come about; in others, jibing will result in faster action. If a spinnaker is in use, it will probably have to be gotten down immediately before the boat can maneuver. For sailboats, man overboard drills are far more important than for power craft, and should be executed under a wide variety of situations.

## Use additional markers

In some circumstances, particularly at night, it may be desirable to throw overboard additional small objects that will float while the boat maneuvers so as to ensure that the path back to the victim can be retraced. A single marker may be lost to sight; multiple objects increase the probability of returning to the proper location.

## Maneuvering for the pick-up

Circumstances will dictate best procedure as to how to approach the man in the water. Although the boat can best be kept under control by approaching from leeward, maneuvering into a position to windward of him will provide a lee as the boat drifts toward him.

The particular maneuver that you use in approaching the victim depends upon common sense and good judgment based on existing conditions such as the sea condition, the temperature of the water, physical condition and ability of the man in the water, boat maneuverability, and the availability of other assistance.

A good procedure is to stop the boat a short distance from the victim in the water, throwing him a light line (such as a skiing tow line of material that floats), and pulling him over to the boat. This will be considerably less hazardous than trying to maneuver the boat right up to him.

## Getting the victim on board

While the boat is being maneuvered back to the victim in the water, make all preparations for getting him back on board. Have a member of the crew, who is physically capable, prepare to go into the water, *if necessary*. He should remove any excess clothing and shoes and *always* put on a life jacket. He will need the added buoyancy in order to save his strength to aid the victim. The rescuer should also have a light safety line; it may be useful in transferring it to the accident victim.

Assisting the unlucky victim back into the boat is a highly individualized matter determined by the craft, the person, and the prevailing sea conditions. The availability of a transom boarding platform if the boat is so equipped will be most helpful. A swimming ladder can usually be quickly rigged if one is carried aboard. Lines with a loop in one end tied with a bowline may be hung over the side for handholds or footholds in climbing back aboard.

Obviously, the propeller should be stopped whenever there is a person in the water near the stern of the boat.

## Call for help if needed

If the victim is not immediately rescued, get on the radio with the urgent communications signal "Pan" to summon assistance from the Coast Guard, marine police, and nearby boats. (Do *not* use "Mayday" as your vessel is not in distress.) Continue the search until released by competent authority.

## Importance of drills

Man overboard drills are most important. It is not necessary for an individual to go over the side, any floating object about the size of a human head can be used as the "victim." For such drills, one crew member should be told to stand aside and take no part in the "rescue" just as if it were he who was in the water. And don't forget that for some drills this non-participant should be the skipper—some day it just might be he who was the "man overboard" and his rescue had to be effected by the rest of the crew without his guidance.

Always hold a "critique" after each drill. Discuss what was done right and what was done wrong, how the procedures could be done better. Learn from your mistakes, and don't repeat them.

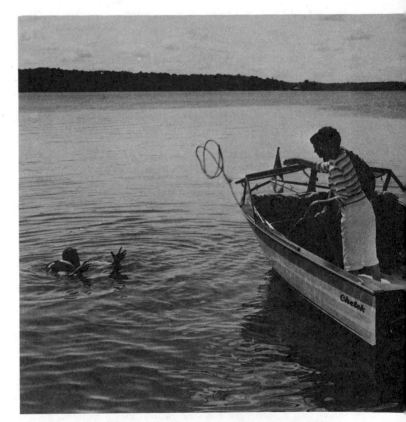

FIG. 924 On every boat, large or small, it is wise occasionally to conduct a "man-overboard" drill. The exact techniques may vary with conditions, but the essence of the idea is: be prepared.

### FIRE EMERGENCIES

Fire on a boat can be a serious experience. A person's surroundings are burning, and he is faced with nowhere to go except into the water. In a sense, he is trapped.

Keep in mind that most fires are preventable. A skipper who keeps his boat in shipshape condition, which includes clean bilges and proper stowage of fuel and gear, will probably never be faced with the emergency condition of fighting a fire. This requires constant attention; whenever a condition is observed that might contribute to a fire, it should be corrected at once.

Despite the skipper's best efforts, fires are a possibility and do occur. Every boatman should be foresighted in this regard. Shipshape conditions include the proper stowage and maintenance of firefighting gear. Having this equipment handy and in good working condition is the first step in combating fire.

### Explosions and fires

Fires may start with either a "bang"—an explosion—or on a much smaller scale. Should your craft have a gasoline explosion, there usually is little that you can do except grab a life preserver, if possible, and go over the side.

When clear of danger, check about and account for all those who were aboard. Render such assistance as you can to those who may be in the water without a buoyant device and those who may have been burned or injured in the blast. Keep all individuals in the water together in a group for morale purposes and to facilitate rescue by other craft.

### Small fires

Should a small fire develop, prompt and effective action will probably control it. Fires require three elements for their existence—fuel, oxygen (air), and heat— remove any one of these and the fire will go out. Thus most fires are fought by smothering them (removing the source of air) or by cooling below the temperature that will support combustion.

FIG. 925 Three elements are needed to support combustion of a fire—fuel, oxygen (air), and heat. If any one is removed, the fire will go out. Fires can be fought by removal of air (smothering), reduction of heat (cooling), or by shutting off of the flow of liquid or gaseous feul.

FIG. 926 Risk of explosion or fire is greatest when the engines are being started or are running. The helmsman should have an extinguisher within easy reach.

### Classes of fires

Fires are classified into three categories:

Class A—fires in ordinary combustible materials such as wood, paper, cloth, etc., where the "quenching-cooling" effect of quantities of water or solutions containing large percentages of water is most effective in reducing the temperature of the burning material below the ignition temperature, and is, therefore, of first importance.

Class B—fires in flammable petroleum products or other flammable liquids, greases, etc., where the "blanketing-smothering" effect of oxygen-excluding media is most effective.

Class C—fires involving electrical equipment where the electrical conductivity of the extinguishing media is of first importance.

### Fire extinguishers

Fire extinguishers are classified on the same "A", "B", "C" system as are fires. Some types of extinguishers, however, have a suitability greater than their basic classification. Extinguishers required by law on boats are in the "B" category, but a carbon-dioxide or dry-chemical extinguisher will also have value in fighting an electrical ("C") fire. On the other hand, a foam-type "B" extinguisher is effective on ordinary Class "A" fires but is *not* safe on Class

"C" electrical fires. Boatmen should remember that for typical Class "A" fires in wood, paper, or bedding, the popular dry-chemical extinguishers are *not* as suitable as an ordinary bucket of water.

Fire extinguishers should be distributed around the boat in relation to potential hazards. One should also be near the boat's control station where it can be grabbed quickly by the helmsman. Another should be mounted near the skipper's bunk so that he can roll out at night with it in his hand. Other locations include the galley (but remember that water is best on a stove alcohol fire!) and any other compartment at some distance from the location of other extinguishers. Fire extinguishers should be mounted where they are clearly visible to all on board as they move about the boat.

## Fighting fires

Burning items such as wood, mattresses, and rags are best extinguished by the cooling effect of an agent such as water. For this reason a bailer or bucket can be a most valuable piece of equipment. You will have an unlimited supply of water available on all sides. Throwing burning materials over the side should not be overlooked.

If a fire occurs in a relatively confined space, the closing of hatches, doors, vents, and ports will tend to keep oxygen from fanning the flames. The hatch or door should not be reopened until fire-fighting equipment is ready for use. In addition, should the fire be in a machinery space, shut off the fuel supply and activate the fixed fire-extinguishing system, if your boat is so equipped.

## Maneuvering the boat

Now let us consider vessel maneuvers that will assist in extinguishing fires. When underway, wind caused by the boat's motion fans the flames; stopping or reducing speed helps to reduce the wind effect. Also it would make sense to keep the fire downwind—that is, if the fire is aft, head the bow of the boat into the wind; if the fire is forward, put the stern of the boat into the wind. Such action helps to reduce any tendency of the fire to spread to other parts of the boat, and may reduce the hazard of smoke enveloping persons on board.

Stow some life preservers well forward in case of fire aft or the necessity of abandoning ship over the bow.

## Summary of actions

The following suggested steps are listed and may be performed, not necessarily in the order shown:
1. If possible, apply the extinguishing agent by:
   a. Using a fire extinguisher,
   b. Discharging fixed smothering system, or
   c. Applying water to wood or materials of this type.
2. If practical, burning materials should be jettisoned (thrown over the side).
3. Reduce the air supply by:
   a. Maneuvering the vessel to reduce the effect of wind, and
   b. Closing hatches, ports, vents, doors, etc. if the fire is in an area where this action will be effective.
4. Make preparation for abandoning ship, which include:
   a. Putting on lifesaving devices, and
   b. Signaling for assistance by radio or any other means available.

## LEAKS AND DAMAGE CONTROL

A boat floats properly only so long as the water is kept outside. A small boat with sufficient built-in flotation ability may stay afloat when filled with water, but it will be rather uncomfortable for the crew and passengers. A skipper who is a good seaman prepares a plan of action to be put into effect should his craft suddenly start taking on water as a result of a collision, striking a submerged object, failure of a through-hull fitting, etc.

## Planning ahead

The circumstances of suddenly taking on water are so varied as to permit only the most generalized advance planning. Drills are usually not possible for this type of emergency, but a checklist of probably desirable actions can be prepared.

## Standard procedures

It should be, to use a military term, SOP (Standard Operating Procedure) to immediately switch on *all* bilge pumps if there is any suspicion of hull damage that might result in taking on water. There are no legal requirements for pumps, as there are for life preservers, fire extinguishers, etc., and many small craft are equipped to handle only a very small inflow of water. The risk of harm to the pumps by running them dry is far less than that of having water in the bilge get a head start on you because of a delay in starting pumping. Remember to turn off the pumps as soon as you are sure that they are not needed.

## Actions of the crew

Members of the crew should be assigned immediately to man the manual bilge pump if you have one (and you certainly should have one!). Another crewman should be told to start at once to inspect for leaks; pull up floor boards and check the bilges, don't wait for the water to rise above the cabin sole.

**FIG. 927 In addition to electrical bilge pumps, a boat should be equipped with at least one manually-operated pump. This can be used even if rising water in the bilge shorts out the boat's batteries.**

If it is determined that the boat is taking on water, it is probably advisable for the skipper to turn over the helm to a qualified member of the crew so that he can go below and personally take charge of the damage control actions.

In most situations, the boat should be slowed or brought to a stop to minimize the inflow of water, but it is possible that a hole in the hull could be in such a location that it would be held above the waterline by maintaining speed.

## Emergency pumping

It is sometimes possible in grave emergencies, where the regular electric and manual bilge pumps cannot keep up with the inflow of water, to use the water pumps of the main engines. Shut off an engine, close the seacock on the raw water intake, break the connection between the seacock and the hose, and move the latter into the now rising bilge water; restart the engine. Engine raw water pumps have quite a capacity and may make the difference between sinking and staying afloat.

Two precautions must be observed. First, there must be enough water already in the bilge and flowing in to meet the engine's needs for cooling. Secondly, caution must be exercised to keep bilge dirt and trash from being sucked into the engine's intake. To lose power if the engine over-heats might be disastrous. These two precautions will usually require that the intake hose be watched and tended at all times by a crew member assigned to that specific duty.

## Operating USCG droppable pumps

Coast Guard aircraft are equipped with pumps that can be dropped in floating containers to boats that need them. The following operating instructions are applicable:

1. Make sure suction hose is tight—connect discharge hose.
2. Fill gas tank.
3. Pull stop switch away from spark plug.
4. Close carburetor choke—turn lever in direction of arrow.
5. Open throttle at base of engine.
6. Attach starting cord and spin engine.
7. After engine starts, open choke.
8. Normally, pumps are self-priming—if difficulty arises, prime.
9. When finished, flush out pump with fresh water.

## Emergency repairs

Almost anything can be stuffed into a hole in the hull to help stop the inflow of water—cushions, pillows, bedding, spare sails—all of these will have some beneficial effect.

Material used to stop a leak will be more effective if it can be applied from the outside where water pressure will aid in holding it in place. This will, of course, require that the boat be stopped while the temporary patch or plug is positioned and secured. If a hole must be plugged from the inside, the pillow, bedding etc., can sometimes be held in place by nailing a batten or bed slat across it. If no better solution can be found, a member of the crew can be assigned to hold the plug in place. In any event, station a crewman or passenger to watch the patched hole and give immediate alarm if the patch or plug fails to hold.

## ASSISTANCE

In any form of emergency, it is well to alert possible sources of assistance without delay. Use your radio with an urgent ("Pan") call to advise the Coast Guard and other craft of your problem. Don't put out a "Mayday" distress call unless you are in obvious danger of sinking, have an uncontrollable fire on board, etc. Don't panic and make a distress call under conditions that do not warrant such action, but also don't fail to alert others to your possible need for assistance soon.

FIG. 928 A radio is probably the primary means of summoning assistance. Do *not* put out a "Mayday" call unless you are in *distress*. If you need help, but are not in danger, use the urgent signal "Pan" on 2182 kc/s or 156.8 Mc/s.

## Summoning assistance

A boat's radio is probably the primary means of obtaining assistance, although it is far from being the only method. Use 2182 kc/s and follow the procedures of Chapter 25.

Other distress signals are listed on pages 67 and 78a.

Any signal that will attract attention and bring help is a satisfactory distress signal. However, if your signal is a known or recognized distress signal, your chances of obtaining assistance are enhanced.

Don't overlook the possible use of a small signal mirror equipped with sighting hole and cross-line target. The reflected mirror signals can be seen as flashes of light for many miles and may be just the device that could attract the attention of aircraft.

There are several recently recognized distress signals for small boats on waters of the United States. A simple orange-red flag may be waved from side to side. Even better is a 72-inch by 45-inch fluorescent orange-red panel cloth bearing an 18-inch black square and an 18-inch black circle, 18-inches apart on the major axis of the flag. This could be tied across a hatch or cabin top as a signal to aircraft. A signal may also be made by slowly and repeatedly raising and lowering arms outstretched to each side. This is a distinctive signal, not likely to be mistaken for a greeting. To be as effective as possible, this signal should be given from the highest vantage point on the boat with consideration given to color contrasts.

## Helicopter rescue

In more and more instances, Coast Guard assistance is being provided by helicopters rather than patrol craft. This new technique requires new knowledge on the part of the boat skipper and is most effective with advance preparations.

## Prior to arrival of helicopter

1. Provide continuous radio guard on 2182 kc/s or specified frequency if possible.
2. Select and clear most suitable hoist area. This must include securing of loose gear, awnings and antenna wires. Trice up running rigging and booms.
3. If hoist is at night, light pick-up areas as well as possible. Be sure you do not shine any lights on the helicopter and blind the pilot. If there are obstructions in the vicinity, put a light on them so the pilot will be aware of their positions.
4. Advise location of pick-up area before the helicopter arrives so that he may adjust for and make his approach as required.
5. Remember that there will be a high noise level under the helicopter, so conversation between the deck crew will be almost impossible. Arrange a set of hand signals between those who will be assisting.

## Rescue by hoist

1. Change course so as to permit the craft to ride as easily as possible with the wind on the bow, preferably on the port bow.
2. Reduce speed if necessary to ease the boat's motion, but maintain steerageway.
3. If you do not have radio contact with the helicopter, signal a "Come on" when you are in all respects ready for the hoist; use a flashlight at night.
4. Allow basket or stretcher to touch down on the deck prior to handling to avoid static shock.
5. If a trail line is dropped by the helicopter, guide the basket or stretcher to the deck with the line; line will not cause shock.
6. Place person in basket sitting with hands clear of sides, or strap person in the stretcher. Place a life

FIG. 929 The Coast Guard is making increased use of helicopters for rescue and assistance work. The gas-turbine powered HH-52A shown can land on the water if necessary. Note the hoisting winch above the door. Skippers should know how to cooperate with helicopter crews. (U.S. Coast Guard photo)

jacket on the person if possible. Signal the helicopter hoist operator when ready for hoist. Person in basket or stretcher nods his head if he is able. Deck personnel give "thumbs up."
7. If necessary to take litter away from hoist point, unhook hoist cable and keep free for helicopter to haul in. *Do not secure cable to vessel or attempt to move stretcher without unhooking.*
8. When person is strapped in stretcher, signal helicopter to lower cable, hook up, and signal hoist operator when ready to hoist. Steady stretcher from swinging or turning.
9. If a trail line is attached to basket or stretcher, use to steady. Keep feet clear of line.

### ABANDONING SHIP

Many boats involved in casualties have continued to float indefinitely. If it becomes necessary to abandon your boat due to fire, danger of sinking, or other emergency, don't leave the area. Generally a damaged boat can be sighted more readily than a person, and it may help to keep you afloat.

Keep in mind that distance over water is deceptive. Usually the estimated distance is much shorter than the actual distance. Keep your head and restrain your initial impulse to swim ashore. Calmly weigh the facts of the situation such as: injuries to passengers, the proximity of shore, and your swimming abilities, before deciding upon your course of action.

Before abandoning your craft, put on your life preserver and give distress signals. Don't foolishly waste signaling devices where small likelihood of assistance exists. Wait until you sight someone or something. If your vessel is equipped with a radio telephone, a distress message should be sent.

# Maintenance

The condition of a boatman's craft can be an indication of his overall seamanship knowledge and abilities. Using a boat is only part of its ownership—maintenance, keeping her shipshape and Bristol Fashion, is the other part.

For most recreational boat owner-skippers, his craft represents a considerable investment of family funds. She must be properly and continuously maintained to keep up the value of this investment. The secret of getting the fullest measure of pleasure from your boat is to make the necessary maintenance effort enjoyable, even fun, and not a grudging chore. The key to this happy situation is proper planning and a low but continuous level of effort.

Don't let your boat get run down; it will not only look worse, but will require more total maintenance than if it had been properly cared for. Deferred maintenance is always more of a burden and more expensive. Maintain the value of your boat—and your pride in her—by continuous attention to maintenance, perhaps peaking in the spring of each year, but not neglected at any time.

### USE AND CARE OF EQUIPMENT

A planned maintenance program can start with the use and care of the boat and its equipment. Let us first consider equipment and supplies. To have one's craft in true shipshape condition means a place for everything and every-

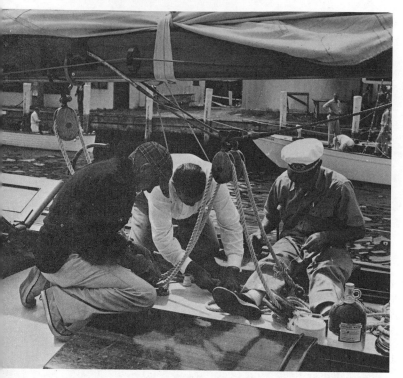

FIG. 930 The key to proper and adequate maintenance, without its becoming a burdensome chore, is a low but continuous level of effort. Do small jobs when they need it—don't put them off. Have a regular schedule for preventive maintenance. (Peter Stackpole photo)

thing in its place; and, too, everything in good working condition.

### Lines and sails

There is nothing that we depend upon so much as lines. We use them to anchor, to tie up, and in fact almost everything we do depends upon their use. For our safety, these must be kept in good condition. We must be sure that lines are dry before stowing; if not, they will rot if they are of manila. And, we must be sure that they are stowed in a well-ventilated compartment, for if it is not, we might just as well have not dried them. While synthetic cordage and sail cloth are not subject to rot, mildew can form from deposited spores of fungus unless these items are clean and dry when stowed. The unseamanlike practice of stowing wet ropes and sails below decks will inevitably result in a damp condition, which is uncomfortable.

The same reasoning goes for cotton sails, foul weather gear, and any other materials of the same sort.

Clean, dry, and well-ventilated compartments not only save lines, sails, etc. but contribute to safety of the hull itself. If these compartments, as well as all other parts of the boat, are not well ventilated, dry rot may set in, and this may involve extensive repairs and a big bill. Nothing could be sadder than the boat that at a distance looks fine with a new coat of paint, but which underneath is a rotting shell.

### Stowage of supplies

Every item of equipment should be well marked and kept in its specific place. Any article with labels should have the contents painted on the bottle or can proper; it is a good idea even to remove any paper labels, as they may come off in any dampness and cause problems. Some skippers use adhesive tape on the articles and print the contents on the tape; others merely place a letter on each different item (A means potatoes, B means beans, C means sunburn ointment) and keep a key list on board. The only trouble with the latter method is if you lose the key list you're in trouble.

The new felt-tip marking pens are excellent for labeling cans and other containers. Experiment with different ones until you find the most moisture-resistant type.

### Use a checklist

If all equipment is clearly marked and always in its proper place it eases the skipper's mind, to say nothing of adding to his safety. Not only is he sure of having everything, but he doesn't worry for the first day trying to remember what he has forgotten. In order to carry this thought out successfully, it is necessary and good seamanship to have and use a sailing checklist. A sailing checklist is a list of all items that a competent skipper will provide for the boat, her equipment, supplies, stores, and condition prior to shoving off from the mooring. If this list is kept aboard, and if the skipper checks off each item before he shoves off, there will never be any need to worry about being without the necessary equipment.

## THE HULL

The hull is, to say the least, a very important part of a boat. No matter how good your superstructure is, if your hull is rotten you just have no boat. In order to preserve a wooden hull, we must keep it well painted. Every year the old coat of paint should be sanded down before new is applied, and every so often, depending on how thick the

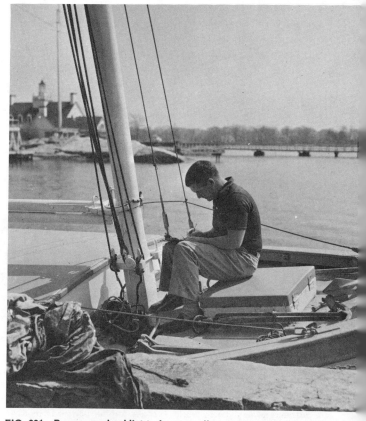

FIG. 931 Prepare a checklist to be sure all necessary supplies and equipment are on board before setting out on a cruise. Use it every time, modifying and updating from experience.

old coats of paint are, all paint should be removed, the hull sanded, and seams and scars filled before a new coat of paint is applied.

## Selection of paint

The number of different types of paint has expanded remarkably in recent years. While there is nothing wrong with "old fashioned" marine paint as used for many years, the modern skipper should give consideration to some of the new paints with exotic names such as polyutherane, epoxy, acrylic, etc. If you don't feel qualified to make a selection, ask the professionals at your boatyard and talk to other skippers about their experiences with various hull finishes.

## Painting techniques

No matter which paint you select, proper surface preparation and application of the paint are *absolutely essential* if the desired results are to be obtained. Follow the manufacturer's directions explicitly from start to finish. Select the proper weather conditions for your work—wait until the morning dew has evaporated, and stop well before sundown.

"Between wind and water," that part of the vessel at or near the waterline, is the most difficult part of the hull to keep protected. This is because it is always getting wet and drying off and also that the water causes a lot of friction at this location. A special quick-drying paint called boot-topping is used here, the principal ingredients of which are varnish and dryer.

## Fiberglass hulls

The above comments have been directed to the owners of boats with wooden hulls. If yours is of fiberglass, you will have less maintenance, but some will still be required. Don't neglect the care of your hull just because it requires less attention.

A fiberglass hull should be cleaned as required to keep it free of dirt and oily scum; more cleaning will be needed near the waterline than higher on the topsides. Try to get the job done using only a detergent without an abrasive powder that can dull a high-gloss finish. If you must use a scouring powder to remove marks and greasy streaks, use a mild one and use it with caution.

Liquid cleaner wax is excellent for fiberglass hulls, particularly for mid-season continuing maintenance. Once a year, usually at spring fitting-out, do a more thorough two-step job with a paste cleaner followed by a paste wax. This is also the time to patch up any hair-line cracks that have appeared in the gel (surface) coat of the fiberglass.

After a few years of use, a fiberglass hull may require painting to restore it to top appearance. Many paints are available for this purpose, most of which are two-part products to be mixed just prior to application. Advances in chemical and plastics technology are now resulting in one-part paints for fiberglass surfaces that are easier to use and will give satisfactory results. The problem is to get proper adhesion to the fiberglass plus a high-gloss finish. As with painting a wooden hull, the best procedure is to ask a professional and talk with people who have used various products to get their opinions. Again, too, it is most important that the manufacturer's instructions for surface preparation and paint application be adhered to exactly.

FIG. 932 **Two secrets to success in painting are proper preparation of the surface and application of the paint in strict conformity with manufacturer's instructions.**

## BOTTOM MAINTENANCE

Special attention must be given to the maintenance of the bottom of the boat; this is a most important item as it is usually available for inspection only once or twice a year.

Except for small boats that are taken out of the water after each period of use, the bottom must be kept covered with anti-fouling paint. This type of paint, usually with a copper base, has properties that tend to keep worms out of the bottom as well as to discourage marine growth that attaches itself to the bottom.

Coming into wider use are bottom paints employing other metals and chemicals toxic to marine life. With these, bottom paints are now available in a wide range of colors.

**FIG. 933** In most locations, antifouling paint must be applied to a boat's underwater surfaces to protect against worms and marine growth. Bottom finishes are available in many colors as well as the old familiar "copper" paint. (Wm. H. Koelbel photo)

## Launching wet or dry

There are two theories about applying bottom paint. Some say that the boat should be put into the water as soon as the paint has been applied, that is, while it is still fairly wet, while others state that the paint should be dry before launching. Follow the manufacturer's directions on the can for the best results.

## BRIGHTWORK

Brightwork, natural wood surfaces finished with varnish or similar products, requires special care. Horizontal areas of brightwork should be wiped clear of morning dew each day to prolong their life. All brightwork will require a good sanding at least yearly followed by a fresh coat of varnish. Those parts of the brightwork that receive a lot of wear or spray will need to be given more than one coat each season. Unless varnished areas are kept well covered, moisture will get into the wood and the result will be that

**FIG. 934** Varnished surfaces, called "brightwork," require more care than painted or natural wood or fiberglass areas, but to many boat owners their added beauty is worth the effort. Often, care of brightwork can be turned over to the "first mate." (Rosenfeld photo)

it will turn dark, in extreme cases, black.

## Wooding down

To keep brightwork looking well is a lot of work, but the beauty of it can make it worthwhile. No matter how much care is taken, it will turn just a little darker each year. Many modern varnishes and synthetic equivalents now include a "filter" to screen out ultraviolet rays of the sun that are most damaging to brightwork. The additive slows down the aging process. Even with this added protection, however, it will be necessary every few years to remove all of the varnish with varnish remover, sand the bare wood, and start with a fresh coat. From four to six separate coats will generally be required.

## Reduction of brightwork

In recent years more and more boats have appeared with almost no brightwork at all. The cabins and spars are painted and in fact the only parts left natural may be the handrails, toerails, and trim around hatches.

This move toward little or no brightwork has even invaded interiors. A few years ago this would have been looked upon as sacrilege. No matter how much oldtimers view this trend with alarm, it does have this advantage—it does not reduce the protective qualities which are the main reasons for keeping surfaces covered, and it does make less work. In many cases, natural, unfinished teak is being substituted for mahogany that must be kept varnished.

## DECK CARE

Canvas decks present a special problem. They must be kept covered with a good deck paint for protection, but the less paint you put on the better. If you get too much paint on the decks, not only will it crack but they will become smooth. This is not good especially on a small boat, as a smooth deck makes for precarious footing in wet weather. This has been overcome on some boats by sprinkling fine sand on the decks while the paint is still wet. Also, some paint manufacturers are putting out a special paint with a non-skid surface.

## Fiberglass decks

Decks of fiberglass require little care other than rinsing off dirt and salt spray. On most boats, anti-slip protection is built in by the manufacturer. In some cases, however, additional non-skid strips or specially painted areas will be required for safety. If it becomes necessary to paint a fiberglass deck, don't fail to provide for continued anti-skid protection where needed.

## Teak decks

Decks on large power and sail craft are often made of unfinished teak. Such decks are attractive, quite non-skid, and require little maintenance. They may be allowed to assume a natural, weathered appearance, or they can be periodically bleached to a lighter color, as the individual skipper prefers.

Teak decks should be washed down to keep them free of dirt that might get ground in when walked upon. Salt sea water is excellent for washing down teak decks. A periodic scrubbing with a special teak cleaner is not a difficult chore and will improve overall appearance, but it should not be done too often.

**FIG. 935 Teak is an excellent material for decks. The wood can be left unfinished or given a light treatment with special preservatives. It weathers well and provides a non-skid surface.** (Rosenfeld photo)

Decks of teak wood are subject to staining from oily liquids or solids—particularly from some types of food such as bits of potato chips or mayonnaise drippings from sandwiches—but special paste or spray cleaners will efficiently remove these spots.

## PAINTING METAL SURFACES

If any metal is to be painted, be sure to use a priming coat of anti-corrosive paint against the metal first. Popular types of such paint include the familiar red lead, zinc chromate, and aluminum. Paints for this purpose will be so labeled on the container; don't use a paint for anti-corrosion protection unless it is so designated.

If your boat has a metal bottom it is specially important that anti-corrosive paint be used before the anti-fouling paint. Ingredients of most bottom paint are oxides of mercury and copper, and if these come in contact with steel, corrosion will result. The anti-fouling paints offer no protection to the hull against sea-water corrosion, but the anti-corrosion paints have no anti-fouling properties, so both must be used.

### Painting aluminum

Boats having aluminum hulls may be painted for protection against corrosive attack although this is not generally required with modern alloys properly selected. Underwater anti-fouling paint will be needed for aluminum bottoms under the same conditions as for wood or fiberglass boats.

Aluminum will hold paint very well *provided* that the metal surface has been properly prepared and a suitable primer has been used. Greater care must be taken with this metal than with others commonly used. The aluminum must be *absolutely clean*, free of all oil, scale, dirt, etc., even free of fingerprints. Sand-blasting or wire brushing will be needed to etch the surface slightly in order to make the paint adhere. Zinc chromate is a suitable primer; two

coats should be used to insulate the aluminum hull from any lead-pigmented paint or copper-bearing bottom coating so as to prevent galvanic action between the dissimilar metals.

When patching up the paint job on any area of an aluminum hull, always be sure to prepare the metal surface thoroughly and use a primer coat next to the aluminum.

## GENERAL RULES FOR PAINTING

There are a few simple rules for painting. If observed, they will make such work simpler and more satisfactory. These are:

1. Never paint over a wet, dirty, or greasy surface.
2. Never paint during wet weather.
3. Never paint before cleaning and sanding.
4. Do not continuously apply new over old coats.
5. Never apply paint heavily.
6. Paint with reasonable frequency.
7. Use surfacing putty (trowel or brushing cement) to fill nicks and gouges after the prime coat of paint, unless manufacturer's instructions indicate otherwise.
8. Never use a blow torch immediately after applying paint remover.
9. Never scrape or sand near fresh paint.

### Sequence for painting

There is a generally preferred order for painting the various parts of a boat as follows:

1. All interiors, including bilge (if painted) and engines.
2. Spars.
3. All deck gear, cockpits, ventilators, hatches, etc.
4. Cabin exterior and decks.
5. Hull topsides.
6. Bottom.
7. Boot-topping.

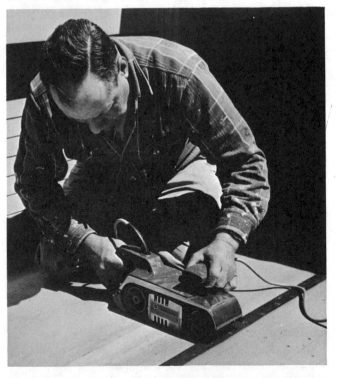

**FIG. 935(a) For boat work, the Black & Decker two-speed belt sander is a versatile tool, eliminating the hard work of hand sanding.** (Photograph by Wm. H. Koelbel)

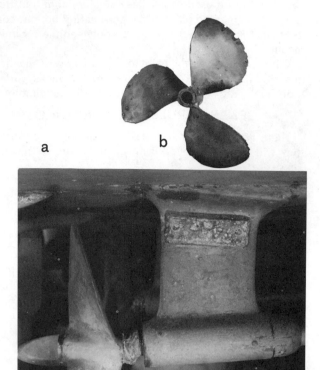

FIG. 936 Whenever your boat is hauled, inspect underwater areas. Zinc blocks and collars, as shown in (a), are used to control galvanic corrosion and must be regularly checked and replaced when needed. Failure to do this may have the results pictured in (b).

## INSPECTION NECESSARY

Besides keeping all appropriate surfaces well covered with paint or varnish, there are many other parts that must be inspected regularly. For example, on some boats you must be constantly on the lookout for galvanic corrosion. This chemical reaction is caused when different metals such as brass or bronze and iron come together or in close proximity to each other in salt or impure water. This is often noticeable on boats between an iron rudder and a bronze propeller. Cases have been known where the rudder is just eaten up. This can be checked by placing a zinc plate nearby so that the zinc, in contact with the part to be protected, will be affected instead of the iron. However, if this is done, care must be taken to watch the zinc plate and replace it whenever necessary. Systems may be installed in which a reverse flow of current is used to equalize and offset any destructive current.

### Make regular checks

Regular checks of shaft logs, stuffing boxes, bearings, underwater fittings, and the propeller are essential. Your steering system and cables should be gone over often. If your steering system goes wrong in a tight place, you will not only damage your own vessel but may also injure some person or another boat.

### Keep your boat clean

All equipment as well as the hull itself must be kept clean at all times. This also includes the bilges. Dirty bilges can result in stopped-up inlets to bilge pumps, and this is sure to happen just when the pump is most needed. There is nothing that gets dirty easier than a boat. Not only is it uncomfortable to try to live on, but it is injurious to the hull and the equipment. Regular cleaning makes for little work to keep your boat spick-and-span; if you let it go, it is a hard job to clean up.

### Inspection checklist

Earlier in this section, a sailing checklist was described that all good skippers use before each run. In order to assist the skipper in preventing breakdowns, every boat should have an *inspection checklist* on board and in use. An inspection checklist is a list of all items that the skipper will regularly inspect, and the scheduled periods for such inspections, with a place for the skipper to write in the date of each inspection in order to keep his boat well found.

## ENGINE CARE

In a motor boat the engine is the only means of propulsion, and in an auxiliary it is the means of getting in and out of tight places. Therefore, the engine is something that should be in the best of shape at all times and should always start at once. All of us are not good mechanics, but all of us should be able to (1) obtain, read, and follow the manufacturer's instruction book; (2) know enough not to fool with something we are not sure of; and (3) get instruction on simple trouble diagnosis and emergency repairs—U.S.P.S. members can and should take the Engine Maintenance Course.

### Routine care

There are, however, a number of things that any skipper can do not only to keep his engine running well for whenever it is needed, but also to keep down the cost of repair bills. All should be done at intervals and in the manner prescribed by the maker's operating manual.

FIG. 937 Regular cleaning makes for little work to keep a boat spick-and-span.
(Rosenfeld photo)

FIG. 938 The average powerboat skipper is not expected to be a mechanic, but he must have an idea of how to maintain his engines. The manufacturer's instruction book should be aboard and its preventive maintenance procedures carried out. (Charles Anderson photo)

Typical routine maintenance items include:
1. Frequently check oil level; change oil regularly.
2. Check cooling system, including intake, regularly.
3. Keep batteries filled and fully charged.
4. Oil starter, generator, and distributor regularly.
5. Keep grease cups filled; turn down and clean regularly.
6. Keep engines clean, especially all filters.
7. Keep fuel lines tight; check for vibration.
8. Check all electric wiring periodically.
9. Do not race a cold motor.
10. Cool down engine before stopping it.
11. Engage clutch only at moderate speeds.
12. Carry spare parts and know how to install them.
13. Carry proper tools.

## CARE OF SAILS

Modern sailboats use nearly all synthetic sailcloth—dacron and nylon. These materials have greatly improved characteristics over canvas, but they do require proper use and maintenance.

### Care in use

Protect sails from chafing—use wooden or rubber protectors over turnbuckles and at the tips of spreaders. Don't let sails slat needlessly; it wears the stitching and tears batten pockets. Use properly fitted battens and remove them when the sail is furled.

### Care in stowage

The greatest enemy of synthetic sailcloth is the sun. Excessive sunlight ultimately causes the material to break down and lose its strength. If sails are left on, they should be furled *and covered*. Water and moisture will not harm dacron and nylon and so such sails can be stored damp if necessary. It is, however, advisable to dry them if you can in order to avoid mildew and the general carrying of mois-

ture below decks.

Wash sails once or twice a season with pure water and soap—no detergents; and never use a washing machine. Hose off, spread to dry, and inspect before folding. Try to keep them as free from salt as possible.

When storing for the winter, wash, clean, and dry. In folding, lay out on the floor, fold lengthwise accordion fashion. When you have a 2- to 3-foot-square bundle, fold head to foot, tie up and store safely or hang to protect from vermin.

### Sail maintenance

Although any major repairs should be left to a professional sailmaker, every sailor should be familiar with four basic emergency repairs: the round stitch, the herringbone stitch, the patch, and sail repair tape.

**Round Stitch.** The round or overhand stitch is used particularly for light sails and in repairing minor tears of from one to four inches. Gather the two sides of the rip, starting about an inch above it. Secure the thread *not* by knotting, but by passing it under the first few stitches; then

FIG. 939 Sails of modern craft are almost entirely synthetic— dacron, nylon, and others. While more resistant to damage from misuse, they still require proper care and maintenance for good service and long life. (Rosenfeld photo)

187

**FIG. 940** When sails are furled on the boom, they should be protected by a cover. Sunshine, more than use, rain, or salt spray, is the greatest enemy of synthetic sails. *(Schwarm, Sheldon photo)*

sew over it and continue round and round, ending about an inch below the tear. Finish your job in the same turn-under way.

**Herringbone Stitch.** This is used for more serious repairs. Before placing the two sides of the rip together, fold under a narrow margin on each and "iron" it like a pair of pants by gently scraping the edge of the sailcloth with your knife. Then make alternate long and short stitches to avoid an even line, starting about a quarter-inch from the end of the tear, and finish a quarter-inch below it. Tuck the end of the twine under the final few stitches as in the round job, and cut it. This is a stitch that is best learned from someone who knows how.

**FIG. 941** A sailboat skipper should be able to make minor repairs, but all major maintenance and alteration work should be referred to a professional sailmaker. The herringbone stitch, above, is used for tears too extensive to permit use of the simpler round stitch. Start ¼-inch from the tear and finish below it. *(Frank Rohr photo)*

**Patch.** Cut your patch, if possible, from the same weight and type of material as the damaged sail. Allow about one and one-half inches of margin on either side of the tear and turn the patch under a half-inch all the way round, "ironing" folds with knife treatment to keep them manageable, especially with heavier weight cloths. Try to get the weave of the patching cloth to run identically with the sail being repaired. Measuring the approximate area and marking the patch material with pencil before cutting will help.

Miter corners of the patch and, pinning it to sail with extra needles, use the round or overhand stitch to sew your patch to the sail. Pound it into submission with a knife handle; turn the whole lot over; miter the corners of the torn sail itself; sew it to the back of the patch, and hoist away.

**Tape.** Spinnaker and white rigging tape can be pressed into service swiftly and efficiently to help you finish—even win—a race, or perhaps withstand the wind in some cruising crisis till you reach port.

In making the repair, separate the sticky part from its guard which comes as part of the roll; then, as you unroll the ready tape, press with your fingers on both sides of the rip or seam. It should hold till you can get to it with needle and thread, or bring it ashore to the sailmaker.

## Sail repair kit

Various sailmakers can supply emergency repair kits suitable for the sails used on your boat. These include sewing twine, needles, beeswax, a sewing palm, and other useful items, including a booklet of instructions on the care and repair of sails.

## WINTER LAY-UP

Perhaps the greatest damage is done to a boat during the long winter months when she is laid up. In the north boats are usually pulled out during the winter, while in the south they are usually left in the water. Of course these call for slightly different techniques.

## Storage on land

In general, these are the things to do when laying up for the winter hauled out on shore:

1. Thoroughly clean the bottom, decks, cockpit, bilge, all compartments, and lockers.
2. Apply a coat of good anti-fouling paint to the bottom, and sand down and prime all other marred surfaces.
3. Drain the fuel system, tanks, lines, pumps, and carburetor.
4. Drain and flush out all water systems and tanks; drain the toilets.
5. Winterize the engine in accordance with the manufacturer's instruction manual. This will normally include draining and flushing the cooling system; draining and refilling the crankcase; applying oil to inside of each cylinder through the sparkplug holes; and other preservative actions. Thoroughly clean the exterior of the engine; sand and touch up with paint any scarred areas to prevent rusting.
6. Remove the batteries from the boat; store in an area not subject to freezing temperatures and place on a "trickle" charge.
7. Place a light coating of grease over all chromeplated

metal surfaces.

8. Leave all floorboards up, doors ajar, ports and skylights open, hatches partly open, drawers and lockers open.
9. Carefully fit a well-made winter cover, provided with ventilation ports, if boat is to be stored outdoors.

## Storage afloat

When making plans for your boat's winter lay-up, don't fail to give consideration to "wet storage." New ice-protection techniques are coming into wider usage, and more owners are leaving their craft in the water for the winter months—it has many advantages.

The cost is often less, but the real gains are in the better storage conditions for the boat. Water temperatures do not fluctuate so widely or rapidly as do those of the air, and so there is less "sweating" inside the hull. Properly protected with antifreeze, the engine can be periodically started and run, which is better for it than standing idle for several months.

Another advantage of wet storage is that there is less danger of the hull's warping or becoming distorted. A boat's structure is designed to be uniformly supported by water; resting on a few blocks, or even in its own special cradle, is distinctly "unnatural" for it. If protected against ice, covered, in-water storage is the best way for your boat to sit out the winter months until the next boating season.

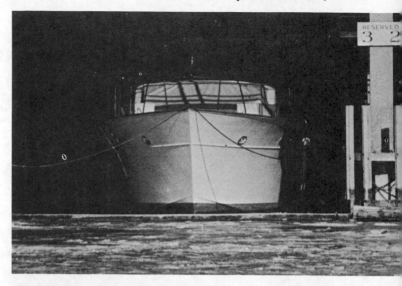

**FIG. 943** More and more boats are being kept in the water over the winter season even where ice normally is a problem. Air pumped through pipes on the bottom brings warmer water to the surface and prevents formation of ice near the hull. (Chicago Sun-Times photo)

**FIG. 944** Black & Decker's variable speed reversible drill is adaptable to a wide variety of boat construction and maintenance jobs.

## Winterizing procedures afloat

The actions to be taken for a winter lay-up afloat will, of course, be somewhat different from those in the list above for when the boat is to be hauled out. The engine should be winterized, but the details, as in connection with the cooling system, will vary. Gas tanks may be filled, to reduce condensation, rather than being drained. Excess gear should be removed from the boat, and all lockers, drawers, etc., should be left open to promote ventilation.

## Getting a head start on fitting out

Some annual maintenance chores may be suitable for accomplishment in the fall at the time of laying-up. Any that can be done at this time will reduce the effort required the following spring and so expedite your next boating season.

### KEEP YOUR BOAT WELL MAINTAINED

Once a boat is "Shipshape and Bristol Fashion" it doesn't take much work to keep her so. It is only when she is allowed to run down that the work is heavy.

**FIG. 942** In northern waters, boats are normally hauled out for dry storage during the winter. Proper blocking and shoring are necessary so that the hull is adequately supported and will not distort in shape. Canvas cover should provide protection and ventilation.

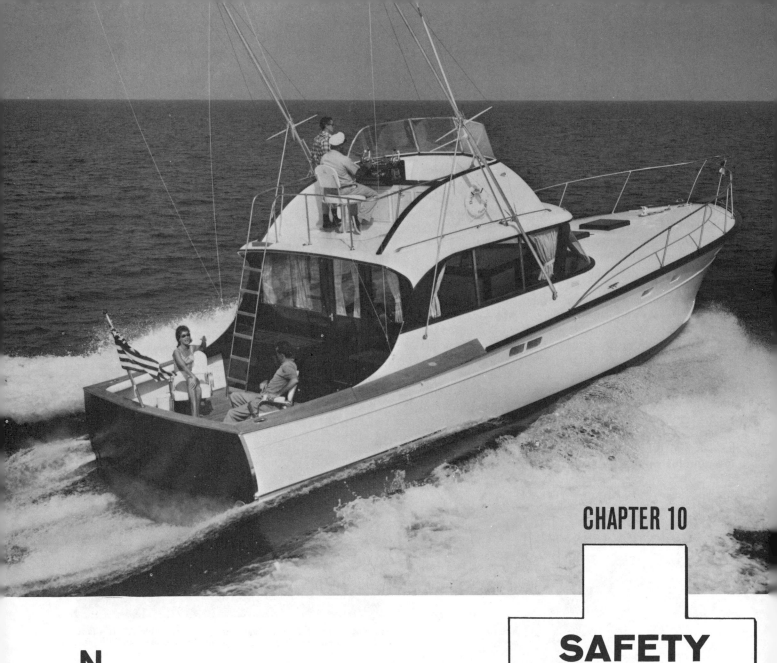

# CHAPTER 10

# SAFETY AFLOAT

**N**o one should ever be deterred from enjoying the wholesome pleasures of boating by hazards that *might* be encountered; neither should he take safety for granted. No one—skipper, first mate, crew, nor guests—need fear the water and recreational boating if it is approached in a sensible manner.

While not allowing it to detract from the enjoyment of boating, the wise skipper practices safety at *all* times while afloat and studies it frequently ashore. He recognizes its importance, and safety is always in the back of his mind, never forgotten nor ignored. He views safety not as an arbitrary set of rules, but rather as the practical application of knowledge, as commonsense requirements and practices that should be thoroughly understood and followed. If "hazards" of any nature are recognized and respected, they largely cease to be hazards.

It is an established fact that most boating accidents and difficulties arise from ignorance, and could have been avoided. A man does not knowingly put his life, and the lives of others, and the safety of valuable property in jeopardy, but he may do so through lack of knowledge. Serious study and thought toward safety can significantly reduce the problems encountered while on the water.

Photograph by Schwarm and Sheldon, Inc.

Safety afloat is a broad topic encompassing essentially all aspects of boating. It is involved in the construction of boats, their equipment, operation, and maintenance. Safety matters are touched on in other chapters of this book in their relationship to government regulations, Rules of the Road, boat handling, seamanship, and other major topics. Here, safety afloat will be the *principal* consideration, with appropriate cross-references to other sections.

## SAFETY ORGANIZATIONS

There are a number of public organizations devoted to the promotion of safety in recreational boating. Several of these approach safety as an educational matter; others are concerned with the material and operational aspects of boats and boating. Each plays an important part in enhancing the safety of small craft, their crews and passengers.

### Educational organizations

The **United States Power Squadrons** is a volunteer organization of more than 75,000 members organized into over 370 local Squadrons. These units, located throughout the United States and in some overseas areas, offer educational programs of basic boating safety and piloting to the public, and more advanced courses to their membership.

The USPS was founded in 1914 primarily to provide training in the proper operation of power boats (most of the "yachts" of those days were sail). This was accomplished by courses of instruction in winter and boat drills during the summer. Over the years since its founding, membership and activities of the USPS have gradually changed and adjusted to the prevailing interests and needs of boatmen. Today, despite the word "Power" in its name, the USPS includes many sailboat skippers in its membership and teaches a "Sail" course.

Although members may wear uniforms, and various levels of the organization are directed by officers with semi-naval ranks, the United States Power Squadrons is a civilian body in every way, not military. It is a nonprofit, self-sustaining, private membership educational organization dedicated to the teaching of better and safer boating. It also provides cooperation with federal, state, and local governments in the broad interests of boating safety. Boats under command of a member can usually be identified by the USPS ensign with its blue and white vertical stripes; see page IXe.

More than 50,000 boatmen and members of their families attend the free USPS Piloting course every year. Information on local classes is published periodically in *Motor Boating* magazine or an inquiry can be addressed to USPS Headquarters, P.O. Box 510, Englewood, New Jersey 07631.

In Canada, the Canadian Power Squadrons are organized in a manner generally similar to the USPS, with modifications to fit that country's laws and customs. The CPS ensign is illustrated on page T. Power Squadron ideals and programs are also spreading to other nations and parallel organizations may be seen in future years.

The **United States Coast Guard Auxiliary** is a voluntary civilian organization of owners of boats, private airplanes, and amateur radio stations; it is a non-military group although administered by the U.S. Coast Guard. Its mission is to promote safety in the operation of small craft through education, boat examinations, and operational activities.

The USCG Auxiliary carries a program of free public in-

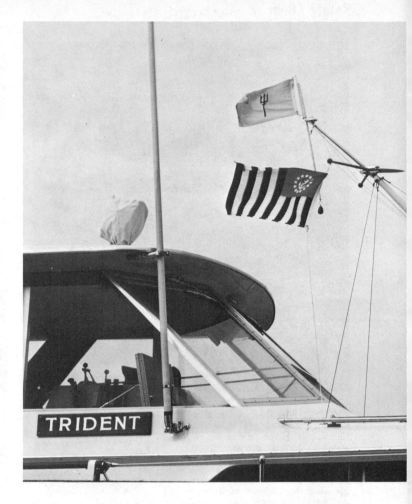

FIG. 1001 The United States Power Squadrons is an organization of volunteers dedicated to making boating safer through education. Craft skippered by USPS members are usually identified by the distinctive flag, with blue and white vertical stripes, shown here at the starboard yardarm. The flag at the masthead identifies the owner as an officer of the USPS; in this case, the blue trident on a white field signifies Rear Commander.

struction through its 1-lesson Outboard Motorboat Handling Course, 3-lesson Safe Boating Course, and 8-lesson Basic Seamanship Course. Members of the Auxiliary also take courses to increase their knowledge and abilities, advancing through qualifications of Basically Qualified Member, Specialist, and Operationally Qualified Member. Although uniformed and organized along military lines, and closely affiliated with the regular Coast Guard, membership in the Auxiliary remains strictly civil in nature and does not in any way constitute inactive or active military service. The Auxiliary has no law enforcement powers. See pages V and W for illustrations of USCGAux (the correct abbreviation for the Auxiliary) flags, pennants, and uniform insignia.

The Coast Guard Auxiliary is well-known for its program of Courtesy Motorboat Examinations, fig. 1002. Specially trained members conduct annual checks of boats only at the owner's request. Boats that meet a strict set of requirements are awarded a decal called the "Shield of Safety." No report to the authorities is made of craft that fail to qualify; the skipper is urged to remedy defects and request re-examination. The CME is provided as a public service for the boat owner's benefit.

Operationally, the Auxiliary promotes safety afloat by assisting the Coast Guard in patrolling marine regattas and

191

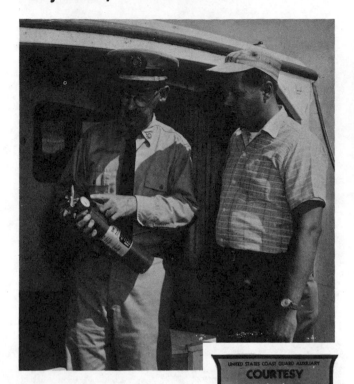

FIG. 1002 The Coast Guard Auxiliary makes Courtesy Motorboat
Examinations, but only at the request of the craft's owner. Boats
meeting all legal requirements
and certain additional safety
standards of the Auxiliary are
awarded the "Shield of Safety"
decal for the current year.
(Official Coast Guard photograph)

FIG. 1003 The Coast Guard Auxiliary is a civilian organization of
boatmen closely affiliated with the USCG. Members conduct public
instruction classes, make courtesy boat safety examinations, and
assist the Coast Guard in near-shore operational missions. The
"Blue Ensign" identifies the boat of a USCGAux member. They frequently supplement regular USCG patrol craft at races, regattas,
and other marine events. When so functioning in the interest of
boating safety, these boats fly the regular Coast Guard flag and
carry an identification sign.

racing events. In many areas, the Auxiliary also carries out
an extensive program of search and rescue for craft that
are in distress, disabled, or reported as overdue. Many
lives have been saved and many skippers have been aided
by the dedicated members of the Coast Guard Auxiliary.

Information on public classes of the Auxiliary or mem-
bership in the organization may be obtained from the
Flotilla in your vicinity or by writing to the appropriate
Coast Guard District Headquarters; see fig. 1502, page 301.

The **American National Red Cross** has a program of
water safety education that includes instruction and the
publication of pamphlets. Topics covered by the Red Cross
include swimming, outboard boating, and small sailboat-
ing. Information on classes and other programs can be obtained from local Red Cross Chapters.

## Equipment organizations

In addition to the national volunteer organizations
working toward greater safety afloat through education,
there are nonprofit groups within and related to the boating industry that promote safety through higher standards
for equipment, including its installation and use.

The **American Boat & Yacht Council, Inc.** is a nonprofit,
public service organization founded for the purpose of
"improving and promoting the design, construction,
equipage, and maintenance of small craft with reference to
their safety." Membership in the Council is open to anyone
interested in furtherance of its objectives. Regular Members may serve in administrative offices and on administra-

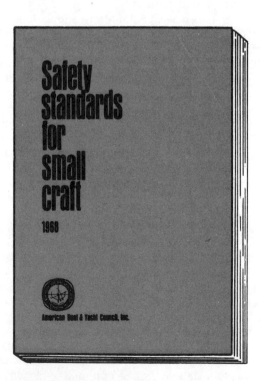

FIG. 1004 The American Boat & Yacht Council, Inc. is a non-profit,
public service organization founded to increase safety in the design,
construction, equipment, and maintenance of small craft. It periodically publishes a compilation of its "Safety Standards"—worthwhile
reading for all skippers.

tive committees, but only Technical Members (highly qualified individuals) may serve on the Council's Technical Board and technical committees.

The American Boat & Yacht Council publishes "Safety Standards." These recommended specifications and practices are intended as good guidance toward making small craft as free from dangerous defect or deficiency as practicable in the interest of minimizing loss of life, injury, and loss of property. Standards are stated largely in terms of desired performance and are not intended to preclude attainment of the desired safety level by other means.

Safety Standards are prepared by Project Technical Committees formed as broadly based groups of recognized authorities with the objective of obtaining a maximum of agreement and acceptance. All technical reports and safety standards are advisory only; the Council has no powers of enforcement.

The AB&YC does not "approve" boats, equipment, materials, or services. Compliance with appropriate standards may be indicated by listings of nationally recognized testing laboratories whose findings may be used as a guide to approval. All standards are reviewed at intervals of three years, or more frequently if necessary because of comments received or advances in technology.

The American Boat & Yacht Council periodically publishes a complete compilation of its "adopted" and "proposed" standards. If needed, supplements are prepared between regular editions of the full publication. Included are standards for such diverse matters as "good visibility from the helm position," "life-saving equipment," "engine exhaust systems," "electrical grounding of DC systems," "lightning protection," "sewerage treatment systems," and "distress signals." The full set of recommended practices is published as "Safety Standards for Small Craft" available for $5 from the Council at 537 Steamboat Road, Greenwich, Conn. 06830. The serious skipper can well devote some spare time to reading this volume; it is a good book to have on hand for reference purposes.

The Yacht Safety Bureau, Inc., for many years a non-profit public service organization under joint sponsorship of the National Association of Engine and Boat Manufacturers and major marine insurance underwriters, has now become the Marine Division of Underwriters Laboratories. This will not change the organization's primary purpose of inspection, testing, and safety evaluation of products intended for use on, in, or in conjunction with small boats, including hulls and entire boats.

Simply stated, the Bureau's objective is to see that marine equipment is available to the boating public that has been measured for safety of operation when used as intended. This objective is based on the logic that safety begins with safe products and continues with how they are used.

The Yacht Safety Bureau does not solicit work. Manufacturers voluntarily submit products for evaluation. Extensive laboratory facilities are maintained in New Jersey; field testing is frequently accomplished at other sites.

The word "approved" is frequently misused in connection with YSB product certification. The Bureau does not approve or disapprove anything. What it does is operate a product listing and labeling service.

Satisfactory completion of safety evaluation results in an item's being "listed" by the Yacht Safety Bureau. Listing of a product, with its related privilege of use of the Bureau's label, means that production samples of it have been evaluated and found acceptable under the Bureau's requirements. Listing is an expression of the Bureau's good faith opinion, based on tests, that the item meets minimum applicable safety standards. It is not a warranty of quality or performance, nor are listed products of the same class necessarily equivalent in quality, performance, or merit.

The Bureau's labels include the words "LISTED PRODUCT" in a copyrighted design, fig. 1005. These symbols may be seen in advertisements and on tags, stickers, etc., on products. This label will gradually be replaced with the well-known UL label widely used on electrical items.

The presence of the YSB or UL label on any device means that a production sample has been successfully evaluated to related safety requirements, and nothing else. The label may, however, be the basis on which "authorities having jurisdiction" grant approval. Such authorities include individuals making judgments for their own purposes, industry people making judgments for components or original equipment installations, marine surveyors for insurance purposes, and administrators of regulations making judgments required by law.

FIG. 1006  Fire Protection Standards for Motor Craft, No. 302, is a small yet valuable safety bulletin issued by the National Fire Protection Association. A copy should be studied by every boat owner and carried aboard as a useful reference document. See text for how a copy may be obtained.

FIG. 1005  Boating products that have passed a safety evaluation are "listed" by the Yacht Safety Bureau. The YSB seal can be used in advertising the items and may be found on it in the form of a sticker, tag, etc. Periodic re-testing ensures the continued safety of all listed products.

Only products commercially available are eligible for listing. New products may be submitted in their model stage for evaluation, but no final listing action is taken until production units are submitted. Continuity of a Bureau listing is provided for by means of its periodic re-inspection service. This is directed only toward confirming that originally tested qualities of listed and labeled products are maintained so long as the listing continues.

The **National Fire Protection Association** is an organization whose activities extend far beyond boating and marine interests to include all aspects of the science and methods of fire protection. NFPA issues codes, standards, and recommended practices for minimizing losses of life and property by fire.

NFPA does not approve, inspect, or certify any installations, procedures, equipment, or materials, nor does it approve or evaluate testing laboratories. It does prepare, by coordinated action of committees of experts, codes and standards for the guidance of all persons in the matter of fire protection. Frequently, NFPA codes and standards are written into law or regulations by various governmental units.

Of interest to boatmen is NFPA Fire Protection Standard No. 302 for Motor Craft (Pleasure and Commercial).

Originally issued in 1925, it has been amended and revised many times. The small booklet, available for 75c from NFPA, 60 Batterymarch Street, Boston, Mass. 02110, is a useful guide to any skipper.

## Construction for Safety

In one respect, safety afloat may be considered to start with the design and construction of the craft itself. The average skipper is not likely to build his own boat, but he should be able to recognize proper design features and sound construction characteristics. He should be at least broadly familiar with safe and unsafe aspects of boat construction—the points that should be checked in determining whether or not a particular craft, new or used, should be bought. There is little the average yachtsman can do directly to influence the design and construction of boats, but he can, through knowledge and careful inspection, avoid those that fail to measure up to desirable standards.

A boatman contemplating purchase of a used boat should seriously consider use of the services of a qualified

FIG. 1008 Anti-slip protection on deck walkways and at boarding areas is a *must* for safety. This can be obtained from the natural qualities of the deck, ingredients added to the deck paint, or by applying special strips of material having a no-slip surface and an adhesive backing.

marine surveyor. He is an expert in determining the condition of the hull, engine, and equipment. He may well discover hidden defects that the would-be buyer overlooked in his enthusiasm. An impartial survey is sound protection for a purchaser; the modest cost involved will be well-justified. Such a survey is often required to obtain insurance, particularly on older boats.

### HULL CONSTRUCTION

Modern boats, built by reputable manufacturers, are basically seaworthy because they are honestly constructed to proven designs. This points out the proper course in the selection of a good, sound boat. There is no necessity of trying some freak of questionable worth. If you have no experience in selecting a boat, it is easy enough to avail yourself of the advice and guidance of others who are better qualified; be sure to talk to several persons to avoid personal biases.

### Construction materials

For seaworthiness and safety, suitable materials for boatbuilding and highgrade construction are equally essential. Use of fire-retardant materials wherever practicable is suggested. Boats may be built equally well of wood, fiberglass, steel, or aluminum. Combinations of materials may also be used, such as a fiberglass superstructure on a wooden hull.

FIG. 1007 Even an experienced yachtsman should make use of the services of a qualified marine surveyor when considering purchase of a used boat. This expert will make a thorough examination of the craft and its equipment, noting defects, weaknesses, missing safety features, etc. His report should guide the would-be buyer in his decision as to whether to buy. A survey report may also be required for insurance purposes.

**FIG. 1009** Lifelines are important on all boats, but are an absolute must on offshore cruising and racing sailboats. The lines must have adequate strength and the stanchions must be securely through-bolted. Note how lines shown above merge into liferails at bow and stern.

(Photograph by Romaine-Skelton)

It should be noted, too, that boats can also be built poorly in any of these materials. Many arguments can be made for and against each hull material, but basically the decision is one for the individual owner, considering the use of the boat, cost factors, maintenance, and not least, his personal preferences.

Water-tight bulkheads (or as tight as practicable) are recommended to isolate bilges of fuel and machinery spaces from those of living quarters. Where feasible, two means of exit should be provided from compartments where persons may congregate or sleep. Thus, in a small craft having only one cabin and cockpit, a forward hatch is a desirable feature.

## Safety on deck

A Class 1 or larger boat may have side decks on which individuals move forward to the bow and back. It is essential that four safety features be present. First, these decks must be wide enough for secure footing. People will attempt to pass forward from the cockpit, around the cabin, and to the forward deck. There must be adequate space for their feet to be placed fully on deck, even though the space may be measured in inches and they have to make their way forward sideways. Secondly, if the deck is of a material that is slippery when wet (and most are), anti-slip protection must be provided at critical points. This may consist of a built-in roughness in fiberglass decks, added material to deck paint, or special anti-slip strips attached to the deck with their own adhesive backing. Any place that a person can or has slipped, even once, is a potential area for anti-slip protection.

Thirdly, there must be adequate hand-holds, places to grab and hold on. These must be sufficient in number and so spaced that no one need be beyond a secure grasp of the boat at any time in moving forward and aft, or when coming aboard or leaving the boat. The old saying "one hand for the boat and one for yourself" is an excellent one —even in calm waters; hold on at all times to something

strong enough to bear your weight.

Lifelines, also referred to as liferails, are the fourth item of deck security for personnel. No boat large enough for lifelines should be without them. These are often carried forward to join a low rail around the bow. Lifelines are important on most small craft, but are of special value on offshore sailboats, fig. 1009.

Inadequate lifelines are worse than none at all; they may impart a false sense of security. Adequate lifelines, on the other hand, are worth whatever cost and bother they may entail. They are a safety measure against an unpredictable sea, perhaps responsible for the saving of more lives than any other safety feature of boats.

Lifelines must be of adequate inherent strength; even more important, they must be properly installed. Stanchions must be internally strong and through-bolted to the deck. The lines themselves must have the necessary strength and be of a material compatible with that of the stanchions.

Detailed information on non-skid deck materials, lifelines, and handrails will be found in the American Boat & Yacht Council Safety Standard H-12 on the security of personnel on deck. There are also nine other AB&YC safety standards relating to hulls of small craft, all of which will make interesting reading to those seriously concerned with safety afloat.

## Superstructure and stability

The mistaken notion that a boat can carry weight anywhere as long as she appears to trim right in the water must be corrected. Addition of more superstructure, such as a flying bridge, is particularly bad, as is the shifting of heavy weights such as motors, ballast, tanks, machinery, etc. Where stability is concerned, no shifts of major weights or changes in design should be considered without the advice of a qualified naval architect. Amateur boatbuilders sometimes ruin boats and reduce their safety factors by deviating from architect's plans in which the proportioning of weights has been given the most painstaking attention.

### Through-hull fittings

Fittings which pass through the hull near or below the water line should have sea-cocks installed internally close to the planking to permit positive closing. It is desirable that solid, seagoing metal pipe extend from the sea-cock to a level above the water line, from which point flexible hoses may be run to the pump or other accessory. Where hose is placed over pipe nipples for connections, hose clamps should be used.

There are now available through-hull fittings and sea-cocks that have been safety evaluated by the Yacht Safety Bureau and "listed" by that organization. AB&YC Safety Standard A-2 furnishes additional information on these.

FIG. 1010  Seacocks are important items of safety equipment on boats of all sizes. Every through-hull fitting should have one for cutting off the entry of water in case of hose leakage or for working on equipment. Seacocks should be tested for easy shut-off action at least twice each year; adjust or replace without delay any seacock stuck in the open position.

# Engines and Fuel Systems

Probably the first thought that comes to mind in connection with safety afloat is that of preventing fire and explosion. Fire is usually traceable to the engine room or galley where improper equipment, faulty installation, or careless operation is the direct cause. All of these are under the owner's control.

## ENGINE INSTALLATION

Engines should be suited to the hulls they power. Extremes of underpowering and overpowering are both bad. Original installations and subsequent changes require the advice of a naval architect or one thoroughly familiar with this phase of boat design.

Conversions of automobile engines for marine duty by amateur mechanics are invariably a source of trouble because of basic differences between the two types. Lubrication and cooling are the chief problems. Selection of an accepted type of marine engine or a commercially-produced conversion is advisable.

Pans, preferably made of copper, are recommended for installation under the engine to catch any oil and grease drippings and prevent these from getting into the bilge. Accumulations should be removed promptly for fire safety.

## FUEL SYSTEMS

The primary aspect of fuel system safety is the prevention of fires and explosion. Not to be forgotten, however, are the reliability aspects of the system that will ensure a continuous flow of clean fuel to the engine.

The discussion that follows will be principally concerned with boats using gasoline engines; exceptions and special requirements relating to diesel fuel systems will be covered separately.

### Fire prevention

It is of primary importance that the entire fuel system be liquid- and vapor-tight with respect to the hull interior. Gasoline fumes, mixed with air, form an explosive combination. These fumes, several times heavier than air, settle to the bottom of the bilge. A concentration of gasoline in air as low as 1¼% can be exploded by a slight spark with tremendous effect—a half-teacup of gasoline can create

enough explosive vapor to totally destroy a large motorboat.

The obvious answer for safety is *prevention*—make it impossible for gasoline, either in liquid or gaseous form, to get into the bilge in the first place. Then keep the bilge clean and ventilate the engine compartment thoroughly, and there will be nothing that can be ignited.

Leakage of liquid gasoline into the bilge can be prevented by proper installation, using strongly built gasoline tanks, copper tubing for fuel lines, leakproof connections, tight fittings, and lengths of flexible metallic fuel hose to take care of vibration. Gasoline vapors created when the tanks are filled must be prevented from finding their way down through open hatches and companionways. Finally, avoidable sparks and flames should not be permitted in the engine room.

### Carburetors

Carburetors must be equipped with flame arresters for protection against backfire; see fig. 1011. If not of the downdraft type, they should also have a pan covered with a fine mesh screen attached under the carburetor to collect any drip. Leakage will be sucked back into the engine if a copper tube is run from the bottom of the pan to the intake manifold. Flame arresters should be kept clean both for safety and best engine operation.

Air intakes to the engine compartment should be directed so that any backfires will not tend to blow into the bilges.

### Fuel tanks

Fuel tanks should be permanently installed in such a manner as to be secure against moving about in a seaway. The use of portable tanks below decks is not good practice.

Fuel tanks must be constructed of a metal that is compatible both with the fuel and a normal marine environment. Copper and copper alloys of certain specific compositions are used for gasoline tanks. The necessary thickness of metal may vary with capacity of the tank in accordance with standards developed by the American Boat & Yacht Council. Seams of a tank may be welded by any one of several methods as listed in the applicable

AB&YC safety standard. Such tanks should not be painted.

Gasoline tanks must not be integral with the hull. The shape of the tank should be such that there are no exterior pockets that would trap moisture after the tank is in its installed position. Tank bottoms must not have sumps or pockets in which water could accumulate.

Internal stiffeners and baffle plates will normally be used to provide necessary rigidity and resistance to surging of liquid in the tanks. Baffles must meet certain specified design criteria to prevent formation of liquid pockets in the bottom of tanks and vapor pockets in the tops.

There should be no drains or outlets for drawing off fuel from the tank, nor outlets or fittings of any type in the bottom, sides, or ends of tanks. Fuel lines to the engine should enter the tank at its top and internally extend nearly, but not quite all the way, to the bottom.

### Fuel filler pipes and vents

One of the most essential requirements in the proper installation of a fuel system is that there be a completely tight connection between the gasoline tank and the filling plate on deck. If the filler is located outside the coaming, spillage will go overboard, while tight pipe connections between deck plate and tank will prevent leakage or spillage below. Fill pipes, at least 1½" inside diameter, should run down inside the tank nearly to the bottom to lessen the production of vapors.

A suitable vent pipe for each tank should lead *outside the hull;* vents should *never* terminate in closed spaces such as the engine compartment or under the deck. Minimum inside diameter of vent pipes should be 9/16". Where a vent terminates on the hull, the outlet should be fitted with a removable flame screen to protect against flash-backs from outside sources of ignition. In boats that normally heel, such as auxiliary sailboats, it may be necessary to have dual vents with the port tank vent led to the starboard side and vice versa.

Non-metallic hose may be used as a coupling between

FIG. 1011 **Carburetors on marine engines (other than outboards) must be equipped with a flame arrester. Out of sight beneath the updraft carburetor shown above is a drip pan for further safety. Downdraft carburetors do not need such a pan.**

sections of metallic piping. The hose must be reinforced or of sufficient thickness to prevent collapse. A grounding jumper wire must be installed across the non-conducting section so as to provide a complete electrical path from the deck fitting to the fuel tank, which in turn is grounded.

A fuel level indicator, if used, should be of an approved type. If the fuel supply for an auxiliary electric plant is not drawn from the main tank, the separate tank should be installed with fillers and vents similar to those of the main tank.

### Fuel lines

Fuel lines should be of seamless copper tubing, run so as to be in sight as much as possible for ease of inspection, protected from possible damage, and secured against vibration by soft non-ferrous metal clips with rounded edges. A short length of flexible tubing with suitable fittings should be used between that part of the fuel line that is secured to the hull and that part which is secured to the engine itself; this will prevent leakage or breakage as a result of vibration.

Reinforced non-metallic hose in the fuel line should be limited to the short flexible section described above, but may be used for the full distance from the tank shutoff valve to the engine if the line is fully visible and accessible for its entire length. Wherever used, non-metallic hose must be dated by the manufacturer and not be used for a period longer than that recommended by the maker.

Tube fittings should be of non-ferrous drawn or forged metal of the flared type, and tubing should be properly flared by tools designed for the purpose, preferably annealing the tube end before flaring.

A shut-off valve should be installed in the fuel line directly at the tank connection. Arrangements should be provided for ready access and operation of this valve from outside the compartment in which tanks are located, preferably from above deck. Where engine and fuel tank are separated by a distance exceeding 12 feet, an approved-type manual stop-valve should be installed at the engine end of the fuel line to stop fuel flow when servicing accessories.

Valves should be of non-ferrous metal with ground seats installed to close against the flow. Types which depend on packing to prevent leakage at the stem should not be used. For fuel, gas, and oil lines a type of diaphragm packless valve is available which is pressure-tight in any position. A YSB-listed electric fuel valve shuts off the flow of gasoline whenever the ignition switch is turned off; it can also be independently turned off in an emergency.

### Fuel pumps and filters

Electric fuel pumps, where used, should be located at the engine end of fuel lines. They must be so connected as to operate only when the ignition switch is on and the engine is turning over.

A filter should be installed in the fuel line inside the engine compartment, properly supported so that its weight is not carried by the tubing. Closure of the filter must be so designed that its opening for cleaning will minimize fuel spillage. It should also be designed so that the unit can be disassembled and reassembled in dim light without undue opportunity for crossing threads, displacing gaskets

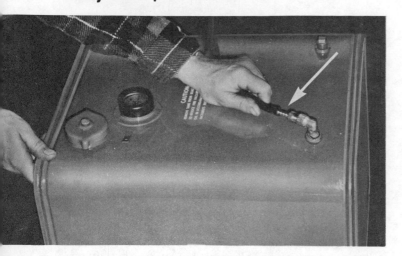

FIG. 1012 Portable gasoline tanks used with outboard motors may have a quick-disconnect fitting on the fuel line. This fitting must be designed so as to minimize leakage of gasoline when it is detached.

or seals, or assembly of parts in an improper order, resulting in seepage of fuel after reassembly. Fuel filter bowls should be highly resistant to shattering due to mechanical impact and resistant to failure from thermal shock.

## Fuel systems for outboards

Fuel tanks and systems permanently installed in the hull of outboard-powered boats should be designed, constructed, and installed in accordance with the above principles. No pressurized tanks should be built into or permanently attached to hulls. A quick-disconnect coupling may be used between motor and fuel line but, when disconnected, it must automatically shut off fuel flow from the tank. Arrangements should be provided so that the operation of making and breaking the connection can be accomplished with a minimum of spillage.

## Plastic containers for gasoline

Extreme caution must be exercised in the use of plastic containers for storing gasoline. Plastic articles can accumulate a heavy charge of static electricity. As plastic material does not allow the charge to be drained off by grounding connections, a spark could ignite fuel vapors in the container.

Some plastic containers are safe, but a boatman should use *only* those approved by a national listing agency or a major city fire department. In case of doubt, *don't* store gasoline in a plastic container.

## Safety first

Every possible precaution must be taken to ensure that not even a single drop of gasoline can find its way into the bilge. Bilge ventilation is most important. It is a strict legal requirement and it is a vital safety measure; see pages 607 to 610.

## Fuel systems of diesel-powered boats

Fuel systems of diesel-powered boats will generally conform to safety standards for gasoline-fueled craft, with a few exceptions as required or permitted by the nature of the fuel and characteristics of diesel engines.

Tanks for diesel fuel may be made of iron or steel as well as nickel-copper. Tanks may be painted if not galvanized externally; iron tanks must not be galvanized internally. Diesel tanks may have a sump or pocket in the bottom for collection of water but, if so, must have a positive means for removal of any accumulations from above deck. Tanks for diesel fuel may be integral with the hull.

Fuel lines for diesel oil may be of iron or steel pipe or tubing in addition to the metals approved for gasoline. A return line to carry excess fuel from the engine back to the tank will be needed.

### Additional information

Many additional technical details on gasoline and diesel fuel systems for boats will be found in AB&YC Safety Standard P-2.

The Yacht Safety Bureau has evaluated and accepted for listing a number of fuel tanks, filters, valves, and related equipment by various manufacturers.

## EXHAUST SYSTEMS

Exhaust lines and pipes should be installed so that they cannot scorch or ignite woodwork. Where necessary, gratings can be used to prevent gear from touching the line. Exhaust systems must be gas-tight, constructed and installed so that they can be inspected and repaired readily along their entire length. Any leaks must be rectified at *once* to prevent escape of exhaust gases into various compartments. *Carbon monoxide is a deadly gas.*

A "wet" exhaust system requires a continuous flow of cooling water (from the heat exchanger or the engine block) discharged through the exhaust line, entering as near the manifold as practicable. Exhaust systems of the "dry" type (no cooling water) operate at considerably higher temperatures and their use is relatively rare except on larger yachts.

An exhaust system should be run with a minimum number of bends. Where turns are necessary, long-sweep elbows or 45° ells are recommended. The exhaust system must not result in back pressure at the exhaust manifold greater than that specified by the engine manufacturer. A $1/8$" pipe tap, located not more than 6" from the exhaust-manifold outlet, should be provided for measuring back pressure.

The exhaust system should be designed to prevent undue stress on the exhaust manifold, particularly where an engine is shock-mounted. All supports, hangers, brackets, and other fittings in contact with the exhaust should be noncombustible and so constructed that high temperatures will not be transmitted to wood or other combustible materials to which fittings are secured.

The exhaust piping or tubing should have a continuous downward pitch of at least $1/2$" per foot when measured with the vessel at rest. It must be so designed and installed as to eliminate any possibility of having cooling water or sea water return to the engine manifold through the exhaust system.

### Exhaust systems for sailboat engines

Exhaust systems for auxiliary sailing craft should be carefully designed to prevent sea or cooling water from running back into the engines because such engines are usually installed close to or below the water line. A riser must

TYPICAL SAILBOAT EXHAUST SYSTEM

WATER JACKETED
EXHAUST RISER

WATER DISCHARGED INTO
EXHAUST AT THIS POINT

EXHAUST MANIFOLD

WATER LINE

FIG. 1013 The AB&YC Safety Standard for small-craft exhaust systems has special provisions for auxiliary-powered sailboats. Unusual precautions must be taken in such installations as the engine is often below the waterline and a normally-sloping exhaust line cannot be installed.

reach sufficiently high above the water line to allow a steep drop-off of at least 12"; the rest of the piping or tubing should have a downward pitch to the outlet of at least 1/2" per foot. The high point of the line should form a gooseneck, with cooling water injected aft of this point; see fig. 1015. The vertical dry section must be either adequately insulated and provided with a metallic bellows flexible section or water-jacketed. As an alternate arrangement, a water-trap silencer is recommended.

## Flexible exhaust lines

Steam hose or other non-metallic material may be used for exhaust lines where greater flexibility is desired. Every flexible line of this type must be secured with adequate clamps of corrosion-resistant metal at each end. Hose used for this purpose must have a wall thickness and rigidity sufficient to prevent panting (internal separation of plies) or collapse. Full-length nonmetallic exhaust tubing may be used in wet exhaust systems providing it is water-cooled throughout its length and is not subjected to temperatures above 280° F. Tubing used for engine exhaust service should be specifically constructed for that purpose and so labeled by the manufacturer. Tubing should be installed in a manner that will not stress or crimp the inner or outer plies, or permit any local impingement of exhaust gases or cooling water.

## Additional information

The AB&YC Safety Standard P-1 provides much additional information on "wet" and "dry" exhaust installations. It should be studied by persons building or rebuilding any boat equipped with an inboard engine.

## ELECTRICAL SYSTEMS

The entire electrical installation should comply rigidly with the best and most modern safety practices. Requirements of marine installations are more exacting than other applications where salt- and moisture-laden atmospheres are not prevalent. Wiring and other electrical equipment should be installed correctly in the beginning and kept safe by frequent inspection.

Information on electrical systems will also be found in chapter 25 on pages 487 and 488.

The sources of electrical power for engine starting, lights, pumps, electronic gear, and other electrical accessories are usually lead-acid storage batteries kept charged by a generator or alternator integral with the main engine. Larger craft equipped with electrical cooking and air-conditioning will have a separate engine-driven generator producing AC electrical power similar to shore current. The discussion in this section will be directed to the more-common 12- and 32-volt DC electrical systems found on all boats, even though also equipped with AC power.

All direct-current electrical systems should be of the two-wire type with feed and return wires parallel throughout the system. Conductors should be twisted together where their magnetic field would affect compasses or automatic pilots. Where one side of a DC system is grounded, connections between that side and ground should be used only to maintain that side at ground potential and should not normally carry current.

## Wiring diagrams

All boats should be provided with a complete wiring diagram of the electrical system as originally installed. It is recommended that the diagram be enclosed in a suitable plastic envelope and secured to an accessible panel door, preferably near the main switchboard. Diagrams should include an indication of the identification provided for each conductor.

Additions to and/or changes in electrical circuits should be drawn in on the wiring diagram without delay so that it is correct at all times.

## Batteries

Storage batteries should be so located that gas generated during charging will be quickly dissipated by natural or mechanical ventilation. They should be located as high as practicable, where they are not exposed to excessive heat, extreme cold, spray, or other conditions which could impair performance or accelerate deterioration. Caution should be taken to avoid locating batteries in areas subject to accumulation of gasoline fumes and also in proximity to any electrical or electronic devices. Engine starting batteries should be located as close to the engine as practicable.

Batteries must be secure against shifting. Care also should be taken to secure a battery against vertical motion which would allow it to pound against the surface on which it is resting while cruising in rough water. Batteries should be chocked on all sides and supported at the bottom by non-absorbent insulating supports of a material that will not be affected by contact with electrolyte. These supports should allow air circulation all around. Where the hull or compartment material in the immediate vicinity of the battery is aluminum, steel, or other material readily attacked by the acid, a tray of lead, fiberglass, or other suitable material resistant to the deteriorating action of electrolyte should be provided.

Batteries should be arranged to permit ready access for inspection, testing, watering, and cleaning. A minimum of 10" clear space above the filling openings should be available.

A non-conductive, ventilated cover or other suitable means should be provided to prevent accidental shorting

**FIG. 1014 Storage batteries should have a cover to protect terminals from being shorted by an accidentally dropped tool or other metal object. Such covers must be ventilated to prevent accumulation of gases during charging.**

of the battery's terminals; fig. 1014.

An emergency switch capable of carrying the maximum current of the system (including starter circuits) should be provided in each ungrounded conductor as close to the battery terminal connection as practicable. This switch should be readily accessible; a switch with a remote operating handle that can be opened or closed from the bridge or other location outside the compartment containing the batteries is highly desirable.

## Generators and motors

Generators, alternators, and electric motors intended for use in machinery spaces or other areas which might contain flammable or explosive vapors must be designed and constructed so as to prevent such devices from becoming a source of ignition of these vapors. These units must be of a type approved for marine service.

Generators, alternators, and electric motors must be located in accessible, adequately ventilated areas as high above the bilge as possible. They must not be located in low or pocketed positions.

Ground connections from battery to starter should be made as close to the starter as possible. It is recommended that all other ground connections to the engine be made at this same point. By making all ground connections at one point, damaging stray-current flow through the metal of the engine will be minimized.

## Distribution panels and switches

Switchboards and distribution panels should be located in accessible, adequately ventilated locations, preferably outside of engine and fuel-tank compartments. They should be protected from rain and spray; where necessary, panels should be provided with a drip shield to prevent wetting of terminals or electrical components from overhead dripping.

Totally enclosed switchboards and distribution panels of the dead-front type are recommended. Metal enclosures are desirable, but wood may be used if all terminal strips,

fuse blocks switches, etc., are mounted on non-absorbent, non-combustible, high-dielectric insulating material. It is recommended that the interior of enclosures be lined with asbestos sheet or other fire-resistant material.

All switches should have suitable electrical ratings for the particular circuits on which they are used; distribution panels should have several spare switches to take care of additional equipment that may be added later.

Switches used in fuel-tank and machinery spaces, or other hazardous locations, must be designed so as to prevent ignition of flammable or explosive vapors. Such switches must be of a type approved for marine use.

## Wiring

Conductors used for general wiring throughout the boat should be approved for marine use to indicate adequate mechanical strength, moisture resistance, dielectric strength, insulation, and current-carrying capacity for the intended marine service.

The table of wire gauges on page 488, fig. 2504, is for an allowable voltage drop of $1/2$ volt on a 12-volt system. For lighting and other non-critical purposes, the wire size shown there may be reduced slightly (wire gauge number one or two *greater*, as gauge number varies *inversely* with conductor size). For more critical applications, such as for some electronic equipment, the voltage drop should be kept to 3% or less by using slightly larger wire in accordance with fig. 1015.

| Current in Amps. | Length of Wire, in feet | | | | | |
|---|---|---|---|---|---|---|
| | 10 | 15 | 20 | 30 | 40 | 50 |
| 5 | 14 | 12 | 12 | 10 | 8 | 8 |
| 10 | 12 | 10 | 8 | 6 | 6 | 5 |
| 15 | 10 | 8 | 6 | 5 | 4 | 3 |
| 20 | 8 | 6 | 6 | 4 | 2 | 2 |
| 25 | 8 | 6 | 5 | 3 | 2 | 1 |

**FIG. 1015 The table above, extracted from the appropriate AB&YC Safety Standard, specifies the wire gauge to be used versus conductor length for a voltage drop of not more than 3% in a 12-volt system. This small drop is required for some critical electronic installations. For less critical applications, the table in Chapter 25, Fig. 2504, may be used.**

All wiring must be routed as high above the bilge as possible with consideration given to protection of wire and connections from physical damage. Wiring should be secured throughout its length, at intervals not exceeding 14 inches, in a manner that will not crush or cut insulation around the conductor. Non-metallic clamps are excellent; if metallic clamps are used, they must be lined with a suitable insulating material. All non-metallic material must be resistant to the effects of oil, gasoline, and water.

Unless absolutely necessary, wire splices should not be made in any circuit vital to the operation of the boat nor in the navigation light circuit. Splices, where made, should be taped to relieve all strain from the joint. If solder is used, it should be a low-temperature resin-core radio solder. Acid-core solder must *not* be used.

## Terminal connections

Terminal connections should be designed and installed so as to insure a good mechanical and electrical joint without damage to conductors. Metals used for terminal studs, nuts, and washers should be corrosion-resistant and galvanically compatible with the wire and terminal lug.

Terminals should be of solderless type, preferably with ring-type ends. Solderless terminals should be attached with crimping tools specified by the manufacturer of the terminal. The holes in ring-type terminals should be of a size that will properly fit the terminal stud. Formed and soldered wire terminal connections should not be used. It is recommended that terminal lugs include a means of clamping the wire insulation for mechanical support. A short length of insulated sleeving over the wire at each terminal connection is desirable.

No more than four conductors should be secured to any one terminal stud. Where additional connections are necessary, two or more terminal studs should be used and connected together with copper jumpers or straps.

Wires terminating at switchboards, in junction boxes or fixtures, etc., should be arranged to provide a surplus length of wire sufficient to relieve all tension, allow for repairs, and permit multiple wires to be fanned at terminal studs, etc.

## Electrical shock hazards

Voltage is only one factor in determining whether a shock will be fatal or only startling. Many people have received shocks from spark-plugs, where the voltage is 10,000 or more, with no more harm than a few bruised knuckles. The actual factors that determine the extent of harm are: (1) the amount of current that flows through the body, the amperage; (2) the path of the current through the body; and (3) the length of time that the current flows.

The effects of different levels of current are not exact and will vary with the individual victim and the path of current through his body. Unfortunately, there is no way of predicting in advance how much current will flow in any given situation—play safe, work only on de-energized circuits.

## Additional information

Further guidance and recommendations for DC electrical systems for boats will be found in Safety Standards E-1, E-3, E-5, E-6, E-9, and E-10 issued by the American Boat & Yacht Council.

## AC electrical systems

More and more boats are being wired for 115-volt AC electrical systems so that larger, home-type appliances and equipment may be used afloat. Power may be obtained from dockside connections only or from such sources plus an engine-driven generator for use while under way. From a safety viewpoint, it is important to recognize the increased hazards from this higher-voltage wiring and devices.

All component parts of a 115-volt AC system must be designed, constructed, and installed so as to perform with safety under environmental conditions of continuous exposure to vibration, mechanical shock, corrosive salt atmosphere, and high humidity. The system must provide maximum protection against electrical shock for persons on the boat, in the water in contact with the boat, or in contact with the boat and a grounded object on shore.

Appliances and fixed AC electrical equipment used on boats must be designed so that current-carrying parts of the device are effectively insulated from all exposed metal parts by a dielectric material suitable for use in damp and/or wet locations as determined by location of the item and its intended use.

Further technical specifications for AC electrical systems on boats will be found in AB&YC Safety Standard E-8. Portions of standards E-3, E-5, and E-6 are also applicable.

## LIGHTNING PROTECTION

One seldom hears of a boat, power or sail, being struck by lightning, yet cases have been reported. A skipper can add to both his physical safety and his peace of mind by obtaining some basic information and taking a few precautionary actions.

**FIG. 1016** Under *certain* conditions, a grounded radio antenna can provide a "cone of protection" from lightning strikes for a boat and its occupants. See text for details. *(from A.B. & Y.C. Safety Standards)*

## Protective principles

A grounded conductor, or lightning protective mast, will generally divert to itself direct lightning strokes which might otherwise fall within a cone-shaped space, the apex of which is the top of the conductor or mast and the base a circle at the water's surface having a radius approximately twice the conductor's height. Probability of protection is considered to be 99.0% within this 60° angle as shown in fig. 1016. Probability of protection can be increased to 99.9% if mast height is raised so that the cone apex angle is reduced to 45°.

To provide an adequately grounded conductor or protective mast, the entire circuit from the masthead to the ground (water) connection should have a conductivity equivalent to a #8 gauge wire. The path to ground followed by the conductor should be essentially straight, with no sharp bends.

If there are metal objects of considerable size within a few feet of the grounding conductor, there will be a strong tendency for sparks or side flashes to jump from the grounding conductor to the metal object at the nearest point. To prevent such possibly damaging flashes, an interconnecting conductor should be provided at all likely places.

Large metallic objects within the hull or superstructure of a boat should be interconnected with the lightning protective system to prevent a dangerous rise of voltage due to a lightning flash.

## Protective measures

For power boats, a radio antenna may serve as a lightning or protective mast provided it is equipped with a transmitting-type lightning arrester or means for grounding during electrical storms, and that the antenna height is sufficient to provide an adequate cone of protection for the length of the craft. Antennas with loading coils are considered to end at a point immediately *below the coil* unless the coil has a suitable gap for bypassing lightning current. The size of the grounding conductor, interconnection, and grounding of metallic masses should be in accordance with principles noted above.

Sailboats with metallic standing rigging will be adequately protected provided that all rigging is grounded and a proper cone of protection exists. Interconnection and grounding of metallic masses should be done as on power boats.

Metal objects situated wholly on a boat's exterior should be connected to the grounding conductor at their upper or nearest end. Metal objects within the boat may be connected to the lightning protective system directly or through the bonding system for underwater metal parts.

Metal objects that project through cabin tops, decks, etc., should be bonded to the nearest lightning conductor at the point where the object emerges from the boat and again at its lowest extreme end within the boat. Spotlights and other objects projecting through cabin tops should be solidly grounded regardless of the cone of protection.

A ground connection for lightning protection may consist of any metal surface, normally submerged, which has an area of at least one square foot. Propellers and metallic rudder surfaces may be used for this purpose; the radio ground plate is more than adequate. A steel hull itself constitutes a good ground connection to the water.

## Protection for personnel

As the basic purpose of lightning protection is safety of personnel, the following precautions should be taken by the crew and guests.

Individuals should remain inside a closed boat as much as practicable during an electrical storm.

Persons should avoid making contact with any items connected to a lightning protective conductor, and especially in such a way as to bridge between two parts of the grounding system. For example, it is undesirable to touch either the reverse lever or spotlight control, particularly in contact with both at the same time.

No one should be in the water during a lightning storm.

# Equipment for Safety

Some items of safety equipment are required by laws and Coast Guard regulations. These are generally written, however, in such broad language that additional knowledge and guidance are required for the greatest degree of safety afloat.

Additional items of equipment above legal minimums are required to receive the approval decal of the Coast Guard Auxiliary Courtesy Motorboat Examination.

Still further pieces of equipment are desirable for safety or convenience, or both. Many of these are discussed in Chapter 3 and other chapters. This chapter will supplement rather than duplicate equipment considerations covered

## LIFESAVING EQUIPMENT

As noted in Chapter 31, each boat must, by law, have a lifesaving device for each person aboard; few specific details are stated. A wise skipper has, in addition to his regular buoyant devices, several jackets of smaller size to protect children. On boats under 40 feet in length, life "jackets" are not required, but a buoyant cushion is not fully safe for a small child who might lose his grasp on the straps.

Although non-commercial boats under 40 feet may carry buoyant cushions, buoyant vests, or special-purpose buoyant devices (ski vests, racing vests, flotation jackets, etc.), the skipper who is really safety-conscious will carry an adequate number of *life jackets,* the canvas jackets with flotation material (usually kapok) sealed in plastic pouches; fig. 1017. These are clearly marked with the words "Approved for use on all vessels and motorboats." Such jackets provide ample buoyancy and, most importantly, float the wearer in the position that will best hold his face clear of the water so that he can breathe adequately even though he may be semi-conscious or unconscious. Jackets of this type (or life rings) are required on Class 3 boats; they are actually of even greater importance on·smaller craft as statistics show that over 97% of all accidents involve boats of the smaller classes. Jackets may be bulkier and harder to stow than vests, and they don't make sitting easier as do cushions (even though these should not be sat upon), but when needed to keep you afloat until help comes, nothing else does the job half so well!

## PUMPS AND BAILERS

Oddly enough, there are no federal legal requirements for a boat (if used exclusively for pleasure) to be equipped with a device of any type for removing water that leaks in or comes aboard as spray. Essentially all boats are, of course, equipped with some form of pump or bailer, but too many skippers place their *full* dependence on electrical bilge pumps, and perhaps on only one of those. Once water rises in the bilge to a level sufficient to short out the battery, there is no way to combat the further rise of water. (Incidentally, on most boats the batteries are placed low in the bilge—excellent for stability, but not for safety if the craft starts taking on water.)

FIG. 1017 Life jackets of the type shown provide a greater measure of safety than other lifesaving devices that may be acceptable on small craft. Properly worn, they will not only provide buoyancy but will float an individual in the best position for breathing. As these are strapped to the person, he cannot lose his grasp as he could with a buoyant cushion. Two children's sizes are also available.
(Courtesy Atlantic-Pacific Mfg. Corp.)

Only the smallest boats should depend on a hand bailer or bucket. Other boats should be equipped with a hand-operated pump of generous capacity. Such an item can be either a fixed installation or a portable pump stowed where it can be quickly and easily reached when needed.

## DISTRESS SIGNALING EQUIPMENT

A boat's radiotelephone is probably the most often used means of summoning assistance in an emergency. Use of the radio for this purpose is covered on pages 382(d) to 382(f).

Without special equipment a distress signal can be made to other craft in sight by standing where one is clearly visible and slowly raising and lowering one's arms. Another visual distress signal is a fluorescent red-orange rectangular panel displayed where most visible to boats and/or aircraft. This item of safety equipment is described more fully on page 180.

Signal flares may be projected several hundred feet into the air by a special type of pistol, or to a lesser height from a pocket "tear gas" gun that resembles an old-fashioned fountain pen. The laws of several states regulate possession of these and similar explosive projectile devices; check carefully before putting one aboard, but if permissible, these are effective and desirable items of safety equipment.

There are also hand-held flares of the single- and double-ended types, the latter producing a bright flame at one end for night use and a dense smoke at the other end for day distress situations. Before using any flare, read all instructions carefully so as to avoid personal injury or aggravation of the emergency. Read carefully *before* any emergency arises, you won't have time then!

## MISCELLANEOUS ITEMS OF SAFETY EQUIPMENT

There are many small items of equipment that serve to increase safety and convenience.

Every boat should be equipped with several **flashlights** and at least one battery-powered **electric lantern,** fig. 1019. If provided with an adjustable head, the beam can be directed where needed. Flashlights should be distributed so as to be quickly available in an emergency. One should be within reach of the skipper's bunk and the first mate's, too. There should also be a flashlight in the guest cabin, if any, and another on the bridge. The electric lantern should be kept in an accessible place. Batteries in all units should be checked at least monthly to be sure that they have sufficient power.

An installed searchlight of adequate intensity is desirable on medium-sized and large boats operated at night. It is useful both in routine navigation and docking, and in emergencies such as man-overboard situations or assisting another boat in distress. On smaller boats, the electric lantern can serve as a hand-held searchlight.

FIG. 1018 A night distress signal will be seen at much greater distances if projected to a height of several hundred feet. Flare pistols and related devices will do this, but in some states these items of boating safety equipment are subject to firearms laws and regulations.
(Courtesy Abercrombie & Fitch)

FIG. 1019 An electric lantern should be aboard every boat. If provided with adjustable head, it projects a stronger beam of light than most flashlights and has the added advantage of being able to be set down with the light directed where needed, thus making both hands available for working.

FIG. 1020 Every boat should have aboard some emergency drinking water and food. The quantity and type of these supplies will vary, of course, with the number of persons aboard and the cruising area. Prepared kits of long shelf-life food and water can be purchased, or the boat owner can assemble his own supplies. (Courtesy Winslow Company Marine Products)

Boats of medium or large size should have on board a small **hand axe** to be used in cutting lines in an emergency. The axe should be stowed on deck, where it might be needed in a hurry.

**Tools** and **spare parts** for the engine and major accessories can be considered parts of a boat's essential safety equipment. Personal experience and conversation with seasoned skippers will offer the best guidance to just what tools and parts should be carried aboard any particular craft. Insofar as practicable, tools should be of rust-proof metal; tools susceptible to rust or corrosion, and all spare parts, should be properly protected from adverse effects of a marine environment.

All but the smallest craft should be equipped with **emergency drinking water** and **food** supplies. The amount will vary with the number of persons normally on board. The type of food is not important—anything will do when you get hungry enough! Non-perishability over a long period is important, but it might be wise once each year to consume your emergency supplies (a shipwreck party?) *after* they have been replaced with a fresh stock. Such items can usually be purchased from marine supply stores or from Army-Navy surplus stores; food should be simple and compact, but sustaining and energy-producing.

**First aid kits** are essential safety items; they will be considered in more detail later in this chapter.

**Navigation equipment, charts,** and **ground tackle** are all items of safety equipment, but each is considered in detail elsewhere in this book, see index.

## SAFETY ASPECTS OF OTHER EQUIPMENT

Several items generally found on boats are not "safety equipment" per se, but have definite aspects of safety about their design, installation, or operation that must be considered by boat owners.

### Galley stoves

All boatmen seem to love to eat, especially when out on the water. Cabin boats will normally have a galley, the de-

gree of size and elaborateness varying with the design and use of the craft.

Galley stoves should be designed, manufactured, and approved for marine use. Types of fuel that are ordinarily used include alcohol, electricity, and liquified petroleum gas (LPG—normally propane or butane). Stoves fueled with kerosene, coal, wood, or canned heat (solidified alcohol) are only rarely seen now. Gasoline is *not* a safe stove fuel and should *never* be used on a boat.

Electricity is probably the safest source of heat for cooking, but an auxiliary generating plant is required to produce the large amounts of AC power required. Because of the inexpensive and simple nature of the equipment,

FIG. 1021 This galley stove installation shows the use of insulating board behind, beside, and below the stove to protect woodwork from unsafe high temperatures. The stove also has a drip pan beneath it, another safety feature.

alcohol stoves are widely used on boats despite their rather high fuel costs; with moderate and reasonable precautions, such installations can be quite safe. Plain water will extinguish alcohol fires.

LPG stoves are excellent for cooking, but can present a serious safety hazard unless installed and operated in accordance with strict rules—their use is prohibited on certain classes of commercial vessels.

Stoves should be permanently and securely fastened in place when in operation. Portable stoves are not recommended; if one must be used, it should be secured temporarily while in use. Adequate ventilation should be provided to prevent any excess rise in temperature of an area in which a stove is operated for extended periods of time (for the sake of safety as well as the cook's comfort!). All woodwork or other combustible material directly above or immediately surrounding a stove, including smoke stacks, must be effectively protected with non-combustible sheathing; see fig. 1021. A recommended means is the use of 1/8-inch asbestos board covered with sheet metal.

Fuel for alcohol and kerosene stoves may be supplied to the burners either by gravity or pressure systems provided fuel tanks cannot be filled while the burners are in operation except where the supply tank is remote from burners and the filling operation will not introduce a fire hazard. A removable or accessible liquid-tight metal drip pan at least 3/4" deep should be provided beneath all burners. Pressure tanks should have suitable gauges and/or relief valves.

## Refrigeration

Ice is used on many boats as a means of keeping food fresh and for cooling beverages. It offers no safety hazards, but water from melting ice should be piped overboard rather than into the bilge. Fresh-water drip tends to promote dry rot. A collection sump, with pump, may be used if desired.

Mechanical refrigeration will normally be of the electric-motor-driven compressor type similar to units found in the home. Occasionally, a compressor will be belt-driven from a main engine, but this is rare.

Safety aspects of mechanical refrigeration include use of a non-toxic and non-flammable refrigerant, non-sparking motors, safety valves on high-pressure portions of the system, and general construction adequate to survive rigors of marine service.

Kerosene and bottled-gas refrigerators have a constant small open flame. This can produce an explosion hazard, and the use of such absorption-type units is presently excluded from the AB&YC Safety Standard A-6.

## Heaters

Cabin heaters are sometimes used on boats in northern waters to extend the boating season or to ward off the chill of a sudden cold snap. Gasoline should never be used as a fuel and portable kerosene or alcohol heaters are not recommended. Built-in electrical heaters are safe; portable electrical heaters should be used only if secured in place while in operation.

Gas-burning heaters should be equipped with an automatic device to shut off the fuel supply if the flame is extinguished. Pilot lights should not be used. Coast Guard regulations prohibit use of LPG fuel for any purpose on certain commercial craft.

Many models of air-conditioning equipment used on boats are of the "reverse cycle" or "heat pump" type and can supply warmth rather than cooling when the former is needed. This is a thoroughly safe method of heating.

# Safety in Operations

Safety should be a part of every aspect of the operation of small craft. Boat handling has been covered in Chapter 8. Safety in such operations as stranding and towing was considered in Chapter 9. Navigation and piloting—essential for safety—are discussed in Chapter 21 and other chapters. The aspects of operational safety afloat to be considered here are those that do not fall under other major headings.

### FUELING PRECAUTIONS

Certain precautions must be carefully and completely observed *every* time a boat is fueled with gasoline. Step by step, these are:

#### Before fueling

1. Make sure that the boat is securely tied to the fueling pier. Fuel before darkness, if possible.

2. Stop engines, motors, fans, and other devices capable of producing a spark. Open the master switch if the electrical system has one. Put out all galley fires and open flames.

3. Close all ports, windows, doors, and hatches so that fumes cannot blow aboard and below.

4. Disembark all passengers and any crew members not needed for the fueling operation.

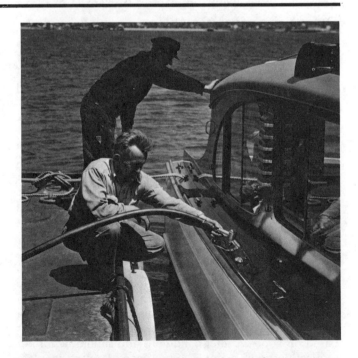

FIG. 1022 Fueling must be accomplished in a safe manner to reduce hazards of gasoline explosion and fire. Refer to the text for a 16-point checklist of actions before, during, and after fueling.

5. Prohibit all smoking on board and in the vicinity.

6. Have a filled fire extinguisher close at hand.

7. Measure the fuel in the tanks and do not order more than the tank will hold; allow for expansion.

## While fueling

8. Keep nozzle or can spout in contact with the fill opening to guard against static sparks.

9. Do not spill gasoline.

10. Do not overfill. The practice of filling until fuel flows from the vents is highly dangerous.

11. For outboards, remove portable tanks from boat and fill on shore.

## After fueling

12. Close fill openings.

13. Wipe up any spilled gasoline; dispose of wipe-up rags on shore.

14. Open all ports, windows, doors, and hatches; turn on bilge power exhaust blower. Ventilate boat this way *at least* five minutes—time it, don't guess.

15. Sniff low down in tank and engine compartments. *If any odor of gasoline is present, do not start engine;* continue ventilation actions until odor can no longer be detected.

16. Be prepared to cast off lines as soon as engine starts; get clear of pier quickly.

## SAFETY IN LOADING

Overloading is probably the greatest cause of accidents in smaller boats and dinghies, and is even a significant factor in medium-size boats such as those of Class 2. Overloading is particularly hazardous as it is not so feared as are fires and explosions. Many a skipper, cautious in his handling of gasoline, will unknowingly load his craft far beyond safe limits. The number of seats in a boat is *not* an indication of the number of persons it can carry safely.

### Determining capacity

"Loading" and "capacity" are terms primarily related to the weight of persons, fuel, gear, etc., that can be safely carried. The safe load of a boat in persons depends on many of its characteristics, such as the hull volume and dimensions; the material of which it is built, if it is an outboard hull, whether there is an effective engine well inboard of the transom notch where the engine is mounted; how heavy the engine is; and other factors. Many small boats now carry a "capacity plate," see fig. 1023, placed on the hull in accordance with standards of the Boating Industry Association. Such plates show the recommended maximum weight capacity, usually in number of persons as well as in number of pounds for persons, motor, fuel, and gear.

The BIA standards are accepted by the Coast Guard for boats in classes A and 1. The capacity is determined by the application of two formulas, one quite complex for determination of the boat's cubic capacity and the other simply length times beam divided by 15. The answer in either case is the maximum number of persons to be carried and the smaller of the two results is the one used. This capacity is based on good weather conditions and should be further reduced in rough water. The presence of a capacity plate does not relieve the boatman of the responsibility for exercising individual judgment. This includes knowledge of

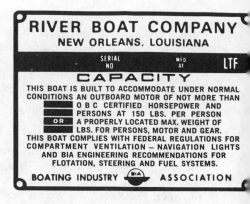

FIG. 1023 The Boating Industry Association has developed standards for safe loading of boats under 23 feet in terms of horsepower and weight-carrying capacity. Boats meeting these standards as determined by an independent testing laboratory will carry the BIA certification plate.

probable future weather conditions as well as those prevailing at the start of a cruise.

The weight-carrying capacity of a small boat having a conventional hull can be computed by multiplying 7.5 x overall length x maximum width x *minimum* effective depth of the boat (the depth of the hull to the lowest point at which water can enter—this penalizes low-cut transoms and recognizes properly designed engine wells). The result is the weight *in pounds* that can be carried; subtract the weight of engine, tanks, fuel, all installed or carried accessories and gear; the remainder is the weight in pounds, of persons that can be safely carried. As between the number of persons computed by weight as above and the number determined from L x B divided by 15, the lower figure should be used.

### Safe loading

It must always be remembered that people represent a "live" load (no pun intended); they move about and affect a boat quite differently than a "dead" or static load such as the engine or fuel tank. If the capacity of the boat is fully utilized, or the weather gets rough, distribute the load evenly, keep it low, and don't make abrupt changes in its distribution. Any shifting of human or other weights should be done only after stopping or slowing the boat so that the change can be made safely.

### Horsepower capacity

A second aspect of the capacity of an outboard boat is the maximum horsepower motor that can be *safely* put on it. This is exceeded perhaps as often as the weight-carrying capacity. The safe maximum horsepower will also be included on the capacity plate of a boat rated to BIA standards. If a boat does not have such a plate, the maximum horsepower can be determined from the graph and instructions on page 583.

The maximum horsepower that is safe need not be used; most boats will give satisfactory, and more economical, service with motors of less horsepower. A larger engine does not always mean more speed. If the horsepower of the engine is doubled, it does not mean that boat speed will be doubled. It does mean, however, that because of the increased weight of the engine, fuel and accessories it will require, the number of persons that can be safely carried will be significantly reduced.

### Boarding a boat

There is a safe way to step aboard a small boat—outboard or dinghy—and an unsafe way. In boarding from a pier, step into the boat as near to the center as possible, keeping body weight low. If you're boarding from a beach, come in over the bow. Keep lines tight or have someone steady the boat.

Never jump into a boat or step on the gunwale (edge of the hull). If you have a motor or other gear to take aboard, pile it on the pier so that you can easily reach it from the center of the boat. Better still, have someone hand it to you after you're aboard.

## SAFETY IN THE WATER

Anyone who goes boating regularly should know how to care for himself in the water. Fortunately, most boatmen and their families do know "how to swim," but this is often limited to taking a few strokes in a calm, relatively warm pool, with safety and rest only a few feet away. More attention should be given to staying afloat under adverse conditions of water temperature, waves, etc. Seldom is it necessary, or even desirable, to "swim" any distance; the problem is that of remaining afloat until help arrives. The skipper and crew should all have instructions in "drown-proofing."

Safety *in* the water can well start with swimming and/or lifesaving class at the local "Y" or community recreation center. Local chapters of the American Red Cross also give instruction in these subjects.

### Lifesaving devices

A person in the water following a boating accident should, of course, have a life jacket or buoyant cushion. It is of extreme importance that these devices be worn or used properly. Buoyant cushions are far from the best flotation device, but are widely used because of their convenience and low cost. Buoyant cushions are *not* intended to be worn. The straps on a buoyant cushion are put there primarily for holding-on purposes and also to aid in throwing the device. Because they must be grasped, cushions are

not suitable for small children or injured persons, and are not desirable for non-swimmers. Cushions should never be worn on a person's back since this tends to force his face down in the water.

As mentioned earlier in this chapter, the lifesaving device providing the greatest safety is the canvas jacket with flotation material in sealed plastic pouches. But the real potential of this most important safety item will be realized *only* if several conditions are met. Life preservers should be stored in several locations about the boat so that fire or other disaster cannot cut you off from all of them, and they must be stowed so as to be easily and quickly accessible. Everyone on board, including guests who may be aboard for only a few hours, *must* know where the life preservers are stowed. The skipper and regular crew must have tried them on and must be able to get into them quickly even in the dark (practice wearing a blindfold). Most importantly, the skipper must not delay in ordering everyone into life preservers in advance of their need if the emergency is of the type that builds up rather than striking suddenly without warning. It is far better to put them on, as bulky and uncomfortable as they may be, when trouble first threatens than it is to wait until near-panic develops. At night, anyone on deck should routinely wear a life jacket; non-swimmers, young children, and persons physically handicapped should wear one at all times—a person with a cast on an arm or leg goes down like a rock without added buoyancy.

The wise skipper never carries non-approved, damaged, or condemned lifesaving devices as "extra"—someone might grab one of them in an emergency.

### Swimming tips

Even with the best of lifesaving equipment aboard, a boatman may find himself in the water without the aid of a buoyant device. If the boat remains afloat or awash, *stay with it*. Search vessels and aircraft can spot a boat or its

**FIG. 1024 Swimming is a fine sport and an excellent capability to have for anyone who goes boating. Every skipper and his crew should know how to stay afloat and swim moderate distances. Take lessons at your local "Y" or Red Cross if you do not have this most desirable ability.**

wreckage far easier than an individual whose head only is above water.

A swimmer may find temporary relief from fatigue by floating or by varying his style of swimming. Cold or tired muscles are susceptible to cramps. A leg cramp can often be overcome by moving your knees up toward your chest so that you can massage the affected area. Save your breath as much as possible; call for help only when there is someone definitely close enough to hear you.

## PRE-DEPARTURE SAFETY

A worthwhile degree of increased safety afloat can be achieved if certain actions are taken routinely before departing on a short cruise. If it is to be an extended cruise of days or weeks, most of these items should be repeated each day.

### Final weather check

Few, if any, boats are of such size for the waters on which they are operated that no heed need be given to possible worsening of weather conditions before return to the home berth or reaching the next port. The wise skipper makes a final weather check just as close as possible to his departure time so as to have the latest weather report of current conditions and most up-to-date forecast. He learns the time of best weather broadcasts, radio and TV, in his home area (such broadcasts vary widely in their scope and suitability for boating); he knows the telephone numbers of agencies that he can call for last-minute information. When away from his home area, he finds on arrival at each overnight stop how he can get early morning forecasts before his departure.

The Coastal Warning Facilities Charts published each year in early summer by the Weather Bureau (see pages 264 and 265) provide information on major radio and TV weather broadcasts as well as the location of day and night storm warning displays. The Weather Bureau also is steadily expanding the number of VHF-FM radio transmitters that broadcast continuous weather information on 162.55 Mc/s.

### Pre-departure check list

Each skipper should prepare his own pre-departure checklist *and use it*. The following items are of general applicability; all may not be needed, and others certainly will have to be added for your own boating.

1. All safety equipment is aboard, accessible, and in good working condition, including one Coast Guard-approved life-saving device for each person embarked.

2. The bilge has been checked for fuel fumes and water. Ventilate or pump out as necessary.

3. Horn and all navigation lights operate satisfactorily.

4. All loose gear is stowed securely. Dock lines and fenders should be stowed immediately after getting under way.

5. All guests aboard have been properly instructed in safety and operational matters, both do's and don'ts.

6. Engine oil levels have been checked, both crankcase and reverse/reduction gears; water level has been checked in closed cooling systems. After starting engines, check overboard flow of cooling water.

7. Fuel tanks have been checked for quantity of gasoline or diesel fuel. Know your tank capacity and fuel consumption at various RPMs, thus knowing your cruising radius.

FIG. 1025 Although boating is generally a leisure-time activity, a skipper often leaves his pier or mooring in a hurry. A "pre-departure checklist" will ensure that no essential preparatory step has been left undone. This is especially important for safety when running single-handed and the skipper cannot leave the helm once underway.

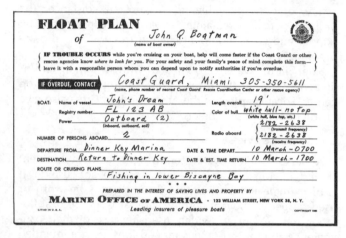

FIG. 1026 A "Float Plan" is a handy means of leaving behind on shore essential information when you go out fishing or for a cruise. Should you become overdue and a search must be made, much valuable time may be saved. Be sure, however, to report in when you return so as to avoid needless concern and wasted action.

Make sure there is enough fuel aboard for your anticipated cruising, plus an adequate reserve if you must change your plans for weather or other reasons.

8. There is a second person on board capable of taking over from the skipper should he become disabled or excessively fatigued.

### Float plan

Before departing on a cruise, the skipper should advise a responsible relative or friend as to where he intends to cruise and when he expects to make port again; make sure that this person has a good description of the boat. Keep him advised of any changes in your cruise plans. By doing these things, this person will be able to tell the Coast Guard where to search and what type of boat to look for if you are overdue. Be sure to advise this relative or friend when you return so as to prevent any false alarms about your safety.

An excellent means of accomplishing the foregoing is through use of "Float Plan" forms made available by the Marine Office of America, a leading insurer of boats. These forms, fig. 1026, provide a simple and convenient way of filing the necessary information. A pad of forms may be obtained by writing to 123 William Street, New York, N. Y. 10038, or from a local agent of the company.

## SAFETY IN WATER SKIING

Water skiing has become an ever more popular sport and its spread brings with it new problems in safety afloat. The following guides should do much to reduce hazards.

1. Allow no one who is not qualified as a basic swimmer to engage in water skiing. A ski belt or vest is intended to keep a stunned or unconscious skier afloat.

2. Water ski *only* in safe areas, out of channels and away from other craft. Some bodies of water will have areas designated for this sport with skiing prohibited elsewhere.

3. Install a wide-angle rear-view mirror or take along a second person to act as lookout. This will permit watching the skier *and* the waters ahead. Some state laws require this mirror or a second person in the boat to assist the operator, or both; check before starting to ski.

4. Make sure that the skier is wearing a proper lifesaving device.

5. If the skier falls, approach him from the lee side; stop your motor before starting to take him aboard.

6. In taking the skier on board, be careful not to swamp the boat. For smaller craft, it is usually safer to take a person aboard at the stern.

### Skiing signals

The following set of signals is recommended by the American Water Ski Association; see fig. 1027. Make sure that the skier, boat operator, and safety observer all know and understand the signals.

**Faster**—palm of one hand pointing upward.

**Slower**—palm pointing downward.

**Speed O.K.**—arm upraised with thumb and finger joined to form a circle.

**Right Turn**—arm outstretched pointing to the right.

**Left Turn**—arm outstretched pointing to the left.

**Return to Drop-off Area**—arm at 45° from body pointing down to water and swinging.

**Cut Motor**—finger drawn across throat.

**Stop**—hand up, palm forward—policeman style.

**Skier O.K. After Fall**—hands clenched together overhead.

**Pick Me Up** or **Fallen Skier, Watch Out**—one ski extended vertically out of water.

FIG. 1027 **This simple set of hand signals will allow adequate communication from the skier to the operator or observer on the towing craft. They must all be thoroughly familiar with the full set of signals if maximum safety is to be achieved.**

(from the USCG Recreational Boating Guide)

# Maintenance for Safety

Safety afloat is achieved, as we have seen in this chapter, by good design, sound construction, proper equipment, and sensible operating practices. The remaining element is continued maintenance for safety. Continual attention is needed for some of the material aspects of safety; for others, periodic checks at weekly, monthly, or annual intervals is sufficient. The important thing is that these checks of safety equipment be made *regularly* when needed.

### Keep your boat clean

Cleanliness aboard a boat is an important aspect of safety. Accumulations of dirt, sawdust, wood chips, and trash in the bilge will soak up oil and fuel drippings and become a fire hazard. Such accumulations may also stop up limber holes and clog bilge pumps. Keep your bilge absolutely free of dirt and trash; check frequently and clean out as often as needed.

## LIFESAVING EQUIPMENT

Lifesaving equipment usually requires no maintenance, but such items should be carefully inspected at the beginning of each boating season and again near its mid-point. These devices are not permanent; they do slowly wear out. Check for cut or torn fabric, broken stitches, and other signs of deterioration. **Do not delay in replacing below-par lifesaving devices;** attempt repairs *only* where *full* effectiveness can be restored. In case of doubt, ask the Coast Guard.

## FIRE EXTINGUISHERS

Portable fire extinguishers and installed systems should be checked at least annually; the best time is at the beginning of the year's activities afloat and again at mid-season if required.

### Dry chemical extinguishers

Pressurized dry chemical extinguishers are widely used on boats. These will have a gauge that should be checked every six months for an indication of adequate pressure—needle in center or green area of scale. Do not, however, merely read the gauge; tap it lightly to make sure that it is not stuck at a safe indication. If it drops to a lower reading, take the extinguisher to a service shop for recharging. Even if the gauge reads O.K., take the unit out of its bracket and shake it a bit to loosen the dry chemical inside to keep it from settling and hardening. Any areas on the exterior of the cylinder showing rust should be cleaned and repainted.

### CO2 extinguishers

Carbon dioxide—$CO_2$—fire extinguishers are checked annually by weight. Both portable units and built-in systems will have a weight stamped on them at the valve housing. If the weight is as much as 10% below the indicated value, the unit *must* be recharged. Weighing is the only check normally required on $CO_2$ extinguishers, but it must be done accurately. Portable units can be checked by the boat owner if he has access to suitably accurate scales. Built-in systems are best checked by a professional serviceman using his specialized knowledge and equipment.

$CO_2$ cylinders should also have verified the date on which the cylinder was last hydrostatically pressure-tested. This should be done every 12 years if the cylinder is not discharged. If the extinguisher is used, it must be pressure-tested if this has not been done within the preceding five years. If a used $CO_2$ extinguisher is purchased, it should be discharged, hydrostatically tested, and recharged before it is installed aboard. Remember that the pressure confined in these cylinders is tremendous, and if the cylinder has been damaged (through rust or corrosion), it is just like having a time bomb aboard, not knowing when it is set to go off!

Carbon dioxide extinguishers should not be installed where bilge or rain water will collect and cause rust. Any exposed metal should be painted at each annual inspection. If a cylinder becomes pitted from rust, have it hydrostatically tested for safety. Replace any damaged hoses or horns on this type of extinguisher.

### Foam-type extinguishers

Foam-type fire extinguishers are acceptable on boats, but are seldom actually installed because they are messy in use and need annual recharging. If you do have one, it must be completely discharged and recharged each year. There is no other method of checking it.

### Periodic discharges

It is a good policy to discharge a fire extinguisher periodically even though it is not needed for fighting a fire. An effective way of doing this would be to discharge one of the portable units each year on a regular rotation basis. This should be done in the presence of the whole crew and preferably in the form of a drill, putting out an actual small fire—off the boat, of course—in a metal pan or tub. Probably 99% or more of all persons who go boating have never discharged a fire extinguisher, let alone used one to put out an actual fire! There is no time to read the instructions carefully and practice after a real fire has started on the boat.

A word of warning with respect to $CO_2$ extinguishers—*never* unscrew the hose from the cylinder and then discharge it openly. This would have the same effect as trying to hang onto a rocket. A strong, heavy man would have trouble in hanging onto the cylinder, and if it were to get loose, it could cause a great deal of trouble.

Make sure that when fire extinguishers are removed for testing or practice discharge they are serviced by a competent shop and reinstalled *as soon as possible*. Sitting empty in the basement or garage at home or in the trunk of your car, an extinguisher cannot protect your boat. It is also wise not to denude your boat of fire protection by removing all extinguishers at the same time for servicing; do a half or a third at a time.

### Log entries

An entry should be made in the boat's log of all inspections, tests, and servicing of fire extinguishers. This will help keep these essential checks from being overlooked and may prove valuable in the event of insurance surveys or claims.

## ENGINE AND FUEL SYSTEM

Frequent safety checks should be made of the engine and fuel system for cleanliness and leaks. Any drippings of oil or grease should be kept wiped up and stopped as soon as possible. Immediate action must be taken in the case of any gasoline leaks—do not use the boat and disconnect the leads from the battery (with all loads turned off so that no spark will jump) in order that the engine cannot be started.

Annually, the entire fuel system should be checked inch by inch, including fuel lines in areas not normally visible. Look for any evidence of weepage of fuel or external corrosion of the lines. If any suspicious joints or lengths of tubing are found, it would be well to call in a qualified mechanic without delay.

## ELECTRICAL SYSTEMS

A thorough annual inspection should be made of a boat's electrical system, including all wiring in areas not normally visible. This should be done by a person qualified to evaluate what he finds—the skipper if he has the necessary knowledge and experience, or an outside expert if needed. A search should be made for any cut or chafed insulation, corrosion at connections, excessive sag or strain on conductors, and other visible signs of deterioration. A leakage test should be made by opening each circuit at the main distribution panel and measuring current flow when all loads are turned off. Ideally there should be no current flow; current of more than a few milliamperes indicates electrical "leakage" that should be traced down and corrected without delay.

### Bonding systems

If all through-hull fittings, struts, shafts, etc., are electrically connected by an internal bonding system, this wiring should be checked annually. Especially careful checks should be made where connections are made to the fitting or other metal part; connections in the bilge are subject to corrosion and development of poor contacts with high electrical resistance.

The skipper can make a visual check of the bonding system, but an electrical expert with specialized equipment is needed for a thorough evaluation. Should any signs of corrosion at points of connection of bonding wires to through-hull fittings be noted, a complete electrical test is recommended.

With respect to possible electrolysis damage, a bonding system with one or more poor connections is worse than no system at all. Electrolysis can and does cause weakening of through-hull fittings, bolts on struts and rudder posts, etc., that could result in serious safety hazards.

## HULL SAFETY MAINTENANCE

Boats that are kept in the water will be hauled out periodically for bottom cleaning and repainting. This occasion should not be overlooked as an opportunity for a *safety* inspection of hull and fittings below the waterline.

Hull planking should be carefully checked for physical damage from having struck floating or fixed objects, and for any general deterioration from age. In general, it is best to call upon the services of an expert if any suspicious areas are found.

### Through-hull fittings

An inspection should be made each time the boat is hauled to see that through-hull fittings and their seacocks are in good condition. This check should include fastenings susceptible to damage from electrolytic action.

### Underwater components

Underwater fittings should get an annual inspection. This includes such parts as shafts, propellers, rudders, struts, stuffing boxes, and metal skegs. Stuffing boxes should be repacked as often as necessary to keep them from leaking excessively, shafting checked for alignment and excessive wear at strut bearings, and propellers examined to see if they need truing up.

## FOLLOW-UP OF INSPECTIONS

Nothing is gained if prompt and thorough follow-up actions are not taken on findings of periodic safety inspections. *Maintenance related to the safety of the craft and those aboard must not be delayed. Do not operate a boat that has a known safety defect.*

# First Aid Afloat

*No one who is not educated and properly qualified to practice medicine should attempt to act as a doctor.* There are, however, many instances where availability of a first aid kit, some knowledge on the part of the boatman, and a ready reference book have materially eased pain or even saved the life of a sick or injured person on a boat. All skippers should prepare themselves and their craft to render emergency first aid, doing no more than is absolutely necessary while getting the victim to a doctor or hospital as rapidly as possible.

## FIRST AID KITS

There are many published guides to the proper contents of a first aid kit. Probably each of these has merit, and the list that follows can, and should, be modified for the size of boat, the number of persons aboard, the length of an average cruise, the area to be cruised, and the hazards likely to be encountered.

The first aid kit must be accessible and each person aboard should be made aware of its location.

### Basic first aid materials

There are certain basic first aid materials that should be carried aboard all classes of boats. Bandages should be ready for instant use—each dressing individually wrapped, a complete dressing in itself. Each should be sterilized and designed to provide protection against infection and contamination.

Antiseptic liquids are preferably packaged so that the solution stays at its original strength until used. This type of packaging is available as a swab that contains a sealed ampoule in a sleeve of multi-layered cardboard; when the ampoule is broken there is no chance for the user to be

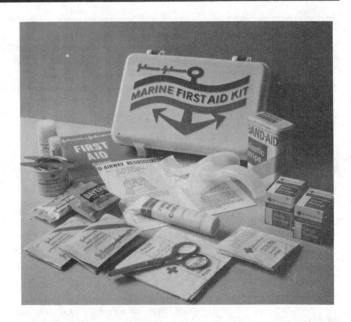

FIG. 1028   All boats should have on board adequate first aid equipment, supplies, and instructions. Kits may be either home-assembled or bought ready-made. See text for recommended items to be included. Skippers should also consider taking a standard first-aid course of instruction.

cut by glass. A close-packed cotton tip saturates instantly and then is applied to the wound area. There is no wasteage, spillage, or deterioration.

Basic first aid materials should also contain burn treatment compounds to take care of sunburn or burns caused by other hazards. Scissors have multiple uses. Forceps, to remove splinters, should be blunt-end, to preclude possi-

# Artificial Respiration

Every boatman should have a working knowledge of the principles of artificial respiration. When the need for it arises, there is no time to search for instructions nor to study each step while, at the same time, attempting to apply the treatment. A boatman who has familiarized himself in advance with one of the accepted methods is more likely to work with calm assurance, saving precious minutes that could mean the difference between success and failure.

Through the courtesy of The American National Red Cross, we reproduce below the simplified illustrated methods they advocate. In recent years the mouth-to-mouth method, illustrated in steps 1 to 5, has come into widespread use. Recognizing, however, that some rescuers cannot or will not apply this method, the Red Cross includes instructions for the older manual chest pressure—arm lift (Silvester) and back pressure—arm lift (Holger Nielsen) methods. Study carefully the additional instructions at the bottom of the page applicable to all methods.

If victim is not breathing, begin some form of artificial respiration at once. Wipe out quickly any foreign matter visible in the mouth, using your fingers or a cloth wrapped around your fingers.

## MOUTH-TO-MOUTH (MOUTH-TO-NOSE) METHOD

Tilt victim's head back. (Fig. 1). Pull or push the jaw into a jutting-out position. (Fig. 2).

If victim is a small child, place your mouth tightly over his mouth and nose and blow gently into his lungs about 20 times a minute. If victim is an adult (see Fig. 3), cover the mouth with your mouth, pinch his nostrils shut, and blow vigorously about 12 times a minute.

If unable to get air into lungs of victim, and if head and jaw positions are correct, suspect foreign matter in throat. To remove it, suspend a small child momentarily by the ankles or place child in position shown in Fig. 4, and slap sharply between shoulder blades.

If the victim is adult, place in position shown in Fig. 5, and use same procedure.

## MANUAL METHODS OF ARTIFICIAL RESPIRATION

Rescuers who cannot, or will not, use mouth-to-mouth or mouth-to-nose technique should use a manual method.

### THE CHEST PRESSURE-ARM LIFT (SILVESTER) METHOD

Place the victim in a face-up position and put something under his shoulders to raise them and allow the head to drop backward.

Kneel at the victim's head, grasp his wrists, cross them, and press them over the lower chest (Fig. 6). This should cause air to flow out.

Immediately release this pressure and pull the arms outward and upward over his head and backward as far as possible (Fig. 7). This should cause air to rush in.

Repeat this cycle about 12 times per minute, checking the mouth frequently for obstructions.

If a second rescuer is available, have him hold the victim's head so that the jaw is jutting out (Fig. 8). The helper should be alert to detect the presence of any stomach contents in the mouth and keep the mouth as clean as possible at all times.

### THE BACK PRESSURE-ARM LIFT (HOLGER NIELSEN) METHOD

Place the victim face-down, bend his elbows and place his hands one upon the other, turn his head slightly to one side and extend it as far as possible, making sure that the chin is jutting out. Kneel at the head of the victim. Place your hands on the flat of the victim's back so that the palms lie just below an imaginary line running between the armpits (Fig. 9).

Rock forward until the arms are approximately vertical and allow the weight of the upper part of your body to exert steady, even pressure downward upon the hands (Fig. 10).

Immediately draw his arms upward and toward you, applying enough lift to feel resistance and tension at his shoulders (Fig. 11). Then lower the arms to the ground. Repeat this cycle about 12 times per minute, checking the mouth frequently for obstruction.

If a second rescuer is available, have him hold the victim's head so that the jaw continues to jut out (Fig. 12). The helper should be alert to detect any stomach contents in the mouth and keep the mouth as clean as possible at all times.

## RELATED INFORMATION FOR ALL METHODS

If vomiting occurs, quickly turn the victim on his side, wipe out the mouth, and then reposition him.

When a victim is revived, keep him as quiet as possible until he is breathing regularly. Keep him from becoming chilled and otherwise treat him for shock. Continue artificial respiration until the victim begins to breathe for himself or a physician pronounces him dead or he appears to be dead beyond any doubt.

Because respiratory and other disturbances may develop as an aftermath, a doctor's care is necessary during the recovery period.

bility of doing further injury by probing, which is *not* a first aid measure.

Pre-packed first aid kits, available at most drug stores and marine supply stores, are generally acceptable, but their contents should be checked against recommendations that follow. Consideration should be given to separate purchase of any significant shortages; such items should be stored in or near the kit.

## The container

The container for a first aid kit for a boat should not be made of a metal that could rust, nor of cardboard that could soak up moisture. A plastic box such as is often used to hold fishing tackle or tools is a good choice. It should close securely and be moisture-tight. It should *never* be locked, although it may be sealed with tape. Keep it on a high shelf out of the reach of small children. The kit may be lightly secured in place for safety in rough weather, but it must be portable and capable of being quickly unfastened and taken to the scene of an emergency.

## Contents (instruments)

First aid kits should contain both simple instruments and consumable supplies. In the first category, the following are recommended:

**Scissors**—small and sharp; if there is room for two pairs, one should be of the blunt-end surgical type. Also a packet of single-edge razor blades.

**Tweezers**—small, pointed; tips must meet exactly to pick up small objects.

**Safety pins**—assorted sizes.

**Thermometer**—inexpensive oral-rectal type, in case.

**Tourniquet**—use only for *major* bleeding that cannot be controlled by compresses; follow instructions *exactly*.

**Eye-washing cup**—small, metal.

**Cross Venti-breather**—resuscitation device for drowned or asphyxiated person; aids in mouth-to-mouth resuscitation; follow directions on box.

**Hot-water bottle** and **ice bag**—these items, or a single unit that will serve both purposes, can do much to ease pain. Use with caution, following instructions in the first aid manual or medical advice book; improper use can aggravate conditions, sometimes seriously.

## Contents (supplies)

The first aid kit should contain approximately the following types, sizes, and quantities of consumable supplies. Within reasonable limits, substitutions can be made to reflect local availabilities, personal preferences, etc.

**Bandages**—1", 2", and 4" sterile gauze squares, individually wrapped. Bandage rolls, 1" and 2". Band-aids (or equivalents) in assorted sizes, plus "butterfly closures." A minimum of one unit of each item, more on larger craft with greater number of persons aboard.

**Triangular bandage**—40" for use as sling or major compress.

**Elastic bandage**—3" width for sprains or splints.

**Adhesive tape**—Waterproof, 1" and 2" by 5 or 10 yards.

**Absorbent cotton**—standard size roll, for cleaning wounds, padding, etc.

**Applicators**—cotton-tipped individual swabs (Q-tips or equivalent) for applying antiseptics, removing foreign objects from cuts, eyes, ears.

**Antiseptic liquid**—Tincture of iodine of merthiolate; or zephiran chloride, aqueous solution, 1:1,000. Antiseptic may be in bottle, but preferably in form of individual crushable ampoule applicators. Also a 4 oz. or larger bottle of antiseptic (70% alcohol) solution, or Phisophex solution.

**White petroleum jelly**—small jar, or preferably tube; plain, not carbolated; for small burns, dressings. An antiseptic burn cream may be substituted. This may be supplemented by a tube or bottle of sunburn remedy and a package of sterile petroleum-jelly-saturated gauze squares.

**Antiseptic ointment**—1 oz. tube of Bacitracin or Polysporin, or as recommended by your physician (prescription required); for general cuts, abrasions, and infections of the skin.

**Nupercainal ointment**—1 oz. tube; for local anesthetic purposes—apply to raw surface before cleaning or if painful. Calamine lotion is good for relief from itching.

**Pain killer**—Aspirin or related compound for ordinary pain. Also Darvon Compound, Codeine, or Demerol tablets or capsules for more severe pain (prescription required).

**Sleeping pills**—Seconal or equivalent as prescribed by your physician; use with caution as directed. If sleeplessness is related to pain, also give aspirin or Darvon Compound.

**Antibiotics**—Use *only* if there will be a delay in reaching a doctor and infection appears serious. Use Achroymcin, Eryothromycin, or similar drug as prescribed by your doctor.

**Ophthalmic (eye) ointment**—small tube of butyn sulphate with metaphen. If necessary to flush out eye, use sterile solution of 1 teaspoon of salt in 1 pint of water; do *not* use sea water.

**Antihistamine**—Pyrabenzamine tablets or as prescribed by your physician; use for allergies and allergic reactions to stings and insect bites. Also an antihistamine ointment.

**Ammonia inhalants**—crushable ampoules; for relief of symptoms of faintness or dizziness.

**Seasickness remedy**—Dramamine, Marezine, Bonamine, or Bonine tablets; may also be obtained in suppository form. Prescription required for all except Bonine. These should be taken before embarking; usually not effective after vomiting starts.

**Anti-acid preparation**—liquid or tablet, or both, for heartburn and indigestion.

**Laxative**—one or two forms for variations in personal preferences; Milk of Magnesia is excellent. Also Fleets disposable enemas are desirable items to have an board.

**Anti-diarrhea drug**—3 oz. bottle of Paregoric (prescription required) or 8 oz. bottle of Kaopectate.

## First aid manual

A compact first aid manual should be packed in the top of the first aid kit. A larger medical-adviser and first aid book may be carried in a book shelf, but there should always be a small booklet of instructions in or immediately adjacent to the container of instruments and supplies.

First aid manuals can be obtained from the American Red Cross and other safety agencies. Books relating specifically to medical problems afloat and their management can be obtained through book stores and at many marine supply stores.

### Replenishment

A first aid kit missing some items does not provide a full measure of safety afloat. As supplies are used, they should be replenished promptly. Further, some drugs do not last indefinitely. They may lose their strength, become unstable and toxic, or evaporate to increased concentrations that could be harmful. Ask your physician about the safe shelf-life of drugs prescribed by him and other supplies carried in your first aid kit. Replace questionably-old supplies whether used or not.

If instruments, or the first aid manual, become lost or damaged, they, too, should be replaced at the earliest opportunity.

### Medicine cabinet

Most cruisers have medicine cabinets in the head where additional first-aid supplies may be found. A word of caution should be sounded here—this cabinet should supplement rather than replace the first-aid kits as outlined above because its contents are not portable to the scene of the emergency. It should contain the items which normally are stocked in a medicine cabinet at home such as aspirin, upset stomach remedies, etc.

### ADMINISTERING FIRST AID

It would be highly impractical to attempt the instruction of first aid in the few paragraphs that can be devoted to that topic in this book. It is the skipper's responsibility to his passengers and crew to acquaint himself with the proper first-aid procedures. This can be done through classes given by each Chapter of the American Red Cross in a standard first-aid course. It should be remembered that when you are aboard your boat and at sea, you are out of immediate touch with professional medical attention and thus advance preparedness is necessary.

**Rule one.** Always take first aid to the victim, not the victim to the first aid. You may well aggravate an injury by attempting to move an accident victim. You will add to a sick person's discomfort by requiring him to move about. Limit movement of the affected individual to that absolutely necessary to get him clear of a hazardous area.

**Rule two.** When giving first aid, take your time. Usually there is more damage done by the well-meaning amateur than was ever caused by the actual injury. Remember, there are only three instances when speed in giving first aid is required: (1) when the victim has stopped breathing; (2) when there is arterial bleeding; and (3) when the victim has been bitten by a poisonous snake. The measures required in these instances are taught in the standard Red Cross first aid course available locally; get a group of your fellow boatmen together and attend one soon.

It should be noted that we have eliminated splints from the first-aid kit. The average first-aider is not qualified to set a broken limb; it is much safer to place the limb in pillows or blankets, tying them securely around the fractured member so that no further damage will be done. And always remember that first-aid should stop at first aid . . . which is administering aid and comfort to avert further complications until professional medical attention can be obtained.

### Radio advice

In many emergency situations, a call to the Coast Guard can bring medical advice for treatment of serious injuries or illnesses. Initial contact should be made on 2182 kc/s, but it is most desirable that the boat be capable of shifting to a Coast Guard working frequency such as 2670 kc/s. On VHF-FM, the initial contact should be on 156.8 Mc/s (Channel 16).

---

**Basic Guides to Boating Safety**

1. Carry proper equipment—know how to use it.
2. Maintain boat and equipment in top condition.
3. Know and obey the Rules of the Road afloat.
4. Operate with care, courtesy, and common sense.
5. Always keep your boat under complete control.
6. Watch posted speeds; slow down in anchorages.
7. Under no circumstances, overload your boat.
8. See that life-saving equipment is accessible.
9. Check local weather reports before departure.
10. Inspect hull, engine, and all gear frequently.
11. Keep bilges clean, electrical contacts tight.
12. Guard rigidly against any fuel system leakage.
13. Have fire extinguishers instantly available.
14. Take maximum precautions when taking on fuel.
15. Be sure to allow adequate scope when anchoring.
16. Request a USCG Auxiliary courtesy examination.
17. Enroll in a US Power Squadrons piloting class.

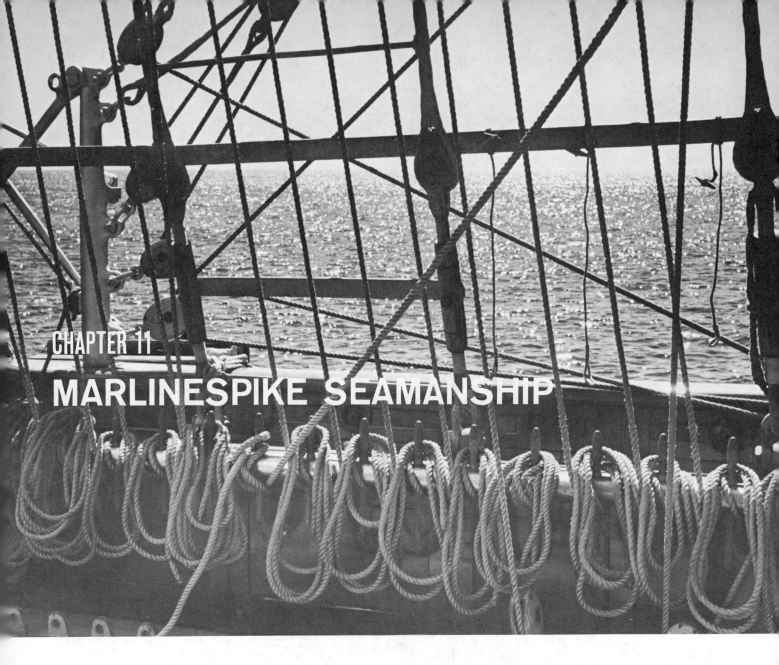

CHAPTER 11

# MARLINESPIKE SEAMANSHIP

**The Selection and Care of Rope—**

**Knots, Bends,**

**Hitches and Splices—**

**Blocks and Tackles—**

**The Bosun's Locker—**

FIG. 1101 Running rigging on a windjammer. Sails are power on wind-ships; their rigging is as important as the engines of motorboats.

## Cordage

Earlier editions of Piloting, Seamanship and Small Boat Handling, before the coming of many types of synthetic cordage, were much concerned with the prevention of rot, which is one of the two worst enemies of natural or vegetable fiber rope. The other is abuse. Abuse rather than proper use, today, is probably the cause of most cordage failure.

In Table 11-1 you will note the variation in weight and strength—size being equal—between ropes made of different fibers or fiber combinations. Manufacturers compare rope of different fibers, or different constructions of the same fiber, by calculating "breaking length." This means the length of rope that would break from its own weight if it were hung on a sky hook. For instance, the "breaking length" of nylon is approximately 100,000 vs. manila at approximately 32,000. The strength of the fiber, the unit weight of the fiber and the rope construction all enter into breaking strength and breaking length.

It would appear that ropes could be substituted on the

basis of strength alone. NOT SO!, except perhaps in some limited applications. A *working* line must have other attributes beyond strength alone. For instance, abrasion resistance; a small line presents less surface area over which to distribute the surface wear. Notice the proportion of cross section area the same size cut or nick makes in two lines of different diameters which might be of the same strength. (Fig. 1102)

**FIG. 1102 Relative effect on strength of cuts or nicks in rope of different diameter.**

Perhaps as important in size selection, even for large hawsers for ships and tugs, is handling convenience. On a small sailboat a *Dacron 3/16" diameter sheet might be strong enough but it would not be easy to hold or grasp. Therefore, a 3/8" main sheet and 5/16" jib sheets are about the smallest that can be handled except in very light wind.

Another factor in the surface area is that twisted rope has "crowns" which reduce this area and abrade more rapidly; as contrasted to double braided rope which essentially is round and presents some 30% greater surface area to distribute the wear. Double braid also provides a visible safety check, because severe abraiding of the cover can be spotted while there is still more than 50% of the strength left in the line from the inner core.

## SELECTION OF SIZE

Now, to select the size synthetic to substitute for manila or cotton lines, and referring to Table 11-1 of weights and strengths, the following method has worked out in practice:

There are two ways to approach selection. The first is a straight synthetic substitute for manila or cotton line. The other is to select a different type and fiber combination such as 2-in-1 double braid, depending on the use. For sheets and halyards, where low stretch is required, you can use Dacron, or a double braid that combines a polyester cover with a polypropylene core that has 25% less stretch than Dacron alone. For mooring, anchor, and tie-up lines, you can select nylon twisted, or double braided nylon for a better stretch and strength combination. For example, a 3/4" diameter, 2 1/4" (2.25") circ. manila rope (@ 16.3 lbs. per 100; 5400 lb. strength) could well be replaced by 9/16" dia. (1 3/4" circ.) or 5/8" dia. (2" circ.) twisted nylon or Dacron; or by a 7/16" dia. 2-in-1 double nylon braided line. Added strength and less weight and

## FIBER CORDAGE – TYPICAL WEIGHTS AND MINIMUM BREAKING STRENGTHS (POUNDS)

| NOMINAL SIZE (inches) | | MANILA Fed. Spec. TR 605 | | | NYLON (High Tenacity—H.T.) | | | DU PONT DACRON or H.T. POLYESTER | | | POLYOLEFINS (H.T.) (Polypropylene and/or Polyethylene) | | | DOUBLE NYLON BRAID | | | POLYESTER/POLYOLEFIN DOUBLE BRAID | | |
|---|---|---|---|---|---|---|---|---|---|---|---|---|---|---|---|---|---|---|---|
| Dia. | Circ. | Net Wt. 100' | Ft. per lb. | Breaking Strength | Net Wt. 100' | Ft. per lb. | Breaking Strength | Net Wt. 100' | Ft. per lb. | Breaking Strength | Net Wt. 100' | Ft. per lb. | Breaking Strength | Net Wt. 100' | Ft. per lb. | Breaking Strength | Net Wt. 100' | Ft. per lb. | Breaking Strength |
| 3/16 | 5/8 | 1.47 | 68 | 450 | 1 | 100 | 1,000 | 1.3 | 77 | 1,000 | .73 | 137 | 750 | NA | NA | NA | .75 | 133 | 900 |
| 1/4 | 3/4 | 1.96 | 51 | 600 | 1.5 | 66.6 | 1,700 | 2.1 | 47.5 | 1,700 | 1.24 | 80 | 1,250 | 1.66 | 60.3 | 2,100 | 1.7 | 60.2 | 1,700 |
| 5/16 | 1 | 2.84 | 35 | 1,000 | 2.5 | 40 | 2,650 | 3.3 | 30 | 2,550 | 1.88 | 53 | 1,850 | 2.78 | 36 | 3,500 | 2.6 | 38.4 | 2,600 |
| 3/8 | 1 1/8 | 4.02 | 25 | 1,350 | 3.6 | 28 | 3,650 | 4.7 | 21.3 | 3,500 | 2.9 | 34.5 | 2,600 | 3.33 | 30 | 4,200 | 3.5 | 28.5 | 3,500 |
| 7/16 | 1 1/4 | 5.15 | 19.4 | 1,750 | 5 | 20 | 5,100 | 6.3 | 15.9 | 4,800 | 3.9 | 25.5 | 3,400 | 5.0 | 20 | 6,000 | 5.1 | 20 | 5,100 |
| 1/2 | 1 1/2 | 7.35 | 13.6 | 2,650 | 6.6 | 15 | 6,650 | 8.2 | 12.2 | 6,100 | 4.9 | 20.4 | 4,150 | 6.67 | 14.9 | 7,500 | 6.8 | 15 | 6,800 |
| 9/16 | 1 3/4 | 10.2 | 9.8 | 3,450 | 8.4 | 11.9 | 8,500 | 10.2 | 9.8 | 7,700 | 6.2 | 16 | 4,900 | 8.33 | 12 | 9,500 | NA | NA | NA |
| 5/8 | 2 | 13.1 | 7.6 | 4,400 | 10.5 | 9.5 | 10,300 | 13.2 | 7.6 | 9,500 | 7.8 | 12.8 | 5,900 | 11.1 | 9 | 12,000 | 11 | 9 | 11,000 |
| 3/4 | 2 1/4 | 16.3 | 6.1 | 5,400 | 14.5 | 6.9 | 14,600 | 17.9 | 5.6 | 13,200 | 11.1 | 9 | 7,900 | 15.0 | 6.7 | 17,000 | 15 | 6.7 | 15,000 |
| 7/8 | 2 3/4 | 22 | 4.55 | 7,700 | 20 | 5 | 19,600 | 24.9 | 4 | 17,500 | 15.4 | 6.5 | 11,000 | 20.8 | 4.8 | 23,700 | 20 | 5 | 20,000 |
| 1 | 3 | 26.5 | 3.77 | 9,000 | 26 | 3.84 | 25,000 | 30.4 | 3.3 | 22,000 | 18.6 | 5.4 | 13,000 | 25.0 | 4 | 28,500 | 28 | 3.6 | 28,000 |
| 1 1/8 | 3 1/2 | 35.2 | 2.84 | 12,000 | 34 | 2.94 | 33,250 | 40.5 | 2.5 | 26,500 | 24.2 | 4.1 | 17,500 | 35.0 | 2.8 | 39,000 | 35 | 2.8 | 35,000 |
| 1 1/4 | 3 3/4 | 40.8 | 2.45 | 13,500 | 39 | 2.56 | 37,800 | 46.2 | 2.16 | 30,500 | 27.5 | 3.6 | 20,000 | 40.0 | 2.5 | 44,000 | 40 | 2.5 | 40,000 |
| 1 5/16 | 4 | 46.9 | 2.13 | 15,000 | 45 | 2.22 | 44,500 | 53.4 | 1.87 | 34,500 | 31.3 | 3.2 | 23,000 | 45.0 | 2.2 | 49,500 | 45 | 2.2 | 45,000 |
| 1 1/2 | 4 1/2 | 58.8 | 1.7 | 18,500 | 55 | 1.8 | 55,000 | 67 | 1.5 | 43,000 | 39.5 | 2.5 | 29,000 | 60.0 | 1.6 | 65,000 | 60 | 1.6 | 60,000 |

Table 11-1

NOTE:—The figures on synthetics, above, are an average of those available from four large cordage manufacturers. Those for the rope you buy should be availabe at your dealers. Check them carefully. Also check the rope. In general a soft, sleazy rope may be somewhat stronger and easier to splice but it will not wear as well and is more apt to hockle or unlay than a firm, well "locked-up" rope. Blended ropes, part polyolefins and part other fibers, may be found. Multifilament (fine filament) polypropylene looks like nylon—don't expect it to be as strong or do the job of nylon. (It floats, nylon doesn't.) Spun, or stapled, nylon and Dacron are not as strong as ropes made from continuous filaments but are less slippery and easier to grasp. Sometimes used for sheets on sailing craft.

*Du Pont registered trademark.

storage room, in addition to long life and other advantages, would be gained.

By similar method, use 80 to 85% factor to find the polyolefin size to use. (2" circ. ⅝" dia. indicated by previous example). The polys are not as strong and have lower melting points, thus are not as abrasion-resistant. They are, however, the lightest weight and they float which are advantages for "female hands" for tie-up lines and towing, such as dinghies and passing a tow line.

Table 11-3 gives the preferred ropes for different uses. Others may be used if care is taken in the selection, and the limitations are taken into account.

## CARE AND PROTECTION OF ROPE

The anchor and mooring lines, standing and running rigging, and similar gear that constitute one of the most important parts of a yachtsman's equipment may be used with intelligent care—to which it will respond with years of useful service—or it may be abused by ignorance and neglect, ruining it in short order.

## TEN RULES TO LENGTHEN ROPE LIFE

These ten commandments for the care of rope may not be all-inclusive, but it is safe to say that if they are observed a boatman may very well, in many cases, be able to double the useful life of his rope.

### 1. Look Out for Kinks

One sure way to destroy the value of a piece of line is to allow it to get a kink in it and then put it under strain. For example, you decide to play the Good Samaritan and break out your new spare line to haul a stranded boat off a bar. The new line is unruly and doesn't handle like the well-used anchor line, so there are a dozen kinks between your quarter bitt and his samson post when you ease the clutch in and open the throttle. In thirty seconds, you'll take more out of that line than you would in thirty weeks of normal service—if you don't shake those kinks out first.

What happens is this: The fibers are overstressed at the sharp bend, weakening fibers of the strands. Rapid wear follows and later the line may part at that spot, right at a critical time—through no fault of its own.

The time to start watching for kinks is in the very beginning when the rope is first taken from the coil or reel. There are right and wrong ways of doing this. The right way is to lay the coil on deck with the inside end down according to direction on the tag attached to the coil. Now reach down into the coil and pull this inner end up through the center, unwinding counter-clockwise. (See fig. 1120.) If it uncoils in the wrong direction, turn the coil over and pull the end out from the other side.

Synthetic rope should be shipped on reels and should be pulled or rolled off, disturbing the lay as little as possible. If it becomes unruly when coiling, try "faking down" in a figure 8. Do not "loop" off over the end of the reel —let it roll.

In natural fiber ropes kinks are most troublesome in wet weather; yachtsmen therefore have more to watch than those who use their rope ashore. Wet manila rope shrinks in length and swells in diameter and the lay shortens, making it more difficult to handle.

Knots have the same effect as a sharp kink. Some knots

Table 11-2

| ROPE AND FIBER COMPARISON CHART | | | | |
|---|---|---|---|---|
| | MANILA | NYLON | DACRON | POLY-OLEFINS |
| Relative Strength | 1 | 4 | 3 | 2 |
| Relative Weight | 3 | 2 | 4 | 1 |
| Elongation | 1 | 4 | 2 | 3 |
| Relative Resistance to Impact or Shock Loads | 1 | 4 | 2 | 3 |
| Mildew and Rot Resistance | Poor | Excellent | Excellent | Excellent |
| Acid Resistance | Poor | Fair | Fair | Excellent |
| Alkali Resistance | Poor | Excellent | Excellent | Excellent |
| Sunlight Resistance | Fair | Fair | Good | Fair |
| Organic Solvent Resistance | Good | Good | Good | Fair |
| Melting Point | 380° (Burns) | 410°F. | 410°F. | about 300°F. |
| Floatability | Only when new | None | None | Indefinite |
| *Relative Abrasion Resistance (*Depends on many factors—whether wet or dry, etc.) | 2 | 3 | 4 | 1 |
| KEY TO RATINGS: 1 Lowest—4 Highest | | | | |

may take 40 to 50 per cent out of a rope's efficiency. (See table 11-4.) A good splice, on the other hand, will allow a rope to retain 85 to 95 per cent of its original strength. Therefore, if a splice is indicated, don't use a knot.

### 2. Keep Your Rope Clean

Simple cleanliness in taking care of rope pays big dividends. In the course of use it is bound to pick up mud and sand. When this occurs, the rope should be draped in loose loops over a rail and hosed down gently, with fresh water if available. Don't use a high pressure stream with the intent of doing a more thorough job, as this will only force dirt and grit deeper into the rope. After washing, allow it to dry and then rap or shake it thoroughly to get out any remaining particles of dirt. Grit cuts the fibers.

### 3. Stow Carefully

Natural fiber rope will rot so it must be dried and carefully stowed in a place with adequate ventilation. This applies to manila, sisal, cotton and, to a lesser extent, linen and flax. Many a yachtman has been embarrassed or worse because of rot. Dry lines on deck before stowing. Hang up light lines. Loosely coil heavier ones on gratings so air can circulate. Don't subject them to intense heat.

Synthetic rope *may* be stowed wet but introduces unpleasant dampness below. Iron rust from rusty chain and thimbles is not good for nylon.

Keep lines away from exhaust pipes and batteries.

### 4. Guard Against Chafe and Abrasion

Chafe and abrasion are among rope's worst enemies. Heavy coils are sometimes dragged along the ground instead of being carried on the shoulder. Dragging over a rough surface causes the outside fibers to be cut or rubbed off while grit works inside the strands and is equally destructive in cutting inside fibers.

Rope should never be allowed to rub on sharp edges, or one rope chafe against another. Surface wear is accelerated and fraying often starts as a result of it. If it is necessary to have a rope pass over a sharp edge like a rail on the deck edge or a badly designed chock, rig a canvas

| RECOMMENDED ROPE FOR VARIOUS USES | | | | | | | | |
|---|---|---|---|---|---|---|---|---|
| | Tie-Up or Mooring Lines | Anchor Ropes or Mooring Pennants | Sheets and Halyards | Flag Halyards | Seizing and Whipping | Bolt Rope Synthetic Sails | Towing | Water Skiing |
| **MANILA** | √ | √ | √ | √ | | | √ | |
| **NYLON** | √ | √ | | √ | | | √ | |
| **DACRON** | √ | | √ | √ | | √ | | |
| **POLYOLEFIN** | √ | | | | | | √ | √ |
| **BRAIDED DACRON** | | | √ | √ | | | | |
| **BRAIDED NYLON** | √ | √ | | √ | √ | | √ | |
| **WIRE (Stainless)** | | Pennants | √ | | | | | |
| **BRAIDED COTTON** | | | | √ | √ | | | |
| **NYLON SEINE TWINE** | | | | | √ | | | |
| **LINEN or FLAX** | | | √ | √ | √ | | | |

pad to prevent excessive wear from damaging the fibers.

When riding to an anchor for considerable periods, it is always well to "freshen the nip" by paying out a little line to bring the chafe of chocks in another place.

Chafing gear of canvas will protect the line from this source of trouble; it is particularly desirable on mooring lines where chafing always comes in one spot. Some boatmen carry a split length of rubber hose which can be readily clapped on the line where required. Specially molded rubber and plastic chafing gear is available.

Another trick to lengthen the life of a line like an anchor line or halyard, where most of the wear comes on one end, is to turn the line end-for-end occasionally. Any rope ends that do not terminate in a splice should be whipped to prevent fraying.

When making fast at a dock, select smooth round piles of good diameter to make fast to, and shun square or rectangular timbers with sharp corners. If there is no alternative, pad the sharp edges.

## 5. Prevent Slipping

When using rope on the drums of winches or hoists it is bad practice to let the rope slip on the drum as it revolves. This not only increases wear on the rope, but the sudden jerks as the rope is snubbed, strain the fibers badly.

Similarly the rope should not be allowed to lie against the revolving drum of a hoist or winch. In addition to objectionable chafe, there is the element of heat from friction to be considered; this may be enough to burn or melt the fibers.

Synthetic ropes that are highly strained and/or repeatedly stretched while around a cleat or winch may melt and grab so they will not run or pay out smoothly.

## 6. Avoid Small Blocks

There are two sources of trouble when rope is expected to run over too small a block. On the one hand there is excessive internal friction. Wear from such friction is always present when rope runs over the sheaves of blocks and the smaller the sheave diameter, the greater the friction. On the other hand, there is the external wear as the rope chafes against the inside of sheave holes providing insufficient clearance. Faulty alignment of blocks which causes the rope to rub against the sides, or cheeks, of the

blocks is also bad. A combination of this internal friction and external chafe breaks down fibers much faster than would be expected in normal use.

One place where trouble of this kind shows up quickly if installation is faulty is in the use of small sheaves in the steering lines or cables. These get a great deal of hard usage and their life can be extended by the use of sheaves of generous diameter.

In tackles, when matching blocks to rope, use a block with a shell length of at least 3 inches for $3/8$-inch (diameter) rope; 4 inches for $1/2$; 5 inches for $5/8$; 6 inches for $3/4$; 8 inches for $7/8$; 9 inches for 1 inch; and 12 inches for $1 1/4$-inch rope. (See table 11-5.)

Care should be exercised to see that sheaves are never allowed to become rough or rusty. See to it that they are well lubricated to reduce friction and to prevent their seizing. A sheave frozen by rust or corrosion on its pin would work havoc on a piece of rope.

## 7. Don't Lubricate

For natural fiber, the manufacturer has already treated the rope with an oil or solution which preserves it and lubricates internal fibers. This may account for roughly 10 per cent of the rope's weight. Even some synthetics have special fiber treatments.

Users are cautioned not to attempt to improve upon the manufacturer's work by using additional lubricant of any kind upon it. The treatment given the rope originally when manufactured prolongs its life and retains its strength.

## 8. Beware of Chemicals

Both acids and alkalis attack vegetable fiber rope and some synthetics. See fiber comparison table 11-2. Consequently it should never be stowed any place where it might be brought into accidental contact with chemicals or even be subject to exposure to the fumes. In testing storage batteries with a hydrometer, for example, acid dropped on a rope will burn it badly. Even paint and drying oils, like linseed, should not be allowed to get in contact with it.

Alkalis and acids burn the fibers and kill the life of rope by rendering the fibers brittle. Wet rope is more susceptible to chemical fumes than if it were dry. Rust, too, is bad for rope. If a line must be used around chemicals, it is essential to check it frequently. Spots of discoloration are a danger sign showing when fibers have broken down.

In the case of double braided rope, excessive wear will show up on the cover (or outside braid) by a parting of the strands. The inner core is rarely, if ever, affected by abrasion and provides 50% strength retention as a safety factor.

## 9. Never Overload

Many tables have already been published giving suitable sizes of anchor and mooring lines for motor and sailing craft of all sizes. See Tables 1 and 2, page 103.

Table 11-1 will serve as a guide in this respect. It shows the minimum breaking strain carried by standard brands of manila, and typical synthetic ropes. It should be understood these strengths are for new cordage.

The factor of safety to be allowed in determining the working load on a rope is commonly taken as 5. That is, if a rope must lift 500 pounds, a rope with tensile strength of 2,500 pounds should be selected. With synthetic ropes the same factor of 5 or sometimes 4 (2,000 lbs. in the example above) may be used. The condition of the rope must be considered when making a selection. If the load ever exceeds 75 per cent of the rope's breaking strength the chances are good that it will be permanently injured. In that case, it may fail unexpectedly, without warning.

## 10. Don't Use Frozen Rope

While this is a problem seldom encountered by the average yachtsman whose boat is normally laid up in freezing weather, it is still a matter of moment to those such as charter boat fishermen, etc., whose activities often run right through the winter. Manila rope that has been allowed to freeze after a wetting is readily broken and therefore cannot be trusted. Since synthetics absorb very little moisture this is not too much of a problem and is one of the reasons tow boats and fishermen are using synthetics. However, reasonable care should be exercised to prevent internal damage of the rope structure by internal ice formation and subsequent heavy loading while frozen. The only practical solution if this happens is to thaw it out and dry it thoroughly before putting it back into service in extreme weather.

## HOW TO INSPECT YOUR ROPE

Careful periodic inspection should, in a practical way, enable you to renew lines long before they have deteriorated to a point where they might be considered unsafe, even though theoretically a scientific breaking test might be insisted upon for some services. Here are things to look out for:

In an external examination of the rope, watch out for abrasion, cuts and broken fibers, variations in size and shape of the strands, and uniformity of the lay. Excessive wear on the outside is revealed when fibers appear to be about half worn out and yarns $1/2$ or $2/3$ worn through. Then, depending on the rope size and percentage of good yarns remaining, it may be time to down-grade to lighter work loads or time to renew the rope. Acid stains, frayed strands and broken yarns should all be revealed in such an examination, which should include the entire length of the rope.

Now twist the strands so as to open the rope up, revealing the condition of interior fibers. Evidence of powdered or melted or fused fiber is a danger signal warning of excessive internal bending, tension and wear. Repeat this test in several places. If yarns (the twisted fibers inside) appear to be clean, bright and free from spots of discoloration or melting (harsh and brittle) the chances are that the rope is still in good condition—assuming the exterior is also OK.

Signs of damage due to overloading are also found in the interior yarns of the strands. A rope in which these inner yarns have been broken or partly broken or melted by excessive or repeat loading can never be trusted.

Natural fibers should have a certain luster, and evidences of dryness or brittleness should be viewed with suspicion. A good manila rope will have a certain feel that distinguishes it from another out of which the life has gone. The sound rope will have a certain pliability, stretch and flexibility that is never present in a limp, dead worn-out rope. A good rope will be free from splinters of fiber—just another earmark of quality in good rope. A rough and ready breaking test that the owner can apply is to unlay about a foot of one yarn and break it, or fibers taken from it, with the hands. If this single yarn breaks easily, or fibers have little strength, the rope undoubtedly has lost strength from old age or perhaps has rotted.

Again scientists may demand more scientific tests. When black or brown discoloration spots reveal the action of acid or chemical fumes, use this breakage test frequently.

Table 11-4

| HOW KNOTS AND SPLICES REDUCE THE STRENGTH OF ROPE | | |
|---|---|---|
| | | % EFF. |
| | Normal rope | 100% |
| KNOTS | Anchor or Fisherman's bend | 76 |
| | Timber hitch | 70-65 |
| | Round turn | 70-65 |
| | Two half-hitches | 70-65 |
| | Bowline | 60 |
| | Clove hitch | 60 |
| | Sheet bend or Weaver's knot | 55 |
| | Square or Reef knot | 45 |
| SPLICES | Eye splice (over thimble) | 95-90 |
| | Long splice | 87 |
| | Short splice | 85 |

Based on a normal rope strength of 100% (without knots) the figures above show what percentage of strength is left in a straight rope after a knot has been tied in it. Under differing conditions of test and stress, results vary. Therefore the percentages of efficiency tabulated are necessarily approximate, but they do serve as a base for general calculations.

219

The real problem in advising the boatman as to the knots he should learn to tie and use is to select the few that are of real utility on the average cruiser and exclude the numerous knots which, although serving a special purpose excellently, are of little practical use to the average boatman.

The short list of knots described below and illustrated in the accompanying sketches will meet all ordinary situations. Better know these knots—practice until they can be tied with certainty in the dark or blindfolded—than to have a superficial knowledge of a greater number of knots, including many that are of little practical value.

A knot or splice is never as strong as the rope itself. See table 11-4. Splices are preferred for heavy loads. It may be of some interest to recall that the strength of a rope is derived largely from the friction that exists between the individual fibers, yarn and strands, of which the rope is made. The twisting of these fibers into yarn, then into strands, hawsers and finally cables is always carried out in such a manner as to increase the amount and effectiveness of the friction between the rope elements. In the tying of knots this principle of making use of friction is also applicable, for in this manner, much more can be accomplished by the use of a simple knot, so tied that the strain on the rope adds to the knot's holding power, than will ever develop from a conglomeration of hitches, many of which serve no useful purpose, and which, moreover, make it more practicable in the end to cut the rope than to untie the knots. From the examples which follow it will be evident that wherever possible the most effective use is made of friction between two or more portions of a knot in order to increase its holding power.

## Knots, Bends and Hitches

#### FIG. 1103a  Overhand

The simple overhand knot (fig. 1103a) used to keep the end of a rope from unlaying. This knot jams and may become almost impossible to untie. A better knot for the purpose is shown in fig. 1103b.

#### FIG. 1103b  Figure Eight

The figure eight knot. This does not jam.

#### FIG. 1103c  Square or Reef Knot

The square or reef knot (fig. 1103c) perhaps the most useful knot known. The rope manipulated by the right hand (this is the rope leading from the left side of the sketch and terminating in the arrow in A) is turned over the other rope in tying both the first and second half of the knot. Learn to always turn this rope over the other and the knot can be tied with certainty in the dark. If the rope manipulated by the right hand is first turned over and then under the other rope the treacherous granny knot will result.

Do not use the square knot to tie together lines of different sizes, as it will slip. The reef or square knot is used for tying light lines together (not for tying heavy hawsers), for tying awning stops, reef points, cord on packages, and in fact is put to such numerous uses by sailors that many landsmen call it the sailor's knot. The knot has one serious fault. It jams and is difficult to untie after being heavily stressed.

#### FIG. 1103d  Sheet or Becket Bend

The sheet or becket bend (fig. 1103d) known to landsmen as the weaver's knot, is used for tying two lines together. It will not slip even if there is great difference in the sizes of the lines. To make the knot secure for connecting hawsers for towing, the free ends of the lines should be stopped down with twine in the manner illustrated in fig. 1103j, the reeving line bend.

#### FIG. 1103e  Bowline

The bowline (fig. 1103e) a knot second in usefulness only to the square knot. The bowline will not slip, does not pinch or kink the rope as much as some other knots, and does not jam and become difficult to untie. By tying a bowline with a small loop and passing the line through the loop the running bowline is obtained. This is an excellent form of running noose.

Bowlines are used wherever a secure loop or noose is needed in the end of a line, such as a line which is to be secured to a bollard in making a boat fast to a pier or wharf. They may also be used in securing lines to anchors where there is no time to make a splice. Hawsers are sometimes connected by two bowlines, the loop of one knot being passed through the loop of the other.

#### FIG. 1103f  Clove Hitch

The clove hitch (fig. 1103f) is used for making a line fast temporarily to a pile or bollard.

**FIG. 1103g   Two Half Hitches**

Two half hitches (fig. 1103g) are used for making a line fast to a bollard, pile, timber, or stanchion. Note that the knot consists of a turn around the fixed object and a clove hitch around the standing part of the line.

**FIG. 1103h   Correct Method of Making Fast to a Cleat**

Correct method of making fast to a cleat (fig. 1103h). The half hitch which completes the fastening is taken with the free part of the line. The line can then be freed without taking up slack in the standing part.

**FIG. 1103i   Incorrect Method of Making Fast to a Cleat**

Common incorrect method of making fast to a cleat (fig. 1103i). The half hitch is taken with the standing part of the line and the line consequently can not be freed without taking up slack in the standing part. Accidents have been caused by the use of this type of fastening on lines which must be freed quickly.

**FIG. 1103j   Reeving Line Bend Free ends must be stopped down with twine**

The reeving line bend (fig. 1103j), so called because it is used to connect lines which must pass through a small opening, such as a hawse pipe.

**FIG. 1103k   Fisherman's Bend**

The fisherman's bend (fig. 1103k), also called the anchor bend, is handy for making fast to a buoy or spar or the ring of an anchor. In some localities it is preferred to the thimble and eye splice for attaching the anchor line to the ring. As is evident from the illustration, it is made by taking two round turns around the ring, then passing the end under both turns to form a half hitch around the standing part of the line. For further security, a second half hitch is taken around the standing part only, or in place of the last half hitch, the end may be stopped down or seized back to the line with twine.

**FIG. 1103l   Two Methods of Whipping a Rope End**

All butt-ended ropes should of course be whipped to prevent raveling of the strands. Two common methods for doing this are shown in fig. 1103l. While these figures are not strictly to scale this has been done purposely to avoid difficulty in following the several steps involved in either of the two methods.

**FIG. 1103m   Sheepshank**

The sheepshank (fig. 1103m) is used to shorten a line. Lay the bight in three parts and take a half hitch around each doubled part.

**FIG. 1103n   Cat's Paw**

The cat's paw (fig. 1103n) used to secure a line to a hook. Make a double loop by twisting two bights of the line as shown.

**FIG. 1103o   Rolling Hitch**

The rolling hitch (fig. 1103o) used to bend a line to a spar or rope. Close turns up tight and take the strain on the arrow-tipped end.

**FIG. 1103p   Timber Hitch**

The timber hitch (fig. 1103p) temporarily secures a line to a spar or timber, as in towing. The half hitch shown is sometimes omitted. If used, it should be taken first. In both hitches, strain should be kept on the line to make it hold.

**FIG. 1103q   Blackwall Hitch**

The Blackwall Hitch is easy to make and practical to use when *temporarily* securing a rope to a hook. It will carry a heavy load, *provided* the tension is constant.

## The Art of Splicing_____

### EYE SPLICE OR SIDE SPLICE

Start the splice by unlaying the strands, about six inches to a foot or more, or 6 to 10 turns of lay, depending on the size of rope you are splicing. Now whip the end of each strand to prevent its unlaying while being handled. If working with synthetic rope, it is sometimes helpful to use masking or friction tape wrapped around the unlaid strands every 4 to 6 inches to help hold the "turn" in the strand. The ends may be fused with a flame or whipped.

Next form a loop in the rope by laying the end back along the standing part. Hold the standing part away from you in the left hand, loop toward you. The stranded end can be worked with the right hand.

The size of loop is determined by the point X (fig. 1104) where the opened strands are first tucked under the standing part of the rope. If the splice is being made around a thimble, the rope is laid snugly in the thimble groove and point X will be at the tapered end of the thimble. The thimble may be temporarily taped or tied in place until the job is finished.

Now lay the three opened strands across the standing part as shown in fig. 1104 so that the center strand B lies over and directly along the standing part. Left-hand strand A leads off to the left; right-hand strand C to the right of the standing part.

Tucking of strand ends A, B and C under the strands of the standing part is the next step. Get this right and the rest is easy. See fig. 1105.

Start with the center strand B. Select the topmost strand (2) of the standing part near point X and tuck B under it. Haul it up snug but not so tight as to distort the natural lay of all strands. Note that the tuck is made from right to left, against the lay of the standing part.

Now take left-hand strand A and tuck under strand (1), which lies to the left of strand (2). Similarly take strand C and tuck under strand (3), which lies to the right of strand (2). Be sure to tuck from right to left in every case.

The greatest risk of starting wrong is in the first tuck of strand C. It should go under (3), from right to left. Of course, strands (1), (2), and (3) are arranged symmetrically around the rope.

It may help to visualize this by referring to fig. 1106, a cross-section through the rope at X, seen from below.

If the first tuck of each of strands A, B and C is correctly made, the splice at this point will look as shown in fig. 1107.

The splice is completed by making at least two additional tucks in manila rope or 4 full tucks in synthetic rope with each of strands A, B and C. As each added tuck is made be sure it passes over one strand of the standing part, then under the strand next above it, and so on, the tucked strand running against the lay of the strands of the standing part. This is clearly shown in fig. 1108, the completed splice. Note C, C¹ and C², the same strand as it appears after successive tucks.

*Suggestions:* The splice can be made neater by tapering. This is done by cutting out part of the yarns from the tucking strands, before the finishing tucks. In any case, the first

3 tucks in manila or 4 tucks in synthetics, are made with the full strands. (Synthetics are slippery and stretchy and thus require at least one extra tuck.) After that, some prefer to cut out one-third of the yarns, make a tuck, then cut out another third of the yarns, and make the last tuck. This produces an even taper. After the splice is finished, roll it on deck under foot to smooth it up. Then put a strain on it and finally cut off the projecting ends of the strands. Do not cut off the "tails" of synthetic rope too short. If possible seat the splice in use or whip down the ends before cutting. The loose fibers may be fused with a match or candle to finish off, but be careful not to melt the rope.

**FIG. 1108** How the eye splice should look when completed. A thimble, if spliced in, would fit as shown by the dotted lines.

From the earliest days of rope, marlinspike seamanship had concerned itself with the splicing of 3-strand or twisted rope. With the increasing use of 2-in-1 double braided rope, however, a new method of splicing has

Fig. 1103r   Tightly tape end with one layer of tape. Mark a big dot one fid length from end of line. From the dot, form a loop the size of the eye you want, and mark with an X as shown.

Fig. 1103s   Bend line sharply at X, and spread strands apart firmly to make opening so center can be pried out. Mark one big line on center where it comes out (this is Mark #1), and use your fingers to pull all the center out of the cover from X to the end. Pull on paper tape inside center until it breaks back at slip knot; you need to get rid of it so you can splice. Put a single layer of tape on end of center.

**Fig.1103t** Pull out more of the center. From Mark #1 measure a distance equal to the short section of the fid, and mark two heavy lines (this is Mark #2). Mark three heavy lines at a distance of one fid length plus one short section of fid from Mark #2. This is Mark #3.

**Fig. 1103u** Insert fid into center at Mark #2, and slide it lengthwise through "tunnel" until point sticks out at Mark #3.

**Fig. 1103v** Cut across taped end of cover to form a point, and re-tape tightly with one layer of tape. Jam this point into open end of the fid. Jam pusher into fid behind the tape. Hold center gently at Mark #3, and push both fid and cover through the center until dot almost disappears at Mark #2.

**Fig. 1103w** Note how center tail must travel through cover. It must go in close to dot, and come out through opening at X. On large eyes several passes may be necessary for fid to reach X. When this occurs simply reinsert fid at exact place it comes out and continue to X. To start, insert fid in cover at dot and slide it through tunnel to X. Form tapered point on center tail, jam it into open end of fid, and push fid and center through the cover. After fid comes out at X, pull all center tail through cover until tight, then pull cover tail tight.

**Fig. 1103x** Unravel cover tail braid all the way to Mark #3, and cut off groups of strands at staggered intervals to form a tapered end. Hold loop at crossover in one hand, and firmly smooth both sides of loop away from crossover. Do this until the tapered tail section completely disappears inside Mark #3.

**Fig. 1103y** Hold rope at slipknot, and gently begin to "milk" or slide the cover slack toward the loop. You'll see the center begin to disappear into the cover. Go back to the knot, and continue sliding cover more and more firmly until all center and the crossover are buried inside the cover.

come into being. The splicing of braided rope is best done by following an 8-step procedure that, in an over-simplified way, starts by extracting the core from inside the cover, then inserting the cover into the core in one direction, inserting the core back into the cover in the opposite direction, and then "milking" a slack section of cover over the core. A fid and pusher are used in the process. The holding power is related to the old Chinese finger trick, and the result is a sure and good looking splice. A thimble can be inserted during the splicing process. The 8 steps for a basic eye splice are shown in the sketches

## HOW TO MAKE A SHORT SPLICE

A short splice is used where two ropes are to be permanently joined, provided they do not have to pass through the sheave hole, swallow or throat, of a block. The splice will be much stronger than any knot.

The short splice enlarges the rope's diameter at the splice, so in cases where the spliced rope must pass through a sheave hole, a long splice should be used.

To start the short splice, unlay the strands of both rope ends for a short distance as described for the eye splice. Whip the six strand ends, or fuse or tape them, to prevent unlaying. A seizing should also be made around each of the ropes to prevent strands from unlaying too far. These seizings can be cut as the splice is completed.

Next "marry" the ends so that the strands of each rope lie alternately between strands of the other as shown in fig. 1109. Now tie all three strands of one rope temporarily to the other. See fig. 1110. (Some omit this step; it is not absolutely essential.)

Working with the three free strands, remove temporary seizing from around other rope and splice them into the other rope by tucking strands exactly as described for the eye splice, working over and under successive strands from right to left against the lay of the rope. When first tucks have been made, snug down all three strands. Then tuck two or three more times on that side.

Next cut the temporary seizing of the other strands and the rope and repeat, splicing these three remaining strands into the opposite rope.

Just as in the eye splice, the short splice can be tapered as desired by cutting out yarns from the strands after the full tucks are made. Figure 1111 shows how the short splice would appear if not tapered, after finally trimming off the ends of strands. Never cut strand ends off too close. Otherwise when a heavy strain is put on the rope, the last tuck tends to work out, especially with synthetics.

Another method which some find easier, is to start as in fig. 1109 and tie pairs of strands from opposite ends in an overhand knot. See fig. 1112. This, in effect, makes the first tuck.

FIG. 1109

FIG. 1111
SHORT SPLICE

FIG. 1110

FIG. 1112

## HOW TO MAKE A LONG SPLICE

The long splice (fig. 1113) is used where the spliced ropes are to reeve through blocks or sheaves. There are several methods of making this splice. Some splicers unlay both ends, marry as in the short splice and work from the center both ways. But by starting as in fig. 1113 you do not lose any of the lay of strands. For a long splice in a 3-inch circumference line allow not less than 6 feet, or about 2 feet for each inch of *circumference,* as the farther apart the three splices are staggered, the stronger will be the completed splice. In the illustration 2-inch circumference rope was used, but the illustration does not show proper spacing of tucks. After seizing or taping the ends of each strand, to start this splice, unlay one strand of one rope for about 6 feet and cut off, leaving about one foot as in Illustration 1, strand C. Then unlay one strand from other rope and lay in space formerly occupied by strand C, allowing a foot for splicing as in Illustration 1 at A.

When laying the first strand A (1), plan the spacing of splices so that B will be about central in the finished long splice. Next unlay a strand from right hand rope and a strand from left hand rope and lay the left hand strand in the respective space formerly filled by the strand from right hand rope as in Illustration 2. Continue strand C until all three strands are about equal distance as in Illustration 3.

Then with all pairs of strands (for example Illustration 4A) tie an overhand knot with all yarns flat and even. Next take spike and tuck strands over one and under one as in 4B, unlaying or untwisting strands sufficient to allow yarns to lay flat when tucked. The overhand knot at 4A and, after tucking as at 4B, should be as near as possible to an original strand in size and volume of fiber by reducing twist in the tucked strand. Make another full tuck with all strands.

You now have an overhand knot and two full tucks. Halve each strand and tuck as in 4C, again halve the re-maining yarns and tuck as in 4E. Roll tucks under foot and stretch before cutting off ends. Here, again, do not cut off too short. Much better a little fuzz or whiskers than tucks starting to pull out.

To make a long splice in fishing line, make the same as above, using a sail needle to tuck the strands. The small sail needle, used in fine work, takes the place of the larger fid.

## SPLICING WIRE ROPE

In general, wire rope is spliced in a similar way except that tucks are made with the lay rather than against the lay. Splicing vises are used to hold the rope and metal tools and hammers are usually needed.

Splices of wire-to-fiber rope should be left to professional riggers. They can usually be found at sail lofts where wire halyards with rope tails can be made to specification. With the right tools and a lot of practice, you can work out a method yourself.

## A FEW TIPS

Practice these knots and splices with a couple of short lengths of line and put them to practical use. Always keep lines dry and clean. Keep ends of lines neatly served or whipped with twine to prevent unlaying. Serving or whipping is preferable to the crown knots or splices sometimes used to prevent unlaying as these knots and splices prevent reeving the line through the openings of a block which would otherwise take the line nicely.

The knots, hitches, bends and splices just described are sufficient for all practical purposes aboard the average pleasure boat. To make them with facility in a seamanlike manner, have some experienced yachtsman, sailor or fisherman show you how he'd do it, especially the bowline, clove hitch and splice.

**LONG SPLICE**

**FIG. 1113  While the short splice is excellent for strength and neat-ness, as compared to a knot, there are times when the spliced line** must reeve through a block. In such cases, the long splice should be used. Illustrated above are steps in the making of a long splice.

# Blocks and Tackles

The use of blocks and tackle (pronounced tay-kle) or, to use a higher sounding name, mechanical appliances, on board a small cruising type boat is very limited. The competent seaman, however, should have a basic knowledge of them, as their use enables one man to do the work of many.

Blocks and tackle on small boats are almost entirely confined to sailboats where the hoisting of heavy sails, as well as setting them, requires some means for one or two men to match the strength of many. No matter how small the sailboat, the sheets usually run through one or more blocks, which means we have a mechanical appliance.

To see how this aids, go for a sail in a 20-foot boat, in a moderate breeze, and bend a line to the boom. While under way attempt to trim in the sail with your improvised sheet. It will come in but it will be a struggle, so try it with the regular system of blocks and tackle and you will see with what ease the sail comes in. About the most common use on a motorboat is in hoisting your dinghy.

A *block* consists of a frame of wood or metal inside of which is fitted one or more *sheaves* (pulleys—the word is pronounced shiv), and is designated according to the number of sheaves it contains, such as single, double, or triple. The size of the block to be used is, of course, de-termined by the size of the rope to be reeved. If a fiber rope is being used, the size of the block should be *about* three times the *circumference* of the rope and the sheave diameter about twice the circumference. Therefore, if 2-inch rope, $^5/_8$" diameter, is being used the block could be 6 inches (three times the circumference) and the sheave diameter 4 inches (twice the circumference). This is an approximation. See Table 11-5, block sizes and rope diameter, for recommended sizes.

Wire rope is also used but usually only as halyards on sailboats. Some larger sailing craft use wire sheets and guys. This should be stainless steel and sheaves should be as large as possible for long rope life. Make sure the rope cannot squeeze between the sheave and the cheeks of the block or a "panic party" may ensue.

The term *tackle* is used for an assemblage of *falls* (ropes) and *blocks*. When you pass ropes through the blocks, you *reeve* them and the part of the fall made fast to one of the blocks, or the weight, as the case may be, is known as the *standing part*, while the end upon which the force is to be applied is called the *hauling part*. To *overhaul the falls* is to separate the blocks; to *round in* is to bring them together; and *chock-a-block* or *two blocks* means they they are tight together.

---

## FIG. 1114  PARTS OF A BLOCK

1. Hook
2. Inner Strap
3. Outer Strap
4. Pin
5. Swallows
6. Cheeks
7. Sheaves — either plain, roller, or self-lubricating
8. Breech
9. Becket
10. Thimble
11. Shell

---

### DEFINITIONS:

**Block**
A frame of wood or metal within which are fitted sheaves or pulleys over which a rope runs. Blocks may be single, double, treble, etc. They are designated by the number of sheaves they contain. The lifting power is multiplied in ratio to the number of sheaves used.

**Tackle**
A combination of blocks, ropes and hooks for raising, lowering or moving heavy objects. A "tackle" increases lifting power but reduces lifting speed.

**Fall Rope**
That part of the tackle to which lifting power is applied.

**Fall Block or Running Block**
The block attached to the object to be moved.

**Fled Block or Standing Block**
Is fixed to a permanent support.

**Standing End**
The end of the fall fixed to the tackle.

**Running End**
The end opposite the standing end.

**Return**
Each part of the fall between the two blocks or between either end and the block.

**Lifting Force**
Is in ratio with the number of times the rope passes to and from the fall block.

**To Overhaul**
Is to separate the blocks.

**To Round In**
Is to bring the blocks closer together.

**Two Blocks**
Means the blocks of the fall are in contact.

**Shell or Frame**
Part which holds sheave or wheel.

*(From Columbia Rope Co. rigger's booklet)*

## KINDS OF TACKLE

Tackles (fig. 1116) are named according to the number of sheaves in the blocks that are used (single, two-fold, three-fold purchases), according to the purpose for which the tackle is used (yard-tackles, stay-tackles, etc.), or from names handed down from the past (luff-tackles, watch-tackles, gun-tackles, Spanish-burtons, etc.). The tackles that may be found aboard cruising boats, and should be known are:

**1. Single Whip**—A single fixed block and fall—no increase in power. Gain only in height of lift or change in direction of pull.

**2. Gun Tackle**—Two single blocks. If lower block is movable, double force is gained. If upper block is movable, triple force is gained.

**3. Luff Tackle**—A double hook-block and single hook-block. Force gained three if single block is movable, four if double block is movable.

**4. Two-Fold or Double Tackle**—Two double sheave hook-blocks. Force gained four or five, depending upon application.

## CALCULATING POWER OF A TACKLE

The force gained as given in all of these tackle combinations is theoretical only, as the friction of the blocks has been ignored. The method of calculating the actual force gained and compensating for this friction is to add

**FIG. 1117  The size of rope should be matched to the block it reeves through. Chafe at blocks can cause serious damage. The second and fourth are swivel blocks.**

A — Hauling part
B — Standing part
C — Fixed block
D — Movable block
W — Weight

RATIO — 1:3      RATIO — 1:4

**FIG. 1115  The number of falls leading to and from the movable block determines the ratio of force to weight necessary for lifting.**

10% to the weight W, for each sheave in the tackle before dividing by the number of falls. Thus, in Illustration 4 (fig. 1116) if W is 1000 lbs.: 10% is 100 lbs.; 4 sheaves × 100 = 400 lbs.; total theoretical W then is 1000 plus 400 = 1400 lbs. With 4 falls the force needed on A to lift W would be 1400 ÷ 4 or 350 lbs. rather than an apparent 250 lbs., disregarding friction. This will vary with the type of bearings and pins and lubrication in the blocks and sheave diameter.

There are, of course, a number of other purchases, the heaviest commonly used aboard ship being a three-fold purchase, which consists of two triple blocks. It must be remembered the hauling part reeved through a triple block should be led through the center sheave. If not, the block will cant causing it to bind and, in extreme cases, to break the block. This is especially true with a three-fold purchase.

## TO OBTAIN GREATEST EFFICIENCY

To get the greatest mechanical efficiency, the hauling part should lead from the block with the most sheaves, and if both blocks have the same number it is best for the hauling part to lead from the movable block. It is also best to have the block with the greatest number of sheaves the movable block, as the number of falls leading to and from the movable block determines the ratio of force-to-weight necessary for lifting.

In the illustration (fig. 1116) showing two arrangements of luff tackles, in one there are three falls leading from the movable block and ratio of force-to-weight would be 1:3. Now change the blocks—the single block fixed and the double block made movable with the weight attached and the hauling part leading from it. Notice that, counting the hauling part, there are four falls leading to or from the now movable block, and the ratio becomes 1:4, which is quite an increase.

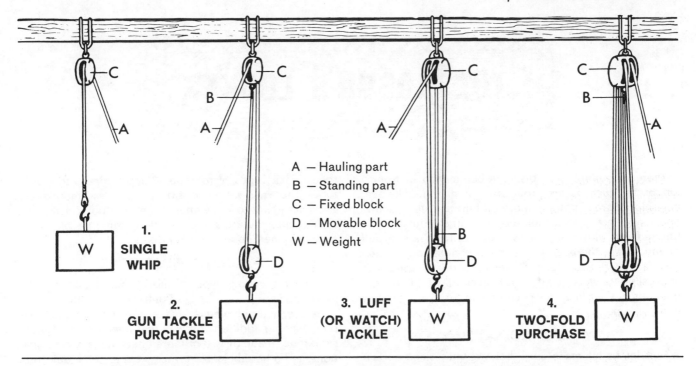

A — Hauling part
B — Standing part
C — Fixed block
D — Movable block
W — Weight

1. **SINGLE WHIP**

2. **GUN TACKLE PURCHASE**

3. **LUFF (OR WATCH) TACKLE**

4. **TWO-FOLD PURCHASE**

FIG. 1116 Some of the common tackles that are found aboard cruising boats.

Table 11-5

| BLOCK AND ROPE SIZES * | | | |
|---|---|---|---|
| Size of Block (Length of Shell) | Diameter of Rope | Size of Block (Length of Shell) | Diameter of Rope |
| 3 | ⅜ " | 8 | ⅞ " – 1 " |
| 4 | ½ " | 10 | 1⅛ " |
| 5 | ⁹⁄₁₆ "–⅝ " | 12 | 1¼ " |
| 6 | ¾ " | 14 | 1⅜ "–1½ " |
| 7 | ¹³⁄₁₆ " | 16 | 1⅝ " |

*NOTE—Some heavy blocks can accommodate larger rope sizes but the use of smaller blocks for larger rope than recommended reduces rope life. Too small diameter sheaves cause extra strain on outer rope fibers and increase internal friction.

## PROPORTIONING BLOCKS TO ROPE SIZE

In using blocks and tackle the utmost care must be taken in having the proper size blocks for the rope used. See Table 11-5. If the rope is too big it will jam and if too small it will slip out of the sheave and jam between the *cheeks* (sides of a block) and the sheave, which will cause untold damage. Also be careful that the proper size of rope and type of tackle is used in reference to the weight to be lifted. There are many tables to give you this. Also your blocks must be lubricated, clean, well painted or varnished (if wooden), and they must be so placed when in use that they will not be crushed or beaten against a spar or other gear.

The entire study of mechanical appliances is a lengthy and technical one, but also immensely interesting. There has been no effort to cover the subject, but only to give a few notes as an introduction. As said before, it allows one man to do many men's work, or it is a case of a "boy doing a man's job."

FIG. 1118 Main sheet tackle rigged with a double block (movable) on the boom, and single block (fixed, with becket) on deck. The extra single block (foreground) does not increase power but serves as a fairlead. Note eye splice around thimble.

# THE BOSUN'S LOCKER

There is nothing that distinguishes a seaman from a lubber as much as his proficiency in marlinespike seamanship. There is nothing more pitiful than seeing someone make fast with a multitude of turns around a pile finished off with many fancy loops only to see a puff of wind cause the boat to tug and the entire conglomeration fall apart and the boat begin to drift. Again, it is impossible to keep a boat shipshape and Bristol fashion, if the ends of your lines have "cow's tails" (frayed or untidy ends of rope).

## TERMINOLOGY

First let us all make sure that we understand certain terms. Marlinespike seamanship deals with rope and the methods of working it. *Rope* is cordage of all types and sizes: fiber, wire, small cordage. *Small stuff* is small cordage, usually made of tarred hemp, such as spun-yarn, seine twine, either cotton, linen or synthetic, marlin, ratline, houseline, roundline, frequently used as seizing for whipping, worming and serving line. *Line* is a general term applied on board ship to a piece of rope in use.

There are few ropes on shipboard. Here is a good question to ask boating friends or to send to a quiz program: "How many ropes are there aboard ship? Name them." There are but nine principal ropes on board ship. These are bell ropes, man ropes, top ropes, foot ropes, bolt

ropes, back ropes, yard ropes, bucket ropes, and tiller ropes. There may be one or two more, of less importance. The main thing to remember is that you don't make fast with a rope, you use a line; you don't trim in a sail with a rope or a sheet-rope, but with a sheet.

## KINDS OF FIBER ROPE

There are various types of fiber rope, mainly manila, nylon, polyesters such as Du Pont Dacron or the English Terrylene, and polyolefins such as polyethylene and polypropylene. In addition you may find linen or flax, cotton, sisal, ropes made of two or more fibers in many combinations, and other fibers. New ones seem to come out every year.

Because the *synthetics* have proved themselves, both as to ultimate cost and ease of handling, they are replacing much of the natural fiber rope. The exception seems to be where the rope is lost by accident or theft or rapidly worn out by abuse and where the higher cost, in most cases, of synthetics cannot be recovered by longer life.

Usually the rope is made from three strands but sometimes four-strand rope is made. A cable is made by twisting three ropes together. To keep rope from unlaying easily, each successive step is twisted in the opposite direction. This is done as follows: yarn—right-handed; strands—left-handed; rope—right-handed; and cable—left-handed. It is possible, however, to get left-handed rope and in this case the procedure is reversed. Left-laid genoa jib sheets and others that are winched hard run more freely (without kinks) when spun off the winch and released for tacking.

**FIG. 1119** Anchor line neatly coiled, clockwise, on deck. Note the grating below it to aid in drying.

**FIG. 1120** Taking line from a new coil, reach down inside and take inner fag end from bottom. Coil clockwise if rope is right-handed.

The newest kind of fiber rope is referred to as 2-in-1 double braid. This consists of an inner braided core of nylon or polypropylene and a braided cover of nylon or polyester. The double braid construction has gained wide acceptance for sheets because its fiber combinations provide very low stretch, and because it is non-rotational so it will always run free (not kink). The double braid also has greater bearing surface, so it holds better on winches and in the hand. It also retains flexibility, whether wet or dry, over extensive periods of use. These same characteristics also make the double braid construction useful for anchor lines where ease of storing, non-kinking, and high stretch/strength ratios are desirable.

## HOW ROPE IS MEASURED AND SOLD

The size of rope is measured in different ways. Marine fiber rope is measured by its circumference, although most yachtsmen have always designated it by its diameter. On the other hand wire rope is designated by its diameter. Therefore, two-inch wire rope is much thicker than two-inch fiber rope (⅝ inch diameter).

The length of fiber and wire rope may be measured in feet or in fathoms. A fathom is 6 feet. Small stuff is sometimes designated by the number of *threads* it contains. The largest of small stuff is ratline stuff, which is usually 3-stranded, right-handed and may have 8 threads to the strand, in which case it would be 24-thread.

Cordage is sold by the foot or fathom or by the pound. Usually standard coils and reels are sold by the pound and cut lengths are sold by the foot or at a higher price per pound. Your dealer is entitled to increase the price for cuts because of the waste involved in fag ends and his investment and time.

Another method that is gaining in acceptance is "prepacked" lines. Double-braided type rope comes as prespliced dock lines of specific lengths and diameters; and as pre-spliced anchor lines, ready to use.

## POINTS TO REMEMBER

Vegetable fiber rope will shrink when wet, and because of this fact it is necessary to loosen all standing fiber rigging whenever wet. If this is not done the shrinking will cause an injurious strain on the rope.

FIG. 1121 Line faked down ready to run out rapidly. Coils, in practice, would lie closer together.

FIG. 1122 Line is flemished down for neatness by laying it down in close concentric coils, one against the other, in the form of a flat mat, free end at the center. If left long in one spot it may discolor the deck. It does not dry as well as a loose coil. Sunlight may damage nylon and poly ropes.

Rope of natural fiber will deteriorate rapidly from continued dampness and therefore should always be dry before stowed. To dry, it is best to coil down loosely and place where the sun can get at the rope and the air can pass freely all about it. Of course, such rope should never be stowed in a locker that is not well ventilated and dry; for if not, there is not much use in drying the rope as it will rot in the locker.

One thing not generally understood about synthetic ropes is *cold flow*. Due to the nature of the fiber, a long sustained load may cause the fibers to stretch or elongate permanently with a consequent reduction in rope diameter and ultimate strength. Some synthetics are worse than others in this respect. Temperature affects the flow. In a surging load such as anchoring in moderate weather, the anchor line can recover. But in a hurricane or a long passage at sea the load might be continuous and cold flow could become a hazard.

## USE AND CARE OF WIRE ROPE

Wire rope or strand is generally used on board cruising boats as standing rigging. On a number of sailboats, however, it is also used as running rigging. Steel is used almost exclusively in making wire rope. To preserve it from corrosion it is sometimes galvanized. Stainless steel is fine, but expensive. Some wire rope has a hemp core. This greatly increases flexibility and also acts as a cushion against sudden stress or heavy pull.

Great care must be taken of wire rope also. It should always be kept on a reel when not in use and must be

229

reeled off and not slipped off over the ends of the reel. If kept in a coil it should be rolled off at all times. If a kink ever gets into a wire rope it is a disaster, as this practically ruins it. As with fiber rope, sharp bends will cause an excessive strain and greatly impair the efficiency.

It is important to note that whenever you see broken wires, "meat hooks" that surely cut up the hands, or when the diameter of the outside wires is worn to one-half the original diameter, it is time to condemn the rope as it is no longer safe.

## COILING, FAKING AND FLEMISHING

When line is left on deck, or put in a locker, it should never be thrown down in a heap. Not only would this give a lubberly appearance, but if you needed to use the line, especially in a hurry, it might kink or tangle. For safety and good seamanship we always either coil, fake, or flemish down a line.

When it must be kept ready for emergency use, clear for running, a line is generally coiled down (figures 1119-1120) always with the lay (clockwise for right lay rope). To make a straight coil, a circular bight of the secured end is laid and successive bights are placed on top. When all the line has been used, the entire coil is capsized to leave it clear for running.

When the entire length of a line must be run out rapidly it is usually faked down (fig. 1121). To do this a short length of the free end is laid out in a straight line and then turned back to form a flat coil. Successive flat coils are then formed, laying the end of each coil on top of the preceding coils, rather like figure 8s.

When great neatness is desired a line is flemished down (fig. 1122). Successive circles of the line are wrapped about each other with the free end at the center. When it is finished it looks like a mat and with an old piece of line can be used as one.

A disadvantage of coiling down is that you must watch out for kinks. With a flemished-down line care must be taken to prevent coils from falling back and fouling the preceding coil. If a line is flemished down and left on deck

for some time it will mark the deck and remain wet on the under side. On small boats lines are usually either coiled down or flemished down.

## KNOTS THE SEAMAN KNOWS

Before a person dares to take a boat out he should be able to make a bowline, two half hitches, clove hitch, square knot and sheet bend. (See figures 1103 c-g.) This is not all he should know, but they are the minimum. The following are those that every competent seaman should know:

**A.—Knots in the end of a rope:**

1. Overhand
2. Bowline
3. Running bowline
4. Bowline on a bight
5. French bowline
6. Sheepshank
7. Blackwall hitch
8. Figure 8
9. Cat's-paw

**B.—Knots for bending two ropes, or two ends of the same rope, together:**

1. Square or reef
2. Two bowlines
3. Single and double sheet or becket bend
4. Single and double carrick bend
5. Reeving line bend

**C.—Knots for securing a line to ring or spar:**

1. Fisherman's bend
2. Timber hitch
3. Timber and half hitch
4. Two half hitches
5. Round turn and two half hitches
6. Rolling hitch
7. Clove hitch
8. Studding sail tack bend
9. Studding sail halyard bend

**D.—Knots worked in the end of a rope:**

1. Wall knot
2. Wall and crown
3. Single Matthew Walker
4. Lanyard knot

**Rope end dip.** A new, effective way to treat rope ends is to dip them into a red vinyl liquid called Whip-End Dip. It seals all rope ends in seconds, setting into a tough, flexible permanent finish that eliminates whipping.

SERVING MALLET

PARCELLING

WORMING

SERVING

FIG. 1123 Worming, parcelling and serving guards against severe chafe. The rule is: Worm and parcel with the lay; turn and serve the other way.

## OTHER ARTS OF THE SAILOR

Besides the general classes of knots and the splices shown earlier, there are other types of work that all seamen should be able to do.

**Back Splice:** To put an enlarged, finished end on a line.

**Stopper on a rope:** A length of rope secured at one end used in securing or checking a running line.

**Strap on a rope:** Turns taken around a standing part with the tackle hooked through the bights.

**Mouse a hook:** A method of closing the open part of a hook with small stuff to assist in preventing the object to which it is hooked from jumping out.

**Grommet strap:** A grommet or continuous loop of rope, used to attach a hook to a block permanently.

**Seizing:** The lashing together of two ends of rope by continuous turns of small stuff. Word sometimes used to mean whipping.

As said before there is nothing more unseamanlike than cow's tails on the end of a line. There are many ways to prevent this such as a back splice, wall knot, etc., but perhaps the best method is by whipping. See fig. 1103-l. Another method, sewed whipping, is preferred as it is easier to get taut and much harder to pull off. Plastic whips that are shrunk on with heat are available but good "fancy" work is preferred over substitutes like friction tape. The advantage of whipping over the other methods of eliminating cow's tails is that it does not increase the size of the rope. This can work as a disadvantage: for example, a sheet can run through all the blocks, making it necessary to re-reeve. Another type, such as a wall and crown, will not allow the end to run through a block.

## HOW TO PREVENT CHAFE

There is nothing that wears rope so fast as chafing. In order to prevent this, it is necessary to rig *chafing gear*. When the chafe is of only temporary nature the rope can be protected by wrapping a piece of canvas around it. However, when the chafe will be more or less permanent

FIG. 1124 **This sail repair kit, created by Ratsey & Lapthorn, contains a sailmaker's palm, bench hook, thread, seven needles, awl, knife, wax, rule, pencil and booklet on sail care and handling.**

FIG. 1125 **Crow's Nest ditty bag contains all the essentials for splicing and sail and canvas repair—palm, assorted needles, marline, sail twine, and 6-inch heavy-duty steel spike.**

or severe, the line should be wormed, parceled, and served or molded rubber gear, leather or rawhide, permanently attached.

**Worming:** consists of following the lay of the rope, between the strands, with small stuff, to keep the moisture out and for filling out the round of the rope.

**Parceling:** consists of wrapping the rope spirally with long overlapping strips of canvas, following the lay of the rope.

**Serving:** consists of wrapping small stuff over the parceling opposite to the lay of the rope to form a taut, protective cover. Should be hard-laid marline or seine twine for the best wear.

## REPAIRS TO CANVAS

All seamen should be able to work with canvas and a needle. You should provide yourself with a sewing kit consisting of a small canvas kit bag, two or three short and long needles, some beeswax, and some small stuff. The long needle, usually triangular, straight, or curved, is generally used for sewing canvas, while the short needle, usually broad, straight or curved, is generally used for rope work.

There are four main types of stitches used in sewing canvas. Flat is used for seams in sails, tarpaulins, etc.; round is for making duffel bags; baseball, where a snug edge-to-edge fit in canvas is desired; and herringbone is for very stiff or painted canvas.

Have the right cordage for the job and take care of it well—then it will take care of you if you use it correctly.

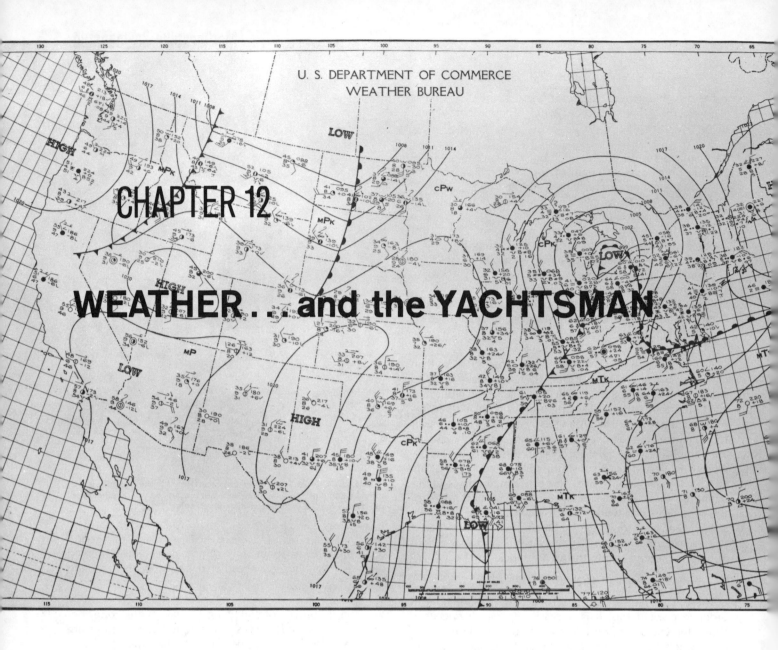

U. S. DEPARTMENT OF COMMERCE
WEATHER BUREAU

# CHAPTER 12

# WEATHER....and the YACHTSMAN

## How to Read a Weather Map

THE WEATHER MAP provides a bird's-eye view of the weather over a large area. With its many figures, symbols and lines, the map at first appears to be puzzling. But with a little study of these markings and an understanding of their meaning, the map becomes a picture of the weather giving you a good idea of what's in store.

Some boatmen may receive the weekly compilations of daily weather maps mailed to subscribers by the Weather Bureau, Washington, D.C. Most, however, must depend upon newspaper maps for their information. These are drawn from Weather Bureau master weather charts. Four times each day, the Weather Bureau in Washington prepares and analyzes surface and upper air weather charts for the entire Northern Hemisphere.

On surface charts, weather data are plotted as received every six hours from more than 750 reporting stations in North America, more than 200 ships at sea, and 1500 stations in other countries. Each station reports the amount of sky covered by cloud, direction and speed of wind,

visibility distance in miles, present weather, weather during the last three hours, sea level barometric pressure, air temperature, kinds of low, middle and high clouds, dew-point temperature, character and amount of pressure change in the last three hours, and the character, duration and amount of rainfall in the last six hours. Many of these stations also furnish twelve-hour reports of pressure, temperature, moisture and wind conditions for several levels of upper air. Thus, the central weatherman with his daily surface and several upper air charts has a detailed picture of the weather occurring at the same time over the entire Northern Hemisphere. These charts are used in issuing the daily weather forecasts and warnings of approaching storms.

Over 150 *symbols* are used in entering data on weather maps. Although you may never need know what all the symbols mean, nor have occasion to plot them on a weather map, a knowledge of those most often used will help you to understand and interpret the daily maps appearing in newspapers. See fig. 1201.

## THE STATION MODEL

Fig. 1202 shows the *"station model,"* a system weathermen the world over developed for entering data on weather maps. It presents a "model" or picture of the weather at a station, using symbols and numbers, which can be understood in any language. Not only the symbols and numbers but their positions around the station circle tell what each item means. Fig. 1202 represents a typical arrangement.

Study these for a few moments. By referring to fig. 1201 and reading the parenthetical explanations in fig. 1202, you can interpret the weather at this particular station.

For example, starting with the "station circle" itself (the black dot in the middle)—the fact that this circle is solid black indicates that the sky is completely covered with clouds here.

Let's go counterclockwise around the station circle to examine and understand what's shown. Take the wind first. The symbol indicates a pretty windy day, the wind being from the northwest at 21 to 25 mph. The wind

arrows always "fly" with the wind.

Next is temperature in degrees Fahrenheit. As you can see, it was relatively cold, the thermometer registering only 31°.

Since we know the sky was completely overcast, the next two markings—Visibility and Present Weather—begin to give us a picture of conditions at the station. It was a nasty day with a stiff, cold wind blowing light snow all over the place.

## PRECIPITATION SYMBOLS

A word about precipitation symbols is in order here. Fig. 1201 shows the symbols used to indicate different forms of precipitation—drizzle, rain, snow, etc. Increasing precipitation is indicated by more than one symbol being plotted, the range being from one to four identical symbols.

In fig. 1202 the use of the two stars (or asterisks) tells you that it is snowing continuously but lightly at this station. If there had been three stars the snow would have

| SYMBOLS | | |
|---|---|---|
| **SKY COVER** | **WEATHER** Present and Past | **WIND** Miles per Hour |

**SKY COVER**

| | | | |
|---|---|---|---|
| 0 | ○ | 5 | ◓ |
| 1 | ◔ | 6 | ◕ |
| 2 | ◔ | 7 | ◑ |
| 3 | ◔ | 8 | ● |
| 4 | ◑ | 9 | ⊗ |

**WEATHER Present and Past**

| | |
|---|---|
| ≡ | FOGGY |
| , | DRIZZLING |
| • | RAINING |
| ✳ | SNOWING |
| ▽ | SHOWERS |
| ℞ | THUNDERSTORMS |

**WIND Miles per Hour**

| | | |
|---|---|---|
| Calm | 21-25 | 50-54 |
| 1-4 | 26-31 | 55-60 |
| 5-8 | 32-37 | 61-66 |
| 9-14 | 38-43 | 67-71 |
| 15-20 | 44-49 | 72-77 |

**FIG. 1201**

FIG. 1202   Illustrating how symbols in fig. 1201 are used by weathermen to show weather conditions at a station.

FIG. 1203   A section of the Atlantic coast from a Weather Bureau Surface Chart with data for several stations.

been moderate to heavy. Now, if the *shower* symbol (a triangle) had been shown instead of the star it would have carried a star symbol above it to indicate that the showers were *snow* showers. If the showers were *rain* the shower symbol would have carried a dot (the rain symbol) above it.

Hail is indicated by a small triangle (inverted shower symbol) above the thunderstorm symbol. Fog is represented by three horizontal lines.

Other symbols around the station circle in fig. 1202 are interesting and important to weathermen and anyone wishing to use the information. They are worth studying but since most of them do not appear on the abbreviated maps appearing in newspapers we won't go into a detailed description here. Fig. 1202 does provide a brief explanation of each.

Fig. 1203 shows a small portion of a Weather Bureau surface chart with data plotted for several stations. By re-

Cold Front ▼▼▼    Occluded Front ▲▲▲    Stationary Front ▲▼▲▼

**FIG. 1205  Section of a weather map with fronts, isobars, HIGHS, LOWS, and direction of fronts plotted on it.**

| Inches | Millibars | Inches | Millibars |
|--------|-----------|--------|-----------|
| 28.44 | 963 | 29.77 | 1008 |
| 28.53 | 966 | 29.86 | 1011 |
| 28.62 | 969 | 29.94 | 1014 |
| 28.70 | 972 | 30.03 | 1017 |
| 28.79 | 975 | 30.12 | 1020 |
| 28.88 | 978 | 30.21 | 1023 |
| 28.97 | 981 | 30.30 | 1026 |
| 29.06 | 984 | 30.39 | 1029 |
| 29.15 | 987 | 30.48 | 1032 |
| 29.24 | 990 | 30.56 | 1035 |
| 29.32 | 993 | 30.65 | 1038 |
| 29.41 | 996 | 30.74 | 1041 |
| 29.50 | 999 | 30.83 | 1044 |
| 29.59 | 1002 | 30.92 | 1047 |
| 29.68 | 1005 | 31.01 | 1050 |

**FIG. 1204  Conversion table for a weather map's millibars.**

ferring to figs. 1201 and 1202 you can tell what the weather conditions at any given station are. Let's take Raleigh, N. C. as a case in point:

You can see that the sky is completely overcast, the wind is south, at 9 to 14 mph, the temperature is 69°F., the dew point is 68°, the numeral 2 indicates the clouds were low, the letter T says that precipitation in the past 6 hours was very slight, T standing for "Trace," the barometer has fallen 1.0 millibar during the past 3 hours, there were thunderstorms at the station during the past 6 hours, and

**FIG. 1206  Typical abridged weather map commonly appearing in newspapers.**

the pressure is 1018.5 millibars or 30.08 inches of mercury.

Fig. 1204 provides a conversion table for changing millibars to inches and vice versa.

## ISOBARS AND FRONTS

When data from all stations are entered on the map, the weatherman draws black lines, called *isobars*. These are lines drawn through points having the same ("iso-" means equal) barometric pressure. For example, a 1020 millibar (30.12 inches) isobar is a line drawn through all points having a barometric pressure of 1020 millibars. Ad-

FIG. 1207 **Diagrams indicate action of cold and warm fronts and show how their interaction forms occluded fronts.**

ditional isobars are drawn for every four millibar intervals. The purpose of the isobars is to position the centers of low and high pressure—the familiar "LOWS" and "HIGHS" which govern our weather. The centers of high pressures are marked "H" or "High" and the low pressures are marked "L" or "Low." It is the movement of these HIGHS and LOWS which enables the weatherman to forecast weather, taking into consideration, of course, the various data supplied by the weather stations.

The heavier lines in fig. 1205 are drawn to indicate "*fronts*"—the boundaries between different air streams. Triangles and half circles are attached to these heavier lines pointing in the direction in which the fronts are mov-

ing. The triangle indicates a "*cold front*," the half circle a "*warm front*." (See also fig. 1207.)

A front which is not moving, one which is "*stationary*," is shown by attaching triangles on one side of the line and half circles on the opposite side. An "*occluded front*" is indicated by attaching both triangles and half circles to one side of the line. Fronts and their significance will be explained later.

## WEATHER OFFICES

If you visit a Weather Bureau office you can see the latest surface and upper air weather maps. Maps prepared at the Washington Weather Bureau are sent to the various stations over a picture (facsimile) transmission circuit. Maps prepared by local stations appear much the same as the Washington maps with a few exceptions. The cold fronts, for instance, will be drawn on the map in blue pencil, warm fronts in red, occluded fronts in purple, while the stationary front will be shown by a line of alternating red and blue dashes.

## NEWSPAPER WEATHER MAP

Because of their reduced size, it is impossible to include on newspaper maps all of the data usually entered on a map prepared at a Weather Bureau office. To permit easier reading, only sky covered by cloud or other forms of present weather, wind direction and speed, and air temperature are plotted for each station. Barometric pressure at each station is omitted because it can be estimated for any place from the nearest isobar (remember—isobars represent lines of equal barometric pressure). Incidentally, on some weather maps, isobars may be drawn for 3 millibar intervals; for example, 996, 999, 1002, etc., rather than the 4 millibar intervals. Some maps show isobars marked at one end with the millibar pressure and at the other end in inches. Symbols used for entry of all this information, including those for types of fronts, are usually shown in the margin of newspaper maps. See fig. 1206.

Morning newspapers usually contain the weather map prepared from data collected the evening before, while afternoon editions publish the early morning chart. The time is noted on the newspaper chart.

# Analysis of the Weather Map

We don't need to know how to draw the isobars and fronts on a weather map in order to be able to read one, but we can review to advantage the method used by the professional weatherman. First, the meteorologist enters on the chart the observations at all stations from which he has received reports. The entries, which include both instrumental and visual observations, are recorded partly in numerical and partly in symbolic form, as illustrated in fig. 1202. Second, he delineates any fronts that may exist, using preceding maps, in addition to present information, as a guide to their locations.

Let's take an actual case as analyzed by the late Dr. B. C. Haynes, Senior Meteorologist with the U.S. Weather Bureau, and published by the Bureau in its booklet "An-

alysis of a Series of Surface Weather Maps." Fig. 1208 is the finished map for 1930 EST Wednesday, 17 April, in the year the analysis was made. Given the observations at each station, how was analysis of the data accomplished?

## LOCATING THE FRONTS

Consider first the location of the fronts. A *front* is the boundary between two contiguous bodies, or masses, of air which have come from different geographical regions and traveled along different routes (see fig. 1209) and which, therefore, have different physical properties. The *position of a front* is marked principally by the difference in the temperatures of the two air masses, the difference

FIG. 1208   The finished weather map for 1930 EST Wednesday, 17 April.

in dew points (the temperature at which the air is saturated with moisture), differences in barometric pressure and pressure tendency, and differences in wind direction and velocity.

To make a start, we examine the plotted data and find that the lowest barometric pressure (998.0 millibars for this map) is at a station in western Indiana. Note that the general wind pattern over Kentucky, Tennessee and the southwestern states is from south to southwest. Over Illinois, Missouri, Kansas and the central plains states the general wind pattern is northwest to north. Different air masses must be over each of these regions and these air masses must be separated by a front. Beginning at our station in western Indiana we will draw this front.

To confirm our finding that a front exists, we look at the next station due west of our starting point; it is located in central Illinois. Here are the salient data at the two stations:

|  | Western Indiana | Central Illinois |
|---|---|---|
| Air temperature ........... | 65° | 37° |
| Dew point ................ | 60° | 36° |
| Pressure .................. | 998.0 mb | 1,004.4 mb |
| Pressure tendency ........ | −2.2 mb | +2.4 mb |
| Wind direction ............ | SW | N |

The differences are sharp; we are on the right track.

We continue southwestward across Illinois, southeastern Missouri, central Arkansas, the northwestern tip of Louisiana, eastern Texas, and into Mexico, all the time comparing the observations at different stations and placing the front between those showing critical contrasts.

## Kinds of Fronts

We have drawn a front on our map, but what kind of front is it? To the west and northwest of this front, the observations show relatively colder air moving from the north or northwest; to the east and southeast they show relatively warmer air moving from the south. The colder air is moving toward the front. As it is colder and heavier, it pushes the warmer, lighter air eastward before it, at the same time driving under this warmer air and lifting it off the ground. Cold air is displacing warm; we have a *cold front.*

Are there any more fronts to be found? Starting again at our station in western Indiana, suppose we work eastward this time. Through southern Michigan and northern Ohio we again find differences in wind direction and velocity, in air temperature and dew point. These differences remain quite sharp all the way to western Pennsylvania. We have located another front, a *warm front* this time as the somewhat colder air north of our line is retreating to the northeast and warmer air south of the line is following and replacing the colder.

As we continue eastward from western Pennsylvania, the front becomes more obscure; the differences between the air masses become less pronounced. On the other hand, reports of rain, overcast skies and fog continue. The winds are lighter. We draw in a *stationary front* (neither air mass moving appreciably against the other), all the way across West Virginia, Virginia, and North Carolina to the sea.

Warm fronts and cold fronts are *active* weather factories; a stationary front is a *potential* weather factory. The latter may gradually dissipate or it may resolve itself into an active front.

Taking a final glance at the map, we notice another wind shift and temperature difference in eastern Montana. Applying the same technique, we locate another, a short, warm front in this region. We now have our frontal analysis complete.

**FIG. 1209  North American Air Masses. Source regions and directions of movement of air masses influencing North American weather are shown. Air remaining in contact with earth's surface gradually acquires properties characteristic of the surface beneath it. Then, as this air mass subsequently moves over the earth, its properties, and its conflicts with other air masses that it may encounter en route, cause changes in weather of the area invaded.**
(Reproduced by courtesy of Aviation Training Division, U.S. Navy)

## ANALYSIS OF PRESSURE INDICATIONS

The third step is to analyze our map for pressure indications; we need to know the pattern of the *isobars,* where high and low pressure centers exist, *the nature of the pressure field.* Because of the earth's rotation, the wind blows, not directly from high to low pressure, but nearly parallel to the isobars and only slightly across them toward low pressure. The more closely spaced the isobars, the stronger the winds in that area. The closely spaced isobars mean that a greater pressure difference exists, hence the winds are stronger, but the earth's rotation still makes them blow almost along the isobars. Observe the wind direction arrow at each station, then note the direction of adjacent isobars. Compare the velocity of the wind, as indicated by the number of feathers on the arrow, with the spacing of the isobars.

To get back to the map for 17 April, we have a low-pressure center in western Indiana. We find a high-pressure center in northeastern Nevada and another off the coast of Maine. There is a high over the central plains states, another over central Canada, and others off the South Atlantic and Pacific coasts. In addition to our western Indiana low, there are lows in the southwest, off the east coast of Texas, and over western Canada.

As we approach our long cold front, the isobars become more closely spaced; the pressure differences are greater and the winds are stronger. It is not too promising a time for a comfortable cruise along the east coast, the Gulf, Mississippi or Great Lakes.

FIG. 1210 Cumulonimbus cloud, indicative of very unstable air. Strong updrafts and severe turbulence are found in and around center of the cloud. Note heavy rain shower falling out of it.

FIG. 1211 A layer of stratus cloud, typical of moist, stable air. In this picture the stratus is very low; shreds of cloud trailing downward from base of the layer are visible against dark hillside.

## LABELING THE AIR MASSES

The fourth step is to determine the *kinds of air masses* on either side of each front. A given air mass has its own individual properties; these properties tell us much about the kind of weather we can expect. Having located our fronts and completed the pressure analysis, we can label these air masses. Look at fig. 1208 again.

In the southeastern United States, the winds and pressure gradient indicate that a broad current of air is flowing from over the warm waters of the Gulf northward across the southeastern states. The high temperatures and high dew points in this area tell us that this air is warm and moist. As this is a late afternoon (1930 EST) map, the air has been further heated for many hours by re-radiation of the sun's heat by the earth, which means that the air probably is unstable. The thunderstorms and showers, cumulus and towering cumulonimbus clouds (see fig. 1210) reported at various stations confirm the diagnosis. We label this air with the symbol mTk, meaning that it is *unstable, tropical maritime air,* air that can result in foul weather.

Looking north of the front along the Atlantic Coast, we note that the winds and pressure gradient indicate an onshore movement of air from over the Atlantic Ocean. Temperatures and dew points are fairly low; fog and low clouds (see fig. 1211) are shown at many stations. These are signs of *maritime, stable polar air* so we label it mPw, the w indicating that it is relatively warmer than the land over which it is moving and hence not given to heating from below. It will lose heat to the earth; more low clouds, fog and light rains are probable.

To the west of our main cold front, we observe northerly winds, low temperatures and low dew points. Many stations report stratocumulus clouds (see fig. 1212) and a few report cumulus clouds. The temperatures recorded tell us that this air mass is being warmed as it moves southward. Again we have unstable air. As it came, however, from the northward over Canada and not from over an ocean, it is unstable, continental, polar air. We label it cPk.

Studying our map further, we find *stable continental polar air* over the Dakotas (cPw) and *unstable moist (maritime) polar air* (mPk) over the northwestern states.

## ESTIMATING EXPECTED CHANGES

We can now make a rough estimate of the changes that will take place during the next 12 hours. The cold front extending from western Indiana to eastern Texas should move eastward in response to the push of the relatively cold northwesterly winds over Illinois, Missouri, Arkansas, Oklahoma and Texas. The warm front across northern Ohio and western Pennsylvania should advance across Lake Erie as the relatively cool air situated to the northeast of the warm front gives way to the moist tropical air flowing from the south. The low-pressure center over western Indiana should be displaced northeastward along the advancing warm front. We should expect this center to move toward the area where the largest negative pressure tendencies are observed, namely, southern Michigan.

A feature of the 1930 EST 17 April map which should not pass unnoticed is the small low-pressure center spotted in the Gulf of Mexico just southeast of the southern tip of Texas. This center appears to be unconnected with the cold front, and its future behavior is hard to judge.

Now let's look at the map for 0730 EST 18 April (fig. 1213). We find that the low-pressure center which was over western Indiana twelve hours earlier has moved in a general northeasterly direction and is situated somewhere between Lake Huron and Lake Ontario. The actual center may be spotted about 100 miles east of the station in eastern Michigan that reports a pressure of 1000.3 millibars, temperature 35°, dew point 35°, and a northwest wind. (Incidentally, twelve hours earlier this same station reported a due north wind, an indication that the cold air there was holding its ground against the advancing warm front. This fact explains why the low-pressure center

# CLOUDS–How they form–What they mean

*Storm warning—the anvil-shaped cumulonimbus cloud associated with thunderstorms. The wind at high altitudes is stronger than lower down, so the top of the cloud is carried ahead of the main body and forms an anvil which points like a finger in the direction toward which the upper wind is blowing. (Photographed, on the Mississippi River, by J. D. Tennison, Jr.)*

Out on the water you have a front row seat at one of the greatest shows on earth: the constantly changing and highly instructive spectacle presented by the clouds. The meteorological information that clouds convey can help you to estimate future weather developments and thereby make your boating safer and more enjoyable.

Everyone knows that clouds are composed of water In order to learn how to interpret them, one must first understand how water behaves in the atmosphere.

There is always a certain amount of water in gaseous form ("water vapor") present in the air, even on a perfectly clear day. However, there is a limit to the quantity of water vapor that can exist in a given volume of air.. When the amount of water vapor actually present in the air is equal to the limit, the air is said to be "saturated," because then no more water can evaporate into it from ocean, river, lake or other sources.

Saturated air can be thought of as air that contains its full quota of water vapor. This quota varies with the temperature of the air. The warmer the air, the more water vapor it can take up. Thus, if a volume of saturated air is heated, some additional water can be evaporated into it because the temperature of the air will be raised and, hence, the allowable proportion of water vapor will be increased.

Suppose, however, the air is cooled, rather than heated, as happens on a clear night. As its temperature is lowered its water-vapor quota is reduced. Eventually the air is cooled to a temperature for which the allowable propor-tion of water vapor is equal to the actual amount in the air. This temperature is called the "dew point"; the air is now at saturation. If the air is cooled some more, its water-vapor content becomes excessive in relation to its temperature, and condensation results. This leads to the formation of liquid water particles, which form a cloud when the condensation process takes place in the air aloft, or fog when it takes place near the ground.

Air is cooled whenever it rises. As air ascends, the weight of the atmosphere above it decreases, and so the pressure upon the air diminishes. The decrease of pressure permits the air to expand and to cool. If the ascent and accompanying expansion is great enough to cool the air to a temperature below its dew point, clouds appear. (There are several other ways in which air may be cooled sufficiently to produce condensation, but they play a minor part in cloud formation.)

Clouds formed at heights greater than 4 miles, where the temperature is *always* below freezing, might be expected to consist solely of ice particles. However, at these altitudes clouds composed of liquid droplets also are found; such droplets are said to be "supercooled." Although unfrozen water clouds can exist at temperatures as low as −20°F, the introduction of a relatively small number of ice particles into a cloud composed of supercooled water droplets will, by means of a sort of chain reaction, transform it into an ice cloud, out of which snow will fall and produce a trail stretching downward from the underside of the cloud.

E

# The Use of Cloud Observations in Weather Forecasting

It would be naive to believe that anyone can forecast weather 24 hours in advance solely from observations of clouds. Even if such a feat were possible it would provide no great advantage, since the universality of radio communication makes the official forecasts issued by the government weather service readily available to the boatman.

However, government forecasters, despite the enormous quantity of weather observations at their disposal, have difficulties. Greatest problem is probably that of timing; for example, estimating the time of arrival of a wind-shift line.

Here is where an understanding of the meaning of the clouds can be helpful. Clouds are the visible manifestations of physical processes that are taking place in the atmosphere. Some of these processes cause clouds to form and grow; others cause existing clouds to break up and disappear. The ability to interpret the clouds in terms of the physical processes that are going on aloft often will enable the boatman to decide for himself whether the latest official forecast is working out or not. In many cases he can amend the forecast and thereby still make use of it when the timing or some other feature has been miscalculated.

The formation and growth of a cloud or cloud system means that there is an upward component of motion of the air at the level of the cloud, because the cooling necessary to produce the cloud has resulted from expansion of the air. The general appearance of the growing cloud is determined by the stability of the air in which it forms. If the air is stable, then the upward motion responsible for the cloud is a "forced" one; characteristically it is uniformly smooth and gentle. Therefore, the clouds formed by the expansion and concomitant cooling of air that ascends in this fashion are layered, and they grow or thicken relatively slowly.

The pattern of cloud growth just described is illustrated by Photographs Nos. 5, 9, and 30, viewed in that order. The processes at work often produce long-lasting steady rain and, hence, this sequence of photographs typifies the evolution of the sky during the approach of a widespread rain area.

If the atmosphere is unstable, portions of it will rise spontaneously. The upward motion in this case is irregular and rapid; the clouds that form are of the cumulus type and are separated by clear spaces. The pattern of cloud growth in unstable air is illustrated by Photographs Nos. 15, 16 and 25, viewed in that order. This sequence is typical of pre-thunderstorm weather.

> This 4-page insert amplifies the discussion of cloud forms and their significance, which appears on pages 241 and 242.

CIRRUS—These are ice clouds in the form of tufts. Snow is falling out of tuft in upper left portion of photograph. Altitude—above 20,000 feet. The elements are isolated. 1

CIRRUS—This is a dense ice cloud. If viewed toward the sun it appears greyish. It appears to be the edge of an "anvil" cloud formed from Cumulonimbus. 2

ALTOSTRATUS — Thin, translucent water cloud sheet, often the forerunner of rain in most parts of the U.S. Small, dark clouds underneath are Cumulus. 7

ALTOSTRATUS — Translucent sheet cloud with fibrous characteristics. Difference in opacity produces a dark band (bottom). Dark clouds below are Cumulus. Alt —8,000 to 20,000 ft. 8

CUMULUS — Typical of fine weather. Appearance of sky indicates good weather continuing for 6 hours at least. Altitude—base of cloud 3,000 to 5,000 feet. 13

CUMULUS—These are less benign than those in Photograph No. 13. However, they do not have a threatening appearance. Altitude of cloud tops about 10,000 feet. 14

STRATOCUMULUS — Another example of an unbroken sheet of Stratocumulus. The elongation and alignment of the rolls suggest that strong wind is blowing. 19

STRATOCUMULUS and CUMULUS — Here is cloud-layer formed from decaying Cumulus. Fresh Cumulus are growing underneath. Altitude—base 5,000 to 8,000 feet. 20

CUMULONIMBUS—This is a "chaotic" sky with Cumulonimbus in the background and growing Cumulus in the foreground. Showers and thunderstorms are occurring nearby. 25

CUMULUS and CUMULONIMBUS — Cumulus are seen in lower portion. Cloud sheet above is part of a vast Cumulonimbus. Scene is typical of thunderstorm weather. 26

**CLOUDS AND THE BAROMETER**—There is very little correlation between individual cloud types and barometric indications. Most clouds shown here can occur in association with either a rising or falling barometer. However, if the sky is filled with Cumulus and the barometer is falling, look for the development of Cumulonimbus and showers. Thickening high-altitude ice clouds accompanying a falling barometer are particularly significant. This combination almost always indicates the approach of wet weather. But *isolated* Cirrus tufts or streaks occur without relation to the barometric trend.

**CIRRUS** — Ice clouds in the form of 3 both tufts and hooks. The hooks are snow trails which are bent when they encounter changes in wind direction and velocity at lower altitudes.

**CIRROSTRATUS** — This cloud covers 4 the whole sky. Individual Cirrus tufts appear, but they merge with a sheet of ice filaments. Altitude—above 20,000 feet.

**CIRROSTRATUS** — Ice cloud in the form 5 of a veil. The halo is caused by refraction of sunlight through the ice crystals composing the veil. The halo is **not** a sure sign of rain.

**CIRROCUMULUS** — Fairly typical in 6 middle section. Cirrus streaks are visible at top. Altitude—above 20,000 feet. This cloud is often difficult to distinguish from Altocumulus.

**ALTOSTRATUS** — This layer is suffi 9 ciently translucent to reveal the position of the sun. Dark patches in vicinity of sun probably are remains of Cumulus.

**ALTOCUMULUS**—This sheet of lightly 10 shaded white to dark grey elements displays the chief characteristics of Altocumulus. Altitude—8,000 to 20,000 feet.

**ALTOCUMULUS** — This layer of Alto 11 cumulus has a wavy appearance. The billows are caused by irregularities in the wind at the altitude of the cloud.

**ALTOCUMULUS**—This is clearly a 12 water cloud, since it shows no signs of hair-like structure. The elements are ragged and apparently are evaporating.

**CUMULUS** — The build-up in the left 15 half of the picture appears to be sprouting rather rapidly. However, development of Cumulonimbus is not imminent.

**CUMULUS**—The Cumulus in the right 16 half of the picture has considerable vertical extent. The bulging upper part indicates strong ascending air currents.

**STRATOCUMULUS** — Appearance indi 17 cates localized rising air currents. Stratocumulus is dark cloud in foreground. Cumulonimbus (white cloud). Altitude—base 3,000 to 5,000 feet.

**STRATOCUMULUS**—This is a solid 18 layer of Stratocumulus formed by the merging of numerous Cumulus clouds. Light showers may fall from it. Often accompanied by gusty winds.

**STRATOCUMULUS**—Typifies Strato 21 cumulus formed during the day and evaporating at sunset. Rising currents have stopped; a clear night can be expected.

**ALTOCUMULUS**—An unusual form of 22 Altocumulus. It might be identified as Cirrocumulus, but absence of streaks means it is a water rather than ice cloud.

**ALTOSTRATUS and CUMULUS** — This 23 combination and the general appearance of the sky suggest that the weather is beginning to improve following a rainstorm.

**CUMULUS and CIRRUS** — The white 24 clouds at top are Cirrus (note the streaks). Cumulus below suggest Cirrus have been derived from distant Cumulonimbus.

**CUMULONIMBUS**—A rain shower can 27 be seen falling from the darkest portion. This feature identifies the cloud as Cumulonimbus even though it is not a thunderstorm cloud.

**CUMULONIMBUS** — Exhibiting hanging 28 protuberances, called "mamma," caused by the descent of blobs of cloud-filled air. Associated with severe thunderstorms.

**CUMULONIMBUS** — The heavy rain 29 shower in the distance identifies the cloud as Cumulonimbus. The scene is common over warm ocean waters in summer.

**STRATUS** — A featureless grey sheet 30 whose base is within a few hundred feet of the ground. If rain falls from it, the cloud is called NIMBOSTRATUS. Note top of tower is obscured.

**STABLE vs. UNSTABLE AIR**—These terms are best explained by first considering stability in a liquid. A light liquid can float on top of a heavier one without mixing, but a heavy liquid will not float on top of a lighter one. The first arrangement is stable, the second unstable. Heating of a kettle of water from below demonstrates the same fact. The water at the bottom of the kettle is heated and becomes lighter than the water above it. The warmed water rises from the bottom, its place being taken by colder water from above. This action occurs because water is unstable when cold water lies above warm. Because air is compressible, the condition for stability in the atmosphere is — *not* that the temperature shall increase with height, but that the temperature shall not decrease at a rate (*for unsaturated air*) greater than 5.4°F per 1,000 feet. If, due to heating at the earth's surface, the temperature decrease with height exceeds this rate, the air is unstable, or top-heavy, and tends to overturn.

G

## BASIC CLOUD FORMS

Although 10 principal cloud types are defined in the International Cloud Classification (see pages 241-242), there are really only three basic cloud forms: (1) "streak" clouds, (2) "sheet" clouds and (3) "heap" clouds. The streak clouds are composed of tiny ice particles which often form trails, giving rise to the picturesque English name "mares' tails." ("Federwolke" is the German name for the same formation.)

## HOW CLOUDS ARE NAMED

In the interest of conformity, however, the cloud designations chosen for international usage are derived from Latin words. Streak clouds are called *cirrus* (a hair or curl) A sheet-like cloud is called *stratus* (a spreading out) and a heap cloud *cumulus* (a heap). When appropriate, other Latin words are joined to these primary ones. Thus, for example, the Latin word *nimbus* (black rain cloud) is combined with *stratus* and with *cumulus* to give *nimbostratus* and *cumulonimbus,* meaning, respectively, "raining cloud sheet" and "raining heap cloud."

## SHEET AND HEAP TYPES

Sheet clouds are produced mainly by a slow widespread ascent of stable air, less commonly by radiative cooling of air moving purely horizontally. Heap clouds, on the other hand, are formed in unstable air permeated with localized, strong updrafts created by spontaneous ascent of buoyant "bubbles" of air.

## EFFECT OF WIND SHEAR

Numerous modifications of the basic cloud forms are observed. These may be caused by complex motions within the clouds or by the twisting effect of "vertical wind shear," that is, changes in the direction and velocity of the wind from one altitude to another. We have a demonstration of the latter in the not-uncommon sight of curving streaks of ice crystals which trail from a parent cirrus (see photograph No. 3).

## IN MIDDLE LATITUDES

In middle latitudes, at elevations greater than about 10,000 feet, the wind velocity generally increases with height but the direction usually remains fairly constant right up to 30,000 feet at least. Tall cumulus clouds in this kind of environment will be bent by vertical wind shear, so that their tops lean forward. A striking example of this is provided in the photograph on page 246 (a). Here the cloud apparently has built up to the base of the stratosphere. At that altitude a temperature inversion has stopped its upward growth, and the stronger wind which exists there has spread the cloud top horizontally off to the right.

## IN TRADE-WIND BELTS

In the tropical trade-wind belts, where easterly winds prevail in the lowest 10,000 feet of the atmosphere, cumulus clouds are sometimes seen to lean backwards. This happens because the easterly winds of the tropics ordinarily do not increase in velocity upward as do the westerlies of middle latitudes. It is not uncommon for the wind velocity to decrease with elevation, so that the vertical wind shear is directed from west toward east. If the top of a tall tropical cumulus cloud is seen to be bent sharply backward, perhaps pointing in an almost horizontal direction, it is probable that the cloud top has penetrated an upper layer where the wind is blowing from the west.

## ROLLS OR BILLOWS

The roll formations, or billows, that often occur in a layer of middle-level clouds (see photograph No. 11) are usually caused by vertical wind shear. The upper part of the layer is moving faster than the lower part but is flowing in the same direction. The sliding of the upper part over the lower part sets up waves on the boundary between the two, with the result that the cloud deck is shaped into rolls which are oriented approximately at right angles to the direction of the air flow.

## CLOUDS AND CLIMATE

The ten cloud types defined in pages 241-242 can be seen the world over. However, the frequency of each type varies considerably from one climate region to another. For example, *cumulus* is far more prevalent in the tropics than in the polar regions, whereas *stratus* occurs more often in middle and high latitudes than in the tropics. Moreover, the predominating cloud types in certain parts of the United States are quite different from those in others.

## HEIGHT— RANGES

The table below gives the approximate height-ranges of the bases of the ten principal cloud types. In this table the overlapping of the upper limits of the middle-level water clouds (Ac and As) and the lower limits of the ice clouds is explained by latitudinal, seasonal, and day-to-day variations in temperature, which occur aloft as well as well as at the earth's surface.

| APPROXIMATE HEIGHT-RANGES AT WHICH BASES OF VARIOUS CLOUDS ARE FOUND | | | |
|---|---|---|---|
| Cloud Type | In polar regions | In middle latitudes | In tropical regions |
| Ci, Cc, Cs | 10,000-30,000 ft. | 16,000-45,000 ft. | 25,000-55,000 ft. |
| Ac, As | 6,000-15,000 ft. | 6,000-23,000 ft. | 6,000-25,000 ft. |
| Ns, Sc, St, Cu, Cb | From near the ground to 8,000 feet | | |

PHOTOGRAPH CREDITS: Figure 1212, W. Humphreys. Figures 1210, 1211, 1218, 1223, 1224, 1228, and 1239, Frank A. Montgomery.

U. S. DEPARTMENT OF COMMERCE
WEATHER BUREAU

FIG. 1212 Stratocumulus clouds in the rear of a LOW.

0730 E. S. T., THURSDAY, APRIL 18

FIG. 1213

239

moved in a slightly more easterly direction than we had expected from our consideration of the pressure tendencies reported at 1930 EST 17 April.)

From the point of lowest pressure north of Lake Erie we can start our diagnosis of the location of the cold front. The front quite clearly runs southwestward through Ohio and Kentucky, between the stations reporting northwest winds and the stations reporting southerly winds. To the east of the front, temperatures are quite uniformly in the low sixties and dew points in the upper fifties. To the west of it both temperatures and dew points decrease rapidly westward, being in the thirties at a distance of 200 miles from the wind-shift line.

In Tennessee the east-to-west contrasts of temperature and dew point become less sharp, but pronounced differences in wind direction still exist, with winds from the south over eastern Tennessee, Alabama and eastern Mississippi, in contrast to winds generally from the north over western Tennessee, northwestern Mississippi and central and western Louisiana.

If we look at the pressure reports from the region near the Gulf Coast we find a barometric reading at New Orleans of 1004.1 millibars (fig. 1213). This indicates the presence of another low-pressure center, which is almost certainly the same one that we noticed southeast of Texas twelve hours earlier. It has now made connections with the original cold front, and is affecting the movement of this front, as we shall now determine.

In drawing the 1008 millibar isobar northward from the Gulf Coast we find that it no longer can be traced with practically no change in direction all the way to western Pennsylvania, as it could on the preceding map (fig. 1208). It intersects the front in northeastern Mississippi and thence must make a sharp turn to the left, with the result that it returns to the Gulf via western Louisiana. It has become separated from the 1008 millibar isobar to the north, which crosses the front in southwestern Ohio and closes around the northern low-pressure center.

### Changes in Wind Pattern

This splitting of the isobaric pattern means that changes in the wind pattern have taken place from Tennessee southward. In eastern Louisiana especially, it can be seen that the winds in the moist tropical air have backed to southeast, while on the other side of the front the winds in the cold air have, in general, veered to a straight northerly, or even north-northeasterly direction. Hence, the winds in the cold air have become more nearly parallel to the front. The result is that the eastward advance of the front has been abruptly stopped; the front has become stationary or is even beginning to reverse its course and to move slowly to the west. Therefore, from the point in Tennessee to just west of New Orleans the front may now be marked a warm front. Southwest of the low-pressure center near New Orleans we assume that the cold air is advancing eastward across the Gulf of Mexico and so we indicate there that the front is acting as a cold front.

### RELOCATING THE WARM FRONT

Let us now see how to locate the warm front that extended eastward across northern Indiana, northern Ohio, and thence southeastward to the Middle Atlantic Coast at

1930 EST of 17 April (see fig. 1208). The determination of the position of this front has to be based largely on temperature differences and dew-point differences, since the contrast of wind directions on either side of it are nowhere near as marked as in the case of the cold front.

Beginning at the center of low pressure just east of Lake Huron (fig. 1212), the warm front runs southeastward and may be found in western New York lying between the station that reports a south-southwest wind, pressure 1001.0 millibars, temperature 60°, dew point 58°, and the station in central New York with a southeast wind, pressure 1006.1 millibars, temperature 52°, dew point 45°.

From this point the front extends southward through western Pennsylvania. We determine that it lies between the station in extreme southwestern Pennsylvania (Pittsburgh) which reports a south-southwest wind, temperature 61°, dew point 58°, and the station in central Pennsylvania reporting a southeast wind, continuous light rain, temperature 54°, dew point 47°. (The temperature-dew point combination of 61°/58° observed at Pittsburgh is characteristic, for that latitude, of the moist tropical air that has come from the Gulf of Mexico.)

Beyond this point the position of the front does not show up clearly, owing to the lack of reports from stations in Maryland and northeastern Virginia. We are on safe ground, however, if we draw it between stations reporting south to southwest winds and places where the winds range from northeast to southeast. On this basis we determine that the front intersects the coastline at about latitude 38°. From there we project it eastward out to sea.

We shall not take time to analyze the weather features over the western part of the United States at 0730 EST of 18 April, since little of interest is occurring there. And so we conclude our brief study of the weather map.

### SUBSEQUENT DEVELOPMENTS— IN RETROSPECT

The reader, however, may be interested to hear what happened to the principal frontal system and its two associated low-pressure centers during the next four days. During the interval between 0730 EST of 18 April and 0730 EST of 19 April the northern low-pressure area continued its northeastward movement and reached a position just north of the St. Lawrence River. But, meanwhile it weakened considerably, its lowest pressure on 19 April being not less than about 1005 millibars. The northern part of the cold front which extended southwestward from it pushed across Pennsylvania, New York and New England, all the way to the Atlantic. Further south, however, the advance of cold air was slowed by the developing low-pressure center which we noted near New Orleans at 0730 EST of 18 April. During the next 24 hours this center moved north-northeastward to Tennessee, all the while strengthening; by 0730 EST of 19 April it had become more prominent than the northern center.

Subsequently it continued to intensify, as it changed course to a more easterly direction, and eventually it developed into a severe storm. At 0730 EST of 22 April it was located about 250 miles east of Nantucket; the pressure at its exact center had fallen to about 972 millibars (28.70″). It caused exceptionally strong northeast gales off the New England coast during 21 April.

# Types of Storms

## EXTRA-TROPICAL CYCLONES

The principal source of rain, winds and generally foul weather in the United States is the *extra-tropical cyclone*. There are other storms—the hurricane, the thunderstorm and the tornado—that are usually more destructive but it is a fact that the extra-tropical cyclone is the ultimate cause of most of our weather troubles. Fog is another enemy not to be taken lightly, as we shall see, but let's concentrate on storms right now. If we would take proper and timely precautions for them, we should know something of their characteristics.

A definition of an extra-tropical cyclone in the Northern Hemisphere is: a traveling system of winds rotating counterclockwise around a center of low barometric pressure and containing a warm front and a cold front.

### How extra-tropical cyclones develop

We saw what one looked like on the daily weather map. Fig. 1214 is a diagram (plan view) of the birth, development and death of an extra-tropical cyclone. Our thanks are due Captain Charles G. Halpine, USN, for permission to reproduce this diagram from his book "A Pilot's Meteorology," published by D. van Nostrand Company.

In part (a) of fig. 1214, we have a warm air mass, typically moist tropical air, flowing northeastward and a cold air mass, typically polar continental, flowing southwestward. They are separated by a heavy line representing the boundary or front between them. The next stage is shown in part (b). The cold air from behind pushes under the warm air; the warm air rushes up over the cold air ahead of it. A cold front is born on the left, a warm front on the right. Where they are connected, the barometric pressure is lowered and the air starts circulating counterclockwise around this LOW. At the rear of the cold front, a high-pressure area

develops. At the same time, the whole system keeps moving in a general easterly direction. The crosshatched area represents rain. When warm, moist air is lifted, as it is when a cold air mass pushes under it or when it rushes up over cold air ahead, it cools by expansion. After its temperature has fallen to the dew point, excess water vapor condenses to form first clouds and then rain.

In parts (c) and (d) of fig. 1214, the storm matures, the low-pressure area intensifying more and more, the clouds and rain increasing and the winds becoming stronger. In part (e), the cold front begins to catch up with the warm front; an occluded front is formed. The storm is now at its height. It will do about one-half of its mischief while in occlusion. In part (f), it has begun to weaken; after a while, the weather should clear, as the high-pressure area reaches us.

Extra-tropical cyclones often occur in families of two, three or four storms. It takes about one day (24 hours) for this disturbance to reach maturity with three or possibly four days more required for complete dissipation. In winter, these storms occur on the average of twice a week in the USA; in summer they occur somewhat less frequently and are less severe. Their movement is eastward to north of east at a velocity in winter of about 700 miles per day and in summer of perhaps 500 miles per day. Finally, this storm usually covers a large area geographically; it can affect a given locality for two days or more.

### Parts of the extra-tropical cyclone

The component parts of an extra-tropical cyclone are:
1. A warm front, with its two conflicting air masses and its weather.
2. A cold front, with its two conflicting air masses, one of which (the warmer) is situated between the cold front and the warm front.

**FIG. 1214 Diagram of development of extra-tropical cyclone.**
(Reproduced by courtesy of Captain C. G. Halpine, U.S.N., and D. van Nostrand Co., Inc.)

(A)

(B)

(C)

(D)

(E)

(F)

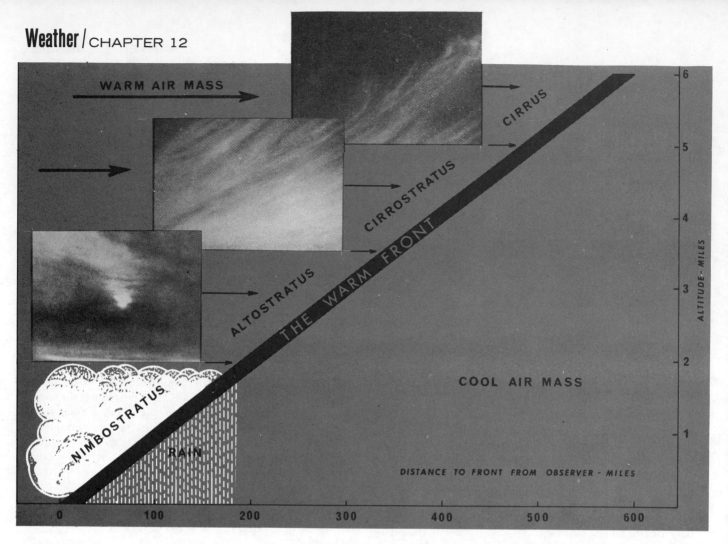

WARM AIR MASS

CIRRUS

CIRROSTRATUS

THE WARM FRONT

ALTOSTRATUS

NIMBOSTRATUS

RAIN

COOL AIR MASS

DISTANCE TO FRONT FROM OBSERVER - MILES

ALTITUDE - MILES

FIG. 1215

3. A center of low barometric pressure with its wind system, at the junction of the fronts.

4. A high pressure area behind the cold front.

## A typical cruising experience

In early May a few years ago we were cruising down the Mississippi. We noticed on the weather map that there was an extra-tropical cyclone far to the WSW, its center moving NE along a path that would leave us SSE of it. The warm front, the warm sector between the fronts, and the cold front would pass over us if we continued our cruise. Being stubborn, we kept on but watched carefully for the approaching trouble.

The first day the weather was fine with gentle winds and light fluffy cumulus clouds. The next morning we observed cirrus (Ci) clouds (fig. 1215) to the westward and noted that the barometer was falling. As these slowly thickened, we knew that the warm front was perhaps 500 miles, about one day, away. As the day wore on, the barometer fell more rapidly, the wind blew increasingly strong from the southeast, and the clouds thickened to the cirrostratus (Cs) of fig. 1215. A halo appeared around the sun.

Altostratus (As) clouds (fig. 1215) next were seen approaching from westward. Knowing that these clouds precede a warm front by about 300 miles and that rain can be expected about 200 miles ahead of the front, it required no magician to tell us that we had better begin securing

ship and breaking out the oilskins. We observed that the spread between the air temperature and dew-point temperature was growing less and less; it looked as though we could also expect fog. We decided to anchor until the warm front had passed over.

Next came the low nimbostratus (Ns) clouds and the rain, the barometer continuing to fall and the temperature slowly to rise. The visibility grew worse and worse. The ship's bell began its clamor and we spent a not too comfortable night. By morning, however, the wind had veered to SSW, the clouds had begun to break, the barometer had stopped falling, the rain had ceased. Knowing that it might be 6 to 12 hours before the cold front struck us, we got under way, keeping our eyes peeled for altocumulus (Ac) clouds to the westward. The watch below was set to airing the cabins and our duffle as we ran through the warm sector.

About 1400 the lookout spotted the altocumulus clouds (fig. 1216); the cold front was perhaps 100 miles away. As the day was hot and quite humid, we thought that thunderstorms were probable and that they might be severe. We decided to anchor early, about 1500, and prepare for the worst. The barometer was again falling, the wind was SW and increasing. Nimbostratus (Ns) clouds with cumulonimbus (Cb) (fig. 1216) towering out of them appeared to the west. Rain set in and the wind rose sharply. We had a busy few hours—and were mighty glad that we had known enough to recognize and time the warning signs. By the

FIG. 1216

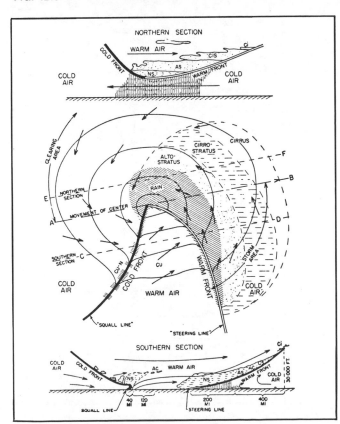

FIG. 1217 **Cross-sections of extra-tropical cyclone.** (Reproduced by courtesy of Captain C. G. Halpine, U.S.N., and D. van Nostrand Co., Inc.)

next morning the storm was over and we continued our cruise with a blue sky and fair winds.

Thus, we passed through an extra-tropical cyclone. Fig. 1217 is a picture of it, again with acknowledgement to Captain Halpine. The central portion is a plan view of the storm; the lower portion is a vertical cross-section along the line CD, our "course" through the storm. The cloud sequences and the rain are clearly shown (Cb symbol omitted). Had we passed north, instead of south, of the center, the upper diagram would represent the clouds and weather.

## HURRICANES

Another type of cyclone which is of concern principally to those of us cruising the Gulf of Mexico and the southeast Atlantic coast is the *tropical cyclone,* which in its most violent (and best known) form is called a *hurricane.* Unlike the extra-tropical cyclone, it does not contain warm and cold fronts, and its occurrence (over waters adjacent to the United States) is restricted to summer and autumn.

The hurricane as a storm type is too well known among sailors to require any description here of the various premonitory signs, the violence of the wind and rain accompanying such a storm and the steps to be taken to minimize the dangers of encounter. These are fully detailed in standard nautical works, such as Bowditch's "American Practical Navigator."

243

FIG. 1218 Wall cloud around eye of a hurricane, as seen from an aircraft within the eye. Upper edge of wall cloud is at an altitude of nearly 40,000 feet. Note clear space in right foreground.

Over the years much statistical information on the frequency of hurricanes in various regions of the world has accumulated. In the Far East hurricanes (or *typhoons,* as they are called in the western Pacific) may occur in any month, although late summer and early autumn are the preferred seasons. In North American waters, however, the period from early December through May is hurricane-free. August, September and October are the months of greatest frequency; in these months hurricanes form over the tropical Atlantic, mostly between latitudes 8°N and 20°N. The infrequent hurricanes of June and November almost always originate in the southwestern part of the Caribbean Sea.

## Development of a hurricane

The birthplace of a hurricane typically lies within a diffuse and fairly large area of relatively low pressure situated somewhere in the latitude belt just mentioned. The winds around the low-pressure area are not particularly strong, and, although cumulonimbus clouds and showers are more numerous than is usual in these latitudes, there is no clearly organized "weather system." This poorly-defined condition may persist for several days before hurricane development commences.

When development starts, however, it takes place suddenly. Within an interval of 12 hours or less the barometric pressure drops 15 millibars or more over a small, almost circular area. Winds of hurricane force spring up and form a ring around the area; the width of this ring is at first only 20 to 40 miles. The clouds and showers become well-organized and show a spiral structure. At this stage the growing cyclone acquires an *eye.* This is the inner area enclosed by the ring of hurricane-force winds, which, by the time the cyclone reaches maturity, has expanded to a width of 100 miles or more. Within the eye we find the lowest barometric reading.

Hurricane eyes average about 15 miles in diameter but may be as large as 25 miles. The wind velocities in the eye of a hurricane are seldom greater than 15 knots and often are less. Cloud conditions vary over a wide range. At times

FIG. 1219 Path of the hurricane, showing positions of the center at 0700 EST, 18-22 September 1938.

there are only scattered clouds, but usually there is more than 50% cloud cover. Through the openings the sky is visible overhead and at a distance the dense towering clouds of the hurricane ring can be seen extending to great heights (fig. 1218). This feature has been given the name *wall cloud.*

## Hurricane tracks

The usual track of an Atlantic hurricane describes a parabola around the semipermanent Azores-Bermuda high-pressure area. Thus, after forming, a hurricane will move westward on the southern side of the Azores-Bermuda HIGH, at the same time tending to work away from the equator. When the hurricane reaches the western side of this HIGH, it begins to follow a more northerly track, and its direction of advance changes progressively toward the right. Thus, the usual movement of Atlantic hurricanes at first is roughly westward, then northwestward, northward, and finally northeastward. The position where the westward movement changes to an eastward movement is known as the *point of recurvature.*

Occasionally when a hurricane is in a position near the southeast Atlantic coast, the Azores-Bermuda HIGH happens to have an abnormal northward extension. In this type of situation the hurricane will fail to execute a complete recurvature in the vicinity of Cape Hatteras. It will skirt the western side of the HIGH and follow a path almost due north along the Atlantic coast, as occurred in the case of the famous New England hurricane of September 1938 (see figs. 1219 and 1220).

The rate of movement of tropical cyclones while they are still in low latitudes and heading westward is about 15 knots, which is considerably slower than the usual rate of travel of extra-tropical cyclones. After recurving they begin to move faster and usually attain a forward speed of at least 25 knots, sometimes 50 to 60 knots, as in the case of the September 1938 hurricane. A small proportion of hurricanes, however, do not recurve at all, and a few of these follow highly irregular tracks which may include a complete loop.

Hurricanes gradually decrease in intensity after they reach middle and high latitudes and move over colder water. Many lose their identity by absorption into the wind circulation around the larger extra-tropical cyclones of the North Atlantic.

## THUNDERSTORMS

We stated at the beginning of this section that the extra-tropical cyclone was the ultimate cause of most of our foul weather. We said this advisedly, because in addition to the strong winds and generally wet weather which it generates, smaller-scale storms, such as *thunderstorms* and *tornadoes,* usually are created by the contrasting air masses and conflicting winds within the large-scale, overall air circulation of the extra-tropical cyclone. Thus, thunderstorms are commonly linked to the cold front of the cyclone. But if the air comprising the warm sector is sufficiently unstable, which is often the case in summer, thunderstorms together with general rain will occur during the approach of a warm front as the warm-sector air ascends over the cold air ahead. They also develop on their own in the middle of an air mass, unaided by frontal activity.

We know a thunderstorm as a storm of short duration, arising only in a cumulonimbus cloud, attended by thunder and lightning, and marked by abrupt fluctuations of temperature, pressure and wind. A *line squall,* now usually referred to in meteorological parlance as a *squall line,* is a lengthy row of thunderstorms stretching for 100 miles or more.

Incidentally, a *shower* (as opposed to gentle, steady rain) is a smaller brother, though the rainfall and wind in it may be of considerable intensity. It characteristically is the product of relatively large cumulus, or small cumulonimbus, clouds separated from one another by blue sky. It is not accompanied by thunder and lightning.

### Features of the thunderstorm cloud

In all cases the prime danger signal is a cumulus cloud growing larger. Every thunderstorm cloud has four distinctive features, although we may not always be able to see all four as other clouds may intervene in our line of sight. Fig. 1221 shows these four features; the anvil top is better illustrated in fig. 1222. These three photographs of an anvil were taken from the same position over a period of one-half hour!

FIG. 1220 Constancy of anticyclonic flow, as shown by unchanged orientation of sea-level isobars from September 19 to September 20. Upper figure of each pair of numbers is barometric reading on September 19, lower figure that on September 20. Although a general fall of pressure took place during the interval, flow pattern remained the same.

**FIG. 1221 Diagram of thunderstorm cloud.**
(Courtesy of Aviation Training Division, U.S. Navy)

*Key to Diagram of Cumulonimbus Cloud*

| | |
|---|---|
| **A** – Anvil Top | **U** – Up Drafts |
| **B** – Dark Area | **R** – Primary Rain Area |
| **C** – Roll Cloud | **R'** – Secondary Area |
| **Cᵤ** – Advance Cumulus Clouds | **W** – Wind Direction |
| **D** – Down Drafts | |

Fig. 1221 is a drawing, by courtesy of the Navy Bureau of Aeronautics from their booklet "Thunderstorms" (Aerology Series Two), of a cumulonimbus cloud; it shows these four features diagrammatically. Starting at the top, we notice the layer of cirrus clouds, shaped like an anvil and consequently called "anvil top," leaning in the direction toward which the upper wind is blowing. This tells us the direction in which the storm is moving.

The next feature is the main body of the cloud; it is a large cumulus of great height with cauliflower sides. It must be of great height, as it must extend far above the freezing level if the cirrus anvil top is to form. Cirrus clouds are composed of ice crystals, not water droplets. The third feature is the roll cloud formed by violent air currents along the leading edge of the base of the cumulus cloud. The fourth and final feature is the dark area within the storm and extending from the base of the cloud to the earth; at the center this is rain, at the edges hail and rain.

## Requirements for thunderstorm formation

There are three requirements for the formation of thunderstorms. One, there must be strong upward air currents such as are caused by a cold front burrowing under and lifting warm air or by heating of the air in contact with the surface of the earth on a summer day. Warm, humid air blowing up a mountain slope also can produce a thunderstorm. Two, the air parcels forming the storm must be buoyant relative to their neighbors outside the storm and willing, therefore, to keep on ascending higher and higher until they pass the freezing level. Third, the air must have a large concentration of water vapor. The most promising thunderstorm air is of tropical maritime origin; whenever it appears in our cruising area, especially when a cold front is approaching, we need to be suspicious.

## Frequency of thunderstorms

Thunderstorms occur most frequently and with the greatest intensity in the summer over all parts of the USA. While they may strike at any hour, they prefer the late afternoon and early evening over inland and coastal waters. The surrounding land has been a good "stove" for many hours, heating the air to produce strong upward currents. Over the ocean, well away from shore, thunderstorms more commonly occur between midnight and sunrise. Finally, thunderstorms are most frequent and most violent in tropical latitudes; they are less common and less intense in the higher latitudes. The southeastern states experience as many as four thunderstorms per week in summer.

Ahead of a thunderstorm the wind may be either steady or variable, but as the *roll cloud* (fig. 1221) draws near, the wind weakens and becomes unsteady. As the roll cloud passes overhead, violent shifting winds, accompanied by strong downdrafts, may be expected. The wind velocity may reach 60 knots. Heavy rain and sometimes hail begins to fall just abaft the roll cloud. However, the weather quickly clears after the passage of the storm, which brings cooler temperatures and lower humidity.

If the cumulonimbus cloud is fully developed and towers to normal thunderstorm altitudes, 35,000 feet or more in summer, the storm will be violent. If the anvil top is low, say only 20,000 feet or so, as is usual in spring and autumn, the storm will be less severe. If the cumulonimbus cloud is not fully developed, particularly if it lacks the anvil top, and the roll cloud is missing, only a shower may be expected.

We can time the approach of a thunderstorm, once the cumulonimbus cloud is visible, by a series of bearings. If we wish, we can estimate its distance off by another

**FIG. 1222** **Growth of the anvil of thunderstorm cloud. Top photograph was taken at 1200, the middle at 1220, the lower at 1230 from same position as storm developed.**
(Courtesy, U.S. Weather Bureau)

method. The thunder and lightning occur simultaneously at the point of lightning discharge, but we see the lightning discharge much sooner than we hear the thunder. Consequently, time this interval, in seconds. Multiply the number of seconds by 0.2; the result will be the approximate distance off in miles.

## TORNADOES

When numerous thunderstorms are associated with a cold front, the storms are apt to be organized in a long, narrow band. The forward edge of this band is usually marked by a *squall line*, along which the cold downdrafts from a series of thunderstorms meet the warm air (see fig. 1221). Here the wind direction changes suddenly in vicious gusts, and a sharp drop in temperature occurs. The importance of squall lines is that they often spawn a most destructive type of storm, the deadly *tornado*. We should keep firmly in mind the fact that tornadoes have wrecked boats on the Mississippi and elsewhere in the southern part of the USA.

Tornadoes formed at squall lines often occur in families and move with the wind that prevails in the warm sector ahead of the cold front. This wind direction is usually from the southwest. The warm air typically consists of two layers, a very moist one (source: Gulf of Mexico) near the

FIG. 1223 The terrifying "funnel" of a tornado is actually a cloud of water droplets mixed with dust and debris. Close to the ground, dust and debris are plentiful, because greatly reduced atmospheric pressure inside funnel (a lowering of pressure of the order of 50 millibars) causes air to whirl violently inward and upward.

FIG. 1224 Waterspout over St. Louis Bay, off Henderson Point, Mississippi. Note cloud of spray just above sea surface.

ground and a relatively dry layer above. The temperature decreases with altitude relatively rapidly in each layer. When this combination of air layers is lifted along a squall line or cold front, excessive instability develops and violent updrafts are created.

A tornado is essentially an air whirlpool of small horizontal extent which extends downward from a cumulonimbus cloud and has a funnel-like appearance (see fig. 1223). The average diameter of the visible funnel cloud is about 250 yards, but the destructive effects of the associated system of whirling winds may extend outward from the tornado center as much as 1/4 mile on each side. The wind speed near the core can only be estimated, but it undoubtedly is as high as 200 knots. This means almost certain death for the occupants of a boat which might have the misfortune to be in the path of a tornado.

Fortunately, the tornado belt in the USA is in the interior section of the country, but still there are boating areas which can be affected. So, if you live in the Midwest or the southern tier of states, keep your radio tuned to your local station, if weather conditions look threatening. The U.S. Weather Bureau now has a highly refined and reliable system for forecasting the likelihood of tornadoes.

## Waterspouts

The marine counterpart of the tornado is the *waterspout*. The conditions favoring the formation of waterspouts at sea are similar to those conducive to the formation of tornadoes over land. Waterspouts are much more frequent in the tropics than in middle latitudes. Although they are less violent than tornadoes, nevertheless they are a real danger to small craft.

A waterspout, like a tornado, forms under a cumulonimbus cloud. A funnel-shaped protuberance first appears at the base of the cumulonimbus and grows downward toward the sea. Beneath it the water becomes agitated and a cloud of spray forms. The funnel-shaped cloud descends until it merges with the spray; it then assumes the shape of a tube that stretches from the sea surface to the base of the cloud (see fig. 1224).

The diameter of a waterspout may vary from 20 feet to 200 feet or more. Its length from the sea to the base of the cloud is usually between 1000 feet and 2000 feet. It may last from 10 minutes to half an hour. Its upper part often travels at a different speed and in a different direction from its base, so that it becomes bent and stretched-out. Finally the tube breaks at a point about one-third of the way up to the cloud base, and the "spout" at the sea surface quickly subsides.

The existence of considerably reduced air pressure at the center of a waterspout can be inferred from visible variations of the water level. A mound of water, a foot or so high, sometimes appears at the core, because the atmospheric pressure on the water surrounding the spout is perhaps 30 to 40 millibars greater than that on the sea surface inside the funnel. This difference causes the rise of water at the center.

Like the tornado, the visible part of a waterspout is composed, on the whole, of tiny water droplets formed by the condensation of water vapor in the air. Considerable quantities of salt spray, however, picked up by the strong winds at the base of the spout, are sometimes carried far aloft. This has been verified by observations of the fall of salty rain following the passage of a waterspout.

# FOG

## How, Why, Where and When It Forms — Its Distribution in the United States

The essential part is not always to know things; it is to know how to reason about them. This truism applies to fog. The basic causes of fog are few in number and easy to understand. What we want is a working knowledge of these causes; then we can judge if and when fog is likely to upset our plans.

Fog is merely a cloud whose base rests upon the earth, be the latter land or water. It consists of water droplets, suspended in the air, each droplet so small that it cannot be distinguished individually, yet present in such tremendous numbers that objects close at hand are obscured.

If we are to have innumerable water droplets suspended in the air, there must be plenty of water vapor originally in that air. If droplets are to form from this vapor, the air must be cooled by some means so that the vapor will condense. If the droplets are to condense in the air next to the earth, the cooling must take place at the surface of the earth. If the fog is to have any depth, successively higher

layers of air must be cooled sufficiently to cause condensation in them. Fog forms from the ground up. Thus, the land or water must be colder than the air next to it; the lower layers of air progressively must be colder than the layers above them.

If water vapor is to condense out of the air, then the temperature of the air must be lowered to or below the *dew-point temperature,* that is, the temperature at which the air is saturated with water vapor and below which condensation of water vapor will occur.

Air is said to be *saturated* with water vapor when its water-vapor content would remain unchanged if it were placed above a level surface of pure water at its own temperature. The amount of water vapor which is required to saturate a given volume of air depends on the temperature of the air, and increases as the temperature increases. The higher the temperature the more water vapor can the air hold before it becomes saturated, and the lower the temperature the less water vapor can the air hold before it becomes saturated.

If a mass of air is originally in an unsaturated state, it can be saturated by cooling it down to a temperature at which its content of water vapor is the maximum containable amount, that is to say, to the dew-point temperature. Or we can saturate it by causing more water to evaporate into it, thereby raising the dew-point temperature to a value equal to the air temperature. In regard to the latter process, unsaturated air, as it passes over rivers and lakes, over the oceans or over wet ground, picks up water vapor and has its dew point raised. Also, rain falling from higher clouds will increase the amount of water vapor in unsaturated air near the earth.

## JUDGING THE LIKELIHOOD OF FOG

In order to judge the likelihood of fog formation, we should periodically measure the air temperature and dew-point temperature and see if the spread (difference) between them is getting smaller and smaller. The Navy, in its Aviation Training booklet "Fog" (Aerology Series 3) has

provided us with a diagram of the change in spread; it is reproduced here as fig. 1225.

Fig. 1226 is a graph of a series of air and dew-point temperatures. By recording these temperatures and plotting their spread over a period of several hours, as is indicated by that part of the curve drawn as a solid line, we have a basis for forecasting the time at which we are likely to be fog-bound. The dot-dash portion of the curve represents actual data but it could just as easily have been drawn by extending the solid portion. If an error were made in this extrapolation, it would probably indicate that the fog would form at an earlier hour. This is on the safe side; we would be secure in our anchorage some time before the fifty-ninth minute of the eleventh hour!

Note that the curve is not a straight line. While the average decrease in spread is about one and one-half degrees (Fahrenheit) per hour, the decrease is at a much greater rate in the earlier hours. So long as we do not make unreasonable allowances for a slowing up in the rate of change of the spread, this also will help to keep us on the safe side.

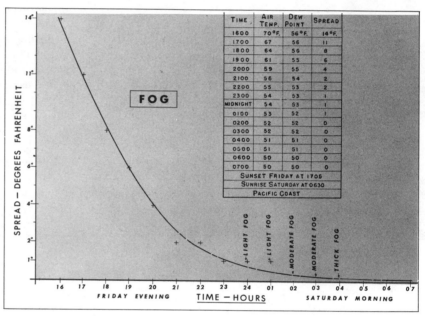

FIG. 1226   Graph of a series of air and dew-point temperatures.

**FIG. 1225   Why fog forms.**
(Reproduced by courtesy of Aviation Training Division, U.S. Navy)

## DETERMINING THE DEW POINT

How do we determine the dew point? By means of a simple-to-operate, inexpensive little gadget known as a *sling psychrometer* (fig. 1227). A sling psychrometer is merely two thermometers, mounted in a single holder with a handle that permits it to be whirled overhead. One thermometer, know as the *dry bulb,* has its bulb of mercury exposed directly to the air. This thermometer shows the actual temperature of the air. The other thermometer, known as the *wet bulb,* has its bulb covered with a piece of gauze. We soak this gauze in water so that the bulb is moistened. If the air is not saturated with water vapor, evaporation then takes place from the wet-bulb thermometer, and the wet bulb is cooled, since the process of evaporation requires the expenditure of heat. The reduced temperature shown by the wet-bulb thermometer, the so-called "wet-bulb temperature," represents the lowest temperature to which the air can be cooled by evaporating water into it.

**FIG. 1227  A pocket-type sling psychrometer, having two 5" etched tubes, 20° to 120° in 1° divisions.**
(Courtesy Taylor Instrument Companies)

When we whirl the psychrometer we create a draft around the instrument. The ventilation so produced increases the efficiency of the evaporation process and makes the wet-bulb reading more reliable than it would be if there were little or no air movement past the wet bulb. This is the reason why the psychrometer is designed for whirling.

From the wet-bulb temperature and dry-bulb temperature, the dew point may be determined by referring to a suitable table. As we are far more interested, however, in knowing the *spread, or difference, between the air temperature and dew point,* we will save ourselves some work by using another table (Table 12-1), its use being explained in the next two paragraphs.

If the air is already actually saturated with water vapor, then no water can evaporate from the gauze and both thermometers must show the same value. The dew point then has this same numerical value and so the spread between air temperature and dew point must be zero. But, as explained above, if the air is not already saturated with

water vapor, the wet-bulb thermometer will give a lower reading than the dry-bulb thermometer. We subtract the wet-bulb temperature from the dry-bulb temperature. With this difference and the dry-bulb (the air) temperature, we consult Table 12-1 and find directly the corresponding spread between the air temperature and the dew-point temperature. This is the figure we want.

If, in the late afternoon or early evening, the spread between the air temperature and dew point is less than approximately 6°F, and the air temperature is falling, fog or greatly restricted visibility will probably be experienced in a few hours. These critical values are emphasized by the heavy line above which they lie in Table 12-1. Incidentally, should we ever want to know the dew-point temperature itself, all we need do is to subtract the spread figure given in the table from the temperature shown by the dry-bulb thermometer. Thus, when the dry-bulb thermometer indicates an air temperature of 70°F and the difference between the dry-bulb and wet-bulb temperatures is 11°F, the spread is 19°F and the dew point is 51°F.

## FOUR TYPES OF FOG

We can distinguish four types of fog: (a) *radiation fog,* formed in near-calm conditions by the cooling of the ground on a clear night as a result of radiation of heat from the ground to the clear sky; (b) *advection fog,* formed by the flow of warm air over cold sea or lake; (c) *steam fog,* or "sea smoke," formed when cold air blows over much warmer water; and (d) *precipitation fog,* formed when rain coming out of warm air aloft falls through a shallow layer of cold air at the earth's surface.

### Radiation fog

There are four requirements for the formation of *radiation fog* (sometimes called "ground fog"). First, the air must be stable, that is, the air next to the earth must be colder than the air a short distance aloft. Second, the air must be relatively moist. Third, the sky must be clear, so that the earth readily can lose heat by radiation to outer space. This enables the ground to become colder than the overlying air, which subsequently is cooled below its dew point both by contact with the ground (conduction of heat) and by radiative loss of heat to the ground.

The fourth requirement is that the wind must be light to calm. If there is a dead calm, the lowest strata of air will not mix with the ones above, and fog will form only to a height of two to four feet. If there is a slight motion of the air (say a wind of three to five knots) and, hence, some turbulent mixing, the cooling is spread through a layer which may extend to a height of several hundred feet above the ground. With strong winds, the cooling effect is distributed through so deep a layer that the temperature nowhere falls to the dew point and fog does not form.

Radiation fog is most prevalent in the middle and high latitudes. It is local in character and occurs most frequently in valleys and lowlands, especially near lakes and rivers where we may be cruising. The cooled air drains into these terrain depressions; the lake or river aids the process of fog formation by contributing water vapor, which raises the dew point.

This type of fog, which may be patchy or uniformly dense, forms only at night. Shortly after sunrise, it will start

**TABLE 12-1**      AIR TEMPERATURE —— DEWPOINT SPREAD

(All figures are in degrees Fahrenheit at 30" pressure)

| Difference Dry-Bulb Minus Wet-Bulb | 35 | 40 | 45 | 50 | 55 | 60 | 65 | 70 | 75 | 80 | 85 | 90 | 95 |
|---|---|---|---|---|---|---|---|---|---|---|---|---|---|
| 1 | 2 | 2 | 2 | 2 | 2 | 2 | 2 | 1 | 1 | 1 | 1 | 1 | 1 |
| 2 | 5 | 5 | 4 | 4 | 4 | 3 | 3 | 3 | 3 | 3 | 3 | 3 | 2 |
| 3 | 7 | 7 | 7 | 6 | 5 | 5 | 5 | 4 | 4 | 4 | 4 | 4 | 4 |
| 4 | 10 | 10 | 9 | 8 | 7 | 7 | 6 | 6 | 6 | 6 | 5 | 5 | 5 |
| 5 | 14 | 12 | 11 | 10 | 10 | 9 | 8 | 8 | 7 | 7 | 7 | 7 | 6 |
| 6 | 18 | 15 | 14 | 13 | 12 | 11 | 10 | 9 | 9 | 8 | 8 | 8 | 8 |
| 7 | 22 | 19 | 17 | 16 | 14 | 13 | 12 | 11 | 11 | 10 | 10 | 9 | 9 |
| 8 | 28 | 22 | 20 | 18 | 17 | 15 | 14 | 13 | 12 | 12 | 11 | 11 | 10 |
| 9 | 35 | 27 | 23 | 21 | 19 | 17 | 16 | 15 | 14 | 13 | 13 | 12 | 12 |
| 10 | - | 33 | 27 | 24 | 22 | 20 | 18 | 17 | 16 | 15 | 14 | 14 | 13 |
| 11 | - | 40 | 32 | 28 | 25 | 22 | 20 | 19 | 18 | 17 | 16 | 15 | 15 |
| 12 | - | - | 38 | 32 | 28 | 25 | 23 | 21 | 20 | 18 | 17 | 17 | 16 |
| 13 | - | - | 45 | 37 | 31 | 28 | 25 | 23 | 21 | 20 | 19 | 18 | 17 |
| 14 | - | - | - | 42 | 35 | 31 | 28 | 26 | 24 | 22 | 21 | 20 | 19 |
| 15 | - | - | - | 50 | 40 | 35 | 31 | 28 | 26 | 24 | 23 | 21 | 21 |

Opposite — Difference Dry-Bulb Minus Wet-Bulb and
Under   — Air Temperature Shown By Dry-Bulb Thermometer
Read    — Value of Spread: Air Temperature minus Dewpoint Temperature

Based on U.S. Weather Bureau Psychrometric Tables

FIG. 1228 Fog bank over Lake Huron. This is basically an advection-type fog which has formed over an area of relatively cold water. When the wind is very light and unsteady, as in this case, fog tends to concentrate in patches, even after it has drifted away from its source.

FIG. 1229 Sea smoke in Great Harbor, Woods Hole, Massachusetts, 0915 EST, 31 December 1962. Water temperature 31.6°F; air temperature (30 feet above sea level) +5°F. Wind NW 20 knots. Height of steaming approximately 15 feet. Rigging of vessel encountering this type of condition will become coated with rime ice. Note frosty deposit on beach grass in lower right corner of photograph.
(Courtesy of P. M. Saunders, Woods Hole Oceanographic Institution)

to evaporate ("burn off") over the land, the lower layers being the first to go. It is slow to clear over water, since the temperature of the water does not vary nearly as much from day to night as does the temperature of the land.

## Advection fog

Radiation fog bothers us chiefly in the late summer and early autumn; *advection fog* can be an annoyance at any season. (Advection means transport by horizontal motion.) Winds carrying warm, moist air over a colder surface produce advection fog. The dew point of the air must be higher than the temperature of the surface over which the air is moving. Thus, the air can be cooled below its dew point by conduction and by radiation of heat to the colder surface. Other requirements for the formation of advection fog are as follows: (a) the air at a height of 100 feet or so must be warmer than the air just above the surface; (b) the temperature of the surface—be it land or water—must become progressively colder in the direction toward which the air is moving. Fig. 1230, again by courtesy of the U.S. Navy from its "Flying the Weather," illustrates the formation of advection fog along the coast and fig. 1231

its formation at sea. Advection fog may form day or night, winter or summer, over the sea.

**Coastal Fog.** For yachtsmen the most bothersome variety is *coastal fog* (fig. 1230). When steady winds blow landward and carry warm oceanic air across cold coastal water, the resulting fog may blanket a great length of coastline and, especially at night, may extend many miles inland up bays and rivers. For example, let's go to the Pacific coast, where the water close to the land is often colder than the water to westward. The prevailing winds in summer are onshore and the air, since it frequently has come from mid-Pacific, usually is nearly saturated with water vapor. Fig. 1230 illustrates the result; the same thing happens when southerly winds carry air across the Gulf Stream and thence northward across the colder Atlantic coastal waters. Advection fog also may form over the larger inland lakes whenever relatively warm and moist air is carried over their colder surfaces.

Advection fog is generally much harder to dissipate than is radiation fog. A wind shift or a marked increase in wind velocity usually is required. Sunshine has no effect on it over the water.

**FIG. 1230  Coastal fogs are common along the West Coast—warm ocean, cool coastal water, frequent winds from the sea.**
(Courtesy Aviation Training Division, U.S. Navy)

**FIG. 1231  Most persistent sea fog is an advection fog that forms when air blows from warm sea to cold sea.**

**FIG. 1233  Formation of precipitation fog.**

American coastal waters are concerned, this variety of steam fog occurs most frequently off the coasts of Maine and Nova Scotia, and in the Gulf of St. Lawrence, where it can be a serious navigational hazard. However, its occurrence is not restricted to the higher latitudes. Off the east coast of the United States it has been observed as far south as Florida and it occurs occasionally over the coastal waters of the Gulf of Mexico.

## Steam fog

On the Mississippi and Ohio rivers, a special type of fog, known as *steam fog* is a particular hazard to late evening or early morning cruising in the autumn. When cold air passes over much warmer water, the lowest layer of air is rapidly supplied with heat and water vapor. Mixing of this lowest layer with unmodified cold air above can, under certain conditions, produce a supersaturated (i.e., foggy) mixture. Owing to the fact that the water is much warmer than the air, vertical air currents are created, and we observe the phenomenon of steaming. Hence, this type of fog is called "steam fog"; it forms in just the same way as steam over a hot bath.

**Sea Smoke.** When, in winter, very cold air (having a temperature less than about 10°F) blows off the land and across the adjacent coastal waters, steam fog may be widespread and very dense. It is then known as "sea smoke" (sometimes called "Arctic sea smoke"). As far as North

## Precipitation fog

As mentioned earlier, we can distinguish a fourth type of fog, which we may call "precipitation fog," or "rain fog." When rain, after descending through a layer of warm air aloft, falls into a shallow layer of relatively cold air at the earth's surface, there will be evaporation from the warm raindrops into the colder air (see fig. 1233). Under certain conditions, this process will raise the water-vapor content of the cold air above the saturation point and fog will form. Its mode of formation is similar to that of the fog produced in the bathroom when one takes a hot shower.

It may be noted that both steam fog and rain fog are basically the result of evaporation from relatively warm water, a process which increases the dew point. These fogs can be placed in the single category of "warm-surface" fogs. Likewise, radiation fog and advection fog come under the single heading of "cold-surface" fogs.

**FIG. 1232  Steam fog forming, then dissipating upwards, over pond near Mount Kisco, N.Y., 0700 EST, 12 October 1964. Air temperature approximately 25°F; water temperature not known, but probably 50°F or higher. Wind less than 1 knot.**
(Photograph by Caroline S. Emmons)

UNITED STATES: DISTRIBUTION OF FOG

Courtesy American Geographical
Society, from "Fog in the U.S. and
Adjacent Regions" by R. G. Stone

GEOGR. REVIEW, JAN. 1936

300 MILES

FIG. 1234  Map showing distribution of fog in the United States. Isopleths show mean annual number of days with "dense fog, i.e., fogs obscuring visibility to 1000 feet or less." In order to bring out more detail in the large portion of the country where fogginess is less than 20 days, an interval of 5 days was selected. For regions with more than 20 days of fog a 10-day interval is used.

## DISTRIBUTION OF FOG IN THE UNITED STATES

Turning our attention now to the distribution of fog (all types included) in the United States, we find that the coastal sections most frequently beset by fog are (1) the area from the Strait of Juan de Fuca to Point Arguello (Calif.), on the Pacific Coast, and (2) the area from the Bay of Fundy to Montauk Point (N.Y.), on the Atlantic Coast. In these waters the average annual number of hours of fog occurrence exceeds 900, that is, more than 10% of the entire year. In the foggiest parts of these areas, namely, off the coast of Northern California and the coast of Maine, fog is present about 20% of the year.

As we go southward along both the Atlantic and Pacific Coasts the frequency of fog decreases, but it does so much more rapidly on the Atlantic Coast than on the Pacific. Hence, we find that the average annual fog frequency over the waters adjacent to Los Angeles and San Diego is about three times that in the same latitude along the Atlantic Coast.

## SEASONAL FREQUENCIES

The *time of maximum occurrence* of fog off the Pacific Coast varies somewhat with the various localities and, of course, with the individual year. In general, however, over the stretch from Cape Flattery (Wash.) to Point Arguello the season of most frequent fog comprises the months of July, August, September and October, with more than 50% of the annual number of foggy days occurring during this period. However, along the lower coast of California, that is, from Los Angeles southward, the foggiest months are those from September through February, and the least foggy from May through July.

On the Atlantic side: Off the coast of New England the foggiest months are usually June, July and August, with a maximum of fog generally occurring during July, in which month fog normally is encountered from one-third to one-half of the time. Off the Middle Atlantic Coast, however, fog occurs mostly in the winter and spring months, with a distinct tendency toward minimum frequency in summer and autumn. Along the South Atlantic Coast (from Cape Hatteras to the tip of Florida) and in the Gulf of Mexico fog rarely creates a problem for the yachtsman. It is virtually non-existent during the summer, and even in the winter and early spring season (December through March), when it has maximum frequency, the number of days with fog hardly anywhere exceeds 20, on the average, during this four-month period.

The *fog regime of the Great Lakes* is essentially like that of the oceanic coastal waters in middle latitudes; the Great Lakes as a whole tend to have more fog in the warmer season. The explanation of this circumstance is to be found in the comparison of the lake temperatures with the air temperatures over the surrounding land. From March or April to the beginning of September the lakes are, on the average, colder than the air. Hence, whenever the dew-point temperature is sufficiently high, conditions are favorable for the formation of advection fog over the water.

The greatest fogginess occurs when and where the lakes are coldest in relation to the air blowing off the surrounding land. On Lake Superior, north-central Lake Michigan, and northwestern Lake Huron the *time* of maximum frequency is late May and June; elsewhere it is late April and May. As to the *location* of maximum fogginess, since the lake temperatures become colder from south to north and from the shores outward, the occurrence of fog increases northward and towards the central parts of each lake.

254

# Observations Afloat—Weather signs

We have already discussed fog and how we can use a sling psychrometer to help us in forecasting its occurrence. There are a few other weather instruments which are practical on shipboard and which provide us with helpful information.

## WIND OBSERVATIONS

Every sailor is familiar with the *wind direction indicators* that may be mounted at the masthead. Because a boat, at anchor or under way, can head in any direction all around the compass, a few mental calculations are necessary before we can use this indicator or an owner's flag or club burgee to determine the true direction of the wind. At anchor, the fly will give us the bearing of the wind relative to the boat's head; this must be converted to the true bearing of the wind itself. We can use our compass to obtain these values, provided we know its deviation on our heading and know the variation for our anchorage. Also, we need to remember that wind direction is always stated as the true direction *from* which, not toward which, the wind is blowing.

FIG. 1235 Danforth/White's anemometer with flush-mounted wind velocity indicator supplies accurate readings on two scales (0-25 and 0-120 knots). Two-wire conductor leads from indicator to masthead or spreader. Wind direction indicator is a matching unit.

## The anemometer

For measuring *wind velocity* we need something else. This is an *anemometer;* the principal parts of the instrument are illustrated in fig. 1235. The anemometer is essentially a speedometer. It consists of a rotor with conical cups attached to the ends of spokes and is designed for mounting at the masthead, where the wind is caught by the cups, causing them to turn at a speed proportional to the speed of the wind. Indications of the rotor's speed are transmitted to an indicator which may be mounted in the cabin.

In the type of instrument illustrated in fig. 1235, the indicator is direct-reading, in two scales from 0 to 25 and 0 to 120 knots for velocity, gusts and variations. Battery drain (.09 amp.) is insignificant. A 60-foot wire cable is supplied to connect the rotor aloft with the illuminated indicator below. At anchor, the reading is the actual or true wind velocity at masthead height.

## True and apparent wind

So far we have been considering the determination of the direction and speed of the wind while at anchor. Under way, the determination is more difficult, but the Oceanographic Office of the Navy has worked out the problem, so we may as well use their results. Table 12-2 is based on wind tables formerly published in Bowditch. Using our true course and speed, we can determine from this table the approximate *true* wind direction and velocity, provided we know the *apparent* direction and velocity. Our wind indicator or owner's flag will give us the apparent direction and our anemometer will give us the apparent velocity.

## The Beaufort Scale

Another method is to estimate the strength of the wind in terms of the *Beaufort Scale* of Wind Force. Visually we can observe the sea condition and note the Beaufort number to which it corresponds (see Table 12-3). The range of wind velocity represented by each force number on the Beaufort scale is shown in the extreme left-hand column of Table 12-3.

*Wind direction* can be judged by observing the direction from which the smallest ripples are coming, since these ripples always run with the wind, responding instantly to changes in wind direction.

We don't need to determine wind direction and velocity with great precision, but reasonable estimates are helpful in preparing our own local forecasts. Estimating direction to two points is sufficient; within one Beaufort number is enough for velocity. By observing wind direction and velocity regularly and making a record of them we can obtain clues concerning potential weather developments as the wind shifts direction and changes its velocity.

**TABLE 12-2**

# TRUE FORCE AND DIRECTION OF THE WIND FROM ITS APPARENT FORCE AND DIRECTION ON A BOAT UNDER WAY

| APPARENT WIND VELOCITY (Knots) | SPEED OF BOAT | | | | | | | |
|---|---|---|---|---|---|---|---|---|
| | **5 Knots** | | **10 Knots** | | **15 Knots** | | **20 Knots** | |
| | TRUE WIND | | TRUE WIND | | TRUE WIND | | TRUE WIND | |
| | Points off Bow | Velocity Knots | Points off Bow | Velocity Knots | Points off Bow | Velocity Knots | Points off Bow | Velocity Knots |
| **I. APPARENT WIND DIRECTION IS DEAD AHEAD** | | | | | | | | |
| Calm | D. As. | 5 K. | D. As. | 10 K. | D. As. | 15 K. | D. As. | 20 K. |
| 4 K. | D. As. | 1 K. | D. As. | 6 K. | D. As. | 11 K. | D. As. | 16 K. |
| 8 K. | D. Ah. | 3 K. | D. As. | 2 K. | D. As. | 7 K. | D. As. | 12 K. |
| 12 K. | D. Ah. | 7 K. | D. Ah. | 2 K. | D. As. | 3 K. | D. As. | 8 K. |
| 16 K. | D. Ah. | 11 K. | D. Ah. | 6 K. | D. Ah. | 1 K. | D. As. | 4 K. |
| 22 K. | D. Ah. | 17 K. | D. Ah. | 12 K. | D. Ah. | 7 K. | D. Ah. | 2 K. |
| 30 K. | D. Ah. | 25 K. | D. Ah. | 20 K. | D. Ah. | 15 K. | D. Ah. | 10 K. |
| 42 K. | D. Ah. | 37 K. | D. Ah. | 32 K. | D. Ah. | 27 K. | D. Ah. | 22 K. |
| 60 K. | D. Ah. | 55 K. | D. Ah. | 50 K. | D. Ah. | 45 K. | D. Ah. | 40 K. |
| **II. APPARENT WIND DIRECTION IS 4 POINTS (BROAD) OFF THE BOW** | | | | | | | | |
| 4 K. | 11 pts. | 4 K. | 14 pts. | 8 K. | 15 pts. | 12 K. | 15 pts. | 17 K. |
| 8 K. | 7 pts. | 6 K. | 11 pts. | 7 K. | 13 pts. | 11 K. | 14 pts. | 15 K. |
| 12 K. | 6 pts. | 9 K. | 9 pts. | 9 K. | 11 pts. | 11 K. | 13 pts. | 14 K. |
| 16 K. | 5 pts. | 13 K. | 7 pts. | 11 K. | 10 pts. | 12 K. | 11 pts. | 14 K. |
| 22 K. | 5 pts. | 19 K. | 6 pts. | 16 K. | 8 pts. | 15 K. | 9 pts. | 16 K. |
| 30 K. | 5 pts. | 27 K. | 6 pts. | 24 K. | 7 pts. | 22 K. | 8 pts. | 21 K. |
| 42 K. | 4 pts. | 39 K. | 5 pts. | 36 K. | 6 pts. | 33 K. | 6 pts. | 31 K. |
| 60 K. | 4 pts. | 57 K. | 5 pts. | 53 K. | 5 pts. | 51 K. | 6 pts. | 48 K. |
| **III. APPARENT WIND DIRECTION IS 8 POINTS OFF THE BOW (ABEAM)** | | | | | | | | |
| 4 K. | 13 pts. | 6 K. | 14 pts. | 11 K. | 15 pts. | 16 K. | 15 pts. | 20 K. |
| 8 K. | 11 pts. | 9 K. | 13 pts. | 13 K. | 14 pts. | 17 K. | 14 pts. | 22 K. |
| 12 K. | 10 pts. | 13 K. | 12 pts. | 16 K. | 13 pts. | 19 K. | 13 pts. | 23 K. |
| 16 K. | 10 pts. | 17 K. | 11 pts. | 19 K. | 12 pts. | 22 K. | 13 pts. | 26 K. |
| 22 K. | 9 pts. | 23 K. | 10 pts. | 24 K. | 11 pts. | 27 K. | 12 pts. | 30 K. |
| 30 K. | 9 pts. | 30 K. | 10 pts. | 32 K. | 10 pts. | 34 K. | 11 pts. | 36 K. |
| 42 K. | 9 pts. | 42 K. | 9 pts. | 43 K. | 10 pts. | 45 K. | 10 pts. | 47 K. |
| 60 K. | 8 pts. | 60 K. | 9 pts. | 61 K. | 9 pts. | 62 K. | 10 pts. | 63 K. |
| **IV. APPARENT WIND DIRECTION IS 12 POINTS OFF THE BOW (BROAD ON THE QUARTER)** | | | | | | | | |
| 4 K. | 14 pts. | 8 K. | 15 pts. | 13 K. | 15 pts. | 18 K. | 15 pts. | 23 K. |
| 8 K. | 14 pts. | 12 K. | 14 pts. | 17 K. | 15 pts. | 21 K. | 15 pts. | 26 K. |
| 12 K. | 13 pts. | 16 K. | 14 pts. | 20 K. | 14 pts. | 25 K. | 15 pts. | 30 K. |
| 16 K. | 13 pts. | 20 K. | 14 pts. | 24 K. | 14 pts. | 29 K. | 14 pts. | 33 K. |
| 22 K. | 13 pts. | 26 K. | 13 pts. | 30 K. | 14 pts. | 34 K. | 14 pts. | 39 K. |
| 30 K. | 13 pts. | 34 K. | 13 pts. | 38 K. | 13 pts. | 42 K. | 14 pts. | 46 K. |
| 42 K. | 12 pts. | 46 K. | 13 pts. | 50 K. | 13 pts. | 54 K. | 13 pts. | 58 K. |
| 60 K. | 12 pts. | 64 K. | 13 pts. | 67 K. | 13 pts. | 71 K. | 13 pts. | 75 K. |

## CONVERSION OF POINTS OFF BOW TO TRUE DIRECTION OF WIND

| POINTS OFF BOW | BOAT'S HEADING—TRUE | | | | | | | |
|---|---|---|---|---|---|---|---|---|
| | 000° | 045° | 090° | 135° | 180° | 225° | 270° | 315° |
| **I. WHEN WIND DIRECTION OBTAINED FROM TABLE ABOVE IS OFF STARBOARD BOW** | | | | | | | | |
| Dead Ahead | N | NE | E | SE | S | SW | W | NW |
| 4 points | NE | E | SE | S | SW | W | NW | N |
| 8 points | E | SE | S | SW | W | NW | N | NE |
| 12 points | SE | S | SW | W | NW | N | NE | E |
| Dead Astern | S | SW | W | NW | N | NE | E | SE |
| **II. WHEN WIND DIRECTION OBTAINED FROM TABLE ABOVE IS OFF PORT BOW** | | | | | | | | |
| Dead Ahead | N | NE | E | SE | S | SW | W | NW |
| 4 points | NW | N | NE | E | SE | S | SW | W |
| 8 points | W | NW | N | NE | E | SE | S | SW |
| 12 points | SW | W | NW | N | NE | E | SE | S |
| Dead Astern | S | SW | W | NW | N | NE | E | SE |

**TO USE THIS TABLE**

Abreviations: D. As. = Dead Astern. D. Ah. = Dead Ahead. K. = Knots. pts. = Points off bow.

1. **With Wind Direction Indicator:** Determine Apparent Wind Direction off the Bow.
2. **With Anemometer:** Determine Apparent Wind Velocity, in Knots.
3. **Enter Upper Part of Table:** Use portion for nearest Apparent Wind Direction Opposite Apparent Wind Velocity and under nearest Speed of Boat, read Wind Direction in Points off Bow and True Wind Velocity in Knots. Note whether True Wind Direction is off Starboard or Port Bow.
4. **Enter Lower Part of Table:** Use portion for proper Bow: Starboard or Port. Opposite Points off Bow and under Boat's True Heading, read True Wind Direction.
5. **Log:** Record True Wind Direction as obtained from Lower Part of Table and True Wind Velocity as obtained from Upper Part of Table in Boat's Weather Log.

**TABLE 12-3**

## DETERMINATION OF WIND SPEED BY SEA CONDITION

| Knots | Descriptive | Sea Conditions | Wind force (Beaufort) | Probable wave height (in ft.) |
|---|---|---|---|---|
| 0-1 | Calm | Sea smooth and mirror-like. | 0 | — |
| 1-3 | Light air | Scale-like ripples without foam crests. | 1 | ¼ |
| 4-6 | Light breeze | Small, short wavelets; crests have a glassy appearance and do not break. | 2 | ½ |
| 7-10 | Gentle breeze | Large wavelets; some crests begin to break; foam of glassy appearance. Occasional white foam crests. | 3 | 2 |
| 11-16 | Moderate breeze | Small waves, becoming longer; fairly frequent white foam crests. | 4 | 4 |
| 17-21 | Fresh breeze | Moderate waves, taking a more pronounced long form; many white foam crests; there may be some spray. | 5 | 6 |
| 22-27 | Strong breeze | Large waves begin to form; white foam crests are more extensive everywhere; there may be some spray. | 6 | 10 |
| 28-33 | Near gale | Sea heaps up and white foam from breaking waves begins to be blown in streaks along the direction of the wind; spindrift begins. | 7 | 14 |
| 34-40 | Gale | Moderately high waves of greater length; edges of crests break into spindrift; foam is blown in well-marked streaks along the direction of the wind. | 8 | 18 |
| 41-47 | Strong gale | High waves; dense streaks of foam along the direction of the wind; crests of waves begin to topple, tumble, and roll over; spray may reduce visibility. | 9 | 23 |
| 48-55 | Storm | Very high waves with long overhanging crests. The resulting foam in great patches is blown in dense white streaks along the direction of the wind. On the whole, the surface of the sea is white in appearance. The tumbling of the sea becomes heavy and shock-like. Visibility is reduced. | 10 | 29 |
| 56-63 | Violent Storm | Exceptionally high waves that may obscure small and medium-sized ships. The sea is completely covered with long white patches of foam lying along the direction of the wind. Everywhere the edges of the wave crests are blown into froth. Visibility reduced. | 11 | 37 |
| 64-71 | Hurricane | The air is filled with foam and spray. Sea completely white with driving spray; visibility very much reduced. | 12 | 45 |

(Courtesy U.S. Weather Bureau)

**FIG. 1236   A modern aneroid barometer, graduated in both millibars (inner scale) and inches of mercury (outer scale). Pointer indicates reading at last setting.**
(Courtesy Airguide Instrument Company)

## THE BAROMETER

Another weather instrument with which we are all familiar is the *aneroid barometer*. The one illustrated (fig. 1236) has several interesting features.

First, there are two *pressure scales*. Not a few of us are accustomed to thinking of barometric pressure in terms of *inches of mercury*, so the outer scale is graduated in these units. Weather maps are now printed with the pressures shown in *millibars* and many radio weather reports specify this value. Consequently, the inner scale is graduated in millibars, and so we don't have to worry about conversions between units.

Second, it is a rugged instrument, a feature not to be despised on board a 40-footer. It has a high order of accuracy.

Third, it has the usual reference hand, so we can keep track of changes in pressure.

The words "Fair—Change—Rain," in themselves, when they appear on the face of an aneroid barometer, are meaningless. It is not the actual barometric pressure that is so important in forecasting; it is the *direction* and *rate of change of pressure*. The words may be misleading if this fact is not clearly understood.

## How it is used

Now, a good barometer is a helpful instrument, *provided* a few things: provided we read it at regular intervals and keep a record of the readings; provided we remember that there is much more to weather than just barometric pressure.

An individual reading of the barometer tells us only the pressure being exerted by the atmosphere on the earth's surface at the particular point of observation. But, suppose we have logged the pressure readings at fairly regular intervals, as follows:

| Time | Pressure | Change |
|------|----------|--------|
| 0700 | 30.02 inches | — |
| 0800 | 30.00 | −0.02 |
| 0900 | 29.97 | −0.03 |
| 1000 | 29.93 | −0.04 |
| 1100 | 29.88 | −0.05 |
| 1200 | 29.82 | −0.06 |

The pressure is falling, at an increasing rate. Trouble is brewing. A fall of 0.02 inch per hour is a low rate of fall; consequently, this figure would not be particularly disturbing. But a fall of 0.05 inch per hour is a pretty high rate.

Next, there is a normal *daily change in pressure*. The pressure is usually at its maximum value about 1000 and 2200 each day, at its minimum value about 0400 and 1600. The variation between minimum and maximum may be as much as 0.05 inch change in these six-hour intervals (about 0.01 inch change per hour). Thus, when the pressure normally would increase about 0.03 inch (0700 to 1000) our pressure fell 0.09 inch.

Suppose, now, around 1200 we also observed that the wind was blowing from the NE with increasing force and that the barometer continued to fall at a high rate. A rocky lee shore close aboard would not be pleasant to contemplate as a severe northeast gale is on its way. On the other hand, given the same barometer reading of about 29.80, rising rapidly with the wind going to west, we could expect improving weather. Quite a difference.

## Barometer rules

A few general rules are often helpful. First, *foul* weather is usually forecast by a *falling* barometer with winds from the *east* quadrants; *clearing* and *fair* weather is usually forecast by winds shifting to *west* quadrants with a *rising* barometer. Second, there are the rules formerly printed on every Weather Bureau daily surface weather map:

"When the wind sets in from points between south and southeast and the barometer falls steadily, a storm is approaching from the west or northwest, and its center will pass near or north of the observer within 12 to 24 hours, with the wind shifting to northwest by way of south and southwest.

"When the wind sets in from points between east and northeast and the barometer falls steadily, a storm is approaching from the south or southwest, and its center will pass near or to the south of the observer within 12 to 24 hours, with the wind shifting to northwest by way of north.

"The rapidity of the storm's approach and its intensity will be indicated by the rate and amount of fall in the barometer."

There are some other generally useful barometer rules.

With our sling psychrometer we can determine the air temperature, so: a falling barometer and a rising thermometer often forecast rain; barometer and thermometer rising together often forecast fine weather. A slowly rising barometer forecasts settled weather; a steady, slow fall of pressure unsettled or wet weather.

## Barometric changes and wind velocity

We shall now give some rules relating barometric changes to changes in wind velocity. First, it is generally true that a *rapidly falling barometer* forecasts the development of strong winds. This is so because a falling barometer indicates the approach or development of a LOW, and the pressure gradient is usually steep in the neighborhood of a low-pressure center. On the other hand, a *rising barometer* is associated with the prospect of lighter winds to come. This is true because a rising barometer indicates the approach or development of a HIGH, and the pressure gradient is characteristically small in the neighborhood of a high-pressure center.

The barometer does not necessarily fall before or during a strong breeze. The wind often blows hard without any appreciable accompanying change in the barometer. This means that a steep pressure gradient exists (isobars close together, as seen on the weather map) but that the well-developed HIGH or LOW associated with the steep pressure gradient is practically stationary. In this case the wind may be expected to blow hard for some time; any slackening or change will take place gradually.

It not infrequently happens that the barometer falls quite rapidly, yet the wind remains comparatively light. If we remember the relation between wind velocity and pressure gradient, we conclude that the gradient must be comparatively small (isobars relatively far apart). The rapid fall of the barometer must be accounted for, then, in either one or both of two ways. Either a LOW with a weak pressure gradient on its forward side is approaching rapidly, or there is a rapid decrease of pressure taking place over the surrounding area, or both. In such a situation the pressure gradient at the rear of the LOW is often steep, and in that case strong winds will set in as soon as the barometer commences to rise. (It will rise rapidly under these circumstances.) The fact, however, that the barometer is now rising indicates that decreasing winds may soon be expected.

## The barometer and wind shifts

Nearly all extra-tropical cyclones display an unsymmetrical distribution of pressure. The pressure gradients are seldom the same in the front and rear of an extra-tropical cyclone. During the approach of a LOW the barometer alone gives no clue as to how many points the wind will shift and what velocity it will have after the passage of the low-pressure system. This is particularly applicable to situations in which the wind blows from a southerly direction while the barometer is falling. The cessation of the fall of the barometer will coincide with a *veering* (gradual or sudden) shift of the wind to a more westerly direction. Unfortunately, an observer having no information other than that supplied by his barometer cannot foretell the exact features of the change.

In using barometric indications for local forecasting it is most important to remember that weather changes are

FIG. 1237 Forecast—Severe Storm. Squall line clouds mark an advancing cold front; storm will be severe, with sharp, violent shift in wind, rain and probably lightning and thunder. (Courtesy U.S. Weather Bureau)

influenced by the characteristics of the earth's surface in our locality. All rules should be checked against experience in our own cruising waters before we can place full confidence in their validity.

## VISUAL WEATHER SIGNS

In addition to our instrumental weather observations there are certain *visual signs* that we can record. First, we should note the *visibility*. Haze, dust and smoke are nearly as important as fog. Many of the tiny particles which are suspended in the air and which reduce the visibility serve as nuclei on which water vapor can condense. Unless the water vapor in the air does condense, we can have no fog nor clouds. If haze thickens to a degree where it restricts the visibility to 3 miles, we have an indication that condensation has begun on the more active condensation nuclei and a warning that fog may soon develop.

Next, we should note the *clouds*. First, we ask ourselves: "What form (or forms) of cloud is (or are) present?" In order to answer this question we need to know the international system of cloud classification. This system resembles the method of classification used in the biological sciences. The different cloud types are given descriptive names which depend mainly upon appearance, but also sometimes upon the processes of formation as seen by an observer on the ground.

### Cloud forms classified

Despite an almost infinite variety of shapes and forms, it is possible to define 10 basic types. The following definitions are taken from the 1956 edition of the International Cloud Atlas.

**1. Cirrus (Ci)**—Detached clouds in the form of white, delicate filaments, or white or mostly white patches or narrow bands. These clouds have a fibrous (hair-like) appearance, or a silky sheen, or both.

**2. Cirrocumulus (Cc)**—Thin, white patch, sheet or layer of cloud without shading, composed of very small elements in the form of grains, ripples, etc., merged or separate, and

H. T. Floreen

FIG. 1238 Cumulus clouds of fair weather, illustrating situation in which atmosphere is stable a short distance above bases of clouds which, therefore, cannot grow vertically. Appearance of sky indicates fine weather will continue for at least another 6 hours.

more or less regularly arranged; most of the elements have an apparent width of less than one degree.

**3. Cirrostratus (Cs)**—Transparent, whitish cloud veil of fibrous (hair-like) or smooth appearance, totally or partly covering the sky, and generally producing halo phenomena.

**4. Altocumulus (Ac)**—White or gray, or both white and gray, patch, sheet or layer of cloud, generally with shading, composed of laminae, rounded masses, rolls, etc., which are sometimes partly fibrous or diffuse, and which may or may not be merged; most of the regularly arranged small elements usually have an apparent width between one and five degrees.

**5. Altostratus (As)**—Grayish or bluish cloud sheet or layer of striated, fibrous or uniform appearance, totally or partly covering the sky, and having parts thin enough to reveal the sun at least vaguely, as through ground glass. Altostratus does not show halo phenomena.

**6. Nimbostratus (Ns)**—Gray cloud layer, often dark, the appearance of which is rendered diffuse by more or less continuously falling rain or snow, which in most cases reaches the ground. It is thick enough throughout to blot out the sun. Low, ragged clouds frequently occur below the layer, with which they may or may not merge.

**7. Stratocumulus (Sc)**—Gray or whitish, or both gray and whitish, patch, sheet or layer of cloud which almost always has dark parts, composed of tessellations, rounded masses, rolls, etc., which are non-fibrous (except for virga) and which may or may not be merged; most of the regularly arranged small elements have an apparent width of more than five degrees.

**8. Stratus (St)**—Generally gray cloud layer with a fairly uniform base, which may give drizzle, ice prisms or snow grains. When the sun is visible through the cloud, its outline is clearly discernible. Stratus does not produce halo phenomena except, possibly, at very low temperatures. Sometimes stratus appears in the form of ragged patches.

**9. Cumulus (Cu)**—Detached clouds, generally dense and with sharp outlines, developing vertically in the form of rising mounds, domes or towers, of which the bulging upper part often resembles a cauliflower. The sunlit parts of these clouds are mostly brilliant white; their bases are relatively dark and nearly horizontal. Sometimes cumulus is ragged.

**10. Cumulonimbus (Cb)**—Heavy and dense cloud, with a considerable vertical extent, in the form of a mountain or huge towers. At least part of its upper portion is usually smooth, or fibrous or striated, and nearly always flattened; this part often spreads out in the shape of an anvil or vast plume. Under the base of this cloud, which is often very dark, there are frequently low ragged clouds either merged

FIG. 1239 Semi-transparent altocumulus clouds. Clouds in this picture clearly show signs of evaporation; edges of individual elements are frayed and indistinct. This indicates continuing fair weather.

FIG. 1240 Altostratus clouds, together with some altocumulus, over Mt. Kisco, New York, 1655 EST, 11 February 1965. (Note aircraft condensation trail in lower left portion of photograph.) At this time a LOW was centered over southeastern Missouri, moving northeastward. Rain began to fall about 7 hours after picture was taken.
(Photograph by Caroline S. Emmons)

with it or not, and precipitation, sometimes in the form of virga (precipitation trails).

## Significance of changing cloud forms

Having identified the cloud form (or forms) present in the sky, we should next note whether the clouds are *increasing* or *decreasing* in amount, and whether they are *lowering* or *lifting*. In general, thickening and lowering of a cloud layer, be it a layer of cirrostratus, altocumulus or altostratus, is a sign of approaching wet weather. On the other hand, when a layer of clouds shows signs of evaporation, that is, when holes or openings begin to appear in a layer of altostratus, or the elements of an altocumulus layer are frayed and indistinct at the edges, we have an indication of improving weather or, at least, delay of the development of foul weather.

Finally, we should note the *sequence of cloud forms* during the past few hours. Cirrus clouds are frequently the advance agents of an approaching extra-tropical cyclone, especially if they are followed by a layer of cirrostratus. In this case the problem is to forecast the track the low-pressure center will take to one side or the other, the nearness of approach of the center and the intensity of the low.

As the clouds thicken steadily from Ci to Cs and from Cs to As, we naturally expect further development to Ns with its rain or snow. There are usually contrary indications if such is not to be the case, or if the precipitation will arrive late, amount to little and end soon, or will come in two brief periods separated by several hours of mild, more or less sunny, weather.

If the northern horizon remains clear until a layer of altostratus clouds overspreads most of the sky, the low-pressure center will probably be passing to the south without bringing precipitation. If the northern horizon is slow in clouding up but becomes covered by the time the cloud sheet is principally As, there will probably be some precipitation but not much. If the cloud sheet, after increasing to As, breaks up into Ac and the sky above is seen to have lost most of its covering of Cs, the low-pressure area is either weakening or passing on to the north.

The approach of a squall line accompanied by thunderstorms may be detected an hour or more in advance by observing the thin white arch of the cirrus border to the anvil top of the approaching cumulonimbus cloud. The atmosphere ahead of a squall line is often so hazy that only this whitish arch will reveal the presence of a moderately distant Cb, for the shadowed air under the dense anvil will be invisible behind the sunlit hazy blue air near the observer. Thus this part of the sky will appear to be clear and will resemble the blue sky above the cirrus arch.

## THE WEATHER LOG

Although the latest Weather Bureau forecasts are readily available to us via the medium of radio, it is often helpful to keep a record of our own observations of clouds and weather as they develop. This procedure will enable us to check the reliability of the latest prediction. Occasionally the professional forecaster misjudges the future rate of travel of the weather pattern, which may move faster or

**TABLE 12-4A Boat Weather Log.**

```
                    BOAT WEATHER LOG


Yacht_____At/Passage_____to_____
Day____Date_____Time Zone_____Skipper_____
1.  Latest Weather Map: Date____Time_____Summary of forecast and
    of principal regional weather features:_____

    _____
    _____
    _____

2.  Radio Weather Reports Received (state source and time):_____

    _____
    _____
    _____
    _____

3.  Local Weather Observations (see over for record)

4.  Remarks and Local Forecast for Next____Hours (state time fore-
    cast effective):_____

    _____
    _____
    _____
    _____
    _____
```

**TABLE 12-4B Local Weather Observations.**

```
                LOCAL WEATHER OBSERVATIONS

Time -- ZT, Navy Style        :   :   :   :   :   :
Latitude - degrees, minutes   :   :   :   :   :   :
Longitude -    "       "      :   :   :   :   :   :
Course - degrees psc          :   :   :   :   :   :
       -   "    true          :   :   :   :   :   :
Speed - Knots                 :   :   :   :   :   :

Barometer - in. or mb.        :   :   :   :   :   :
          - tendency          :   :   :   :   :   :
Clouds - form                 :   :   :   :   :   :
       - moving from          :   :   :   :   :   :
       - amount               :   :   :   :   :   :
       - changing to          :   :   :   :   :   :
Sea - condition               :   :   :   :   :   :
    - swells                  :   :   :   :   :   :
    - moving from             :   :   :   :   :   :
Temperatures - air, dry bulb  :   :   :   :   :   :
             - dewpoint       :   :   :   :   :   :
             - water          :   :   :   :   :   :
Visibility                    :   :   :   :   :   :
Wind - direction, true        :   :   :   :   :   :
     - shifting to            :   :   :   :   :   :
     - velocity, true         :   :   :   :   :   :
     - force (Beaufort)       :   :   :   :   :   :
Weather - present             :   :   :   :   :   :
```

more slowly than anticipated. (This is known as an error of timing.) Or there may occur a new, unforeseen development in the pattern.

Table 12-4 shows a form of *Weather Log* which is similar to that used in the Weather Course of the United States Power Squadrons. Table 12-4 A is the face sheet, Table 12-4 B the reverse side. The first weather items recorded are based on a perusal of the latest weather map (if available to us) and a summary of radio reports received. Then we use the reverse side to jot down our local observations. Sufficient columns are available to permit the entry of these data six times during one 24-hour day, or at four-hour intervals. Entries may be made using the standard weather code symbols or any other way we choose, provided we use the same system consistently.

From these records we can estimate in what way and to what extent the actual weather during the next few hours is likely to differ from the official forecast.

FIG. 1241 Semi-transparent layer of altostratus clouds over Mt. Kisco, New York, 1445 EST, 14 February 1965, looking south-southwestward. Sun is dimly visible. Later in the afternoon, altostratus layer thickened and lowered. Light snow began to fall about 6 hours after picture was taken.     (Photograph by Caroline S. Emmons)

FIG. 1241-A Squall line approaching Mt. Kisco, N.Y., late afternoon of 27 July 1965. View at left looking toward WNW, center and right toward NW. Time interval between pictures approximately three minutes. Thunderstorm overhead one hour later.
(Photographs by Caroline S. Emmons.)

## Appendix

DISSEMINATION OF STORM WARNINGS
AND ROUTINE WEATHER INFORMATION

After much preparatory work and consultation with marine groups, yacht clubs, shipping agencies and other coastal interests, a new and simplified system of Coastal Warning Displays was put into effect January 1, 1958 by the U. S. Weather Bureau.

Under this method, only four separate signals are used during the day. During the night, only four comparable lantern signals are used for Small Craft, Gale, Storm, and Hurricane warnings.

The Weather Bureau emphasizes that these visual storm warnings displayed along the coast are supplementary to —and not a replacement for—the written advisories and warnings given prompt and wide distribution by press, radio and television. In most cases, important details of the forecasts and warnings in regard to the time, intensity, duration, and direction of storms cannot be given satisfactorily through visual signals alone.

Following is a detailed explanation of the new signals:

**Small Craft Warning:** One red pennant displayed by day and a red light above a white light at night to indicate winds up to 38 mph (33 knots) and/or sea conditions dangerous to small craft operations are forecast for the area.

**Gale Warning:** Two red pennants displayed by day and a white light above a red light at night to indicate winds ranging from 39 to 54 mph (34 to 47 knots) are forecast.

**Storm Warning:** A single square red flag with black center displayed by day and two red lights at night to indicate winds 48 knots (55 mph) and above *(no matter how high the velocity)* are forecast for the area. NOTE—If winds are associated with a tropical cyclone (hurricane) the *storm warning* display indicates forecast winds of 48 to 63 knots (55 to 73 mph). The *hurricane warning* is displayed only in connection with a tropical cyclone (hurricane).

**Hurricane Warning:** Two square red flags with black centers displayed by day and a white light between two red lights at night to indicate that winds 74 mph (64 knots) and above are forecast for the area.

The term *Small Craft Warning* needs some explanation. In the first place, small craft, as defined by the Weather Bureau, consist of "small boats, yachts, tugs, barges with little freeboard, or any other low-powered craft." In the second place, a small-craft warning does not distinguish between the expectation of a general, widespread, all-day blow of 25 knots or more and, for example, a forecast of the occurrence of isolated, late-afternoon thunder-squalls in which winds dangerous to small craft will be localized and of short duration. It is up to the individual skipper to deduce from his own observations, supplemented by any information he can obtain from radio broadcasts about the current over-all weather picture, to which type of situation the warning applies and to plan his day's cruise accordingly.

Storm warnings and storm advisories issued by the U.S. Weather Bureau are broadcast by designated United States Naval and Coast Guard radio stations. A large number of commercial radio stations also broadcast storm warnings, although at somewhat irregular intervals.

In 1945 the display of storm warning signals from lightships was authorized. These signals consist of the standard Weather Bureau flag hoists, displayed by day. No night signals are displayed. The storm warning signals are flown only while the lightships are on station, not while proceeding to and from station.

**VHF-FM Broadcasts:** The Weather Bureau now has a service at many locations of *continuous* broadcasts on 162.55 MHz of reports and forecasts with particular emphasis on marine use. New tapes are prepared every few hours.

These can be received on regular VHF sets, on inexpensive transistor receivers, and on some newer AM-FM receivers and MF-band radiotelephones. The broadcasts are of excellent quality and are most useful to boatmen.

FIG. 1242 **SMALL CRAFT, GALE, STORM AND HURRICANE WARNINGS**

RED

RED and BLACK

**DAY**

SMALL CRAFT     GALE     STORM     HURRICANE

**NIGHT**

RED

WHITE

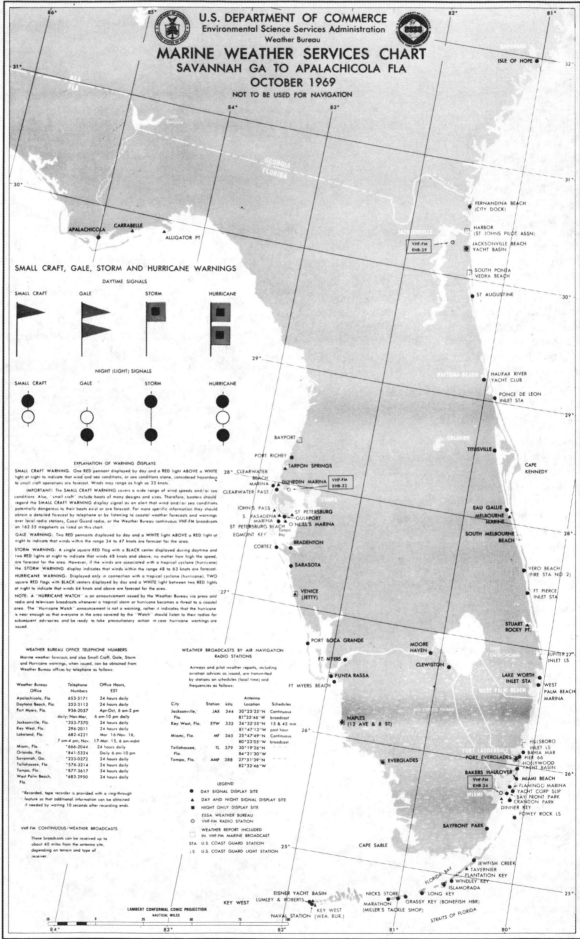

## MARINE WEATHER SERVICES CHARTS

Coast Guard vessels now display storm warning signals. Headquarters of the Coast Guard are supplied with weather information by the Weather Bureau and Coast Guard vessels receive instructions to fly the proper signals when bad weather is approaching.

The shore stations where storm warning signals are displayed are prominently marked on the *Marine Weather Services Charts,* a series which is published annually by the Weather Bureau. These charts, of which fig. 1243 is an example, also contain detailed information concerning the times of weather broadcasts from commercial stations, the radio frequencies of marine broadcast stations, the specific type of storm warnings issued and the visual display signals (already described and illustrated in the text above) which are used in connection with the warnings. This series consists of fourteen charts, twelve of which cover the coastal waters of the United States and the Great Lakes. The remaining two charts are for (a) the Hawaiian Islands, and (b) Puerto Rico and the Virgin Islands. They can be purchased from the Superintendent of Documents, Government Printing Office, Washington, D. C. 20402.

Yachtsmen will find much interesting weather information on the various Pilot Charts of the North Atlantic and North Pacific Oceans issued by the Oceanographic Office of the Navy Department. The Pilot Charts show average monthly wind and weather conditions over the oceans and in addition contain a vast amount of supplemental data on subjects closely allied to weather.

## WIND FORCE—AND ITS EFFECT ON THE SEA

Boatmen, like mariners at sea, frequently use the Beaufort Scale to log wind speed and the condition of the sea. Too often the description of sea conditions relies solely upon a verbal statement like "moderate waves, large waves, moderately high waves" (column 3, Table 12-3) which leaves the boatman pretty much "at sea" in trying to visualize exactly what these relative terms imply.

England's Meteorological Office has solved this problem by issuing a State of Sea card (M.O. 688A) with photographs to accompany each of the descriptions of thirteen wind forces of the Beaufort Scale. Thus the observer has a guide in estimating wind strength (*in knots*) when making weather reports or in logging sea conditions. Fetch, depth of water, swell, heavy rain, tide and the lag effect between the wind getting up and the sea increasing, may also affect the appearance of the sea. Range of wind speed and the mean wind speed are given for each force. By special permission, we are privileged to reproduce (figure 1244, page 248) seven of these photographs (Forces 1, 3, 5, 6, 8, 10, 12). Forces 0, 2, 4, 7, 9, and 11, though not illustrated, may be estimated in relation to those above and below them in the scale.

→

This table shows the velocity of sound at various air temperatures. Strictly speaking, the table is valid only for dry air, i.e., air containing no water vapor. However, the effect of water vapor on the speed of sound is quite small, so that the values in the table are entirely suitable for use in ordinary, rough calculations.

---

| TABLE 12-5 |
|---|
| **WIND PRESSURE AT VARIOUS WIND VELOCITIES** |
| (Air temperature 50°F, barometric pressure 1000 mbs.) |

| WIND VELOCITY (Knots) | WIND PRESSURE (Lbs. Per Square Foot) |
|---|---|
| 0 | 0.0 |
| 5 | 0.1 |
| 10 | 0.3 |
| 15 | 0.8 |
| 20 | 1.3 |
| 25 | 2.1 |
| 30 | 3.1 |
| 35 | 4.2 |
| 40 | 5.5 |
| 45 | 6.9 |
| 50 | 8.5 |
| 55 | 10.3 |
| 60 | 12.3 |

This table gives the wind pressure exerted on the windward side of a flat surface oriented at right angles to the wind. The values in the table have been computed for air temperature equal to 50°F and barometric pressure equal to 1000 millibars. At greater barometric pressures and lower air temperature the wind pressure corresponding to a given wind velocity will be somewhat greater; at higher air temperatures and lower barometric pressures, somewhat less.

---

| TABLE 12-6 |
|---|
| **VELOCITY OF SOUND IN DRY AIR** |

| AIR TEMPERATURE | SOUND VELOCITY | |
|---|---|---|
| °F | Feet per second | Knots |
| 100 | 1160 | 687 |
| 95 | 1155 | 684 |
| 90 | 1149 | 681 |
| 85 | 1144 | 678 |
| 80 | 1139 | 675 |
| 75 | 1133 | 671 |
| 70 | 1128 | 668 |
| 65 | 1123 | 665 |
| 60 | 1117 | 662 |
| 55 | 1112 | 659 |
| 50 | 1107 | 656 |
| 45 | 1101 | 653 |
| 40 | 1096 | 649 |
| 35 | 1090 | 646 |
| 30 | 1084 | 642 |
| 25 | 1079 | 639 |
| 20 | 1073 | 635 |
| 15 | 1067 | 632 |
| 10 | 1062 | 629 |
| 5 | 1057 | 626 |
| 0 | 1051 | 622 |
| −5 | 1045 | 619 |
| −10 | 1040 | 616 |
| −15 | 1034 | 613 |
| −20 | 1028 | 609 |
| −25 | 1022 | 605 |
| −30 | 1016 | 601 |
| −35 | 1010 | 598 |
| −40 | 1004 | 595 |

**FORCE 1**—Wind speed 1-3 kt.; mean 2 kt.

**FORCE 3**—Wind speed 7-10 kt.; mean 9 kt.

**FORCE 5**—Wind speed 17-21 kt.; mean 18 kt.

**FORCE 6**—Wind speed 22-27 kt.; mean 24 kt.

**FORCE 8**—Wind speed 34-40 kt.; mean 37 kt.

**FORCE 10**—Wind speed 48-55 kt.; mean 52 kt.

## FIG. 1244 — HOW THE SEA LOOKS IN WINDS OF VARYING FORCE

Wind forces used in these illustrations are based on the Beaufort Scale. See column 3, table 12-3, for verbal description of the state of the sea for Forces 0-12.

(All photographs Crown Copyright, by R. R. Baxter, except Force 10, J. Hodkinson, and Force 12, G.P.O. Reproduced by permission of the Controller of Her Brittanic Majesty's Stationery Office.)

**FORCE 12**—Wind speed 64-71 kt.; mean 68 kt.

FIG. 1301  Typical spherical compass

# CHAPTER 13

*Planning a voyage,*
*or when under way,*
*the navigator or the*
*small boat pilot is always*
*concerned with direction*
*and distance.*
*Methods of determining*
*and recording distance*
*are thoroughly*
*covered elsewhere in*
*this book. This chapter*
*is about direction*
*and, more particularly,*
*about the most commonly*
*used direction*
*indicator afloat,*
*the mariner's compass.*

# THE MARINER'S COMPASS

FIG. 1302  Lines of force, bar magnet

## Why It Works

The operating principle is the behavior of a freely suspended bar magnet.

A permanent bar magnet has two poles, conventionally labeled north or south, in accordance with usage. The so-called force of the magnet is apparently concentrated at each of these poles. Actually it exists in the three-dimensional space, called the field, around the bar, roughly as shown in fig. 1302 and is presumed to consist of innumerable *lines of force,* a few of which are pictured. Another smaller magnet, brought into this field and free to move, will align itself along a line of force of the larger magnet.

The earth has only some of the properties of a large bar magnet. Fig. 1303. A bar magnet freely suspended in the

FIG. 1303  Lines of force, earth

267

earth's magnetic field will align itself along one of the earth's lines of force and thus establish a *direction*. As will appear later this direction will not necessarily be north or south, but at any particular point on the earth, for practical navigation, it may be considered relatively constant for periods of several years. It is true that the direction is always changing, has even a diurnal oscillation, but with occasional exceptions *(see the discussion of variation)* these movements are of an order far too miniscule to affect what is indicated by the best of mariner's compasses at any given location. The changes in the indicated direction when the compass is moved many miles to another place will be discussed in due course.

This fact, that a freely suspended bar magnet stably indicates a direction, is the secret of the operation of the mariner's compass. It should be remembered such an indicated direction is generally neither geographic north or south, nor the true direction of the magnetic pole. Nonetheless, it is relatively *constant at a place*. The navigator usually has at hand ready information and rapid means of converting what his compass shows to true directions. He knows that if the magnetic effects of his ship be

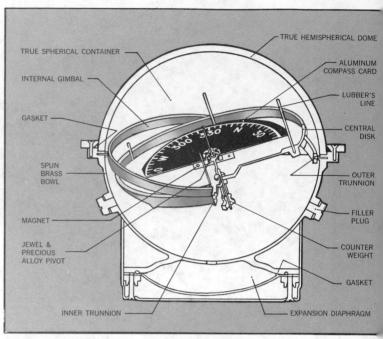

FIG. 1304 Compass with internal gimbal ring
Courtesy DANFORTH/WHITE

neutralized *(see Chapter 14)* his compass is a magnetic direction finder; that its 'pointer' is aligned with one of the earth's lines of force. This line of force is called the *magnetic meridian* of the place; it will be referred to later.

## Construction

Few wearers can describe or need to know the construction of a watch. Some know it contains a motor, an escapement and a gear train. All know it has a dial and hands. A compass has a dial and a hand too. Unlike a watch, the 'hand' of a typical mariner's compass *moves around the periphery of its 'dial.'* The 'hand' is a mark called the *lubber's line,* painted on the inside of the compass bowl or is a stile or a pointer fastened to its upper edge. The 'dial' is the compass card.

Several long thin permanent magnets, each enclosed in a non-magnetic tube, are affixed, parallel to each other, to a light non-magnetic wire frame. Like poles of the magnets are adjacent. In some modern instruments there is a different type of magnetic element. An annular disk, bearing suitable graduations, *the card,* is fastened to the frame above the magnets. Centrally placed under the frame is a bearing. Usually a float is attached to the frame to reduce wear on the pivot and bearing. This whole assembly serves as the dial. The user looks at its peripheral graduations.

The bowl, with its lubberline 'hand,' has a pivot atop a post in its center. See fig. 1306. The frame bearing rests on this pivot. A top of transparent material, either flat or hemispherical, is rigidly fastened with a liquid-proof seal to the top of the bowl. Through a pluggable aperture, the bowl is filled with a non-freezing liquid, formerly alcohol, but now usually a special oil. An expansion chamber is provided to allow for the effects of temperature changes. The sealed unit is mounted in gimbals so as to remain level in a seaway. In some instruments the gimbal mounting is inside the bowl. See fig. 1304.

FIG. 1305 Navy-type 7½" compass

FIG. 1306 Cross section, typical compass

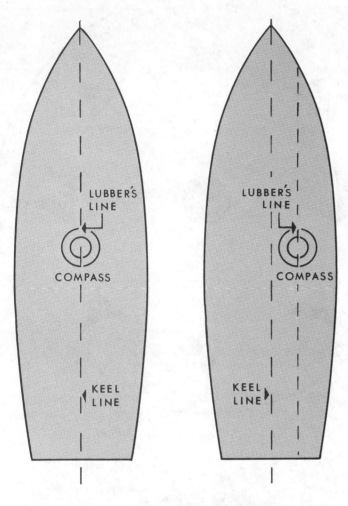

FIG. 1307 Mounting parallel to keel

## Mounting ───────────

These are principles only. Most strongly is it suggested that pages 287-291 be read before using *any* tools.

The compass should be securely fastened aboard. A line through the lubber's line and the center of the card must be parallel to the keel. See fig. 1307. The instrument should be level, and so placed that it is within easy and unobstructed view of the helmsman. See fig. 1308. It must be lighted for night use with a minimum of illumination, preferably red. Magnetic material in its vicinity should be minimal. Wires near it, carrying direct current, should be twisted. Equipment generating strong magnetic fields should be as far away from it as is practical.

A box compass, fig. 1309, not permanently mounted, should have some permanent receptacle to receive it, so that upon each occasion of use it is correctly positioned.

Ships and larger yachts mount the compass in a stand called the binnacle, fig. 1404 though the term binnacle list does not indicate the need to shore up one side.

Photo by Dale Phillips

FIG. 1309  Box Compass

FIG. 1308  Cruiser "bridge" or steering station showing compass mounted amidships and off centerline

## The Card

As previously stated the card serves as a dial; the lubber's line as a hand. A clock has a zero reference point. Time is told by observing the position of two or more hands relative to the twelfth or zero hour. Actually we observe an angle, but long ago each of us learned to ignore the angle, to read immediately what we see as time. The lubber's line indicates an angle, a direction relative to that of the north or zero point of the card, though most of us think not of the angle but of the direction. We think of east as a direction, paying no thought to the fact that it is one-quarter of a single clockwise rotation from north.

Modern compass cards are graduated in degrees, clockwise from north. Marks may be at each degree or for smaller craft at five-degree intervals. Numerals may be printed every ten degrees from 10° to 350°; every fifteen degrees from 15° to 345° or every thirty degrees from 30° to 330°, see figs. 1301, 1310 and 1311.

Still extant are older compasses with cards graduated only ninety degrees to the east and to the west from north and from south. In that system N 90°E means the same as S 90°E, i.e. East.

For many years the card bore only points. There are eight points to a quadrant; thus a point equals 11¼°. As the building of better hulls and the development of the fore and aft rig enabled vessels to hold course with greater accuracy, came need to use smaller units of arc. Each point was divided into fourths, giving rise to quarter-points, about 2¾°. There were various methods of naming these quarter-points. There was a time when no man was a salt unless he could recite them forwards and backwards all around the card starting from any given one. The age of steam brought the ability to hold a course regardless of all but the stronger winds and the need for a smaller division of the 'dial.' So the sexagesimal system came to the helmsman.

The cardinal points, North, East, South and West, and the intercardinals, Northeast, Southeast, Southwest and Northwest are still in common use as rough directions and as descriptions of wind direction. The combination points, as ENE, NNE and so on are but little used and as for the by-points, NxE, NExN, they and their like seem but to embellish (often erroneously) some TV or radio

**FIG. 1310  Compass Card—degrees, cardinals and intercardinals**

**FIG. 1311  Compass Card—degrees, points and quarter points**

drama. For those who do not wish to forget the past, and for those neophytes in sail who must learn points for ease in steering their wind-driven craft, there is included a table of comparisons of the various systems of nomenclature, fig. 1312.

Many modern compasses do label the cardinal and the intercardinal points, see fig. 1310, but the ensuing work here will be carried out in degrees.

## CONVERSION TABLE—POINTS TO DEGREES

| | Points | Angular measure | | Points | Angular measure |
|---|---|---|---|---|---|
| **NORTH TO EAST** | | ° ′ ″ | **SOUTH TO WEST** | | ° ′ ″ |
| North | 0 | 0 00 00 | South | 16 | 180 00 00 |
| N¼E | ¼ | 2 48 45 | S¼W | 16¼ | 182 48 45 |
| N½E | ½ | 5 37 30 | S½W | 16½ | 185 37 30 |
| N¾E | ¾ | 8 26 15 | S¾W | 16¾ | 188 26 15 |
| N by E | 1 | 11 15 00 | S by W | 17 | 191 15 00 |
| N by E¼E | 1¼ | 14 03 45 | S by W¼W | 17¼ | 194 03 45 |
| N by E½E | 1½ | 16 52 30 | S by W½W | 17½ | 196 52 30 |
| N by E¾E | 1¾ | 19 41 15 | S by W¾W | 17¾ | 199 41 15 |
| NNE | 2 | 22 30 00 | SSW | 18 | 202 30 00 |
| NNE¼E | 2¼ | 25 18 45 | SSW¼W | 18¼ | 205 18 45 |
| NNE½E | 2½ | 28 07 30 | SSW½W | 18½ | 208 07 30 |
| NNE¾E | 2¾ | 30 56 15 | SSW¾W | 18¾ | 210 56 15 |
| NE by N | 3 | 33 45 00 | SW by S | 19 | 213 45 00 |
| NE¾N | 3¼ | 36 33 45 | SW¾S | 19¼ | 216 33 45 |
| NE½N | 3½ | 39 22 30 | SW½S | 19½ | 219 22 30 |
| NE¼N | 3¾ | 42 11 15 | SW¼S | 19¾ | 222 11 15 |
| NE | 4 | 45 00 00 | SW | 20 | 225 00 00 |
| NE¼E | 4¼ | 47 48 45 | SW¼W | 20¼ | 227 48 45 |
| NE½E | 4½ | 50 37 30 | SW½W | 20½ | 230 37 30 |
| NE¾E | 4¾ | 53 26 15 | SW¾W | 20¾ | 233 26 15 |
| NE by E | 5 | 56 15 00 | SW by W | 21 | 236 15 00 |
| NE by E¼E | 5¼ | 59 03 45 | SW by W¼W | 21¼ | 239 03 45 |
| NE by E½E | 5½ | 61 52 30 | SW by W½W | 21½ | 241 52 30 |
| NE by E¾E | 5¾ | 64 41 15 | SW by W¾W | 21¾ | 244 41 15 |
| ENE | 6 | 67 30 00 | WSW | 22 | 247 30 00 |
| ENE¼E | 6¼ | 70 18 45 | WSW¼W | 22¼ | 250 18 45 |
| ENE½E | 6½ | 73 07 30 | WSW½W | 22½ | 253 07 30 |
| ENE¾E | 6¾ | 75 56 15 | WSW¾W | 22¾ | 255 56 15 |
| E by N | 7 | 78 45 00 | W by S | 23 | 258 45 00 |
| E¾N | 7¼ | 81 33 45 | W¾S | 23¼ | 261 33 45 |
| E½N | 7½ | 84 22 30 | W½S | 23½ | 264 22 30 |
| E¼N | 7¾ | 87 11 15 | W¼S | 23¾ | 267 11 15 |
| **EAST TO SOUTH** | | | **WEST TO NORTH** | | |
| East | 8 | 90 00 00 | West | 24 | 270 00 00 |
| E¼S | 8¼ | 92 48 45 | W¼N | 24¼ | 272 48 45 |
| E½S | 8½ | 95 37 30 | W½N | 24½ | 275 37 30 |
| E¾S | 8¾ | 98 26 15 | W¾N | 24¾ | 278 26 15 |
| E by S | 9 | 101 15 00 | W by N | 25 | 281 15 00 |
| ESE¾E | 9¼ | 104 03 45 | WNW¾W | 25¼ | 284 03 45 |
| ESE½E | 9½ | 106 52 30 | WNW½W | 25½ | 286 52 30 |
| ESE¼E | 9¾ | 109 41 15 | WNW¼W | 25¾ | 289 41 15 |
| ESE | 10 | 112 30 00 | WNW | 26 | 292 30 00 |
| SE by E¾E | 10¼ | 115 18 45 | NW by W¾W | 26¼ | 295 18 45 |
| SE by E½E | 10½ | 118 07 30 | NW by W½W | 26½ | 298 07 30 |
| SE by E¼E | 10¾ | 120 56 15 | NW by W¼W | 26¾ | 300 56 15 |
| SE by E | 11 | 123 45 00 | NW by W | 27 | 303 45 00 |
| SE¾E | 11¼ | 126 33 45 | NW¾W | 27¼ | 306 33 45 |
| SE½E | 11½ | 129 22 30 | NW½W | 27½ | 309 22 30 |
| SE¼E | 11¾ | 132 11 15 | NW¼W | 27¾ | 312 11 15 |
| SE | 12 | 135 00 00 | NW | 28 | 315 00 00 |
| SE¼S | 12¼ | 137 48 45 | NW¼N | 28¼ | 317 48 45 |
| SE½S | 12½ | 140 37 30 | NW½N | 28½ | 320 37 30 |
| SE¾S | 12¾ | 143 26 15 | NW¾N | 28¾ | 323 26 15 |
| SE by S | 13 | 146 15 00 | NW by N | 29 | 326 15 00 |
| SSE¾E | 13¼ | 149 03 45 | NNW¾W | 29¼ | 329 03 45 |
| SSE½E | 13½ | 151 52 30 | NNW½W | 29½ | 331 52 30 |
| SSE¼E | 13¾ | 154 41 15 | NNW¼W | 29¾ | 334 41 15 |
| SSE | 14 | 157 30 00 | NNW | 30 | 337 30 00 |
| S by E¾E | 14¼ | 160 18 45 | N by W¾W | 30¼ | 340 18 45 |
| S by E½E | 14½ | 163 07 30 | N by W½W | 30½ | 343 07 30 |
| S by E¼E | 14¾ | 165 56 15 | N by W¼W | 30¾ | 345 56 15 |
| S by E | 15 | 168 45 00 | N by W | 31 | 348 45 00 |
| S¾E | 15¼ | 171 33 45 | N¾W | 31¼ | 351 33 45 |
| S½E | 15½ | 174 22 30 | N½W | 31½ | 354 22 30 |
| S¼E | 15¾ | 177 11 15 | N¼W | 31¾ | 357 11 15 |
| South | 16 | 180 00 00 | North | 32 | 360 00 00 |

**FIG. 1312**

**Conversion Table: points and degrees**

*(From BOWDITCH)*

## Variation

The point has been made that a freely suspended permanent magnet indicates a direction. That direction is, at any place, the vertical plane of the magnetic meridian. That the magnet may not be strictly horizontal and may dip slightly at one end is of no moment in the use of a mariner's compass.

In his normal day's work the navigator, or the small boat pilot, plotting his track on the chart, has need to know true directions, directions relative to the earth's geographic north. His courses and bearings are recorded with respect to the true north. His directional instrument, his mariner's compass, rarely indicates a direction as an angle referred to true north; always indicates an angle referred to the north point of the compass card, or compass north.

In a non-magnetic ship, one like the now non-existent CARNEGIE, a magnetic compass is subject only to the effect of the earth's magnetic field. In this unusual condition the north point of the compass card lies in the magnetic meridian. In general, the magnetic meridian does not coincide with the true meridian (which is the direction of the plane passing through the place and the geographic poles). There is an angle between them. This angle is termed variation. (V or Var)

The variation at any place is the angle there between the true meridian and the magnetic meridian. See fig. 1313. When that part of the magnetic meridian running towards the north magnetic pole lies to the east of the northern half of the true meridian, the variation is termed easterly. When it is to the west, the variation is westerly. Currently variation is expressed in degrees and minutes and labelled east or west, e.g. 7°30'W or 16°45'E. See fig. 1315. Its value may range from 0° to 180°.

Contrary to popular ideas the location of the magnetic poles is of little interest to the pilot or navigator. (Should he cruise in their vicinity he must perforce rely for directions on some instrument other than the magnetic compass.)

Variation is *not* the angle between the direction of the true and the magnetic poles. This supposition, a fictitious construct, useful in helping students to realize that true and magnetic north are usually in different directions, has been accepted by many as truth. Emphatically it is not so. It must be recognized as merely a learning aid, not a factual representation. The magnetic pole does not control the compass. The controlling force, as previously stated, is the earth's magnetic field. The compass magnet does not point to the magnetic pole.

Actually two antipodean points on the earth which are magnetic poles do not exist. There are north and south *magnetic polar areas* containing many magnetic poles, places where a dip needle would stand vertically. If this seems strange, give thought to pin-pointing the pole in the end of a bar magnet having a cross-sectional area of one square inch.

For scientific purposes rough approximate positions of theoretical north and south magnetic poles are computed from a large number of continuing observations made the

FIG. 1313 Defines Variation

FIG. 1315 Typical chart rose, modern

world over through many years. In 1955 these adopted positions were respectively in latitude 74°N, longitude 101°W and latitude 68°S, longitude 144°E. In 1960 the adopted positions were in latitude 75°N, longitude 101°W and latitude 67°S, longitude 143°E.

Several facts become obvious. A magnetic compass in 79°N, 101°W would show north in a direction to the southward of the instrument! The magnetic poles are not stationary. They are not diametrically opposed as one conceives of the geographic poles. They are far from the geographic poles. A magnetic meridian is generally not a segment of a great circle passing through the magnetic poles, since but one great circle passes through any two surface points not at the end of a diameter. Not so obvious but nonetheless true is that, again generally, the magnetic meridian is not part of a great circle from the place to the adjacent magnetic pole.

**Variation changes with location.** Cognizance of this is part of the duty of every navigator or pilot. If he neglects it he will be in trouble, see fig. 1314. At any place the amount of the variation is relatively constant, though there is usually a small annual change. The navigator finds this data on the chart he is using. On U.S. Coast and Geodetic Survey coastwise and harbor charts and on Lake Survey charts are printed compass roses suitably spaced for convenient use in plotting. See figs. 1315 and 1316. The rose has two concentric circular scales. The outer one is graduated in degrees and is oriented so that its zero point indicates true or geographic north. The inner one is graduated in degrees and points. Its zero point, identified by an arrow, shows the direction of the northern half of the magnetic meridian at that place. The angle at the center of the rose, between this arrow and the zero point of the outer, or true, rose, is the variation at *that place* for the year stated. This information is printed on the rose to the nearest 15', as "Var 14° 45'W (1964)," together with a further notation on the annual rate of change, to the nearest 1', and whether the variation increases or decreases as "ANNUAL INCREASE 2'," "ANNUAL DECREASE 10' or "NO ANNUAL CHANGE." See fig. 1315.

**Fig. 1314.**

The course from X to Y is 039° true. At X the variation is zero, so the magnetic course is also 039°. Because the variation changes with location, the magnetic course steered must be changed as the vessel enters regions having different variations. This must be done for each 1° change in the variation.

An airplane leaving X headed 039° magnetic for Y and held on this magnetic course would follow the curved track and ultimately be at Z, 150 miles from Y. To remain on the track XY, the magnetic course is altered in successive increments of 1°

On smaller scale charts covering larger areas, variation is shown by labeled *isogonic lines*. Every point on such a line has the same variation. That line joining all the points having zero variation is called the agonic line.

The annual rate of change printed on chart roses permits the chart user to estimate the variation to be expected at some date subsequent to the publishing of the chart. Estimates based on information more than five years old should be used with caution. The annual rate of change is not due to the motion of the magnetic poles. It cannot be predicted accurately. The rate on the chart *is the best guess* of its trend, based upon prior observations of the gradual alterations in the earth's ever-changing magnetic field. Within the suggested time limit the prediction is adequate

for nautical use. It is well to know that there are recorded instances of sudden major changes and indeed reversals in the rate. Here then is another reason for not using old charts. Charts are cheap. Stranding is not.

## LOCAL ATTRACTION

In some localities, fortunately few, over relatively small areas, the compass is subject to irregular magnetic disturbances in the earth's field. A striking example is found in Kingston Harbor, Ontario, Canada, where deflection of the compass may be as great as 45° in a distance of a mile and a half. This phenomenon is called local attraction. Charts of the area bear warnings to this effect.

**FIG. 1316** Typical chart rose, older type

## Deviation

Usually the mariner's compass is subject to magnetic forces additional to those of the earth. Magnetic materials aboard the vessel cause the compass to deviate from its ideal position in the magnetic meridian. This angular swing or rotation on its pivot is called *deviation* (*D* or *Dev*) fig. 1317.

Deviation is the angle between the magnetic meridian and a line from the pivot through the north point of the compass card. Its amount can range from 0° to 180°, though large values are not to be tolerated. It is described east or west as the compass north lies to the east or west of the north branch of the magnetic meridian, fig. 1317.

It will be recalled that variation changes with geographic position. *Deviation changes with the ship's heading.* The causes will be explained subsequently. To cope with these changes a vessel carries a deviation table, a tabulation of the respective deviations, usually for every 15° of heading by the ship's compass. (See page 282.) For added convenience a table is made on the basis of magnetic headings (page 285), or the two combined in a direct reading table (page 285).

Reducing deviation to a minimum brought into existence professional compass adjusters. A yachtsman may avail himself of their expert services, but with common sense and an understanding of the causes, may *compensate* his compass himself. *(See Chapter 14.)* Note that a compass is not 'corrected'; its deviations are reduced; the process is called *compensating*. Rarely is a compensated compass entirely free of deviation on all headings. As will be seen, there will be residuals, quite possibly of small practical significance.

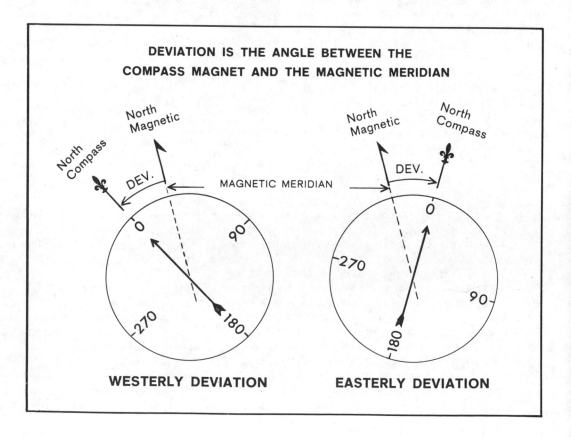

**FIG. 1317**
**Deviation defined**

# Compass Error _____

Because variation depends upon location and deviation upon the ship's heading, there are various possible combinations of the two, fig. 1318. The algebraic sum of the variation and the deviation is termed the *compass error,* CE. This is a semantic term. The compass is not in error. It is operating according to the forces that control its behavior. Compass error is merely another angle, that one between the direction of true north and the direction north as shown by the compass. Similarly to variation and deviation it is expressed in degrees and direction, i.e., 5°E or 7°W. The accomplished navigator uses this combined figure frequently in his work.

## THE APPLICATION OF VARIATION AND DEVIATION

A course is merely an angle. It is the angle which the keel, or a line on a chart, makes with some other line of reference. Three lines of reference have been established: the direction of true north or the true meridian; the direction of the magnetic meridian; and the direction of the north point of the compass. Thus *there are three ways to name a course,* true, magnetic or compass. Always to be kept in mind, and sometimes this is difficult for the novice, is that no matter how the course be named among these three, *it applies to only one track, one direction,* fig. 1319.

The helmsman steers by compass. Bearings are observed by, or relative to, a compass. On the other hand, the navigator customarily plots and logs his courses, bearings and lines of position as true. Hence there is need for continual interconversion between the three systems of nomenclature.

Like learning to read, to tell time by a watch, to finger a musical instrument, facility in making these conversions comes with practice. At first one reasons out the steps. Later, reasoning is dropped as the process becomes one of habit.

Two of the many mnemonic aids available to help the student master conversion will be described. Both are applicable only when courses are stated in the conventional 0° to 360° system now in most common use. One is verbal, the other pictorial.

FIG. 1318  Variation, Deviation and Compass Error

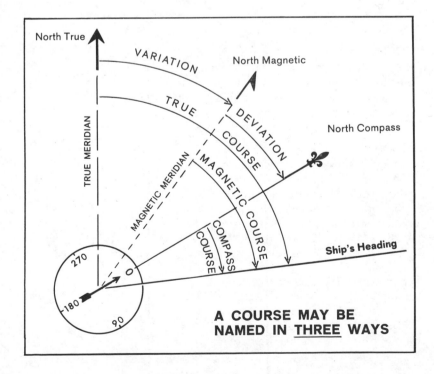

FIG. 1319  Three ways to name a Course

## VERBAL AID

Assume the correct method of expressing a course as true, since no variable is involved. See fig. 1320. Assume the magnetic course to be less correct an expression because variation is involved and finally for a similar reason assume the compass course to be the least correct method of expression. Call the conversion of a course from compass to magnetic and from magnetic to true 'correcting.' Then the rule is: *"When correcting, add easterly errors"* which may be shortened to *"Correct add east."*

*Example 1.* The magnetic course is 061° and the variation is 11°E.
*Required:* The true course, TC.
The conversion is one of 'correcting' and the variation is easterly, so the basic rule, *"Correct add east"* is used.
061° + 11° = 072°
*Answer:* TC 072° See fig. 1321.

The rule is easily altered for application to the three other operations of conversion by remembering that *always two and only two* words are to be changed for any application.

*Example 2.* The magnetic course is 068° and the variation is 14°W.
*Required:* The true course, TC.
The conversion is 'correcting,' and the variation is westerly. The rule becomes: *"Correct subtract west."* Two words were changed in the basic rule.
068° − 14° = 054°
*Answer:* TC 054°. See fig. 1322.

Call the process of conversion from true to magnetic, or from magnetic to compass 'uncorrecting.' Now the two other forms of the rule are: *"Uncorrect east subtract"* and *"Uncorrect west add."* Two and only two words have been changed in each case.

*Example 3.* The true course is 088°. The variation is 18°W and the deviation 12°W.
*Required:* The compass course, CC.
Both conversions are 'uncorrecting' and both 'errors' are westerly. The rule is: *"Uncorrect west add."*
088° + 18° + 12° = 118°
*Answer:* CC 118°. See fig. 1323.

*Example 4.* The true course is 107°. The variation is 14°E and the deviation is 11°E.
*Required:* The compass course, CC.
Both conversions are 'uncorrecting' and both 'errors' are easterly. The rule: *"Uncorrect east subtract."*
107° − 14° − 11° = 082°
*Answer:* CC 082°. See fig. 1324.

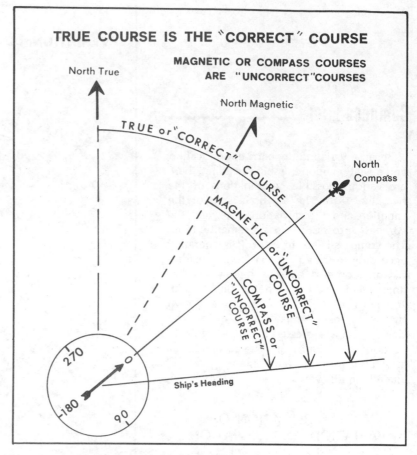

FIG. 1320  True Course is the "Correct" Course

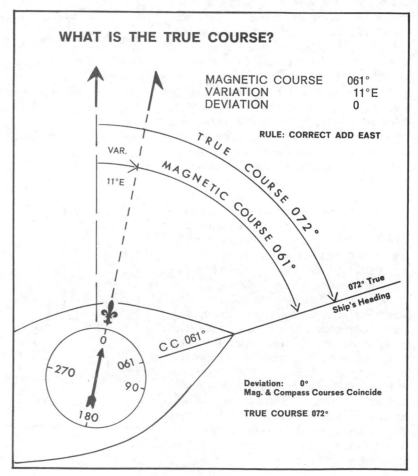

FIG. 1321  Problem What is the True Course Var E

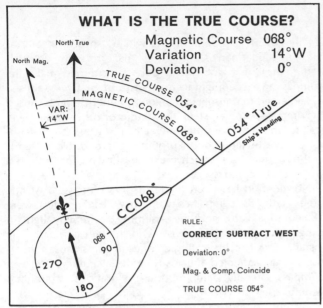

## WHAT IS THE TRUE COURSE?

Magnetic Course   068°
Variation   14°W
Deviation   0°

RULE:
**CORRECT SUBTRACT WEST**

Deviation: 0°

Mag. & Comp. Coincide

TRUE COURSE 054°

**FIG. 1322**   Problem What is the True Course Var W

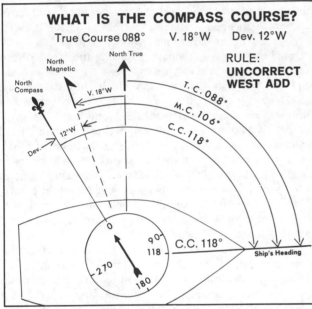

## WHAT IS THE COMPASS COURSE?

True Course 088°    V. 18°W    Dev. 12°W

RULE:
**UNCORRECT
WEST ADD**

C.C. 118°

**FIG. 1323**   Problem What is the Compass Course Var W, Dev W

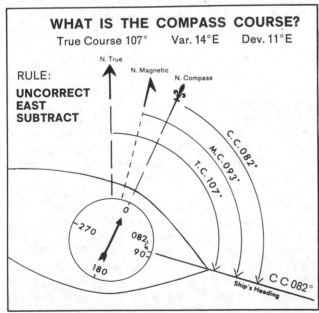

## WHAT IS THE COMPASS COURSE?

True Course 107°    Var. 14°E    Dev. 11°E

RULE:
**UNCORRECT
EAST
SUBTRACT**

CC 082°

**FIG. 1324**   Problem What is the Compass Course Var E, Dev E

$$W- \leftarrow T\ V\ M\ D\ C \rightarrow -E$$

## PICTORIAL SCHEMA

Vertically arrange the letters representing the three ways of naming a course, true, magnetic and compass, with the respective differences variation and deviation between them. Memorizing the reversal, Can Dead Men Vote Twice, may help to keep this arrangement in mind. On each side of the letters draw an arrow indicating the kind of conversion: on the left true to compass, on the right compass to true. Write in the appropriate arithmetic processes to be used with either easterly or westerly errors. The right side represents what has been called 'correcting' and the left side the reverse process, "uncorrecting." See fig. 1325. Memorize *DAW, DOWN ADD WEST* or WEST DOWN PLUS.

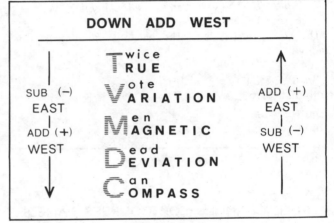

### DOWN ADD WEST

| | | |
|---|---|---|
| SUB (−) EAST | **T**wice **T**RUE | ADD (+) EAST |
| ADD (+) WEST | **V**ote **V**ARIATION | SUB (−) WEST |
| | **M**en **M**AGNETIC | |
| | **D**ead **D**EVIATION | |
| | **C**an **C**OMPASS | |

**FIG. 1325**   Verbal Aid, Down Add West etc

*Example 5(a).* From the chart the true course is 107° and the variation in the locality is 25°E.

*Required:* The magnetic course, MC.

The conversion is 'down' the picture. Use the left side. Easterly variation is to be subtracted.

107° − 25° = 082°

*Answer:* MC 082°. See below.

| DOWN | T | 107° |
|---|---|---|
| SUBTRACT | V | (−) 25°E |
| EAST | M | 082° |

*Example 5(b).* For this magnetic heading the deviation aboard this ship is 11°W.

*Required:* The compass course, CC.

The conversion is again 'down' the picture. Use the left side. Westerly deviation must be added.

082° + 11° = 093°

*Answer:* CC 093°. See below.

| DOWN | M | 082° |
|---|---|---|
| ADD | D | (+) 11°W |
| WEST | C | 093° |

Note that the so-called *compass error*, CE, the difference between true and compass, is 25°E − 11°W = 14°E. For any bearings taken over the ship's compass, while she is on the compass course 093°, applying the correction of 14°E yields the true bearing to be plotted on the chart.

*Example 6(a).* A ship is on compass course (CC) 193°. The deviation aboard this ship, for this compass heading is 11°E.
*Required:* The magnetic course, MC.
The conversion is 'up' the picture. Use the right side. Easterly deviation is to be added.
193° + 11° = 204°
*Answer:* MC 204°. See below.

| ADD | T | 178° |
|---|---|---|
| EAST | V | (−) 26°W |
| SUBTRACT | M | 204° |
| WEST | D | (+) 11°E |
| | C | 193° |

*Example 6(b).* The variation in the locality is 26°W.
*Required:* The true course, TC.
The conversion is 'up.' The westerly variation is subtractive.
204° − 26° = 178°
*Answer:* TC 178°
Note that CE is 26°W − 11°E = 15°W.

## RULE CHANGES FOR COURSES NAMED IN POINTS

When courses are named in points and quarter points, the terms add and subtract should not be used. For this application the shortened rules become:

**Correct easterly** errors **clockwise**

**Correct westerly** errors **counter clockwise**

**Uncorrect easterly** errors **counter clockwise**

**Uncorrect westerly** errors **clockwise**

The serious student by this time has an understanding of the existence of variation and deviation and the means of making allowances for them in operating his craft. From what has been presented he should know that a chart will give him the variation and that if he has reliable deviation tables he can interconvert courses.

Before explaining why deviation changes with the ship's heading, how to determine the deviations and how to prepare deviation tables it seems well to present a little general information.

**Always trust your compass.** Failure to do this may be disastrous. The so-called errors of the compass, you have learned, are not errors. A compass does not usually exhibit erroneous behavior. It is subject to natural laws which

totally govern its operation. As will be shown, insofar as the small boatman is concerned, its errors are determinable; may be reduced and once determined make the compass an exceedingly accurate instrument. Unless abused or subjected to unusual extraneous magnetic effects caused by wrenches, knives, steel cans, radio or other equipment, it is far more reliable than a watch. For years it will faithfully indicate direction, if properly guarded. No watch is without some rate, which must be allowed for; not so a well treated compass.

No mention has been made of dry compasses. At one time mariner's compasses were dry. The needles were affixed to a card, and the assembly, extremely light in weight, supported on a pivot as in the wet compass. The installation of reciprocating engines in ships caused vibrations which affected the instruments' accuracy. The wet compass, literally damping these vibrations, came into general use.

Do not attempt to use the rules for conversion with a compass having a free needle supported above a card. In this type of compass the card and the magnet do not move as a unit. Such a compass has no lubber's line and is useful only for estimating directions from its center.

Detail on the gyro compass is outside the scope of this book. Interested readers are referred to texts such as: American Practical Navigator, Bowditch, published by the U.S. Oceanographic Office or to Dutton's Navigation and Piloting, The U.S. Naval Institute, publisher. The gyrocompass is a complex device designed to maintain a fixed direction in space. Contrary to the usual belief it is not without "errors." Aboard ship allowances have to be made for changes in geographic latitude and for rapid changes in the speed of the vessel. Its great advantages, of course, are the absence of the magnetic effects, variation and deviation. Gyro error is termed east or west and applied exactly as is deviation.

The sun compass is not a compass. It is an instrument for taking bearings of the sun. The observer looks, not at the sun, but at a shadow cast by a small pin in the center of a card. The card is graduated clockwise through 360° from a zero point at South. Thus the shadow marks the sun's true bearing. If the instrument be properly oriented with the vessel's heading, the shadow will show the vessel's true course. The difference between it and the ship's compass course is the compass error, CE. Applying the variation yields the deviation of the ship's own compass on that heading. Accuracy depends on knowledge of the sun's true bearing. Since latitude, date and time affect this and moreover since the rate of change of the sun's true bearing is inconstant, the method is not recommended to the uninitiate. Spherical compasses have been made with a shadow pin mounted centrally on the card directly above the pivot. The knowing navigator uses this device in checking deviation by azimuths of the sun.

A pelorus (see pages 378 and 379) is an instrument having sight vanes and a compass card, either of which may be clamped in a fixed position. Sometimes referred to as a dumb compass, it is used to take bearings when, because of obstructions, sighting across the compass is impossible. The pelorus is placed in a position suitable for observations, its zero point either on the ship's heading, or oriented to compass north depending on whether relative or compass bearings are desired.

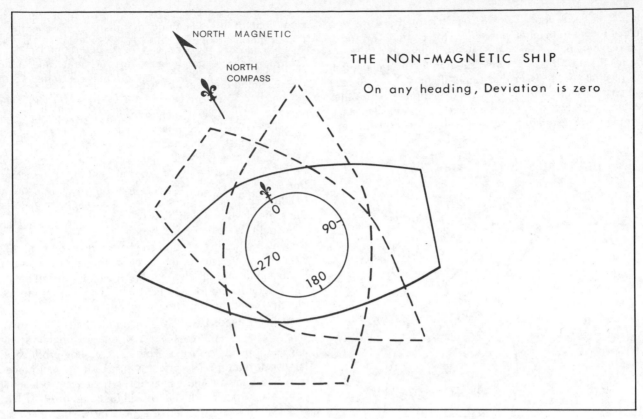

NORTH MAGNETIC

NORTH COMPASS

THE NON-MAGNETIC SHIP

On any heading, Deviation is zero

0

90

270

180

**FIG. 1326  The Non-magnetic Ship**

## WHY DEVIATION DEPENDS ON THE SHIP'S HEADING

Aboard ship the mariner's compass is subject to two magnetic forces, that of the earth and that of the vessel. Were the vessel absolutely free of magnetism, there would be no deviation, regardless of her heading, fig. 1326. The earth's force depends upon geographic location. The compasses of all the ships in a harbor are subject to the same variation. The deviations aboard these ships will be unlike because of the magnetic characteristics of each hull. Further, if all these ships be put on identical magnetic courses, their corresponding compass courses will differ, except in the exceedingly remote circumstance that each compass be completely compensated.

*Deviation*, it was stated, *varies with the ship's heading,* because of the magnetic material aboard. A little investigation will demonstrate this. Refer again to fig. 1326, the non-magnetic ship. No heading of the vessel affects the compass card; its north point always lies in the magnetic meridian. The compass has no deviation. As the ship changes course, the lubber's line, turning with the ship's head, indicates on the "dial," the card, the magnetic course.

Now put aboard this ship, anchors, chain, rigging, pipe berths, steering gear, galley fittings, gas tanks, water tanks, stanchions, life lines, a host of similar magnetic material, not forgetting the all-important engine. The vessel has acquired a magnetic field of her own. To consider how this may affect the compass, assume the same field is created by fastening a large permanent magnet, slightly askew, in the vessel's stern. This artifact is exceedingly applicable; it simulates the magnetic condition aboard most wood or

NORTH MAGNETIC

NORTH COMPASS

M 000°
D   7°E
C 353°

DEV: 7°E

CC 353°

0

90

270

180

S

N

**FIG. 1327  Heading North Magnetic aboard ANACHRONISM**

plastic pleasure craft. Two forces, that of the earth and that of the stern magnet, now affect the compass magnets. The magnets behave as if they were subject to one force, the resultant of the two. When the two forces are aligned, the resultant force is in that same alignment; so are the compass magnets and there is no deviation. On all other headings the two forces are applied at an angle to each other and the resultant force will be in a direction different from that of the magnetic meridian. Consequently, on these other headings, north by compass (000° CC) will not be north magnetic, (000° M), but north by compass will be stable on any specific heading if no changes be made in the magnetic material aboard.

Consider a typical vessel, the yacht ANACHRONISM. Headed North (000°) magnetic, fig. 1327, the forces referred to cause the compass magnets and hence the card, to come to rest with compass north slightly to the right, or east, of the magnetic meridian. There is an easterly deviation. Its magnitude is of no moment in this instance. Important to realize is that whenever she is put on this heading, with no changes made in her magnetic materials, the same deviation will exist.

Swinging to the eastward the ship steadies on a course for which it has been found she has no deviation, fig. 1328. Now the earth's force, the force of the stern magnet and the resultant are all aligned. The compass magnets lie in the magnetic meridian. The direction compass north is identical with the direction magnetic north.

Next she heads East (090°) Magnetic, fig. 1329. Now the ship's force is applied from a direction roughly at right angles to the earth's force. This 90° coupling produces the largest deviations. The effect is just as if a small piece of iron had been brought near the left or west side of the compass north. The deviation will be large. In ANACHRONISM it is westerly. Had the polarity of the theoretical stern magnet been reversed, the deviation on this heading would likewise have been large, but in the opposite direction, to the east.

Coming now to head South (180°) Magnetic, fig. 1330, the stern magnet's force is approaching alignment with the earth's force, but in a direction diametrically opposite to that of the heading 000° Mag. shown in fig. 1327. The large westerly deviation so evident on the heading East mag-

| M | 017.5° |
| D | 0 |
| C | 017.5° |

FIG. 1328  Heading with zero deviation aboard ANACHRONISM

| M | 090° |
| D | 14°W |
| C | 104° |

FIG. 1329  Heading East Magnetic aboard ANACHRONISM

netic is greatly reduced.

As the swing continues there will be a heading on which the two forces and their resultant will be again in line and the deviation zero. (In ANACHRONISM, as will appear later in this chapter, this occurs on the heading 187.5° Mag.)

Heading West (270°) Magnetic, fig. 1331, once more puts the two forces roughly at right angles, but the stern magnet's force is applied from the other side of the compass. The effect, now, is similar to that brought about by putting a small piece of iron close to the right or east side of the compass's north point. Again, as on the heading East, Magnetic, the deviation will be large, but now in the opposite direction, easterly.

Do not assume that on any other vessel these same deviations will exist. A ship's magnetic field does not necessarily lend itself to depiction as that of a single magnet. Indeed, changing the skew of the assumed magnet aboard ANACHRONISM a trifle would have altered the deviations.

To reiterate, were the ship non-magnetic, it would have no magnetic field, no deviation on any heading. Compensating a compass is an endeavor to so neutralize the magnetic field of the ship as to produce this non-magnetic environment for the mariner's compass. It is done by placing small magnets close to the compass in such positions as may be required. For this purpose many modern compasses have small magnets, adjustable as to position, built into their stands or binnacles. By their use and, if necessary, by adding other compensating magnets in the vicinity of the compass, the deviation on small boats is usually reducible to zero on most headings and leaving not more than three or four degrees in the others. Sailing craft, heeling out of the horizontal, frequently require heeling magnets to reduce their deviations. Iron and steel craft are subject to changes in deviation upon large changes in their geomagnetic latitude. This is outside the scope of this work.

It is not difficult for the small boat operator to ascertain and record the deviations for a number of headings. Such a record becomes a ready reference deviation table good until structural changes or other movements of magnetic material are made aboard.

| M | 180° |
| D | 2°W |
| C | 182° |

FIG. 1330  **Heading South Magnetic aboard ANACHRONISM**

| M | 270° |
| D | 14°E |
| C | 256° |

FIG. 1331  **Heading West Magnetic aboard ANACHRONISM**

## DETERMINING THE DEVIATIONS

Deviation is the angle between the compass card axis and the magnetic meridian, fig. 1317, page 274.

Aboard any craft the direction of compass north is sighted at a glance. Not so the direction of the magnetic meridian or, as it is loosely termed, magnetic north. So it is not possible to compare, visually, the deviation angle between these two reference directions. But the difference between an observed compass bearing, and its magnetic equivalent yields the same angle. The bearing is sighted over, or with reference to, the compass. The magnetic equivalent is taken from the chart. The navigator does this by observing celestial bodies, the piloting boatman by running ranges, or by crossing a range on different headings.

Two visible objects, preferably ashore or fixed to the bottom, both accurately charted, are selected. From the chart the magnetic range, i.e. the magnetic course, from the fore to the after mark is recorded. See fig. 1332. A and B are two visible objects; B is visible behind A. The magnetic bearing of the range is 075°. A vessel sails on the range, keeping A and B visibly in line. While held on this course, the compass heading is noted. It is 060°. The amount of the deviation is the difference between 075° and 060° or 15°. Reference to either of the conversion rules makes clear that its direction is East.

A buoy and a fixed object or even two buoys may be used if a range of fixed objects is unavailable. The charted position of a buoy is that of its anchor. Thus wind, or current, or both may move a buoy from its charted position. Large ships have been known to move buoys inadvertently by collision in thick weather. Steering a visible course from buoy to buoy and noting the heading by compass, will, if the observation be made at the *start of the run,* give reasonably accurate results. (See fig. 1333.) Easiest perhaps is to swing the ship about its compass by sailing different headings across a range, recording the compass bearing of the range on each crossing.

Two prominent objects ashore are on a range bearing 087° from seaward. On a calm day the yacht ANACHRONISM sails across this range on compass headings successively 15° apart. Using sight vanes and an azimuth ring mounted on the compass (page 378) the compass bearing of the range is taken at each crossing. The results are recorded and tabulated. *(See below.)*

The navigator, noting the average compass bearing, 086.9°, was unusually close to the magnetic bearing of the range, decided the table was valid.

| Ship's Head Compass | Range bears Compass | Range bears Magnetic | Deviation |
|---|---|---|---|
| 000° | 082° | 087° | 5°E |
| 015° | 086° | 087° | 1°E |
| 030° | 091° | 087° | 4°W |
| 045° | 096° | 087° | 9°W |
| 060° | 100° | 087° | 13°W |
| 075° | 104° | 087° | 17°W |
| 090° | 106° | 087° | 19°W |
| 105° | 106° | 087° | 19°W |
| 120° | 104° | 087° | 17°W |
| 135° | 101° | 087° | 14°W |
| 150° | 097° | 087° | 10°W |
| 165° | 093° | 087° | 6°W |
| 180° | 089° | 087° | 2°W |
| 195° | 085° | 087° | 2°E |
| 210° | 082° | 087° | 5°E |
| 225° | 079° | 087° | 8°E |
| 240° | 076° | 087° | 11°E |
| 255° | 073° | 087° | 14°E |
| 270° | 070° | 087° | 17°E |
| 285° | 069° | 087° | 18°E |
| 300° | 070° | 087° | 17°E |
| 315° | 072° | 087° | 15°E |
| 330° | 075° | 087° | 12°E |
| 345° | 078° | 087° | 9°E |

The first and last columns in this tabulation now constitute a deviation table for ANACHRONISM'S compass provided *no changes are made in the magnetic environment of the compass.* Clearly indicated is the manner in which the deviation changes with the vessel's heading. To paraphrase Lecky, when on the heading 045° *magnetic* the ship's bow points in a direction quite different from where it does when she heads 045° by *compass.* The deviations in this table are applicable immediately to compass headings. It would not be difficult to interpolate visually for courses between the tabular values.

There is another problem. The navigator determines from the chart the magnetic course, wishes to know the compass course to steer. Use of this table for that purpose requires tedious, repetitive and time-consuming trial-and-error steps. To avoid these he makes a second table listing the deviations for *magnetic* headings. The second table is prepared without further observations by plotting a graph of the first. This nomogram or interconversion curve may be prepared in various forms. The simplest to plot and to use is still that of Admiral Sir Charles Napier, R.N., devised early in the nineteenth century, and bearing his name.

NORTH MAGNETIC

NORTH COMPASS

Dev 15°E

075° MAG

A  B

CC 060°

0

90

270

180

M   075°

D   15°E

C   060°

**FIG. 1332  Determining the Deviation, sailing on a range**

# The Napier Diagram

The Napier Diagram is used to this day in most of the world's navies, including our own. One cannot now agree with Squire Lecky's statement that "it requires a man who has lived on the same street as a draughtsman to produce" it. Napier arranged his co-ordinates at angles of 60° instead of the usual 90° so that in place of a rectilinear grid, his is a series of equilateral triangles on a common base. This singularly simple device (see fig. 1334) makes the single scale, that of the base line, equally applicable to the inclined lines. The base line is laid off to represent 360°, with a dot every degree of its length. Every fifth dot is slightly heavier, for ease in identification. Every 15° along the base line is printed an angular value. Through these fifteen-degree stations are drawn the lines of the grid. Those sloping downward to the right are dotted every degree and like the base line, have the fifth dot accented. Those sloping downward to the left are solid.

Note that in the improved form of Napier diagram shown, the base line is not continuous but divided into two sections. To simplify its use for courses near the ends of these sections, this one, prepared by the United States

Power Squadrons, has 15° extensions at both ends of each section. When points were in vogue the base and dotted lines were spaced in quarter-points. Perhaps this, the difficulty of dividing 11¼° accurately into quarters, may have occasioned Lecky's caustic comment. Deviations for compass headings are plotted on the dotted lines, easterly deviations to the right of the base line, westerly ones to its left.

Consider now plotting a Napier curve of ANACHRONISM'S deviation table from the observations previously made. For the heading 000° CC the deviation is 5°E. On the dotted line passing through the point marked North or 000° on the base line, circle the fifth dot to the right. For the heading 015° CC the deviation is 1°E. Circle the first dot to the right on the dotted line passing through 015° on the base line. For 030° CC the deviation is 4°W. Circle the fourth dot *to the left* on the dotted line passing through 030° on the base line. Continue in this fashion, plotting each one of the deviations listed in the table. Stations 345°, 195°, 165° and 015° are plotted twice, once in each of their respective positions on the base line.

**FIG. 1333  Chart Segment showing magnetic headings from buoy to buoy**

FIG. 1334  Napier Diagram

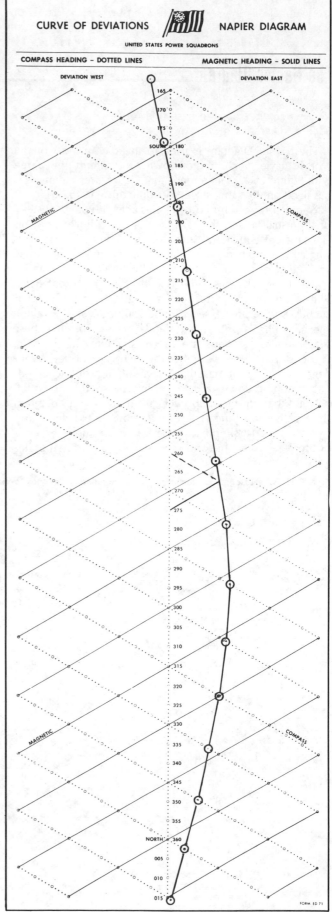

Now draw a fair curve through the plotted points. It may not pass exactly through every point because of observational or other errors, but if most of the points lie on the curve and those few which do not are within $\frac{1}{2}°$ of the curve, it will be sufficiently accurate. Should there be larger discrepancies the original observations or their subsequent computations are repeated. This is the conversion curve. All possible deviations of ANACHRONISM'S compass lie between this curve and the base line.

The length, from the base line to the curve, of any line of the diagram's grid, represents, to the baseline's scale, the magnitude of a deviation. Measured on the *dotted* lines are deviations for *compass* headings. Measured on the *solid* lines are deviations for *magnetic* headings. Where the curve is to the east (right) of the baseline, the deviations are east; where it is to the west (left), the deviations are west.

Making the second table, that of deviations for the magnetic headings, is now easy. The lengths of the respective solid lines are measured. Start with north. The curve is east of the baseline, hence this deviation will be east. See fig. 1334. Place one point of a pair of dividers on the center line at 000°. Adjust the dividers so that the other point is on the curve at its intersection with the solid line passing through 000°. Without changing the setting of the dividers' legs and keeping one leg on the base line, swing back to the base line. Record the number of degrees on the baseline between the divider points. It is 7° and the deviation for the heading 000° magnetic is 7°E.

Doing this for stations 15° apart produces the required second table for ANACHRONISM. It looks like this:

| Ship's Head Magnetic | Deviation |
|---|---|
| 000° | 7°E |
| 015° | 1°E |
| 030° | 6°W |
| 045° | 12.5°W |
| 060° | 17°W |
| 075° | 19°W |
| 090° | 18°W |
| 105° | 17°W |
| 120° | 14°W |
| 135° | 11°W |
| 150° | 8°W |
| 165° | 5°W |
| 180° | 2°W |
| 195° | 2°E |
| 210° | 4°E |
| 225° | 6°E |
| 240° | 9°E |
| 255° | 11.5°E |
| 270° | 14°E |
| 285° | 16°E |
| 300° | 17.5°E |
| 315° | 17°E |
| 330° | 15°E |
| 345° | 11°E |

Reverting to the Napier diagram, note that in swinging the dividers back to the base line it matters not, insofar as the amount of deviation is concerned, which way they are swung. If they be swung so that the two points on the baseline and the point on the curve form an equilateral triangle, the swung leg will indicate not only the deviation, but the corresponding compass course. Direct course conversion is arrived at this way, or by drawing lines parallel to the grid lines. See fig. 1334 showing the inter-relationship between a magnetic course of 275° and a compass course of 260° aboard ANACHRONISM. This old jingle outlines procedure.

*From compass, the magnetic course to gain,*

*Depart by dotted and return by plain.*

*But from magnetic, to gain the course allotted,*

*Depart by plain and then return by dotted.*

From the Napier diagram a third table listing deviations in increments of 1°, applicable to either compass or magnetic headings, may be made. Appended is a portion of such a table, to the nearest integral degree, for ANACHRONISM. It has the advantage that no interpolations are required. For a known magnetic or a known compass course the deviation is immediately available.

| Magnetic Heading | Deviation | Compass Heading |
|---|---|---|
| 017°-018° | 0° | 017°-019° |
| 019°-021° | 1°W | 020°-022° |
| 022° | 2°W | 023°-025° |
| 023°-025° | 3°W | 027°-028° |
| 026°-027° | 4°W | 029°-031° |
| 028° | 5°W | 032°-034° |
| 029°-031° | 6°W | 035°-038° |
| 032°-033° | 7°W | 039°-041° |
| 034°-035° | 8°W | 042°-044° |
| 036°-037° | 9°W | 045°-046° |
| 038°-039° | 10°W | 047°-050° |

For a compass with deviations as large as those of ANACHRONISM, such a table would be quite extensive, but nonetheless useful. For a compensated compass the table will be shorter because the deviations will be greatly reduced. *See: ANACHRONISM Compensated, Chapter 14.*

Instead of the three tables shown, some pilots prefer a circular deviation card, fig. 1335. The outer rose represents magnetic directions; the inner one directions by compass. Lines are drawn connecting corresponding values, as, for example, one between 275° on the outer rose and 260° on the inner. This really says that to make good 275° magnetic, ANACHRONISM must steer 260° by her compass or, conversely, that when she is steering 260° by compass she is making good 275° magnetic.

Some prefer a columnar arrangement. One column is headed: "For Magnetic"; the other: "Steer, Compass" and the corresponding values tabulated.

Using either of these two, conversion is performed by direct reading. No arithmetic is necessary and, with respect only to courses, not bearings, the user need know neither the amount nor the direction of the deviations.

Let the reader not infer that a Napier diagram or any similar conversion graph is to be used in daily piloting. That would be impractical. The diagram has but one function, to serve as a means of conversion in the preparation of those tables which the pilot chooses to use afloat.

*See Chapter 14 for a further discussion of the compass*

285

# COMPASS DEVIATION CARD

MAGNETIC COURSE
FROM CHART
ON OUTER
ROSE

COURSE TO STEER
BY COMPASS
ON INNER
ROSE

MOTOR BOATING

YACHT _____     OWNER _____

PORT _____     DATE _____

Read only MAGNETIC courses on the OUTER rose; only COMPASS courses on the inner one. For each compass heading (inner rose) apply the known deviation and draw a line from that degree or point to the corresponding magnetic heading (outer rose).

**TO FIND THE COMPASS COURSE:** Locate the magnetic course on the outer rose. Follow the lines to the inner rose and read the compass course.

**TO CONVERT COMPASS COURSE TO MAGNETIC COURSE:** Locate the compass course on the inner rose. Follow the lines to the outer one and read the magnetic course.

DO NOT CONVERT BEARINGS with this card. To do this find first the deviation for the boat's heading when the bearing was taken. Apply this deviation to the bearing.

**FIG. 1335  Deviation Card**

# CHAPTER 14

# THE MARINER'S COMPASS

**SELECTION,
INSTALLATION,
MAINTENANCE
and
COMPENSATION**

A VESSEL'S SAFETY may depend upon her compass. Cruising under conditions of poor visibility, the small craft pilot may have no other means of keeping to his desired track and, crossing a body of open water, no other means of making a good landfall. Running out the time on a given course in thick weather and neither seeing nor hearing the expected aid to navigation is not conducive to peace of mind. There is little comfort in a chain of soundings that does not match what the chart shows in the expected vicinity. Stranding because of unexpected contact with rock, shoal or any bottom is unnerving.

The preceding chapter gave some ways of ascertaining and using variation and deviation. Here will be discussed compensating, the reduction of deviations to a minimum, after some remarks on the choice of a compass and some further details as to its mounting aboard.

**FIG. 1401 Inspecting the pivot action and instrumentally zeroing-in the compensators of a compass, prior to packaging for shipment.**

## Selecting a Compass

Almost any new compass looks fine in the store, or aboard in the quiet motion of the mooring or the marina slip. Its behavior under way, when the sea makes up and the little ship rolls, pitches and yaws, is of supreme importance. Will the card stick at some angle of heel? Will its apparent motion be jerky or smooth and easy? Are the card graduations legible and different headings easily distinguished? Is the instrument to be subject to large temperature changes? What if under its glass appears a bubble which may distract the helmsman? Answers depend on the quality of the compass.

No aviator will knowingly accept a cheap parachute, no sailor a bargain in life-jackets or fire extinguishers. No boatman should settle for a cheap compass. Select one adequate for your expected needs, erring on the side of luxury. Look at a number of them before buying. Pick them up, tilt and turn them, simulating motions to which they would be subject afloat. The card should have a smooth and stable reaction, come to rest without oscillations about the lubber's line. Reasonable tilting, comparable to the rolling and pitching of your boat, should not materially affect the reading. In fairness to the compass, if it has internal compensators, they must be zeroed-in (see below) before making these tests.

Pay particular attention to the card. Its graduation should be suited to the intended use. That a large craft may be held more easily on course than a small one is axiomatic. Hence the larger the ship, the greater is the number of divisions required on the card periphery. Owners of large ocean-going auxiliaries and cruisers seem to prefer cards which can be read to single degrees. Many of them also use quarter-point cards for long runs under sail.

Except under ideal conditions a small boat cannot long be held on a course with single-degree accuracy. The varying effects of wind, sea and indeed of trim brought about by the movement of a person aboard, swing her off the desired heading. Admittedly in the planning of a voyage, in the chart work, in the application of variation and deviation, accuracy to the nearest degree is essential. It gives the helmsman a goal. The experienced seaman knows little vessels cannot be steered so closely. Their track is an average, made up of headings at times on course, at times off to the right and to the left.

The novice, trying to steer 'too fine,' attempts to achieve the unachievable, to keep constantly on one heading. He cannot do so and, in the endeavor, repeatedly shifting his rudder, he overdoes it, makes steering needlessly laborious and is much less efficient than he would have been in a less effortful and more relaxed operation. Far from the smooth and easy performance of the skilled helmsman, his is that of the learner, most inept and suffering from a self-defeating concentration on precise control.

Steering is a bodily skill. The helmsman's brain, processing information received through his eyes, sends a signal to his muscular system to act in a certain way, to move the wheel or tiller. Lest the boat swing in a circle this muscular action must be stopped and a new one initiated to return the wheel to its previous position. Should the first action be too violent or too long continued, the vessel's head swings past the desired course, causing need for stronger action in the opposite direction in attempted rectification. There is little reason to believe the second action will be less violent than the first. Now the heading is off course in the opposite direction and the whole cycle must be repeated. The ship's head wanders from side to side about the course desired. (The modern science of control, of reducing in many operations this oscillating about a desired end, Norbert Wiener named cybernetics, using Plato's term for the steersman's art.)

Though most machines and electrical circuits respond much faster than man to specific orders, it cannot be denied that man does well when the orders allow him some latitude in performance. Consider attempting to steer 113° for a short 30-minute trick at the wheel using a small compass card. Close to the lubber's line are the graduations representing 111°, 112°, 113°, and 114° not in any way distinguishable from each other, except by position. More easily recognizable, because their marks are somewhat longer and perhaps heavier than the other four, are 110° and 115°. fig. 1402. Under any but the calmest conditions holding on 113° will not be possible. The effort of identifying 113° among the other close and cluttered marks will be difficult. Handling the wheel or tiller to keep the lubber's line on it for 30 minutes will be impossible.

To the best of his ability, the experienced small craft captain will hold the lubber's line midway between the more prominent graduations 110° and 115°, each clearly recognizable, and steer this course with the admonition "nothing to the left," gauging his handling to give her just

FIG. 1402 Segment of a card graduated in degrees, the lubber's line indicating a course of 113°. Compare fig. 1403.

FIG. 1403 Another card, graduated every 5°. Most helmsmen find this type of graduation easier to use.

"a little to the right." The orders to the operator of the boat's steering mechanism, a man, are not too specific and can be carried out with relative ease. The amount of error, the amount that the track sailed will wander from 113°, will be less than it would have been under rigorous endeavors to keep the lubber's line exactly on that course mark. Moreover the operation will be easier visually when there are no intermediate marks on the card between 110° and 115°. Thus a card graduated only every 5° is ideal for the small boatman's purpose. See fig. 1403.

## CRITERIA FOR SELECTION

1. The card should remain level and not stick through reasonable angles of pitch and roll.

2. The card should move but slightly during any course change made by rotating the box or case through 90° or more. Some small motion due to the inertia of the fluid is permissible, but the card should be dead-beat, swinging but once to a steady position, not oscillating about the lubber's line.

3. The card should be easily read and graduated to your preference.

4. Provision should be made for lighting.

5. Hemispherically shaped, rather than a flat top plate.

6. Internally gimballed card and lubber's line.

7. Sturdy waterproof case.

8. Internal compensators, that is, built into the case.

9. Expansion bellows in the assembly to prevent bubbles in the liquid in lowered temperature.

10. For a larger boat a deck-mounted binnacle (fig. 1404), means for taking bearings and frequently for small steel boats soft iron compensators, those hollow iron balls you may have seen mounted on binnacles.

11. Do not consider a dry marching compass nor a dry tank compass. This is pure folly, inviting later disaster.

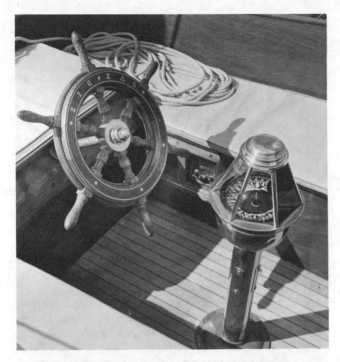

FIG. 1404  Deck-mounted binnacle.

Above all do not be niggardly. Buy an instrument made by a manufacturer of repute and pay his price. Hidden in the construction of a compass are things that make for accuracy and long life. Among them are: precise positioning of the magnetic element or the magnets under the card, so that its 000°-180° axis indicates exactly the direction of the magnetic meridian; the permanency of the markings on the card, of the expansion bellows, of the case seals; the life of the pivot bearing, its resistance to wear or to warping or distention from being, in the case of many little ships, tied up on one heading for five days every week. Here quality will pay off. In the long run the best is the least expensive.

## ZEROING-IN

A modern compass having built-in compensators should be zeroed-in before being mounted aboard. If necessary such a compass already installed may be demounted and taken ashore for this purpose. Zeroing-in is nothing more than adjusting the compensators so that they have no effect on the compass. A compass subject only to the earth's field has no need of compensation; there are no deviations to remove. Therefore **before being installed, any deviation caused by improper positioning of the compensators themselves must be removed** and the unit go aboard just as an old-fashioned compass, ready for what magnetic changes may be wrought upon it by the ship's field. Setting the compensators by aligning screws with marks on the case or housing may not be sufficient for accurate navigation. Zeroing-in by trial-and-error is simple and effective, does not require any knowledge of the direction of magnetic North.

Do it in an area well away from any known magnetic influence: iron, steel girders, pipes, and ductwork concealed in walls, floors or ceilings; loud-speakers, radios, motors, refrigerators, freezers and so on. Don't work wearing a steel belt buckle, bracelet or watch band, nor a

yachtsman's cap containing a steel top grommet.

Using non-magnetic screws or tacks mount the compass temporarily on a small board having two parallel edges. Placing the lubber's line closely parallel to these edges is helpful but not essential. On a level flat board—be wary of a table or card table as it may have hidden steel screws or fittings—place a large book and the compass on its small board. Set the compass board with one of its parallel sides firmly against the edge of the book. Turn book and board as a unit until the compass reads North, fig. 1405. Hold the book steady. It serves as a fixed direction marker. Bring the opposite edge of the compass board snugly against the book. The lubber's line is now exactly reversed. If, now, the compass reads South, the N-S compensator is already zeroed-in and needs no adjustment.

If the reading is not South, half the difference must be removed. With a non-magnetic screw driver (a dime may do), slowly turn the N-S screw. Should the card move farther away from South, turn the screw in the opposite direction. With half the difference removed, realign the book and compass board, again as a unit, to the compass heading, South. Then without moving the book, reverse the compass.

If it does not now read North, halve the difference by turning the N-S adjusting screw. Again realign the book and compass on North, reverse the compass and if it does not read South, again halve the difference. Continue this process until the reversal is as nearly perfect as possible. When these adjustments are concluded, the direction of

FIG. 1405  Zeroing-in with book and board. Note that this type of compass is to be mounted so that the lubber's line is between the card and the helmsman.

the magnetic meridian (see Chapter 13) is that of the North-South axis of the compass card.

Next adjust the E-W compensators in the same way: line up on either an East or West heading, reverse and if the resultant heading is not exactly opposite, remove half the difference and continue working on East and West headings just as was done on North and South.

If exact reversals are not attainable move to a different

site; some magnetic influence may be at work.

If the adjusting screws are accessible and if the compass fits tightly in its packing box, zeroing-in can be done with the compass in its box instead of mounted on a board. If the compass, however, has to be removed from its box to adjust the screws, it is difficult to halve the differences and the chance of the compass not being exactly reversed is more probable.

Do not discard the temporary mounting board. It may be useful in testing the proposed permanent site aboard.

## Installation

Intentionally Chapter 13 made only brief reference to the principles of mounting a compass. Now those should be amplified. There are definite steps to a good compass installation: inspect, test, mount, compensate and maintain.

Look critically at the proposed location. Clearly the compass should be directly in front of the helmsman, placed so that he may view it without bodily stress as he sits or stands in a posture of relaxed alertness. Give thought to his comfort in heavy weather and, in conditions of poor visibility, day or night. His position is fairly well determined by the wheel or tiller he handles. The compass is to be brought into what one might term his zone of comfort. Too far away, he bends forward to watch it. Too close, he rears backward for relief. Much of the time he may be not only the helmsman, but the forward and after lookout. So put the compass where he can bring his eyes back to it with a minimum of bodily movement. A distance of 22 to 30 inches from his eyes with the head tilted forward not more than 20° is about right, see fig. 1406.

Now inspect the site. It should be at least two feet away from engine indicators, bilge vapor detectors, other mag-netic instruments and any steel or iron. Six or more feet is better than two, but there may have to be compromise on the small boat. When one or more of these magnetic influences is too close, either it or the compass must be moved. Vertical magnetic material is to be particularly avoided.

When, from this cursory inspection, the location seems satisfactory, test it. There may be magnets or magnetic influences concealed under the cabin top, forward of the cabin's after bulkhead, within the cockpit ceiling or in a wood-covered stanchion. You will test with the compass. If the compass has internal compensators, be sure, before testing, that they have been zeroed-in. If this has not been done, rotary motion of the case will make the card move, nullifying the test procedure.

Move the compass all around the area of the proposed site. Watch the card. One thing only will make it turn, a magnetic influence. Find it with the compass. If it cannot be moved away or replaced by non-magnetic material, test to determine whether it is merely magnetic, a random piece of iron or steel, or is magnetized. Successively bring the North and South poles of the compass near it. Both

**FIG. 1406    Consider the helmsman's comfort when installing a compass.**

FIG. 1407 Keep magnetic materials away from the compass. This light meter would cause deviation.

poles will be attracted if it is unmagnetized. If it attracts one pole and repels the other, it is magnetized. Demagnetization (see page 295), should be attempted.

Next hold or tape down the compass where you expect to mount it. Now the temporary mounting board used in zeroing-in will be helpful. Test everything that might affect the compass. Turn the wheel, switch on and off all the lights, radios, radio direction finder, radio telephone, depth finder and, if there is one, the shipboard intercom. Sound the electric 'whistle,' turn on the windshield wipers. Start the engine, work the throttle, move the gear shift. When there is an auxiliary generator, start it. In short, one at a time test everything that might cause deviation. When, on any one of these tests, the card moves, ideally the compass should be relocated or the cause demagnetized. Some of these things, windshield wipers, for example, you may

have to settle for, making a different deviation table to use when they are operating.

Be sure the site is firm. Vibration not only increases pivot wear, but may initiate that disconcerting phenomenon, a slowly spinning card!

Now prepare to mount the compass, following the principles given on page 269. The line through the lubber's line and the compass card pivot must be exactly parallel to the boat's keel to forestall an error constant on all courses. Establish the fore-and-aft line of the ship with stout cord or string. Carefully transfer this line to the compass site. If necessary shim the base so that a stile-type lubber's line affixed to the case and not gimballed, is vertical when the ship is on an even keel. Drill one hole, only. If, during compensation, the instrument has to be skewed slightly to counteract disalignment of the card or the fore-and-aft line, more than one hole will present problems.

# Maintenance

Maintenance has two aspects. The first is the preservation of the magnetic environment of the compass. Except for occasional testing, no piece of iron or steel is to be brought or installed near it. An ashtray, a beverage can, camera, light meter, freon-powered horn, a portable radio, steel tools and a host of other common magnetic materials must be kept well away from the compass while it is in use. See fig. 1407. They will cause unknown deviations.

The second consists mainly of getting to know your compass. Watch how it appears to swing. Check that its readings are consistent on frequently sailed courses. Note if it appears to become sluggish and above all if it becomes erratic—these two warn you of alien magnetism or a damaged pivot bearing.

Test for a damaged pivot bearing or for undue pivot friction by deflecting the card a few degrees from the lubber's line with a piece of steel. There is need for repair

should the card not return to its former heading.

A bubble is removed by adding some liquid but the liquid must be that with which the compass is filled. No alcohol or water should be added to an oil-filled compass, no oil added to an alcohol-water-filled one lest the card, gaskets and internally painted marks be damaged.

Lightning and electric welding aboard may change the ship's own magnetic field. After exposure to either of these, test to see whether the deviations have changed.

On small welding jobs, placing the ground connection close to the weld limits the electric current flow and the resultant magnetic field to a small area, rendering large changes less likely.

Do read and follow the manufacturer's recommendations for winter storage. They may add years to the instrument's useful life.

## PRINCIPLES OF COMPENSATION

It should be understood that what follows applies to compensation in the craft of the average pleasure boat owner. Though in these vessels deviations may be large initially (see ANACHRONISM, Chapter 13) and indeed the compass may even lock and swing with the ship after the ill-considered installation of some useful but strongly magnetic article, the causative factors are limited. With common sense, care in procedure and occasional ingenuity, the causes can be removed or their effects largely neutralized by the average boat owner if he will methodically follow the steps laid out in this chapter.

Usually absent in these craft are complications due to permanent hull magnetism acquired during building; the variable transient magnetism induced in vertical iron or steel members: the ship's sides, bulkheads, stanchions, masts; not forgetting those arising from a magnetic cargo. Solution of these and other problems should be left to an expert skilled and experienced in that field, a professional compass adjuster. The reader interested in the magnetic conditions aboard larger steel vessels is again referred to Dutton or Bowditch (page 278) or to still more technical treatises.

Compensating a compass is the process of reducing its deviations to a minimum. Deviation is caused by the magnetic field of the vessel. Compensation, then, is the elimination of the effects of this ship's magnetism on the compass. A small magnet very near the compass can negate the effect of more remote large magnetic masses.

In wooden or plastic power craft compensation is usually achieved by firmly fastening two small permanent bar or needle magnets, one parallel to the keel, the other athwartship, close to the compass. These two compensators need not be in the same horizontal plane, but there is one restriction upon their placement. Each must be centered on a line passing through the compass pivot. Thus the one parallel to the keel, called the fore-and-aft magnet, is placed to the right or left of the compass, with its center on a line running accurately athwartship through the compass pivot. The athwartship one is positioned forward or aft of the compass with its center on a truly fore-and-aft line through the pivot.

When, and only when, the compensators are placed that way, a unique condition exists which greatly simplifies the process of compensation. The athwartship compensator will not materially affect the compass on east or west magnetic headings, nor the fore-and-aft one on north or south headings.

A ship is headed east magnetic. An athwartship magnet, centered on a fore-and-aft line through the compass pivot and placed at A or B, fig. 1408, is approximately parallel to the compass's magnetic element. Irrespective of the direction of the compensator's poles, north to starboard or to port, it will exert no force bringing about any practical change in the deviation.

A compensator, centered on an athwartship line through the compass pivot, placed fore-and-aft at D or F, fig. 1409, is roughly at right angles to the compass magnet, exerts a strong torque or turning force upon it, and causes it to move, either increasing or decreasing the deviation.

Obviously similar conditions obtain on a heading of

**FIG. 1408  On E-W headings athwartship magnets have no effect.**

**FIG. 1409  On E-W headings fore-and-aft magnets have maximum effect.**

west magnetic. In the same way on north-south headings the effectivity of athwartship compensators and the nullity of those placed fore-and-aft could be demonstrated.

Of course both compensators come into use when sailing other than cardinal directions. The great value of the phenomena just explained is that they permit the pleasure craft operator to divide the causes of deviation into only two component parts and, without knowledge of their magnitude, remove each of them separately and uncomplicated by the other.

When the compensators have been fastened in what is found to be their most effective positions they could be replaced by one single horizontal magnet centered exactly under the pivot, at a specific distance from it and fixed at

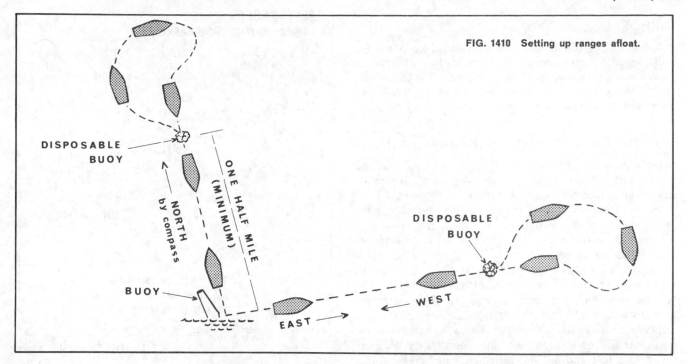

FIG. 1410  Setting up ranges afloat.

some necessary angle to the ship's fore-and-aft line. This, the Admiralty method at one time used in the British Navy, is, to quote Lecky, "very elegant, . . . but somewhat more difficult than the ordinary one in vogue on merchant vessels." For "merchant vessels" read present-day pleasure craft and that understatement made twenty years before the twentieth century began still holds good.

Internal compensators, built in by the manufacturer, are so arranged that when the compass is installed they will be in the proper relative positions previously outlined. They are adjusted, as was shown in the discussion of zeroing-in, by means of a slotted bolt head, usually called a compensating screw. Casual inspection will show that one of the compensating screws is aligned with the lubber's line, the other at right angles to it. On some instruments the screws are marked N-S and E-W. Turning the screw varies the magnet's influence on the compass card from zero to maximum. Aboard many pleasure craft proper setting of these compensators will bring about compensation. When this does not suffice, because of powerful magnetic forces aboard, additional means, to be described later, will be necessary.

The astute reader will have perceived that compensation is analogous to zeroing-in. In zeroing-in, the book and board served to make certain that, at each reversal of the compass, its lubber's line turned exactly 180°. It was as if the compass had been aboard a ship, which, on each reversal, sailed an exactly reciprocal magnetic course.

Zeroing-in ashore began by using an unknown magnetic direction or course, identified only as North (000°) by compass. Zeroing-in was successful because this, or any other unknown magnetic heading, could be accurately reversed. Afloat, compensation may be started in the same way. Afloat, the nub of the problem is achieving accurate reversal, putting and holding the vessel on a course over the bottom, exactly the reciprocal of the original unknown magnetic heading. This, as will be shown, is not as difficult as one might surmise.

## SAILING A RECIPROCAL COURSE

Between any two visible marks, or on a range, reversing the magnetic heading is obviously easy. In compensating there is need ultimately to sail at least the four cardinal magnetic directions North, South, East and West. Cardinal directions are seldom defined by aids to navigation or by landmarks in cruising waters. In a yacht anchorage or in waters adjacent to a marina, ranges may be built on these bearings and vessels easily steadied on them.

This then becomes a do-it-yourself project. *The skipper makes his own range.* Departing from a fixed mark (a buoy will do) he sails on a steady compass heading until ready to reverse course, then drops his own disposable buoy clear of the screw, creating the required range. Next he executes a buttonhook turn, lines up the disposable buoy and the original departure point, steadies on this range visually and, ignoring the compass, heads for the starting point, runs down the disposable buoy and continues back toward the mark originally left, fig. 1410. The turn is made as tightly as possible, keeping the buoy in sight, and is completed before the buoy has time to drift. The skipper, knowing the characteristics of his boat, will choose a right or a left turn.

This maneuver has accurately put the ship on a reciprocal course, providing that the buoy remained where it was dropped and that no wind or current sets the ship to either side of her heading on the outward or inward courses. Compensation will be inaccurate if she has moved crabwise over the bottom, going one way, but headed another; therefore the requisite courses are sailed where the current is negligible and when the wind or sea produces no leeway.

The skipper who has qualms about running the buoy down should take it very close alongside, touching it. On a range of $1/2$ nautical mile, 1000 yds, when the buoy is $6^1/4$ feet to one side of the vessel's center line the course error will be 8', less than 1/7 of 1°.

## DISPOSABLE BUOYS

Excellent disposable buoys are plastic bleach bottles ballasted about one-quarter full of sand, fig. 1411. Newspapers wadded into a ball about the size of a basketball, tied with light string—no heavy stuff or wire, please—and weighted at the end of a four-foot cord with an old bolt, spark plug, washer or similar gear will also serve.

## ADDITIONAL MATERIALS AND PREPARATIONS

For a compass without internal compensators or for one whose internal compensators are insufficient to remove deviation, two compensating magnets will be needed. Each is an encased permanent magnet having two holes for screw fastening. Modern units are small, but equally as effective as the original tubular types in which the magnets were either long steel wires or rods. The ends of the compensators will either be stamped N and S or be colored, blue on the south and red on the north end. Adhesive tape will be ideal for temporarily fastening the external compensators. Carefully mark their longitudinal centers. Lay out carefully in chalk in the areas where the external compensators will be located, two lines through the compass pivot, one fore-and-aft, the other athwartship, fig. 1412.

For the internally compensated compass a non-magnetic screw driver will be needed. A thin coin may do. The compass has been previously zeroed-in.

Every magnetic article of ship's gear should be stowed in its accustomed place, the windshield wiper blades be in their normal position of rest, no magnetic material near the compass, either obviously or hidden in the clothing of the helmsman or others. Realize that steel partial dentures, or the steel grommet of a yachting cap brought within a few inches of the compass may produce deviation. Someone may be working that close to the instrument during compensation. Keep external compensators far from the compass until they are to be installed.

## COMPENSATION ON THE CARDINAL HEADINGS

With due regard for the conditions of wind, sea and current already mentioned steer 000° by compass from the

FIG. 1411 Disposable buoys.

chosen mark, holding rigorously to this course by the compass for half a mile or more. Next, have a crew member drop the disposable buoy over the stern, execute the turn and sail the reciprocal course, fig. 1410. This course, the reader will recall, is not sailed by compass, but by heading for the original departure point. The helmsman must hold this course visually. The compass heading is noted. If it is 180° there is no deviation on either the north or south compass headings. The athwartship internal compensator is not touched and no athwartship external compensator is necessary.

If the compass heading is not 180° compensation is required. Exactly as in the process of zeroing-in, half the difference between 180° and the observed compass course is to be removed. Halving the difference is based on the assumption that the deviation on reciprocal courses is equal and opposite. It may not be exactly so (see again ANACHRONISM, Chapter 13), but it serves well as an approach.

Assume the compass heading is observed to be 200°. Then one half of the 20° difference, or 10°, is to be removed; adjustment is made until 190° is on the lubber's line while the helmsman continues to hold the course by steering for the buoy.

On an internally compensated compass turn the N-S adjusting screw. This controls the concealed athwartship magnet. If the compass course becomes more than 200°, turn the screw in the opposite direction. Move the screw slowly until the compass course is 190°.

For the externally compensated compass the correction will be made by *centering* a compensator athwartship on the chalked fore-and-aft line. If there is room, place a compensator forward of the compass in the position D, A or C, fig. 1413. Should the course become more than 200° the compensator is increasing the deviation and must be turned end-for-end. The card will move in the desired direction.

Should the card stop moving before 190° reaches the lubber's line, the compensator, in a position as at D, is too far from the compass. On the other hand, should the card

FIG. 1412 Chalk lines for positioning external compensators, laid out through the compass pivot.

swing past 190° the compensator is in the position as at C, too close to the compass. Move the compensator aft or forward as necessary until the course is 190°. Now tape the compensator firmly down; no screws yet. If there is no room for the compensator forward of the compass, place it in the vicinity shown as A'. *Do not place it off the center line as at E.*

In zeroing-in, the compass was next oriented so that 180° was on the lubber's line. This maneuver is not usable here before returning to the buoy because there is no means of laying out a reciprocal course. Return to the buoy, then run either south or north, repeat the procedure: outbound again on 000° (though the track will be 10° away from the original one), drop the disposable buoy, make the turn, head visually for the marker. If the observed course is not now 180° again remove only half the difference by turning the adjusting screw or moving the external compensator, as the case may be. Repeat if necessary until the N-S headings are error-free. Screw down the external magnet in its place, being careful not to move it. Do not touch

**FIG. 1413  How compensating magnets are placed.**

the internal compensator screw again. The smallest shift will nullify the careful work and re-introduce some deviation.

A similar method is pursued on east-west headings. Run from a buoy to the eastward on 090° or to the westward on 270°, drop the buoy, make the turn, head back visually for the departure point. Remove half the apparent error. On the internally compensated compass, adjust the E-W screw. With external compensation, place the compensator in a fore-and-aft position and *centered* on the athwartship chalk line, similar to B or B', fig. 1413, following the same techniques as on the north-south headings. When, after sufficient trials, the deviations are zero, *or as near to zero as is attainable,* screw down the external compensator with utmost care. Leave the internal compensator screw alone.

An alternate method of sailing reciprocal courses, credited to Darrach, uses a vertical shadow pin in the center of a horizontal graduated disc, preferably gimbal-mounted.

As the vessel heads north by the compass, the disc is rotated by hand so that the shadow falls on its zero point.

The ship comes about, steadies on a course such that the shadow falls on the opposite edge of the disc, exactly on the 180° mark. Now the course shown on the compass is noted. If it is 180° there is no deviation on N-S headings. If it is not, the procedure for compensation is undertaken, halving the difference and similarly on the E-W headings.

This appears to be simple. The vessel need not run far on any course. No departure mark nor disposable buoy is necessary. Neither wind nor current alters the result. But, reader, wait before you exclaim "this is for me." That shadow is not a fixed direction. The earth turns under the sun. While the ship holds a constant heading for a few minutes, that shadow moves. So time becomes a factor in the operation. Compensators must be adjusted or taped down before the shadow moves appreciably, taking the ship off the reciprocal heading. A navigator knows how to make the needed changes in his course by the shadow pin. The novice would best plan to use this method of course reversal only near the time of the summer solstice when the rate of change of the shadow movement is less than 1° in ten minutes of time, depending on the latitude.

## COMPENSATION ON INTERCARDINAL HEADINGS

This is not for the amateur. However, in the average wooden, plastic or aluminum hull after cardinal compensation, the deviations on the intercardinals are usually small, not exceeding 4°.

Steel hulls may present problems whose solution may require installing soft iron spheres on the binnacle, use of Flinders bars and possibly heeling magnets. All this is for the professional, or for the exceptional amateur who, by study and practice in methods not discussed in this book, has achieved professional competence.

## RESIDUALS ON INTERCARDINAL HEADINGS

The deviations remaining on the intercardinal headings may be determined by the methods discussed in Chapter 13 or estimated by making reciprocal runs on these headings. In the latter method half the difference between the outward course steered by compass and the observed inward course will be the deviation for the heading. Proper attention should be paid to the direction of the deviation, East or West.

## FAILURE TO ACHIEVE COMPENSATION

When compensation cannot be achieved there is a strong magnetic field nearby. If care was used to remove or relocate the more obvious culprits in view of or hidden from the compass as earlier advised, look to the existence of a magnet nearby. Always suspect are tachometer cables and the steering mechanism. Test them with a thin piece of steel; a machinist's thickness gauge .001" thick is ideal. Touch one end to the part being tested and gently pull it away. If the thin piece of steel tends to stick to the part, the latter is magnetized. Test thoroughly. Open the wheel housing and test all its metal parts. Finding a magnet, demagnetize it.

## DEMAGNETIZATION

Robert C. Beard wrote: "When the offending part has been located, you can demagnetize it by borrowing from an electronics service shop either his color TV degaussing coil or his magnetic tape bulk erasing coil. Before doing any demagnetizing, *remove the compass from the boat* to prevent accidentally demagnetizing the compass needle.

"Connect the demagnetizing coil to the shore line. Holding it about one foot from the part to be demagnetized, turn it on and keep it on! Do not let it turn off for any reason, until this procedure is finished. Move the coil slowly toward the part until it is in contact with it. Then, still slowly, move it all over the part and around it. Finally, very slowly draw the coil away from the part for about five feet before turning it off. If your finger slipped and allowed the coil to turn off momentarily during the process, you will have to repeat the whole process to be sure of complete demagnetization."

Now test once more, with the thin piece of steel, the previously discovered permanent magnet or magnets. Inaccessibility may have precluded their complete demagnetization. Ideally, such parts should be disassembled, taken ashore, demagnetized and reassembled. Steel used in some linkages may be replaced by non-ferrous metals, aluminum or bronze.

Remount the compass, positioning the lubber's line with care and follow the procedure of compensation.

When the compass has been compensated preserve its magnetic environment as was suggested earlier in this chapter.

## WORKING DEVIATION TABLE

Now that the compass has been non-professionally compensated a new deviation table must be made. That of ANACHRONISM is here reproduced.

### ANACHRONISM COMPENSATED

| Compass Heading | Deviation | Compass Heading | Deviation |
|---|---|---|---|
| 000° | 2.0°W | 180° | 2.0°E |
| 015° | 2.5°W | 195° | 2.5°E |
| 030° | 3.0°W | 210° | 3.0°E |
| 045° | 3.0°W | 225° | 3.0°E |
| 060° | 3.0°W | 240° | 3.0°E |
| 075° | 2.5°W | 255° | 2.5°E |
| 090° | 2.0°W | 270° | 2.0°E |
| 105° | 1.5°W | 285° | 1.5°E |
| 120° | 1.0°W | 300° | 1.0°E |
| 135° | 0° | 315° | 0° |
| 150° | 0.5°E | 330° | 1.0°W |
| 165° | 1.5°E | 345° | 1.5°W |

From this the direct-reading table in the next column was prepared. Slight discrepancies, due to rounding, have no practical significance.

Either table makes quite evident those courses on which deviations are larger. In planning a voyage and in keeping track of position under way, using accurate deviation is essential. The knowing pilot, seeing at a glance where in ANACHRONISM the deviations are maximum, will be aware of those courses upon which compass bearings differ widely from their magnetic equivalents. Bearings taken on these headings must, before plotting, be converted by applying the deviation for the ship's heading. Bearings taken on headings in the vicinity of 135° and 315° may be plotted immediately as magnetic.

| Magnetic | Deviation | Compass |
|---|---|---|
| 133°-144° | 0° | 133°-145° |
| 145°-153° | 0.5°E | 146°-153° |
| 154°-163° | 1.0°E | 154°-162° |
| 164°-176° | 1.5°E | 163°-174° |
| 177°-187° | 2.0°E | 175°-185° |
| 188°-211° | 2.5°E | 186°-208° |
| 212°-251° | 3.0°E | 209°-248° |
| 252°-264° | 2.5°E | 249°-262° |
| 265°-279° | 2.0°E | 263°-277° |
| 280°-294° | 1.5°E | 278°-292° |
| 295°-303° | 1.0°E | 293°-302° |
| 304°-310° | 0.5°E | 303°-309° |
| 311°-319° | 0° | 310°-319° |
| 320°-326° | 0.5°W | 320°-327° |
| 327°-335° | 1.0°W | 328°-336° |
| 336°-352° | 1.5°W | 337°-353° |
| 353°-006° | 2.0°W | 354°-008° |
| 007°-018° | 2.5°W | 009°-021° |
| 019°-061° | 3.0°W | 022°-064° |
| 062°-078° | 2.5°W | 065°-080° |
| 079°-097° | 2.0°W | 081°-099° |
| 098°-109° | 1.5°W | 100°-110° |
| 110°-120° | 1.0°W | 111°-121° |
| 121°-132° | 0.5°W | 122°-132° |

## TESTING FOR RANDOM DEVIATIONS

Random deviations are those existent only when some auxiliary equipment is put to use. They will not have normally been present during the compensation process, but may show up with the use of windshield wipers, radio-telephone, radio direction-finder, depth sounder, any lights or other electrical device used intermittently.

Testing is simple. Any single electro-magnetic influence that affects a fully compensated compass will cause a maximum deviation on two diametrically opposed headings. On the two headings midway between these there will be no deviation. A compass having residual deviations, as ANACHRONISM, may exhibit departure from this rule.

## DEVIATION CAUSED BY WINDSHIELD WIPERS

Put the ship on a compass heading of 000° for a buoy or a landmark. Hold the course by steering, not by the compass, but visually for the mark. Repeatedly turn on the windshield wipers for five to ten seconds. Watch the compass closely. If the card swings even slightly, the wipers are affecting it. No motion of the card does not, at this point, support the conclusion that the wipers have no magnetic influence. By coincidence this might be the heading of zero deviation.

To continue the test, position the boat so that on a compass heading of 090° or 270° it may be steered visually for a buoy or landmark. Again turn on the wipers repeatedly for five- to ten-second periods. If the card is again motionless, the wipers cause no deviation.

When deviation does occur, the headings of maximum and zero deviations must be found. The opinion of experts is that rarely will these be cardinal points. The wise skipper is concerned with the maximum amount of deviation the wipers may cause. To find the maximum he looks first for a minimum, that heading on which the wiper-caused deviation is zero. Should this be hard to pinpoint he knows the maximum will be small and then hunts for it. He is dealing no longer with the whole 'magnetic mass' of the ship but with one small additional field either present or not present as the wipers are turned on or off.

The magnetic situation is as if, closely enough to affect the compass, a small magnet were sometimes placed in a definite position and orientation. When the wipers are off, the magnet is not there. When the wipers are on, the magnet is there—always in the same place and position, always exerting a deviation force on the compass, constant for any particular heading. Reason says eliminate the magnet. Practice says wipers are necessary; compensating for their magnetic effect is impractical and therefore allowance is to be made for their use. The allowance will be listed in a subsidiary deviation table to be used only when the wipers are running.

Slowly swing the boat, testing with the wipers for deviation on successive headings 15° apart. This is not too tedious. In any quadrant a point of either maximum or minimum deviation must occur. Hunt for a heading of no deviation, a null. Finding it, record the compass heading. If, as may well be, the precise null heading is not determinable, find and record the two headings on which the deviation is respectively 1°E and 1°W or 2°E and 2°W. Now determine arithmetically the mid-point between either of these pairs. Put the ship on a heading 90° from this mid-point. Now turn on the wipers and observe and record the deviation. It should be maximum. Further trial may be necessary to ascertain precisely the heading of maximum deviation.

When the maximum deviations are small, the values for the intermediate headings may be calculated by simple interpolation.

*Example.* Aboard EVOTZ the deviation is zero on the compass heading 060° and is maximum at 6°W on the compass heading 150°.

*Required:* The deviations for the intermediate headings at 15° intervals.

*Answer.* In 90° the deviation changes 6°. Therefore in 15° it will change $\frac{15 \times 6}{90}$° or 1° and the required deviations will be:

075° 1°W;    090° 2°W;    105° 3°W;    120° 4°W;    135° 5°W

As long as the wiper deviations are small, even though the headings of maximum and minimum are not exactly 90° apart (in the case of a not fully compensated compass), it is safe to estimate the intermediate values. A curve of deviations plotted on a Napier diagram would yield a table more accurate, but only in insignificant fractions of degrees.

A round of observations in ANACHRONISM produces these tables.

## WIPERS OPERATING

| Compass Heading | Deviation | Compass Heading | Deviation |
|---|---|---|---|
| 000° | 6°W | 180° | 6°E |
| 015° | 5.5°W | 195° | 5.5°E |
| 030° | 5°W | 210° | 5°E |
| 045° | 3°W | 225° | 4°E |
| 060° | 2°W | 240° | 2°E |
| 075° | 0.5°W | 255° | 0 |
| 090° | 1°E | 270° | 2°W |
| 105° | 3°E | 285° | 3.5°W |
| 120° | 5°E | 300° | 5°W |
| 135° | 7°E | 315° | 6°W |
| 150° | 7°E | 330° | 6°W |
| 165° | 6°E | 345° | 6°W |

| Magnetic | Deviation | Compass |
|---|---|---|
| 072°-085° | 0° | 073°-084° |
| 086°-095° | 1°E | 085°-093° |
| 096°-103° | 2°E | 094°-101° |
| 104°-112° | 3°E | 102°-109° |
| 113°-122° | 4°E | 110°-117° |
| 123°-130° | 5°E | 118°-124° |
| 131°-137° | 6°E | 125°-131° |
| 138°-163° | 7°E | 132°-156° |
| 164°-201° | 6°E | 157°-195° |
| 202°-223° | 5°E | 196°-218° |
| 224°-233° | 4°E | 219°-229° |
| 234°-239° | 3°E | 230°-236° |
| 240°-246° | 2°E | 237°-244° |
| 247°-252° | 1°E | 245°-251° |
| 253°-259° | 0° | 253°-260° |
| 260°-266° | 1°W | 261°-267° |
| 267°-274° | 2°W | 268°-276° |
| 275°-282° | 3°W | 277°-285° |
| 283°-292° | 4°W | 286°-296° |
| 293°-303° | 5°W | 297°-308° |
| 304°-010° | 6°W | 309°-015° |
| 011°-028° | 5°W | 016°-033° |
| 029°-040° | 4°W | 034°-043° |
| 041°-053° | 3°W | 044°-055° |
| 054°-062° | 2°W | 056°-064° |
| 063°-071° | 1°W | 065°-072° |

The existence of other random deviations which cannot be eliminated is unusual in small craft, but tests should be made for them. If present, knowledge of their existence first promotes safety, and second may impel the skipper to remove them.

Using alternate deviation tables is not difficult, particularly if they are made of different colored stock. With a little practice the skipper soon learns those headings on which wipers introduce important changes in deviation or, as in ANACHRONISM, those few headings where the change is slight. Turning on the wipers is an automatic order to recheck the compass course to be steered.

It is well to keep in mind the result of sailing off course. With a 10° error the ship will be set off course 1 mile for every 5.7 miles run. This may be serious when making a landfall in poor visibility. More hazardous are the risks of stranding when running a narrow channel through shallow water in fog or heavy rain. Note the following table.

| Error in Course | Number of feet off course after sailing one nautical mile | Miles sailed to be one mile off course |
|---|---|---|
| 1° | 106 | 57.3 |
| 2° | 212 | 28.6 |
| 3° | 318 | 19.1 |
| 4° | 424 | 14.3 |
| 5° | 530 | 11.5 |
| 6° | 635 | 9.6 |
| 7° | 740 | 8.2 |
| 8° | 846 | 7.2 |
| 9° | 950 | 6.4 |
| 10° | 1055 | 5.7 |

Properly installed, understood and used, the magnetic compass is the finest, least troublesome, inexpensive direction indicator obtainable by the small-craft sailor. Study and mastery of the principles and methods covered in these two chapters will be richly rewarding. A review of the highlights appears in the following two pages.

297

# COMPASS BRIEFS

→ The heart of the compass is a magnetic element so mounted that on any heading of the ship, it lies in a constant direction in a horizontal plane. A card is rigidly attached to the magnetic element. To the helmsman the card may appear to move, but this is not so. The compass bowl, carrying the lubber's line, the 'hand,' moves around the card, the 'dial,' to mark the course. Except for movements caused by deviation, *the card is stationary.* The ship rotates about the card.

Card graduations are in degrees or points, or in various combinations of the two. Scales read from 000° at North clockwise through 360° or in points logically named by their positions relative to the cardinal or intercardinal points. There are eight points to a quadrant, thus a point is 11¼° and a quarter-point approximately 2¾°.

→ Buy the best compass you can afford or one a little better. A large card makes for easy steering. By virtue of its optical magnification, so does a spherical compass. Card graduations should suit your needs. Many craft sail on only short coastwise, lake or river voyages. On most of these, 'open' cards graduated every 5°, are adequate. Skippers of larger boats or of small ones making blue-water passages prefer graduations in single degrees and points. Many wind sailors still use quarter-points.

→ Before buying, test the compass by simulating the motions of rolling, pitching, yawing and deliberate course change. A good one behaves well under these conditions. It is also 'dead beat,' showing minimum over-swing as the vessel steadies on a new course.

→ Before taking it aboard, zero-in a compass having built-in compensators. Zeroing-in is done by adjusting the compensators so that they do not affect the compass. This is imperative if the unmounted compass is to be moved about its projected site testing for ship's magnetism or magnetic influences.

→ Mount the compass as far as possible from any known shipboard magnetic influences and yet where the helmsman may watch it without strain. There may have to be compromise here. Be sure that a line through the pivot and the lubber's line is parallel to the keel's fore-and-aft direction. See that the instrument is level at cruising speed and *particularly not canted* to port or starboard.

Once mounted, preserve the compass's magnetic environment, except for the adjustments made during compensation.

→ Keep the bowl filled with liquid. Should additions be made, check the tightness of the seals and top-off with nothing foreign to the original contents lest the card, bellows, seals and even the pivot and bearings be damaged. Watch the compass in operation. If it becomes sluggish, test for pivot friction. Should it oscillate in a seaway, look for and consider removing vertical iron aboard.

→ Magnetic meridians are lines of force of the earth's magnetic field. A compass, influenced by this field alone, aligns its N-S axis along a magnetic meridian. Such a compass *does not point to a magnetic pole* but does show accurately the direction of the magnetic meridian. Generally, the magnetic and the true meridians do not coincide. The angle between their similar parts is called variation. It is labelled East or West as the (magnetic) northerly part of the magnetic meridian lies to the east or the west of the true meridian. Variation ranges in amount from zero to 180°.

→ Variation exists where there is no compass. It is an attribute of the earth. Variation changes with geographical position. It is relatively constant in a locality. The small annual changes noted on charts are not persistent. The annual rate of change may itself change. The chart bears at best an educated guess, based on past observations. Therefore do not rely on computations projected from obsolete charts.

→ Magnetic materials aboard ship or alongside cause the compass magnet and card to swing out of the magnetic meridian. The resulting angle between the north-indicating branch of the magnetic meridian and the compass's N-S axis is called deviation. It, too, can range in amount from zero to 180° and, like variation, is termed East or West as the North point of the compass card deviates to the East or West of the magnetic meridian. Deviation exists only where there is a compass and some magnetic force additional to that of the earth. It is an attribute of the compass, not of the earth. Deviation changes with the ship's heading.

Though often so-called, variation and deviation are not errors of the compass, but are simply predictable magnetic effects to be reckoned with in course conversion.

→ A course may be named in three ways: true (TC), magnetic (MC) and compass (CC). A course (or a bearing) is a fixed direction. The scale zero, the line of reference for the angle, may be in one of three directions: the true meridian, the magnetic meridian or the direction of the north point of the compass. Hence courses have to be converted, that is, expressed with respect to the three different reference lines.

Converting courses expressed in degrees is simple.

| True | | Conversion from true through |
|---|---|---|
| Variation | | magnetic to compass is in |
| Magnetic | | the rule: *Down Add West* or |
| Deviation | | *DAW,* which should be |
| Compass | | memorized. The changes in the rule are obvious: |

Down Subtract East, Up Subtract West, Up Add East.

→ When courses are expressed in points and quarter-points "add" and "subtract" can be confusing instructions. (Try adding ½ pt E to E ¾ N and you will be 1 point in error!) The direction in which the deviation or variation is to be applied is substituted. For 'add' use 'clockwise' and for 'subtract' use counterclockwise. Call conversion from compass to magnetic to true 'correcting' and the reverse conversion 'uncorrecting.' Then a basic rule emerges, Correct Easterly Errors Clockwise, shortenable to *Correct Easterly Clockwise, CEC.* With this in memory, remember further that in any change of this basic, *only two and always two* of the terms are changed. Thus there are UWC, UECC and CWCC. UWC is immediately recognizable as the DAW of the degree system.

→ Deviation changes with the heading because the ship

rotates about the compass card. Hence magnetic material aboard located in the compass's first quadrant while the vessel heads North, will be moved into the compass's fourth quadrant when she heads West. Similarly all the other magnetic material aboard shifts its position relative to the compass on this 90° course change. The compass card, subject to two influences, that of the earth and that of the moved field of the ship, may deviate from its original direction on CC north. Thus it should be seen that any change in heading may change the deviation.

→ Among the methods of determining deviation are running ranges or sailing across one range on different headings. Recording the deviations so observed yields a deviation table for compass headings. Plotting these on a Napier diagram and taking therefrom the deviations for magnetic headings gives a table of deviations on magnetic headings.

Thence for everyday use, deviation cards of various types, pictorial or tabular, are constructible, as the user desires.

→ A word of warning. *Never enter a deviation table with a bearing.* The deviation to be applied to a bearing is that of the ship's head at the time of bearing. For convenience in plotting bearings the proper deviation and the variation are algebraically combined to give one quantity, the so-called compass error (CE). CE = Var + Dev. When the two are in the same direction they are added, when opposite in direction the smaller is subtracted from the larger and the remainder takes the name of the larger.

→ Compensating, often called adjusting, a compass is the act of neutralizing, by small magnets near the compass, the effect on the compass of the ship's own magnetic field. Many compasses are equipped with two small magnets, whose position is adjustable, built into their cases. Adjust-

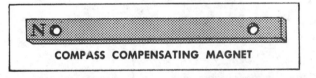

**COMPASS COMPENSATING MAGNET**

ment or compensation consists of positioning these compensators so that they negate the action of the ship's field. A compass not so equipped is compensated by fastening one or two small magnets near the compass. The proper position of these magnets is most important. Each must be centered on a line passing through the compass pivot. The athwartship magnet is centered on such a line running truly fore-and-aft; the fore-and-aft one on such a line running truly athwartship.

→ A table of deviations may be analyzed to ascertain approximately its components or coefficients and so determine, again approximately, the position of the compensators. This is usually unnecessary in small craft.

→ Compensation in small craft is not difficult. Run from a fixed mark on compass course North, establishing a range with a disposable buoy. Reverse course by sailing the range, ignoring the compass. Now observe the course the compass shows. The difference between 180° and the compass-indicated course is approximately twice the deviation. Remove half of this by adjusting the N-S internal compensator or temporarily taping down an athwartship

external compensator on the fore-and-aft line through the compass pivot. Repeat this operation on N-S and S-N headings until the deviations reach a minimum. Then do the same on the E-W compass headings, adjusting the E-W internal compensator or taping down, on the athwartship line through the pivot, a fore-and-aft external compensator. Permanently fasten the external compensators or leave the internal ones in the optimum positions found.

With a thin piece of steel (.001″) locate any strong magnetic influence which prevents reasonable compensation. Demagnetize it or remove it from the boat and re-compensate. *Caution. Do not subject the compass to demagnetization.* Before turning on any demagnetizer unship the compass, take it ashore, well away from the influence of this powerful equipment.

Swing the ship for residuals and make a working deviation table or tables as desired.

Reasonable compensation is obtainable by this method. There may be residuals near the intercardinal points which merit some explanation here.

→ Broadly, deviations may be classified as observational, semicircular and quadrantal. The student need not be fearful of these names.

Observational deviation is that part of the total deviation due to errors in observation. It includes errors caused by lack of parallelism of the pivot-lubber's line axis and the keel. Observational deviation exists when a Napier diagram is symmetrical with respect not to its base line, but to a line parallel to the base line.

Semicircular deviation waxes and wanes, so to speak, in a semicircle. It increases from zero to maximum and decreases again to zero through a course change of 180°.

Quadrantal deviation does the same thing in one quarter of a circle. It increases from zero to maximum and decreases to zero through a course change of 90°.

A plotted curve of deviations includes all these elements. It follows, then, that when a Napier or other curve of deviations is unsymmetrical (i.e. of different shape on the opposite sides of its base line or a base line adjusted for observational error) quadrantal deviation exists. Fore-and-aft and athwartship compensators may not remove all the quadrantal deviations. Those remaining appear as residuals on the intercardinals. Generally, in wooden or plastic craft, they are not large enough to be troublesome.

Removing these residuals by hollow iron spheres, called quadrantal correctors, attached to the binnacle may not be within the competence of the amateur, is best left to the professional.

→ Windshield wipers in operation may cause significant deviations. Test for these. When existent, make a deviation table for use only when they are turned on. In reduced visibility, fog, rain or snow, comes greater need for trying to be sure that the course steered is the one desired to be made good.

→ Preserve the compass's magnetic environment. When it is altered by the installation of a new motor or other equipment, or by electric welding aboard, check the deviations.

→ Know your compass. Know its deviations. Above all, trust it. Not without good reason has it been dubbed the mariner's best friend.   *   *   *

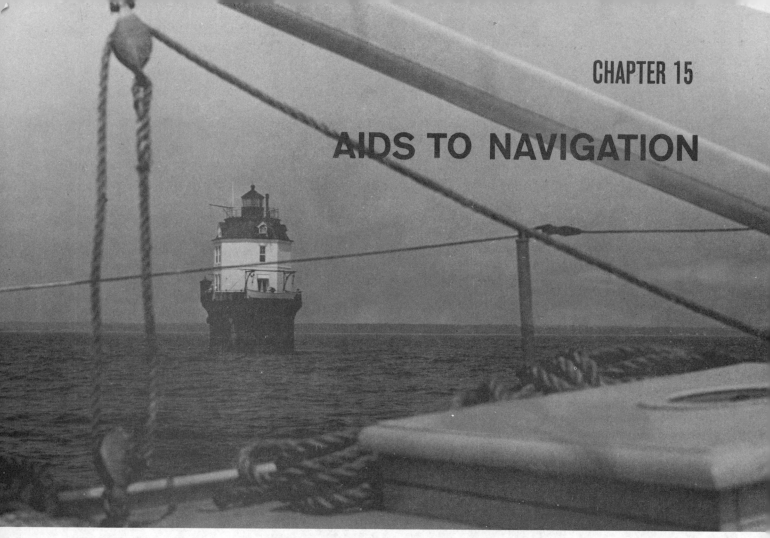

# CHAPTER 15

# AIDS TO NAVIGATION

**FIG. 1501** The skipper of a boat of any size is highly dependent on aids to navigation to warn him of unseen underwater hazards. He must be able to recognize such aids and know their significance.

# Buoyage Systems

Although few mariners or boatmen may be aware of it, directing the movements of a vessel of any size in near-shore waters is closely akin to "flying blind" in an aircraft. It is not the few visible obstacles that are dangerous, but rather the more numerous shoals and rocks that lie unseen beneath the surface.

Natural landmarks may be used as reference points for navigation, but these are often few and far between, and may not be located to best advantage. It is to protect the mariner from these unseen dangers, and to allow him to safely direct his course, that government agencies and private individuals establish and maintain *aids to navigation*.

Figures 1502-1510, 1512, 1514, 1516 and 1517 reproduced from official U. S. COAST GUARD photographs.

The term *aid to navigation* may be applied to any man-made object prepared and located so as to indicate to a mariner the location of his vessel or the safe and proper course on which to proceed. The term includes buoys, day-beacons, lights, lighthouses, lightships, radiobeacons, fog signals, and loran, consolan, and other electronic systems. It covers unlighted objects, floating and non-floating; and visible, audible, and electronic signals and their supporting structures.

The term "aid to navigation" should always be stated thus, and not as "navigational aid". The latter term has been more broadly defined as also including "charts, instruments, devices, methods, etc., intended to assist in the navigation of a craft."

## PURPOSE OF AIDS TO NAVIGATION

Aids to navigation are placed at various points along the coasts and navigable waterways as markers and guides to enable mariners to determine their position with respect to the shore and to hidden dangers. They assist mariners in making landfalls when approaching from the high seas, mark isolated dangers, make it possible for pilots to follow natural and improved channels, and provide a continuous chain of charted marks for coast piloting.

Establishment and maintenance of any aid must have economic justification. Aids established by the Federal government must, by law, be needed for the safety of a reasonable amount of water traffic, not just the occasional craft or the coming and going of a few local boats.

Within the bounds of actual necessity and reasonable cost, every aid to navigation is designed to be seen or heard over the greatest practicable area. As all aids serve the same broad purposes, such structural differences as those between an unlighted buoy or beacon, a minor light, or a major lighthouse with radiobeacon, are solely for the purpose of meeting requirements and conditions of the particular location at which the aid is established.

## OPERATING AGENCIES

The United States Coast Guard, since 1967 a part of the Department of Transportation, is the agency responsible for maintenance of the system of aids to navigation on waters of the United States subject to Federal jurisdiction. Federal "navigable waters" are legally defined as coastal waters; rivers, bays, sounds, lakes, etc. navigable from the sea; and rivers, canals, and lakes *not* lying wholly within the boundaries of a single state. Such areas include the Atlantic, Gulf, and Pacific coasts of the continental United States, the Great Lakes, the Mississippi River and its tributaries, Puerto Rico, the Hawaiian Islands, and Alaskan waters. Aids to navigation may also be maintained by the Coast Guard at other places where required to serve the needs of our armed forces.

The senior officer of the Coast Guard is its Commandant, with headquarters in Washington, D.C. Functions of planning, procurement, establishment, operation, and maintenance of aids to navigation are carried on under his direction. Because of the wide geographic distribution of such aids on our coasts and inland waters, actual field work is executed by district organization.

There are 12 Coast Guard Districts. They maintain the system of aids to navigation and carry out other Coast Guard functions. The ten continental Districts are numbered from 1 to 13, omitting 4, 6, and 10; see fig. 1502. Hawaii is in the 14th Coast Guard District, Alaska in the 17th. Each District has its Commander, assisted by a suitable engineering and administrative force. Each District has the necessary supply and buoy depots, and specially designed and equipped vessels for the maintenance of aids to navigation. See fig. 1503.

### "Private" aids to navigation

Aids to navigation may, with prior approval, be established in waters subject to Federal jurisdiction by agencies other than the Coast Guard. Information on procedures for obtaining such permission may be obtained from any Coast Guard District office. These aids must be patterned after Federal aids, and if a fixed structure is to be erected in navigable water, a permit must also be obtained from the Army Corps of Engineers.

All such aids to navigation—whether established by an individual, a corporation, a state or local government, or even a Federal agency other than the Coast Guard, such as the Navy—are termed "private" aids. These will have the same appearance as Coast Guard-maintained aids, but will be specially designated in the Light Lists.

### State-maintained aids

On bodies of water wholly within the boundaries of a single state, and not navigable to the sea, the state government has the responsibility for the establishment and maintenance of aids to navigation.

Although each state retains authority over its waters, agreement has been reached on a uniform system of aids

**FIG. 1502  Maintenance of aids to navigation is a district responsibility in the Coast Guard organization. There are ten districts covering the continental 48 states. District boundaries and headquarters are shown. Note that there are no districts numbered 4, 6, or 10.**

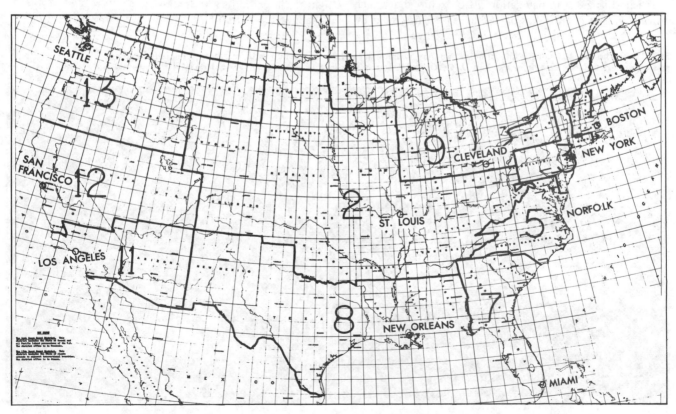

to navigation and regulatory markers. These will be described and discussed in detail later in this chapter.

## PROTECTION BY LAW

Whether established by the Coast Guard or by another agency, all aids to navigation are protected by law. It is not only a violation of common sense, but also a criminal offense, to cause any damage or hindrance to the proper operation of any aid. Do not deface, alter, move, or destroy any aid to navigation. Never tie your boat to a buoy, daybeacon, or light structure. Avoid anchoring so close to a buoy that you obscure the aid from the sight of other passing craft.

If you should unintentionally or unavoidably collide with or damage an aid to navigation, this fact must be reported to the nearest Officer in Charge, Marine Inspection, U.S. Coast Guard in full detail and without delay.

For your own safety and that of others, cooperate with the Coast Guard and other agencies by promptly reporting any missing or malfunctioning aid. This will normally be done immediately after returning to port; if the safety of navigation is threatened seriously, the report should be made by radio without delay.

## Types of Aids to Navigation

The term "aid to navigation" encompasses a wide range of fixed and floating objects from a single pile with a pointer or a small sixth-class buoy to manned lightships and lighthouses with an array of visible, audible, and electronic signals. Conspicuous shapes and objects on shore, such as mountain tops, radio antennas, smoke stacks, etc., may be charted and used to assist in piloting, but these are generally grouped under the term *landmark* and are excluded from the definition of an aid to navigation. This latter term is applied to objects that have been *primarily* established to assist in navigation. Also excluded are such informal aids as bush stakes placed in many side creeks by local watermen to mark minor natural channels or hazards. These do indeed help the skipper to pilot his boat safely, but they are not a part of the organized system of aids to navigation.

## MAJOR TYPES

**Buoys** are floating objects moored or anchored to the bottom as aids to navigation; lightships fit this overall definition, but they are excluded as they form a separate category of aids. Buoys will have a distinctive shape and color as determined by their location and purpose. They may be equipped with visual, audible, and/or electronic signals.

**Daybeacons** are unlighted fixed structures established to aid navigation. They may be a single pile or a multiple-pile structure. Clusters of piles are called dolphins. Daybeacons will normally be equipped with a pointer, signboard, or other marker ("daymark"). These pointers or daymarks may be of a distinctive color and shape as determined by the information that they indicate.

**Lights** are aids to navigation that have active visual signals. These are fixed aids (lighted floating aids are designated as lighted buoys or lightships). Lights are classified by the Coast Guard and other authorities as *primary seacoast lights, secondary lights,* or *minor lights,* as determined by their location, importance, and physical characteristics; the intensity of the light and its visible range will vary with the classification. The shape and color of the structure supporting the light source may be distinctive for purposes of identification, but will not convey information as, for example, in the case of buoys. The term *lighthouse* is often applied to primary seacoast lights and to some secondary lights.

**Fog signals** are audible signals transmitted to assist mariners during periods of low visibility, primarily fog. Occasionally they may be separate aids, as when located on the end of a jetty, but more often they will be part of a buoy, light, or larger aid to navigation.

**Ranges** are pairs of unlighted or lighted fixed aids so

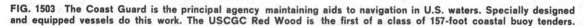

**FIG. 1503 The Coast Guard is the principal agency maintaining aids to navigation in U.S. waters. Specially designed and equipped vessels do this work. The USCGC Red Wood is the first of a class of 157-foot coastal buoy tenders.**

FIG. 1504 "Super buoys" are now in use at some offshore locations. The one shown, built of high-strength low alloy steel plate, is 40 feet in diameter with a 5,000 candlepower light 33 feet above the water. It replaces the old Scotland Lightship in the approaches to New York Harbor.

located that when observed in line the pilot is on the centerline of a channel. The individual structures may, in some cases, also serve as separate aids to navigation marking a turn in a channel.

**Lightships** are specially equipped vessels moored or anchored at specific locations to serve as aids to navigation. They are of distinctive shape and color, and will have lights and sound signals, and radiobeacons.

**Radiobeacons** are transmitters broadcasting a characteristic signal specifically to aid navigation at night, in fog, or at distances exceeding normal visibility. These, too, are usually at another aid, but may at times be located separately.

**Electronic navigation systems** are radio transmitters, usually in groups, which emit special signals that may be used for assistance in navigation when in fog or otherwise out of sight of land or offshore aids. Such systems include *Loran-A* and *Loran-C*, operated by the Coast Guard, *Consolan* operated by the Federal Aviation Agency, and other systems operated by various government or private interests. Only the USCG and FAA systems will be of general interest and use to boatmen.

## Buoys

Buoys are floating objects, other than lightships, anchored or moored to the bottom at specific locations so as to serve as aids to navigation. They are shown on charts by special symbols and lettering that will indicate their shape, color, and visual and/or sound signals. They will vary widely in size from sixth-class buoys projecting only a few feet above the surface of the water to the new "super buoys" that are some 40 feet in diameter with a superstructure rising to 30 or more feet in height; see fig. 1504.

The buoyage system adopted for waters of the United States consists of several different types of buoys, each kind designed to serve under definite conditions. Broadly speaking, all buoys serve as daytime aids; those having lights are also available to aid navigation at night, and

those having sound signals are especially useful in time of fog as well as at night.

The shape, color, and light characteristic, if any, will convey to a pilot information as to his location and the proper guidance of his vessel to remain in safe waters. The size of a buoy does *not* indicate such information and is usually determined by the importance of the waterway and size of vessels using it. The size of a buoy need not be taken into consideration by a skipper, except when estimating distances.

Buoys are normally anchored to the bottom using chain and heavy concrete sinkers weighing from one to five tons, fig. 1505. The length of chain will vary with the location, but will generally be two to three times the depth of water.

FIG. 1505 Buoys are anchored with cast concrete blocks called "sinkers." They range in size from one-ton, shown above, to as heavy as five tons. Normally, only a single sinker of appropriate size is used for any buoy.

### BUOY CHARACTERISTICS

Buoys may be subdivided into types as lighted or unlighted, sound buoys, or combination buoys. This latter type is comprised of buoys that have both an audible and a visual signal.

The Coast Guard maintains about 21,000 unlighted and 3,700 lighted and combination buoys in waters under its jurisdiction. Many others are maintained by state and private agencies in non-federal waters.

#### Buoy shapes

Unlighted buoys may be further classified by their shape.

**Can buoys** are objects made up of steel plates so that the above-water appearance is cylindrical, like a can or drum floating with its axis vertical and flat end upward; see fig. 1506. Two lifting lugs may project slightly above the flat top of a can buoy, but these will not significantly alter its appearance.

**Nun buoys** are objects made up of steel plates so that the above-water appearance is that of a cylinder topped

(a)

(b)

FIG. 1506 Can buoys have a cylindrical shape with a flat top. An older-type, still used, is shown on the left. Newer can buoys have integral radar reflectors as shown in (b) above.

FIG. 1507 Nun buoys have a conical shape coming to a near-point at the upper end. This is a modern nun buoy with radar reflector plates in its upper section.

with a cone, pointed end up, fig. 1507. The cone may come to a point or the tip may be slightly rounded. Smaller nun buoys will have a single lifting ring at the top; larger buoys will have several lugs around the sides.

Unlighted buoys come in standardized sizes. These are designated as classes — first through sixth — and as tall, standard, or special. Knowledge of the various sizes is not important to the boatman, although it may be of general interest to note that the above-water visible portion of a nun buoy may vary from 2'-6" for a sixth-class standard to 14'-0" for a first-class tall. Can buoys are somewhat shorter, ranging from 1'-4" to 9'-9" above the waterline. The smaller buoys are, of course, lesser in diameter also, with a range of 1½ to 5 feet. Pilots should remember that a considerable portion of a buoy is under water, and that they are really much larger and heavier objects than they would appear to be from a casual observation.

The Coast Guard has now eliminated the use of *spar* buoys, but they may be found in some private or foreign systems of aids. These are usually large logs, trimmed, shaped, and appropriately painted; they are anchored from one end with a suitable length of chain.

Special shapes will sometimes be found in use as markers, but these are not regular aids to navigation. Spherical buoys are the most generally used of the special shape category.

Lighted, sound, and combination buoys are described by their visual and/or audible signals rather than by their shape.

## Sound buoys

Buoys are often equipped with a characteristic sound signal to aid in their location during periods of reduced visibility, chiefly fog. Several different sound signals are available and are used to distinguish between different aids to navigation that may be within audible range of each other.

**Bell buoys** are steel floats surmounted by short skeleton towers in which a bell is mounted, fig. 1512. They serve

with considerable effectiveness both by day and night, and especially in fog; they are much used because of their moderate maintenance costs. Most bell buoys are operated by the motion of the sea—four tappers, loosely hung externally around the bell, are readily set in motion. When the buoy rolls as a result of waves, ground swells, or the wake of passing vessels, a single note is heard at irregular intervals. Some bell buoys are operated by electric batteries, their strokes sounding at regular intervals. These are particularly useful in sheltered waters where wave action is often insufficient to sound the signal.

**Gong buoys** are similar in construction to bell buoys, except that a set of gongs is substituted for the bell, fig. 1512. Gong buoys are used to give a distinctive character-

(a)

FIG. 1508 Buoys equipped with both a light and a sound signal are called combination buoys. Shown above in (a) is a lighted buoy with a whistle below the radar reflector. In (b) at the right, the lighted buoy has an electric horn fog signal.

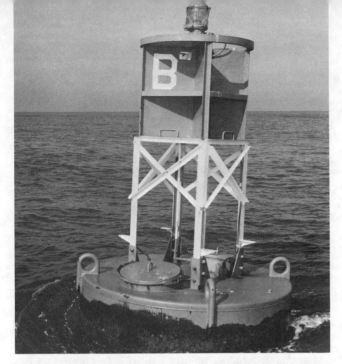

FIG. 1509 This is a late design of lighted buoy without sound signal. Note the straight sides of the tower-like superstructure; older designs had towers that first tapered in and then out near the top.

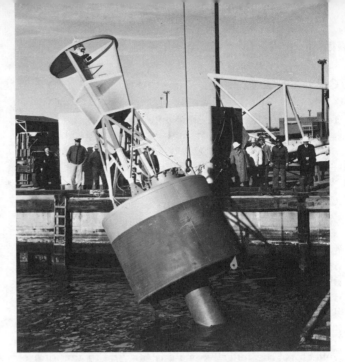

FIG. 1510 The Coast Guard is experimenting with an atomic power source for a buoy. This buoy is lighted from a strontium-90 thermo-electric system. It is hoped that the use of atomic power will increase the reliability of remote buoys and decrease the number of servicing visits required.

FIG. 1511 The Coast Guard has equipped many lighted buoys with "daylight controls." These electric-eye devices turn off the light during daylight to conserve battery power. Such buoys are often marked in white with the symbol shown above; in the future when all buoys are so equipped, this symbol will be discontinued.

FIG. 1512 Shown here are models, all to the same scale, of four typical buoys. Note the range of sizes and large mass of the lighted buoys that is below the waterline. The smaller lighted buoy has a bell and the larger one four gongs; both have external "tappers" to strike and sound the fog signal. These are all of the so-called "1962" design, many of which are in use.

istic when there are several sound buoys in one vicinity. In these buoys, four gongs of different tones are mounted, with one tapper for each gong. As the sea rocks the buoy, the tappers strike against their respective gongs, sounding four different notes in an irregular sequence.

**Whistle buoys** provide yet another distinctive audible signal useful at night or in fog. The whistle is sounded by compressed air produced by the motion of the buoy in the sea. For this reason, such buoys are used principally in open and exposed locations where a ground swell normally exists, fig. 1508.

## Lighted buoys

Buoys may be equipped with lights of various colors, intensities, and flashing characteristics (called "phase characteristics"). The color and characteristics of the light are used to convey information to the mariner. Intensity of the light will be determined by the distance at which the aid must be detected, influenced by such factors as background lighting, normal atmospheric clarity, etc.

**Lighted buoys** are constructed as metal floats with a short skeleton tower at the top of which the light is placed; see fig. 1509. The light is powered by electric batteries placed inside the lower body of the buoy below the waterline. Lighted buoys are designed to operate for many months without servicing.

Lighted buoys are now generally equipped with "daylight controls" that automatically turn the light on and off as darkness falls and lifts. Buoys equipped with such electric eye controls are specially marked with a white-paint symbol consisting of a circular spot with horizontal bar running through its center; see fig. 1511.

Lights on buoys, as on other lighted aids, are either red, green, or white. The colors red and green have specific applications as will be discussed later in this chapter. White lights are prescribed for certain specific functions, and may also be substituted for red or green where a greater range of visibility is desired.

## Color of buoys

Buoys used for navigation may be painted red, black, red-and-black, or black-and-white. Buoys for special purposes will use these colors and also yellow, green, orange, and blue. The specific meanings of the various colors will be discussed later in this chapter when buoyage systems are considered.

## Optical reflectors

Many unlighted buoys are fitted with optical reflectors. These greatly facilitate the locating of the buoys at night when using a searchlight. Optical reflectors may be white, red, or green, and have the same significance as lights of these colors.

Reflective sheeting is used extensively by the Coast Guard for marking buoys. This flexible plastic film is easily attached to any reasonably smooth surface and has improved reflective characteristics over conventional glass reflectors. The reflective material may be in the form of square "patches" or as bands around the buoy.

Although primarily intended to make unlighted buoys more visible at night, reflective material is also placed on lighted buoys to aid in their detection by searchlight between flashes. Numerals of reflective material are now being placed on buoys, and these will aid in their nighttime identification as well as detection.

## Radar reflectors

Many buoys are equipped with radar reflectors, vertical metal plates set at right angles to each other in such a manner as to greatly increase the echo returned to a radar receiver on a ship or boat. The plates are shaped and mounted so as to preserve the overall characteristic shape of an unlighted buoy or the general appearance of a lighted buoy. See fig. 1512.

## LIGHT PHASE CHARACTERISTICS

The lights on lighted buoys will generally flash in one of several specific patterns. The flashing-light type of operation serves a number of useful purposes:

(1) It conserves the energy source within the buoy by having the light on only a small portion of the total time. Fixed lights, continuously lit with no variation of color or intensity, are not used on Coast Guard buoys, and only occasionally on buoys maintained by other agencies.

(2) Flashing assists in the detection of the lighted aid against a background of other lights.

(3) Flashing allows the signaling during hours of darkness of a limited amount of information, such as the need to exercise special caution at a certain point in a channel.

(4) The flashing characteristic of the light can be selected from a number of available patterns so as to be able to distinguish between several buoys of the same general function that may be within visible range of each other.

Lights are classed as *flashing* when the light comes on for a single brief flash at regular intervals; the period of light is always *less* than the period of darkness. Coast Guard-maintained buoys designated as of the flashing type will flash their light not more than 30 times per minute. This is the more-generally used characteristic for buoys. It is sometimes termed "slow flashing," but the official and correct description is simply "flashing."

Flashing (Fl)

Quick Flashing (Qk Fl)

Interrupted Quick Flashing (I Qk Fl)

Morse Code "A" (Mo A)

FIG. 1513 Buoys show various light phase characteristics which help in conveying information and assist in distinguishing between buoys of the same type located near each other.

**Quick flashing** lights will flash not less than 60 times each minute. These buoys are used for special situations where they will be more quickly spotted and where particular attention to piloting is required.

**Interrupted quick flashing** lights are characterized by a series of quick flashes separated by dark intervals of about four seconds' duration. This light characteristic, too, is used in special situations as will be described later.

**Morse code "A"** flashing lights have a cycle consisting of a short flash, a brief dark interval, a longer flash, and a longer dark interval. This is the "dot-dash" of the letter "A" in the International Morse Code; the characteristic was formerly known as "short-long flashing." The color of the light is always white.

The above light phase characteristics are shown diagramatically in fig. 1513. The *period* of a light is the time required for the completion of one full cycle of flash and dark interval, or flashes and dark intervals. A light de-

FIG. 1514 Buoys should be used with caution because of natural hazards to which they are exposed. A Coast Guardsman is seen here removing ice from a large lighted buoy; such ice may have interferred with the buoy's normal operation.

scribed as "Flashing 4 seconds" has a period of four seconds. One flash and one dark interval lasts just that long before the cycle is repeated.

### Standardized flashing rates

As noted earlier, "flashing" lights may have various repetition rates for individual buoy identification, provided that there are not more than 30 flashes each minute. Over the years, the Coast Guard has used various characteristics involving different flash lengths and intervals. Buoys have been operated in the past that flashed at intervals of 2, 2½, 3, 4, 5, and 6 seconds; individual flashes have varied in length from 0.05 to 1.0 second. Standardization has now been introduced into the system of lighted buoys to reduce the number of different light phase characteristics.

Three standard characteristics will be used—flashing at intervals of 2.5, 4, and 6 seconds. These correspond to 24, 15, and 10 flashes per minute. These three light phase characteristics will provide sufficient differences for individual buoy identification and will provide economic battery service periods.

Another part of the Coast Guard's continuing effort to improve the reliability of its aids to navigation is the replacement of motorized mechanical flashers with solid-state (transistorized) electronic equipment having no moving parts. The use of precision moulded acrylic plastic lenses on buoys and minor lights has made possible substantial increases in the candlepower of such aids.

### CAUTIONS IN USING BUOYS

A pilot should not rely on floating aids to navigation to always maintain their charted positions, or to constantly and unerringly display their specified characteristics. Obstacles to perfect performance are of such magnitude that complete reliability is manifestly impossible. The Coast Guard makes a continuous effort to keep aids working properly, but cannot be completely successful with all of the many thousands to be checked and maintained.

Buoys are heavily anchored, but they may shift in location, be carried away, capsized, or sunk as a result of violent storms or of having been struck by passing ships. A pilot must be prepared for the possible absence of a buoy he planned to use in his navigation, or its displacement off-station.

Buoys that have been placed to mark shifting shoals may not always be properly located in relation to the hazards they are meant to mark. This is particularly true during and immediately after heavy storms when shoals are liable to shift their positions relative to the buoys.

Lighted buoys may become extinguished, or their control apparatus become broken or deranged causing them to show improper light characteristics. Essentially all audible signals on buoys are operated by action of the sea, and may consequently be silent during periods of calm water. They may fail to sound, regardless of wave activity, due to mechanical defects in their sound-producing mechanism. Even if functioning properly, a sound buoy may not be heard at relatively close range due to erratic transmission of sound in air.

Buoys do not maintain their position directly over their anchors as they must be provided with some scope on their anchor chains; they swing in small circles around the anchor, which is the charted location. (See Chapter 18 for how buoys are charted.) For this reason, buoys are inferior

to fixed aids to navigation when precise bearings are desired.

Moored as they are, buoys have a tendency to yaw about under the influence of wind and current. This action is unpredictable, and a vessel attempting to pass close aboard risks collision with a yawing buoy. In extremely strong currents, buoys may even be pulled beneath the surface.

Buoys are sometimes removed to make way for dredging operations, or for other reasons. In northern waters, buoys may be discontinued for the winter, or smaller unlighted buoys substituted for lighted and combination buoys to prevent damage or loss from ice floes. The dates shown in the Light Lists for seasonal buoys, or seasonal changes in buoys, are only approximate and may vary slightly due to weather or other conditions.

Temporary or permanent changes in buoys may be made between editions of charts. A wise skipper keeps informed of existing conditions through reading Notices to Mariners or Local Notices to Mariners—see Chapter 17.

All buoys (especially those located in exposed positions) should, therefore, be regarded as warnings or guides, and not as infallible navigation marks. Whenever possible, a boat should be navigated by bearings or angles on fixed objects on shore (see Chapter 21), and by soundings, rather than by total reliance on buoys.

FIG. 1515 The simplest daybeacon is a single pile with a pointer or daymark. This one, on a Gulf Coast River Channel, has a numbered black pointer on a white pile with green reflector that will show up brilliantly at night in a boat's searchlight. (Florida State News Bureau photograph)

## Daybeacons

**Daybeacons** are unlighted structures established as an aid to navigation; they are "fixed" rather than "floating" aids. Daybeacons may be located either on shore or in waters up to perhaps 12 to 15 feet deep.

Daybeacons vary greatly in design and construction, depending upon their location and the distance at which they must be seen. A continuing effort is now being made by the Coast Guard to standardize daybeacon structures and markings for easier identification as aids to navigation.

FIG. 1517 A minor light may consist of a single-pile structure with the light itself at the top and number identification on the daymark below. The light shown here is receiving periodic maintenance from a Coast Guard crew.

FIG. 1516 Buoys must be periodically hauled out for servicing. A new buoy is placed on station, and the old one is taken in to a depot for scraping and repainting.

## CHARACTERISTICS

The simplest daybeacon is a single pile with a pointer or number sign, called a "daymark," at or near the top, fig. 1515. The pile may be wood, concrete, or metal.

A larger, more visible, and more sturdy daybeacon is the "three-pile dolphin" type. Here the single pile is replaced by three piles separated a few feet at their lower ends, but coming together at their tops where they are strongly held together with wire cables. Such structures are equipped with a daymark at the top, or more likely two daymarks facing in opposite directions. (Some dolphins may be made of five piles, four around one central pile.)

### Daymarks and pointers

The daybeacon must be properly identified if it is to serve its purpose as an aid to navigation. Daymarks are widely used for this purpose; in some areas, pointers are placed on single-pile daybeacons in lieu of the daymark.

Daymarks are normally either square or triangular in shape, corresponding to can and nun buoys; see page 292. In some special applications, the daymark may be octagonal (eight-sided) or diamond-shaped. Pointers are all of the same shape, but are painted red or black in accordance with their use. The pointers always point toward the channel, or safe side of the daybeacon.

Daybeacon pointers and daymarks are normally equipped with reflective material to enhance their visibility at night. The reflective material is usually applied to the end of the pointer or around the border of the daymark.

## THE USES OF DAYBEACONS

For obvious reasons, the use of daybeacons is restricted to relatively shallow waters. Within this limitation, however, a daybeacon is often more desirable than a buoy. From a navigator's point of view, it is a superior aid to navigation — firmly fixed in position, and more readily seen and identified. From the Coast Guard's viewpoint, a daybeacon is more desirable too—once established, it is in position and requires but little maintenance (buoys must be regularly hauled out for scraping and repainting, fig. 1516).

Daybeacons are used primarily for channel marking and serve in the same manner as buoys in the buoyage systems to be described later in this chapter.

## Minor Lights

Just as daybeacons are sometimes substituted for unlighted buoys, so may lighted buoys be replaced with *minor lights*. These are fixed structures of the same overall physical features as daybeacons, but equipped with a light generally similar in characteristics to those found on buoys. Most minor lights are part of a series marking a channel, river or harbor; also included, however, are some isolated single lights if they are of the same general size and characteristics. The term "minor light" does not include the more important lights marking harbors, peninsulas, major shoals, etc.; these have lights of greater intensity and/or special characteristics — these are designated as "secondary" or "primary seacoast" lights and are discussed in detail in Chapter 16.

## CHARACTERISTICS

Minor lights are placed on single piles, fig. 1517, on multiple-pile dolphins, fig. 1518, or on other structures in the water or on shore. Daymarks are placed on the structures for their identification, and reflective material is added for nighttime safety should the light be extin-

FIG. 1518 Structures for daybeacons or minor lights may also consist of three or more piles driven in a few feet apart and then bound together at their top.   (Morris Rosenfeld photograph)

guished. In general, the description of daybeacons is applicable plus the addition of the light mechanism.

### Light characteristics

A minor light will normally have the same color and flash with the same phase characteristics that a lighted buoy would have if the aid were of floating rather than fixed type. Intensity of the light will generally be of the same order as that of a lighted buoy, occasionally somewhat greater, but visibility may be increased by its greater height above water and its more stable platform.

Flashing characteristics of minor lights have been standardized with flashes at intervals of 2.5, 4 and 6 seconds. This is part of the same light modernization program as previously described for lighted buoys.

### Sound signals

Minor lights may, in some locations, have an audible fog signal. These cannot, of course, be of a type operated by wave action, as in the case of bell and gong buoys. A bell, horn, or siren will be electrically operated on the structure, in some cases continuously for months during which fog may be expected.

## Buoyage Systems

The primary function of buoys is to warn the mariner of some danger, obstruction, or change in the contours of the bottom, and to delineate channels leading to various points, so that he may avoid hazards and continue on his course safely. The greatest advantage is obtained from buoys used to mark specifically defined spots, for if a pilot knows his precise position at the moment and is properly equipped with charts, he can plot a safe course. Such features as shape, coloring, and signaling characteristics of buoys are but means to these ends of warning, guiding, and orienting the navigator.

Most maritime nations use either the *lateral system of buoyage* or the *cardinal system*, or both. In the lateral system, the buoys indicate the direction to a danger relative to the course that should be followed. In the cardinal system, characteristics of buoys indicate location of the danger relative to the buoy itself. The term "cardinal" relates to cardinal points of the compass, see Chapter 13, page 270.

## The Lateral System of Buoyage

In the United States, the lateral system of buoyage is uniformly used in all Federal-jurisdiction areas and on many other bodies of water where it can be applied. In this system, the shape, coloring, numbering, and light characteristics of buoys are determined by their position with respect to the navigable channel, natural or dredged, as such channels are entered and followed from seaward toward the head of navigation. The lateral system is described in detail in the subsequent sections covering each of the basic characteristics.

### THE BASIC U. S. SYSTEM

The lateral system of buoyage employs a simple arrangement of shapes, colors, numbers, and light characteristics to indicate the side on which a buoy should be passed when proceeding in a given direction. The system is easily learned and should be known in detail by all boatmen.

As all channels do not lead from seaward, certain arbitrary assumptions must be made in order that the lateral system may be consistently applied. In coloring and numbering offshore buoys along the coasts, the following system has been adopted: proceeding in a southerly direction along the Atlantic Coast, in a northerly and westerly direction along the Gulf Coast, and in a northerly direction along the Pacific Coast will be considered the same as coming in from seaward. This can be remembered as proceeding around the coastline of the United States in a clockwise direction.

On the Great Lakes, offshore buoys are colored and

numbered as proceeding from the outlet end of each lake toward its upper end. This will be generally westerly and northward on the Lakes, except on Lake Michigan where it will be southward. Buoys marking channels into harbors are colored and numbered just as for channels leading into coastal ports from seaward.

On the Mississippi and Ohio Rivers and their tributaries, characteristics of aids to navigation are determined as proceeding from seaward toward the head of navigation, although local terminology describes "left bank" and "right bank" as proceeding with the flow of the river.

## Coloring

All buoys are painted distinctive colors to indicate the side on which they should be passed, or their special purpose. In the lateral system, the significance of colors is as shown below.

| TABLE 15-1 | | | | LATERAL SYSTEM IN U.S. AND CANADIAN WATERS | | |
|---|---|---|---|---|---|---|
| **Returning from sea*** | **Color** | **Number** | **Unlighted Buoy Shape** | **Lights or Lighted Buoys** | | **Daymark Shape** |
| | | | | **Light Color** | **Light Phase Characteristic** | |
| **Right side of channel** | Red | Even | Nun | Red or White | Flashing or Quick Flashing | Triangular |
| **Left side of channel** | Black | Odd | Can | Green or White | Flashing or Quick Flashing | Square |
| **Channel Junction or Obstruction** | Red-and-black horizontally banded** | Not Numbered; May be Lettered | Nun or Can** | Red, Green or White** | Interrupted Quick Flashing | Triangular or Square** |
| **Midchannel or Fairway** | Black-and-white vertically striped | May be lettered | Nun or Can | White | Morse Code "A" | Octagonal |

*or entering a harbor from a larger body of water, such as a lake.
**Preferred channel is indicated by color of uppermost band (shape of unlighted buoy), color of light, if any.

**Black buoys** mark the left (port) side of a channel when entering from seaward, or the location of a wreck or other obstruction that must be passed by keeping the buoy on the left hand.

**Red buoys** mark the right (starboard) side of a channel, or the location of a hazard to navigation that must be passed by keeping the buoy to starboard. It is from this color designation that the often-used phrase "Red — Right — Returning" is derived, meaning that *red* buoys should be kept on the *right* side of the boat when *returning* to harbor from the sea or other large body of water.

**Red-and-black horizontally banded buoys** mark junctions in a channel, or wrecks or obstructions that may be passed on *either* side. If the topmost band is black, the preferred channel will be followed by keeping the buoy on the left (port) hand. If the topmost band is red, the preferred channel is followed by keeping the buoy on the right (starboard) side of the vessel. (Note: When proceeding *toward* the sea, it may *not* be possible to pass such buoys safely on either side. This is particularly true in situations where you are following one channel downstream and another channel joins in from the side, see fig. 1519; always consult the chart for the area.)

**Black-and-white vertically striped buoys** mark the fairway or midchannel; they should be passed close to, but on either side.

It should be noted that when the areas of color run horizontally, they are "bands"; when they are arranged

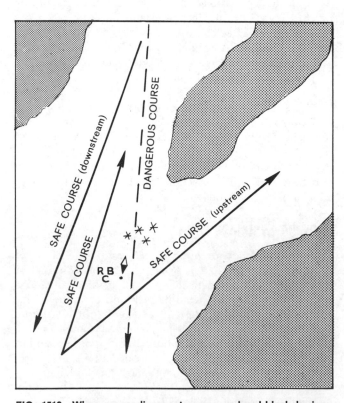

**FIG. 1519 When proceeding upstream, a red-and-black horizontally-banded junction buoy may be safely passed on either side. This is not true, however, when going downstream, as examination of the above situation will quickly show.**

vertically, they are "stripes." These terms are used in other color combinations in the case of special-purpose buoys.

## Shapes of buoys

In the lateral system of buoyage, definite shape characteristics are given to the unlighted buoys to indicate which side of the channel they mark. The use of shapes is particularly valuable when a buoy is first sighted in line with the sun and only its silhouette rather than its color can be distinguished.

**Can buoys,** painted black, mark the left (port) side of the channel when returning from seaward, or the location of a wreck or shoal that must be passed by keeping the buoy on the left hand.

**Nun buoys** are used to mark the right (starboard) hand side of channels, or hazards that must be passed by keeping the buoy to starboard.

Channel junction and obstruction buoys may be of *either* can or nun shape. If the uppermost band is *black,* the buoy will be a *can;* if the uppermost band is *red,* it will be a *nun.*

Black-and-white vertically striped midchannel buoys may be either nuns or cans, and in this situation the shape has no significance.

No special significance is to be attached to the shape of spar buoys, bell buoys, gong buoys, whistle buoys, lighted buoys, or combination buoys. The purpose of these is indicated by their coloring, number or the characteristic of the light.

## Numbering

Most buoys are given "numbers" that actually may be numbers, letters, or a combination of numbers and letters. These markings facilitate identification and location of buoys on charts.

In the lateral system, numbers serve as yet another indication of which side the buoy should be passed. The system is as follows:

**Odd numbered buoys** mark the left hand side of a channel leading in from seaward. In accordance with the rules stated above, these will be black buoys, cans if they are unlighted.

**Even numbered buoys** mark the right (starboard) side of a channel; these will be red (nun) buoys.

Numbers increase from seaward and are kept in approximate sequence on the two sides of a channel by omitting numbers as appropriate if buoys are not uniformly placed in pairs. Occasionally, several numbers will be omitted on longer stretches without buoys in order to allow for possible later additions.

Numbers followed by letters, such as 24A, 24B, 24C, etc., indicate buoys that have been added to a channel with the series not being immediately renumbered.

A buoy marking a wreck will often be designated with a number derived from the number of the buoy next downstream from it, preceded by the letters "WR". Thus, a buoy marking a wreck on the left-hand side of a channel between buoys 17 and 19 would be numbered "WR17A". A wreck buoy not related to a channel may be designated by one or two letters relating to the name of the wrecked vessel or a geographic location.

Letters, without numbers, are applied in some cases to black-and-white vertically striped buoys marking fairways, and to red-and-black horizontally banded buoys marking channel junctions or obstructions.

Numbers followed by letters may be used on some buoys marking offshore dangers. An example of this usage is the buoy marked "2TL" where the number has the usual sequential significance and the letters "TL" indicate the place as a shoal known as "Turner's Lump." This form of marking buoys is now more traditional than necessary.

## Color of lights

For all buoys in the lateral system that have lights, the following system of colors is used.

**Green lights** on buoys are used only on those marking the left-hand side of a channel returning from seaward (black, odd-numbered buoys) or on red-and-black horizontally banded buoys that have the topmost band painted black.

**Red lights** on buoys are used only on those marking the right-hand side of a channel when entering from sea (red, even-numbered buoys) or on red-and-black horizontally banded buoys having a red topmost band.

**White lights** on buoys may be used on either side of channels in lieu of red or green. White lights are frequently employed where a greater visible range is desired, such as at a change in the direction of the channel. No special significance is derived from a white light, the purpose of the buoy being indicated by its color, number, or its light phase characteristic.

## Light phase characteristics

Fixed lights (lights that do not flash) may be found on either red or black buoys, but are rare.

**Flashing lights** (flashing at a rate of not more than 30 flashes per minute) are placed only on black or red buoys, or on special purpose buoys.

**Quick flashing lights** (not less than 60 flashes each minute) are placed only on channel-edge-marking black and red buoys; these are used at points where it is desired to indicate that *special caution* in piloting is required, as at sharp turns or changes in the width of the waterway, or where used to mark wrecks or dangerous obstructions that must be passed only on one side.

**Interrupted quick flashing lights** are used only on buoys painted with red-and-black horizontal bands. These are the buoys at channel junctions and obstructions that can be passed on either side.

**Morse code "A" flashing lights** (short-long flashing) are placed only on black-and-white vertically striped buoys that mark a fairway or midchannel; these are passed close to, on either side. The lights are always white.

## WRECK BUOYS

Buoys established by the Coast Guard to mark dangerous wrecks are generally placed on the seaward or channel side of the obstruction and as near to it as conditions permit. Wreck buoys are *not* placed directly over a wreck; they must be placed in position by a vessel and it is usually impossible for such vessel to maneuver directly over the hazard without incurring underwater damage to herself.

Caution must be exercised when navigating in the vicinity of buoys marking wrecks because, due to sea action, the wreck may shift in location between the time that the buoy is established and when it is later checked or serviced.

## STATION BUOYS

Important buoys, usually large combination buoys, with both light and sound signals, are sometimes accompanied by *station buoys*. These are smaller, unlighted buoys, see fig. 1520, placed in the vicinity of the main buoy on the side away from marine traffic. They are colored and numbered the same as the main buoy. Station buoys are not charted; their existence is noted, however, in the Light Lists in the remarks column for the major aid to which they are related.

The purpose of the station buoy is to mark the location should the main buoy be sunk or carried away for any reason, such as being struck by a passing ship. The station buoy serves as a temporary substitute and aids in the replacement of the main buoy on the correct location.

## DAYBEACONS AND MINOR LIGHTS

Although the lateral system of buoyage has been described in terms of unlighted and lighted buoys, the use of comparable daybeacons and minor lights is fully applicable.

Daybeacons with red triangular daymarks or red pointers may be substituted for nun buoys, and structures with black square daymarks or black pointers may replace can buoys where the water is shallow enough to make such installations practicable. Minor lights likewise may be used in place of lighted or combination buoys. It is not unusual to find a channel marked with a mixture of unlighted and lighted buoys, daybeacons, and minor lights.

Occasionally, daybeacons will be used to indicate a channel junction or obstruction. In such a case, the daymark will be red-and-black horizontally banded with the color of the uppermost band indicating the main or preferred channel. The shape of the daymark will be either square or triangular as determined by the color or the top band, similar to the use of a can or nun buoy for this purpose.

Daybeacons used to mark fairways or the middle of a channel will have an octagonal-shaped daymark, painted with the normal black-and-white vertical stripes.

A diamond-shaped daymark has *no* significance in the lateral system. A typical application might be to increase the daytime detectability of a minor light which is not a part of a channel or waterway series.

## INTRACOASTAL WATERWAY AIDS

The Coast Guard maintains the system of aids to navigation along the Atlantic and Gulf Intracoastal Waterway (ICW). The coloring and numbering of buoys and daybeacons, and the color of lights on buoys and light structures, is in conformity with the lateral system of buoyage as described above. The system is applied by considering passage from north to south along the Atlantic coast, and from south to north and east to west along the Gulf coast, as corresponding to returning from sea in an entrance channel. Thus, red buoys and fixed aids are on the right side of the channel when proceeding from New Jersey toward Florida and then on to Texas; black aids are on the left hand side of the Waterway when proceeding in the same direction. This rule is applied in a uniform manner from one end of the Intracoastal Waterway to the other, regardless of widely varying compass headings on

FIG. 1520  Station buoys are occasionally used in conjunction with major combination buoys. These are placed near the main buoy on the side away from ship traffic. Such buoys are not separately charted, but they are mentioned in the Light Lists. The older tapered "wasp-waist" design of buoy superstructure is giving way to a newer straight-sided design.

many stretches, and the fact that rivers and other waterways marked by the seacoast system are occasionally followed.

The aids to navigation do differ in one respect, however, in that they carry on additional distinctive marking to identify the ICW route. This special marking is applied to the so-called "inside route" and to those portions of all connecting waterways that must be crossed or followed to make a continuous passage.

### Distinctive ICW markings

All buoys, daybeacons, and light structures marking the Intracoastal Waterway have some portion of them painted *yellow*. This is the distinctive coloring adopted for the ICW. Buoys and single piles have a band of yellow at the top; daymarks and pointers have a band or border of yellow. For examples of these markings, see the color illustrations on page 324.

The numbering of Intracoastal Waterway aids follows the same basic rule as for entrance channels, with numbers increasing in the direction from New Jersey toward Florida and Texas. Aids are numbered in groups, usually not exceeding 99, beginning again with "1" or "2" at specified natural dividing points.

Lights on buoys follow the standard system of red or white lights on red buoys, and green or white lights on black buoys. The color of lights on fixed structures follows the same general system. Range lights, not being a part of the lateral system, may be any of the three standard colors.

### Dual marking

In order that vessels may readily follow the Intracoastal Waterway where it coincides with another route such as an important river marked on the seacoast system, special *dual markings* are employed. These are applied to the buoys or other aids that mark the river channel for other traffic. Special marks consist of a yellow square or a yellow

*continued on page 313*

triangle painted on a conspicuous part of the dual-purpose aid. The yellow square, in outline similar to a can buoy, indicates that the aid on which it is placed should be kept on the left-hand side when following the ICW in the direction from New Jersey to Texas. The yellow triangle, in outline similar to a nun buoy, indicates that the aid should be kept on the right hand side when traveling in the same direction.

The yellow squares may appear on *either* a black can or a red nun of the river channel marks (or comparable daybeacons and light structures). Similarly, the yellow triangle dual markings may appear on any type of lateral aid. These similarly contradictory markings result from the fact that in some situations a southbound ICW route (red nuns on the right side) will be *up* a river channel from seaward (red nuns on the right side); and in other situations, the same ICW route will be down a river toward the sea where black cans will be on the skipper's right side. In both of these situations, however, the yellow triangle will be kept to the right. See page 311.

Where the yellow squares and triangles are added to regular river or harbor aids to navigation, the ICW yellow band or border is omitted.

Where dual marking is employed, the boatman following the ICW disregards the shape and coloring of the aid on which the yellow square or triangle is placed and pilots his craft solely by the shape of the yellow markings. The numbers on the aids will be those of the river's lateral system, and in some instances where the southward ICW proceeds down a river, the numbers will be temporarily decreasing rather than increasing. See page 311.

By this system of dual marking, the mariner approaching a body of water such as the Cape Fear River, and realizing that he must follow it for some distance before again entering a dredged land cut of the Intracoastal Waterway, knows that his course lies along such buoys or other aids as are specially marked in yellow. He determines the side of his craft on which these aids should be passed by the shape of the yellow marks, keeping always in mind the basic direction of his ICW travel.

## Special Purpose Buoys

In addition to the lateral system of buoyage maintained by the Coast Guard in Federal-jurisdiction waters, several special-purpose buoy characteristics, having no lateral significance, are used to mark dredging areas, anchorages, quarantine areas, fish net areas, race courses, experiments or tests, etc.

The meaning of special-purpose buoys is indicated by their colors as follows:

**White buoys** mark *anchorage* areas.

**Yellow buoys** mark *quarantine anchorage* areas.

Note carefully the difference between an *anchorage* buoy and a *mooring* buoy — an anchorage buoy is an aid to navigation marking the boundary of an area in which vessels may be anchored in accordance with prescribed regulations; a mooring buoy is a strong, heavily anchored buoy to which vessels can be made fast in lieu of anchoring.

**White buoys with green tops** are used in connection with *dredging* and *survey* operations.

**White-and-black horizontally banded buoys** mark fish net areas. Particularly, but not exclusively, in the Chesapeake Bay area, such buoys are used to mark the boundaries of areas in which fish nets and traps may be placed; such areas and buoys are indicated on charts. (See fig. 1521.) These buoys may be cans or nuns, the shape has no significance; they carry identification numbers and letters.

**White-and-international-orange buoys,** with either horizontal bands or vertical stripes, are used for special purposes to which neither the lateral-system colors nor the other special-purpose colors are applicable. (See fig. 1522.)

Special-purpose buoys are illustrated in color at the bottom of page 309.

**Yellow-and-black vertically striped buoys** mark seaplane operating areas and have no marine significance other than to indicate the need for caution and a sharp lookout for aircraft.

**FIG. 1521 A black-and-white horizontally banded buoy is charted here at the intersection of lines (long and short dash) indicating outer limits of a fish trap area.**

**FIG. 1522 Positions of white-and-orange horizontally banded special purpose buoys near Choptank River Light are indicated on this chart. These are lettered for identification and it is indicated that they are privately maintained.**

Special-purpose buoys may be lighted or unlighted, and some may have a fog signal. These buoys may be of any shape if unlighted—can, nun, or spherical.

### SPECIAL—TYPE BUOYS

Special-type buoys may be encountered in all waters. Typical of these in inland waters are the buoys used in current surveys. The shape, size, color, lights (if any), markings, etc., vary too widely to be described here, but will be completely listed in the public notices that are always published before such buoys are placed in navigable waters.

Offshore boatmen may occasionally encounter large sea buoys used for gathering meteorological or oceanographic data, or those employed in naval defense operations.

## Uniform State Buoyage System

Each state has authority over control of navigation on waters that lie wholly within its boundaries. This includes the responsibility for the establishment and maintenance of aids to navigation. Each state is free to mark its waters according to any system that it desires. Initially, the result of this freedom was a considerable variance in the ways that inland waters not subject to Federal jurisdiction were marked. More recently, however, although the states still retain their authority, they have agreed to adopt a single consistent system of markers. With trailer-borne craft traveling freely over the highways from state to state, the gain for boatmen from the uniform system is too obvious to discuss in detail. The rambling skipper no longer has to try to decipher the significance of what had been intended to serve him as an "aid to navigation."

By Act of Congress, the Uniform State Waterway Marking System (USWMS) may be extended to cover waters subject to Federal jurisdiction, but which have not been marked with aids by the Coast Guard. Agreements may be entered into between a Coast Guard District Commander and state officials for the designation of "state waters for private aids to navigation." In such waters, state or local governments may establish and maintain aids to navigation which comply with the standards of the USWMS.

### MAJOR FEATURES OF THE USWMS

The Uniform State Waterway Marking System has been

developed to provide a means to convey to the small craft operator, in particular, adequate guidance to indicate safe boating channels by indicating the presence of either natural or artificial obstructions or hazards. The USWMS also provides means for marking restricted or controlled areas and for providing directions. The system is suited for use in all water areas and designed to satisfy the needs of all types of small vessels. It supplements and is generally compatible with the lateral system of aids to navigation maintained by the Coast Guard.

The USWMS consists of two categories of aids to navigation:

(1) A system of regulatory markers to indicate to the pilot the existence of dangerous areas as well as those which are restricted or controlled, such as speed zones and areas set aside for a particular use, or to provide general information and directions.

(2) A system of aids to navigation to supplement the Federal lateral system of buoyage.

### Regulatory markers

On Federal waters, the boatman can turn to his charts, Light Lists, Coast Pilots, and other publications for information on natural hazards, zoned areas, directions, distances, etc., to supplement the knowledge that he gets from buoys, daybeacons, and other aids. On state waters, he now has a uniform system of water signs or markers that, in themselves, convey their message without reference to any publication — an obvious advantage, especially for inexperienced boatmen.

Just as Intracoastal Waterway markers are distinguished by their special yellow borders or other yellow marks, state regulatory markers are identified by international-orange-and-white colors. On buoys, an orange band will be seen near the top and bottom; on the white area between these bands, a geometric shape, also in orange, will be noted. An open diamond shape indicates danger. A diamond with a cross inside indicates a prohibited area; vessels are excluded from the area marked by such buoys. A circle signifies zoning or control; vessels operating in such areas are subject to certain operating restrictions. A square or rectangular shape signals the conveying of information, the details of which are spelled out within the shape. (See fig. 1523.)

Where the regulatory marker consists of a square or

**FIG. 1523** Uniform state regulatory markers convey their meaning to the boatman without need for reference to charts or other publications.

| | |
|---|---|
| **DANGER!** Warns of rocks, reefs, dams, snags, or other hazards. | **BOATS KEEP OUT!** Marks waterfalls, swim areas, rapids, and other restricted areas. |

| | |
|---|---|
| **CAUTION!** Type of control is indicated within the circle such as No ski, speed zone, No anchoring. | **INFORMATION!** Tells distances, locations, other official information. |

FIG. 1524 Running upstream, in state waters, a boat passes between black buoys (on port side) and red buoys (to starboard), outside of (away from shore) a red-and-white striped obstruction buoy, south (or west) of a white buoy with red top, and north (or east) of a white buoy with black top.

How buoys might be placed in a
typical waterway under state jurisdiction

| Black | White | Red | Blue |

rectangular shaped sign displayed from a structure, the sign is white with an international orange border. If a diamond or circular shape is associated with the meaning of the marker, it will be centered on the signboard.

The geometric shape displayed on a regulatory marker is intended to convey the basic idea of danger, or control, etc., so that the boatman can tell at a distance whether he should stay away or may safely approach for more information. To convey a specific meaning, spelled-out words or recognized abbreviations appear within the shape. The sole exception to this is the cross within the diamond shape that is used to absolutely prohibit boats from entering an area, because of danger to the boat, swimmers in a protected area, or for any other reason sufficient to warrant exclusion by law.

To minimize the risk of misinterpretation, initials, symbols, and silhouettes have not been used. In some cases, words may be needed outside the geometric shape to give the reason, authority, or some clarification of the specific meaning.

## Aids to navigation

The second category of marker in the USWMS is the aid to navigation having lateral or cardinal meaning. In selecting types of buoys for use on waters not marked by the Coast Guard, the principal objective was to make the state system compatible with the Federal.

On a well-defined channel, including a river or other relatively narrow natural or improved waterway, an aid to navigation of the USWMS is normally a solid-colored buoy. A buoy that marks the left side of a channel viewed *looking upstream* or toward the head of navigation is colored *solid black*. A buoy that marks the *right* side, looking in the same direction, is colored *solid red*. (This, it will be noted, is the same as the Coast Guard lateral system.) On a well-defined channel, solid-colored buoys will be found

in pairs, one for each side of the channel that they mark, and opposite each other, leaving no doubt that the channel lies between the red and the black buoys, and that the skipper should pilot his boat between them.

On irregularly defined channels, solid-colored buoys may be used singly in staggered fashion on alternate sides provided that they are spaced at sufficiently close intervals to clearly inform the skipper that the channel lies between the buoys and that he should pass between them.

Where there is no well-defined channel, or when a body of water is obstructed by objects whose nature or location is such that the hazard might be approached from more than one direction, a *cardinal* system is used. The use of cardinal system aids to navigation is strictly limited to waters wholly subject to state jurisdiction or waters covered by a Coast Guard-state agreement. This restriction is necessary as the Coast Guard's lateral system makes no provision for markers of the cardinal system.

**A white buoy with red top** indicates that a boat must pass to the *south or west* of the buoy.

**A white buoy with black top** indicates that the safe water is to the *north or east* of the buoy.

**A buoy with alternate red and white vertical stripes** indicates that an obstruction extends from the nearest shore to the buoy, and that the boat must not pass between the buoy and that shore. The number of red and white stripes may vary, but the width of the white stripes will always be twice that of the red ones. See fig. 1524.

## Characteristics of markers and aids

The size, shape, material, and construction of all markers, fixed or floating, is discretionary with the state authorities. They must, however, be such as to be observable under normal conditions of visibility at a distance such that the significance of the marker or aid will be recognizable before a craft stands into danger.

## Numbers

State aids to navigation and regulatory markers may carry numbers, letters, or words. These must be placed in a manner so as to be clearly visible to approaching and passing boats, with characters in block style, well proportioned and as large as the available space permits. Numbers and letters on red or black backgrounds will be in white; on white backgrounds, they will be black. The use of numbers on buoys is optional, but if used will conform to the following system:

**Odd numbers** will be used on *solid black* buoys and on *black-topped* buoys.

**Even numbers** will be used on *solid red* buoys and on *red-topped* buoys.

All numbers will *increase* in an *upstream* direction or toward the head of navigation.

Letters only may be used to identify regulatory markers and red-and-white vertically striped obstruction buoys. If used, letters will follow an alphabetical sequence in the upstream direction; the letters "I" and "O" will not be used to prevent possible confusion with numbers.

## Reflectors

The use of reflectors or reflective tape is discretionary with the local authorities maintaining the markers and aids. If used, red reflectors or reflective material will be used on solid red buoys, and green on solid black buoys.

All other buoys will have white reflectors or reflective material, as will regulatory markers, except that orange reflectors may be placed on the orange portions of such markers.

## Lights

Lights may be used on USWMS regulatory markers and aids to navigation if desired by the state authorities. When used, lights on solid colored buoys will be regularly flashing, regularly occulting, or equal interval. (An "occulting" light is one that is on more than it is off.) For ordinary purposes, the rate of flashing will not be more than 30 times per minute.

When lights have a distinct cautionary significance, such as at sharp bends in a channel, the light may be quick flashing, not less than 60 flashes each minute.

When a light is placed on a cardinal system buoy or a red-and-white vertically striped buoy, it will always be quick flashing.

Red lights are used only on solid red buoys, green lights only on solid black buoys. White lights will be used on all other buoys and on regulatory markers.

## Ownership markings

The use and placement of ownership identification is discretionary. If used, such markings must be worded and placed in such a manner that they will not detract from the meaning being conveyed as a regulatory marker or aid to navigation.

## Mooring buoys

Mooring buoys in waters covered by the Uniform State Waterway Marking System will be white with a horizontal blue band around them midway between the waterline and the top of the buoy.

A lighted mooring buoy will normally show a slow flashing white light. If, however, its location is such that it is an obstruction to craft operating during hours of darkness, the light will be quick flashing white.

A mooring buoy may carry ownership identification provided that such markings do not detract from the meaning intended to be conveyed by the color scheme and identification letter, if assigned.

---

### Illustration of the USWMS

The Uniform State Waterway Marking System is illustrated in color on page 292j

---

# Other Buoyage Systems

Buoyage on the "Western Rivers of the United States" (the Mississippi and its tributaries, and certain other designated rivers) conforms to the lateral system, but includes some additional shapes and daymarks not found in other areas. See the color illustration on page K.

On these rivers, unlighted buoys are not numbered, while the numbers on lighted buoys have no lateral significance, rather indicating the number of miles upstream from a designated reference point.

Additional details on the buoyage of the Western Rivers will be found in Chapter 28.

## Foreign waters

Boatmen who carry their cruising into foreign waters should, prior to departure, fully acquaint themselves with the buoyage systems to be encountered. Significant differences from the U. S. lateral system may be found, and there will be variations between the systems used in different countries.

In Canadian waters, the lateral system of buoyage is essentially the same as in the United States. Minor differences in the physical appearance of buoys may be noted, but these should not be great enough to result in any confusion. Chart symbols, likewise, may be slightly different from those standardized for use on U. S. charts.

In British waters, however, quite a different situation exists. A lateral system of buoyage is employed, but the coloring, light characteristics, etc. are entirely at variance with the U. S. system. The "red-right-returning" rule becomes "black-right-returning." Buoys on the right side of entering channels are conical (nun), but they are painted black or black-and-white checkered; lights will flash in sequences of 1, 3, or 5. On the left side of such a channel, there are can buoys, as an American boatman might expect, but they are painted red or red-and-white checkered; lights will flash in sequences of 2, 4, or 6.

Junction (obstruction) buoys in British waters are spherical in shape and are horizontally banded, red-and-white or black-and-white, according to the general system for indication of the main or preferred channel as used in the United States. Midchannel buoys are of a distinctive shape — a shape other than can, nun, or spherical — and vertically striped in either black-and-white or red-and-white colors.

# CHAPTER 16

# AIDS TO NAVIGATION —
# Lighthouses and Other Aids

The preceding chapter covered the many thousands of aids to navigation that mark rivers and channels for watercraft of all sizes. These constitute the majority in the system of aids in U.S. waters, but there are other, major aids to serve the mariner. These other aids and systems provide guidance to the navigator making a landfall after a sea voyage or piloting his vessel along a coast. Electronic systems serve to help the navigator fix his position when he is out of sight of land because of darkness, fog, or distance. Primary and secondary lights, lightships and offshore tower light stations, fog signals, and ranges and directional lights will be considered in this chapter to complete the topic of aids to navigation. Electronic navigation systems are covered in Chapter 25.

## Primary Seacoast and Secondary Lights

*Primary seacoast* and *secondary lights* are so designated because of their greater importance as aids to navigation. In general, they differ from the minor lights considered in Chapter 15 by their physical size, intensity of light, and complexity of light characteristics. These lights are more individual in nature than minor lights and buoys; only broad, general statements can be made about them as a group.

Primary seacoast lights are maintained to warn the high-seas navigator of the proximity of land. They are the first aids to navigation to be seen when making a landfall (except where there may be an offshore lightship). A coastwise pilot can use these lights to keep farther offshore at night than if he were using other visual aids. These are the most powerful and distinctive lights in the U.S. system of aids to navigation.

Primary seacoast lights may be located on the mainland or offshore on islands and shoals. When located offshore, they may mark a specific hazard or they may serve merely as a marker for ships approaching a major harbor.

Many primary seacoast lights are so classified from the importance of their location, the intensity of the light, and the prominence of the structure. Other aids will be classed as *secondary lights* because of their lesser qualities in one or more of these characteristics. The dividing line, however, is not clear cut, and lights that may seem to be more properly in one category may be classified in the other group in the Light Lists (see page 331). The difference in classification is of no real significance to boatmen and it can be ignored in practical piloting situations.

### STRUCTURES

The physical structure of a primary seacoast light and many secondary lights is generally termed a *lighthouse*, although this is not an official designation used in the Light Lists. The principal purpose is to support a light source and

Figures 1606-1609
from official U. S. COAST GUARD
photographs

lens at a considerable height above water. The same structure may also house a fog signal, radiobeacon, equipment, and quarters for the operating personnel. In many instances, however, the auxiliary equipment and personnel are housed in separate buildings nearby; such a group of buildings is called a *light station*.

Lighthouses vary greatly in their outward appearance, determined in part by their location, whether in the water or on shore, the importance of the light, the kind of soil on which it is constructed, and the prevalence of violent storms; see fig. 1601.

Lighthouses also vary in appearance with the distance at which their lights must be seen. Where the need is for a relatively great range, a tall tower with a light of high candlepower is erected. Conversely, at points intermediate to the principal lights, where ship traffic is light, and where long range is not so necessary, a less expensive structure of more modest dimensions is constructed.

The terms, "secondary light" and "minor light," indicate in a general way a wide variety of lights, one class shading imperceptibly into the other. These lights may be displayed from towers resembling the most important seacoast lights, or from a relatively inexpensive structure. The essential features of a light structure where operating personnel are not in residence are: best possible location as determined by the physical characteristics of the site, sufficient height for the requirements of the light, a rugged support for the light itself, and proper shelter for the power source. Many
(Text continued on page 320)

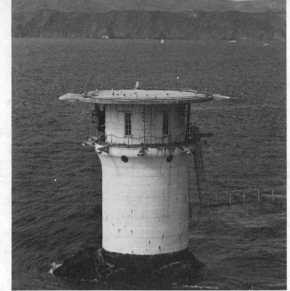

**MILE ROCKS LIGHT,** at the entrance to San Francisco harbor, was built in 1906. In 1966, its tower superstructure was cut off to provide a landing platform for helicopters. No longer manned, operation is automatic. A horn fog signal is remotely controlled from Pt. Bonita Light.

During periods of low visibility, **CHARLESTON LIGHT** on south side of Sullivans Island (S.C.) shows a 28,000,000 candlepower flash visible 26 miles seaward. Built in 1962, this modern 140-foot elevator-equipped structure is one of the world's tallest lights. ▲

New and old lights at **CAPE HENRY,** Va., at the entrance to Chesapeake Bay. The old tower, no longer lighted, was the first built by the Federal Government.

# AMERICAN LIGHTS –

On the lower coast of Maine, **CAPE NEDDICK LIGHT** is situated on a small rock islet called The Nubble, separated by a narrow channel from Cape Neddick, a headland which juts out a mile into the Atlantic.

▲ **PEMAQUID POINT LIGHT** (Maine) is a secondary light of 10,000 candlepower, visible 14 miles from a white pyramidal tower, 79 feet above water. Originally established in 1827, the rebuilt structure dates to 1857.

◄ **SPLIT ROCK LIGHT,** on a rocky cliff in Minnesota on Lake Superior, is one most frequently visited. Standing 178 feet above water, its 1,000,000 candlepower beam is visible 23 miles.

▲ EASTERN POINT LIGHT (Mass.) has guided Gloucestermen for more than a century. Its white brick tower, built in 1890, replaces one built in 1832.

▲ PORTLAND HEAD LIGHT, at Cape Elizabeth, Me., guards the entrance to Portland harbor with a 200,000 candlepower beam. The original station dates back to 1791.

◄ Isolated CAPE SPENCER LIGHT, 150 miles from a town, marks the northern entrance from the Pacific into the Inside Passage of southeastern Alaska. It is a primary light, fog signal and radiobeacon station.

►

FOWEY ROCKS LIGHT, a skeleton iron structure, is typical of those used on the Florida Reefs at Carysfort Reef, Alligator Reef, Sombrero Key, American Shoal and Sand Key.

# —Safeguards of Coastal Navigation

PHOTO CREDITS—Cape Henry, Sullivan's Island, Fowey Rocks, Dry Tortugas, Galveston, and Mile Rocks Official U.S. Coast Guard photos. Portland Head, Cape Neddick and Pemaquid from Kodachromes by Wm. H. Koelbel.

GALVESTON (Texas) JETTY LIGHT flashes white and red alternately from a height of 91 feet. Resident personnel attend it. Fog signal is a diaphone. There is a radiobeacon, with special RDF calibration service. ▼

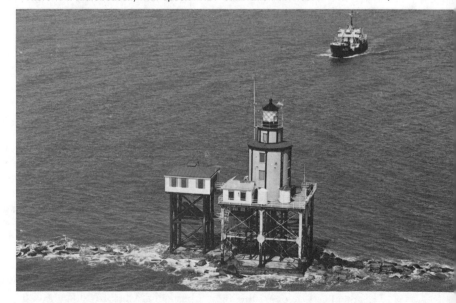

◄ DRY TORTUGAS LIGHT on Loggerhead Key in the Gulf of Mexico was established in 1826, rebuilt in 1858. The conical black and white tower is 157 feet high, the light visible 19 miles.

forms of structures meet these requirements—small houses topped with a short skeleton tower, a cluster of piles supporting a battery box and light, and countless others.

Many lights originally tended by resident keepers are now operated automatically because of the availability of commercial electric power and reliable equipment. There are also a great many automatic lights on inexpensive structures, cared for by periodic visits of Coast Guard cutters or by attendants who are in charge of a group of such aids.

The recent introduction of much new automatic equipment means that the relative importance of lights can no longer be judged on the basis of whether or not they have resident personnel; a number of powerful lights in towers of great height are now operated without continuous attention.

## Coloring of structures

Lighthouses and other light structures are marked with various colors for the purpose of making them readily distinguishable from the backgrounds against which they are seen, and to make possible the identification of individual lights among others that are in the same general area. Solid colors, bands of color, stripes, and various other patterns are used, fig. 1602.

## LIGHT CHARACTERISTICS

Primary seacoast and secondary lights are assigned distinctive light characteristics so that one may be distinguished from another. These characteristics are achieved by using lights of different colors, and by having some that show continuously while others go on and off in regular patterns of great variety. Actually, in these days of modern electronic navigation there is much less need for special distinctive characteristics of major lights—those were necessary when a navigator making a landfall might have been in doubt as to whether he was approaching the coast of Maryland or Virginia, or even farther to the north or south.

The three standard colors used for the lights of major aids to navigation are white, red, and green.

### Light phase characteristics

By varying the length of the intervals of light and darkness, a considerable number of individual *light phase characteristics* may be obtained.

The term "flashing" has already been defined in Chapter 15 as a light that is on less than it is off in a regular sequence of single flashes occurring less than 30 times each minute. Some primary seacoast and secondary lights will "flash" in accordance with such a definition although their characteristics will have no relation to the flashes of buoys and minor lights. In general, a flashing major light will have a longer period (time of one complete cycle of the characteristic) and may have a longer flash; for example, Cape Hatteras Light flashes once every 15 seconds with a 3-second flash. On the other hand, some of the newer aids are equipped with xenon-discharge-tube lights that give a very brilliant, but very brief, flash. The intensity of these lights can be varied for periods of good or bad visibility. A few major lights may be "fixed"—a continuous light without change of intensity or color.

Typically, however, the light phase characteristic of a primary seacoast or secondary light will be more complex. These are described below and are illustrated in fig. 1603.

MASONRY STRUCTURE    CYLINDRICAL TOWER SQUARE HOUSE ON CYLINDRICAL BASE    SKELETON IRON STRUCTURE

**TYPICAL LIGHT STRUCTURES** —————

**FIG. 1601.** Primary seacoast and secondary lights are mounted on a wide variety of structures. The location of the light, whether on shore or rising from the water; the degree of exposure to violent storms; the need for great height; and many other factors determine the type of structure. Physical characteristics of the structures are described in the Light Lists.

**Group flashing (Gp. Fl.)**—the cycle of the light characteristic consists of two or more flashes separated by brief intervals and followed by a longer interval of darkness.

**Alternating flashing (Alt. Fl.)**—flashes of alternating color, usually white and red, or white and green.

**Occulting (Occ.)**—the light is on more than it is off. The interval of time that the light is *lighted* is greater than the time that it is *eclipsed*.

**Equal interval (Eq. Int.)**—the periods of light and darkness are equal; the light will be described in the Light List or on charts in terms of the period, the lighted and eclipsed portions each being just half of that time interval.

**Group Occulting (Gp. Occ.)**—intervals of light regularly broken by a series of two or more eclipses. This characteristic may have all eclipses of equal length or one may be greater than the others.

**Fixed and Flashing (F. and Fl.)**—a fixed light varied at regular intervals by a flash of greater intensity. The flash may be of the same color as the fixed light (usually white) or of another color. This characteristic may also appear as *fixed and group flashing (F. and Gp. Fl.)*.

### Complex characteristics

The above light phase characteristics may be combined. Examples might include "Group flashing white, alternating flashing red" (Gp. Fl. W. Alt. Fl. R.)—Gay Head Light—with three white and one red flash in each 40-second period; or "Gp. Fl. W., (1 4 3)"—Minots Ledge Light where 1½-second flashes occur at 1½-second intervals in groups of one, four, and three separated by 5-second intervals and followed by a 15½-second longer interval to indicate the proper starting point of the 45-second period; or others of a generally similar nature.

Perhaps one of the most complex characteristics is that of Halfway Rock Light off the Maine Coast where the description is "Alternating fixed white, red, and flashing red" (Alt. F. W., R., and Fl. R.)—in a 90-second period, the light shows fixed white for 59 seconds, fixed red for 14 seconds, a high-intensity red flash for 3 seconds, and fixed red again for the final 14 seconds—this is certainly a distinctive enough characteristic to avoid any confusion.

# AIDS TO NAVIGATION ON NAVIGABLE WATERWAYS
## except Western Rivers and Intracoastal Waterway

## LATERAL SYSTEM AS SEEN ENTERING FROM SEAWARD

### PORT SIDE
ODD NUMBERED BUOYS OR STRUCTURES
WITH ☐ WHITE OR ■ GREEN LIGHTS

FIXED
FLASHING
OCCULTING
QUICK FLASHING

BELL OR WHISTLE

LIGHTED BUOY "9"

CAN "C"7"

"1" DAYMARKS "3"

POINTER "5"

### MID CHANNEL
NO NUMBERS   MAY BE LETTERED
☐ WHITE LIGHT ONLY

MORSE CODE

BW "N"
Mo(A)

T  CAN  BW C"T"  LIGHTED  NUN  BW N"B"

A  MID CHANNEL DAYMARK  BW

### JUNCTION
MARKS JUNCTION AND OBSTRUCTIONS. NO NUMBERS
PASS ON EITHER SIDE. MAY BE LETTERED
INTERRUPTED QUICK FLASHING

☐ WHITE OR ■ GREEN     ☐ WHITE OR ■ RED

M     RB LIGHTED     D

N PREFERRED CHANNEL STARBOARD TOPMOST BAND BLACK

L PREFERRED CHANNEL PORT TOPMOST BAND RED

CAN RB C"N"     NUN RB N"L"

L RB     J RB

### STARBOARD SIDE
EVEN NUMBERED BUOYS OR STRUCTURES
WITH ☐ WHITE OR ■ RED LIGHTS

FIXED
FLASHING
OCCULTING
QUICK FLASHING

BELL OR WHISTLE

LIGHTED BUOY "8"

NUN N"6"

DAYMARK "4"

POINTER "6"

## BUOYS HAVING NO LATERAL SIGNIFICANCE—ALL WATERS

NO SPECIAL SHAPES, NO NUMBERS
(MAY BE LETTERED)
☐ WHITE LIGHTS ONLY

FIXED
FLASHING
OCCULTING

WOr C  SPECIAL PURPOSE

Y C  QUARANTINE ANCHORAGE

N  W C"N"  ANCHORAGE

BW C  FISH NET

GW C  DREDGING

## RANGE DAYMARKS

## DANGER     DAYMARKS NON-LATERAL SIGNIFICANCE

SUBMERGED DANGER JETTY     M     M

# AIDS TO NAVIGATION ON WESTERN RIVERS

## AS SEEN PROCEEDING IN THE DIRECTION (DESCENDING) OF RIVER FLOW

### LEFT SIDE
□ WHITE OR ■ RED LIGHTS
GROUP FLASHING (2)

**LIGHTED BUOY**

**NUN**

**PASSING DAYMARK**

**CROSSING DAYMARK**

**123.5**

**MILE BOARD**

### JUNCTION

MARKS JUNCTIONS AND OBSTRUCTIONS
PASS ON EITHER SIDE
INTERRUPTED QUICK FLASHING

□ WHITE OR      □ WHITE OR
■ RED LIGHTS    ■ GREEN LIGHTS

**LIGHTED**

**NUN**      **CAN**

**PREFERRED CHANNEL**  **PREFERRED CHANNEL**
**TO THE RIGHT**      **TO THE LEFT**

TOPMOST BAND RED   TOPMOST BAND BLACK
WHITE OR RED LIGHT  WHITE OR GREEN LIGHT

### RIGHT SIDE
□ WHITE OR ■ GREEN LIGHTS
FLASHING

**LIGHTED BUOY**

**CAN**

**PASSING DAYMARK**

**CROSSING DAYMARK**

**176.9**

**MILE BOARD**

## BUOYS HAVING NO LATERAL SIGNIFICANCE—ALL WATERS

**NO SPECIAL SHAPES, NO NUMBERS**
(MAY BE LETTERED)
□ WHITE LIGHTS ONLY

FIXED ═══
FLASHING ▬ ▪ ▪
OCCULTING ▬▬ ▪

**SPECIAL**    **QUARANTINE**    **ANCHORAGE**    **FISH NET**    **DREDGING**
**PURPOSE**    **ANCHORAGE**

K

# UNIFORM STATE WATERWAY MARKING SYSTEM

## AIDS TO NAVIGATION

**PORT (left) SIDE**

COLOR – Black
NUMBERS – Odd
LIGHTS – Flashing green
REFLECTORS – Green

**THE LATERAL SYSTEM**—In well-defined channels and narrow waterways, USWMS aids to navigation normally are solid-colored buoys. Though a can and a nun are illustrated here, SHAPES may vary. COLOR is the significant feature. When proceeding UPSTREAM or toward the head of navigation, BLACK BUOYS ← mark the *left* side of the channel and must be kept on the left (port) hand. RED BUOYS → mark the *right* side of the channel and must be kept on the right (starboard) side. This conforms with practice on other federal waterways. On waters having no well-defined inlet or outlet, arbitrary assumptions may be made. Inquire in the locality for further information and charts when available.

**STARBOARD (right) SIDE**

COLOR — Red
NUMBERS — Even
LIGHTS — Flashing red
REFLECTORS — Red

---

**THE CARDINAL SYSTEM**—Used where there is no well-defined channel or where an obstruction may be approached from more than one direction.

**BLACK-TOPPED WHITE BUOY** indicates boat should pass to NORTH or EAST of it. Reflector or light, if used, is white, the light quick-flashing.

**RED-TOPPED WHITE BUOY** indicates boat should pass to SOUTH or WEST of it. Reflector or light, if 'used, is white, the light quick-flashing.

**RED-AND-WHITE VERTICALLY STRIPED BUOY** indicates boat should not pass between buoy and nearest shore. Used when reef or obstruction requires boat to go *outside* buoy (away from shore). White stripes are twice the width of red stripes. Reflector or light, if used, is white, the light quick-flashing.

**MOORING BUOY**—White with horizontal blue band. If lighted, shows slow-flashing light unless it constitutes an obstruction at night, when light would be quick-flashing.

**NOTE**—The use of lights, reflectors, numbers and letters on USWMS aids is discretionary.

**LIGHTS**—On solid-colored (red or black) buoys, lights when used are flashing, occulting, or equal interval. For ordinary purposes, *slow-flashing* (not more than 30 per minute). *Quick-flashing* (not less than 60 per minute) used at turns, constrictions, or obstructions to indicate *caution.*

**REFLECTORS**—On lateral-type buoys, *red* reflectors or retro-reflective materials are used on solid-red buoys, *green* reflectors on solid-black buoys, *white* on all others including regulatory markers (except that *orange* may be used on orange portions of markers).

**NUMBERS**—*White* on red or black backgrounds. *Black* on white backgrounds. Numbers increase in an upstream direction.

**LETTERS**—When used on regulatory and white-and-red striped obstruction markers, letters are in alphabetical sequence in an upstream direction. (Letters I and O omitted.)

---

## UNIFORM STATE REGULATORY MARKERS

Diamond shape warns of DANGER! Suggested wording for specific dangers: ROCK (illustrated), DAM, SNAG, DREDGE, WING-DAM, FERRY CABLE, MARINE CONSTRUCTION, etc.

Circle marks CONTROLLED AREA "as illustrated." Suggested wording to control or prohibit boating activities: 5 MPH (illustrated), NO FISHING, NO SKI, NO SWIM, NO SCUBA, NO PROP BOATS, SKI ONLY, FISHING ONLY, SKIN DIVERS ONLY, etc.

Diamond shape with cross means BOATS KEEP OUT! Explanatory reasons may be indicated outside the crossed diamond shape, for example SWIM AREA (illustrated), DAM, WATERFALL, RAPIDS, DOMESTIC WATER, etc.

Square or rectangle gives INFORMATION, names, activities. May give place names, distances, arrows indicating directions, availability of gas, oil, groceries, marine repairs, etc.

**REGULATORY MARKERS** are *white* with *international orange* geometric shapes. Buoys may be used as regulatory markers. Such buoys are *white* with two horizontal bands of *international orange*—one at the top, another just above the waterline. Geometric shapes, colored *international orange*,  are placed on the white body of the buoy between the orange bands. When square or rectangular *signs* are displayed on structures as regulatory markers, they are *white* with *international orange* borders. Diamond and circular shapes, when used, are centered on the signboard.

L

BOSTON, MASS.    ST. AUGUSTINE, FLA.    CAPE HENRY, VA.    TYBEE, GA.

**FIG. 1602.** The physical structure supporting a primary seacoast light, usually referred to as a lighthouse, may be painted in a number of different patterns for better daytime identification. The colors are usually black and white. Details are given in the Light Lists.

**COLORING OF TYPICAL LIGHTHOUSES**

## Sectors

Many lights will have *sectors,* portions of their all-around arc of visibility in which the normally white light is seen as red. These mark shoals or other hazards, or warn mariners of nearby land.

Lights so equipped show one color from most directions, but a different color or colors over definite arcs of the horizon as indicated on charts and in the Light Lists. A sector changes the color of a light when viewed from certain directions, but *not* the flashing or occulting characteristic. For example, a flashing white light having a red sector, when viewed from within the sector, will appear as flashing red, fig. 1604.

Sectors may be a few degrees in width, as when marking a shoal or rock, or of such width as to extend from the di-

**FIG. 1604.** Many lights that are basically white in color have one or more **red sectors** to mark areas of shoal water or other hazards. The light will have the same phase characteristics in both the white and red sectors. Red sectors will be indicated on charts and described in the Light Lists.

rection of deep water to the shore. Bearings referring to sectors are expressed in degrees as *observed from a vessel toward the light.*

In the vast majority of situations, water areas covered by red sectors should be avoided, but in all cases the extent of the hazard should be determined from an examination of the chart for the vicinity. A few lights are basically red (for danger) with one or more white sectors marking the direction of safe passage through the hazards. A narrow white sector may also be used to mark a turning point in a channel.

Lights may also have sectors in which the light is *obscured* and cannot be seen. These will be shown graphically on charts and described in words and figures in the Light Lists, fig. 1605.

## THE VISIBILITY OF LIGHTS

The theoretical visibility of a light in clear weather depends upon two factors, its intensity and its height above water. The intensity of the light fixes its *nominal range.* The height determines what is known as the *geographic range* which is not affected by the intensity (provided

| Illustration | Symbols and meaning | | Phase description |
| --- | --- | --- | --- |
| | Lights which do not change color | Lights which show color variations | |
| | F. = Fixed . . . | Alt. = Alternating. | A continuous steady light. |
| | F. Fl. = Fixed and flashing | Alt. F. Fl. = Alternating fixed and flashing. | A fixed light varied at regular intervals by a flash of greater brilliance. |
| | F. Gp. Fl. Fixed and group flashing. | Alt. F. Gp. Fl. = Alternating fixed and group flashing. | A fixed light varied at regular intervals by groups of 2 or more flashes of greater brilliance. |
| | Fl. = Flashing | Alt. Fl. = Alternating flashing. | Showing a single flash at regular intervals, the duration of light always being less than the duration of darkness. |
| | Gp. Fl. Group flashing. | Alt. Gp. Fl. = Alternating group flashing. | Showing at regular intervals groups of 2 or more flashes. |
| | Gp. Fl. (1+2) = Composite group flashing. | — | Light flashes are combined in alternate groups of different numbers. |
| | E. Int. Equal interval. | — | Light with all durations of light and darkness equal. |
| | Occ. = Occulting. | Alt. Occ. Alternating occulting. | A light totally eclipsed at regular intervals, the duration of light always greater than the duration of darkness. |
| | Gp. Occ. Group Occulting. | — | A light with a group of 2 or more eclipses at regular intervals. |
| | Gp. Occ. (2+3) = Composite group occulting. | — | A light in which the occultations are combined in alternate groups of different numbers. |

**FIG. 1603.** Primary seacoast and secondary lights flash with specific **light phase characteristics.** These permit rapid and positive identification at night. The time for a light to go through one full cycle of changes is called its **period.**

that the light is bright enough to be seen at the full distance of the geographic range). These ranges are given in the Light Lists in nautical miles; both are important factors about a major light.

As a rule, the nominal range of major lights is greater than the geographic, and the distance from which such aids can be seen is limited only by the earth's curvature. Such lights are often termed "strong"; conversely, a light limited by its luminous range can be called a "weak light."

Often, the glare, or *loom*, of strong lights may be seen far beyond the stated geographic range. Occasionally, under rare atmospheric conditions, the light itself may be visible at unusual distances. On the other hand, and unfortunately more frequently, the range of visibility may be lessened by rain, fog, snow, haze, or smoke.

FIG. 1605. Some lights — particularly those on shore—will have sectors in which they cannot be seen at all. The light is said to be "obscured" in these sectors which are indicated on the chart and described in the Light Lists.

The Light Lists show the nominal range when such is 5 miles or more. Instructions are given for conversion of nominal range to *luminous* range, the maximum distance at which a light may be seen in *existing* visibility. Luminous range may be found from either nominal range or intensity of the light, also given in the Lists. For lights of complex characteristics, nominal ranges and intensities are given for each color and/or intensity.

The geographic range is given in the Light Lists for an observer whose eye level is 15 feet above the water surface. Boatmen should know their eye height when at the controls of their craft. A height of eye of 5 feet decreases the geographic range of a light by 1.8 miles; a height of eye of 10 feet decreases it by 0.8 mile. On the other hand, an eye level height of 20 feet adds 0.7 mile to the geographic range of any light.

Lights on inland waters, where their radius of usefulness is not great, are frequently "weak" lights of insufficient intensity to reach the full limit of their geographic range.

## IDENTIFICATION OF LIGHTS

Charts can only briefly describe the characteristics of a primary seacoast or secondary light by means of abbreviations and a notation of the total period of the light cycle. It will often be necessary to consult the Light List for the details of the characteristic that may be needed for positive identification.

When a light is first observed, its color should be noted, and, by means of a watch or clock with a second hand, a check made of the time required for the light to go through its full cycle of changes. If color, period, and number of flashes per cycle agree with the information in the Light

List, correct identification has been accomplished. As a further check, however, the charts and Light List should be examined to see if any other light in the vicinity might have such similar characteristics that there could be a case of mistaken identity. If there is any doubt, a careful timing of the length of all flashes and dark intervals should be made and compared with the Light List entries; this will normally be conclusive.

## CAUTIONS IN USING LIGHTS

Complex lights with several luminous ranges may appear differently at extreme distances where, for example, a white fixed (or flashing) light could be seen but a red flash of the same light was not yet within luminous range. Examination of a Light List will show that ordinarily the candlepower of a red or green light is only 1/4 or 1/5 that of a white light from the same aid. Caution must be exercised in light identification under such circumstances.

The effect of fog, rain, snow, haze, etc., on the visibility of lights is obvious. Colored lights are more quickly lost to sight than are white lights under weather conditions that tend to reduce visibility. On the other hand, refraction may cause a light to be seen at a greater distance than would normally be expected.

Caution must also be applied when using light sectors. The actual boundaries between the colors are not so sharp and distinct as indicated on the chart; the lights shade gradually from one color into the other. Allow an adequate margin for safety when piloting by colored light sectors.

The increasing use of brilliant shore lights for advertising, illuminating bridges, and other purposes may cause marine navigational lights, particularly those in densely populated areas, to be outshone and difficult to distinguish from the background lighting.

There is always the possibility of a light's being extinguished. In the case of unattended lights, this condition may not be immediately detected and corrected. If lights are not sighted within a reasonable time after prediction from the course and speed of the boat, a dangerous situation may exist requiring prompt action to ensure the safety of the craft and its crew.

Do not rely on any *one* light, except perhaps for making a landfall. Use several lights *together* as a system, checking each against the others.

At many lights, rip-rap mounds are maintained to protect the structures against ice damage and scouring action, fig. 1606. Skippers should not attempt to pass close to light structures rising out of the water in order to be sure of avoiding collision with uncharted, submerged portions of such rip-rap or with the structure itself.

### Standby lights

Standby lights of reduced candlepower are displayed from many light stations when the main light is inoperative. These standby lights may or may not have the same characteristics as the main light. The existence of the standby light, if any, and its characteristics, are noted in the Light Lists.

# Fog Signals

Any sound-producing instrument operated in time of fog from a definite point shown on a chart serves as a useful fog signal. To be effective as an aid to navigation, a pilot must be able to identify it and know from what location it is sounded.

The simpler fog signals used on buoys and at minor lights have been covered in Chapter 15. There it was noted that such signals operated by the action of the sea cannot be entirely depended upon and identification might be difficult. At all lighthouses and lightships equipped with fog signals, these devices are operated by mechanical or electrical means and are sounded on definite time schedules during periods of low visibility to provide the desirable feature of positive identification.

## SIGNAL CHARACTERISTICS

Fog signal characteristics are described in terms of the length of a total cycle consisting of one or more *blasts* of specific length and one or more *silent intervals,* also of definite lengths. These times are shown in the Light Lists to aid in identification. (Normally, only type of fog signal, without further details, is indicated on charts.) Where counting the number of blasts and the total time for the signal to complete a cycle is not sufficient for identification, reference may be made to the details in the Light List.

### Fog signal equipment

The various types of fog signals differ in tone, and this also aids in identification. The type of fog signal for each station is shown in the Light Lists and on charts.

**Diaphones** produce sound by means of a slotted reciprocating piston actuated by compressed air. Blasts may consist of two tones of different pitch, in which case the first part of the blast is higher pitch and the latter is lower. These alternate-pitch signals are termed "two-tone."

**Diaphragm horns** produce sound by means of a disc diaphragm vibrated by compressed air or electricity. Duplex or triplex horn units of different pitch are sometimes combined to produce a more musical signal.

**Sirens** produce sound by means of either a disc or cup-shaped rotor actuated by compressed air, steam, or electricity. These should not be confused with what might be called "police sirens"; these may produce a sound of constant pitch much like a diaphragm horn or a whistle.

**Whistles** produce sound by compressed air, emitted through a circumferential slot into a cylindrical bell chamber.

**Bells** are sounded by means of a hammer actuated by an electric solenoid.

### Operation of signals

Fog signals at stations where a continuous watch is maintained (identified in the Light Lists by the words "Resident Personnel") are sounded whenever the visibility decreases below a limit set for that particular station; typically, this might be two to five miles. The audible fog signals at certain stations are synchronized with the radiobeacon signals of these stations for distance-finding; see page 506.

Fog signals at locations where no continuous watch is maintained may not always be sounded promptly when fog conditions occur, or may operate erratically due to mechanical difficulties.

Where fog signals are operated continuously on a seasonal basis or throughout the year, this information will be found in the Light Lists.

**FIG. 1606.** Light structures rising out of the water are often protected by piles of rocks known as "rip-rap." Skippers should keep well clear as obstructions below the surface may extend far out. This is the light shown in the chart extract of fig. 1604—note there how the rip-rap is indicated around the light.

## CAUTIONS IN USING FOG SIGNALS

Fog signals depend upon the transmission of sound through air. As aids to navigation, they have certain inherent limitations that *must* be considered. Sound travels through air in a variable and unpredictable manner. It has been established as fact that:

(a) Fog signals can be heard at greatly varying distances, and the distance at which such an aid can be heard may at any given instant vary with the bearing of the signal, and may be different on different occasions.

(b) Under certain conditions of the atmosphere, when a fog signal has a combination of high and low tones, it is not unusual for one of them to be heard but not the other. In the case of sirens which produce a varying tone, portions of the blast may not be heard.

(c) There are occasionally areas close to the signal in which it will not be heard. This is particularly true when the fog signal is screened by intervening land masses or other obstructions, or when the signal is on a high cliff.

(d) The apparent loudness of a fog signal may be greater at a distance than in the immediate vicinity.

(e) A patch of fog may exist at a short distance from a manned station but not be seen from it. Thus the signal may not be placed in operation.

(f) Some fog signals require a start-up interval.

(g) A fog signal may not be detected when the vessel's engines are in operation, but may be heard when they are stopped, or from a quieter location on deck.

Based on the above established facts, a mariner must *not* assume:

(1) That he is out of ordinary hearing distance from a fog signal because he fails to hear it.

(2) That because he hears a fog signal faintly, he is at a greater distance from it.

(3) That he is near to it because he hears it loudly.

(4) That the fog signal is not sounding because he does not hear it, even when in close proximity.

(5) That the detection distance and sound intensity under any one set of conditions is an infallible guide for any future occasion.

In summary, fog signals are valuable as warnings, but the boatman should not place implicit reliance upon them in navigating his vessel. They should be considered solely as warning devices.

### Standby fog signals

Standby fog signals are sounded at some of the more important stations when the main signal is inoperative.

The standby signals may be of a different type and characteristic than the main signal. Details of such auxiliary apparatus, where they exist, are given in the Light Lists.

## Lightships and Offshore Towers

Lightships are vessels of distinctive design and markings, equipped with lights, fog signals, and radiobeacons. They are anchored or moored at specific, charted locations to serve as aids to navigation; see fig. 1607.

### Purpose

Lightships mark the entrances to important harbors, warn of dangerous shoals lying in much-frequented waters, and serve as departure marks for both ocean and coastwise traffic.

Lightships serve the same essential purposes as lighthouses. They take the form of vessels only because they are at locations where it is (or has been until recently) impracticable to build lighthouses. As will be noted later, modern construction technology has now made possible the replacement of all but a few of the traditional lightships with more efficient fixed structures.

### LIGHTSHIPS

The hulls of lightships in U. S. waters are almost invariably painted red with the name of the station in large white letters on each side. All the signals—the light, fog signal, and radiobeacon—have distinctive characteristics so that the lightship may be identified under all conditions. As with lighthouses, details regarding these signals are shown briefly on charts and more completely in the Light Lists. A riding light on the forestay indicates the direction that the ship is heading, and since lightships ride to a single bow anchor, this also indicates the direction from which the current is flowing, whenever the current is stronger than the wind.

Modern U. S. lightships are self-propelled, capable of proceeding to and from their stations under their own power. All are diesel-powered and can use their main engines to either relieve the strain on their moorings during storms or work their way back to station if blown off by high winds and seas. Each lightship carries a crew of about 15 men.

**FIG. 1607.** Lightships are used to mark both offshore hazards and the entrance to major harbors. The entrance to the Golden Gate has been marked by lightships since 1898. The San Francisco Lightship is shown here anchored in 108 feet of water; her 450,000 candlepower light is 55 feet above the surface and can be seen 14 miles on clear nights. She is also equipped with two-tone diaphone fog signal and a radiobeacon.

### Identification

A lightship underway to or from its station will fly the International Code flags "LO" signifying "lightship not at anchor on her station," fig. 1608. She will not show or sound any of the signals of a lightship, but will display the lights prescribed by the International or Inland Rules for a vessel of her class.

When on station at night, a lightship shows only the aid to navigation and riding lights. By day, lightships will display the International Code signal of the station whenever a vessel is in the vicinity and there are any indications that her crew fails to recognize the station, or whenever a vessel asks for information. The International Code signal for each lightship station is stated in the Light Lists.

### Relief lightships

Whenever the regular lightship must be withdrawn from her station for maintenance, she is temporarily replaced with a *relief lightship*. These are painted the same colors as regular lightships, but have the word "RELIEF" on each side in lieu of a station name.

Relief lightships will generally exhibit lights and sound signals having the regular characteristics of the station. They may differ in outward appearance from the regular lightship in minor details. Changes in lightships are announced in advance by Notices to Mariners.

### Station buoys

*Station buoys*, also referred to as "watch buoys," are used to mark the position of lightship stations. These buoys are located from several hundred yards to as much as a mile from the station as shown on the chart; the distance and direction are given in the Light Lists. They are *not* separately charted.

Station buoys serve as a substitute if the lightship is forced to seek shelter in extreme weather, and they aid in later returning the lightship to its correct position. They are always of an unlighted type and are marked with "LS" and the initials of the lightship station.

### Cautions in using lightships

A skipper should set his course so as to pass a lightship with sufficient clearance to avoid the possibility of collision from any cause. It should be borne in mind that most lightships are anchored by a very long scope of chain and as a result the radius of their swinging circle is considerable. The charted position is the location of the anchor.

It must also be remembered that during extremely heavy weather lightships may be carried off station despite the best efforts of their crews, and perhaps without their knowledge. A navigator should not, therefore, implicitly rely on the position of a lightship during and immediately after severe storms. A lightship known to be off station will secure her light, fog signal, and radiobeacon, and will fly the International Code signal "LO."

A craft steering toward a radiobeacon on a lightship, "homing" on it, should exercise particular care to avoid collision. Sole reliance should *never* be placed on sighting the lightship or hearing her fog signal in time to prevent hitting her. The risk of collision will be lessened by ensuring that the radio bearing does not remain constant.

Skippers must also use care in passing lightships so as

**FIG. 1608.** A lightship flies the International Code flags "LO" when she is not on her station. These are seen above flying from the foremast. The vessel shown here is used as a temporary substitute for other lightships when those must return to port for maintenance, hence the name "RELIEF" in white letters on the red hull rather than the name of a specific station.

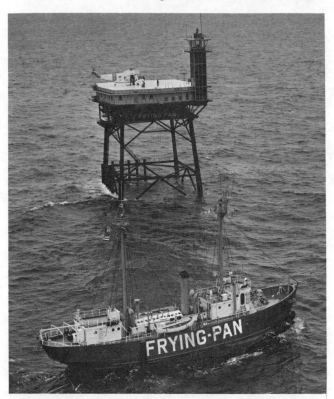

**FIG. 1609.** The old and the new in offshore aids to navigation. Lightships have been used since 1820, but in 1961 the Coast Guard started their replacement along the Atlantic Coast with tower structures. The fixed towers offer many advantages over lightships and will be constructed wherever hydrographic conditions permit. Frying Pan Shoals Light off the coast of North Carolina stands in 46 feet of water.

to not collide with the station buoy, remembering that it is unlighted and may be at a considerable distance from the lightship. Particular caution must be exercised in fog and at night.

### OFFSHORE LIGHT TOWERS

Along the Atlantic Coast, lightships are being gradually replaced with offshore light structures, fig. 1609. The first of these was placed in operation in 1961 and others will be added until only a few lightships remain. On the Pacific Coast, lightships will remain in use as the greater depths of water make tower construction impractical.

### Characteristics

A typical tower deckhouse is 60 feet above the water, 80 feet square, and supported by steel legs in pilings driven nearly 300 feet into the ocean bottom. The deckhouse accommodates living quarters, radiobeacon, and communications and oceanographic equipment. The top serves as a landing platform that will take the largest helicopters flown by the Coast Guard. On one corner of the deckhouse is a 32-foot radio tower supporting the radiobeacon antenna and a 3½-million candlepower light. At an elevation of 130 feet above the water, it is visible for 18 miles. The construction details of other towers will vary slightly, but all are of the same general type.

### Advantages

Fixed offshore light stations have five major advantages over lightships:

(1) Lower operating costs. The annual operating, personnel, and maintenance expenses of a tower light station are only about one-third of those of a lightship.

(2) Greater light range. Greater luminous range is made possible by more efficient optics, and greater geographic range results from the increased height of the light above the water—some 50 to 70 feet higher than one on a lightship.

(3) Better fog signal projection. By eliminating the swinging to which a lightship is subject, fog signals may be projected specifically in the most useful directions under all circumstances.

(4) More accurate guidance for ships. The location of a tower light is fixed; it does not swing about the charted position and cannot be blown off station in violent storms.

(5) Longer life. Towers are expected to last 75 years, as compared with the average 50-year lifespan of lightships.

### Unmanned light towers

In addition to the manned offshore light stations, the Coast Guard is also building unmanned light towers such as the one which replaced Brenton Reef Lightship at the entrance to Narragansett Bay.

## Ranges and Directional Lights

Ranges and directional lights serve to indicate the centerline of a channel and thus aid in the safe piloting of a vessel. Although they are frequently used in connection with channels and other restricted waterways, they are not a part of the lateral system of buoyage and so were not covered in Chapter 15.

### RANGES

A *range* consists of two fixed aids to navigation so positioned with respect to each other that when seen in line they indicate that the observer's craft *may* be in safe waters, fig. 1610. The aids may be lighted or unlighted as determined by the importance of the range, and may take a wide variety of physical appearances.

The conditional phrase "may be in safe waters" is used in the definition above since observation of the two markers in line is *not* an absolute determination of safety. A range is "safe" only within specific limits of distance from the front marker; a vessel too close or too far away may be in a dangerous area. The aids that comprise the range do not in themselves indicate the usable portion of the range; reference *must* be made to a chart of the

**FIG. 1610.** The principle of range markers. A boat B follows a safe mid-channel course between shoals S and S' by aligning the front marker directly below the rear marker. If the range opens and the rear marker shows to the **left** of the front marker, the boat is off course, displaced toward B'. If the rear marker shows to the **right** of the front marker, she is displaced toward B". Ranges may be lighted or unlighted.

area and to other aids.

Ranges are described in the Light Lists by first giving the position of the front marker, usually in terms of geographic coordinates—latitude and longitude; and then stating the location of the rear marker in terms of direction and distance from the front marker. This direction, given in degrees and minutes, true, need not be used in ordinary navigation, but is useful in making checks of compass deviation. The rear daymark (and light, if used) is always higher than the one on the front aid.

Because of their fixed nature, and the accuracy with which a vessel can be positioned by using them, ranges are among the best aids to navigation. Preference should always be given to using a range when one is available; buoys should be referred to only in order to determine the beginning and end of the usable portion of the range.

## Unlighted ranges

Although any two objects may be used as a range, the term is properly applied only to those pairs of structures built specifically for that purpose. Special shapes and markings will be used for the front and rear markers of a range for easier identification and more accurate alignment. Many different designs will be found in use today—front and rear daymarks of different shape, such as one round and the other diamond-shaped; both markers of the same overall shape, but with painted centers of different designs; and many others. To make ranges more easily identifiable, and easier to use, the Coast Guard has standardized on the use of rectangular daymarks, longer dimension vertical, painted in vertical stripes of contrasting colors, see page 310. The design of range daymarks will normally be described in the Light Lists.

## Lighted ranges

Because of their importance and high accuracy in piloting, most range markers are equipped with lights to extend their usefulness through the hours of darkness. Entrance channels are frequently marked with range lights; the Delaware River on the Atlantic Coast and the Columbia River on the Pacific Coast are examples of this.

*Range lights* may be of any color used with aids to navigation—white, red, or green—and may show any characteristic. See fig. 1611. The principal requirement is that they be easily distinguished from shore backgrounds and from other lights. Front and rear lights will, however, often be of the same color (white is frequently used because of its greater visibility range), with different phase characteristics. Since both lights must be observed together for the proper steering of the craft, range lights will generally have

a greater "on" interval than will other lights. Range rear lights will normally be on more than their front counterparts. Fixed or occulting lights are typical for range rear aids, equal interval or quick flashing for range front lights.

Many range lights will be fitted with special lenses that result in a much greater intensity being shown on the range center line than off of it; the lights rapidly decrease in brilliance when observed from only a few degrees to either side. In some cases, the light will be visible only from on or very near to the range line; in other cases, a light of lesser intensity may be seen all around the horizon—this can be either from the main light source or from a small auxiliary "passing" light. Light is shown around the horizon when the front aid also serves to mark the side of a channel at a turn of direction.

Often range lights will be of such high intensity that they can be seen and used for piloting in the daytime, being of more value than the painted daymarks.

**FIG. 1611.** Lighted range markers are extensively used on the Connecticut River. When aligned by an observer in mid-channel, Rock Landing Range Front Light (flashing white, height 54 feet) shows below Rock Landing Range Rear Light (fixed red, height 70 feet). A similar range leads through Haddam Island Bar. Their daymarks are white diamonds with black centers. Details are given in the Light List.

## DIRECTIONAL LIGHTS

The establishment of a range requires suitable locations for two aids, separated adequately both horizontally and vertically. In some areas, this may not be possible and a single light of special characteristics will be employed.

A *directional light* is a single light source fitted with a special lens so as to show a white light in a narrow beam along a desired direction, with red and green showing to either side. The width of the sectors will depend upon the local situation, but red will be seen if the pilot is to the right of the center line as he approaches the aid from seaward, and green if he is to the left of the desired track. A typical directional light, at Deer Island, Massachusetts, shows white for a sector of 2.4° with red and green showing for 8.5° to either side. Another directional light in Delaware Bay has a white beam width of 1° 40' with red and green sectors of 6½° to either side.

Directional lights will normally have an occulting or equal interval characteristic, so they are easily followed.

### Caution regarding directional lights

A pilot should not place too great reliance on the various colors of a directional light for safe positional information. As noted for light sectors, the boundaries between colors are not sharp and clear; the light shades imperceptibly from one color to the other along the stated directional lines.

# CHAPTER 17

# GOVERNMENT PUBLICATIONS

The typical boatman undoubtedly thinks first of charts when considering the publications that are issued by governmental agencies to aid his safe boating. This is certainly a valid thought—so much so that another chapter is devoted entirely to charts—but he should not overlook the many other publications that are available to make his boating safer and more enjoyable. Generally, these are issued by the same governmental agencies as are charts. Such publications will be considered in this chapter.

## PUBLISHING AGENCIES

Agencies of the Federal Government that issue publications valuable to the boatman include:

U.S. Coast & Geodetic Survey (now a part of the Environmental Science Services Administration, Department of Commerce).

United States Coast Guard (transferred in 1967 from the Treasury Department to the Department of Transportation).

U.S. Navy Department—the Naval Oceanographic Office and the Naval Observatory.

U.S. Army, Corps of Engineers (through its Lake Survey District and other District Offices).

The Weather Bureau (also a part of the Environmental Science Services Administration, Department of Commerce).

### Government Printing Office

The Government Printing Office, an independent agency, does much of the actual printing of the publications prepared by the agencies listed above. The Superintendent of Documents is responsible for the sale of most of these publications, but not all of them. Unfortunately, there seems to be no rule for the determination of whether a publication is sold by the GPO, or by the preparing agency —for example: H.O. 9 can be purchased from the GPO, but H.O. 103 cannot be bought there, only from the Naval Oceanographic Office and its sales agents.

Publications that are sold by the GPO can be purchased by mail. The address is Superintendent of Documents, Government Printing Office, Washington, D.C. 20402. There is also a retail bookstore in the GPO building at North Capital and H Streets in Washington where over-the-counter purchases can be made. Personal checks for the purchase of publications are acceptable; they should be made payable to the "Superintendent of Documents."

### State agencies

Publications of interest to boatmen are also prepared by many State agencies, so many that it is not possible to list them all in this book. Boatmen should check with local authorities in their own state and write ahead to other states when they expect to cruise into new waters. Information may be obtained that will add to safety and convenience, possibly avoiding legal embarrassment as well. "Ignorance is no excuse" applies both afloat and ashore!

The name of the state agency to be addressed will vary widely from state to state. Consult page 618 for the name and address of an office to which inquiries may be sent. Requests for information and literature should be as specific as possible.

### SALES AGENTS

Various boating supply stores, marinas, and similar activities have been designated by governmental agencies as official *sales agents* for their publications. These agents accept responsibility for maintenance of adequate stocks of the various charts and documents of interest to mariners and boatmen in their respective areas.

Authorized sales agents may carry stocks of Coast & Geodetic Survey publications, Naval Oceanographic Office publications, Coast Guard publications, or combinations of two or three of these. It does *not* hold true that because an activity is an agent for one type of publication it will have those of other governmental agencies. Lake Survey charts and publications may be sold by local marinas and stores, but there is no formal system of sales agents.

### Other information

Additional information on where to obtain certain specific government publications will be found on pages 571 and 611-613.

## Coast & Geodetic Survey Publications

The Coast and Geodetic Survey (C&GS) is charged with the survey of the coasts, harbors, and tidal estuaries of the United States and its insular possessions. It issues the following publications relating to these waters as guides to navigation: Charts, Coast Pilots, Tide Tables, Tidal Current Tables, Tidal Current Charts, and chart catalogs.

The Coast and Geodetic Survey has now been combined with the Weather Bureau and the Central Radio Propagation Laboratory to comprise the Environmental Science Services Administration (ESSA) within the Department of Commerce.

### TIDE TABLES

Tide Tables, fig. 1701, are of great value in determining the predicted height of the water at almost any place at any given time. These tables are calculated in advance and are published annually in four volumes, one of which covers the East Coast of North and South America and another the West Coast of these continents.

The Tide Tables give the predicted times and heights of high and low waters for each day of the year at a number of important points known as *reference stations*. The East Coast Tide Tables include 48 sets of detailed listings for such points as Portland, Boston, Sandy Hook, Baltimore, Miami, Pensacola, and Galveston. Additional

data are tabulated showing the differences in times and heights between these reference stations and thousands of other points, termed *subordinate stations*. From these tables, the tide at virtually any point along the coast can be easily computed.

The C&GS Tide Tables also include other useful data including tables of sunrise and sunset, reduction of local mean time to standard zone time, and moonrise and moonset.

The Tide Tables and their use in piloting are discussed at length in Chapter 20, pages 397-402.

### TIDAL CURRENT TABLES

The Tidal Current Tables are in much the same format as the Tide Tables, see fig. 1702. However, instead of times of high and low waters, these tables give the times of maximum flood and ebb currents and times of the two slacks when current direction reverses. The times of slack water do *not* correspond to times of high and low tides, and the Tide Tables *cannot* be used to predict current situations. Velocity of the current at maximum strength is given in terms of knots (nautical miles per hour).

Tidal Current Tables are published in two volumes—Atlantic Coast of North America and Pacific Coast of North America and Asia. Included in each volume are tables from

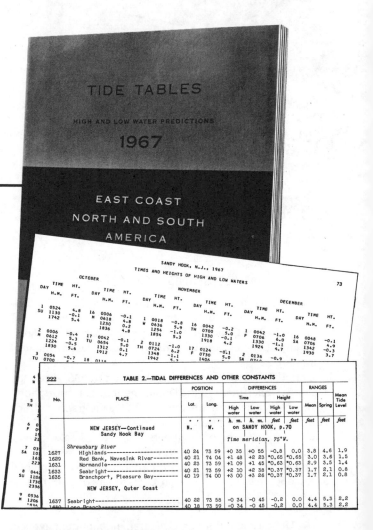

FIG. 1701   Tide Tables published by the Coast & Geodetic Survey provide necessary data for predicting height of tide at thousands of coastal points for any desired day and hour. Separate volumes are issued for the Atlantic-Gulf and Pacific Coasts.

**FIG. 1702** Tidal Current Tables are prepared in much the same format as the Tide Tables. A system of a limited number of reference points together with thousands of subordinate stations permits calculation of current strengths and slacks at virtually any location of navigational interest.

which may be calculated current velocity at any intermediate time and the duration of slack water or weak currents.

Tidal Current Tables and their use in piloting are covered in detail in Chapter 20, pages 406-409.

## TIDAL CURRENT CHARTS

Tidal Current Charts are available for eight bodies of water—Boston Harbor, Narragansett Bay to Nantucket Sound, Narragansett Bay, Long Island Sound and Block Island Sound, New York Harbor, Delaware Bay and River, San Francisco Bay, and Puget Sound (in two parts on separate charts). These are made up in sets of a series of twelve reproductions of the chart of the locality, each of which indicates graphically the direction and velocity of tidal currents for a specific hour with respect to the state of the tide or current prediction for a major reference station. Currents in the various passages are indicated with red arrows and velocities are noted at numerous points; see fig. 1703. By following through the sequence of charts, hourly changes in velocity and direction are easily seen. These charts make it possible to visualize just how tidal currents act in various passages and channels throughout every part of the entire twelve-hour-plus cycle.

Where currents run at considerable velocity, and espe-

cially where tidal currents are complex, often flowing in opposite directions at the same stage of tide, a real advantage can be gained in consulting one of these charts. A few minutes' study may well be the means of carrying a favorable current through the entire passage, instead of needlessly bucking an opposing flow for much or all of the time. As is the case for all current predictions, it must be remembered that these charts indicate normal conditions; a strong wind from certain directions may have a decided influence on both the strength of currents and the times that maximums are reached.

The New York Harbor Tidal Current Charts are used in conjunction with the annual tide tables. All other Tidal Current Charts are used with the annual tidal current tables for their respective areas. See also pages 409 and 410.

**FIG. 1703** Tidal Current Charts are available for a number of major bodies of water where such flows are of significance in piloting. A series of twelve charts, for hourly intervals in the cycle of ebb and flood, comprise each Tidal Current Chart.

## COAST PILOTS

The amount of information that can be printed on nautical charts is limited by available space and the system of symbols that is used. Additional information is often needed for safe and convenient navigation. The Coast and Geodetic Survey publishes such information in the *Coast Pilots*. These are printed in book form, covering the coastline in eight separate volumes.

Each Coast Pilot, see fig. 1704, contains sailing directions

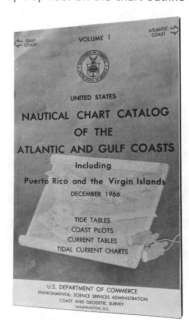

FIG. 1704 The Coast Pilot is issued in eight volumes for various sections of the coastline. Each includes sailing directions, courses and distances between ports; information on hazards and aids to navigation; data on facilities for supplies and repairs; and much other useful information that cannot be conveniently shown on nautical charts.

154                    9. WESTERN LONG ISLAND SOUND

There are several marinas and boatyards in the harbor. Craft up to 12 tons can be hauled out for engine and hull repairs. Gasoline, diesel fuel, water, ice, storage facilities, lifts, and marine supplies are available. The town of Huntington maintains several launching ramps.

Lloyd Harbor extends westward from Huntington Bay nearly to Oyster Bay, from which it is separated by a narrow strip of beach at high water. Vessels drawing less than 7 feet can anchor just inside the entrance, where the depths are 7 to 11 feet. An abandoned light tower is about in the middle of the entrance.

Oyster Bay, on the south side of the sound about 5 miles westward of Eatons Neck Light, lies between Lloyd Neck and Rocky Point. The entrance and harbor are characterized by extensive shoals, boulder reefs, and broken ground making off from the shores. Vessels should proceed with caution if obliged to approach or cross shoal areas. The bay south of Cold Spring Harbor Light is a secure harbor, available for vessels of less than 18-foot draft. A fog signal is sounded at the light.

Lloyd Neck, between Huntington and Oyster Bays, is high and wooded, and has a high, yellow bluff on its north side 0.8 miles eastward of Lloyd Point. Many patches of boulders having least depths of 2 to 8 feet extend 0.2 to 0.5 mile offshore from East Fort Point to Lloyd Point. Small craft skirting this shore should keep well

Currents.—About 0.2 mile north of Cold Spring Harbor Light the velocity is about 0.5 knot; about 0.2 mile north of Cove Point, 1.2 miles southwestward, it is about 0.8 knot. For predictions, the Tidal Current Tables should be consulted.

Ice.—During severe winters ice has been known to extend the full length of the bay during part of January and February.

Plum Point, the easternmost point of Centre Island, is marked at its south end by a small stone tower; boat landings are on the southwest side of the point. A yacht club with a prominent flagstaff is about 0.3 mile west of Plum Point. The yacht club landing has depths of about 9 feet. See appendix for storm warning display.

Cooper Bluff, at the northeast end of Cove Neck is prominent. A boulder reef extends nearly 0.3 mile northward from Cove Point at the northwest end of Cove Neck, and is marked by a lighted buoy.

Cold Spring Harbor, the southeasterly end of Oyster Bay, extends about 2.3 miles southward of Cooper Bluff. The seminary on the hill of West Neck, on the east side of the harbor, is prominent. The harbor is free of dangers if the shores be given a berth of about 0.3 mile, the depths being 15 to 18 feet to near its head.

The village of Cold Spring Harbor is on the eastern shore near the head of the harbor. An oil company

between ports in its respective area, including recommended courses and distances. Channels, with their controlling depths, and all dangers and obstructions are fully described. Harbors and anchorages are listed, with information on those points at which facilities are available for boat supplies and marine repairs. Information regarding canals, bridges, docks, etc., which cannot be adequately expressed on charts due to limitations of space, is provided in full in the Coast Pilots. Information on the Intracoastal Waterways is contained in the various applicable volumes.

The various volumes of the Coast Pilot cover areas as follows:

Atlantic Coast
No. 1  Eastport to Cape Cod
No. 2  Cape Cod to Sandy Hook
No. 3  Sandy Hook to Cape Henry
No. 4  Cape Henry to Key West
No. 5  Gulf of Mexico, Puerto Rico, and
         Virgin Islands
Pacific Coast
No. 7  California, Oregon, Washington,
         and Hawaii
Alaska
No. 8  Dixon Entrance to Cape Spencer
No. 9  Cape Spencer to Beaufort Sea

Note: Currently there is no Volume No. 6.

*Annual supplements* are issued for each volume of the Coast Pilot. A volume for which a supplement has been issued should be used *only* in conjunction with the *latest* supplement. Each supplement is cumulative, complete in itself and superseding all prior supplements.

Annual supplements to the Coast Pilot are available without charge at local C&GS sales agents or from the Coast and Geodetic Survey, ESSA, Rockville, Md. 20852. On a

rotating basis, the C&GS reprints the various Coast Pilots to include all up-to-date data; the reprintings of any specific volume occur about every seven years.

## CHART CATALOGS

The Coast and Geodetic Survey issues free *Chart Catalogs,* fig. 1705, in three volumes for the Atlantic and Pacific Coasts, including offshore islands, and for Alaska. These are actually small-scale outline charts with diagrams delineating the area covered by each nautical chart published by the C&GS. These catalogs are also sources of much additional information regarding charts and publications of other agencies, and the location of sales agents (shown both by a listing of the name and address of the agent and by a symbol on the chart-outline diagrams).

FIG. 1705 The Coast & Geodetic Survey issues catalogs of their nautical charts; these also include listings of other useful publications of the C&GS and other agencies. These catalogs show the area covered by each chart, the scale, price, etc. They are updated at intervals of 6 to 12 months.

## C&GS OFFICES

Nautical charts, Tide and Tidal Current Tables, Coast Pilots, and other publications of the Coast and Geographic Survey can be purchased over-the-counter at the Distribution Office in Washington, D.C. at Connecticut Avenue and Van Ness Street, N.W., or by mail (prepaid) to the address shown in fig. 1817.

### Obtaining information

Information regarding C&GS charts, publications, and activities can be obtained by addressing the Coast and Geodetic Survey, Rockville, Md. 20852. Field offices in various major port cities, formerly sources of information, were closed in mid-1969.

> Distribution Division (C44)
> U.S. Coast and Geodetic Survey
> Washington, D.C. 20235

**FIG. 1706 If not available at local sales agents, publications and charts of the Coast & Geodetic Survey can be purchased by mail from the office listed above. A check or money order for the total price should accompany the order; the material will be sent postpaid.**

# Coast Guard Publications

The United States Coast Guard prepares a major navigational publication and a number of minor ones. All of these are worthy of a boatman's serious consideration.

### LIGHT LISTS

The Light Lists are useful to any boatman, but particularly so to those who cruise into unfamiliar waters. These Lists provide more complete information concerning aids to navigation than can be conveniently shown on charts, see fig. 1707. They are *not* intended to be used in navigation in place of charts and Coast Pilots, and should not be so used. Charts should be consulted for the location of all aids to navigation. It may be dangerous to use aids to navigation without reference to charts.

The Light Lists describe, for the use of mariners, the lightships, lighthouses, lesser lights, buoys, and daybeacons maintained in all navigable waters of the United States by the Coast Guard and various private agencies. (In this usage, the Navy and all other non-USCG governmental organizations are considered to be "private agencies.") The data shown in the Lists includes the official name of the aid, the characteristics of its light, sound, and radio signals, its structural appearance, position, and other significant factors.

Light Lists are published in five volumes as follows:

Volume I—Atlantic Coast from St. Croix River,
　　　　　Maine to Little River, S.C.
Volume II—Atlantic and Gulf Coasts from Little
　　　　　River, S.C. to Rio Grande, Texas
Volume III—Pacific Coast and Pacific Islands
Volume IV—Great Lakes
Volume V—Mississippi River System

Within each volume, aids to navigation are listed by Coast Guard Districts in the following order: seacoast, major channels, Intracoastal Waterway, minor channel, and miscellaneous. Lighted and unlighted aids appear together in their geographic order, with amplifying data on the same page.

Seacoast aids are listed in sequence from north to south along the Atlantic Coast, from south to north and east to west along the Gulf Coast, and from south to north along the Pacific Coast. On the Atlantic and Gulf Coasts, aids along the Intracoastal Waterway are listed in the same sequence. For rivers and estuaries, the aids to navigation are shown from seaward to the head of navigation. Where an

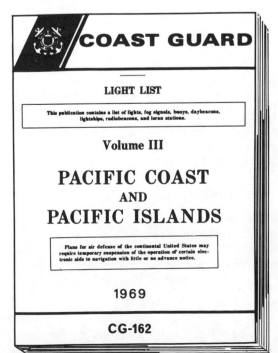

**FIG. 1707 Light Lists, published by the U.S. Coast Guard, provide more detailed information on aids to navigation than can be shown on charts. Five volumes cover all coasts, the Great Lakes, and the Mississippi River system. Light Lists are to be used with, not as a substitute for, nautical charts.**

aid serves both a channel leading in from sea and the ICW, it will be listed separately in both sequences.

All volumes of the USCG Light Lists are for sale by the Superintendent of Documents, Government Printing Office; the volume for the local area concerned is sold by many of the authorized chart and publication sales agents.

## RULES OF THE ROAD

The Coast Guard issues a series of free pamphlets setting forth the Rules of the Road for various bodies of water. These include the general "Inland Rules" (Publication CG-169), fig. 1708, the "Great Lakes Rules" (CG-172), and the "Western Rivers Rules" (CG-184). The International Rules

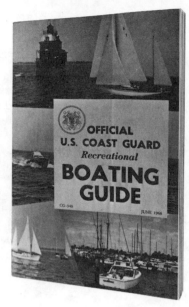

FIG. 1709 The official U.S. Coast Guard Recreational Boating Guide contains excellent summaries of information relating to legally required equipment, other items that should be aboard a boat, registration and numbering, responsibilities of a skipper, and services rendered boatmen by the Coast Guard Auxiliary.

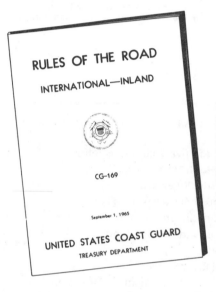

FIG. 1708 Separate pamphlets are issued by the U.S. Coast Guard covering Rules of the Road for Inland Waters, the Great Lakes, and the Western Rivers. The International Rules, used on the high seas, are included in the pamphlet covering Inland Rules.

of the Road, used on the open seas and outside of specified boundaries. at major ports, are included with the Inland Rules in CG-169 in a convenient parallel column format.

Copies of the Rules of the Road pamphlets may be obtained from Coast Guard Marine Inspection Offices in the major ports, or by writing to the Commandant (CHS), U.S. Coast Guard Headquarters, Washington, D.C. 20226.

## RECREATIONAL BOATING GUIDE

An excellent collection of information on boat numbering, legal minimum equipment requirements, other equipment that should be carried, responsibilities when operat-

ing a boat, emergency procedures, and U.S. Coast Guard Auxiliary services is published as the *Official U.S. Coast Guard Recreational Boating Guide* (CG-340), fig. 1709.

This publication also contains an example of a boating accident report, a Distress Information Sheet, and guides to the safe loading capacity of small boats.

The USCG Recreational Boating Guide is revised periodically when required by changes in the applicable laws and regulations. Copies may be purchased by mail from the Superintendent of Documents, or frequently may be found for sale at marinas or boating supply stores; the price is 45¢.

## OTHER USCG PUBLICATIONS

The Coast Guard issues a number of publications relating to the safety of navigation and covering such topics as aids to navigation, applicable rules and regulations, general safety matters, etc. See pages 611-612 for a more complete listing and information on where they may be obtained. Some of these are free, others are available for a nominal charge.

A USCG publication of more-than-usual interest is *Ventilation Systems for Small Craft* (CG-395). This free pamphlet explains the Coast Guard requirements for the ventilation of engine and fuel tank compartments on gasoline-powered boats.

# Oceanographic Office Publications ————————————

The U.S. Naval Oceanographic Office (formerly the Hydrographic Office) is responsible for several publications of considerable value to boatmen.

Charts, publications, and other products of the Naval Oceanographic Office will be identified with a prefix to the individual chart or publication number as follows:

Nautical charts, publications, and other products used primarily for navigational purposes, and which are clearly not oceanographic in nature, will be identified with the letters "H.O." as a prefix to the chart or publication number as was done when such items were issued by the Hydrographic Office.

Oceanographic products, primarily publications, related to the dynamic nature of the oceans or the scientific aspects of oceanography will be identified with the letters "N.O.O." as a prefix to the publication or chart number.

## BOWDITCH (H.O. 9)

The *American Practical Navigator,* originally written by Nathaniel Bowditch.in 1799, and generally referred to simply as "Bowditch," is an extensive treatise on piloting, celestial navigation and other nautical matters. It is Publication No. H.O. 9, last revised in 1958 and reprinted with

H.O. Pub. No. 9

# AMERICAN
# PRACTICAL NAVIGATOR

## AN EPITOME OF NAVIGATION

ORIGINALLY BY
NATHANIEL BOWDITCH, LL.D.

1966—Corrected Print

PUBLISHED BY THE
U.S. NAVY HYDROGRAPHIC OFFICE
UNDER THE AUTHORITY OF THE
SECRETARY OF THE NAVY

U.S. GOVERNMENT PRINTING OFFICE
WASHINGTON : 1966

**FIG. 1710** "Bowditch" is the name by which this popular and highly useful government publication is usually known. It contains a wealth of material on piloting, electronic and celestial navigation, and related topics. The mathematical tables contained in it are also available as a separate publication.

minor corrections in 1962 and 1966, see fig. 1710.

"Bowditch" has long been accepted as an authority on questions of piloting and navigation; a copy will be found useful on all but the smallest of boats. In addition to the lengthy text, the basic volume contains many mathematical tables as appendices. These tables alone are also available as a separate publication.

## OTHER H.O. PUBLICATIONS

Other Oceanographic Office publications that may be found useful to a boatman include H.O. 117A, *Radio Navigation Aids;* H.O. 118A, *Radio Weather Aids;* and H.O. 103, *International Code of Signals, Visual* (see Chapter 26).

The Oceanographic Office publishes a series of *Sailing Directions* which provide supplementary information for foreign coasts and ports in a manner generally similar to the Coast Pilot for U.S. waters.

The *Lists of Lights* published by this agency likewise cover foreign waters and so are not duplicatory of the Coast Guard Light Lists. These are H.O. 111A through H.O. 116.

The Oceanographic Office's catalog of its charts is Publication No. H.O. 1N. It has an Introduction in three parts plus lists of charts subdivided into ten "regions." It may be purchased as a whole or separately by regions. Regions 0, 1, and 2 would be of the most interest to American boatmen. See fig. 1710a.

Other H.O. publications include a number of tables for the reduction of celestial observations, and tables and charts for plotting lines of position from Loran-A and Loran-C measurements. These are of interest only to those yachtsmen making extensive voyages on the high seas.

Additional Oceanographic Office publications are listed on page 613.

## Obtaining Oceanographic Office Publications

Branch Offices of the Naval Oceanographic Office are located at Norfolk, Va.; Wilmington, Calif.; Honolulu, Hawaii; Rodman, C.Z.; and Yokosuka, Japan.

Charts and publications of the Naval Oceanographic Office are available for sale through authorized sales agents, and purchases should be made through these agents whenever possible. If not so available, charts may be purchased from the Branch Oceanographic Offices listed above, or by mail from the U.S. Naval Oceanographic Office, Washington, D.C. 20390, or from either of the Oceanographic Distribution Offices listed below. Mail orders from purchasers located west of the Mississippi River (except Gulf of Mexico and the Canal Zone area) should be sent to:

U. S. Naval Oceanographic Distribution Office, Clearfield, Utah 84016

Mail orders from all other localities should be sent to:

U.S. Naval Oceanographic Distribution Office, U.S. Naval Supply Depot, 5801 Tabor Ave., Philadelphia, Penna. 19120

Orders submitted to the U.S. Naval Oceanographic Office or to a Naval Oceanographic Distribution Office must be accompanied by a check or money order made payable to the "U.S. Naval Oceanographic Office" for the amount of the purchase. Material will be mailed at Government expense in regular printed-matter postal service. The added cost of requests for any special handling, such as air mail, special delivery, etc., must be borne by the purchaser.

## Naval Observatory Publications

The U.S. Naval Observatory, Washington, D.C. publishes the *American Nautical Almanac.* This publication contains astronomical data necessary to boatmen who are concerned with celestial navigation, but is not needed for piloting. It can be purchased, in annual editions, from the Superintendent of Documents.

The Naval Observatory also participates in and assists the publication of other navigational documents such as the Tide Tables and celestial sight reduction tables, but it is not the agency directly responsible for them.

**FIG. 1710a.** The Oceanographic Office catalog indexes charts by regions. Of these, Region O (United States) is of particular interest.

333

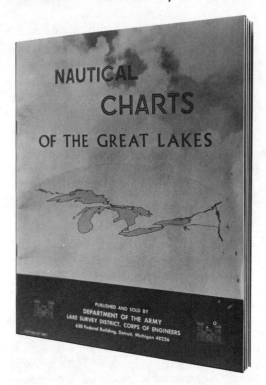

FIG. 1711 The new U.S. Lake Survey chart catalog covers not only the Great Lakes, but also its outflow rivers, Lake Champlain, N.Y. State Barge Canal system, and Minnesota-Ontario border lakes.

CORPS OF
ENGINEERS
U.S. ARMY

## U. S. LAKE SURVEY

# GREAT LAKES PILOT
# 1967

## BEARINGS ARE TRUE AND DISTANCES ARE EXPRESSED IN STATUTE MILES

The text of this Pilot has been edited and its publication supervised by the U.S. Lake Survey. It is a complete revision compiled from former Pilots; from surveys made by the U.S. Lake Survey; from publications of the U.S. Coast Guard; from information supplied by the Environmental Science Services Administration (U.S. Weather Bureau), the Department of Health, Education and Welfare, the St. Lawrence Seaway Development Corp., the New York State Department of Public Works, the Canadian Departments of Transport, of Public Works and of Energy, Mines and Resources (Mines and Technical Surveys), and the St. Lawrence Seaway Authority; and from revisory data related to the river and harbor improvements carried on in these waters, by the Corps of Engineers, U.S. Army.

FIG. 1712 The Great Lakes Pilot is a comprehensive volume prepared to supplement information given on charts published by the U.S. Lake Survey. It is revised annually and kept up-to-date by supplements issued monthly during the navigation season (May-November).

## Army Engineers Publications

The Corps of Engineers of the U.S. Army has the responsibility for navigational and informational publications on the Great Lakes, major inland (non-tidal) rivers such as the Tennessee, Ohio, and Mississippi, and many lakes and reservoirs behind the large dams.

### GREAT LAKES CHART CATALOGS

An excellent free catalog of Nautical Charts of the Great Lakes, fig. 1711, is available from the Lake Survey District, Corps of Engineers, 630 Federal Building, Detroit, Mich. 48226, where mail orders and counter sales of Lake Survey charts are handled. Lake Survey charts are also sold, over the counter only, at their sales offices in Sault Ste. Marie, Mich.; Buffalo, N.Y.; Cleveland, Ohio; Chicago, Ill., and Massena, N.Y.

Included in the waterways listed in the Lake Survey catalog, in addition to the Great Lakes and its outflow rivers, are Lake Champlain, the New York State Barge Canal System, and the Minnesota-Ontario Border Lakes. The catalog also supplies information on the Lake Survey's recreational chart series, designed especially for the operators of small pleasure boats, and other Lake Survey publications, such as the Great Lakes Pilot.

### THE GREAT LAKES PILOT

For the Great Lakes and other waters covered by U.S. Lake Survey charts, the publication corresponding to the Coast Pilots is called the *Great Lakes Pilot,* fig. 1712. This is an annual publication, kept up to date during the navigation season by seven monthly supplements issued from May to November.

### INTRACOASTAL WATERWAY BOOKLETS

The Army Engineers has prepared two paperbound booklets on the Intracoastal Waterway, which comes under its jurisdiction. These booklets contain descriptive material, photographs, small-scale charts, and tabulated data. Caution must be exercised, however, when using the distance tables as considerable differences exist between these publications and the C&GS charts of the Atlantic ICW. The Army Engineers use statute (not nautical) miles, and their zero point is at Trenton, N.J. rather than Norfolk, Va. Mileage differences will also be noted along the Gulf Intracoastal Waterway.

Unfortunately, these publications are *not* periodically updated, and they are of far less value than the corresponding volumes of the C&GS Coast Pilots with their annual supplements.

Bulletins on the Intracoastal Waterways are issued periodically by the Engineers' District Offices. Addresses of these offices are given on page 612.

### RIVERS AND LAKES INFORMATION

*Regulations* relating to the use of many rivers and lakes (reservoirs), *Navigational Bulletins,* and *Notices to Navigation Interests* are issued by various offices of the Corps of Engineers, U.S. Army, as listed on page 571. Other government publications relating to inland river and lake boating are also listed on that page, together with information as to where they may be obtained.

## Weather Bureau Publications

The U.S. Weather Bureau, an element of ESSA, Department of Commerce, publishes *Daily Weather Maps* (see Chapter 12), but these are directly used by relatively few boatmen. Much greater reliance is placed on radio and television broadcasts of current weather conditions and predictions.

To assist mariners and boatmen in knowing when and where to listen for radio and TV weather broadcasts, the Weather Bureau publishes a series of *Marine Weather Services Charts* in annual editions. These are discussed in more detail in pages 264-265 and 498.

## Keeping Publications Up to Date

It is essential that certain navigational publications, as well as charts, be kept corrected and fully up to date with respect to the information contained in them. Incorrect, outdated information can be considerably more harmful than no information at all; a false sense of knowledge and confidence can easily lead to a dangerous situation.

Coast Pilots and Light Lists are the primary publications that need continual correction. Fortunately, the government has provided a convenient means for executing this most necessary function. The time and effort required are not great, provided a skipper keeps at it regularly and does not permit the work to build up a backlog.

### NOTICE TO MARINERS

The U.S. Naval Oceanographic Office publishes a weekly *Notice to Mariners* which is prepared jointly with the Coast & Geodetic Survey and the Coast Guard; see fig. 1713. These pamphlets advise mariners of important matters affecting navigational safety, including new hydrographic discoveries, changes in channels and navigational aids, etc. Besides keeping mariners informed generally, the Notice to Mariners also provides information specifically useful for updating the latest editions of nautical charts and publications produced by the Naval Oceanographic Office, the Coast & Geodetic Survey, and the Coast Guard.

Each issue contains instructions on how it is to be used to correct charts and other publications. Certain supplementary information is published at the beginning of each year, and portions are repeated at mid-year or at quarterly intervals.

### LOCAL NOTICES TO MARINERS

The Commander of each Coast Guard District issues *Local Notices to Mariners,* fig. 1714. These are usually better suited to the needs of boatmen who do not need information on remote or foreign waters. The Local Notices are reproduced and mailed from the respective District Headquarters, and corresponding items of information will reach boatmen several weeks in advance of the weekly Notices that are printed in Washington, D.C. and mailed from there.

### Report all useful information

All boatmen are urged to cooperate with governmental agencies in keeping the buoyage system up to its highest

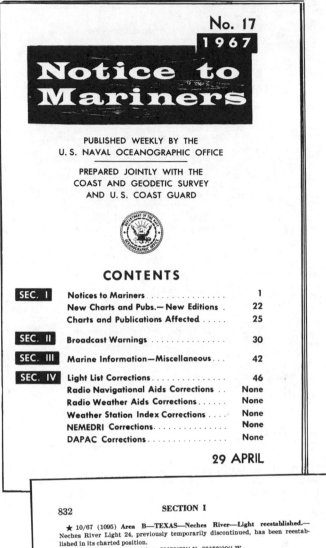

FIG. 1713. Notice to Mariners is a free weekly publication used to correct charts and other navigational publications. A single volume covers the major navigable waters of the world. Information appears in the form of descriptive paragraphs, inserts for pasting on charts, and cut-outs for insertion in volumes such as Light Lists. Information is limited to waters used by ocean-going vessels; for inland waters, Local Notices to Mariners must be used.

efficiency and helpfulness by reporting any facts that may come to their attention concerning damage to aids, malfunctioning of lights, shifting of shoals and channels, new hazards, etc. Defects in navigational aids and new hazards should be reported to the nearest Coast Guard activity by the fastest means available, including radio if the situation is of sufficient urgency. Suggestions for the improvement of aids to navigation should be sent to the Commandant, U.S. Coast Guard, Washington, D.C. 20226.

Data concerning dangers to navigation, changes in shoals and channels, and similar information affecting charts or publications of the C&GS should be sent to the Director, Coast and Geodetic Survey, ESSA, Washington Science Center, Rockville, Maryland 20852.

**FIG. 1714   Local Notices to Mariners are published by each Coast Guard District on a "when required" basis, often several times per week. Information in Local Notices often reaches boatmen several weeks before it appears in weekly Notices from Washington. Check your local yacht club or marina for its file of Local Notices.**

## Quasi-Governmental Publications

In addition to the governmental agencies and their publications noted above, there are several activities that can be best described as "quasi-governmental." Publications issued by them are of considerable interest to boatmen.

## RADIO TECHNICAL COMMISSION FOR MARINE SERVICES

This organization with the long name is for obvious reasons better known by its initials, RTCM. It includes representatives of governmental agencies such as the FCC, the Coast Guard, ESSA, Maritime Administration, and others; user organizations, such as ocean steamship operating groups, Great Lakes shipping interests, and the United States Power Squadrons; equipment manufacturers; labor organizations; and communications companies such as the Bell System. The RTCM does not have authority to make binding decisions, but it wields considerable influence through its function as a meeting place for the presentation and resolution of conflicting views and interests.

The RTCM publishes *Marine Radio Telephony,* a booklet presenting a simplified interpretation of the FCC Rules and Regulations relating to the use of radios on ships and boats. This small booklet can be most useful to a skipper with a set on board in the 2-3 Mc/s marine band. See fig. 2517.

The RTCM also publishes a companion operator's manual, *Maritime Mobile VHF-FM Radio Telephony—Usage in the United States.* This volume, as well as that for the 2-3 Mc/s marine band, may be purchased from the Executive Secretary, RTCM, P.O. Box 764, Washington, D.C. 20044.

## NAVAL INSTITUTE PUBLICATIONS

The United States Naval Institute is not a governmental agency; rather it is a private association "for the advancement of professional, literary, and scientific knowledge in the Navy." One of its principal activities is the publication of books on naval and maritime matters.

The Naval Institute publishes a large number of books, but none will be more familiar to boatmen than *Dutton's Navigation and Piloting.* Like Bowditch, this volume has come to be an accepted authority on matters of piloting and navigation. Again like Bowditch, the current volume is an outgrowth of many years of development from an early work; the book was initially known as "Navigation and Nautical Astronomy" by Benjamin Dutton. This useful book can be purchased in boating supply and book stores, or directly by mail from the U.S. Naval Institute, Annapolis, Maryland, 21402.

⚓

# CHAPTER 18

# THE NAUTICAL CHART

## ...Indispensable Aid to Safe Piloting

IN ORDER to travel anywhere safely in his boat, a skipper must have knowledge of the depths of the water, the shoals and the channels. He must also know the location of aids to navigation and landmarks, and where ports and harbors can be found. At any given position, he can generally measure the depth, and he sees some landmarks; but for true safety he has to know the depth ahead, the actual location of those aids to navigation which he can presently see, and where more aids are located relative to the course he plans to follow. For the best route to his destination, he must know where it lies with respect to his present position, and the dangers to navigation which may be along the way.

All of this information can only be determined from charts, one of the most essential and important items of equipment for piloting a boat. It would take a skillful boatman indeed to cruise any distance into strange waters without the necessary charts, even if he were equipped with all the other needed devices—and it would be foolhardy of him to attempt it. The skipper must not only have the required charts; he must know how to use them.

**FIG. 1801** You are at Buoy "4" and the water is measured to be 18 feet deep, but what is the course to your destination, and how deep is the water along the way? Only a chart can give you this information —be sure that you have the right charts on board, and that you know how to use them.

**FIG. 1802** A nautical chart is a representation in miniature of a portion of the earth's surface with emphasis on natural and man-made features of particular interest to the navigator of a ship or boat.

## CHARTS VS. MAPS

A *nautical chart,* fig. 1802, is a representation in miniature, on a plane surface, of a portion of the earth's surface emphasizing natural and man-made features of particular interest to a navigator. A map, fig. 1803, is a similar miniature representation for use on land in which the emphasis is on roads, cities, political boundaries, etc. For a boatman to refer to a chart as a "map" is to reveal his lack of nautical knowledge and experience.

A chart covers an area which is primarily water and includes such information as the depth of water, obstructions and other dangers to navigation, and the location and type of aids to navigation. Adjacent land areas are portrayed only in such detail as will aid a navigator—the shoreline, harbor facilities, prominent natural or man-made features, etc. Charts are printed on heavy-weight, durable paper so that they may be used as worksheets on which courses may be plotted and positions determined.

A basic requirement of a nautical chart is to provide the navigator with the proper information to enable him to make the *right* decision *in time to avoid danger.* Charts are prepared by various agencies of the Government to furnish the pilot or navigator with absolutely accurate representations of navigable bodies of water showing the depths, aids to navigation, shorelines, and other essential features. They differ from road maps both in the great amount of detailed information that they contain and in the precision with which they are constructed. The need for this accuracy can be appreciated when it is realized that an error of only a small amount in charting the position of a submerged obstruction could constitute a serious menace to navigation.

Several major oil companies produce a series of "cruising guides" which cover important boating areas, fig. 1804. These are useful in planning a nautical trip, but lack the detail, accuracy, and provision for revisions between printings (by means of Notices to Mariners) required for actual navigational use. Do *not* try to substitute them for official government charts.

## GEOGRAPHIC COORDINATES

Charts will also show a grid of intersecting lines to aid in the description of a position on the water. These lines are the charted representations of a system of *geographic coordinates* which exist on the earth's surface, although in an unseen, imaginary sense like state boundaries.

The earth is nearly spherical in shape—it is slightly flattened along the polar axis, but the distortion is slight and

© General Drafting Co., Inc.

FIG. 1803 A map differs from a nautical chart in that the emphasis is on towns, roads, political boundaries, etc. It is designed primarily for motorists and should never be used for navigation.

FIG. 1804 The major oil companies issue "cruising guides" which may be of great value in planning a cruise, but should never be depended upon for the actual navigation of a boat.

339

need be of concern only to scientists, not boatmen. A *great circle*, fig. 1805a, is the line traced out on the surface of a sphere by a plane cutting through the sphere at its center. This is the largest circle that can be drawn on the surface of a sphere. A *small circle,* fig. 1805b, is one marked on the surface of a sphere by a plane that does not pass through its center.

### Meridians and parallels

Geographic coordinates are defined by two sets of great and small circles. One is a set of great circles each of which passes through the north and south geographic poles — these are the *meridians of longitude,* fig. 1806. The other set is a series of circles each established by a plane cutting through the earth perpendicular to the polar axis. The

For greater precision in position definition, degrees may be subdivided into *minutes* (60 minutes = 1 degree) and *seconds* (60 seconds = 1 minute).

From figures 1808b and 1809, it will be seen that the meridians of longitude get closer together as one moves away from the equator in either direction, and eventually converge at the poles. Thus the distance on the earth's surface between adjacent meridians is not a fixed quantity but varies with latitude. On the other hand, the parallels of latitude are essentially equally spaced and the distance between successive parallels is nearly the same. One degree of latitude is, for all practical purposes, 60 nautical miles: and *one minute of latitude may be taken as one nautical mile,* a relationship which we will later see is quite useful.

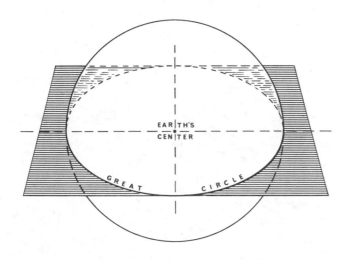

**FIG. 1805 a    A GREAT CIRCLE is the line traced out on the surface of a sphere by a plane cutting through the center point of the sphere.**                (From Dutton)

**FIG. 1805 b    A SMALL CIRCLE is the line traced on the surface of a sphere by a plane which cuts through the sphere but does NOT pass through the center point of the sphere.**

largest of these is midway between the poles and thus passes through the center of the earth, becoming a great circle; this is the *equator,* fig. 1807a. Other parallel planes form small circles which are known as the *parallels of latitude,* fig. 1807b.

Geographic coordinates are measured in terms of degrees (one degree is 1/360th of a complete circle). The meridian that passes through Greenwich, England is the reference for all measurements of longitude and is designated as the *prime meridian,* or *0°.* The longitude of any position on earth is described as —° East or West of Greenwich, to a maximum in either direction of 180°. The measurement can be thought of as either the angle at the north and south poles between the meridian of the place being described and the prime meridian, or as the arc along the equator between these meridians, fig. 1808a. The designation of "E" or "W" is an essential part of any statement of longitude, abbreviated as "long." or "λ" (the Greek letter lambda).

Parallels of latitude are measured in degrees North or South from the equator, from 0° at the equator to 90° at each pole. The designation of latitude (abbreviated "L") as "N" or "S" is necessary for a complete description of position, fig. 1808b.

**FIG. 1806    MERIDIANS of LONGITUDE are formed on the earth's surface by great circles which pass through the North and South Poles.**
                                                (From Bowditch)

FIG. 1807 a    The great circle that cuts through the earth perpendicular to the polar axis traces out the EQUATOR at the earth's surface.

FIG. 1807 b    PARALLELS of LATITUDE are the small circles formed at the earth's surface by planes perpendicular to the polar axis but not passing through the center of the earth. They are parallel to the plane of the Equator.

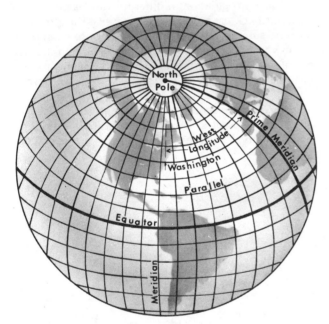

FIG. 1808 a    Longitude is measured in degrees from the Prime Meridian (0°), which passes through Greenwich, England, East or West to a maximum of 180°. The designation of "E" or "W" is an essential part of any statement of longitude.

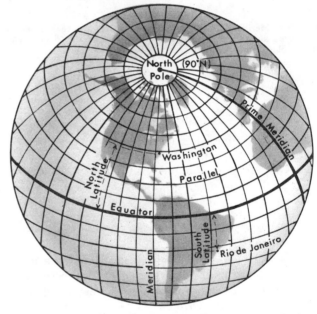

FIG. 1808 b    Latitude is measured in either direction, North or South, from the Equator (0°) to the Poles (90°). Statements of latitude, abbreviated "L", must be labeled either "N" or "S" to be complete.

(From Bowditch)

## CHART CONSTRUCTION

The construction of a chart for a portion of the earth's surface immediately produces the problem of representation of a spherical, three-dimensional surface on a plane, two-dimensional sheet of paper. Actually, it is impossible to accomplish this exactly. A certain amount of distortion is inevitable, but various methods, called *projections,* have been developed which provide practical and sufficiently accurate results.

The transfer of information from the sphere to the flat surface of the chart should be accomplished with as little distortion as possible in the shape and size of land and water areas, the angular relation of positions, the distance between points, and other more technical properties. Each of the different projections is superior to others in one or

more of these qualities; none is superior in all characteristics. In all projections, as the area covered by the chart is decreased, the distortion diminishes, and the difference between various types of projections lessens.

Of the many techniques of projection that might be used, two are of primary interest to boatmen. The *Mercator projection* is an example of the most common; it is used for charts of ocean and coastal areas. The *polyconic projection* is employed for charts of the Great Lakes and inland rivers. The average skipper can quite safely navigate his boat using either type of chart without a deep knowledge of the techniques of projection. (For those who would know more of the various projection methods, see pages 359-362.

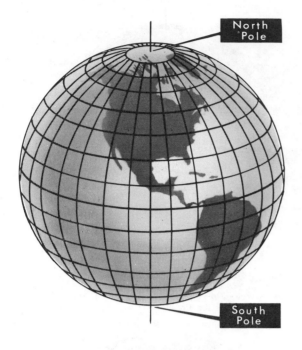

FIG. 1809 Meridians of longitude converge toward each other as one moves away from the Equator in the direction of either pole. All meridians meet at the North and South Poles.

## DIRECTION

*Direction* is defined as the angle between a line connecting one point with another point and a base, or reference, line extending from the origin point toward the true or magnetic north pole; the angle is measured in degrees clockwise from the reference line. Thus direction on charts may be described as so many degrees "True" (T) or so many degrees "Magnetic" (M). The difference between these directions is "variation" and must be allowed for as described in Chapter 13. The principal difference in the use of charts on the Mercator projection and those on the polyconic projection lies in the techniques for measuring direction; this will be covered in Chapter 19 when the use of piloting instruments is considered.

### Measurement of direction

To facilitate the measurement of direction, as in plotting bearings and laying out courses, most charts will have compass roses printed on them. A *compass rose*, fig. 1810, consists of two or three concentric circles, several inches in diameter and accurately subdivided. The outer circle has its zero at *true* north; this is emphasized with a star. The inner circle or circles are oriented to magnetic north. The middle circle, if there are three, is *magnetic* direction expressed in degrees, with an arrow printed over the zero point to indicate magnetic north. The innermost circle is also magnetic direction, but in terms of "points," and halves and quarters thereof; its use by modern boatmen will be limited. (One point = 11¼ degrees.) This innermost circle using the point system of subdivision may be omitted on some charts of the "small-craft" series.

The difference between the orientation of the two sets of circles is, of course, the magnetic variation at the location of the compass rose. The amount of the variation and its direction (Easterly or Westerly) is given in words and figures in the center of the rose, together with a statement of the year that such variation existed and the annual rate of change. When using a chart in a year later than the date shown on the compass rose, it *may* be necessary to modify the variation shown by applying the annual rate of change. Such cases are, however, relatively rare as rates are quite small and differences of a small fraction of a degree may be ignored from a practical standpoint.

Each chart will have several compass roses printed on it at convenient locations where they will not conflict with navigational information. Roses printed on land areas may cause the elimination of topographical features in these regions.

Until a skipper has thoroughly mastered the handling of compass "errors," he should use only true directions and the true (outer) compass rose. Later, the magnetic rose may be used directly, thus simplifying computations.

*Several cautions* are necessary when measuring directions on charts. When large areas are covered, it is possible for the magnetic variation to differ for various portions of the chart. Check each chart when you first start to use it, and, to be sure, always use the compass rose nearest the area for which you are plotting. Depending upon the type and scale of the chart, graduations on the compass rose circles may be for intervals of 1°, 2°, or 5°. On some charts, the outer circle (true) is subdivided into units of 1° while the inner (magnetic) circle, being smaller, is subdivided into steps of 2°. Always check carefully to determine the interval between adjacent marks on each compass rose scale.

FIG. 1810 A compass rose graphically illustrates true and magnetic directions. The outer circle is in degrees with zero at true north. The inner circles are in degrees and "points" with their zero oriented to the magnetic north. Several will be found on each chart conveniently located for plotting courses and bearings.

**FIG. 1811** C&GS charts at scales of 1:80,000 or larger will have two sets of graphic scales. Each set consists of a scale of nautical miles and a scale of yards. On Intracoastal Waterway Charts, a scale of statute miles will also be shown.

## DISTANCE

*Distances* on charts may be measured in statute or in nautical miles. The *statute (land) mile* of 5280 feet is the same as used on road maps; its use in boating is limited to the Great Lakes, inland lakes and rivers, and, since 1969, the Atlantic and Gulf Intracoastal Waterways. The *nautical mile* of 6076.1 feet is used on ocean and coastal waters.

It is sometimes necessary to convert from one unit to the other. This is not difficult—*1 nautical mile = 1.15 statute miles,* or roughly 7 nautical miles = 8 statute miles.

In navigation, distances of up to a mile or so usually are expressed in *yards,* a unit that is the same no matter which "mile" is used on the chart.

## SCALE

As a chart is a representation in miniature of an area of navigable water, actual distances must be "scaled down" to much shorter dimensions on paper. This reduction is termed the *scale* of the chart. The basic way of describing the scale of a chart is its so-called *natural scale,* an expression of the relationship between a given distance on the chart to the actual distance that it represents on the earth. This may be expressed as a ratio, 1:80,000 meaning that 1 unit on the chart represents 80,000 units on the actual land or water surface, or as a fraction $\frac{1}{80,000}$ with the same meaning.

The ratio of chart to actual distance can also be expressed as a *numerical* or *equivalent scale.* This is such a statement as "1 inch = 1.1 miles," another way of expressing a 1:80,000 scale. Equivalent scales are not as commonly used on nautical charts as on maps, but they may be encountered from time to time on such publications as cruising guides.

It is important that at all times the pilot have clearly fixed in his mind the scale of the chart then being used—in order that he will not misjudge the distance to aids to navigation, dangers, etc. Quite often in a day's cruise, a skipper will use charts of different scales, changing back and forth between small-scale coastal charts and larger-scale harbor charts. Unless he is keenly aware of the scale

of the chart being used at the moment, a pilot may find himself unexpectedly in a dangerous position.

### Large-scale and small-scale

When chart scales are expressed fractionally, confusion sometimes results from the use of the terms "large-scale" and "small-scale." Since the number that is varied to change the scale is in the *denominator* of the fraction, as it gets larger, the fraction, and hence the scale, gets smaller. For example, $\frac{1}{80,000}$ is a smaller fraction than $\frac{1}{40,000}$, and thus a chart to the former scale is termed a smaller-scale chart. The terms "large-scale" and "small-scale" are relative and have no limiting definitions. Scales may be as large as 1:5,000 for detailed harbor charts, or as small as 1 to several million for charts of large areas of the world.

Charts at a scale of 1:80,000 or larger will normally carry, in addition to a statement of scale, two sets of *graphic scales,* fig. 1811, each subdivided into conveniently and commonly used units. Note that one basic unit is placed to the *left* of the scale's zero point and is subdivided more finely than is the main part of the scale. The use of these graphic scales will be covered in Chapter 19.

When using Mercator charts, the navigator can take advantage of the fact that one minute of the *latitude* scale on each *side* of the chart is essentially equal to one nautical mile. On charts of a scale smaller than 1:80,000, the latitude scale will be the only means of measuring distance.

A *logarithmic speed scale,* fig. 1812, is printed on all charts of 1:40,000 or larger scale. Its use is explained in Chapter 19.

## SOURCES OF CHARTS

### Who issues charts

Charts are prepared and issued by several agencies of the Federal Government. This is not duplication, however, as different areas and types of charts are the responsibility of each office. The majority of boatmen will use charts prepared by the Coast & Geodetic Survey of the Environ-

**FIG. 1812** C&GS charts of 1:40,000 or larger scale will have a **LOGARITHMIC SPEED SCALE** from which a graphic calculation of speed may be made if the time of run is measured between two known points. See Chapter 19 for a detailed discussion of its use.

mental Science Services Administration, Department of Commerce. C&GS charts cover the coastal waters of the United States, including harbors and rivers extending inland to the head of tidal action.

The Naval Oceanographic Office of the Department of Defense (formerly the Hydrographic Office) publishes charts of the high seas and foreign waters based on its own surveys and on charts originally produced by other countries. Boatmen will become familiar, for example, with HO charts when sailing to Bermuda or cruising in the Bahamas. (The designation "HO" was retained for charts and publications despite the change in the name of the agency.) Canadian waters, however, are charted by that nation's Hydrographic Service.

Charts of the Great Lakes and major inland rivers, such as the Ohio and the Mississippi, are issued by several activities of the U.S. Army Corps of Engineers. The Lake Survey District is the issuing agency for charts of the Great Lakes; their charts are identified by the letters "LS" preceding the chart numbers. Also available from the Army Engineers are charts for many of the inland lakes and canal systems. These are issued by various Division and District Offices.

## Where to buy them

Charts may be purchased directly from the headquarters or field offices of the issuing agencies, or from retail sales agents. The government offices may be addressed as shown in fig. 1813. Sales agents are widely located in boating and shipping centers. Lists of sales agents for C&GS and HO charts are published in each Coast Pilot and periodically in Notices to Mariners as discussed in Chapter 17. Lake Survey charts are sold by designated offices of the Army Engineers as listed in their Chart Catalog and the Great Lakes Pilot. The Lake Survey is also establishing a system of local sales agents for their publications.

The cost of charts is amazingly little for the vast amount of information furnished to the navigator. The prices charged for charts include only a small part of the cost to the government for their production. Traditionally, it has been the duty of a country to aid safe navigation by publishing low-cost charts and nautical guides. Recent increases in chart prices have reflected only the general rise in costs, not a change in pricing policy.

C&GS, HO, and Lake Survey charts are sold by government offices or local sales agents at the price printed on

---

**CHART ISSUING AGENCIES**

⚓ U.S. Coast and Geodetic Survey, ESSA
Washington Science Center
Rockville, Maryland 20852

⚓ U.S. Naval Oceanographic Office
Washington, D.C. 20390

⚓ U.S. Army Engineer District,
Lake Survey
630 Federal Building
Detroit, Michigan 48226

FIG. 1813 Information on nautical charts can be obtained by writing to the appropriate headquarters at the address shown above. Regional and District Offices may also be able to provide answers to questions on charts.

---

them, a discount being allowed to the dealer for his quantity purchases. Yacht clubs, boating organizations, etc. also may purchase charts in quantity for a discount; get details from the issuing agency.

The prudent skipper carries on his boat a full set of charts covering the waters that he cruises, and he regularly replaces worn-out or outdated charts with new ones. Charts are among his best boating bargains!

## Chart catalogs

Catalogs are available from issuing agencies which indicate the area covered by each chart, the scale used, and the price. These will be found useful when planning a cruise into unfamiliar boating waters.

The C&GS catalog is issued in three volumes, each a large, accordion-folded sheet; they are free. Volume 1 covers the U.S. Atlantic and Gulf coastal waters. Volume 2 is for the West Coast and Pacific Islands. Volume 3 covers the Alaskan Coast.

The HO chart catalog, publication number 1-N, is issued in "Regions" at a price of 25¢ each. Region "0" covers U.S. coastal waters; Region "2" includes the Bahamian and West Indian cruising areas as well as the waters bordering Central and South America.

The Lake Survey annually publishes its chart catalog covering the Great Lakes, Lake Champlain, the New York Barge Canal System, and other waters. It is available without charge upon request.

---

# What Charts Show

Charts include a great amount of information and a boatman should carefully study each chart soon after he purchases it, certainly well before he must use it to safely navigate his craft.

## BASIC INFORMATION

Located at some convenient place on the chart, where space is available, will be found the *general information block,* fig. 1814. Here is the chart title which is descriptive of the waters covered (the chart number will not appear

here, but rather in several places around the margins), a statement of the type of projection used and the scale, the unit of measurement of depth (feet or fathoms — one fathom equals six feet), and the datum plane for such soundings.

Elsewhere on the chart where there is space available (normally in land areas), other information will be found, such as the meaning of abbreviations used on this chart, special notes of caution regarding dangers, the units of measurement of heights and the reference plane from

UNITED STATES—WEST COAST

# SAN FRANCISCO TO CAPE FLATTERY

Mt. Shasta
14/62

Mercator Projection
Scale 1:1,200,000 at Lat. 49°00'

SOUNDINGS IN FATHOMS
AT MEAN LOWER LOW WATER

**FIG. 1814** The title block shows the official name of the chart, the type of projection, scale, and datum and unit of measurement for depths. Printed nearby will be much valuable information—be sure to read all notes and data before using any chart.

which measured, tidal information, references to anchorage areas, and many other useful bits of data. *All* notes on charts should be read carefully and fully, as they may cover important information that cannot be graphically presented, such information applying to an extended length of a river or channel; see fig. 1815.

### Editions and revisions

The edition number and date appear in the margin at the lower left-hand corner; immediately following these figures will be the date of the latest revised printing, if any. Figures 1816a and b illustrate these two cases. The typical nautical chart is printed to supply the normal demand for one or two years; quantities are so limited to provide for bringing it up to date as frequently as practicable. Charts may be reprinted as-is when the stock runs low, but a revised printing is more likely. Revisions include all changes that have been printed in Notices to Mariners since the preceding issue of the chart. When major changes in hydrography occur, such as new surveys revealing significant differences between charted depths and actual conditions, a new edition is published; it, too, will include all other changes which have been made in aids to navigation, etc.

Special charts, for which there is an urgent need, are printed directly from smooth drafting without engraving; these are designated as "Provisional Charts" and are so labeled in the title block. A chart constructed from unverified information will be marked as a "Preliminary Chart."

*It is of the utmost importance that only the latest edition of a chart be used.* All new editions supersede older issues, which should be discarded. New editions contain information published in Notices to Mariners, *plus* all other corrections that were too extensive for hand-application and so were not published in the Notices. Skippers are cautioned against using superceded charts that may not contain all information essential to safe navigation.

Between editions, charts should be corrected from information published in Notices to Mariners (see page 305). Charts are no longer kept corrected by the Coast and Geodetic Survey while in stock awaiting sale. The pur-

chaser of a chart should make every effort to check all Notices subsequent to the printed edition date and enter all applicable corrections. The safest chart is the one that is fully corrected up to date.

## LATITUDE AND LONGITUDE SCALES

Nautical charts of the conventional type with the geographical north direction toward the top of the sheet will have latitude scales in each side border and longitude scales in the top and bottom borders. The meridians and parallels will be drawn across the chart as fine black lines at intervals of 2', 5', or 10' as determined by the scale of the particular chart.

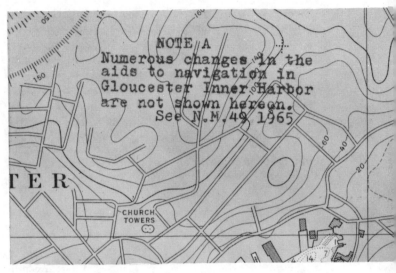

**FIG. 1815** Charts will often have printed notes with information of considerable importance. These may concern navigation regulations, hazardous conditions at inlets, information on controlling depths that cannot be conveniently printed alongside the channel (as above), or other matters. Check each chart that you buy for such notes and read them carefully.

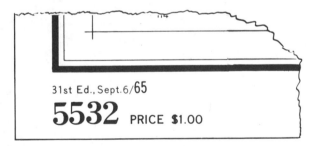

31st Ed., Sept. 6/65

**5532** PRICE $1.00

**FIG. 1816 a** The edition number and date are printed in the margin of each C&GS chart in the lower-left corner. Also shown here are the chart number and price.

**FIG. 1816 b** Between editions, revised printings are made of charts to include all changes that have been published in Notices to Mariners. Be safe—do not use obsolete charts!

35'

8th Ed., Aug. 10/64 ; Revised 7/19/65

On C&GS charts having a scale larger than 1:49,000, such as on harbor charts, the subdivisions in the border scales are in terms of minutes and seconds of latitude and longitude, fig. 1818a.

On smaller-scale charts, the subdivisions are in minutes and fractions of minutes—charts at a scale of 1:80,000, such as 1210Tr, use minutes and tenths of minutes, fig. 1818b. Still smaller scale charts will use fifths or halves of minutes.

Where skewed projections are used, and north is not toward the top of the sheet, as on Intracoastal Waterway charts, the subdivisions of latitude and longitude are indicated along parallels and meridians at several convenient places.

## USE OF COLOR

Nearly all charts use color, pages M and N, to emphasize various features, and thus facilitate chart reading and interpretation. The number of different colors will vary with the agency publishing the chart and with its intended use. The Coast & Geodetic Survey makes use of five colors (and several shades of some of these) on their regular charts.

Land areas are shown in buff or yellowish color; water areas are white, the color of the paper, except for the shallower regions which are in blue. Areas that may be submerged at some tidal stages, but which uncover at others, are represented in green. Sand bars, mud flats,

coral reefs, and marshes are typical of such green areas on charts. On some charts, water areas that have been swept with wire drags to ensure the absence of isolated rocks or coral heads may be shown in a greenish half-tone with the depth of the sweep indicated. This shade of green is lighter than the solid color used for uncovering areas and no confusion should result.

Magenta, a purplish-red color, is used for many purposes; it was selected for its visibility under red light which is used on many vessels for reading charts during darkness because it does not destroy night vision as white light would. Red buoys are printed in this color, as are red day-beacon symbols. Lighted buoys of any color have a magenta disc superimposed over the dot portion of the symbol to enhance its identification as a lighted aid to navigation. This same scheme is used with lighthouses, lights, lighted ranges, etc. Caution and danger symbols and notes are printed in magenta; also compass roses and recommended courses where shown. Black, of course, is used for most symbols and the bulk of printed information.

## LETTERING STYLES

In order to convey to the chart reader as much information as possible in the clearest form, a system has been adopted whereby certain classes of information are printed in one style of lettering and other classes in another style.

**FIG. 1817 U.S. Coast and Geodetic Survey and Navy Department Oceanographic charts, as well as Light Lists and Coast Pilots, are corrected by Notices to Mariners. Illustrated is a typical extract showing a new marina and hydrography changes in Northport Harbor, Long Island, N.Y. Not all corrections require a reproduction from the chart affected (in this case No. 224). The amended section of chart shown is provided in the Notice as a loose insertion. The notes indicate which chart and Coast Pilot are affected.**

★ (2295) **LONG ISLAND SOUND—Northport Bay—Northport Harbor—Chart amendment.**—The accompanying reproduction of a portion of C. & G.S. Chart 224 shows a recently constructed marina and changes in hydrography in Northport Harbor. Approx. position: 40°54′ N., 73°21′ W. (N.M. 17/65.)

Correction to C. & G. S. Chart 224

73°21′          NM 17 – Apr. 24, 1965

FIG. 1818 a   On charts with scales of 1:49,000 or larger, the longitude and latitude scales in the borders are subdivided into minutes and seconds. On this extract from a 1:40,000 harbor chart, meridians are drawn at 5-minute intervals, tick marks are placed every minute, and one 1-minute interval is subdivided into units of 5 seconds each.

**FIG. 1818(b)**   On charts with relatively small scales, the latitude and longitude border markings will be in minutes and fractions of minutes. On this 1:80,000 chart, meridians are drawn in every 10 minutes and the subdivisions are in minutes and tenths of minutes. On yet smaller scale charts, the smallest subdivision might be fifths, halves, or whole minutes of latitude and longitude.

FIG. 1819   This chart excerpt illustrates the use of vertical lettering for features above water—"TOWERS," and leaning letters for underwater features—"hrd S", a hard sand bottom of the river at that point. Note also the designation of a CABLE AREA.

By knowing what type of lettering is used for which class of information, one can more easily and quickly grasp the data being presented.

VERTICAL lettering is used for features which are dry at high water and are not affected by movement of the water, except for the height of the feature above the water, which may be changed by tidal action. See the use of vertical lettering for the power line towers and the bell fog signal in fig. 1819.

LEANING, or slanting, lettering *(such as this)* is used for water, underwater, and floating features, except depth figures. Note the use in fig. 1819 of leaning lettering for *"hrd S"* meaning a hard sand bottom at that point.

On smaller-scale charts, a small reef (covering and uncovering with tidal action) often cannot be distinguished by symbol from a small islet (always above water); the proper name for either might be "— Rock." Following the standard of lettering, the feature in doubt is an islet if the name is in vertical letters, but is a reef if lettered in leaning characters.

Similarly, a piling visible above water at all tidal stages will be charted as "Pile," but one beneath the surface will be noted as *"subm pile."*

Periods after abbreviations are omitted in water and in land areas, but the lower-case *i* and *j* are dotted. Periods are used only where needed for clarity, as, for example, in certain notes.

## WATER FEATURES

The information shown on charts is a combination of the natural features of the water and land areas and various selected man-made objects and features. Each item shown will have been carefully chosen for its value to those navigating vessels of all sizes.

### Depths

The principal feature of concern to boatmen and mariners regarding water areas is the *depth.* For any system of

depth information, there must be a reference plane, or *datum.* This is obvious in coastal areas where depths may change hourly as a result of tidal action; it is likewise true in inland areas where lake or river levels may also change, though more slowly on a seasonal basis. Each chart will have printed on it a statement of the datum from which all depths, also called *soundings,* are measured. The choice of the reference plane is based on many factors, most of them technical, but the primary consideration is that of selecting a datum near to normal low-water levels.

### Planes of reference

Different planes of reference are used on charts of various boating areas. For charts along the Atlantic seaboard, the Coast & Geodetic Survey uses *mean low water* as the datum for soundings. On the Pacific Coast, it is the *mean lower low water* that is used as a reference plane. (In some areas, one of the two daily low tides is markedly lower than the other—see Chapter 20 for a detailed discussion of tides.) Lake and river charts will generally use a datum which is based on past records of variations in level over many years. When entering strange waters, always be sure to check the chart for the statement of the datum used for depths.

Since by definition, "mean low water" is an average of low tide stages over a period of time, it can be seen that on approximately half the days individual low-water levels may be lower than the datum. This will result in actual depths being shallower than the charted figures. However, these variations are not often great enough to affect navigation. Many charts will have a small box with a tabulation of the extreme variations from charted depths that may be expected for various points, fig. 1820. Prolonged winds from certain directions, or persistent extremes of barometric pressure, may cause temporary local differences from charted depths. *It must always be remembered that exceptional conditions may occur at which time the water may be much shallower than indicated on the chart.*

| TIDAL INFORMATION | | | | |
|---|---|---|---|---|
| Place | Height referred to datum of soundings (MLW) | | | |
| | Mean High Water | Mean Tide Level | Mean Low Water | Extreme Low Water |
| | feet | feet | feet | feet |
| Wilmington, Del. | 5.3 | 2.9 | 0.0 | −4.0 |
| Chester, Pa. | 5.4 | 2.9 | 0.0 | −4.0 |
| Billingsport, N.J. | 5.5 | 3.0 | 0.0 | −4.5 |
| Phila. Pier 9N., Pa. | 5.8 | 3.1 | 0.0 | −5.0 |

**FIG. 1820 Coast and Harbor Charts will usually have information on the normal range of tides and the extreme variations from charted depths that may be expected. Check all newly-purchased charts for this important information.**

**FIG. 1821 The side limits of "improved" (dredged) channels are marked by dashed lines. Information on the depth (and date of measurement) will often be printed between or alongside the dashed lines. In some cases, information on the width of the channel will also be shown.**

## How depths are shown

Depth information is shown on the chart by many small printed figures. These indicate the depth at that point measured in units of feet or fathoms as stated in the basic information block of the chart. A few charts may mix these units of measurement, using feet in the shallower areas and fathoms offshore in deeper water; such charts, however, are relatively rare. The depth figures are only a small part of the many soundings taken by survey teams. Only the more significant and representative depths are selected for printing on the final chart.

The boatman can form some opinion of the characteristics of the bottom by noting the density of the depth information. Where depth figures are rather widely spaced, he can be assured of a reasonably flat or uniformly sloping bottom. Wherever the depths vary irregularly or abruptly, the figures will be more frequent and more closely spaced.

## Fathom curves

Most charts will have *contour lines,* sometimes called *fathom curves,* connecting points of equal depth. Such lines will appear at certain depths as determined by the scale of the chart and the relative range of the depths. Typically, fathom curves are shown for 1, 2, 3 5, 10, and multiples of ten fathoms. Continuous solid lines or various combinations of dots and dashes are used to code the depth along each line, but it is often easier to learn a line's significance by inspection of the depth figures on either side of it.

On many charts, a blue tint is shown in water areas out to the curve that is considered to be the danger curve for that particular chart. In general, the 6-foot curve is considered the danger curve for small-craft and Intracoastal Waterway charts, the 12- or 18-foot curve for harbor charts, and the 30-foot curve for coast and general charts. (These types of charts are discussed in more detail on pages 356-358.) In some instances, the area between the 3-fathom and the 5- or 6-fathom curves may be tinted in a lighter shade of blue than the shallower areas. Thus it can be seen that while blue tint means shallow water, this symbolism does not have the same exact meaning on all charts. Check each chart that you use to determine at just what depth the coloring changes.

Charts on which no fathom curves are marked for water areas must be regarded with some suspicion and used with caution as this may indicate that soundings are too scarce to allow the lines to be drawn with accuracy.

Isolated soundings, shoaler than surrounding depths, should always be avoided, particularly if ringed around, as it is doubtful how closely the spot may have been examined and whether the least depth has been found.

## Dredged channels

Dredged channels are shown on a chart by two dashed lines to represent the side limits of the improvement. The depth of the channel and the date on which such data were obtained will be shown within the lines or close alongside, see fig. 1821. A dredged basin will be similarly outlined with printed information on depths and date.

The depth shown, such as "6 feet 1965," is the controlling depth through the channel on the date shown but does not mean that this depth exists over the full width of the channel.

Channels are sometimes described on charts in terms of specific width as well as depth; for example, "8 feet for width of 100 feet." The printing of such depth information does not insure that it may not have subsequently changed due to either shoaling or further dredging. Such changes do occur, and therefore if your craft's draft is close to the depth shown for the channel, local information on existing conditions should be obtained if possible before entering.

Detailed information for many dredged channels is shown in tabular form on the applicable charts, with revisions of the data published in Notices to Mariners as changes occur.

## Nature of the bottom

The nature of the bottom, such as sand, rocky, mud, grass, etc., or a more general description such as "hard" or "soft," will be indicated for many areas by means of abbreviations. This information is of value when anchoring, and advantage should be taken of it wherever it appears. The meanings of these and other abbreviations are usually given on the face of the chart near the basic identification block; many are self-evident, the more frequently encountered ones should be memorized.

## The shoreline

The shoreline shown on charts is the mean high-water line except in marsh or mangrove areas where the outer edge of vegetation (berm line) is used. It is represented by a solid line which gradually decreases in width up streams and rivers. Unsurveyed shoreline, or shoreline connecting two surveys that do not join satisfactorily, is represented by a dashed line. The outer limits of marsh are indicated by a fine solid line. On some large-scale charts, a low-water line will be indicated by a single row of dots.

The region between the high- and low-water lines will be tinted green, and may be labeled "Grass," "Mud," "Sand," etc.

## FEATURES OF LAND AREAS

Features and characteristics of land areas are shown on nautical charts in only such detail as will be of assistance to a navigator. Details are usually confined to those near the shoreline or of such a prominent nature as to be clearly seen for some distance offshore.

### How topography is shown

The general topography of land areas will be indicated by contours, form lines, or hachures. *Contours* are lines connecting points of equal elevation. The specific height, usually measured in feet, of such contour lines may be shown by figures placed at suitable points along the lines. The interval of height between adjacent contours is uniform over any one chart.

*Form lines,* or *sketch contours,* are shown by broken lines and are approximations of contours intended to give an indication of terrain formations without exact information on height. They are used in areas where accurate data are not available in sufficient quantity to permit the exact location of contours. The interval between form lines is not necessarily uniform and no height figures are given.

*Hachures* are short lines, or groups of lines, indicating approximately the location of steep slopes. The lines follow generally the direction of the slope, the length of the lines indicating the height of the slope.

### Cliffs, vegetation and the shore

Cliffs are represented by bands of irregular hachures. The symbol is not an exact "plan view," but rather somewhat of a "side elevation"; its extent is roughly proportional to the height of the cliff. For example, a perpendicular cliff of 100 feet height will be shown by a hachured band wider than one representing a cliff of 15 feet with

**FIG. 1822 Information on the elevation of hills or mountain summits, or the tops of conspicuous landmarks, is often printed on a nautical chart. Heights are usually measured from Mean High Water.**

**FIG. 1823 a** On relatively large-scale charts, detailed information may be shown of the streets and buildings of a city or town, particularly near the waterfront. Some street names may be given, also the location of public buildings such as a customhouse and post office.

slope. According to the principles of "plan" drawing (viewing from directly above), a perpendicular cliff would be shown by one line only and could not be distinguished from an ordinary shoreline.

Spot elevations are normally given on nautical charts only for summits or the tops of conspicuous landmarks, fig. 1822. Heights are measured from mean high water.

The type of vegetation on land will sometimes be indicated by symbols or wording where such information may be of use to the mariner.

The nature of the shore is indicated by various symbols—rows of fine dots denote a sandy beach, small circles indicate gravel, irregular shapes mean boulders, etc.

## MAN-MADE FEATURES

Man-made features on land will be shown in detail where they relate directly to water-borne traffic. Examples of these are piers, bridges, overhead power cables, and breakwaters. Other man-made features on land, such as built-up areas, roads, streets, etc., will be shown in some detail or will be generalized as determined by their usefulness to navigation and the scale of the chart. On large-scale charts, the actual network of streets will at times be depicted, with public buildings such as the post office and customs house individually identified, fig. 1823a. On less detailed charts, the town or city may be represented by a halftone shaded area for the approximate limits of the built-up area with major streets and roads shown by single heavy lines, see fig. 1823b. Prominent isolated objects, tanks, stacks, spires, etc., will be shown accurately

**FIG. 1823 b** On smaller-scale charts, cities, towns, and other built-up areas are generalized by "screening," a shading process that shows up as a darker, but not black, area. Only principal roads and streets are shown, these by a single, heavy solid line.

located in order that they may be used for taking bearings.

Specific descriptive names have been given to certain types of landmark objects for the purpose of standardizing terminology. Among the more often used are the following:

**Building** or **House**—the appropriate one of these terms is used when the entire structure is the landmark, rather than any individual feature of it.

**Spire**—a slender, pointed structure extending above a building. It is seldom less than two-thirds of the entire height of the structure, and its lines are rarely broken by intermediate structures. Spires are typically found on churches.

**Dome**—a large, rounded, hemispherical structure rising above a building; for example, the dome of the United States Capitol in Washington.

**Cupola**—a dome-shaped tower or turret rising from a building, generally small in comparison with the size of the building.

**Chimney**—a relatively small projection for conveying smoke from a building to the atmosphere. This term is used when the building is more prominent than the chimney, but a better bearing can be taken on the smaller feature.

**Stack**—a tall smokestack or chimney. This term is used when the stack is more prominent as a landmark than the accompanying buildings.

**Flagpole**—a single staff from which flags are displayed. This term is used when the pole is not attached to a building.

**Flagstaff**—a flagpole arising from a building.

**Radio Tower**—a tall pole or structure for elevating radio antennas.

**Radio Mast**—a relatively short pole or slender structure for elevating radio antennas; usually found in groups.

**Tower**—any structure with its base on the ground and high in proportion to its base, or that part of a structure higher than the rest, but having essentially vertical sides for the greater part of its height.

**Lookout Station** or **Watch Tower**—a tower surmounted by a small house from which a watch is regularly kept.

**Tank**—a water tank elevated high above ground by a tall skeleton framework. *Gas Tank* and *Oil Tank* are terms used for distinctive structures of specialized design.

**Standpipe**—a tall cylindrical structure whose height is several times its diameter.

**Tree**—an isolated, conspicuous tree useful as a navigational landmark.

When two similar objects are so located that separate landmark symbols cannot be used, the word "TWIN" is added to the identifying name or abbreviation. When only one of a group of similar objects is charted, a descriptive legend is added in parentheses; for example, ("TALLEST OF FOUR)" or "(NORTHEAST OF THREE)".

Radio broadcasting station (AM) antennas are shown on charts where they may be used for taking visual or radio bearings. The call letters and frequency are often shown adjacent to the symbol marking the location of the towers.

# Symbols and Abbreviations

The vast amount of information to be shown on a chart, and the closeness with which many items appear, necessitate the extensive use of symbols and abbreviations. It is essential that a boatman have a high degree of familiarity with the symbols and abbreviations encountered on the charts that he uses. A skipper must be able to read and interpret his charts quickly and accurately; the safety of his boat may depend on this ability. Knowledge will come with use, but dependence upon a build-up from experience alone may be costly—specific study is recommended.

## INTERNATIONAL STANDARDS

*Symbols* are conventional shapes and designs which indicate the presence of a certain feature or object at the location shown on the chart. No attempt is made at an accurate or detailed representation of the object, but the correct location is shown. Symbols and abbreviations used on charts prepared by the Coast & Geodetic Survey, the Naval Oceanographic Office, and the Army Engineers' Lake Survey have been standardized. These are published in a small pamphlet designated as Chart No. 1, available at 50¢ per copy. The same information is also printed on the reverse side of Training Chart No. 1210Tr. These standardized symbols and abbreviations are in general conformance with world-wide usage as adopted by the International Hydrographic Bureau.

The standardized symbols and abbreviations are shown in figures 1844 a-o; they are grouped into *classifications* and are *numbered* in accordance with Chart No. 1. In these designations, vertical figures indicate that the symbol or abbreviation is in conformity with the standards of the International Hydrographic Bureau. Slanting figures mean that the symbol or abbreviation shown either differs from that of the IHB or else that it does not appear in its standards; those items which differ from the IHB standard are underlined. Where letter designations are enclosed in parentheses, the symbol or abbreviation is in addition to those on the international list.

These standardized abbreviations will be used on all new charts or new editions by the Coast & Geodetic Survey, the Oceanographic Office, and the Lake Survey. Older charts may continue to show other symbols and abbreviations until they are next revised and brought into conformity with the standards.

## Classification

In Chart No. 1, the standardized symbols and abbreviations are grouped into classifications as follows:

| | |
|---|---|
| A—The Coast Line | K—Lights |
| B—Coast Features | L—Buoys and Beacons |
| C—The Land | M—Radio Stations |
| D—Control Points | N—Fog Signals |
| E—Units | O—Dangers |
| F—Adjectives | P—Various Limits |
| G—Harbors | Q—Soundings |
| H—Topography | R—Depth Contours |
| I—Buildings | S—Quality of the Bottom |
| J—Miscellaneous | T—Tides and Currents |
| Stations | U—The Compass |

Chart No. 1 also includes a table for the conversion of meters, fathoms, and feet.

### BASIC SYMBOLS & ABBREVIATIONS

Simple inspection of many symbols will reveal a pattern or system to the way that they are formed. Knowledge of the general principles of chart symbols will facilitate learning of the details.

### Buoys

Buoys, except mooring buoys, are shown by a diamond-shaped symbol and a small dot; the dot indicates the position of the buoy. To avoid interference with other features on the chart, it is often necessary to show the diamond shape at various angles to the dot; in some instances, the symbol might even appear "upside down." The symbol for a mooring buoy is number L22 in fig. 1844i; the small circle on the base line of the symbol indicates the position of the buoy.

A *black buoy* is shown as a solid black symbol without further identification of color. On charts using the normal number of colors, *red buoys* are shown in magenta; the

FIG. 1824 Ranges are excellent aids to navigation. They are charted by showing the front and rear markers with a line denoting the center of the range. This line is solid over the portion that is to be navigated, and dashed elsewhere.

FIG. 1825 This is a section from a "sailing chart." These charts, at scales of 1:600,000 or less, are the smallest scale series and cover long stretches of coastline. They are used by vessels approaching the coast from the high seas or when voyaging between distant coast ports.

A portion (slightly less than half) of the U. S. Army Engineers' chart for Sandusky Bay (eastern end), south shore of Lake Erie, from the U. S. Lake Survey Recreational Craft Series chart No. 360—Port Clinton to Sandusky, Ohio. The spiral-bound volume includes 35 charts—lake, rivers, harbors, and islands—and much data of value to the boatman. As reproduced above, the scale differs slightly from that (1:40,000) on which the original chart is drawn. Only charts as published by official sources should be used for navigation.

Inset 9 reproduced full-size from the U. S. Coast & Geodetic Survey's Small-Craft series chart number 117 (A, B, C, D, E)—New Haven Harbor Entrance and Port Jefferson to Throgs Neck—Long Island Sound, Connecticut, New York. Scale of this inset is 1:20,000, in which one mile (see distance on latitude scale from 40°53' to 40°54') measures about 3⅛ inches. The Small-Craft series of charts is produced in a format of maximum convenience to the operator of small boats. For more detailed information, see page 357.

# INTERNATIONAL FLAGS AND PENNANTS

| ALPHABET FLAGS | | | NUMERAL PENNANTS |
|---|---|---|---|
| **A**lfa — Diver Down; Keep Clear | **K**ilo — Desire to Communicate | **U**niform — Standing into Danger | 1 |
| **B**ravo — Dangerous Cargo | **L**ima — Stop Instantly | **V**ictor — Require Assistance | 2 |
| **C**harlie — Yes | **M**ike — I Am Stopped | **W**his-key — Require Medical Assistance | 3 |
| **D**elta — Keep Clear | **N**ovem-ber — No | **X**ray — Stop Your Intention | 4 |
| **E**cho — Altering Course to Starboard | **O**scar — Man Overboard | **Y**ankee — Am Dragging Anchor | 5 |
| **F**oxtrot — Disabled | **P**apa — About to Sail | **Z**ulu — Shore Stations | 6 |
| **G**olf — Want a Pilot | **Q**uebec — Request Pratique | **REPEATERS** — 1st Repeat | 7 |
| **H**otel — Pilot on Board | **R**omeo — Require a Tug | 2nd Repeat | 8 |
| **I**ndia — Altering Course to Port | **S**ierra — Engines Going Astern | 3rd Repeat | 9 |
| **J**uliett — On Fire; Keep Clear | **T**ango — Keep Clear of Me | CODE — Code and Answering Pennant (Decimal Point) | 0 |

*NOTE: From revised International Code of Signals effective 1 April 1969.*

O

# How International Code Flags are Used in Signaling

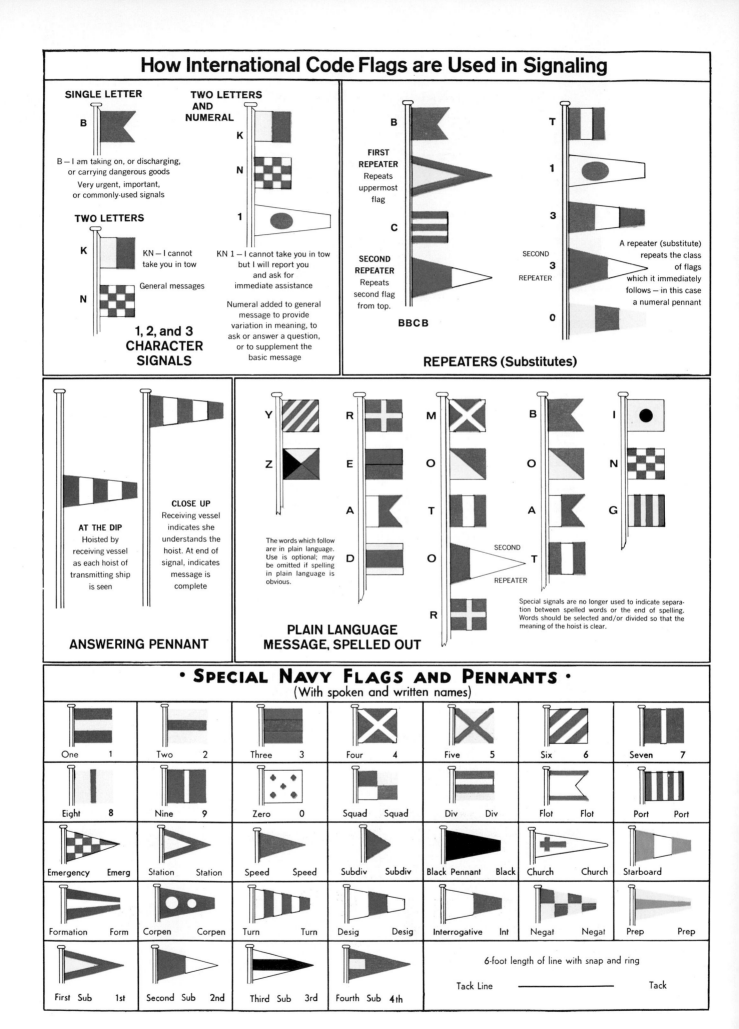

### SINGLE LETTER

B

B – I am taking on, or discharging, or carrying dangerous goods

Very urgent, important, or commonly-used signals

### TWO LETTERS

K

N

KN – I cannot take you in tow

General messages

### TWO LETTERS AND NUMERAL

K

N

1

KN 1 – I cannot take you in tow but I will report you and ask for immediate assistance

Numeral added to general message to provide variation in meaning, to ask or answer a question, or to supplement the basic message

### 1, 2, and 3 CHARACTER SIGNALS

B

FIRST REPEATER
Repeats uppermost flag

C

SECOND REPEATER
Repeats second flag from top.

BBCB

T

1

3

SECOND REPEATER

3

0

A repeater (substitute) repeats the class of flags which it immediately follows — in this case a numeral pennant

### REPEATERS (Substitutes)

AT THE DIP
Hoisted by receiving vessel as each hoist of transmitting ship is seen

CLOSE UP
Receiving vessel indicates she understands the hoist. At end of signal, indicates message is complete

### ANSWERING PENNANT

Y
Z

R
E
A
D
R

M
O
T
O

SECOND REPEATER

B
O
A
T

I
N
G

The words which follow are in plain language. Use is optional; may be omitted if spelling in plain language is obvious.

Special signals are no longer used to indicate separation between spelled words or the end of spelling. Words should be selected and/or divided so that the meaning of the hoist is clear.

### PLAIN LANGUAGE MESSAGE, SPELLED OUT

## • SPECIAL NAVY FLAGS AND PENNANTS •
### (With spoken and written names)

| One 1 | Two 2 | Three 3 | Four 4 | Five 5 | Six 6 | Seven 7 |
|---|---|---|---|---|---|---|
| Eight 8 | Nine 9 | Zero 0 | Squad Squad | Div Div | Flot Flot | Port Port |
| Emergency Emerg | Station Station | Speed Speed | Subdiv Subdiv | Black Pennant Black | Church Church | Starboard |
| Formation Form | Corpen Corpen | Turn Turn | Desig Desig | Interrogative Int | Negat Negat | Prep Prep |
| First Sub 1st | Second Sub 2nd | Third Sub 3rd | Fourth Sub 4th | | | |

6-foot length of line with snap and ring

Tack Line ———————————— Tack

letter "R" may also be shown adjacent to the symbol. Other buoys are shown by open outline symbols with the color indicated by an appropriate abbreviation, such as "Y" for yellow, "W Or" for white and orange, etc. On charts without colors, red buoys are printed as open symbols with the identifying abbreviation "R."

A buoy symbol with a line across its shorter axis indicates a *horizontally banded buoy.* For a junction buoy, if colors are used, the upper half (away from the dot) will be red and the lower half black. This is true whether in actuality the uppermost band is red (as on a nun buoy) or black (as on a can buoy). The letters "RB" will appear near the symbol. Other kinds of horizontally banded buoys, such as white-and-orange *special purpose buoys,* will be shown by an open symbol with appropriate letters for the colors.

A buoy symbol with a line across its longer axis represents a *vertically striped buoy.* No colors will be used on this symbol; the colors of such a buoy will be indicated by abbreviations, usually "BW" for black and white.

The type and shape of *unlighted buoys* is often indicated by an abbreviation such as "C" for can, "N" for nun, or "S" for spar.

*Lighted buoys* are indicated by the placing of a small magenta disc over the dot which marks the buoy's position. The color and characteristics of the light are indicated by abbreviations near the symbol. Buoys equipped with a *reflector* to increase their detection by radar are often indicated by the abbreviation "Ra Ref" in addition to other identification.

## Daybeacons

The symbol for *daybeacons,* unlighted aids to navigation, is a small triangle. In general, the same scheme for indicating color is used as for buoys except that two colors are not combined in a single symbol. The occasional red-and-black horizontally banded daybeacon is printed as an open symbol with the description of colors abbreviated, "RB."

## Lighthouses

*Lighthouses and lights* are shown as black dots each with a small magenta disc as for lighted buoys. In addition to the color and characteristics of the light, there may be shown, in abbreviated form, information on the height of the light and its range of visibility (for a height of observer's eye of 15 feet above the water).

The type of *fog signal* on buoys, lights, and lighthouses so equipped will be indicated by a descriptive word or abbreviation adjacent to the chart symbol.

## Identification by number

Buoys and lights are usually *numbered* (or less-frequently, designated with letters or combinations of letters and numbers). This identification is placed on the chart near the symbol and is enclosed in quotation marks to distinguish the figures from depth data or other numbers. Lighthouses and some major lights are named; the words

FIG. 1826 A small portion of C&GS Chart 1108. This is at a larger scale than Fig. 1825, but it still lacks many details. "General charts" should be used only for offshore navigation. Only major aids to navigation are shown. For comparison purposes, Figs. 1827 and 1828 show portions of this same area at progressively larger scales.

**FIG. 1827  A portion of C&GS Chart 1215.** "Coast charts," uusally at a scale of 1:80,000, are used for close-in coastwise navigation, entering and leaving harbors, and for cruising on some large inland bodies of water. The scale of this series is such that many more buoys and other aids to navigation can be shown. The depth of water is given in greater detail, the soundings being given in feet.

or abbreviations will be printed near the symbol where space permits.

### Ranges

*Ranges* are indicated by the two symbols of the front and rear markers (lights or daybeacons), plus a line joining them and extending beyond. This line is solid over the distance for which the range is to be used for navigation; it continues on as a dashed line to the front marker and on to the rear marker, see fig. 1824.

### Radiobeacons

*Radiobeacons* are indicated by a magenta circle around the basic symbol for the aid to navigation at which the beacon is located plus the abbreviation "R Bn." Aeronautical radiobeacons are shown only if they are useful for marine navigation; the same symbol is used and the iden-

tification "AERO" is added. The frequency, in KiloHertz, is given, as is the identifying signal in dots and dashes of the Morse code. Aeronautical radio ranges use the same symbol as beacons plus "AERO R Rge."

### Dangers to navigation

Symbols are also used for many types of *dangers to navigation*. Differentiation is made between rocks that are awash at times and those which remain below the surface at all tides, between visible wrecks and submerged ones, and between hazards which have been definitely located and those whose position is doubtful. There are a number of symbols and abbreviations for objects and areas dangerous to navigation. The prudent skipper will spend adequate time studying them, with the greatest emphasis being placed on those types commonly found in his home waters.

## Chart "Series"

### FOUR C & G S SERIES

As previously mentioned, charts are published in a wide range of scales. For general convenience of reference, the issuing agencies have classified charts into "series" as follows:

**1. Sailing Charts**—the smallest scale charts covering long stretches of coastline; for example, Cape Sable, Newfoundland to Cape Hatteras, N. C.; or the Gulf of Mexico; or San Francisco to Cape Flattery, Washington; see fig.

1825. The charts of this series are published at scales of 1:600,000 and smaller. Sailing charts are prepared for the use of the navigator in fixing his position as he approaches the coast from the open ocean, or when sailing between distant coast ports. They show the offshore soundings, the principal lights and outer buoys, and landmarks visible at great distances. Other than for ocean cruising races, the average boatman will have little use for charts in this series, except perhaps to plot the path of hurricanes and other tropical disturbances.

FIG. 1828 Portion of C&GS Chart 369. This extract shows some of the same area as the preceding three figures but at a greater scale and with more detail. "Harbor charts" at a scale of 1:40,000 or larger include all hazards and aids to navigation, some of which may have been omitted from smaller-scale charts. More details of features on land are also shown.

**2. General Charts** — the second series comprises charts with scales in the range of 1:100,000 to 1:600,000. These cover more limited areas, such as Cape May, N. J. to Cape Hatteras; or Mississippi River to Galveston Bay; or San Francisco to Point Arena, Calif. General charts are intended for coastwise navigation outside of offshore reefs and shoals when the vessel's course is mostly within sight of land and her position can be fixed by landmarks, lights, buoys, and soundings. Fig. 1826 is a portion of a general chart.

**3. Coast Charts**—this next larger scale series consists of charts for close-in coastwise navigation, for entering and leaving harbors, and for navigating large inland bodies of water. The scales used range from 1:50,000 to 1:100,000 with most at 1:80,000. See fig. 1827. Typical examples of coast charts are the widely-used training chart No. 1210Tr, and such navigational charts as the series of five which cover Chesapeake Bay or No. 5142 which takes the California boatman from Long Beach or Newport to Santa Catalina Island and back. The average boatman will use several charts from this series.

**4. Harbor Charts** — this is the largest-scale and most-detailed series, see fig. 1828. Scales will range from 1:40,000 to 1:5,000, with an occasional insert of even larger scale. The scale used for any specific chart is determined by the need for showing detail and by the desired area to be covered by a single sheet. Skippers of small craft will find this the most generally useful type of chart.

## Stowage and use

C&GS charts in the four series above are printed by accurate techniques on highly durable paper. Individual charts will range in size from approximately 19x26 to 36x54 inches. As they are among the most important tools of the navigator, they should be given careful handling and proper stowage. If circumstances permit, they should be stowed flat or rolled, and in a dry place. Charts should never be folded if this can be avoided.

*It is advisable that permanent corrections be made in ink* so that they will not be inadvertently erased; all other lines and notations should be made lightly in pencil so that they may be erased when no longer applicable without removing permanent information or otherwise damaging the chart.

## Lake Chart series

Charts of the Great Lakes published by the Lake Survey office of the Army Corps of Engineers are likewise grouped into series.

The *"general chart"* series includes one of all of the Great Lakes at a scale of 1:1,120,000, Chart No. 0. There are also separate charts for each lake at 1:500,000 or 1:400,000 scales; these are numbered 2, 3, 5, 7, and 9 from east to west.

*Coast charts* at a scale of 1:80,000 or 1:120,000 are designated with two-digit numbers, the first of which is the number of the general chart for that lake.

*Harbor charts* at scales of 1:60,000 to 1:5,000 comprise the most detailed series; these have three-digit numbers, the first two of which indicate the related coast chart. For example: Chart No. 2 covers all of Lake Ontario; Chart No. 23 is a coast chart from east of Sodus Bay, N. Y. to Rochester Harbor, N. Y.; and Chart No. 238 is the harbor chart of Rochester Harbor itself, see fig. 1829. (Note: an exception to this system occurs in upper Lake Michigan where the number series 701-706 is used for coast charts.)

**FIG. 1829** This page from the Lake Survey Chart Catalog illustrates the numbering system used in the Great Lakes and adjacent waters. Chart 2 covers all of Lake Ontario, Chart 23 a portion of the coast thereof, and Chart 238 a harbor within that portion. The charts are of a progressively larger scale, showing an increasing amount of detail.

## SELECTING THE PROPER CHART

From a consideration of the four categories of charts discussed above, it will be noted that most boating areas will appear on two charts of different series, and that some will be covered by three or four charts of different scales. Such charts will vary widely in the extent of the area covered and the amount of detail shown. The selection of the proper chart to use is important.

The chart catalogs (fig. 1830 is an example of one published by the Coast & Geodetic Survey) indicate graphically the area covered by each chart. Also included is a listing giving the name, scale, and price of each chart. These catalogs provide a starting point for the selection of the proper charts for your cruise. In general, the closer you will be to shoal water and dangers to navigation, the larger you will want the scale of the chart that you are using.

### What coast charts show

Coast charts show only the *major* hazards and aids to navigation, and give generalized information on depths. Some charts in this series will omit entirely any details on portions thereof which are covered by larger scale charts. For example, Narragansett Bay appears on Chart 1210, but no details at all are given, merely a small note "(Chart 353)." Other 1200 series coast charts include in their area coverage portions of the Atlantic Intracoastal Waterway, but the navigator is referred to the 800-SC ICW charts for all information on the inland route. Many coast charts

include a small diagram outlining the areas covered by each larger scale chart—on No. 1210, this amounts to all or portions of 13 more-detailed charts.

### What harbor charts show

Harbor charts will show more numerous soundings and *all* aids to navigation, and will permit the most accurate fixing of position from plotted bearings. The question may arise as to why ever select any but the largest-scale chart. The answer lies in the fact that as the scale is increased, the area that can be covered on a given size sheet of paper is proportionately reduced. Thus, for a cruise, many more charts of the harbor series would be required than from the coast series. Further, in some areas, continuous coverage from port to port is not possible from harbor charts alone. Another problem is that the increased number of larger-scale charts complicates the task of laying out a long run between ports.

The selection of the proper charts will usually result in a mixture of coast charts for the longer runs and harbor charts for entering ports and exploring up rivers and creeks. For some areas, one or more general charts, in addition to the coast and harbor charts, may be found useful. For example, the best route down Chesapeake Bay is more easily plotted on Charts 77 and 78 than on the series of coast charts 1226 to 1222. When you have a variety of charts on board, duplication of area coverage may result but the right chart is available for the various specific requirements.

In the margin of many charts, you will find helpful information regarding the next chart to use when you are going in a particular direction. This note will take the form of a statement such as "(Joins Chart 264)" or "(Continued on Chart 251)."

## "SMALL-CRAFT" CHARTS

The charts in the four series just discussed are referred to as "conventional" charts and are intended for flat or rolled stowage. There is another category, a fifth series, which is of special interest to boatmen — these are the *Small-craft Charts* of the Coast & Geodetic Survey, designed for more convenient use in the limited space available on boats, and for folded stowage, fig. 1831. (See also color plate, page K.) The letters "SC" following the chart number identify charts published in this series.

The first chart in this series was 101-SC of the Potomac River. It was introduced in 1957 and immediately was popular beyond all expectations. Requests were soon received from hundreds of boatmen throughout the United States for similar coverage of their waters. The years since 1959 have seen a steadily increasing number of "SC" charts published, as well as revised editions for those already out. As of January 1970, there were 64 Small-craft editions published, with more in the planning stage.

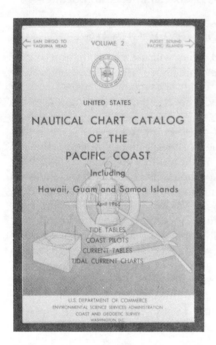

FIG. 1830 Chart Catalogs published by the various issuing agencies show the area coverage of each chart and greatly aid the skipper in the selection of the proper charts to be used in cruising unfamiliar waters. The title, scale, and prices are listed in tabular form. Shown here is one of the three volumes issued by the Coast & Geodetic Survey; all are available free upon request.

### SC chart number groups

Small-craft Charts are listed in the C&GS Nautical Chart Catalog as they become available, and are placed in one of the following number groups:

**1. 100-SC to 199-SC:** Small-craft folios, consisting of three or four sheets printed front and back, accordion-folded, and bound in a suitable cover. (Size folded in cover 9" x 14³/₄".)

**2. 600-SC to 699-SC:** Small-craft route charts (rivers and narrow waterways).

**800-SC to 899-SC:** Small-craft route charts (Intracoastal Waterway).

Route charts consist of an accordion-folded single sheet printed front and back, and isued in a suitable jacket. (Size

FIG. 1831 "Small-craft" Charts are a special series designed for the boatman. They are easier to use and stow, and contain added information of particular interest to the operators of power and sail boats. Included are data on boating facilities, tides and currents, weather broadcasts, etc.

folded in jacket 7³/₄" x 15¹/₂".)

**3. 70-SC to 9500-SC** (except for the number groups above): Small-craft area charts, generally conventional charts printed on a lighter-weight paper with additional information for small craft operators. They are folded once on a horizontal axis and then accordion-folded; they are issued in a protective jacket. (Size folded in jacket 7³/₄" x variable.)

### Facilities data

A unique feature of these most-modern charts is the variety of data printed on the chart and its protective jacket, fig. 1832. No longer is it necessary to use other sources to locate repair yards and marinas; their locations are clearly marked on the chart, and the available services and supplies are tabulated on the jacket. A tide table for the year, current and marine weather information, rules of the road, signals, and warning notes are included for ready reference.

Small-craft charts make frequent use of "insets" to show such features as small creeks and harbors in greater detail. Fig. 1833 shows an inset from Chart 101-SC of the Potomac River.

### Courses indicated

Many of the folio and route types of Small-craft charts will indicate a recommended track to be followed. The longer stretches of these tracks will be marked as to true course (some older charts showed magnetic courses; check each chart used) and the distance in miles and tenths. Route charts of the Atlantic Intracoastal Waterway also have tick marks every five miles indicating the accumulated distance southward from Norfolk, Virginia to Florida, fig. 1834. Facilities along the Atlantic ICW are designated in accordance with a numbering system that starts at Norfolk, Virginia and progresses southward.

### Revised annually

Small-craft charts are revised and reissued annually, usually to coincide with the start of the boating season in each locality. SC charts are *not* hand-corrected by the C&GS after they are printed and placed in stock. The skipper should keep his chart up-to-date between yearly editions by applying all critical changes as published in the local and weekly editions of Notices to Mariners—this is not a great chore, *if* you keep up with the changes and don't get behind!

## OCEANOGRAPHIC OFFICE (HO) CHARTS

Charts of the Naval Oceanographic Office will be used by boatmen making long ocean voyages or visiting foreign waters (except Canada). In general, the presentation of information will not differ much from the more familiar C&GS charts, and few difficulties will be encountered. Symbols and abbreviations will be familiar to the coastal boatman, but land areas will be found to be tinted gray rather than buff. A standardized border has been adopted, and on charts with scales of 1:50,000 and larger, graphic scales of distances in yards and kilometers will be found in the right side and top borders respectively.

The Oceanographic Office issues special charts for the major ocean sailing races. These are regular editions of the applicable charts overprinted with additional information for the yachtsman, including the direct rhumb line, typical sailing tracks for seasonal winds, additional current data, and other useful items. The publication of these special charts is well-publicized in Notices to Mariners and boating periodicals.

It must be remembered that many HO charts are based on foreign surveys, fig. 1835. The authority for the charted information will always be given as will the date of the surveys. Check for this information, and apply appropriate judgment and caution when using charts of foreign waters; their accuracy and completeness will almost invariably be poor in comparison with C&GS charts of U.S. waters.

## LAKE SURVEY CHARTS

As mentioned before, the polyconic method of projection is used for Army Engineer charts, and certain other small differences between these and C&GS charts will be noted. LS charts may use as many as four different shades of blue in denoting various depths of water nearest the shore — the deeper the shade, the shallower the water. Often courses and distances (in statute miles) will be shown for runs between important points.

FIG. 1832 Small-craft Charts are printed on lighter weight paper than those in the conventional series. These "SC" charts are then folded and placed in protective jackets. Some are bound-in (114-SC on the left) and others are merely slipped into their jackets (831-SC on the right).

The Lake Survey also issues special editions of charts for the small-craft operator. These are called "Recreational Craft Charts" and are issued in a bound volume of large-scale individual charts of special interest to boatmen.

## INLAND RIVER CHARTS

Boatmen on inland rivers will use charts that are different in many respects from those used in coastal waters. Often these will be called "navigational maps" and be issued in book form with several pages covering successive stretches of a river.

Probably the most obvious difference is the usual lack of depth figures. In lieu of these, there will generally be a broken line designating the route to be followed. In order to make the best use of the paper sheet, each page may be oriented differently; north will seldom be toward the top, its actual direction being shown by an arrow. Some symbols may vary slightly in appearance from those on "salt water" charts, and additional ones may be used as required by local conditions. Distances are often designated in terms of statute miles upriver from a specified origin point.

More detailed information on river charts will be found in Chapter 28, particularly on pages 550, 556, and 562 to 569. A complete listing of where river charts and related publications can be obtained is presented on page 571.

FIG. 1833 Insets are used liberally on Small-craft Charts to show local cruising areas in greater detail. This inset, No. 1 from Chart 101-SC, for the Little Wicomico River, is typical. Depths under six feet are tinted blue. Channel markers (black triangles in this reproduction) are in red and black on the original.

the thousands, and there are, in addition, the many Army Engineer charts.

It can easily be seen that the task of keeping so many charts up-to-date is literally staggering. Surveys are constantly being made in new areas and must be rechecked in old areas. An extensive program of cooperative reporting by boatmen is used by the Coast & Geodetic Survey and the Lake Survey to supplement the information-gathering capability of the Government.

Every effort is made by the charting agencies to keep their products accurate and up-to-date with changing editions. Major disturbances of nature such as hurricanes along the Atlantic coast and earthquakes in the Pacific Northwest cause sudden and extensive changes in hydrography, and destroy aids to navigation. The everyday forces of wind and wave cause slower and less obvious changes in channels and shoals.

All boatmen must be alert to the possibility of changes in conditions and inaccuracies in charted information. Most charts will cite the authorities for the information presented and frequently the date of the information will be given. Use additional caution when the surveys date back many years.

**FIG. 1834 Charts of the Atlantic Intracoastal Waterway show a fine magenta line indicating the route to be followed. Tick marks are placed at five-mile intervals along this course line and are labeled with the accumulated mileage southward from Norfolk, Virginia. Since 1969, distances have been measured in statute miles. Passages over larger bodies of water may show information on true course and distance. The "2–2" line on the chart extract above is a matching indicator to facilitate shifting from one page to another.**

## CAUTIONS REGARDING USE

The production of charts is a major undertaking for the vast coastline and contiguous waterways of the United States. Our Atlantic coastline exceeds 24,500 nautical miles, the Gulf Coast 15,000 miles, the Pacific Coast 7,000 miles, and the Alaskan and Hawaiian shorelines total more than 30,000 nautical miles. The Coast & Geodetic Survey publishes more than 800 charts covering over two million square miles, and both of these figures continue to increase each year. In meeting its global responsibilities, the Naval Oceanographic Office puts out charts numbered in

WEST INDIES
BAHAMA ISLANDS
GRAND BAHAMA ISLAND

# FREEPORT HARBOR
## AND APPROACHES

From a British survey in 1959
with corrections to 1964

**FIG. 1835 Many charts issued by the Naval Oceanographic Office (HO Charts) are based on foreign surveys. This fact will be noted in the title block. Such charts should be used with caution, particularly if the surveys date back many years, as is often the case.**

# Chart Projections

The small craft skipper can safely navigate his boat without extensive knowledge of the various types of projection used in the preparation of charts. It is adequate to know that the projection of a spherical surface onto a plane surface inevitably results in some distortions; for small areas, these can be safely neglected.

As in almost any field, however, greater knowledge of the "how" and "why" will assist in understanding and using nautical charts. Hence the following paragraphs will provide additional detailed information on chart projections for those who would extend their knowledge in that direction.

The Mercator projection used in ocean and coastal waters and the polyconic projection used in inland lakes and rivers have been mentioned earlier in this chapter. These, plus the gnomonic projection used in polar regions, will now be presented in more detail. There are many other systems of projection, but each has limited application and need not be considered here.

## MERCATOR PROJECTION

The Mercator projection is often illustrated as a projection onto a cylinder. Actually, the chart is developed mathematically to allow for the known shape of the earth, which is not quite a true sphere. The meridians appear as straight, vertical lines, fig. 1836a. Here we have our first example of distortion, and it is quite obvious—the meridians no longer converge, but are now shown as being

FIG. 1836 a    A Mercator projection starts with the placement of a cylinder around the earth parallel to the polar axis and touching the earth at the Equator. The meridians are projected out onto the cylinder and appear as a series of parallel straight lines when the cylinder is unrolled into a flat plane.

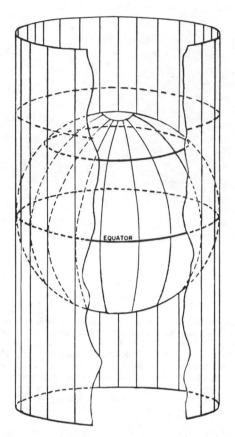

FIG. 1836 b    Parallels of latitude are projected onto the enveloping cylinder. They appear as parallel straight lines intersecting the meridians at right angles. The actual spacing of the meridians and parallels is adjusted to account for the true shape of the earth which is not an exact sphere. See text.

parallel to each other. This changes the representation of the shape of objects by stretching out their dimensions in an East-West direction.

To minimize the distortion of shape, one of the qualities that must be preserved as much as possible, there must be a stretching-out of dimensions in a North-South direction. The parallels of latitude appear as straight lines intersecting the meridians at right angles. Their spacing increases northward from the Equator, fig. 1836b, in accordance with a mathematical formula that recognizes the slightly oblate shape of the earth. This increase in spacing is not obvious in the case of charts of relatively small areas, such as in the harbor and coastal series, but it is quite apparent in Mercator projections of the world, fig. 1837, or of a large area such as covered by a sailing chart.

The Mercator projection is said to be "conformal," which means that angles are correctly represented and the scale is the same in all directions from any point.

By the Mercator technique of distortion, then counter-distortion, the shape of areas in high latitudes is correctly shown, but their size appears greater than that of similar areas in lower latitudes. An island, for example, in 60° latitude (Alaska) would appear considerably larger than an island of the same size located 25° above the equator (Florida). Its shape, however, would still be true to the actual proportions.

## Advantages and disadvantages

The great value of the Mercator chart is that the meridians of longitude appear as straight lines all intersecting the parallels of latitude, also straight lines, at right angles to form an easily-used rectangular grid. Directions can be measured with reference to any meridian or any compass rose. The geographic coordinates of a position can easily be measured from the scales along the four borders of the chart. *We can draw upon a Mercator chart a straight line between two points and actually sail that course* by determining the compass direction between them; the heading is the same all along the line. Such a line is called a *rhumb* line. However, a great circle, the shortest distance between two points on the earth's surface, is a curved line on a Mercator chart; this is more difficult to calculate and plot. For moderate runs, the added distance of a rhumb line is insignificant, and this is the track that is used. Radio waves follow great circle paths and radio bearings on stations more than about 200 miles distant will require correction before being plotted on a Mercator chart.

The scale of a Mercator chart will vary with the distance away from the equator as a result of the N-S expansion. The change is unimportant on charts of small areas such as harbor and coastal charts, and the graphic scale may be used. The change in scale with latitude does become signi-

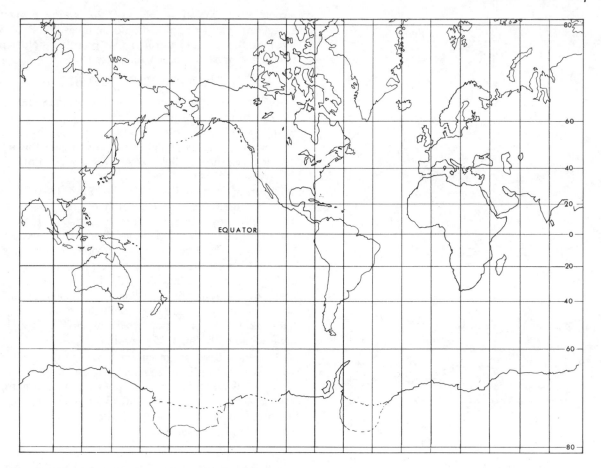

**FIG. 1837** This Mercator projection of the world shows the considerable distortion in near-polar latitudes. Note that the spacing between parallels is not uniform, but increases as the distance from the Equator increases.

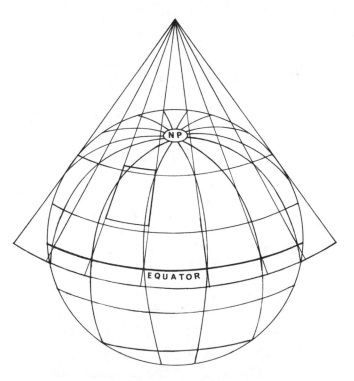

**FIG. 1838** Polyconic projections are developed onto a series of cones tangent to the earth. Separate cones are used for each parallel of latitude. For clarity, the drawing above shows only one of these cones.

ficant, however, in charts covering greater areas, as on general and sailing charts. On such charts, it is necessary to measure distances using the latitude scale on either side margin, remembering that 1′ of latitude is essentially 1 nautical mile. *Take care that distance is measured at a point on the latitude scale directly opposite the region of the chart being used. Never use the longitude scale at the top and bottom of the chart for measuring distance.*

## POLYCONIC PROJECTION

Another form of chart construction is the *polyconic* projection. This method is based on the development of the earth's surface upon a series of cones, a different one being used for each parallel of latitude, fig. 1838. The vertex of the cone is at the point where a tangent to the earth at the specified latitude intersects the earth's axis extended. At the edges of the chart, the area between parallels is expanded to eliminate gaps.

*The polyconic projection yields little distortion in shape, and relative sizes are more correctly preserved than in the Mercator projection.* The scale is correct along any parallel and along the central meridian of the projection. Along other meridians, the scale increases with increased difference in longitude from the central meridian.

Parallels appear as nonconcentric arcs of circles and meridians as curved lines converging toward the pole, concave toward the central meridian, see fig. 1839. These characteristics contrast with the straight-line parallels and meridians of Mercator charts, and are the reasons why this

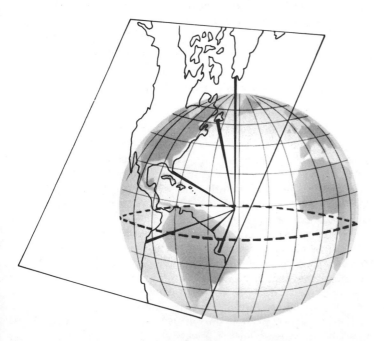

**FIG. 1839** This polyconic projection of a large area emphasizes the curved characteristics of the parallels and meridians on this type of chart. Such curvatures exist on smaller area charts but are not so noticeable.

**FIG. 1840** A Gnomonic projection is made by placing a plane surface tangent to the earth. Points on the earth's surface are then projected onto this plane. The point of tangency may be at any location.

projection is not so widely used in marine navigation. Directions from any point should be measured relative to the meridian passing through that point; in actual practice, the nearest compass rose is used.

## GNOMONIC PROJECTION

A *gnomonic* chart results when the meridians and parallels of latitude are projected onto a plane surface tangent to the earth at one point, fig. 1840. For the oblique case, meridians appear as straight lines converging toward the nearer pole; the parallels, except for the equator, appear as curves, fig. 1841.

Distortion is great, but this projection is used in special cases because of its unique advantage—*great circles appear as straight lines,* which of course is not so with the other two projections discussed above. Probably the easiest way to obtain a great circle track on a Mercator or polyconic chart is to draw it as a straight line on a gnomonic chart and then transfer points along the line to the other chart using the geographic coordinates for each point. The points so transferred are then connected with short rhumb lines and the result will approximate, closely ough, the great circle path, fig. 1842a and b.

A special case of gnomonic chart projection occurs when a geographic pole is selected as the point of tangency. Now all meridians will appear as straight lines, and the parallels as concentric circles. The result is a chart easily used for polar regions where ordinary Mercator charts cannot be used.

**FIG. 1841** A chart made on the Gnomonic projection shows meridians as straight lines converging toward the nearer pole. The parallels, other than the Equator, appear as curves.

**FIG. 1842 a**   A great circle provides the shortest distance between two points on the earth's surface, but is difficult to plot directly on a Mercator chart. An easier procedure is to draw it as a straight line on a Gnomonic chart, noting the latitude of each intersection of the track with a meridian.

**FIG. 1842 b**   Using the geographic coordinates of each point previously marked on the track, it is reconstructed on the Mercator chart by joining the points with short straight (rhumb) lines. This approximation can then be steered without great difficulty.

## THE LAMBERT CONFORMAL PROJECTION

A projection can be made onto a single cone tangent to the earth at a single specified parallel of latitude; this is termed a *simple conic projection*. It is generally a poor projection as the scale is not correct except along the standard parallel. Areas not projected equally and correct angular relationships are not preserved.

The polyconic projection, previously considered, avoids some of these distortions, but only at the cost of the complexity of using a series of cones. Another technique to minimize the distortions of the simple conic projection is to have the cone *intersect* the earth's surface at two parallels. This general type is called a *conic projection with two standard parallels*.

If the spacing of the parallels is altered so that the distortion is the same along them as along the meridians, the projection becomes conformal, that is, the angular relationships are correctly represented, a highly desirable chart quality. This is known as the *Lambert conformal projection*. It is the most widely used conic projection,

although its use is more common among aviators than navigators. Its appearance is very much the same as the simple conic or polyconic projections. If the chart is not carried far beyond the standard parallels, and these are not a great distance apart, the distortion over the entire chart is small.

A straight line on this projection so nearly approximates a great circle that the two can be considered identical for most purposes of navigation. Radio bearings, from signals which are considered to travel great circle paths, can be plotted on a Lambert conformal chart without the correction needed when using a Mercator chart. This feature, gained without sacrificing conformality, has made this projection popular for aeronautical charts, since aircraft make much use of radio aids to navigation. It has made little headway in replacing the Mercator projection for marine navigation, except in high latitudes. In a slightly modified form, the Lambert conformal projection is sometimes used for polar charts.

## PILOT CHARTS

No discussion of nautical charts would be complete without at least brief mention of a unique but valuable chart issued each month by the Naval Oceanographic Office. *Pilot Charts* present in graphic form information on ocean currents and weather probabilities for that month, plus other data of interest to a navigator. Timely articles are printed on the reverse side of each chart. They are issued in three editions—

    **(1) the North Atlantic Ocean,**
    **(2) the Greenland and Barents Seas,**
    **(3) the North Pacific Ocean.**

Fig. 1843 below, is a portion of the front side of a North Atlantic Pilot Chart.

## NAUTICAL CHART MANUAL

Those desiring to know more about the basic essentials of nautical chart construction and details of the current charting practices of the Coast & Geodetic Survey might wish to purchase the "Nautical Chart Manual," 6th Edition. This 213-page manual is available from the Superintendent of Documents, U.S. Government Printing Office, Washington, D.C. 20402. The price is $6.75.

⚓

**FIG. 1843** This is a small portion of the pilot chart of the North Atlantic for the month of May 1966. Dotted lines in blue on the original indicate the percentage of days in which fog can be expected for the month. The full lines represent the accepted tracks for full-powered and low-powered steamers. The wind rose (in blue on the original) in each 5-degree square shows the character of prevailing winds. Arrows fly with the wind. Length of the arrow gives percentage of the total number of observations in which the wind has blown from that point. The number of feathers shows the average force (Beaufort scale). Figures inside the circle give percentage of calms, light airs, and variable winds. Ocean station vessels (lettered red circles) supply meteorological information. The (red) long-short dashed line indicates extreme limit of ice. Outside this limit, triangles show where and when bergs have been sighted. Growlers are shown as small circles. Small (green) arrows indicate currents; velocity given in miles per day.

# STANDARDIZED CHART SYMBOLS AND ABBREVIATIONS

The nautical chart can convey much or little to its user, depending upon the extent of his understanding of all those many small, odd shapes, marks, and lines. A great amount of information must be shown on a chart for safe navigation and, in many areas, there is little room for it. Thus, extensive use is made of *symbols* and *abbreviations*. To make chart reading easier, quicker, and surer, the various U.S. agencies that produce nautical charts have adopted a standardized system of abbreviations and symbols.

It is essential that a boatman have the ability to read and understand his charts rapidly and accurately. Knowledge of symbols and abbreviations is a "must" for this ability.

The standardized symbols and abbreviations are broadly grouped into classifications as follows:

**A—The Coast Line
B—Coast Features
C—The Land
D—Control Points
E—Units
F—Adjectives
G—Harbors
H—Topography
I—Buildings
J—Miscellaneous Stations
K—Lights
L—Buoys and Beacons
M—Radio Stations
N—Fog Signals
O—Dangers
P—Various Limits
Q—Soundings
R—Depth Countours
S—Quality of the Bottom
T—Tides and Currents
U—The Compass**

Most of the symbols used on nautical charts published by the Coast & Geodetic Survey and the Naval Oceanographic Office conform to the standards of the International Hydrographic Bureau (IHB), but a few do not. In the numbering of the symbols and abbreviations in fig. 1844 a to 1844(o) on this and the following pages, vertical figures indicate that

the designated symbol or abbreviation is in conformity with the IHB standards. Slanting figures mean that it either differs from the standard or does not appear in the international list. Where the figures are enclosed in *parentheses*, the symbol or abbreviation is in addition to those included in the IHB standards.

The symbols and abbreviations shown in fig. 1844 will be used on all CS and HO charts produced in the future. Cases may occur where older symbols still appear on charts that have not yet been revised and reissued in new editions.

COLOR KEY:

| Blue | Green |
|---|---|
| Yellow | Red |

FIG. 1844 a    SYMBOLS—The coastline

## F. Adjectives, Adverbs and other abbreviations

| # | Abbr | Term |
|---|------|------|
| 1 | gt | Great |
| 2 | lit | Little |
| 3 | lrg | Large |
| 4 | sml | Small |
| 5 | | Outer |
| 6 | | Inner |
| 7 | mid | Middle |
| 8 | | Old |
| 9 | anc | Ancient |
| 10 | | New |
| 11 | St | Saint |
| 12 | conspic | Conspicuous |
| 13 | | Remarkable |
| 14 | D.. Destr | Destroyed |
| 15 | | Projected |
| 16 | dist | Distant |
| 17 | abt | About |
| 18 | | See chart |
| 18a | | See plan |
| 19 | | Lighted; Luminous |
| 20 | sub | Submarine |
| 21 | | Eventual |
| 22 | AERO | Aeronautical |
| 23 | | Higher |
| 24 | exper | Experimental |
| 25 | discontd | Discontinued |
| 26 | prohib | Prohibited |
| 27 | explos | Explosive |
| 28 | estab | Established |
| 29 | elec | Electric |
| 30 | priv | Private; Privately |
| 31 | prom | Prominent |
| 32 | std | Standard |
| 33 | subm | Submerged |
| 34 | approx | Approximate |
| (Fa) | unverd | Unverified |
| (Fb) | AUTH | Authorized |
| (Fc) | cl | Clearance |
| (Fd) | maintd | Maintained |
| (Fe) | aband | Abandoned |
| (Ff) | cor | Corner |
| (Fg) | concr | Concrete |
| (Fh) | fl | Flood |
| (Fi) | extr | Extreme |
| (Fj) | mod | Moderate |
| (Fk) | bet | Between |
| (Fl) | 1st | First |
| (Fm) | 2nd | Second |
| (Fn) | 3rd | Third |
| (Fo) | 4th | Fourth |

## D. Control Points

| # | Symbol/Abbr | Term |
|---|-------------|------|
| 1 | △ | Triangulation point (station) |
| 2 | ⊙ | Fixed point (landmark) (See L-63) |
| 3 | ·256 | Summit of height (Peak) (when not a landmark) |
| (Da) | | Peak, accentuated by contours |
| (Db) | | Peak, accentuated by hachures |
| (Dc) | | Peak, elevation not determined |
| (Dd) | | Peak, when a landmark |
| 4 | Obs Spot | Observation spot |
| 5 | BM | Bench mark |
| 6 | See View | View point |
| 7 | | Datum point for grid of a plan |
| 8 | | Graphical triangulation point |
| 9 | Astro | Astronomical |
| 10 | Tri | Triangulation |
| (De) | C of E | Corps of Engineers |
| 12 | | Great trigonometrical survey station |
| 13 | | Traverse station |
| 14 | Bdy. Mon | Boundary monument |
| (Df) | ◇ | International boundary monument |

## E. Units

| # | Abbr | Term |
|---|------|------|
| 1 | hr | Hour |
| 2 | m: min | Minute (of time) |
| 3 | sec | Second (of time) |
| 4 | m | Meter |
| 4a | dm | Decimeter |
| 4b | cm | Centimeter |
| 4c | mm | Millimeter |
| 4d | m² | Square meter |
| 4e | m³ | Cubic meter |
| 5 | km | Kilometer |
| 6 | in | Inch |
| 7 | ft | Foot |
| 8 | yd | Yard |
| 9 | fm | Fathom |
| 10 | cbl | Cable length |
| 11 | M | Nautical mile |
| 12 | kn | Knot |
| 12a | t | Ton |
| 12b | cd | Candela (new candle) |
| 13 | lat | Latitude |
| 14 | long | Longitude |
| 15 | pub | Publication |
| 16 | Ed | Edition |
| 17 | corr | Correction |
| 18 | alt | Altitude |
| 19 | ht: elev | Height; Elevation |
| 20 | ° | Degree |
| 21 | ' | Minute (of arc) |
| 22 | " | Second (of arc) |
| 23 | No | Number |
| (Ea) | St. M | Statute mile |
| (Eb) | Msec | Microsecond |

**FIG. 1844 c   Control points, units, adjectives, adverbs**

**FIG. 1844 b   Features of the coast and natural features of the land**

## B. Coast Features

| # | Abbr | Term |
|---|------|------|
| 1 | G | Gulf |
| 2 | B | Bay |
| (Ba) | B | Bayou |
| 3 | Fd | Fjord |
| 4 | L | Loch; Lough; Lake |
| 5 | Cr | Creek |
| 5a | C | Cove |
| 6 | In | Inlet |
| 7 | Str | Strait |
| 8 | Sd | Sound |
| 9 | Pass | Passage; Pass |
| | Thoro | Thorofare |
| 10 | Chan | Channel |
| 10a | | Narrows |
| 11 | Entr | Entrance |
| 12 | Est | Estuary |
| 12a | | Delta |
| 13 | Mth | Mouth |
| 14 | Rd | Road; Roadstead |
| 15 | Anch | Anchorage |
| 16 | Hbr | Harbor |
| 16a | Hn | Haven |
| 17 | P | Port |
| (Bb) | P | Pond |
| 18 | I | Island |
| 19 | It | Islet |
| 20 | Arch | Archipelago |
| 21 | Pen | Peninsula |
| 22 | C | Cape |
| 23 | Prom | Promontory |
| 24 | Hd | Head; Headland |
| 25 | Pt | Point |
| 26 | Mt | Mountain; Mount |
| 27 | Rge | Range |
| 27a | | Valley |
| 28 | | Summit |
| 29 | Pk | Peak |
| 30 | Vol | Volcano |
| 31 | | Hill |
| 32 | Bld | Boulder |
| 33 | Ldg | Landing |
| 34 | | Table-land (Plateau) |
| 35 | Rk | Rock |
| 36 | | Isolated rock |
| (Bc) | Str | Stream |
| (Bd) | R | River |
| (Be) | Slu | Slough |
| (Bf) | Lag | Lagoon |
| (Bg) | Apprs | Approaches |
| (Bh) | Rky | Rocky |

## C. The Land (Natural Features)

| # | Term |
|---|------|
| 1 | Contour lines (Contours) |
| 1a | Contour lines, approximate (Contours) |
| 2 | Hachures |
| 2a | Form lines, no definite interval |
| 2b | Shading |
| 3 | Glacier |
| 4 | Saltpans |
| 5 | Isolated trees (⊙ TREE) |
| 5a | Deciduous or of unknown or unspecified type |
| 5b | Coniferous |
| 5c | Palm tree |
| 5d | Nipa palm |
| 5e | Filao |
| 5f | Casuarina |
| 6 | Cultivated fields / Cultivated |
| 6a | Grass fields / Grass |
| 7 | Paddy (rice) fields / Rice |
| 7a | Park; Garden |
| 8 | Bushes / Bushes |
| 8a | Tree plantation in general |
| 9 | Deciduous woodland / Wooded |
| 10 | Coniferous woodland / Wooded |
| 10a | Woods in general / Wooded |
| 11 | Tree top elevation (above height datum)   2560 |
| 12 | Lava flow |
| 13 | River; Stream |
| 14 | Intermittent stream |
| 15 | Lake; Pond |
| 16 | Lagoon (Lag)   Symbol used in small areas |
| 17 | Marsh; Swamp / Swamp |
| 18 | Slough (Slu.) |
| 19 | Rapids |
| 20 | Waterfalls |
| 21 | Spring |

**1844 e    Artificial features of topography**

**FIG. 1844 d    Ports and harbors**

## I. Buildings and Structures (continued)

| No. | Symbol | Abbr. | Name |
|---|---|---|---|
| 61 | | Inst | Institute |
| 62 | | | Establishment |
| 63 | | | Bathing establishment |
| 64 | | Ct Ho | Courthouse |
| 65 | | Sch | School |
| (Ig) | | H.S | High school |
| (Ih) | | Univ | University |
| 66 | | Bldg | Building |
| 67 | | Pav | Pavilion |
| 68 | | | Hut |
| 69 | | | Stadium |
| 70 | | T | Telephone |
| 71 | ● | | Gas tank; Gasometer |
| 72 | GAB | °Gab | Gable |
| 73 | | | Wall |
| (Ii) | | Ltd | Limited |
| (Ij) | | Apt | Apartment |
| (Ik) | | Cap | Capitol |
| (Il) | | Co | Company |
| (Im) | | Corp | Corporation |
| (In) | ⊙ | | Landmark (conspicuous object) |
| (Io) | o | | Landmark (position approx.) |

## J. Miscellaneous Stations

| No. | Symbol | Abbr. | Name |
|---|---|---|---|
| 1 | | Sta | Any kind of station |
| 2 | | Sta | Station |
| 3 | C.G. | | Coast Guard station (Similar to LS. S.) |
| (Ja) | C.G. LS.S | | Coast Guard station (when landmark) |
| 4 | ⊙LOOK.TR | | Lookout station; Watch tower |
| 5 | | | Lifeboat station |
| 6 | LB.S | | Lifesaving station (See J-3) |
| 7 | | Rkt. Sta | Rocket station |
| 8 | ⊙PIL. STA | | Pilot station |
| 9 | | Sig Sta | Signal station |
| 10 | | Sem | Semaphore |
| 11 | | S Sig Sta | Storm signal station |
| 12 | | | Weather signal station |
| (Jb) | ⊙W.B. SIG. STA | | Weather Bureau signal station |
| 13 | | | Tide signal station |
| 14 | | | Stream signal station |
| 15 | | | Ice signal station |
| 16 | | | Time signal station |
| 17 | | | Time ball |
| 18 | | | Signal mast |
| 19 | FS | °FP | Flagstaff; Flagpole |
| (Jc) | F. TR | °F.Tr | Flag tower |
| 20 | | | Signal |
| 21 | | Obsy | Observatory |
| 22 | | Off | Office |
| (Jd) | °BELL | | Bell (on land) |
| (Je) | °HECP | | Harbor entrance control post |

FIG. 1844 g    Other buildings and structures, and miscellaneous stations

FIG. 1844 f    Buildings and structures

## I. Buildings and Structures   (see General Remarks)

| No. | Symbol | Abbr. | Name |
|---|---|---|---|
| 1 | | | City or Town (large scale) |
| (Ia) | | | City or Town (small scale) |
| 2 | | | Suburb |
| 3 | | Vil | Village |
| 3a | | | Buildings in general |
| 4 | | Cas | Castle |
| 5 | | | House |
| 6 | | | Villa |
| 7 | | | Farm |
| 8 | | Ch | Church |
| 8a | | Cath | Cathedral |
| 8b | ⊙SPIRE | Spire | Spire; Steeple |
| 8c | | | Christian Shrine |
| 9 | | | Roman Catholic Church |
| 10 | | | Temple |
| 11 | | | Chapel |
| 12 | | | Mosque; Minaret |
| (Ib) | | | Moslem Shrine |
| 13 | | | Marabout |
| 14 | | Pag | Pagoda |
| 15 | | | Buddhist Temple; Joss-House |
| 15a | | | Shinto Shrine |
| 16 | | | Monastery; Convent |
| 17 | | | Calvary; Cross |
| 17a | | | Cemetery, Non-Christian |
| 18 | Cem | | Cemetery, Christian |
| 18a | | | Tomb |
| 19 | | | Fort (actual shape charted) |
| 20 | | | Battery (Same as 1-19) |
| 21 | | | Barracks |
| 22 | | | Powder magazine |
| 23 | | | Airplane landing field |
| 24 | Airport | | Airport, large scale (See P-13) |
| (Ic) | | | Airport, military (small scale) |
| (Id) | | | Airport, civil (small scale) |
| 25 | | | Mooring mast |
| 26 | King St | St | Street |
| 26a | Locust Ave | Ave | Avenue |
| (Ie) | Grand Blvd | Blvd | Boulevard |
| 27 | | Tel | Telegraph |
| 28 | | Tel. Off | Telegraph office |
| 29 | | P.O | Post office |
| 30 | | Govt. Ho | Government house |
| 31 | | | Town hall |
| 32 | | Hosp | Hospital |
| 33 | | | Slaughterhouse |
| 34 | | Magz | Magazine |
| 34a | | | Warehouse; Storehouse |
| 35 | ⊙MON | °Mon | Monument |
| 36 | ⊙CUP | °Cup | Cupola |
| 37 | ⊙ELEV | °Elev | Elevator; Lift |
| (If) | | Elev | Elevation; Elevated |
| 38 | | | Shed |
| 39 | | | Zinc roof |
| 40 | Ruins | °Ru | Ruins |
| 41 | ⊙TR | °Tr | Tower |
| 42 | ✕WINDMILL | | Windmill |
| 43 | ✿ | | Watermill |
| 43a | ✕WINDMOTOR | | Windmotor |
| 44 | ⊙CHY | °Chy | Chimney; Stack |
| 45 | ⊙S'PIPE | °S'pipe | Water tower; Standpipe |
| 46 | ● | | Oil tank |
| 47 | ☐ Facty | | Factory |
| 48 | | | Saw mill |
| 49 | | | Brick kiln |
| 50 | ✕ | | Mine, Quarry |
| 51 | °Well | | Well |
| 52 | | | Cistern |
| 53 | ⊙TANK | °Tk | Tank |
| 54 | | | Noria |
| 55 | | | Fountain |

## K. Lights (continued)

| | | |
|---|---|---|
| 69 | | Unwatched light |
| 70 | Occas | Occasional light |
| 71 | Irreg | Irregular light |
| 72 | Prov | Provisional light |
| 73 | Temp | Temporary light |
| (Kg) | D:Destr | Destroyed |
| 74 | Exting | Extinguished light |
| 75 | | Faint light |
| 76 | | Upper light |
| 77 | | Lower light |
| 78 | | Rear light |
| 79 | | Front light |
| 80 | Vert | Vertical lights |
| 81 | Hor | Horizontal lights |
| (Kh) | VB | Vertical beam |
| (Ki) | RGE | Range |
| (Kj) | Exper | Experimental light |
| (Kk) | TRLB | Temporarily replaced by lighted buoy showing the same characteristics |
| (Kl) | TRUB | Temporarily replaced by unlighted buoy |
| (Km) | TLB | Temporary lighted buoy |
| (Kn) | TUB | Temporary unlighted buoy |

## L. Buoys and Beacons (see General Remarks)

| No. | Description |
|---|---|
| 1 | Position of buoy |
| 2 | Light buoy |
| 3 | Bell buoy |
| 3a | Gong buoy |
| 4 | Whistle buoy |
| 5 | Can or Cylindrical buoy |
| 6 | Nun or Conical buoy |
| 7 | Spherical buoy |
| 8 | Spar buoy |
| 8a | Pillar buoy |
| 9 | Buoy with topmark (ball) (See L-70) |
| 10 | Barrel or Tun buoy |
| (La) | Color unknown |
| (Lb) | Float |
| 12 | Lightfloat |
| 13 | Outer or Landfall buoy |
| 14 | Fairway buoy (BWVS) |
| 14a | Mid-channel buoy (BWVS) |
| 15 | Starboard-hand buoy (entering from seaward) |
| 16 | Port-hand buoy (entering from seaward) |
| 17 | Bifurcation buoy (RBHB) |
| 18 | Junction buoy (RBHB) |
| 19 | Isolated danger buoy (RBHB) |
| 20 | Wreck buoy (RBHB or G) |
| 20a | Obstruction buoy (RBHB or G) |
| 21 | Telegraph-cable buoy |
| 22 | Mooring buoy (colors of mooring buoys never carried) |
| 22a | Mooring |
| 22b | Mooring buoy with telegraphic communications |
| 22c | Mooring buoy with telephonic communications |
| 23 | Warping buoy |
| 24 | Quarantine buoy |
| 25 | Explosive anchorage buoy |
| 25a | Aeronautical anchorage buoy |
| 26 | Compass adjustment buoy |
| 27 | Fish trap buoy (BWHB) |
| 27a | Spoil ground buoy |
| 28 | Anchorage buoy (marks limits) |
| 29 | Private buoy (maintained by private interests, use with caution) |

**FIG. 1844 i    Other lights, buoys and beacons**

**FIG. 1844 h    Lights**

## K. Lights

| No. | Abbr. | Description |
|---|---|---|
| 1 | | Position of light |
| 2 | Lt | Light |
| (Ka) | | Riprap surrounding light |
| 3 | Lt. Ho | Lighthouse |
| 4 | AERO | Aeronautical light (See F-22) |
| 4a | | Marine and air navigation light |
| 5 | Bn | Light beacon |
| 6 | | Light vessel; Lightship |
| 8 | | Lantern |
| 9 | | Street lamp |
| 10 | REF | Reflector |
| 11 | Ldg Lt | Leading light |
| 12 | | Sector light |
| 13 | | Directional light |
| 14 | | Harbor light |
| 15 | | Fishing light |
| 16 | | Tidal light |
| 17 | | Private light (maintained by private interests; to be used with caution) |
| 21 | F | Fixed light |
| 22 | Occ | Occulting light |
| 23 | Fl | Flashing light |
| 24 | Qk Fl | Quick flashing (scintillating) light |
| 24a | I Qk Fl / Int Qk Fl | Interrupted quick flashing light |
| (Kb) | E Int | Equal interval (isophase) light |
| 25a | S Fl | Short flashing light |
| 26 | Alt | Alternating light |
| 27 | Gp Occ | Group occulting light |
| 28 | Gp Fl | Group flashing light |
| 28a | S-L Fl | Short-long flashing light |
| 28b | | Group short flashing light |
| 29 | F Fl | Fixed and flashing light |
| 30 | F Gp Fl | Fixed and group flashing light |
| 31 | Rot | Revolving or Rotating light |
| (Kbb) | Mo | Morse code |
| 41 | | Period |
| 42 | | Every |
| 43 | | With |
| 44 | | Visible (range) |
| (Kc) | M | Nautical mile (See E-11) |
| (Kd) | m: min | Minutes (See E-2) |
| (Ke) | sec | Seconds (See E-3) |
| 45 | Fl | Flash |
| 46 | Occ | Occultation |
| 46a | | Eclipse |
| 47 | Gp | Group |
| 48 | Occ | Intermittent light |
| 49 | SEC | Sector |
| 50 | | Color of sector |
| 51 | Aux | Auxiliary light |
| 52 | | Varied |
| 61 | Vi | Violet |
| 62 | Pur | Purple |
| 63 | Bu | Blue |
| 64 | G | Green |
| 65 | Or | Orange |
| 66 | R | Red |
| 67 | W | White |
| 67a | Am | Amber |
| 68 | OBSC | Obscured light |
| (Kf) | Fog Det Lt | Fog detector light (See Nb) |

## M. Radio and Radar Stations

| No. | Symbol | Description |
|---|---|---|
| 1 | ∘R. Sta | Radio telegraph station |
| 2 | ∘R. T | Radio telephone station |
| 3 | R. Bn | Radiobeacon |
| 4 | R. Bn | Circular radiobeacon |
| 5 | R.D | Directional radiobeacon; Radio range |
| 6 | | Rotating loop radiobeacon |
| 7 | R.D.F | Radio direction finding station |
| (Ma) | TELEM ANT | Telemetry antenna |
| 9 | R. MAST / R. TR | Radio mast / Radio tower |
| (Mb) | TV TR | Television tower |
| 10 | R. TR. (WBAL) 1090 Kc | Radio broadcasting station (commercial) |
| 10a | ∘R. Sta | Q.T.G. Radio station |
| 11 | Ra | Radar station |
| 12 | Racon | Radar responder beacon |
| 13 | Ra Ref | Radar reflector (See Li) |
| 14 | Ra (conspic) | Radar conspicuous object |
| 14a | | Ramark |
| 15 | D.F.S | Distance finding station (synchronized signals) |
| (Mc) | AERO R. Bn 302 | Aeronautical radiobeacon |
| (Md) | AERO R. Rge 342 | Aeronautical radio range |
| (Me) | Ra Ref Calibration Bn | Radar calibration beacon |
| (Mf) | CONSOL Bn 190 Kc MMF | Consol (Consolan) station |
| (Mg) | Loran Sta Venice | Loran station (name) |
| (Mh) | LORAN TR SPRING ISLAND | Loran tower (name) |
| (Mi) | 10 | Radio calling-in point for traffic control |

## N. Fog Signals

| No. | Symbol | Description |
|---|---|---|
| 1 | Fog Sig | Fog-signal station |
| 2 | | Radio fog-signal station |
| 3 | GUN | Explosive fog signal |
| 4 | | Submarine fog signal |
| 5 | SUB-BELL | Submarine fog bell (action of waves) |
| 6 | SUB-BELL | Submarine fog bell (mechanical) |
| 7 | SUB-OSC | Submarine oscillator |
| 8 | NAUTO | Nautophone |
| 9 | DIA | Diaphone |
| 10 | GUN | Fog gun |
| 11 | SIREN | Fog siren |
| 12 | HORN | Fog trumpet |
| 13 | HORN | Fog horn |
| 14 | BELL | Fog bell |
| 15 | WHIS | Fog whistle |
| 16 | HORN | Reed horn |
| 17 | GONG | Fog gong |
| 18 | | Submarine sound signal not connected to the shore (See N-5,6,7) |
| 18a | | Submarine sound signal connected to the shore (See N-5,6,7) |
| (Na) | HORN | Typhon |
| (Nb) | Fog Det Lt | Fog detector light (See Kf) |

**FIG. 1844 k    Radio and radar stations, fog signals**

**FIG. 1844 j    Buoys and beacons (continued)**

## L. Buoys and Beacons (continued)

| No. | Symbol | Description |
|---|---|---|
| 30 | | Temporary buoy (See Kk,l,m,n) |
| 30a | | Winter buoy |
| 31 | HB | Horizontal stripes or bands |
| 32 | VS | Vertical stripes |
| 33 | Chec | Checkered |
| (Lc) | Diag | Diagonal buoy |
| 41 | W | White |
| 42 | B | Black |
| 43 | R | Red |
| 44 | Y | Yellow |
| 45 | G | Green |
| 46 | Br | Brown |
| 47 | Gy | Gray |
| 48 | Bu | Blue |
| (Ld) | Am | Amber |
| (Le) | Or | Orange |
| 51 | | Floating beacon |
| 52 | RW Bn, W Bn, R Bn | Fixed beacon (unlighted or daybeacon) |
| | Bn | Black beacon |
| | Bn | Color unknown |
| (Lf) | MARKER | Private aid to navigation |
| 53 | Bn | Beacon, in general (See L-52) |
| 54 | | Tower beacon |
| 55 | | Cardinal marking system |
| 56 | Deviation Bn | Compass adjustment beacon |
| 57 | | Topmarks (See L-9, 70) |
| 58 | | Telegraph-cable (landing) beacon |
| 59 | Piles | Piles (See O-30, H-9) |
| | | Stakes |
| 59 | Stumps | Stumps (See O-30) |
| | | Perches |
| 61 | CAIRN Cairn | Cairn |
| 62 | | Painted patches |
| 63 | | Landmark (conspicuous object) (See D-2) |
| (Lg) | | Landmark (position approximate) |
| 64 | REF | Reflector |
| 65 | MARKER | Range targets, markers |
| (Lh) | W Or, W Or | Special-purpose buoys |
| 70 | Note: | TOPMARKS on buoys and beacons may be shown on charts of foreign waters. The abbreviation for black is not shown adjacent to buoys or beacons. |
| (Li) | Ra Ref | Radar reflector (See M-13) |

## Q. Soundings

| No. | Symbol | Description |
|---|---|---|
| 1 | SD | Doubtful sounding |
| 2 | 6̄5̄ | No bottom found |
| 3 | | Out of position |
| 4 | | Least depth in narrow channel |
| 5 | 30 FEET APR 1958 | Dredged channel (with controlling depth indicated) |
| 6 | 24 FEET MAY 1958 | Dredged area |
| 7 | | Swept channel (See Q-9) |
| 8 | | Drying or uncovering height in feet above chart (sounding) datum |
| 9 | | Swept area, not adequately sounded (shown by green tint) |
| 9a | | Swept area adequately sounded (swept by wire drag to depth indicated) |
| 10 | | Hair-line depths |
| 10a | $8_2$ | Figures for ordinary soundings |
| 11 | $8_2$ | Soundings taken from foreign charts |
| 12 | $8_2$ | Soundings taken from older surveys or smaller scale charts |
| 13 | $8_2$ | Soundings taken by echo |
| 14 | $8_2$ | Sloping figures (See Q-12) |
| 15 | $8_2$ | Upright figures (See Q-10a) |
| 16 | (25) | Bracketed figures (See O-1, 2) |
| 17 | | Underlined sounding figures (See Q-8) |
| 18 | $3_2$  $6_1$ | Soundings expressed in fathoms and feet |
| (Qa) | | Stream |

## P. Various Limits, etc.

| No. | Symbol | Description |
|---|---|---|
| 1 | | Leading line, Range line |
| 2 | | Transit |
| 3 | | In line with |
| 4 | | Limit of sector |
| 5 | | Channel, Course, Track recommended (marked by buoys or beacons)(See P-21) |
| (Pa) | | Alternate course |
| 6 | | Leader cable |
| 7 | | Submarine cable (power, telegraph, telephone, etc.) |
| 7a | Cable Area | Submarine cable area |
| 8 | Pipeline | Submarine pipeline |
| 8a | Pipeline Area | Submarine pipeline area |
| 9 | RESTRICTED AREA | Maritime limit in general |
| 9a | | Limit of restricted area |
| 10 | | Limit of fishing zone (fish trap areas) |
| 11 | | Limit of dumping ground, spoil ground (See P-9, G-13) |
| 12 | | Anchorage limit |
| 13 | | Limit of airport (See I-23, 24) |
| 14 | | Limit of sovereignty (Territorial waters) |
| 15 | | Customs boundary |
| 16 | | International boundary (also State boundary) |
| 17 | | Stream limit |
| 18 | | Ice limit |
| 19 | | Limit of tide |
| 20 | | Limit of navigation |
| 21 | | Course recommended (not marked by buoys or beacons)(See P-5) |
| 22 | | District or province limit |
| 23 | COURSE 055°00' TRUE — RANGE MARKERS | Reservation line |
| 24 | | Measured distance |
| 25 | PROHIBITED AREA | Prohibited area (See G-12) |

**FIG. 1844 m   Various limits, and soundings**

**FIG. 1844-l   Dangers**

## O. Dangers

| No. | Symbol | Description |
|---|---|---|
| 1 | ⌁(25) | Rock which does not cover (elevation above MHW) (See general remarks) |
| | *Uncov 2 ft   ⌁Uncov 2 ft   *(2)   ⌁(2) | |
| 2 | | Rock which covers and uncovers, with height in feet above chart (sounding) datum |
| 3 | | Rock awash at the level of chart (sounding) datum |
| | | When rock of O-2 or O-3 is considered a danger to navigation |
| 4 | | Sunken rock with less than 6 feet of water over it (Same as O-26) |
| 5 | | Sunken rock with between 6 and 33 ft. of water over it (Same as O-26) |
| 5a | ⌁Rk | Shoal sounding on isolated rock (replaces symbol) |
| 6 | | Sunken rock with more than 66 feet of water over it (Same as O-26) |
| 6a | ⌁Rk  ⌁Wk  ⌁Obstr | Sunken danger with depth cleared by wire drag (in feet or fathoms) |
| 7 | Reef | Reef of unknown extent |
| 8 | Sub Vol | Submarine volcano |
| 9 | Discol Water | Discolored water |
| 10 | Coral  Co  Co | Coral or Rocky reef, covered at sounding datum (See A-11d, 11g) |
| | Co 3↑ Reef Line | Coral reef, detached (uncovers at sounding datum) |

| No. | Symbol | Description |
|---|---|---|
| 11 | (5.) Obstr | Obstruction |
| | | Wreck showing any portion of hull or superstructure above sounding datum |
| 12 | Masts | Wreck with only masts visible above sounding datum |
| 13 | | Old symbols for wrecks |
| 13a | | Wreck always partially submerged |
| 14 | | Sunken wreck which may be dangerous to surface navigation (See O-6a) |
| 15 | (5.) Wk | Wreck over which depth is known |
| 16 | | Sunken wreck, not dangerous to surface navigation |
| 17 | Foul | Foul ground |
| 18 | Tide Rips | Overfalls or Tide rips (Symbol used only in small areas) |
| 19 | Eddies | Eddies (Symbol used only in small areas) |
| 20 | Kelp, Seaweed | Kelp (Symbol used only in small areas) |
| 21 | Bk | Bank |
| 22 | Shl | Shoal |
| 23 | Rf | Reef (See A-11d,11g; O-10) |
| 23a | Le | Ledge |
| 25 | | Breakers (See A-12) |
| 26 | | Sunken rock (depth unknown) |
| | | When rock is considered a danger to navigation |

| No. | Symbol | Description |
|---|---|---|
| 27 | Obstr | Obstruction |
| 28 | Wks | Wreck (See O-11 to 16) |
| 29 | Wreckage | Wreckage |
| 29a | | Wreck remains (dangerous only for anchoring) |
| 30 | Subm piles | Submerged piling (See H-9, L-59) |
| 30a | Snags  Stumps | Snags; Submerged stumps (See L-59) |
| 31 | | Lesser depth, possible |
| 32 | Uncov | Dries(See A-10; O-2, 10) |
| 33 | Cov | Covers (See O-2, 10) |
| 34 | Uncov | Uncovers (See A-10; O-2, 10) |
| 35 | (3.) Rep (1958) | Reported (with date) |
| | Eagle Rk (rep 1958) | Reported (with name and date) |
| 36 | Discol | Discolored (See O-9) |
| 37 | | Isolated danger |
| 38 | | Limiting danger line |
| 39 | Rk | Limit of rocky area |
| 41 | PA | Position approximate |
| 42 | PD | Position doubtful |
| 43 | ED | Existence doubtful |
| 44 | P Pos | Position |
| 45 | D | Doubtful |
| (Oa) | Subm Crib  Crib (above water) | Crib |
| (Ob) | Platform (lighted) HORN | Offshore platform (unnamed) |
| (Oc) | Hazel (lighted) HORN | Offshore platform (named) |

## U. Compass

Compass Rose — VAR 14° 45' W (1963) ANNUAL INCREASE 2' — MAGNETIC

The outer circle is in degrees with zero at true north. The inner circles are in points and degrees with the arrow indicating magnetic north.

| No. | Abbr. | Description |
|---|---|---|
| 1 | N | North |
| 2 | E | East |
| 3 | S | South |
| 4 | W | West |
| 5 | NE | Northeast |
| 6 | SE | Southeast |
| 7 | SW | Southwest |
| 8 | NW | Northwest |
| 9 | N | Northern |
| 10 | E | Eastern |
| 11 | S | Southern |
| 12 | W | Western |
| 21 | brg | Bearing |
| 22 | | True |
| 23 | mag | Magnetic |
| 24 | var | Variation |
| 25 | | Annual change |
| 25a | | Annual change nil |
| 26 | | Abnormal variation; Magnetic attraction |
| 27 | deg | Degrees (See E-20) |
| 28 | dev | Deviation |

## T. Tides and Currents

| No. | Abbr. | Description |
|---|---|---|
| 1 | HW | High water |
| 1a | HHW | Higher high water |
| 2 | LW | Low water |
| (Ta) | LWD | Low water datum |
| 2a | LLW | Lower low water |
| 3 | MTL | Mean tide level |
| 4 | MSL | Mean sea level |
| 4a | | Elevation of mean sea level above chart (sounding) datum |
| 5 | | Chart datum (datum for 'sounding reduction) |
| 6 | Sp | Spring tide |
| 7 | Np | Neap tide |
| 8 | MHWS | Mean high water springs |
| 8a | MHWN | Mean high water neaps |
| 8b | MHHW | Mean higher high water |
| (Tb) | MHW | Mean high water |
| 9 | MLWS | Mean low water springs |
| 9a | MLWN | Mean low water neaps |
| 9b | MLLW | Mean lower low water |
| (Tc) | MLW | Mean low water |
| 10 | ISLW | Indian spring low water |
| 11 | | High water full and change (vulgar establishment of the port) |
| 12 | | Low water full and change |
| 13 | | Mean establishment of the port |
| 13a | | Unit of height |
| 14 | | Equinoctial |
| 15 | | Quarter; Quadrature |
| 16 | Str. | Stream |
| 17 | | Current, general, with rate |
| 18 | | Flood stream (current) with rate |
| 19 | | Ebb stream (current) with rate |
| 20 | | Tide gauge; Tidepole; |
| 21 | | Automatic tide gauge |
| 23 | vel. | Velocity; Rate |
| 24 | kn. | Knots |
| 25 | ht. | Height |
| 26 | | Tide |
| 27 | | New moon |
| 28 | | Full moon |
| 29 | | Ordinary |
| 30 | | Syzygy |
| 31 | fl. | Flood |
| 32 | | Ebb |
| 33 | | Tidal stream diagram |
| 34 | | Place for which tabulated tidal stream data are given |
| 35 | | Range (of tide) |
| 36 | | Phase lag |
| (Td) | | Current diagram, with explanatory note |

**FIG. 1844 o   Tides and currents, the compass**

**FIG. 1844 n   Depth contours and tints, quality of the bottom**

## R. Depth Contours and Tints (see General Remarks)

| Feet | Fathoms |
|---|---|
| 0 | 0 |
| 6 | 1 |
| 12 | 2 |
| 18 | 3 |
| 24 | 4 |
| 30 | 5 |
| 36 | 6 |
| 60 | 10 |
| 120 | 20 |
| 180 | 30 |
| 240 | 40 |
| 300 | 50 |
| 600 | 100 |
| 1,200 | 200 |
| 1,800 | 300 |
| 2,400 | 400 |
| 3,000 | 500 |
| 6,000 | 1,000 |
| 12,000 | 2,000 |
| 18,000 | 3,000 |

Or continuous lines, with values

black … 5 … 100 (blue or)

## S. Quality of the Bottom

| No. | Abbr. | Description |
|---|---|---|
| 1 | _ | Ground |
| 2 | S | Sand |
| 3 | M | Mud; Muddy |
| 4 | Oz | Ooze |
| 5 | Ml | Marl |
| 6 | Cl | Clay |
| 7 | G | Gravel |
| 8 | Sn | Shingle |
| 9 | P | Pebbles |
| 10 | St | Stones |
| 11 | Rk; rky | Rock; Rocky |
| 11a | Blds | Boulders |
| 12 | Ck | Chalk |
| 12a | Ca | Calcareous |
| 13 | Qz | Quartz |
| 13a | | Schist |
| 14 | Co | Coral |
| (Sa) | Co Hd | Coral head |
| 15 | Mds | Madrepores |
| 16 | Vol | Volcanic |
| (Sb) | Vol Ash | Volcanic ash |
| 17 | La | Lava |
| 18 | Pm | Pumice |
| 19 | T | Tufa |
| 20 | Sc | Scoriae |
| 21 | Cn | Cinders |
| 22 | Mn | Manganese |
| 23 | Sh | Shells |
| 24 | Oys | Oysters |
| 25 | Ms | Mussels |
| 26 | Spg | Sponge |
| 27 | | Kelp |
| 28 | Wd | Seaweed |
| 29 | Grs | Grass |
| 30 | | Seatangle |
| 31 | | Spicules |
| 32 | Fr | Foraminifera |
| 33 | Gl | Globigerina |
| 34 | Di | Diatoms |
| 35 | Rd | Radiolaria |
| 36 | Pt | Pteropods |
| 37 | Po | Polyzoa |
| 38 | | Cirripeda |
| 38a | | Fucus |
| 38b | | Mattes |
| 39 | fne | Fine |
| 40 | crs | Coarse |
| 41 | sft | Soft |
| 42 | hrd | Hard |
| 43 | stf | Stiff |
| 44 | sml | Small |
| 45 | lrg | Large |
| 46 | stk | Sticky |
| 47 | brk | Broken |
| 47a | grd | Ground |
| 48 | | Rotten |
| 49 | | Streaky |
| 50 | spk | Speckled |
| 51 | gty | Gritty |
| 52 | | Decayed |
| 53 | fly | Flinty |
| 54 | glac | Glacial |
| 55 | | Tenacious |
| 56 | wh | White |
| 57 | bk | Black |
| 58 | vi | Violet |
| 59 | bu | Blue |
| 60 | gn | Green |
| 61 | yl | Yellow |
| 62 | or | Orange |
| 63 | rd | Red |
| 64 | br | Brown |
| 65 | ch | Chocolate |
| 66 | gy | Gray |
| 67 | lt | Light |
| 68 | dk | Dark |
| 70 | | Varied |
| 71 | | Uneven |
| 76 | | Fresh water springs in sea-bed |

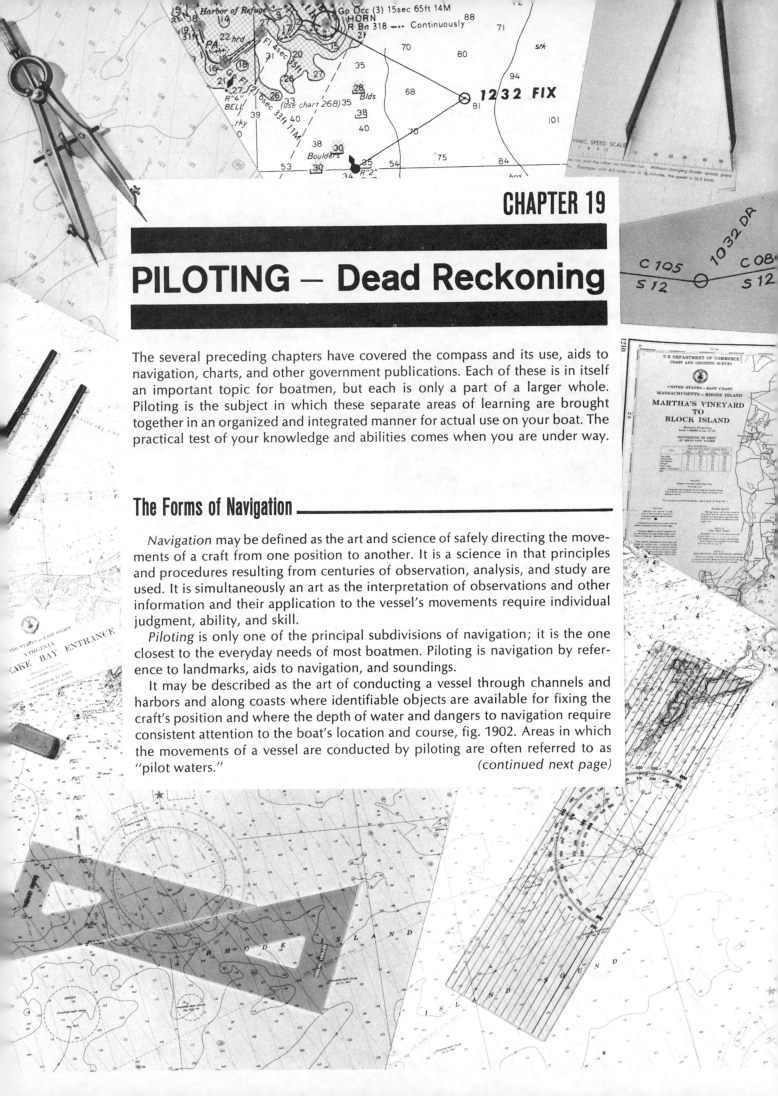

# CHAPTER 19

# PILOTING — Dead Reckoning

The several preceding chapters have covered the compass and its use, aids to navigation, charts, and other government publications. Each of these is in itself an important topic for boatmen, but each is only a part of a larger whole. Piloting is the subject in which these separate areas of learning are brought together in an organized and integrated manner for actual use on your boat. The practical test of your knowledge and abilities comes when you are under way.

## The Forms of Navigation

*Navigation* may be defined as the art and science of safely directing the movements of a craft from one position to another. It is a science in that principles and procedures resulting from centuries of observation, analysis, and study are used. It is simultaneously an art as the interpretation of observations and other information and their application to the vessel's movements require individual judgment, ability, and skill.

*Piloting* is only one of the principal subdivisions of navigation; it is the one closest to the everyday needs of most boatmen. Piloting is navigation by reference to landmarks, aids to navigation, and soundings.

It may be described as the art of conducting a vessel through channels and harbors and along coasts where identifiable objects are available for fixing the craft's position and where the depth of water and dangers to navigation require consistent attention to the boat's location and course, fig. 1902. Areas in which the movements of a vessel are conducted by piloting are often referred to as "pilot waters."

*(continued next page)*

# Dead Reckoning / CHAPTER 19

Along with piloting, the boatman will often use another form of navigation, *dead reckoning,* a procedure by which the craft's approximate location at any time is deduced from its movements since the last accurate determination of position.

Other subdivisions of navigation are *electronic,* which will be touched on briefly in the following chapters insofar as specific systems are applicable to small craft, and *celestial,* which will be left to more advanced students and texts.

## The importance of piloting

Piloting is a most important part of navigation, and perhaps the form requiring the least study but the most experience and best judgment. It is used by boatmen in

FIG. 1902 Piloting, by reference to landmarks and aids to navigation, is most often done in waters restricted by shoals and other dangers and which are relatively heavily traveled by other boats.

FIG. 1901 Piloting is the principal form of navigation used by boatmen. It requires study and practice, but it often becomes one of the major sources of enjoyment in boating.          M. Rosenfeld.

rivers, bays, lakes, and close alongshore when on the open oceans. In such waters, the hazards to safe navigation may be quite frequent and the density of traffic quite high. The navigator of a craft of any size in pilot waters must have adequate training and knowledge; he must give his task close attention and constant alertness. Frequent determinations of position are usually essential, and changes in course or speed may be necessary at relatively short intervals.

## The high seas vs. pilot waters

On the high seas, or well offshore in such large bodies of water as the Great Lakes, navigation can be more leisurely and relaxed. An error or uncertainty of position of a few miles will present no immediate hazard to the safety of the boat and its crew. But when one approaches the shore line, or the water shoals, a greater degree of accuracy is required. An error of only a few yards can result in running aground with certain embarrassment, and possibly much more serious consequences. The proximity of other craft requires constant knowledge of where the dangers lie and where one's own boat can be safely steered.

## The enjoyment of piloting

Piloting can be "fun" for a boatman, but it will be most enjoyable when done without tension or anxiety; this happy state can be achieved only with a sound background of study and practice. The wise skipper "overnavigates" in times of fair weather so as to acquire the skill that will let him navigate his boat safely through fog or rain or night without fear or nervous strain.

# The Dimensions of Piloting

The basic "dimensions" of piloting are direction, distance, and time. Other quantities which must be measured, calculated, or used, include speed, position, and depths and heights. A qualified pilot must have a ready understanding of how each of these dimensions is measured, expressed in units, used in calculations, and plotted on charts.

## DIRECTION

*Direction* is the position of one point relative to another point without reference to the distance between them. As discussed earlier in the chapters on compasses and charts, modern navigation uses the system of angular measurement in which a complete circle is divided into 360 units called "degrees." Although each degree can in turn be subdivided into 60 minutes, the more common practice

in angular measurement in piloting is to use ordinary fractions such as $\frac{1}{2}$ and $\frac{1}{4}$, or decimal fractions in tenths.

## True, magnetic, or compass

Directions are normally referred to a base line running from the origin point toward the geographic North Pole. Such directions can be measured on a chart with reference to the meridians of longitude and are called "true" directions. Measurements made with respect to the direction of the earth's magnetic field at that point are termed "magnetic" directions, and those referred to local magnetic conditions as measured by the craft's compass are designated "compass" directions, see fig. 1903. *It is of the utmost importance to always designate the reference used for directional measurement, true (T), magnetic (M), or compass (C).*

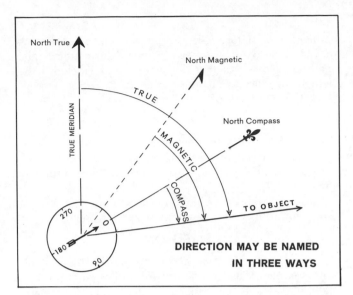

FIG. 1903 Direction is one of the basic "dimensions" of piloting. It can be measured with respect to True, Magnetic, or Compass North. Always be sure to designate the reference used.

## Directions and angles

The basic system of measurement uses the reference direction as 0° (North) and measures clockwise through 90° (East), 180° (South), and 270° (West) around to 360° which is North again. Directions are expressed in three-digit form such as 005°, 030°, 150°, etc. Note that zeros are added before the figures denoting direction if necessary to make a three-digit number, for example, 005° or 030°, fig. 1904a. *Angles* which are *not* directions are expressed in one, two, or three digits as appropriate, 5°, 30°, 150°, etc., fig. 1904b.

Occasionally, directions will be expressed as so many degrees east or west of North or South, such as N30°E (030°), S20°E (160°), S40°W (220°), or N15°W (345°), fig. 1905. This form of expression, "direction in quadrant," is useful for some types of computations, but it is not employed for general navigational purposes.

## Directions in the "point" system

The "point" system of angular measurement, so widely used in the days of sailing ships, has now fallen almost completely from practical use in navigation. It divided a complete circle into 32 points of 11¼ degrees each which could then be further subdivided fractionally. It is cumbersome to use and complicates calculations; with respect to the piloting of modern small craft, it is now of historical interest only.

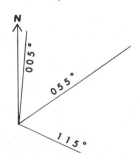

FIG. 1904a Directions are always designated by a *three-digit* number. Add zeros before a single or double-digit number as shown here.

FIG. 1904b An angle between two directions, as distinguished from the directions themselves, is *not* expressed as a three-digit number. An angle such as BAC above is shown as simply 50°, not as 050°.

FIG. 1905 Directions may be described "in quadrant," but this technique is rarely used in modern boating. In this obsolete procedure, angles are measured in either direction from North or South to a maximum of 90°.

FIG. 1906a                    FIG. 1906b

The *reciprocal* of a direction is simply the opposite direction, shown here as a broken line. To find a reciprocal, add 180° to the given direction. If the total exceeds 360°, subtract that amount. Alternatively, subtract 180° from the given direction if it is greater than that amount.

## Reciprocals

For any given direction, there is its *reciprocal*. This latter direction is the direct opposite, differing by 180°. Thus the reciprocal of 030° is 210°, and the reciprocal of 300° is 120°. To find the reciprocal of any direction, simply add 180° if the given direction is less than the amount; or subtract 180°, if it exceeds that figure, as shown in fig. 1906.

## DISTANCE

This is the second of the basic dimensions of piloting. *Distance* is defined as the spacial separation between two points without regard to the direction of one from the other. It is commonly thought of as the length of the shortest line that can be drawn between the two points.

## Nautical and statute miles

The basic unit of distance in piloting is the *mile,* but, as noted in Chapter 18, there are two types of miles that a boatman may encounter. The *statute mile* is used on inland bodies of water such as the Mississippi River and its tributaries, the Great Lakes, etc. (also the Atlantic and Gulf Intracoastal Waterways since 1969). It is 5280 feet in length, the same mile commonly used on land.

On the high seas and connecting tidal waters, the unit of measurement is the *nautical mile* of 6076.1 feet. This "salt-water" mile is essentially equal to one minute of latitude, and this relationship is often used in navigation. Nautical miles are slightly longer than statute miles, and the comparison is usually taken as 7 nautical miles equals 8 statute miles. More accurately, the conversion of nautical miles into statute miles is done by using the factor of 1.15.

It is quite possible to cruise from an area using one kind of mile into waters where the other kind is used. Care must be exercised at such times to determine which type of mile is being used and so specify in calculations.

For shorter distances, a few miles or less, the unit of measurement may be the *yard*. This is the same unit of three feet as commonly used on land. Roughly, a nautical mile can be considered as being 2000 yards although this introduces a small error of about 1¼%. Feet are seldom used as a measure of horizontal distance in navigation.

## TIME

The third basic dimension of piloting is *time*. Although the pilot does not need so accurate a knowledge of the exact time of day as does a celestial navigator, ability to determine the passage of time and to perform calculations with such *elapsed time* is essential. A boat should have aboard a clock or watch of reasonable time-keeping accuracy; a second one in reserve is desirable. For many practical problems in piloting, a stop watch will be found useful.

### Units of time

The units of time used in boating are the everyday ones of *hours* of 60 *minutes* each. In piloting, measurements will not often be carried to the preciseness of *seconds* of time although decimal fractions of minutes may occassionally occur in calculations. Seconds and fractions of minutes may be used in competitive events such as races and predicted log contests, but seldom otherwise.

### The 24-hour clock system

In navigation, including piloting, the time of day is expressed in a 24-hour system that eliminates the necessity for using the designations of "am" and "pm." Time is written in four-digit figures; the first two are the hour and the second pair represent the minutes. The day starts at 0001, one minute after midnight, 12:01 am in the old system. 0100 would be 1 am, 1000 is 10 am, and 1200 is noon. The second half of the day continues in the same pattern with 1300 being 1 pm, 1832 being 6:32 pm, etc., to 2400 for midnight. Time is spoken as "zero seven hundred" or "fifteen forty." The phrase "hours" should *not* be used. The times of 1000 and 2000 are correctly spoken as "ten hundred" and "twenty hundred," *not* as "one thousand" or "two thousand."

When performing arithmetic computations with time caution must always be exercised to remember that when "borrowing" or "carrying" there are *60* minutes in an hour, and not 100. As obvious and simple a matter as this may be, the mistake occurs all too often.

### Time zones

A navigator in pilot waters must also be alert to *time zones*. Even in coastal or inland waters, it is possible to cruise from one zone to another resulting in the necessity for changing clocks, the plot on the chart, and the log; plus one's arrival time at the next port.

A further complication in time is the prevalence of "daylight time" in many boating areas during the summer months. Government publications are in standard time; local sources of information such as newspapers and radio broadcasts will undoubtedly use daylight time if it is in effect. Daylight time is one hour *later* than standard time. When going from standard time to daylight, *add* one hour; from daylight to standard, *subtract* one hour.

## SPEED

No matter how fast or slow one's craft may be, speed is an essential dimension of piloting. *Speed* is defined as the number of units of distance that would be traveled in a specified unit of time.

The basic unit of speed is *miles per hour,* whether these be nautical or statute miles, as determined by location. A special name, *knot,* has been given to the nautical mile per hour. Note well that the word "knot" includes the element of time—to say "knots per hour" is not only incorrect, it is a mark of ignorance.

### Conversion of knots and MPH

The conversion factors between statute miles per hour (MPH) and knots are the same as for the corresponding units of distance—1 knot = 1.15 MPH, or 7 knots roughly equals 8 MPH.

The unit "knot" may be abbreviated either as "kt." or "kn."; the former has a somewhat greater usage.

## POSITION

The ability to describe accurately the position of his craft is an essential requirement for a pilot, and one that marks him as well qualified. To realize the importance and the difficulties of this seemingly simple task, one has only to listen to his radio on 2182 kc/s on a weekend afternoon during the boating season. The hesitant, inadequate, and inaccurate attempts by skippers to simply say where they are must surely irritate the Coast Guard and embarrass all competent boatmen!

### Relative and geographic coordinates

*Position* may be described in relative terms or by geographic coordinates. When defined as a *relative position,* the location of the craft is described as being a certain distance and direction from a specified identifiable point such as a landmark or aid to navigation. A boat's position may be described with varying degrees of preciseness as determined by the accuracy of the data on which it is based. A skipper might say that he was "about two miles southwest of Brenton Reef Light"; or if he had the capability of being more precise, he could say, "I'm 2.2 miles, 230°. True from Brenton Reef Light." In relative positioning, the distance may, of course, be essentially zero, as would be the case with a position report such as "I am at Lighted Whistle Buoy 2." See fig. 1907.

**FIG. 1907 A boat's position may be described in "relative" terms. It is stated to be at a certain distance and direction from an identifiable object such as an aid to navigation. In this example, it would be "1.8 miles, 120 degrees True from Point Judith Light."**

FIG. 1908 The position of a boat can be described in terms of "geographic coordinates." Using the subdivisions of the chart's borders, the latitude and longitude of the plotted position are measured and recorded. (from DUTTON'S NAVIGATION AND PILOTING)

FIG. 1909 Depth is a "dimension" of piloting that is often of the greatest importance to the safety of a boat and its crew. Be sure that you know whether the charted depths on the chart you are using are shown in feet or fathoms.

The preceding examples of position description have all used visible identifiable objects. It is also possible to state one's *geographic position* in terms of *latitude* and *longitude* using those nice straight, uniformly-spaced lines on charts which so unfortunately do not appear on the surface of the water. Using this procedure, the position is measured from the markings on either side and the top or bottom of the chart.

The units of measurement for geographic coordinates are *degrees* and *minutes,* but this degree is not quite the same unit as used in the measurement of direction, nor is this minute the same as the unit of time. Care must be used to avoid confusion between these units of position and other units with similar names. For precise position definition, one may use either *seconds* or *tenths of minutes* as determined by the chart being used. Typically, the smallest unit on the marginal scales of C&GS coast charts will be tenths of minutes, but for harbor charts it will be seconds; see page 355.

In a statement of geographic position, latitude is given first, before longitude, and the figures must be followed by "North" or "South" as appropriate. In U.S. waters, the latitude is, of course, always "North," even for the most unreconstructed "rebel." Similarly, longitude must be designated "East" or "West" to be complete; all U.S. waters are in West longitude, fig. 1908.

## DEPTHS

The *depth* of the water is important both for the safety of a boat in preventing grounding and for navigational purposes. Thus, this vertical measurement from the surface of the water to the bottom is an essential dimension of piloting. Measurements may be made continuously or only occasionally as determined by the circumstances, but you can be sure that at some time or another on almost any cruise, knowledge of the depth will become critically important.

In pilot waters, depths will normally be measured in *feet.* In open ocean waters, the small craft operator may find himself on charts indicating depths in *fathoms* of six feet each. It is important to check each chart when purchased and again when used to note the unit of measurement of depth, fig. 1909.

In many areas, depths will fluctuate somewhat from the printed figures on charts due to tidal changes. Charts will indicate the *datum* used, the reference plane from which measurements were made. They will also indicate the normal range of tidal variations and the extreme low-water condition that must be considered.

## HEIGHTS

The height, or elevation, of certain objects will be of concern to the pilot. The height of some landmarks and lighted aids to navigation may determine their range of visibility. Of more critical importance, however, are such vertical measurements as the clearance under a bridge, fig. 1910. *Heights,* or vertical dimensions upward from the surface of the water, are measured in *feet.* It should be noted that in tidal areas, the datum, or plane of reference, for heights is *not* the same as for depths. Examine each chart closely and note the datum from which heights are measured.

The usual datum for the measurement of heights is *mean high water.* This will be an imaginary plane surface above the mean low-water datum for depths by an amount equal to the *mean tide range;* the height of mean high water will usually be shown on a chart.

FIG. 1910 Charts will show the heights of bridges or other structures that will affect navigation. Heights are measured vertically in feet, usually from mean high water (MHW).

# The Instruments of Piloting

The practice of piloting in coastal and inland waters requires the use of a few simple tools or instruments, fig. 1911. These are not particularly expensive items, but they should be of good quality, well cared for, and used with the proper respect. A skilled man in any profession or trade is known by his tools, when that term is used in its broadest sense. A navigator may well be judged by his instruments and how he uses them.

FIG. 1911 Only a few simple instruments are needed for piloting, but these should be of good quality, used with respect, and properly maintained.

## DIRECTION

Many instruments are used in the measurement of direction. Some are concerned with such measurement directly, and others with its measurement on a chart. Still other instruments are used to both measure direction from a chart and to plot directions from observations.

### Determining Direction

The basic instrument on a boat for the determination of direction is a *compass*. With rare exceptions, this will be a *magnetic* compass as shown in fig. 1912 and described in Chapter 13. Directions obtained from this instrument will be "compass" directions and will require correction for deviation and variation as covered in that chapter.

A *gyro* compass is a complex device capable of indicating the true north direction without regard to magnetic conditions. However, its size, weight, electrical power requirements, and particularly its high cost, limit its use to the largest and most luxurious yachts. The average boatman must make do with a magnetic compass, but, properly used, this traditional piloting instrument will serve him well.

The compass is used primarily to determine the direction in which the craft is headed. Depending upon its loca-

tion, and how it is mounted, the steering compass may also be used for determining the direction of other objects from the boat. Rough readings may be taken by sighting across the compass itself and estimating the reading of the compass card. More exact readings can be taken if a pair of *sight vanes* can be mounted on the compass as illustrated in fig. 1913. Sights taken with a steering compass are satisfactory as to accuracy, but are generally limited by physical considerations to objects forward of the beam.

**Pelorus.** A more flexible instrument for measuring the direction of objects from the boat is the *pelorus*, fig. 1914. This simple device consists of a set of sighting vanes mounted over a circular scale calibrated in degrees like a compass card. A means must be provided for mounting or temporarily locating the pelorus so that it may be properly oriented to the fore-and-aft center line of the boat. Peloruses may be purchased or made in the home workshop; see fig. 1915.

The circular scale of a pelorus is usually made so that it may be rotated to a desired position and there clamped in place. With the scale so set that 000° is dead ahead, over or parallel to the center line of the boat, the directions that are then measured are termed *relative bearings*.

FIG. 1912 A magnetic compass is the basic instrument for measuring direction on a boat. See Chapters 13 and 14 for detailed coverage of the compass.

FIG. 1913 The compass can be used to determine the direction from the boat to an object such as an aid to navigation. Greater accuracy will be obtained if *sight vanes* are used as shown here.

FIG. 1914 A *pelorus* is used to take bearings on objects from a boat. It consists of a set of sights mounted over an angular scale calibrated like a compass card.

The sight vanes placed on a compass, or those of a pelorus, may be replaced with a small telescope having cross-hairs. Greater accuracy will be achieved, but the telescope must be of low power in order to have a wide enough field of view to pick up and hold objects at a distance despite the movements of the boat.

Even greater flexibility of use can be obtained with one of several patented instruments now on the market. Each of these consists of a small magnetic compass conveniently mounted for holding in front of one's eyes, plus a set of sights and a prismatic optical system for simultaneously observing a distant object through the sights and reading the compass card. Internal lighting for night use is usually provided. Typical of these instruments is the Hand Bearing Compass (fig. 1916) with open sights. Fig. 1917 illustrates how some small compasses may be unshipped from their mounting and held at eye level to take a bearing.

## Plotting directions

Once direction has been determined by compass, pelorus, or other device, it must be plotted on the chart. For this action, there are a number of instruments available. These same tools will be used when the problem is the determination of direction from the chart itself.

**Course plotters.** These are pieces of clear plastic, usually rectangular in shape, with one or more semi-circular angular scales marked thereon, see fig. 1918. The center of these scales is at or near the center of one of the longer sides of the plotter and is usually emphasized with a small circle or "bull's-eye." There are normally two main scales, one from 000° to 180° and the other from 180° to 360°; each is calibrated in degrees. There may also be smaller auxiliary scales offset 90° from the main scales. Lines are marked on the plotter parallel to the longer sides. Some instruments have distance marks along the edges corresponding to the more commonly-used chart scales.

Course plotters are used in the following manner:

1. *To determine the direction of a course or bearing from a given point,* place the plotter on the chart so that one of its longer sides is along the course or bearing line and slide the plotter until the bull's-eye is over a *meridian.* The true direction is then read on the scale where it is intersected by the meridian. Easterly courses are read on the scale that reads from 000° to 180°, and westerly courses are read on the other main scale, see fig. 1919.

These may be converted to compass directions or compass bearings, by numerically adding the heading of the boat as read from the steering compass at the instant of observation (subtract 360° from this sum if it exceeds that amount). A steady hand at the wheel is required, and the observer should call "Mark" at the time that he reads the pelorus so that the helmsman may simultaneously read the boat's compass. Alternatively, the helmsman may call a series of "marks" as he is on the prescribed heading, remaining silent if the boat falls off to either side. When using this technique, the observer takes his reading only when the helmsman is indicating that he is directly on the correct heading.

A second method of using a pelorus is to set the scale so that it matches the compass for the heading being steered. Readings then taken with the pelorus are directly compass bearings without further conversion. Two cautions must be observed—the craft must be directly on course at the time of observation; and, when correcting for *deviation,* the value used is that for the *heading* of the boat, *not* that for the observed direction. Because of these possible errors, particularly the latter one, this technique should be avoided, or used only with much practice and great care.

FIG. 1915 A pelorus may be purchased or it is easily made in a home workshop. A compass rose or card diagram such as Fig. 1310 or 1335 is cut out and mounted on a wooden or metallic base. A set of rotatable sighting vanes completes the pelorus.

FIG. 1916 A hand bearing compass has the advantage that it may easily be used from almost any place on a boat. Be careful, however, of using it near large masses of magnetic material that will introduce deviation errors.

FIG. 1917 Some compasses, like this Corsair, are so mounted (particularly on small boats) that they can be easily unshipped and held at eye-level for taking bearings. The same precautions regarding deviation must be observed as for a hand bearing compass.

If it is more convenient, the course or bearing may be lined up with one of the marked parallel lines rather than the edge of the course plotter. In measuring courses and bearings, it is not absolutely necessary to actually draw in the line connecting the two points, the plotter can be aligned using only the two points concerned. Usually, however, it will be found easier and safer to draw in the connecting line.

When the direction to be measured is within 20° or so of due North or South, it may be difficult to reach a meridian by sliding the course plotter across the chart. The small inner auxiliary scales have been included on the plotter for just such cases. Slide the plotter until the bull's-eye intersects a *parallel of latitude* line. The intersection of this line with the appropriate *auxiliary* scale indicates the direction of the course or bearing, see fig. 1920.

2. *To plot a specified direction (course or bearing) from a given point,* put a pencil on the origin point, keep one of the longer edges of the course plotter snug against the pencil, and slide the plotter around until the center bull's-

FIG. 1918 A *course plotter* is a single rectangular piece of transparent plastic ruled with circular scales and a set of lines parallel to its longer sides. Shown here is the model used by the U.S. Power Squadrons.

FIG. 1919 The course plotter is lined up with the course line along one of the longer sides, and then is moved until a meridian cuts through the "bull's eye." Direction can then be read from the appropriate main scale.

eye and the desired mark on the appropriate main scale both lie along the same meridian. With the plotter thus positioned, draw in the specified direction from the given point.

Alternatively, the plotter may first be positioned using the bull's-eye and scale markings without regard to the specified origin point. The plotter is then carefully slid up or down the meridian until one of the longer edges is over the origin point and then the direction line is drawn in.

For directions nearly North or South, one of the small auxiliary scales can be used in conjunction with a parallel of latitude.

3. *To extend a line* which must be longer than the length of the course plotter, place a pair of dividers, opened to three or four inches, tightly against the edge of the plotter and then slide the plotter along using the divider points as guides. Draw in the extension of the course or bearing line after the plotter has been advanced.

4. In piloting, it is sometimes necessary *to draw a new line parallel to an existing course or bearing line.* For such situations, the parallel lines marked on the course plotter may be used as guides.

**Course protractors.** Many pilots use a *course protractor,* fig. 1921, as their primary plotting tool. This instrument, with its moving parts, is not as easily used as the course plotter described above; but, when it is employed with care, it gives as satisfactory results.

In using the course protractor *to measure the direction of a course or bearing,* its center should be placed on the chart exactly over the specified origin point, such as the boat's position or an aid to navigation. The arm of the protractor is then swung around to the nearest compass rose on the chart, making the upper edge of the arm (which is in line with the center of the compass part of the course protractor) pass directly over the center of the compass rose.

Holding the course protractor arm firmly in this position, the compass part of the protractor is then turned around until the upper edge of the arm cuts across the same degree marking of the protractor compass as it does at the compass rose. The compass and the rose are now parallel. Holding the protractor compass firmly against the chart, the protractor arm is then moved around until its edge cuts across the second point involved in the course

FIG. 1920 If a meridian cannot be easily reached, as may be the case with courses within a few degrees of North or South, use the *auxiliary* inner scales and a *parallel* of latitude as shown here.

Main Scale

Auxiliary Scale

or bearing. The direction in degrees can then be read directly from the protractor compass scale.

*To lay off a line in a specified direction from the given point,* the protractor rose is first lined up with the compass rose on the chart as in the preceding instructions. Then the arm is rotated until the desired direction is indicated on the compass scale, and the line is drawn in; this line will have to be extended back to the origin point after the course protractor has been lifted off the chart.

**Parallel rulers.** A traditional instrument for measuring and plotting directions on charts is a set of *parallel rulers.* Their use on boats has declined somewhat in recent years, but they are still capable of giving good results if the navigator is careful to avoid slippage. Parallel rulers may be

FIG. 1922 *Parallel rulers* are a traditional charting instrument. The two straightedges are kept in parallel alignment by the connecting links. Directions are transferred from one place to another by "walking" the rulers across the chart.

FIG. 1921 Some skippers prefer to use a *course protractor* as their primary plotting tool. It consists of two pieces of plastic movable with respect to each other.

FIG. 1923 A pair of ordinary drawing triangles can be used for transferring a direction from one part of a chart to another, but not for great distances. See text for method of their use.

made of black (as shown in fig. 1922) or clear transparent plastic material. The two rulers are connected by metal linkages so that the edges always remain parallel. To measure the direction of a line, one ruler is lined up with the desired objects on the chart and then the pair is "walked" across the chart to the nearest compass rose by alternately holding one ruler and moving the other. To plot a line of stated direction, the process is essentially reversed; the procedure is started at the compass rose and worked to the desired origin point.

**Drawing triangles.** A pair of ordinary plastic *drawing triangles* can also be used for transferring a direction from one part of a chart to another, although not for very great distances. The two triangles need not be similar in size or shape. The two hypotenuses (longest sides) are placed together and one of the other sides of one triangle is lined up with the course or bearing line, or with the desired direction at the compass rose, fig. 1923. The other triangle is held firmly in place as a base, and the first one is slid along in contact with it, carrying the specified line to a new position while maintaining its direction. If necessary, the triangles may be alternately held and slid for moving somewhat greater distances.

**Courser.** One rather unique direction instrument, particularly useful in outboards or other situations of limited space, is a "Courser," a patented device consisting of a sheet of flexible plastic upon which are ruled a series of parallel lines, fig. 1924. One line is placed over the course or bearing to be measured and another will fall across or near the center of a compass rose on the chart. By slight adjustments to the Courser, directions can be read off the

FIG. 1924 A "Courser" is a sheet of soft flexible transparent plastic on which parallel lines have been ruled. It is simple and convenient to use in smaller boats, and the accuracy obtained with it is adequate for such applications.

rose with sufficient accuracy for practical use in a small boat.

An ordinary *drawing protractor* may find some use aboard a boat for measuring angles, but it is not a highly useful instrument and can be omitted. A chart compass rose can always be used for angle measurement if this becomes necessary.

**FIG. 1925** A *radar set* on a boat can measure the direction and distance to other boats, aids to navigation, prominent structures and terrain features, etc. The use of radar is covered more fully in Chapter 25.

**FIG. 1926** A *patent log*, used for determining distance run and speed. A log line connects the rotator to a registering device near the stern of the boat. The log line must be long enough to clear the wake as it is towed astern. In use, the rotator revolves as it is towed through the water, and the line transmits this rotary motion to the registering device which is calibrated so that the distance can be read directly from the dial.

**FIG. 1927** A more modern patent log consists of a much smaller impeller mounted on the bottom of the boat connected to a dialed instrument for measuring speed and distance run through the water.

## DISTANCE

Distance to an object can be measured directly by *radar*, fig. 1925; and distance traveled can be measured directly by a *summing log*, figs. 1926 and 1927. However, few boats are equipped with either of these items of equipment. Distance is usually measured in piloting by taking it from a chart.

### Chart measurements for distance

**Dividers.** Distance is measured on a chart with a pair of *dividers*, fig. 1928a. The two arms of this small drafting instrument can be opened as desired, and the friction at the pivot is sufficient to hold them in place with the same separation between the points. Most dividers have some means for adjusting this friction; it should be enough to hold the arms in place, but not so much as to make opening or closing difficult. A special type of dividers has a center cross-piece (like the horizontal part of the capital letter "A") which can be rotated by a knurled knob to set and maintain the opening between the arms, fig. 1928b; thus the distance between the points cannot accidentally change. This type of dividers is particularly useful if kept set to some standard distance, such as one mile to the scale of the chart being used.

The dividers are first opened to the distance between the two points on the chart, then they are transferred without change to the chart's graphic scale, figs. 1929a and b. Note that the zero point on this scale is *not* at the left-hand end, but rather is one basic unit up the scale. This unit to the left of zero is more finely divided than are the remaining basic units. For the measurement of any distance, the right-hand point of the dividers is set on the basic unit mark that will result in the left-hand point falling somewhere on the more-finely-divided unit to the left of the zero. The distance measured is the sum of the basic units counted off to the right from the scale's zero point plus the fractional unit to the left from zero. In the illustration, the distance is 2½ units.

If the distance on the chart cannot be spanned with the dividers opened widely (about 60° is the maximum practical opening), set them at a convenient opening for a whole number of units on the graphic scale or latitude subdivisions, step this off the necessary number of times, then measure the odd remainder. The total distance is then the simple sum of the parts stepped off and measured separately, fig. 1930.

To mark off on the chart a desired distance, set the right point of the dividers on the nearest lower whole number of units, and the left point on the remaining fractional part of a unit measured leftward from zero on the scale. The dividers are now properly set for the specified distance at the scale of the chart being used and can be applied to the chart. If the distance is too great for one setting of the dividers, it may be stepped off in several increments.

Charts at a scale smaller than 1:80,000 will not have a graphic scale. In lieu thereof, distances are measured on the latitude scales at either side of the chart. Care should be taken to measure on these scales near the same latitude as the portion of the chart being used; in other words, move directly horizontally across the chart to either of its sides to use the scales.

With a little experience, dividers can be set and used

FIG. 1928 Dividers are used to measure distances on a chart. A—Friction at the pivot holds the arms to the desired opening. B—In this type of dividers, an adjustable center cross-arm maintains the separation between points and avoids accidental changes. C—Long-legged dividers enable the pilot to step off long runs on a chart, without "walking" them.

FIG. 1929 After the dividers have been set for the distance on the chart between the points concerned, they are moved to the graphic scale or latitude subdivisions at the edge of the chart. Distance is measured on these scales as described in the text.

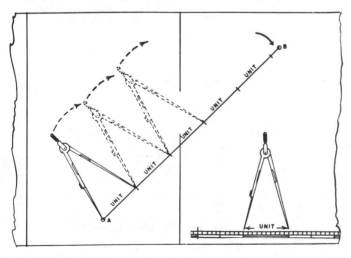

FIG. 1930 When a chart distance is too great to be measured with a single setting of the dividers, open the points to a convenient whole number of units. Step these along the chart for the required number of times and then measure any small left-over distance (arrow) in the usual manner. (Figs. 1908 and 1930 are based on DUTTON'S NAVIGATION AND PILOTING, copyright © 1957 and 1958 by U. S. Naval Institute, Annapolis, Maryland.)

With a little experience, dividers can be set and used with one hand. Making sure that the friction at the pivot is properly adjusted, practice this technique until it can be used with ease; such ability will add convenience and speed to your piloting work.

An instrument that looks much like a pair of dividers, except that a pencil lead or pen is substituted for one point, is called a *compass* (or *drawing compass* to distinguish it from a magnetic compass). This is used primarily for drawing arcs or circles.

Distance can also be measured across a chart with reduced, but generally acceptable, accuracy by using a *chart measurer*, fig. 1931. This device has a small wheel that is rolled along the chart; the wheel is internally geared to an indicating dial. Chart measurers will read distances directly in miles at various typical chart scales; separate models are available for charts using statute and nautical miles. They are particularly useful in measuring distances up rivers with many bends and changes of direction.

## TIME

Every pilot, no matter how small his craft, should have a dependable and reasonably accurate timepiece. This can be a clock, wrist watch, or pocket watch. Long-term accuracy is of secondary importance in piloting, but short-term errors, those accumulated over the length of a day or half-day, should be small. A knowledge of the time of day within a few minutes will usually be sufficient. A clock, if used, should be mounted where it is clearly visible from the helm-seat or plotting table. If two clocks are used, be sure that they show the same time.

*Elapsed* time is usually of greater interest than *absolute* time. A stop watch will often be handy although it cannot be classed as a necessary instrument of piloting. Most stop watches have a second hand that makes one revolution for each minute, but there are some that sweep completely around in 30 seconds, and even a few that have a 10-second period. Know for sure the type of stop watch that you are using.

383

FIG. 1931 If a *chart measurer* is rolled across a chart, between two points, an indicating dial will show the distance directly for typical chart scales. It is especially useful in measuring distances on waterways with many bends and curves.

FIG. 1933 Many small boats are fitted with a simple device that measures speed by the pressure built up in a probe as a result of the movement of the boat through the water. Accuracy is quite good, but it must be remembered that it is speed through the water that is measured, and not speed made good over the bottom.

## SPEED

Speed is a dimension that can be measured directly or calculated from knowledge of distance and time. Direct reading instruments are convenient, but they give only the relative speed through the water, and not the speed made good between two geographic points.

In years gone by, speed through the water was measured by use of a *chip log*, fig. 1932. More modern marine speedometers use the static pressure built up in a small tube by motion of the boat, fig. 1933, an impeller turned by the passing water, or a finger-like strut projecting below the bottom of the boat, fig. 1934. Many different models are available in a wide variety of speed ranges from those for sailboats to models reading high enough for fast speedboats.

Speed can be calculated from a knowledge of the distance covered and the elapsed time, to be discussed later in this chapter, or by the use of special calculating devices. These calculators are specialized adaptations of slide rules used for general mathematical calculations; they may be either linear or circular in form, figs. 1935a and b.

## DEPTH

This most important dimension of piloting can be measured manually or electronically. A hand *lead line*, fig. 1936, is simple, accurate, and not subject to breakdowns. It does have the disadvantages, however, of being awkward to use, inconvenient in bad weather, and capable of giving only one or two readings per minute; a lead line can be used only at quite slow speeds.

Many small craft today are equipped with an *electronic depth sounder*. These devices can clearly, accurately, and most conveniently provide measurements of the depth of water beneath the boat. Moreover, soundings are indicated many times each second, so frequently that they appear to be a smooth, continuous measurement of depth. For more information on these relatively inexpensive but most useful piloting aids, see Chapter 25, pages 499 to 501.

FIG. 1934 This speedometer, designed primarily for sailboats, is actuated by a strut or finger which projects below the bottom of the boat. A modern solid-state electronic instrument, it measures speed variations to 1/100 knot. An optional feature measures distance up to 999.9 nautical miles.

FIG. 1932 The old chip log, consisting of the log-chip, log-line, and log-glass. The log-chip is a thin piece of wood, weighted so that it will float vertically. The chip is thrown from the stern and the log-line is allowed to flow freely over the rail. The line is marked at intervals of 47 feet 3 inches, called "knots," and the number of knots that pass over the rail in the time that it takes the glass to empty is a direct measure of the speed.

FIG. 1934 a Unipas-300, a versatile 12-volt solid-state navigational instrument, measures depth on 25- or 100-foot scales; speed, on various scales from 0-2.5 or 0-25 knots, with sensitivity as fine as .01 knot; and distance logged, in steps of .001 mile. Plug-in modules provide for twin-engine synchronization, wind-speed measurement, detection of gasoline vapors, and a battery check. At anchor, it will even measure current velocity.

## MISCELLANEOUS PILOTING TOOLS

Among the most important of all piloting tools are the ordinary *pencils* and *erasers*. Pencils should be neither too hard nor too soft. If too hard, there will be a tendency to score into the chart paper; if too soft, smudging may result. A medium, or No. 2, pencil will often be found to be satisfactory, but personal preferences may cause some variation. Pencils should be kept well sharpened, and several should be handy to the piloting table.

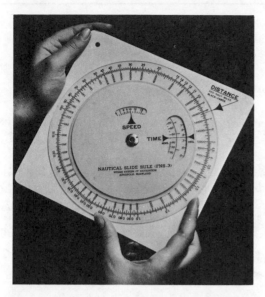

FIG. 1935a Speed need not be measured directly; it may be calculated from a knowledge of distance and time. A circular calculator as shown here will make all speed-time-distance computations quickly and accurately.

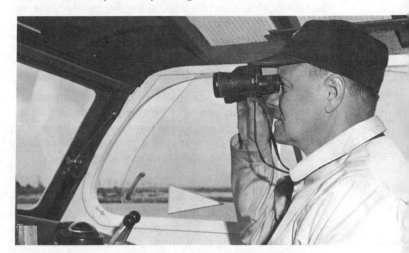

FIG. 1937 A good pair of binoculars is almost a necessity on a boat. The size most often recommended is designated "7 x 50." The eyepieces may be individually or centrally focused.

A soft eraser of the "Pink Pearl" type will be satisfactory for most erasures; an art gum eraser can be used for general chart cleaning.

**Binoculars.** A good pair of *binoculars* will be found essential for most piloting situations, fig. 1937. In selecting a pair of binoculars, it should be remembered that higher powers will result in greater magnification, bringing distant objects closer, but only at the cost of a more limited field of view. An adequate field of view is essential on small boats with their rapid and sometimes violent motion. Binoculars are designated by two figures, such as "6x30" or "10x50." The first figure indicates the power of magnification, the second is the diameter of the front lens in millimeters. This latter characteristic is important in night use. Most authorities recommend a 7x50 set of binoculars as best suited for marine use.

The binoculars may be individually focused (IF) for each eye, or centrally focused (CF) for both eyes, with a minor adjustment on one eyepiece to balance any difference between a person's two eyes. The choice between IF and CF glasses is a matter of personal preference.

Binoculars should be kept in their case when use is not imminent. When taken out, they should be carefully placed where they cannot be thrown from a table or ledge to the deck and damaged; protect your binoculars from any rough usage.

A boat should be equipped with several *flashlights* for emergency use. One of these should have a red lens or filter in order that it may be used to read charts and other printed matter at night without undue loss of night vision by a person who must both check the chart and act as helmsman or lookout.

FIG. 1935b This calculator enables the pilot to solve 18 different types of navigational problems—speed-time-distance, conversions and measurement, and includes special aids for the sailboatman, even a plotting board on the reverse side.

FIG. 1936 Depth can be measured manually with a marked weighted line—a lead line. Markings can be of the traditional type with strips of leather and rags, or with modern direct-reading plastic tags.

## MEASUREMENTS

In considering the measurement of various quantities in piloting, and the calculations in which they are used, some attention must first be given to standards of accuracy and precision. Statements of distance as 32 miles or 32.0 miles are not quite the same thing. The former merely says that to the best of observation and measurement the distance is not 31 nor 33 miles; the latter says that it is not 31.9 nor 32.1 miles. Note the difference in the degree of preciseness of these two statements of the same distance. Never write 32.0 for 32 unless your measurements are sufficiently precise to warrant such action.

### STANDARD LIMITS OF ACCURACY

The navigation of various sizes of vessels naturally involves different standards of precision or accuracy as befitting the different conditions encountered. The piloting of small craft does not permit so high a degree of accuracy as on large ships that offer a more stable platform.

### Direction

Direction is measured in small-craft navigation to the nearest whole degree. It is not reasonable to measure or calculate directions to a finer degree of precision when a boat is seldom steered with an accuracy closer than 2° or 3°.

### Distance

Distances are normally expressed to the nearest tenth of a mile. This degree of precision, roughly 200 yards, is reasonable in consideration of the size of the craft and other measurement standards.

### Time

Time is measured and calculated to the nearest minute. Fractions of a minute are rarely of any significance in routine piloting. In contests, however, time will be calculated to decimal fractions and used in terms of seconds.

### Speed

Speed is calculated to the nearest tenth of a knot or mile-per-hour. It is seldom measurable to such fine units, but a calculation to the nearest tenth is not inconsistent with the expressed standards of accuracy of distance and time. This same degree of precision is used in calculations of current velocity.

### Position

Geographic coordinates will be expressed to the nearest tenth of a minute of latitude and longitude, or to the nearest second, as determined by the scale of the chart. As explained in Chapter 18, latitude and longitude markings will be subdivided into minutes and seconds on the larger-scale charts (1:49,000 and larger) and in fractions of minutes on smaller-scale charts (1:50,000 and smaller).

### Depths and heights of tide

Tidal variations in the depth of water are normally tabulated to the nearest tenth of a foot, fig. 1938; calculations are carried out to the same degree of precision. It must be recognized, however, that modifications to tidal action resulting from winds and atmospheric pressure variations make such a degree of precision hardly warranted.

PORTLAND, MAINE, 1966

TIMES AND HEIGHTS OF HIGH AND LOW WATERS

| | OCTOBER | | | | | | NOVEMBER | | | | |
|---|---|---|---|---|---|---|---|---|---|---|---|
| DAY | TIME H.M. | HT. FT. | DAY | TIME H.M. | HT. FT. | DAY | TIME H.M. | HT. FT. | DAY | TIME H.M. | | |
| 1 SA | 0542 1148 1806 | 0.3 9.1 0.1 | 16 SU | 0600 1212 1836 | -1.0 10.9 -1.8 | 1 TU | 0024 0618 1230 1854 | 8.3 0.8 9.4 -0.2 | 16 W | 0118 0712 1330 2000 | | |
| 2 SU | 0012 0612 1224 1836 | 8.7 0.5 9.1 0.1 | 17 M | 0048 0648 1300 1924 | 9.8 -0.5 10.6 -1.3 | 2 W | 0100 0654 1306 1936 | 8.1 0.9 9.3 -0.1 | 17 TH | 0212 0806 1418 2048 | | |
| 3 M | 0048 0648 1254 1918 | 8.5 0.7 9.1 0.1 | 18 TU | 0142 0742 1354 2024 | 9.2 0.1 10.0 -0.8 | 3 TH | 0148 0736 1354 2024 | 7.9 1.1 9.2 0.0 | 18 F | 0306 0900 1512 | | |
| 4 TU | 0124 0724 1336 | 8.2 0.9 | 19 | 0236 | 8.6 | 4 | | | | | | |

FIG. 1938 **Heights of tides are tabulated in the tables of daily predictions to the nearest tenth of a foot. However, local conditions of wind and barometric pressure will often cause variations of greater magnitude.**

## Arithmetic Calculations and Rounding of Numbers

Any mathematical expression of a quantity will have a certain number of "significant figures." These can perhaps be better explained through the use of examples rather than by a complicated definition. The quantity "4" has one significant figure; 4.0 or 14 has two significant figures; 5.12, 43.8, or 609 each has three significant figures, etc.

A quantity ending in one or more zeros may have a varying number of significant figures as determined by the degree of precision with which it was measured. The number 150 may have either two or three significant figures; 2000 may have one, two, three, or four significant figures.

Consideration must be given to the number of significant figures occurring in the result of mathematical calculations, especially multiplication and division. Results should not have an excessive and unwarranted number of significant figures. For example, if 83 is multiplied by 64, the result is 5312. But note that this quantity has four significant figures whereas each of the input quantities had only two significant figures. A more meaningful statement of the result would be 5310 or even 5300.

The process of reducing the number of significant figures is called "rounding." In order to have uniform results, rules have been established for the rounding of numbers.

1. If the digit to be rounded off is "4" or less, it is dropped or changed to a zero.

8.23 can be rounded to 8.2

432 can be rounded to 430

2. If the digit to be rounded off is "6" or larger, the preceding digit is raised to the next higher value and the rounded digit is dropped or changed to a zero.

8.27 can be rounded to 8.3

439 can be rounded to 440

3. If the digit to be rounded off is a "5," the rounding is to the nearest *even* value.

8.25 is rounded to 8.2

435 is rounded to 440

This rule may seem somewhat arbitrary, but it is followed

for consistency in results; it has the advantage that when two such rounded figures are added together and divided by two for an average, the result will not present a new need for rounding.

4. Rounding can be applied to more than one final digit; but all such rounding must be done in *one* step. For example: 6148 is rounded to 6100 in a single action; do not round 6148 to 6150, and then round 6150 to 6200.

In many of the statements of accuracy requirements in the preceding section, the phrase "to the nearest ———" has been used. Rounding is used to reduce various quantities to such limitations. For example: if you calculated the distance traveled in 5 minutes at 13 knots, you would get 1.08 miles. However, distance is normally stated to the nearest tenth of a mile, and so the proper expression for distance run would be 1.1 mile.

**FIG. 1939 A Dead Reckoning plot should always be maintained when a boat is off-shore or cruising in large, open bodies of water.**
M. Rosenfeld.

# Dead Reckoning

When operating his boat offshore in large bodies of water, a pilot should have at all times at least a rough knowledge of his position on the chart. Basic to such knowledge is a technique of navigation known as *dead reckoning,* usually abbreviated to *DR.* This is the advancement of the boat's position on the chart from its last accurately determined location, using the course (or courses) steered and the speed (or speeds) through the water. No allowance is made for the effects of wind, waves, current, or steering errors.

## Terms used in dead reckoning

At this point, we will deal with only those terms related to *dead reckoning.* Later, when the influence of current is being considered, additional terms will be introduced and defined.

The *DR track* (or *DR track line)* is the path that the boat is expected to follow (no current) represented on the chart by a line drawn from the last known position using courses and speeds through the water. The path the boat actually travels may be different due to one or more offsetting influences, to be considered later.

Course, abbreviated as "C" (but not to be confused with "C" as used to designate a compass direction), is the direction of the DR track line. Courses are normally plotted in terms of the true direction stated as a three-digit figure.

*Heading* is the direction in which the boat is pointed at any given time. The term is usually used in connection with the direction in which a boat must be steered in order to make good a desired path, allowing for various offsetting influences. Headings are often stated in terms of magnetic or compass directions.

*Speed,* abbreviated as "S," is the rate of travel through the water. This is the DR track speed; it is used, together with elapsed time, to determine *DR positions* along the track line.

## The Basic Principles of Dead Reckoning

It is important that the pilot adhere to certain basic principles of dead reckoning.

**1. A DR track is always started from a known position.**

**2. Only true courses steered are used for determining a DR track.**

**3. Only the speed through the water is used for determining distance traveled and a DR position along the track.**

Although it may appear unusual to ignore the effects of a current that is known to exist, this is always done for reasons that will be established later.

## The importance of dead reckoning

A DR track should always be plotted when navigating in large, open bodies of water. It is the primary representation of the path of the boat, the base to which other factors, such as the effect of current, are applied. Dead reckoning can be considered to be the basic method of navigation to which corrections and adjustments from other sources of information are applied.

At the same time, it must be remembered that this DR track is rarely a representation of the boat's actual progress. If there were no steering errors, speed errors, or external influences, the DR track could be used as a means of determining the craft's position at any time desired, as well as the ETA (Estimated Time of Arrival) at a stated destination. Despite the fact that this will rarely, if ever, be the case, a DR plot is highly desirable at all times as a safety measure in the event of unexpected variations in current, and it is most useful in the event of a sudden fog or other loss of visibility.

### PLOTTING

Fundamental to the use of dead reckoning is the use of charts and plots of the craft's intended and actual positions.

**FIG. 1940a** The course is labeled above the line as shown here. The letter "C", followed by a space roughly equal to one character, and then the direction, in degrees True, as a three-digit number. Omit the degree symbol "°".

**FIG. 1940b** Speed is labeled below the course line. Write in the letter "S", a space, and the speed in knots or MPH as appropriate (but do not show the unit used).

## Basic requirements

The basic requirements of plotting are *accuracy, neatness,* and *completeness*. All measurements taken from the chart must be made carefully, all direct observations must be made as accurately as conditions on a small craft will permit, and all calculations should be made in full and in writing. If time permits, each of these actions should be repeated as a check; errors can be costly!

Neatness in plotting is essential to avoid confusion of information on the chart. The drawing in on charts of excess or overly-long lines, or the scribbling of extraneous notes, may obscure small bits of vital information.

In addition to being neat, information on a chart must be complete. Often a pilot will have need to refer back to information that he placed on the chart hours, or even days, ago. It could be dangerous if he should have to rely on memory to supply part of the details. In some cases, the piloting duties may be shared among several persons; here it is obvious that all plotted information must be fully identified.

The use of standardized procedures for identifying information on charts will ensure neatness, completeness, and understandability to any person who uses it.

## Labeling

Lines on charts should be drawn lightly and no longer than necessary. Be alert to the fact that a straightedge must be placed a slight distance off the desired position of the line to be drawn to allow for the thickness of the pencil point, no matter how finely it is sharpened.

The requirements of neatness and completeness combine to establish a need for *labeling*. To meet these requirements, certain rules and procedures have been established. The proper labeling of any plot is essential.

Immediately after any line is drawn on a chart, or any point is plotted, it should be labeled. The basic rules for labeling are:

**1. The label for any *line* is placed *along* that line.**

**2. The label for any *point* should *not* be along any line;** it should make such an angle with any line that its nature as the label of a point will be unmistakably clear.

The above basic rules are applied in the labeling of DR plots in the following manner:

1. The label indicating the direction of a DR track is placed *above* the track as a three-digit number preceded by the letter "C," fig. 1940a. Note that the degree symbol "°" is omitted.

2. The speed along the track is indicated by numerals placed *under* the track line, usually directly beneath the direction, fig. 1940b. Units, knots or MPH, are omitted.

3. A known position at the start of a DR track, a *Fix*, to be discussed later, is shown as a circle across the track line. It is labeled with the time, in four-digit notation (24-hour clock system) followed by "FIX," fig. 1941.

4. A DR position, calculated as a distance along the track at the set speed through the water, is shown as a circle on the track line; it is labeled with the time in four-digit notation plus the letters "DR"; see fig. 1942.

5. When planning and pre-plotting a run, speed, which is often affected by sea conditions, may not be known in advance. In this case, distance, D, may be labeled below the course line; as before, units are not shown.

Further applications of the basic rules of labeling will be given as additional piloting procedures and situations are introduced in subsequent chapters.

All lines on a chart should be erased when no longer needed to keep the chart clear. Erasures should be made as lightly as possible to avoid damage to the surface of the chart and its printed information.

**FIG. 1941** A known position of the boat is plotted as a dot with a small circle around it. If it is along a line, the dot will not show separately. Label the position with the time as a four-digit number in the 24-hour system plus the word "FIX".

**FIG. 1942** A dead reckoning position along a track is plotted as a circle across the track line and labeled with the time followed by "DR"

## D, T, AND S CALCULATIONS

As mentioned earlier, calculations involving distance (D), time (T), and speed (S) are often done by means of a small calculator. The use of such a device is perfectly acceptable, but the good pilot can accurately and quickly make his calculations without one, using only a simple set of equations and ordinary arithmetic. An ability to make arithmetical computations is necessary as a calculating device may not always be available.

The three basic equations are:

$$D = ST \qquad S = \frac{D}{T} \qquad T = \frac{D}{S}$$

Where D is distance in miles, T is time in *hours*, and S is speed in knots or miles per hour as determined by the type of mile being used. Note carefully that T is in hours in these basic equations. To use time in *minutes*, as is more normally the case, the equations are modified to read:

$$D = \frac{ST}{60} \qquad S = \frac{60D}{T} \qquad T = \frac{60D}{S}$$

Examples of the use of these practical equations may serve to make them clearer:

1. You are cruising at 14 knots; how far will you travel in 40 minutes?

$$D = \frac{ST}{60} \qquad D = \frac{14 \times 40}{60} = 9.3 \text{ miles}$$

Note that the calculated answer of 9.33 is rounded to

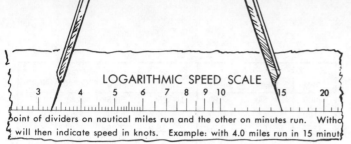

LOGARITHMIC SPEED SCALE

3   4   5   6   7  8  9 10      15      20

point of dividers on nautical miles run and the other on minutes run. Witho
will then indicate speed in knots.  Example: with 4.0 miles run in 15 minut

FIG. 1943a  On some charts, a logarithmic speed scale may be used to graphically determine speed. First, set one point of your dividers on the scale division indicating the miles traveled, and the other on the number corresponding to the time in minutes.

HMIC SPEED SCALE

7  8  9 10      15      20      25      30      40      50    60

es run and the other on minutes run.  Without changing divider spread, place
ts.  Example: with 4.0 miles run in 15 minutes, the speed is 16.0 knots.

FIG. 1943b  With the dividers maintaining the same spread, transfer them so that the right point is on the "60" of the scale (right end). The left point will indicate the speed in knots or MPH, as determined by the type of mile used.

the nearest tenth according to the rule for the degree of accuracy to be used in stating distance.

2. On one of the Great Lakes, it took you 40 minutes to travel 11 miles; what is your speed?

$$S = \frac{60D}{T} \qquad S = \frac{60 \times 11}{40} = 16.5 \text{ MPH}$$

3. You have $9\frac{1}{2}$ miles to go to reach your destination, your cruising speed is 11 knots; how long will it take you to get there?

$$T = \frac{60D}{S} \qquad T = \frac{60 \times 9.5}{11} = 52 \text{ minutes}$$

Note again the rounding of results; the calculated answer of 51.8 minutes would be used as 52 minutes, except in contests where it would probably be used as 51 minutes 48 seconds.

The three practical equations of distance, time, and speed should be carefully memorized. Practice using them until you become thoroughly familiar with them and can obtain your answers to typical problems quickly and accurately.

## Use of logarithmic scale on charts

Charts of the Coast and Geodetic Survey at scales of 1:40,000 and larger will have printed on them a *logarithmic speed scale. To find speed,* place one point of your dividers on the mark on the scale indicating the distance in nautical miles, and the other point on the number corresponding to the time in minutes, fig. 1943a. Without changing the spread between the divider arms, place the right point on the "60" at the right end of the scale; the left point will then indicate on the scale the speed in knots, see fig. 1943b.

This same logarithmic scale can also be used *to determine the time* required to cover a given distance at a specified speed (for situations not exceeding one hour). Set the two divider points on the scale marks representing speed in knots and distance in miles. Move the dividers, without changing the spread, until the right point is at "60" on the scale; the other point will indicate the time in minutes.

Likewise, *distance can be determined* from this logarithmic scale using knowledge of time and speed. Set the right point of the dividers on "60" and the left point at the mark on the scale corresponding to the speed in knots. Then, without changing the spread, move the right point to the mark on the scale representing the time in minutes; the left point will now indicate the distance in nautical miles.

CS charts will have instructions for determining speed printed beneath the logarithmic scale, but not the procedures for determining distance or time. In all cases, you must know two of the three quantities in order to determine the other.

## Use of S-D-T calculators

It is not possible here to give detailed instructions for the operation of all models of speed-distance-time calculators. In general, such devices will have two or more scales, each logarithmically subdivided. The calculator will be set using two of the factors and the answer, the third factor, will be read off at an index mark.

If you have a calculator for S-D-T problems, read the instructions carefully and practice with it sufficiently, using simple, self-evident problems, to be sure of obtaining reliable results, even under the stress of difficult situations or emergencies.

## SPEED CURVES

Although some boats may be equipped with marine speedometers, the more-often used method of determination of speed is through the use of engine speed as measured by the *tachometer* in revolutions per minute (RPM). A *speed curve* is prepared as a plot on cross-section (graph) paper of the boat's speed in knots or MPH for various engine speeds in RPM.

### Factors affecting speed curves

The speed that a boat will achieve for a specified engine setting may be affected by several factors. The extent of each effect will vary with the size of the boat, type of hull, and other characteristics.

*Load* is a primary factor influencing a boat's speed. The number of persons aboard, the amount of fuel and water in the tanks, and the amount and location of other weights on board will affect the depth to which the hull sinks in the water and the angular trim. Both displacement and trim may be expected to have an effect on speed.

Another major factor affecting speed is the *underwater hull condition.* Fouling growth, such as barnacles or moss, increases the drag, the resistance to movement through the water, and slows the speed of the boat at any given engine RPM.

Whenever preparing speed data on a boat, the loading and underwater hull conditions at the time of the trials should be noted with the figures for RPM and speed. If a speed curve is made at the start of a boating season when the bottom is clean, it should be checked later on in the season if the boat is used in waters where fouling is a problem. A new speed curve may be required, or it may be possible to determine what small corrections can be applied to get a more accurate measure of speed. A good skipper also knows what speed differences he may expect from full tanks to half to nearly empty; the differences can be surprising in many boats.

### Obtaining speed curves

Speed curves are obtained by making repeated runs over a known distance using different throttle settings and timing each run very accurately. Any reasonable distance can be used. Ordinarily, it should not be less than a half-mile in order that small timing errors will not excessively influence the results; it need not be more than a mile, to avoid excessive time and fuel requirements for the trials.

The run need not be an even half-mile or mile if the distance is accurately known. Do not depend upon floating aids to navigation — they may be slightly off-station, and, in any event, they have some scope on their anchor chains and will swing about under the effects of wind and current. Many areas will have *measured miles* (or half-miles), fig. 1944. These are accurately surveyed distances with each end marked by ranges. Use these courses whenever possible; they can be depended upon for accuracy and calculations are made easier by the even-mile distance. But do not let the absence of such a measured mile in your local waters keep you from having a speed curve for your boat. Use accurately charted wharves, fixed aids to navigation, points of land, etc.

In most speed trials, it will be necessary to run the known distance twice, once in each direction, in order to allow for the effects of current. Even in waters not affected by currents, it is advisable to make round-trip runs for each throttle setting to allow for wind effects.

For each *one-way* run, measure the time required; steer the boat carefully so that the most direct, the shortest run is made. Compute the speed for each run by the equations previously used. If a measured mile is used for the speed trials, speeds can be found easily by use of the table on page 622. If the measured distance is an exact half-mile, the tabulated speeds must be divided by two. Then average the *speeds* of each run of a pair at a given RPM to determine the true speed of the boat through the water. The strength of the current is one-half the difference between the speed in the two directions of any pair of runs. *Caution:* do *not* average together the *times* of a pair of runs to get a single time for use in the calculations; this will *not* give the correct value for speed through the water.

If time is measured with a regular clock or watch, be

careful in making the subtractions to get elapsed time. Remember that there are 60 seconds in each minute, not 100, and likewise 60 minutes in one hour. Most people are so used to decimal calculations that foolish errors are sometimes made when "borrowing" in the subtraction of clock times.

If one is willing to use a slightly more complex equation, the boat's speed through the water (or the strength of the current) can be found from a single calculation using the times of the two runs of each pair.

$$S = \frac{60D(Tu + Td)}{2TuTd} \qquad C = \frac{60D(Tu - Td)}{2TuTd}$$

Where S is speed through the water in knots or MPH
C is current in knots or MPH
Tu is time upstream, in minutes
Td is time downstream, in minutes
D is distance, in nautical or statute miles

In the preparation of a speed curve for a boat, sufficient pairs of runs should be made to provide points for a plot of speed versus RPM; some six or eight points will usually be enough for a satisfactory curve. With some types of hulls, there will be a break in the curve at a critical speed when the hull changes from displacement action to semi-planing action. At this portion of the curve, additional, more closely-spaced measurements may be required. For this reason, it is often a good idea to calculate speeds during runs and make a rough plot as you go along.

| RPM | N-S Time | N-S Speed | S-N Time | S-N Speed | Average Speed | Current |
|---|---|---|---|---|---|---|
| 900 | 7m 54s | 7.60 | 11m 25s | 5.26 | 6.43 | 1.17 |
| 1100 | 6 53 | 8.72 | 9 14.2 | 6.50 | 7.61 | 1.11 |
| 1300 | 6 08.8 | 9.76 | 7 36.8 | 7.88 | 8.82 | .94 |
| 1500 | 5 35.8 | 10.72 | 6 40.4 | 9.00 | 9.86 | .86 |
| 1700 | 5 10.8 | 11.59 | 5 54.2 | 10.17 | 10.88 | .71 |
| 1900 | 4 38.0 | 12.96 | 5 06.4 | 11.76 | 12.36 | .60 |
| 2150 | 3 48.6 | 15.75 | 4 05.6 | 14.73 | 15.24 | .51 |

FIG. 1945 Tabulated results of speed trials made for "Trident." Note that runs were made in each direction to account for the effect of current. Entries were made in the log as to fuel and water loads aboard and condition of the bottom of the hull.

FIG. 1944 Many boating areas have *measured mile* courses established for making accurate speed trials. These will be shown on the chart of the area.

FIG. 1946 The speed curve for "Trident" plotted from the data of fig. 1945. This curve is truly accurate only for load and underwater hull conditions similar to those on the day of the trials.

It may also be found desirable to calculate the strength of the current for each pair of runs. It will probably be noted that the current values will vary during the speed trials, but such variations should be small and in a consistent direction, either steadily increasing or decreasing, or going through a slack period. The best results will normally be obtained if the trials are run at a time of minimum current.

## Example of a Speed Curve

A set of speed trials was run for the motor yacht "Trident" over the measured mile off Kent Island in Chesapeake Bay, fig. 1944. This is an excellent course as it is marked both by buoys offshore and by ranges on land. The presence of the buoys aids in steering a straight run from one end of the course to the other; the ranges are used for greater accuracy in timing.

On this particular day, it was not convenient to wait for slack water, but a time was selected that would result in something less than maximum ebbing current. A table was set up in the log, and runs were made in each direction at speeds of normal interest from 900 RPM to 2150 RPM which was maximum for the 6-71 diesels.

The results of the runs are shown in fig. 1945. An entry was also made in the log that these trials were made with fuel tanks 0.35 full, the water tanks approximately 1/3 full, and a clean bottom. The column of the table marked "Current" is not necessary, but it serves as a "flag" to quickly expose any inconsistent data. Note that on these trials the current is decreasing at a reasonably consistent rate.

After the runs had been completed, a plot was made on cross-section paper of the boat's speed as a function of engine RPM. This resulted in the speed curve shown as fig. 1946.

## DEAD RECKONING PLOTS

With knowledge of dead reckoning terms and principles, the rules for labeling points and lines, and the procedures for making calculations involving distance, time, and speed, it is possible to consider now the use of DR plots.

There are several specific rules for making and using DR plots.

1. A DR plot should be made when leaving a known position, fig. 1947.

2. A DR position should be shown whenever a change is made in course, fig. 1948a, or in speed, fig. 1948b.

3. A DR position should be plotted each hour on the hour, fig. 1949.

4. A new DR track should be started each time the boat's position is fixed. The old DR position for the same time as the fix should also be shown at the end of the old DR track, see fig. 1950.

FIG. 1948b  If a variation in speed is made without a change in direction, a DR position is plotted on the track and new labels of course and speed are entered following it.

FIG. 1949  A DR position should be plotted each hour on the hour along the track even though there is no change in course or speed. These plots will keep the pilot informed of his progress and are useful in sudden emergencies.

FIG. 1947  A dead reckoning plot is started when leaving a known position. The time of that position is plotted as a Fix; course and speed are labeled along the DR track.

FIG. 1948a  Whenever a change in course is made, a DR position is plotted for that time; the new course and speed are labeled along the new track.

FIG. 1950  Whenever the boat's position is fixed, such as by passage close by a buoy as shown here, a DR position is plotted for that time, calculated from speed and distance information. The fix is also plotted and a new DR track is started. The difference between the DR position and the Fix for the same time indicates the effect of offsetting influences such as current.

# CHAPTER 20

*Tides and currents are of much interest and concern to the skipper who does his boating on coastal waters. Time invested in mastering their theory and practice will pay dividends in the form of increased safety, convenience, and economy. And too, there is the satisfaction of developing an ability to deal with natural phenomena that you can't change, but which can often be used to your advantage.*

# PILOTING
# —Tides
# and
# Currents

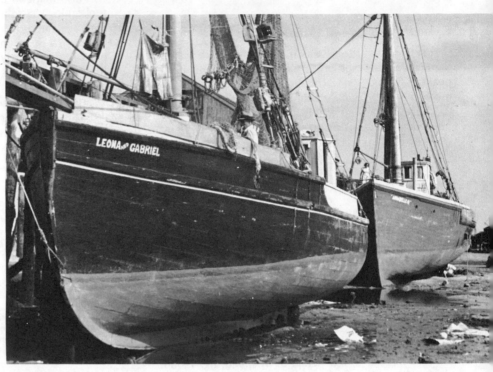

FIG. 2001 Boatmen in coastal regions must learn to cope with tidal conditions. The range from high water to low may be only inches, or it may be many feet.

## Dead Reckoning and Currents

In the preceding chapter, it was noted that a dead reckoning plot is based upon the course steered and the boat's speed through the water. Even though offsetting factors were known to exist, they were *not* included in a DR plot. Thus, it can readily be seen that while a DR plot is a basic representation of a boat's motion, it fails to account for all existing circumstances.

Offsetting influences that will make the boat's actual path diverge from the DR track include current, leeway from wind and waves, and steering errors. Of these, the one that can be most easily and accurately handled is current. The extent of its effect will vary widely with the relative values of current strength and boat speed through the water, but often the influence of current can be a major factor in piloting.

## Tides vs. Current

Perhaps at this point we should pause to make clear the proper meaning and use of several terms that are often loosely and incorrectly used. *Tide* is the rise and fall of the ocean level as a result of changes in the gravitational attraction between the earth, moon, and sun. It is a *vertical* motion only. *Current* is a *horizontal* motion of water from any cause. *Tidal current* is the flow of water from one point to another that results from a difference in tidal heights at those points. How often have you heard others say (or perhaps even said it yourself) that "The tide is certainly running strongly today!" This is not correct, for tides may be high or low, but they do not "run." Obviously, the correct expression would have been "The (tidal) current is certainly strong today." Remember—tide is vertical change; current is horizontal flow.

## Tides

As tidal action is a primary cause of currents, let us consider it first, and save our consideration of currents for later. Actually, tides in themselves are important factors in the safe navigation of watercraft as will be discussed in the following pages.

Tides originate in the open oceans and seas, but are only noticeable and significant close to shore. The effect of tides will be observed along coastal beaches, in bays and sounds, and up rivers generally as far as the first rapids,

waterfall, or dam. Curiously, the effect of tides may be more noticeable a hundred miles up a river than it is at the river's mouth. Coastal regions in which the water levels are subject to tidal action are often referred to as "tidewater" areas.

### Definition of Terms

In addition to the basic definition of tide as given above, certain other terms used in connection with tidal action must be defined. The *height of tide* at any specified time is the vertical measurement between the surface of the water and the *tidal datum* or reference plane. Do not confuse "height of tide" with "depth of water." The latter is the total distance from the surface to the bottom. The tidal datum for an area is selected so that the heights of tide are normally positive values, but the height can at times be a small negative number when the water level falls below the datum.

*High water,* or *high tide,* is the highest level reached by an ascending tide. Correspondingly, *low water,* or *low tide,* is the lowest level reached by a descending tide, fig. 2003. The difference between high and low waters is termed the *range* of the tide.

The change in tidal level does not occur at a uniform rate; starting from, say, low water, the level builds up slowly, then at an increasing rate which in turn tapers off as high water is reached. The decrease in tidal stage from high water to low follows a corresponding pattern of a slow buildup to a maximum rate roughly midway between stages followed by a decreasing rate. At both high and low tides, there will be periods of relatively no change in level; these are termed *stand. Mean sea level* is the average level of the open ocean and corresponds closely to mid-tide levels offshore.

## TIDAL THEORY

Tidal action can be studied both from a theoretical view and in terms of actual conditions. It is perhaps best approached from an initial consideration of basic principles, with practical departures from theory being noted afterwards. As briefly mentioned earlier, tidal theory is based on the gravitational attraction between the earth on one hand, and the moon and sun on the other. In order to simplify the presentation of these effects, they will be described separately, although, of course, in actual practice, they both act simultaneously. Although the sun has a lesser effect on tides than the moon, its gravitational

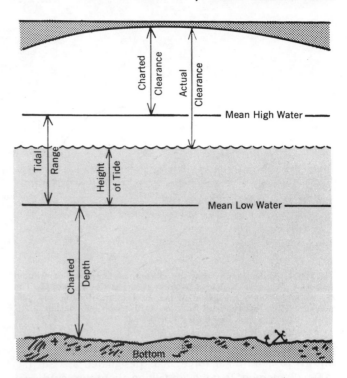

**FIG. 2003** This diagram illustrates the relationship between some of the terms used to describe tidal conditions. Terms are defined in the text. Mean lower low water may be substituted for mean low water in some areas.

action is easier to visualize, and so it will be considered first.

### Earth-Sun Effects

Each year the earth and the sun revolve around a common point located close to the center of the sun; for all practical considerations, the earth can be thought of as revolving around the sun. Just as a stone tied to the end of a string tends to sail off when a young boy whirls it about

**FIG. 2002** The rise and fall of ocean tidal levels will cause a flow first into and then out of inland bodies of water such as bays, sounds, and the lower reaches of rivers. These tidal currents may have important effects on the piloting of boats in such waters. (from Kodachrome by Wm. H. Koelbel)

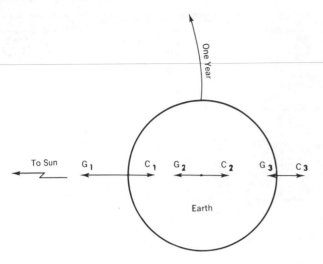

FIG. 2004 Tides result from the differences between centrifugal forces—$C_1$, $C_2$, and $C_3$—and gravitational forces—$G_1$, $G_2$, and $G_3$. The forces shown here are those of the interaction of earth and sun; corresponding forces result from the earth-moon relationship.

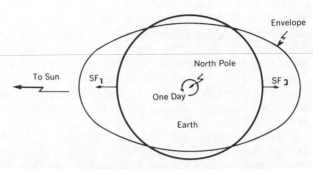

FIG. 2005 Inequalities of gravitational and centrifugal forces result in high tides on opposite sides of the earth at the same time, on the side away from the sun as well as the side toward it. Low tides will occur midway between these areas.

his head, so the earth tends to fly off into space. This is known as centrifugal force; it is designated as C in fig. 2004. (Remember that we are talking about the centrifugal force related to the sun-earth system, and not that of the day-night spinning of the earth on its axis.)

The earth is kept from flying off into space by the gravitational attraction of the sun, designated G in fig. 2004. Now, since the earth does not fly off into space, nor does it fall into the sun, $C_2$ and $G_2$ (at the center of the earth) must be equal.

Keeping mathematics at a minimum, we need only note that gravitational attraction varies inversely with the square of the distance between the objects, and centrifugal force varies directly with the radius of rotation—the distance from the sun in this case. Thus $G_1$ is greater than $G_2$ and $G_3$ is less. Likewise, $C_1$ is less than $C_2$ or $C_3$. With $G_2$ equal to $C_2$, there will be unbalanced forces at both sides—$G_1$ being greater than $C_1$ and $C_3$ being greater than $G_3$. These differences called $SF_1$ and $SF_3$ in fig. 2005, are the vertical tidal forces. Note that $SF_1$ points toward the sun and $SF_3$ away, and that $SF_1$ is essentially equal to $SF_3$.

Continuing our theoretical analysis, we can think of the earth as being a smooth sphere uniformly covered with water (no land areas). The two forces $SF_1$ and $SF_3$ will cause a flow of water toward their locations building up a bulge on either side of the earth in line with the earth-sun line; this is marked as "envelope" in fig. 2005. These points would accordingly experience a rising of the water level, a high tide. Between those two points, around the earth, the water would be drawn away, and such places would have a low tide.

As the earth turns on its axis, once in twenty-four hours, inside this envelope of water, each point on the earth's surface would then have two high and two low tides each day, following each other in alternate and regular succession.

## Earth-Moon Effects

The moon is commonly thought of as revolving about the earth; actually, the two bodies revolve around a common point on a monthly cycle. This point is located about 2900 miles from the center of the earth toward the moon (about 1100 miles deep inside the earth). By just the same logic as applied to the earth-sun system, a second set of tidal forces is developed. In explaining tidal forces in the earth-moon system, however, one must always remember to think of both the earth and the moon as revolving around a common point, rather than the moon merely going around the earth. It is only by the former concept that we can get the necessary centrifugal forces for tides on the earth.

## Spring and Neap Tides

Let us now combine the earth-sun and earth-moon systems. Due to the fact that the moon is much closer to the earth (about 238,860 miles away), its tidal forces are approximately $2\frac{1}{2}$ times greater than those of the sun (roughly 92,900,000 miles distant). The result is that the observed tide usually "follows the moon," but the action is somewhat modified by the sun's relative position. The two high and two low waters each day occur about 50 minutes later

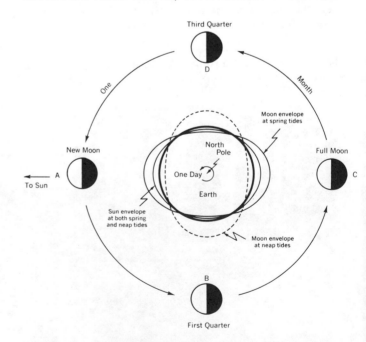

FIG. 2006 At new and full moon, combined gravitational "pull" of sun and moon acts to produce maximum effect; at these times, tidal ranges are greatest. At first and third quarters of the moon, the two gravitational forces partially offset each other and the net effect is at a minimum; tidal ranges are then least.

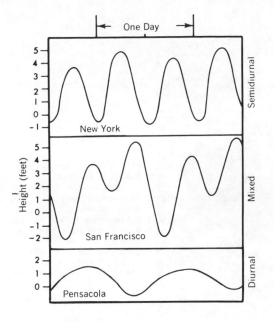

FIG. 2007 **Characteristics of the daily cycle of tides vary widely at different places. Shown here are three basic types—from the top, semi-diurnal, mixed, and diurnal.**

than the corresponding tides of the previous day.

In the course of any one month, the three bodies line up sun-moon-earth (position A in fig. 2006) and sun-earth-moon (position C). These are the times of the new and full moon, respectively. In both cases, the sun's effect (or "envelope") lines up with and reinforces the moon's effect, tending to result in greater-than-average tidal ranges (about 20%), called *spring tides;* note carefully that this name has nothing to do with the season of the year.

At positions B and D in fig. 2006, when the moon is at its first and third quarters, the tidal "bulge" due to the sun is at right angles to that caused by the moon (they are said to be "in *quadrature*"). The two tidal effects are in conflict and partially cancel each other, resulting in smaller-than-average ranges (again about 20%); these are *neap tides.*

It should also be noted that the tidal range of any given point varies from month to month, and from year to year. The monthly variation is due to the fact that the earth is not at the center of the moon's orbit. When the moon is closest to the earth, the lunar influence is at its maximum; tides at these times will have the greatest ranges. Conversely, when the moon is farthest from the earth, its effect, and tidal ranges, are the least.

In a similar manner, the yearly variations in the daily ranges of the tides are caused by the changing gravitational effects of the sun as that body's distance from the earth becomes greater or less.

## ACTUAL TIDES

We have been considering the tidal forces and their envelope rather than the actual tide as we observe it in the sea. Why do they differ? The following are the main reasons:

1. Great masses of land, the continents, irregularly shaped and irregularly placed, act to interrupt, restrict, and reflect tidal movements.

2. Water, although generally appearing to flow freely, is actually a somewhat viscous substance and therefore

lags in its response to tidal forces.

3. Friction is present as the ocean waters "rub" against the ocean bottom.

4. The depth to the bottom of the sea, varying widely, influences the speed of the tidal motion horizontally.

5. The depths of the ocean areas and the restrictions of the continents often result in "basins" which have their own way of responding to tidal forces.

Although these reasons account for great differences between theoretical tidal forces and actual observed tides, there nevertheless remain definite, constant relationships between the two at any particular location. By observing the tide, and relating these observations with the movements of the sun, moon, and earth, these constant relationships can be determined. With this information, tides can be predicted for any future date at a given place.

### Types of Tides

A tide which each day has two high waters approximately equal in height, and two low waters also about equal, is known as a *semidiurnal* type. This is the most common tide, and, in the United States, occurs along the east coast (fig. 2007, New York).

In a monthly cycle, the moon moves north and south of the Equator. Fig. 2008 illustrates the importance of this action to tides. Point A is under a bulge in the envelope. One half-day later, at point B, it is again under the bulge but the height is not as large as at A. This situation, combined with coastal characteristics, tends to give rise to a "twice daily" tide with unequal high and/or low waters in some areas. This is known as the *mixed* type of tide; see fig. 2007, San Francisco. The term "low water" may be modified to indicate the more pronounced of the two lows. This tidal stage is termed *lower low water* and is averaged to determine the *mean lower low water* (MLLW); this is used as the tidal datum in many areas subject to mixed tides. Likewise, the more significant of the higher tides is termed *higher high water.*

Now consider point C in fig. 2008. At this place, it is still under the bulge of the envelope. One half-day later, at point D, however, it is above the low part. Hence, the tidal forces tend to cause only one high and one low water each day (actually each 24 hours and 50 minutes approximately). This is the *diurnal* type, typified by Pensacola in fig. 2007.

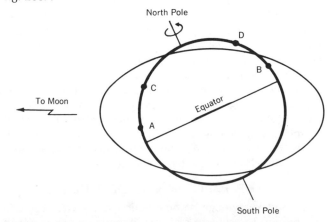

FIG. 2008 **The moon travels north and south of the earth's equatorial plane. This change results in variations in the daily tidal cycle at any given location. Similar, but lesser, effects result from changes in the sun's position with respect to the earth.**

**FIG. 2009** Watch out for falling tides! A prudent skipper knows not only the depth of water when he anchors, but also how it is going to change over the next 12 hours or so. In this river in Nova Scotia, the river bed will be exposed for about five hours; in the sixth hour the flood will rush in as a "bore" and rise 20 feet.
(from Kodachrome by Wm. H. Koelbel)

Whenever the moon is farthest north (as in fig. 2008) or south, there will be a tendency to have the diurnal or mixed type. When the moon lies over the Equator, we tend to have the semidiurnal type. These are *Equatorial tides* and the tendency toward producing inequality is then at a minimum.

The above theoretical considerations are, however, modified by many practical factors such as the general configuration of the coastline.

## Special Tidal Situations

Peculiarities in the tide can be found almost everywhere, but none compare with those in the Bay of Fundy. Twice each day, the waters surge in and out of the Bay, producing, at Burntcoat Head, the highest tidal range in the world —a typical rise and fall of nearly 44 feet. At springs, according to Sailing Directions for Nova Scotia, it rises 51½ feet —on perigee springs, 53 feet.

This great range is often attributed to the funnel-like shape of the Bay, but this is not the main cause. Just as the water in a wash basin will slosh when you move your hand back and forth in just the right period of time, depending upon the depth of water and the shape of the basin, so the tide will attempt to oscillate water in bays in cycles of 12 hours and 25 minutes. It would be a coincidence indeed if a bay were of such a shape and depth as to have a complete oscillation with a period of exactly 12 hours and 25 minutes. A bay, however, can easily have a part of such an oscillation; such is the case in the Bay of Fundy.

A further factor in creating the large tidal ranges in the Bay of Fundy is the circumstance that they are controlled by the Gulf of Maine tides which, in turn, are controlled by the open ocean tides. The relationships between these tides are such as to exaggerate their ranges.

## THE IMPORTANCE OF TIDES

A good knowledge of tidal action is essential for safe navigation. The skipper of a boat of any size will be faced many times with the need for knowledge of the time of high water and low water, and their probable heights. He may be faced with the desirability or necessity of crossing some shoal area, passable at certain tidal stages but not at others. He may be about to anchor, and the scope to pay out will be affected by the tide's range. He may be going to make fast to a pier or wharf in a strange harbor and will have need of tidal information if he is to adjust his lines properly for overnight.

## Tidal effects on vertical clearances

The rise and fall of the tide will change the vertical clearance under fixed structures such as bridges or overhead power cables. These clearances are stated on charts and in Coast Pilots as heights measured from a datum which is *not* the same plane as used for depths and tidal predictions. The datum for heights is normally mean high water (MHW).

It will thus be necessary to determine the height of MHW above the tidal datum. On the East Coast, where the tidal datum is mean low water (MLW), the plane of mean high water is above MLW by the "mean range" which is listed in Table 2 of the Tide Tables, fig. 2010, for each reference and subordinate station.

On the West Coast, or in any area where the tidal datum is mean lower low water (MLLW), slightly more complicated calculations are required. Here, MHW is above the tidal datum by an amount equal to the sum of the "mean tide level" plus one-half of the "mean range"; both of these values appear in Table 2 for the West Coast.

If the tide level at any given moment is below MHW, the vertical clearance under a bridge or other fixed structure is then greater than the figures shown on the chart; but if the tide height is *above* the level of MHW, then the clearance is *less*. Calculate the vertical clearance in advance if you anticipate a tight situation, but *also* observe the clearance gauges usually found at bridges. Clearances will normally be greater than the charted MHW values, but will occasionally be less.

## SOURCES OF TIDAL INFORMATION

The basic source of information on the time of high and low water, and their heights above (or below) the datum, is the *Tide Tables* published by the U.S. Coast and

Geodetic Survey, fig. 2010. Any predictions appearing in newspapers, or broadcast over radio and TV stations, will have been extracted from these tables. The cover jackets of charts in the small-craft series will also include excerpts from the Tide Tables as applicable to the area covered by the chart, fig. 2011.

Not to be overlooked is the possibility of "local knowledge." Never be hesitant to ask experienced local watermen when you are in unfamiliar waters and need information of any kind. The best of tables prepared by electronic computers sometimes cannot compare with a knowledge of what to expect that is based on years of local experience.

## TIDE TABLES

The Coast and Geodetic Survey Tide Tables are of great value in determining the height of water at any place at a given time. These are calculated in advance and published annually. There are four volumes, one of which covers the East Coast of North and South America, and another the West Coast of these continents.

These Tables can usually be bought at any authorized sales agent for C&GS charts. The price for each volume is $2.00.

The Tide Tables give the predicted times and heights of high and low water for each day of the year at a number of important points known as *reference stations*. Portland, Boston, Newport, and Sandy Hook are examples of points for which detailed information is given in the East Coast Tables. Reference stations in the West Coast Tables include

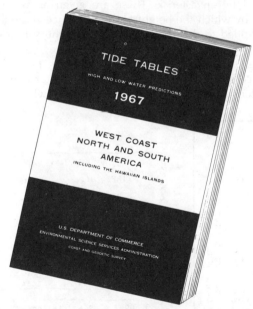

**FIG. 2010  The Coast and Geodetic Survey uses modern electronic computing equipment to prepare advanced predictions of tidal levels at many points. These are published in the annual Tide Tables.**

San Diego, the Golden Gate at San Francisco, and Aberdeen, Washington.

Additional data are tabulated showing the difference in times and heights between these reference stations and thousands of other points termed *subordinate stations*. From these tables, the tide at virtually any point of significance along the coasts can easily be computed. The West Coast Tide Tables contain predictions for reference sta-

tions and differences for about 1100 subordinate stations in North and South America.

The heights given in Tide Tables must, of course, be reckoned from some plane of reference, or tidal datum. From the discussion earlier in this chapter, it is evident that there are a number of different planes to which the heights might be referred. In actual practice, the predictions in the Tables are based on the same datum as that used in making the charts for any given locality. The datum used for the Atlantic Coast is *mean low water* (MLW), which is the average of *all* low-water levels. On the Pacific Coast, where the mixed type of tide is more prevalent, it is the average of the lower of the two low waters occurring each day (MLLW).

All of the factors that can be determined in advance are taken into account in tide predictions, but in the use of the tables, it must be remembered that certain other factors which have a pronounced influence on the height of tides, cannot be forecast months or years in advance. Such influences include barometric pressure and wind. In many areas, the effect of a prolonged gale of wind from a certain quarter is sometimes sufficient to offset all other factors. Tidal rivers may be affected by changes in the volume of water flowing down from the watershed. Normal seasonal variations of flow are allowed for in the predictions, but unexpected prolonged wet or dry spells may result in significant changes to the predictions of tidal heights. Intense rainfall upriver may result in changes to both the heights and times of tides; these effects may not appear downstream for several days.

Caution should therefore be exercised whenever using the Tide Tables, especially since low waters may at times go considerably lower than the level predicted.

### Explanation of the Tables

Table 1 of the Tide Tables, fig. 2012, gives the predicted times and heights of high and low water at the main reference stations and is practically self-explanatory. Where no sign is given before the predicted height, the quantity is positive and is to be added to the depths as given on the chart. When the value is preceded by a minus (−) sign, the "heights" are to be *subtracted* from charted depths.

Time is given in the four-digit system from 0001 to 2400 (see page 376). In many areas, caution must be exercised regarding *daylight time.* The Tide Tables are published in terms of local *standard* time, and a correction must be applied if you are in a DT locality.

While there are normally two high and two low tides each date, they are, on an average, nearly an hour later each succeeding day. Consequently, there will be instances when a high or low tide may skip a calendar day, as indicated by a blank space in the Tide Tables, fig. 2013. If it is a high tide, for example, that has been skipped, it will be noted that the previous corresponding high occurred late in the foregoing day, and the next one early in the following day; see the sequence for the late evening high tides of 1, 2, and 3 February in fig. 2013.

It may also be noted from a review of the Tide Tables that at some places there will be only one high and one low tide on some days, with the usual four tides on other days. This is not a diurnal tide situation, where a single high and low would occur every day. The condition considered here arises when the configuration of the land and the periods between successive tides are such that one tide is reflected back from the shore and alters the effect of the succeeding tide.

Sometimes the diurnal inequality (the difference in the height of the two high or two low waters of a day) is so increased as to cause only one low water each day. These tides are not unusual in the tropics and consequently are called *tropic tides.*

Table 2, Tidal Differences and Constants, fig. 2014, gives the information necessary to find the time and height of tide for thousands of subordinate stations by the application of simple corrections to the data given for the main reference stations. The name of the applicable reference station in each case is given in bold-face type at the head of the particular section in which the subordinate station is listed. The following information is given in separate columns of Table 2:

a. Latitude and longitude of the subordinate station.

b. Differences in time and height of high (and low) waters at the subordinate station and its designated reference station.

c. Mean and spring (or diurnal) tidal ranges.

d. Mean tide level.

Note carefully that the existence of a "minus tide" means that the actual depths of water will be *less* than the figures on the chart.

To determine the time of high or low water at any station in Table 2, use the column marked Differences, Time. This gives the hours and minutes to be added to (+) or subtracted from (−) the time of the respective high or low water at the reference station shown in bold-face type next *above* the listing of the subordinate station. Be careful in making calculations near midnight. The application of the time difference may result in crossing the line from one day to another. Simply add or subtract 24 hours as necessary.

The height of the tide at a station in Table 2 is determined by applying the height difference or ratio. A plus sign (+) indicates that the difference, in feet and tenths, is to be added to the height at the designated reference station for the same time; a minus sign (−) indicates that it should be subtracted.

Where height differences would give unsatisfactory predictions, *ratios* may be substituted for heights. Ratios are identified by an asterisk. These are given as a decimal fraction by which the height at the reference station is to be multiplied to determine the height at the subordinate station.

In the columns headed Ranges, the *mean range* is the difference in height between mean high water and mean low water. This figure is useful in many areas where it may

FIG. 2011 Small-craft charts give annual tidal predictions for reference stations covered by that chart. Information tabulated for marinas and other boating facilities includes tidal ranges at such locations and time differences from a reference station.

FIG. 2012 Table 1 of the Tide Tables lists daily predictions of the time and height of high and low tides at selected reference stations.

FIG. 2013 An extract from Table 1 showing how a high tide may occasionally be omitted near midnght; see text for explanation. Similarly, a low tide near midnight may be skipped about once each two weeks.

### TABLE 2.—TIDAL DIFFERENCES AND OTHER CONSTANTS

| No. | PLACE | POSITION Lat. | POSITION Long. | DIFFERENCES Time High water | DIFFERENCES Time Low water | DIFFERENCES Height High water | DIFFERENCES Height Low water | RANGES Mean | RANGES Diurnal | Mean Tide Level |
|---|---|---|---|---|---|---|---|---|---|---|
| | | ° ' N. | ° ' W. | h. m. | h. m. | feet | feet | feet | feet | feet |
| | **WASHINGTON—Continued** **Admiralty Inlet—Continued** | | | on PORT TOWNSEND, p.94 | | | | | | |
| | | | | Time meridian, 120°W. | | | | | | |
| 897 | Port Townsend (Point Hudson) | 48 07 | 122 45 | -0 04 | -0 04 | +0.3 | +0.1 | 5.3 | 8.6 | 5.2 |
| 899 | Marrowstone Point | 48 06 | 122 41 | +0 09 | +0 07 | +0.5 | 0.0 | 5.6 | 8.8 | 5.3 |
| 901 | Oak Bay | 48 01 | 122 43 | +0 15 | +0 29 | +1.0 | +0.1 | 6.0 | 9.4 | 5.6 |
| | **Hood Canal** | | | on SEATTLE, p.98 | | | | | | |
| 903 | Port Ludlow | 47 55 | 122 41 | -0 27 | -0 18 | *0.88 | *0.88 | 6.4 | 9.9 | 5.9 |
| 905 | Port Gamble | 47 51 | 122 35 | -0 17 | -0 17 | *0.91 | *0.91 | 6.7 | 10.3 | 6.2 |
| 907 | Bangor Wharf | 47 45 | 122 44 | -0 20 | +0 04 | -0.3 | 0.0 | 7.3 | 10.9 | 6.4 |
| 908 | Zelatched Point, Dabob Bay | 47 43 | 122 49 | -0 10 | -0 05 | 0.0 | +0.1 | 7.5 | 11.3 | 6.6 |
| 909 | Seabeck | 47 38 | 122 50 | -0 03 | +0 03 | +0.3 | +0.1 | 7.8 | 11.6 | 6.6 |
| 911 | Union | 47 21 | 123 06 | -0 09 | +0 04 | +0.4 | 0.0 | 8.0 | 11.7 | 6.8 |
| | **Puget Sound** | | | | | | | | | |
| 913 | Point No Point | 47 55 | 122 32 | -0 16 | -0 16 | *0.92 | *0.92 | 6.7 | 10.4 | 6.1 |
| 915 | Port Madison | 47 42 | 122 32 | -0 08 | -0 08 | +0.1 | 0.0 | 7.7 | 11.4 | 6.6 |
| 917 | Poulsbo, Liberty Bay | 47 44 | 122 39 | +0 08 | +0 08 | +0.6 | +0.1 | 8.1 | 11.9 | 6.9 |
| 919 | Brownsville, Port Orchard | 47 39 | 122 37 | +0 02 | +0 08 | +0.4 | 0.0 | 8.0 | 11.7 | 6.8 |
| 921 | SEATTLE (Madison St.), Elliott Bay— | 47 36 | 122 20 | Daily predictions | | | | 7.6 | 11.3 | 6.6 |
| 923 | Eighth Ave. South, Duwamish River--- | 47 32 | 122 19 | +0 05 | +0 07 | -0.1 | 0.0 | 7.5 | 11.1 | 6.5 |
| 925 | Port Blakely | 47 36 | 122 30 | +0 02 | +0 03 | +0.2 | 0.0 | 7.8 | 11.5 | 6.7 |
| 927 | Pleasant Beach, Rich Passage | 47 36 | 122 32 | +0 01 | +0 07 | +0.2 | 0.0 | 7.8 | 11.5 | 6.7 |
| 929 | Bremerton, Port Orchard | 47 33 | 122 38 | +0 07 | +0 12 | +0.4 | 0.0 | 8.0 | 11.7 | 6.8 |
| 931 | Tracyton, Dyes Inlet | 47 37 | 122 40 | +0 30 | +0 56 | +1.0 | +0.3 | 8.6 | 12.3 | 7.1 |
| 933 | South Colby, Yukon Harbor | 47 31 | 122 32 | +0 01 | +0 07 | +0.3 | 0.0 | 7.9 | 11.6 | 6.7 |
| 935 | Des Moines | 47 24 | 122 20 | +0 03 | +0 09 | +0.4 | 0.0 | 8.0 | 11.7 | 6.8 |
| 937 | Burton, Quartermaster Harbor | 47 23 | 122 28 | +0 07 | +0 13 | +0.6 | 0.0 | 8.2 | 11.9 | 6.9 |
| 939 | Gig Harbor | 47 20 | 122 35 | +0 06 | +0 14 | +0.6 | 0.0 | 8.2 | 11.8 | 6.9 |
| 941 | Tacoma, Commencement Bay | 47 17 | 122 25 | +0 07 | +0 06 | +0.5 | 0.0 | 8.1 | 11.8 | 6.8 |
| 943 | Arletta, Hale Passage | 47 17 | 122 39 | +0 23 | +0 36 | +1.7 | 0.0 | 9.3 | 13.0 | 7.4 |
| 945 | Home, Von Geldern Cove, Carr Inlet-- | 47 16 | 122 45 | +0 27 | +0 39 | +2.3 | +0.2 | 9.7 | 13.6 | 7.8 |
| 947 | Wauna, Carr Inlet | 47 23 | 122 38 | +0 20 | +0 36 | +1.8 | 0.0 | 9.4 | 13.1 | 7.6 |
| 949 | Stellacoom | 47 10 | 122 36 | +0 22 | +0 35 | +1.8 | 0.0 | 9.4 | 13.1 | 7.5 |
| 951 | Hyde Point, McNeil Island | 47 12 | 122 39 | +0 23 | +0 41 | +2.1 | +0.1 | 9.5 | 13.4 | 7.7 |
| 953 | Sequalitchew Creek, Nisqually Reach- | 47 07 | 122 40 | +0 24 | +0 42 | +2.1 | +0.1 | 9.6 | 13.4 | 7.7 |
| 955 | Longbranch, Filucy Bay | 47 13 | 122 45 | +0 26 | +0 39 | +2.2 | +0.1 | 9.7 | 13.5 | 7.7 |
| 957 | Henderson Inlet | 47 09 | 122 50 | +0 27 | +0 45 | +2.5 | +0.2 | 10.0 | 14.0 | 8.0 |
| 959 | Vaughn, Case Inlet | 47 20 | 122 46 | +0 35 | +0 47 | +2.8 | +0.2 | 10.2 | 14.1 | 8.1 |
| 961 | Allyn, Case Inlet | 47 23 | 122 49 | +0 27 | +0 46 | +2.8 | +0.2 | 10.2 | 14.1 | 8.1 |
| 963 | Walkers Landing, Pickering Passage-- | 47 17 | 122 56 | +0 35 | +0 47 | +2.9 | +0.2 | 10.3 | 14.3 | 8.1 |
| 965 | Arcadia, Pickering Passage | 47 12 | 122 56 | +0 35 | +0 54 | +3.0 | +0.2 | 10.4 | 14.4 | 8.2 |
| 967 | Shelton, Oakland Bay | 47 13 | 123 06 | +1 12 | +1 54 | +2.8 | -0.2 | 10.4 | 14.4 | 7.9 |
| 969 | Burns Point, Totten Inlet | 47 07 | 123 03 | +0 36 | +0 54 | +3.6 | +0.2 | 11.0 | 15.0 | 8.5 |
| 971 | Rocky Point, Eld Inlet | 47 04 | 123 01 | +0 34 | +0 52 | +3.3 | +0.1 | 10.6 | 14.7 | 8.4 |
| 973 | Dofflemyer Point, Budd Inlet | 47 08 | 122 54 | +0 29 | +0 47 | +3.1 | +0.2 | 10.5 | 14.4 | 8.2 |
| 975 | Olympia, Budd Inlet | 47 03 | 122 54 | +0 31 | +0 46 | +3.1 | +0.2 | 10.5 | 14.4 | 8.2 |
| | **Possession Sound and Port Susan** | | | | | | | | | |
| 977 | Mukilteo | 47 57 | 122 18 | -0 08 | -0 12 | -0.3 | -0.1 | 7.4 | 11.0 | 6.4 |
| 979 | Everett | 47 59 | 122 13 | -0 09 | -0 11 | -0.2 | 0.0 | 7.4 | 11.1 | 6.5 |
| 981 | Tulalip | 48 04 | 122 17 | +0 02 | -0 02 | 0.0 | 0.0 | 7.6 | 11.2 | 6.6 |
| 982 | Kayak Point | 48 08 | 122 22 | -0 04 | -0 01 | -0.4 | -0.1 | 7.3 | 10.9 | 6.3 |
| 983 | Stanwood,¹ Stillaguamish River | 48 14 | 122 22 | +0 18 | +2 10 | *0.63 | *0.29 | 5.7 | 7.4 | 3.6 |

*Ratio.
¹The low water seldom falls below the chart datum.

FIG. 2014 Table 2—Tidal Differences and Other Constants. Data are given for hundreds of subordinate stations so that predictions can be made for almost any point of significance to navigation.

FIG. 2015 Table 3—Height of Tide at Any Time. This table is used in determining tide level at intermediate times between low and high waters.

be added to mean low water to get mean high water (MHW), the datum commonly used for the measurement of vertical heights above water, bridge and other vertical clearances, etc. The *spring range* is the average semidiurnal range occurring twice monthly when the moon is new or full. It is larger than the mean range where the type of tide is either semidiurnal or mixed, and is of no practical significance where the tide is of the diurnal type. Where this is the situation, the table gives the *diurnal range,* which is the difference in height between mean higher high water and mean lower low water.

Table 3, fig. 2015, is provided in order that detailed calculations can be made for the height of the tide at any desired moment between the times of high and low waters. It is equally usable for either reference stations in Table 1 or the subordinate stations of Table 2. Note that Table 3 is not a complete set of variations from one low to one high. Since the rise and fall are assumed to be symmetrical, only a half-table need be printed. Calculations are made from a high or low water, whichever is nearer to the specified time. In using Table 3, the nearest tabular values are used; interpolation is not necessary.

If the degree of precision of Table 3 is not required (it seldom is in practical piloting situations), a much simpler and quicker estimation can be made by using the following one-two-three rule of thumb. The tide may be assumed to rise or fall 1/12 of the full range during the first and sixth hours after high and low water stands, 2/12 during the second and fifth hours, and 3/12 during the third and fourth hours. The results obtained by this rule will suffice for essentially all situations and locations, but should be compared with Table 3 calculations as a check when entering new areas.

The table shown at the bottom of page 352p has been prepared from the above rule of thumb to supply multiplying factors for half-hour intervals of a rising or falling tide.

The Tide Tables also include four other minor tables which, although not directly related to tidal calculations, are often useful. Table 4 provides sunrise and sunset data at five-day intervals for various latitudes. Table 5 lists corrections to convert the local mean times of Table 4 to standard zone time. Table 6 tabulates times of moonrise and moonset for certain selected locations. Table 7 lists other useful astronomical data such as the phases of the moon, solar equinoxes and solstices, etc.

Each Table is preceded by informative material which should be read carefully prior to its use.

## EXAMPLES OF TIDAL CALCULATIONS

The instructions in the Tide Tables should be fully adequate for the solution of any problem. However, examples will be worked out here for various situations as guides to the use of the various individual tables. Comments and cautions relating to the solution of practical problems involving the Tide Tables will also be given.

### Example 1. Determination of the time and height of a high or low tide at a reference station.

**Problem:** What is the time and height of the evening low tide at Seattle on Sunday, 1 October 1967?

**Solution:** Using Table 1, fig. 2012, it will be seen directly that the evening low water occurs at 2124 Pacific Standard Time on this date and that the height is 4.2 feet above the tidal datum of mean lower low water.

**Notes:** a. Observe that if the date had been 3 November, the tide level at low water stand would have been a *minus* figure, —3.0 feet. At this time, the water level is predicted to be *below* the datum and actual depths will be *less* than those printed on the charts of this area.

b. Observe that if the date had been 4 November, there would have been no solution as the normal progression of the tides on a cycle of roughly 24 hours and 50 minutes has moved the normal evening low tide past midnight and into the next day. Thus, Saturday, 4 November has only three tides rather than the usual four.

c. It should be further noted that the reference stations are also listed in Table 2 and additional information is shown there. This table, fig. 2014, indicates, for reference stations as well as subordinate stations, the specific location for which predictions are given, the mean and spring (or diurnal) tidal ranges, and the mean tide level.

d. Remember to add one hour if you are in an area using daylight saving time.

### Example 2. Determination of the time and height of a high or low tide at a subordinate station.

**Problem:** What is the time and height of the morning low water at Shelton on Oakland Bay, Puget Sound on Tuesday, 5 December 1967?

**Solution:** From the Index to Table 2 in the back of the Tide Tables, Shelton is found to be Subordinate Station No. 967. It is then located in Table 2 (fig. 2014). First, note that the Reference Station shown next *above* this place is "Seattle." Then note the time and height differences for Shelton for *low* waters; be sure to use the correct columns.

Th differences are then applied as follows:

| Time | | Height |
|------|---|--------|
| 00 48 | At Seattle | —2.5 feet |
| 1:54 | Differences | —0.2 |
| 02 42 | At Shelton | —2.7 feet |

Thus, at Shelton on 5 December 1967, the predicted morning low water will occur at 0242 PST with a height of —2.7 feet (2.7 feet *below* the tidal datum).

**Notes:** a. If the date had been 5 October, the morning low water at Seattle for that date is at 1130. Adding the time difference of $1^h 54^m$ would have resulted in a time prediction for Shelton of 1324, which is *not* a *morning* tide at the subordinate station. In this case, it would be necessary to use the low water at the reference station that occurs before midnight on the *preceding* day. At Seattle on *4* October, there is a low water at 2318; adding the time difference gives a morning low tide at Shelton of 0112 on *5* October.

b. Observe that if the subordinate station had been Port Gamble on Hood Canal, the height would be determined by multiplying the height at the reference station by the *ratio* of 0.91 rather than adding or subtracting a difference in feet. (Ratios may be either greater or less than 1.) Note also that here the time differences are *negative;* the high and low waters at the subordinate station occur *earlier* than at the reference station of Table 1.

c. The use of minus time differences with predictions of

---

FIG. 2016 **Table 4—Local Mean Time of Sunrise and Sunset. Times are tabulated for various dates and latitudes, usually at intervals of 5 days and 2°; interpolation is used for exact dates and locations.**

| Date | 30° N. Rise | 30° N. Set | 32° N. Rise | 32° N. Set | 34° N. Rise | 34° N. Set | 36° N. Rise | 36° N. Set | 38° N. Rise | 38° N. Set | 40° N. Rise | 40° N. Set |
|------|------|-----|------|-----|------|-----|------|-----|------|-----|------|-----|
| | h. m. | h. m. | h. m. | h. m. | h. m. | h. m. | h. m. | h. m. | h. m. | h. m. | h. m. | h. m. |
| Jan. 1 | 6 56 | 17 11 | 7 01 | 17 07 | 7 06 | 17 02 | 7 11 | 16 57 | 7 16 | 16 51 | 7 22 | 16 44 |
| 6 | 6 57 | 17 15 | 7 02 | 17 11 | 7 06 | 17 06 | 7 11 | 17 01 | 7 17 | 16 56 | 7 22 | 16 49 |
| 11 | 6 57 | 17 19 | 7 02 | 17 15 | 7 06 | 17 10 | 7 11 | 17 05 | 7 16 | 17 00 | 7 22 | 16 54 |
| 16 | 6 57 | 17 23 | 7 01 | 17 19 | 7 05 | 17 15 | 7 10 | 17 10 | 7 15 | 17 05 | 7 20 | 17 00 |
| 21 | 6 56 | 17 27 | 6 59 | 17 24 | 7 04 | 17 20 | 7 08 | 17 15 | 7 12 | 17 11 | 7 18 | 17 05 |
| 26 | 6 54 | 17 32 | 6 57 | 17 28 | 7 01 | 17 25 | 7 05 | 17 21 | 7 09 | 17 16 | 7 14 | 17 11 |
| 31 | 6 51 | 17 36 | 6 55 | 17 33 | 6 58 | 17 29 | 7 02 | 17 26 | 7 06 | 17 22 | 7 10 | 17 17 |
| Feb. 5 | 6 48 | 17 40 | 6 51 | 17 37 | 6 54 | 17 34 | 6 58 | 17 31 | 7 01 | 17 27 | 7 05 | 17 23 |
| 10 | 6 45 | 17 44 | 6 48 | 17 42 | 6 50 | 17 39 | 6 53 | 17 36 | 6 56 | 17 33 | 7 00 | 17 29 |
| 15 | 6 41 | 17 48 | 6 43 | 17 46 | 6 45 | 17 44 | 6 48 | 17 41 | 6 50 | 17 39 | 6 54 | 17  |
| 20 | 6 36 | 17 52 | 6 38 | 17 50 | 6 40 | 17 48 | 6 42 | 17 46 | 6 44 | 17 44 | 6 4  | 17  |
| 25 | 6 31 | 17 56 | 6 32 | 17 55 | 6 34 | 17 53 | 6 36 | 17 51 | 6 39 |  |  | 16 52 |
| | | | | | | | | | | | | 16 47 |
| Mar. 2 | 6 26 | 17 59 | 6 27 | 17 58 | 6 28 | 17 57 | 6 29 |  |  |  | 6 47 | 16 43 |
| 7 | 6 20 | 18 03 | 6 21 | 18 02 | 6 22 | 18 0 |  |  | 6 48 | 16 52 | 6 52 | 16 39 |
| 12 | 6 14 | 18 06 | 6 14 |  |  |  |  | 16 47 | 6 53 | 16 42 | 6 58 | 16 37 |
| 17 | 6 09 | 18 09 |  |  |  |  |  |  |  |  |  |  |
| 22 | 6 02 |  |  |  |  | 6 48 | 16 51 | 6 53 | 16 46 | 6 58 | 16 41 | 7 03 | 16 35 |
| 27 |  | 00 |  |  | 6 52 | 16 51 | 6 57 | 16 46 | 7 02 | 16 40 | 7 08 | 16 35 |
|  | 49 | 17 01 | 6 51 | 16 56 | 6 56 | 16 52 | 7 01 | 16 46 | 7 07 | 16 41 | 7 12 | 16 35 |
|  |  | 17 03 | 6 54 | 16 58 | 6 59 | 16 53 | 7 04 | 16 48 | 7 10 | 16 42 | 7 16 | 16 36 |
|  | 6 52 | 17 05 | 6 56 | 17 00 | 7 01 | 16 55 | 7 07 | 16 49 | 7 12 | 16 44 | 7 18 | 16 38 |
| 27 | 6 54 | 17 08 | 6 59 | 17 03 | 7 04 | 16 58 | 7 09 | 16 53 | 7 15 | 16 47 | 7 20 | 16 41 |
| Jan. 1 | 6 56 | 17 11 | 7 01 | 17 07 | 7 06 | 17 01 | 7 11 | 16 56 | 7 16 | 16 50 | 7 22 | 16 44 |

Local mean time. To obtain standard time of rise or set, see Table 5.

---

FIG. 2017 **Table 5—Reduction of Local Mean Time to Standard Time. A correction, obtained from this table, is applied to the time of sunrise or sunset computed from Table 4 to get the time of the event in standard zone time. A further correction of one hour is needed for Daylight Saving Time.**

| Difference of longitude between local and standard meridian | Correction to local mean time to obtain standard time | Difference of longitude between local and standard meridian | Correction to local mean time to obtain standard time | Difference of longitude between local and standard meridian |
|---|---|---|---|---|
| ° ' ° ' | *Minutes* | ° ' ° ' | *Minutes* | ° |
| 0 00 to 0 07 | 0 | 7 23 to 7 37 | 30 | 15 |
| 0 08 to 0 22 | 1 | 7 38 to 7 52 | 31 | 30 |
| 0 23 to 0 37 | 2 | 7 53 to 8 07 | 32 | 45 |
| 0 38 to 0 52 | 3 | 8 08 to 8 22 | 33 | 60 |
| 0 53 to 1 07 | 4 | 8 23 to 8 37 | 34 | 75 |
| 1 08 to 1 22 | 5 | 8 38 to 8 52 | 35 | 90 |
| 1 23 to 1 37 | 6 | 8 53 to 9 07 | 36 | 105 |
| 1 38 to 1 52 | 7 | 9 08 to 9 22 | 37 | 120 |
| 1 53 to 2 07 | 8 | 9 23 to 9 37 | 38 | 135 |
| 2 08 to 2 22 | 9 | 9 38 to 9 52 | 39 | 150 |
| 2 23 to 2 37 | 10 | 9 53 to 10 07 | 40 | 165 |
| 2 38 to 2 52 | 11 | 10 08 to 10 22 | 41 | 180 |
| 2 53 to 3 07 | 12 | 10 23 to 10 37 | 42 | |
| 3 08 to 3 22 | 13 | 10 38 to 10 52 | 43 | |
| 3 23 to 3 37 | 14 | 10 53 to 11 07 | 44 | |
| 3 38 to 3 52 | 15 | 11 08 to 13 32 | 55 | |
| 3 53 to 4 07 | 16 | 13 53 to 14 07 | 56 | |
| 4 08 to 4 ?? | | | | |
| 6 38 to 6 52 | 27 | 14 08 to 14 22 | 57 | |
| 6 53 to 7 07 | 28 | 14 23 to 14 37 | 58 | |
| 7 08 to 7 22 | 29 | 14 38 to 14 52 | 59 | |

If local meridian is east of standard meridian, subtract the tion from local time.
If local meridian is west of standard meridian, add the co to local time.

tides to occur shortly after midnight at the reference station may result in a change of date backward into the preceding day. Always be careful in making calculations close to 2400.

## Example 3. Determination of the level of the tide at a reference station at a given time between high and low waters.

**Problem:** What is the height of the tide at Seattle at 1820 on Saturday, 2 December 1967?

**Solution:** From Table 1, we first note that the given time of 1820 falls between a high tide at 1554 and a low tide at 2318. We compute the time difference and range as follows:

| Time | Height |
|---|---|
| 23 18 | 11.8 feet |
| 15 54 | −3.6 |
| 7:24 time difference | 15.4 feet range |

Thus our desired tide level is on a falling tide whose range is 15.4 feet (since the low water height is a negative value, we are subtracting a minus number which is arithmetically equivalent to adding the numerical values).

The desired time is nearer to the time of the high water, so calculations will be made in Table 3, fig. 2015, using this starting point.

| 18 20 | Desired time |
|---|---|
| 15 54 | Time of nearest high or low water |
| 2:26 | Difference |

The given time is $2^h 26^m$ after the nearest high water. Table 3 is used to the nearest tabulated value; do not interpolate. Entering the *upper* part of the Table on the line for Duration of rise or fall of $7^h 20^m$, (nearest value to $7^h 24^m$), read across to the entry nearest $2^h 26^m$; this is $2^h 27^m$ in the tenth column from the left. Follow *down* this column into the *lower* part of Table 3 to the line for Range of Tide of 15.5 feet (nearest value to actual range of 15.4 feet). At the intersection of this line and column is found the correction to the height of the tide; in this case, 3.9 feet.

Since we have noted that in this example the tide is falling, and we are calculating from high water, the correction is subtracted from the height of high water: 11.8 − 3.9 = 7.9.

The predicted height of the tide at Seattle at 1820 PST on 2 December 1967 is 7.9 feet above the tidal datum.

**Notes:** a. Be sure that calculations are made for the right pair of high and low tides; be sure that the calculations are made for the *nearest* high or low water.

b. Be careful to apply the final correction to the nearest high or low water as used in its computation; do not apply it to the range; apply it in the right direction, down from a high, or up from a low.

## Example 4. Determination of the height of tide at a subordinate station at a given time.

**Problem:** What is the height of the tide at Port Ludlow at 0930 on Saturday, 2 December 1967?

**Solution:** First, the times of the high and low waters on either side of the stated time must be calculated for the subordinate station using Tables 1 and 2. This is done as follows:

| High water | 06 06 | At Seattle | 12.8 feet |
|---|---|---|---|
| | −:27 | difference/ratio | 0.88 |
| | 05 39 | At Point Ludlow | 11.3 feet |
| Low water | 11 06 | At Seattle | 7.7 feet |
| | −:18 | difference/ratio | 0.88 |
| | 10 48 | At Point Ludlow | 6.8 feet |

Next, we calculate the time difference and range:

| 10 48 | 11.3 |
|---|---|
| 05 39 | 6.8 |
| 5:09 time difference | 4.5 feet range |

The time from the nearest high or low is calculated:

| 10 48 |
|---|
| 09 30 |
| 1:18 time from nearest low |

With the data from the above calculations, enter Table 3 for a Duration of rise or fall of $5^h 09^m$ (use $5^h 00^m$), a time from nearest high or low of $1^h 18^m$ (use $1^h 20^m$), and a range of 4.5 feet. From these data, we find a correction to height of tide of 0.7 feet. We know that the tide is falling and that the nearest time of stand was the low water at 1048. From these facts, we can see that the correction is to be *added* to the low water height; 6.8 + 0.7 = 7.5.

The height of the tide at Port Ludlow at 0930 PST on 2 December 1967 is predicted to be 7.5 feet above the datum.

**Note:** Be sure to use the high and low tides occurring *at the subordinate station* on either side of the given time. It may be that in some instances with large time differences, a correction of times from the reference station to the subordinate station will show that you have selected the incorrect pair of tides; in this case select another high or low tide so that the pair used at the subordinate station will bracket the given time.

## Example 5. Determination of the time of the tide reaching a given height at a reference station.

**Problem:** At what time on the afternoon of 4 October 1967 will the height of the rising tide reach 10 feet at Seattle?

**Solution:** This is essentially Example 3 in reverse. First, determine the range and duration of rise (or fall).

| 16 48 | High water | 11.9 feet |
|---|---|---|
| 10 48 | Low water | 2.3 |
| 6:00 | Duration | 9.6 feet range |

It is noted that the desired difference in height of tide is 11.9 − 10.0 = 1.9 feet. Enter the *lower* part of Table 3 on the line for a range of 9.5 feet (nearest value to 9.6) and find the column in which the correction nearest 1.9 feet is tabulated; in this case, the nearest value (2.0) is found in the ninth column from the left. Proceed *up* this column to the line in the upper part of the Table for a Duration of $6^h 00^m$ (here the exact value can be used). The time from nearest high or low found on this line is $1^h 48^m$. Since our desired level is nearer to high water than low, this time difference is subtracted from the time of high water; 1648 − 1:48 = 1500.

Thus the desired tidal height of 10 feet above datum is predicted to occur at 1500 PST on 4 October.

**Note:** A similar calculation can be made for a subordinate station by first determining the applicable high and low water times and heights at that station.

401

## Example 6. Determination of vertical clearance.

**Problem:** What will be the vertical clearance under the fixed west span of the bridge across the Hood Canal near Port Gamble, Washington, at the time of morning high tide on 2 December 1967?

**Solution:** Chart 185-SC states the clearance to be 35 feet. The datum for heights is mean high water; the tidal datum is mean lower low water.

From Tables 1 and 2, we determine the predicted height of the tide at the specified time:

| | |
|---|---|
| At Seattle | 12.8 feet |
| ratio | 0.91 |
| At Port Gamble | 11.6 feet |

From Table 2, we calculate the height of mean high water for Port Gamble:

| | |
|---|---|
| Mean tide level | 6.2 feet |
| ½ mean range | 3.4 |
| Mean high water | 9.6 feet above tidal datum |

The difference between predicted high water at the specified time and MHW is 11.6 − 9.6 = 2.0 feet. The tide is above MHW and the bridge clearance is reduced, 35 − 2.0 = 33 feet.

On the morning of 2 December 1967, the clearance at high tide under the fixed west span of the bridge across Hood Canal near Port Gamble is predicted to be 33 feet; this is *less* than the clearance printed on the chart.

## ASTRONOMICAL DATA FROM THE TIDE TABLES

Table 4 gives sunrise and sunset information for various latitudes at five-day intervals. If more precise times are needed, interpolation can be used. Times are *local* meridian and must be corrected to standard zone time.

## Example 7. Determination of the time of sunrise at a specified location.

**Problem:** What is the time of sunrise at Catalina Harbor, Santa Catalina Island on 12 February 1967?

**Solution:** From Table 2, we note that the latitude and longitude of the given point are 33° 26′N, 118° 30′W.

Fig. 2016 is an extract from Table 4; the applicable entries are set up as follows:

| | 32°N | 34°N |
|---|---|---|
| Feb 10 | 0647 | 0650 |
| Feb 15 | 0643 | 0645 |

Then we interpolate to the nearest minute vertically for the desired date:

| | 32°N | 34°N |
|---|---|---|
| Feb 10 | 0647 | 0650 |
| **Feb 12** | **0645** | **0648** |
| Feb 15 | 0643 | 0645 |

Next, interpolation is done horizontally for the latitude of the given point:

| | 32°N | **33° 26′N** | 34°N |
|---|---|---|---|
| Feb 12 | 0645 | **0647** | 0648 |

This time of 0647 is local meridian time and must be corrected to zone time by Table 5, fig. 2017. The meridian of Pacific Standard Time is 120° W (from Table 1, bottom of any page).

$$\begin{array}{r} 120°\ 00' \\ \underline{118°\ 30'} \\ 1°\ 30'\ \text{Longitude difference} \end{array}$$

From Table 5, the time correction for 1°30′ is 6 minutes. Since Catalina Harbor is *east* of the zone meridian, the correction is *subtracted*; 0647 − 6$^m$ = 0641.

On the morning of 12 February 1967, the time of sunrise at Catalina Harbor is 0641 PST.

**Notes:** a. Interpolation can be done first horizontally for the latitude difference and then vertically for the desired date. The results may vary slightly due to rounding to the nearest minute, but the difference should not exceed one minute.

b. Calculations for the time of sunset are made in exactly the same manner.

c. Latitude and longitude data may be taken from a chart or any other source.

d. Times must be corrected for daylight time, if in effect.

### Times of moonrise and moonset

Table 6 gives daily times for moonrise and moonset for selected points. Correction or interpolation for other points is *not* possible.

# Currents

*Current* is the horizontal motion of water. This motion may be the result of any one of several factors, or of a combination of two or three. Although certain of these causes are of greater importance to a boatman than are others, he should have a general understanding of all.

## TIDAL CURRENTS

Boatmen in coastal areas will be most affected by *tidal currents*. The rise and fall of tidal levels is a result of the flow of water to and from a given locality. This flow results in tidal current effects.

The normal type of tidal current, in bays and rivers, is the *reversing* current that flows alternately in one direction and then the opposite. Off-shore, tidal currents may be of the *rotary* type, flowing with little change in strength, but slowly and steadily changing direction.

A special form of tidal current is the *hydraulic* type such as flows in a waterway connecting two bodies of water. Differences in the time and height of the high and low waters of the two bays, sounds, etc., cause a flow from one to the other and back again. A typical example of hydraulic current is the flow through the Cape Cod Canal with Massachusetts Bay at one end and Buzzards Bay at the other.

Remember to use the terms correctly—tide is the *vertical* rise and fall of water levels; current is the *horizontal* flow of water.

FIG. 2018  The major ocean currents of interest to boatmen are the Gulf Stream off the East Coast and the California Current along the Pacific Coast.

## OTHER TYPES OF CURRENT

Although most piloting situations involving current are concerned with tidal currents, there will be times when river, ocean, and wind-driven currents must be considered.

### River currents

Boatmen on rivers above the head of tidal action must take into account *river currents*. (Where tidal influences are felt, river currents are merged into tidal currents and are not considered separately.) River currents will vary widely with the width and depth of the stream, the season of the year, recent rainfall in the river basin, etc.

### Ocean currents

Off-shore piloting will frequently require knowledge and consideration of *ocean currents*. These result from regions of relatively constant winds such as the often-mentioned "trade winds" and "prevailing westerlies." The rotation of the earth and variations in water density are also factors in the patterns of ocean currents.

The ocean currents of greatest interest to boatmen are the Gulf Stream and the California Current, fig. 2018. The *Gulf Stream* is a northerly and easterly flow of warm water along the Atlantic Coast of the United States. It is quite close to shore along the southern part of Florida, but moves progressively further to sea as it flows northward, where it both broadens and slows.

The *California Current* flows generally southward and a bit eastward along the Pacific Coast of Canada and the United States, turning sharply westward off Baja California (Mexico). It is a flow of colder water and, in general, is slower and less sharply defined than the Gulf Stream.

### Wind-driven currents

In addition to the consistent ocean currents caused by sustained wind patterns, local *wind-driven currents* may be established by temporary conditions. The effect of wind blowing across the sea is to cause the surface water to move. The extent of the effect varies with many factors, but generally a steady wind for 12 hours or longer will result in a discernible current.

For a rough rule-of-thumb, the strength of a wind-driven current can be taken as 2% of the wind's velocity. The direction of the current will *not* be the same as that of the wind, a result of the earth's rotation. In the Northern Hemisphere, the current will be deflected to the right to a degree determined by the latitude and the depth of the water. The deflection may be as small as 15° in shallow coastal areas, or as great as 45° on the high seas; it is greater in the higher latitudes.

## DEFINITIONS OF CURRENT TERMS

Currents have both strength and direction. The proper terms should be used in describing each of these characteristics.

The *set* of a current is the direction *toward* which it is flowing. A current that flows from North to South is termed a southerly current and has a set of 180°. (Note carefully the difference here from the manner in which wind direction is described—it is exactly the opposite: a wind from North to South is called a northerly wind with a direction of 000°.)

FIG. 2019  In some narrow passages, tidal currents are so strong that a lightly powered boat could not make headway against them, and must wait for slack water. Here, an auxiliary races through Cobscook Falls in Maine, propelled by a 10-knot "down-hill" current.
(Photograph courtesy Donald W. Gardner)

**FIG. 2020** Table 1 of the Tidal Current Tables. Daily predictions are listed for the times and strengths of maximum flood and ebb currents, and the time of slack water, at major reference stations.

### CHESAPEAKE BAY ENTRANCE, VA., 1967

F–FLOOD, DIR. 305 TRUE    E–EBB, DIR. 125 TRUE

#### SEPTEMBER

| DAY | SLACK WATER TIME H.M. | MAX CURRENT TIME H.M. | VEL. KNOTS | DAY | SLACK WATER TIME H.M. | MAX CURRENT TIME H.M. | VEL. KNOTS |
|---|---|---|---|---|---|---|---|
| 1 F | 0400 | 0030 | 1.1E | 16 SA | 0448 | 0130 | 1.3E |
|  | 0800 | 0554 | 0.4F |  | 0942 | 0718 | 0.7F |
|  | 1542 | 1224 | 1.4E |  | 1700 | 1336 | 1.6E |
|  | 2154 | 1836 | 1.1F |  | 2254 | 1954 | 1.0F |
| 2 SA | 0436 | 0118 | 1.3E | 17 SU | 0524 | 0206 | 1.3E |
|  | 0906 | 0648 | 0.6F |  | 1030 | 0754 | 0.8F |
|  | 1630 | 1312 | 1.6E |  | 1742 | 1418 | 1.6E |
|  | 2236 | 1924 | 1.3F |  | 2324 | 2024 | 1.0F |
| 3 SU | 0512 | 0200 | 1.4E | 18 M | 0554 | 0242 | 1.4E |
|  | 1006 | 0736 | 0.8F |  | 1112 | 0830 | 0.9F |
|  | 1718 | 1400 | 1.8E |  | 1824 | 1454 | 1.6E |
|  | 2318 | 2012 | 1.4F |  | 2348 | 2100 | 0.9F |
| 4 M | 0554 | 0236 | 1.6E | 19 TU | 0630 | 0318 | 1.4E |
|  | 1100 | 0824 | 1.1F |  | 0906 | 0906 | 0.9F |
|  | 1806 | 1442 | 1.9E |  | 1148 | 1530 | 1.5E |
|  | 2354 | 2054 | 1.4F |  | 1854 | 2124 | 0.9F |
| 5 TU | 0630 | 0318 | 1.7E | 20 W | 0012 | 0342 | 1.4E |
|  | 1148 | 0906 | 1.2F |  | 0700 | 0936 | 1.0F |
|  | 1854 | 1530 | 2.0E |  | 1224 | 1606 | 1.5E |
|  |  | 2136 | 1.4F |  | 1930 | 2154 | 0.8F |
| 6 W | 0036 | 0400 | 1.8E | 21 TH | 0030 | 0412 | 1.3E |
|  | 0712 | 0954 | 1.4F |  | 0730 | 1006 | 1.0F |
|  | 1242 | 1618 | 1.9E |  | 1300 | 1642 | 1.4E |
|  | 1942 | 2218 | 1.4F |  | 2006 | 2224 | 0.7F |
| 7 TH | 0112 | 0442 | 1.8E | 22 F | 0054 | 0442 | 1.3E |
|  | 0800 | 1042 | 1.4F |  | 0806 | 1042 | 1.0F |
|  | 1336 | 1712 | 1.8E |  | 1336 | 1718 | 1.2E |
|  | 2030 | 2306 | 1.2F |  | 2048 | 2254 | 0.6F |

#### OCTOBER

| DAY | SLACK WATER TIME H.M. | MAX CURRENT TIME H.M. | VEL. KNOTS | DAY | SLACK WATER TIME H.M. | MAX CURRENT TIME H.M. | VEL. KNOTS |
|---|---|---|---|---|---|---|---|
| 1 SU | 0400 | 0042 | 1.4E | 16 M | 0454 | 0136 | 1.3E |
|  | 0854 | 0624 | 0.8F |  | 1018 | 0730 | 0.9F |
|  | 1612 | 1248 | 1.6E |  | 1718 | 1354 | 1.5E |
|  | 2200 | 1854 | 1.2F |  | 2236 | 1954 | 0.8F |
| 2 M | 0436 | 0124 | 1.6E | 17 TU | 0524 | 0206 | 1.4E |
|  | 0954 | 0712 | 1.1F |  | 1054 | 0806 | 0.9F |
|  | 1700 | 1336 | 1.8E |  | 1800 | 1430 | 1.5E |
|  | 2236 | 1942 | 1.3F |  | 2300 | 2024 | 0.8F |
| 3 TU | 0518 | 0206 | 1.7E | 18 W | 0554 | 0242 | 1.4E |
|  | 1048 | 0800 | 1.3F |  | 1136 | 0836 | 1.0F |
|  | 1748 | 1424 | 1.9E |  | 1830 | 1506 | 1.4E |
|  | 2318 | 2030 | 1.4F |  | 2324 | 2054 | 0.7F |
| 4 W | 0600 | 0248 | 1.9E | 19 TH | 0624 | 0306 | 1.4E |
|  | 1142 | 0848 | 1.5F |  | 1206 | 0906 | 1.1F |
|  | 1836 | 1512 | 2.0E |  | 1906 | 1542 | 1.4E |
|  |  | 2112 | 1.3F |  | 2342 | 2118 | 0.7F |
| 5 TH | 0000 | 0330 | 1.9E | 20 F | 0654 | 0336 | 1.4E |
|  | 0648 | 0936 | 1.6F |  | 1242 | 0942 | 1.1F |
|  | 1236 | 1606 | 1.9E |  | 1942 | 1618 | 1.3E |
|  | 1924 | 2154 | 1.2F |  |  | 2148 | 0.6F |
| 6 F | 0036 | 0418 | 1.9E | 21 SA | 0006 | 0406 | 1.3E |
|  | 0736 | 1024 | 1.6F |  | 0730 | 1012 | 1.1F |
|  | 1330 | 1654 | 1.8E |  | 1318 | 1654 | 1.2E |
|  | 2018 | 2242 | 1.1F |  | 2024 | 2224 | 0.5F |
| 7 SA | 0118 | 0506 | 1.8E | 22 SU | 0030 | 0436 | 1.3E |
|  | 0824 | 1118 | 1.5F |  | 0806 | 1054 | 1.0F |
|  | 1424 | 1748 | 1.6E |  | 1400 | 1730 | 1.1E |
|  | 2112 | 2330 | 0.9F |  | 2106 | 2300 | 0.4F |

The *drift* of a current is its velocity, normally in knots (except for river currents which will be in MPH). As noted in the preceding chapter, current drift is stated to the nearest tenth of a knot.

A tidal current is said to *flood* when it flows in from the sea and results in higher tidal stages. Conversely, a tidal current *ebbs* when the flow is seaward and water levels fall.

## Slack vs. Stand

As these currents reverse, there are brief periods of no discernible flow, called *slack,* or *slack water.* The time of occurrence of slack is *not* the same as the time of *stand,* when the vertical rise or fall of tide has stopped. Tidal currents do *not* automatically slack and reverse direction when tide levels stand at high or low water.

High water at a given point simply means that the level there will not get any higher. Further up the bay or river, the tide will not have reached its maximum height and water must therefore continue to flow in so that it can continue to rise. The current can still be flooding after stand has been passed at our given point and the level has started to fall.

For example, let us consider the tides and currents on Chesapeake Bay. High tide occurs at Baltimore some 7 hours after it does at Smith Point, roughly half way up the 140 miles from Cape Henry at the entrance to Baltimore. On a certain day, high water occurs at 1126 at Smith Point, but slack water does not occur until 1304. The flooding current has thus continued for 1h 38m after high water was reached.

Corresponding time intervals occur in the case of low water stand and the slack between ebb and flood currents.

In many places, the time lag between a low or high water stand and slack water is not a matter of minutes but hours. At The Narrows in New York Harbor, flood current continues for about 2 hours after high water is reached and the tide begins to fall, ebb for 2½ hours after low water stand. After slack, the current increases until mid-flood or mid-ebb, then gradually decreases. Where ebb and flood last for about six hours—as along the Atlantic seaboard—current will be strongest about three hours after slack. Thus, the skipper who figures his passage out through The Narrows from the time of high water, rather than slack, will start about two and a half hours too soon and will run into a current at nearly its maximum strength.

## NEED FOR KNOWLEDGE

Currents, primarily of the tidal type, will affect many boating situations. Currents will be a definite factor in piloting in tidal rivers, bays, and sounds. Coastal currents, resulting from waves striking the beaches at an angle, will often influence coastal piloting problems.

### Effect on course and speed made good

A current directly in line with a boat's motion through the water will have a maximum effect on the speed made good, but with no off-course influence. The effect can be of real significance in figuring your ETA at your destination. It can even affect the safety of your craft and its crew if you have figured your fuel too closely and run into a bow-on current.

A current that is nearly at a right angle to your course through the water will have a maximum effect on the course made good and a minor effect on the distance you must travel to reach your destination. The off-course effect can be of great importance if there are shoals or other hazards near your desired track.

Knowledge of current set and drift can be applied to assist your cruising. Departure times can be selected to take advantage of favorable currents, or at least to minimize adverse effects. A 12-knot boat speed and a 2-knot current, reasonably typical situations, can combine to result in either a 10-knot or a 14-knot speed made good—the 40%

gain of a favorable current over an opposing one is significant both in terms of time en route and fuel consumed.

Even lesser currents have some significance. A half-knot current would hinder a swimmer and make rowing a boat noticeably more difficult. A one-knot current can seriously affect a sailboat in light breezes.

## Difficult locations

In many boating areas, there will be locations where current conditions can be critical.

Numerous ocean inlets are difficult, or even dangerous, in certain combinations of current and onshore surf. In general, difficult surf conditions will be made more hazardous by an outward-flowing (ebbing) current. The topic of inlet seamanship is covered in more detail on pages 396–415.

There are a number of narrow bodies of water where the maximum current velocity is such as to make passage impossible at times for boats of limited power, and to seriously slow boats of greater engine power, fig. 2019. Such narrow passages are particularly characteristic of Pacific Northwest boating areas, but do occur elsewhere. Currents in New York City's East River reach a maximum of 4.6 knots, and at the Golden Gate of San Francisco velocities greater than 5 knots occur. Velocities of 3½ to 4 knots are common in much-traveled passages like Woods Hole, Mass., and Plum Gut, at the eastern end of Long Island, N. Y.

**FIG. 2021 Table 2— Current Differences and Other Constants. Data are given for hundreds of subordinate stations so that predictions for current may be made for many points of navigational significance.**

| No. | PLACE | POSITION | | TIME DIFFERENCES | | VELOCITY RATIOS | | MAXIMUM CURRENTS | | | |
|---|---|---|---|---|---|---|---|---|---|---|---|
| | | | | | | | | Flood | | Ebb | |
| | | Lat. | Long. | Slack water | Maximum current | Maximum flood | Maximum ebb | Direction (true) | Average velocity | Direction (true) | Average velocity |
| | | ° ′ N. | ° ′ W. | h. m. | h. m. | | | deg. | knots | deg. | knots |
| | **DELAWARE BAY and RIVER—Continued** | | | on DELAWARE BAY ENTRANCE, p.58 | | | | | | | |
| | | | | *Time meridian, 75°W.* | | | | | | | |
| 1091 | Fisher Point | 39 59 | 75 04 | +5 45 | +5 25 | 0.8 | 0.9 | 40 | 1.4 | 225 | 1.7 |
| 1093 | Torresdale, west of channel | 40 02 | 74 59 | (1) | +5 50 | 0.5 | 0.8 | 45 | 0.9 | 225 | 1.6 |
| 1095 | Rancocas Creek, off Delanco | 40 03 | 74 58 | +6 15 | +6 15 | 0.6 | 0.5 | 90 | 1.0 | 270 | 0.9 |
| 1097 | Bristol, south of | 40 05 | 74 52 | (2) | (2) | 0.7 | 0.8 | 25 | 1.3 | 200 | 1.6 |
| 1099 | Burlington Island, channel east of | 40 06 | 74 50 | (3) | (3) | 0.5 | 0.9 | 20 | 0.9 | 205 | 1.8 |
| 1101 | Whitehill | 40 08 | 74 44 | ----- | 4+7 00 | ---- | 0.7 | ---- | ---- | 235 | 1.4 |
| | **DEL., MD. and VA. COAST** | | | | | | | | | | |
| 1103 | Indian River Inlet (bridge) | 38 37 | 75 04 | +0 10 | +0 10 | 1.0 | 1.1 | 265 | 1.8 | 85 | 2.1 |
| 1105 | Fenwick Shoal Lighted Whistle Buoy 2 | 38 25 | 74 46 | See table 5. | | | | | | | |
| 1107 | Winter Quarter Shoal Lightship5 | 37 55 | 74 56 | See table 5. | | | | | | | |
| | | | | on CHESAPEAKE BAY ENTRANCE, p.64 | | | | | | | |
| 1109 | Cape Charles, 70 miles east of | 37 05 | 74 51 | See table 5. | | | | | | | |
| 1111 | Smith Island Shoal, southeast of | 37 05 | 75 43 | -2 10 | -2 10 | 0.3 | 0.3 | 300 | 0.3 | 70 | 0.4 |
| 1113 | Chesapeake Lightship | 36 59 | 75 42 | (6) | (6) | ---- | ---- | ---- | ---- | ---- | ---- |
| 1115 | Cape Henry Light, 2.2 miles SE. of | 36 54 | 75 59 | -1 15 | -1 30 | 1.0 | 0.6 | 345 | 1.0 | 165 | 0.9 |
| | **CHESAPEAKE BAY** | | | | | | | | | | |
| 1117 | Cape Henry Light, 1 mile north of | 36 56 | 76 00 | 0 00 | -0 25 | 1.1 | 1.3 | 280 | 1.1 | 90 | 2.0 |
| 1119 | Cape Henry Light, 1.8 miles north of | 36 57 | 76 00 | -0 05 | -0 15 | 1.2 | 1.0 | 290 | 1.2 | 100 | 1.5 |
| 1121 | CHESAPEAKE BAY ENTRANCE | 36 59 | 76 00 | Daily predictions | | | | 305 | 1.0 | 125 | 1.5 |
| 1123 | Cape Henry Light, 4.6 miles north of | 37 00 | 75 59 | -0 35 | -0 50 | 1.3 | 0.9 | 295 | 1.3 | 105 | 1.3 |
| 1124 | Cape Charles Light, 9.5 mi. WSW. of | 37 04 | 76 05 | +0 10 | 0 00 | 1.5 | 0.9 | 320 | 1.5 | 125 | 1.4 |
| 1125 | Cape Henry Light, 8.3 mi. NW. of | 37 02 | 76 07 | -0 05 | -0 10 | 1.0 | 0.7 | 330 | 1.0 | 135 | 1.1 |
| 1126 | Lynnhaven Roads | 36 55 | 76 05 | -0 35 | -0 40 | 0.8 | 0.6 | 280 | 0.8 | 70 | 0.9 |
| 1127 | Lynnhaven Inlet bridge | 36 54 | 76 06 | -2 05 | -2 35 | 0.6 | 0.9 | 180 | 0.6 | 0 | 1.4 |
| | *Chesapeake Bay Bridge Tunnel* | | | | | | | | | | |
| 1128 | Chesapeake Beach, 1.5 miles N. of | 36 57 | 76 07 | -0 15 | -0 20 | 0.8 | 0.6 | 305 | 0.8 | 100 | 0.9 |
| 1129 | Thimble Shoal Channel | 36 58 | 76 07 | -0 40 | -0 40 | 1.4 | 0.9 | 310 | 1.4 | 95 | 1.3 |
| 1130 | Tail of the Horseshoe | 37 00 | 76 06 | -0 25 | -0 40 | 0.9 | 0.7 | 300 | 0.9 | 110 | 1.0 |
| 1131 | Middle Ground, channel west of | 37 03 | 76 05 | -0 25 | -0 10 | 1.6 | 0.9 | 335 | 1.6 | 150 | 1.3 |
| 1132 | Chesapeake Channel | 37 02 | 76 04 | -0 15 | -0 10 | 1.8 | 1.0 | 335 | 1.8 | 145 | 1.5 |
| 1133 | Fisherman I., 3.2 miles WSW. of | 37 04 | 76 02 | -0 55 | -1 05 | 1.2 | 1.1 | 330 | 1.2 | 135 | 1.4 |
| 1134 | Fisherman I., 1.4 miles WSW. of | 37 05 | 76 00 | (7) | -1 15 | 1.8 | 0.7 | 330 | 1.8 | 140 | 1.1 |
| 1135 | Fisherman I., 1.8 miles south of | 37 04 | 75 59 | -0 45 | -1 10 | 1.6 | 0.9 | 320 | 1.6 | 120 | 1.4 |
| 1136 | Fisherman I., 0.4 mile west of | 37 06 | 75 59 | -0 45 | -1 10 | 2.0 | 1.3 | 5 | 2.0 | 175 | 2.0 |
| 1137 | Fisherman I., 1.1 miles NW. of | 37 06 | 76 00 | (8) | -0 40 | 1.8 | 1.1 | 355 | 1.8 | 165 | 1.6 |
| 1139 | Cape Charles, off Wise Point | 37 07 | 75 58 | (9) | (9) | 0.7 | 0.1 | 305 | 0.7 | 75 | 0.2 |
| | *Little Creek* | | | | | | | | | | |
| 1141 | North of east jetty | 36 56 | 76 11 | -1 50 | -2 00 | 0.9 | 0.7 | 280 | 0.9 | 75 | 1.0 |
| 1143 | 0.5 mile north of west jetty | 36 56 | 76 11 | -1 10 | -1 15 | 0.9 | 0.6 | 275 | 0.9 | 110 | 0.9 |
| 1145 | Old Plantation Flats Light, west of | 37 14 | 76 04 | +1 10 | +0 50 | 1.2 | 0.9 | 5 | 1.2 | 175 | 1.3 |
| 1146 | York Spit Channel | 37 13 | 76 09 | +0 55 | +0 55 | 0.8 | 0.7 | 10 | 0.8 | 195 | 1.1 |
| 1147 | Wolf Trap Light, 0.5 mile west of | 37 23 | 76 12 | +1 05 | +1 05 | 1.0 | 0.8 | 15 | 1.0 | 190 | 1.2 |
| 1148 | Wolf Trap Light, 5.8 miles east of | 37 23 | 76 04 | +1 45 | +1 45 | 0.9 | 0.9 | 15 | 0.9 | 175 | 1.3 |
| 1149 | Stingray Point, 5.5 miles east of | 37 35 | 76 10 | +1 50 | +2 20 | 1.0 | 0.6 | 345 | 1.0 | 180 | 0.9 |
| 1150 | Stingray Point, 12.5 miles east of | 37 34 | 76 02 | +1 40 | +2 05 | 1.0 | 1.0 | 30 | 1.0 | 175 | 0.8 |

1 Flood begins, +6ʰ 55ᵐ; ebb begins, +5ʰ 00ᵐ.

2 Flood begins, +6ʰ 55ᵐ; maximum flood, +5ʰ 30ᵐ; ebb begins, +4ʰ 55ᵐ; maximum ebb, +6ʰ 10ᵐ.

3 Flood begins, +7ʰ 30ᵐ; maximum flood, +5ʰ 45ᵐ; ebb begins, +4ʰ 15ᵐ; maximum ebb, +6ʰ 45ᵐ.

## TIDAL CURRENT PREDICTIONS

Without experience or official information, local current prediction is always risky. East of Badgers Island in Portsmouth, Maine, for example, the average ebb current flows at a maximum velocity of less than a half-knot. Yet, southwest of the same island, it averages 3.7 knots.

One rule is fairly safe for most locations—the ebb is stronger and lasts longer than the flood. Eighty percent of all reference stations on the Atlantic, Gulf, and Pacific coasts of the U.S. report currents stronger at the ebb. This is normal because river flow adds to the ebb, but hinders the flood.

On the Atlantic coast, expect to find two approximately equal flood currents and two similar ebb currents in a cycle of roughly 25 hours. On the Pacific coast, however, two floods and ebbs will differ markedly. On the Gulf coast, there may be just one flood and one ebb in 25 hours. In each case, these patterns are, of course, generally similar to tidal action in the respective areas.

Don't try to predict current velocity from the time that it takes a high tide to reach a given point from the sea's entrance. Dividing the distance from Cape Henry to Baltimore by the time that it takes high water to work its way up Chesapeake Bay gives a speed of 13 knots. True maximum flood current strength is only about one knot.

Another useful truism about tidal currents is that tidal currents at different places *cannot* be forecast from their tidal ranges. You would expect strong currents at Eastport, Maine, where the difference between successive high and low waters reaches as much as 20 feet. And you would be right; there are three-knot currents there. But Galveston, Texas, with only a two-foot range of tides has currents up to more than two knots. So has Miami with a three-foot range, and Charleston, S. C. with a six-foot range—these are stronger currents than Boston where the range is often more than 10 feet and as strong as at Anchorage, Alaska where it's as much as 35 feet from some highs to the next low.

A good forecasting rule for all oceans: expect strong tidal currents where two bays meet. The reason: tidal ranges and high water times in the two bodies of water are likely to be different.

For the coasting skipper, here is another tidal current fact that may be useful: near the beach, flood and ebb don't usually set to and from the land, but rather parallel with the coast. This is as true off New Jersey and Florida as it is off California and Oregon. A few miles offshore, however, and in some very large bays, the current behaves quite differently—the rotary current mentioned previously in this chapter.

## TIDAL CURRENT TABLES

At any given place, current strength varies with the phases of the moon and its distance from the earth. It will be strongest when tidal ranges are greatest—near new and

### TABLE A

Interval between slack and maximum current

| Interval between slack and desired time (h. m.) | 1 20 | 1 40 | 2 00 | 2 20 | 2 40 | 3 00 | 3 20 | 3 40 | 4 00 | 4 20 | 4 40 | 5 00 | 5 20 | 5 40 |
|---|---|---|---|---|---|---|---|---|---|---|---|---|---|---|
| | f. | f. | f. | f. | f. | f. | f. | f. | f. | f. | f. | f. | f. | f. |
| 0 20 | 0.4 | 0.3 | 0.3 | 0.2 | 0.2 | 0.2 | 0.2 | 0.1 | 0.1 | 0.1 | 0.1 | 0.1 | 0.1 | 0.1 |
| 0 40 | 0.7 | 0.6 | 0.5 | 0.4 | 0.4 | 0.3 | 0.3 | 0.3 | 0.3 | 0.2 | 0.2 | 0.2 | 0.2 | 0.2 |
| 1 00 | 0.9 | 0.8 | 0.7 | 0.6 | 0.6 | 0.5 | 0.5 | 0.4 | 0.4 | 0.4 | 0.3 | 0.3 | 0.3 | 0.3 |
| 1 20 | 1.0 | 1.0 | 0.9 | 0.8 | 0.7 | 0.6 | 0.6 | 0.5 | 0.5 | 0.5 | 0.4 | 0.4 | 0.4 | 0.4 |
| 1 40 | ----- | 1.0 | 1.0 | 0.9 | 0.8 | 0.8 | 0.7 | 0.7 | 0.6 | 0.6 | 0.6 | 0.5 | 0.5 | 0.4 |
| 2 00 | ----- | ----- | 1.0 | 1.0 | 0.9 | 0.9 | 0.8 | 0.8 | 0.7 | 0.7 | 0.6 | 0.6 | 0.6 | 0.5 |
| 2 20 | ----- | ----- | ----- | 1.0 | 1.0 | 0.9 | 0.9 | 0.9 | 0.8 | 0.7 | 0.7 | 0.7 | 0.6 | 0.6 |
| 2 40 | ----- | ----- | ----- | ----- | 1.0 | 1.0 | 1.0 | 0.9 | 0.9 | 0.8 | 0.8 | 0.7 | 0.7 | 0.7 |
| 3 00 | ----- | ----- | ----- | ----- | ----- | 1.0 | 1.0 | 1.0 | 0.9 | 0.9 | 0.8 | 0.8 | 0.8 | 0.7 |
| 3 20 | ----- | ----- | ----- | ----- | ----- | ----- | 1.0 | 1.0 | 1.0 | 0.9 | 0.9 | 0.9 | 0.8 | 0.8 |
| 3 40 | ----- | ----- | ----- | ----- | ----- | ----- | ----- | 1.0 | 1.0 | 1.0 | 0.9 | 0.9 | 0.9 | 0.9 |
| 4 00 | ----- | ----- | ----- | ----- | ----- | ----- | ----- | ----- | 1.0 | 1.0 | 1.0 | 1.0 | 0.9 | 0.9 |
| 4 20 | ----- | ----- | ----- | ----- | ----- | ----- | ----- | ----- | ----- | 1.0 | 1.0 | 1.0 | 1.0 | 0.9 |
| 4 40 | ----- | ----- | ----- | ----- | ----- | ----- | ----- | ----- | ----- | ----- | 1.0 | 1.0 | 1.0 | 1.0 |
| 5 00 | ----- | ----- | ----- | ----- | ----- | ----- | ----- | ----- | ----- | ----- | ----- | 1.0 | 1.0 | 1.0 |
| 5 20 | ----- | ----- | ----- | ----- | ----- | ----- | ----- | ----- | ----- | ----- | ----- | ----- | 1.0 | 1.0 |
| 5 40 | ----- | ----- | ----- | ----- | ----- | ----- | ----- | ----- | ----- | ----- | ----- | ----- | ----- | 1.0 |

### TABLE B

Interval between slack and maximum current

| Interval between slack and desired time (h. m.) | 1 20 | 1 40 | 2 00 | 2 20 | 2 40 | 3 00 | 3 20 | 3 40 | 4 00 | 4 20 | 4 40 | 5 00 | 5 20 | 5 40 |
|---|---|---|---|---|---|---|---|---|---|---|---|---|---|---|
| | f. | f. | f. | f. | f. | f. | f. | f. | f. | f. | f. | f. | f. | f. |
| 0 20 | 0.5 | 0.4 | 0.4 | 0.3 | 0.3 | 0.3 | 0.3 | 0.3 | 0.3 | 0.2 | 0.2 | 0.2 | 0.2 | 0.2 |
| 0 40 | 0.8 | 0.7 | 0.6 | 0.6 | 0.5 | 0.5 | 0.5 | 0.4 | 0.4 | 0.4 | 0.4 | 0.3 | 0.3 | 0.3 |
| 1 00 | 0.9 | 0.8 | 0.8 | 0.7 | 0.7 | 0.6 | 0.6 | 0.5 | 0.5 | 0.5 | 0.4 | 0.4 | 0.4 | 0.4 |
| 1 20 | 1.0 | 1.0 | 0.9 | 0.8 | 0.8 | 0.7 | 0.7 | 0.6 | 0.6 | 0.6 | 0.5 | 0.5 | 0.5 | 0.5 |
| 1 40 | ----- | 1.0 | 1.0 | 1.0 | 0.9 | 0.9 | 0.8 | 0.8 | 0.7 | 0.7 | 0.7 | 0.6 | 0.6 | 0.6 |
| 2 00 | ----- | ----- | 1.0 | 1.0 | 0.9 | 0.9 | 0.9 | 0.8 | 0.8 | 0.7 | 0.7 | 0.7 | 0.7 | 0.6 |
| 2 20 | ----- | ----- | ----- | 1.0 | 1.0 | 1.0 | 0.9 | 0.9 | 0.8 | 0.8 | 0.8 | 0.7 | 0.7 | 0.7 |
| 2 40 | ----- | ----- | ----- | ----- | 1.0 | 1.0 | 1.0 | 0.9 | 0.9 | 0.9 | 0.8 | 0.8 | 0.8 | 0.7 |
| 3 00 | ----- | ----- | ----- | ----- | ----- | 1.0 | 1.0 | 1.0 | 0.9 | 0.9 | 0.9 | 0.9 | 0.8 | 0.8 |
| 3 20 | ----- | ----- | ----- | ----- | ----- | ----- | 1.0 | 1.0 | 1.0 | 1.0 | 0.9 | 0.9 | 0.9 | 0.9 |
| 3 40 | ----- | ----- | ----- | ----- | ----- | ----- | ----- | 1.0 | 1.0 | 1.0 | 1.0 | 0.9 | 0.9 | 0.9 |
| 4 00 | ----- | ----- | ----- | ----- | ----- | ----- | ----- | ----- | 1.0 | 1.0 | 1.0 | 1.0 | 0.9 | 0.9 |
| 4 20 | ----- | ----- | ----- | ----- | ----- | ----- | ----- | ----- | ----- | 1.0 | 1.0 | 1.0 | 1.0 | 1.0 |
| 4 40 | ----- | ----- | ----- | ----- | ----- | ----- | ----- | ----- | ----- | ----- | 1.0 | 1.0 | 1.0 | 1.0 |
| 5 00 | ----- | ----- | ----- | ----- | ----- | ----- | ----- | ----- | ----- | ----- | ----- | 1.0 | 1.0 | 1.0 |
| 5 20 | ----- | ----- | ----- | ----- | ----- | ----- | ----- | ----- | ----- | ----- | ----- | ----- | 1.0 | 1.0 |
| 5 40 | ----- | ----- | ----- | ----- | ----- | ----- | ----- | ----- | ----- | ----- | ----- | ----- | ----- | 1.0 |

FIG. 2022 Table 3—Velocity of Current at Any Time. Using the appropriate part, A or B, of this table, the velocity of current at intermediate times between maximum strength and slack may be calculated for either a reference or a subordinate station. Table B is for use at Cape Cod Canal, Hell Gate, or Chesapeake and Delaware Canal only; use Table A for all other locations.

### DURATION OF WEAK CURRENT NEAR TIME OF SLACK WATER

#### Table A

| Maximum current | Period with a velocity not more than— | | | | |
|---|---|---|---|---|---|
| | 0.1 knot | 0.2 knot | 0.3 knot | 0.4 knot | 0.5 knot |
| Knots | Minutes | Minutes | Minutes | Minutes | Minutes |
| 1.0 | 23 | 46 | 70 | 94 | 120 |
| 1.5 | 15 | 31 | 46 | 62 | 78 |
| 2.0 | 11 | 23 | 35 | 46 | 58 |
| 3.0 | 8 | 15 | 23 | 31 | 38 |
| 4.0 | 6 | 11 | 17 | 23 | 29 |
| 5.0 | 5 | 9 | 14 | 18 | 23 |
| 6.0 | 4 | 8 | 11 | 15 | 19 |
| 7.0 | 3 | 7 | 10 | 13 | 16 |
| 8.0 | 3 | 6 | 9 | 11 | 14 |
| 9.0 | 3 | 5 | 8 | 10 | 13 |
| 10.0 | 2 | 5 | 7 | 9 | 11 |

#### Table B

| Maximum current | Period with a velocity not more than— | | | | |
|---|---|---|---|---|---|
| | 0.1 knot | 0.2 knot | 0.3 knot | 0.4 knot | 0.5 knot |
| Knots | Minutes | Minutes | Minutes | Minutes | Minutes |
| 1.0 | 13 | 28 | 46 | 66 | 89 |
| 1.5 | 8 | 18 | 28 | 39 | 52 |
| 2.0 | 6 | 13 | 20 | 28 | 36 |
| 3.0 | 4 | 8 | 13 | 18 | 22 |
| 4.0 | 3 | 6 | 9 | 13 | 17 |
| 5.0 | 3 | 5 | 8 | 10 | 13 |

FIG. 2023 Table 4—Duration of Slack. Although actual slack water is only a momentary event, current velocity is quite small for a significant period while the direction is reversing. Part A or B of this table is used in the same situations as for Table 3.

SPEED LINES   Chesapeake Bay

Bound Northward      Bound Southward

6 7 8 9 10 11 12 13 14 15    15 14 13 12 11 10 9 8 7 6

KNOTS              KNOTS

full moon—and weakest when tidal ranges are least—near first and last quarters. Current velocity may vary as much as 40 percent above and below its average value.

The relationship between currents and tides makes possible the prediction of tidal currents. The Coast and Geodetic Survey publishes two volumes of predictions annually; one covers the Atlantic Coast of North America and the other the Pacific Coast of North America and Asia.

Each volume includes for its area, predictions of tidal currents in bays, sounds, and rivers, plus ocean currents such as the Gulf Stream. General information on wind-driven currents is also included although these, of course, result from temporary, local conditions and so cannot be predicted a year or more ahead. Your own past experience and "local knowledge," the advice of experienced watermen of the area, will be the best source of information regarding the effect of storm winds on local waters and their currents.

Tidal Current Tables are available at authorized sales agents for C&GS charts. The cost of each volume is $2.00.

### Description of the Tables

The format and layout of the *Tidal Current Tables* is much the same as for the *Tide Tables* discussed earlier in this chapter. A system of reference stations, plus constants and differences for subordinate stations, is used to calculate the predictions for many points.

**Table 1.** There are 20 *reference stations* in the Atlantic Coast volume and 10 for the Pacific Coast. The Gulf of Mexico is included in the Atlantic Coast volume. For each station, there are tabulated the predicted times and strengths of maximum flood and ebb currents, plus the times of slack water. The direction of the flood and ebb currents is also listed, see fig. 2020.

**Table 2.** Time differences and velocity ratios are listed for hundreds of *subordinate stations*, fig. 2021. The location of these stations is described in terms of place names or position relative to identifiable points; the latitude and longitude are also given as an aid to their precise location. The direction and strength of typical maximum currents for each station are also tabulated. A number of subordinate stations will have only the footnoted entry "Current too weak and variable to be predicted." This information, even though negative in nature, is useful in planning a cruise.

**Table 3.** This table, fig. 2022, provides a convenient means for determination of the strength of the current at times intermediate between slack and maximum velocity. Use nearest tabulated values without interpolation.

**Table 4.** Although slack water is only a momentary event, there is a period of time on either side of slack during which the current is so weak as to be negligible

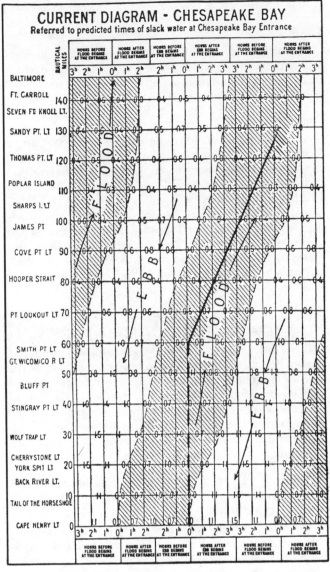

FIG. 2024. Tidal Current Diagrams from the Tidal Current Tables (East Coast volume only) provide a quick and simple way of determining the best speed and time of departure for a run up or down several of the major waterways subject to tidal currents.

for practical piloting purposes. This period, naturally, varies with the maximum strength of the current, being longer for weak currents. Two sub-tables, fig. 2023, predict the duration of currents from 0.1 to 0.5 knot by tenths for normal reversing currents and for the hydraulic currents found at certain specified locations.

**Table 5.** For the Atlantic Coast only, information is given on rotary tidal currents at various offshore points of navigational interest. These points are described in terms of general location and specific geographic coordinates. Predictions of velocity and direction are referred to times after maximum flood at designated reference stations.

### Current Diagrams

For a number of major tidal waterways of the United States, a *current diagram,* such as fig. 2024, is provided in the Tidal Current Tables. These give a graphic means of quickly and easily selecting a favorable time for traveling in either direction along these routes.

# Tides and Currents / CHAPTER 20

### Time

The Tidal Current Tables list all predictions in *local standard time.* Be sure to make a conversion to daylight time if you are piloting in an area using such "fast" time; this is done by adding one hour to the tabulated times.

### Cautions

As with tidal predictions, the data in the Tidal Current Tables may often be upset by sustained abnormal local conditions such as winds or rainfall. Use the current predictions with caution during and immediately after such weather abnormalities.

It should also be noted carefully that tidal current predictions are generally for a *spot location only;* the set and drift may be quite different only a mile or less away. This is at variance from predictions of high and low tides which can usually be used over fairly wide areas in the vicinity of the reference or secondary station.

## EXAMPLES OF TIDAL CURRENT CALCULATIONS

The Tidal Current Tables contain all the information needed for the determination of such conditions as the time of maximum current and its strength, the time of slack water, the duration of slack (actually, the duration of the very weak current conditions), etc. Examples will be given of typical problems and their solution, plus comments and cautions to be used in connection with such situations.

### Example 1. Determination of the time and strength of maximum current, and the time of slack, at a reference station.

**Problem:** What is the time and strength of the maximum ebb current at Chesapeake Bay Entrance during the afternoon of 17 October 1967?

**Solution:** As with the Tide Tables, the answer is available for a reference station by direct inspection. Fig. 2020 is a typical page from the Tidal Current Tables; we can see that the maximum ebb current on the specified afternoon is 1.5 knots setting 125° True; it is predicted to occur at 1430 EST.

**Problem:** What is the time of the first slack before ebb at this station on 17 October 1967?

**Solution:** Table 1 does not directly identify the slacks as being "slack before ebb" or "slack before flood"; this must be determined by comparison of the slack time with the nature of the next occurring maximum current.

From fig. 2020, we can see that the earliest slack that will be followed by an ebbing current at Chesapeake Bay Entrance on 17 October is predicted for 1054 EST.

**Notes:** a. Times obtained from the Tidal Current Tables are *standard;* add one hour for daylight time if in effect.
b. The set of the current for a reference station is found at the *top* of the page in Table 1; it is also given in Table 2 where further information, such as the geographic coordinates of the station, and the average velocity of maximum flood and ebb currents, is listed.
c. The normal day at Chesapeake Bay Entrance, where the tide is of the semi-diurnal type, will have four slacks

and four maximums. The tidal cycle of 24$^h$ and 50$^m$ will result in the occasional omission of a slack or maximum.

### Example 2. Determination of the time and strength of maximum current, and the time of slack, at a subordinate station.

**Problem:** What is the time and strength of the morning flood current in Lynnhaven Inlet at the bridge on 21 September 1967?

**Solution:** Table 2, fig. 2021, gives time differences and velocity ratios to be applied to the predictions at the appropriate reference station. There is an Index to Table 2 in the rear of the Tidal Current Tables if it is needed to locate the given subordinate station.

In this problem, the time difference and velocity ratio are applied as follows:

|  |  |  |
|---|---|---|
| 10 06 | at Chesapeake Bay Entrance | 1.0 knot |
| −2:35 | difference/ratio | 0.6 |
| 07 31 | at Lynnhaven Inlet | 0.6 knot |

The set (direction) of the current is also noted from the appropriate column of Table 2; in this case, it is 180° True.

Thus the predictions are for a maximum current of 0.6 knot setting 180° True at Lynnhaven Inlet bridge at 0731 EST on 21 September 1967.

**Problem:** What is the time of the first afternoon slack water at Lynnhaven Inlet bridge on 6 September 1967?

**Solution:** From Table 2, the time difference is found to be −2:05. This is applied to the time of slack at the reference station:

|  |  |
|---|---|
| 19 42 | at Chesapeake Bay Entrance |
| −2:05 | difference |
| 17 37 | at Lynnhaven Inlet bridge |

The time of the first afternoon slack water at Lynnhaven Inlet bridge on 6 September 1967 is 1737 EST.

**Notes:** a. Observe that often there may be two separate time differences, one for slack and the other for maximum current, either flood or ebb. More complex situations with varied time differences will be shown by special footnotes to Table 2 where required. Note also that the velocity ratios may differ between ebb and flood.
b. Note that the direction of the current at a subordinate station must be taken from Table 2. It will nearly always differ from that at the reference station. No statement of current is complete without giving direction as well as strength.
c. The locations in Table 2 are usually a point some distance and direction from a landmark or aid to navigation. There may be several subordinate stations referred to the same base point (see subordinate stations 1117 to 1124, and 1149-1150 in fig. 2021); be sure to use the correct subordinate station.

### Example 3. Determination of the current at an intermediate time at a reference station.

**Problem:** What is the velocity and set of the current at Chesapeake Bay Entrance at 1300 EST on 3 October 1967?

**Solution:** The time of slack and maximum current (ebb or flood) which bracket the desired time are found from Table 1. The interval between these times is determined, as is the interval between the desired time and the slack.

```
  14 24
  10 48
```
3:36  interval, slack—maximum current

```
  13 00
  10 48
```
2:12  interval, slack—desired time

With these time intervals, Table 3A is used to determine the ratio of the velocity of the current at the desired time to its maximum velocity. The nearest tabulated values are used, no interpolation. In this example, the ratio at the intersection of the line for $2^h 20^m$ and the column for $3^h 40^m$ is found to be 0.8. Multiply the maximum current by this decimal factor, $1.9 \times 0.8 = 1.5$.

From the times used, we note that the current is ebbing. From the top of Table 1, we determine that the direction is 125° True.

Thus, at 1300 EST on 3 October 1967, the current at Chesapeake Bay Entrance is predicted to have a velocity of 1.5 knots and be setting 125° True.

**Notes:** a. Except as specially indicated, use Table 3A, the upper portion of Table 3. The lower, B, portion is for use in designated waterways only.

b. Be sure that the interval is calculated between the desired time and the time of *slack,* whether or not this time is nearer to the given time than the time of maximum current.

c. Note that calculations of current velocity are rounded to the nearest tenth of a knot.

## Example 4.  Determination of the current at an intermediate time at a subordinate station.

**Problem:** What is the velocity and set of the current at a point 5½ miles east of Stingray Point at 1700 EDT on 5 October 1967?

**Solution:** First, the predictions for slack and maximum current must be found for the subordinate station after converting 1700 EDT to 1600 EST for entering the Tables.

| Slack | | Maximum | |
|---|---|---|---|
| 12 36 at Chesapeake Bay | | | |
| Entrance | | 16 06 | 1.9 knots, Ebb |
| +1:50 difference/ratio | | +2:20 | 0.6 |
| 14 26 at subordinate station | | 18 26 | 1.1 |

With the information developed above, and the desired time, further calculations are made as follows:

```
  18 26
  14 26
```
4:00  interval, slack—maximum current

```
  16 00  (EST)
  14 26
```
1:34  interval, slack—desired time

Using Table 3A, fig. 2022, the velocity ratio is found to be 0.6; then $1.1 \times 0.6 = 0.7$. From Table 2, the direction is seen to be 180° True.

The current at 1700 EDT at a point 5½ miles east of Stingray Point on 5 October 1967 is predicted to be 0.7 knot setting 180° True.

**Note:** Calculations for the strength at an intermediate time of a hydraulic current, such as in the Cape Cod Canal or at Hell Gate in East River, New York City, are handled

exactly as above, except that the lower, B, part of Table 3 is used.

## Example 5.  Determination of the duration of slack (weak current) at a designated point.

**Problem:** For how long will the current be less than 0.4 knots around the time of slack before ebb on the morning of 4 October 1967 at Chesapeake Bay Entrance?

**Solution:** From Table 1 (fig. 2020), for this date, the maximum currents on either side of this slack (at 1142) are 1.5 knots flood at 0848 and 2.0 knots ebb at 1512.

Using Table 4A (fig. 2023), the duration of current less than 0.4 knot is determined for each maximum. One-half of each such duration is used for the period from 0.4 to 0 knots and then 0 to 0.4 knots.

The value for the ending flood current is one-half of 62, or 31 minutes; for the beginning ebb current, it is one-half of 46, or 23 minutes.

On 4 October 1967 at Chesapeake Bay Entrance, the predicted duration of a current less than 0.4 knot is $31 + 23 = 54$ minutes; from $1142 - 31 = 1111$ until $1142 + 23 = 1205$. **Notes:** a. If the maximum strengths of the ebb and flood currents are essentially the same, only one figure need be taken from Table 4. Interpolate as necessary.

b. Use the A or B portion of Table 4 in the same manner as for Table 3.

## Example 6.  Use of a Tidal Current Diagram.

**Problem:** For an afternoon run up Chesapeake Bay from Smith Point to Sandy Point Light at 10 knots on 20 October 1967, what time should you depart from Smith Point for the most favorable current conditions?

**Solution:** We use the current diagram for Chesapeake Bay and a graphic solution, fig. 2024. Draw a line on the diagram parallel to the 10-knot northbound speed line so that it fits generally in the center of the shaded area marked "Flood." Project downward from the intersection of this line with the horizontal line marked Smith Point Light to the scale at the bottom of the diagram. The mark here will be seen to be "$0^h$ after ebb begins at the entrance."

Referring to Table 1, it will be seen that on the given date, the afternoon slack before ebb occurs at 1242.

For a run up Chesapeake Bay to Sandy Point Light at 10 knots on the afternoon of 20 October 1967, it is predicted that the most favorable current conditions will be obtained if you leave Smith Point Light at about 1242 EST or 1342 EDT.

**Notes:** a. Similar solutions can be worked out for southbound trips, but it is likely that on longer runs you will be faced with both favorable and unfavorable current conditions. Selection of starting time may be made, however, to minimize adverse conditions.

b. Conditions shown on Tidal Current Diagrams are averages and for typical conditions; small variations should be expected in specific situations.

## TIDAL CURRENT CHARTS

The Coast and Geodetic Survey also publishes a series of *Tidal Current Charts.* These are available for eight bodies of water, from Boston Harbor around to Puget Sound (see complete listing on page 299).

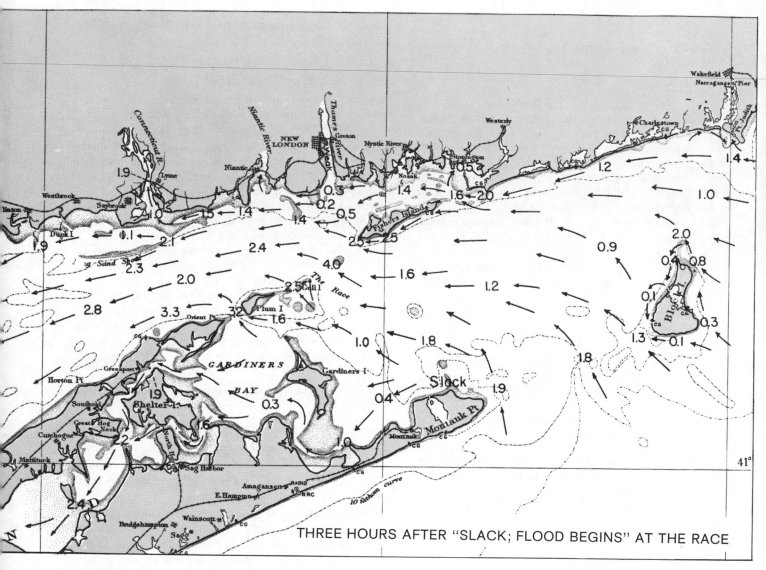

**FIG. 2025** Tidal Current Charts are published for certain major bodies of water. Each is a set of 12 small-scale chartlets showing currents existing at hourly intervals throughout a complete cycle of flood and ebb.

Tidal Current Charts are made up in the form of a series of 12 reproductions of a small-scale chart of the area. Each of the charts depicts the direction and velocity of the current for a specific time in terms of hours after the predicted time of the beginning of flood or the beginning of ebb at the appropriate reference station. See fig. 2025. The currents in various passages and portions of the body of water are indicated by arrows and numbers. By following through the sequence of the charts, the hourly changes in strength and direction are easily seen.

These charts must be used with caution as tidal current strengths may vary widely between points separated by only a short distance.

Tidal Current Charts are periodically updated from new surveys and only the latest edition should be used.

## RIVER CURRENTS

River currents, above tidal action, will consistently flow in one direction, but the velocity may vary widely. In some instances, information can be obtained from the U.S. Army Engineers, but usually your best source will be local personnel. Experience has shown, however, that such persons will more often than not overestimate current strength.

Usually, the strongest currents will occur in the deepest part of the channel. Near the banks, the current will be weaker; you may even find a counter-current running weakly in the opposite direction. In a bend of a river, expect the strongest current on the outside of the turn. Where a river narrows, or the flow is restricted by a shoal, an island, or man-made structure, the current will accelerate.

For further consideration of river current, refer to Chapter 29.

## SUPPLEMENTARY SOURCES OF INFORMATION

The ultimate source of current information is your own eyesight and past experience, fig. 2026. These are most helpful even where there are predictions from the C&GS tables. As noted before, the tabular data are to be expected under "normal" conditions, and may be easily upset by unusual circumstances. Strong winds will, for example, drive water into or out of bays and modify tidal levels and currents.

◀ **0.6 KNOT**

Note (far left) how at 0.3 knot a wake is evident and the buoy inclines slightly. Doubling the velocity (0.6 knot, at left) increases the disturbance on both sides of the buoy. At 1.0 knot (below, left) it leans over and a whirlpool-like eddy has developed. Finally, at 2.2 knots (below), the wake has whitened. Buoy shapes affect the pattern and inclination.

**2.2 KNOTS** ▼

▲ **0.3 KNOT**

These photographs by Larry Riordan show clearly how buoys can be a helpful aid in estimating the direction and strength of current. Even though some data are available in Current Tables, predictions may be in error because of wind. Turbulence and eddies around a buoy increase with current velocity. In very strong currents, buoys may tow completely under.

**1.0 KNOT** ▶

**FIG. 2026** Tidal current predictions are often upset by temporary local conditions of wind or rainfall. There is no substitute for an ability to interpret currents from visual observations. This excellent set of photographs shows visible indications on a buoy of currents of various strengths. Be careful; do not overestimate current velocity.

## Currents and Piloting

One of the most interesting problems in small-craft piloting is the matter of currents, their effect upon boat speed, the determination of courses which must be steered to make good a desired path, and the time required to reach a destination. This is often know as *current sailing.*

Contrary to popular belief, the solution of current problems is really comparatively simple and does not require the use of higher mathematics to obtain results of practical accuracy. Indeed, when the fundamental principles have been mastered, the working out of current problems can be fun.

As a boat is propelled through the water, by oars, sails, or motor, and as it is steered, it moves with respect to the water. At the same time, the water may be moving with respect to the bottom and the shore as a result of current. The resultant motion of the boat is the net effect of these two motions combined, with regard to both velocity and direction. The actual track made good over the bottom will not be the same as the DR track, neither in terms of course nor speed.

The importance of tidal currents should not be underestimated. Unexpected current is always a threat to the skipper because it can carry his craft off course, possibly into dangerous waters. The risk is greater with slower boat speeds and under conditions of reduced visibility. A prediction of current effect can be added to a plot of a DR

track to obtain an *estimated position (EP)* plotted as a small square with a dot in the center, fig. 2027.

### Leeway

Before proceeding further with current effects, let us here introduce, and then dispense with, the term *leeway.* By definition, leeway is the leeward (away from the wind)

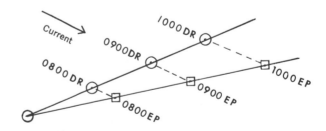

**FIG. 2027** If the current is known, or can be estimated, a DR plot can be modified to show a series of Estimated Positions (EP) showing the effect of current.

motion of a vessel due to the wind. The term is most applicable to sailing craft, but it can be appreciable on larger motorboats and yachts. Its effect, however, need not be considered separately from current; the two may be lumped together, plus such factors as wave action on the boat, and the total offsetting influence termed "current."

Sailing Directions emphasize the necessity of taking such influences into account. A typical caution might read: "The directions 'steer' or 'make good' a course mean, without exception, to proceed from a point of origin along a track having the identical meridional angle as the designated course. Vessels following the directives must allow for every influence tending to cause deviation (not to be confused with compass deviation—Ed) from such track, and navigate so that the designated course is continuously being made good."

## DEFINITION OF CURRENT SAILING TERMS

The terms "Course" and "Speed" were used in DR plots for the motion of the boat through the water without regard to current. Now this most important influence will be studied and additional terms must be introduced.

The *intended track* is the expected path of the boat, as plotted on a chart, after consideration has been given to the effect of current.

*Track,* abbreviated as TR, is the direction (true) of the intended track line.

*Speed of advance, SOA,* is the intended rate of travel along the intended track line.

It must be recognized that the intended track will not always be the actual track, and so two more terms are needed.

*Course over the ground, COG,* is the direction of the *actual* path of the boat, the track made good.

*Speed over the ground, SOG,* is the actual rate of travel along this track.

## CURRENT SITUATIONS

A study of the effects of current resolves itself into two basic situations, as follows:

1. When the direction of the current, its *set,* is in the same direction as the boat's motion, or is in exactly the opposite direction.

2. When the direction of the current is at an angle to the boat's course, either a right or an oblique angle.

The first situation is, of course, the simplest and most easily solved. The velocity of the current, the *drift,* is added to, or subtracted from, the speed through the water to obtain the speed over the ground. The course over the ground (or intended track) is the same as the DR course—COG equals C, as does TR.

## CURRENT DIAGRAMS

When the boat's motion and the set of the current form an angle with each other, the solution for the resultant course and speed is more complex, but still not difficult. Several methods may be used, but a graphic solution using a *current diagram* will usually be found to be the easiest to understand.

Basically, a current diagram represents the two component motions separately, as if they occurred independently and sequentially, which, of course, they do not. These diagrams can be drawn in terms of velocities or distances. The former is easier and is usually used; current diagrams in this book will be drawn in terms of velocities and labeled as shown in fig. 2028. If distances are plotted, be sure to use the same period of time for each component motion—one hour is commonly used since the units of distance will then be the same numerically as the units of speed.

### Accuracy of current diagrams

The accuracy with which the resultant course and speed can be determined depends largely on the accuracy with which the current has been determined. Values of the current usually must be taken from tidal current tables or charts, or estimated by the skipper from visual observations; see fig. 2026.

Current diagrams may also be called "vector triangles of velocity," a profound title for a simple graphic procedure. The term "vector" in mathematics means a quantity that has both magnitude and direction. Directed quantities are important things. In current sailing, the directed quantities are the motions of the boat and the water (the current).

### Vectors

A vector may be represented graphically by an arrow, a segment of a straight line with an arrowhead indicating the direction, and the length of the line scaled to the velocity, fig. 2029. If we specify that a certain unit of length is equal to a certain unit of speed—e.g., that 1 inch equals 1 knot—then two such vectors can represent graphically two different velocities. Any speed scale may be used, the larger the better for accuracy. The size of the available paper and working space will normally control the scale.

Current diagrams may be drawn on a chart either as part of the plot or separately. They may also be drawn on plain paper; in this case, it is wise to draw in a north line as the

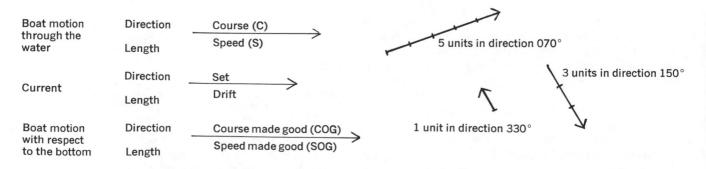

**FIG. 2028** The component lines of a current diagram must always be correctly and completely labeled. Direction is shown above the line; velocity is noted below the line. Typical labels are shown above.

**FIG. 2029** A vector is a line representing a *directed quantity*. It has direction (shown by the arrowhead) and magnitude (length). Any convenient scale may be selected to indicate magnitude.

reference for measuring directions.

Since boats are subject to two distinct motions—the boat through the water, and the water with respect to the bottom—we will now consider how the resultant motion, or vector sum, is obtained by current diagrams.

## Vector triangles

When the two motions are not in line with each other, they form two sides of a triangle, fig. 2030. Completing the triangle gives the third side which will be a vector representing the resultant motion or velocity. Thus, when any two velocity vectors are drawn to the same scale and form the sides of a velocity triangle, the third side will be the resultant velocity vector (the vector sum of the other two), and its direction and magnitude may be measured from the diagram.

It may be an aid to the visualization of the component motions if a time period of one hour is used and the points that are the corners of the triangle are considered as positions of the boat before and after certain motions, as follows:

O—the origin.

DR—the DR position of the boat as a result solely of its motion through the water.

W—the position of the boat solely as a result of the motion of the water.

P—the position (intended or actual) of the boat as a result of the combined action of the component motions.

(It should be noted that, in some cases, two of the above letters are applicable to a position; it is customary to use only one.)

**"Tail-to-head" relationship.** Note very carefully how the vectors for boat motion through the water and the current are drawn. These vectors are always drawn "tail-to-head," *not* so that both are directed out from the same source. (This rule applies only when one of the vectors is current; not when they both represent boat's motion.)

If both boat motion through the water and current are known, either may be drawn first from the origin; fig. 2031b will give the same resultant motion as fig. 2031a.

## The four "Cases" of current problems

There are four typical current problems, different combinations of known and unknown factors. For convenience, we will call them Case 1, 2, etc.

CASE 1—Known: Boat's course (C) and speed (S) through the water; current set and drift.
To be determined: The intended (expected) track (TR) and speed of advance (SOA).
This is the determination of the effect of a known current if no allowance is made for its effect.

CASE 2—Known: Boat's course (C) and speed (S) through the water; the course (COG) and speed made good (SOG).
To be determined: The set and drift of the current.
This is the determination of the nature of an unknown current from observation of its effect.

CASE 3—Known: Boat's speed through the water (S), the set and drift of the current, and the intended track (TR).
To be determined: The course to be steered (C) and the speed of advance (SOA) along the intended track.
This is the determination of corrected course to be steered, but without regard for the effect on speed or ETA.

CASE 4—Known: The set and drift of the current, the intended track (TR), and the speed of advance desired (SOA).
To be determined: The course to be steered (C) and speed to be run through the water (S). This is the "rendezvous" or "contest" case where the destination and the time of arrival are specified.

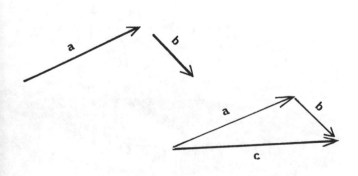

FIG. 2030 Vectors may be combined graphically to determine the vector sum. Typically, vectors *a* and *b* above, representing component motions, are combined as vector *c*, the resultant motion of the two components.

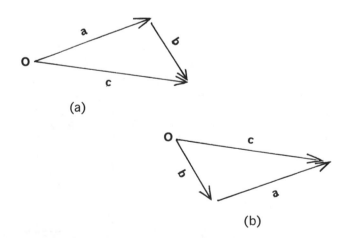

(a)

(b)

FIG. 2031 The two vector triangles shown above appear to be different because in one vector *a* was drawn before vector *b*, and in the other, *b* was drawn before *a*. The resultant vector, *c*, however, is exactly the same for either procedure.

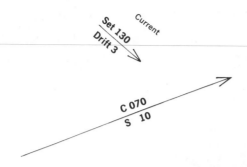

FIG. 2032 If a boat is traveling through the water on a course of 070°, and the current is setting in the direction 130°, it is obvious that the craft will be set off course to starboard. The question of how much, and the effect on speed over the bottom, is what must be determined. A current diagram will provide the answers.

## Illustrative examples

Let us first consider **Case 1**—the effect of current on a boat's course and speed. If the set of the current is as shown in fig. 2032, then the boat will be set off to the right of the direction in which it is being steered. We will use a current diagram to determine the exact extent of this effect, the path the boat can be expected to follow and its speed (the intended track and speed of advance).

We first draw in a north line as a reference for measuring directions, fig. 2033a, and then the vector for the boat's speed through the water, O-DR, a line drawn from the origin in the direction 070° for a length of 10 units, fig. 2033b. Next we add the vector for current, DR-W, three units in the direction 130°, fig. 2033c. Note that we have remembered to observe the "tail-to-head" relationship rule. (Either of these two vectors could have been drawn first; the triangle would appear differently, but the result will be the same.) Because these vectors form two sides of a triangle of velocities, the third side O-W, fig. 2033d, is the resultant velocity at which the boat moves with respect to the bottom under the combined influences of its propulsion and the current. The point W can now be relabeled "P." The intended (or expected) track (TR) and the speed of advance (SOA) can be measured from the O-P line. In this example, it turns out that the boat can be expected to sail a course over the ground of 083° and to have a speed of advance of 11.8 knots. Note that the directions of these vectors are always plotted as *true* directions.

Summarizing briefly, we have drawn vectors to indicate independently the motion of the boat from two different influences, its own propulsion and the current. Actually, of course, the boat will *not* go first from O to DR and then on to P. All the time, it will travel directly along the intended track O-P. The boat is steered on course C, the direction of O-DR, but, due to the effect of current, it is expected to travel along the intended track O-P. This is the route that must be considered for shoals and other hazards to navigation.

→

Cruising men can never afford to ignore the effect of current. Down East, for example, in Maine waters big tidal ranges often cause baffling current conditions, compounded by unusual influences of headlands and river currents. Fog in such areas places a special premium on piloting skill.

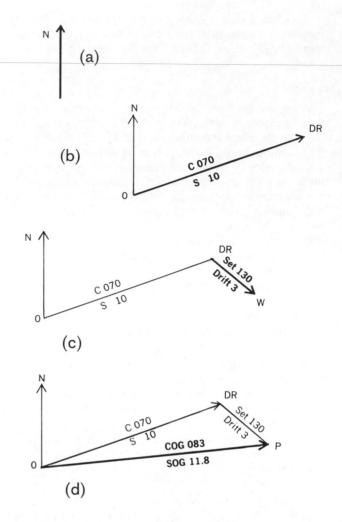

FIG. 2033 Current Diagram—CASE 1. These diagrams illustrate the step-by-step graphical solution: (a) the reference North line; (b) the vector for boat's motion through the water; (c) the vector for current, the motion of the water with respect to the bottom; and finally (d) the vector for the resultant motion of the boat with respect to the bottom.

**FIG. 2034 Current Diagram — CASE 2. The prevailing current (actually the net effect of all offsetting influences) can be found graphically from a vector triangle of velocities.**

Now for a **Case 2** situation in which you know the course you have steered and the speed through the water from either the speed curve of your boat or a marine speedometer. It is also obvious to you that you did not arrive at your DR position. From your chart plot, you have been able to determine the course and speed over the ground. Current has acted to set you off your course—you desire to know its set and drift.

After again drawing a north reference line, plot vectors for your motion through the water—C 255°, S 12 knots; and your motion with respect to the bottom—COG 245°, SOG 13.4 knots. See fig. 2034. These vectors are both drawn outward from the origin, O, to points DR and P respectively. The "tail-to-head" rule is not applicable as neither of these vectors represents current. The action of the current has been to offset your boat from DR to P (which is also point W in this case), thus the set is the direction *from* DR *toward* P, and the drift is the length of this line in scale units.

In fig. 2034, the current is found to be setting 192° with a drift of 2.6 knots. This is the *average* current for the time period and location of the run from O to P for which the calculations were made; it is not the current at P. For the next leg of your cruise, these current values can be used as is, or modified as required by the passage of time and/or the continuing change in position of the boat.

**Case 3** is a typical cruising situation—here, you know the track you desire to make good (TR 080°), you have decided to run at your normal cruising speed through the water (S 10 knots), and you have calculated (or estimated) the current's set (140°) and drift (4 knots). What you desire to know is the course to be steered (C) and the speed of advance (SOA) which can be used to figure your estimated time of arrival (ETA).

Draw in a north line and measure directions from it, fig. 2035a. Plot the current vector, O-W, at the specified direction and length, and a line (not a vector yet) in the direction of the intended track—this line should be of indefinite length at this time. From point W, swing an arc, with dividers or drawing compass, equal in length to the speed through the water in scale units. The point at which this arc intersects the intended track line is point P and the vector triangle has been completed. The direction of W-P is the course to be steered (C 060°); the length of the vector O-P is the speed over the ground (SOG 11.4) and from this the ETA can be calculated.

Let us look at the reasoning behind this graphic solution of Case 3. Again considering the component motions separately for the sake of simplicity, the boat is moved by current from O to W. It is to move from W at the specified speed through the water, but must get back on the intended track line; the problem is to find the point P on the track which is "S" units from point W. The solution is found by swinging an arc as described above.

Remember that all vectors are plotted as *true* directions, including C, the course to be steered in the preceding solution. This must be changed to a compass direction (course) for actual use at the helm.

In accordance with the principles of dead reckoning, it is desirable to plot the DR track even though a current is known to exist. This line, drawn from point O in the direction C and with a length of S scale units, forms a basis for consideration of possible hazards if the current is not as calculated or estimated, fig. 2035b.

**FIG. 2035 Current Diagram — CASE 3. If you know your desired track, and have decided upon your speed through the water, a graphical solution (a) can be used to determine the course to be steered and the speed of advance. For safety's sake, a DR plot from the origin should be added as in (b).**

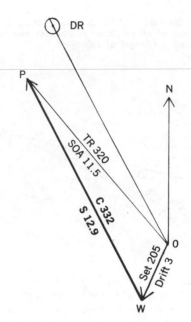

FIG. 2036 Current Diagram—CASE 4. This problem concerns the course to be steered and the speed at which to run in order to arrive at a specified destination at a predetermined time. This could be useful in a predicted log contest or in rendezvousing with another boat.

A **Case 4** situation is an interesting variation of Case 3— you desire to arrive at a specified point at a given time. It may be that you are competing in a predicted log contest, or merely that you have agreed to meet friends at that time and place. In addition to the data on current that you have, you have decided upon your track and your speed of advance. For fig. 2036, let us assume that the current sets 205° at 3 knots. You need to make good a track of 320°, and a quick distance-time-speed calculation sets your required speed of advance at 11.5 knots.

From the north reference line, draw the current vector O-W and the intended track vector O-P. Complete the triangle with the vector W-P which will give you the course to be steered (C 332 True) and the speed to run through the water (S 12.9) to arrive at the destination at the desired time. Line O-DR should be drawn in from the origin as a dead reckoning track for the sake of safety.

Solutions of Cases 1, 2, 3, and 4 using tabular data, rather than graphic plots, are given in pages 441-447.

These tables should not be used without a clear understanding of the fundamentals of current sailing, the component motions and their relationships to each other. These fundamentals, and the terms and symbols used, should be learned from simple graphic solutions as presented above.

FIG. 2037 Ability to estimate the set and drift of currents on a proposed course is of paramount importance to contestants in a predicted log race, where accuracy of the highest order is required to win.

# CHAPTER 21
# PILOTING—Position Determination

The art of piloting reaches its climax in *position determination*. Underway on a body of water of any size, where the safety of your boat and its crew is at stake, it's not "where you ought to be," or "where you think you are," but your knowledge of "where you are for sure" that counts. The development of an ability to determine your position quickly and accurately under a wide range of conditions should be one of your primary goals as a skipper.

## The need for position determination

In three of the current sailing situations covered in the preceding chapter, the set and drift of the current were taken as known values. In everyday cruising, it is more than likely that the strength and direction of the actual current will be somewhat different from that calculated or estimated. Local wind conditions or abnormal rainfall will frequently upset tabular predictions; estimates based on visual observations of current will often be inaccurate unless the boatman has had considerable experience. Because of these uncertainties, current sailing solutions can be considered only as *estimates* of present positions and of future motions and positions.

Buoy positions are usually reliable; the Coast Guard expends much effort in keeping them on station and operating properly. They are, however, not infallible, and the position of a boat should be determined by other means as often as practicable.

Accurate position determination whenever the opportunity presents itself is essential in order that the safety of the craft can be verified, or corrective action taken promptly. By so doing, the true effects of the current may also become known. Further, such fixing of position makes possible the start of a new DR plot, fresher and more accurate than the old one.

Frequent position determination is an essential safety precaution. No matter how safe your boat is, no matter how experienced you are in boating, no matter how good the weather nor how calm the seas, emergencies can arise, and suddenly, too. Knowledge of where you are, extended from a *recent* position determination, can be of the greatest value when you must call for help. Or, if it is another boat that has trouble, you can set the most direct course to render assistance if you are sure of where you are.

### THE SKIPPER'S RESPONSIBILITIES

*It is the duty of a skipper to fix the position of his craft with such degree of precision and at such frequent intervals as is required by the proximity to hazards to safe navigation.* This is an absolute requirement of the person in charge of the vessel, whether he is personally doing the piloting or this is being done by another person. He can assign the function, but he cannot delegate his responsibility.

The actual procedures in position determination will vary widely in practice. Proceeding down a narrow channel, positioning will be informal and a chart plot will not be maintained. But this does not mean that position de-

St. Petersburg Times Photo by Dan Hightower

**FIG. 2101 The skipper of any boat is responsible for the safety of it and of all persons on board. He must be able to determine his position accurately, and do so as often as required by prevailing conditions.**

termination is being omitted; indeed, it is being done essentially continuously by visual reference to the aids to navigation. On the other hand, during an open ocean passage, a plot will be maintained, but positions will be determined, other than by DR calculations, perhaps only three or four times each day.

Between the extremes cited above, there will be found the normal cruising situations in pilot waters. Cruising just offshore, or in the larger inland bodies of water, a skipper will usually maintain a plot of his track with periodic checks on its accuracy, perhaps every 15 or 20 minutes, perhaps at hourly intervals.

*The ability to determine the position of his craft to an acceptable degree of accuracy under any condition of visibility is essential to safe boating. The absence of this ability, or any limitation on it, should restrict the extent of a person's boating activities, setting the boundaries of the water areas and weather conditions into which he will enter.*

## DEFINITION OF TERMS

*A line of position (LOP)* is a line, in actuality or drawn on a chart, at some point along which an observer is presumed to be located, fig. 2102. A LOP may result from observation or measurement; from visual, electronic, or celestial sources. It may be straight or curved; a circular LOP is sometimes referred to as a *circle of position*, fig.

2103. A line of position may be *advanced* (moved forward) or *retired* (moved backward) in time according to the movement of the vessel during the time interval involved. In piloting, the more usual situation will be the advancement of a previously taken LOP to the time of another LOP just taken.

A *bearing* is the direction of an object from the observer, expressed in degrees as a three-digit number—005°

FIG. 2102 Position determination is based on "lines of position." These are lines, in actuality or on a chart, along which the observer is presumed to be located. A single line will not determine position, but it does tell the observer where he is *not* located, and such information is often useful.

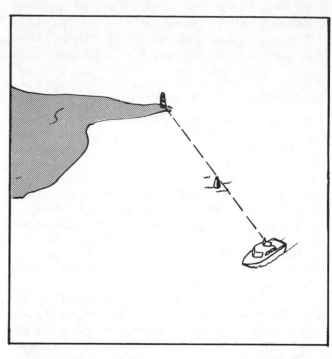

FIG. 2104 When two objects can be observed in line, an excellent line of position is established. Such "ranges" may have been set up with specific aids to navigation, or they may be any two identifiable objects such as ordinary navigational aids, landmarks, or natural or man-made features.

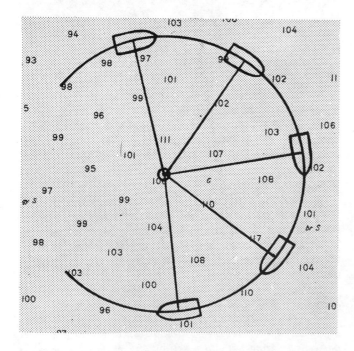

FIG. 2103 Lines of position may be curved as well as straight. A measurement of distance from an identified object yields a circular LOP. It may be plotted as a complete circle or as only a partial arc.

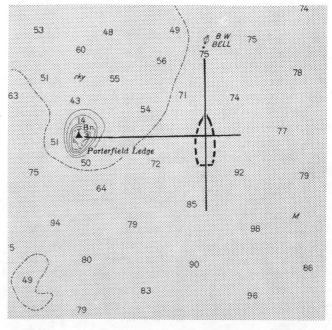

FIG. 2105 A "fix" is an accurately determined position for the observer and his craft. It is not based on any prior position, but is determined from currently observed lines of position or other data.

418

062°, 157°, etc. A *true bearing* is a bearing measured with reference to the true north direction as 000°. *Magnetic* and *compass bearings* are, respectively, observations with reference to the local magnetic north direction or to the craft's steering compass as it is affected by deviation at that moment. A *relative bearing* is a bearing measured with reference to the ship's heading—it is measured clockwise from the fore-and-aft line with 000° being dead ahead,

090° broad on the starboard beam, 180° dead astern, etc. (An older method of measuring relative bearings 180° to port or starboard is seldom used any more; it made calculations more complicated than necessary.)

A *range* consists of two objects that can be observed in line with each other and the observer, fig. 2104.

A *fix* is an accurately located position determined without reference to any prior position, fig. 2105. A *running fix* is a position that has been determined from LOPs at least one of which has been taken at a different time and advanced or retarded to the time of the other observation.

An *estimated position (EP)* is the best position obtainable short of a fix or good-quality running fix. It is the most probable position, determined from incomplete data, or from data of questionable accuracy.

FIG. 2106 **The correct labeling of lines of position is most important; unlabeled lines on a chart can only be a source of confusion. The time is always shown above the line (in 24-hour clock system) and direction below the line as a three-digit number without the "○" symbol.**

## Lines of Position

Lines of position are the basic elements of position determination. By definition, the observer, and his craft, are located somewhere along a LOP. If two LOPs intersect, the only position at which the vessel can be, and be on both lines, is their intersection. Thus, the usual fix is determined by the crossing of two lines of position.

### Labeling

Since LOPs are also lines that are drawn on a chart, it is essential that they be labeled immediately, and that such labels conform to a standardized system. A label should contain all information necessary for identification, but nothing further that might cause confusion or clutter up the chart. The information to be recorded for each line of position is the time that it was observed or measured and its basic dimension, such as direction toward, or distance from, the object used.

A bearing is a LOP that has time and direction. Fig. 2106 shows several examples of correctly labeled bearings. Time is always shown *above* the line of the bearing, and direction *below* the line. Time is given as a four-digit figure in the 24-hour clock system. Directions are *true* and are written as a three-digit group with zeros prefixed as necessary.

A circle of position has dimensions of time and distance; it may be plotted as a complete circle, fig. 2107a, or merely as a partial circle, an arc, as in fig. 2107b. Time is labeled above the curved line and distance, with units, is shown below the line.

A range is a line of position whose direction is self-evident from the two points which define it. In this case, only time need be shown; it is placed above the line as for other LOPs; see fig. 2108.

Do not draw the line completely through the chart symbols for the two objects used as the range; this will avoid the necessity for subsequent erasure across the symbols. Draw the line neatly and no longer than necessary; it need not extend all the way to the front range marker or other object if the two features used to form the range are clearly evident.

A line of position that has been advanced (or retired) in time is labeled with *both* times above the line, the time of original observation or measurement and the time to which it has been advanced (or retired). The time of the original LOP is written first, followed by a dash and then

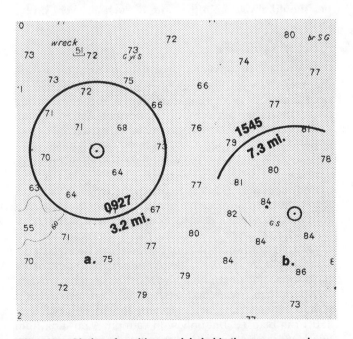

FIG. 2107 **Circles of position are labeled in the same general manner as straight lines of position. The time is placed above the line and the distance below, as it would normally be viewed and read. Thus, the time may be "inside" or "outside" the circle as determined by the curvature of the arc.**

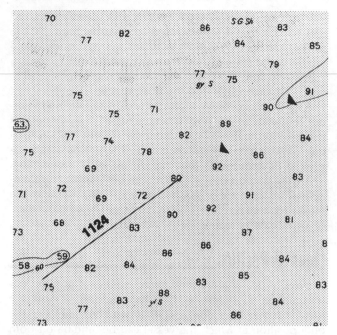

FIG. 2108 Since a range is based on the relationship between the two sighted objects, it is often used without a measurement of its actual direction. Ranges need be labeled only with the time of the observation.

the second time, fig. 2109.

*Always label lines of position as soon as they are drawn.* Unmarked lines on a chart can easily be a source of confusion. If labeling is put off until a later time, mistakes may be made.

## FIXES

As previously defined, a fix is an accurately located position for a vessel. On many occasions in small-craft piloting, position will be established by passing close by an

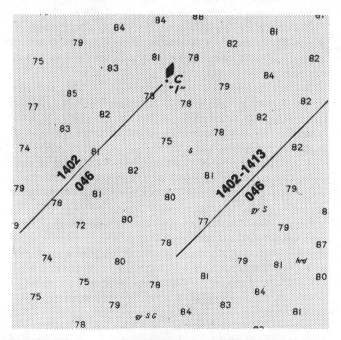

FIG. 2109 A line of position may be "advanced," that is, used at a later time than when it was observed if it is replotted to account for the movement of the boat since the time of observation. An advanced LOP is labeled with the original time and the time for which it is replotted. The direction, of course, remains the same.

FIG. 2110 A simple, but excellent, determination of position occurs when a boat passes close alongside an aid to navigation or other identifiable point. A good pilot always notes the time of such an event on his chart.

identifiable object, usually an aid to navigation. This is, of course, a fix of the highest possible accuracy, and a skipper should always note the time of such an event on his chart plot, fig. 2110.

### Fix from two LOPs

The typical fix obtained from lines of position will be the intersection of two such lines. It is important to consider the effect of the angle of intersection between the two LOPs on the accuracy of the position determination. Let us look first at the situation where the two lines cross at right angles, 90°, fig. 2111a. If there should be an error of, say, 2° in one LOP, the resulting fix from this mistake would be off only a short distance.

Consider now fig. 2111b in which the intersection angle is only 30°. An error of 2° in one LOP would result in a considerably greater change in the location of the intersection.

*Two lines of position should intersect as nearly as possible at right angles; the angle of intersection should never be less than 60° nor more than 120° if this can be avoided.*

Where there is no alternative, a fix from two lines of position intersecting at angles of 30° to 60° (120° to 150°) can be used, but only with caution. A position from two LOPs intersecting at less than 30° (more than 150°) is of too dubious accuracy for safe navigation. **Areas of uncertainty.** Lines of position will normally be stated as having a specific direction, such as 072°, 147°, etc. In actuality, there may be an uncertainty in each line of two or three, or even more, degrees. This condition can be shown graphically on the chart by additional lines drawn lightly on either side of the basic LOP; this should always be done if such uncertainty could mean the difference between a safe position and a hazardous one.

Lines of position from various sources and techniques will have different degrees of uncertainty. Only experience will give the pilot the ability to judge various methods and assign relative values of probable accuracy.

If two LOPs, each with its graphic representation of uncertainty, are drawn, the result is an *area of uncertainty* about the intersection of the lines of position; there is an element of doubt about the location of the fix. Figs. 2112a and b show how the angle of intersection alters this area of uncertainty and why it is desirable to have the LOPs cross as nearly as possible at 90°. Based on the mathematics of statistics and probability, the area of uncertainty is elliptical (circular if the LOPs cross at 90°) rather than the quadrilateral formed by the outside limiting lines for each bearing. In actual piloting, this distinction is more theoretical than practical. A detailed discussion of this topic, including the additional complexities that arise if one line of position can be considered to be more accu-

rate than the other, is beyond the scope of this book, but may be found in Bowditch, Chapter 29.

### More than two LOPs

Since most lines of position obtained in small-craft piloting (except possibly ranges) are reasonably, but certainly not exactly, accurate, it is highly desirable to use more than two LOPs to reduce the uncertainty of position. There is no theoretical upper limit to the number of lines of position that can be used, but practical considerations with a boat underway will normally limit the pilot to three LOPs.

Ideally, since the observer is presumed to be on all three lines of position, they will intersect in a common point, fig. 2113a. The much more likely result is that when the observations are plotted, the lines will form a triangle, fig. 2113b.

The use of three LOPs results in a modification of the previously stated rule about the desirable intersection angle of the lines. For optimum results, the three lines should each differ in direction as closely as possible to 60° (or 120°), fig. 2114. In this configuration, an inaccuracy in any of the LOPs will result in the minimum net error of position.

An alternative technique to the above is to obtain two

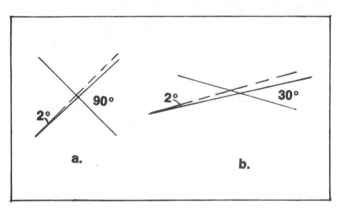

FIG. 2111 Lines of position taken from a small craft are seldom precisely accurate. Selection of an optimum angle of intersection between LOPs reduces the uncertainty of position. Shown here is the difference that a change of 2° in one LOP makes in the intersection point when the lines cross at 90° or at 30°.

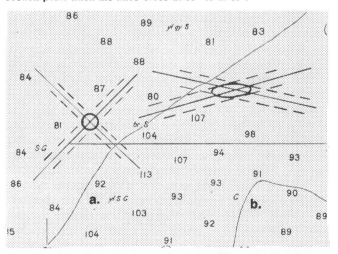

FIG. 2112 When each of two LOPs may have an inaccuracy of several degrees, there is an *area of uncertainty* around the intersection point. This is least, a circle, when the angle of intersection is 90°. Angles of 60° to 90° are satisfactory; those of 30° to 60° may be used with caution.

FIG. 2113 The use of more than two LOPs will enhance confidence in the resulting fix. Ideally, three lines of position will intersect at a common point, as in *a* above. More often in actual piloting, a triangle will be formed as shown in *b*. If the triangle is unreasonably large for the prevailing conditions, the observations should be checked or discarded.

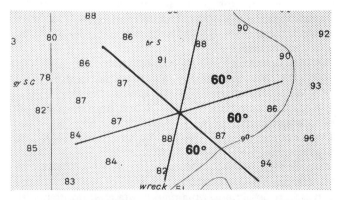

FIG. 2114 For an optimum set of three observations, the lines of position should cross at 60° to each other. This will seldom be exactly possible in actual piloting situations, but should be kept in mind as fundamentally desirable.

lines of position at nearly 90° to each other, and then a third LOP making an angle of approximately 45° with those of the original pair, figs. 2115a and b. This procedure has the advantage of providing an optimum two-LOP plot in the event that a change of visibility or other circumstance should suddenly prevent the third observation.

## Triangles of position

As noted above, three lines of position will usually form a *triangle of position*. If this triangle is quite large, it is probable that there is a significant error in one or more of the LOPs, and a check should be made of the observations, calculations, and plotting.

If, however, the triangle is relatively small (and "relatively" will have to be defined in each situation as determined by the techniques used, the experience of the observer, the size of the boat, sea state, and other conditions), it can be assumed that no more than normal inaccuracies and uncertainties exist. In the everyday practice of piloting on boats, it is customary to use the center of the triangle of position, as estimated by eye, for the fix.

## Labeling fixes

A fix is shown on a chart plot as a small circle with a dot in its center; it is labeled with the time followed by the letters "FIX"; see fig. 2116a. A running fix is labeled with the time and "R FIX"; fig. 2116b.

Often the dot in the center of the circle is not seen separately, as when the fix lies along a line or at the intersection of two lines. If the fix is obtained by passing close to a buoy or other aid to navigation, the dot or center of the chart symbol is used for the plot. The usual distance off, 50 to 100 yards or so, is not significant at typical chart scales; greater distances are estimated and the fix is plotted in the correct direction from the aid at a scaled distance.

## THE VALUE OF A SINGLE LOP

The preceding discussion has centered on the use of two or more lines of position for obtaining a fix. While admittedly this is the most desirable situation, the value of a single LOP should not be overlooked.

Basically, a single line of position cannot tell a pilot where he is at the moment, but it can, within the limitations of its accuracy, tell him where he is *not*. If he is presumed to be somewhere along the LOP, then he cannot be at a position appreciably distant from the line. This information, although lacking in detail and negative in sense, may often be of value to a navigator concerned with the safety of his vessel.

A single line of position can frequently be combined with a DR position to obtain an "estimated position." This EP is the point along the LOP that is closest to the DR position for the same time. A line is drawn from the DR position perpendicular to the LOP until it intersects that line. The estimated position is marked with a small square and labeled with the time followed by "EP"; see fig. 2117a. Note that if a beam bearing is used, the EP will fall along the DR track line, fig. 2117b.

It is also possible to obtain an "estimated position with current" from a single LOP if the set and drift of the current have been determined from predictions or from its effect on the boat's course and speed made good. From

**FIG. 2115** An alternative procedure for taking three observations is to select the first two objects so that their LOPs will cross at as near 90° as possible, *a* above. Then the third sight is taken so that its plotted LOP will cross the other two at approximately 45°, as in *b* above. If circumstances prevent the pilot from getting the third sight, he will still have a near-optimum two-LOP fix.

**FIG. 2116** A *fix* is labeled with the time followed by "FIX" not written parallel to any line. A *running fix* is labeled with the time and "R FIX".

the DR position for the specified time, a line is drawn to scale to represent the effect of the current since the DR track was started from the last fix. This line is drawn in the direction of the set of the current and for a length equal to the "total drift," the distance found by multiplying the drift by the elapsed time since the last fix. This total drift line is labeled and from its end another line is drawn perpendicular to the LOP until it intersects that line; see fig. 2117c. The intersection is the *EP with current;* it is labeled in the same manner as before (the fact that current has been included is obvious from the plot).

In using an EP, make generous allowances for the uncertainty of the position; always err on the side of safety.

In some piloting situations, a single bearing on an object can be advanced and crossed with a later LOP on the same object. This will result in a running fix, not as desirable as a fix from two independent lines of position, but far better than a DR position or the pilot's "best guess."

Running fixes, and the use of a single LOP with depth measurements, will be discussed later in this chapter.

FIG. 2117 An *estimated position* can be obtained from a single line of position. It is the point on the LOP closest to the DR position for that time, see *a* above. If a beam bearing is used, the EP will fall along the DR track, as in *b* above.

FIG. 2117c If information about the current is available, an improved "estimated position with current" can be plotted. The off-setting effect of the current since the start of the DR track is calculated and plotted; the nearest point on the LOP from this current-influenced point is the EP.

FIG. 2118 A very simple, yet fully accurate method of taking bearings is to "aim" the boat directly at the sighted object and read the compass. Brief off-course swings for this purpose will not materially affect the DR plot but be sure that there are no hazards close alongside your course. Correct such compass bearings to true directions before plotting them.

# Visual Observations

For the pilot of a typical motorboat or sailboat, the primary source of lines of position will be visual observations. These will include direct and relative bearings, ranges, and horizontal and vertical angle measurements. Correct identification of the sighted object is essential. Other methods and equipment may lead to LOPs such as those from radio direction finding, radar, and depth measurements, but these will normally be secondary to visual observations.

## SIMPLE VISUAL BEARINGS

It will amaze the novice pilot (and perhaps some of the more experienced ones, too) how much navigational information can be obtained from the most simple of visual bearings, those directly ahead or broad on the beam.

### Bearings dead ahead

Bearings taken directly ahead require no auxiliary equipment; the boat's steering compass will suffice. Only insignificant effects will be made on the DR track of a boat if the bow is momentarily swung off course and pointed toward an object on which it is desired to take a bearing. The craft should be held on this new heading long enough for the helmsman to properly line up on the object and for the compass to settle down and be read. This is normally a matter of less than a minute, perhaps only 20 or 30 seconds.

To use this technique, the pilot must be sure enough of his general location that the off-course swing can be made safely. But if such is the situation, he should not hesitate to use this quick and simple way of getting a line of position. The accuracy of bearings obtained by this method will normally be considerably greater than those of the more complex techniques to be discussed later.

The procedure of taking bearings dead ahead by "aiming" the boat at the object sighted upon has an additional advantage in that it can be accomplished by the helmsman alone, without the assistance of another person. Other methods will generally require the services of a second individual as the bearing-taker while the helmsman continues his normal duties, plus reading the steering compass at the time of the observation.

### Beam bearings

If the observed aid to navigation or landmark is well around on either beam, it may not be feasible to make so great a deviation from the normal heading being steered in order to take a dead-ahead bearing. Or perhaps the limited width of the available deep water does not permit so large an excursion from the DR track. In this case, the other simple bearing technique may be used.

Determine some portion of the boat that is at a right angle to the fore-and-aft axis of the craft. Among the possibilities are bulkheads, seat backs, deck seams, etc. Sights taken along these features will determine when the observed object is directly abeam—a relative bearing of 090° or 270°.

The boat may be held on course and the passage of time awaited until sighting along the pre-selected portion of the boat indicates that the aid to navigation or other object is exactly broad on the beam. Its direction then is, of course, 90° greater or less than the direction read from the boat's compass at that moment.

If waiting until the object comes abeam in the normal course of events is not feasible or desirable, then the heading of the craft can sometimes be temporarily altered slightly as needed to bring the sighted object directly on the beam more quickly. Should such a temporary change of heading be made, the pilot must be sure that the 90° is added to, or subtracted from, the compass reading at the exact moment that the sighted object is abeam; do not use the normal base course.

### Correction of compass bearings

The pilot should always remember that in either of these types of observations the bearings that are taken are *compass bearings*. It will be necessary to correct them for deviation and variation (see Chapter 13) and then plot them as *true* bearings. Any of the plotting instruments and techniques described in Chapter 19 may be used.

Beam bearings are obtained by adding 90° to or subtracting 90° from the boat's *true* heading. Be sure to correct the boat's compass heading for deviation and variation *first,* and *then* add the 90° if the observation was to starboard or subtract the 90° if the sighting was on the port beam. Do not use the direction of the bearing for entering the craft's deviation table; use the heading.

### Plotting bearings

The direction measured by the visual observation is *from the boat toward the object*. When plotting is being done, the position of the boat is not known, but it is still possible to draw the line so that it will have the correct direction and lead toward, to, or through the chart symbol for the sighted object. The particular plotting instrument used will determine the exact procedures used.

It is also possible to plot a line of position outward from the sighted object by using the *reciprocal* of the corrected observed bearing. (In fact, this is the formally correct procedure, but it is usually by-passed in favor of the more direct technique mentioned in the paragraph above.) Here, caution must be taken to *first* correct the observed compass (or relative) bearing to a true direction, and then add or subtract 180° to obtain the reciprocal; do not reverse this sequence.

## MORE SOPHISTICATED BEARINGS

The procedures just described above for bearings dead ahead and broad on the beam will suffice in many situations, but not in all. It may be neither safe nor convenient to alter the boat's heading for the purpose of taking a bearing.

Greater flexibility of navigation is obtained if bearings can be taken in any direction without a change in the normal heading of the craft. Such bearings will involve the use of the boat's compass, a pelorus or hand bearing compass, or some combination of these instruments.

### Using the boat's compass

On many boats, it will be possible to take bearings directly over the steering compass, at least through a limited angle on either side of the bow. As determined by the construction of the compass, it may be feasible to sight directly over the card and get bearings of acceptable accu-

racy. On other models, a set of sighting vanes may be placed on the compass for greater precision in direction measurement. The directions in which bearings may be taken using the boat's steering compass will normally be limited by the nearby superstructure of the boat. Bearings taken using the boat's compass must be corrected for the deviation on the heading of the boat, *not* that for the bearing direction, and for the variation of the locality.

### Using a hand-held compass

Direct visual bearings can also be taken using a hand-bearing compass, or even with the boat's compass if it is a model that has been designed for quick and easy dismounting with accurate remounting. It is normally not feasible to prepare a deviation table for such hand compass use because of the many different positions and circumstances connected with this procedure. Careful tests should be made to determine the locations about the boat, if any, at which a hand-held device can be used without deviation errors. These tests are best made from known positions by taking bearings on objects whose actual direction can be established from the chart. If deviation-free locations can be found on board, then correction will be required for magnetic variation only, to obtain true bearings for plotting.

### Using a pelorus

Alternatively, a pelorus may be used to measure directions, usually as relative bearings. This instrument is, of course, not affected by magnetic disturbances on the boat and may be used at any location from which the desired object can be seen. The caution to be observed in this case is that the pelorus must be accurately aligned with the fore-and-aft axis, the keel-line, of the vessel. The correct positioning of the pelorus should be worked out for several locations on the boat so that sights may be taken on an object regardless of its relative position with respect to the boat.

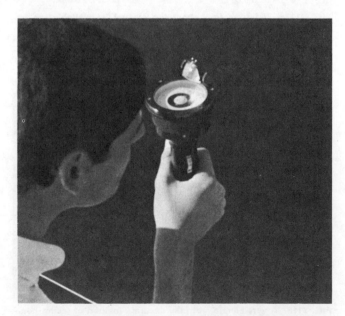

FIG. 2119 A hand bearing compass can be used to take direct readings on objects that cannot be sighted over the boat's steering compass. Before using such an instrument on your boat, however, make checks to find locations at which it will not be affected by local magnetic influences.

The scale of the pelorus can be aligned to the boat's heading and observations made directly in terms of compass bearings, but this procedure is generally less desirable than the technique of relative bearings to be described below. In all cases, the compass bearings must be converted to true bearings before plotting.

An exception to the above statement can be made in the case of an *experienced* pilot. It is possible to omit the step of correction from magnetic to true direction and plot in terms of magnetic bearings. This procedure, while appearing to be a handy short cut, has two pitfalls. First, it requires the use of the magnetic directions circle of the compass roses printed on the chart plus the use of a plotting instrument that determines direction from these compass roses rather than from the meridians and parallels; this rules out use of the convenient and accurate course plotter. Secondly, this technique requires the use of magnetic directions for all purposes, such as courses, ranges, set of current, etc., or else a confusing mixture of directions. Because of these two serious disadvantages, the possibility of plotting bearings as magnetic directions will be noted here, but will be discarded immediately in favor of the "old reliable" procedure of using only true directions on the chart.

## RELATIVE BEARINGS

Relative bearings are those taken with respect to the vessel alone, without reference to geographic directions. Relative bearings offer some advantages, but also have some built-in problems.

The instrument for taking relative bearings is the pelorus. As noted before, it has the advantage of being usable anywhere on the boat if properly oriented. Its disadvantage is that close coordination is required between two persons, the bearing-taker and the helmsman. The heading of the boat at the instant of observation must be known, and direct communication between these two individuals is required.

To take a relative bearing, the scale of the pelorus is set with 000° dead ahead. The helmsman is alerted to the fact that a bearing is about to be taken; he concentrates on steady steering and continuously reads the compass. When the observation is made, the bearing-taker calls out "Mark," and reads the scale of the pelorus. (It is very helpful if the bearing-taker calls out "Stand by" a few seconds before his "Mark.") At the word "Mark," the helmsman notes the reading of the steering compass and calls it off to the observer or other person who will compute the bearing. If the compass should be swinging at the moment, so that an accurate reading cannot be taken, the helmsman calls out that information and the pelorus reading is discarded; another attempt is then made to take the bearing.

As noted in Chapter 19, an alternative technique is to have the helmsman call a series of "Marks" when, but only when, he has the boat directly on course. The bearing-taker makes his observation only when it is so indicated that the boat is on the specified heading.

When the relative bearing has been taken by either of the above techniques, it must be converted to a true bearing for plotting. This is done by adding the numerical values of the relative bearing and the *true* heading of the boat at the instant of observation. If the sum so obtained is more than 360°, that amount is subtracted. The true bearing can then be plotted and labeled.

If the true heading is not known for any reason, such as the boat's being momentarily off-course when the bearing was taken, it is, of course, necessary that it be determined before the addition of the preceding paragraph can be accomplished. *Always be sure to use the deviation value for the heading of the boat, and not for the bearing angle.* This is an often-made error, and one that must be continually guarded against.

In fig. 2121a, an observer on a boat heading 047° takes a relative bearing on a buoy of 062°. To determine the true bearing of this aid to navigation, these two numbers are added, 047° + 062° = 109°.

FIG. 2120 A pelorus eliminates the magnetic difficulties that may be experienced with a hand-held compass. It can be used at any point from which the target object can be seen. A pelorus must, however, be properly oriented to the fore-and-aft axis of the boat.

FIG. 2121 Relative bearings must be converted to true bearings before they are plotted. To do this, the relative bearing is added to the true heading of the craft at the moment of observation. If the sum exceeds 360°, that amount is subtracted.

In fig. 2121b, the boat is heading 306° by its compass when a relative bearing of 321° is measured. The variation is 6°W and the deviation (for the compass heading of 306°) is 2°E. The true heading of the boat is thus 306° − 6° + 2° = 302°. The sum of the relative bearing, 321° and the true heading 302° is 623°; therefore 360° is subtracted and a value of 263° is found to be the true bearing of the object.

If the pilot is so fortunate as to have multiple objects on which to take bearings, he should select the nearer ones (provided, of course, that desirable angles of intersection between the LOPs will result). An angular error of 1° will result in a lateral error of about 100 feet at a distance of one mile—at two miles, the *same* angular error will cause a lateral displacement of 200 feet; at three miles, 300 feet, etc.

## RANGES

Lines of position from ranges are of exceptional value in position determination. They are free from all of the magnetic effects that might cause errors in bearings taken with a compass or a pelorus. Such LOPs are also easily obtained, much more so than those from bearings. Ranges can be absolutely accurate, as accurate as the charted positions of the two objects lined up in the observation. No matter how small the boat, how rough the water, or how poor the visibility, if you can see the objects come into line, you can plot a good line of position on your chart and so have half of an accurate fix.

Ranges can be classified into two groups. First, there are those that consist of two aids to navigation constructed specifically to serve as a range and are charted with a special symbol, see fig. 1824, page 352. The true direction of such ranges can be determined from the information in the Light List for the rear marker. Ranges are particularly useful in determining compass deviation because of their high accuracy.

It is not necessary, however, to have an especially constructed pair of aids to navigation in order to have a range. Any two objects that can be identified by sight and on the chart form a natural range and can be used in the same manner as one consisting of two formally established navigational aids. Among such objects are ordinary aids to navigation of all types; spires, radio towers, flagpoles, stacks, etc.; identifiable portions of bridges, such as center spans; and other prominent, isolated features; see fig. 2122. Caution should be exercised in using points of land as either a front or rear range mark; errors may be made in attempting to sight on the exact end of the point, particularly if it is of low elevation.

The taking of a LOP from a range requires no more than the observation of the time that the two objects came into line. The LOP is plotted on the chart by lining up the symbols for the two objects with a straightedge and drawing a light solid line over such portion of the chart where the LOP has significance. The line will normally not be drawn all the way back to the two objects that established the range. Its actual direction will not ordinarily need to be determined. The line should be labeled as soon as it is drawn on the chart.

This line of position can be crossed for a fix with another range, or with any other form of LOP. If such is not available at the time, the LOP from the range may often be advanced later and used as part of a running fix.

**FIG. 2122** Pilots are not limited to those ranges that have been established as such by the Coast Guard or other authorities. Any two identifiable objects can be used. Here, a skipper northbound in Buzzards Bay can get an excellent line of position when light "2" lines up with the standpipe ashore.

**FIG. 2123** Ranges are excellent means of keeping your position centered in a channel, but caution must be exercised not to follow them beyond their proper limits. One or two buoys may be used to mark the beginning or end of a range-marked channel, the point at which to make a change of course.

Never pass up an opportunity to obtain a line of position from a range; there are none better. And there is no better fix than one obtained from the intersection of two ranges.

Ranges are often established by the Coast Guard or other authority to mark the center of important waterways, usually dredged channels or natural channels with hazards close on either side. When so established, the range center line will be printed on the chart, see fig. 1827, page 354. Such ranges will normally be used for direct steering rather than as a line of position, but there is no reason that they should not be used for the latter purpose if desired.

Two cautions should be observed in steering up or down a channel marked by a range. A vessel traveling in the opposite direction on the range will be on a collision course, or will pass too close aboard for comfort. Secondly, the beginning and end of the range, the ends of the solid portion of the line on the chart, must be noted carefully—a range can be followed for too great a distance on either end. Buoys will often be used to mark the spot at which to turn onto or off of the range line, fig. 2123. Always study your chart carefully when using a range.

## HORIZONTAL ANGLES

A fix may also be obtained by measuring the two horizontal angles between the lines of sight to three identifiable objects, without a measurement of the relative or geographic direction to any of them. This procedure avoids the inaccuracies involved in relative or compass bearings. Such horizontal angles can be measured to a high degree of accuracy (as close as $1/2°$) with a sextant.

For plotting these horizontal angles, a *three-arm protractor*, fig. 2124, is the preferred instrument. Each side arm is set for the angle measured to its side of the line of sight to the center object. Then the instrument is moved about on the chart until the arms line up with the symbols for the objects sighted upon in measuring the angles. There is a small hole in the center of the protractor through which a pencil point can be placed to mark the fix on the chart.

The same general technique can be used without a special instrument by drawing lines with the proper angles between them on a piece of transparent paper, fig. 2125. This is then moved about as before until the lines and points are properly related.

FIG. 2125  If a three-arm protractor is not available, the angles can be drawn on a sheet of transparent paper. This is then moved about on the chart until correctly positioned.

Some caution must be exercised in selecting the objects between which the angles are to be measured. Three points, not in a straight line, will all lie on the circumference of a specific circle, such as points X, Y, and Z in fig. 2126a. An angle measured between X and Y, or Y and Z, will be the same measured at A or B, or at any point on the circular arc from X around through A and B to Z. Thus,

FIG. 2124  A three-arm protractor is a specialized plotting instrument used with the two-horizontal-angles technique of position determination. When the angles have been set, the arms are lined up with the appropriate chart symbols; then the position is marked with a pencil point through a hole in the center of the device.

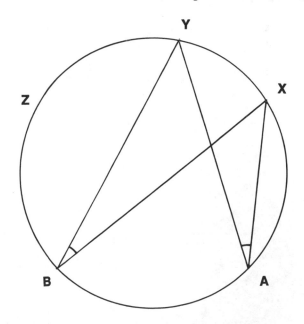

FIG. 2126a  In using the two-horizontal-angles method of positioning, the center of the three objects, Y in this illustration, should *not* be farther away from the observer than the other two. If this caution is neglected, the result may be an indeterminate solution called a "revolver," as shown above, where the boat may be at any point on a circle containing the three objects.

if the observer should be on the circle, his position will be indeterminate. This situation, known as a "revolver," can occur if the center object sighted upon is farther away from the observer than the other two. By selecting three objects so that they are essentially in line, or that the center one is closer to the observer, an indeterminate situation is avoided. (If the center object is closer, a circle still exists, but it curves away from the observer, and he could not possibly be on it.) See fig. 2126b.

A "revolver" should be avoided; but if one does develop, it can be made determinate by the addition of another LOP, such as a single bearing on one of the three objects, or on any other point.

This technique of using the two horizontal angles is not often used in practical piloting, but it does offer excellent results when high accuracy is needed. Fig. 2127 illustrates an instrument developed especially for the measurement of horizontal angles and bearings.

## VERTICAL ANGLES

A circular line of position represents points at a constant distance from a specific object. Such distances are often found by the measurement of vertical angles with a marine sextant, or with a specialized device for such purposes alone.

The height of many natural and man-made features is

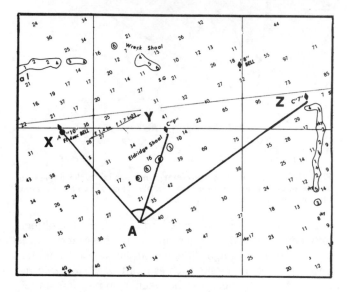

FIG. 2126b   If the center object is on line with the other two, or is nearer to the observer, as Y is above, an indeterminate solution is avoided and a fix is found.

FIG. 2127   The Ilon position finder is a specialized instrument that determines a fix from a combination of the compass bearing to an object and the horizontal angle between that line of sight and the line to a second object.

FIG. 2128   A marine sextant, most commonly used for celestial navigation sights, may also be used in piloting for the measurement of vertical or horizontal angles.

FIG. 2129   If a vertical or horizontal dimension of a distant object is known, this simple optical rangefinder can make an accurate measurement of the distance to it.

shown on charts. Such objects include lighthouses, bridges, radio towers, and generally similar features. Caution must be exercised to determine if the height shown is that above the structure's base on land or the vertical distance above the chart's datum for heights, usually mean high water. Frequently, a correction may be required for the tidal level at the time of observation, its difference from MHW, see Chapter 20. On such features as lighthouses, the height usually given is that of the *light,* not that of the top of the structure.

Using a sextant, the vertical angle is measured between the base and the top or other part of the structure, fig. 2128. This angle and the known height can be used to de-

termine the distance from the observer to the object. Solution can be had from plane geometry formulas, or from specially prepared tables such as Table 9 in Bowditch.

Special range finder instruments are now being marketed which use the principle of matching images much like the focusing mechanism of many cameras. It is still necessary, however, to know the height (or a horizontal dimension) of the object on which the observation is made. Fig. 2129 shows one such instrument.

## DANGER BEARINGS AND ANGLES

The safety of navigation can often be insured without the establishment of a complete fix. As noted earlier, a single line of position has value—if it is of reasonable accuracy, it can assure you that you are somewhere along it and not elsewhere. A line of position can be chosen, in many piloting situations, that will keep a boat in safe water without precisely defining its position.

### Danger bearings

A bearing line can be established so that positions on one side will assure the craft's being in safe waters, while a position on the other side may signify a hazardous situation; such a *danger bearing* is shown in fig. 2130. Here, a shoal, unmarked by any aid to navigation, lies offshore; the problem is to pass it safely. A lighthouse is observed on shore just beyond the shoal, and is identified on the chart. The danger bearing is a line from the lighthouse just tangent to the shoal on the safe side. This line is drawn on the chart and its direction is measured. The line is labeled with the direction preceded by the letters "DB." (No time is shown as it is not an actual observation.) For greater emphasis, short hachures may be added on the side toward the danger; and, if available, the use of a red pencil for this line is desirable to make it stand out from other lines on the chart.

As the boat approaches the hazardous area, a series of observations are made on the selected object. In the example shown in fig. 2130a, any bearing on the lighthouse *less* numerically than the danger bearing indicates a *safe* position; any bearing *greater* than the danger bearing indicates that the boat is in or approaching the shoal area if it continues on the same course. Should the danger area lie to starboard, rather than to port as in fig. 2130b, the "greater" and "less" factors above would be reversed.

Danger bearings cannot always be established for the safe passage of hazardous areas, but their use should be considered whenever conditions permit. It is necessary to have a prominent object, although it need not be an aid to navigation, that can be seen from the boat and positively identified on the chart. This object should lie beyond the danger area in the same general direction as the course of the boat as it approaches and passes the area to be avoided.

## HORIZONTAL DANGER ANGLES

A horizontal angle measured between two identifiable fixed objects defines a circle of position. In fig. 2131, an observer at *X* or *Y* would measure the same angle between *A* and *B*; he would also measure the same angle at any point along that semi-circular arc. If the observer were on the other side of the center of the circle, at *X'* or *Y'*, or

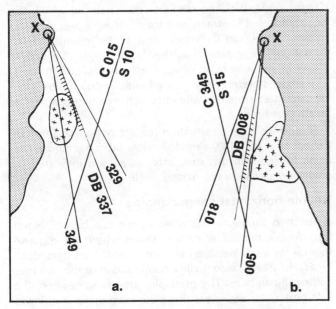

FIG. 2130 A *danger bearing* can be established so as to avoid an unmarked hazardous area. In *a* above, any bearing on object *X* that is more than 337° indicates a potentially hazardous position for the boat. In *b*, the reverse is true, bearing less than 008° are indications of possible danger if the craft continues on the same course.

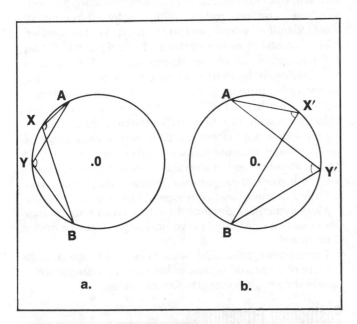

FIG. 2131a and b  The various points at which there is a constant angle between the lines of sight to two objects form a circle. The angle between the lines to *A* and *B* is the same at *X* or *Y*. At points *X'* and *Y'*, the angle is likewise the same.

other point on that arc, a constant angle also would be observed. This angle, however, is not the same as that measured across the circle at X and Y. Note that the angle will be greater than 90° if the sighted objects are on the same side of the circle as the observer, as in fig. 2131a, and less than 90° if they are on the opposite side as in fig. 2131b.

Such a circle may be established to indicate the boundary between positions of safety and those of possible danger. When such a LOP is set up, the angle defined by the circle is termed the *horizontal danger angle*.

Fig. 2132 illustrates the use of a single horizontal danger angle to avoid an unmarked shoal area. The problem is to

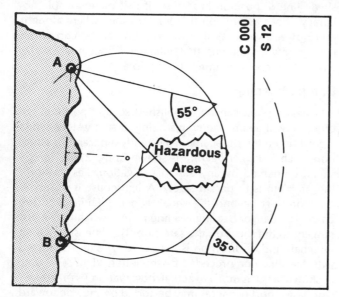

**FIG. 2132** Horizontal angles between *A* and *B* are measured as the boat approaches the hazardous area. Any angle *less* than the *horizontal danger angle* of 55° indicates that the boat is in safe waters.

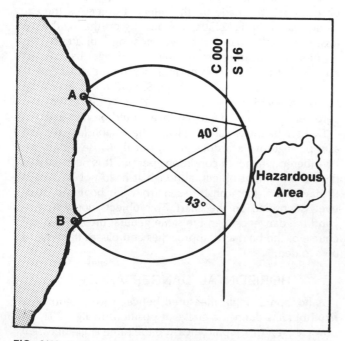

**FIG. 2133** In this situation, it is desired to pass inshore of an unmarked hazardous area. The horizontal danger angle is established as before, but now the safe angular measurements are those *greater* than the horizontal danger angle.

stay sufficiently offshore to miss the hazard. The horizontal danger angle is found by drawing a circle that includes two prominent identifiable objects ashore, *A* and *B* in fig. 2132, and the shoal area. The circle is established by drawing a line between the sighted objects, and then drawing a second line at right angles to the first line at its midpoint. The center of the circle is found by trial-and-error along this second line so that the arc includes the desired points.

Lines are then drawn to *A* and *B* from any point on the circle near the shoal area and the angle between them is measured; in this example, it is 55°.

If the angle between the objects, measured from the boat as it approaches the area, is *less* than the horizontal danger angle, then the radius of the circle on which the boat is located is larger, and the boat is farther offshore in *safe* waters. On the other hand, if the measured horizontal angle is greater than the danger angle, the boat is closer in and may be in or approaching a hazardous area. The angle is preferably measured with a sextant, but it can be calculated from the difference between two compass or relative bearings.

Should the piloting situation require passage inshore of a shoal area, fig. 2133, a single horizontal danger angle can again be used. In this case, *safe* waters are indicated by angles *greater* than the danger angle.

## Double horizontal danger angles

The two situations described above can be combined into *double horizontal danger angles* where the requirement is for a safe passage between two offshore hazardous areas. Fig. 2134 is essentially a combination of the two preceding illustrations. The principles are the same; here the safe horizontal angles are those *between* upper and lower danger limits.

## Vertical danger angles

A circle of position, obtained from a vertical angle measurement, can also be used to mark the boundary between safe and hazardous waters. With a selected prominent object identified visually and on the chart, a circle is drawn using that object as the center and having a radius that will just include all of the hazardous area. The radius is measured from the chart and converted to a vertical angle by geometric formula or Table 9 in Bowditch. The danger circle is then labeled with the *vertical danger angle*. Fig. 2135 shows such a circular LOP outlining a shoal area.

As the boat approaches the dangerous area, a series of vertical angle measurements are taken on the selected object. Measurement of a vertical angle *less* than that specified as the vertical danger angle indicates that the observer is farther offshore, and consequently he is in *safe* waters.

Measurements of distance directly from an optical range finder can be substituted for vertical angles if such a device is on board.

Corresponding situations would prevail for safe passage inshore of a hazardous area, or between two danger areas, as was shown for horizontal danger angles.

## Positioning Procedures

As mentioned earlier, the "basic" fix is obtained by crossing two lines of position. A third LOP is desirable, but this can be obtained in only a limited number of situations. It is assumed for the fix that the observations or measurements for these LOPs are made simultaneously, and this may often be the procedure on a naval ship or other large vessel. On small craft, however, the normal situation will be that of a single bearing-taker and one piece of equipment. Of necessity, therefore, observations will be taken sequentially rather than concurrently. If the observations are taken quickly, the distance traveled between them will be negligible, and adherence to the procedures to be described here will minimize the error from sequential observations.

As a result of the movement of the boat along its course, the observed bearing angles will be changing. Consider the relative *rate of change* of the bearing to each object to be sighted upon; those on the beam will be changing at a more rapid rate than those nearly dead ahead or astern; those on nearer objects will be changing more rapidly than those at greater distances.

For the most accurate determination of a fix from two lines of position, first take a sight on the object with the *least* rate of change, then on the other object, and finally a repeat on the first object. Use the second observation and the average of the first and third bearings (which are, of course, on the same object). If circumstances permit only one observation on each object, it is usually preferable to take the more rapidly changing bearing last and then make an immediate chart plot of both bearings.

If you are able to take observations on three objects, take them in descending order of rate of change of bearing and consider taking a repeat of the first bearing, if possible, for averaging as before.

The time of the fix should be that of the approximate middle of the series of observations. At typical boat cruising speeds and chart scales, a difference of a minute or two will not be significant. At 12 knots, a boat will travel 1/5 mile in one minute; on a 1:80,000 scale chart, this distance of approximately 400 yards is less than 3/16 inch.

## Positioning standards of precision

As set forth in Chapter 19, there are generally accepted standards of precision in describing position of a vessel. If geographic coordinates are used, latitude and longitude, in that sequence, are stated to the nearest tenth of a minute on charts with scales of 1:50,000 or smaller, and to the nearest second on charts of larger scale.

If the position is stated with respect to some aid to navigation or landmark, direction from that point is given to the nearest degree (true) and distance is given to the nearest tenth of a mile.

## THE RUNNING FIX

The lack of a second object on which to make an observation may at times prevent the immediate determination of the boat's position by a normal fix, even though one good line of position has been established. In such situations, a somewhat less accurate determination of position may be made by a *running fix (R Fix)*. In this technique there is one line of position at the time of the running fix and another from a different time, usually earlier. This latter LOP must be replotted from its position at the time of its measurement to account for the movement of the boat during the intervening time. The act of advancing the first LOP brings it to a common time with the second obser-

vation so that their intersection may be considered as a determination of position. It should be noted that this line so advanced (or retired) may have resulted from an observation on the *same* object as that used for the second sighting at the time of the running fix, or on a different object.

## Advancing a line of position

A line of position is advanced as follows:

(1) A point is selected on the original LOP. This can be

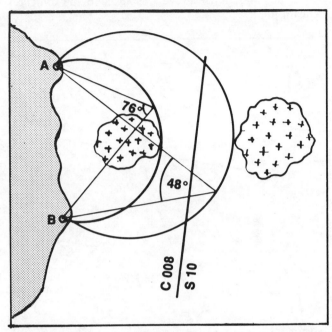

**FIG. 2134** For passage between two unmarked hazardous areas, *double horizontal danger angles* may be used. This technique is essentially the combination of the two preceding situations; a safe passage is indicated by measurement of horizontal angles between specified upper and lower limits.

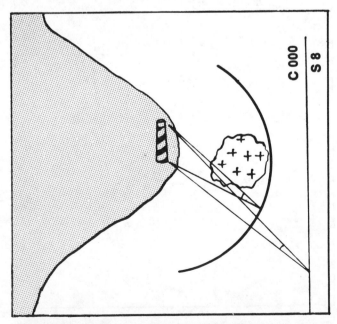

**FIG. 2135** A measurement of vertical angle establishes a circle of position at a specific distance from a point. Such an angle can be calculated for an object of known height so as to insure that a boat does not get too close. Safe vertical angles are those *less* than the *vertical danger angle*.

the intersection of the line with the DR track, X in fig. 2136, or any point on the LOP, such as X'.

(2) The selected point is moved in an amount equal in distance and direction to the boat's motion during the time interval involved. This is most easily measured from the DR position at the time of observation to the DR position for the advanced time.

(3) The new LOP is drawn in through the advanced point parallel to the original LOP.

(4) The advanced LOP is labeled as soon as it is drawn: both times are shown above the line and the direction beneath it.

FIG. 2136 A line of position is *advanced* by moving forward any point on it an amount equal to the boat's motion during the time interval and re-drawing the line through this advanced point.

FIG. 2137 A circle of position, or circular LOP, is advanced by merely moving the center point an amount equal in direction and distance to the motion of the boat during the time interval, and redrawing the circle on the new center. In the illustration above, C = C' is equal to the spacing between the two DR positions.

## Advancing a circular LOP

If the LOP to be advanced is circular, as would be the case with a distance measurement by vertical angle or range finder, the center of the circle is the point advanced by the procedure described above, fig. 2137. The circle or arc is redrawn using the new center, and is then labeled as for any other advanced LOP.

## Advancing a LOP with course and/or speed changes

The advancement of the selected point on the initial LOP must take into account all changes in course and/or speed of the boat during the time interval. It is frequently a convenient procedure to calculate and plot the DR positions for the time of the initial observation and for the advanced time. The movement of the selected point on the initial LOP should parallel and equal a line drawn between these two DR positions. This technique is particularly useful if there has been more than one change in course and/or speed, fig. 2138.

## Advancing a LOP with current

The advancement of a line of position may take into account current effects if they are adequately known or can be estimated. The selected point on the initial LOP is first advanced for DR speeds and courses, and then for the set and drift of the current, both calculations using the elapsed time interval between the two observations; see fig. 2139.

## The accuracy of advanced LOPs

The accuracy of an advanced line of position can be only as good as the accuracy of the initial observation *decreased* by any errors or uncertainties in the navigator's data for the boat's course and speed (and current data, if used). Obviously, the longer the time interval over which

FIG. 2138 The advancement of a LOP must take into consideration all changes of course and/or speed during the time interval. The net effect can be determined by drawing a light line between the DR positions for the two times concerned. The selected point on the original LOP is advanced in the same direction and distance as this net effect line.

the sight is advanced, the greater the uncertainties become. The interval should, therefore, be the minimum possible, and, in piloting, should rarely exceed 30 minutes. (In navigation on the high seas, celestial lines of position are often advanced several hours, but the accuracy of positioning is less critical in these circumstances.)

The same criteria for the angle of intersection of lines of position apply to running fixes as were discussed previously for normal fixes. Running fixes involving three lines of positions (two of them advanced) are possible but are unusual in actual piloting practice.

Lines of position may be retired, moved back to an earlier time, in a similar manner. Such retrograde movement is, however, quite rare in piloting situations.

### Running fixes and DR plots

The DR plot may be interrupted and restarted from a running fix if it is considered of reasonable accuracy. In all cases, however, a fix obtained from two or more essentially simultaneous observations or measurements is to be preferred over a running fix.

## OBSERVATIONS ON A SINGLE OBJECT

In addition to the technique of the running fix using advanced lines of position, position information can be obtained from successive observations on a single object by means of several other more specialized procedures. These include: bow-and-beam bearings, doubling the angle on the bow, two bearings and run between, and two relative bearings.

### Bow-and-beam bearings

Position determination is easily accomplished by the technique of taking two particular successive bearings on an object to one side or the other of the craft's course. The first bearing is taken when the object sighted upon

bears either 45° to starboard (RB 045°) or to port (RB 315°). The second bearing is taken when the same object is broad on the respective beam (RB 090° or 270°), fig. 2140. The time of each bearing having been noted, the time interval is found, and then the distance traveled between the two sightings is calculated using the boat's speed. Because of the nature of the triangle established by the two bearings and the course line, the boat is away from the sighted object at the time of the second (beam) bearing at the same distance as that traveled during the time interval. This distance is that traveled *over the bottom*; correction to the DR track should be made for any current or other offsetting influence if such information is known or can be estimated. Since there is a LOP (the beam bearing) and a distance, the position of the craft has been determined. It should be noted that this position is *not* necessarily the intersection of the second bearing and the course line; the craft may be off its intended track.

The principal advantage of this procedure is the ease with which it can be accomplished. Beam bearings are easily taken, and 45° relative bearings can be quickly set up using crude sights oriented with an ordinary plastic drafting triangle. On some boats, it may be possible to make the 45° sight over the steering compass. The bow-and-beam technique often can be done by the helmsman without assistance.

### Doubling the angle on the bow

This is a more generalized application of the same principles as those involved in bow-and-beam bearings, in which a 45° angle was doubled to 90°. Geometric principles establish that whenever an angle on the bow is doubled, the distance from the position at which the second bearing is taken to the object sighted upon is equal to the distance traveled (over the bottom) during the time

FIG. 2139 If the LOP is to be advanced with allowance for current, the same procedure as before is followed, except that a further movement is made from the second DR position to account for the current during the time interval and obtain an estimated position.

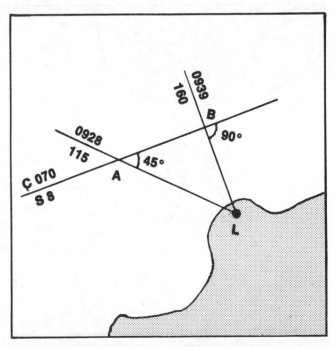

FIG. 2140 If a bearing is taken when an object bears 45° on either bow (RB = 045° or 315°), and again when the same object is broad on the beam (RB = 090° or 270°), the distance to the object at the time of the second bearing will be equal to the distance run (over the bottom) between the bearings; B-L = A-B.

interval between the two observations, fig. 2141. The angle referred to above is the relative bearing to starboard or to port. A relative bearing of, say 340° measured in the conventional manner, must be converted to an angle of 20° to port for the purpose of "doubling"; in this case, the doubled angle would be RB 320° (40° to port).

The doubling-of-the-bow-angle technique has the advantage of determining the boat's position *before* the sighted object is abeam. With information as to the boat's position at such an earlier moment, the course can be projected ahead on the chart. Should the craft be traveling too close to shore for passing a headland, a more adequate warning of the dangerous course will thus be in hand, and corrective action can be taken sooner.

This technique does, however, have a disadvantage in that it requires the possession and use of a pelorus or other instrument for measuring relative bearings with reasonable accuracy. Another disadvantage is that a second person is needed as a bearing-taker.

## Two-bearings-and-run-between

With only a single object upon which sights can be taken, another method, known as "two-bearings-and-run-between" for lack of a better name, may be used. In this procedure, a bearing is taken on the object, the boat proceeds along her course, and a second bearing is taken after the angle has changed by at least 30°. This second bearing may be taken before or after the sighted object is passed abeam. From the times of each bearing, the time interval is calculated, and from this, the distance run is determined.

Both bearings are plotted, as is the course of the boat, fig. 2142. A pair of dividers is opened to the distance run between the two bearings and is then moved parallel to the course line until the points fall on the bearing lines.

**FIG. 2142** If two bearings are taken on a single object as the boat passes it, and are plotted on the chart, then only one point can be found on each LOP so that the course and distance made good will fit between these LOPs.

The divider points now indicate the positions of the boat at the times of the first and second bearings.

As before, the distance run must be that *over the bottom;* suitable corrections must be made for any current. The accuracy of this technique depends upon many factors: the accuracy of each of the two bearings, the accuracy of the calculation of the distance run over the bottom, and the accuracy with which the boat was steered during the interval between the two sightings. The net effect of this compounding of accuracies is to make the positions so determined somewhat less certain than the other techniques described above.

## Two relative bearings

A more generalized solution from two relative bearings can be used if a copy of "Bowditch" is on board. Table 7 of that book uses two items of information—the angle between the course and the first bearing (the first relative bearing) and the difference between the course and the second bearing (the second relative bearing). Columns of the Table are in terms of the first item and lines are in terms of the second item above; the interval between tabular entries is two degrees in both cases.

For any combination of the two relative bearings within the limits of Table 7, two factors will be found. The first

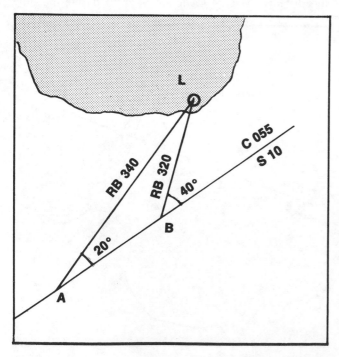

**FIG. 2141** If two observations are made so that the second relative bearing is twice that of the first (as measured from the bow to either starboard or port), then the distance to the sighted object at the time of the second bearing is the same as the distance made good between the sightings; again, **L-B = A-B.**

number is a factor by which the distance run between the bearings is multiplied to obtain the distance away from the sighted object at the time of the second bearing. The second factor of the same entry in Table 7 is the multiplier to be used to determine the distance off when the object is abeam, assuming, of course, that the same course and speed are maintained. See fig. 2143.

# Electronic Piloting

Although electronic navigation is essentially a topic in itself, and outside of the scope of piloting, brief mention will be made here of two techniques which have direct comparability and applicability to visual piloting.

## RADIO BEARINGS AND DISTANCES

With relatively simple equipment, observations can be made of the direction to radio stations, even though such "objects" lie far beyond visual range, either as a result of night, fog, or simply great distance. See fig. 2144. Bearings can be taken on radiobeacons operated by the Coast Guard as aids to navigation; some aeronautical ranges and beacons operated by the FAA; on standard AM radio broadcast stations; and on stations in the 2-3 Mc/s marine band, including both shore and ship stations. In general, the desirability for use in radio direction finding is in descending order as listed above. Radio bearings can be taken under any condition of visibility, and on stations at ranges as great as hundreds of miles; accuracies will, of course, be more favorable with nearer stations.

Radio bearings are taken with a *radio direction finder*, usually referred to as an RDF. This item of electronic equipment is discussed more fully in Chapter 25, pages 502 to 506.

### Using radio bearings

Radio bearings are plotted in essentially the same manner as visual bearings. They are not as sharp as visual observations, however; an accuracy of 2° to 3° is the best that can be expected, and this precision will be achieved only with experience. Accordingly, it is advisable to obtain three radio LOPs, and even so, the position so determined should not be considered as precise as one from visual bearings.

Accurate identification of the station being received is essential, and the exact location of the transmitting antenna must be plotted on the nautical chart if it is not already shown there.

Radio bearings taken on a station more than approximately 200 miles distant must be corrected if they are to be plotted on a Mercator chart. (The exact distance will vary with latitude and the relative position of the vessel and the radio station.) This correction is required because radio waves travel via the most direct route, a great circle path, and this does not plot as a straight line on a Mercator chart; see page 363. Table 1 in Bowditch provides the correction factor and instructions on how it should be applied. No correction is needed for nearer stations, or on stations at any distance if the plotting is done on a gnomonic chart.

### Labeling RDF bearings and fixes

In view of the lesser accuracy of RDF bearings as com-

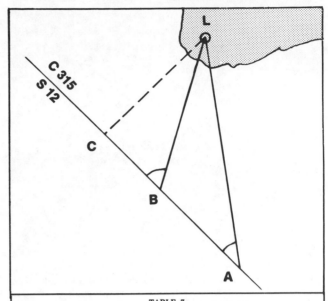

**TABLE 7**
Distance of an Object by Two Bearings

| Difference between the course and second bearing | Differences between the course and first bearing | | | | | | | | | | | | |
|---|---|---|---|---|---|---|---|---|---|---|---|---|---|
| | 34° | | 36° | | 38° | | 40° | | 42° | | 44° | | 46° | |
| 44 | 3.22 | 2.24 | | | | | | | | | | | | |
| 46 | 2.69 | 1.93 | 3.39 | 2.43 | | | | | | | | | | |
| 48 | 2.31 | 1.72 | 2.83 | 2.10 | 3.55 | 2.63 | | | | | | | | |
| 50 | 2.03 | 1.55 | 2.43 | 1.86 | 2.96 | 2.27 | 3.70 | 2.84 | | | | | | |
| 52 | 1.81 | 1.43 | 2.13 | 1.68 | 2.54 | 2.01 | 3.09 | 2.44 | 3.85 | 3.04 | | | | |
| 54 | 1.63 | 1.32 | 1.90 | 1.54 | 2.23 | 1.81 | 2.66 | 2.15 | 3.22 | 2.60 | 4.00 | 3.24 | | |
| 56 | 1.49 | 1.24 | 1.72 | 1.42 | 1.99 | 1.65 | 2.33 | 1.93 | 2.77 | 2.29 | 3.34 | 2.77 | 4.14 | 3.43 |
| 58 | 1.37 | 1.17 | 1.57 | 1.33 | 1.80 | 1.53 | 2.08 | 1.76 | 2.43 | 2.06 | 2.87 | 2.44 | 3.46 | 2.93 |
| 60 | 1.28 | 1.10 | 1.45 | 1.25 | 1.64 | 1.42 | 1.88 | 1.63 | 2.17 | 1.88 | 2.52 | 2.18 | 2.97 | 2.57 |
| 62 | 1.19 | 1.05 | 1.34 | 1.18 | 1.51 | 1.34 | 1.72 | 1.52 | 1.96 | 1.73 | 2.25 | 1.98 | 2.61 | 2.30 |
| 64 | 1.12 | 1.01 | 1.25 | 1.13 | 1.40 | 1.26 | 1.58 | 1.42 | 1.79 | 1.61 | 2.03 | 1.83 | 2.33 | 2.09 |
| 66 | 1.06 | 0.96 | 1.18 | 1.07 | 1.31 | 1.20 | 1.47 | 1.34 | 1.65 | 1.51 | 1.85 | 1.69 | 2.10 | 1.92 |
| 68 | 1.00 | 0.93 | 1.11 | 1.03 | 1.23 | 1.14 | 1.37 | 1.27 | 1.53 | 1.42 | 1.71 | 1.58 | 1.92 | 1.78 |
| 70 | 0.95 | 0.89 | 1.05 | 0.99 | 1.16 | 1.09 | 1.29 | 1.21 | 1.43 | 1.34 | 1.58 | 1.49 | 1.77 | 1.66 |
| 72 | 0.91 | 0.86 | 1.00 | 0.95 | 1.10 | 1.05 | 1.21 | 1.15 | 1.34 | 1.27 | 1.48 | 1.41 | 1.64 | 1.56 |
| 74 | 0.87 | 0.84 | 0.95 | 0.92 | 1.05 | 1.01 | 1.15 | 1.10 | 1.26 | 1.21 | 1.39 | 1.34 | 1.53 | 1.47 |
| 76 | 0.84 | 0.81 | 0.91 | 0.89 | 1.00 | 0.97 | 1.09 | 1.06 | 1.20 | 1.16 | 1.31 | 1.27 | 1.44 | 1.40 |
| 78 | 0.80 | 0.79 | 0.88 | 0.86 | 0.96 | 0.94 | 1.04 | 1.02 | 1.14 | 1.11 | 1.24 | 1.22 | 1.36 | 1.33 |
| 80 | 0.78 | 0.77 | 0.85 | 0.83 | 0.92 | 0.91 | 1.00 | 0.98 | 1.09 | 1.07 | 1.18 | 1.16 | 1.28 | 1.27 |

**FIG. 2143  Distance off at time of second bearing, L-B, and distance off when abeam, L-C, can be found by applying multiplying factors to the distance run, A-B. These factors for various pairs of angles will be found in Table 7 of Bowditch.**

**FIG. 2144  Radio direction finders (RDFs) can be used to take bearings on transmitters located a fraction of a mile, or several hundreds of miles, distant. Lines of position can be found at night, in fog, or when visibility is good but the station is too far away to be seen.**

FIG. 2145a  Because the accuracy of a fix derived from radio bearings is usually less than that of one obtained from visual observations, it should be labeled "RDF FIX".

FIG.2145b  If a combination of LOPs includes one from an RDF measurement, it may be well to add the letters "RDF" above the line where applicable.

**Distance finding stations.** At certain stations the radiobeacon and sound signal are synchronized for distance finding. The beginning of the ten-second radio dash and the beginning of the five-second blast of the fog signal are synchronized for this purpose. The ten-second radio dash and the long (5 second) blast of the fog signal commence at the same instant. Therefore, when within audible range of the sound signal, navigators on vessels with radio receivers capable of receiving the radiobeacon signals may readily determine their distance from the station by observing the time in seconds which elapsed between first hearing the beginning of the ten-second radio dash and the beginning of the five-second sound blast and dividing the result by 5.5 for nautical miles. The error of such observations should not exceed 10 percent.

The two seconds of silence preceding the long radio dash is a stand-by or warning signal as is also the one-second fog signal blast.

Observations for distance from these stations are not **restricted to vessels with direction finders**, but may be made by any vessel having a radio receiver capable of receiving in the band 285 to 325 kilocycles. An example of these synchronized signals follows:

|  | For 5 minutes | | For 1 minute | |
|---|---|---|---|---|
| **R B N** | Off | 48<br>Code | 2 | 10<br>■ |
| | | 3<br>17 ■ 33 | ■1 | 1   5<br>■ 5 |
| **F S** | 1 blast ev 20ˢ (3ˢbl) | ■ Shows dash of RBN or<br>blast of fog signal.<br>‖ Figures show seconds. | | |

If the interval between hearing the beginning of the long radio dash marking the end of the radiobeacon minute and the beginning of the long blast of the diaphone is 33 seconds, the observer is 33 + 5.5 = 6 miles from the light station.

FIG. 2146  Radiobeacons whose transmissions are periodically synchronized with the blasts of a fog signal are designated as *Distance Finding Stations (DFS).* The Light Lists give detailed information on the synchronization pattern.

| (1) | (2) | (3) | (4) | (5) | (6) | | (7) |
|---|---|---|---|---|---|---|---|
| | Name | Location | Light<br>or day-<br>beacon | Candle-<br>power | Structure, vessel, or buoy | | |
| No. | Character and period of light | Latitude, N.   Longitude, W. | above<br>water | *Miles seen,* | Top of lan-<br>tern above<br>ground | Established.<br>Moved or<br>rebuilt | Radiobeacon, fog signal, sectors<br>and remarks |
| | (*Duration in italics*) | Deg. Min.     Deg. Min. | Feet | *in italics* | Feet | *Year* | |
| FIRST DISTRICT | | **MAINE** | | | | | |
| | **GULF OF MAINE**<br><br>**Penobscot Bay**<br>MONHEGAN ISLAND APPROACH | | | | | | |
| 168<br>3<br>*J128* | **MONHEGAN ISLAND LIGHT**<br>**Fl. W.,** 30ˢ (*2.8ˢfl*) | Near center of island..<br>43 45.9      69 19.0 | 178 | 190,000<br>*20* | Gray conical tower covered<br>way to white dwelling.  1824<br>47               1850 | | Within 3 miles of island<br>the light is obscured<br>between west and south-<br>west. |
| 169<br>4<br>*J130* | Manana Island Fog Signal Station...<br>*Resident Personnel.* | On west side of island,<br>close to Monhegan<br>Island.<br>43 45.8      69 19.7 | ... | ......... | Brown brick house .........<br>1855<br>1870 | | **RADIOBEACON:** An-<br>tenna 2,880 feet 259°<br>from Monhegan Island<br>Light tower. **Distance<br>finding station.** (See p.<br>XVII for explanation.)<br>**HORN,** diaphragm; *gp* of<br>3 blasts ev 60ˢ (*2ˢbl-<br>8ˢsi-2ˢbl-8ˢsi-2ˢbl-38ˢsi*). |

pared to visual sighting, and particularly those radio bearings taken on distant stations, it is desirable that the fix obtained from such lines of position be so identified. The location should be labeled with the time and "RDF FIX"; see fig. 2145a. If radio lines of position are mixed with visual bearings, the former may be identified by adding the letters "RDF" above the line following the time of observation, fig. 2145b.

## Radio distance finding

Certain of the radiobeacons operated by the Coast Guard have the transmissions of their radio signals synchronized with the audible blasts of their fog signal. These are designated as *Distance Finding Stations*. The letters "DFS" will appear on the chart near the symbol for the basic aid to navigation, such as a lighthouse or major light. Aids to navigation operated as distance finding stations will be designated in the Light List as "DFS" in the remarks column and details of the exact synchronization scheme will be given, fig. 2146.

Because of the difference in the speed of travel of radio waves (essentially instantaneous over short distances) and the speed of sound (roughly 1100 feet per second) the two signals transmitted at the same instant will be received sequentially on a boat up to several miles distant. The distance from the aid to navigation, in nautical miles, to the observer can be calculated, to an accuracy of approximately 10%, by dividing the time difference, in seconds, between the arrival of the radio "beep" and the fog signal blast by 5.5.

The measurement of distance from the radiobeacon gives, of course, a circular line of position. This can be plotted and combined with a LOP from any other source or even with depth measurements. Because of the ±10% accuracy of the DFS technique, the result should be considered as an estimated position rather than a fix.

The use of this technique is confined to periods of reduced visibility when the fog signal is operating, and is limited to audible ranges of a few miles. Within these limitations, however, distance finding procedures of this type can be very useful.

## RADAR BEARINGS AND DISTANCES

Radar is another item of electronic equipment that is covered in greater detail in Chapter 25, but which will be considered here in connection with piloting situations. Radar has unique advantages in that a single instrument can measure both direction and distance (range), and that these measurements can be accomplished under visibility conditions that would preclude visual observations.

## Radar observations

Measurements of direction by radar are *not* as accurate as those by visual sightings, but radar will penetrate darkness; light and moderate rain without difficulty, and heavy rain with some reduction in effectiveness; fog; and other restrictions that would prohibit visual bearings or range measurements.

On the other hand, measurements of distance by radar can be quite accurate, much more so than such observations taken by vertical sextant angles or with simple optical range finders.

## Use of radar information

Radar data are used in the same manner as information from visual observations. Lines of position are combined to obtain fixes—typical combinations include two bearings, a bearing with a distance measurement to the same or another object, or two distance measurements. A fix obtained by radar bearings and/or distance measurements is labeled with the time and "RAD FIX"; see fig. 2147.

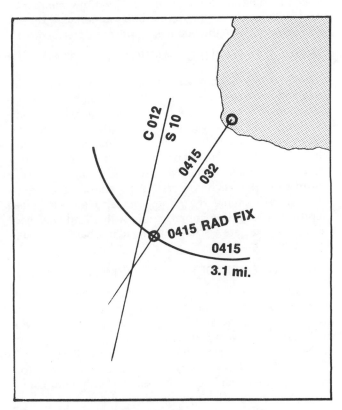

FIG. 2147 A fix obtained from radar lines of position is labeled on the chart as "RAD FIX". In the example above, a fix has been obtained on a single object by measurement of both bearing and distance.

When visibility conditions permit, a frequent combination, and an excellent one, is that of a visual bearing on an object and a radar measurement of distance to that same point.

Radar distance measurements also may be used in the same manner as distance determinations by vertical sextant angle to avoid a shoal area delineated by a circular LOP from a prominent object identifiable on the radarscope.

Radar observations on isolated objects such as buoys, offshore lighthouses, etc., usually are made without difficulty in identification of the object on the radarscope. When the radar target is on shore, however, some problems may be encountered in picking out the exact object on which the bearing and range information is to be obtained. Navigate with caution when using radar information from such objects. Even more so than other types of piloting, radar requires practice and the building up of experience. If you have a radar, use it often in non-critical times so that you can employ it and have the advantage of its unique capabilities when its use is essential. You must be capable of using it with competence and confidence when it is needed.

# Depth Information in Piloting

Information on the depth of water under a vessel is usually considered to be merely a safety matter for the prevention of running aground. In actuality, such data can be of considerable value in piloting. The essential characteristic of depth information is the fact that although it cannot tell the pilot where he is, it can tell him *positively* where he is *not*. If an accurate measurement of depth gives a reading of 26 feet, you may be at any number of places where such is the depth, but you certainly are not at a position where the depth is significantly greater or less.

## HOW DEPTH INFORMATION IS OBTAINED

Data on the depth of the water beneath a craft can be obtained manually or electronically. A hand lead line, see page 385, is a time-honored instrument of piloting, and every boat should have one of a length suitable for the waters usually sailed. It is accurate and dependable in use, although far from efficient or convenient. The modern-day trend is toward electronic depth sounders that can provide information at a much faster rate and with the convenience of reading a simple dial. They can also measure great depths that would be impracticable with a lead line. Electronic sounders are discussed in detail in Chapter 25, page 499 to 501.

## USE OF DEPTH INFORMATION

In using depth information, regardless of how obtained, a correction for the height of tide may be required. The use of Tide Tables and the necessary calculations with their data are covered in Chapter 20.

Depth data can be combined with a line or lines of position obtained from other means to yield positional information. Under some circumstances, depth information alone may be of value in position determination.

### Depth information and a single LOP

If the bottom of the body of water being navigated has some slope, and this slope is reasonably uniform, it may be possible to get positional information from a single LOP, typically a beam bearing, and a depth reading. The bearing line is plotted and then examined for a spot where the depth figure on the chart agrees with the measured depth as corrected for the tidal stage; be sure that there aren't several such depths along the LOP, fig. 2148. Such a location should be considered as an Estimated Position (EP) rather than a Fix.

### Matching measured depths to the chart

In some instances, a rough estimate of the position of a boat can be obtained by matching a series of depth readings, appropriately corrected for the prevailing height of the tide, with depths printed on the chart. Depth readings are taken and recorded at regular time intervals, such as those corresponding to intervals of distance of one-tenth to one-half mile, as determined by the scale of the chart concerned, the density of printed depth figures, etc. (Electronic depth sounders can provide far more depth measurements than can be used.) These depths are marked on a piece of transparent paper at intervals determined by the scale of the chart, fig. 2149a. This piece of paper is then moved about on the chart, keeping the line of sound-

depth sounder reading 23 ft. corrected to MLW

**FIG. 2148 Depth information can often be used with a single LOP, such as a simple beam bearing, to determine an estimated position.**

ings parallel to a line representing the course steered while they were being taken. A maximum degree of match is sought between the observed depths and the charted depths; exact concurrence should not be expected.

In the example shown here, the 60-foot depth as measured is aligned with the 10-fathom curve on the chart, and a search for a match is started. If the line of soundings is moved north of the position shown in fig. 2149b, the depths at the outer end would still be in general agreement, but the mismatch at the inshore end would generally show that the line was incorrectly placed. If the line were moved down the chart, keeping it parallel to the course sailed, then the 37-foot measurement near the inshore end would mismatch with the actual 48-foot depth. The matching found by the location shown in fig. 2149b is as close as may be expected, and this position of the line can be considered to fairly well indicate the track of the craft as the soundings were made.

Position determination by the use of depth data is not well suited to shorelines that are foul with offshore rocks, or areas that have varying, irregular depths. Nor can this technique be used where the depth is quite uniform with few or no variations. There are, however, many situations where it can, and should, be used.

### Position checking by depth data

If an EP has been determined by some other method or combination of methods, consideration should be given to checking it by a depth measurement. Remember that confirmation cannot be positive, but that denial can be quite

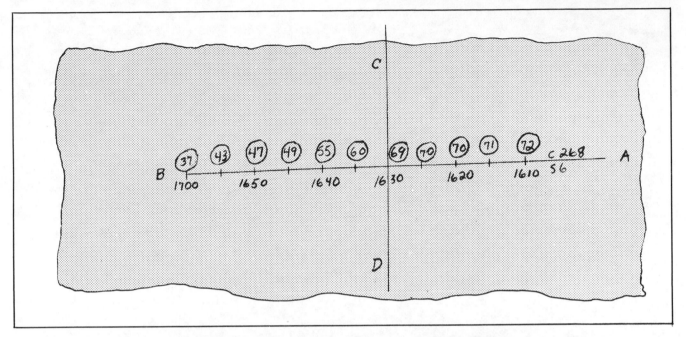

**FIG. 2149a   Position by a line (or chain) of soundings. The sound-ings are taken at regular intervals and plotted on transparent paper as shown.**

**FIG. 2149b   The paper is then moved about on the chart until meas-ured depths correspond with the charted depths.**

certain if there is a significant difference between the depth at the boat's actual location and that charted for the estimated position. If such should be the case, a further verification of the estimated position is a necessity, per-haps even an urgent necessity!

### Fathom curve sailing

When cruising along a coast that has a fairly uniformly sloping bottom offshore, piloting can often be simplified by an examination of the chart for a fathom curve that will keep the craft in safe waters generally and will avoid any specific hazards. The boat is then steered so as to keep the

reading of the electronic depth sounder within a few feet of the selected depth. If readings increase, the boat is gently steered toward shore; if they decrease, the wheel is put over a bit to edge farther offshore.

For the sake of safety, the chart should be checked for the *full* distance that this technique is to be used to be sure that there are no sudden changes in depth, or bends in the depth curve, that might result in an unexpectedly hazardous situation. For added safety, this examination of the chart should be carried beyond the intended end of fathom-curve sailing to prevent unexpected hazards from arising should your speed over the bottom be greater than anticipated.

439

**FIG. 2150** As a general rule, it is better practice to lay two short courses between buoys than one long one. This is especially true in thick weather.

## Practice — and More Practice

Position determination is the part of piloting that truly cannot be learned "from the book." Study is important, it is essential, but the skipper must put into actual practice the various procedures and techniques. He must know the rules and principles involved, but he must also be able to *apply* them. Make a habit of "over-navigating" during daylight and good weather conditions so that you will be experienced and capable at night or in foul weather.

| TABLE FOR FINDING HEIGHT OF TIDE ABOVE LOW WATER AT ANY HOUR OF THE EBB OR FLOOD | | |
|---|---|---|
| FALLING TIDE<br>Hours after high water | RISING TIDE<br>Hours after low water | CONSTANT<br>Rising or Falling |
| 0 | 6 | 1.0 |
| ½ | 5½ | 0.98 |
| 1 | 5 | 0.92 |
| 1½ | 4½ | 0.84 |
| 2 | 4 | 0.75 |
| 2½ | 3½ | 0.63 |
| 3 | 3 | 0.50 |
| 3½ | 2½ | 0.38 |
| 4 | 2 | 0.26 |
| 4½ | 1½ | 0.16 |
| 5 | 1 | 0.08 |
| 5½ | ½ | 0.025 |

1. Find rise of tide for given day in Tide Tables (difference between heights of nearest high and low tides)
2. Enter column 1 or 2 on line corresponding to time for which height of tide is to be calculated
3. In column 3, find constant given for that time
4. Multiply constant obtained in (3) by total rise of tide (1)

*Preceding pages in this chapter have provided all of the basic information required for the safe navigation of a boat in pilot waters —the dimensions and instruments of piloting, the procedures of dead reckoning, calculations involving tides and currents, and position determination. The material to be presented in this supplementary section extends beyond these fundamentals. These are techniques that will be useful in specialized situations, or which may provide a quicker or easier solution to a piloting problem. The material of this section might be considered as "graduate study" in small-craft piloting. These techniques should not be approached without a thorough understanding of Chapters 19 and 20, and the basic methods already discussed in Chapter 21. FIG. 2152 (left): Current problems, for example, may be solved with the aid of precomputed speed factors and course corrections—but first understand the principles.*

# PILOTING—Specialized Techniques

## Current Problem Solutions from Tabulated Factors

When a boat moves in water that is in itself in motion with respect to the bottom as a result of current, two effects must be considered. One of these is the difference in speed over the bottom as compared with speed through the water. The other effect is the variation between the course steered and the path actually traveled.

### THE VARIOUS CURRENT SAILING PROBLEMS

The effects mentioned above can be approached from several viewpoints:

(a) with a selected course and speed, together with a known or estimated current, *determining the track and speed of advance* that may be expected;

(b) with a desired track and speed to be run through the water, plus knowledge of the current, *determining the course to steer and the speed of advance* that may be expected; and

(c) with a desired track and speed of advance to be made good, and knowledge of the current, *determining the course to steer and the speed to run through the water.*

In all current situations, there are three pairs of direction and speed values—*boat with respect to the water, water with respect to the bottom,* and *boat with respect to the bottom.* For the solution of current sailing problems, in general, four of the above six quantities will be known (or estimated) and the other two are to be determined.

In Chapter 20, graphic solutions using vectors were used, see pages 392 to 416.

Such current problems can also be solved using data derived from an electronic digital computer. Solutions from these tables of data should not be attempted, however, without a thorough understanding of the relationships between the various quantities involved, as are shown in the graphic plots of Chapter 20. An understanding of the graphical procedure will reduce the chances of

misinterpreting the tables, or of using the factors incorrectly. For easier understanding, the same terms, abbreviations, and designations of problems (Case 1, Case 3, etc.) will be used here as in Chapter 20.

### DISTANCE, TIME, AND SPEED CALCULATIONS

Where no current is present, the pilot's problem is a simple matter of *determining the time required to run a given distance in slack water.* Even where there is current, slack water speed (or speed through the water without reference to current) is a basic factor. The formulas for D, T, and S, see page 388, can be used, but the table of fig. 2151 is a handy means of achieving the same results. It was developed primarily for the cruising boatman who is interested in relatively long runs involving hours and minutes of time.

#### Slack water speed solutions

The use of fig. 2151 is simple, as the following examples will illustrate:

**Example A.** At 13 knots, how long does it take to go 36 miles?

*Answer:* Reading directly from the table, $2^h 46^m$.

**Example B.** At 11 knots, how long does it take to go 43.6 miles?

*Answer:* Reading from the table—

| | |
|---|---|
| to go 43. miles, | $3^h 55^m$ |
| to go .6 miles, | $3^m$ |
| to go 43.6 miles | $3^h 58^m$ |

**Example C.** At 14.3 knots, how long does it take to go 26.4 miles?

*Answer:* From the table, in the same manner as for Example B:

| | |
|---|---|
| to go 26.4 miles at 14 knots, | $1^h 53^m$ |
| to go 26.4 miles at 15 knots, | $1^h 46^m$ |
| Difference in time for 1 knot, | $7^m$ |

Hence, to go 26.4 miles at 14.3 knots requires $1^h 53^m - (0.3 \times 7^m) = 1^h 51^m$.

DISTANCE—.1 TO 90—IN MILES

| Dist. miles | 6.0 | 7.0 | 8.0 | 9.0 | 10.0 | 11.0 | 12.0 | 13.0 | 14.0 | 15.0 | 16.0 | 17.0 | 18.0 | 19.0 | 20.0 | 21.0 | 22.0 | 23.0 | 24.0 | 25.0 | 26.0 | 27.0 |
|---|---|---|---|---|---|---|---|---|---|---|---|---|---|---|---|---|---|---|---|---|---|---|
| .1 | 01 | 01 | 01 | 01 | 01 | 01 | 01 | 00 | 00 | 00 | 00 | 00 | 00 | 00 | 00 | 00 | 00 | 00 | 00 | 00 | 00 | 00 |
| .2 | 02 | 02 | 02 | 01 | 01 | 01 | 01 | 01 | 01 | 01 | 01 | 01 | 01 | 01 | 00 | 00 | 00 | 00 | 00 | 00 | 00 | 00 |
| .3 | 03 | 03 | 02 | 02 | 02 | 02 | 02 | 01 | 01 | 01 | 01 | 01 | 01 | 01 | 01 | 01 | 01 | 01 | 01 | 00 | 00 | 00 |
| .4 | 04 | 03 | 03 | 03 | 02 | 02 | 02 | 02 | 02 | 02 | 02 | 01 | 01 | 01 | 01 | 01 | 01 | 01 | 01 | 01 | 01 | 01 |
| .5 | 05 | 04 | 04 | 03 | 03 | 03 | 03 | 02 | 02 | 02 | 02 | 02 | 02 | 02 | 02 | 01 | 01 | 01 | 01 | 01 | 01 | 01 |
| .6 | 06 | 05 | 05 | 04 | 04 | 03 | 03 | 03 | 03 | 02 | 02 | 02 | 02 | 02 | 02 | 02 | 02 | 02 | 01 | 01 | 01 | 01 |
| .7 | 07 | 06 | 05 | 05 | 04 | 04 | 04 | 03 | 03 | 03 | 03 | 02 | 02 | 02 | 02 | 02 | 02 | 02 | 02 | 02 | 01 | 01 |
| .8 | 08 | 07 | 06 | 05 | 05 | 04 | 04 | 04 | 03 | 03 | 03 | 03 | 03 | 03 | 02 | 02 | 02 | 02 | 02 | 02 | 02 | 02 |
| .9 | 09 | 08 | 07 | 06 | 05 | 05 | 05 | 04 | 04 | 04 | 03 | 03 | 03 | 03 | 03 | 03 | 02 | 02 | 02 | 02 | 02 | 02 |
| 1.0 | 10 | 09 | 08 | 07 | 06 | 05 | 05 | 05 | 04 | 04 | 04 | 04 | 03 | 03 | 03 | 03 | 03 | 03 | 02 | 02 | 02 | 02 |
| 2.0 | 20 | 17 | 15 | 13 | 12 | 11 | 10 | 09 | 09 | 08 | 08 | 07 | 07 | 06 | 06 | 06 | 05 | 05 | 05 | 05 | 05 | 04 |
| 3.0 | 30 | 26 | 23 | 20 | 18 | 16 | 15 | 14 | 13 | 12 | 11 | 11 | 10 | 09 | 09 | 09 | 08 | 08 | 08 | 07 | 07 | 07 |
| 4.0 | 40 | 34 | 30 | 27 | 24 | 22 | 20 | 18 | 17 | 16 | 15 | 14 | 13 | 13 | 12 | 11 | 11 | 10 | 10 | 10 | 09 | 09 |
| 5.0 | 50 | 43 | 38 | 33 | 30 | 27 | 25 | 23 | 21 | 20 | 19 | 18 | 17 | 16 | 15 | 14 | 14 | 13 | 13 | 12 | 12 | 11 |
| 6.0 | 1 00 | 51 | 45 | 40 | 36 | 33 | 30 | 28 | 26 | 24 | 23 | 21 | 20 | 19 | 18 | 17 | 16 | 16 | 15 | 14 | 14 | 13 |
| 7.0 | 1 10 | 1 00 | 53 | 47 | 42 | 38 | 35 | 32 | 30 | 28 | 26 | 25 | 23 | 22 | 21 | 20 | 19 | 18 | 17 | 16 | 16 | 15 |
| 8.0 | 1 20 | 1 09 | 1 00 | 53 | 48 | 44 | 40 | 37 | 34 | 32 | 30 | 28 | 27 | 25 | 24 | 23 | 22 | 21 | 20 | 19 | 18 | 18 |
| 9.0 | 1 30 | 1 17 | 1 08 | 1 00 | 54 | 49 | 45 | 42 | 39 | 36 | 34 | 32 | 30 | 28 | 27 | 25 | 24 | 23 | 22 | 21 | 20 | 20 |
| 10.0 | 1 40 | 1 26 | 1 15 | 1 07 | 1 00 | 55 | 50 | 46 | 43 | 40 | 38 | 35 | 33 | 32 | 30 | 29 | 27 | 26 | 25 | 24 | 23 | 22 |
| 11.0 | 1 50 | 1 34 | 1 23 | 1 13 | 1 06 | 1 00 | 55 | 51 | 47 | 44 | 41 | 39 | 37 | 35 | 33 | 31 | 30 | 29 | 28 | 26 | 25 | 24 |
| 12.0 | 2 00 | 1 43 | 1 30 | 1 20 | 1 12 | 1 05 | 1 00 | 55 | 51 | 48 | 45 | 42 | 40 | 38 | 36 | 34 | 33 | 31 | 30 | 29 | 28 | 27 |
| 13.0 | 2 10 | 1 51 | 1 38 | 1 27 | 1 18 | 1 11 | 1 05 | 1 00 | 56 | 52 | 49 | 46 | 43 | 41 | 39 | 37 | 35 | 34 | 33 | 31 | 30 | 29 |
| 14.0 | 2 20 | 2 00 | 1 45 | 1 33 | 1 24 | 1 16 | 1 10 | 1 05 | 1 00 | 56 | 53 | 49 | 47 | 44 | 42 | 40 | 38 | 37 | 35 | 34 | 32 | 31 |
| 15.0 | 2 30 | 2 09 | 1 53 | 1 40 | 1 30 | 1 22 | 1 15 | 1 09 | 1 04 | 1 00 | 56 | 53 | 50 | 47 | 45 | 43 | 41 | 39 | 38 | 36 | 35 | 33 |
| 16.0 | 2 40 | 2 17 | 2 00 | 1 47 | 1 36 | 1 27 | 1 20 | 1 15 | 1 09 | 1 04 | 1 00 | 56 | 53 | 51 | 48 | 46 | 44 | 42 | 40 | 38 | 37 | 36 |
| 17.0 | 2 50 | 2 26 | 2 08 | 1 53 | 1 42 | 1 33 | 1 25 | 1 18 | 1 13 | 1 08 | 1 04 | 1 00 | 57 | 54 | 51 | 49 | 46 | 44 | 43 | 41 | 39 | 38 |
| 18.0 | 3 00 | 2 34 | 2 15 | 2 00 | 1 48 | 1 38 | 1 30 | 1 23 | 1 17 | 1 12 | 1 08 | 1 04 | 1 00 | 57 | 54 | 51 | 49 | 47 | 45 | 43 | 42 | 40 |
| 19.0 | 3 10 | 2 43 | 2 23 | 2 07 | 1 54 | 1 44 | 1 35 | 1 28 | 1 21 | 1 16 | 1 11 | 1 07 | 1 03 | 1 00 | 57 | 54 | 52 | 50 | 48 | 46 | 44 | 42 |
| 20.0 | 3 20 | 2 51 | 2 30 | 2 13 | 2 00 | 1 49 | 1 40 | 1 32 | 1 26 | 1 20 | 1 15 | 1 11 | 1 07 | 1 03 | 1 00 | 57 | 55 | 52 | 50 | 48 | 46 | 44 |
| 21.0 | 3 30 | 3 00 | 2 38 | 2 20 | 2 06 | 1 55 | 1 45 | 1 37 | 1 30 | 1 24 | 1 19 | 1 14 | 1 10 | 1 06 | 1 03 | 1 00 | 57 | 55 | 53 | 50 | 48 | 47 |
| 22.0 | 3 40 | 3 09 | 2 45 | 2 27 | 2 12 | 2 00 | 1 50 | 1 42 | 1 34 | 1 28 | 1 23 | 1 18 | 1 13 | 1 09 | 1 06 | 1 03 | 1 00 | 57 | 55 | 53 | 51 | 49 |
| 23.0 | 3 50 | 3 17 | 2 53 | 2 33 | 2 18 | 2 05 | 1 55 | 1 46 | 1 39 | 1 32 | 1 26 | 1 21 | 1 17 | 1 13 | 1 09 | 1 06 | 1 03 | 1 00 | 58 | 55 | 53 | 51 |
| 24.0 | 4 00 | 3 26 | 3 00 | 2 40 | 2 24 | 2 11 | 2 00 | 1 51 | 1 43 | 1 36 | 1 30 | 1 25 | 1 20 | 1 16 | 1 12 | 1 09 | 1 05 | 1 03 | 1 00 | 58 | 55 | 53 |
| 25.0 | 4 10 | 3 34 | 3 08 | 2 47 | 2 30 | 2 16 | 2 05 | 1 55 | 1 47 | 1 40 | 1 34 | 1 28 | 1 23 | 1 19 | 1 15 | 1 11 | 1 08 | 1 05 | 1 03 | 1 00 | 58 | 56 |
| 26.0 | 4 20 | 3 43 | 3 15 | 2 53 | 2 36 | 2 22 | 2 10 | 2 00 | 1 51 | 1 44 | 1 38 | 1 32 | 1 27 | 1 22 | 1 18 | 1 14 | 1 11 | 1 08 | 1 05 | 1 02 | 1 00 | 58 |
| 27.0 | 4 30 | 3 51 | 3 23 | 3 00 | 2 42 | 2 27 | 2 15 | 2 05 | 1 56 | 1 48 | 1 41 | 1 35 | 1 30 | 1 25 | 1 21 | 1 17 | 1 14 | 1 10 | 1 08 | 1 05 | 1 02 | 1 00 |
| 28.0 | 4 40 | 4 00 | 3 30 | 3 07 | 2 48 | 2 33 | 2 20 | 2 09 | 2 00 | 1 52 | 1 45 | 1 39 | 1 33 | 1 28 | 1 24 | 1 20 | 1 16 | 1 13 | 1 10 | 1 07 | 1 05 | 1 02 |
| 29.0 | 4 50 | 4 09 | 3 38 | 3 13 | 2 54 | 2 38 | 2 25 | 2 14 | 2 04 | 1 56 | 1 49 | 1 42 | 1 37 | 1 32 | 1 27 | 1 23 | 1 19 | 1 16 | 1 13 | 1 10 | 1 07 | 1 04 |
| 30.0 | 5 00 | 4 17 | 3 45 | 3 20 | 3 00 | 2 44 | 2 30 | 2 18 | 2 09 | 2 00 | 1 53 | 1 46 | 1 40 | 1 35 | 1 30 | 1 26 | 1 22 | 1 18 | 1 15 | 1 12 | 1 09 | 1 07 |
| 31.0 | 5 10 | 4 26 | 3 53 | 3 27 | 3 06 | 2 49 | 2 35 | 2 23 | 2 13 | 2 04 | 1 56 | 1 49 | 1 43 | 1 38 | 1 33 | 1 29 | 1 25 | 1 21 | 1 18 | 1 14 | 1 12 | 1 09 |
| 32.0 | 5 20 | 4 33 | 4 00 | 3 33 | 3 12 | 2 55 | 2 40 | 2 28 | 2 17 | 2 08 | 2 00 | 1 53 | 1 47 | 1 41 | 1 36 | 1 31 | 1 27 | 1 23 | 1 20 | 1 17 | 1 14 | 1 11 |
| 33.0 | 5 30 | 4 43 | 4 08 | 3 40 | 3 18 | 3 00 | 2 45 | 2 32 | 2 21 | 2 12 | 2 04 | 1 56 | 1 50 | 1 44 | 1 39 | 1 34 | 1 30 | 1 26 | 1 23 | 1 19 | 1 16 | 1 13 |
| 34.0 | 5 40 | 4 51 | 4 15 | 3 47 | 3 24 | 3 05 | 2 50 | 2 37 | 2 26 | 2 16 | 2 08 | 2 00 | 1 53 | 1 47 | 1 42 | 1 37 | 1 33 | 1 29 | 1 25 | 1 22 | 1 18 | 1 16 |
| 35.0 | 5 50 | 5 00 | 4 23 | 3 53 | 3 30 | 3 11 | 2 55 | 2 42 | 2 30 | 2 20 | 2 11 | 2 04 | 1 57 | 1 51 | 1 45 | 1 40 | 1 35 | 1 31 | 1 28 | 1 24 | 1 21 | 1 18 |
| 36.0 | 6 00 | 5 09 | 4 30 | 4 00 | 3 36 | 3 16 | 3 00 | 2 46 | 2 34 | 2 24 | 2 15 | 2 07 | 2 00 | 1 54 | 1 48 | 1 43 | 1 38 | 1 34 | 1 30 | 1 26 | 1 23 | 1 20 |
| 37.0 | 6 10 | 5 17 | 4 38 | 4 07 | 3 42 | 3 22 | 3 05 | 2 51 | 2 39 | 2 28 | 2 19 | 2 11 | 2 03 | 1 57 | 1 51 | 1 46 | 1 41 | 1 37 | 1 33 | 1 29 | 1 25 | 1 22 |
| 38.0 | 6 20 | 5 26 | 4 45 | 4 13 | 3 48 | 3 27 | 3 10 | 2 55 | 2 43 | 2 32 | 2 23 | 2 14 | 2 07 | 2 00 | 1 54 | 1 49 | 1 44 | 1 39 | 1 35 | 1 31 | 1 28 | 1 24 |
| 39.0 | 6 30 | 5 34 | 4 53 | 4 20 | 3 54 | 3 33 | 3 15 | 3 00 | 2 47 | 2 36 | 2 26 | 2 18 | 2 10 | 2 03 | 1 57 | 1 51 | 1 46 | 1 42 | 1 38 | 1 34 | 1 30 | 1 27 |
| 40.0 | 6 40 | 5 43 | 5 00 | 4 27 | 4 00 | 3 38 | 3 20 | 3 05 | 2 51 | 2 40 | 2 30 | 2 21 | 2 13 | 2 06 | 2 00 | 1 54 | 1 49 | 1 44 | 1 40 | 1 36 | 1 32 | 1 29 |
| 41.0 | 6 50 | 5 51 | 5 08 | 4 33 | 4 06 | 3 44 | 3 25 | 3 09 | 2 56 | 2 44 | 2 34 | 2 25 | 2 17 | 2 09 | 2 03 | 1 57 | 1 52 | 1 47 | 1 43 | 1 38 | 1 35 | 1 31 |
| 42.0 | 7 00 | 6 00 | 5 15 | 4 40 | 4 12 | 3 49 | 3 30 | 3 14 | 3 00 | 2 48 | 2 38 | 2 28 | 2 20 | 2 13 | 2 06 | 2 00 | 1 55 | 1 50 | 1 45 | 1 41 | 1 37 | 1 33 |
| 43.0 | 7 10 | 6 09 | 5 23 | 4 47 | 4 18 | 3 55 | 3 35 | 3 18 | 3 04 | 2 52 | 2 41 | 2 32 | 2 23 | 2 16 | 2 09 | 2 03 | 1 57 | 1 52 | 1 48 | 1 43 | 1 39 | 1 36 |
| 44.0 | 7 20 | 6 17 | 5 30 | 4 53 | 4 24 | 4 00 | 3 40 | 3 23 | 3 09 | 2 56 | 2 45 | 2 35 | 2 27 | 2 19 | 2 12 | 2 06 | 2 00 | 1 55 | 1 50 | 1 46 | 1 42 | 1 38 |
| 45.0 | 7 30 | 6 26 | 5 38 | 5 00 | 4 30 | 4 05 | 3 45 | 3 28 | 3 13 | 3 00 | 2 49 | 2 39 | 2 30 | 2 22 | 2 15 | 2 09 | 2 03 | 1 57 | 1 53 | 1 48 | 1 44 | 1 40 |
| 46.0 | 7 40 | 6 34 | 5 45 | 5 07 | 4 36 | 4 11 | 3 50 | 3 32 | 3 17 | 3 04 | 2 53 | 2 42 | 2 33 | 2 25 | 2 18 | 2 11 | 2 05 | 2 00 | 1 55 | 1 50 | 1 46 | 1 42 |
| 47.0 | 7 50 | 6 43 | 5 53 | 5 13 | 4 42 | 4 16 | 3 55 | 3 37 | 3 21 | 3 08 | 2 56 | 2 46 | 2 37 | 2 28 | 2 21 | 2 14 | 2 08 | 2 03 | 1 58 | 1 53 | 1 48 | 1 44 |
| 48.0 | 8 00 | 6 51 | 6 00 | 5 20 | 4 48 | 4 22 | 4 00 | 3 42 | 3 26 | 3 12 | 3 00 | 2 49 | 2 40 | 2 32 | 2 24 | 2 17 | 2 11 | 2 05 | 2 00 | 1 55 | 1 51 | 1 47 |
| 49.0 | 8 10 | 7 00 | 6 08 | 5 27 | 4 54 | 4 27 | 4 05 | 3 46 | 3 30 | 3 16 | 3 04 | 2 53 | 2 43 | 2 35 | 2 27 | 2 20 | 2 14 | 2 08 | 2 03 | 1 58 | 1 53 | 1 49 |
| 50.0 | 8 20 | 7 09 | 6 15 | 5 33 | 5 00 | 4 33 | 4 10 | 3 51 | 3 34 | 3 20 | 3 08 | 2 56 | 2 47 | 2 38 | 2 30 | 2 23 | 2 16 | 2 10 | 2 05 | 2 00 | 1 55 | 1 51 |
| 51.0 | 8 30 | 7 17 | 6 23 | 5 40 | 5 06 | 4 38 | 4 15 | 3 55 | 3 39 | 3 24 | 3 11 | 3 00 | 2 50 | 2 41 | 2 33 | 2 26 | 2 19 | 2 13 | 2 08 | 2 02 | 1 58 | 1 53 |
| 52.0 | 8 40 | 7 26 | 6 30 | 5 47 | 5 12 | 4 44 | 4 20 | 4 00 | 3 43 | 3 28 | 3 15 | 3 04 | 2 53 | 2 44 | 2 36 | 2 29 | 2 22 | 2 16 | 2 10 | 2 05 | 2 00 | 1 56 |
| 53.0 | 8 50 | 7 34 | 6 38 | 5 53 | 5 18 | 4 49 | 4 25 | 4 05 | 3 47 | 3 32 | 3 19 | 3 07 | 2 57 | 2 47 | 2 39 | 2 31 | 2 25 | 2 18 | 2 13 | 2 07 | 2 02 | 1 58 |
| 54.0 | 9 00 | 7 43 | 6 45 | 6 00 | 5 24 | 4 55 | 4 30 | 4 09 | 3 51 | 3 36 | 3 23 | 3 11 | 3 00 | 2 51 | 2 42 | 2 34 | 2 27 | 2 21 | 2 15 | 2 10 | 2 05 | 2 00 |
| 55.0 | 9 10 | 7 51 | 6 53 | 6 07 | 5 30 | 5 00 | 4 35 | 4 14 | 3 56 | 3 40 | 3 26 | 3 14 | 3 03 | 2 54 | 2 45 | 2 37 | 2 30 | 2 23 | 2 17 | 2 12 | 2 07 | 2 02 |
| 56.0 | 9 20 | 8 00 | 7 00 | 6 13 | 5 36 | 5 05 | 4 40 | 4 18 | 4 00 | 3 44 | 3 30 | 3 18 | 3 07 | 2 57 | 2 48 | 2 40 | 2 33 | 2 26 | 2 20 | 2 14 | 2 09 | 2 04 |
| 57.0 | 9 30 | 8 09 | 7 08 | 6 20 | 5 42 | 5 11 | 4 45 | 4 23 | 4 04 | 3 48 | 3 34 | 3 21 | 3 10 | 3 00 | 2 51 | 2 43 | 2 35 | 2 29 | 2 23 | 2 17 | 2 12 | 2 07 |
| 58.0 | 9 40 | 8 17 | 7 15 | 6 27 | 5 48 | 5 16 | 4 50 | 4 28 | 4 09 | 3 52 | 3 38 | 3 25 | 3 13 | 3 03 | 2 54 | 2 46 | 2 38 | 2 31 | 2 25 | 2 19 | 2 14 | 2 09 |
| 59.0 | 9 50 | 8 26 | 7 23 | 6 33 | 5 54 | 5 22 | 4 55 | 4 32 | 4 13 | 3 56 | 3 41 | 3 28 | 3 17 | 3 06 | 2 57 | 2 49 | 2 41 | 2 34 | 2 28 | 2 22 | 2 16 | 2 11 |
| 60.0 | 10 00 | 8 34 | 7 30 | 6 40 | 6 00 | 5 27 | 5 00 | 4 37 | 4 17 | 4 00 | 3 45 | 3 32 | 3 20 | 3 09 | 3 00 | 2 51 | 2 44 | 2 37 | 2 30 | 2 24 | 2 18 | 2 13 |
| 61.0 | 10 10 | 8 43 | 7 38 | 6 47 | 6 06 | 5 33 | 5 05 | 4 42 | 4 21 | 4 04 | 3 49 | 3 35 | 3 23 | 3 13 | 3 03 | 2 54 | 2 46 | 2 39 | 2 33 | 2 26 | 2 21 | 2 16 |
| 62.0 | 10 20 | 8 51 | 7 45 | 6 53 | 6 12 | 5 38 | 5 10 | 4 46 | 4 26 | 4 08 | 3 53 | 3 39 | 3 27 | 3 16 | 3 06 | 2 57 | 2 49 | 2 42 | 2 35 | 2 29 | 2 23 | 2 18 |
| 63.0 | 10 30 | 9 00 | 7 53 | 7 00 | 6 18 | 5 44 | 5 15 | 4 51 | 4 30 | 4 12 | 3 56 | 3 42 | 3 30 | 3 19 | 3 09 | 3 00 | 2 52 | 2 44 | 2 38 | 2 31 | 2 25 | 2 20 |
| 64.0 | 10 40 | 9 09 | 8 00 | 7 07 | 6 24 | 5 49 | 5 20 | 4 55 | 4 34 | 4 16 | 4 00 | 3 46 | 3 33 | 3 22 | 3 12 | 3 03 | 2 55 | 2 47 | 2 40 | 2 34 | 2 28 | 2 22 |
| 65.0 | 10 50 | 9 17 | 8 08 | 7 13 | 6 30 | 5 55 | 5 25 | 5 00 | 4 39 | 4 20 | 4 04 | 3 49 | 3 37 | 3 25 | 3 15 | 3 06 | 2 57 | 2 50 | 2 43 | 2 36 | 2 30 | 2 24 |
| 66.0 | 11 00 | 9 26 | 8 15 | 7 20 | 6 36 | 6 00 | 5 30 | 5 05 | 4 43 | 4 24 | 4 08 | 3 53 | 3 40 | 3 28 | 3 18 | 3 09 | 3 00 | 2 52 | 2 45 | 2 38 | 2 32 | 2 27 |
| 67.0 | 11 10 | 9 34 | 8 23 | 7 27 | 6 42 | 6 05 | 5 35 | 5 09 | 4 47 | 4 28 | 4 11 | 3 56 | 3 43 | 3 32 | 3 21 | 3 11 | 3 03 | 2 55 | 2 48 | 2 41 | 2 35 | 2 29 |
| 68.0 | 11 20 | 9 43 | 8 30 | 7 33 | 6 48 | 6 11 | 5 40 | 5 14 | 4 51 | 4 32 | 4 15 | 4 00 | 3 47 | 3 34 | 3 24 | 3 14 | 3 05 | 2 57 | 2 50 | 2 43 | 2 37 | 2 31 |
| 69.0 | 11 30 | 9 51 | 8 38 | 7 40 | 6 54 | 6 16 | 5 45 | 5 18 | 4 56 | 4 36 | 4 19 | 4 04 | 3 50 | 3 38 | 3 27 | 3 17 | 3 08 | 3 00 | 2 53 | 2 46 | 2 39 | 2 33 |
| 70.0 | 11 40 | 10 00 | 8 45 | 7 47 | 7 00 | 6 22 | 5 50 | 5 23 | 5 00 | 4 40 | 4 23 | 4 07 | 3 53 | 3 41 | 3 30 | 3 20 | 3 11 | 3 03 | 2 55 | 2 48 | 2 42 | 2 36 |
| 71.0 | 11 50 | 10 09 | 8 53 | 7 53 | 7 06 | 6 27 | 5 55 | 5 28 | 5 04 | 4 44 | 4 26 | 4 11 | 3 57 | 3 44 | 3 33 | 3 23 | 3 14 | 3 05 | 2 58 | 2 50 | 2 44 | 2 38 |
| 72.0 | 12 00 | 10 17 | 9 00 | 8 00 | 7 12 | 6 33 | 6 00 | 5 32 | 5 09 | 4 48 | 4 30 | 4 14 | 4 00 | 3 47 | 3 36 | 3 26 | 3 16 | 3 08 | 3 00 | 2 53 | 2 46 | 2 40 |
| 73.0 | 12 10 | 10 26 | 9 08 | 8 07 | 7 18 | 6 38 | 6 05 | 5 37 | 5 13 | 4 52 | 4 34 | 4 18 | 4 03 | 3 51 | 3 39 | 3 29 | 3 19 | 3 10 | 3 03 | 2 55 | 2 48 | 2 42 |
| 74.0 | 12 20 | 10 34 | 9 15 | 8 13 | 7 24 | 6 44 | 6 10 | 5 42 | 5 17 | 4 56 | 4 38 | 4 21 | 4 07 | 3 54 | 3 42 | 3 31 | 3 22 | 3 13 | 3 05 | 2 58 | 2 51 | 2 44 |
| 75.0 | 12 30 | 10 43 | 9 23 | 8 20 | 7 30 | 6 49 | 6 15 | 5 46 | 5 21 | 5 00 | 4 41 | 4 25 | 4 10 | 3 57 | 3 45 | 3 34 | 3 25 | 3 16 | 3 08 | 3 00 | 2 53 | 2 47 |
| 76.0 | 12 40 | 10 51 | 9 30 | 8 27 | 7 36 | 6 55 | 6 20 | 5 51 | 5 26 | 5 04 | 4 45 | 4 28 | 4 13 | 4 00 | 3 48 | 3 37 | 3 27 | 3 18 | 3 10 | 3 02 | 2 55 | 2 49 |
| 77.0 | 12 50 | 11 00 | 9 38 | 8 33 | 7 42 | 7 00 | 6 25 | 5 55 | 5 30 | 5 08 | 4 49 | 4 32 | 4 17 | 4 03 | 3 51 | 3 40 | 3 30 | 3 21 | 3 13 | 3 05 | 2 58 | 2 51 |
| 78.0 | 13 00 | 11 09 | 9 45 | 8 40 | 7 48 | 7 05 | 6 30 | 6 00 | 5 34 | 5 12 | 4 53 | 4 35 | 4 20 | 4 06 | 3 54 | 3 43 | 3 33 | 3 23 | 3 15 | 3 07 | 3 00 | 2 53 |
| 79.0 | 13 10 | 11 17 | 9 53 | 8 47 | 7 54 | 7 11 | 6 35 | 6 05 | 5 39 | 5 16 | 4 56 | 4 39 | 4 23 | 4 09 | 3 57 | 3 46 | 3 35 | 3 26 | 3 18 | 3 10 | 3 02 | 2 56 |
| 80.0 | 13 20 | 11 26 | 10 00 | 8 53 | 8 00 | 7 16 | 6 40 | 6 09 | 5 43 | 5 20 | 5 00 | 4 42 | 4 27 | 4 13 | 4 00 | 3 48 | 3 38 | 3 29 | 3 20 | 3 12 | 3 05 | 2 58 |
| 81.0 | 13 30 | 11 34 | 10 08 | 9 00 | 8 06 | 7 22 | 6 45 | 6 14 | 5 47 | 5 24 | 5 04 | 4 46 | 4 30 | 4 16 | 4 03 | 3 51 | 3 41 | 3 31 | 3 23 | 3 14 | 3 07 | 3 00 |
| 82.0 | 13 40 | 11 43 | 10 15 | 9 07 | 8 12 | 7 27 | 6 50 | 6 18 | 5 51 | 5 28 | 5 08 | 4 49 | 4 33 | 4 19 | 4 06 | 3 54 | 3 44 | 3 34 | 3 25 | 3 17 | 3 09 | 3 02 |
| 83.0 | 13 50 | 11 51 | 10 23 | 9 13 | 8 18 | 7 33 | 6 55 | 6 23 | 5 56 | 5 32 | 5 11 | 4 53 | 4 37 | 4 22 | 4 09 | 3 57 | 3 46 | 3 37 | 3 28 | 3 19 | 3 12 | 3 04 |
| 84.0 | 14 00 | 12 00 | 10 30 | 9 20 | 8 24 | 7 38 | 7 00 | 6 28 | 6 00 | 5 36 | 5 15 | 4 56 | 4 40 | 4 25 | 4 12 | 4 00 | 3 49 | 3 39 | 3 30 | 3 21 | 3 14 | 3 07 |
| 85.0 | 14 10 | 12 09 | 10 38 | 9 27 | 8 30 | 7 44 | 7 05 | 6 32 | 6 04 | 5 40 | 5 19 | 5 00 | 4 43 | 4 28 | 4 15 | 4 03 | 3 52 | 3 42 | 3 33 | 3 24 | 3 16 | 3 09 |
| 86.0 | 14 20 | 12 17 | 10 45 | 9 33 | 8 36 | 7 49 | 7 10 | 6 37 | 6 09 | 5 44 | 5 23 | 5 04 | 4 47 | 4 32 | 4 18 | 4 06 | 3 55 | 3 44 | 3 35 | 3 26 | 3 18 | 3 11 |
| 87.0 | 14 30 | 12 26 | 10 53 | 9 40 | 8 42 | 7 55 | 7 15 | 6 42 | 6 13 | 5 48 | 5 26 | 5 07 | 4 50 | 4 35 | 4 21 | 4 09 | 3 57 | 3 47 | 3 38 | 3 29 | 3 21 | 3 13 |
| 88.0 | 14 40 | 12 34 | 11 00 | 9 47 | 8 48 | 8 00 | 7 20 | 6 46 | 6 16 | 5 52 | 5 30 | 5 11 | 4 53 | 4 38 | 4 24 | 4 11 | 4 00 | 3 50 | 3 40 | 3 31 | 3 23 | 3 16 |
| 89.0 | 14 50 | 12 43 | 11 08 | 9 53 | 8 54 | 8 05 | 7 25 | 6 51 | 6 21 | 5 56 | 5 34 | 5 14 | 4 57 | 4 41 | 4 27 | 4 14 | 4 03 | 3 52 | 3 43 | 3 34 | 3 26 | 3 18 |
| 90.0 | 15 00 | 12 51 | 11 15 | 10 00 | 9 00 | 8 11 | 7 30 | 6 55 | 6 26 | 6 00 | 5 38 | 5 18 | 5 00 | 4 44 | 4 30 | 4 17 | 4 05 | 3 55 | 3 45 | 3 36 | 3 28 | 3 20 |

FIG. 2151 Time required to run a known distance at a specified speed. Time is shown in hours and minutes. Distances and speeds may be in nautical miles and knots, or in statute miles and MPH. Times for whole miles and fractions may be combined. See text.

The technique of interpolating between speeds in Example C is not precisely correct from a pure mathematics viewpoint. The error, if any, however, will be negligible in practical piloting situations, and the procedure is quite acceptable.

## CURRENT PROBLEM SOLUTIONS

In solving current sailing problems with tabulated data, the pilot will still use the terminology developed in earlier chapters. For review, these terms are as follows:

**Course (C)**—the direction of the DR track, the direction the boat is steered through the water.

**Speed (S)**—the speed of the boat through the water, the DR track speed.

**Set**—the direction *toward* which the current is flowing.

**Drift**—the velocity of the current.

**Track (TR)**—the direction of the desired (expected) track line.

**Speed of Advance (SOA)**—the desired (expected) speed along the intended track line.

The terms *Course over the Ground (COG)* and *Speed over the Ground (SOG)* are used only with Case 2 problems which will not be considered in these tabular solutions.

Whenever distance and speed appear in the above definitions, and in the examples to follow, the units may be either statute miles and MPH, or nautical miles and knots.

## Special terms

In the solution of current problems by tabulated factors, it is necessary to introduce certain additional terms not previously employed in the graphic solution of such problems.

$$\text{Drift, in percent} = \frac{\text{Drift} \times 100}{\text{Speed, or SOA, as specified}}$$

*Relative set* is the angle measured from the course steered (C), or from the desired (expected) track (TR), to the set of the current, measured either clockwise or counter-clockwise so that the angle is less than 180°. When measured in a *clockwise* direction, relative set is *positive;* when measured in a *counter-clockwise* direction, relative set is *negative*. In some cases, relative set will be figured with respect to course (C); in other cases, with respect to track (TR).

Fig. 2153 shows graphically the relationship of relative set and course change (CC) to the previously used terms of course, track, set, etc. for Case 1 problems.

Relative set is calculated as shown in the examples shown below:

Relative set = Set − Course, 180° or less
to starboard or port.

| | | |
|---|---|---|
| Set | 060 | 300 |
| Course | −025 | −340 |
| Relative set | +035 | −040 |

If (Set − C) is numerically greater than 180°, and positive, subtract 360° obtaining a *negative* relative set less than 180°.

| | |
|---|---|
| Set | 240 |
| Course | −030 |
| | +210 |
| | −360 |
| Relative set | −150 |

If (Set − C) is numerically greater than 180°, and negative, add 360°, obtaining a *positive* relative set less than 180°.

| | |
|---|---|
| Set | 060 |
| Course | −300 |
| | −240 |
| | +360 |
| Relative set | +120 |

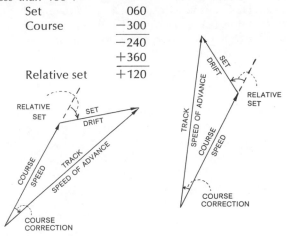

**FIG. 2153 The tabular solution of current problems introduces two new terms—*relative set* and *course correction* (CC). The relationship of these terms to the more familiar directions and velocities are shown above for Case 1 problems.**

Fig. 2154 and subsequent tables will yield a multiplying quantity, termed Speed Factor (SF), and an angle, called Course Change or Course Correction (CC). The use of these factors will be explained in connection with each of the three types of current problems to be solved by the tables.

## Case 1 solutions by tabular factors

In Case 1, the pilot has selected the course that he will steer and the speed at which he will operate his boat with respect to the water (the engine rpm setting that he will use). He also has information on the set and drift of the current from predictions or visual observations. He desires to know *the direction of the path that the boat may be expected to follow with respect to the bottom (TR) and*

**FIG. 2154 Case 1—To find Track and Speed of Advance from knowledge of Course and Speed through the water, plus relative set and percent drift. This table yields Speed Factors (SF) and Course Corrections (CC).**

DRIFT—in percent of speed over water

| 2 | | 4 | | 6 | | 8 | | 10 | | 12 | | 14 | | 16 | | 18 | | 20 | | 22 | | 24 | | 26 | | 28 | | 30 | | 32 | | 34 | | 36 | | 38 | | 40 | |
|---|---|---|---|---|---|---|---|---|---|---|---|---|---|---|---|---|---|---|---|---|---|---|---|---|---|---|---|---|---|---|---|---|---|---|---|---|---|---|---|
| SF | CC | SF | CC | SF | CC | SF | CC | SF | CC | SF | CC | SF | CC | SF | CC | SF | CC | SF | CC | SF | CC | SF | CC | SF | CC | SF | CC | SF | CC | SF | CC | SF | CC | SF | CC | SF | CC | SF | CC |
| 1.020 00 | | 1.040 00 | | 1.060 00 | | 1.080 00 | | 1.100 00 | | 1.120 00 | | 1.140 00 | | 1.160 00 | | 1.180 00 | | 1.200 00 | | 1.220 00 | | 1.240 00 | | 1.260 00 | | 1.280 00 | | 1.300 00 | | 1.320 00 | | 1.340 00 | | 1.360 00 | | 1.380 00 | | 1.400 00 | |
| 1.020 00 | | 1.040 00 | | 1.060 00 | | 1.080 00 | | 1.100 01 | | 1.120 01 | | 1.140 01 | | 1.159 01 | | 1.179 01 | | 1.199 01 | | 1.219 01 | | 1.239 01 | | 1.259 01 | | 1.279 01 | | 1.299 01 | | 1.319 01 | | 1.339 01 | | 1.359 01 | | 1.379 01 | | 1.399 01 | |
| 1.019 00 | | 1.039 00 | | 1.058 01 | | 1.079 01 | | 1.099 01 | | 1.118 01 | | 1.138 01 | | 1.158 01 | | 1.178 02 | | 1.197 02 | | 1.217 02 | | 1.237 02 | | 1.257 02 | | 1.277 02 | | 1.296 02 | | 1.316 02 | | 1.336 03 | | 1.356 03 | | 1.376 03 | | 1.396 03 | |
| 1.019 00 | | 1.039 01 | | 1.058 01 | | 1.077 01 | | 1.097 01 | | 1.116 02 | | 1.136 02 | | 1.155 02 | | 1.175 02 | | 1.194 02 | | 1.214 03 | | 1.233 03 | | 1.253 03 | | 1.273 03 | | 1.292 03 | | 1.312 04 | | 1.331 04 | | 1.351 04 | | 1.371 04 | | 1.390 04 | |
| 1.018 00 | | 1.036 01 | | 1.055 01 | | 1.073 02 | | 1.091 02 | | 1.110 03 | | 1.128 03 | | 1.147 03 | | 1.166 04 | | 1.184 04 | | 1.203 04 | | 1.222 05 | | 1.241 05 | | 1.259 05 | | 1.278 06 | | 1.297 06 | | 1.316 06 | | 1.335 07 | | 1.354 07 | | 1.373 07 | |
| 1.017 01 | | 1.035 01 | | 1.052 01 | | 1.070 02 | | 1.088 03 | | 1.106 03 | | 1.123 04 | | 1.141 04 | | 1.159 04 | | 1.177 05 | | 1.196 05 | | 1.214 06 | | 1.232 06 | | 1.250 06 | | 1.269 07 | | 1.287 07 | | 1.306 07 | | 1.324 08 | | 1.343 08 | | 1.361 08 | |
| 1.016 01 | | 1.033 01 | | 1.050 02 | | 1.067 02 | | 1.083 03 | | 1.100 04 | | 1.118 04 | | 1.135 05 | | 1.152 05 | | 1.169 06 | | 1.187 06 | | 1.204 07 | | 1.222 07 | | 1.240 07 | | 1.258 08 | | 1.275 08 | | 1.293 09 | | 1.311 09 | | 1.329 09 | | 1.347 10 | |
| 1.015 01 | | 1.031 01 | | 1.047 02 | | 1.063 03 | | 1.079 03 | | 1.095 04 | | 1.111 05 | | 1.127 05 | | 1.144 06 | | 1.160 06 | | 1.177 07 | | 1.194 07 | | 1.211 08 | | 1.228 08 | | 1.245 09 | | 1.262 09 | | 1.279 10 | | 1.297 10 | | 1.314 11 | | 1.331 11 | |
| 1.014 01 | | 1.029 02 | | 1.043 02 | | 1.058 03 | | 1.073 04 | | 1.088 04 | | 1.103 05 | | 1.119 06 | | 1.134 06 | | 1.150 07 | | 1.166 08 | | 1.182 08 | | 1.198 09 | | 1.214 09 | | 1.231 10 | | 1.247 10 | | 1.263 11 | | 1.280 11 | | 1.297 12 | | 1.314 12 | |
| 1.013 01 | | 1.026 02 | | 1.040 03 | | 1.053 03 | | 1.067 04 | | 1.081 05 | | 1.095 06 | | 1.110 06 | | 1.124 07 | | 1.139 08 | | 1.154 08 | | 1.169 09 | | 1.184 10 | | 1.199 10 | | 1.215 11 | | 1.230 11 | | 1.246 12 | | 1.262 13 | | 1.278 13 | | 1.294 14 | |
| 1.012 01 | | 1.023 02 | | 1.036 03 | | 1.048 04 | | 1.061 04 | | 1.073 05 | | 1.086 06 | | 1.100 07 | | 1.113 08 | | 1.127 08 | | 1.141 09 | | 1.155 10 | | 1.169 11 | | 1.183 11 | | 1.198 12 | | 1.212 12 | | 1.227 13 | | 1.242 14 | | 1.257 14 | | 1.272 15 | |
| 1.010 01 | | 1.021 02 | | 1.031 03 | | 1.042 04 | | 1.054 05 | | 1.065 06 | | 1.077 06 | | 1.089 07 | | 1.101 08 | | 1.114 09 | | 1.126 10 | | 1.139 11 | | 1.152 11 | | 1.166 12 | | 1.179 13 | | 1.193 13 | | 1.206 14 | | 1.220 15 | | 1.235 15 | | 1.249 16 | |
| 1.009 01 | | 1.018 02 | | 1.027 03 | | 1.036 04 | | 1.046 05 | | 1.056 06 | | 1.067 07 | | 1.077 08 | | 1.088 09 | | 1.100 09 | | 1.111 10 | | 1.123 11 | | 1.135 12 | | 1.147 13 | | 1.159 14 | | 1.172 14 | | 1.184 15 | | 1.197 16 | | 1.211 17 | | 1.224 17 | |
| 1.007 01 | | 1.014 02 | | 1.022 03 | | 1.030 04 | | 1.038 05 | | 1.047 06 | | 1.056 07 | | 1.065 08 | | 1.075 09 | | 1.085 10 | | 1.095 11 | | 1.105 12 | | 1.116 13 | | 1.127 14 | | 1.138 14 | | 1.149 15 | | 1.161 16 | | 1.173 17 | | 1.185 18 | | 1.197 18 | |
| 1.005 01 | | 1.011 02 | | 1.017 03 | | 1.024 04 | | 1.030 05 | | 1.038 06 | | 1.045 07 | | 1.053 08 | | 1.061 09 | | 1.069 10 | | 1.078 11 | | 1.087 12 | | 1.096 13 | | 1.106 14 | | 1.116 15 | | 1.126 16 | | 1.136 17 | | 1.147 18 | | 1.158 18 | | 1.169 19 | |
| 1.004 01 | | 1.008 02 | | 1.012 03 | | 1.017 04 | | 1.022 06 | | 1.028 07 | | 1.034 08 | | 1.040 09 | | 1.046 10 | | 1.053 11 | | 1.061 12 | | 1.068 13 | | 1.076 14 | | 1.084 15 | | 1.093 16 | | 1.102 17 | | 1.111 18 | | 1.120 18 | | 1.130 19 | | 1.140 20 | |
| 1.002 01 | | 1.004 02 | | 1.007 03 | | 1.010 05 | | 1.014 06 | | 1.018 07 | | 1.022 08 | | 1.026 09 | | 1.031 10 | | 1.037 11 | | 1.042 12 | | 1.049 13 | | 1.055 14 | | 1.062 15 | | 1.069 16 | | 1.076 17 | | 1.084 18 | | 1.092 19 | | 1.100 20 | | 1.109 21 | |
| 1.000 00 | | 1.001 02 | | 1.002 03 | | 1.003 05 | | 1.005 06 | | 1.007 07 | | 1.010 08 | | 1.013 09 | | 1.016 10 | | 1.020 11 | | 1.024 12 | | 1.028 13 | | 1.033 15 | | 1.038 16 | | 1.044 17 | | 1.050 18 | | 1.056 19 | | 1.063 20 | | 1.070 21 | | 1.077 22 | |
| .998 01 | | .997 02 | | .997 03 | | .996 05 | | .996 06 | | .997 07 | | .998 08 | | .999 09 | | .999 10 | | 1.001 10 | | 1.003 11 | | 1.005 13 | | 1.008 14 | | 1.011 15 | | 1.015 16 | | 1.019 17 | | 1.023 18 | | 1.028 19 | | 1.033 20 | | 1.038 21 | |
| .997 01 | | .994 02 | | .991 03 | | .989 05 | | .988 06 | | .986 07 | | .985 08 | | .985 09 | | .985 10 | | .985 12 | | .986 13 | | .987 14 | | .989 15 | | .991 16 | | .993 17 | | .996 18 | | .999 20 | | 1.002 21 | | 1.006 22 | | 1.010 23 | |
| .995 01 | | .990 02 | | .986 03 | | .982 05 | | .979 06 | | .976 07 | | .973 08 | | .971 09 | | .969 10 | | .968 12 | | .967 13 | | .966 14 | | .966 15 | | .966 16 | | .967 17 | | .968 19 | | .969 20 | | .971 21 | | .973 22 | | .976 23 | |
| .993 01 | | .987 02 | | .981 03 | | .976 04 | | .970 06 | | .966 07 | | .961 08 | | .957 09 | | .954 10 | | .950 11 | | .948 13 | | .945 14 | | .943 15 | | .942 16 | | .941 17 | | .940 19 | | .940 21 | | .940 22 | | .942 22 | | .941 24 | |
| .992 01 | | .984 02 | | .976 03 | | .969 04 | | .962 05 | | .955 07 | | .949 08 | | .944 09 | | .938 10 | | .933 11 | | .929 12 | | .925 14 | | .921 15 | | .917 16 | | .915 17 | | .912 19 | | .910 20 | | .908 21 | | .907 22 | | .907 24 | |
| .990 01 | | .981 02 | | .971 03 | | .962 04 | | .954 05 | | .946 06 | | .938 07 | | .930 09 | | .923 10 | | .917 11 | | .910 12 | | .904 13 | | .899 15 | | .894 16 | | .889 17 | | .885 18 | | .881 20 | | .877 21 | | .874 22 | | .872 23 | |
| .989 01 | | .978 02 | | .967 03 | | .956 04 | | .946 05 | | .936 06 | | .927 07 | | .918 08 | | .909 09 | | .900 10 | | .892 12 | | .884 13 | | .877 14 | | .870 15 | | .864 17 | | .858 18 | | .852 19 | | .847 20 | | .842 22 | | .837 23 | |
| .987 01 | | .975 02 | | .963 03 | | .951 04 | | .939 05 | | .927 06 | | .916 07 | | .905 08 | | .895 09 | | .885 10 | | .875 11 | | .865 12 | | .856 13 | | .848 15 | | .839 16 | | .831 17 | | .824 18 | | .817 20 | | .810 21 | | .804 22 | |
| .986 01 | | .972 02 | | .959 03 | | .945 03 | | .932 04 | | .919 05 | | .906 06 | | .894 07 | | .882 08 | | .870 09 | | .859 10 | | .847 12 | | .837 13 | | .826 14 | | .816 15 | | .806 16 | | .797 18 | | .788 19 | | .779 20 | | .770 22 | |
| .985 01 | | .970 02 | | .955 02 | | .940 03 | | .926 04 | | .911 05 | | .897 06 | | .883 07 | | .870 08 | | .856 09 | | .843 10 | | .831 11 | | .818 12 | | .806 13 | | .794 14 | | .782 15 | | .771 16 | | .760 18 | | .750 19 | | .740 20 | |
| .984 01 | | .968 01 | | .951 02 | | .936 03 | | .920 04 | | .904 04 | | .889 05 | | .874 06 | | .859 07 | | .844 08 | | .829 09 | | .815 10 | | .801 11 | | .787 12 | | .774 13 | | .760 14 | | .747 15 | | .735 16 | | .722 18 | | .710 19 | |
| .983 01 | | .966 01 | | .949 02 | | .932 02 | | .915 03 | | .898 04 | | .882 05 | | .865 05 | | .849 06 | | .833 07 | | .817 08 | | .801 09 | | .786 10 | | .770 10 | | .755 11 | | .740 12 | | .726 14 | | .711 15 | | .697 16 | | .684 17 | |
| .982 01 | | .964 01 | | .946 02 | | .928 02 | | .910 03 | | .893 03 | | .875 04 | | .858 05 | | .840 05 | | .823 06 | | .806 07 | | .789 07 | | .772 08 | | .756 09 | | .739 10 | | .723 11 | | .707 12 | | .691 13 | | .675 14 | | .660 15 | |
| .981 01 | | .963 01 | | .944 01 | | .925 02 | | .907 02 | | .888 03 | | .870 03 | | .851 04 | | .833 04 | | .815 05 | | .797 05 | | .779 06 | | .761 07 | | .743 07 | | .725 08 | | .708 09 | | .690 10 | | .673 11 | | .656 11 | | .639 12 | |
| .981 01 | | .961 01 | | .942 01 | | .923 01 | | .904 02 | | .885 02 | | .866 02 | | .846 03 | | .827 03 | | .808 04 | | .790 04 | | .771 05 | | .752 05 | | .733 06 | | .714 06 | | .696 07 | | .677 07 | | .659 08 | | .641 09 | | .622 10 | |
| .980 01 | | .961 00 | | .941 01 | | .921 01 | | .902 01 | | .882 01 | | .862 02 | | .843 02 | | .823 02 | | .804 02 | | .784 03 | | .765 03 | | .745 03 | | .726 04 | | .706 04 | | .687 05 | | .668 05 | | .648 06 | | .629 06 | | .610 07 | |
| .980 00 | | .960 00 | | .940 00 | | .920 00 | | .900 01 | | .881 01 | | .861 01 | | .841 01 | | .821 01 | | .801 01 | | .781 01 | | .761 02 | | .741 02 | | .721 02 | | .702 02 | | .682 02 | | .662 03 | | .642 03 | | .622 03 | | .603 03 | |
| .980 00 | | .960 00 | | .940 00 | | .920 00 | | .900 00 | | .880 00 | | .860 00 | | .840 00 | | .820 00 | | .800 00 | | .780 00 | | .760 00 | | .740 00 | | .720 00 | | .700 00 | | .680 00 | | .660 00 | | .640 00 | | .620 00 | | .600 00 | |

*the speed of advance over the bottom (SOA)* that will result from the current's effect.

Fig. 2154 can be used to solve the above problem. The tables of this figure are entered with the drift, in percent of speed through the water, at the top (columns labeled 2 to 40), and the relative set of the current (lines labeled 000° to 180° at the left side). The intersection of the appropriate column and line yields a Speed Factor (SF) and Course Change (CC).

In Case 1 problems, speed (S) is a known value; it is multiplied by SF to get the value for the speed of advance (SOA). In this type of current problem, the Course steered (C) is also a known value. Thus, "CC" is "Course Change," the angle by which the boat is set off course by the current. It is applied as follows:

Track (TR) = C + CC, when relative set is positive.

= C − CC, when relative set is negative.

Three examples will be used to illustrate the application of these tabular factors. Graphic plots of each example are shown as aids to understanding, but they are not required, and are not normally drawn.

**Example D.** (Fig. 2155)

Known: Course = 076° True
Speed = 8 knots
Set = 324°
Drift = 3 knots

To be determined: Track and Speed of Advance

Solution: Relative set = 324° − 076° = +248°
248° − 360° = −112°

Percent drift = $\frac{3 \times 100}{8}$ = 38

From the table: for 110°, CC = 22°, SF = 0.940
for 115°, CC = 22°, SF = 0.907
by interpolation, for 112°, CC = 22°, SF = 0.927
Thus: Track = 076° − 22° = 054° True
Speed of Advance = 8 × 0.927
= 7.4 knots

**Example E.** (Fig. 2156)

Known: Course = 331° True
Speed = 9 knots
Set = 021°
Drift = 2.5 knots

To be determined: Track and Speed of Advance

Solution: Relative set = 021° − 331° = −310°
+360°
+050°

Percent drift = $\frac{2.5 \times 100}{9}$ = 28

From the table: CC = 10°
SF = 1.199
Thus: Track 331° + 10° = 341°
Speed of Advance = 9 × 1.199
= 10.8 knots

FIG. 2155 Example D—a Case 1 problem: Course 076° True, Speed 8 knots; Set 324°, Drift 3 knots. Find Track and Speed of Advance. See text for solution by tabular factors of fig. 2154.

FIG. 2156 Example E— a Case 1 problem with positive relative set. See text for solution.

**Example F.** (Fig. 2157)

Known: Course = 015° True
Speed = 10 knots
Set = 156°
Drift = 2 knots

To be determined:
Track and Speed of Advance
Solution:
Relative set = 156° − 015° = +141°

Percent drift = $\frac{2 \times 100}{10}$ = 20

From the table: CC = 9
SF = 0.854
Thus: Track 015° + 9° = 024°
Speed of Advance = 10 × 0.854
= 8.5 knots

FIG. 2157 Example F—a Case 1 problem with Course 015° True, Speed 10 knots; Set 156°, Drift 2 knots.

## Case 3 solutions by tabular factors

In Case 3 current sailing problems, the pilot has determined the direction of the track line that he desires to make good (TR) and has selected his rpm speed (S). He also has information on the set and drift of the current. He desires to determine *what course he should steer through the water (C) and to know what speed of advance (SOA) will be achieved* at this throttle setting.

In this Case (and in Case 4 problems to be examined later), relative set is the angle between the current and the desired track; see fig. 2158.

Relative set = Set − Track, 180° or less
to starboard or port.

As before, relative set is positive when measured clockwise and negative when measured counter-clockwise. Follow the same rules as for Case 1 if the subtraction gives you an angle greater than 180°.

Fig. 2159 may be used for the solution of this particular current sailing problem. As speed (S) is again a known quantity, it is multiplied by SF as before to obtain speed of advance (SOA).

FIG. 2158 In Case 3 and 4 current sailing problems, the relative set is measured between the current and the intended track. The course correction remains as the angle between track and course as in Case 1.

In Case 3, the course to be steered (C) is a desired rather than a known value, and it must be determined by the application of a correction to the desired track (TR). Thus the tabulated angle "CC" is termed "Course Correction" and is used as follows:

Course to be steered (C)
= TR − CC, when the relative set is positive.
= TR + CC, when the relative set is negative.

**FIG. 2159 Case 3—To find Course to be steered and Speed of Advance from knowledge of desired Track and Speed through the water, plus relative set and percent drift. This table yields Speed Factors (SF) and Course Corrections (CC) to be applied as shown in text.**

Drift 2–20 (each cell = SF CC):

| 2 | 4 | 6 | 8 | 10 | 12 | 14 | 16 | 18 | 20 |
|---|---|---|---|---|---|---|---|---|---|
| 1.020 00 | 1.040 00 | 1.060 00 | 1.080 00 | 1.100 00 | 1.120 00 | 1.140 00 | 1.160 00 | 1.180 00 | 1.200 00 |
| 1.020 00 | 1.040 00 | 1.059 01 | 1.079 01 | 1.098 01 | 1.118 01 | 1.138 01 | 1.157 01 | 1.177 01 | 1.199 01 |
| 1.020 00 | 1.039 00 | 1.058 01 | 1.077 01 | 1.096 01 | 1.115 02 | 1.135 02 | 1.154 02 | 1.173 02 | 1.192 03 |
| 1.019 00 | 1.039 01 | 1.056 01 | 1.075 02 | 1.093 02 | 1.112 02 | 1.130 03 | 1.149 03 | 1.167 04 | 1.186 04 |
| 1.018 00 | 1.036 01 | 1.054 02 | 1.072 02 | 1.090 02 | 1.107 03 | 1.125 03 | 1.143 04 | 1.160 04 | 1.178 05 |
| 1.017 01 | 1.034 01 | 1.052 02 | 1.068 02 | 1.085 03 | 1.102 03 | 1.119 04 | 1.135 05 | 1.152 05 | 1.168 06 |
| 1.016 01 | 1.033 01 | 1.049 02 | 1.064 03 | 1.080 03 | 1.096 04 | 1.111 05 | 1.127 05 | 1.142 06 | 1.157 07 |
| 1.015 01 | 1.030 01 | 1.045 02 | 1.060 03 | 1.075 04 | 1.089 04 | 1.103 05 | 1.117 06 | 1.131 07 | 1.145 07 |
| 1.014 01 | 1.028 02 | 1.042 02 | 1.055 03 | 1.068 04 | 1.081 05 | 1.094 06 | 1.107 06 | 1.119 07 | 1.131 08 |
| 1.013 01 | 1.025 02 | 1.038 03 | 1.050 04 | 1.061 04 | 1.073 05 | 1.084 06 | 1.095 07 | 1.106 08 | 1.117 09 |
| 1.011 01 | 1.022 02 | 1.033 03 | 1.044 04 | 1.054 04 | 1.064 06 | 1.074 07 | 1.083 08 | 1.092 08 | 1.101 09 |
| 1.010 01 | 1.019 02 | 1.029 03 | 1.038 04 | 1.046 05 | 1.055 06 | 1.063 07 | 1.070 08 | 1.078 09 | 1.085 10 |
| 1.008 01 | 1.016 02 | 1.024 03 | 1.031 04 | 1.038 05 | 1.045 06 | 1.051 07 | 1.057 08 | 1.063 09 | 1.068 10 |
| 1.007 01 | 1.013 02 | 1.019 03 | 1.025 04 | 1.030 05 | 1.035 06 | 1.039 08 | 1.043 09 | 1.047 10 | 1.051 11 |
| 1.005 01 | 1.010 02 | 1.014 03 | 1.018 04 | 1.021 06 | 1.024 07 | 1.027 08 | 1.029 09 | 1.031 10 | 1.033 11 |
| 1.003 01 | 1.006 02 | 1.009 03 | 1.011 05 | 1.013 06 | 1.014 07 | 1.015 08 | 1.015 09 | 1.015 10 | 1.015 11 |
| 1.002 01 | 1.003 02 | 1.003 03 | 1.004 05 | 1.004 06 | 1.003 07 | 1.002 08 | 1.001 09 | .999 10 | .997 11 |
| 1.000 01 | .999 02 | .998 03 | .997 05 | .995 06 | .993 07 | .990 08 | .987 09 | .984 10 | .980 12 |
| .998 01 | .996 02 | .993 03 | .990 05 | .986 06 | .982 07 | .978 08 | .973 09 | .968 10 | .963 11 |
| .996 01 | .992 02 | .988 03 | .983 05 | .978 06 | .972 07 | .966 08 | .960 09 | .953 10 | .946 11 |
| .995 01 | .989 02 | .983 03 | .976 04 | .969 06 | .962 07 | .955 08 | .947 09 | .938 10 | .929 11 |
| .993 01 | .986 02 | .978 03 | .970 04 | .961 05 | .953 06 | .943 08 | .934 07 | .924 10 | .914 11 |
| .991 01 | .982 02 | .973 03 | .964 04 | .954 05 | .943 06 | .933 07 | .922 08 | .911 09 | .899 10 |
| .990 01 | .979 02 | .969 03 | .958 04 | .946 05 | .935 06 | .923 07 | .910 08 | .898 09 | .885 10 |
| .988 01 | .977 02 | .964 03 | .952 04 | .939 05 | .926 06 | .913 07 | .900 08 | .886 08 | .872 09 |
| .987 01 | .974 02 | .960 03 | .947 04 | .933 04 | .919 05 | .904 06 | .890 07 | .875 08 | .860 09 |
| .986 01 | .971 02 | .957 02 | .942 03 | .927 04 | .912 05 | .896 06 | .880 06 | .865 07 | .849 08 |
| .985 01 | .969 01 | .953 02 | .937 03 | .921 04 | .905 04 | .889 05 | .872 06 | .855 07 | .838 07 |
| .984 01 | .967 01 | .950 02 | .933 03 | .916 03 | .899 04 | .882 05 | .865 05 | .847 06 | .830 07 |
| .983 01 | .965 01 | .948 02 | .930 02 | .912 03 | .894 03 | .876 04 | .858 05 | .840 05 | .822 06 |
| .982 00 | .964 01 | .945 01 | .927 02 | .908 02 | .890 03 | .871 03 | .853 04 | .834 04 | .815 05 |
| .981 00 | .962 01 | .943 01 | .924 02 | .905 02 | .886 02 | .867 03 | .848 03 | .829 04 | .810 04 |
| .981 00 | .961 01 | .942 01 | .923 01 | .903 01 | .884 02 | .864 02 | .845 02 | .825 03 | .805 03 |
| .980 00 | .961 00 | .941 01 | .921 01 | .901 01 | .882 01 | .862 01 | .842 02 | .822 02 | .802 02 |
| .980 00 | .960 00 | .940 00 | .920 00 | .900 00 | .880 00 | .860 00 | .841 01 | .821 01 | .801 01 |
| .980 00 | .960 00 | .940 00 | .920 00 | .900 00 | .880 01 | .860 01 | .840 00 | .820 00 | .800 00 |

Drift 22–40 (each cell = SF CC):

| 22 | 24 | 26 | 28 | 30 | 32 | 34 | 36 | 38 | 40 |
|---|---|---|---|---|---|---|---|---|---|
| 1.220 00 | 1.240 00 | 1.260 00 | 1.280 00 | 1.300 00 | 1.320 00 | 1.340 00 | 1.360 00 | 1.380 00 | 1.400 00 |
| 1.219 01 | 1.239 01 | 1.259 01 | 1.279 01 | 1.299 01 | 1.318 02 | 1.338 02 | 1.358 02 | 1.378 02 | 1.398 02 |
| 1.216 02 | 1.235 02 | 1.255 03 | 1.275 03 | 1.294 03 | 1.314 03 | 1.333 03 | 1.353 04 | 1.372 04 | 1.392 04 |
| 1.211 03 | 1.230 04 | 1.249 04 | 1.268 04 | 1.287 04 | 1.306 05 | 1.325 05 | 1.343 05 | 1.362 06 | 1.381 06 |
| 1.204 05 | 1.222 05 | 1.240 05 | 1.259 05 | 1.277 06 | 1.295 06 | 1.313 07 | 1.331 07 | 1.349 07 | 1.366 08 |
| 1.195 05 | 1.212 05 | 1.230 06 | 1.247 07 | 1.264 07 | 1.281 08 | 1.298 08 | 1.315 09 | 1.331 09 | 1.348 10 |
| 1.184 06 | 1.201 07 | 1.217 07 | 1.233 08 | 1.248 09 | 1.264 09 | 1.280 09 | 1.295 10 | 1.311 11 | 1.326 12 |
| 1.172 07 | 1.187 08 | 1.202 09 | 1.216 09 | 1.231 10 | 1.245 11 | 1.259 11 | 1.273 12 | 1.287 13 | 1.301 13 |
| 1.158 08 | 1.172 09 | 1.185 10 | 1.198 10 | 1.211 11 | 1.224 12 | 1.236 13 | 1.249 13 | 1.261 14 | 1.273 15 |
| 1.143 09 | 1.155 10 | 1.167 11 | 1.178 11 | 1.189 12 | 1.200 13 | 1.211 14 | 1.222 15 | 1.232 16 | 1.242 16 |
| 1.127 10 | 1.137 11 | 1.147 11 | 1.157 12 | 1.166 13 | 1.175 14 | 1.184 15 | 1.193 16 | 1.201 17 | 1.209 18 |
| 1.110 10 | 1.118 11 | 1.126 12 | 1.134 13 | 1.141 14 | 1.149 15 | 1.155 16 | 1.162 17 | 1.168 18 | 1.174 19 |
| 1.092 11 | 1.098 12 | 1.104 13 | 1.110 14 | 1.116 15 | 1.121 16 | 1.126 17 | 1.130 18 | 1.134 19 | 1.138 20 |
| 1.073 12 | 1.077 13 | 1.082 14 | 1.086 15 | 1.089 16 | 1.092 17 | 1.095 18 | 1.097 19 | 1.099 20 | 1.101 21 |
| 1.054 12 | 1.056 13 | 1.059 14 | 1.061 16 | 1.062 16 | 1.063 17 | 1.064 19 | 1.064 20 | 1.064 21 | 1.063 22 |
| 1.034 12 | 1.035 13 | 1.035 15 | 1.035 16 | 1.035 16 | 1.034 18 | 1.033 19 | 1.031 20 | 1.029 22 | 1.026 23 |
| 1.014 13 | 1.013 14 | 1.012 15 | 1.010 16 | 1.007 17 | 1.005 18 | 1.001 20 | .998 21 | .993 22 | .989 23 |
| .995 13 | .992 14 | .989 15 | .985 16 | .980 17 | .976 19 | .971 20 | .965 21 | .959 22 | .952 23 |
| .976 13 | .971 14 | .966 15 | .960 16 | .954 17 | .947 19 | .940 20 | .933 21 | .925 22 | .917 24 |
| .957 13 | .950 14 | .943 15 | .936 16 | .928 17 | .920 19 | .911 20 | .902 21 | .892 22 | .882 22 |
| .938 13 | .930 14 | .922 15 | .913 16 | .903 17 | .893 18 | .883 20 | .873 21 | .861 22 | .850 23 |
| .920 12 | .911 13 | .901 15 | .890 16 | .879 17 | .868 18 | .857 19 | .844 20 | .832 22 | .819 23 |
| .903 12 | .892 13 | .881 14 | .869 15 | .857 16 | .844 17 | .831 19 | .818 20 | .804 21 | .790 22 |
| .887 12 | .875 13 | .862 14 | .849 15 | .836 16 | .822 17 | .808 18 | .793 19 | .778 20 | .763 21 |
| .872 11 | .858 12 | .844 13 | .830 14 | .816 15 | .801 16 | .786 17 | .770 18 | .754 19 | .738 20 |
| .857 10 | .843 11 | .828 12 | .813 13 | .797 14 | .781 15 | .765 16 | .749 17 | .732 18 | .715 19 |
| .844 10 | .829 11 | .813 11 | .797 12 | .780 13 | .764 14 | .747 15 | .730 16 | .712 17 | .695 18 |
| .832 09 | .816 10 | .799 11 | .782 11 | .765 12 | .748 13 | .730 14 | .712 15 | .695 16 | .676 16 |
| .821 08 | .804 09 | .787 10 | .769 10 | .751 11 | .733 12 | .715 13 | .697 13 | .679 14 | .660 15 |
| .812 07 | .794 08 | .776 09 | .758 09 | .739 10 | .721 11 | .702 11 | .684 12 | .665 13 | .646 13 |
| .803 06 | .785 07 | .766 07 | .748 08 | .729 09 | .710 09 | .691 10 | .672 10 | .653 11 | .633 12 |
| .796 05 | .777 06 | .758 06 | .739 07 | .720 07 | .701 08 | .681 08 | .662 09 | .643 09 | .623 10 |
| .790 04 | .771 05 | .752 05 | .732 05 | .713 06 | .693 06 | .674 07 | .654 07 | .634 07 | .615 08 |
| .786 03 | .766 04 | .747 04 | .727 04 | .707 04 | .687 05 | .668 05 | .648 05 | .628 06 | .608 06 |
| .783 02 | .763 02 | .743 03 | .723 03 | .703 03 | .683 03 | .663 03 | .644 04 | .624 04 | .604 04 |
| .781 01 | .761 01 | .741 01 | .721 01 | .701 01 | .681 01 | .661 02 | .641 02 | .621 02 | .601 02 |
| .780 00 | .760 00 | .740 00 | .720 00 | .700 00 | .680 00 | .660 00 | .640 00 | .620 00 | .600 00 |

In other words, the course correction is toward the current.

Again, three examples will be used to illustrate the application of the tabular factors; these will actually be the same situations as the previous examples, but with different known and unknown elements.

**Example G.** (Fig. 2160)
*Known:* Track = 054° True
Speed = 8 knots
Set = 324°
Drift = 3 knots
*To be determined:* Course and Speed of Advance
*Solution:* Relative set = 324° − 054° = 270°
−360°
−090°

$$\text{Percent drift} = \frac{3 \times 100}{8} = 38$$

From the table: CC = 22°
SF = 0.925
Thus: Course = 054° + 22° = 076°
Speed of Advance = 8 x 0.925
= 7.4 knots

**Example H.** (Fig. 2161)
*Known:* Track = 341° True
Speed = 9 knots
Set = 021°
Drift = 2.5 knots
*To be determined:*
Course and Speed of Advance
*Solution:*
Relative set = 021° − 341° = −320°
+360°
+040°

$$\text{Percent drift} = \frac{2.5 \times 100}{9} = 28$$

From the table: CC = 10°
SF = 1.198
Thus: Course 341° − 10° = 331°
Speed of Advance = 9 x 1.198
= 10.8 knots

FIG. 2161 Example H—a Case 3 problem with positive relative set. Note that relative set is measured with respect to the desired Track.

**Example I.** (Fig. 2162)
*Known:* Track = 024° True
Speed = 10 knots
Set = 156°
Drift = 2 knots
*To be determined:*
Course and Speed of Advance
*Solution:*
Relative set = 156° − 024° = +132°

$$\text{Percent drift} = \frac{2 \times 100}{10} = 20$$

From the table: for 130°, CC = 9°, SF = .860
for 135°, CC = 8°, SF = .849
by interpolation, for 132°, CC = 9°, SF = .856
Thus: Course = 024° − 9° = 015°
Speed of Advance = 10 x 0.856
= 8.6 knots

FIG. 2162 Example I—a Case 3 problem with desired Track 024° True; Speed 10 knots; Set 156°, Drift 2 knots. To be determined: Course to be steered and Speed of Advance.

FIG. 2160 Example G—a Case 3 problem: Track 054° True; Speed 8 knots; Set 324°, Drift 3 knots. Desired: Course and Speed of Advance. See text for solution by tabular factors of fig. 2159.

DRIFT—in percent of speed of advance

RELATIVE SET—000 TO 180

| Rel. Set | 2 SF | 2 CC | 4 SF | 4 CC | 6 SF | 6 CC | 8 SF | 8 CC | 10 SF | 10 CC | 12 SF | 12 CC | 14 SF | 14 CC | 16 SF | 16 CC | 18 SF | 18 CC | 20 SF | 20 CC | 22 SF | 22 CC | 24 SF | 24 CC | 26 SF | 26 CC | 28 SF | 28 CC | 30 SF | 30 CC | 32 SF | 32 CC | 34 SF | 34 CC | 36 SF | 36 CC | 38 SF | 38 CC |
|---|---|---|---|---|---|---|---|---|---|---|---|---|---|---|---|---|---|---|---|---|---|---|---|---|---|---|---|---|---|---|---|---|---|---|---|---|---|---|
| 000 | .980 | 00 | .960 | 00 | .940 | 00 | .920 | 00 | .900 | 00 | .880 | 00 | .860 | 00 | .840 | 00 | .820 | 00 | .800 | 00 | .780 | 00 | .760 | 00 | .740 | 00 | .720 | 00 | .700 | 00 | .680 | 00 | .660 | 00 | .640 | 00 | .620 | 00 |
| 005 | .980 | 00 | .960 | 00 | .940 | 00 | .920 | 00 | .900 | 01 | .881 | 01 | .861 | 01 | .841 | 01 | .821 | 01 | .801 | 01 | .781 | 01 | .761 | 02 | .741 | 02 | .721 | 02 | .702 | 02 | .682 | 02 | .662 | 03 | .642 | 03 | .622 | 03 |
| 010 | .980 | 00 | .961 | 00 | .941 | 01 | .921 | 01 | .902 | 01 | .882 | 01 | .862 | 02 | .843 | 02 | .823 | 02 | .804 | 02 | .784 | 03 | .765 | 03 | .745 | 03 | .726 | 04 | .706 | 04 | .687 | 05 | .668 | 05 | .648 | 06 | .629 | 06 |
| 015 | .981 | 00 | .961 | 00 | .942 | 01 | .923 | 01 | .904 | 02 | .885 | 02 | .866 | 02 | .846 | 03 | .827 | 03 | .808 | 04 | .790 | 04 | .771 | 05 | .752 | 05 | .733 | 06 | .714 | 06 | .696 | 07 | .677 | 07 | .659 | 08 | .641 | 09 |
| 020 | .981 | 00 | .963 | 01 | .944 | 01 | .925 | 02 | .907 | 02 | .888 | 03 | .870 | 03 | .851 | 04 | .833 | 04 | .815 | 05 | .797 | 05 | .779 | 06 | .761 | 07 | .743 | 07 | .725 | 08 | .708 | 09 | .690 | 10 | .673 | 11 | .656 | 11 |
| 025 | .982 | 00 | .964 | 01 | .946 | 02 | .928 | 02 | .910 | 03 | .893 | 03 | .875 | 04 | .858 | 05 | .840 | 05 | .823 | 06 | .806 | 07 | .789 | 07 | .772 | 08 | .756 | 09 | .739 | 10 | .723 | 11 | .707 | 12 | .691 | 13 | .675 | 14 |
| 030 | .983 | 01 | .966 | 01 | .949 | 02 | .932 | 02 | .915 | 03 | .898 | 04 | .882 | 05 | .865 | 05 | .849 | 06 | .833 | 07 | .817 | 08 | .801 | 09 | .786 | 10 | .770 | 10 | .755 | 11 | .740 | 12 | .726 | 14 | .711 | 15 | .697 | 16 |
| 035 | .984 | 01 | .968 | 01 | .951 | 02 | .936 | 03 | .920 | 04 | .904 | 04 | .889 | 05 | .874 | 06 | .859 | 07 | .844 | 08 | .829 | 09 | .815 | 10 | .801 | 11 | .787 | 12 | .774 | 13 | .760 | 14 | .747 | 15 | .735 | 16 | .722 | 18 |
| 040 | .985 | 01 | .970 | 02 | .955 | 02 | .940 | 03 | .926 | 04 | .911 | 05 | .897 | 06 | .883 | 07 | .870 | 08 | .856 | 09 | .843 | 10 | .831 | 11 | .818 | 12 | .806 | 13 | .794 | 14 | .782 | 15 | .771 | 16 | .760 | 18 | .750 | 19 |
| 045 | .986 | 01 | .972 | 02 | .959 | 03 | .945 | 03 | .932 | 04 | .919 | 05 | .906 | 06 | .894 | 07 | .882 | 08 | .870 | 09 | .859 | 10 | .847 | 12 | .837 | 13 | .826 | 14 | .816 | 15 | .806 | 16 | .797 | 18 | .788 | 19 | .779 | 20 |
| 050 | .987 | 01 | .975 | 02 | .963 | 03 | .951 | 04 | .939 | 05 | .927 | 06 | .916 | 07 | .905 | 08 | .895 | 08 | .885 | 10 | .875 | 11 | .865 | 12 | .856 | 13 | .848 | 15 | .839 | 16 | .831 | 17 | .824 | 18 | .817 | 20 | .810 | 21 |
| 055 | .989 | 01 | .978 | 02 | .967 | 03 | .956 | 04 | .946 | 05 | .936 | 06 | .927 | 07 | .918 | 08 | .909 | 09 | .900 | 10 | .892 | 12 | .884 | 13 | .877 | 14 | .870 | 15 | .864 | 17 | .858 | 18 | .852 | 19 | .847 | 20 | .842 | 22 |
| 060 | .990 | 01 | .981 | 02 | .971 | 03 | .962 | 04 | .954 | 05 | .946 | 06 | .938 | 07 | .930 | 09 | .923 | 10 | .917 | 11 | .910 | 12 | .904 | 13 | .899 | 15 | .894 | 16 | .889 | 17 | .885 | 18 | .881 | 20 | .877 | 21 | .874 | 22 |
| 065 | .992 | 01 | .984 | 02 | .976 | 03 | .969 | 04 | .962 | 05 | .955 | 07 | .949 | 08 | .944 | 09 | .938 | 10 | .933 | 11 | .929 | 12 | .925 | 14 | .921 | 15 | .917 | 16 | .915 | 17 | .912 | 19 | .910 | 20 | .908 | 21 | .907 | 22 |
| 070 | .993 | 01 | .987 | 02 | .981 | 03 | .976 | 04 | .970 | 06 | .966 | 07 | .961 | 08 | .957 | 09 | .954 | 10 | .950 | 11 | .948 | 13 | .945 | 14 | .943 | 15 | .942 | 16 | .941 | 17 | .940 | 19 | .940 | 20 | .940 | 21 | .940 | 22 |
| 075 | .995 | 01 | .990 | 02 | .986 | 03 | .982 | 05 | .979 | 06 | .976 | 07 | .973 | 08 | .971 | 09 | .969 | 10 | .968 | 12 | .967 | 13 | .966 | 14 | .966 | 15 | .966 | 16 | .967 | 17 | .968 | 19 | .969 | 20 | .971 | 21 | .973 | 22 |
| 080 | .997 | 01 | .994 | 02 | .991 | 03 | .989 | 05 | .988 | 06 | .986 | 07 | .985 | 08 | .985 | 09 | .985 | 10 | .985 | 12 | .986 | 13 | .987 | 14 | .989 | 15 | .991 | 16 | .993 | 17 | .996 | 18 | .999 | 20 | 1.002 | 21 | 1.006 | 22 |
| 085 | .998 | 01 | .997 | 02 | .997 | 03 | .996 | 05 | .996 | 06 | .997 | 07 | .997 | 07 | .998 | 08 | .999 | 09 | 1.001 | 10 | 1.003 | 11 | 1.005 | 13 | 1.008 | 14 | 1.011 | 15 | 1.015 | 16 | 1.019 | 17 | 1.023 | 18 | 1.028 | 19 | 1.033 | 20 |
| 090 | 1.000 | 01 | 1.001 | 01 | 1.002 | 03 | 1.002 | 05 | 1.003 | 05 | 1.005 | 06 | 1.007 | 07 | 1.010 | 08 | 1.013 | 09 | 1.016 | 10 | 1.020 | 11 | 1.024 | 12 | 1.028 | 13 | 1.033 | 15 | 1.038 | 16 | 1.044 | 17 | 1.050 | 18 | 1.056 | 19 | 1.063 | 20 |
| 095 | 1.002 | 01 | 1.004 | 02 | 1.007 | 03 | 1.010 | 05 | 1.014 | 06 | 1.018 | 07 | 1.022 | 08 | 1.026 | 09 | 1.031 | 10 | 1.037 | 11 | 1.042 | 12 | 1.049 | 13 | 1.055 | 14 | 1.062 | 15 | 1.069 | 16 | 1.076 | 17 | 1.084 | 18 | 1.092 | 19 | 1.100 | 20 |
| 100 | 1.004 | 01 | 1.008 | 02 | 1.012 | 03 | 1.017 | 04 | 1.022 | 06 | 1.028 | 07 | 1.034 | 08 | 1.040 | 09 | 1.046 | 10 | 1.053 | 11 | 1.061 | 12 | 1.068 | 13 | 1.076 | 14 | 1.084 | 15 | 1.093 | 16 | 1.102 | 17 | 1.111 | 18 | 1.120 | 18 | 1.130 | 19 |
| 105 | 1.005 | 01 | 1.011 | 02 | 1.017 | 03 | 1.024 | 04 | 1.030 | 05 | 1.038 | 06 | 1.045 | 07 | 1.053 | 08 | 1.061 | 09 | 1.069 | 10 | 1.078 | 11 | 1.087 | 12 | 1.096 | 13 | 1.106 | 14 | 1.116 | 15 | 1.126 | 16 | 1.136 | 17 | 1.147 | 18 | 1.158 | 18 |
| 110 | 1.007 | 01 | 1.014 | 02 | 1.022 | 03 | 1.030 | 04 | 1.038 | 05 | 1.047 | 06 | 1.056 | 07 | 1.065 | 08 | 1.075 | 09 | 1.085 | 10 | 1.095 | 11 | 1.105 | 12 | 1.116 | 13 | 1.127 | 14 | 1.138 | 14 | 1.149 | 15 | 1.161 | 16 | 1.173 | 17 | 1.185 | 18 |
| 115 | 1.009 | 01 | 1.018 | 02 | 1.027 | 03 | 1.036 | 04 | 1.046 | 05 | 1.056 | 06 | 1.067 | 07 | 1.077 | 08 | 1.088 | 09 | 1.100 | 09 | 1.111 | 10 | 1.123 | 11 | 1.135 | 12 | 1.147 | 13 | 1.159 | 14 | 1.172 | 14 | 1.184 | 15 | 1.197 | 16 | 1.211 | 17 |
| 120 | 1.010 | 01 | 1.021 | 02 | 1.031 | 03 | 1.042 | 04 | 1.054 | 05 | 1.065 | 06 | 1.077 | 06 | 1.089 | 07 | 1.101 | 08 | 1.114 | 09 | 1.126 | 10 | 1.139 | 11 | 1.152 | 11 | 1.166 | 12 | 1.179 | 13 | 1.193 | 13 | 1.206 | 14 | 1.220 | 15 | 1.235 | 15 |
| 125 | 1.012 | 01 | 1.023 | 02 | 1.036 | 03 | 1.048 | 04 | 1.061 | 04 | 1.073 | 05 | 1.086 | 06 | 1.100 | 07 | 1.113 | 08 | 1.127 | 08 | 1.141 | 09 | 1.155 | 10 | 1.169 | 11 | 1.183 | 11 | 1.198 | 12 | 1.212 | 12 | 1.227 | 13 | 1.242 | 14 | 1.257 | 14 |
| 130 | 1.013 | 01 | 1.026 | 02 | 1.040 | 03 | 1.053 | 03 | 1.067 | 04 | 1.081 | 05 | 1.095 | 06 | 1.110 | 06 | 1.124 | 07 | 1.139 | 08 | 1.154 | 08 | 1.169 | 09 | 1.184 | 10 | 1.199 | 10 | 1.215 | 11 | 1.230 | 11 | 1.246 | 12 | 1.262 | 13 | 1.278 | 13 |
| 135 | 1.014 | 01 | 1.029 | 02 | 1.043 | 02 | 1.058 | 03 | 1.073 | 04 | 1.088 | 04 | 1.103 | 05 | 1.119 | 06 | 1.134 | 06 | 1.150 | 07 | 1.166 | 08 | 1.182 | 08 | 1.198 | 09 | 1.214 | 09 | 1.231 | 10 | 1.247 | 10 | 1.263 | 11 | 1.280 | 11 | 1.297 | 12 |
| 140 | 1.015 | 01 | 1.031 | 01 | 1.047 | 02 | 1.063 | 03 | 1.079 | 03 | 1.095 | 04 | 1.111 | 05 | 1.127 | 05 | 1.144 | 06 | 1.160 | 06 | 1.177 | 07 | 1.194 | 07 | 1.211 | 08 | 1.228 | 08 | 1.245 | 09 | 1.262 | 09 | 1.279 | 10 | 1.297 | 10 | 1.314 | 11 |
| 145 | 1.016 | 01 | 1.033 | 01 | 1.050 | 02 | 1.067 | 02 | 1.083 | 03 | 1.100 | 04 | 1.118 | 04 | 1.135 | 05 | 1.152 | 05 | 1.169 | 06 | 1.187 | 06 | 1.204 | 07 | 1.222 | 07 | 1.240 | 07 | 1.258 | 08 | 1.275 | 08 | 1.293 | 09 | 1.311 | 09 | 1.329 | 09 |
| 150 | 1.017 | 01 | 1.035 | 01 | 1.052 | 02 | 1.070 | 02 | 1.088 | 03 | 1.106 | 03 | 1.123 | 04 | 1.141 | 04 | 1.159 | 04 | 1.177 | 05 | 1.196 | 05 | 1.214 | 06 | 1.232 | 06 | 1.250 | 06 | 1.269 | 07 | 1.287 | 07 | 1.306 | 07 | 1.324 | 08 | 1.343 | 08 |
| 155 | 1.018 | 01 | 1.036 | 01 | 1.055 | 01 | 1.073 | 02 | 1.091 | 02 | 1.110 | 03 | 1.128 | 03 | 1.147 | 03 | 1.166 | 04 | 1.184 | 04 | 1.203 | 04 | 1.222 | 05 | 1.241 | 05 | 1.259 | 05 | 1.278 | 06 | 1.297 | 06 | 1.316 | 06 | 1.335 | 07 | 1.354 | 07 |
| 160 | 1.019 | 01 | 1.038 | 01 | 1.057 | 01 | 1.076 | 01 | 1.095 | 02 | 1.114 | 02 | 1.133 | 02 | 1.152 | 03 | 1.171 | 03 | 1.190 | 03 | 1.209 | 04 | 1.228 | 04 | 1.247 | 04 | 1.267 | 04 | 1.286 | 05 | 1.305 | 05 | 1.325 | 05 | 1.344 | 05 | 1.363 | 05 |
| 165 | 1.019 | 01 | 1.039 | 01 | 1.058 | 01 | 1.077 | 01 | 1.097 | 01 | 1.116 | 02 | 1.136 | 02 | 1.155 | 02 | 1.175 | 02 | 1.194 | 02 | 1.214 | 03 | 1.233 | 03 | 1.253 | 03 | 1.273 | 03 | 1.292 | 03 | 1.312 | 04 | 1.331 | 04 | 1.351 | 04 | 1.371 | 04 |
| 170 | 1.020 | 01 | 1.039 | 00 | 1.059 | 01 | 1.079 | 01 | 1.099 | 01 | 1.118 | 01 | 1.138 | 01 | 1.158 | 01 | 1.178 | 02 | 1.197 | 02 | 1.217 | 02 | 1.237 | 02 | 1.257 | 02 | 1.277 | 02 | 1.296 | 02 | 1.316 | 02 | 1.336 | 03 | 1.356 | 03 | 1.376 | 03 |
| 175 | 1.020 | 01 | 1.040 | 00 | 1.060 | 01 | 1.080 | 00 | 1.100 | 00 | 1.120 | 01 | 1.140 | 01 | 1.159 | 01 | 1.179 | 01 | 1.199 | 01 | 1.219 | 01 | 1.239 | 01 | 1.259 | 01 | 1.279 | 01 | 1.299 | 01 | 1.319 | 01 | 1.339 | 01 | 1.359 | 01 | 1.379 | 01 |
| 180 | 1.020 | 00 | 1.040 | 00 | 1.060 | 00 | 1.080 | 00 | 1.100 | 00 | 1.120 | 00 | 1.140 | 00 | 1.160 | 00 | 1.180 | 00 | 1.200 | 00 | 1.220 | 00 | 1.240 | 00 | 1.260 | 00 | 1.280 | 00 | 1.300 | 00 | 1.320 | 00 | 1.340 | 00 | 1.360 | 00 | 1.380 | 00 |

FIG. 2163 Tabulation of Speed Factors (SF) and Course Corrections (CC) for the solution of Case 4 current sailing problems. Be careful to use the proper set of tabular factors for a Case 1, 3, or 4 problem; there is a separate table for each Case.

It might be supposed that the course corrections and speed factors above would be the same as those found in the preceding table and used in the examples for Case 1, but a careful comparison of the tables will reveal that this is not so. To illustrate, let us suppose that the drift is 20 percent and the relative set is 90°. Using the table of fig. 2154 for Case 1, we find that the current sets us off course by 11°. From the table of fig. 2159, however, we find that we must alter course 12° to compensate for the same current situation.

Also, when the course is not corrected, the speed factor is 1.020, which means that our speed of advance is two percent greater than our speed through the water (but, of course, it isn't getting us where we want to be). If, as in Case 3, we do "crab" into the current by the required 12°, the speed factor is 0.980, meaning that our actual speed of advance is two percent less than our speed through the water. Obviously, the two cases, and their respective tabulated factors, are different.

## Case 4 solutions by tabular factors

This is a variation of Case 3 in which the pilot knows both where he wants to go and when he desires to arrive. Thus he has a desired track (TR) and speed of advance (SOA) in addition to the known or estimated set and drift of the current. He needs to determine the course to be steered (C) and the necessary speed through the water (S).

Fig. 2163 enables the pilot to determine these desired quantities without the construction of a vector diagram. Instead, he uses another set of course corrections (CC) and speed factors (SF). These factors are not the same as in either of the preceding tables and must be used for Case 4 problems only.

The speed to run through the water (S) is determined by multiplying the desired speed of advance (SOA) by the tabular factor SF. The course to be steered is found by adding the correction angle CC to, or subtracting it from, the track (TR) in the same manner as for Case 3.

Course to be steered (C)
= TR − CC, when the relative set is positive.
= TR + CC, when the relative set is negative.

The same basic examples as before will be used, but again with different combinations of known and unknown elements.

**Example J.** (Fig. 2164)

Known: Track = 054° True
SOA = 7.4 knots
Set = 324°
Drift = 3 knots

To be determined: Course and Speed

Solution: Relative set = 324° − 054° = 270°
                                                     −360°
                                                     −090°

Percent drift = $\frac{3 \times 100}{7.4} = 40$

From the table: CC = 22°
SF = 1.077

Thus: Course = 054° + 22° = 076°
Speed = 7.4 x 1.077 = 8 knots

FIG. 2164 Example J—a Case 4 problem: Track 054° True, Speed of Advance 7.4 knots; Set 324°, Drift 3 knots. To be found: Course to be steered and Speed to be run through the water. See text for solution by tabular factors of fig. 2163.

**Example K.** (Fig. 2165)

*Known:* Track = 341° True
SOA = 10.8 knots
Set = 021°
Drift = 2.5 knots
*To be determined:*
Course and Speed
*Solution:*
Relative set = 021° − 341° = −320°
$$+360°$$
$$\overline{+040°}$$

Percent drift = $\dfrac{2.5 \times 100}{10.8}$ = 23

From the table: for 022%, CC = 10°, SF = 0.843
for 024%, CC = 11°, SF = 0.831
by interpolation, for 023%, CC = 10.5°, SF = 0.837
Thus: Course = 341° − 10.5° = 330.5°
= 330°
Speed = 10.8 × 0.837 = 9.04
= 9 knots

FIG. 2165 Example K—a Case 4 problem in which both the Track and Speed of Advance are specified. The Course to be steered and the Speed to be run through the water are the values to be found by the application of tabulated course correction and speed factor.

FIG. 2166 Example L—a Case 4 problem to be solved by use of the factors from fig. 2163. Given: Track 024° True, Speed of Advance 8.6 knots; Set 156°, Drift 2 knots. To be found: Course and Speed.

**Example L.** (Fig. 2166)
*Known:* Track = 024° True
SOA = 8.6 knots
Set = 156°
Drift = 2 knots
*To be determined:*
Course and Speed
*Solution:*
Relative set = 156° − 024° = +132°
Percent drift = $\dfrac{2 \times 100}{8.6}$ = 23
From the table, by double interpolation,
for 132°/23% : CC = 8.3°
SF = 1.167
Thus: Course = 024° − 8.3° = 015.3°
= 015°
Speed = 8.6 × 1.167 = 10 knots

Course Correction

| PILOTING IN CURRENTS: GENERAL RESUME OF THE THREE CASES | | CASE 1 | CASE 3 | CASE 4 |
|---|---|---|---|---|
| KNOWN: Set and Drift, plus | | Course | Track | Track |
| | | Speed Through Water | Speed Through Water | Speed of Advance |
| DESIRED: | | Speed of Advance | Speed of Advance | Speed Through Water |
| | | Track | Course | Course |
| Calculate Before Using Table | % Drift | $\dfrac{\text{Drift} \times 100}{\text{Speed Through Water}}$ | $\dfrac{\text{Drift} \times 100}{\text{Speed Through Water}}$ | $\dfrac{\text{Drift} \times 100}{\text{Speed of Advance}}$ |
| | Relative Set | SET—COURSE (180° or less to port or starboard) | SET—TRACK (180° or less to port or starboard) | SET—TRACK (180° or less to port or starboard) |
| Read from table, interpolating, if necessary | SF | Speed factor | Speed factor | Speed factor |
| | CC | Course Change | Course Correction | Course Correction |
| ANSWERS | | Speed of Advance = (Speed through water) X SF | Speed of Advance = (Speed through water) X SF | Speed Through Water = (Speed of Advance) X SF |
| | If Rel. Set is positive (to St'bd.) | TRACK = COURSE + CC | COURSE = TRACK − CC | COURSE = TRACK − CC |
| | If Rel. Set is negative (to Port) | TRACK = COURSE − CC | COURSE = TRACK + CC | COURSE = TRACK + CC |

FIG. 2167 Summary of the procedures for the solution of certain current sailing problems by the use of pre-computed factors and corrections.

### Summary of tabular factor solutions

Fig. 2167 is a consolidated presentation of the procedures used in the solution of current sailing problems using tabulated factors of course and speed corrections. The numbering of the cases corresponds to the basic presentation of current problems in Chapter 20 and the examples above.

In all of the cases presented here, the set and drift of the current were considered to be known values, as determined from the Tidal Current Tables or Charts, or from visual observations. Thus, Case 2 of the current sailing problems—the determination of the characteristics of an unknown current from the measurement of its effects—is omitted from this tabular technique.

# Specialized Positioning Procedures

In addition to the generally used procedures for position determination previously described in this chapter, there are other, more specialized, techniques. These should not be scorned as "short cuts"; they will provide valid position information and fixes under the particular circumstances that permit their use.

## COMBINATIONS OF RELATIVE BEARINGS

The bow-and-beam-bearings technique has already been described, fig. 2140. This was a particular set of two relative bearings, 045° and 090° (or 315° and 270°). It was included there because of its basic simplicity and the ease with which such a pair of bearings could be obtained. There are other combinations of relative bearings, not so easily obtained, but quite easily used.

### Special pairs of bearings

The following sets of bearings have such a relationship to each other that the run between the first bearing and

the second will nearly equal the distance away from the sighted object when it is passed abeam:

20°-30°, 21°-32°, 22°-34°, 23°-36°, 24°-39°, 25°-41°, 27°-46°, 29°-51°, 30°-54°, 31°-56°, 32°-59°, 34°-64°, 35°-67°, 36°-69°, 37°-71°, 38°-74°, 39°-77°, 40°-79°, 41°-81°, 43°-86°, 44°-88°.

There are also additional pairs of angles that could theoretically be used, but these involve half-degrees and have been omitted here as such precision is not usually obtainable on small craft.

It should be noted that these are pairs of relative bearings to port as well as to starboard. In the table above, "20°-30°" can be either relative bearings 020° and 030°, or 340° and 330°; "31°-56°" can be either RB 031° and 056°, or RB 329° and 304°; etc.

### The 7/8th rule

If observations are made when the relative bearings are 30° and 60° on either bow, simple calculations will give *two* useful items of information. The distance run between the two bearings is equal to the distance to the object at the time of the second bearing (doubling the angle on the bow). Also, this same distance, fig. 2168, multiplied by $7/8$ is the distance that the craft will be off from the sighted object when it is broad on the beam, provided that course and speed are not changed.

## The 7/10th rule

A situation comparable to the preceding rule is that which exists when the two relative bearings are $22\frac{1}{2}°$ and $45°$ to port or starboard (assuming that bearings can be taken to a half-degree). In this case, as before, the distance away from the sighted object at the time of the second bearing is equal to the distance run between bearings, but the multiplier is $7/10$ to determine the distance off the sighted object when it is abeam.

## THREE BEARINGS AND RUN BETWEEN

The technique of using *two* bearings and the run between them was illustrated in fig. 2142. The positional information derived from this procedure was dependent upon the assumption that the course and speed made good with respect to the bottom during the run between bearings was accurately known. Along strange coasts, without current predictions or means of estimating current effects, this assumption is often of doubtful validity.

By taking a *third* bearing and timing a second run (between the second and third bearings), enough additional known factors are entered into the problem so that no assumption need be made about the course made good nor the actual speed over the bottom. All that is required for this technique is a prominent object or mark on shore, plus the means for taking bearings and measuring time intervals.

As soon as you spot the object, "X" in fig. 2169, take a bearing on it and note the exact time; record both items of information. Plot the bearing line on your chart, line XA in fig. 2169(a). Next, when the object is exactly broad on the beam, note the time. Plot this line of position on the chart. Later, when the bearing to X has changed enough to give a good angle of intersection, take a third bearing and again note the time carefully. Plot this line, XC. Be sure that throughout this procedure you are maintaining a steady course and speed through the water.

Since you have recorded the time of each bearing, you can determine the two elapsed times, and compute the *ratio* between these intervals.

For example, if you ran for $32\frac{1}{2}$ minutes between the first and second (beam) bearings, and then for $22\frac{1}{2}$ minutes more to the third bearing, the ratio would be $32\frac{1}{2}/22\frac{1}{2}$, which can be reduced to $6.5/4.5$.

Through a convenient point, B, on the beam bearing line, draw a light "construction" line in the direction of your course (C) as steered. Using point "B" as the reference or zero point, measure off to each side, along the construction line, distances proportional to the ratio of the time intervals using any convenient scale, fig. 2169(b).

Erect perpendiculars to the construction line at the spots determined by these proportionate distances. These lines, drawn at $90°$ angles to the construction line, intersect the bearing lines XA and XC at points A' and C' respectively, fig. 2169(c).

Connect points A' and C' with a line and you have your answer. Line A'-C' is the course you are making good and

**FIG. 2168** If observations are made when the relative bearings of a fixed object are $30°$ and $60°$, and the distance made good between these observations is calculated, the pilot can determine his distance from the object both at the time of the second bearing and when it is abeam by the "$7/8$th Rule."

includes the effects of currents, wind, and errors in steering. Its direction may be taken from the chart and compared with the intended course. It should be noted that this is *not the actual track*—the selection of the scale to represent the two time intervals would determine the location of points A' and C', and hence the line's location, although not its direction.

It is *because ratios* are used, and not actual speeds, that an accurate speed over the bottom is not needed here as it was in the case of the technique of *two* bearings and run between. Although it does not allow the navigator to determine his position nor his speed over the bottom, this technique does show plainly whether he is making good his intended course, or is being set onto or off the shore; it helps determine whether the actual track parallels the beach or not.

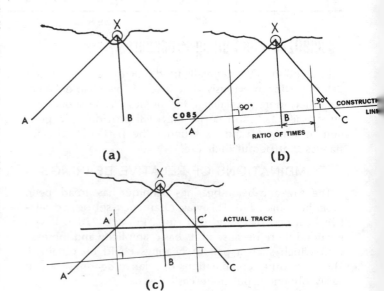

**FIG. 2169** The actual track of a boat under unknown conditions of current can be determined by taking three bearings on a single object. See text for details of this technique.

# FLAGS

## When and How to Fly Them

*This illustration shows the Union Jack flying at the port yardarm. Correct practice dictates that this flag can be flown only on Sundays or Holidays.*

*Diagrams illustrating how to fly various flags on a yacht club mast ashore will be found on page 360.*

NOTE:—*While it is true that no naval or other authority can be quoted for the display of the Union Jack on a yacht club mast ashore, a long-standing precedent has been established in its widespread use by the better yacht clubs.*

To be rated a 100% boatman—in other words, a "Seasoned Skipper" — the owner or captain of a boat must know flags, what they mean, and how to fly them.

In this connection, it has always been my feeling that yachtsmen would gladly comply with the protocol associated with the display of flags if they understood it.

With these thoughts in mind, the editors of Motor Boating have prepared this special section containing illustrations of flags in full color and authoritative information concerning their use.

There is a right way to fly every flag. Following this guide, you can be sure you are displaying your flags correctly.

As a long-time proponent of propriety in the flying of flags aboard ship, it gives me considerable pleasure to recommend this feature to our readers.

*Charles F. Chapman*

# U.S. GOVERNMENT and ARMED SERVICES FLAGS

Except for those of the Army, Navy and Coast Guard, the flags illustrated on this page won't often be seen flying from small craft. Nevertheless, they are presented here with the thought that every American will want to be able to identify whatever flag he may see afloat—or ashore. For a complete discussion of flag etiquette, see pages 354-371.

PRESIDENT OF THE UNITED STATES

NATIONAL
ENSIGN AND MERCHANT FLAG

VICE PRESIDENT

SECRETARY OF STATE

SECRETARY OF TREASURY

SECRETARY OF DEFENSE

ATTORNEY GENERAL

COAST GUARD ENSIGN

JOINT CHIEF OF STAFF

POSTMASTER GENERAL

SECRETARY OF LABOR

COAST GUARD COMMANDANT

SECRETARY OF THE NAVY

SECRETARY OF THE ARMY

SEC. OF AGRICULTURE

SEC. HEALTH, ED. & WELF.

COAST GUARD REAR ADMIRAL

ADMIRAL, U. S. NAVY

CORPS OF ENGINEERS
(U. S. Army)

SEC. OF INTERIOR

FISH AND
WILD LIFE SERVICE

U. S. CUSTOMS

NAVAL RESERVE
YACHT PENNANT

U. S. ARMY TRANSPORT

SEC. OF COMMERCE

COAST & GEODETIC SURVEY

UNITED STATES
IMMIGRATION SERVICE

U. S. MARINE CORPS

SECRETARY, AIR FORCE

NOTE—Caption, third flag, third row, should read CHAIRMAN, JOINT CHIEFS OF STAFF. Fifth flag, sixth row—Army Transport not in current use.

R

# YACHTING FLAGS

**NATIONAL**
ENSIGN AND MERCHANT FLAG

**UNION JACK**

**YACHT ENSIGN**

**U. S. POWER SQUADRONS'
ENSIGN**

**YACHT CLUB
PENNANT**

**NAVAL RESERVE**
YACHT OWNERS'
DISTINGUISHING PENNANT

**YACHT
PRIVATE SIGNAL**

**YACHT
OWNER ABSENT**

**YACHT
GUEST FLAG**

**YACHT
OWNER'S MEAL**

**YACHT
CREW'S MEAL**

**QUARANTINE
INTERNATIONAL Q**

**TRANSPORTATION**

**YACHT PROTEST**

**DIVER**

*NOTE: Navy Department regulations provide that the Union Jack should be the same size as the union of the ensign flown from the stern. See page 360 on two types of Naval Reserve pennant.*

## GENERAL COMMENTS

**COLORS:** Though the term "colors" is frequently used to include all flags on a boat, a strict interpretation would restrict its use to the national flag which identifies the nation to which the boat belongs. The term "colors" or "making colors" is also used to refer to the ceremony of hoisting the boat's flags at 8 A.M. and lowering at sunset.

**WHEN TO FLY FLAGS:** A boat's flags should be flown from 8 A.M. to sundown, except as otherwise noted in the chart opposite. At sundown flags should be lowered, whether the boat is underway, at anchor, or made fast. However, if you *enter* or *leave* port *before* 8 A.M., it is permissible to hoist your flags while there is sufficient light for them to be seen. Likewise, if you are *entering* or *leaving* port after sundown, the same holds true. During bad weather at sea, flags may or may not be flown, at the captain's discretion.

At 8 A.M. the national ensign should be hoisted first, followed by the USPS ensign (*if* you are a member of the U.S. Power Squadrons in good standing, and in command of the boat), the yacht club burgee, officer's flag, and/or private signal. For C.G. Auxiliary vessels the same procedure holds, but C.G. Auxiliary blue ensign and officer's flag are substituted for yacht club flags. Flags are hoisted smartly, but lowered ceremoniously. Flag officers' flags, though displayed day and night, may be temporarily lowered and hoisted at colors.

At U.S.P.S., C.G. Auxiliary, or Club rendezvous, marine parades, etc., on order of the Commanding Officer, flags may be flown after sundown but must be lowered at or before midnight, as ordered.

**SIZE OF FLAGS:** The national ensign, yacht ensign, USPS ensign, whichever is flown (See Footnote 1, opposite), should be a minimum of 1" on the fly per foot of overall length of boat. The hoist should be two-thirds the fly. The burgee, private signal, and flag officer's flag should be a minimum of ½" on the fly for each foot of the highest truck above the water on sailing yachts, and ⅝" on the fly for each foot of overall length for motorboats.

When the USPS ensign is flown from the starboard yardarm on motorboats, the fly should be ⅝" per foot of overall length of boat.

**SALUTING:** Never salute, or answer a salute, by dipping the U.S. national ensign. Salute by dipping the yacht ensign, or the USPS ensign, when flown at the stern or gaff of motor craft, stern staff of sailing vessels, under power or at anchor. Never salute by dipping a flag flown from the yardarm or spreader.

## MISCELLANEOUS

**CHARTER:** When a boat is chartered, use flags of the charterer.

**DISTRESS:** Though not official, flying the U.S. Ensign upside down is universally recognized as a distress signal.

**OPTIONAL:** Flags authorized by naval, military, government, or yachting organizations, may be displayed at option, providing the procedure for flying such flags specified by these organizations is followed. No other flag should be displayed, except when making signals with international code flags or when dressing ship.

**COCKTAIL:** The cocktail flag, etc., being signals, may be flown where best seen.

**QUARANTINE:** The square yellow quarantine flag is a signal meaning "I request pratique." Fly entering foreign port—or return to U.S.

**TRANSPORTATION:** Code flag "T" is used to call club tender.

**PROTEST:** For sailors who race. See illustration.

**DIVERS:** Display when diving is in progress. See illustration. Do not fly underway.

**STRIKING:** "Striking colors" is a naval term meaning surrender. *Never* use in yachting.

# UNITED STATES POWER SQUADRONS FLAGS and INSIGNIA

## USPS ENSIGN

The Ensign of United States Power Squadrons may be displayed only by enrolled members of USPS. It is an outward and visible sign that the vessel displaying it is under the charge of a person who has made a study of piloting and small boat handling, and will recognize the rights of others and the traditions of the sea. The Squadrons' Ensign also marks a craft as being under the command of a man who has met certain minimum requirements and is so honored for meeting them. This honor may not be bought, sold, rented, loaned or given away. The USPS Ensign is displayed, during the hours from 0800 to sundown, from the stern staff or from the starboard yardarm of a power vessel. On craft under sail, it is flown from the leach or peak of the mainsail or aftermost sail.

## USPS OBJECTIVES

Shall be to establish a high standard of skill in handling and navigation of yachts, to encourage the study of the science of navigation, and small boat handling, to cooperate with the agencies of the United States Government charged with the enforcement of the laws and regulations relating to navigation and to stimulate interest in activities which will tend to the upbuilding of our Army, Navy, Coast Guard and Merchant Marine.

T

# Relative Motion

The easiest way to acquire what is often called a "sailor's eye" is to learn the simple, but basic, principles of *relative motion*. The term "relative motion" scares some people, but it is really quite a simple subject to master. It is also one of the most useful skills that a boatman can acquire as it gives quick and accurate answers to problems involving moving vessels.

For example, you find that your motorboat is converging on another boat that has the right of way. If you hold your present course and speed, will you clear her? Or your sailboat is beating to windward on a port tack, and you find a boat coming in on the starboard tack. Will you cross safely ahead, or must you pass astern? Or you have laid a course for a buoy, making allowance for the current. Have you made the right allowance? Relative motion will give you the answers to all such questions.

When a boat is under way, its movement across the water is termed *actual motion*. If it is anchored, the movements of another craft appear in their actual relationship to the earth's surface; you are observing that boat's actual motion. But if you get under way, the movement of the other boat appears to be different because you are now observing *relative motion*. Some objects, especially moving ones, seem to be doing things that are not actually happening; elements of what may be almost an optical illusion can exist.

Let us suppose that you are under way and proceeding north at 5 knots up a marked channel. You sight another boat coming directly toward you; this other craft is also making 5 knots. The two boats are converging at a *relative speed* of 10 knots which is simply the sum of your speed and his. Both craft are passing the stationary channel markers at the same actual speed, but the distance between them is lessening at a rate which is the sum of the individual speeds.

As the other boat approaches, you recognize the skipper as a friend and turn around to join him on his southerly course. As soon as the boats are alongside each other on the same course and at the same speed, *relative motion* ceases to exist because the other boat stays in the same place relative to your boat. Only *actual motion* remains—that of your boat past the buoys and over the bottom. If the other craft develops engine trouble and slows down, there is again relative motion between the two vessels. He will appear to be moving aft because of his reduced speed. Thus, the rule may be stated as follows: *relative motion is present only when the actual movements of two or more objects are not the same.*

## Relative bearings

The bearing of an object is usually taken as a relative bearing; these were discussed in pages 352a, b. See fig. 2170. With practice, the relative bearing of an object can be estimated within five or ten degrees. It must be remembered that a change in course of your own boat will change the relative bearings of all objects around it. Thus, if you are on a course of 050° True and sight an object bearing 090° relative, the true bearing of that object will be 140°, fig. 2171a. Come left to a course of 020°, and although the true bearing will remain unchanged at 140°, the rela-

FIG. 2170 In determining relative motion in small-craft piloting, much use is made of relative bearings measured clockwise from 000° dead ahead.

tive bearing will now become 120°, fig. 2171b.

In small craft piloting, approximations will usually suffice in relative motion problems and special instruments are not needed. A steady hand at the wheel or tiller, a clear eye, and a rough mental diagram are all that are needed. A pelorus can be used, but seldom is, in actual practice.

## TO CROSS OR NOT TO CROSS

When determining the relative motion of another boat, it is necessary either to convert relative bearings to compass (or true) bearings, or to maintain a steady course. In practice, it is easier to maintain a steady course, with the result that any change in relative bearing will be the result of a change in the positions of the boats relative to each other, rather than the result of the changing course of your craft. Since the desired information is the changing positions of the boats relative to each other, the actual value of the relative bearing is of far less importance than the direction and rate of change, if any.

## Collision bearings

What we want to know in any crossing or converging situation is: will we cross ahead of, or astern of, the other boat, or will we hit her? Because the two boats are considered relative to each other, it is convenient to think of one's own boat as stationary—relative to the other boat. Thus, we have three basic situations:

1. The relative bearing of the other boat moves ahead (toward the bow), or
2. The relative bearing of the other boat moves aft, or
3. The relative bearing of the other boat remains constant.

Fig. 2172a illustrates the first situation, that of a boat passing ahead. This illustration indicates the actual successive positions of the two boats. Fig. 2172b represents

FIG. 2171 If a boat's heading changes, the relative bearing of an object is changed by the same amount. From the situation in *a* below to that in *b*, the true heading of the boat has changed from 050° to 020°; the relative bearing has changed by the same amount, from 090° to 120°. (Note that the sum of the heading and the relative bearing remains constant.)

(a)                                        (b)

FIG. 2172  The positions of two boats are shown for three intervals of time separated by five minutes each. In *a*, the actual positions of each craft are shown. In *b*, the motion of the other boat is shown *relative* to our craft. In both cases, the relative bearings move forward on our boat and the other craft will cross ahead of us. The distance *x* is the separation at the *point of closest approach*.

the same situation shown in terms of motion relative to our own boat as stationary. The bearing change is then more clearly seen.

The line connecting the positions of the other boat in fig. 2172b is the *line of relative movement*, the relative course and relative distance traveled by the other boat in relationship to our boat. Provided both boats maintain course and speed, it is a straight line. In this situation, when the line of relative motion is extended, it passes the bow of our "stationary" boat; therefore, the other boat following that line relative to us will cross ahead. The distance "x" fig. 2172b is the distance apart that the two boats will be at the *closest point of approach* (CPA).

The second case, in which the relative bearing moves aft, is the opposite of the first situation. The relative mo-

FIG. 2173  In this crossing situation, the relative bearings move aft, and the other boat will pass astern of us (we will pass ahead of her). The actual successive positions of each craft are shown in *a*, and relative motion is shown in *b*.

tion line passes astern, and so will the other boat. Figs. 2173a and b illustrate this situation.

If the relative bearing does not change, the line of relative motion will pass through our boat's position, the distance "x" is zero, and the two boats will collide unless one or both changes course or speed. See figs. 2174a and b.

It is important to note that figs. 2172-2174 are intended to illustrate situations rather than actual chart plots on a boat. The position of the other craft could not be plotted unless distance as well as bearing information was available, and this is unlikely unless your boat has radar. The significance here is that *bearing information only*, which is available to any pilot, will by its change, if any, tell him whether he will pass ahead, astern, or "through" the other craft. The closest point of approach can be determined only if an actual plot based on distances is made, but lack of this information is not significant.

## Rules for crossing situations

The foregoing discussion, formulated into rules, results in the following procedures for a crossing situation:

1. Maintain a reasonably steady course and speed.
2. Observe the relative bearing of the other boat only when you are on your specified compass course. You must be on the *same* course each time you take a relative bearing.
3. Watch the other boat for changes in course or speed which would obviously upset the relative motion conditions.
4. (a) If the relative bearing moves ahead, the other boat will pass ahead.
   (b) If the relative bearing moves aft, the other craft will pass astern.
   (c) If the relative bearing is steady, there is a dangerous possibility of collision.

FIG. 2174  Here is a crossing situation in which the relative bearing does *not* change! A collision will result if both craft maintain course and speed. Note that in *b* the line of relative movement passes *through* our boat and the value of *x* is reduced to zero.

## Offsetting effects of current or wind

There is another useful application of relative motion in the case of allowances for offsetting the effects of current and/or wind.

In fig. 2175, the boat has been put on a course that her skipper believes will put her close aboard the buoy marking the shoal. At the time of the first bearing, "0" minutes, the buoy bears 340° relative. Five minutes later, the relative bearing has changed to 350°. It is clear from this change that the boat is being set down more than expected and that the relative movement line of the buoy will pass ahead of the boat, i.e., the boat will pass on the shoal side of the buoy. If the bearings on the buoy remained steady, the boat would pass close to it; and if the bearings shifted gradually away from the bow, the skipper would know that he would clear the shoal safely.

In fig. 2175a, the problem is shown in terms of the boat moving relative to the buoy. In fig. 2175b, the boat is considered to be stationary and the relative movement line is that of the buoy. Note that the relative movement lines in the two representations are parallel, equal, and opposite.

FIG. 2175  Relative motion considerations are also applicable when the other "craft" is stationary, such as a buoy. The change, if any, of the relative bearings on the object can be used to determine on which side of it you will pass. In *a* and *b* below, the motion is considered relative to the buoy and to your boat, respectively.

# The Maneuvering Board

Since 1920, the U.S. Naval Oceanographic Office (formerly the Hydrographic Office) has published a plotting sheet known as the *Maneuvering Board (H.O. 2665)*. This device is used by all maritime services for the solution of relative motion problems. Complicated movements of large task forces, as well as the tracking of a single ship, are plotted on maneuvering boards to facilitate the solution of problems of interception and the determination of the course and speed of radar contacts.

## Use on boats

Here we will consider a few of the simpler, though useful, applications of the maneuvering board, using only the plotting sheet, parallel rulers or equivalent, and a pair of dividers. For the fortunate yachtsman who has radar aboard, however, the applications are increased ten-fold.

## Description of the sheet

To observe the physical appearance of a maneuvering board, examine fig. 2176 which shows one reduced about 40% from its original size of approximately 12 inches square. On it is printed, in green, a large circle with bearing lines radiating outward from the center every 10 degrees, and 10 concentric circles ½ inch apart to indicate speed or distance. At the right and left sides are lines of scale with numbered marks spaced equal to the distance between the concentric circles. Thus, a speed line drawn out to the fifth circle could indicate 5, 10, 15, 20, or 25 knots as determined by your choice of scale.

At the bottom of the sheet are three lines divided into logarithmic scales for use in solving time, distance, and speed problems. If two of these quantities are known, the third may be found by drawing a line between the known values on the appropriate scales, and finding the answer at the intersection of this line with the third scale.

In fig. 2177, observe the solution to three problems: (1) if you run 6 miles in 30 minutes, your speed is 12 knots; (2) to run 6 miles at 12 knots will require 30 minutes; or (3) running at 12 knots for 30 minutes, you will cover 6 miles. Distance, time, speed—knowing two, you can quickly, easily, and accurately solve for the third. This alone makes the maneuvering board a handy device, but it is only a small sample of its usefulness.

FIG. 2176  The U.S. Navy Oceanographic Office (formerly the Hydrographic Office) publishes pads of a useful plotting sheet known as a *maneuvering board*. These sheets are particularly handy when plotting situations or relative motion.

FIG. 2177  Extract from a maneuvering board showing the logarithmic distance-time-speed scales. The problem illustrated by the line drawn across the scales is discussed in the text.

The bearing lines and circles of distance facilitate the plotting of positions of other craft or objects relative to the boat on which the maneuvering board is being used. These radial lines and concentric circles can also be used for vector diagrams with lines drawn to represent actual and relative motion. Each vector, according to its length and direction, depicts a statement of fact in the problem. For example: a vector line to indicate a course of 040° and a speed of 5 knots would be drawn outward along the 40° bearing line to a length of 5 units, i.e., to the fifth circle. If the speed is greater than 10 units (knots or MPH), use is made of the 2:1, 3:1, 4:1, or 5:1 scales at the sides of the chart.

A vector line indicates graphically the direction and velocity of an element of the problem, such as the course and speed of your boat, another boat, the wind, or the current. In some instances, the vector will not be drawn from the center of the sheet, but its direction is always measured with reference to the center point and the outer circular scale.

Points on diagrams of positions are labeled with upper-case (capital) letters; points on vector diagrams are labeled with lower-case letters.

Maneuvering boards come in pads of 50 sheets. Each sheet is printed on both sides, and the paper is sufficiently heavy that both sides may be used. The fifth edition of H.O. 2665 includes condensed instructions in each of the four corners, outside the circular scale. The pad comes with a cover sheet on which is printed a "sample problem" but this, unfortunately, is a problem of interest to naval task force commanders, not boatmen.

## USE OF THE MANEUVERING BOARD

The H.O. 2665 sheets may well be used for plots of the relative motion of two vessels in a crossing situation as shown in figs. 2172-2174. These sheets are particularly useful on board radar-equipped craft where distance as well as bearing can be measured. Fig. 2178, for example, is a re-plot of fig. 2173b on a maneuvering board sheet.

FIG. 2179  A vector triangle of relative motion. The course and speed of your own craft is plotted as e - r and the apparent (relative) motion of the other craft as r - m. The triangle can be closed with the line e - m which is the *actual* course and speed of the other craft.

From a plot such as fig. 2178, with successive relative positions of the other craft plotted at recorded times, the direction of relative movement (DRM) and speed of relative movement (SRM) can be found. SRM is determined from the logarithmic scales at the bottom of the sheet using distance and time as the known factors. Knowing these relative motion quantities, and the course and speed of your own boat, a *vector triangle* can be used to determine the *actual* course and speed of the other craft. The relationships between these quantities are shown in fig. 2179. Point e, always at the center of the maneuvering board, represents earth, the reference for actual motion. Point r is the outer end of the speed vector, e-r, for the reference craft (your boat). The vector r-m represents the relative motion of the maneuvering (other) craft. By completing the triangle with the vector e-m, always outward from the point e at the center, the actual course and speed of the other boat are found. When such a vector triangle is drawn on a maneuvering board sheet, as in fig. 2180, the actual course can be read directly from the outer circular scale, and the actual speed can be read from the convenient concentric circles of the sheet, remembering to apply the same scale factor as used in plotting the speed of your own boat.

### True wind problem

Fig. 2181 illustrates what is called a *true wind problem*.

**Situation:** Your sailboat is close-hauled on true course 080°, speed 5 knots. The apparent (relative) wind is coming over the starboard side from 125° true with a velocity of 15 knots.

**Problem:** You want to sail your boat as close to the wind as possible, say at an angle of 45° off the true wind. You wish to know the direction and velocity of the *actual* wind so as to be able to determine whether you can lay the mark on the next tack, and the best course that you will be able to make to windward.

**Solution:** Draw your course and speed vector, e-r, along the bearing line for 080° outward from the center for 2½ circles (5 knots at a scale of 2:1). From point r, draw a line for the relative wind in the direction *toward* which the wind is traveling; use parallel rulers or another plotting instrument to transfer this direction from the bearing line out to the point r. With dividers, measure off the length for 15 knots along the 2:1 scale at the left side of the chart; lay off this distance along the relative wind line and so obtain the vector for that element of the problem. Where this vector ends is point w.

Next, draw a line from point e at the center to point w;

FIG. 2178  This is a re-plot of the situation of fig. 2173b on a Maneuvering Board sheet. Note that the plot has been rotated so that the direction of one's own boat is toward the top of the sheet (RB 000° dead ahead). The direction of relative motion (DRM) can be readily taken from the sheet, and the point of closest approach (CPA) and "miss distance" easily determined.

FIG. 2180 This is a re-plot of the preceding illustration on a Maneuvering Board sheet. The actual course of the other craft can be read directly from the outer scale of figures and the speed from the concentric rings; note that in this example the speed ratio is 2:1, each circle represents 2 knots or MPH.

this vector, e-w, represents the direction and velocity of the *true wind*. Since wind direction is never expressed in terms of where it is going (blowing toward), we look directly across the board and see that it is blowing *from* 142°. The velocity of 12 knots is read directly from the circles, the sixth circle at a scale of 2:1. Now it can be seen that the motion of your boat through the water has caused the apparent wind to come from a direction 17° counterclockwise from its true direction. (The actual wind velocity is seen to be less than the apparent velocity, but this information is not pertinent to this particular problem.)

To determine our course for sailing at an angle of 45° to the actual wind on the next, port, tack, it is merely a matter of adding 45° to the true wind direction of 142° to get 187°.

## Current sailing problems

One problem common to both sail boats and motor boats is that of choosing the correct course in traversing an area where the current will set the craft off her intended track if allowances are not made. In fig. 2182 we have the graphic solution of two questions. What is the current doing? What course do we take to correct for it?

Assume that your boat is on course 320° at a speed of 6 knots to pass close aboard a light vessel that now, at 0800, is dead ahead, 9 miles distant. As you progress through the water on your specified course, you notice that the light vessel appears to be moving to your left. This indicates that a current is at work on your port side.

To learn the set and drift of the current, and the course needed to correct for it: Plot the 0800 position of the light vessel from you—320°, 9 miles. Fix your present position and determine from the chart the new relative position of the light vessel. In fig. 2182 this is 310° and 7 miles; label this position with the time, 0829.

Now, draw in your boat's course and speed vector, e-r, of 320° and 6 knots, using a 2:1 scale ratio and the third circle. Note that the same scale ratio does not have to be used for both distance and speeds; it must, however, be constant within either category.

With parallel rulers or other plotting instrument, transfer the direction of the line of relative movement between the two plots of the light vessel's position to point r and draw in a line to some convenient length. After measuring the distance "traveled" by the light vessel, solve for its relative speed using the distance-time-speed logarithmic

scales. In this case, 2.4 miles in 29 minutes gives 5.2 knots.

Using the speed scale factor of 2:1, the speed of 5.2 knots is laid off along the line drawn from r. The point so found is labeled m and a line drawn *from m* to e at the center represents the set and drift of the current. This is found to be 080° and 3 knots.

With this information, we can now determine a new course to correct for the effect of the current. Remembering that our vessel *never* leaves the center of the maneuvering board, we must make the light vessel "come to us." A line drawn from the 0829 position of the light vessel, the broken line in fig. 2182, is the line that we wish the light vessel to follow on its way to us.

Parallel a line to this, starting at a convenient distance out, beyond the third circle (6 knots at our 2:1 speed scale), and draw toward point m in the same direction as the intended track of the light vessel; this is line a-m in the illustration. Where this relative movement line crosses the third circle is the course to steer for a speed of 6 knots —287°. It should be noted that there are many possible

FIG. 2181 The maneuvering board can be used to determine the velocity and direction of the true wind to aid in setting a new course on the next tack. See the text for details of this technique.

FIG. 2182 In this problem, a maneuvering board sheet enables the pilot to determine the current setting the boat off the desired track. It is also possible to graphically determine the necessary new course to be steered for any given speed.

combinations of courses and speeds available along this line, and that any increase in speed would bring a lesser course change, and vice versa. For example: looking out along the line *a-m,* we would find that for 8 knots, the course would be 293°; for 10 knots, 297°; for 12 knots, 299°.

## Other uses for the maneuvering board

The examples above have barely touched on the many uses of the maneuvering board sheets. There are many more applications—all interesting, but of lesser direct use in small-craft boating. Those interested in this topic in more detail can satisfy their curiosity in the many pages of *Bowditch* and *Dutton* devoted to the maneuvering board and its uses.

A pad of 50 maneuvering boards (H.O. 2665-10) may be obtained almost anywhere that Oceanographic Office publications are sold. The cost is only a few cents for each sheet, a small price to pay for safety and interesting, easy piloting!

# Longshore Piloting

There are a number of specialized techniques that might well be a part of every skipper's piloting skills. Their practicability has been thoroughly tested.

## DELIBERATE OFFSET OF COURSE

One of these specialized piloting techniques is used in making a landfall. The essence of it is this—lay your course, *not* for your objective, but decidedly to one side to allow for possible inaccuracies in the offsetting effect of the current, or to account for possible uncertainties of position. The advantage of this procedure lies in the fact that should you not arrive at your destination at the scheduled time, you have a near-certainty, rather than considerable doubt, as to which way you should turn to reach your objective.

The technique is best explained by use of an example.

### Situation

Let us assume that you have been fishing somewhere in the area between Block Island and Martha's Vineyard. After several hours of trolling, drifting, and just circling around, your position is quite problematical. Just as you decide that your fishing luck has run out for the day and it is time to head for Block Island Harbor, fog sets in to make the situation more interesting.

Your best "guesstimate," in the absence of any positional information, is that you are somewhere to the east of bell buoy "1", marked as point *B* in fig. 2183; you believe that you are somewhere in the vicinity of point *A* on the chart.

### Solution with deliberate offset of course

It's a good plan to lay your course for the off-lying bell buoy—as a matter of fact, that's what they are there for—but even if there were no such buoy, there can be merit in laying the course decidedly off to one side of the ultimate objective, Block Island Harbor.

Suppose you lay your course AB to the bell buoy and miss it by ⅛ mile to the north. When you pick up the 3-fathom (18-foot) curve, at *C,* you know you are north of

**FIG. 2183  If you are caught in a fog somewhere offshore in the vicinity of point A, the inclination might be to head directly for the harbor entrance at E. It is much safer, however, to deliberately head for a point more to the north on a course that will take you past the bell buoy at B. The text explains why.**

the harbor—a fact confirmed by the realization that you would have picked it up much sooner if you were south of the harbor entrance.

Had you missed it by ⅛ mile to the south, and picked up the 3-fathom curve at *D,* you could still follow the curve southeastward to buoy *C "3".* Even if your position were ¼ mile south of *A* when you laid your course westward, you would still pick up the 3-fathom curve at the harbor entrance.

You find added assurance of your general position above the harbor entrance when you find depths holding generally at 3 fathoms on your course southeastward. If your calculations were completely wrong and you ran southeastward from any point below the harbor entrance, depths would increase.

### Solution without deliberate offset of course

Consider, however, what could happen if you missed your objective E by ¼ mile to the south if the course had been laid direct to buoy *C "3".* Picking up the 3-fathom curve at *F,* you could not be sure whether you were north or south of the entrance.

Your first conclusion might be that, since you have run a few minutes overtime before reaching the 3-fathom curve, you are north of the harbor. But don't forget that you didn't accurately know your starting point. Suppose you had been several minutes eastward of where you thought you were when the fog set in. In this event, the additional few minutes running time before reaching 18-foot depths is reasonable.

On the assumption that you are indeed somewhat to the north of the harbor, you turn south, proceeding slowly and carefully. A few minutes pass, but still no buoy or harbor entrance. How far to continue? That buoy may be just ahead, obscured by the fog. On the other hand, doubt creeps in. You couldn't have been that far off in your reckoning—or could you? So there you are, in a fog—literally and figuratively.

### General procedures

In the first example above (where we laid a course for the bell) the intended track was laid about ⅜ mile to the north of the objective (the harbor entrance). How much deliberate offset of course is made in any given case varies within limits determined by what you feel would be a maximum error under the circumstances. On a long run in from offshore, making a landfall on a beach that trends in a straight line for miles in either direction with few marks of identification even if visibility is good, you may prefer to make an allowance of a mile or more. It adds little to the total run, but eliminates much uncertainty. But don't use this technique blindly, without regard to possible dangers that may line the beach. Study the chart carefully and adapt the procedure to the situation at hand.

## Crossing the Gulf Stream

This same procedure may be used in crossing the Gulf Stream. Rather than attempting to make an exact allowance for the distance you will be set northward, a somewhat overly-generous allowance is made, with the knowledge that if you don't pick up your target landmark after the allotted passage time, you have only to turn northward. It can be comforting to know the proper direction in which to turn, rather than to have to make a choice with perhaps a 50-50 chance of being wrong.

The same technique can be used in recrossing the Gulf Stream on your westward passage back to Florida. Again, over-allow for the northward offsetting influence of the Stream and plan to turn northward as you approach the coast if you see no identifiable landmarks.

## NIGHT PILOTING BY TIMETABLE

Another specialized piloting technique that will go far toward increasing the pleasure of nighttime piloting is the establishment of a "timetable" for your particular cruise.

### Preparing the timetable

When you anticipate a night run, don't wait until you are on your way before studying out courses, distances, running times, etc. Go over the entire trip in advance and acquaint yourself thoroughly with the separate legs of the cruise, the aids to navigation that you will pass, the characteristics of the lights, and other items of piloting interest.

Then set up a timetable, assuming that you will leave your point of departure at exactly 0000, and note in orderly fashion the predicted time of arrival abeam of every light and buoy on both sides of your intended track. Alongside each entry, show the characteristics of the navigational aid and the compass course at the time. You can also enter into your timetable the approximate times that major lights can be expected to become visible.

### Using the timetable

Invest in an alarm clock or watch with a luminous dial and set it for 12 o'clock when you start your run from the point of departure on which your predetermined timetable is based. Then as the flashing, occulting, or other lights successively wink over the horizon, you won't have to dash below to puzzle out characteristics and identify each in turn. The elapsed time from your start will clue you as to the identity of the aid to navigation.

The timetable will aid you in knowing where you are at any time, what light you just passed, what the characteristics will be of the next light to appear, and when that should happen. The use of elapsed time, rather than actual clock time, allows flexibility in the starting time; it is not necessary to revise your entire timetable if you take your departure earlier or later than originally planned. If any discrepancy creeps in consistently between when events should happen and when they actually do, the hands of the clock or watch can be shifted as needed.

## NIGHT COASTWISE PILOTING BY SHORE LIGHTS

For night piloting alongshore, the lights of towns and settlements along the beach can be used to estimate distances offshore. An experienced boatman reports that he has been able to maintain a course approximately 5½ miles offshore going down the Jersey coast simply by keeping in sight of the reflected glow in the sky above lights in towns along the shore.

The appearance of direct rays of light would be a signal indicating that the distance offshore was decreasing to 5 miles or less, whereupon it would be advisable to haul off until only the reflected glow was visible once more. The objective of keeping so far offshore was to avoid the extensive areas of fish net stakes, and yet not lose contact with land.

The distance that the direct rays will be seen will be determined by the height of the observer's eye, and should be determined by the individual skipper for his own boat. The principles involved, however, remain the same for all craft.

## FOLLOWING THE BEACH

Elsewhere, we have considered how a boat may be piloted along a coast by following a constant depth, or fathom curve. It is possible, however, that the sounder might be inoperative or not available for some other reason. It is well to have another means of following the shoreline approximately when visibility conditions permit the observation of objects on the beach.

Let's say that you wish to parallel the Jersey or Long Island beach (or any average coast where there are no hills or mountains ashore to stand out prominently at long range). Fig. 2184 shows such a coastline. From the deck of a typical small boat at sea, you will be unable to see the beach if you are more than about 4½ miles offshore, due to the earth's curvature. If you can just make out the beach, you are approximately 4 miles out. This, naturally, will not hold true if there is haze or fog.

**FIG. 2184  With just a little effort, you can determine for your height of eye on your boat the distances off shore at which you can see the beach and certain features of the buildings. Your distances shouldn't vary much from those shown here for a typical boat.**

## Distance off by visibility of details

Now as you follow the coast, you will probably trend in closer without realizing that you are off your intended track. Buildings appear, and you find that you can distinguish detail enough to make out individual windows of houses. This means that you are roughly within 2 miles of the beach.

Thus, you have established two limits, by keeping within sight of the beach, but far enough off that you cannot count windows, you are averaging 2 to 4 miles offshore. Meticulous pilots may object that this is too loose, but there are many cruises that do not require any higher degree of precision.

## Check for your height-of-eye

The 2-mile distance at which windows can be counted will not vary with the observer's height of eye. This is a matter of distance and detail. The 4- to 4½-mile limits of visibility for the beach itself, however, are subject to variation from one boat to another. These are average figures; establish more exact distances for your own craft by using the bow-and-beam bearings technique or any other positioning procedure.

## A NEW POSITION FINDER

Earlier in this chapter, we considered a positioning technique using two horizontal angles between the lines of sight to three identifiable objects. See figs. 2124-2126. Although this is a standard method, it has not been widely used on small boats because a sextant is normally required to measure the angles and a three-arm protractor to plot them accurately. As a sextant would be a relatively large investment for this use only, those who do not venture onto the high seas and use celestial navigation do not normally have one aboard.

The Weems Position-Finder is a combination instrument that can be used both to measure the angles and do the chart plotting. It eliminates the need for a sextant for making observations, and the attendant steps of reading angles from the sextant scale and setting these values on the protractor. This results in a saving of time, effort, and risk of error. As the observations are taken, the arms of this instrument are locked in position, and the device becomes, in effect, a three-arm protractor with the angles already set. The actual values of the angles need never be known. The solution is entirely independent of the compass or other instruments. The optical principle employed is shown in fig. 2185.

FIG. 2187 The position-finder in place on a chart. The arms are set directly as the observations are made, and no angles need be read in order to determine the fix. The three arms are aligned with the chart symbols for the objects sighted upon; the observer's position is at the center of the instrument.

The observing portion of the device, fig. 2186, consists of a fixed horizon mirror, A, in which the reflected image of one object is seen immediately below the true image of the center object viewed over the top of the mirror. This is called a horizon mirror because it has the same function as the horizon mirror of a marine sextant.

The rotatable index mirror, B, is moved by the index arm, C, to reflect the image of the right or left object into the fixed mirror. By viewing through the slot in the center of this mirror, it is possible to use this one mirror for both the right and left angles. This is not possible with a sextant, where the index mirror is offset and can be used for only one horizontal angle at a time.

The plotting portion of the position-finder consists of three arms, pivoted at one center point, at which a pencil mark can be made through a hole onto the chart. The center arm is permanently located with an etched centerline at 90° to the plane of the horizontal mirror. The two movable arms can be locked in position during the observations, avoiding the need for any reading of scales and subsequent setting of the arms before plotting. The inside edges of the movable arms are used for plotting.

## Using the position-finder

Three objects are selected that can be identified visually and on the chart. The procedure is to measure the angle between the line of sight to the center object and those to the right-hand and left-hand objects. The two angles cannot be measured simultaneously. If it is apparent that one angle is changing at a more rapid rate than the other, the angle changing more slowly should be measured first and the angle changing more rapidly last; otherwise, it is not important which angle is measured first.

Each angle is measured in accordance with the detailed instructions furnished with the instrument. As the angles are measured, the movable arms are locked into place. The instrument is then transferred to the chart and used as a conventional three-arm protractor, lining up each arm with the respective chart symbol and marking the position with a pencil through the hole in the center of the device. Fig. 2187 shows the Position-Finder in place on a chart.

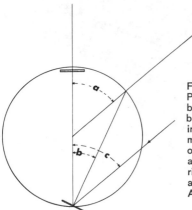

FIG. 2185 Optical principle of Position Finder. Angle *a* is angle between two objects on shore being observed. Angle *b* is amount index arm, and therefore index mirror, is turned. This is always one-half of angle *a*. Angle *c* is angle of light rays coming from right hand object to index mirror and reflected to horizon mirror. Always the same as angle *a*.

FIG. 2186 The observing portion of the position finder. A, fixed horizon mirror. B, rotatable index mirror. C, index arm. See text for a description of the use of this instrument.

## ECHO PILOTING

An approximate method of determining distance, in passages or other bodies of water where there are sheer cliffs that will produce echoes, is to sound a short blast of the whistle or horn, and time, preferably with a stop watch, the interval before the echo is received.

Divide this interval in seconds by two (because the sound has to travel to the shore and return as the echo), and multiply that figure by 1100, a rough value for the speed of sound in air in feet per second. (Actually, at 32°F, the speed is 1088 feet per second and at 72°F it is 1132 fps, but the figure of 1100 is close enough for the accuracy of the timing method used.)

For example, you sound a short blast on your horn and time the interval until the return of the echo as five seconds. Half of this time is 2½ seconds; multiply by 1100, and you have 2650 feet or a distance off of slightly less than one-half nautical mile.

This is sometimes called "dog-bark navigation" and is used to a limited extent in the inside passage to Alaska on the British Columbia coast. If an echo can be received from both shores, a vessel can be kept in the approximate middle of the passage by holding such a course that an echo will be received simultaneously from both sides.

## THE RULE-OF-SIXTY

Another useful specialized piloting technique is the *Rule-of-Sixty*. It provides a simple, practical way of changing course to clear an off-lying danger area without a lot of chart work. Again, the technique is best explained with an example.

Let's assume in this case that you have come out of Portsmouth Harbor and are running a southerly course down the coast to Cape Ann. See fig. 2188. Somewhere out off Newburyport you pick up dead ahead the light on Straitsmouth Island, marked *C* in the figure. Your course made good along the line *AC* has been 164° True. A bell buoy has been placed a mile and a half eastward of the light to mark a number of rocks and ledges that must be cleared. It is obvious that you must make a change of course for safety. The problem is how much?

Instead of getting out the chart and plotting a position and a new course to clear the bell buoy, you can apply the Rule-of-Sixty and get a new course with a simple mental calculation. You know from the chart or Light List that the light on Straitsmouth Island is visible for 8 miles, assuming good visibility. (With less than perfect visibility, you will have to establish your distance from the light by other means. But on this night, the visibility is good and you can accept the distance as 8 miles when the light appears on the horizon.)

The procedure is to divide 60 (the rule) by 8 (the distance); the result is 7.5. Since you want to clear the light by a mile and a half, you multiply 7.5 by 1.5 and get 11.25. This is rounded to 11, and is the number of degrees that you must change your course. Thus, your new course is 164° − 11° = 153° True. Long before you need to be concerned about the rocks and ledges, you will pick up the bell buoy north of Flat Ground and then the light on the bell buoy at *D*.

Although this technique is quite valid and acceptable as a specialized procedure, it should not be considered a full

FIG. 2188 The Rule of Sixty can guide you in determining how much to change course to clear an obstacle seen ahead at a known distance. The rule can be applied without making a chart plot of the situation.

FIG. 2189 The length of the several straight courses required to pass around a point of land can be added graphically and measured all at one time, rather than measuring them separately and adding the distances numerically.

substitute for the basic and conventional procedure of accurately determining your position and plotting a revised course. There may be circumstances where the Rule-of-Sixty will be useful, such as on a single-handed passage or under conditions too rough for accurate plotting, but consider it a "secondary" method rather than a first-choice method.

## DETERMINING THE DISTANCE AROUND A HEADLAND

A pilot may be confronted with the problem of determining the total distance to be covered when rounding a headland or point of land in a series of short, straight courses. There is a graphic method that will give a quick and accurate solution.

In fig. 2189, the boat is at *A*. You want to know the total run to *F* on the other side of the point if you proceed to *B*, then *C*, *D*, and *E* in turn.

In the figure, lines are drawn from point to point, but after you become familiar with the technique, you can merely swing the legs of your dividers from point to point so as to ensure that the invisible line determined by the points will be far enough offshore to be safe.

### Step-by-step procedures

The starting point is *A*; use a pair of dividers and measure the distance to *B*. Keep the dividers' leg point that is at *B* on that point, and swing the other leg around from *A* to the right until it touches the broken line extended backwards from *C* to *B* at $A^1$. Hold this dividers' point on $A^1$, and extend the other leg from *B* to *C*.

Now hold the point at *C* fast and swing the other point around from $A^1$ until it touches the broken line extended backward from *D* to *C* at $A^2$. Hold this point fast at $A^2$ and open the dividers further, as before, until the point at *C* reaches to *D*.

This same step-by-step procedure is repeated to find $A^3$ and $A^4$. When the dividers have been finally extended from $A^4$ to *F*, they are set to measure the total distance around the headland using the chart's graphic scale or latitude markings.

This technique saves much time and is more accurate than the usual procedure of measuring each leg separately and adding the distance together to get the total run.

Fig. 2201
*Mastless motor boat.* Aft, US or USPS ensign (not yacht ensign). Forward, yacht club burgee, Squadron pennant or USCG Aux. blue ensign.

Fig. 2202 *(above)*
*Typical outboard cruiser or open boat, with temporary staff placed on forward deck.* Same flags at bow and stern as Fig. 2201 (except USCG Aux. blue ensign). At deck staff may be flown an officer's flag, a private signal or the USCG Aux. blue ensign.

Fig. 2203 *(left)*
*Mastless cruiser with temporary staff on deck.* Same flags as Fig. 2202.

# Chapter 22

# FLAG ETIQUETTE

**How to fly your flags afloat—**

**Where and when to fly them—**

**Flag, pennant or burgee, which?—**

**Origin of the national and yacht ensigns—**

**Flags for masts ashore—**

**Etiquette in foreign waters**

Fig. 2204
*Cruiser with bow and stern staffs, with signal mast and yardarm.* At bow, Squadron pennant or club burgee. Aft, US ensign or USPS ensign. At main truck, officer's flag or private signal. At starboard yardarm, USPS ensign (if not flown aft), absent flag or guest flag.

Fig. 2205
*Typical mastless outboard boat. Same flags as Fig. 2201.*

**Fig. 2206**
*Cruiser with signal mast, gaff and yardarm.*
Same flags as Fig. 2205 except, when under way, ensigns should be flown at gaff (at the stern, when at anchor).

**Fig. 2207**
*Two-masted documented motor boat, at anchor, with jack staff and 2 yardarms.* Union jack at jack staff (when at anchor, only). Club burgee, Squadron pennant, USCG Aux. blue ensign at fore truck. Private signal or officer's flag at main truck. Yacht ensign at stern staff. USPS ensign at main starboard yardarm. Crew's meal pennant at fore port yardarm.

**Fig. 2208**
*Single-masted sailing vessel, under way.* Club burgee, Squadron pennant or officer's flag at the truck. Ensign at the leech of the main, approximately ⅔ the length of the leech above the clew.

**Fig. 2209**
*Single-masted sailing vessel, at anchor.* Same flags as Fig. 2208 except US ensign flown from stern and USPS ensign from starboard yardarm or spreader. Note USPS officer's flag at main truck.

Fig. 2210
*Two-masted sailing vessel under way.* Ensign at leech of main. Club burgee or Squadron pennant at the fore truck. Officer's flag or private signal at the main truck.

Fig. 2211
*Dress-ship.* Flags of the International Code arranged as shown. Union jack at jack staff. Club burgee or Squadron pennant at the fore truck. Officer's flag or private signal at main truck. Guest flag at starboard main yardarm or spreader. Crew's meal pennant at port fore spreader. Ensign at stern staff. (Dress-ship only at anchor. See text for order of displaying code flags.)

Fig. 2212
*Yawls and ketches.* Club burgee or Squadron pennant at the main truck. Private signal or officer's flag at the mizzen truck. Ensign at the leech of the mizzen. (Same flags at anchor, except US ensign flown from staff at stern and USPS ensign from starboard main spreader.)

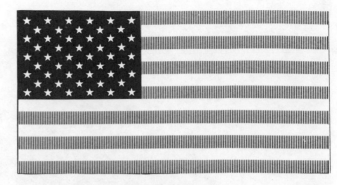

**U.S. ENSIGN,** the one and only U.S. National flag, proper for all yachts, without reservation. Old Glory, the flag with 50 stars and 13 stripes. Flown, when at anchor, at the stern staff. When under way in inland waters, and when meeting or passing other vessels on the high seas, weather and rig permitting, by: motor yachts at the stern staff; by motor yachts with mast and gaff at the gaff.

Marconi-rigged sailboats, when under sail, fly the ensign at the leech of the mainsail, or when there's more than

U.S. ENSIGN

U.S. POWER SQUADRON ENSIGN

U.S. YACHT ENSIGN

U.S. COAST GUARD AUXILIARY ENSIGN

one mast, at the leech of the aftermost sail, approximately ²/₃ the length of the leech above the clew.

Gaff-rigged sailboats, when under sail, fly the ensign at the peak of the mainsail gaff, or when there's more than one mast, at the peak of the aftermost gaff. In the case of a schooner with Marconi main and gaff foresail, the ensign flies from the leech of the mainsail.

Under power alone, or when at anchor or made fast, the ensign should be flown from the stern staff of all sailboats. *(The English practice is to fly the ensign at a stern staff, on all sailing craft at anchor, under way, under sail and under power.)*

On yawls and ketches, the ensign is flown from the mizzen.

At 8 A.M., the national ensign should be hoisted first, followed by the USPS ensign (if you are a member of the U.S. Power Squadrons in good standing, and in command of the boat), the yacht club burgee, officer's flag, and/or private signal. For C.G. Auxiliary vessels the same order holds, but C.G. Auxiliary blue ensign and officer's flag are substituted for yacht club flags. Flags are hoisted smartly, but lowered ceremoniously. Flag officer's flags, though displayed day and night, may be temporarily lowered and hoisted at colors.

At U.S.P.S., C.G. Auxiliary, or club rendezvous, marine parades, etc., on order of the Commanding Officer, flags may be flown after sundown but must be lowered at or before midnight, as ordered.

**U.S. POWER SQUADRONS ENSIGN** is flown as an outward and visible signal to other craft that the boat is commanded by a member of the USPS in good standing, one who is an able seaman, with a knowledge of things nautical, and competent to handle his craft.

Flown from the stern staff (or gaff under way) or from

starboard yard arm (the latter preferred) at the option of the member, on motor craft under way and on both motor and sailing craft at anchor.

On sailing vessels under way it's flown at leech of the Marconi's main or at the mainsail gaff peak (aftermost mast on vessels with more than two masts).

**U.S. YACHT ENSIGN,** by custom and by rulings of government authorities, may be flown on yachts of all sizes in place of the U.S. Ensign. Strictly speaking, the Yacht Ensign is not the American flag. Originally the flying of the Yacht Ensign was restricted to documented vessels of a special classification. However, all such restrictions have now been removed. Most Yacht Clubs now provide in their club by-laws that the Yacht Ensign be flown from the stern staff of power vessels, both at anchor and underway; at the stern on sailing craft when at anchor and at the leech of the mainsail when underway. (See page X)

**U.S. COAST GUARD AUXILIARY ENSIGN,** known as the "Blue Ensign" is flown only from 8 A.M. to sunset when a qualified Auxiliarist is in charge of an approved facility. Here's how:

☐ On a vessel without a mast—at the bow staff.
☐ On a vessel with one mast—at the truck.
☐ On a vessel with two or more masts—at the main truck.
☐ NEVER in place of the national ensign.

The USPS ensign may be flown at its proper location on boats displaying the U.S.C.G. Aux. ensign to indicate that the owner is a member of both organizations.

**YACHT CLUB BURGEE,** generally triangular in shape, sometimes swallow tail.

Flown from the bow staff of mastless and single-masted vessels (foremost truck of vessels with two or more masts); at the main truck of yawls and ketches.

YACHT CLUB BURGEE     SQUADRON PENNANT     OWNER'S PRIVATE SIGNAL     USPS OFFICER'S FLAG

COLOR KEY

RED

BLUE

WHITE

OPTIONAL

UNION JACK

OWNER'S ABSENT FLAG     GUEST FLAG DIVER (Red)

U.S.C.G. AUXILIARY OFFICER'S PENNANT     OWNER'S MEAL FLAG     CREW'S MEAL PENNANT

Burgee may be flown under way and at anchor. It is, however, permissible to substitute the private signal for the burgee on single-masted yachts without bow staff when under way.

**SQUADRON PENNANT.** A distinguishing Squadron pennant which has been approved by the District and authorized by the U.S. Power Squadrons' Governing Board, may be flown between morning and evening colors, in place of and instead of the club burgee.

NOTE: Color reproductions of all Squadron pennants will be found on the end papers of this book.

**OWNER'S PRIVATE SIGNAL,** generally swallow tail in shape, sometimes rectangular or pennant, flown from masthead of single-masted motor boats, at the main truck of motor boats with two masts, at the main truck of single-masted sailing vessels when under way and at the aftermost truck of sailing yachts with two or more masts. Mastless motor yachts may display, on a staff erected on the superstructure, the flag designated by this code to be flown from the truck of single-masted yachts.

**OFFICER'S FLAG,** rectangular in shape, blue (with white design) for senior officer(s); red for next lower in rank; white (with blue design) for lower rank. Other officer's flag (except fleet captain) may be swallow tail or triangular in shape, as provided in the regulations of those organizations making provisions for such flags. Flown in place of private signal on all rigs of motor and sailing vessels except on single-masted sailing vessels, when it is flown in place of burgee at truck.

**UNION JACK,** a rectangular blue flag with 50 white stars. The Union Jack may be displayed *only* at the jackstaff on sailing yachts and at the jackstaff on motor yachts with more than one mast, between morning and evening colors,

and only while at anchor on Sundays or holidays, or when dressing ship. The Union Jack shall never be substituted for or replace the club burgee.

**ABSENT FLAG,** rectangular blue flag, flown during owner's absence in daylight hours. Flown from starboard yardarm, starboard main spreader or equivalent, provided USPS ensign is not flown at this hoist, with a USPS member in command. (Replaced at night, at anchor, by blue light.)

**GUEST FLAG,** a rectangular blue flag, crossed diagonally by a white stripe, flown during daylight, when owner is absent but guests are on board. Flown from the starboard yardarm, starboard main spreader or equivalent, provided USPS ensign is not being flown from this hoist. Guest flag should also be flown when owner is absent but a member of his family is aboard.

**U.S.C.G. AUXILIARY OFFICER'S PENNANT,** or a past officer's burgee (same design except swallow-tail shape), flies day and night when officer is on board. On a vessel without a mast, flown at the bow staff in lieu of the Auxiliary flag. On a vessel with one mast, at starboard spreader. On a vessel with two or more masts, at main starboard spreader.

Only *one* officer's pennant or burgee may be flown at one time. An incumbent officer's pennant takes precedence. When the Blue Ensign is displayed, it is improper to hoist a guest, owner absent, meal, cocktail, or novelty flag.

**OWNER'S MEAL FLAG,** a white rectangular flag, flown at anchor, during daylight meal hours of owners, from the main starboard spreader or yardarm, if the USPS ensign is not at this hoist. (Replaced by white light at night.)

**CREW'S MEAL PENNANT,** red, flown during daylight, at anchor, during the meal hours of the crew at the fore port yardarm or spreader.

# FLYING FLAGS AT YACHT CLUB HOISTS ASHORE

**These diagrams illustrate how flags can be displayed for a variety of situations and on different types of yacht club masts and poles.**

NOTES: The flag of the Senior Club Officer present on the club grounds or aboard his boat in the club anchorage, or Storm Signal flags can be substituted for the International Code Flags shown in the diagrams, except in the case illustrated at bottom left. The diagrams show hoists as if you were standing ashore facing seaward.

If only a Yacht Club single pole with no yard or gaff, only the U.S. Flag should be flown, at the truck.

If a pole with yardarm only, the U.S. Flag should be flown at truck, Club burgee at starboard yardarm, USPS Ensign or other organizational flag may be flown at port yardarm during activities ashore of such organization.

On national holidays and on days of special yachting significance, it is permissible to fly the flags of the International Code.

The code for "flying flags ashore at Yacht Clubs" may be followed for flags flown ashore at the homes of yachtsmen.

Signal flags, such as storm and weather flags, etc. should be flown from a conspicuous hoist.

Flags of yachting organizations should not be flown from commercial establishments, except by special permission.

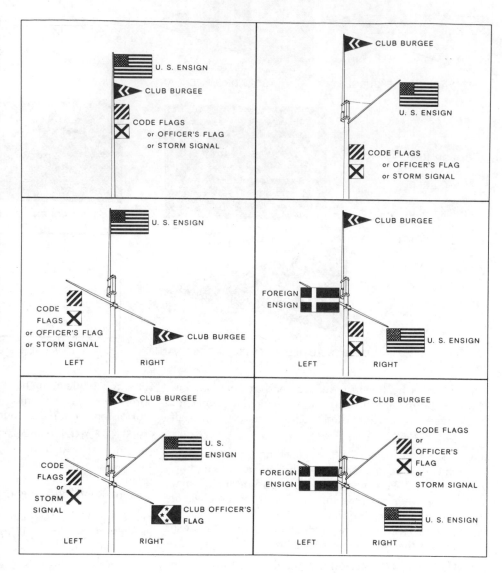

## About Pennants

**Pennant or Burgee.** Adrift in a foggy sea of semantics, a sea lawyer could easily founder, groping for the right terms to describe those bits of bunting he flies from the truck and bow staff. Basically, there are four shapes his signals may take—rectangular, triangular, rectangular swallow-tailed, and triangular swallow-tailed. What to call them? Pennants or burgees?

We can't go far wrong if we think of a *pennant* as a flag smaller at the fly than at the hoist which is (1) commonly pointed, triangular (2) often truncated, as in some Navy signals (3) sometimes swallow-tailed (4) occasionally a long thin streamer.

The *burgee* we might regard as a swallow-tailed flag which is (1) often rectangular (2) may be pennant-shaped (3) by popular usage, the identifying signal of a yacht club, regardless of shape.

**Naval Reserve Pennants.** There are two types of Naval Reserve pennant. (See illustrations, pages R and S.) The *Naval Reserve Yacht Pennant* is displayed at the fore truck by yachts and vessels commanded or owned by Naval Reserve Officers, designated by the Secretary of the Navy as suitable for service as naval auxiliaries in time of war. The *Naval Reserve Yacht Owners Distinguishing Pennant* is a personal flag flown, preferably at the fore truck, on yachts owned by, or under the command of, individuals who donated yachts or other craft for use by the Navy during World War II. Those awarded this pennant are not necessarily members of the U.S. Naval Reserve.

**Racing Pennant.** A distinctive pennant has been designed by the Sea Cliff (N.Y.) Yacht Club as an identifying signal for racing boats. The field is blue, with white fluorescent strip in the middle, and red anchor superimposed. Cruising yachts carry it at the starboard spreader; smaller boats fly it from the leech of the mainsail. It aids race committees in distinguishing contesting boats; other boats, hopefully, will give them a wide berth. It is suggested that other clubs follow Sea Cliff's lead, standardizing on the design illustrated below.

*"And yet, though silent, it speaks to us—speaks to us of the past, of the men and women who went before us, and of the records they wrote upon it."* —PRESIDENT WILSON

## The Flag of Your Country

THE FLYING of flags and colors on motor craft, sailing and other yachts is governed largely by custom. Few, if any, laws or government regulations have ever been enacted on this subject. Mention has seldom if ever been made by Congress in all of its years, of any requirements for the flying of any flag on numbered, undocumented or unlicensed vessels or yachts. Documented yachts are expected to fly the yacht ensign but the enforcement of even this regulation is questionable.

A review or a brief history of the United States National Flag should permit one to better understand some of the fundamentals on which many of the customs of flags and colors are based, especially their evolution for use on the water.

The origin and early history of the use of national flags is very indefinite. This is especially true of the national ensign of the United States. Early Colonial and American history makes very little mention of our flag or flags. Our Navy seems to have begun the use of the Stars and Stripes immediately after the Continental Congress had passed an Act in June, 1777, establishing the Stars and Stripes as the flag of this country. However, it was not until 1895 or some 30 years after the close of the Civil War, that the United States cavalry was given the right to carry the Stars and Stripes as the national standard. It was in 1841 that the infantry first used the national colors. Not until 1876 did the Marines carry the Stars and Stripes.

As the Navy made use of the national flag from the beginning and the other branches of the U.S. government were slow in adopting it, it emphasizes that the Stars and Stripes as the national ensign is a flag of the sea and its right to be flown from yachts is clearly established.

On the subject of the origin and development of the flag from which the Stars and Stripes has been evolved, accounts are too conflicting to warrant placing much credence in them. Prince Edward, afterwards Edward I of England, about the middle of the last half of the 13th century, adopted the Red Cross of St. George, on a white field, as the national flag of England. After James VI of Scotland ascended the throne of England in 1603, as James I, he was much annoyed by the wrangling between the masters of English and Scotch ships when they met at sea as to which one should dip its colors to the other. Therefore, in 1606, he stopped this annoyance and to help unite the two kingdoms into one country, combined the two crosses into a new flag, which subsequently became known as the Union

Jack. This he required all vessels of both countries to carry at their mainmast. A century later when the two countries agreed upon their union, a national agreement required the union of the crosses to be used on flags, banners, standards, and ensigns both at sea and on land.

Near the beginning of the revolution, General Washington assigned to the various officers as a distinction of rank, ribbons varying in color and these were worn by them until something more formal was designed. There were practically no flags or colors although some of the individual companies of the Colonial Army are supposed to have brought with them those which they had previously used. Later General Washington urged the various Colonels to provide for their regiments colors of such design as might appeal to them. This was frequently done and in many instances, some designs of 13 units were used to represent the 13 colonies.

Some of the colonies adopted flags of their own. Massachusetts adopted the Pine Tree, with the motto An Appeal to Heaven. Rhode Island selected one having an anchor and the word Hope and within the canton a union of 13 white stars on a blue field, said to be the first flag on which the 13 colonies were represented by 13 stars.

South Carolina's flag has an interesting history. In September 1775, the Committee of Safety of Charleston instructed Colonel William Moultrie to take possession of Fort Johnson on James Island, which he did. The uniforms of their troops were blue with a silver increscent in the cap. Soon realizing that a flag was needed, he improvised one having a blue field with a white increscent in the canton. This was the flag which sergeant Jasper so gallantly rescued on June 28, 1776, when the fort of palmetto logs on Sullivans Island was attacked by the British Fleet under Admiral Sir Peter Parker. It was under this flag that the Declaration of Independence was read to the people of Charleston on August 8, 1776. When the state came to officially adopt a flag, it took the one which Colonel Moultrie had designed and in recognition of the good services of the palmetto logs, placed upon it a palmetto tree.

While our first flag act was adopted June 14, 1777, by resolution of the Continental Congress and reading as follows: "Resolved, That the flag of the United States be thirteen stripes, alternate red and white; that the union be thirteen stars, white in a blue field, representing a new constellation" yet there is nothing to show that the Revolutionary Army ever carried any flags furnished by the American Congress. Those which were carried were purely personal, each made by or for some officer, company or regiment, and represented the sentiments of the makers. However, the United States Navy began to use the flag immediately after it was authorized by the Continental Congress.

History records only one Stars and Stripes that was carried by the American Army during the Revolutionary War. It was carried by the North Carolina Militia at the Battle of Guilford Courthouse, March 15, 1781, but the stripes were blue and red and the union had a white field with 13 eight-pointed stars. There is also another flag hanging in the State House at Annapolis, which it is claimed was carried by the Third Maryland Regiment in 1781. It has 13 five-pointed stars, one in the center, and 12 arranged in the form of a circle around it. In both of these cases, the flags were purely personal, not official.

The Stars and Stripes preserved in the State House of Boston is claimed to have flown over Fort Independence during the American Revolution but was not carried by the Army. In 1863 each battery of artillery and each company of cavalry was allowed to carry a small flag consisting of Stars and Stripes but that privilege was revoked at the end of the Civil War. The U.S. Marines did not carry the Stars and Stripes as national colors until 1876, yet those which they carried as such in the Mexican and Civil Wars had an eagle in the union.

In none of the three acts adopting the United States national flag is there any mention as to how the stars should be arranged or how many points they should have. In one of the first flags, the stars were sometimes arranged in a circle or with one star in the center and the remaining 12 either in the form of a circle or hollow square, or three horizontal rows of 4, 5 and 4 stars respectively. In a later flag, they were also arranged in several different orders, three horizontal rows of five each or three vertical rows of five each; sometimes in the quincunx order as was the flag that floated over Fort McHenry when Key wrote the Star Spangled Banner.

Apparently about 1841, when the United States Infantry was first given the right to carry the Stars and Stripes, there was a desire on the part of some to preserve their old national colors in the union of the new flag. One of these had an eagle with a bunch of arrows in one claw and the Indian pipe of peace in the other with 13 stars above and a like number below. During the Mexican War, the Fourth Indiana Volunteers carried a flag having in the union an eagle standing on a segment of the globe with a bunch of arrows in one claw, as though intending to conquer the earth.

Near the beginning of the 20th Century, the different departments of our National Government appointed representatives to confer and see if they could not bring order out of chaos. The proportions of Naval flags and Army colors were quite different, the former being much longer in proportion to its height, the latter being much shorter to avoid interfering with the color or standard bearer. It was decided to leave the Army colors alone but to fly the Naval flag from flagstaffs and from Government buildings.

Accordingly, following the recommendations of this committee, President Taft, in 1912, issued an executive order defining minutely the proportions and other details of the Stars and Stripes, at the same time approving a cus-

tom which had existed in the Navy of placing on their small boats flags having only 13 stars instead of the full complement. The use of only 13 stars on our small or boat flags was discontinued by an executive order of President Wilson, dated May 29, 1916, and now all flags, colors, etc., used by the United States Government are required to have their full complement of 50 stars. In all of the discussion by the conference it does not appear that there was any mention whatsoever of the yacht ensign or the rights or duties of yachts or any other vessels to fly any particular flag.

From the foregoing it will be seen that the United States has only one flag. The use of the yacht ensign is misleading. England has, by law, created a flag for its navy, another for its merchant service, another for yachts and another for its land forces; each is a national flag and entitled to the position and courtesy due the colors of a nation. But, in the United States, wherever, whenever and for whatever purpose the national colors are flown, there is but one flag to fly.

The place of honor for the national colors on land and sea is as follows: on land on a straight mast, at the head; on a mast with a gaff, at the gaff. At sea and at anchor on a steam or motor vessel, at the flag staff aft; on vessels under sail, at the peak; and on vessels with a gaff, at this gaff when under way.

There has never been passed a law compelling boats to fly the national flag or none at all from the place of honor. It has probably never been contemplated that a loyal citizen would ever do otherwise. Yet, we are free to do as we

The American flag is flying here, properly, from the gaff at a yacht club station. The club burgee is at the masthead.

M. Rosenfeld.

like and in the use of this freedom there has grown the custom of flying the yacht ensign at the point of honor at shore stations and aboard yachts. There are today ardent yachtsmen in high places who believe this custom aboard yachts should be continued.

The yacht ensign had its beginning on August 7, 1848, when the Congress passed "an act to authorize the Secretary of the Treasury to license yachts and for other purposes" providing for the enrollment and licensing of yachts and exempting them from entering and clearing at Customhouses. The third paragraph of the act provided "that all such licensed yachts shall *use a signal* of the form, size and colors prescribed by the Secretary of the Navy." (This paragraph has been subsequently reenacted as Sec. 4215 Revised Statutes of the United States.) The Secretary of the Navy acted promptly, and on August 26, 1848, he requested the New York Yacht Club to submit a design for this signal. The design they submitted on January 9, 1849, was the then adopted American ensign, which carried thirteen stars in a circle in the blue field and the thirteen red and white stripes (the Betsy Ross flag), in which they placed a fouled anchor in the center of the circle of stars. The Secretary of the Navy accepted the suggestion of the New York Yacht Club and authorized the adoption of the design.

It is the design of the yacht "signal" that has resulted in the present confusion because its similarity in appearance to the national ensign promptly led yachtsmen to fly the "signal" now known as the yacht ensign in place of the national ensign and the custom has grown until at present nearly all pleasure craft, from outboard speedsters up, are flying the "signal" as an ensign. The yacht ensign was created only as a signal for yachts enrolled and licensed (documented) and exempted them from entering and clearing at Custom-houses. Presumably it was to be flown in addition to the national ensign on documented yachts. To fly it from a club mast ashore signifies nothing.

Under present law it is the general rule that "the ownership of a vessel determines its national character." Several cases bear upon this and explain also how else a vessel's nationality may be proved.

In one called the Merritt (17 Wall 582, 21 L.Ed. 682) Mr. Justice Hunt, writing for the U.S. Supreme Court in October 1873, observed that "The documents a vessel carries furnish the only evidence of her nationality."

In the 1880's, U.S. v. Seagrist (27 F. Cas. No. 16,245) held that the register of a vessel, while proper evidence of nationality, is not indispensable, and the flag and ownership of the vessel may be proved by *any* competent evidence.

In 1894 in St. Clair v. United States (154 U.S. 134) the Supreme Court ruled not only that the "certificate of the vessel's registry, and its carrying the American flag, was admissible in evidence," but that "such evidence made, at least, a *prima facie* case . . . of the nationality of the vessel. . . ." This means that such evidence is sufficient to prove the points for which it is introduced unless it is contradicted by other evidence.

Conclusion: Generally the nationality of a vessel is determined by the nationality of her owner. Her papers or her flag may indicate otherwise, however, but neither is conclusive on the issue. Both elements are entitled to prima facie weight—that is, they will stand unless overcome by other evidence. Obviously there are no exclusive ways

Never fly the American flag from the masthead of a mast equipped with a gaff, as illustrated here. Just as on a ship, the gaff, even though lower in height, is the place of honor.

to prove this matter in a court of law; all material and relevant evidence on the issue will be allowed.

## DRESSING SHIP

On national holidays, at regattas, and on other special occasions, yachts often dress ship with International Code signal flags. Flag officers' flags, club burgees, and national flags are not used. The ship is dressed at 8:00 A.M. and remains so dressed from morning to evening colors. (While at anchor only.) See fig. 2211, page 461.

In dressing ship, the yacht ensign is hoisted at the peak or staff aft, and the jack at the jackstaff. Then a rainbow of flags of the International Code is arranged, reaching from the waterline forward to the waterline aft, by way of the bowsprit end to the foretop masthead, then across to the main topmast, and down to the main boom end, allowing several flags to touch the water line from both the bowsprit end and the main boom end. To keep the flags in position, a weight should be attached to the end of each line. Where there is no bowsprit, flags will start at the stemhead. Flags and pennants should be bent on alternately, rather than in any indiscriminate manner. Since there are twice as many letter flags as numeral pennants, it is good practice, as in the Navy, to follow a sequence of two flags, one pennant, etc., etc., throughout. In order to effect a degree of uniformity in yacht procedure, the following arrangement has been proposed:

Starting from forward, AB2, UJ1, KE3, GH6, IV5, FL4, DM7, PO Third Repeater, RN First Repeater, STo (zero), CX9, WQ8, ZY Second Repeater.

The arrangement here proposed is designed to effect a harmonious color pattern throughout.

467

# The Evolution of the United States Flag

**GRAND UNION:**
Before the American Revolution, the Colonies used a flag with a British ensign as the canton, plus 13 alternate red and white stripes signifying the original Colonies.

**GADSDEN FLAG:**
Even before 1776, there were those who resented anything in our flag resembling the British ensign. The Gadsden flag was developed about this time with a coiled rattlesnake on a yellow field with the words "Don't Tread On Me." Other flags used by some of the Colonies carried such slogans as "Liberty or Death."

**BUNKER HILL FLAG:**
In the New England area, the pine tree of Maine was the popular flag emblem. This appeared on the banner hoisted by the Colonies at Bunker Hill. It showed a red background with the pine tree in the canton. Another was the British blue ensign with a pine tree in the canton.

**FIRST "STARS AND STRIPES":**
Congress passed the first flag resolution on June 14 (now flag day), 1777. The battle of Bennington in August of the same year is believed to mark the first display of Old Glory with 13 stars and 13 stripes, with 11 stars arranged in a semi-circle and one in each corner. The 76 denotes the year of Independence.

**COWPENS FLAG:**
This flag, consisting of 12 white stars in a circle with one in the center, with 13 alternate red and white stripes, was first carried in the battle of Cowpens, January 1781.

**BETSY ROSS FLAG:**
The legend has it that Betsy Ross of Philadelphia was asked in 1776 to design a national flag suggested by General Washington. She is credited with making the stars 5-pointed and arranging them in a circle on the national flag.

**FLAG OF 1795:**
This flag had 15 stripes and 15 stars indicating the 15 States at that time. Five new stars were added during the five years this flag flew, but no additional stripes. This flag is credited with being the first official flag to fly over the Capitol in Washington.

**FLAG OF THE CONFEDERACY:**
Of the four Confederate flags, the one shown was most popular and best known; it consisted of a blue cross arranged diagonally across a red field. On the cross were 13 stars.

**FLAG OF 1912:**
Two stars were added to the flag when this design became offical, representing the new States of Arizona and New Mexico. The stars were arranged in six rows of 8 stars each and remained unchanged for 47 years.

**OLD GLORY OF TODAY:**
With the admission of the 49th and 50th States, Alaska and Hawaii, 2 more stars were added to the flag, making a total of 50, arranged in 5 rows of 6 stars each and 4 rows of 5 stars each. The flag became official on July 4, 1960.

**The United States ensign proudly flies from the tallest single-masted, unguyed flagpole in the world (172 ft.) at the United States Merchant Marine Academy, Kings Point, N. Y.**

# Suggested Flag Ceremonies and Etiquette at Yacht Club and Squadron Meetings

## FLAG CEREMONIES AT SQUADRON MEETINGS

It is better to place the flags with ceremony than to consider them merely a part of the decorations and equipment.

The route of march in advancing the colors will depend upon the size and layout of the meeting place, width of aisles, etc. In the following it is assumed that the flag of the United States and the USPS flag are to used, mounted on staffs, and with stands properly located in advance.

In small or congested rooms the following is recommended.

The bearer of the flag of the United States stands at the right side of the room, as viewed by the audience, with the bearer of the USPS flag on the opposite side of the room, in the open space between the first rows of chairs and the speaker's platform. If there is no raised platform for the head table or speaker, the bearers of the U.S. and USPS flags take positions opposite from the positions indicated (see paragraph 4 Display of Flags at Squadron Meetings).

The Commander raps his gavel for order, and as soon as obtained announces "We will now have the presentation of the colors. All please rise and stand at attention."

As soon as this is accomplished the Commander orders, "Color Guard—Present the colors." The Color Guard, on the order, marches in opposite directions across the room in front of the speaker's platform. At the center point and just before passing, each comes to a distinct stop facing each other. The bearer of the USPS flag dips his flag slightly and as soon as his flag is back up in carrying position both bearers continue their march and place the flags in their respective stands.

As soon as each flag is placed both bearers step back and come to the position of breast salute, facing the flag of the United States.

Referring back in the above, as soon as the bearers start their march across the room, the Commander orders all present "Breast Salute."

As soon as the bearers have come to the position of breast salute as above, the Commander orders "Two." (Second count of the salute routine.) On this order all present return to the position of attention and the color bearers retire.

The Commander then raps his gavel and orders all present "Be seated" or calls for the Invocation, after which he seats the audience.

If a larger hall is used or more formal ceremonies are desired, the flags may be marched up the center aisle or right aisle. If in single file, with the United States flag in the lead, if abreast with the U.S. flag on the right of marchers.

If marching up the center aisle, at the point where the cleared space between the front seats and the table is reached, the bearer of the USPS flag stops momentarily and allows the bearer of the U.S. flag to cross in front of him. The flag dip is used only when the flags meet from opposite directions as in the first method above.

The Commander follows the same sequence of orders as for the first method above.

## COLOR RETIRING CEREMONIES

Color retiring ceremonies may properly and easily be followed at all formal business meetings, where there is a definite moment of official closing. It is not recommended at social gatherings.

Color retiring ceremonies are as follows:

Just before declaring the meeting adjourned the Commander gives the order "Color Guard, stand by to retire the colors." On receiving this order, the Color Guard advances and stands directly in front of their respective colors. When both are in position the Commander orders "Attention" and all present rise and stand at attention. When this is accomplished the Commander orders "Color Guard, secure the colors."

Each color bearer at this command removes his flag from the stand and together do an about-face to face the audience, and then hoist the flags to carry position.

As soon as this is accomplished the Commander orders "Breast salute" and all present except the color bearers comply. As soon as the position of breast salute is accomplished, the color bearers step off together to retrace their presentation march. If the first method described for presenting colors is used, the dipping ceremony is repeated just before they cross in the center of the room. In this method, as soon as the colors reach the side of the room, or if the aisle method is used, as soon as the colors pass from sight or reach the back of the room, the Commander orders "Two" and all present return to the position of attention.

The Commander may now order the meeting adjourned, or may seat the audience first if there are to be informal activities following.

On a shore mast equipped with gaff, at yacht clubs and similar marine installations such as marinas, USPS and USCG Auxiliary shore headquarters, etc., the U.S. Ensign should be flown from the gaff, the position of honor. The illustration above, made from a poster issued by the U.S. Government, shows Old Glory flying from the gaff. Even though there may be positions at a greater height above the ground, yet the flying of the ensign from the gaff is not a violation of the statutes that "no flag should be displayed 'above' the U.S. Ensign."

# CODE OF FLAG ETIQUETTE FOR U.S. BOATS IN FOREIGN WATERS

## Motor Boats*

MASTLESS VESSELS (with bow and stern staffs)

Foreign national flag at bow staff.

Own ensign at stern staff.

ONE-MAST MOTOR VESSELS (with yard-arm)

Foreign national flag at bow staff.

Own ensign at stern staff.

Club flag at starboard yard-arm.

Private signal or flag officer's flag at masthead.

TWO-MAST MOTOR VESSELS

Underway:—

Club pennant at bow staff.

Foreign national flag at fore-truck.

Private or flag officer's flag at main-truck.

Own ensign at stern staff.

At anchor or dock:—

The practice outlined above for two-mast motor vessels under way is also correct when at anchor, or at a dock.

## Sailing Vessels

SLOOPS AND CUTTERS

Own ensign at peak when under sail and at stern staff when at anchor or under power.

Club signal at masthead when at anchor.

Private signal at masthead when underway.

Flag officer's flag in place of club flag or private signal.

Foreign flag on forestay at anchor, and forestay or forward starboard shroud one-third mast height when underway.

YAWLS AND KETCHES

Own ensign at mizzen peak when under sail and at stern staff when at anchor or under power.

Club pennant at main-truck.

Private signal at mizzen-truck.

Flag officer's flag in place of private signal.

Foreign flag on forestay at anchor, and forestay or forward starboard shroud one-third mast height when underway.

## SCHOONERS OF TWO OR MORE MASTS

Own ensign at after peak when under sail and at stern staff when at anchor or under power.

Club signal at fore-truck at anchor.

Private signal at main-truck.

Flag officer's flag at main-truck in place of private signal.

Foreign flag at bow staff or forestay at anchor, and fore-truck or forward starboard shroud while underway.

## All Vessels

Hoist your own ensign first and lower last if you are shorthanded.

Show your own colors if entering or leaving port before 8:00 A.M. or after sunset, but do not pay honors except from 8:00 A.M. to sunset.

---

* NOTE: Motor boats with a gaff should fly their own ensign at gaff while underway, but at stern staff while at anchor or tied to a dock.

---

## DISPLAY OF FLAGS AT YACHT CLUB AND SQUADRON MEETINGS

1. The flag of the United States should be displayed either from a staff, or flat against the wall above and behind the speaker's table.

2. The flag of the United States should never be draped or laid over anything except a casket, at which time special rules apply.

3. When displayed flat against a wall it should be fastened along the upper edge only, with the union to the flag's right, to the left as viewed by the audience. This applies whether the flag is hung with stripes vertical or horizontal. The horizontal position of the stripes is preferable.

4.* When displayed on a staff indoors, in an enclosure where there is no platform at the head of the room, the U.S. ensign is stood at the right of the audience; but if there is a platform, the U.S. ensign is displayed on a staff at the left of the audience, namely, at the right of the speaker. The USPS ensign, if also displayed, is stood at the left of the audience where there is no platform, and at the right of the audience (left of the speaker) if there is a platform. If the Canadian ensign is also to be so displayed, it should be at the right of the audience where there is no platform, and at the right of the speaker where there is a platform but just inboard of the U.S. ensign.

5. If the flag of the United States, and another, are displayed with crossed staffs, as at the head of a room, the flag of the United States should be at the flag's right, to left as viewed by the audience, and with its staff in front of the other.

6. If the flag of the United States is displayed with other flags in a group, from staffs, it should be in the center and slightly higher or in front of the other flags.

7. If the USPS flag is to be displayed flat against a wall, it is hung as prescribed for the Flag of the United States, as in paragraph 3 above, but on the opposite wall.

* See USPS Officers Manual.

## DISPLAY OF STATE FLAGS

Any citizen of any state, according to P/C William B. Matthews Jr., Boating Administrator for the State of Maryland, may fly the flag of that state unless it is specifically prohibited by law. On a *vessel with one or more masts,* the State flag is flown at the main truck in place of the private signal, officer's flag or Coast Guard Auxiliary ensign. On a *mastless boat,* the State flag would be flown at the bow staff in place of a club burgee. It should be understood that, when a State flag displaces a Coast Guard Auxiliary ensign at the truck, an Auxiliary officer cannot fly his officer's pennant from the starboard yardarm. When the State flag at the truck displaces the flag of an officer of a yacht club or the USPS, he cannot fly his officer's flag at any hoist.

# Honoring Other National Flags_____

Just as a certain code of etiquette has been adopted to govern the display of flags by American yachts on the waterways of our own nation, so too there is a certain accepted procedure to which pleasure boats should properly adhere when they cross international boundaries into the waters of another nation.

There are only a limited number of positions from which flags may be properly displayed on motor boats and consequently when a foreign flag is to be flown, it must displace one of the flags commonly flown in home waters.

The United States Power Squadrons has adopted a code of flag etiquette which might well be followed by all American pleasure craft cruising in foreign waters.

## MOTOR BOATS

For the purposes of this flag code, motor boats may be divided into three general groups: (1) mastless vessels, having bow and stern staffs only; (2) single-masted motor vessels, with yardarm; and (3) vessels with two masts.

**Mastless vessels.** A motor boat having only bow and stern staffs, if in home waters, would fly the yacht club burgee forward and her own ensign aft. In foreign waters, she must obviously keep her own ensign at the place of honor aft. Therefore she has no alternative but to display the national flag of the foreign country which she is visiting at the bow staff in place of her own club burgee. Under no circumstances should she try to fly both flags from one staff at the same time. That principle holds consistently true throughout all flag etiquette.

**Motor vessels with one mast.** Considering next the motor vessel with one mast and yardarm—possibly the most common of all arrangements aboard cruising motor boats—her own ensign remains at the stern staff and her private signal or officer's flag at the masthead. Her club flag, flown at the bow staff in home waters, is now displayed at the starboard yardarm, giving way to the foreign national flag, which is properly displayed at the bow staff.

**Motor vessels with two masts.** Some of the larger motor craft have two masts. Assuming that the mainmast has no gaff, then the practice is as follows. Her own ensign is at the stern staff as usual, and her private signal or officer's flag stays at the main truck. The club pennant goes to the bow staff, making way for the foreign national flag at the fore truck. This is correct practice whether the vessel is under way or lying at anchor, or at a dock.

The only variation of this procedure for two-masted vessels is found when the mainmast is equipped with a gaff. In such cases, the gaff takes precedence over the stern staff as the position of honor when the vessel is under way. Therefore the vessel's own ensign flies at the gaff instead of the stern staff when under way. However, when she comes to anchor or ties up to a dock, then the ensign should appear at the stern staff just as it would in vessels without a gaff both at anchor and under way.

NOTE:—National flags should never be flown at a yard arm for any reason. Correct method of flying a foreign flag (illustrated in this article) applies only when waters of that nation are entered.

Ashore, it is common practice among U. S. yacht clubs on the border to fly the Canadian flag at the masthead, with the U.S. flag at the gaff, when they have Canadian entries in races or Canadian flag officers officially in the club house.

## SAILING VESSELS

Sailing vessels can also be divided into general classifications, insofar as the display of flags is concerned. This classification is based on the arrangement of their masts, and is as follows: (1) sloops and cutters; (2) yawls and ketches; and (3) schooners, whether they have two masts or more.

**Sloops and cutters** have only one mast, the basic distinction being that the cutter's mast is further aft. Sailing vessels of this type show their own ensign at the peak when under sail, but at the stern staff when at anchor or under power. Most sailboats today have the jib-headed (Marconi) rig. Since such a rig has no gaff, the ensign is flown from the leech of the sail in a position which would correspond with the peak if there were a gaff.

Sloops and cutters fly the club signal when at anchor only, from the masthead. When under way, the private signal takes the place of the club pennant at the masthead. In the event that the owner is a club officer, then his officer's flag is flown instead of the club flag at anchor or the private signal when under way. All of this practice is identical whether the vessel is in home waters or abroad.

There is no need to displace any of these flags when going abroad. In foreign waters, the sloop or cutter flies the foreign ensign from her forestay when at anchor, and from the forestay or from the forward starboard shroud (one-third mast height) when under way.

**Yawls and ketches** have two masts, the larger of which is forward. Their ensign flies at the mizzen peak when under sail, at the stern staff when at anchor or running under power without sails. The club pennant is at the main truck, private signal at the mizzen truck. If the owner is a flag officer of a club, the officer's flag flies at the mizzen truck in place of the private signal. Again, this part of flag practice is identical for home or foreign waters.

To take care of the foreign flag, yawls and ketches, like sloops and cutters, fly it on the forestay when at anchor, and on the forestay or forward starboard shroud (one-third mast height) when under way.

**Schooners.** The third category of sailing vessels embraces schooners, having two masts or more. Perhaps the best way to show the distinction between the practice in home and foreign waters for them is to outline first the procedure in home waters and then point out the differences in practice when abroad.

At home, the schooner has her own ensign at the after peak when under sail, but at the stern staff when at anchor or under power, without sails set. The club signal is at the fore truck, private signal at the main truck. The flag officer's flag would be flown in place of the private signal at the main truck.

Now, when the schooner is in foreign waters, the practice is the same except that the club signal is flown at the fore truck when at anchor only, (not when under way.) Also, when at anchor, the foreign flag is flown at the bow staff or forestay, but when under way the foreign flag should be at the fore truck or the forward starboard shroud.

See page 470 for tabulation of USPS code of flag etiquete for boats in foreign waters, and page ix(e) for complete flag code adopted by the USPS.

SLOOPS AND CUTTERS — UNDER WAY — AT ANCHOR

YAWLS AND KETCHES — AT ANCHOR — UNDER WAY

THREE-MASTED SCHOONERS — UNDER WAY — AT ANCHOR

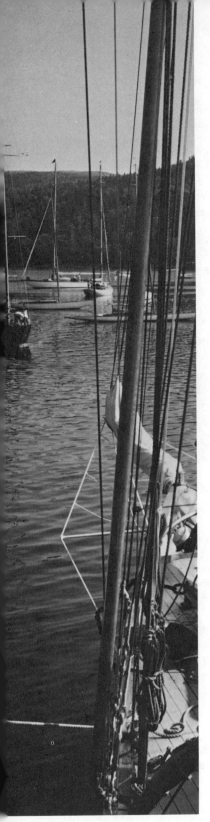

Many boatmen spend their time afloat with little or no thought to the customs and etiquette of yachting. This is regrettable, for their activities can be more enjoyable both to themselves and to others with some knowledge and practice of doing things "the proper way."

A *custom* is defined in one dictionary as "the habitual practice; the usual way of doing a thing in given circumstances." Such long-standing practices and procedures have usually developed out of trial and error over many years into the "best," or "safest," or "most appropriate" method. By adhering to yachting customs, a boatman is benefiting from long years of others' experience — to defy custom is really to miss a fine opportunity. A love of boats and the water should be accompanied by respect for the traditions and long-established customs of the sea.

*Etiquette* has been described as "a prescribed or accepted code of usage as established for any occasion." Since recreational boating is a purely voluntary activity, let us drop the "prescribed" aspect of that description and emphasize the "accepted" qualities of the usages. If etiquette were regarded as no more than blind adherence to certain set conventionalities and amenities of social life, there might be sound reasons why one could question the need for, or desirability of, conforming to relatively rigid rules of conduct.

Just as soon, however, as one realizes that these principles of etiquette are not mere arbitrary laws demanding conformity on the part of all individuals—that they are basically the natural expressions of those who instinctively conduct themselves in a sincerely considerate manner toward all others, regardless of rank or race—it becomes quite obvious why anyone should seek to follow the practices that distinguish the true gentleman and yachtsman.

# YACHTING CUSTOMS and ETIQUETTE

## CHAPTER 23

## Customs in general

In the varied relationships of people in many walks of life, a natural body of customs and accepted procedures inevitably develops to govern such relationships. Nowhere is this better exemplified than in the various branches of government service. In the departments that are concerned with diplomacy and statesmanship, observance of the correct form is inextricably woven into the act itself. In the military services, it is safe to say that efficient functioning could not be achieved without the many established customs and procedures.

## Customs in Boating

The direct application of all naval customs and forms of etiquette to boating activities would be quite inappropriate and quickly rejected by most boatmen. There are, however, many customs and items of service etiquette that can be used as-is or modified for the circumstances of non-military small craft. Other boating customs derive directly from the ways of the sea and seafaring men.

## The Skipper

By custom and by law, the skipper of a craft has the sole ultimate responsibility and authority aboard, especially in emergencies. These are spelled out in some detail in Chapter 7; here it is enough to note that these duties and powers have developed over the years, first as desirable and necessary practices, then as customs, and finally, in many cases, into legal requirements.

## Leadership

Even on non-military and non-commercial small craft leadership is an important requirement. Getting things done by a willing and happy crew is a large step forward in putting the "pleasure" into pleasure boating. Proper attention to customs and etiquette provides a basis for effective leadership.

Leadership is said to be largely a matter of intelligent and just administration of authority. Knowledge along technical lines and of practical matters does not automatically provide the capability for leadership. This involves a study and cultivation of such qualities as self-control, judgment, courage, earnestness, sympathy, and loyalty, to name just a few of the many necessary attributes. One of the best methods of acquiring these qualities is to consciously take stock of one's own shortcomings with a view toward eliminating deficiencies and developing the desired characteristics—do this rather than demand in one's crew a degree of perfection that one has not himself attained.

## Discipline

Leadership and discipline, including self-discipline, are logically considered in conjunction with each other—they are inseparable. Given a group of individuals in which all have the qualities of leadership developed to a greater or lesser degree, discipline will give each person an appreciation of the authority and responsibilities of their appointed or elected leader. Consequently, they will each work at assigned tasks in mutual cooperation, and will not waste time or mental effort in envy of their superior's position. The leader, in turn, will have the ability to inspire his subordinates to self-development and the voluntary

acceptance of higher responsibilities. It is an error for any leader to believe that he can grow no more; the effective leader grows as well as the men he leads.

It should be quickly apparent that the principles above have great applicability to the world of boating. The yacht club, Power Squadron, or unit of the Coast Guard Auxiliary that reflects an understanding of these ideas will flourish. Of all places, there is none where the demand for capable leadership and discipline is more vital than aboard a vessel, whether it be a large yacht, an ocean-racing sailboat, or a motorboat of any size. The skipper has, and must have, the final authority; he must be equal to that responsibility. If he is worthy of his trust as a "leader," he will get the cooperation of his crew by "leading" and not by driving.

## PERSONAL SALUTES

Hand salutes are not often given by civilian boatmen, although they may be used in some formal ceremonies. In a way, this lack of personal saluting is unfortunate, for what better way is there to say "thank you" to a cooperative bridge tender or to the skipper of a boat that slowed down in passing you than to give him a snappy—but not exaggerated—hand salute. Its meaning will never be misunderstood and it will often be much appreciated. It is more of a show of appreciation than merely a wave of the hand in greeting.

## Origins

The practice of hand salutes is believed to have had its origins at least as far back as the days of the Romans, when the raising of one's hand, palm forward, was a gesture to show that no dagger was concealed in it. The native American Indians used much the same gesture to indicate a lack of harmful intent. Today, happily, we have other motives when showing respect for superiors.

Uncovering the head also dates back to ancient days. Certain types of headgear, however, were not easily removed, and so the present day salute evolved as a gesture in which the hand is raised to the visor of the cap in much the same manner as if the visor of a helmet were going to be lifted.

## Exchanging salutes

Etiquette prescribes that in ceremonies a person junior in rank or seniority should salute first. It is emphasized that this deference to superiors does not imply an admission of inferiority, no more than one could logically be accused of cowardice when displaying a wholesome respect for laws. Those who might take the attitude that a salute is undemocratic should recognize that such an act is merely an extension of the courtesies of everyday life. The salute, thus understood, becomes an opportunity to respect the authority an official represents with no thought of personal inferiority.

## BOARDING AND LEAVING GOVERNMENT SHIPS

It is not inappropriate for a civilian boatman in an organizational uniform, or even in informal clothing but wearing a uniform or visored cap, to observe the proper naval etiquette when boarding and leaving a ship of the Navy, Coast Guard, Coast & Geodetic Survey, or other gov-

**FIG. 2301  By law as well as long-established custom, the skipper of a boat has the sole ultimate responsibility and authority for the actions of the craft and the safety of all those aboard.**

FIG. 2302 Of all places, there is none where the demand for capable leadership and discipline is more vital than aboard an ocean-racing sailboat. The skipper must have final authority.

ernmental agency. He can be assured that his actions will be promptly and properly responded to by the personnel of the watch.

## Procedures

When reaching the upper platform of the gangway or accommodation ladder, the person about to board, and before stepping aboard, should stop, then turn toward the stern of the vessel and salute the national ensign. He then turns back to the Officer of the Deck (O.O.D.), salutes, and says: "Request permission to come aboard, sir." The O.O.D. returns both salutes as they are given and with the second one says "Permission granted."

When leaving the vessel, the individual first salutes the Officer of the Deck and says: Request permission to leave ship, sir." The O.O.D. returns the salute and grants permission. At the top of the gangway or other platform, the departing person stops, faces aft, and salutes the U.S. Flag; the O.O.D. returns this salute also, but says nothing.

If the individual is *not* wearing a cap, the *salutes* are *omitted,* but the request for permission to board or depart is made as noted above.

### DAILY COLOR CEREMONIES

If a boatman is at a yacht club, or a military or naval base, where formal morning and evening color ceremonies are held, he should follow the actions of local personnel who are not in formation. If he is outdoors when the flag is raised or lowered, and he is wearing a uniform or visored cap, he should face the flag and give a hand salute, holding it until the ceremony is completed. If he is wearing a civilian hat, this should be removed and held over the left breast. If no headgear is worn, the right hand should be placed over the left breast. This is the "breast salute." Women not in uniform stand at attention and give the

breast salute. Automobiles are stopped and personnel remain inside.

The above rules do not, of course, apply if the boatman is engaged in hoisting or lowering his own colors. He should complete his actions and then, if the official ceremonies have not ended, he should stand at attention, and salute if appropriate.

On official occasions, the same salutes as above are given for the playing of the Star Spangled Banner or national anthem of another country.

## Yachting Etiquette

Etiquette in yachting takes many forms, but all are essentially the act of showing consideration and courtesy to others. The range of correct etiquette extends from simple everyday actions to formal daily routines and official ceremonies.

### Boarding another boat

The etiquette to be observed when coming on board another person's boat is derived from that explained above for boarding a naval vessel. Salutes are seldom exchanged, but a simple request for permission to come aboard is always in good taste. An occasion for saluting might be if the individual boarding were wearing a uniform cap and the craft were that of the commodore of the yacht club or the commander of a Power Squadron.

When leaving another's boat, the naval form of requesting permission is not used. A simple statement of thanks for the hospitality or best wishes for a pleasant cruise is sufficient.

### SALUTES BETWEEN VESSELS

In formal ceremonies such as a rendezvous of a yacht club or Power Squadron, the fleet of boats present may pass in review before the flagship of the commodore or USPS commander. In such cases, each craft will salute as it passes. In other isolated instances, joining a club cruise or passing a ship with a high public official embarked, salutes may be exchanged between vessels.

### Dipping the ensign in salute

Federal law prohibits dipping the Flag of the United States (the 50-star flag) to any person or thing, and only government vessels are permitted to dip the national ensign in reply to a dip.

The law does, however, permit organizational or institutional flags to be dipped. Thus the U.S. Power Squadrons Ensign, when flown from stern or gaff, may be dipped to salute another craft, or dipped in reply to a dip.

The status of the Yacht Ensign (13 stars in a circle around an anchor on a blue field) is not spelled out clearly, but since the law specifically covers only the Flag of the United States, the assumption has been made that the Yacht Ensign may be dipped.

In a fleet review of a unit of the Power Squadrons, the USPS Ensign should be flown from the stern staff or gaff if a suitable size flag is available. In this way, the flag dipped would be that of the organization holding the review.

All vessels in any review, flying either the USPS or Yacht Ensign at the stern or gaff, should dip that flag when their

FIG. 2303 "Dressing ship" is an old custom applicable to yachts as well as to naval and merchant vessels. This is done only on special occasions and the proper procedures must be followed to be correct.

## YACHT ROUTINES

The following regulations, particularly applicable to a consideration of yachting etiquette, are taken from that portion of the New York Yacht Club code entitled *Yacht Routine*. These deal with salutes, boats (meaning tenders and dinghies), and general courtesies. Other sections, not given here, relate primarily to the display of flags, signaling, and lights.

The routines of other yacht clubs may be considerably less formal and detailed than that which follows, but whatever routines are used they are likely to have been derived from the procedures of the New York Yacht Club.

### Salutes

All salutes shall be made by dipping the ensign once, lowering the ensign to the dip and hoisting it when the salute is returned. All salutes shall be returned.

Whistles shall never be used in saluting.

Guns may be used to call attention to signals, but their use otherwise shall be avoided as much as possible.

Vessels of the United States and foreign navies shall be saluted.

When a flag officer of the Club comes to anchor, he shall be saluted by all yachts present, except where there is a senior flag officer present.

When a yacht comes to anchor where a flag officer is present, such officer shall be saluted. A junior flag officer anchoring in the presence of a senior shall salute.

Yachts passing shall salute, the junior saluting first.

All salutes shall be answered in kind.

A yacht acting as Race Committee boat should neither salute nor be saluted while displaying the Committee flag.

### Boats

Upon entering and leaving boats, deference is shown seniors by juniors entering first and leaving last.

When in boats, flag officers display their flags, captains (owners) their private signals, and members (non-owners) the club burgee. When on duty, the fleet captain and race committee display their distinctive flags. The flag of the senior officer embarked takes precedence. A flag officer embarked in a boat not displaying his distinctive flag should be considered as present in an unofficial capacity.

When two boats are approaching the same gangway or landing stage, flag officers shall have the right of way in order of seniority.

Whenever possible, boat booms shall be rigged in at night. Otherwise, a white light shall be shown at the end. All boats made fast to the stern of a yacht at anchor shall show a white light at night.

### Courtesies

When a flag officer makes an official visit, his flag, if senior to that of the yacht visited, shall be displayed in place of the burgee while he is on board.

A yacht may display the personal flag of a national, state, or local official when such individual is on board, or the national ensign of a distinguished foreign visitor. This flag should be displayed in place of the private signal or officer's flag for the President of the United States, and in place of the burgee for all other officials and visitors.

On Independence Day, and when ordered on other occasions, a yacht shall, when at anchor and the weather

bow comes abreast of the stern of the flagship and return it to full height when their stern clears the bow of the flagship.

On this occasion, the Flag of the United States should *not* be flown, but if it is, *do not dip it* and use only the hand salute described below. Do not dip any flag other than the flag being flown at the stern staff or the gaff (including the equivalent position on a Marconi sail).

### Hand saluting

When a vessel is officially reviewing a parade of other vessels, the senior officer present stands on the deck of the reviewing ship with his staff in formation behind him. Only he gives the hand salute in return to salutes rendered him.

On a boat passing in review, if the skipper has his crew and guests in formation behind him, only he gives the hand salute. If the crew and guests are in uniform and standing at attention at the rail facing the reviewing boat as they pass, they all give the hand salute. The criterion is whether or not the other persons aboard are in formation. If in formation, only the skipper salutes; but if not in formation, all salute.

For both situations, the hand salute is given as the flag is dipped and is held until it is raised again.

### Gun salutes

Guns should not be used in salutes between yachts unless ordered by a national authority or by the senior officer present.

FIG. 2304 Cruising will usually take a boatman well away from familiar home waters. He should be alert to the peculiarities of local customs and should conform to the way in which things are done at the club or harbor he is visiting.

permits, *dress ship* from morning to evening colors. See pages 461 and 467.

After joining the Squadron during the Annual Cruise, a yacht shall request permission before leaving.

# Cruising

When cruising away from home waters, the wise skipper keeps a sharp eye out for local customs. It is a mark of courtesy to conform to local procedures and practices.

While visiting at a yacht club of which you are not a member, observe the actions and routines of the local owner-members, and particularly the club officers. This is especially important with respect to evening colors. Not all clubs strictly calculate the daily time of sunset, and some may be earlier than you would normally expect.

If you will be off your boat at the time of evening colors —in the clubhouse for dinner, for example—be sure to take down your flags before you leave your craft.

### Be a good neighbor

Consideration of the other skipper is an important element of yachting etiquette. Don't anchor too close to another boat so as to give cause for concern for the safety of both craft; consider the state of the tide and the effect of its range on the radius about which you will swing. Use a guest mooring only with permission; tie up to a fuel pier only briefly.

In the evening hours at an anchorage, don't disturb your neighbors on other boats. Sound travels exceptionally well across water and many cruising boatmen turn in early for dawn departures. Keep voices down and play radios only at low levels. If you should be one of the early departees, leave with an absolute minimum of noise.

Be a good neighbor in other ways, too. Don't throw trash and garbage overboard. Secure flapping halyards; they can be a most annoying source of noise for some distance. When coming into or leaving an anchorage area, do so at a dead slow speed to keep your wake and wash at an absolute minimum.

### Passing other boats

A faster boat overtaking and passing a slower one in a narrow channel should slow down *sufficiently* to cause no damage or discomfort. Often overlooked is the fact that it may be necessary for the *slower* boat itself to reduce speed. If that boat is making, say, 8 knots, the faster boat can only slow down to about 10 knots in order to have enough speed differential left to get past. At this speed, the passing boat may unavoidably make a wake that is uncomfortable to the other craft. In such cases, the overtaken boat should slow to 4 or 5 knots to allow herself to be passed at 6 or 7 knots with little wake.

If adequate depths of water extend outward on one or both sides of the course, it is the courteous thing for the passing boat to swing well out to a safe side to minimize the discomfort of the overtaken boat.

Proper etiquette calls for power boats to pass sailing craft astern or well to leeward.

## GUESTS ABOARD

If you are invited to go cruising for a day, a weekend, or a more extended period, there are many things to be considered—clothes, promptness, gifts, aids, noise, smoking, privacy, and time.

FIG. 2305 Whenever circumstances such as the depth of water permit, power boats should observe the proper etiquette of passing sailboats on their lee side or crossing under their stern. Consideration of the other skipper is a mark of a good yachtsman. The wake must always be kept down to a reasonable level.

Take a minimum of *clothes*, packed in collapsible containers, or at least in suitcases that will nest inside each other when empty—storage space is severely limited aboard boats. Bring one outfit of "city clothes" for use at those places ashore requiring such dress. Bring two bathing suits if you plan to do much swimming—at times, things dry slowly around a boat. For additional comments on boating clothing and shoes, see Chapter 24.

For the *stowage of clothing* you bring aboard, the skipper may assign a special locker which he has cleared for your convenience. Don't scatter gear and clothing all over the boat. Use the locker provided, keep it orderly, and thus help the skipper keep things shipshape.

When a *sailing time* is given, be there ahead of time. The skipper generally chooses a time with a purpose in mind—the tides and currents, normal weather patterns, the length of the planned run, etc.

*Meal times* are set for the convenience of the galley hand. It is inconsiderate for a tardy guest to delay meals. In any event, it is bad manners to be late for a meal.

*Rising* and *bedtimes* are a matter of convenience to everyone aboard because of the generally limited washing and toilet facilities. Get up promptly when the skipper or paid hands are heard moving about. Use the head as expeditiously as possible, make up your bunk, stow any loose gear about the cabin, and appear on deck. When the skipper suggests that it is time to retire for the evening, take the hint and bed down.

*Noise* on a boat seems to amplify, so walk and speak softly and your shipmates will be glad you're aboard.

*Smoking* is stopped, of course, when gasoline is to be taken aboard, but care is the order of the day even when smoking is permissible. A carelessly flicked cigarette ash or butt has started many a fire in a chair, awning, or compartment. Cigars leave a particularly unpleasant after-odor and should be enjoyed only in the open air.

Many small particles—pipe tobacco and ashes, peanut shells, bits of potato chips, crumbs, etc.—have a way of getting into cracks, crevices and corners, and there defying the ordinary cleaning facilities found on a boat. Use care with all of these things.

*Privacy* becomes valuable on a protracted cruise. Part of every day should be set aside for getting away from everyone else aboard. Your cruisemates will be more glad of your company if it is not constant.

Should occasions arise where you board the boat from a *dinghy*, or have an opportunity to use the skipper's dinghy (with his permission, of course) use care in coming alongside. Unship oarlocks which could scar the boat's planking, and stow oars in the boat; never leave them in the oarlocks.

*Gifts* are certainly not expected, but are always acceptable. Be sure, however, that they are appropriate for boating—if in doubt, make it liquid and consumable. When invited on board for a day or a week, ask what you can bring. If the owner wants to provide all of the food and drink, the guest might take the cruising party ashore for a good dinner at the first port of call. Buying part of the fuel is looked upon as a partial charter by some government agencies, but bringing food or liquid refreshment is not so regarded.

*Assistance* on board a boat can be useful, or it can do more harm than good. If you don't know what to do, sit down out of the way and be quiet. Always keep out of the line of vision of the helmsman and be particularly quiet and unobtrusive when the craft is being docked or undocked.

If being on board is not a new experience, or you wish to learn to be more useful, you may ask what you can do to help. Ask, however, when things are calm and uneventful; don't ask in the midst of getting under way or coming alongside a pier.

Above all, if you are assigned to do something, do exactly that. If you think that the instructions were wrong, say so, but don't go off on your own when the skipper thinks that you are doing what he asked.

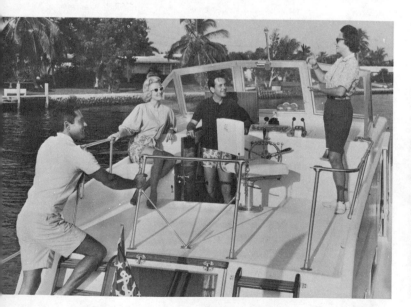

FIG. 2306  Having guests aboard for a day's cruise or longer period can add to a boat owner's enjoyment of his recreation by sharing his enjoyment with others. Guests can do their part by "fitting in" with the routine of the craft.

FIG. 2307  Guests aboard for a cruise may offer their assistance in the operation of the craft or in the daily chores. They should not, however, tackle work without the skipper's knowledge and should work under proper supervision.

# CHAPTER 24

# BOATING CLOTHING and UNIFORMS

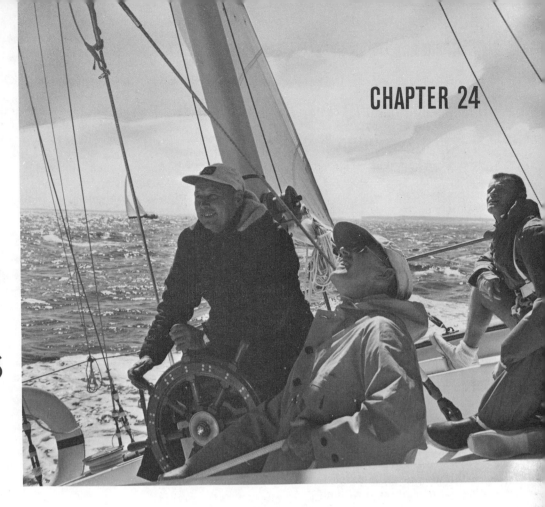

**FIG. 2401** Many boatmen find an informal visored cloth cap the most practical form of headgear afloat. It is comfortable, provides good shade for the eyes, and stays on well in a breeze. Club emblems, but no insignia of rank, may be worn on such caps.
(Photograph by Frank Rohr)

The subject of "clothing and uniforms" encompasses both the matter of wearing or not wearing a uniform and that of safe, sensible apparel for today's boating. In each of these areas rather strong differences of opinion will be found to exist.

When it comes to clothing, most boatmen have rather strong convictions as to whether or not they should, or must, abide by any arbitrary set of regulations. The spokesmen of one faction argue that they go afloat for pleasure and relaxation, and propose to dress as they please—for comfort and practicability. The other group advocates strict adherence to all the proprieties, frowning on those who do not conform to the dictates of etiquette, whether it be in dress, the display of flags, or other areas.

Who is right? Actually neither, in the sense that the other would be wrong. There is room for differences of opinion, and no logical reason why each group and individual should not be entitled to his own position and actions.

## Good taste

Few boatmen would deliberately violate the principles of good taste in regard to dress aboard their craft. In some cases, it is merely a matter of not realizing that such principles exist. Errors are often made in the use of various devices and insignia worn on uniforms, and in the choice of articles of uniforms themselves. Generally these practices would be corrected if the wearer knew that he was in error.

One thing is certain. The clothing that might be appropriate and acceptable in one situation may be decidedly in bad taste in another. It would be hard to say who would be more uncomfortable—the outboarder in shorts at a yacht club dinner party or the commodore in spotless whites tinkering with a balky engine under a blazing sun.

## Origins of present-day clothing

The clothing that is worn while boating today has developed over the years from the quite stiff and formal uniforms of the late 1800's and early years of this century. The steady trend toward smaller, owner-operated craft has taken its toll on the rigid customs of yachting circles—the "dressing for dinner" routine. The establishment of many small, much less formal yacht clubs and boating clubs has likewise supported the gradual change to a more informal mode of attire. A third factor is the general trend of modern life to an easier, more casual mood.

These developments all combine to make a full yachting uniform something of a rarity aboard present-day craft or at typical yacht clubs.

## Yacht Club Uniforms

Essentially all yacht clubs provide in their by-laws for uniforms and insignia of rank. In actual practice, however, there will be found a wide variance in the degree to which such apparel is worn. In a very few clubs, the officers, many members who are boat owners, and even some non-owner members have uniforms and will wear them on formal occasions. Hardly ever will full uniforms be worn while cruising or at every-day activities around the clubhouse. It should be noted, though, that members are not required to have uniforms; their purchase and use are purely optional.

### Uniforms in typical clubs

In most yacht and boating clubs, the officers will own uniforms, but few members will have them. Rare indeed in these clubs would be a uniform on a member who did not own a boat.

In the smaller and even less formal clubs, the uniforms of officers and members may be limited by general agreement and custom to the wearing of a uniform cap only, worn with any boating clothes of good taste. This is not "wrong" although it may be viewed with disfavor by older, more tradition-minded yachtsmen. It is well in tune with the informality of modern life and family-style boating, particularly outboarding.

### When uniforms are worn

Yacht and boating club uniforms are typically worn only on special occasions, although it is quite reasonable to wear a uniform cap with regular clothing while engaged in ordinary activities while afloat or at the club piers. Formal occasions for uniform wearing might include the ceremonies at the beginning of a new season, the installation of officers, holiday regattas, and the like. The best guidance at any club regarding the wearing or non-wearing of the full uniform or cap only is the policy adhered to by the majority of the officers and members.

On board and under way, the cap will probably be the only item of uniform worn on owner-operated boats. On larger craft where there are paid hands to take care of the operation of the yacht, a uniform for the owner would seem to be in far better taste, as well as more sensible, than on a small boat where the owner-captain must break out his own anchor, swab his own deck, and attend to numerous other chores both clean and dirty.

### Derivation of the uniform

On one point, at least, there can be little argument. For the occasions where a uniform is appropriate, it should certainly follow the style prescribed by yacht clubs as correct. For authority, no better source can be found than the code to which the New York Yacht Club has adhered for many years. While there may be minor deviations in the practices of other clubs, the N.Y.Y.C. rules are the basic form on which the others are patterned.

### Basic uniforms

The service dress uniform prescribed for yacht club officers and members is normally a double-breasted sack coat of navy blue or white cloth, serge or flannel, with trousers of the same material or of white drill. The cap is of navy blue cloth and has a patent leather visor, black chin strap, and black buttons. The white cap is of the same style with a fixed or removable cover. White shirts with black or dark ties are appropriate; some clubs have ties of their own design. White or black shoes are worn to match the trousers; boating shoes are not worn with a uniform except under limited circumstances afloat when advisable for safety.

### Cap emblems

There are a number of styles of yachting caps offered by the manufacturers of uniforms. In every case, an emblem or device will be found on the front of the band over the visor. This identifies the club to which the individual belongs and indicates his status in the club. See figures 2402(a), (b), (c), (d). The central part of the device will be an enameled metal or silk embroidered disc showing the distinctive emblem of the club, basically its burgee. This is placed at the intersection of two crossed fouled anchors in gold embroidery.

### Insignia of rank

If the yachtsman holds the office of commodore, there will be three gold stars around the anchors, one at the top and one at each side. See fig. 2402(a).

**COMMODORE** ★ ★ ★

Trefoil with 4 additional black stripes; 3 gold stars within loops.

**VICE COMMODORE** ★ ★

Trefoil with 3 additional black stripes; 2 gold stars within side loops.

**REAR COMMODORE** ★

Trefoil with 2 additional black stripes; 1 gold star in center loop.

FIG. 2402(a)   Yacht club officers are distinguished by insignia on sleeve and cap. Stars of current officers are gold, those of past officers, when used, are silver.
(All insignia illustrations courtesy Commodore Uniform Company, Inc.)

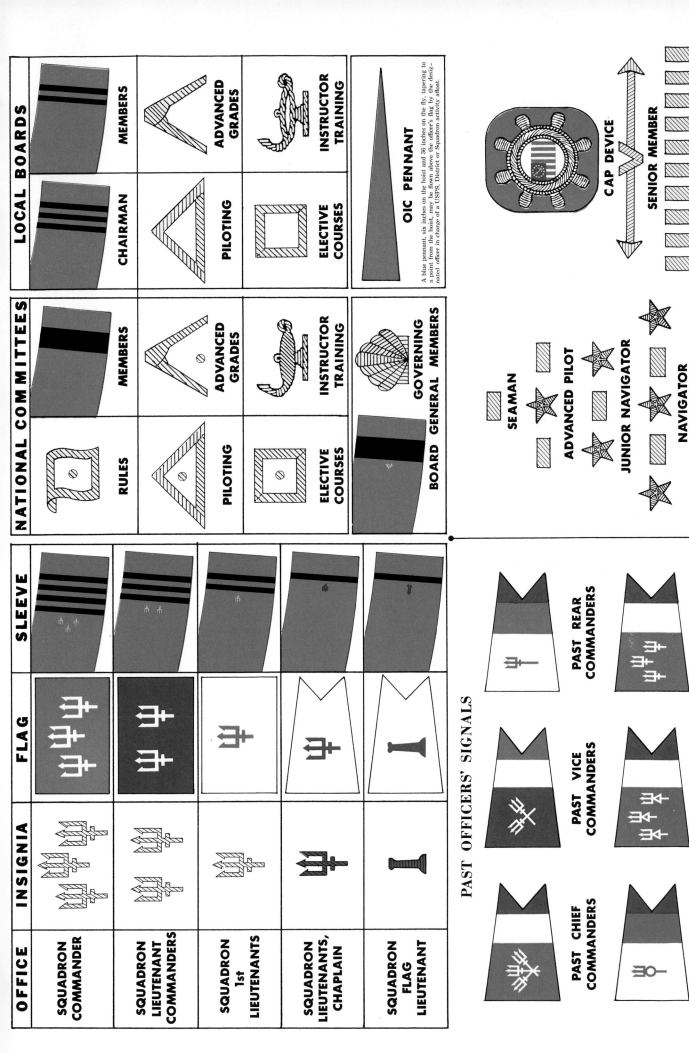

# LOCAL BOARDS

| | |
|---|---|
| CHAIRMAN | MEMBERS |
| PILOTING | ADVANCED GRADES |
| ELECTIVE COURSES | INSTRUCTOR TRAINING |

**OIC PENNANT**

A blue pennant, six inches on the hoist and 36 inches on the fly, tapering to a point from the hoist, may be flown above the officer's flag by the designated officer in charge of a USPS, District or Squadron activity afloat.

# NATIONAL COMMITTEES

| | |
|---|---|
| RULES | MEMBERS |
| PILOTING | ADVANCED GRADES |
| ELECTIVE COURSES | INSTRUCTOR TRAINING |
| GOVERNING BOARD GENERAL MEMBERS | |

CAP DEVICE

SENIOR MEMBER

MERIT MARKS
WORN ON LEFT SLEEVE ONLY

SEAMAN

ADVANCED PILOT

JUNIOR NAVIGATOR

NAVIGATOR

| OFFICE | INSIGNIA | FLAG | SLEEVE |
|---|---|---|---|
| SQUADRON COMMANDER | | | |
| SQUADRON LIEUTENANT COMMANDERS | | | |
| SQUADRON 1st LIEUTENANTS | | | |
| SQUADRON LIEUTENANTS, CHAPLAIN | | | |
| SQUADRON FLAG LIEUTENANT | | | |

## PAST OFFICERS' SIGNALS

PAST CHIEF COMMANDERS

PAST VICE COMMANDERS

PAST REAR COMMANDERS

PAST STAFF COMMANDERS

PAST DISTRICT COMMANDERS

PAST SQUADRON COMMANDERS

U

# U.S. COAST GUARD AUXILIARY FLAGS

COAST GUARD ENSIGN

COAST GUARD AUXILIARY

THE AUXILIARY FLAG, known as the "Blue Ensign" (at left), is flown only from 8 A.M. to sunset when a qualified Auxiliarist is in charge of an approved facility. **Never** in place of the national ensign.

When the Blue Ensign is displayed, it is improper to hoist a guest, owner absent, meal, cocktail, or novelty flag.

AN OFFICER'S PENNANT, or a past officer's burgee flies day and night when officer is on board:

NATIONAL COMMODORE

NATIONAL VICE COMMODORE

(With small star, Nat. Rear Commodore)

CHIEF OF DEPARTMENT

3 Bars—Division Chief
2 Bars—Branch Chief
1 Bar—Aide to National Commodore

DISTRICT COMMODORE

DISTRICT VICE COMMODORE

(White field, blue markings: Dist. Rear Commodore)

DISTRICT STAFF OFFICER

DIVISION CAPTAIN

DIVISION VICE CAPTAIN

DIVISION STAFF OFFICER

FLOTILLA COMMANDER

FLOTILLA VICE COMMANDER

FLOTILLA STAFF OFFICER

## U.S. COAST GUARD AUXILIARY PAST OFFICERS' BURGEES

Past elected officers who are not currently holding office, but are active or permanent members of the U. S. Coast Guard Auxiliary, may display the burgee of the highest office held in the same manner as prescribed for officers' pennants. Past officers' burgees are of the same design as present officers' pennants, except for their shape.

PAST DIVISION CAPTAIN

Past staff officers of the U. S. Coast Guard Auxiliary who are not currently holding appointive office, but who are active members, may display the burgee of the highest appointed office held, in the same manner as prescribed for staff officers' pennants. Burgees have the same hoist dimensions as pennants, with the fly 1½ times the hoist.

# U.S. COAST GUARD AUXILIARY INSIGNIA

| OFFICER | METAL COLLAR and SHOULDER INSIGNIA [1] | SHOULDER BOARDS [2] | SLEEVE [3] |
|---|---|---|---|
| National Commodore | | | |
| National Vice Commodore District Commodore | | | |
| District Vice Commodore With Red "A": Department Chief | | | |
| District Rear Commodore With Red "A": Division Chief | | | |
| Division Captain With Red "A": Branch Chief Division Staff Officer | | | |
| Division Vice Captain Flotilla Commander With Red "A": Aide | | | |
| Flotilla Vice Commander | | | |
| Flotilla Staff Officer (Red "A") | | | |

Notes: 1. Large metal shoulder insignia is worn on blue raincoats; the same insignia in smaller size is worn on khaki, blue flannel, and khaki tropical shirts.

2. Shoulder Marks are worn on khaki coats, blue overcoats, and white tropical shirts.

3. Sleeve Grade stripes are worn on blue coats; braid goes only halfway around the sleeve.

CAP DEVICE

SHIELD
Current Officer

SHIELD
Staff Officer

SHIELD
Past Officer

Silver Collar
Insignia Member

AUXILIARY AVIATOR

W

# WHEN AND WHERE TO FLY FLAGS ON BOATS

FLAG CODE OF THE UNITED STATES POWER SQUADRONS

| FLAG | WHEN FLOWN | Power Boat with Bow and Stern Staffs Only | Power Boat with Bow and Stern Staffs and Signal Mast | Single-Masted Sailing Yacht | Power Boat or Sailing Yacht With Two Masts |
|---|---|---|---|---|---|
| U.S. ENSIGN OR U.S. YACHT ENSIGN[1] | 0800 to Sundown | Stern Staff | Stern Staff | At Anchor or Under Power Alone: Stern Staff[3] Under Way: From Peak or Leech of Mainsail | At Anchor or Under Power Alone: Stern Staff[3] Under Way: From Peak or Leech of Aftermost Sail |
| USPS ENSIGN[1] | 0800 to Sundown | Stern Staff | Stern Staff or Starboard Yardarm[2] | At Anchor or Under Power Alone: Stern Staff[3] Under Way: From Peak or Leech of Mainsail | At Anchor or Under Power Alone: Stern Staff[3] Under Way: From Peak or Leech of Aftermost Sail |
| SQUADRON PENNANT OR YACHT CLUB BURGEE | 0800 to Sundown | Bow Staff | Bow Staff | At Bow Staff If Yacht So Equipped; Otherwise At Masthead | Foremost Masthead |
| PRIVATE SIGNAL OR USPS PAST OFFICER'S SIGNAL | 0800 to Sundown | Not Flown | At Masthead | At Masthead | Aftermost Masthead |
| FLAG OFFICER'S (RECTANGULAR) | Day and Night While Boat Is In Commission | Not Flown | At Masthead Instead of Private Signal | At Masthead Instead of Squadron Pennant or Yacht Club Burgee | Aftermost Masthead Instead of Private Signal |
| APPOINTED OFFICER'S (SWALLOWTAIL) | 0800 to Sundown | Not Flown | At Masthead Instead of Private Signal | At Masthead Instead of Squadron Pennant or Yacht Club Burgee | Aftermost Masthead Instead of Private Signal |
| UNION JACK | 0800 to Sundown, At Anchor Only, On Sundays and Holidays or When Dressing Ship | Not Flown | Not Flown | Not Flown | Jack Staff |
| ABSENT FLAG | 0800 to Sundown When Owner Is Absent | Not Flown | Starboard Yardarm | Starboard Spreader | Starboard Main Spreader |
| GUEST FLAG | 0800 to Sundown When Owner Is Absent, But Guests Are on Board | Not Flown | Starboard Yardarm | Starboard Spreader | Starboard Main Spreader |
| OFFICER-IN-CHARGE (OIC) PENNANT | See USPS By-Laws Art. XVI, Sec. 9 | Not Flown | At Masthead Above Officer's Flag or Private Signal | At Masthead Above Officer's Flag or Private Signal | Aftermost Masthead Above Officer's Flag or Private Signal |

**Footnotes:**

[1] A USPS Member has the Option of Flying the U.S. Ensign, the U.S. Yacht Ensign or the USPS Ensign.

[2] If the USPS Ensign is Flown from the Yardarm, the U.S. Ensign or the U.S. Yacht Ensign should be Flown from Stern Staff.

[3] On Sailing Yachts with Overhanging Booms, the Stern Staff should be located on the Starboard Side of the Boom.

Where the Same Hoist Is Indicated for More Than One Flag or Signal, the Choice Is Optional. The Flying of Two Flags or Signals From the Same Hoist Is **Not Authorized**, Except In the Case of the OIC Pennant or International Code Flags.

NOTE—When a motor yacht with mast and gaff is under way, the ensign (U.S., USPS or U.S. Yacht) should be flown at the gaff instead of the stern staff. A mastless boat may display, on a staff erected on the superstructure, the flag designated by this code to be flown from masthead of single-masted boats.

The vice-commodore of the club, next lower in rank, has the same device except that he is entitled to two stars, one on each side of the anchors.

The third-ranking officer, the rear commodore, rates one star, placed above the device the same as the top star of the commodore.

## Members and staff officers

The N.Y.Y.C. code prescribes that captains (owners of boats) and ex-flag officers rate only the two gold fouled anchors without the gold stars of incumbent officers. In some clubs, however, this practice is modified to authorize past officers to wear silver stars of the same number and in the same locations.

In most yacht clubs, a member who is not a boat owner uses a cap device with a *single* fouled anchor placed vertically, fig. 2402(c). Some clubs, however, omit this separate insignia and allow the wearing of two crossed fouled anchors for all members not holding office.

Other officers of a club (often referred to as "staff officers") are distinguished by certain symbols in gold placed above the regular cap emblem, fig. 2402(b). A fleet captain, for example, is identified by a horizontally placed anchor. The secretary is entitled to a maple leaf; the treasurer, an acorn; the measurer, a short bar; and a member of the race committee, a half-inch anchor placed vertically. A fleet surgeon is identified by a red cross.

Variations exist in some clubs—the letter M for the measurer; the letters RC for race committeemen.

## Sleeve insignia

Rank and status are also indicated by stripes on each sleeve of the uniform coat, fig. 2402(a). On blue uniforms, the stripes are black; on white coats, they are white.

A commodore wears five stripes of mohair braid, the upper one taking the shape of what is known as a trefoil—this might be described as a triple loop, one part vertical and the others horizontal. In each loop of the trefoil, the commodore wears a gilt star. Regulations, of course, prescribe the width of the braid, how far from the cuff the lower stripe is and how far apart the others are, the size of the stars, etc.

The vice-commodore wears four stripes, the upper one being a trefoil, and there are two stars, one in each horizontal loop.

The rear-commodore has three stripes with one star in the upper loop of the trefoil formed by the top stripe.

Boat owners and staff officers are entitled to two stripes, the upper one having the trefoil; they, of course, have no stars. Members not owning boats wear a single stripe which has the trefoil.

Ex-flag officers continue to wear the stripes designating their former rank, but omit the stars that they were entitled to while holding office.

## *No* gold braid

Note particularly that in all of the uniform descriptions above there is *no* mention of *gold braid* for the yachtsman, whether member, owner, or officer. The only gold permissible is the gold fouled anchors of the cap device, the stars on cap and sleeve, and the insignia of the staff officers.

The yachtsman does *not* wear a gold chin strap on his cap, nor is there any sanction for the wearing of gold embroidery on the cap visor as is worn by senior Navy and Coast Guard officers—the so-called "scrambled eggs." This has been seen in some boating circles in recent years, but is entirely incorrect and improper for a boatman.

## Formal dress

In some of the older clubs, the uniform regulations prescribe a mess jacket for the most formal occasions. This might be compared with a tuxedo or dinner jacket of civilian dress. The yacht club mess jacket is single-breasted, of blue undress worsted, with rolling collar made with a long roll, and pointed lapels. It is trimmed with black silk braid and appropriate collar and sleeve ornaments.

In most clubs, however, the more formal uniform will consist of the regular service dress coat with a bow tie substituted for the usual four-in-hand tie.

**STAFF OFFICERS' INSIGNIA**

RACE COMMITTEE    FLEET CAPTAIN    FLEET SURGEON

SECRETARY    TREASURER    MEASURER

**FIG. 2402(b)** Cap insignia worn by staff officers are illustrated at the right. Sleeve insignia is shown above—trefoil with one additional black stripe, and insignia of officer in the center loop (in this case the gold anchor of the Race Committee).

## Blazers

A relatively recent development in boating clothing is the wearing of a blazer jacket with matching or contrasting slacks. This is a comfortable and attractive alternative to the full club uniform except on formal occasions. It has been widely adopted and its use continues to spread.

Blazers are dark blue, two- or three-button style, single-breasted with a left upper and two lower patch pockets. Either black or gilt buttons may be prescribed by the club's rules for the front and sleeves of the jacket.

A patch of the club burgee on crossed fouled anchors, or other design derived from the club insignia, is worn on the upper left pocket. The blazer is not, however, an item of uniform and thus no insignia of rank is worn on the sleeve or elsewhere on the blazer. The club uniform cap should be worn with the blazer only if authorized by the club's rules.

## UNIFORMS OF PAID CREW

The uniform regulations of the New York Yacht Club, from whence most other clubs' procedures are derived, include a complete set of descriptions of uniforms for various *paid* crew members. Crews, in general, are much smaller today than they were in the days of very large sail and steam yachts when the regulations were originally drafted, but logical adaptations to current conditions can easily be made.

Rare indeed will be the yacht paid captain—"sailing master" in NYYC terminology—in blue uniform with four gold sleeve stripes, or chief engineer with three red stripes, overseeing a crew of mates, assistant engineers, boat-swains, oilers, coxswains, and launchmen. If blue crew uniforms are seen, it will be noted that the trefoil device of club members is not worn by professionals.

The typical work and cruising uniform of paid crew is khaki. Blue coats and trousers may be worn in port or for more formal occasions. White uniforms may be worn in warm or hot climates.

### Caps for paid crew

The cap is the distinguishing device of the professional. See fig. 2402(d). The use of gold for the chin strap is as proper for the paid crewmen as it is improper for the owner. Further, the insignia above the gold strap is always quite different. There is no single accepted design for the cap ornament for the professional. Many owners have adopted an embroidered design consisting of their club burgee and their personal flag crossed and partially surrounded by a gold wreath. Others use a more simple design of crossed clear anchors (*not* the fouled anchors of the owner's emblem) within a plain gold circle. Engineering personnel would wear a three-bladed propeller in lieu of the anchors.

Skippers and mates of charter fishing boats may be seen using the last design described above with or without the word "captain" or "mate" embroidered in gold above the circle.

## CLUB UNIFORMS IN GENERAL

Having read all of the above, one might reach the conclusion that most boatmen own a wardrobe full of uniforms and never relax in anything less formal. That, how-

ever, is not at all true. While the formal occasions mentioned contribute in large measure to the general good fellowship and enjoyment found in yachting circles, if the sport were ever to lose its basic character as a freedom from shore-based conventions, it would very rapidly lose some of its virtues, and most likely many of its followers.

**OWNER - CLUB MEMBER**

**MEMBER (non-owner)**

**OWNER (non-member)**

**FIG. 2402(c)** While practice varies among yacht clubs, the cap and sleeve insignia illustrated here satisfy the dictates of etiquette. Above—the boat-owning yacht club member has a trefoil with one additional black stripe on the sleeve; the member who owns no boat has the trefoil without additional stripes.

**CAP INSIGNIA FOR YACHTING PROFESSIONALS**

**FIG. 2402(d)** Traditionally correct devices for paid hands aboard yachts. Crossed flags in gold wreath may be used, at the yacht owner's discretion, by professional officers and crewmen. Crossed anchors in gold wreath often designate the paid captain. Crossed anchors (in circle) are worn by deck officers, propeller in circle by engineer officers. Lettering in gold wreath (below) is self-explanatory.

FIG. 2403 Officers and members of the U.S. Power Squadrons may wear a variety of uniforms for different climates and occasions. Uniform "C" shown here with long-sleeve white shirt, black tie, and long white trousers is typical of those worn at outdoor summer ceremonies such as flag-raisings. The Sea Explorer Scouts forming the color guard are not a part of the USPS, but many Squadrons do sponsor such units.
(Photograph by Frank P. Beauchamp)

# USPS Uniforms

Although the United States Power Squadrons is not a military organization, it has a rather full set of uniforms, winter and summer, formal and informal. These are not required to be worn by all members, and many do not, but they are authorized and specified if desired. Most officers will wear uniforms for meetings, rendezvous ceremonies, and other special occasions. Uniforms are not generally worn to various USPS educational classes.

## Uniform combinations

The USPS uniforms range from informal white Bermuda shorts worn with open-neck, short-sleeve shirt to regular dark blue coat and trousers that can be worn with four-in-hand tie during the day or with bow tie for evening events. In between are uniforms consisting of the short-sleeve shirt and long white trousers, or a long-sleeve white shirt and black tie worn with the same trousers. See fig. 2403. The blue uniform coat may also be combined with white trousers for more formal affairs in warm climates. Although not a part of the uniform series, there is a USPS blazer that may be worn for many occasions.

## Insignia of rank

Officer's rank in the United States Power Squadrons is indicated on the uniform coat by sleeve braid and embroidered insignia. A varying number of black stripes, up to four, is used as on yacht club uniforms, but in addition there are three different widths of braid used in combination. The long-sleeved white shirt also carries the sleeve insignia but not the braid.

## Uniform cap

As with yacht clubs, there is a uniform cap that is worn both with the various uniforms and by itself with informal boating clothes. The rank of various local, District, and National officers is also indicated on the cap. A USPS cap ornament may be worn on non-uniform boating caps, but in such cases no insignia of rank is shown.

## Further information

Details of the USPS uniforms and insignia of rank are spelled out in the by-laws of that organization and are illustrated in the officers' manual. A table of information on officers' sleeve braid and insignia, cap insignia, and flags will be found on page U.

# Coast Guard Auxiliary Uniforms

The uniforms worn by officers and members of the Coast Guard Auxiliary have evolved through several distinct phases over recent years. The uniforms are now more "military" than "yachting" although the organization remains basically civilian in nature. Its supervision and administration by the regular Coast Guard does not change the Auxiliary's non-military status. The title of "Commodore" in various combinations remains in use also as a carry-over from earlier days.

## Uniform combinations

The uniforms of the USCGAux—and that is the correct abbreviation, not USCGA—include a "service dress" in blue, khaki, and combination (blue coat with white trousers); working uniforms in blue and khaki (with boating shoes optional); and tropical whites. Members of the Auxiliary would not, of course, need all of these uniforms, only those appropriate to their area and normal duties. A black bow tie may be worn with the combination service dress uniform for formal evening events. There are also uniform jackets, raincoats, and overcoats.

## Insignia of rank

The rank of various officers is now indicated by sleeve braid, shoulder boards, and pin-on insignia, all patterned after those worn by regular Coast Guard officers, but with differences designed to distinguish the Auxiliarist.

Braid on sleeves and shoulder boards is of silver rather than gold and is worn in stripes, half-stripes, and broad stripes in a series comparable to those worn by Ensigns to Rear Admirals of the Coast Guard and Navy. The Auxiliary, however, does not use rank titles like those of the regular and reserve services. Braid is prescribed for the office held rather than for rank titles. Sleeve braid rings go only half-way around each sleeve.

Shoulder boards worn with khaki uniforms carry the same number of stripes as the sleeves of blue coats; these are also used with the overcoat. Shoulder boards of the most senior officers are solid silver braid with one or two stars as appropriate.

The Auxiliary shield is worn above the stripes of both shoulder boards and sleeve rings.

Collar insignia, worn on the khaki and blue shirts, consist of the same series of designs used for officers of the Armed Forces, but with a letter "A" in blue or red super-

**FIG. 2404 Eyeglasses, if accidentally dropped overboard, are likely to be lost. To prevent this, "keeper" cords or holders are available. Light flotation devices may also be attached to the frames.**
(Courtesy Commodore Uniform Company, Inc.)

imposed. Similar insignia in slightly larger size are worn on the uniform raincoat.

Rank insignia of the Coast Guard Auxiliary are illustrated on page W.

## Uniform caps

Officers and members of the Auxiliary wear frame caps similar to those used by regular officers; white and khaki covers are used—the blue cover is no longer used by the Coast Guard and Navy.

The chin straps of members' frame caps are black, those of officers are silver. Visor ornamentation in silver is worn on the caps of senior officers.

A "working cap" of boating style is authorized in blue and khaki. The fore-and-aft "garrison" cap has been reduced to an optional item only.

## INFORMAL CLOTHING

Informal boating clothing varies widely with the individual, the area, and the activities engaged in. Essentially the only degree of uniformity exists at the two extremes—

top and bottom, cap and shoes. In between, the individual is "on his own," guided only by good sense and good taste. "Gag" or extreme uniforms and clothing do not meet the latter criterion and should be avoided.

## Caps

The yachtsman who is particular to wear the correct style of yachting cap on formal occasions may often go hatless in the summer time. The sun is strong around the water, however, and protection of some kind for head and eyes is usually necessary, which probably gives rise to the custom of wearing the yachting cap even when other parts of the uniform are omitted. See fig. 2401.

When informal boating caps of the visored style, often referred to as "flat-top" or "flight deck" type, are worn, the careful skipper adds no organizational or rank insignia except as prescribed by the organization concerned.

Especially among the sailing enthusiasts a white cloth hat with wide brim all around, frequently with green underneath or with a green transparent visor, is popular.

## Sun glasses

Sun glasses are widely used afloat to prevent eye strain from sun glare. Glasses with Polaroid lenses are among the best as they are particularly efficient in glare reduction.

Those individuals who must wear glasses with prescription lenses for distant vision will find it highly desirable to have a pair made with the prescription in tinted glass. The tint must be dark enough to cope adequately with the extreme degrees of brightness found on and near the water. Persons using bifocals for both near and distant vision correction will also find the use of tinted glass most desirable while afloat.

Regular eyeglasses or sun glasses must be protected from accidental loss overboard. See fig. 2404. A keeper chain or cord can be worn around the back of the person's neck, or a light flotation device can be attached to the frames to keep them from sinking if dropped into the water.

## Foot-gear

Shoes that cannot be relied upon to give you a sure, slip-proof footing on a wet or slippery deck are highly dangerous on a boat. Coupled with this is the necessity of using a type of sole and heel that will not scratch fine decks.

For all-around use afloat, the best informal footwear available is a sneaker type of shoe with cloth uppers and soles of special material and designs that can be depended upon to give a grip on a wet, heeling deck. Slits in the soles of Sperry Topsiders, Randy Boatshus, and others provide an effective "squeegee" action. For more dressy occasions, shoes with leather uppers, but the same non-slip soles, are available.

Cork soles and special designs are available that will not pick up grit and sand when worn ashore, to be tracked back on deck when returning to the boat. Ordinary sneakers or tennis shoes may be worn provided they do not have a smooth sole that would permit slipping on a wet deck. Crepe-soled shoes, though comfortable, are doubtful items on a boat.

Women may wear much the same footgear as men. High heels, obviously, have no place on a boat.

FIG. 2405 Foul weather gear is essential for most boatmen, especially those on sailing craft. It should provide full protection from wind-driven rain and spray. The type shown above is of international orange color to provide the greatest visibility should the wearer fall overboard. Matching boots with non-slip soles complete the outfit.

## Foul-weather gear

Wet weather clothing is essential afloat. You may have a closed-in deckhouse for protection while under way, but there will be occasions when you must go on deck regardless of rain to make fast to a pier, handle an anchor, or pick up a mooring.

Oilskin slickers and sou'westers were the traditional heavy-weather garments, but now foul-weather gear is made of more modern materials and in a variety of styles. See fig. 2405. Articles are available that are light-weight and comfortable to wear. Check your boating store or mail order catalog for the protective clothing best suited to your boating activities.

The secret of greater comfort is to put on foul-weather gear *before* you get wet. It is equally effective in keeping moisture *in* as well as out if you delay in donning it until after you are partially or thoroughly wet.

## Clothing for warmth

Boating activities are often extended into months of chilly weather. Special parka-style coats with hood attached are made for yachtsmen, where warmth and light weight, together with wind- and water-resistant qualities, are prime requisites. These are made of soft waterproof canvas or synthetic material, backed up with a lining for warmth.

A recent development is the flotation jacket which will not only provide warmth on deck but also a considerable measure of buoyancy should the wearer fall overboard. See fig. 2406.

## BAGGAGE

Closely related to clothing for boatmen is the luggage that they and their guests use to bring aboard such apparel and related personal items. Storage space always seems to be at a premium on boats, and baggage should be soft and collapsible if possible. Canvas duffel bags are probably the most practical luggage, but other types that will fold and stow flat can be used.

## IN SUMMARY

Summing up on the question of what to wear while boating, it would seem reasonable to say that if the occasion requires the use of a uniform, then the uniform should be correct in detail according to the regulations and customs of the organization concerned. If, on the other hand, the clothing is being chosen for informal wear, comfort and utility would seem to be the major considerations.

FIG. 2406 A flotation jacket is comfortable, light weight and functional, serving not only as a practical garment but providing buoyancy like a life preserver if the wearer should fall overboard.
(Courtesy Commodore Uniform Company, Inc.)

## Don't mix uniforms

Since the insignia and devices used by yacht clubs differ from those prescribed for the USPS, it is evident that breaches of etiquette would result from wearing, at the same time, articles associated with two different organizations. This might be compared with wearing two socks that were not mates, or a brown shoe and a black one. For example, fouled anchors belong on the cap of an amateur yachtsman, the member of a yacht club. In the center of these anchors belong the yacht club insignia, not the USPS emblem. Again, the sleeve braid with trefoil identifies the member of a yacht club; USPS insignia of rank or merit marks would definitely be improper in combination with such braid.

Similarly, items of the USCGAux uniform, or rank insignia of that organization, should never be mixed with USPS or yacht club apparel or insignia.

The key to correct practice, of course, is to wear the insignia of only one organization at any one time. And, naturally, to avoid the use of any uniform item or insignia to which you are not entitled.

# CHAPTER 25

# ELECTRONIC EQUIPMENT AND ITS USE

FIG. 2501 Electronic equipment now makes boating safer and more pleasurable — radiotelephones, direction finders, depth sounders, radar sets, loran receivers, fuel vapor detectors, and many others.

THE EVER-INCREASING variety of electronic equipment that is available for small craft places on all boatmen the burden of knowing more about this subject. "Electricity" and "electronics" are generally mysterious topics to the average person on the water; you can't see or feel them, but you know that they exist from their effects. The typical boatman shrinks from technical details on electricity and electronics, yet if he fails to put them to work for him on his boat, he is seriously neglecting valuable assistance easily available to him.

The owner of a boat of any size should know four things about electronic equipment—(1) what items are available for his craft, see fig. 2501, (2) how, in very general terms, such equipment operates, (3) how it should be used for greatest effectiveness, and (4) what he should and should not do regarding its maintenance. Such knowledge and understanding will mean not only greater safety on the water, but also increased convenience and pleasure. There is no intention or expectation of making an electronics technician out of Mr. Average Boatman, but he will be surprised how much can be understood and how much better his equipment will serve his requirements when used with greater knowledge of its capabilities and limitations. Technical language will be kept at a minimum in this chapter; only enough details will be included as are needed to make the necessary explanations.

"Electrical" and "electronic" are terms often used in an overlapping manner. In this chapter, *electronic* will be the term applied to equipment primarily employing tubes and transistors. *Electrical* equipment will be considered to include such things as motors, generators, lights, etc. The items of electronic equipment to be covered here are radiotelephones, direction finders, depth sounders, radar, loran, consolan, automatic steering devices, and several minor items.

# Electrical Systems

Electrical power must be considered briefly before electronic equipment for this is the life-blood of such devices as radios, direction finders, and the like. Although a few transistorized items may operate from self-contained batteries, the bulk of electronic equipment is powered from the boat's electrical system. With many of today's outboard motors having generators or alternators, there is almost no lower limit to the size of boat which can have one or more electronic devices, but the total load must not exceed the electrical system's capacity.

## Voltages

Electronic equipment is available for input voltages of 6, 12, 32, or 115, the first three being for direct current (DC) systems, and the last for alternating current (AC) operation. By far the most popular voltage is 12; its primary advantages are the widest selection of items and generally the lowest cost.

Six-volt systems are regarded today as obsolete; the lower voltage requires higher currents for the same power, and this results in heavier wiring or excessive voltage drops

FIG. 2502  Basic source of electrical power for operation of electronic equipment is a generator (A) or alternator (B) driven by main engine. Most electrical systems are 12-volts DC; some older boats have 6-volt. Larger craft may use 32 volts.

between the battery and the load. The use of 32-volt equipment has the advantage of requiring even smaller currents for a given load than do 12-volt systems, but many items such as low and medium power radios, depth sounders, etc., are largely unavailable in this voltage rating. A 32-volt electrical system also has the disadvantage of requiring a larger and more expensive battery.

The current popularity of 12-volt systems in automobiles makes economical the use of such generators, batteries, and regulators on boats. Equipment powered by 115 volts AC can be used, but the primary power must be continuously generated as AC cannot be stored in batteries as can DC. Thus, except where specifically mentioned as being different, it will be assumed throughout this chapter that

items of electronic equipment being discussed are powered from a 12-volt DC electrical system.

## Generators and Alternators

On essentially all boats, the basic source of electrical power will be a generator or an alternator driven by a main engine. See fig. 2502. The difference between these electrical devices is technical and the boat owner need not concern himself with them, except to know that the alternator is the more modern of the two and has the advantage of a greater output at low engine rpm. The external result is the same with both devices: a DC voltage somewhat greater than that of the battery (about 14 volts for a 12-volt system) so that energy can be put into the battery against its natural tendency to discharge into a completed circuit.

The flow of electricity from the generator or alternator into the battery will be through a *voltage regulator*. This device prevents the generator from charging at a rate in excess of its capacity, prevents the battery from being overcharged, and cuts out the generator from the circuit when the engine is not running in order to prevent the generator from acting as a load on the battery and running it down. For more on the operation of such generators and alternators, see books and pamphlets on engine electrical systems.

For boats that are in port with people aboard for a considerable portion of the time, it may be necessary to install a *charger*. This electrical device takes 115-volt AC shore power, *transforms* it to a lower voltage, and then *rectifies* it to DC. Thus as energy is taken from the boat's battery, it is replaced from shore power and the battery is completely or partially protected from becoming discharged.

## Storage Batteries

Fortunately, DC electrical energy can be stored in batteries, and electronic equipment can be used without the operation of the main engine. See fig. 2503. There are several types of storage batteries that might be used in a boat but cost, that most practical of considerations, eliminates all but the lead-acid type used in automobiles.

In connection with electronic equipment, the basic question may be stated as "Is there enough storage capac-

FIG. 2503  Direct current (DC) electrical energy can be stored in a battery. Boats commonly use automobile-type lead-acid batteries.

ity in the boat's electrical system for me to add this new equipment?" Capacity is measured in *ampere-hours*—the product of current drain in amperes multiplied by time in hours. This must be computed for all electrical loads, lights, motors, pumps, etc., as well as for electronic equipment. And there must be enough left over to start the main engine if only one set of batteries is installed! If the estimate of demand exceeds capacity (or if this has been found out the hard way!), a larger battery is needed. The installation of a larger battery may or may not require a larger generator and new regulator. The ratio of running time to idle time will determine this.

## Wiring

If the generator and battery are the heart of a boat's electrical system, then the wires supplying the power to the electronic equipment are the veins and arteries. The wires must be heavy enough, of sufficient cross-sectional area, to carry the current of the loads connected to that

**Fig. 2504**
**RECOMMENDED WIRE GAUGE SIZES**
**12-Volt Systems**

**Distance in feet — Source to Load**

| Current in Amps | 10 or less | 15 | 20 | 30 | 40 | 50 |
|---|---|---|---|---|---|---|
| 5 | 14 | 14 | 12 | 12 | 10 | 8 |
| 10 | 12 | 12 | 10 | 8 | 6 | 6 |
| 15 | 10 | 10 | 8 | 6 | 6 | 4 |
| 20 | 10 | 8 | 6 | 6 | 4 | 2 |
| 30 | 8 | 6 | 6 | 4 | 2 | 2 |

FIG. 2504 Table indicates minimum size of wire for various combinations of current and distance, based on voltage drop of not more than ½-volt in wiring exclusive of connectors. Distances are measured along path followed by wires. For 6-volt systems, substract 2 from each gauge number; for 32-volt systems, 4 may be added, but do not use wire smaller than 14-gauge for any circuit.

circuit. Adequate size is determined by two factors: heating effect and voltage drop. The passage of current through a wire increases its temperature; obviously it must not become so hot that it is a fire hazard. As a general rule of thumb, a wire should not become appreciably warm to the touch when carrying its full load.

The voltage drop problem is the more common one. The heating losses just mentioned result in a lower voltage being delivered to the load than is put into the wire at the generator/battery end. The voltage drop increases with a greater load, being directly proportional to the current in the wire. If the conductors are not of adequate size, the voltage delivered may be too low to operate the electronic device or other load efficiently.

Most, but not all, boats are delivered with wiring adequate for the installed equipment. The problem normally arises as additional accessories are installed. The solution requires either the replacement of existing wires with larger conductors, or the installation of additional main circuits back to the battery (assuming, always, that the various load combinations have been calculated and the

battery capacity is adequate).

The *gauge number* of wire runs opposite to its size; the larger the wire, the smaller the gauge number. Wires of smaller diameter than 14 gauge should not be used for any purpose in a boat's electrical system; most circuits should have heavier wire. The voltage drop is proportional to the length of the circuit between source and load. The longer the circuit, the larger the wire must be to prevent an excessive drop. Figure 2504 provides information to determine the minimum size of wire to be used for various loads and lengths of circuits in a 12-volt system. The insulation of wiring used on boats should be suitable for the damp conditions which will be found below decks; thermoplastic insulation, type T or TW, is best.

## Switches, Fuses, Circuit Breakers

Of the utmost importance in the electrical system providing power to the boat's electronic equipment are the various protective devices, including *switches, fuses,* and *circuit breakers*. Every marine electrical system should have a *main distribution center* where there are switches and overload protective devices. In addition to the switches on the individual pieces of electronic gear which are used to turn them on and off in regular operation, the various loads should be connected together into several *branch circuits,* each with a protective element and a means of shutting off power. This is necessary in order that a short-circuit or other failure on one branch circuit will not require turning off all electrical power.

The combining of loads into branch circuits should be carefully considered, as should the selection of the existing circuit to which a new accessory is to be connected. Loads which are likely to be used at the same time should be connected to different branch circuits; likewise, the loads that are most vital to the boat's safety should be connected to different branch circuits.

Further, there should be a *master switch* by means of which all electrical power can be cut off in case of fire, for working on the electrical system, or when the boat is to be left unattended. An excellent type of master switch is an enclosed, explosion-proof, heavy-duty switch which can be mounted directly at the battery and operated remotely from the instrument panel by means of a cable such as is used on engine chokes and throttles.

Overload protection may be by means of either fuses or circuit breakers. Fuses are less expensive initially, but are a one-time-use device. The cartridge type which fits into clips is preferred over the screw-in plug type often found on shore. The cartridge type is less subject to loosening under vibration, with resulting poor contact. On circuits with motors, be sure to use a "slow-blow" type of fuse in order to withstand the initial starting current surge without going to an overly large capacity fuse for the wiring to be protected. Circuit breakers are a greater initial expense, but there are no spares to be bought and carried aboard as there are with fuses. Many types of circuit breakers can be tripped manually and thus can additionally serve as switches.

With this consideration of electrical systems as the primary power source, we can now turn our attention to the actual items of electronic equipment suitable for use on recreational small craft, and desirable for greater safety and convenience.

# Radiotelephones

When the subject of electronic equipment for boats arises, the first thought probably will be "radio." See fig. 2505. The principal purpose of a radio on any recreational boat is *safety*. Certain other uses are authorized, but by law these are secondary to safety communications.

## Safety Communications

A boat's radio may be used to summon assistance in a wide variety of situations. A leak may have started, involving risk of sinking; the motor may have failed in the face of worsening weather; or there may have been illness or injury to some person aboard. The possibilities of radio's adding to the safety of a boat and its crew are virtually unlimited.

There are many stations listening on the distress frequency—Coast Guard shore facilities, lighthouses, and craft of all sizes, plus many commercial stations on shore. In addition, the regulations of the Federal Communications Commission (FCC) require that a listening watch be maintained when the radio equipment of a boat is turned on but is not actively being used to communicate with another station. Thus there is a high degree of likelihood— a near certainty—that someone (probably many) will hear your distress call and either come to your assistance or get help for you.

## Operational Communications

In addition to its safety value, a radio on a boat may be used for contacts with other boats for "operational" communications. The large number of marine band stations, and the few radio channels available, have made it necessary for the government to impose severe restrictions on the use of radios. As defined by the FCC, operational communications are limited to matters relating to "navigation, movement, and management." *Navigation* includes the actual piloting of a vessel, while *movement* relates to future moves of the boat such as might occur during a club cruise. Radio messages of the *management* category pertain to the obtaining of fuel, dockage, repairs, etc., and are limited to matters too urgent to permit handling by slower means of communication.

## Business Communications

A third type of operational radio traffic is called "business communications," but this is limited to commercial and government craft, and so need not be considered here. Note that for talking between recreational boats, the *only* permitted kinds of radio transmission are *safety* and *operational* communications as narrowly defined by the FCC. Social and personal conversations between boats— any "superfluous" communications—are strictly prohibited.

## Ship-to-shore Communications

In most areas of the United States, a radio on a boat also makes possible contact with various commercial shore stations on channels designated for that purpose. Through these stations, the boat becomes part of the nationwide telephone system; calls may be placed to, or received from, any home or business telephone. The restrictions placed on boat-to-boat contacts do not apply on these channels; calls placed through a "Marine Operator" may

FIG. 2505 A radiotelephone, properly selected, installed, and used, can provide safety and operational communications to other boats, the Coast Guard, and to shore stations.

be of a personal or social nature. The charges for ship-to-shore calls are quite reasonable — the regular land telephone rates from the location of the shore station plus a dollar or two depending upon the position of the boat.

## Frequency Bands

Radiotelephones for ships and boats operate on two frequency bands. Generally speaking, these can be called medium frequency (MF) and very high frequency (VHF). (We say "generally speaking" because many MF sets will also cover some high frequency (HF) channels, but these are quite different from VHF.) Equipment operating in the Citizens Band may also be used on boats; these sets, however, are not in the "maritime service" as established by the FCC and must be considered separately.

Probably 98% or more of the radios now on boats operate in the MF band, on frequencies between 2 and 3 megacycles. (One megacycle (Mc/s) equals 1,000 kilocycles (kc/s).) The discussion which follows will be focused on MF equipment; VHF will be discussed later.

## Choosing a Set

The selection of a radiotelephone is much like that of a new automobile—there are many manufacturers and many models. A number of factors must be weighed in determining which is the right set for your boat.

Almost certainly, the first question that will be asked is "How powerful a set should I get?" A decision should be based on the intended use of the boat and its radio, and on the electrical power available on board. See fig. 2506. The legal power limits are 15 watts to 150 watts (400 watts is permitted for coastal ship-to-shore contacts). These are input powers to the final amplifier stage of the transmitter.

Choosing a too-powerful set for the electrical system of your boat will only lead to trouble, while placing too much emphasis on economy and picking a radio of insufficient power will surely result in disappointment. The battery drain may be roughly calculated as follows: multiply the transmitter input power rating by 3 for a transistorized set or by 4½ for a vacuum tube set. This will give the approximate drain on the boat's electrical system when the transmitter is on the air. Divide this power in watts by the voltage of the electrical system and you will have the drain in amperes. This is, of course, the maximum, and not the average, drain, but the wiring and the battery capacity must be adequate for the greatest load to be imposed. The average load will be less; how much less is determined by the ratio of transmitting time to listening time. The above calculations are intended to give only a rough indication of maximum battery drain. When considering any specific radio, consult the advertising literature or instruction book to learn the specific primary power requirements of that set.

## Power and Range

"How far can I talk with a transmitter of a certain power?" Unfortunately, there is no clear and specific answer. The limitations result much more from the degree of congestion on the radio channels than on transmitter power. Very roughly, the following daytime ranges over salt water might be expected under average interference conditions:

| | |
|---|---|
| 20 watts | 30 miles |
| 35 watts | 40 miles |
| 65 watts | 50 miles |
| 150 watts | 65 miles |

At night, signals will be heard at greater distances, but the interference level rises correspondingly as additional stations come within reception range. Transmission over fresh water will reduce operating range, and if land areas lie between the two stations, an even greater reduction will occur.

The setting of a marine radio to the desired frequency is simplicity itself; all tuning is done at the time that the set is installed. Thereafter, the boat owner merely turns a selector knob to the desired channel or pushes the proper button. Most marine radiotelephones have from four to eight channels, the larger number being found on the more powerful and more expensive sets. Thus the boat owner must determine his requirements for different channels and use this as the second factor in selecting the radio for his boat.

## Number of Channels

The legal minimum number of channels, set by the FCC, is three—these are the 2182 kc/s distress and calling channel plus two working frequencies. The boat owner may also want to have the ability to talk with the Coast Guard on their frequency of 2670 kc/s, and with one or more marine operators. Except for the boat that travels very widely, six channels will probably prove sufficient. Excess channel capability in your set is not harmful, but it does add to the purchase price without being of any value to you.

## Antenna and Ground

The overall radio installation includes an antenna and ground system as well as the basic set. These are important

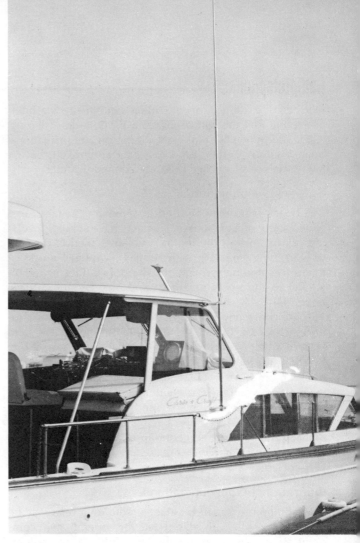

FIG. 2506  Select antenna of good quality, as large as can be safely mounted. Install clear of other metallic objects, as high as possible.

FIG. 2507  Marine radios come in wide variety. This 150-watt unit, maximum power for inland waters, has eight channels and provision for remote operation. "Squelch" control silences normal background noise.

FIG. 2508 Although range is not as great, VHF (Very High Frequency) reception is relatively free from static and man-made electrical noises. VHF channels are less congested, interference between stations rare.

FIG. 2509 Copper sheet secured to wooden keel provides adequate ground; consult service technician as to size. On carvel hulls, ground plate may be attached to planking.

items and deserve careful consideration. An antenna for a boat should be as large as can be properly mounted and of high quality. See fig. 2506. The ground system must have an adequate size plate properly installed. See fig. 2509. Money invested in the best possible antenna and ground system will pay off in results far more than if it had been spent for greater transmitter power.

## The VHF Band

The characteristics of the VHF band, 156-162 Mc/s, are in general the reverse of the MF band discussed above. There is little congestion on the various channels, but the range is quite limited. The principal advantage is more reliable communication with almost interference-free reception. The normal range is only about 20 miles, but it is unchanged whether by day or night. There is also a desirable freedom from static caused by lightning and local electrical noises since VHF sets use frequency modulation (FM). See fig. 2507.

In the past, the major obstacle to VHF installations has been their greater cost. Now, however, sets are on the market at prices comparable to those of 2-3 Mc/s equipment. This development should expedite the move to the more technically desirable VHF channels. In recent years, the Coast Guard has greatly expanded the number of its boats and shore stations that can operate on VHF as

well as MF. Thus there is now some coverage for emergency calls and this will continue to grow but, for the foreseeable future, MF (2182 kc/s) offers the better chance of getting assistance when it is needed.

## Installation and Maintenance

Radio equipment may be physically installed and electrically connected by the boat owner or any person. Before it is put on the air, however, the set must be checked out by a person holding a first or second class license who will make certain tests required by the FCC rules. Radio installations on gasoline-powered boats will generally require some form of ignition noise suppression or shielding; this is a job for a technician. With regard to maintenance, an unlicensed person is limited to matters which will not affect the quality of the signal on the air. For example, he can replace bad fuses, tubes, etc., but cannot change crystals or adjust antenna loading.

## RADIO LICENSES

With over 100,000 marine radio stations operating on a very few channels in the 2-3 Mc/s band, the need for licensing and regulations can easily be seen. The FCC issues its Rules and Regulations in various "Parts," of which "Part 83—Stations on Shipboard in the Maritime Service" is applicable to recreational boats.

To control the use of radio stations, holding down interference and making possible emergency and essential communications, a system of licenses is used. Recognizing that harmful interference could result from either malfunctioning equipment or from misuse of a properly operating set, licenses are required for both the station (see fig. 2510) and the person operating it. Although it is termed a station license, the FCC authorization is essentially concerned with the transmitting component only. The set owner need not concern himself with the many technical requirements for equipment provided that he has a set that is "type accepted."

### The Station License

To obtain a station license, an individual must be a citizen of the United States. (If the applicant is a corporation, the situation is more complex; see Section 83.23 of the FCC Rules.) Application is made on Form 502 which is either mailed to the FCC, Gettysburg, Penna. 17325, or taken to one of the more than 30 FCC field offices. The fee for a station license is $10 for the five-year term. The actual issuance of the license will take perhaps as long as 30 days, but if the application is personally taken to an FCC office, you will be given an interim authorization which will permit immediate use of your set; the fee for station license plus interim authorization is $13.

Radio station licenses are issued in the name of the *owner* and the *vessel*. A station license is not automatically transferred to another person upon sale of the boat, nor may a license be moved with the radio set to a new craft owned by the same person. A simple change in the name of the boat or licensee (but not a change in ownership), or his address does *not* require license modification. Just send a letter to the FCC advising them of the change; a copy of this letter must be posted with the license. Neither modification of license nor letter is required for a change

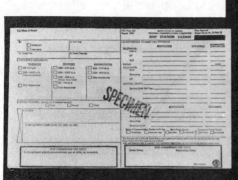

**FIG. 2510** Transmitter on boat must have radio station license issued by Federal Communications Commission (FCC). No license required for receiver, radio direction finder, or depth-sounder.

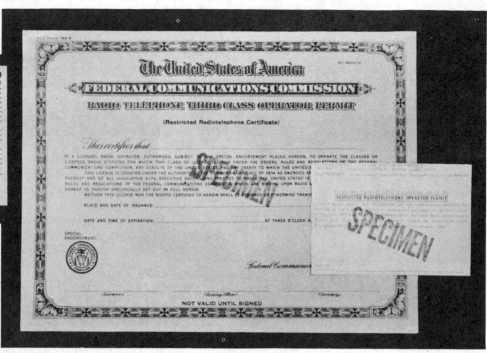

**FIG. 2511** In addition to station license, person in charge of set must have operator's permit. Either Restricted Radiotelephone Operator Permit or Third Class Radiotelephone Operator Permit is satisfactory for voluntarily equipped boat.

in type-approved equipment operating in the same frequency band. If VHF is to be added to a 2-3 Mc/s station, a modification is needed.

The regulations require that a station license be conspicuously posted aboard the vessel. At the end of its five-year term, it must be renewed if continued operation of the station is desired. Form 405-B is used for renewal; it should be sent to Gettysburg with a $4 renewal fee before the expiration of the license. If, but only if, timely application for renewal has been made, operation may continue even should the renewed license not be received before the expiration date. If the use of the radio station is permanently discontinued at any time, the license must be returned to the FCC in Washington for cancellation.

## The Operator's Permit

A personal license is required for the operation of any marine band radio station. The average boatman will obtain either a *Restricted Radiotelephone Operator Permit* or a *Third Class Radiotelephone Operator Permit*. See fig. 2511. Higher class licenses are available for persons with technical training and experience, but they are needed only for making tuning adjustments and repairs. An unlicensed person may talk into the microphone of a radio, but a licensed operator must be present and responsible for the use of the station.

With certain specified exceptions, an applicant for any grade of license must be a U.S. citizen. A Restricted Permit is obtained by submitting an application on FCC Form 753. This form contains all necessary instructions, including where to mail it; there is no need to appear in person at any FCC office. The permit is issued, without test or examination, by "declaration." The applicant must be at least 14 years old and "certify" that he (1) can receive and transmit spoken messages in the English language; (2) can keep a rough log in English, or in a foreign language translatable into English; (3) is familiar with the applicable laws, treaty provisions, rules, and regulations; and (4) understands his responsibility to keep currently informed of the regulations, etc. The Restricted Permit, fee $2, is valid for the lifetime of the person to whom issued, unless, of course, it is suspended or revoked.

For the Third Class Operator Permit, there is no age limit, but an examination is required. This test is nontechnical, covering only operating rules and procedures; questions are all of the multiple-choice type. You will find the examination not at all difficult if you prepare yourself for it properly. A free Study Guide is available from FCC offices. The privileges of this higher class of license are currently no greater than those of the Restricted Permit, but it has become a matter of pride for many boat owners to qualify for it and post it on their boat. Boats carrying more than six passengers for hire, however, are "compulsorily equipped" and must have a crewman with at least a Third Class Permit. The fee for a Third Class Permit is $3, and it is issued for a five-year term.

If your radio operator permit is lost, or becomes so mutilated that it is illegible, you should immediately apply for a duplicate. Use the same form as for the original application, and include a $2 fee regardless of the grade of the permit. The circumstances must be clearly stated and, if the license has been lost, you must certify that a reasonable search has been made. Continued operation is authorized if a signed copy of the application for a duplicate is posted. Should a lost license be found later, either it or the duplicate must be sent at once to the FCC for cancellation.

**FIG. 2512  The FCC Rules require that a radio transmitter be secure against use by unauthorized persons. A set in an exposed location, as above, can be fitted with a key-operated switch for its electrical power. Physical security may also be used, such as a lock for the panel door in fig. 2513.**

## RADIO OPERATING RULES

Hand in hand with licensing, radio operating rules have been established to bring order out of chaos on the air and reduce the interference that would inevitably result from the overcrowded conditions on the few frequencies available. Actually, the legally required procedures are only a bare minimum and must be supplemented with voluntary procedures for the most efficient communications.

As stated before, radio communications (other than ship-shore telephone calls) must be necessary and of a "safety" or "operational" nature. Even within these limitations, a system of priorities has been established to make sure that the more important messages get through. First, of course, are *distress* calls and related follow-up messages; these are identified by the signal "Mayday" and receive "absolute priority" over other communications. Second are *urgent* messages; these are defined as relating to the safety of a ship, aircraft, or other vessel, or of some person on board or in sight. Urgent communications are identified by the signal "Pan." In third place on the priority list are *safety* messages, those concerning the safety of navigation or giving important weather warnings; these transmissions are identified by the safety signal, "Security."

The system of priorities has been established to ensure that the message that *has* to get through does so without delay. No station or operator has any exclusive rights to any frequency; the nature of his traffic determines whether he should transmit or keep silent. One of the most important FCC regulations requires that an operator *listen before transmitting* to ensure that he will not interfere with the communications of others, and particularly not with distress or other priority traffic. See fig. 2518.

### 2182 kc/s for Calling and Distress

The most important channel in the MF band is 2182 kc/s —the International Radiotelephone Distress Frequency. In order to keep one channel relatively clear of traffic so that even a weak distress call can be heard, the use of this frequency is limited to distress traffic and the initial contact between vessels. This latter use as a "Calling Frequency" is permitted to ensure that when a station is not working on another channel, it is listening on 2182 kc/s for calls. Thus many stations are constantly monitoring the distress frequency and a call for help is much more likely to be heard.

Listening on 2182 kc/s is not only a logical procedure, it is legally required. A "voluntarily equipped" boat need not have its radio turned on, but if it is, it must be tuned to the distress and calling frequency when not being actively used on another channel. A "compulsorily equipped" boat must have its radio on and tuned to 2182 kc/s when not communicating on another frequency.

**FIG. 2513  Radio station license must be posted near equipment. On voluntarily-equipped boats, an Operator Permit may be posted. Alternatively, a Restricted Permit or a Verification Card for a Third Class Permit may be carried in one's personal possession.**

### Ship-to-ship and Ship-to-shore Channels

The second group of frequencies covers the ship-to-ship "working" channels. After making their initial contact on 2182 kc/s, stations desiring to communicate with each other must shift from the calling channel to a working frequency. These frequencies are:

```
2638 kc/s............All areas
2003 kc/s............Great lakes only
2830 kc/s............Gulf of Mexico only
2738 kc/s............All areas other than Great
                       Lakes and Gulf of Mexico
2142 kc/s............Pacific Coast south of 42°
                       North latitude; daytime only.
```

For ship-to-shore calls, a third series of channels is provided. These assignments will vary for the different Marine

Operators located along the coasts and the Great Lakes. The channels for your area can be found in Part 83 of the FCC Rules.

On the Great Lakes and adjacent waters, the various frequencies are normally referred to by "channel numbers"; in Canada, some are designated by "range numbers." Those most used are:

| 2182 kc/s | Channel 51 | Range 1 |
|---|---|---|
| 2003 kc/s | Channel 52 | Range 4 |
| 2638 kc/s | Channel 54 | |
| 2670 kc/s | Channel 56 | |

## Legal Requirements

Legal operation of a radio station aboard a boat requires four things. First, a license for the station, properly posted.

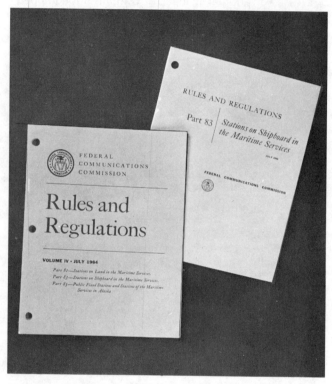

**FIG. 2514** Every radio station licensed in Marine Service must have current copy of Part 83, FCC Rules and Regulations. See text for details.

**FIG. 2515** Every radio station on a boat must have radio log. Requirements are simple, but don't neglect them!

Second, an operator's license. This may be posted, or a Restricted Permit or a Verification Card for a Third Class Permit may be carried on one's person. Third, a station log. Fourth, an up-to-date copy of Part 83 of the FCC Rules on board or in a secure place on shore.

Part 83 will be found with two other parts in Volume IV of the FCC Rules and Regulations. See fig. 2514. This volume may be purchased by mail from the Superintendent of Documents, Government Printing Office, Washington, D. C. 20402. The price is $2 which includes a subscription to changes to this volume as issued. Changes are mailed in the form of reprinted pages; it is a simple task to remove old pages and insert new ones.

## The Radio Log

Log keeping for a radio station on a voluntarily equipped boat has been made much easier than it used to be, but don't let this simplification stop you from meeting the present minimum requirements of the FCC. See fig. 2515. Each page of the log must show the name of the vessel and the radio call sign; each entry must be signed by the person making it. Entries are required for all distress calls heard or transmitted, for all urgent and safety communications transmitted, and any information related to maritime safety. The log must also show the time of starting and ending a listening watch on 2182 kc/s, *but remember that the keeping of such a watch is not mandatory on recreational boats.*

All installation, service, and maintenance work performed on the radio equipment must be logged. It is *not* necessary to make entries for ordinary communications to other boats, the Coast Guard, or shore stations. Logs must be retained for one year following the last entry, except for unusual circumstances described in the Rules. Logs must be made available for inspection upon request from any authorized FCC representative. Inspection of the station by such an official must be permitted at any reasonable hour, and at such frequent intervals as may be determined necessary in the discretion of the FCC.

## Rules Governing Transmissions

Transmissions on the calling channel must be limited to the securing of an agreement as to the working frequency to be used, and this may not take longer than two minutes. Any one calling transmission must not take longer than 30 seconds and, if no reply is heard, you must wait two minutes before calling again. Another two minutes must separate a second and a third attempt to make contact and, if these fail, a delay of 15 minutes is required before a new calling cycle can be started (the 15 minutes may be reduced to 3 if other stations will not receive interference from the calls).

Once contact is made on a working frequency, the exchange of transmissions (between boats) must (1) be of a legally proper nature, (2) be of the minimum length possible, and (3) not exceed three minutes in length. After concluding the contact, neither boat shall re-contact the other until 10 minutes have elapsed. The stations may, however, communicate with others during this time. These time limitations do not apply in emergency situations, nor do they apply to ship-shore telephone calls.

The Communications Act of 1934, together with the FCC Rules, strictly prohibit the use on the air of any language which is "obscene, indecent, or profane." This is watched as closely as possible by various government monitoring stations and violators have been taken into court a number of times. Special, more severe, penalties are specifically provided for this offense.

## Procedure for Station Identification

The FCC has established certain procedures to be followed in identifying your station on the air. Such identification must be given in the English language by stating the official call sign. Phonetic words for the letters may be used but are not legally required; any understandable word may be employed, but use of the international aviation and military alphabet is recommended. See fig. 2516. If the station is operating under an interim authorization, it will not have received its call sign. In this case, identification must be made by announcing the name of the craft *and the name of the licensee.* The licensee's name is required because of the great number of boats with identical or similarly sounding names. It is often erroneously omitted, but this is a violation subject to penalties.

Radio stations must be identified, as a minimum, at the beginning and end of an exchange of transmissions with another station, but identification of *each* transmission is *not* required. If both 2182 kc/s and a working frequency are used, the beginning and ending identification is required on each frequency. The station's call sign or interim identification must be made with each transmission for any other purpose, such as a test. If the exchange of transmissions exceeds 15 minutes (which would be legal only on ship-to-shore telephone calls), the station must identify itself at least once each 15 minutes.

## Secrecy Requirements

The Communications Act of 1934 and the Rules of the FCC protect the *secrecy* of communications. No person may divulge to another person, except the addressee or his authorized agent, any knowledge gained from receiving or intercepting radio transmissions not addressed to himself, *nor shall he use such knowledge for his own benefit.* This basic point of law should be carefully noted by all who operate radios on boats. It does not apply to distress communications nor to broadcasts for the general use of the public, but it does apply to *all* other conversations heard on the air. It could even be construed to apply to the fellow who listened to find out where the fish were biting and then moving in on the good spots.

## OPERATING PROCEDURES

The FCC Rules contain only a few instances of specific operating procedures, chiefly in connection with emergency communications. The various examples of operating procedures given below are in conformance with the regulations, but go further than the legal requirements; they are offered as examples of good practices on the air. See fig. 2517.

## How to Make a Call

Listen carefully to make sure that the channel you want to use is not busy. If it is busy, you will hear voices, or from most public shore stations, an intermittent busy tone. Except in a safety emergency, don't interrupt.

### Standard Phonetic Spelling Alphabet

| | | | |
|---|---|---|---|
| **A** | ALFA | **N** | NOVEMBER |
| **B** | BRAVO | **O** | OSCAR |
| **C** | CHARLIE | **P** | PAPA |
| **D** | DELTA | **Q** | QUEBEC |
| **E** | ECHO | **R** | ROMEO |
| **F** | FOXTROT | **S** | SIERRA |
| **G** | GOLF | **T** | TANGO |
| **H** | HOTEL | **U** | UNIFORM |
| **I** | INDIA | **V** | VICTOR |
| **J** | JULIETT | **W** | WHISKEY |
| **K** | KILO | **X** | X-RAY |
| **L** | LIMA | **Y** | YANKEE |
| **M** | MIKE | **Z** | ZULU |

FIG. 2516  **When receiving conditions are poor, use phonetic equivalents for individual letters in spelling out difficult words such as name of boat or person.**

When the conversation is to take place on a ship-to-ship frequency—unless you have reached an agreement in advance as to the time and frequency, establish contact on 2182 kc/s and then shift to the agreed-upon intership channel.

When the conversation is to take place through a commercial shore station—make your initial contact on a working frequency of that station; this will speed your call.

Both of these practices are designed to relieve the load on 2182 kc/s so that its utility for safety purposes will not be jeopardized.

## Steps to Follow in Making a Call (other than a Distress, Urgency, or Safety Call)

*Boat-to-boat calls*—Listen to make sure 2182 kc/s is not busy. If it is free, put your transmitter on the air and say—

"(Name of boat called) This is (Name of your boat and call sign), Over." To avoid confusion, always observe the proper sequence of call signs—state the name or call sign of the *other station first,* then give your own identification after saying 'This is'—don't reverse the sequence.

(If necessary, the identification of the station called, and your boat's name and call sign may each be given two or three times, but not more; the entire calling transmission must not take longer than 30 seconds.)

Listen for a reply. If no contact is made, repeat the above after an interval of at least two minutes. After establishing contact switch to the agreed upon intership working channel. One exchange of communications shall not exceed three minutes after establishing contact on the working frequency. After conversation is completed, say—

"This is (name of your boat and call sign), Out."

You shall not establish contact thereafter with the same boat until 10 minutes has elapsed.

## Ship-to-shore Service

Listen to make sure that the working channel you wish to use is not busy. See fig. 2518. If it is clear, put your transmitter on the air and say—

"(Location) Marine Operator This is (Name of your boat and call sign), Over."

Listen for a reply. If no contact is made, repeat after an interval of at least two minutes.

When the Marine Operator answers, say—

"This is (Name of your boat and call sign) calling (telephone number desired), Over."

After the telephone conversation is completed, say—

"This is (Name and call sign of your boat), Out."

## How to Receive a Call

Your boat can be reached only when your receiver is turned on and tuned to the frequency over which you expect to receive calls.

The receiver you use to maintain watch on 2182 kc/s

FIG. 2518 To minimize interference, FCC has established strict rules. Listen before transmitting and do not interfere with communications in progress. Keep contacts short and observe time limitations.

FIG. 2517 Booklet "Marine Radio Telephony" contains extracts from FCC Rules plus explanations to make them easily understood. Available from Radio Technical Commission for Marine Services, c/o FCC, Washington, D.C.

will assure that you get calls addressed to you by other boats. For calls from public shore stations, you will generally need to keep a receiver tuned to a working frequency of the station for that area. It is urged that you have one receiver for watch-keeping and a second one to ensure that you can be reached by a public shore station over a working channel. This will help to keep 2182 kc/s free for its primary purpose of securing help.

## Steps in Receiving a Call

*Boat-to-boat calls*—When you hear your boat called, put your transmitter on the air and say—

"(Name of boat that called) This is (Name of your boat and call sign), Over."

Switch to the agreed upon intership channel. After the conversation is completed, say—

"This is (Name of your boat and call sign), Out."

*Shore-to-ship calls*—When you hear the name of your boat called, put your transmitter on the air and say—

"(Name of station that called) This is (Name of your boat and call sign), Over."

After the conversation is completed, say—

"This is (Name of your boat and call sign), Out."

FIG. 2519 RADIOTELEPHONE ALARM SIGNAL (two alternate audio tones of different pitch) attracts attention to boats in trouble. Some larger radios now have built-in generator for this signal; separate units available for other sets.

## Distress, Urgency, Safety

*In an emergency* as a part of the marine safety and communications system, you have help on 2182 kc/s at your fingertips wherever you may be.

Only when grave and imminent danger threatens your boat and immediate help is required, use the distress procedure—radiotelephone alarm signal (if available) and MAYDAY. Transmitted on 2182 kc/s, it should be heard by many boats, as well as by the Coast Guard and public shore stations within range.

FIG. 2520 Prudent skipper tunes in latest weather bulletins before plotting day's course, especially when considering long run offshore.

The *Radiotelephone Alarm Signal* consists of two audio tones, of different pitch, transmitted alternately. The purpose of this signal is to attract the attention of persons on watch, and, at some stations, to actuate automatic devices giving an alarm. It shall be used *only* to announce that a distress call or message is about to follow. (Exception: it may be used with the Urgency Signal in two specified instances. See FCC Rules.) Coast Guard shore radio stations are now equipped with devices to generate this signal, and such devices are now being built into some larger models of boat radios. See fig. 2519.

### The Distress Procedure—"Mayday"—2182 kc/s

Distress communications include the following actions:

1. The RADIOTELEPHONE ALARM SIGNAL (whenever possible) followed by—
2. The DISTRESS SIGNAL "MAYDAY."
3. The DISTRESS MESSAGE.
4. Acknowledgment of Receipt of Distress Message.
5. Further Distress Messages and other communications.
6. Transmission of the Distress Procedure by a boat or shore station not itself in distress.
7. Termination of Distress Situation.

*The DISTRESS CALL* consists of:

—the Distress Signal MAYDAY, spoken three times;
—the words THIS IS;
—the identification (name and call sign) of the craft in distress, spoken three times.

*The DISTRESS MESSAGE follows immediately* and consists of:

—the Distress Signal MAYDAY, spoken three times;
—the identification of the craft;
—particulars of its position (latitude and longitude, or true bearing and distance in miles from a known geographical position);
—the nature of the distress and the kind of assistance desired;

—any other information that might facilitate the rescue; especially a description of the boat: length, color, type, etc.; and the number of persons aboard; OVER.

### Example of Distress Procedure

"(Alarm Signal, if available, for one minute). Mayday, Mayday, Mayday This is Yacht Blue Duck, WZ 1234, Yacht Blue Duck, WZ 1234, Yacht Blue Duck, WZ 1234:

Mayday, Yacht Blue Duck, WZ 1234, 133 degrees true, 12 miles from Montauk Point. Struck submerged object, taking on water fast, engine disabled, estimate cannot stay afloat more than one hour. Four persons on board. Blue Duck is 26-foot cabin cruiser, white hull. Maintaining watch on 2182 kc/s. This is Yacht Blue Duck, WZ 1234, Over."

### General Rules for Distress

With your life at stake, you have a far better chance by following the correct procedure, but the provisions of the International Radio Regulations authorize a vessel in distress to use *any means* at its disposal to attract attention, make known its position, and obtain help.

Stay on 2182 kc/s; but if no answer to a distress call is received, repeat it on any other available frequency on which attention might be attracted.

Speak slowly and distinctly. Use phonetic words for letters when necessary, especially when giving the letters of your call sign.

You may be requested to transmit a "long count" or other suitable signals to permit direction finding stations to determine your position; always end your transmission with the name and call sign of your boat.

If you have to abandon ship, the radio transmitter should be locked on the air, if considered necessary and conditions permit. The purpose of this is to locate you by radio direction finding bearings. If you have already been visually located, do not lock your transmitter on the air as the signal would interfere with rescue operations.

All vessels having knowledge of distress traffic, and

497

which cannot themselves assist, are *forbidden* to transmit on the frequency of the distress traffic; but they should listen and follow the situation until it is evident that assistance is being provided. Always listen before transmitting. It is *unlawful* for any radio operator to *willfully* or *maliciously interfere with* or cause interference to *any radio communication or signal*. No person shall knowingly transmit, or cause to be transmitted, any *false* or *fraudulent signal of distress* or *communication* relating thereto.

## Radio Silence

The signal "Seelonce Mayday" has been adopted internationally to control transmissions on the distress frequency, telling all other stations to leave the air and maintain radio silence. The companion signal "Seelonce Feenee" indicates the end of radio silence and permission to resume normal operations.

## If You Hear a MAYDAY Call

If you are not in distress, but hear a "Mayday" call, this is what you should do:

1. *Listen—Do Not Transmit.*
2. Try to determine if you are the craft in the best position to take action, or if some other vessel is better located or better equipped.
3. *If* yours is the logical boat to render assistance, reply to the distress message as follows:
"(Name of craft in distress) This is (Name of your boat and call sign), Received Mayday (your position, your course and speed toward the scene of the distress, and your estimated time of arrival), Over."
4. If yours is not the logical boat to take action, maintain radio silence, but continue to monitor the frequency closely for any further developments—make an entry in your radio log of the Mayday call and your actions.

When another station retransmits a distress message, the words "Mayday Relay" must be spoken three times before station identification.

## Test Transmissions

Always remember, when making tests, to take every precaution not to cause interference to others. Listen before testing, to make sure that the frequency is not busy. You must obtain the consent of any station affected before proceeding. If the air appears clear, put your transmitter on the air and say—
"This is (name of your boat and call sign) Test."
If you hear no station tell you to "Wait," you may proceed, saying "Testing" followed by a number count or other phraseology that will not confuse listeners.
At the end of the test, announce the name and call sign of your boat, and your general location.
Calls may not be made to Coast Guard stations on 2182 kHz for "radio checks." If a two-way communication is *necessary*, a call may be made to another ship station, preferably on a working frequency. General calls—those not addressed to a partiffcular station—may be made *only* for test purposes.

## Weather Reports

When aboard your boat, you can keep up to date on weather and other marine information by listening to the working frequencies of public or U.S. government shore stations. See fig. 2520. Coast Guard stations transmit weather and other information on 2670 kc/s after a preliminary announcement on 2182 kc/s.

The U.S. Weather Bureau publishes a series of *Marine Weather Services Charts* at only 15¢ each. In addition to showing where weather warnings are displayed day and night, these charts give the frequency and schedules of radio (AM and FM) and TV stations broadcasting weather reports and forecasts. See fig. 1243 on page 246.

Don't take chances—the information on weather conditions is there—get it.

## VIOLATIONS AND PENALTIES

Hopefully, you will never be in violation of the FCC Rules and will have no need for knowledge of the procedures and penalties involved. Yet things do not always work out that way, so it is just as well to be informed.

If you receive a citation of violation from the FCC, you must reply in duplicate within 10 days, to the office that issued the citation. See fig. 2522. If a complete reply cannot be given in that time, an interim reply must be sent and supplemented as soon as possible. If for reasons beyond your control, you cannot reply at all within 10 days, do so at the earliest date practicable, and fully support your reasons for the delay. Each letter to the FCC must be complete and contain all the facts without cross-reference to other correspondence. The answer must contain a full explanation of the incident and describe the actions taken to prevent a recurrence of it. If personnel errors are involved, your reply must state the name and license number of the operator concerned.

You may be lucky, however, and receive a "warning notice" rather than a citation. In this instance, no reply is required. The FCC form that you receive will indicate whether or not an answer is necessary. If one is required, don't get yourself into further trouble by failing to answer *within 10 days*.

## Revocation and Suspension of License

A station license may be revoked for any one of a number of specified violations of the Communications Act or the FCC Rules. Operator licenses and permits normally are not revoked but are suspended for varying periods of time.

**FIG. 2522  If you receive citation for violation of FCC Rules and Regulations, submit written reply within ten days. No reply required if you receive "warning," rather than citation.**

Notice of suspension must be given in writing and is not effective until 15 days after receipt. Within this period, you can apply for a hearing, and this automatically defers the suspension until after the hearing has been held and the FCC has ruled.

## Fines Imposed

In addition to the revocation or suspension of licenses, the FCC can prosecute violators in the Federal District

Courts. Any violation of the Communications Act may be punished by a fine of not more than $10,000, or imprisonment for not more than one year, or both. A second offense, not necessarily a repeat of the first, increases the maximum limit on the prison term to two years. For a violation of any FCC rule, regulation restriction, or condition, or of any treaty provision, a court may additionally impose a fine of not more than $500 for *each and every day* during which the violation occurred.

### Administrative Forfeitures

To avoid the delays, costs, and general cumbersomeness of formal court prosecutions, the FCC has the authority to levy its own "administrative forfeitures," actually small fines, for 12 specified violations. These fines are in addition to any other penalties that may be imposed by law.

Among these twelve, the violations of principal concern to the operators of radio stations of boats are:

—Transmission of any unauthorized communications on a distress or calling frequency.

—Failure to identify the station at the times and in the manner prescribed by the Rules.

—Interference with a distress call or distress communications.

—Operation of a station without a valid permit or license of the proper grade.

—Transmission of any false call contrary to the Rules.

—Failure to respond to official communications from the FCC.

The maximum forfeiture for a single violation, or a series of violations all falling within a single category as listed above, is $100. If, however, more than one category is involved, the maximum liability is raised to $500 for a station licensee, or $400 for an individual operator. It should be noted that the term "operator" may be applied to any person using the equipment, whether or not licensed by the FCC. In some cases, if two different persons are involved, forfeitures may be assessed against both the station licensee and the person who was operating the station.

The procedures for the imposition of these administrative fines have been kept simple, yet ample protection is afforded to the rights of individuals. Upon receipt of a "notice of apparent liability for forfeiture," the addressed person has open to him three courses of action. He can pay the fine and so close the incident; or he may, within 30 days, submit a written statement to the FCC giving reasons why he should be allowed to pay a lesser fine, or none at all; or he may request an interview with an FCC official. These last two courses of action can be combined, submitting both an explanation and a request for an interview. If either or both of these actions are taken, the FCC will review all of the information relative to the case, and make a final determination.

There is no judicial appeal from the FCC's ruling, and you had best pay up as there are established procedures for turning over cases of non-payment to a District Attorney for prosecution.

# Depth Sounders

Depth sounders (fig. 2523) closely rival radiotelephones as the most popular item of electronic equipment for boats; they have a wide range of use—lakes, rivers, bays, and off-shore. Your sounder can be one of the most interesting and useful devices on your boat.

Depth sounders are a modern replacement for the hand-held lead line used for uncounted centuries to determine the depth of water beneath a ship. This electronic device furnishes a vastly greater amount of information, and does it with much greater ease, especially in nasty weather. It provides safety as well as convenience in boating, and so is doubly advantageous to have on board.

### How Depth is Measured

Depth is determined by measuring the round-trip time for a pulse of ultrasonic energy to travel from the boat to the bottom of the water and be reflected back to the point of origin. See fig. 2524. The frequency of the audio pulses generally lies between 50,000 and 200,000 cycles per second, too high to be heard by human ears. Their average velocity through the water is approximately 4800 feet per second; slight variations in speed will occur between salt and fresh water and with different temperatures. The resulting small errors, however, can be safely ignored for the relatively shallow depths of interest to the operators of recreational boats.

Probably the greatest advantage of the electronic device over the hand-held lead line is the essentially continuous nature of the information furnished. Depth sounders vary

**FIG. 2523  Depth sounders are popular on all waters. This compact, inexpensive device gives many indications of depth each second.**

widely in the rate at which readings are taken, but in all cases many more soundings are taken than could be accomplished by hand. Current equipment takes readings at rates between 1 and 30 *each second*.

### Components of a Depth Sounder

The major components of a depth sounder are a source of energy (transmitter), a means of sending out the pulses and picking up the echoes (transducer), a receiver to amplify the weak echoes, and a visual presentation of the information. See fig. 2525. The transducer usually takes the form of a round block of hard ceramic material several inches in diameter and an inch or so thick. In many cases, it is given an oblong, streamline shape to reduce drag.

The visual presentation of information on the depth of the water is accomplished by either an "indicator" or a "recorder." The indicator provides a non-permanent indication of the depth, in most cases by the use of a flashing light, although in a few units an ordinary electric meter is used with a suitably calibrated dial. The flashing light is mounted on the end of an arm which rotates around a scale much like the second hand of a clock, only much faster. The zero of the scale is usually at the top of the dial and a flash of light occurs there when the outgoing pulse leaves the transducer on the boat's bottom. A second flash

FIG. 2524 An electronic depth sounder measures depth by sending pulses of high frequency sound waves, reflected back from bottom. Distance measured by time taken by pulses for round-trip.

occurs when the pulse is received back at the transducer, having been reflected back from the bottom of the water. The deeper the water, the longer it will take for the echo to return to the boat; the longer this takes, the farther the arm will have rotated around the dial. (Fig. 2526.) Thus the scale of depths increases clockwise around the face of the indicator.

FIG. 2525 Typical depth sounder consists of two units, transducer on bottom of boat and electronics package with indicator near helmsman. Model shown has calibrated meter with two ranges.

## Principle of the Depth Sounder Illustrated

An example may make this clearer. If the sounder has a depth range of 240 feet, at full scale the sound pulses will have traveled a round-trip distance of 480 feet. Taking the speed of sound in water at 4800 feet per second, the round-trip will have taken 1/10 second. Therefore the arm carrying the flashing light must make one full rotation in 1/10 second; this is 10 rps or 600 rpm.

If the depth is only, say, 80 feet, the echo will cause the light to flash when the arm has made only 1/3 of a full revolution, and the flash will occur at a position corresponding to four o'clock on a clock dial. In many models, it is possible to detect greater than full-scale depths by turning up the sensitivity control until a flash is seen on the "second trip around" of the rotating arm. Using the same sounder as in the preceding example, if the water was known to be quite deep, and a weak reading of 60 feet was seen with the sensitivity control well advanced, it could mean an actual depth of 300 feet (full scale plus 60 feet). Some models are now calibrated with two sets of numbers around the dial for first and second revolutions of the flashing light. Caution is essential to avoid reading the depth as much greater than is actually the case.

With the recording type of sounder, a permanent record is made of the depths, and notations as to the boat's position can be made directly on the paper tape. See fig. 2527. The paper moves horizontally from a supply roll to a take-up spool at the rate of one inch in several minutes. A dry method of chemically marking the paper is normally used to avoid the messiness of ink. A recording type of depth sounder has some advantages, but this type is more expensive. Some models are now available with both flashing light indicator and a permanent paper tape record of the depths.

## Correction to "Zero" Depth

If you have a sounder on your boat, you must know its "zero" depth. In most instances, the transducer is mounted on the hull several feet below the water surface and, as

FIG. 2526 On this sounder, indicator shows flash of light at "O" on scale and another opposite depth.

FIG. 2527  With recording type of sounder, depth is measured many times each second and presented as series of dots on scaled tape.

FIG. 2528  Navigator notes that Cove Point Light is abeam at 2137 but can get no other line of position. Depth sounder showing depth of 72 feet gives Estimated Position (EP).

depths are measured from the transducer, the indications will be neither the depth of water from the surface nor the depth beneath the keel of the boat. On some models, the zero flash can be offset on the dial to its depth below the surface, then the indicated depths are correspondingly increased to show directly the full distance between the water surface and the bottom without need for adding a correction. This is advantageous when the sounder is used for navigation.

The nature of the bottom of the body of water will have an effect on the appearance of the flash which indicates the depth. Learn how to determine roughly the nature of the bottom by the characteristics of the flashing light; a surprising amount of information can be obtained. Sharp, clear indications mean a hard bottom. Conversely, broad and fuzzy flashes indicate a soft, muddy bottom. Multiple flashes, each fairly sharp, can result from rocky bottoms; the ultrasonic pulses are reflected more or less horizontally to adjacent rocks before being returned upward. The added time delays for these sideward bounces make them show up as if they were at greater depths. Additional flashes at multiples of the least depth indicated may result, in shallow water with a hard bottom, from pulses being reflected downward again by the craft's hull following the first round-trip. Two or even three round-trips may occur; the cure for this is to turn back the sensitivity control until only the first indication is seen. In *all* cases of multiple flashes, play it safe and assume that the minimum reading is the true depth! As the depth indication flash will always have some width, be sure to read the "trailing" edge, or least indicated depth. This is the correct value.

## Application in Piloting

The primary application of an electronic depth sounder is to assist in the safe navigation of the boat in unfamiliar waters. It can provide much useful information, but must be used with care as *it makes no predictions ahead.*

Information on the depth of water is reassuring in itself; furthermore, it can be used to assist in determining the

boat's position. It can be used to make rough position data somewhat more exact. For example, if only a single line of position (LOP) is available, an estimated position (EP) can often be obtained from the additional knowledge of the depth of the water. See fig. 2528. This requires a fairly uniform sloping bottom and some knowledge of the state of the tide. Many times, a rough EP can be obtained from indications of an abrupt change in depth.

A line of soundings can sometimes be matched with chart figures to locate the boat's track. See pages 439 and 543. This is most easily done on depth recorders, but is also possible on indicating types by logging depths at regular time intervals. Depths are plotted on a strip of paper with their distance apart matched to the scale of the chart and the speed of the boat. The paper strip is moved about on the chart parallel to the boat's course until the depths match. This technique is not possible in all locations and should be used with caution lest an erroneous conclusion as to the boat's position lead to danger. Often in conditions of low visibility, a boat can be navigated to a desired destination by using the depth sounder to follow along a path of roughly constant depths. This is the technique of "following a fathom curve."

A depth sounder may also be used navigationally in a negative sense. If your depth indication agrees with the charted depth for your estimated position, you may, *or may not,* be there; the same depth figures occur in many places on any chart. If, however, your sounder shows a considerably different value than that charted for your DR (dead reckoning) position, it is an almost sure indication that your DR is *not* correct. Thus, while a depth sounder cannot positively confirm a DR plot, it can surely call it wrong.

The location of fish with a depth sounder is possible, but you may be disappointed with your results at first. Experience is required and you will improve with practice. Detection will generally be limited to schools of fish or quite large single fish. The echoes are quite weak and the sensitivity control will have to be advanced.

## Radio Direction Finders

On the seacoasts of the United States, and on the Great Lakes and other large inland bodies of water, a *radio direction finder* (RDF) is an important piece of electronic equipment. See fig. 2529. Primarily installed as a safety item, it can also be a great convenience to the boat operator. It is the primary radio aid to navigation for small craft.

A complete radio direction finding system consists of four components:

1. One or more radio transmitters at known locations.
2. An RDF set on the boat.
3. Charts covering both the location of the transmitters and the area of operation of the boat.
4. A person who knows the operation of the system.

To be fully effective, the RDF system must be used with competence and confidence — an incorrect radio bearing can lead to disaster; a correct bearing that is ignored because of mistrust can be equally disastrous.

### Special RDF Features

Basically, an RDF is a radio receiver with two additional features. First and vitally important is the directional antenna. Usually, this antenna is rotatable so that the set may be secured firmly in a convenient location. The directional antenna employed with an RDF set is an improved version of the simple loop used on portable receivers, the directional characteristics of which are familiar to most boatmen. This antenna may take the form of a loop a foot or so in diameter or it may appear as a plastic bar measuring about an inch square by some six inches in length. Both types will be mounted on top of the set; either will do the job.

**FIG. 2529  When visibility is poor, RDF can help fix position, or navigator may "home in" on transmitter near his destination.**

As the antenna is rotated through 360°, these directional antennas show two positions of maximum signal strength and two positions of minimum sensitivity called "nulls." With properly balanced construction and no local interfering objects, the two maximum signal positions will be separated by 180°, as will be the nulls which are found 90° in either direction from the maximums. It is characteristic of these antennas that the maximum signal points are broad and poorly defined, while the nulls are marked and precise. For this reason, the nulls are used for direction finding.

The second special feature of RDFs is a visual null indicator. While the operator can judge by ear the position of the antenna at minimum signal with fair accuracy, a more precise bearing can be obtained by observing a visual indicator. This is normally a small electric meter, read for either a maximum or minimum deflection of its needle in accordance with the instructions for the particular set being used.

**FIG. 2530  Radiobeacon charts are published in Light Lists. As reproduced here, not to be used for navigation. The frequency, identification signal, and schedule of operation are shown on this chart.**

| (1) | (2) | | (3) | | (4) | (5) | (6) | | (7) | |
|---|---|---|---|---|---|---|---|---|---|---|
| | Name | | Location | | Nominal Range | Geographic | Structure | | | |
| | | | | | | | Ht. above | Ht. above | | |
| No. | Characteristic | | Lat, N. | Long. W. | Intensity | Range | ground | water | Remarks | Year |
| | | | | **FLORIDA** | | | | | **EIGHTH DISTRICT** | |
| 137 | CAPE SAN BLAS LIGHT.......... FI. W., 20$^s$ Resident Personnel. | | On cape ............ 29 40. 3 | 85 21.4 | 25 800,000 | 16 | White, square skeleton tower, inclosing stair cylinder; with black lantern house. 96 | 101 | Obscured from 211° to 231°. RADIOBEACON: Antenna 702 feet 208° from lighthouse. See p. XVII for method of operation. 1849–1919 | |
| 138 | *Cape San Blas Outer Shoal Lighted Bell Buoy 30.* FI. W., 6$^s$(1$^s$ fl) | | In 60 feet, off shoals. 29 28.5 | 85 29.8 | .......... | .... | Red ........................ | | Ra ref. | |

**FIG. 2531 The location of the antenna of a radiobeacon is shown in the Light List under the listing of the basic aid to navigation with which it is associated.**

## RDF Frequency Bands

Radio direction finders normally cover three frequency bands: a low frequency (LF) beacon band, the standard AM radio broadcast band, and the 2-3 Mc/s MF communications band. The LF beacon band is of primary interest for the marine radiobeacons operated by the Coast Guard on frequencies between 285 and 325 kc/s at locations along or just off our coastlines and the Great Lakes. See fig. 2530. Aeronautical beacons, somewhat lower and higher in frequency, are also within the tuning range of these sets and can be used for direction finding. (These aero beacons, or "ranges" as they are called, are an excellent source of weather information at 15 and 45 minutes past each hour.)

Coverage of the standard AM radio broadcast band is desirable because of the large number of stations on which bearings can be taken. It should be noted, however, that the accuracy of bearings on this band will not be quite as good as it will on the LF beacon band. The 2-3 Mc/s marine band is generally used only for special purposes such as "homing" since the accuracy of bearings is still less on these higher frequencies.

A direction finder can readily double as an entertainment receiver, particularly if it is of the low-drain transistor type. Coverage of the marine band permits the RDF to be used to monitor a second communications channel when the radiotelephone's receiver is tuned to 2182 kc/s. Usually, a direction finder is tunable to any frequency in the band rather than being crystal-controlled on spot channels. This characteristic permits the monitoring of frequencies to which the boat's radio is not tuned. The pre-tuned spot-frequency feature may also be present on the more expensive models to permit more accurate tuning and quicker frequency changes.

Precise knowledge is required of the antenna location of the radiobeacon or other type of station. For the low frequency band, the locations of Coast Guard operated beacons are shown on standard navigation charts and are listed in Light Lists published by the U.S. Coast Guard. (Fig. 2531.) The *Coastal Warning Facilities Charts* previously described list many broadcast band radio station antenna locations by latitude and longitude. If not already shown

**FIG. 2532 For accurate RDF bearings, you must have table of radio deviation corrections. RDF shown here has built-in sighting vanes for visual bearings, or separate pelorus may be used.**

on your area's nautical charts, these locations may be plotted from this information. Aeronautical radio ranges and beacons are similarly listed and may be plotted if not already shown on your charts.

## Marine Radiobeacons

Marine radiobeacons are divided into four classes according to their power and normal reliable range:

Class A ........................ 200 miles
Class B ........................ 100 miles
Class C ........................ 20 miles
Class D ........................ 10 miles
(marker beacons)

A few of the primary beacons, and the short-range markers, operate continuously. The others are "sequenced"; up to six beacons operating in turn on the same frequency, each being on the air for one minute and then off while the others take their turn. The sequence of operation can be determined from the charts or by reference to the Light List. It is indicated by a Roman numeral immediately following the frequency; if no Roman numeral is shown, the beacon operates continuously.

## Radio Deviation

All RDFs are subject to local deviation errors caused by the reflection of the radio signals by nearby wires and other metallic objects. This is generally similar to the effect of masses of iron on a magnetic compass. One important difference, however, is that the radio bearing errors vary with respect to the *relative* bearing angle; the heading of the boat is not the deciding factor as it is with compass deviation. A table, or curve, must be prepared to show the corrections for RDF error on various relative bearings. Separate tables will generally be required for each of the frequency bands.

## Determining RDF Deviation Error

RDF deviation errors are determined by comparison of observed radio bearings with known correct bearings. Either of two methods may be used. The simplest is to take radio bearings on a radiobeacon or other type of transmitting antenna within sight, at the same time having another person take direct visual bearings. See fig. 2532. The difference between these readings is the radio deviation error. If no radio station is within sight, take radio bearings from a known location and compare them with correct bearings as taken from a chart. Avoid doing this while made fast to the club pier; erroneous readings may result from reflections caused by adjacent boats. In both cases, the deviation corrections have the same numerical value as the errors, but with the opposite sign.

Calibration readings should be taken of a strong local station which is received clearly without interference. A complete deviation correction table, preferably in steps of not more than 15°, should be prepared for the low frequency band. Then spot checks can be made to determine if the same corrections will apply on higher frequency bands or if separate tables must be made for each band. Correction tables should be checked at least annually, and additionally if the direction finder is relocated on the boat or major changes are made in the electrical wiring, rigging, etc.

## Direct and Reciprocal Bearings

Due to the technical characteristics of a loop antenna, two nulls can be found 180° apart. In most situations, the navigator's general knowledge of his approximate position will suffice to eliminate the reverse reading. If this is not

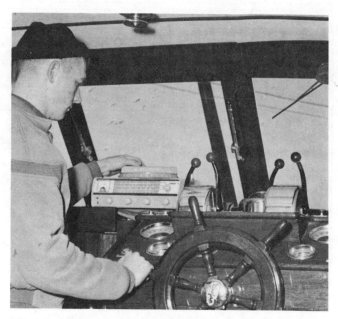

FIG. 2534  Taking radio bearing, antenna is rotated to locate null, angle read from scale. Reading, normally, is a relative bearing.

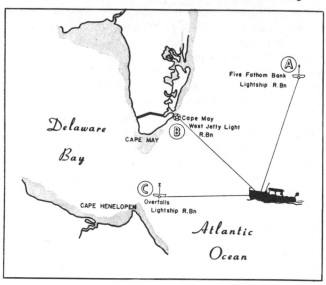

FIG. 2535  Boat shown here could determine position by bearings on any two radiobeacons at "A," "B" and "C." Better fix would be obtained by using all three beacons.

possible, or to be absolutely sure, special measures can be taken. Nearly all direction finders have either an integral auxiliary "sense" antenna or a connection terminal for an external antenna. By operating a switch, this antenna is connected into the circuit to change the directional characteristics to a single null and single maximum pattern. Simple procedures will then indicate which of the previous nulls is the direct bearing and which is the reciprocal reading. (The sense antenna is not left in the circuit all the time as more precise readings are obtained from the loop alone.)

Always use a portable RDF set from the same position on the boat; a change in location may require a completely new deviation table. See fig. 2533. As an RDF contains strong magnets in the speaker and meter, be sure to keep it at least several feet away from the boat's compass, both while in and out of use.

FIG. 2533  To ensure accuracy always use portable RDF from same position. Do NOT, however, place it too close to compass. Speaker magnet may affect it; three feet is safe minimum separation.

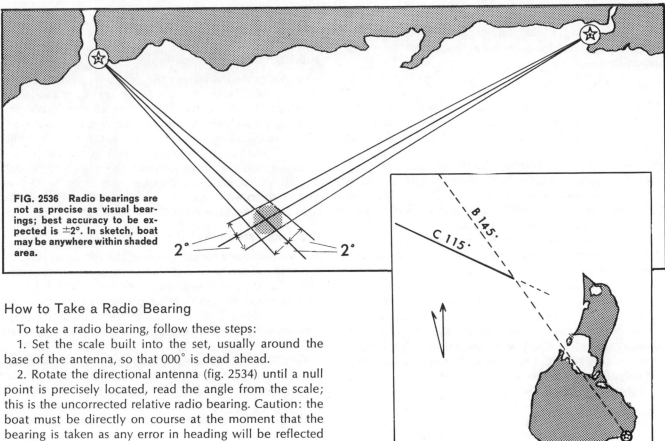

FIG. 2536 Radio bearings are not as precise as visual bearings; best accuracy to be expected is ±2°. In sketch, boat may be anywhere within shaded area.

FIG. 2537 Using single radio bearing, skipper notes bearing of 145° on Southeast Pt., Block Island, will bring him safely to Great Salt Pond. He holds his 115° heading, taking frequent radio bearings. When they increase to 145°, he changes course and homes on signal to entrance buoy.

## How to Take a Radio Bearing

To take a radio bearing, follow these steps:

1. Set the scale built into the set, usually around the base of the antenna, so that 000° is dead ahead.

2. Rotate the directional antenna (fig. 2534) until a null point is precisely located, read the angle from the scale; this is the uncorrected relative radio bearing. Caution: the boat must be directly on course at the moment that the bearing is taken as any error in heading will be reflected in the resultant radio bearing.

3. If there is any doubt as to whether the reading just taken is the direct or reciprocal bearing, use the sense antenna to identify it. If the reading is the reciprocal, do *not* add or subtract 180°, take a new bearing.

4. Having determined the direct bearing angle, apply the proper deviation correction; the sum is the corrected relative radio bearing.

5. Add the boat's *true* heading, subtracting 360° if the sum exceeds that amount; this is now the true radio bearing from the boat, plot in the same manner as a visual bearing.

The above steps outline in basic terms the correct procedures to be followed in taking a radio bearing. In the use of any particular RDF set, however, the manufacturer's manual should be studied and the instructions followed closely.

## Plotting the Radio Bearing

If the transmitting station is more than 200 miles away, and the plotting is to be done on a Mercator chart, a further correction is necessary before plotting. This small correction is required because the great circle path along which radio waves travel does not plot as a straight line on this type of chart. The amount of correction, and the procedure for applying it, can be found in Table 1 of Bowditch.

Radio bearings are plotted in the same manner as visual bearings, and the use of an RDF requires the same degree of piloting knowledge and plotting skill. Radio bearings do not have as high a degree of precision as visual bearings, and for this reason a three-bearing fix is desirable. See fig. 2535. The best probable accuracy for radio bearings is on the order of plus or minus 2°, and some experience and

practice are required to reach this precision. In situations involving close proximity to dangerous waters, a careful navigator will draw additional lines 2° to either side of the corrected bearing; these will indicate graphically the probable limits of his position; see fig. 2536.

## Position-finding by Radio Bearings

Radio bearings can also be used in any of the other forms of position plotting—bow and beam bearings, doubling the angle, danger angles, etc. If only a single radio bearing can be obtained, it is possible to combine this with a visual bearing, an astronomical line of position, or a depth reading to determine an estimated position. (Fig. 2537.) Remember that this EP will be no better than the accuracy of the poorest method used, and navigate accordingly.

In order to ensure the most accurate position from radio bearings:

1. Take bearings from as strong signals as possible.

2. Use the low frequency band in preference to higher frequencies.

3. Avoid taking bearings on radio stations located inland, particularly those behind coastal hills or mountains.

4. Take three or more bearings on different stations if possible; make sure that you identify the station correctly

and know the location of the transmitting antenna.

5. Take bearings so that the intersection angle is at least 30°, preferably 90° for two-station fixes or 60° for three-station fixes.

## Factors Affecting Accuracy

There are two circumstances which tend to degrade the accuracy of radio bearings. "Night effect" is the term applied to the fact that all radio bearings taken at night, but particularly those made near sunset and sunrise, show a broader and sometimes shifting null. This makes less precise any bearing taken at these times, and efforts should be made to take bearings under these conditions only on stations less than 30 to 40 miles distant. If this is not possible, the next best procedure is to take a series of readings on each station and average them for a mean reading; but still consider the accuracy to be less than that of a reading taken in the daytime.

The second special circumstance of lessened accuracy comes into effect when the radio waves travel approximately parallel to a coastline for any appreciable portion of the distance from the transmitting station to the RDF. There is a bending effect on the signals which can be as much as 10°, pulling the waves in toward the land. Fortunately, the effect is to make the boat appear closer to land than it actually is.

## Homing with an RDF

In addition to determination of the position of a boat, an RDF can be used in several other interesting ways. When the directional antenna is set on 000° relative, the craft may be directed toward a radio station by steering so as to keep the signal strength at the deepest point of the null. One RDF model has a direct-reading meter which shows the helmsman whether he is to the right or left of his course. This homing procedure provides a simple navigational technique for getting into port when visibility conditions are bad or other navigational aids are not available; but be sure that the direct course doesn't lead into shoal water or other dangerous areas. It also makes possible the steering of the most direct course to the scene of a distress situation.

These applications usually make use of signals in the 2-3 Mc/s marine communications band. Here the accuracy of radio bearings is less than on lower frequency bands, but the homing process works satisfactorily because the signal strength gets stronger as the source is approached. Caution must be exercised not to run directly into the source of the signals (this may seem like rather obvious advice, but it has happened!).

## The RDF as a Distance-finder

Certain of the marine radiobeacons are operated as *Distance Finding Stations* (shown as DFS on charts and in the Light List). For these stations, fog sound signals and the radio signals are periodically synchronized. Due to the difference in the speed of travel of these two signals, the radio pulse is heard before the sound signal. The time difference, in seconds, of the arrival of the two signals at the boat, divided by 5.5, gives the distance away from the DFS in nautical miles with an accuracy of about 10%. Consult the Light List to learn the exact scheme of synchronism.

## Use and Care of an RDF

Throughout any consideration of the purchase, installation, and use of a radio direction finder, it must be remembered that such an item of electronic equipment is first of all a safety device. Any other planned use, such as an auxiliary receiver, is a bonus feature only, and must not be allowed to detract from readiness for its primary use when needed.

An RDF should be used often in periods of good visibility so as to gain familiarity with its operation under circumstances permitting visual checks on the radio bearings which are obtained. Frequent practice reduces the personal error component of the total error in radio bearings, thus improving the overall accuracy. If these procedures are followed, there is every reason for a boat owner to trust his RDF to bring him safely into port under any conditions of visibility.

## Automatic Radio Direction Finders

An automatic radio direction finder (ADF) indicates on a dial the direction to a transmitter once it has been tuned in—no swinging of a loop, no 180° ambiguity.

ADFs cover the same frequency bands as manual RDFs and use the same types of transmitting stations. They are, of course, more complex in circuitry and thus more expensive. The antenna is continuously rotated, either mechanically or electronically, whenever the set is turned on. Often such equipment is a fixed installation with a remote antenna, but portable models are available.

The advantages of ADFs lie in their ease and speed of operation. They are, however, subject to the same radio deviation as manual RDFs and a correction table must be prepared.

**FIG. 2539  A marine radar set operates by sending brief pulses of super high frequency radio waves, reflected back by other ships, navigational aids and land masses. Sketch shows pulse traveling outward and echo returning. Speed is so great echoes are received before next pulse is transmitted.**

FIG. 2540 Most radars have two major sections. Shown is antenna and upper electronics unit containing transmitter and portion of receiver. Antenna must be mounted high to have clear "look" in all directions.

# Radar

*Radar* is an excellent means of marine navigation and is used on vessels of all sizes down to boats about 30 feet in length. Although size, power requirements, and cost limit its use on recreational boats, its capabilities and limitations should be known to all boatmen for their own safety when cruising on waters navigated by radar-equipped vessels.

## Radar Principles

A radar set sends out brief pulses of super-high frequency radio waves that are reflected by objects at a distance. The time that it takes for the pulse to go out and the echo to return is a measure of the distance to the reflecting object. See fig. 2539. In broad principles, this is the same technique as previously described for depth sounders, except that transmission is through air rather than water, and radio waves have been substituted for ultrasonic pulses. A refinement has been made in that the radar pulses are sent out in a very narrow beam which can be pointed in any direction around the horizon and used to determine direction as well as distance.

## Components of a Radar Set

The major components of a radar set are:

1. The *transmitter* which generates the radio waves; it includes the *modulator* which causes the energy to be sent out in brief pulses.

2. The *antenna* which radiates the pulses and collects the returning echoes. See fig. 2540. The antenna is highly directional in its horizontal characteristics, but 8 to 10 times wider vertically. The beam pattern can be thought of as being like a fan turned up on edge. The beam's narrow horizontal directivity gives it a fairly good angle-measuring capability, while its broadness in the vertical plane helps keep the beam on an object despite any rolling or pitching of the vessel.

3. The *receiver* which detects the returned reflections and amplifies them to a usable strength. See fig. 2541.

4. The *indicator* which provides a visual display of objects sending back reflections.

Radars operate at frequencies far above the usual radio communications bands. At such super-high frequencies, radar pulses act much like light waves in that they travel in essentially straight lines. They travel at the speed of light, 186,000 miles per second. For each nautical mile of distance to the target, only a fraction more than 12 microseconds are required for the round-trip of the outgoing pulse and the returned echo. Pulses, each of which lasts for only a fraction of a microsecond (one millionth of a second), are sent out at a rate of from 600 to 4000 each second depending upon the design of the equipment. The directional antenna rotates at a rate of one revolution in about 4 seconds. The round-trip time for a pulse is so short that the antenna has not appreciably moved before the reflection is returned.

## The Plan Position Indicator (PPI)

Marine navigational radars use a Plan Position Indicator (PPI) type of display. A circular cathode ray tube of a special type from 5 to 20 inches in diameter is used. See fig. 2542. The center of the face represents the position of the radar-equipped vessel and the presentation is roughly like that of a navigational chart.

A bright radial line on the face of the tube represents the radar beam; it rotates in synchronism with the antenna. Reflections show up as points or patches of light depending upon the size of the echo-producing object. The persistence of the screen is such that the points and patches of light do not completely fade out before the antenna has made another rotation and they are restored to brilliance. Thus the picture on the radarscope is repainted every few seconds.

## Radar Range Scales

The relative bearing of an object is indicated directly on the screen; a position corresponding to the "12" on a clock face is directly ahead. The distance to the object is proportional to the distance from the center of the screen to the point of light which is the echo. On most radars, concentric circles of light are used as range markers to make the estimation of distances both easier and more accurate. All radar sets have multiple range scales which may be selected to suit the purpose for which the radar is being used. Longer range scales provide coverage of greater areas, but at a cost of less detail and poorer definition.

Radar sets have both a maximum and a minimum range, each of which is of importance in the operation of the equipment. The maximum range is determined by the transmitter power and the receiver sensitivity, provided, of course, that the antenna is at a sufficient height above water that the range is not limited by the distance to the horizon. See fig. 2543. (The radar pulses normally travel with just a slight amount of bending; thus the radar horizon is about 15% farther away than the visual horizon.)

Because a radar pulse has a definite duration, and therefore occupies a definite length in space as it moves outward from the antenna, there is a minimum range within which objects cannot be detected. This minimum range, usually between 20 and 50 yards, is important when maneuvering in close quarters, as when passing buoys at the side of a narrow channel.

## Units for Small Craft

Radar sets for small craft usually consist of two units. Modern design of the components makes it possible to combine the antenna, transmitter, and a portion of the receiver into a single unit installed on a mast or on the pilothouse. This unit, usually weighing between 60 and 120 pounds, should be located as high as possible in order to avoid limiting the range of the set. The antenna should have an unobstructed "look" in all directions. The remainder of the receiver and the indicator are located near the helmsman's position. Improved design techniques have resulted in indicator units so small that they may be fitted into a pilothouse in any number of positions.

Because radar sets radiate radio frequency energy, they must be licensed by the FCC, but this is not difficult to do for commercially produced equipment. No license is required to operate a radar, but for its installation and maintenance, the technician must have a second- or first-class radio operator's license with a special "ship radar" en-

dorsement. The owner and station licensee of a marine radar installation is responsible that only a properly licensed individual does all of the technical work on the equipment.

## Principal Applications

Radars have two principal applications aboard ships and small craft. They are often thought of primarily as anti-collision devices, but are even more often used to assist in the piloting of the vessel.

Radar was originally conceived for the detection and tracking of ships and aircraft. It offers an excellent means of extending the coverage of a visual lookout, especially at night and under conditions of reduced visibility. This greater range of detection affords more time for a ship to maneuver to avoid another craft or an obstacle.

Radar serves another valuable function in the piloting of a vessel approaching a coastline or traveling in confined waters. It has real advantages even in the daytime, and, of course, becomes particularly helpful at night or in fog.

## Fixes by Radar

The daytime advantages of radar stem from its ability to measure distance. Often a landmark or navigation aid can be seen and a visual bearing easily obtained. If, however, only one such object can be seen, only a single line of position is obtained and a fix is not possible. With a measurement of distance by radar, a fix becomes possible. See fig. 2544. The bearing could have been made by radar simultaneously with the range measurement, but a visual bearing is more precise and should be used if possible. The capability of getting a fix from a single object is often of great importance to the navigator.

Fixes may also be obtained in low visibility situations—from a single radar bearing and range measurement, from crossed bearings (fig. 2545—but this is not too accurate due to the finite width of the radar beam), and preferably from distance measurements to two or more points that can be identified on both the radar screen and the chart. More than two ranges or bearings should be taken and plotted to prevent the possibility of a false fix which might occur if one of the echoes on the scope were incorrectly

FIG. 2541 (Left) Lower section of radar set contains remainder of receiver, indicator, and all operating controls, located within easy view of helmsman, but not too close to compass.

FIG. 2542 (Right) Marine radars present information on ships, buoys, shorelines, etc. as patches of light on face of PPI scope. Radar-equipped boat is at center of scope.

FIG. 2543 Maximum range of radar set on small craft is more likely to be limited by antenna height than by transmitter power. Radar waves bend slightly but distance to radar horizon is only 15% greater than to optical horizon.

FIG. 2544 Radar fix may be obtained from single object, using both distance and bearing measurements. Navigator must be sure he has correctly identified object on both radar scope and chart.

FIG. 2545 Getting navigational fix by plotting distance to two identifiable objects as measured by radar. Radar measurements of distance provide more accurate fix than do radar bearings. Ranges to more than two objects are desirable.

identified. In all cases, the use of radar lines of position and fixes is the same as for visual plotting, giving due consideration to the lesser accuracy of bearing information. See figs. 2546 and 2547 for additional illustrations of radar plotting.

## Coastline Pictures on the PPI

The use of radar to determine a vessel's approximate position from observation of the presentation of a coastline on a radarscope is not a safe procedure. The image seen on the PPI will often vary appreciably from the appearance of a chart. This is true despite some widely publicized photographs of radar screens showing such distinctive patterns as New York harbor appearing nearly identical with the actual scene. Because the radar beam, as narrow (1° to 4°) as it is, does have a finite width, and because the pulse, as brief (0.1 to 0.5 microsecond) as it is, does have a definite length in space, the picture on a radar PPI scope is not an exact replica of the land area or other object returning the echoes. Normally, radar echoes will be returned from buildings, hills, etc., some distance inland from the shorelines shown on charts.

FIG. 2546 For greatest benefit, radar information must be plotted. Here two successive measurements of bearing and range of a fixed point on shore provide data to plot track and speed made good by radar-equipped boat. Track can be projected ahead to give estimated time of arrival (ETA) at any point. Effect of currents may be determined by comparison of heading and slack-water speed with track and speed made good.

## Passive Radar Reflectors

The motorboat owner who does not have a radar can still do something to increase his safety in relation to this item of electronic equipment. He can equip his craft with a *passive radar reflector*. See fig. 2548. This simple and inexpensive item consists of thin lightweight metal sheets, or areas of fine-mesh metal screening, arranged in mutually perpendicular planes. These may fold for storage, but must remain rigid with respect to each other when opened for use. A relatively small reflector with each metal surface only about two feet square will provide a radar reflection as strong as that from a medium-sized steel ship. The echo from the wooden hull of a small craft is so weak as to be easily overlooked in the echoes from the waves if a reflector is not used. With a passive reflector hoisted as high as possible, the operator of a small craft can be sure that his boat will be detected on the radar screens of passing ships. Often Coast Guard or other rescue craft searching for a boat in distress are radar-equipped; the use of a passive radar reflector greatly increases the chances of being quickly spotted.

FIG. 2547 Because radar is changing position with your boat, you cannot depend upon appearance of radar-scope to give indication of course and speed of another vessel. It is necessary to make radar plot. Shown are track and speed of your vessel as established in fig. 2546, plus actual track and speed of another craft based on two successive radar measurements of relative bearing and distance. Both tracks may be projected ahead to evaluate possibility of collision should neither craft change course or speed.

## Electronic Navigation Systems

There are two electronic navigation systems which will be of interest to boatmen. These are *Consolan* and *Loran*. In general, the advantages of one are the disadvantages of the other, and vice versa. Consolan requires only simple, inexpensive equipment on the boat (indeed, if you have a good RDF, nothing else will be required except charts or tables), but this system is useful only in limited areas. Loran stations are many and widespread, but the receiving equipment required is rather expensive and its operation is somewhat more complex.

### CONSOLAN

A Consolan station sends out a pattern of dots and dashes, the relative number and sequence of which will provide a line of position. See fig. 2549. (Strictly speaking, "Consolan" applies to stations with two antenna towers, and "Consol" to stations with three towers; to the boatman on the receiving end, there is no difference, and Consolan will be used as the inclusive term.) The pattern is repeated every 20° to 30°, and the boatman must know his approximate position in order to recognize which sector he is in, but this should present no practical difficulty.

For the proper reception of the dots and dashes, it is almost essential that the receiver or direction finder be equipped with a beat frequency oscillator (BFO), and most RDFs are now so designed. Good selectivity is also neces-sary to prevent interference from other signals on nearby frequencies. It is not necessary that the RDF have a meter (visual null indicator), but if it does, this feature can also be of use in receiving Consolan signals.

Consolan signals are easily used by boatmen, but there are only two stations—at San Francisco, call letters SFI, frequency 192 kc/s; and at Nantucket, TUK, 194 kc/s. These are frequencies just below the marine radiobeacon band, but within range of most RDFs. The lack of stations is a limitation, but it is not as great as it might seem as Consolan signals can be received at distances as much as 1500 miles. On the other hand, there are two zones within reception range where the signals are not usable. The first covers an area within 30 to 50 miles of the station in all directions, and the other extends outward to all distances for about 20° on either side of a line running through the antenna towers. See fig. below for illustration of the dot and dash sectors, and the sectors of unreliability.

Consolan signals are heard in cycles of 75 seconds each. First the station identification letters are transmitted in Morse code for 7½ seconds, then there is a 2½-second silent period, followed by 30 seconds of dots and dashes, 2½ seconds of silence, another 30 seconds of dots and dashes, and a final 2½-second silent period; the cycle is then repeated. Operation is continuous day and night, fair weather and foul.

**FIG. 2549   Portion of Consolan chart (HO 16510) published by Oceanographic Office of the Navy. Consolan bearings are not dependent on compass, on steering, or on an antenna, and can be picked up farther out than regular radio bearings (up to approximately 800 miles). Information on Consolan is published in HO 117 (A and B), Radio Navigational Aids.**

**FIG. 2548 In waters frequented by radar-equipped ships, every boatman should use a passive radar reflector. It makes the boat's echo many times brighter on scope of ship using radar as its "eyes."**

## Finding a Line of Position

A line of position (LOP) is found by determining whether dots or dashes are heard first in each 30-second period, and how many of each there are (all 30-second periods are alike at any position). There is always a total of 60 dashes and dots in each 30 seconds of transmission, but the transition from one to the other is blurred into a brief period of continuous signal known as the *equisignal*. Count the dashes that can be heard distinctly, and do likewise for the dots; subtract the total of these from 60 to determine the ones lost in the equisignal. Divide these lost counts equally between dots and dashes, and add them to those counted. For example:

Dashes counted (first heard) . . . . . . . . . . . . . 15
Dots counted . . . . . . . . . . . . . . . . . . . . . . . . 39
     Total . . . . . . . . . . . . . . . . . . . . . . . . . . 54
Remainder not heard 60 − 54 = 6
Corrected number of dashes 15 + 3 = 18
Corrected number of dots 39 + 3 = 42

Since dashes were heard before dots, you are in a dash sector with a count of 18. Care must be exercised when you are near the border between sectors; you may hear all dots or all dashes with an equisignal. Consult H.O. 117A for guidance in computing the correct dot or dash count.

Determination of the LOP may be made from either tables (fig. 2550) or directly from certain charts. H.O. 117A (117B for West Coast) includes information of Consolan station locations, frequencies, etc., plus tables giving true bearings for each number of dots and dashes in all sectors. These are great circle bearings from the station and must be corrected for plotting on Mercator charts; tables of such corrections are in H.O. 117A and B or Bowditch may be used.

To avoid the trouble of determining the LOP from tables and then plotting it, special charts are available for the East and West Coasts showing Consolan lines.

## Accuracy of Consolan LOPs

The accuracy of Consolan LOPs will vary with the receiver's position with respect to the station as well as with the care with which the counting of dots and dashes is done. The greatest accuracy is achieved at right angles to the line through the antenna towers; also daytime reception will usually be somewhat more accurate than at night. In all cases, accuracy will be better than 1°, and often better than 1/2° if the counting has been done carefully. However, at distances of hundreds of miles, these small angular errors represent uncertainties of position of up to 10 miles. Thus, Consolan is an excellent offshore navigation system, but is not to be used when nearing a coastline.

It is unfortunate that the scarcity of Consolan stations prevents the obtaining of two or more lines of position from this electronic navigation system, and thus a "Consolan Fix." However, an LOP derived from Consolan signals can, of course, be combined with other positional information for the determination of a fix or EP.

## LORAN

Loran is the basic navigation system for ocean-going ships. Its coverage is extensive and includes all offshore boating areas. Loran is a passive system; there is no transmitter aboard the vessel, but a relatively complex and ex-

FIG. 2550 Excerpts from tables of Consolan bearings from Oceanographic Office publication 117A. Note several bearings are given for each dot or dash count. You must know roughly where you are in relation to transmitting station to select proper bearing.

FIG. 2551 Here navigator uses special radio receiver to pick up loran signals. Loran, simple to operate, provides quick fixes of good accuracy. One reading gives line of position from special chart or tables. Another on second pair of signals gives information for loran fix.

pensive receiver is required. See fig. 2551. Loran is a valuable supplement to celestial navigation, particularly when weather prevents the taking of sights.

Loran stations operate on frequencies between 1750 and 1950 kc/s. A pair of transmitters send out pulses of radio waves which are received on board the vessel. The difference in time of arrival of the pulses from each station is measured electronically, and this information is used to determine a line of position. The pulses are not sent out simultaneously, but are synchronized in a predetermined manner. A second pair of pulses is used to determine another LOP and the result is a Loran fix. Normally, one station is common to each of the two pairs; it is called the "master" and the others are "slaves."

Loran has different day and night ranges because of the radio frequencies involved. Daytime reception using "ground waves" is the most accurate and average ranges are about 500 miles. This can be extended by the use of "sky waves" to as much as 1200 miles as determined by the power of the transmitter. Reception at night, also using sky waves, may extend out to 1400 miles, but with lessened accuracy. Range is considerably reduced when the radio waves must cross over land.

### Accuracy of Loran LOPs

The accuracy of a Loran LOP varies over the coverage area of the pair of stations being used; it is greatest near the base line (line between the two stations) or base line extended. Ground wave LOPs should give a fix within 1½ miles accuracy over 80% of the normal coverage area. The accuracy when using sky waves will be degraded to a position uncertainty of from 5 to 7 miles. These accuracies are not affected as much by the passage of the pulses over land as for other systems which determine the direction of arrival of the radio waves.

A line of position can usually be determined in about two minutes; training in the use of a Loran receiver is required, but skill is soon acquired with practice. Loran stations must be accurately identified and the controls of the receiver manipulated properly to measure the time difference in arrival of the pulses. Thereafter, the position may be obtained from tables or plotted directly on readily available charts. As with other navigational techniques, three LOPs will give a better fix than two; coverage is such as to make this possible in many areas.

# Automatic Steering Devices

Automatic steering devices are electrical or electro-hydraulic equipment used to hold a boat on a predetermined heading. They are often, but erroneously, referred to as "automatic pilots"; they do no part of the piloting of a boat.

In lieu of the direct application of human muscle power to the steering mechanism of a boat, electric or hydraulic motors may be used to move the rudder to the desired angle and to hold it there. See fig. 2552. The control of these motors may be made automatic by the addition of a direction-sensing element and suitable electronic amplifiers. Either magnetic or gyroscopic compasses can be used to sense heading changes, but the former is nearly always used because of its lower cost.

Most automatic steering devices have controls which allow temporary manual over-riding of the automatic controls with the boat returning to the preset heading when the over-ride switch is released. This permits brief course changes to avoid obstructions or other boats without having to reset the desired heading. Local control boxes on long cords make possible the maneuvering of the boat while away from the normal helm position. This control of the craft, however, does not include throttle changes or forward-reverse shifting.

The use of automatic steering devices is simple. They do much to relieve boredom and fatigue on long, straight stretches. The device can, under most circumstances, steer

FIG. 2552 Automatic steering mechanism can do better job than human helmsman! Components are shown—magnetic compass with sensing attachments, electronic amplifier, steering motor, and control boxes.

a straighter course than a human helmsman. The disadvantage in this equipment lies in its misuse, excessive reliance on the device and failure to keep a person at the helm as a lookout ready to take over immediately if a dangerous situation should develop. It must also be remembered that the sensing element is usually no more "intelligent" than a magnetic compass; it is subject to all of the same outside corrupting influences such as tools, portable radios, beer cans, etc., if they are placed too close.

# Citizens Band Radio

Citizens Band (CB) radio operations must be considered separately from those of the 2-3 Mc/s and VHF bands as they come under an entirely different set of FCC Rules. The CB sets are relatively inexpensive, easy to install, and simple to operate. See fig. 2553.

The Citizens Radio Service (CRS) is unique; it is not intended to duplicate any other radio service. It is *not* a substitute for the safety features of the regular marine radio service in the 2-3 Mc/s band, nor for the ship-to-shore connections into the public telephone system. Likewise, it is *not* a new type of hobby or amateur service for casual contacts at great distances. The CRS has its own particular functions and these do not overlap or conflict with other established services. As the result of widespread misuse of CB sets, the FCC, in April 1965, tightened its rules to control CRS operations more strictly.

Citizens Band communications can relate to either the business or social activities of the licensee, but they must be "necessary"—messages which could be sent by other means, or which need not be sent at all, are not permitted by FCC regulations. CB stations may not, of course, be used to further any illegal activity.

## CB LICENSES

Licenses for stations in the Citizens Band have been made as easy as possible to obtain, and operator permits are not required at all. There are only a minimum of legal restrictions on the applicant and the equipment. To get a station license, a person must be a U.S. citizen and at least 18 years old. Licenses may also be issued to corporations provided that they meet certain rules regarding the U.S. citizenship of their officers and owners or members. Licenses may not be transferred to another person; prompt report by letter is required for a change in address (but not for a change in approved equipment). Licenses are good for 5 years; renewal requires the same form and fee.

Application for a CB station license is made on Form 505 available from any FCC office. A portion of the application is returned as the station license, and this must be received before the equipment can be used. A check or money order for $8 must accompany each application for a station license, which may, at no additional cost, include any number of sets owned by the same individual or organization.

In licensing equipment to be used on the Citizens Band, the FCC primarily envisions separate complete communications systems to meet the needs of individual licensees. This system would normally communicate within itself, and contacts with other stations heard on the air would be the exception rather than the normal mode of operation. In this connection, a "station" is all of the equipment used by a licensee in his system, and a "unit" is the term applied to a particular transmitter-receiver combination. Thus a *station* normally consists of at least two *units,* although it may consist of many more. Only in well-justified instances will the FCC license a single-unit station in the Citizens Band. The planned use of a Class D set by a boat owner belonging to a group operating a CB system would be an example of justification for licensing a single unit.

## AUTHORIZED CHANNELS

The FCC has authorized 23 channels for the Citizens Band; they are generally referred to by channel number rather than frequency in megacycles. Any of them may be used by any licensee *for communications between units of one station.* For contacts between different stations, *only* channels 10 through 15, plus 23 may be used. Channel 9 is reserved for "emergency communications involving the

FIG. 2553  Citizens Band radios find many applications in boating, car, home or summer cottage. Model shown is specially designed for marine use.

immediate safety of life or the immediate protection of property." It is also available for "communications necessary to render assistance to a motorist" (but *not* for aid to boatmen!). Two points *must* be noted: (1) Although Channel 9 may be used for marine emergencies, it is *not* a substitute for the regular maritime distress frequencies of 2181 kHz and 156.8 MHz; and (2) Channel 9 is *not* to be used for "calling" to make initial contact with another station or unit in a manner similar to 2182 kHz in the marine band.

Class D stations in the Citizens Band are limited to 5 watts input power and, without special approval, an antenna must not extend more than 20 feet above the building on which it is mounted. With these restrictions, the usual reliable range is on the order of five miles, but may extend to 15 miles or more. These are groundwave ranges; skywave transmission of CB signals will often occur and cause signals to be heard at distances of several thousand miles despite their low power. The FCC Rules prohibit exchanges between stations more than 150 miles apart.

## OPERATING PROCEDURES

Operation of a Citizens Band station is quite simple. No specific operating procedures need be learned and used; no log is required. However, there are regulations which must be known and obeyed.

The FCC Rules require that *all* communications be restricted to the *minimum practicable transmission time,* but no time limits are placed on intercommunications between units of the same station. Between different stations, however, an exchange must be limited to a maximum of 5 minutes; after its completion, both stations must remain off the air for an additional 5 minutes, monitoring the frequency just used. A station called during this waiting period may break silence to advise the other station to stand-by. Avoidance of this waiting period by changing to another channel is prohibited.

Station identification must be given at the beginning and end of each exchange of transmissions on each frequency used. If the contact continues for more than 15 minutes (legal only between units of the same station), identification must be made at least each 15 minutes. The Rules

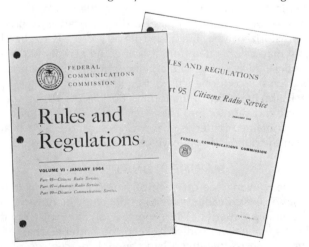

FIG. 2554  Each CB licensee must have on hand CURRENT copy of Part 95 of FCC Rules and Regulations. See text for details.

specifically require that *each letter and digit* of the call sign must be transmitted separately and distinctly. For example, 2951 must be said as "two nine five one," not as "twenty-nine fifty-one"; and 4500 as "four five zero zero," not as "forty-five hundred." Only standard phonetic alphabets may be used for the letters of the call sign.

The CB Rules now provide priority for transmissions involving the immediate safety of life of persons or protection of property. Under such conditions, the regulations restricting inter-station contacts to certain channels, limiting the durations of exchanges, etc., are waived, provided that a report is made to the FCC after the emergency is over. There are no priorities for other types of communications.

The usual prohibitions against profane, obscene, and indecent language apply to the Citizens Band. Plain language must be used, except that abbreviations and normal operating signals (such as the "10" Code) are permitted, provided that a list of such signals and their meaning is kept in the station records. Although no operator permit is required, CB stations may be operated only by the licensee, members of his immediate family, his employees, and certain other individuals specifically authorized in the regulations. CB stations may *not* be operated by a person who has had his own license revoked or has surrendered it for cancellation as the result of rule violations. The licensee must remember that he retains full responsibility for all use of all units of his station. The same system of administrative forfeitures (small fines) that applies to marine band radio operations is also applicable to CB.

The FCC now requires that a CB licensee have a *current* copy of the applicable Rules, now Part 95. See fig. 2554. The only practicable way of complying is to purchase a copy of the FCC Rules and Regulations, Volume VI, from the Superintendent of Documents, Government Printing Office, Washington, D.C. 20402. The price of $2.00 includes a subscription to the mailing service for changes as they are issued.

## Miscellaneous Electronic Equipment

There are many small items of electronic equipment that can be installed on a boat for the greater safety and convenience of the owner and his guests. The boatman should consider each for possible installation on his craft, not forgetting that each item will usually add a bit to the load on the battery and electrical wiring.

### FUEL VAPOR DETECTORS

A *fuel vapor detector* is considered by many boatmen to be an essential piece of safety equipment aboard any craft using gasoline as fuel. See fig. 2555. These devices provide a visual warning of the build-up of any dangerous concentration of fuel vapors in the bilges. Frequently, such a device also provides an audible alarm in addition to the visual warning.

The installation of a fuel vapor detector is not difficult electrically or mechanically, but it is essential that it be done correctly. The location of the detector unit is important if the maximum safety benefit is to be obtained. Have your installation checked by a surveyor or safety inspector from your insurance company. Even the best fuel vapor detector is no substitute for electric bilge blowers, forced ventilation fans that pull air and fumes out of the lower parts of your boat's interior.

### AUXILIARY RECEIVERS

If your boat does not have a direction finder that can be used as an *auxiliary receiver,* the boat owner should consider the purchase of one of several compact and lightweight receivers that are available at a reasonable price. See fig. 2556. This additional receiver can serve the functions previously mentioned of monitoring a second communications channel or of backing up the regular receiver in case of its failure. If the auxiliary receiver is of the transistorized type, the added battery drain is negligible, or it may be operated from its self-contained dry batteries. Models are available with either continuous tuning or several crystal-controlled fixed frequencies. This latter type lacks the flexibility of the former, but has the advantage of quick and sure tuning. These small receivers, if they have self-contained batteries, may be taken ashore on a beach or in the dinghy if you leave your boat for any reason.

### MARINE CONVERTERS

The growing use of electrical equipment on boats has resulted in a steadily increasing demand for power from the craft's batteries. The generator or alternator on the boat's engine will suffice to keep the batteries charged if the engine is operated a large enough percentage of the time that the electrical equipment is in use. There is no way to state a general figure as to what proportion of the

FIG. 2555 Fuel vapor detector, properly installed and used, will warn of explosive vapors in bilge. Models available with audible alarm and visual indicator.

FIG. 2556 With auxiliary receiver, second marine band channel may be monitored, or you can listen to frequency for which your radio-telephone does not have a crystal. Model shown operates from self-contained batteries.

FIG. 2557 Boat batteries are normally charged by generator or alternator driven by main engine. At dockside, marine converter keeps batteries up by converting shoreside AC power to DC at proper voltage for boat's electrical system.

time is required as individual conditions will vary too widely.

It you are one of the boat owners who finds that all too often his battery is down so far that it won't start the engine, then you are a candidate for a *marine converter*. See fig. 2557. This relatively simple electrical device converts the 115-volt AC dockside electricity into the 6, 12, or 32 volts DC required for the boat's electrical system. It is essentially a continuous-duty battery-charger with control circuits to permit it to operate safely left unattended.

## INVERTERS

It may seem a bit contradictory to immediately discuss a means of getting 115-volt AC electrical power from the boat's low voltage DC system just after having considered the reverse process, but there is a reason. There is no way to store AC in a battery, and if AC is needed when under way, the only means of getting it (without installing an engine-driven auxiliary generating plant) is to "invert" the DC power from the batteries into AC.

Alternating current aboard a boat of any size is useful for the powering of television or hi-fi sets, tape recorders, electric razors, electric mixers or other small household appliances. Small inverters are available using vibrators or transistors and these will quietly and efficiently supply you with small amounts of "shore-type" electricity. These DC to AC converters are *not* suitable for use with electrical devices whose function is to produce heat, such as toasters and irons; the power required for such items is beyond the capacity of inverters.

## AUXILIARY GENERATING PLANTS

Inverters using vibrators or transistors are usually limited to a power rating of not more than 250 watts. If greater amounts of 115-volt AC power are required for cooking, air conditioning, or heating, the installation of a small

FIG. 2558 Inverters can change DC electrical power of boat's batteries to 115-volts AC for operation of shore-type electrical equipment, up to a few hundred watts. For heavier loads, install auxiliary electric plant driven by its own gasoline or diesel engine. (Diagram from Technical Bulletin T-021, Installation of Onan Marine Generating Plants.)

auxiliary generating plant should be considered. See fig. 2558. These units are available in sizes from 500 watts to 10 kilowatts or more, with either gasoline or diesel engines to match the type of fuel used in the main engines.

Calculation of the size of generator you will need is not difficult as nearly all items of electrical equipment are plainly rated in watts of power consumed. Be careful, however, about loads that are not constant. For example, an electric refrigerator unit may consume only about 100 watts *average* power since it does not run continuously, but while it is running it may require 400 watts, and the momentary starting load will be even greater. Be generous and be safer; install an electric plant with an adequate excess or reserve capacity. You will soon think of more electrical and electronic gear to add to your boat.

## INTERCOM SYSTEMS

While most people think of a boat as being too small and compact to have internal communications problems, there are numerous possible applications for simple intercom systems. See fig. 2559. The interior of many larger cruisers, particularly those of the double-cabin type, are so divided that voices do not carry well from one compartment to another. A simple three-station intercom system connecting the bridge, forward cabin, and after cabin will

FIG. 2559 Small intercom system permits easy communication between all areas aboard cruisers and yachts. Master unit shown controls five substations, including one on foredeck, useful when anchoring or docking.

make possible easy conversation between these locations and save many steps. On a boat with a small crew, such as a couple living aboard by themselves, a quick and easy means of internal communications is truly a safety item as the helmsman need not leave the controls or divert his attention to carry on a conversation or summon assistance.

On a larger boat, the intercom system can be extended to include a unit in a weather-proof box on the foredeck.

Then you can have constant contact between the person at the boat's controls and the person raising or lowering the anchor, or handling the docking lines. Just try to get up a badly fouled anchor without communicating with the helmsman, and you will quickly appreciate this small electronic device.

## RUDDER POSITION INDICATORS

A simple and inexpensive, but very useful, item is a *rudder position indicator*. See fig. 2560. These are standard equipment of large vessels and tugboats, but are seldom found on recreational boats. This small degree of use probably results from a lack of knowledge of the availability of the device and how it works. A small unit is in-

FIG. 2560 Rudder position indicators are always found on large ships and tugs, infrequently on small craft. They deserve wider use. Knowledge of rudder angle helps when docking, undocking, entering canal locks, etc.

stalled at the rudder post and wires are run forward to a meter located within easy view of the helmsman. This meter is calibrated in degrees of right or left rudder. A quick glance will instantly tell the exact position of the rudder at that moment; such information is of considerable value when getting under way or docking with little steerageway. Once you have and use one of these electronic items, you will never be without it.

---

### New Unit of Frequency Measurement

The familiar units of radio frequency measurement—cycles, kilocycles, and megacycles—are being gradually replaced with new units. Scientific organizations are now using the term "Hertz" to replace "cycles per second." This new unit is named for a pioneer in the field of radio waves, Heinrich Hertz, 1857-1894. (Did you know that the familiar units of Ohms, Amperes, Volts, Watts, and many others were all derived from the names of persons who developed early theories and laws of electricity?) The FCC has accepted the definition of "Hertz," abbreviated as "Hz," and this unit along with kilohertz (kHz) and megahertz (MHz) may be found in increasing use.

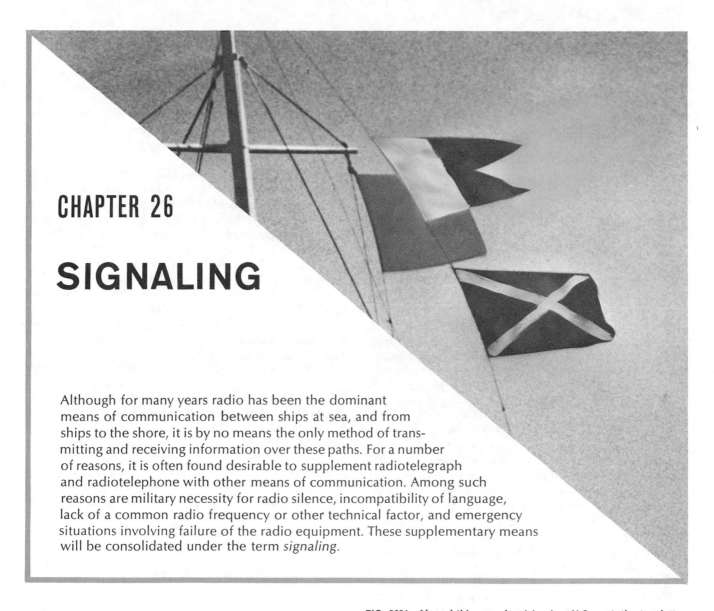

# CHAPTER 26

# SIGNALING

Although for many years radio has been the dominant means of communication between ships at sea, and from ships to the shore, it is by no means the only method of transmitting and receiving information over these paths. For a number of reasons, it is often found desirable to supplement radiotelegraph and radiotelephone with other means of communication. Among such reasons are military necessity for radio silence, incompatibility of language, lack of a common radio frequency or other technical factor, and emergency situations involving failure of the radio equipment. These supplementary means will be consolidated under the term *signaling*.

FIG. 2601 Aboard this vessel arriving in a U.S. port, the two-letter International Code flag signal AM (Alfa Mike) at the masthead signifies "Have you a doctor?" and the single-letter Q (Quebec) at the starboard yardarm is flown to "request pratique." (Rosenfeld photo)

## The forms of signaling

The principal forms of signaling are: (1) flag-hoist, (2) flashing light, and (3) semaphore. These are all visual means; signaling by audible methods, such as by Morse code on the boat's horn, is of little practical use. Sound signals as used in the Rules of the Road are covered elsewhere and will not be repeated here.

### VISUAL SIGNALING

Visual signaling should not be a new or strange concept to the average boatman, although he probably lacks the detailed knowledge to read such signals. The yachtsman crossing a busy harbor will certainly see many ships flying signal flags; and should it be a naval harbor, such as Hampton Roads or San Diego, he will undoubtedly also see flashing signal lights, and perhaps sailors sending semaphore.

## The value of visual signaling

The time taken to acquire a rudimentary knowledge of visual signaling can be of value to a boatman in at least two ways. Not the least of these is the pleasure and satisfaction of knowing what is going on and being able to explain it to the other crew members and guests aboard his boat. Merchant ships, fig. 2602, will be flying signal flags indicating the presence of a pilot aboard, the handling of dangerous cargoes, an imminent sailing, and other interesting facts. Naval and Coast Guard vessels, fig. 2603, probably will be flying many more flags, some signifying simple facts like those noted above, and others signaling more complex naval messages and maneuvers. Being able to read and know the meaning of at least a portion of these signal flags, or other types of signals, will give the boatman a greater sense of "belonging" to the maritime world around him.

The greater value, however, in a knowledge of signaling lies in the added margin of safety that it can provide. So much dependence is placed today on the boat's radio-telephone that one often overlooks the possibility of its not being available when needed. It need not be an electronic failure that precludes your communicating with another craft; it could be merely a lack of a common frequency or type of modulation. Radio will undoubtedly remain your primary means of boat-to-boat and boat-to-shore communications, but don't overlook the added possibilities of signaling.

## Signal Codes

For more than two thousand years, information and orders have been communicated between ships by means of flags. In the days of the ancient Greeks and Romans, battles were begun by the hoisting of streamers of various colors. These were first raised on the vessel carrying the commander of the naval force—hence the term "flagship."

The development of modern flag-hoist signaling may be said to date from 1340 when the British Navy officially listed two signals—one for all captains to come to the flagship and the other that the enemy had been sighted. By 1530, the French Navy was using a signal code with five meanings.

Signal books first appeared in 1673 when an English system was established using flags of different colors hoisted at various places to give a series of meanings. The 1738 French signal code used ten numerical flags in groups of three for transmitting prearranged messages. By 1780, this technique had been expanded by the addition of two "repeaters" so that only 12 flags, rather than 30, would be needed for all combinations, 000 to 999. The code book was prepared in both alphabetical and numerical sections for encoding and decoding. This is essentially the same format as is used for signal books today. The French system also provided for the relaying of signals to the more distant ships in a formation, again just as is currently done in naval forces at sea.

The first American flag code was proposed in 1797 em-

**FIG. 2602 Merchant ships are often seen flying a single flag from the International Code of Signals. This vessel has the "H" flag hoisted to signify that there is a pilot aboard. The "G" flag woud have indicated a request for a pilot. All of the alphabet flags have a special meaning when flown singly as well as when used in groups of two or more.**

ploying numeral pennants and repeaters for 290 signals, and in 1802 a modified version was adopted for use by the Continental Navy. Flag-hoist signaling has been used by the American Navy continuously since then.

In 1817, the British adopted a code of signals for merchant ships different from that used by the Royal Navy. In other countries, non-naval vessels used various signal systems that usually were published by private individuals or groups. These prevailed until 1857 when a new English "commercial code" was established that was gradually adopted by other countries. Because more combinations were needed than could be obtained with ten pennants in combinations of three, a new set of 18 flags was adopted and named after letters of the alphabet—the consonants, less X, Y, and Z. These flags could not be used for spelling out words as the vowels were missing; coded meanings were still employed for geographical locations, common words and phrases, combinations of letters or single letters, and numbers. More than a dozen of these flags are still used in the original design as adopted in 1857; others have been changed to increase their readability under difficult conditions of visibility.

In 1897, the alphabet was filled out with flags for the missing letters and was officially designated as the International Code of Signals. Experience with this code during World War I revealed many deficiencies, and it was subsequently revised in a series of conferences and meetings. Numeral pennants were added to eliminate the need for using code groups of letters for sending numbers, and three substitutes (repeaters) were added to expand the possible combinations of four-flag hoists. The 1930 Code was made truly international by being standardized in official versions in seven languages. Since 1955, the flags have been associated with the phonetic alphabet now so widely used in radio-telephone communications.

### THE REVISED INTERNATIONAL CODE

Between 1961 and 1964 an international committee met periodically and drew up a new Code of Signals. The revised Code is intended primarily for situations related to the safety of navigation and persons, especially where language difficulties arise. Official versions of the new Code are now published in nine languages. It is suitable for transmission by *all* means of communications, including radiotelephony.

#### H.O. 102

The revised International Code of Signals became effective on 1 April 1969. For American use, it has been published by the Naval Oceanographic Office as H.O. 102. This new volume replaces both the old H.O. 103 used for visual signaling and H.O. 104 used for radio. The book can be purchased from local sales agents, or it can be ordered by mail from the U.S. Naval Oceanographic Office, Washington, D.C. 20390.

H.O. 102 includes both general procedures applicable to all forms of communication and specific rules for flag signaling, flashing light signaling, sound signaling, radiotelegraphy, radiotelephony, and signaling by hand flags, using either semaphore or the Morse code.

#### Principles of coding

The revised Code is based on the principle that each

**FIG. 2603** Naval and Coast Guard ships make much use of signal flags for communicating with other vessels. Each flag represents a letter, number or special meaning. Government ships always hoist the flags of their call letters when entering or leaving port.

signal will have a complete meaning. It thus omits the vocabulary method that was a part of the old Code. The Geographical Section, not being considered essential, was dropped. By these means, it was possible to reduce considerably the volume of the Code and achieve greater simplicity.

The signals used consist of: (1) single-letter signals allocated to meanings which are very urgent, important, of very common use; (2) two-letter signals for general messages; and (3) three-letter signals (all beginning with "M") for medical messages.

In certain cases, *complements* are used—an added nu-meral following the basic two-letter signal. Complements express: (1) variations in the meaning of a basic signal; (2) questions and answers related to the meaning of the basic signal; and (3) supplementary, specific, or more detailed meanings.

## Spelling

When names must be sent, or other words for which there are no signal groups in the International Code, they must be spelled out. The signal group YZ *may* be used to indicate that the groups which follow are plain language words rather than code signals; it can, however, be omitted if the spelling is obvious. The "alphabetical signals" formerly used have been discontinued.

## Special procedures

The International Code of Signals provides special procedures for many purposes such as signaling time, courses and bearings, geographical coordinates, etc. The details of these procedures are too lengthy for inclusion in this book; the boatman needing such knowledge will find it in full in H.O. 102. This volume is a "must" for a boatman who may need to communicate with foreign ships or shore stations; it is a necessity for any skipper who carries a full set of signal flags and uses them to communicate with other yachts or with Naval and Coast Guard vessels. It is an interesting book to have aboard even if such signaling is not contemplated.

The problem of compiling a code from which expressions in any one of nine languages might be taken was a difficult one, and certain principles must be followed in its use. These are outlined in the instructions in H.O. 102 and should be read carefully before attempting to use the code itself. Otherwise, because of the form used, erroneous interpretations might be placed on a message sent in code.

## Typical code signals from H.O. 102

The simple single-letter signal codes are shown beneath the flags on page 0. Typical two-letter groups are listed in fig. 2615.

**FIG. 2604** Flags and pennants of the International Code of Signals are joined together with snaps and rings. The "tail line" extending below each flag provides the spacing beween them in each group; the "tack line" provides a greater spacing between two groups hoisted on the same halyard.

**FIG. 2605** Signal flags are normally hoisted on halyards rising to the yardarms. In some situations, particularly on naval vessels, hoists may be made at more than one location simultaneously. See text for sequence in which such multiple hoists are read.

# Flag-hoist Signaling

The set of international code flags prescribed for flag-hoist signaling consists of 26 alphabetical flags, 10 numeral pennants, three substitutes, and the answering pennant. The names "substitute" and "repeater" are used interchangeably in publications on flag-hoist signaling. In either case, they are pennants that are employed as replacements for flags (or pennants) already used once in a hoist, since there is only one of each letter or number in a set.

Five standardized colors are used for signal flags—red, white, blue, yellow, and black. Most of the flags are of two colors, selected and arranged for maximum contrast. Two flags are of a single solid color, several use three colors, and one uses four colors. Each flag and pennant has a piece of line sewn into its hoist edge, extending slightly above the cloth to a metal ring, and for several inches below the cloth ending in a snap hook. This "tail line"

provides the spacing between the flags of a hoist; the combination of snaps and rings permits the rapid joining together of the individual flags and their connection onto a signal halyard. See fig. 2604.

The flags and pennants of the International Code are shown in full color on page 0. Also indicated here are the meanings of the flags when flown singly. Of these, probably the most often seen will be the "B" flag, displayed while a ship is carrying or handling an explosive cargo, and the "H" flag flown when a pilot is on board.

## Special naval flags and pennants

The boatman may sometimes see vessels of the U. S. Navy and Coast Guard flying signals that include flags and pennants not found in the International Code. The Navy uses a set of *numeral flags* as well as the regular pennants for numbers. In addition, special flags and pennants have been adopted for naval formations and maneuvers.

The U. S. Navy uses the three substitutes of the International Code and has added its own fourth substitute.

The special naval flags and pennants are shown in color at the bottom of page P.

### FLAG SIGNALING PROCEDURES

Signal flags are flown singly and in combinations of two or more; see page P. Flags and pennants may be mixed as required.

When signaling by means of the flags and pennants of the International Code, it is advisable to show only a single *hoist* at a time. A hoist means one or more *groups* displayed from a single halyard. The signal is read from the top down. Each group of letters and/or numerals constitute a separate signal; when several groups are used on a single hoist, they must, of course, be separated to convey the correct meaning. A *tackline,* a six-foot length of line with a snap hook in one end and a ring in the other, is used as a spacer to separate the groups.

**FIG. 2606** Flag hoists are read from the top flag down. If there should be more than one halyard in use from the same yardarm at the same time, the hoists are read from outboard inward as shown above.

### TYPICAL SIGNALS
### FROM A YACHT CLUB SIGNAL CODE

A — The course will be _____.
H — Communicate with me via radiotelephone.
L — Come within hail.
Q — Race will finish off _____.
T — Send club launch.
BF — Anchor for night at _____.
CQ — Captains and guests are invited on board this yacht at _____.
CZ — Congratulations, well done.
DC — Mail for you ashore at _____.
IR — Monday
JQ — 0730
NG — Bangor, Maine
SG — Newport, R. I.
AQP — N.N.E.
ARU — S.W.

**FIG. 2607** In a typical yacht club signal code, single letters will consist of special, racing, and emergency signals; two-letter groups will represent general and designating signals, and days of the week and hours of the day; three-letter groups are compass signals.

Signals should be kept flying until acknowledged. There are occasions when more than one hoist need be displayed simultaneously; in such cases, an order of sequence must be followed in order to interpret the message correctly. The hoists are read in the following order: (1) masthead, (2) triatic stay, (3) starboard yardarm, and (4) port yardarm, fig. 2605.

In cases where more than one hoist is flown from a yardarm, they are read from outboard inward, fig. 2606. When a vessel displays more than one hoist from a triatic stay, they are read from the foremost one aft.

The terms *superior* and *inferior* are often used in relation to signals. A signal is superior to another if hoisted

FIG. 2608 On boats equipped with a full set of signal flags and pennants, a flag chest or locker may be built in, with letter or name plates to identify code flags in their individual pigeonholes.

before the latter, either in point of time or hoist. If hoisted after, it is inferior.

Obviously, a visual signal is going to fail in its purpose if it is not clearly visible. For that reason, signals should always be flown where they can be seen best by the receiving vessel or shore station. This means that each flag must stand out clearly, not fouled by the halyard, sails, etc.

## Signal groups

If every message transmitted by flag signals had to be spelled out letter by letter, it is obvious that the procedure would become impossibly lengthy, wasting much time and effort. Many typical messages have been given two-letter signals in the revised Code. One of the first steps in gaining proficiency in visual signaling is to become thoroughly familiar with the code book. With such knowledge, one will naturally frame his messages so as to use phrasing for which code groups have been provided, lessening the number of words that must be spelled out.

## Calling and answering

When calling a particular vessel, her signal letters are hoisted superior to the message that is to follow. Otherwise, in the absence of such signal letters, the message would be understood to be addressed to all vessels in sight of the signal. If the vessel's signal letters are not

known, she can be requested to hoist them by displaying the code letter group CS and hoisting your own signal letters at the same time. As another alternative, display of the code group YQ would convey the message: "I wish to signal to the vessel on bearing indicated from me." This signal would, of course, be accompanied with another hoist indicating the bearing concerned so as to distinguish between several vessels that might be within sight.

In order to understand the procedure followed in answering a signal, there are several terms that should be explained. A signal is said to be *at the dip* when it is hoisted only about half as high as the halyard will permit. It is said to be *close up* when it has been hoisted as high as possible. See page P center left.

In receiving signals, the vessel or vessels addressed should hoist the answering pennant at the dip when each hoist is seen, closing up to indicate that the signal is understood. Then when the hoist on the transmitting ship is hauled down, the answering pennant on the receiving vessel is lowered to the dip again so as to be ready to acknowledge the next hoist in a similar manner when that one is understood. This continues until the message is completed, at which time the answering pennant alone is hoisted aboard the transmitting ship; this signal is acknowledged by the receiving ship as before, after which the answering pennants are hauled down.

When a hoist can not be clearly distinguished, the answering pennant is kept at the dip on the receiving ship and a signal is hoisted to convey the reason for the difficulty. If, on the other hand, the signal can be distinguished but not understood, the letters ZL are hoisted.

## Substitutes or Repeaters

With every set of code flags there are included three *substitutes*. These permit the repetition of a signal flag in a group without carrying extra sets of flags. In the procedures of the International Code, substitutes repeat the same *class* of flag that precedes them; that is, following alphabetical flags they repeat them, but if used with numeral pennants they repeat such pennants.

Considering then only the class of flag directly preceding the substitute, the first substitute repeats the top such flag; the second substitute, the second flag from the top; and the third substitute, the third flag from the top. An answering pennant used as a decimal point is disregarded. For example: if the signal were T1330, the hoist would be: T, 1, 3, second substitute, 0. See the illustration on page P, upper right. A particular substitute is never used more than once in the same group. If the signal were BBCB, the hoist would read: B, first substitute, C, second substitute. Note that the first substitute has been used once in place of the second letter and cannot be used again. However, as used it represented the letter B, and so it can be repeated by use of the second substitute; see page P.

## Naval procedures

Flag-hoist signaling procedures between Naval and Coast Guard vessels will vary from that used by merchant ships and yachts. These differences stem from the different and special requirements of naval formations and maneuvers. They need not cause any concern to boatmen, however, for in communications with non-naval craft, these vessels will use International Code procedures.

## YACHT CLUB SIGNAL CODES

Many yacht clubs have adopted signal codes of their own that are not in conformity with the International Code. The purpose of the signals prescribed in such codes is principally to provide a means of communication between craft of the club's fleet. These local codes permit quicker and easier signaling for matters of particular interest to that group. See fig. 2607.

While the codes do vary between different clubs, there is a tendency toward standardization of both the signals and the procedures. The interpretation of club signals will generally require the availability of that club's signal code as published in its year book.

Most clubs provide that when using the club code the burgee is hoisted over the code flags; the absence of the burgee indicating that the hoist should be read from the International Code of Signals. In other cases, the procedures provide that the three signal flags YV 1 can be hoisted to indicate specifically that the International Code is being used, its absence indicating the use of the club code. It is necessary to know the procedures of the particular club concerned.

### General yachting uses of signal flags

Most boats will not carry a full set of signal flags and pennants, fig. 2608, but may carry one or more for special use under certain conditions.

The flying of the single flag "Q" when returning from a foreign port is correct and desirable in accordance with its International Code meaning "My vessel is healthy and I request free pratique." See fig. 2601. *Pratique* is the formal term for permission to use a port.

The code flag "T" is often seen flying on boats at yacht club moorings. Its meaning at such times is a request for "transportation"—a call for the club launch to come alongside and pick up passengers for shore. This is not in accordance with the International Code of Signals, but has general acceptance and understanding through wide usage.

Another single code-flag signal is the flying of the letter "M" to signify "Doctor on board"; this differs from the revised International Code meaning. Not yet in general use, its value is gradually being recognized and the practice is spreading. While most, if not all, doctors look to their boating hours as a time "to get away from it all," knowledge that a boat has a doctor on board is of great importance should an accident happen within sight; it is to be hoped that the practice of flying the "M" flag will be adopted by more and more physicians and surgeons.

## SPECIAL FLAGS

Many flags will be seen on boats that undoubtedly "signal" a meaning, but nonetheless will not be found in any signal code, International or yacht club.

The more official of these flags include the owner absent, guest aboard, and meal flags described on page 463. Next in line would come the cocktail flag, the meaning of which is never in doubt, closely followed by a newer flag bearing a foaming mug of beer. For the non-alcoholically inclined, there is now a flag decorated with a pot of coffee, obviously inviting the beholder to "come on over and have one."

Boats operating out of sport-fishing ports will often be seen flying flags bearing the likeness of various game fish, indicating their catch for that day. Unhappily, you may also see boats flying the "skunk" flag signifying "no luck today."

A special flag that must be strictly honored is the "diver down" flag—rectangular red with a single white diagonal stripe. Keep well away from any boat or float displaying this signal.

There seems to be an ever-expanding list of what might be called "comic" flags. These are not particularly in good taste in yachting circles, but as they can be considered as signaling information, their existence will be noted here. Among such flags are the ball-and-chain (wife aboard), witch-on-a-broom (wife not on board), battle-axe (mother-in-law aboard), and two sleeping rabbits (do not disturb). See fig. 2609.

There is also the skull-and-crossed-bones "pirate" flag that is often seen, but which apparently has no standardized meaning, if indeed it has any meaning beyond its decorative (?) value.

BATTLE-AXE
MOTHER-IN-LAW ABOARD

SKUNK
(NO FISH CAUGHT)

COCKTAIL

COFFEE

BALL & CHAIN
WIFE ABOARD

WITCH—
WIFE ASHORE

BEER

BUNNIES—SLUMBER
DO NOT DISTURB

FIG. 2609 Many boats will be seen flying the so-called "novelty" or "gag" flags. While in somewhat questionable taste in strict yachting circles, it must be admitted that, properly used, they do "signal" information to other craft.

FIG. 2610 For short-range signaling, naval vessels will use small searchlights not much larger than those found on motorboats. The flashes of light are formed by opening and closing shutter vanes in front of the light source. The Navy also uses several larger sizes of signal searchlights up to 36-inch carbon-arc lights.

Courtesy—U. S. Navy Publications Center

Courtesy—United States Coast Guard

## Flashing Light Signaling

Signaling by short and long flashes of light is widely used by naval forces. It is much faster than hoists of code flags and has a much greater range than semaphore signaling. It maintains the radio silence sometimes needed for security.

Navy vessels may use small or large signal searchlights, yardarm or masthead lights, or special security devices. For normal ranges from one ship to another, a small searchlight about the size of those mounted on medium-sized boats will be used, fig. 2610. These lights will be bright enough for signaling during the day or night. To communicate over greater distances, which may be several miles or more, large and powerful arc-light searchlights will be found on major naval vessels.

Searchlights of all sizes are normally used to communicate with another specific vessel or with a shore station. For signaling to all ships around a harbor or in a formation at sea, use will be made of the yardarm or masthead blinker lights, less powerful but capable of being read

from any direction, fig. 2611. Security can be achieved by using cones over the signal searchlight to restrict the light pattern, or by using infrared devices that require special receiving equipment to read the signals being sent.

### Small-craft use

Flashing light signaling is useful also to boatmen. It has the advantage of needing little or no special equipment; an ordinary flashlight is usually used as the signaling light. There is, however, the disadvantage that a knowledge of the Morse code is required.

Generally, flashing light signals from a boat are limited to nighttime use by the low power of the light source. The boat's searchlight cannot be turned on and off fast enough for the practical transmission of Morse code dots and dashes—the Navy's signal searchlights are left on continuously during use, with shutters being rapidly opened and closed to make the short and long flashes of light. The short but definite time for the filament of a boat's searchlight to come up to brilliance and die out is too great for message sending, but would be satisfactory for such special use as the three shorts, three longs, and three shorts of an SOS signal. (••• — — — •••)

### THE INTERNATIONAL MORSE CODE

As noted above, the International Morse Code of *dots* and *dashes* is used for flashing light signaling. The flashes and the spaces between them are defined in terms of *units* —a *dot* is *one* unit long; a *dash* is *three* units; the space between the dots and dashes of a single character (letter or number) is one unit long, between characters it is three units, and between words or groups it is five units in length. The length of a "unit" is roughly set by the skill of the operator and the speed at which he can transmit accurately; it is always well to transmit somewhat more slowly than one's maximum capability to minimize errors and, in

NONDIRECTIONAL BLINKER LIGHTS

FIG. 2611 For non-directional flashing light signaling, a vessel may be equipped with yardarm blinker lights. They may also be located as a pair at a masthead. With these lights the range over which signals can be sent is much less than that of a searchlight.

| | | | | | | |
|---|---|---|---|---|---|---|
| A | • — | J | • — — — | R | • — • |
| B | — • • • | K | — • — | S | • • • |
| C | — • — • | L | • — • • | T | — |
| D | — • • | M | — — | U | • • — |
| E | • | N | — • | V | • • • — |
| F | • • — • | O | — — — | W | • — — |
| G | — — • | P | • — — • | X | — • • — |
| H | • • • • | Q | — — • — | Y | — • — — |
| I | • • | | | Z | — — • • |

Period • — • — • —
Comma — — • • — —
Interrogative • — • — — • — (RQ)
Distress Call • • • — — — • • • (SOS)
From — • • (DE)
Invitation to transmit (go ahead) — • — (K)
Wait • — • • • (AS)
Error • • • • • • • • (EEEE etc.)
Received • — • (R)
End of each message • — • — • (AR)

| | | | | | |
|---|---|---|---|---|---|
| 1 | • — — — — | 2 | • • — — — | 3 | • • • — — |
| 4 | • • • • — | 5 | • • • • • | 6 | — • • • • |
| 7 | — — • • • | 8 | — — — • • | 9 | — — — — • |
| | | | | 0 | — — — — — |

NOTE:
A dash is equal to three dots.
The space between parts of the same letter is equal to one dot.
The space between two letters is equal to three dots.
The space between two words is equal to five dots.

FIG. 2612 The International Morse Code, with certain simple procedure signals.

case of doubt, it is better to exaggerate slightly the lengths of dashes and spaces than it is to shorten them.

The letters of the alphabet, numbers, and punctuation marks are signaled in Morse code by combinations of dots and dashes. Letters have from one to four components, numbers have five, and punctuation symbols have six. The basic Morse code is shown in fig. 2612.

Time is required to memorize the Morse code characters for the letters, numbers, and simple punctuation marks; but it *can* be done by anyone, and it is well worth the effort required. Once learned, and occasionally used, it will not be forgotten and may prove extremely valuable some day in an emergency.

## FLASHING LIGHT PROCEDURES

Formal procedures have been prescribed for the establishment and carrying out of communications by flashing light. The boatman need know only the barest fundamentals, enough for emergencies, leaving the full details, as described in H.O. 102, to the professional signalman.

### Establishing contact

A vessel desiring to establish flashing light communications with another trains its light on the other and sends the other's call letters, if known, or the signal AA, AA, etc. (• — • —, • — • —, etc.). This is discontinued when the vessel called answers.

TTTTT, etc. (— — — — —, etc.) is the signal used to answer the above call; it is discontinued when the first ship stops calling.

### Procedure signals

Certain letters and combination of letters have been given special procedural meanings. They are, in effect, brief messages in themselves. Some of the more basic signals are given below with their meanings; the bar over the letters means that they are run together and transmitted as a single character.

T (—) is the single dash flash signifying the receipt of each word or code group in a message.

R (• — •) means "Message received."

EEEEEE, etc. (• • • • • •, etc.) is the erase sign, signifying that a mistake has been made. It is answered by the receiving ship with the same signal. When answered, the sending ship repeats the *last word or group sent correctly* and then goes ahead with the rest of the message.

RQ   Interrogative, or "The significance of the previous group should be read as a question."

C   Affirmative, or "The significance of the previous group should be read in the affirmative."

N   Negative, or "The significance of the previous group should be read in the negative. When used with voice transmissions, the procedure signal is 'NO'."

"C" and "N" (or "NO") can be used singly to indicate an affirmative or negative statement or reply. When "N" (or "NO") or "RQ" are used to change an affirmative signal into a negative statement or a question, they are sent after the main signal.

OK   Acknowledging a correct repetition, or "It is correct."

CS   "What is the name or identity signal of your vessel (or station)?"

DE   "From" (used to precede the name or identity signal of the calling station.

RPT   Repeat signal: "I repeat" or "Repeat what you have sent" or "Repeat what you have received."

Many of the above procedure signals may be used with means of communication other than flashing light. When used by voice, the letters are spoken from the phonetic alphabet, except for "NO" which is spoken as the word.

### Using the repeat sign

When the repeat sign is sent singly, it means "Repeat all of the last message." It can be used in conjunction with the signs AA, AB, WA, or WB and an identifying word or the signals AA, AB, BN, WA, and WB plus an identifying group or groups (or word or words) to request the repetition of a portion of a message.

AA   All after . . .
AB   All before . . .
BN   All between . . . and . . .

WA   The word or group after . . .
WB   The word or group before . . .
For example:
RPT alone means to repeat the entire message.
RPT AA RED means "Repeat all after the word Red."
RPT AB MJ means "Repeat all before the group MJ."
RPT WA EY means "Repeat the group after the group EY."
RPT WB BOY means "Repeat the word before the word Boy."
RPT BN FR TX means "Repeat the groups between the groups FR and TX."

Repeat signs are not to be used when a message is not understood or when a message as decoded is unintelligible. In such cases, suitable signals taken from the Code are to be used.

## Use of International Code groups

YV is the international code group indicator, used in messages transmitted by Morse code as the first group of the coded text and signifies that the message that follows consists of code groups, not plain language.

## FLASHING LIGHT SIGNALING BY BOATS

Although the average boatman may have little regular use for flashing light signaling, this means of communications may prove of great value in emergencies. Take, for example, the situation in which a boat is aground at night. It may be unsafe for another boat to approach close enough for shouting back and forth across the gap between them—there may be uncertainty as to where the shoal water lies, or the other craft may draw considerably more water and thus have to stand off at a distance. Knowledge of the Morse code, being able to receive as well as send, will permit the exchange of vital information using nothing more than an ordinary flashlight. Knowledge of plain language is used and numbers are spelled out.

Use of the signal YV (or "INTERCO" by voice) and groups from the International Code of Signals will provide a means of getting around a language barrier.

## Semaphore Signaling

Semaphore signaling may make a boatman think of his Boy Scout days, but actually this means of communication is used more at sea than on land. A pair of skilled naval signalmen "talking" rapidly back and forth with semaphore flags is an interesting sight and a thoroughly practical one.

Semaphore signaling is normally done with a pair of hand flags for greater visibility. Such flags can be omitted for signaling over short distances, although the use of handkerchiefs, rags, etc. will aid in the reading of the signals.

### The semaphore alphabet

Information is transmitted in semaphore signaling by the position of the sender's two hands. For each character, each hand will be in one of eight possible positions, vertically up or down, straight out to either side, or at positions midway between, fig. 2613.

The semaphore alphabet is shown in fig. 2614. The *break sign* (or *front*, as shown in the illustration) is most important; it is used between words and, without a pause, between double letters appearing in a word. In semaphore plain language is used and numbers are spelled out.

### SEMAPHORE PROCEDURES

The desire to communicate by semaphore is indicated by sending the signal K 1 by any means. The other ship hoists the answering pennant at the dip to acknowledge the signal, and closes it up when she is ready to receive. If unable to communicate by semaphore, the reply is the signal YS 1. For simple boating situations, it is sufficient to use the attention sign, waving both arms from straight out to vertically upward.

Courtesy—United States Coast Guard

**FIG. 2613 The semaphore signaling code is based on the position of the sender's two hands (flags). There are eight basic positions as shown; for any character, one hand is at a position and the other hand is at one of the seven remaining positions.**

Each letter is sent distinctly with the sender's flags (or hands) moving directly from the positions of one letter to those of the next, and then dropping to the break (front) position at the end of the word. The sender then waits for the receiver to send "C" indicating that the word has been received and the message should be continued. At the end of the message, the signal AR is sent; if at any time a mistake is made, a series of Es is made, then the *full last word sent correctly* is retransmitted followed by the word in which the error was made and the rest of the message.

### SEMAPHORE SIGNALING BY BOATMEN

Semaphore signaling has its advantages and its disadvantages for use from recreational boats. It permits communications over greater distances than a voice will carry, even when amplified through a loud-hailer; it is effective where wind or breakers would drown out sound. A typical use of semaphore might be from a stranded boat to a Coast Guard rescue craft that could not approach close enough for shouting back and forth.

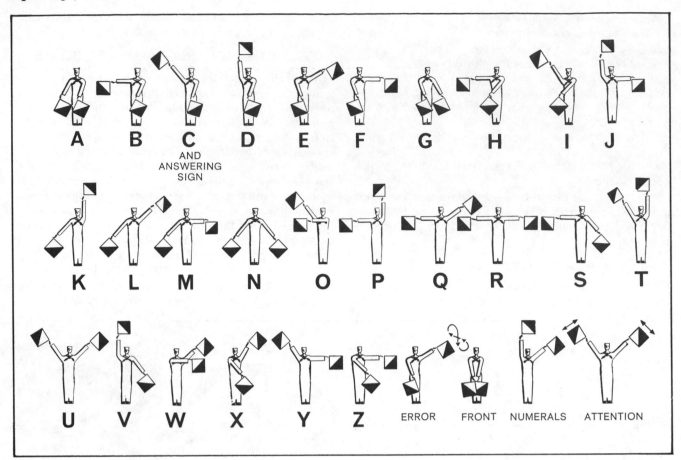

**FIG. 2614   The Semaphore Signaling Code.**

Courtesy: U. S. Navy Training Publications Center

Semaphore requires no special equipment, as does flag-hoist signaling. It is probably more satisfactory for day use than flashing light. On the other hand, it requires learning a new code and regular practice to develop *any* degree of competence. Another disadvantage is that it is not usable for communications at night.

Even though a boatman does not develop a full qualification in semaphore signaling, a knowledge of the letter "R" is often useful. "R" has wide recognition (as "Roger" on radiotelephone circuits) as meaning "received and understood." The semaphore "R"—both arms stretched straight out to the sides—is a simple, but highly effective, way of signaling to another person that you "got the message." Clearly and distinctly given, it is a much more satisfactory means of acknowledging information or instructions than a careless wave of one hand.

## Sound Signaling

Signaling by sound using the boat's horn or whistle is possible, but has severe limitations.

Sound signaling should be used only with the greatest of caution, due to the confusion that it might create with passing or fog signals. A good rule for boatmen would be to become familiar with its principles and procedures, but never to use it except in emergencies or situations in which one was certain that no misunderstandings could possibly arise from its use.

A sound signal should be as brief as possible, and, except in an emergency, communications should be limited to the single-letter signals. In fog or on inland waters, where traffic is heavy, sound signals must be kept to an absolute minimum.

### SOUND SIGNALING PROCEDURES

The Morse code is used for signaling by sound, with calling and answering procedures generally similar to those used for flashing light. The receiving craft makes no signal as the message is sent unless a character is missed in which case the repeat signal RPT is immediately signaled. When the message is completed, the sending ship signals AR; if the message has been fully received, the other ship acknowledges by sending R.

Further details on signaling by sound will be found in H.O. 102.

**Two-letter groups
from the International Code of Signals.**

(Effective 1 April 1969.)

| | | | |
|---|---|---|---|
| AE | I must abandon my vessel. | PD | Your navigation light(s) is (are) not visible. |
| CJ | Do you require assistance? | PT | What is the state of the tide? |
| CN | I am unable to give assistance. | QX | I request permission to anchor. |
| JI | Are you aground? | RY | You should proceed at slow speed while passing me (or vessels making this signal). |
| JL | You are running the risk of going aground. | | |
| JW | I have sprung a leak. | UF | You should follow pilot boat (or vessel indicated). |
| KN | I cannot take you in tow. | UO | You must not enter harbor. |
| LN | Light (name follows) has been extinguished. | UT | Where are you bound for? |
| LO | I am not in my correct position. (To be used by a lightship.) | YK | I am unable to answer your signal. |
| | | YX | I wish to communicate by radiotelephony on frequency indicated. |
| LR | Bar is not dangerous. | | |
| LS | Bar is dangerous. | ZM | You should send (or speak) more slowly. |
| MF | Course to reach me is . . . | ZP | My last signal was incorrect. I will repeat it correctly. |
| MG | You should steer course . . . | | |
| NF | You are running into danger. | ZQ | Your signal appears incorrectly coded. You should check and repeat the whole. |
| NG | You are in a dangerous position. | | |

**FIG. 2615**

## Signaling and the Boatman

Knowledge and ability in signaling can bring both added pleasure and safety to a boatman. Pleasure can be had from being able to recognize and understand simple flag hoists or other visual signals. Safety will surely result from being able to use such methods of communications in an emergency, his or someone else's. Visual signals can often mean the difference between the communication of vitally necessary information, even though slowly and tediously, and no communication at all. Such signals are particularly valuable when one's boat has no radio, or the set on board fails to work when needed.

The more knowledge and ability in signaling the better, but expertness is neither expected nor needed. Simple knowledge of the code flags, the Morse alphabet, or the semaphore code, plus the rudiments of procedure, are all that are required. The boatman should make the effort to learn the fundamentals of signaling, and he should keep in practice. Some day when least expected, it could mean a great difference to all on board his boat.

# Seamanship in Breaking Inlets

# CHAPTER XXVII

FOR a motor boat to proceed in safety at sea and to carry its passengers and crew in security and comfort from port to port along the coast, such a craft must possess certain hull characteristics. These are:

1. Stability    3. Propulsion    5. Strength
2. Buoyancy     4. Steering      6. Endurance

In the modern well-designed motor boat all of these six items of construction characteristics were designed and inbuilt into the craft by its creators when its lines were laid down on the drafting board. The elastic limits of safety in each case have been mathematically and accurately computed and are known with a proven degree of exactitude by test. Knowing that the boat would roll and might even capsize in violent sea conditions when immersed in her native element, her creators placed within her hull an invisible but powerful mechanical servant —her righting arm. Sufficient length and weight were given to this physical force to insure that the boat would return to an even keel in her struggles to constantly stabilize herself at sea and to withstand the ordinary rigors of wave formations, consideration having been given to the individual motor boat's size.

In these articles we are not concerned with ordinary wave conditions of the so-called trochoidal type met commonly off shore and far at sea but rather with the confused maelstrom found during a summer on-shore gale or strong wind before any breaking coastal inlet. The deceiving appearance of these seas, from an off-shore aspect, might overwhelm the unwary, the novice or the careless should he enter them in his boat unprepared or inexperienced. Under these conditions and upon entry into such surf, should a single one of the elements of boat construction enumerated above fail or become destroyed as a result of poor seamanship or inexperience, it is almost axiomatic that the destruction of the remaining five elements will rapidly follow and the boat and its crew may be lost.

The characteristics listed above are set down in order of importance as related to surf running in broken water and it becomes obvious, upon inspection, that the first requisite for a motor boat's safe passage through a breaking inlet is the *preservation of the boat's stability*. In other words, the boat must be handled with that degree of seamanship, as she drives through the racing inlet, that will insure that she will remain in an upright position.

Little that is comprehensive and authentic as to collective detail covering the many and varied phases of this subject's widely scattered components has been written. An effective treatise of all of them would be material for volumes. In our consideration of the subject as a whole we must keep in mind that all inlet conditions vary greatly and the speed, shape, cadence, and height

# A Master Surfman Discusses the Technique of

# Handling Motor Boats in Breaking Seas

with which the seas crash onward to the land in violent crescendo are largely governed by the great compressive influence of bottom contour, bottom declivity and bottom channels.

It is difficult, therefore, to set down didactic direction for the guidance of the seaman when he enters broken water before a coastal inlet with his motor boat. The manufacturing of a norm of explanation must be approached with caution on account of the ever-changing wave behavior encountered in the field's dissimilar scope and the seamanship requirements and surf practices that are required by the many varied types of motor boat hull construction and speeds. The truth is that there is no norm. Safety and success in running broken surf depends almost wholly on the individual motor boat captain's brand of seamanship as suited to the particular hull under him.

In order to correctly evaluate most of the known components of adequate seamanship in breaking inlets, in relation to our research, we are forced to use applicable portions of the knowledge and experience of the master surfman, the naval architect and the engineer. Such a combination of human avocations fertilized in the brain of one individual during a single lifetime is rare indeed. No scientific studies, of record, of wave formations, heights, velocities, currents and counter-currents in any breaking inlet have ever been made.

We do know, however, from the collective experience of those who have spent their lives in surf, that as these great trochoids approach the beach from the sea, owing to the influence of bottom declivity, friction and compression are initiated and the sea wave rushing along at some 40 knots starts to decelerate but that its crest starts to climb and may reach a height of 50 to 60 feet with

a crest speed of 25 to 30 or more knots, in some cases.

Imagine, then, in an ordinary on-shore gale, the difficulty of safe passage that confronts the motor boat captain as he lies before a breaking coastal inlet contemplating the cadence of the seas. Heaving in the trough in a hull whose water-planes, projected rudder area and shaft torque were designed for maximum efficiency at some 15 knots in the long and regular swells at sea, he now reflects, as he watches, that the ability of the same boat to now turn Mr. Hyde and carry him through the racing white mass off there to leeward, rests with his skill as a seaman, the strength and endurance of his boat and the integrity of his power and gear under stress.

Sensitive to the realization that when his boat was built her designers created her to go to sea and that it was not intended that she should cruise in steep, short seas whose height of crest might attain some 50 feet and roar along at a speed of 30 to 35 knots, he realizes that his boat was built as a compromise of naval architecture. He knows that the hiatus of difference between the required characteristics of the motor cruiser and those of the professional surf-boat were too great for the engineer's art to successfully bridge.

One of the illustrations shows a motor surf boat used commonly on both European and American coasts. It is impossible, in breaking surf, to destroy this motor boat's stability or impair her buoyancy—provided she is not holed. The illustration demonstrates her general hull lines; a future illustration will show the extent of her water-tight integrity—she is self-bailing and self-righting. Should sea water in any tonnage enter the motor boat in either of her open compartments that are exposed to the sea (passenger space forward and cockpit aft) these compartments would immediately free themselves through

When heavy seas are breaking on an inlet bar, the thing to avoid at all costs is a broach.
Here a sea has caught the boat on the port quarter and she is starting to go into a broach.

With nothing to hold her stern up to the sea, the boat illustrated on the previous page is shown here swinging broadside into broach. In this position, water will start to pour over the deck and coaming into the cockpit. When necessary to enter an inlet through heavy seas, it is imperative to keep the boat square before the seas, and avoid breaking crests

freeing ports that are provided along her sides in the way of these spaces. Her deck under these compartments is water-tight and extremely strong. There is one case of record in which one of these boats, crossing a bad bar in extremely boisterous weather and bad surf conditions, rolled over three times and yet brought her crew through, hurt but alive.

In her short 36 feet of length she has six transverse bulkheads and two longitudinal ones. She has tremendous strength and weight (12 tons) in comparison with the ordinary motor boat of similar dimensions. She has a bar keel made up of two tons of cast lead. The boat has generous beam, 10 feet 8 inches. She is rather deeper than similar motor boats of her length, 5 feet 6 inch draft; she has moderate power for her size, 100 h.p., direct connected internal combustion engine. Her oak ribs are about half the distance on center as are those of the ordinary motor boat's frames and about 100 percent larger in size. Through heavy cypress planking she is put together with wood screws and her cost of construction with gear is in excess of $30,000—quite a price for a 36-foot boat with a speed of 9 knots. There is no boat in the world that is her equal or her better in surf, breaking or surging. She is sharp on both ends and her controls are water-tight.

Her items of equipment are simply but efficiently arranged and it is pertinent to note that her twin drogue pawls are mounted *on the center line aft;* more will be heard of this arrangement later. The boat has positive stability under any sea conditions and even though, with inexpert handling, she may turn over, she most surely will come back to an upright position as a result of the placement of her heavy bar keel and consequent low center of gravity. Her entire bottom is completely water-tight with the exception of her machinery space and she has buoyancy voids even above the water line, a cross section of which will be shown later on. To sink her she would have to be holed through about 80 percent of her bottom.

For the motor boat yachtsman or small boat operator it is obvious that it is neither desirable or possible to own or attempt to build a motor boat of the type described above. The cost of construction alone is prohibitive and the boat's ability to perform successfully in surf has been obtained by great sacrifice of other important seagoing qualities that are commonly found in comfortable and

able boats of similar dimensions. Considerations of weight, economy, maneuverability, speed and leg-room would prohibit ownership of such a craft either as a yacht or workboat. Further than this, the boat is extremely lively at sea owing to her rapid and whip-like gyrations from one roll to another since the low and concentrated placement of her heavy keel results in an unnaturally low center of hull gravity which produces an extremely short rolling period.

For the average motor boat owner the designer is put to the task of creating a motor boat whose stability, while not the equal of the motor surf-boat, or positive under all of the conditions met in broken surf, is sufficient to insure the safety of the boat at sea under all wave conditions, provided she is handled with a reasonably good degree of seamanship, and will successfully cope with unfavorable wave conditions and even dangerous ones for a reasonable period of time.

It becomes apparent now that the motor boat owner who may, through emergency or other uncontrollable circumstance at sea, be forced to attempt passage of a breaking inlet in his boat, should understand something of, or sufficient of, the nature of the stability in the craft under him since his boat's stability plays so great a part in her performance the moment she enters the outer edge of the breakers.

Consider now the diagram illustrating the stern view of a motor boat rolling freely, easily and deeply in a seaway—actually the boat's action simulates that of a pendulum. Like the pendulum her hull has been set in motion by some exterior force. In this case the physical energy that is stored up in the sea waves has spent a portion of its force against the sides and bottom of her hull and precipitated motion in the form of rotation similar to that of the pendulum.

In the case of the pendulum the mechanical couple of force that is stored up between the suspended weight and the pivoted pendulum (which is capable of oscillation) has produced rotation, when an exterior force, such as the touch of a finger, has initiated motion. Now in a motor boat hull there exists a similar couple of forces which also produce rotation, the result and manifestation of which is rolling, the degree of the roll being controlled by the boat's center of gravity in relation to the boat's center of buoyancy.

Referring again to the diagram (right) of a boat rolling freely in a seaway, B is the center of buoyancy if the boat were in an upright position and immersed in still water. B' represents the boat's new center of buoyancy as related to the new position she assumed in a deep starboard roll from her original vertical state. CG is the center of gravity of the boat's mass. CG-M is called the motor boat's metacentric height and is a measure of her initial stability or safety against capsizing. The higher M is above CG the greater will be the value of the righting arm and consequently the greater will be the tendency of the boat to right herself. GZ is the righting arm and the greater the length of this line, the greater will be the couple of forces tending to right or capsize the boat. Arrow W pointing downward through CG is the thrust of gravity tending to force the boat back to an even keel. Arrow W' pointing upward through B' is the center of the force of buoyancy and tends to lift the boat back to even keel—the force of buoyancy lift being centered through B'.

Now it is axiomatic that as long as the vertical line drawn through B' intersects the line BM above CG, the center of gravity, the boat is in a stable condition and will return to an even keel. Since the force of gravity acting through the arrow W is downward and the lift of buoyancy concentrated through the point B' is upward, a mechanical couple of forces is set up and will produce rotation in the direction of the arrow above the sketch at D. If, however, the vertical through B' should intersect the line B-CG below CG, the couple will produce rotation in the opposite direction than shown in the diagram at D, and the boat will capsize or, in surf, will go into a broach. This is clearly illustrated in the diagram showing the boat on her beam ends.

### Preserve the Stability

It is apparent from the foregoing that the motor boat captain entering a coastal inlet where white crests are seen to be breaking must first *know what he is trying to accomplish* if he is to bring his boat and crew through it safely. His first consideration, then, in this direction, is the *preservation of the stability of his boat.* In the accomplishment of this, his personal skill as an able seaman is so intertwined and bound up with his boat's construction characteristics and her resultant behavior in boisterous surf that it is extremely difficult, or impossible, to separate the two.

That the boat must be kept squarely before the seas now as she approaches the outer breakers is an obvious mandate of good seamanship—that both of her bilges must rest squarely immersed on the back of the sea that will carry

A modern motor surf boat. Unless she is holed, it is impossible to destroy her stability or impair her buoyancy

her through the inlet is an imperative necessity for insurance that her rudder will act instantly and that her propeller will not beat the air. That her bulwarks must not dip into the spume so that she takes sea water aboard which would immediately affect her *stability* and buoyancy is a consideration of major import.

Her speed must now be carefully gauged. The boat must not be allowed to approach a crest, for once she

Below: Diagram to illustrate the stern view of a motor boat rolling freely, easily and deeply in a normal seaway. The boat's action simulates that of a pendulum (right)

Right: The same boat when she has been thrown over on her beam ends, shown in a broach broadside to a breaking sea

climbs near one of these racing tufts of scud there is no power on earth that will stop her run—neither must she be allowed to slowly slide downwards towards the slatch or hollows—if she should be overwhelmed in the trough the forces of hundreds of tons of sea water might tear her apart—the seas must be kept breaking ahead and astern of her at all costs.

The above are all considerations of the master seaman in broken surf. They are closely allied to all effort to preserve the motor boat's stability in a breaking inlet. Yet there are other important construction characteristics inbuilt into motor boats, the effect of which bears considerably on the performance of the small boat in surf. These effects must be explored fully before further considering methods of inlet seamanship. A concise understanding of all of the collective purpose of these details must be had in order that the dictates of good seamanship in breaking inlets may be more readily applied at the proper time.

Buoyancy! The submarine chasers of World War I withstood the incredible pounding of the short steep seas of the English Channel

# A Discussion of the Differences in Handling

# Various Types of Boat, Depending on Their Design

# And the Speeds At Which They Can Be Driven

BUOYANCY is defined, according to Webster, as the resultant upward pressure of a fluid on an immersed object floating on the surface of a still liquid. When 35 cubic feet of water are displaced by any motor boat hull floating in salt water, sufficient buoyancy exists under the boat to support one ton of weight. Boats of generous beam and draft, with bottom area distributed over a large area of water, are usually found to be not only the most stable boats but also the buoyant ones.

The modern motor boat, therefore, with a good turn of speed, comes into its own in breaking surf in this respect and among the motor boats of the work boat class probably the Jersey beach fishing skiff from 18 to 40 feet in length, when properly handled, has no peer in breaking inlets. What this type of hull might lack in length of water planes underway it gains in freeboard and beam, the fullness of which, in most cases, is carried from the hull's point of entry of wetted surface, in operation, in almost a straight line to the stern.

Beyond this, these motor boats are powered with high horsepower for their size and tonnage which, transmitted to the propeller shaft, results in the production of tre-
mendous shaft torque. This becomes a large stabilizing influence in an open surf-boat which depends largely on its natural buoyancy and freeboard for its preservation in breaking seas, where safe and stable flotation together with sufficient fairness of hull contour must be depended upon to cope with the high wave speeds that are encountered at the entrance of coastal inlets in moderate on-shore gales. The upward thrust of buoyancy in these motor boat hulls at an immersion of 3 feet is roughly 192 pounds to the immersed square foot.

Now the location of the position of the center of buoyancy in any hull has a great influence on the manner in which she is handled in steep or breaking seas. The position of this center is largely controlled by the motor boat's designed water planes underway, the location and extent of her hull weights (machinery, equipment, etc.), her general dimensions, hull contour and shaft torque. There are other considerations affecting the location of her center of buoyancy but these are the main ones that concern us here.

Notice, now, the illustration showing a longitudinal section of the ordinary round-bilged surf boat whose dimen-

Longitudinal section of the ordinary round-bilged surf boat. The center of buoyancy is about where spotted. Numerous watertight compartments would serve to localize any threat to buoyancy by the entrance of water

Above: Section of a conventional round-bilge slow-speed cruiser (10 knots). In steep seas she is handled like the surf boat (left, above) but, because she has no watertight compartmentation, great care must be exercised to prevent entrance of sea water into hull

Center of buoyancy, longitudinally and transversely, falls about at point X, somewhat abaft of amidships when underway

Much of the reserve buoyancy forward in newer, faster semi-displacement types of hull is gained by flare (shaded area, above, left) and sheer (black area "A", above right). Buoyancy aft is great due to extreme beam at the transom. Note, in the plan at left and drawing below, how her water planes underway differ from those of slower types of hull. The slow and fast types call for different methods of handling

sions are roughly 36 feet by 10 feet 6 inches by 5 feet 6 inches. Compare this with the illustration showing a typical section of the conventionally arranged and designed motor boat hull of similar dimensions with the exception of somewhat smaller beam and slightly less draft. Each hull is equipped with about 100 h.p. at 1000 r.p.m. motors. In both of these motor boats the center of buoyancy is in about the same locational plane and since the power and speed of both hulls are about equal (9-10 knots), it is evident that in steep seas both motor boats should be handled with about the same method of sea-

manship, due allowance being made for the great strength of the professional motor surf boat.

It is mandatory, for safe seamanship, that each boat of the type described should have the full length of its water planes in immersion at all times, regardless of sea condition, so that the center of buoyancy of each will remain as near as possible to its designed location. The center of buoyancy in all motor boats of the type described is approximately about the midship section, transversely and longitudinally, and your hull's greatest flotation effort therefore is centered through her midship section aided by the reserve

The faster type of modern cruiser, due to its design and speed, must be handled differently from the surf boat

buoyancy on the motor boat's ends produced by sheer and flare.

It is worthy of note in passing that all of the motor surf boat's areas of natural buoyancy are profusely and heavily compartmented. This, of course, gives to the hull great rigidity and strength in withstanding the crushing strains encountered in a boisterous seaway and also enhances the motor boat's ability to withstand for an indefinite length of time the tremendous pounding with which cycloidal seas will punish a small motor boat.

She will wear out her crew before she tires herself.

The great boon, however, of this profuse compartmentation is her security from the hazard of free surface should a leak develop in any portion of her bottom. In this case, such an entering volume of seawater, that would otherwise surge at will over her bilges creating a hazard to her buoyancy and a threat to her stability through its rapidly shifting weight, is immediately localized by the water-tight compartments constructed within her bilges. If half of her bottom were ripped out she would still float on her water-tight decks with the aid of her secured reserve buoyancy from the water line to the top of her deck erections.

Should her passenger well forward and her cockpit aft become filled by a sweeping sea she would immediately free herself, for both spaces are self-bailing. No sea water can enter her bilges through any topside source since all her deck erections are water-tight against 100 pounds pressure and any apertures in her deck structures are secured by heavy dogs setting her hatch door knife-edges deeply in heavy rubber. There are no deck transoms or skylights installed. Any hatches are made of heavy bronze screwed into heavy recess rings installed in her deck. This motor boat was designed and built to steam *out of* a breaking inlet and into the face of seas that may reach 40 feet in height whose crest speed might exceed 30 knots. She is homely as a hedge fence but she is perfection in buoyancy, stability and security; even with lubberly hand-ling she is practically indestructible as she waddles her way through the breakers.

Look for a moment at the illustration of the motor boat with no watertight compartmentation. In the event that a cross sea either ripped her skylight open or tore the hatches from their coamings on either her trunk cabin or cockpit deck and three or four tons of sea water entered the hull, disaster would surely follow in the violence of the breakers. With the first roll that the boat took this uncontrolled mass of seawater, surging about the interior of the hull, would immediately seek the lowest level of the hull's depression, the boat would be hove down on its beam ends, and the chances are that the boat would never again be able to rise since her propeller would be jerked out of the water, her rudder control totally lost, her buoyancy invaded and her stability destroyed, which would insure her capsize. She has, of course, no bilge compartmentation and in the case of an uncontrollable leak developing in steep or broken seas the seawater would course through the entire length and breadth of her interior, rendering her, to say the least, uncontrollable.

The moral is, of course, that whenever you enter broken seas with this type of boat be sure that all deck hatches, transoms and vents are well secured and tight; all deck appurtenances such as anchors, life buoys and deck boxes should be securely lashed and no loose line or ends of lines should be above decks *any place*. It should all be stowed securely below—any loose line left about the decks or cockpit might end up in one of your screws. Any loose gear that might come adrift might go through your transom.

Extreme care and judgment as to the time of entry into the breakers should be used with these round-bilged slow boats. In an inlet that is breaking white across its entire width such an entry should only be made in the most pressing emergency and then only if the motor boat is equipped with an efficiently built drogue. Never attempt

Do not allow your boat to get close to the top of a crest. She might be hurled over the crest and pitch-poled into the trough below

to tow swamped dinghies or the ends of unsecured lines over the stern of your boat—you may not be able to get rid of the dink when you anticipated you should and it may be that the tender might board your boat and either kill some one or so damage the gear of your boat that you might lose control of her. This has actually happened.

A heavy or light line towed over the stern will always float and most certainly will find its way into your propeller in heavy surf. It is impossible either to see or anticipate what an unsecured bight of line hanging over your stern will do next or what direction it may take. It is also impossible to keep a strain on such a line for the reason that you are constantly engaged in the rapid manipulation of your throttle, to keep the seas breaking either ahead or astern of her and you are using radical and frequently large degrees of rudder angle in an attempt to keep her squarely before the seas.

### Seas Have a Regular Cadence

It is true that all breaking seas before a coastal inlet during a strong onshore breeze have a regular cadence and, as the bottom slope starts to slow down the great ocean trochoids and build up their crests, smaller waves form after the passage of the large ones. Usually the smaller seas form in well defined locations and appear in regular cadence after several large seas have passed. If you are going to enter the surf you should do so at a time when you are sure of operating and maneuvering your way through the inlet in an area of seas of this type, keeping a close eye on the color of the water ahead of you and attempting, as best you can, to keep your boat in the darkest green of the water and measuring the break of the crests both ahead and astern of you.

The sea crests must be kept breaking ahead and astern of your boat for if you allow a sea to break aboard your motor boat, she might survive one such break if she were extremely well constructed and did not fill but it is difficult to imagine she would live through the second one to come aboard. Do not allow your boat to gather speed that might become uncontrollable. In this respect you must keep a close watch on the vertical movement of your bow and stern. Should your stern start to rise under you and your bow begin to descend, slow down your motor and let the sea roll under the total length of your immersed water planes and let it break ahead of you.

Do not try to ride the back of a sea with a full bilged boat; your hull was not designed to be efficient at the wave speed with which the sea is travelling and your torque is too low in value to give you much effective rudder control. If your stern begins to descend rapidly and your bow starts to rise, increase your r.p.m. and do so radically immediately; this is a sure sign that you are falling back into the trough and should your boat be sucked into the counter-current *travelling in the opposite direction than that of the crests* a sea may break on your boat at any time. Such counter-currents exist in the hollows of these steep seas and more will be heard of them later.

### Using the Drogue As a Brake

Should your boat begin to run and you feel that you cannot stop her by closing the throttle, do not attempt to reverse her if seas are very bad; you may kite your stern around to port in an instant and hopelessly broach her. Use your drogue to break her. Keep your drogue lines clear and free and when you give the word to set the drogue keep everyone clear of the stern except the drogue tender. When your drogue "roots," its towline will straighten out like an iron bar and sing like a bow-string. Your boat will immediately start to slow down and you may find that by keeping your drogue rooted (set) and blasting your power wide open you have better control of her.

If you do not find this to be so, trip your drogue by simply releasing the tow line and the drogue will spill the instant it feels the touch of the trip line on its apex. Do not allow your boat to get close to the top of any crest; wave speed in this type of cycloidal sea is highest just before the crest is reached and in this position not even a drogue will stop her. Your boat might be hurled over the crest and pitch-poled (see the illustration) into the trough below. When you arrive in less boisterous water, slow down your boat and get your drogue aboard by slacking out on your tow line and heaving in on your trip line while you are going slowly ahead.

Remember that all of the foregoing are the usual tactics applied in breaking surf by experienced surfmen in *full displacement, round bilged* and normally slow boats. You could not apply this practice successfully to modern, well designed semi-displacement and fairly fast types of hull; all surf running in broken seas simply amounts to keeping a motor boat's center of buoyancy somewhere near its designed position in an attempt to preserve her stability and this is accomplished by keeping the boat, while she is maneuvering through breaking surf, on her designed water planes underway. The designed wetted surfaces of the modern motor cruiser differ greatly from those of the slow round-bilged boat in respect to length, breadth, contour and depth.

### Handling the Modern Motor Boat

Now let us consider the modern type of motor boat. From simple inspection of the illustration of this type, it immediately becomes apparent that to attempt to handle boats of this type in breaking seas in a similar manner to those boats of the slow round-bilged types which we have discussed would be only to tempt fate. We first note that as a result of carrying out her lines of flotation in almost a straight line from her widest breadth somewhat forward of amidships to the stern her center of buoyancy underway has been shifted from the amidships section and falls somewhere abaft of the center section of the boat, somewhere about the point X. From an inspection of the illustrations, we note that the length of the modern boat's immersed water-planes is considerably shorter but that she has relatively greater beam than her slower type sister. We see that much of the reserve buoyancy in the newer type of hull forward is gained by deck sheer, flare and contour; her buoyancy aft is very great on account of her extreme beam at the transom. The exact length of her designed and operational water-planes underway is governed primarily by her trim and amount of shaft torque applied at her strut or struts.

It is well to remember here that, when you are about to enter breaking seas with your semi-displacement type hull, this is not the time to start monkeying with your normal trim. This statement is made *all books and articles on the subject to the contrary notwithstanding.* As you have found your boat's trim to be correct at sea under normal conditions—so it should remain when you start through a breaking inlet. Do not go shifting weights to the stern; by so doing you might slow down your boat at a time when all of the speed you can possibly get out of the hull might be the only requisite for a safe passage through the inlet. Once your correct trim has been established both by design and your own experience with your boat, let the boat alone. There are very definite reasons for the foregoing statement as applied to the modern semi-displacement type motor boat.

### Throttle the Key to Control

The one variable over which you have direct and manual control, which will determine whether or not you shall keep your boat immersed fairly on its designed water-planes during your passage through the inlet is the *amount of shaft torque* (turning effort) that is applied to your shaft through the manipulation of your engine throttle. Your degree of judgment in the handling of your throttle and your dexterity and sensitivity to the urge of your helm are now the factors that are going to see you safely through the tumbling seas about you. Remember that your stern controls your bow and that your rudder's greatest point of efficiency is reached only as the highest shaft torque is applied to your screw and your rudder is fed a literal wall of hydraulic pressure surrounding both sides of its vertical surfaces against which its motion becomes effective at the instantaneous touch of your hand.

Again you must watch the seas closely and patiently before you attempt to enter the area of breakers. Judge, if you can, the speed of the slowest of the seas and make a decision as to whether or not you can handle your hull at the speed that the smallest groups of waves to leeward are traveling. You know from past experience with your hull, before a following sea, just about how much of a run your boat will take before she starts to become unmanageable. If you should decide that there is any element of doubt as to your ability to handle your craft at the speed with which the inlet seas are crashing onward to the land do not, under any conditions, attempt to enter the inlet. It is by far better to go to sea and spend a miserable night hove to than risk loss of life. Ordinarily, a hull whose designed full power is produced between 12 and 16 knots will stand a run in a seaway of about 17 to 22 knots before she starts to become difficult to control, provided she is not pounding. Twin screw boats will do somewhat better than this in steep seas that are traveling from astern.

When you have decided to enter the breakers, have streamed

your drogue, and selected your point of entry on the back (seaward side) of one of the smallest and slowest of the seas, approach the surf as near as possible at the speed of the sea that is going to take you through the inlet. Your drogue tow line should be secured over the center line of your transom; your trip line can be made fast to any cleat or samson post about the quarter—it does not matter as long as your lines have no chance of fouling. Mentally measure the length of the sea you are about to ride and so manipulate your throttle and rudder that your eventual position upon it will place you squarely on its horizontal center with your stern directly before the following seas.

### Keep Clear of Breaking Crests

Watch her now and note her behavior as you gather speed; there is a possibility that you might ride the sea, if you have made a selection in the right group of seas, clear through the inlet without it showing any tendency to break. Should the sea show a proclivity to gather sufficient speed and accelerate itself to the point of breaking keep its crest well ahead of your bows. Take a quick glance astern now and then and note your position with respect to the sea that is breaking over your quarter. Should you find your boat uncomfortably close to the one that is breaking astern open your throttles immediately—don't wait until you can feel the suction of the slatch (undertow) pulling your hull back into the yawning hollow that lays just beyond your stern. Remember that that suction is travelling in a reverse direction to your own forward motion and there is a possibility that you might lose rudder control if you allow your boat to slide down the back of the sea and too close to this hollow vortex.

As you gather speed on your opened throttles and regain your correct and safe position on the sea's back, attempt to synchronize your speed to that of the sea as you race through; should your hull show a tendency to dip either gunwale or become tender at the quarters to the sea action racing from the direction of the stern slow her down again and straighten her up with your helm immediately. When she straightens up again and regains her normal position gun her again and keep her scudding along resting squarely on the full length of her normal water planes.

### Breaking a Run

When she is out before it again and should she show a tendency to run and you feel that she might get out of control due to the great speed which you are now making, set your drogue immediately by simply releasing the trip line; by manipulation of your throttles, in bursts if necessary, keep sufficient torque applied to your shafts to guarantee you steerage in attempting to keep her squarely before the seas. As the drogue breaks her run and pulls you back from the crest, cautiously open your throttles without tripping the drogue. You may find that you have better control of her by keeping your drogue set and blasting the full discharge of her fast-turning screws into her rudders. In twin screw installations this is often found to be the case for your keel, held in the vise-like mechanical center of the slip-streams of both screws, now resists any tendency of the flying seas to broach her.

As she roars along, approaching the quiet water which can now be seen on the other side of the breakers, her speed seems to increase—20 . . . 21 . . . 22 knots the speed indicator clocks, her motors thundering under you, while the drogue digs a valley in the breakers astern and the tow rope sings in the spume. This is a thrill supreme. Its only equal in the world perhaps is the performance of the beach boys *riding the forward face* of the steeply breaking surf before the Waikiki Beach Hotel. Like the surfboard of the aborigine some of these modern hulls, intelligently handled and properly powered, are marvels in breaking surf.

### Secure the Dinghy Aboard

Before closing this part of the discussion, it may be well to mention a word of caution regarding the towing of tenders upon the entrance to a coastal inlet under the conditions previously described. If the tender cannot be taken aboard and lashed down securely, bottom up, it is by far safer to cast the tender adrift and lose it rather than to attempt to tow it through the breakers. Once you enter the breakers you have no control over its gyrations whatsoever; your attention is necessarily bent in the direction of keeping your boat in a stable condition and it is impossible for a crew member to exercise any control of it at all while your boat is charging through the surf. A towed tender may capsize, interfere with your drogue lines or actually come aboard of your boat. There is a case of record in which a fisherman (200 tons and 92 feet in length) towing a heavy seine boat, in which a large seine was being carried, while crossing a badly breaking bar on the southeastern coast of the United States, was broached and beached with a loss of six of her crew. This happened as a result of the seine boat boarding the ship, due to the unequal speeds of the two craft in the breakers, killing the engineer and two of the crew members on deck, while the seine fouled the vessel's screw and the ship became helpless in heavily breaking seas. She was beached ultimately with the loss of three more of her crew from the decks.

Should the tender capsize, it would immediately act as a stern anchor as a result of which your motor boat would be immediately swept by a sea and the water-tight integrity of your hull would be instantly invaded, to say the least. If it should foul your drogue lines it might take charge of the operation of the drogue and set it at a time when such an occurrence might result in disastrous disadvantage to your motor boat, laboring in the breakers, or, vice-versa, it might release the drogue at a time when operation advantage might require that the drogue be set and deeply rooted. A tender, therefore, should either be brought aboard and securely lashed bottom side up to the deck or if this is impractical the tender should be cast adrift.

The modern fast sea skiff is among the ablest of small boats in breaking inlets

# How Waves Are Generated—The Trochoidal Type

# Of the Open Sea and the Breaking Cycloid in Shallow

# Water on the Coastal Shelf and at Inlet Bars

AS a motor boat skipper, you are not likely to get into difficulty with your craft in steep, following seas until the speed of those seas approaches and exceeds the speed of your boat.

Sea speed and wave height in breaking inlets depend largely on the depth of breaking, depth to the bottom, rapidity and degree of bottom compression, depth and disposition of bottom obstructions, and state of the tide and currents. Sea contour and shape, in conjunction with the foregoing, are in the main controlled by direction and force of the winds; angular approach of the swells to the inlet bars; and the direction and positional relation of bars (when a number of them are present) to the

are present or where multiple bars extend in divergent directions. To go back to the beginning, sea waves, in general, are creatures begot from the winds over the oceans. Their speed and direction at sea are directly dependent upon the speed and direction of the winds. In a Western Ocean winter gale, as a result of the wind's blowing heavily in one direction for several days, storm waves of over 1,000 feet in length with wave speeds of 71.6 feet per second (about 42.5 to 43 knots) are commonly met by large express passenger vessels. Progress of even the largest and most powerful of these ships is seriously hampered, if not stopped, by these graybacks— trochoidal seas.

The cycloidal type of wave breaking on a bar. Hitting it obliquely, it starts to break where it first feels the effect of shoaling. Note especially the steepness of the crest

others, plus the direction and dimensions of bottom channels.

Knowing the speed of the wind and with an intimate knowledge of local bottom conditions, the type of breaker, approximate wave height and wave speed can be predicted with a fair degree of accuracy in individual localities. However, the statement contained in Part One of this series regarding the futility of attempting to prescribe didactic directions for the motor boat man about to enter breaking seas before a shallow coastal inlet is still true. The bottom approach to every inlet varies widely as to depth, declivity, bottom contour, number of bars and their position in relation to each other and bottom obstructions.

The most difficult of these coastal inlets to run before steeply peaked seas are those where outer and inner bars

It is a common occurrence for these great ships to be forced to heave to in the heavy gusts and the largest of the seas. Hull strains encountered in storm waves reaching heights of 37 to 44 feet are such that even the largest of these powerful vessels might suffer severe damage if not navigated with caution. A ship is but an extended steel girder and it *is* possible to bend it.

The waves of such a storm area at sea travel rapidly out of the locality of the gale and approach the land after a passage of many hundreds of miles in the form of swells. That these swells travel great distances in a relatively short time can be attested by any boatman who has observed the heavy swells outside of the breaker line and surf pounding on the Jersey beaches 650 to 1,000 miles in advance of a tropical hurricane the center of which might be located in the West Indies, a couple of days previous to the actual arrival of the gale itself.

Where such a storm changes its direction, the tendency of these trochoidal swells, as they advance toward the beach, is to decrease both in length and height. As they arrive at the outer inlet coastal bars in rapid succession, even with no storm winds driving them onward, their speed and volume are still considerable and thus, even in fine cruising weather beyond the breaker line, extremely heavy surf may be seen pounding the beaches while high, confused breakers assault the inlet jetties. Should the storm continue in the direction in which the swells have approached the land, such inlets become impassable except to the professional surf-boat.

Basically, then, breaking seas in coastal inlets are precipitated by winds either of the local area variety or may be caused by those of some distant storm area. The characteristics, contour, speed and condition of wave heights before a breaking coastal inlet, however, are another matter.

For his own safety the cruising motor boat man should learn to identify the two primary classes into which sea waves fall. See illustrations. The storm sea that we described in the first part of this series, racing at 30 or more knots beyond the 90-fathom curve and attaining

are met at sea as well as before breaking inlets. These are creatures of wide shoal water areas where shoalness exercises a great effect in the steepening of wave crests and the shortening of seas into vicious cycloids as the result of the wind's blowing over the sea for a prolonged period in one direction. Southern reaches of the North Sea and the westerly portion of the English Channel are world famous for their creation of breakers of this type for sustained periods. Such waves, like their inlet cousins (of the breaker type) are dangerous to small boats. Equally, they constitute a hazard to large ocean freighters. Owing to the length of these vessels, they may be forced to straddle three to four such seas, thereby setting up within hull structures severe sagging and hogging strains under which their collective girder strength might buckle.

With regard to the above, in passing, it is interesting to note the record of the American submarine chaser of World War I in those tumultuous breakers in the English Channel and North Sea during the winters of 1917 and '18. The chaser itself was probably an accident of birth—she was never meant to be a surf boat—but she acquitted herself in those distant and seething breakers as probably the greatest motor surf-boat of all time.

Deep-sea wind waves, as they advance to the shore,

In steep seas, the boat must be kept away from the crests. With sufficient power, this skiff can ride the back of one sea right through the inlet

wave heights of over 40 feet, are generated from swells of the trochoidal type as a result of wind pressure in some distant or local area. They attain great lengths but seldom break except under the influence of storm winds and become confused only as a result of winds of hurricane force; in gusts or squalls, they become dangerous to large ships. It is possible to find these trochoidal type swells present in a delightful cruising area, beyond the beach line, where no wind is apparent. Should you find such a situation you had best watch your barometer for these swells may easily portend difficulty for your boat upon return to your inlet if such return is to be delayed more than three to six hours. Slopes approaching the peaks of such sea waves are long and gradual.

In the second or cycloidal type of sea wave, with which we are mainly concerned, it is well to know that these

do not progress landward as phalanxes of motional regularity or in consistent direction. In the course of their travel, they may either lose or gain some of the speed of transmission, and they may approach the beach from divergent directions. Since they advance over great distances from the locality of their origin they may travel either in the same direction in which the winds were moving that generated them or, having passed through areas where swells advancing from other localities were met, they may take on a new direction. It is entirely possible, therefore, that an observer on the beach may, at times, behold heavy breakers crashing into an inlet entrance against the prevailing local winds. In other words the direction of the prevailing off-shore winds in the locality in which the motor boat captain might be cruising offers no assurance that he will not be confronted

Coast Guardsmen are experienced in the handling of boats in heavy weather. At Yaquina Bay, Ore., this 52' motor lifeboat goes out on routine winter patrol

with badly breaking inlet conditions upon his return to his particular inlet.

Ordinarily, any motor boat operator who must return to his home port through any coastal inlet should keep himself generally informed as to over-all weather conditions, even those existing far at sea, as a hedge against what he can expect for inlet sea conditions between the time of his departure from the jetties and the time of his return. Lacking such knowledge, he should consult his barometer frequently and should any deviation from its ordinary height be observed he must view this occurrence as a cause for caution.

From storm areas trochoidal seas and swells move in the direction of the land in groups or, as some observers have put it, in trains of swells. Deep-water waves advancing on the land from any wind area are not uniform as to wave height, wave period or speed. As they approach and pass over the coastal shelf their entire complexion as to contour and characteristic rapidly changes to that of the shorter-period steep cycloid, owing to the influence of rapid bottom shoaling and other various bottom conditions and obstructions peculiar to the locality.

A 1,000-foot storm wave, for instance, after it crosses the 100-fathom curve, begins a rapid process of slow-down mainly owing to bottom friction and the compression of declivity but it starts to build up in height and steepness, as a result of decreased depth and compression, from a wave speed of some 42.4 knots and a wave period of 14.0 seconds (passing of two successive crests by a fixed point) until it finally crashes into the outer bar of a coastal inlet perhaps reduced in length to some 400 to 600 feet and slowed down to a speed of 26.8 to 32.7 knots. The wave period has now been shortened to, roughly, 11 seconds. A lot can happen in a period of 11 seconds to a motor boat operating in breakers — you have little time to change your mind.

Two-hundred-foot sea waves (typical of a mid-August blow in northern latitudes) approach the inlet bars at a speed of about 20 knots and with a shortened wave period of about 6.2 seconds. In the case of the 1,000-foot wave pounding into any coastal inlet bar at a wave speed of 42 knots such a confused sea and steep breakers would result as to definitely preclude inlet navigation to small boats. The inlet would be impassable. Were it possible to place a 35-foot motor boat on the back (seaward side) of one of these roaring cycloids, its captain would find that his bow had risen some 45 to 50 degrees from its normal horizontal plane. The motor boat would probably go into a reverse pitchpole and upend backwards as a result of its fore and aft stability being destroyed. Of course, it would be entirely unmanageable as a result of the excess of wave speed over that of its own top hull speed.

In the latter case, considering the breaking effect of the 200-foot wave, depending on bottom depths, number and related positions of inlet bars, bottom declivity and channel contour, the inlet would very likely be passable, but extremely dangerous. Such seas are fast enough to produce breakers of the so-called plunging type which, owing to their speed, height, shortness of wave period and steepness, are capable of producing chaotic conditions to confront the small boat operator contemplating entrance through them.

Even sea waves of 100 feet in length with a surface speed of 13.4 knots and a wave period of 4.4 seconds, passing over a bar whose submerged depth is 15 feet, have been known to produce a plunging type breaker with a height of 14 feet, almost equal to the depth. Now a 15-foot breaker with another one 4.4 seconds behind it is a dangerous proposition to the small boat captain who finds himself scudding before it. If he ever needs that old propeller torque blasting its solid and uninterrupted stream of water down onto his rudder surfaces, he

Confused inlet conditions are created when seas strike a bar at several angles. In some cases it is impossible to keep a boat squarely before the sea

needs it now! Should you consider this statement slightly extravagant, just go up to the gutters on your roof and visualize what would happen to a 5- or 6-ton mass of wooden construction, capable of being moved in four directions at once but advancing at a speed of 15 to 20 knots over the ground, should it be hurled down from such a height. Do not forget in a situation of this type that, unless your boat is expertly handled, you may have a portion or all of the speed of translation here to contend with (speed of the wave plus the speed of the boat).

### Factors Affecting Breaker Height

Breaker height, it has now been seen, depends on the height of deep water waves approaching the coast, the depth of the water over bars which they must pass before coursing into an inlet, the strength of local winds (at times), and general bottom topography. Tides, state of the tide and currents also affect their height in a contributory sense. Practically the same components govern their speed with the exception that influence of currents and the state of tide has a more pronounced effect on the speeds of breakers *before inlets* than they do on height. The *depth* of breaking also influences their speed. Any or all of these components might operate in conjunction before inlets whose contour and general topography or bar condition produces them all. On the other hand, but a single one or two of them might be present and yet produce the greatest of breaker confusion.

Direction and contour of the breakers meeting bottom bars from the sea are often governed largely by the angular approach of the ocean waves to such bars as they meet before inlets. Should the swells arrive in an oblique direction to that of the submarine bars, that end of the swell which makes first contact with these obstructions will break sharply over the bar end and the remaining portion of the wave may swing about the bar, in a wide turn, refracting as it breaks against the remaining length of bar. We have already seen that bottom channels, the shape of submarine shelves and bottom obstructions such as ledges and heavy boulders lying in diverse directions also contribute their influence to the contour of inlet breakers.

### Effect of Outer and Inner Bars

Now knowing all of the foregoing it would seem reasonable to conclude that the most hazardous inlet conditions that the entering motor boat captain might expect to meet will be encountered before inlets where outer and inner bars are present on the ocean's floor. A submerged outer bar lying at a depth of 35 to 40 feet upon impact of such seas immediately slows down the first portion of the on-rushing trochoid to a speed of probably 20 to 22 knots and at the same time bottom compression deflects a large portion of its volume upwards and the wave "breaks" upon the surface of the sea. When it peaks up to the point that its top becomes unstable, the wind whips off its crest and the wall of solid water, now risen to a height of 18 to 20 feet, crashes into the trough.

Its crest having been formed and its contour well defined, the breaker, driven on by the remainder of its initial sea-speed, now roars across the intervening space of sea until it again begins to feel the shoaling over the inner bar and the compression of its shallower declivity. As a result of this further compression or squeeze and the wave's meeting the inner bar at a different angle of approach and contact, a perfect welter of confusion now exists on the surface of the sea and it may well be possible that the observing motor boat man offshore would not be able to find *any safe path* or channel through such confused breakers before the inlet jetties.

### Where Channels Are Oblique to the Sea

Years ago, before it was protected by a jetty, Jones Inlet was a notorious example of this type of breaker confusion, resulting, in a driving southeaster, from the presence of outer bars lying on the ocean's floor in divergent directions, thus forcing the seas to meet them at different angles of approach. Even in quite mild weather where ocean swells were present and were rolling in

here at speeds varying between 12 and 15 knots, passage of such an inlet channel was difficult and even hazardous. No small boat operator should enter such an area without a reliable local pilot unless he possesses an intimate knowledge of the bottom contour of the vicinity in which he proposes to operate in breakers. Low-powered motor boats, small boats with hydroplane-type bottoms, outboard-driven boats with low freeboard and flat bottom sections, and small sailboats should use extreme caution in attempting to navigate in such areas. Their operators should be watchful of weather conditions and cognizant of local forecasts. It should be pointed out here that where a winding and angular channel presents itself as the only navigable path through confused breakers, high freeboard in motorboat construction is a prime essential, high propeller torque is a vital necessity, and instantly responsive engine power in large amounts must be available. Almost any type of sailboat in breakers is a bad risk.

Breaker cadence before such inlets as these is entirely unrecognizable during the times of a heavy on-shore blow. The changing direction of the channel and the presence of the outer bar in angular relation to the inner obstruction (bar) simply destroy the contour and recognizable profiles of any wave trains between the two bars under the influence of heavy, onshore winds.

### Breaker Cadence Destroyed

The entrance to Scituate Harbor on the coast of Massachusetts is a similar locality in which breaker cadence disappears and becomes unrecognizable in any wind that is blowing hard from the eastward, onshore. The same effect that was produced before Jones Inlet in relation to the destruction of well-defined breaker and swell cadences is repeated before the jetties at Scituate, however, from differing bottom conditions. Though the channel before the jetties at Scituate runs in lengths that are fairly straight, the bottom that surrounds this pathway through the gradually rising ocean floor is strewn with giant boulders and long and irregular bottom ledges lying close to the channel edges, scattered in all directions in a wide area of open sea before the inlet. These ledges are barely submerged, during periods of low water, and under the influence of a driving easterly, across the full sweep of Massachusetts Bay, a mass of breaking and white confusion is produced that may easily awe even the hardiest local professionals.

A trochoidal sea (upper)
and cycloidal type (lower)

### Watch Surface Swells

So—get out your chart, irrespective of the direction of the local wind as you lie before a breaking inlet—watching. Remember: the breakers hold their secrets well, and the winds that blow before these breaking inlets are fickle indeed. During the summer months on the Atlantic seaboard they have been recorded as changing as many as twenty times in twenty-four hours. So, when you lie around fishing before one of these inlets, keep one eye peeled on the nature of the surface swells as they lazily roll in from over the horizon, and the other on your barometer. Don't wait "until it starts to get rough." An inspection of your bottom chart may assist you in making the correct decision, right now.

(Use the chart for all the information it can give you, but remember that channels and shoals shift so fast at many inlets that buoys cannot be indicated on the chart, and buoys at times may not mark the best water.—Ed.)

Leaving the "I-love-you" (1—4—3) flash of lonely Minot's over the quarter and picking up the long, piercing fingers of the Highland about a point off the starboard bow and coursing it down until we bring it abaft the beam a few degrees, we turn west and south down past the booming beaches of the southerly side of Cape Cod—the natives call it "the back side." Down over the shoals we run, wind northwest, force 2, and picking up a little, barometer slowly rising. She's making good time—getting a little push from the light northwester and rolling easily in the swells that seems to be coming from a general northerly direction. We cross the gulley (Hudson River Canyon) and seem to lose some of the swell. In the early hours of the morning Atlantic City Light stabs through the loom of the half-twilight in staccato sweepings and gleams, between periods, in friendly beckoning. Swell rising somewhat now, as we roll along over the coastal shelf.

## Use Judgment Before Entering

The beach line into which Atlantic City Inlet cuts its long length of passage runs roughly in a north-northeast and south-southwest direction. Ordinarily therefore, a northwester, even though it may be blowing force 3 to 4, may not compel the small boat captain to seek shelter on any course to the northward provided he just clears the seaward end of the fish trap stakes in his progress up the beach. Should he mistakenly reason, however, that *since the wind is off the beach* either Atlantic City or Manasquan would offer convenient shelter in the event of the wind's hardening, he will be well warned to inspect bar conditions off both inlets before attempting entrance. In a moderately fresh offshore breeze, where strong flooding tides or currents run heavily against the wind, breaker heights and speeds build up in certain long inlets that, at times, may preclude passage of such channels even to the professional surf-boat man. Under such weather conditions, even in the upper reaches of Atlantic City Inlet, half a mile from the entrance and well inside, breakers clear and solid may be observed going over the railroad structure.

In spite of assurances by local professionals and beach captains that this popular inlet is never impassable to those who possess an intimate knowledge of local bar conditions, this simply is not so. The inlet is a long and dangerous one and, owing to the duration of time that the motor boat captain must spend traversing its extended

length through the short steep breakers, his boat may take a severe drubbing before she rides her last sea on through the other side of the bridge structure. In this inlet one must make the correct decision first; you cannot turn around when you are half way through it, should you decide you cannot control your boat in the steepness and speed with which the breakers are roaring up the inlet, or as you see the light buoy dip its lantern. The beach over there on the westerly side of the inlet is very hard and you have a long way to go to find a worse spot to be in, if you attempt to turn the bow of your boat into the breakers.

## Where the Beach Is Steep

A few miles up the beach, to the northward, lies another artful Charybdis jutting her jettied fingers out into the surf—Manasquan. An ebb tide and the arrival of heavy sea swells off the inlet bar here simply create a havoc of white confusion; heavy wind need not be present. However, as opposed to the bottom topography off Scituate, which destroys the cadence and natural contour of sea swells on their arrival over the shoals, before Manasquan the average motor boat man can recognize the swells arriving in their trains and groups even in moderately boisterous weather. Beach declivity here is steep, and high-speed breakers start to build up in height about the 30-foot curve. From that point shoreward the wedge of rapidly shoaling bottom accelerates their tendency to climb until, at less than $\frac{1}{8}$ mile to seaward of the jetties, breakers of 8 to 10 feet in height have been observed with speeds over the bottom of about 14 to 15 knots in weather off the beach that might be considered moderately good cruising weather, offshore. Even if you were able to pass successfully through these seas, with a period of less than 5 seconds and a degree of steepness that would probably put the bows of your boat at an angle of about 35 to 40 degrees from her normal horizontal plane, the seas as they pass over the 16-foot shelf crossing the mouth of the inlet drop abruptly down into 7 feet of channel depth between the jetties and roar up the alley formed by the stone buttresses, their hollows sometimes exposing the bottom of the inlet between crests. Any boat, if she did not become unmanageable before her nose got inside the stone breakers, would be smashed here, on contact with the bottom, in seas like this.

If you intend to do any inlet running in bad weather, look to your gear. Confidence in the craft under you is the supreme requisite.

Sailboats and auxiliaries, as a rule, should be kept out of breaking inlets. The Friendship sloop (above) does fairly well in breakers up to five or six feet in height

Approaching the bar, look for the dark water, indicating the best depth, and keep out of the white water of the breakers

Some Thoughts on Bottom Design;

Effect of Currents on Breakers;

Use of Oil and the Drogue;

Handling a Skiff in the Breakers;

Suggestions for Sailing Craft

Much information has been made available to the motor boat man, both scientific and practical, concerning static surf conditions on open beaches and procedures for safe landing through them. Men have made professions of the surf's mastery and many texts are replete with knowledge of such tactics. Not so the inlet, however. Breakers, both of the coastal variety and those surging before a coastal inlet, offer difficult situations for the procurement of exact scientific data, since this is attended by considerable risk.

The motor boat captain must not confuse recommended practices for landing through beach surf with the running of coastal inlets before which white water is surging. Static surf conditions on open beaches are widely dissimilar to the almost organized confusion of wild breakers coursing over an inlet bar. Neither is the regularity of surf or the cadence of its swells affected by so many unseen but compelling components of force, and factors of form, speed, height and direction, as is the inlet breaker.

Never attempt to back your boat into a breaking inlet. Were you to try this in a modern semi-displacement hull, your quarter would be seized by the seas and you would be broached long before your beam was parallel to them. Should you escape this situation and ultimately find your bows facing the breakers, you would immediately lose steering control; if you attempted to gun your motor to give you sufficient rudder effect to hold her head up to the breakers, you would either plunge her nose under a breaker or stave in your bows.

Oil, before a badly breaking inlet, is valueless. The action of bottom declivity in forcing seas to break at such precipitous heights allows the wind to get under their crests and scatter the crest spume in all directions. The shortness of the breaker period continuously breaks the hold of the oil's viscosity upon the surface and scatters the oil with the spume in all directions. The use of oil in breakers on the coastal shelf is another matter and has much to recommend it, since the breaker period is much longer. This is particularly true where towing operations are imminent or in progress. Placing a tow line aboard a disabled boat or taking the crew off a distressed craft is often facilitated by using an oil slick to windward. If you think, however, that the condition of the breaking inlet is so bad as to warrant the use of oil, stay out of it if possible. Go to sea and heave her to, if necessary, for there never was a boat built, that was capable of keeping the sea, that will not heave to on some quarter and in some direction.

Do not attempt to tow another boat (especially a sailboat) through a breaking inlet. Collision is almost a certainty.

The use of a surf line as an aid in entering a breaking inlet is attended with danger to those who might be tending the line. Should you attempt to hold your boat's head up with such an arrangement you might jerk the

542

samson post out of her or shatter the bow section. Cross seas or current might fling the stern of your boat across the jetties, for you have no control of her at the end of a line. Unlike beach surf, the direction of breaking seas before a coastal inlet is by no means constant. Remember that high surf on open beaches is influenced and precipitated to a much greater degree than are the breakers before a coastal inlet by the local direction of the winds. Surf in beach localities is usually at its greatest height during the course of an on-shore gale or high wind. The steepness of these beach breakers is ordinarily governed by declivity, the length of the swell train as it arrives on the beach from the ocean, and the length of time the wind has been blowing in force in one direction. The cadence of such beach surf is usually much more regular and discernible.

We have discussed elsewhere the proclivity of Manasquan to break with no wind present in its vicinity or with the wind blowing off the beach, yet precipitating breakers before its entrance of such short period and height as to preclude safe passage through it in an ordinary motor boat. Likewise, before Atlantic City, combinations of bottom topography, channel contour, tides, currents and obstructions produce collateral effects on breakers that the surfman operating on an open beach may never meet.

A three or four-knot current flowing in heavy volume out of a narrow inlet and funneled into a restricted opening will bore into the base of a concaved on-rushing breaker and all but stop the turbulent water there. At the same time it tends to force the crest higher while the residual speed of the breaker drives that crest on over its stalled hollow, which may have reversed its direction now in obedience to the current's influence. Rising in great height to the point of instability, it crashes down into the trough—this, every 4.5 seconds. Add to this the natural flow of recession—for the pounding breakers ascending the bar must find their way back to the sea—and you can see why counter-currents in the trough may travel in a direction directly opposite to that of the breaker's crest.

In surf on open beaches where such currents exist in lesser extent it is called undertow. You can feel it seething about your ankles as your feet sink into the beach sands. As the current flows back in recession to the sea, it undermines the sand that bears the weight of your body. Should you advance too close to the breaker zone the undertow might seize your body and draw it into the vortex of the pounding surf.

In heavy breakers before a coastal inlet you can feel that current clutching at your boat's bottom. The laboring exhaust will warn you as it changes its note. With one eye watching the seas over the side you can see her slow down and feel a tension peak in the hull vibrating under you. Naturally, therefore, the best position for your boat as you enter the breaker zone is about the horizontal center of the sea's broad back. Should you ever sense the clutch of that counter-current, *open your throttle wide, instantly.* You understand, now, why we said that plenty of power *must* be available at the touch of your finger tips.

If you have a drogue set, trip it right now. Every drogueman that knows his business always carries a sharp, heavy knife or has an axe within reach. She may labor a little in the twenty seconds (that seem an hour) it takes to claw her way clear, but keep forcing her. As she shakes herself free and you feel the tension on her hull slacken a bit, be careful to close the throttle some. If you approach the top of the crest where the speed of the breaker is highest, you risk being hurled over in a pitchpole.

In inlet areas where the range of the tide may vary between 6 and 12 or more feet the state of the tide exerts a strong influence on the breakers. Here, between the two extremes of tide, there exists a varied condition of sea contour, speed and height. This may be due to differing degrees of beach declivity being presented to the breakers between the two tide depths or to the increased or lessened effect of bottom obstructions before the inlet. In approaches to those inlets where the bottom has no submerged obstructions such as bars, ledges or both scattered about and where the degree of beach declivity is almost pleateau-like, breakers of less steepness can usually be expected at low water than at higher states of the tide. Scituate and Manasquan are both affected by rapid rise of the ocean floor at high stages of the tide. Before Scituate, though, this characteristic is complicated by the presence of large ledges and huge boulders, lying all over the bottom.

The effect on an inlet breaker's wave period and its height produced by currents flowing into it, across it or in a direction oblique to it is always greatest when the current is at its maximum strength in either direction. No general rules can be laid down for the guidance of the motor boatman confronted with the confusion of white water created where steep breakers and cross seas tear about the inlet's mouth as a result of such

The sketch below illustrates how waves of the open sea, encountering shallow water on bars at the entrance to inlets, may form breakers which must be avoided at all costs by the boatman running an inlet. At A and B, at the crests, the velocity is the highest—in this case, 22 knots for waves that are advancing with a speed, at C and D, of 15 knots. At E a swell is shown starting to peak up as it feels the effect of the beach declivity, G. At F, the direction of currents of recession and the undertow is reversed, with a speed of 2 to 3 knots. The boat is shown with drogue set, the tow line attached to a bridle at the large end. The trip line to the smaller aft end is slack, and if the boat must gain speed to escape a breaker astern, the trip line will be hauled in to upset the drogue bottom topography, current and tidal effects. Safe passage of the inlet *must* take all of these considerations into account. It is mandatory to enter the breakers at a time when the wave period is at its greatest length and the lessened wave heights are at their lowest value of steepness. This period occurs about twenty minutes before reversal of the tides in either direction. We cannot separate the effect of any single one of these varied components on inlet breakers. We must consider them collectively, since we are dealing with a complicated collateral result on a fluid substance that moves in all directions at the whim of winds, tides and currents. Wave cadence, in most cases at this time, seems to be more regular and discernible.

It is of interest to record here a few impact pressures of inlet breakers accurately obtained as a result of dynamometer tests in shoal water areas, in pounds per square foot.

| Height of breaker | Pressure per sq. foot (pounds) |
|---|---|
| 4-foot | 406 lbs. |
| 6 " | 3,000 " |
| 10 " | 4,562 " |
| 20 " | 6,083 " |

The height of one of the highest cycloidal type breakers was recorded in the North Sea—43 feet. Sea trochoids will *also* break under the lash of prolonged winds of gale force or the hurricane. Bars they meet far off shore will produce breaking seas. The Pacific probably produces the highest of such breakers for over the long reaches or fetch of that ocean, winds blow for thousands of miles in one direction for protracted periods, commonly building up crest lengths of over 1,000 feet during the winter period. The Columbia River bar, during periods of high on-shore winds or protracted gales in the same direction, commonly produces breakers of between 55 and 60 feet in height. These prohibit the passage of 10,000-ton ships. Green water descending on a ship of this size in such tonnage as a breaker that high would produce would tear apart any assembled structure similar to a ship floating on the ocean's surface, with the exception of a sphere—*contour* again.

The highest sea trochoid, whose height was ever accurately computed, was observed by the navigating officer of the USS Ramapo during a protracted gale in the North Pacific during the winter season of 1933. The method of computation and circumstances under which the observation was made were recorded in Naval Institute Proceedings some years ago. In the English Channel strong currents alone have been known to produce breakers some 25 feet in height and about 250-270 feet in length. They can give the staunchest steel ship an astonishing punishment. A series of unending breakers of such dimensions assaulting the hull structure of a ship or boat about its forward flat keel sections with trip-hammer blows, delivering a wallop of about 4,500 pounds per square foot every 7.7 seconds, has been a fatal test for many a ship at sea, of either wooden or steel construction.

Looking back at the table showing the force of breakers crashing against any flat surface at an angle of 90 degrees, one marvels that any kind of vessel can withstand the impact of such blows. The answer lies in the designer's dexterity to fashion hull contour so it will deflect such blows and distribute the force of impact, or divert it from the hull. Sturdiness of hull structure is also paramount. Demands for speed and comfort tend to interfere, at times, with the accomplishment of such a purpose. Often the designer, as a result, has been forced to compromise, and to deviate from the age-old principle of the strongest type of construction ever known—spherical or ring-type.

The frigate United States, built about 1800, is an example of this kind of construction. Were she to be placed in a drydock and you viewed her from astern you could trace around her stern section a perfect circle. Her bulwarks were given tumble-home; even the vital sections of her decks were heavily cambered, thus completing a connected circle. Her broad stern sections (transom) and her bows show pronounced curvature. Her transom was curved outboard to break the force of following seas and to prevent her from being pooped in high breakers or seas. Her bows were fined up only enough to give her deflective entrance to the impact of waves. Ships of such construction as this made a tremendous fuss as they swept through the seas. Their bulbous underbodies set up large areas of submerged frictional resistance end eddy currents. They were exasperatingly slow in light airs and threw stern waves as high as a house when driven by the gale. All this is granted, but they cruised the seven seas both in high latitudes and low; few, if any, were ever lost as a result of destruction by sea waves.

A wooden ship of this type of ring construction even circumnavigated the Polar ice pack—around the top of the world. Her entire hull structure was forced above the surface of the sea time and again by the crushing action of the heaviest ice known to man. Yet she lived to *sail* her intrepid crew home in safety. There was not one inch of area about the weather surfaces of these old veterans that the full force of a breaker could clutch at to obtain leverage to start an opening as a lever to

In the sketch above, drawn to scale, the bottom lines of a World War I subchaser are shown. There was no flat spot anywhere in the hulls of these remarkably able boats

Two views of the hull of a comparatively modern type of semi-displacement motor boat, showing the flared bow sections forward and the underbody aft designed for good cruising speeds

An older type of full displacement cruiser, showing the roundness of lines, both in profile and section. The dotted lines show how nearly her midship section approaches a semicircle

weaken her hull structure. Unlike their more modern sisters with sweeping, graceful speed lines, their bottoms were of such contour as to make them sufficiently stable in high seas and give enormous strength in breakers. They were built about the postulate that they *must* weather any gale in any ocean.

Those were strong ships but their manner of construction could not be applied with success to modern motor boats nor could their "system" of curvature cope with demands for speed in present day motor-driven craft. About the only relic of this example of floating construction left in modern motor boat building may be observed under the turtle deck of the modern motor surf boat. Here speed has necessarily been sacrificed. You cannot have both, and your brand of seamanship plus your ability to utilize to advantage the highly contoured surfaces of your craft in breakers must take the place of the great strength of connected ring construction. Remember that the professional motor surf boat was built to steam out of any breaking inlet where she can find sufficient depth for her propeller, and for effective steering. Your pleasure boat was never designed to do this, so look over inlet conditions before you go to sea.. You can always get authentic reports on bar conditions—don't take a chance and "try it."

Perhaps the most successful compromise of modern motor boat construction in respect to contour-build and retained ring strength was, again, the little American chaser of World War I. Coupled with these qualities was the dependable placement of continuous high torque and its position under her quarter. There was not a flat spot in her entire hull structure (see illustration of the chaser's bottom); she had a modified degree of flare forward and her deck, to complete the connected circle of ring construction, was cambered.

Yet she possessed considerable speed. The placement of her balanced rudder was so expert in relation to her screws that there was no possible position she might assume in the breakers that could deprive her of effective rudder control. Her enormous delivery of torque was available on her shafts 2.5 seconds after the demand for it was rung down. So great was the effect of her high torque on rudder surfaces that the unwary quartermaster was often shocked to attention by having the helm jerked from his hands, when either of her two wing motors were started, despite the fact that her rudder operating linkage passed through a system of gearing.

## Some Aspects of Bottom Design

Now of the various resistances which oppose a motor boat's progress through the water, those of greatest detriment and ever-present obstruction to the designer are frictional resistance and wave-making. To the motor boat captain, struggling in steep breakers, where either of these twin elements is present in exaggerated degree, both work as a double-edged hindrance to safe passage through breaking seas. The frictional wake which is the result of the confluence of the two is usually greater in velocity in full displacement type hulls about the center section of the boat; it may be defined as water having forward motion in the direction in which your craft is traveling. Where it is observed at the stern of your boat, surging about in high turbulence, your propellers are being forced to deliver their power in water that already has forward motion. This results in high slip and propeller thrust losses. Since it interferes with instantaneous delivery of high torque in breakers the designer has resorted to streamlining of bottom sections. Any abrupt termination of hull contour or poorly faired bottom sections handicap you in breakers. In part, the designer is relying on your knowledge of seamanship and good sense in the handling of your craft in breakers in his admonishment of *never pounding* any of your streamlined bottom sections. Such contour has been necessary to produce the speed that *you* demanded.

In the evolution of boat contour, the designer has evolved a hull form whose bottom section, limits of wetted surface (underway), and stern profiles are highly streamlined. These are aimed at decreasing the length of frictional resistance and minimizing effects of frictional wake. Thus additional speed is gained for less weight of horsepower. Greater comfort, extra stability athwartship, and roominess aft also result from carrying out much of the boat's full beam almost to the stern. To the extent that a design is intended for greater speed, a higher caliber of seamanship is called for when handling the boat in rough, breaking seas.

As we study the modern motor boat's underbody (see illustration) we note that the patterned ends of her wide quarter are somewhat flatter in section than the steeper curves of her runs forward. Viewing her forward, from the forefoot knuckle to the top of her

stem post, the graceful curves of her bow flares are pleasing. By the stern we note her broad transom is brought in at the bilge in a sharp but graceful turn. Her rudders look small for the job but the propellers just ahead of the rudder post look business-like. Many elements of her design reveal a similarity to the famous Jersey beach skiff which, intelligently handled, is one of the most able of modern boats in inlet or beach breakers.

## Handling a Skiff

The skiffman well realizes the necessity of keeping his stern squarely before the break of the seas when he enters the breakers. He learned the hard way and he knows that if his boat should become tender at the quarters as a result of inattention or lack of realization of his position, as he roars along on the back of a sea, the submerged portion of his transom and waterline section of his planking aft will instantly produce rudder effect. Since the projected area in friction against the sea in that portion of his hull is far greater than that of his rudders, he can only expect the breakers to seize that portion of his hull and throw him into a broach.

He is deeply conscious of the presence and force of the pressure wave surging along at his bottom's entrance to the sea just forward of his 'midship section and he uses his controls to keep the force of that pressure wave constant and surging evenly down over the outer surfaces of his bottom planking *in a fore and aft direction. He never pounds it.* To do so would immediately destroy the continuity of the stabilizing effect of his high and continuous torque; in exaggeration it might even fracture a plank. It's risky, and *bad* seamanship.

He can feel the force of that pressure wave through the soles of his shoes and he can judge its degree by the vibrations of his hull as his reflexes tell him to move his throttle ahead slightly when they decrease and to ease it back a bit if the rumblings beneath him become excessive.

He rarely uses his drogue for he is not the fool to get caught out there when the breakers are high before the inlet. But, should his boat start to run, its pretty to see his "drugman" go to work and break her out of it. He knows his boat is so constructed aft that she'll stand the whipping strain of that shattering jerk of the drogueline as the drogueman spins off the turns of the trip and the tow-line's red markers fly in the spume—ripping out of the sea as his 2-inch drogueline takes the entire load of his roaring motor's output plus the speed of the breaker's advance.

His skiff now broken out of her run, the Jerseyman knows he cannot ease off and allow a following sea to assault the broad face of his transom. His racing hull now being in a high state of tension, a breaker packing a two-ton wallop reaching his transom might demolish the whole after section of his boat. The chaser's transom was concaved outboard; a sea just couldn't hit it a solid jolt. Not so his skiff, however—so he runs from the breaker and holds her where the tumbling sea cannot reach him.

## Dodge the Cross Seas

Contour construction in small boats in breaking inlets is a mighty important element of design for none better than the Jerseyman realizes those sweeping sections of bow flare forward become flat when faced with the impact of the sea as it attempts to pound them. Should he see a cross sea tearing across his course he'll slow her down or dodge it if he senses that his bows are on a collision bearing with it, for you might as well hit the jetty full tilt as collide with that breaker.

Such cross seas are grave risks to motor boats with bow cockpits, whether or not these are supposed to be self-bailing.

It will be gleaned, as the reader follows through the text, that drogues and their use assume an important stature at times of emergency in breakers. Reference to the *details* of their use and the manner of *adaptation* of the different types of drogues to specific types of hulls have been left unexplained—largely for the reason that pages of explanation might divert the attention of the reader from the subject at hand. Limitations of space might not do that field of seamanship full justice in a discussion where so many elements of boat construction and sea condition are fused together and must be separated in part and then placed back together again for the purposes of full understanding. The amateur boatman has a long voyage to make on the course we have set here. It must not be complicated any more than necessary. Use of drogues and their adaptation is simply another field of seamanship.

In these days of great, responsive and dependable power, able and staunch motor craft and rapid, accurate, reliable weather and bar forecasts, the use of a drogue in breakers is all but a lost art. Only a few of the older beach denizens are left now who were expert in their use. Yet it is a great comfort to have one aboard suited to your own particular boat both in inlet breakers and for the purpose of lying to it in bad weather at sea.

### Forward Cockpits

Before leaving the subject of handling modern motor boats in breaking seas, perhaps a word should be said concerning the vulnerability of open forward cockpits. It is not meant to infer that motor boats of such construction must always be restricted from entrance to the breakers before a coastal inlet. However it seems rather a contradiction of good seagoing sense to otherwise construct a boat whose strength, hull contour, and power are equal to the challenge of the breakers and then to vitiate these good qualities by placing in vulnerable ends a deep, open compartment capable (if filled) of throwing the craft into an immediate broach. Rarely do forward cockpits have adequate means of freeing themselves as fast as demands of safe operation in breakers press upon such a craft. Remember that breaking seas may be encountered in other waters than those of coastal inlets. They may occur at any place on the coastal shelf where the force of wind, depth of water, and combinaton or strength of currents are conducive to their formation.

### Flat Surfaces Vulnerable

Looking back over the taffrail, we have also noted the vulnerability of flat-surfaced structures exposed to waves and weather. We know something of the force *in tons* that assaults these non-contoured weather surfaces. Therefore, if you plan a cruise along the coast, see to it that you have a stout hatch that can be battened down over your forward cockpit—or at least carry aboard materials from which you can quickly construct a suitable cover, if conditions necessitate your bringing the boat's head into heavy seas.

Among the modern materials that have found increasing use in boat construction is flat sheet plywood. Primarily, of course, it is used in the hulls of small craft that are not expected to run breaking inlets. It also lends itself to use in bulkheads, interior joiner work, etc. Properly framed, it has tremendous strength—as in decks, which can often be made stronger than those planked in the conventional manner. But it certainly should not be expected, in either hulls or superstructure, to be able to withstand the full impact of breaking seas, if used in the form of flat surfaces with inadequate framing to back it.

Remember—if you are confronted with the necessity of running breakers before a coastal inlet—every portion of the weather surfaces of your ship becomes a strength member. Collectively, they must be tied into your main framing in a secure and rigid fashion—your deck carlins, cabin sides and bulwarks, weather bulkheads and transoms—flat deckhouse structures, even your cabin and cockpit decks all bear their proportion of the sea-load in the breaker. The breakers will *always* attack the weakest link in the construction chain of your motor boat *first*.

### Fast Boat Runs Bahia Honda

We have mentioned that the amount of punishment some of these well built modern high-speed motor boats will take in breakers is little short of amazing when handled with confidence and the certainty of experience. As a case in point, it might be recalled that some years ago, running the inlet off Bahia Honda with an injured sailor aboard, in one of the more modern, strong, high-speed motor boats a little over 38 feet in length and capable of a speed of about 28 knots with her two big engines full out, on her passage through the inlet she turned completely over in a period of (as near as could be calculated) 2.5 seconds. She righted herself inside the breakers on the inlet side of the bar and came up with her crew in the cockpit and with her port motor still pounding out its 3200 r.p.m. Her two-man crew had been lashed on short bights to her cockpit stanchions previous to her entry into the breakers. The injured sailor had been lashed to the cabin floor.

It looked like only a 50-50 chance, as her crew watched on the seaward side of the breaker line, and from what could be seen of the breakers in the darkness through the flying spume of the gale, the inlet breakers appeared to be about seven to eight feet in height but their period was extremely short. The sailor's life was at stake

and the chance had to be taken. If the boat had a drogue aboard and set when she laid down on her port side and started to run, her mad speed might have been broken and stopped but, like the Dutchman's anchor, old faithful Charlie wasn't there that time. This boat was capable of an honest 28 knots. Her engines, at the time she entered the outer breakers, were not quite full out and she was being handled by a sailor who had spent many years of his life in small boats in the breakers. You can imagine the speed those inlet seas were making!

A few days later the boat was hauled out—the couplings connecting both engines to the tailshafts were checked for alignment, both machines carefully gone over, holding down bolts and all framing in the way of her power plant was checked. Except for three of her six tailshaft flange bolts on the starboard coupling that were found to have slacked up and were only hand-tight, there was nothing amiss with her power plant. A tight wire was run over her hull and she was carefully trammed by two experts both in her center section and at her ends. Her hull was as fair as the day she first met the sea. The only evidence of the mauling she took and damage sustained in her wild passage through Honda was the tearing from their flanges of two 1¼-inch pipe stanchions that supported and stiffened her cabin top. These two were badly twisted. She had no forward cockpit.

### The Auxiliary in Breakers

The difficulties in breakers of the sail boat with auxiliary engine are complicated by the general contour of both its submerged and exposed body plan, its rigging and lofty sparring. In any coastal inlet where breakers are present over three feet in height in conjunction with strong winds blowing on the land, a breaker length of roughly 100 feet and wave periods of less than five seconds, entrance may be attended with extreme difficulty and should only be attempted in extreme emergency, with the auxiliary type of boat. Unless such a boat, contemplating the entrance of a coastal inlet where breakers are seething across its mouth, is extremely high-powered, has a body and topside form that will easily assimilate a sea speed in excess of 15 knots, has very short ends and is very moderately sparred, she should not attempt any such entrance. Rather she should be taken to sea and hove to even in the face of worsening weather; her chance for survival is far better.

It should be borne in mind that the inlet breaker is no respecter of size and great length of hull. A 90-foot Gloucesterman, probably one of the most able types of small sailing vessels afloat, in consideration of its heavy power installation, rig and hull contour, excepting perhaps the world famous Ramsgate trawler and Dutch Pilot boat, found this out one night in a roaring southeaster and a snowstorm while attempting to enter Cold Spring Inlet on the Jersey coast. With the wind almost dead astern, force 5, and approaching the narrow entrance to the inlet under power and bare poles, excepting a rag of riding trysail set flying on the main, she took a heavy squall just off the entrance to the jetties. A cross sea struck her under the flare of her port bow and forced her bows to starboard and slowed her down; she was then pooped by a following breaker, losing her dog-house over the wheel box. Her starboard nest of dories went by the board across the deck and demolished her fish pens as they went, tearing loose from the chainplates her forward, port side, mainmast shroud. The vessel now being in a deep port roll, the wind from astern, driving at her lofty spars and rigging, simply took charge of her steering arrangements and directed her course squarely at 90 degrees to the direction of the gale (while the ship was making an estimated speed of better than 15 knots) into the immovable bulk of the north jetty. She rode clear to the top of the jetty before the cold stone stopped her mad run.

### Auxiliaries Need Sea Room

Many qualified and authoritative persons have written, in a general sense, of the hazards connected with the driving of such auxiliary craft before high following seas and winds of gale force from astern. Every experienced captain of such motor-sail boats senses this danger. The wise sailor, therefore, even though he may be entirely uninitiated or have no conception whatever of the forces at work aloft and those acting on his hull, will watch his chance and, using his power if necessary, will bring his bows to the seas at the earliest opportunity before he dismasts his vessel or she is hopelessly pooped or broached. This can only be done where sea room is available. It cannot be accomplished where the captain of such a boat is threatened with loss of control of his ship in a breaking inlet.

Maneuvering through a breaking coastal inlet the captain of the strictly motor-driven craft has none of these problems to deal with. A clear understanding, however, of the effect of the elements of construction, general contour of hull form and the possibilities of lofty rig leverages must be possessed by the operator of an auxiliary. He should realize how these components are so closely connected with the difficulties of handling his straining hull in breakers before high winds, and, in particular, when his hull is cramped for sea room and maneuvering space when an attempt is made to force her through the narrow channel of a breaking inlet.

Now as the size and lateral plane of auxiliary craft are reduced, the general ratio of the combined qualities of weatherliness, in such types, falls off in almost direct proportion to the degree in size to which the boat is reduced. In other words, it does not necessarily follow, because a big auxiliary might be an able craft in breakers on the coastal shelf, that a smaller vessel of similar design will retain her ability to keep the sea and handle reliably under identical sea conditions.

### How Size Affects Craft of Similar Design

In moderate weather and reasonably smooth going, an exact counterpart of the larger craft but only half her size might possibly outclass her larger sister in ability to work to windward under sail, would probably be fast in stays and possess the general rapid response to her helm which the overall design of her larger counterpart makes possible. However, when the smaller version is brought before heavy seas, alternately breaking, or where it is necessary to bring her bows head to the seas in an attempt to heave her to—the abilities of the larger auxiliary and her diminutive counterpart part company.

To begin with, the righting moments of such small craft when heeled at any angle of inclination near the crest of a breaker are far less than when such a boat is making headway on her normal water planes. Consequently, this factor of tenderness augmented by the gyrations of lofty rigging weights, reeling aloft under the influence of high windage, creates a situation where extreme watchfullness, in heavy breakers, becomes the pass-word of safety. Despite their other attributes of speed, grace and quick response to rudder motion in moderate weather, there is no heaving-to of these ships, with the wheel hard down in a becket, and going below to a pinochle game. By reason of their short keels and resultant quickness in stays, they are also quick under boisterous sea conditions and must be constantly "handled." Resorting to the use of power, before high following breakers, is liable to complicate the situation and in most cases combinations of motor and canvas should only be used when such boats are riding head-to or just off the seas, or to aid in bringing them head to the seas. Despite all of the above (since such motor-sail craft must always be "handled") they must have sea-room, and the forcing of one of these sensitive craft into the tumultuous confines of a breaking inlet channel is fraught with danger to the boat and its crew.

### The Underbody Design

Answering the constant demands for speed, speed and more speed out of such motor auxiliaries particularly on windward legs and in stays, the designer has constantly cut away at the bottom sections of these boats until in some cases there is little evidence of such a boat's keel sections left, and the forefoot has all but disappeared. This has to be done in the interest of reducing the amount of frictional area in contact with the sea, an elimination of frictional wake and eddy-making and, where a boat's forefoot has disappeared, a lessening of the slowing effects of lee bow surge and rapidity of motion in stays. That the designer has achieved his objective there is not the least doubt, but such success has been bought at the cost of creating a craft whose action under power in almost any type of cycloid, unless handled with extreme care, does not emulate, in any sense, the predictable action of a modern motor boat in heavy following breakers before high winds.

There are few boats of any type devoid of forefoot or forefoot gripe, that will "hang on" when hove to or lie without fretfulness to the end of a drogue line in heavy cycloids. This applies equally to both motor and sailing vessels, and combinations of the two. Boats of such construction all evince a tendency to pivot on the after sections of their keel while their bows are at the whim of

surface forces of the sea and are shoved higher and yon by them, making the boat uncomfortable when stemming breakers and resulting in the necessity of having to "sail" such craft constantly. Before the breakers and running, this tendency is exaggerated in the opposite direction, for now the boat's stern, which is the first portion of the ship's bulk to feel the force and direction of the waves from astern, seems to want to proceed off in one direction unmindful of the fact that it might be pushing the overhanging and lightly displaced bows off in another direction. There are several components of hull shape, sectional displacement and rigging plan that are responsible for this alarming tendency of such craft before steep breakers and high winds from astern. They are difficult to separate.

### Tendency to Broach

Auxiliary craft whose straight keel section is but a third or less of their waterline length seem to be more prone to this yawing proclivity before heavy breaking seas and are more likely to be thrown into a broach than are their long, straight-keeled and extended-forefoot sisters. As a result of their deep draft aft and the pulling aft of concentrated keel weights (aft of designed centers of buoyancy) to offset the tendency of their sail plans to depress shallow bows, the inertia built up in that section of the vessel where displacement is greatest and weights are heaviest tends to follow the natural physical law of proceeding in a straight line. Unfortunately, this submerged section of the ship about the keel knuckle and slightly forward of it, feels the violence of the breakers least while the exposed topsides (transom) of the vessel, directly above the keel knuckle, are first to meet the onslaught of breakers and to be attacked from diverse directions. At sea, such forces tearing at the hull produce wild twisting strains. In the narrow confines of an inlet channel, if the breakers are more than four feet high, her actions are likely to be so unpredictable as to make the passage difficult, if not hazardous. You just could not get power enough in her to control her and, under power alone, she could never hope to approach the performance of the modern motor boat in breakers. The inlet just is no place for her.

In my opinion, about the ablest thing in a small auxiliary that has been produced in this country that will stay with you in breakers of up to about six feet in height is the Friendship sloop. Her keel, though sloping, runs her full length; she has short ends, and she'll waddle through small breakers like the professional surfboat. There *are* sailboats in the world that will run breakers—the planing type sailboats of the South Sea natives which, like the modern semi-displacement motor boat, has none of the foregoing complications of contour to beset them in the breakers. These native craft attain speeds of 15 knots and higher sailing against the wind.

### Keep the Auxiliary Out of Breaking Inlets

When you attempt to make a motor boat out of the average auxiliary, and take her through a badly breaking inlet, you are forcing your vessel into a situation which her creators never intended she should be pushed into. If you want to run breakers, tell your architect. What he designs for you will have few of the characteristics of the auxiliary.

We have pointed out the restlessness of this type of ship when you attempt to heave it to in breakers on the coastal shelf. She *will* heave to and she *will* lay to a drogue line, but you can't put the gyro-pilot on her when the wind is force 6 and the seas are 5 and breaking. She won't do the thinking, for that lies in the department of your seamanship and good judgment.

Many sailboat rudders are relatively inefficient. Under sail, the bottom third of such rudders is the position where their greatest projected area should be placed. That section of the rudder, however, is often cut away to preserve contour and reduce eddy-making. Under power, it is the vertical center section of the rudder directly abaft the discharge from your wheel where such rudders should be given their greatest lateral area. But here steering control has been reduced by the cutting away of the rudder blade to make room for the propeller. If you run your shaft out through either of the bilges you are faced with a worse situation in the breakers for then you have the directional effect of your wheel to fight and you do not have the influence of high shaft torque to mitigate the effect of any of these constructional deficiencies. Your power, of necessity, is low. She just doesn't belong in breaking inlets.

547

Piloting on Our Fresh-Water Inland Waterways Can
Be a Rewarding Experience—a Pleasant Change,
for the Salt-Water Boatman, from Coastal Cruising.

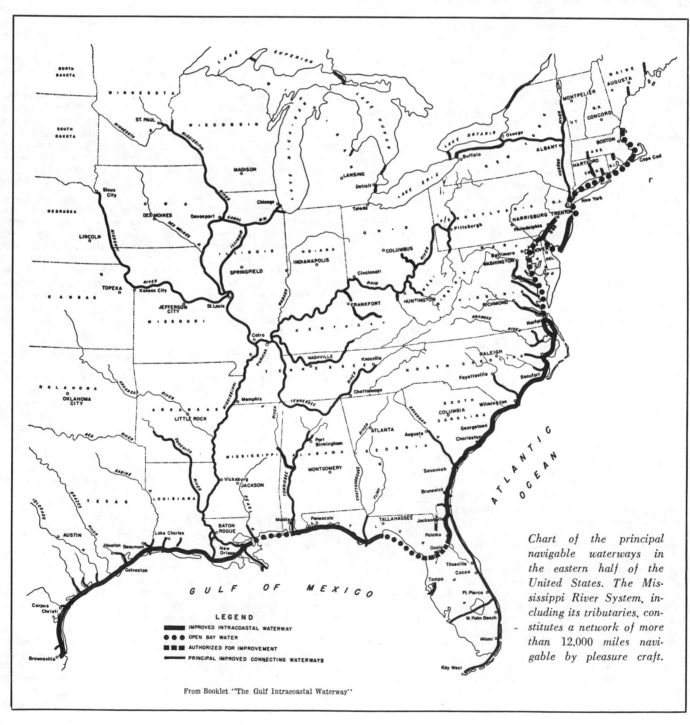

*Chart of the principal navigable waterways in the eastern half of the United States. The Mississippi River System, including its tributaries, constitutes a network of more than 12,000 miles navigable by pleasure craft.*

**LEGEND**
▬▬▬ IMPROVED INTRACOASTAL WATERWAY
●●● OPEN BAY WATER
■■■ AUTHORIZED FOR IMPROVEMENT
▬▬▬ PRINCIPAL IMPROVED CONNECTING WATERWAYS

From Booklet "The Gulf Intracoastal Waterway"

548

*A typical river scene on the Ohio, made from the Kentucky side below Louisville. Deep water favors the outside of the bend.*

FOR the cruising yachtsman who has never laid his course inland, there are surprises in store. Many a coastal boatman is likely to regard the inland waterways as little better than glorified "canals" to be used only as links between large bodies of salt water. Cruising them for their own sake might never occur to him, and canalling, in his mind, is synonymous with "ditch-crawling."

As a matter of fact, some of the finest cruising this country affords can be found on the vast network of interconnected rivers and lakes which give access to areas far removed from tidal waters. Throughout the United States there are nearly 30,000 miles of improved inland waterways. The Mississippi River system alone embraces more than 12,000 miles of waterways navigable by small craft —the largest network of navigable inland waterways, in fact, in all the world. Of these 12,000 miles, the greater part provides depths of better than 6 feet. Using the Mississippi, the Great Lakes, the New York State Barge Canal and other waterways linking these with the Atlantic and Gulf Intracoastal Waterways, the boatman can circumnavigate the entire eastern portion of the United States, a cruise of more than 5,000 miles. Only a comparatively small portion of this would be in the open sea, although the Great Lakes, of course, are sizable bodies of water, comparable to the ocean insofar as small boat cruising is concerned.

While rivers as a rule seldom offer great open expanses common to the coast where the usual techniques of piloting are called into play, they do demand unique piloting skills. On the rivers, local lore often outweighs some of the fundamental piloting principles which are the coastal pilot's law. Ever-changing conditions on the rivers put a premium on local knowledge and elevate river navigation to the status of an art.

One of the first things to impress the salt water boatman on his cruise inland is the perpetual change of scenery as he threads mile after scenic mile of sinuous cross-country course—over hills, into the valleys, through farmlands, forests and cities. Basically the transition is one from salt water to fresh, from tidal to nontidal waters. "Fresh" water does not necessarily imply clear, pure water. In the Missouri, river water is freighted with silt that clogs water strainers and wears out strut bearings and shafts. But in Lake Champlain, you can stop in mid-lake and top off your fresh water tanks.

Because inland water may be designated as non-tidal, it does not follow that there are no fluctuations in level. On the coast we are accustomed to daily changes in height —normally two highs and two lows each day. Inland, the variation in rivers is more apt to be of a seasonal nature, as spring freshets, loaded with debris, flood down from the headwaters, overflow banks, and course down to the sea at surprising velocities. At St. Louis, the seasonal fluctuation in river level from flood conditions in the late winter and early spring to normal levels in the late summer and fall may range from 40 to 50 feet. And in some of the navigable streams, sudden hard rains may raise the level several feet in a matter of hours.

In the passes at the mouth of the Mississippi, there is generally one high and one low water in 24 hours, with a range of about 18 inches. At New Orleans the diurnal range of the tide during low water stages averages about

Section of a typical Mississippi River chart. On the original, the shaded areas appear in blue tint. Channel lines, lights and mileages are printed in red. River stages, or heights, are given on the bulletin boards, locations of which are indicated on the chart in red. Note the revetment which Army Engineers have constructed on the outside of the bend to protect the bank from erosion. Small circles are 1 statute mile apart. Parallels of latitude and meridians of longitude appear, but no compass rose, as used on coastal charts. New charts in sheet form are now available for the Upper Mississippi River, replacing older bound books.

9 inches, with no periodic tide at high river stages. Current in this area is negligible from a piloting standpoint. High water stages occur around April, low in October, with extreme differences in level up to 21 feet.

In the larger lakes, a strong wind will lower levels to windward and pile up the water to leeward. Lake levels vary from year to year and show a seasonal rise and fall as well, low in the winter, high in the summer. Barometric pressure also exerts an influence on lake levels, sometimes causing a sudden temporary oscillation of considerable magnitude. This lake phenomenon is called a seiche.

Usually the cruise inland from the coast does mean a change from exposed to sheltered waters. That, however, is purely relative. While it is true that you can cruise hundreds of miles continuously on streams where shelter from bad weather is seldom more distant than the nearest bank, the larger lakes must be treated with respect. Lake Superior, for example, is the largest body of fresh water in the world. Deep, with rock-ribbed coasts and subject to storm and fog as well, it presents a challenge to even

## AIDS TO NAVIGATION

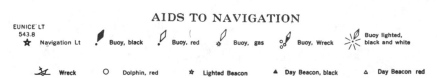

Symbols used on Mississippi River charts. Navigation lights, black buoys and red buoys are in red on original. Solid red distinguishes black buoys—open red, red buoys.

### HYDROGRAPHIC

Hydrographic notations from the legend given in a book of Mississippi River charts. Miles above Head of Passes in red on the original, the river gage in red and black. Most river charts show few soundings, if any. Black arrow is used to indicate direction of current flow, as in illustration at right.

### TYPICAL CROSSING CHANNEL

Crossing channels marked by buoys during low water - See Memphis, Vicksburg and New Orleans Districts latest Navigation Bulletin for detailed sailing directions. Navigation lights identified by name and river mile.

Typical crossing channel, as illustrated in chart book, Cairo to Gulf of Mexico. Note how channel sweeps toward outside of bend. Channel line, lights and mileages in red on original.

*Locks and dams make rivers navigable by changing levels in successive stages. Here a group of cruisers on the Tennessee ascend to a higher level, as they pass through Wilson Dam Lock in Alabama. Coiling lines, the crew make ready to sail out of the lock.*

the saltiest pilot. Lake Erie, though smaller than Superior, is comparatively shallow. In a gale of wind, seas cannot shape up in the normal pattern of ocean waves. Consequently, they are short and steep, frequently breaking in heavy squalls. Even New York's Lake Oneida, only 20 miles in length, can build up seas that will test the ability of an offshore boat.

Broadly speaking, river currents, though they may fluctuate in velocity, will trend always in one direction—from headwaters to mouth. Despite this, tidal rivers connecting with the sea may feel the effect of tidal conditions at the mouth, backing the water up so that the cruiser can take advantage of a favorable current going upstream when tidal conditions are right. On the Hudson, for example, a 10-mile cruiser, starting at The Battery at the beginning of the flood, can carry a favorable current all the way to Albany, 150 miles inland. Tides, here, even this far inland, may range in excess of 6 feet, yet at Newburgh and West Point far down the river, the mean range will be only half that.

Shoaling is a serious problem in most rivers. Spring floods build up current velocities, stir up silt in river bottoms, wash more down from the banks, and carry this load in suspension to be deposited in the form of mud flats and sand bars that present navigational hazards by closing off channels. The Connecticut River on the East Coast is a good example of this, where heavy expenditures are required annually to keep channels dredged to project depths. In the Mississippi, a jellied mass of muck called flocculation is deposited as a sediment on the river bed to a depth of 10 or 15 feet. Deep-draft vessels plow through

it, and high water stages of the river flush it out into the Gulf so Army Engineers do not bother to dredge it at low water stages.

Often where a river discharges into a bay or sound, current velocities are no longer sufficient to hold the silt in suspension and a bar or shoal is built up across the river mouth, much as creeks and streams behave when they flow into the ocean, creating an obstacle against free passage into open water, unless a channel is dredged and protected by breakwaters. On bars of this kind, bad seas may build up in strong currents opposed by the wind. As a matter of fact, at the confluence of some rivers, disturbed surface conditions may be encountered, even where there is seemingly no wind to account for it.

River currents have been the subject of extensive studies and their vagaries are of utmost importance to the masters of deep-draft commercial craft. The surface current acting on a small pleasure boat may in fact be actually contrary to that which grips the keel of a large ship near the river bottom. Even with respect to surface currents alone, there is a variation from bank to mid-stream. Friction of the banks and bottom retards velocity. The skipper of the commercial boat—where fuel costs and hours of operation are of vital import—knows this as he carries the strength of a mid-river current downstream with him. Returning he runs close under the bank to escape the strength of flow opposing him—even turning slightly into coves behind points to take advantage of the counter-current that tends opposite to the trend of the river's flow.

Perhaps the factors which the professional pilot weighs so carefully are less significant to the small boatman.

*A lone cruiser passes out of one of the highest lift locks in the nation, having been raised 80 feet at Fort Loudon Lock as she proceeds up the Tennessee toward Knoxville, Tenn.*

Nevertheless, the pleasure boatman can profitably take a leaf from the river pilot's log and cut his running time and fuel bills merely by running courses that make elemental factors work for him, rather than against him.

Again, speaking broadly, unless there is something in the bottom contour or man-made structures to alter them, river channels have a natural trend somewhat akin to the configurations in creeks along the marshes of our coasts, where the flow of water tends to carry across the stream on the outside of bends, scouring out a natural channel at the outside while depositing a bar on the points.

Study a river chart which gives the depths (those of the Coast & Geodetic Survey do) and notice the trend. Then when you are piloting a river where the navigational "maps" give no clue to depths (as in the Ohio and Mississippi) you can begin to develop an instinct with regard to interpretation of the river's natural course. Try to visualize the whole picture, if you can, as it would appear to you if you were looking down on the river *and* your boat from a plane. This way you will be less likely to run straight courses from buoy to buoy, cutting corners, with obvious risk of piling up on a point. You will appreciate better the problems of the agency which buoys the waterway, where a pair of buoys are used to mark a point and the channel edge opposite, with a similar pair abreast of the next point. Between the two points the river may be taking a natural curve and a mid-channel course would be represented, not by a straight line between the two pairs of buoys, but by a curved line conforming roughly to the trend of the river as a whole.

Gradually developing this sense of perspective, you'll be more acutely conscious of the actual track you make good over the bottom relative to nearby shoals and side limits of the channels. Where currents do occasionally flow diagonally across your

Corps of Engineers, U. S. Army

*Two big tows pass on the Mississippi at Vicksburg bridge.*

course, you will allow for them instinctively and look astern frequently to help maintain that sense of position.

As you glance astern in unfamiliar waters, your wake will provide a clue to the safety of your course. When the natural sequence of waves in your wake is broken, there must be something to disturb it. As it rolls off into shallow water, the smooth undulation will give way to a sharper formation, even cresting on the flats in miniature "breakers." When they encounter a reef or flooded area where submerged stumps lie close to the surface, the wake will show the difference. But when that short peaked unnatural wake closes up toward your stern, sheer off . . . . fast!—away from the side where the telltale wake builds up.

On some river charts, even the curves showing the topography ashore supply clues to what may be expected in the river itself. Frequently contour curves crowded close together on land at the water's edge indicate a cliff rising sheer from the surface, with prospects of good depths close under such a bank. The cliff or hill, as the case may be, may at the same time provide a prominent landmark as a guide to steer by.

Piloting the rivers and canals, encountering bridges, locks and guard gates in rapid succession, you will soon acquire a new awareness of controlling vertical and horizontal clearances. On tidewater you were, no doubt, acutely conscious of depths as a critical consideration. Navigating a waterway where you normally could be assured a 6-foot depth, you automatically exercised extra caution around inlets where rapid shifting of the

*Cruiser entering Kentucky Dam Lock. Note striping on wall.*

shoals might cut your controlling depth to a couple of feet. On the rivers, you will have the clearance overhead on your mind. There may be places on some streams where a fixed bridge will arbitrarily determine your "head of navigation." Beyond that point, your cruising may be restricted to an exploratory trip in the dinghy.

On some of our principal waterways—the New York State Barge Canal System, for example—overhead clearance is restricted to 15½ feet. Masts on auxiliaries must be unstepped and carried on deck, and outriggers and radiotelephone antennas hinged down out of the way. Commercial craft are built with regard for limiting clearance under bridges and in locks. Superstructures are kept low and pilot houses may even be made retractable, to lower for passage under bridges. Fixed overhead power cables are generally high enough to provide clearance for masted vessels, and this clearance is noted on the chart. High water stages on the rivers naturally cut overhead clearances under bridges by the amount of rise above normal pool levels. Chart books for the Ohio give examples of how to calculate existing clearances at open river stages from the vertical clearances at normal pool stage, and at 1936 high water stage, shown on the charts.

Signals for the opening of drawbridges, lift bridges, etc., are not uniform in all waters so it will be necessary to consult local regulations. For the Great Lakes area, for example, they

Photograph by George Yater

*The wandering Ohio from the campus of Hanover College*

*Five cruisers, bound upstream, leave Pickwick Dam Lock located in southern Tennessee. Note the long guide wall.*

are covered in detail in the Great Lakes Pilot. Elsewhere, as on the Illinois Waterway, information may be had from Army Engineer District Offices. On the New York Barge Canal, the signal is three short distinct blasts of the whistle.

Before the days of locks and dams, many of our rivers were unnavigable. Water coursing down valleys at the land's natural gradient, dropping perhaps hundreds of feet in a score of miles, runs too fast and encounters too many natural obstacles. To overcome them, engineers dam the natural waterways at strategic spots, creating a series of "pools" or levels that may be likened to a stairway. Good examples of how closely these can resemble a flight of stairs will be found at places like Waterford, N. Y., and the Rideau Canal at Ottawa, where vessels descend or ascend a series of locks in quick succession.

To a river pilot, the term "pool stage" indicates the height of water in a pool at any given time with reference to the datum for that pool. On the rivers pool stages are posted on conspicuous bulletin boards along the river banks so as to be easily read from passing vessels. Locations of the bulletin boards are given on the river charts. On the Ohio, gage readings are displayed at the powerhouses of the dams. These indicate depths of the pool impounded by the dam next below. A depth of 9 feet is uniformly taken to indicate the pool at normal elevation. A reading of 8.7 feet would indicate that the lower pool at the dam is 0.3 foot below normal elevation. These readings are preceded by the letters NP (normal pool) in white on a green background.

Photograph courtesy J. D. Tennison, Jr.

*At Mile 715.0 on the Lower Mississippi River, just a few miles below Memphis, pleasure craft anchor on the back side of a bar in slack water with complete protection from the wake of passing towboats. There are many such bars along the Mississippi from Baton Rouge on north. The river boatman will find them a snug haven for anchorage at night or during severe weather.*

Locks and Dams, and the Part They Play in Making Rivers Navigable. The Proper Handling of Pleasure Craft in Passing Through Locks, and Some Special Problems of Meeting and Passing Commercial Traffic in Narrow Canals and Congested Waterways.

Photograph from Corps of Engineers, U. S. Army

*A fleet of pleasure craft, locking through together, almost fill all of the available space in a lock chamber of the Inner Harbor Navigation Canal Lock in New Orleans, as they head east on the Gulf Intracoastal Waterway. Gates recess into the lock walls.*

**D**AMS on our inland waterways, without locks, would restrict river cruising to the individual pools and prevent through navigation except to small craft light enough to be portaged around the dams. Locks, in conjunction with the dams, provide the means for watercraft to move from level to level. Locks vary in size but since they must invariably handle commercial traffic, their limiting dimensions offer no restriction to the movement of pleasure craft. On the New York State Barge Canal, a tanker will almost fill a lock, with little space to spare.

Locks are practically water-tight chambers with gates at each end. Valves are provided to admit water as re-

quired. When a vessel is about to be locked upstream to a higher level, the upstream gate is closed, the downstream gate opened, and the water stands at the lower level. The vessel enters the lock through the open gates at the lower end, the gates close behind her and water is valved in until the chamber is full to the upstream level. Now the upstream gate is opened, and the boat is free to resume her course upstream. Locking down is naturally the reverse of this procedure.

Signals are provided for vessels approaching a lock (commonly a long and a short blast) answered by signals from the lock tender. The river boatman should familiarize himself with the special signals applicable to the particular waterway he is using. The Army Engineers at Pittsburgh publish an informative little illustrated leaflet entitled "Locking Through," which sets forth, in a nutshell, the main essentials as they apply to the Ohio.

On the Ohio, vessels sound a long and short blast on the whistle from a distance of not more than one mile from the lock. (On the New York State Barge Canal, they signal with three distinct blasts.) When approaching a lock, boats must wait for the lockmaster's signal before entering. When bound downstream, stay in the clear at least 400 feet upstream from the end of the guide wall leading along the bank into the lock. Approach through the buoyed channel directly toward the lock and keep clear of spillway sections of the dam. Be particularly careful not to obstruct the movement of any large commercial craft that may be leaving the lock. When bound upstream, keep well clear of the turbulent water invariably found below a dam.

On the Mississippi, signs are painted on the river face of the guide wall warning small craft not to pass a given point until signalled by the lock attendant. Near this sign a signal cord is placed. Small craft may use this to alert lock attendants, in lieu of signals used on other waters.

Traffic signal lights at the Ohio locks resemble those you find on the highway—red, amber and green, vertically arranged. Flashing red warns: do not enter, stand clear. Flashing amber signifies: approach, but under full control. Flashing green gives you the all-clear signal to enter. (On N. Y. State Canals, a fixed green light gives clearance to enter; fixed red requires the vessel to wait. U. S. and commercial vessels take precedence; pleasure boats may be locked through with commercial craft if a safe distance may be maintained between them.)

Where locks are in pairs (landward and riverward) the lockmaster on the Ohio may also use an air horn, the significance of his blasts as follows: 1 long, enter landward lock; 2 long, enter riverward lock; 1 short, leave landward lock; 2 short, leave riverward lock.

The Secretary of the Army has established an order of priority with respect to the handling of traffic at locks, giving precedence in this order: 1, U. S. military craft; 2, mail boats; 3, commercial passenger craft; 4, commercial tows; 5, commercial fishermen; and 6, pleasure boats. This means that small pleasure craft may sometimes have to wait to be locked through with other vessels. In deciding on an order of precedence, the lockmaster also takes into account whether vessels of the same class are arriving at landward or riverward locks, and whether they are bound upstream or downstream.

The concrete walls of locks are usually rough and dirty. Consequently a boat will need adequate fender protection. Ordinary cylindrical fenders will pick up dirt and roll on the wall to smear the topsides. Fender boards, consisting of a plank (2-by-6 perhaps, several feet long) suspended horizontally outside the usual fenders, work well amidships or aft where sides are reasonably straight. Bags of hay have the same objection as cylindrical fenders, except

*A view of the wickets at one of the Ohio River movable dams. Wickets are held in an upright position during low water stages of the river. At high water, they can be lowered, creating a navigable pass which river boats use without locking.*

Photograph from J. M. Wallace

Photograph from Corps of Engineers, U. S. Army

*At Mile 633 on the Mississippi, Army Engineers' equipment works on bank protection. Such floating equipment should be passed with caution. Day signal (extreme right) is a black-and-white vertically striped ball over a red ball; at night, equipment of this kind will show three red lights in vertical line.*

Photograph from N. Y. State Department of Public Works

*A westbound tug and barge (pushed ahead) enter the empty Erie Canal Lock No. 4, where they will be raised 34½ feet to the upper level. Propellers on large commercial craft throw a lot of water astern—something for small craft to watch.*

on heavily flared bows at the edge of deck where they flatten down and work pretty well. Auto tires wrapped with burlap would be ideal except that their use is illegal in some canals. As you can't be sure which side of a lock you'll be using, it's wise to fender both sides.

Another essential in locking is adequate line. How heavy it is to be depends on the size of boat; how long depends on the depth of the locks. Good ½" manila is generally

adequate for average sized cruisers. In general, each line (bow and stern) will have to be at least twice as long as the depth of lock. The object of this is to permit your running the bight of a line around a bollard on the top of the lock wall, using it double. Then, on the lower level, when you're read to cast off, you can haul the line in without assistance from above. At Little Falls, N. Y., the drop is roughly 40 feet, so 100 feet is not too much for

*Reproduction of a portion of an Ohio River chart. Arrow (top) indicates true north, seldom at top of chart. Arrow at left indicates direction of river flow. Note symbols for cans and nuns (see legend, next page). Location of bulletin board showing river gages is shown on chart.*

the length of each of the two lock lines in such cases.

Ladders are often recessed into lock walls and on some canals small craft by choice will follow the ladder up, rung by rung, with boat hook or lock lines. On the Ohio, this is frowned upon and boats are requested not to use the ladders. In addition to big bollards along the top of the lock wall, some locks have other recessed posts at intervals in the walls in vertical line. Locking up, lines can be cleared successively from lower posts and transferred to higher ones within reach. In other locks, floating mooring hooks move up and down to follow the pool levels.

Rising or falling, stand by your lock lines at all times and tend them carefully. This requires a hand forward and another aft, though with only two aboard the helmsman could handle the after line. One of the most dangerous practices is to make fast to a bollard above and then secure to a bitt or cleat on deck. If the level drops, your craft is "hung," with risk of serious damage.

Entering and leaving locks, it's always imperative to throttle down and keep the boat under complete control. This is especially true when locking through with other boats. Sometimes, on fleet cruises, it will be necessary to tie up two abreast at each lock wall. This is entirely feasible as long as all boats are intelligently handled. On sail-away cruises to New York from the plant of a western New York State boatbuilder, fleets of twenty or more were handled successfully without damage to any.

Occasionally one hears cautions concerning the possibility of a boat's being tossed about as water boils into locks from the open valves. Actually, lock tenders on our inland waters are careful to control this flow, and there is little cause for apprehension on this score. With a light craft, however, some thought should be given to placement in a lock when passing through with large commercial craft. A light hull, directly astern of a powerful tug, can take quite a tossing around when her big wheel starts to throw the water astern.

There are various kinds of locks, all of which accomplish the same end of effecting a change of level. Gates may swing or roll back and in cases are hoisted in vertical lift, permitting traffic to pass through under the gate. Such is the case at Little Falls, N. Y. On the Trent Waterway in Canada, a hydraulic lock lifts the boat in a water-filled chamber and in another instance a marine railway actually hauls the boat out to get her up over a hill. Through passage on a waterway like the Trent, then, is obviously

| U.S. Light | ☀ |
| Daymark | ♦ |
| Temporary buoys: | |
| Can (black) | • |
| Nun (red) | ○ |
| Permanent type buoy: | |
| Can (black) | ◉ |
| Nun (red) | ◉ |
| Flasher buoys: | |
| Can (white flash) | ☀◉ |
| Nun (red flash) | ☼◉ |
| Radar buoy | ◆ |
| Gage | ⊖ |
| Arrival Point for Lockages | AP |
| General bank line | ∼∼ |
| Water's edge at pool stage | |
| Bar, with less than project 9' depth at pool stage | ▨▨▨ |
| Aerial crossings: | |
| Power | •••••• |
| Telephone | − − − − |
| Seaplane Base | ✝ |

*Legend of symbols used on navigation charts of the Ohio River. Some of these are illustrated on the chart shown on preceding page.*

limited to craft within the capacity of the ways to haul. At Troy, N. Y., a Federally operated time lock opens only at slated intervals—on the hour—occasionally causing a slight delay in lockage.

Lock permits, once necessary for pleasure boats, are no longer required to navigate the New York State Barge Canal. On Western Rivers, no special permission or clearance is required for passage through the locks. There are regulations to be observed, however, and copies of these should be obtained from Army Engineer Offices at Chicago or St. Louis.

The point made by Army Engineers as to the necessity

*Longest vessels in the world are not the big ocean liners but the tows on Western Rivers made up of barges propelled by a towboat at the stern. Length often exceeds 1000 feet. They should always be passed with great care, especially at bends.*

*West of Rochester the New York State Barge Canal passes through a rock cut. Speed limit is 6 statute miles per hour.*

*At Lockport, New York, lock tenders open the gates for craft ready to lock down. The locks here are double.*

for caution when approaching locks is well taken. They emphasize the importance of following the buoyed channel closely. Some years ago, a cruiser bound down the Hudson missed the lock at Troy, which lies far over on the east bank, and went *over* the dam. By rare good fortune, she was able to continue her cruise to New York under her own power. Looking down the river from above the dam, it's virtually impossible to see any break in the water's surface, yet there's no excuse for such an occurrence if one pays attention to the buoys as indicated on the chart.

Actually, there are times and places when it is proper to go *over* a dam, strange as that may sound. On the Ohio, they use a movable type of dam having a lock chamber on one side and "bear traps" on the other. In the middle, between them, there are movable wickets which can be held in an upright position during low water stages and lowered at times of high water. When the wickets are up, traffic necessarily passes through the lock. With the wickets down, at high water, boats run through the navigable pass, over the dam, without locking. By day, it is important to watch the bulletin boards at the locks to know whether the lock or the navigable pass is to be used. By night, distinguishing lights are used on the guide walls. When the navigable pass is being used, the gage reading on the powerhouse bulletin board shows the depth of water over the pass sill at the dam. The reading is in white on a scarlet background, and is preceded by the word PASS.

One point that needs careful watching is the strong current set when bear traps are open. These bear traps are devices used to regulate pool levels within certain limits without having to lower the wickets in the navigable pass. In your passage downstream, while waiting for a lock to open, the set may tend to draw you away from the lock approach toward the dam.

One other caution—approach each lock with care and heed the signals at every one. The fact that the navigable pass is in use at one dam is no assurance that it will be at the next.

Be on guard against current set anywhere near a spillway.

Not all waterways are merely improved versions of natural rivers and lakes. Artificial land cuts are often used to connect navigable waterways and provide continuous passage between major bodies of water. Lake Champlain is accessible from the upper reaches of the Hudson only because of a 24-mile land cut connecting the two. A dredged land cut is also encountered at the western end of the Erie Canal to connect Lake Erie with mid-state rivers.

Narrow cuts of this kind pose problems of their own. A typical earth section of dredged canal might have a bottom width of only 75 feet, at the surface perhaps 125 feet, and a depth, let's say, of 12 feet. If normal cruising speeds were maintained through such sections, the bank would be quickly washed down into the channel and maintenance problems would be aggravated. Consequently in such artificial waterways, speed limits are rigidly enforced. In New York canals, the limit is 6 statute mph in the land lines, 10 mph in canalized rivers and lake sections. It's wise to heed the regulations as lock keepers use their phone connections between locks to check on running times.

Some of the land lines are cut through solid rock, perhaps only 100 feet or less in width. This makes a virtual trough with ragged walls of blasted rock. Anyone who has ever run in company with other craft in a confined channel like this knows full well how the wakes of a group of boats may synchronize at times and build up out of all proportion to that of a single craft running alone. Unless serious thought is given to maintenance of moderate speed, regardless of legal limits, small craft can get out of control under such conditions and yaw exactly as they would in a steep swell over an inlet bar. We've seen it happen, with damage to the boat, when the boat's run was ultimately checked by the rock walls.

Most of our inland waterways handle considerable commercial traffic. In a narrow dredged cut a big tug or tanker requires the better part of the channel. As she approaches, you'll see a sizable bow wave built up, practically running ahead of her, and the water drawn away by suction to lower the level at both her sides amidships. Give such traffic as wide a berth as safety with respect to channel widths permits.

Tugs with tows astern in narrow waterways present a real problem to approaching small craft. Fortunately, most of the "towing" today is done by pushing scows and barges ahead of the tug. This keeps the whole tow under better control as a single unit. In times past we have, however, seen a single file of a dozen or more pleasure boats following the right hand edge of a channel, start to pass a tug with tow astern at a bend. The first boats would get through nicely with

Photo by Paul A. Moore, Tennessee Conservation Dept.
*A pleasure steamer locking through one of the TVA locks.*

*Signal lights and air horn signals used on the Western Rivers to control traffic at locks. (From "Locking Through," prepared by Army Engineers, St. Louis.)*

ample passing room but the swinging barges would gradually cut down the passing room to starboard to such an extent that boats bringing up the rear would be forced to pass to port. Even with the tow ahead, this swinging effect must be taken into account at narrow bends so it's generally wise to pass on the inside of the bends.

Big rafts of barges bunched together on the Mississippi in one vast tow may cover many acres in extent. The prudent pleasure boat pilot will appreciate the problems of handling such colossal floats and never jeopardize their activities, regardless of any considerations of right of way. Integrated tows are often made up of a bowpiece, a group of square-ended barges, and a towboat (at the stern) lashed together in one streamlined unit 1000 feet or more in length. At night, to an observer in a small boat, the towboat's lights may be more conspicuous than those on the tow far out ahead. Consequently, special caution is indicated when attempting to run the rivers at night, even though the river itself be so well lighted as to make this feasible. When commercial traffic is using powerful searchlights their blinding beams may make it impossible for the small boatman to see anything at all. Shore lights add to the difficulty, because of reflections in the water. Then, too, in some rivers, especially in flood, there's the hazard of floating and partially submerged debris.

On all the rivers, recreational craft should give commercial tows a wide berth. In particular they should stay away from the front of tows when under way. If you happen to stall in such a spot, it might be impossible for the tow to stop or steer clear. With the way she carries, a commercial tow may at times travel half a mile or more before she can come to a full stop.

The need for keeping a boat under control on approach to locks has already been mentioned. The same applies to bridges, especially when strong currents tend to sweep a boat down toward the bridge structure. This takes on increased significance when vessels must wait to allow a bridge to open after signalling. Unless care is exercised the current may carry a boat down and put her in a position from which it may be virtually impossible to extricate her without twin-screw power. It is on this principle that Western River Rules grant right of way to a "descending" vessel (one proceeding downstream) since the "ascending" vessel is under far better control. Difficulty of maneuvering is aggravated when vessels are trying to handle tows.

River currents sometimes attain such speed that navigation upstream is unfeasible though capably handled boats may safely be taken down. Such is the case in the Galop Rapids of the St. Lawrence where the velocity may run around 12-13 mph. Some river boats have power enough to ascend certain rapids. As a general rule, it is best to avoid them by using canals and locks that by-pass them, unless the skipper has local knowledge or engages the services of a local pilot.

*From Kodachrome by Wm. H. Koelbel*

*A guard gate on the Champlain Canal. Gates of this kind can be lowered when work is being done on the locks below.*

*Photograph courtesy J. D. Tennison, Jr.*

*Just below the Memphis bridges, vessels work over a wreck caused when a barge got out of control in the river current and sank after striking bridge piers at high water. Day signal (double frustums of a cone, base to base, in vertical line) indicating vessel at work on wreck, is prominently displayed.*

*Guntersville (Ala.) Yacht Club on TVA's Guntersville Lake.*

Photograph from TVA

Finding an Anchorage or Mooring for Overnight Stops on the Rivers. River Charts and How They Differ from Those of Coastal Waters. Local Knowledge for Boatmen Running the Mississippi River.

**P**ROBLEMS of where to tie up or anchor for the night are always with us when cruising, whether on coastal or inland waters. On coastal waters, it may be essentially a matter of finding a sheltered cove or basin to avoid risk of a rough night in an exposed anchorage. As a rule on the rivers, shelter from blows is closer at hand, yet there are areas great enough in expanse to work up sizable seas, especially with the wind opposing the current. Then too, there is the matter of finding protection in narrow waterways from passing river traffic and the wake it throws. Finally, there's always the question of personal preference as to whether one seeks the seclusion of quiet anchorages off the beaten track or prefers the activity usually associated with cities and centers of population.

The development in recent years of new marinas on some of the inland waterways—the TVA, for example—has been of great help in this respect. Not only do they provide a place to tie up for the night, but fuel supplies and other necessities are generally available at the marina or near at hand.

On the Tennessee River, safety harbors and landings have been provided for use in case of bad weather, mechanical failure or other contingencies. Their locations are shown on the charts. Safety harbors are usually coves off the navigable channel. Direction boards on shore define the entrance, and cross boards mark the upper limits.

## THE TENNESSEE VALLEY

PROFILE OF THE TENNESSEE RIVER

*Map of the Tennessee Valley showing location of dams in the TVA system. Dams impound water, creating vast lakes for recreational boating, while locks permit through traffic to by-pass dams on cruises throughout the system. Potential flood waters are stored in wet seasons, released in dry seasons, and minimum depth of 9 feet is maintained for navigation.*

Safety landings are areas where banks have been cleared of stumps, boulders and snags, so vessels may land safely. Upper and lower limits are marked by direction boards— white if a 9′ depth is available at all pool stages; orange if the depth is 9′ at all except low water stages of the river.

The New York State Barge Canal provides terminals at intervals along the route, though these may be occupied by commercial craft. Of concrete, the terminals require adequate fendering when used by small pleasure craft. In order to allow for the seasonal range in levels, or stages, on Western rivers, most yacht clubs are afloat,

on strings of barges, necessitating a long climb up the river bank at low-water stages to get to town.

Frequently a glance at the chart (or navigational map) will reveal a likely place to anchor for the night. A widening of the river may offer an opportunity to get out of the reach of traffic, a small tributary or slough may invite exploration (with caution, sounding as you go), or the natural configuration of river banks and bars may provide a natural harbor with complete protection. Islands in mid-river frequently leave a secondary channel fine for small craft of easy draft, while heavy-draft commercial

Photograph from Joliet Assn. of Commerce

*The Illinois Waterway provides a navigable connecting waterway between the Great Lakes at Chicago on Lake Michigan to Grafton, Ill., on the Mississippi by way of the Chicago, Des Plaines and Illinois Rivers. View at left shows a tow passing through bridges at Joliet, Illinois.*

*Extract from one of the Illinois Waterway charts. With wicket-type dams which can be lowered at high-water stages, traffic uses the navigable pass through the dam, indicated by "high water sailing line." System of lights, explained on chart, shows whether lock or navigable pass is to be used. Below, the symbols. Lights and nun buoys in red on original.*

| LEGEND OF SYMBOLS | | AIDS TO NAVIGATION | |
|---|---|---|---|
| GENERAL | | | |
| SHORE LINE | ▬▬▬ | FLASHING POST LIGHT IN PEORIA LAKE | ⊛ |
| LEVEE | ⊥⊤⊥ | POST LIGHT | ☀ |
| 9-FOOT CONTOUR | ------- | FLOAT LIGHT | ⊚◇ |
| MILES FROM GRAFTON | [150] | DAYMARK | ◈ |
| VERTICAL BRIDGE CLEARANCE FOR 80 FOOT HORIZONTAL CLEARANCE | ⊖ | BLACK (CAN) BUOY | ◄ |
| MOVABLE TYPE BRIDGE NO OPERATING MACHINERY INSTALLED | • | RED (NUN) BUOY | ◇ |
| U.S. GAGE | ⊕ | BRIDGE CLEARANCE GAGE | ◐ |
| | | FLASHING SIGNAL LIGHTS ON BRIDGE | ▪ |

traffic is confined to the main channel. When a river cuts a channel behind a section of bank, a "towhead" is formed. Sometimes these are filled in at the upper end by river deposits, forming a natural protected anchorage in the lower end. At times you can get behind a pile dike, a type of structure used on rivers to protect banks from washing away. The dike juts out into the river and, by tying up to one of the piles just inside the outer end, on the downstream side, you have protection not only from passing traffic but from floating debris as well. When entering sloughs between islands in search of an anchorage, beware of submerged wing dams at the upstream end. To be safe, enter and leave from the downstream end.

In some cases sufficient protection for an overnight anchorage can be obtained behind a mid-river bar. Occasionally one can find a tiny cove (like Partridge Harbor on Lake Champlain) where there's room for only a few boats, and no room to swing at anchor, so you anchor the bow off and run a stern line to the nearest tree ashore.

One trick they use on Western rivers is the so-called river hitch. To tie up to a bank for the night, the boat's bow is held up to the bank with power while a line is run to a nearby tree. Then a sapling is cut, 15 to 20 feet long, and lashed from bank to stern to hold the stern off. Another line ashore holds the stern in.

As a rule when tying up for the night on inland rivers, lines need not be laid with allowance for the tidal range common on the coasts. On tidal rivers, it is of course a factor (6-foot range at Albany) and even on the inland rivers there's always the chance of a change in level with hard rainstorms, etc. It pays to observe the practices of local craft and to be guided accordingly. Tied to a barge or float which will itself rise and fall with changing levels, the boatman need provide only such slack in lines as may be required for comfort if a passing craft happens to throw a disturbing wake.

The character of the bottom varies widely on inland waterways. Especially in their lower courses, river bottoms are often soft mud, pointing to the desirability of carrying, in your complement of ground tackle, at least one anchor with broad flukes of a design that will dig down till it reaches good holding bottom. In such spots, the anchor with spidery arms and flukes will cut through and provide no holding power at all, whereas on a hard bottom the same anchor might be highly efficient. When you get into rocky bottoms or areas infested with roots and snags, you will want to resort to one of the tricks for being prepared to recover the anchor if fouled. One easy way is to use a light line from the anchor crown long enough to reach the surface, where the end of line is buoyed. If the anchor snags, pick up the buoy and raise the anchor with the trip line, crown first. Some anchors are provided with slip rings, shear pins or other device to make them snag-proof.

On the subject of anchoring, there's a point to bear in mind when piloting in bodies of water like Lake Champlain. Along some shores, which may be particularly inviting because of their scenic attractions, you may find a depth of a couple of hundred feet running up to sheer cliff shores. If your power fails, your anchor would be of little use in such depths, and if the breeze is toward those cliffs you're on a bad lee shore.

When anchoring on the big rivers near a sand bar or island, or, for that matter, when beaching the boat to go ashore in such a place, a good rule to follow is to pick the downstream rather than the upper end. If an anchor drags or if for any reason you get aground on the upstream end, it's practically like being on a lee shore except that in this case the current, instead of the wind, is constantly working to drive you harder aground. Water at the downstream end is likely to be quieter and the eddies encountered there may help to free a grounded boat. Grounding hard on the rivers may be more troublesome than it is on tidewater, where the next rising tide will generally free a craft without any other assistance.

One of the points likely to strike the tidewater boatman most forcefully when he takes to the Western rivers is the radical difference between river charts and the Coast and Geodetic Survey charts to which he is accustomed. River charts are commonly in the form of books of "navigational maps," each page covering successive short stretches of the river in strip form. A typical example is the bound volume prepared by the Mississippi River Commission, Vicksburg, Miss., to cover the Mississippi from Cairo, Ill., to the Gulf of Mexico. This is on a scale of 1:62,500 (approximately 1 inch to the mile). All of the soundings (with a few exceptions) and detailed positions of rocks, reefs, ledges and shoals so familiar on

Photograph from Corps of Engineers, U. S. Army

*A view of the upstream side of Alton Lock and Dam No. 26 on the Mississippi River above St. Louis, Missouri. Note the double locks (extreme left). The landward lock of the pair is considerably larger than the riverward lock. Signals indicate which to use.*

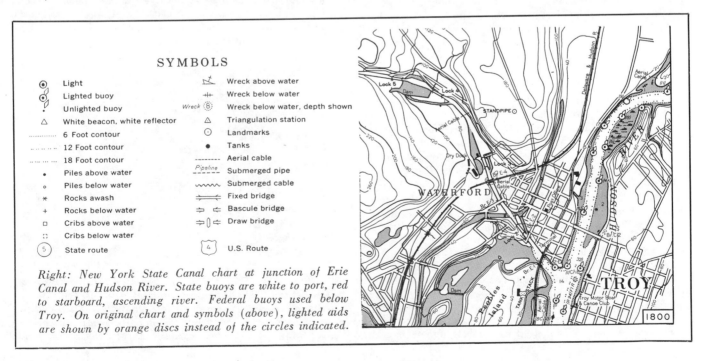

### SYMBOLS

| | | | |
|---|---|---|---|
| ⊙ | Light | ⌐ | Wreck above water |
| ⊙ | Lighted buoy | ⊬ | Wreck below water |
| ⊙ | Unlighted buoy | Wreck ⊗ | Wreck below water, depth shown |
| △ | White beacon, white reflector | △ | Triangulation station |
| ......... | 6 Foot contour | ⊙ | Landmarks |
| -------- | 12 Foot contour | ● | Tanks |
| -·-·-·- | 18 Foot contour | -------- | Aerial cable |
| • | Piles above water | Pipeline | Submerged pipe |
| ○ | Piles below water | ⌇⌇⌇ | Submerged cable |
| ✳ | Rocks awash | ⇥⇤ | Fixed bridge |
| + | Rocks below water | ⇌⇌ | Bascule bridge |
| □ | Cribs above water | ⇌〇⇌ | Draw bridge |
| ⸬ | Cribs below water | | |
| ⑤ | State route | ④ | U.S. Route |

*Right: New York State Canal chart at junction of Erie Canal and Hudson River. State buoys are white to port, red to starboard, ascending river. Federal buoys used below Troy. On original chart and symbols (above), lighted aids are shown by orange discs instead of the circles indicated.*

coastal charts are omitted. In their place the course of the river is traced in blue tint between heavy black lines which delineate the banks. A broken red line is used to indicate the channel line. Navigation lights are denoted by a red star with white dot in the center together with a number which designates its distance upstream above a fixed reference point—in this case A.H.P., "Above the Head of Passes." The Head of Passes is the point not far above the mouth where the river splits into separate channels leading through the delta into the Gulf. Mileages are given in red every five miles, with red circles at one-mile intervals. Mileages above and below the Head of Passes are printed in red. A detailed table is given in the book, listing in alphabetical order all towns, cities, bridges, mouths of rivers, and other important features adjacent to the main channel, with distances (AHP) in miles and map numbers on which the features appear.

Before starting a cruise on the lower Mississippi, the pilot should make a careful study of the legend which appears on the inside front cover of the chart book. Symbols used to designate the various aids to navigation are given, with abbreviations, topographic and hydrographic features, and an illustration of a typical crossing channel (the latter marked by buoys during periods of low water). Charts are on the polyconic projection and elevations refer to mean level.

### On the Illinois Waterway

The book of charts for the Illinois Waterway is prepared by the Chicago District of the Army Engineers. A page of general information in this volume covers practically everything the pilot needs to know in navigating the waterway as he follows his charts. Attention should be paid to the legend of symbols, which differ in some respects from those found on coastal charts. The main channel is shown in white, shoal areas in blue tint. The "sailing line" is indicated by a broken line, the miles from Grafton in brackets in black. Scale is 1 inch to 1000 feet.

Aids to navigation include post lights or range lights with fixed white lights, and some flashing lights. Daymarks are white diamonds on posts without lights. Red nuns are found on the left edge of the channel, black cans on the right edge, proceeding downstream. Detailed information on the operation and lighting of bridges and locks and locking regulations are all given in the Illinois Waterway chart book.

Charts for the Middle and Upper Mississippi from Cairo to Minneapolis (also prepared by the Chicago District of the Army Engineers) resemble those for the lower river except that they are done in black and white with no color to help distinguish significant features. Mileages are reckoned above Cairo. A separate book is available for the Mississippi from Cairo at the mouth of the Ohio to Grafton at the mouth of the Illinois Waterway.

A small booklet of charts for Navigation Pools 25 and 26 of the Mississippi River and Illinois Waterway (published by the St. Louis Engineer Office) is distinguished primarily by the fact that it shows hazard areas (under 6-foot depth) in bright red shading, harbors or anchorage areas with an anchor symbol, and the availability of fuel, water, railways, launching ramps, repairs and docking facilities at specified locations.

When the salt water pilot turns to the book of charts of New York State Canals (published by the U. S. Lake Survey, Detroit, Mich.) he finds himself on more familiar ground. Land areas are tinted a light buff, channels in white, depths of 12 feet or less in a light blue tint with dotted depth curves for 1 and 2 fathoms and distinct black lines delineating the banks. Here, too, are the buoy symbols (diamond and dot) with orange disc signifying lights. Buoys and other aids on shore have their identifying numbers given and rough scattered soundings appear to give the pilot a good idea as to whether he dare venture out of the channel to seek an anchorage in some bend behind an island. Buoy symbols appear in white

to port and red to starboard, entering from seaward, to correspond with the white and red lights they carry at night. Even rocks and wrecks are indicated with symbols similar to those used on coastal charts. The scale in this series of charts, with a few exceptions, is 1:21,120 (3 inches to the mile). Reference plane is normal pool level. Arrows indicating direction of current flow, used on other river charts, do not appear on those of New York waterways.

### Tennessee Easy to Navigate

Commercial towboat pilots consider the Tennessee River channel to be one of the best marked and easiest to navigate of all the inland waterways. The Tennessee itself is navigable for cruisers for 650 continuous miles from Paducah, Kentucky, to Knoxville, Tenn. The channel is marked with buoys, lights and dayboards so that it can be navigated both day and night. Locks in each of the nine main stream dams are open 24 hours a day every day and may be used without charge. Pleasure boats are locked through with commercial tows when there is room, or are entitled to separate lockage at the end of each hour. In addition to the main navigation channels, there are about 225 miles of feeder channels, marked by buoys and dayboards, which are used by recreational craft.

Navigation charts are available in two sizes for the entire length of the Tennessee, as well as navigation maps for the thirteen major tributary reservoirs, from the Tennessee Valley Authority, Knoxville, Tenn. The charts, on scales of 1 inch to the mile, and 1 inch to the half-mile, are multi-colored, showing sailing lines and aids to navigation, including buoys, lights, daymarks, safety harbors, hazards, and depths of water at all reservoir pool stages. Other important features are highways, railroads, bridges, wire crossings, terminals, docks, piers, landings and towns. Many private boat docks offering a variety of services and accommodations are scattered along the 10,000 miles of TVA shoreline. A survey of these is available in a folder from the TVA Information Office at Knoxville. Bound sets of charts of the Tennessee are also available from District Engineers at Cincinnati, Nashville and Louisville.

Charts of the Ohio River, in the form of bound sets of continuous multilith charts, are available from District Engineers at Pittsburgh, Huntington and Louisville. There are three sets—Pittsburgh to Powhatan Point, Ohio; Powhatan Point to Aberdeen, Ohio; and Aberdeen to Cairo, Ill. On a scale of one inch to 2000 feet, they show sailing lines, lights, daymarks, arrival point markers for locks, normal pool elevations, mouths of tributary systems, location of bars, channel buoys, bridges, aerial crossings, seaplane bases, docks, terminals, landings, and navigation structures. No soundings are given. Mileages zero at Pittsburgh.

*At River Mile 775 AHP in Tennessee on the Mississippi a towboat with 23 barges passes a channel dredge. Small craft are advised to pass such dredges with caution and to avoid areas upstream from the dredge and floating discharge pipe line which usually extends several hundreds of feet.*

In addition to these, there is also a set of photolithographic charts of the Ohio from Pittsburgh to the mouth in 281 sheets, on a scale of one inch to 600 feet. These show topographic features, sailing lines, 5-foot contours, high water, low water, normal pool lines, bench marks, etc.

A detailed list of all charts of the Ohio and its navigable tributaries—the Allegheny, Big Sandy, Cumberland, Green, Barren, Nolin, Rough, Kanawha, Kentucky, White and Eel— is available from the Division Engineer, Ohio River Division, in Cincinnati. This list is in the form of a mimeographed Division Bulletin and contains much other valuable data on navigation of the Ohio.

Missing from the river map is the compass rose of coastal charts which enables the pilot to lay a compass course and determine true and magnetic bearings and courses. River charts generally show instead a simple arrow to indicate true north, and on strip charts north may not necessarily be at the top of the page. On charts of the Lower Mississippi, parallels of latitude and meridians of longitude are given. The compass is little used on river boats and the binoculars take its place to aid the pilot in sighting from one navigational aid to the next. In fog, this means that pleasure boat traffic comes pretty much to a standstill, though the big commercial craft carry on using radar for their eyes. This is not to imply that the compass can be dispensed with on all rivers and lakes. In the lower reaches of larger tidal rivers, like the Connecticut, compass courses are occasionally laid in fog, and on the Great Lakes where straight-line courses of 100 miles or more are not unusual, the compass is an indispensable accessory.

### Charts of the Great Lakes

Piloting problems on the Great Lakes are much the same as they are along the coast because of the great expanse of water involved. Charts of the Great Lakes, published by the U. S. Lake Survey, are excellent, covering features of the navigable waters in great detail. They show depths of water (the lesser depths in blue tint), safe channels, submerged reefs and shoals, aids to navigation, adjacent shorelines with topographic features and landmarks, types of bottom, and much additional related information. Scales of the charts vary from as large as 1:2,500 to 1:20,000 for harbor charts and insets, down to 1:80,000 to 1:130,000 for coast charts, and 1:400,000 or 500,000 for general charts of individual lakes. Smallest scale used is the general chart of all the Great Lakes, at 1:1,200,000. For close work on the rivers, the scale varies from 1:15,000 to 1:40,000.

On Lake charts, the familiar compass rose is available, showing in magenta tint both true and magnetic directions, with the variation stated. In parts of the Lakes, variation reduces to zero, where, except for deviation, which is always with us, magnetic and true courses are alike. Elsewhere on the Lakes, great deposits of iron ore in the earth produce a strong local attraction, most pronounced along the north shore of Lake Superior where variation has been observed to change from 26° to 7° in a distance of 650 feet.

Most Lake charts are on the polyconic projection and show some of the principal courses between ports, giving the course in degrees true with the distances in statute miles. Comparative elevations are referred to mean tide as calculated at New York.

To supplement the information available on Lake charts, cruising boatmen should have a copy of the Great Lakes Pilot (published by the U. S. Lake Survey, Detroit). Corresponding to the Coast Pilots used on coastal waters, it provides detailed information which cannot be given on the charts. Included are full descriptions of the waters charted, laws and regulations governing navigation, bridge clearances, signals for locks and bridges, dimensions and capacities of marine railways, and weather information. Purchasers of the Pilot get, free, seven monthly supplements (May-November) to keep the Pilot up to date.

### Local Knowledge on the Mississippi River

The Army Engineers at Vicksburg, Miss., publish an informative pamphlet, "Mississippi River Navigation," which contains not only a great deal of interesting background information on navigation of the Mississippi, but also a few pages with explicit instructions "For Part-Time Pilots," the pleasure boatmen who are using the great river in increasing numbers.

Among other things, the Engineers caution against regarding the Mississippi with insufficient respect. The lower river, they point out, is very large, with low-water widths of ½ mile and bankfull widths up to 9000 feet. These bankfull stages generally occur between December and July, most frequently in March or April. Low-water stages occur in the fall months, October and November.

Lake Pepin typifies the kind of exposed area that may be encountered even on the upper river. This lake, a broadening of the river proper, is 21 miles long and up to 2½ miles in width. Sizable seas build up in such areas. Current velocities on the Mississippi average 4 to 6 mph. At extreme high stages of the river, velocities may be even greater in the narrower sections. At low and medium stages velocities range from 2 to 2½ mph.

River Engineers call special attention to the many kinds of floating equipment constantly at work on construction and maintenance projects along the river. Hydraulic pipeline dredges may have long lengths of floating pipeline which must be avoided. Bank protection equipment carried on barges may extend several hundred feet from shore into the stream, frequently in the swiftest part of the current. Small craft should keep well clear of all such equipment because of the hazard of being swept under it. As a matter of fact, on all waters, river traffic should exercise caution and consideration when passing dredges and similar equipment, slowing down to avoid doing damage with the wake. Army Engineers have prepared regulations governing lights and day signals displayed by all types of craft working on river projects, and the passing of such equipment by other vessels. These will be found in full detail in one section of the Pilot Rules for Western Rivers.

Though in some areas small craft do tie up to the river banks, the Engineers urge caution here, too. Avoid, they advise, vertical banks which may be in a stage of active caving. Exposed tree roots in the banks should be viewed with suspicion as a possible evidence of recent erosion. Such areas obviously are places to avoid when seeking a place to tie up along the bank. Rock riprap can be rough on a boat's bottom.

As for navigation of the river itself, the Engineers point out, too, that sand bars encountered during periods of low water may be quite unstable. Consequently, caution should be exercised in using them for camping or swimming. Floating and partially submerged debris, such as tree trunks and branches, constitute a navigational hazard for small craft, requiring a sharp lookout at all times. The same applies to piloting in the shallower areas, to avoid submerged stumps and snags. Floating debris is generally at its worst in the spring months under flood conditions, when high water and drifting logs may also shift buoys from their charted locations.

River currents sometimes flow so fast that buoys are towed under, leaving only a V-shaped eddy on the surface to reveal their location. Coastal boatmen have sometimes experienced this condition at inlets. Sometimes the top of the buoy will be visible to a boat bound upstream, or the wake of a passing boat may expose it momentarily.

The V-shaped surface eddy left by a buoy partially or totally submerged in a strong current will necessarily point upstream, as the wake divides downstream from the buoy. Any surface wake like this is to be mistrusted, as a submerged obstacle may lurk beneath. This is not to be confused with the condition where two currents meet at the downstream end of a middle bar where converging surface eddies may also show as a V shape, pointing downstream.

Photograph from Corps of Engineers

*One of the major aids to navigation along the Mississippi is the light on shore. In this view, illustrating the position of a typical light used for marking bends and upper and lower ends of crossings, the steamer Mississippi approaches Four Mile Bayou Light, River Mile 728 A.H.P. Number board visible just above the light shows the mileage on the river side.*

Piloting on the Mississippi River. Aids to Navigation on the Rivers.

Light Lists and Other Publications of Interest to the River Boatman.

Some Special Rules of the Road Applicable to River Cruising.

ON its meandering way to the Gulf, the Mississippi winds and twists and bends in a sinuous course that adds many miles to the airline distance. The river is eternally changing, and Army Engineers are everlastingly at work to maintain and improve the navigable channels. Sometimes, a single loop in the river will necessitate a 10-mile run to gain one mile on the route south.

At some of the bends, when the river goes on a rampage under flood conditions, it will cut a channel across the narrow neck of land, forming what is called a chute and creating an island from what was once a peninsula. With-

out local knowledge it is usually wise to avoid the chutes and stick to the main channel. To save distance and straighten navigable channels, the Army Engineers have dredged cut-offs, like the chutes, and these become the new navigable channel.

This constant changing of the Mississippi's course, both by nature and by dredging, has left old channels as dead-end arms of the new, and elsewhere, by closing them off, has created horseshoe-shaped ("oxbow") lakes with no connection with the new channel. River piloting always demands close attention to the chart to avoid being shunted

## ILLINOIS WATERWAY—Illinois River

*Extract from the Mississippi River Light List, showing some of the lights and daymarks on the Illinois Waterway. Distances are given in statute miles, above Grafton. These agree with mileages given on aids to navigation. Note the data given on visibility of directional lights.*

| Name of aid<br>Character and period of light | Number of miles from Grafton | Bank or side of channel | Remarks |
|---|---|---|---|
| Grist Island Bend Daymark | 258.9 | Left | |
| Grist Island Light<br>Fl. W., 2 sec. | 258.8 | Right | Visible 360° with 3° directional light oriented downstream. |
| Barry Island Light<br>Fl. W., 2 sec. | 256.0 | Right | Visible 360° with 3° directional light oriented upstream. |
| Heule Light<br>Fl. W., 2 sec. | 255.1 | Right | 3° directional light oriented downstream; daymark. |
| C., R. I. & P. Ry Bridge, vertical lift. Clearances: Horizontal, 141 feet; vertical, closed 19.9 feet, open 47.5 feet, above pool stage. | 254.1 | | |
| Rock Island Bridge Daymark | 254.1 | Left | Painted on bridge pier. |

into one of the unnavigable arms, or a dead-end heading.

On the Mississippi, as on most rivers, the deepest water and the fastest current are usually found on the outside of bends, at the end of dikes and along the steep banks. As a rule, gently shelving shores should be given a wide berth. Always be wary of unusual surface conditions, especially at high water. A smooth slick or a line or broken water may reveal the presence of a submerged dike or wing dam, used to control the direction of flow of river current. As these wing dams are often submerged even at normal river stages, they constitute a real hazard unless close attention is paid to the chart.

No flat statement can be made as to the relative depth of water indicated by certain sets of surface conditions. This requires a river sense the pilot must develop with experience. On the one hand, where there is a chop in the channel there may be areas of relatively smooth slicks over the bars, especially if there is any weed growth present. As against this, there will be combinations of wind-current conditions where the channel will be comparatively smooth with ripples to reveal the bars. In some narrow river channels, with wind against the current, a small sea builds up in which the larger waves disclose the deeper water, growing progressively smaller until there is no sea at all on the bars at channel's edge. But under any given set of conditions, the boatman with an eye peeled for natural signs will, with the aid of his chart and the buoys, quickly learn to read the signs the river has for those eager to understand its secrets.

Boatmen running the rivers bring back widely conflicting reports of hazards encountered, or the absence of them. Perhaps this may be attributed to the fact that one made his cruise in the early spring, encountering high water, flood conditions, racing currents and drifting trees posing a constant threat to propellers, even to hulls. Another, no doubt, has made his trip under ideal conditions in September or October, possibly as the first leg of a cruise down to the Gulf and Florida for the winter season. With water levels at a low stage and currents at reasonable velocities, no obstacles have been encountered on the entire cruise from Lakes to Gulf. There is that much difference in seasonal conditions. River navigation at extreme flood stages, as a rule, is not to be recommended without the services of an experienced pilot.

A typical example of this conflict in reports of conditions observed is the story of "sand boils" in the Mississippi caused by sand piling up on the river bed. One reports these whirlpool-like disturbances so violent that they practically throw the boat out of control. Others, in more favorable months, find them no worse than surface eddies felt at the helm, but certainly with no element of danger for a boat. (For a swimmer, it might be otherwise.)

Some river boatmen have reported underwater bearings ruined, jackets filled with silt, and water pump gears worn out at the end of one river run. Others have observed no difficulty whatever on this score. As a general rule, as in all other places where waters are laden with silt, the logical course is to provide, in advance, what protection is available in the form of effective water strainers, fresh water cooling systems, cutless type underwater bearings, and pump impellers of a type that will handle mud and sand better than bronze gears.

Discounting all the stories of violent current disturbances, the fact remains, of course, that current is a real factor to be reckoned with on the rivers. When one stream of some velocity flows out into another, a small boat crossing the current at the mouth will feel the effect of this set and will probably have to allow

LEGEND

Government Light

Government Daymark

Government Light—Daymark

Government Lighted Buoy

Levee or Embankment

Bank Protection

Contraction Works<br>(Dotted indicates works are submerged)

Gage

Submerged Island

County Line

State Boundary

Lock and Dam

River Terminal

River Landing

Moorings

*Symbols used on charts of the Middle and Upper Mississippi River—Cairo to Minneapolis—all in black and white, no distinguishing colors.*

A fleet of pleasure craft heading downstream on the Mississippi River after leaving the lock chamber at Harvey Lock, on the west bank at New Orleans. About two dozen craft have passed through at one time in a single locking. Note the towboats standing by waiting their turn to enter lock. Gate (lower right corner) is closed; other (center) is open.

### LEGEND

▬ HAZARD AREA (LESS THAN 6 f1 BELOW EL 418.0 POOL 26)

///// SNAG, STUMPS, AND UNDERWATER HAZARDS

---- SUBMERGED GOVERNMENT DIKE

⊗ GOVERNMENT GAGE

²¹⁰ RIVER MILEAGE

⚓ HARBOR OR TIE UP POINT

On charts of Pools 25 and 26 (Mississippi River and Illinois Waterway) hazard areas are shown in bright red.

somewhat by heading up into it. Pilots of heavy commercial craft are keenly aware of the way they carry with the current under their vessel. To the small boat operator it's a factor of relatively less importance, yet significant enough to be remembered at all times.

Since conditions on the river are in a constant state of flux, with channels changing and levels fluctuating, the river boatman should keep posted on the latest available data at all times. Just as the coastal boatman has his *Notices to Mariners* to turn to for authoritative information, so, too, the river boatman can refer to the *Navigation Bulletins* issued by the district offices of the Army Engineers at Memphis, Vicksburg and New Orleans. They show latest sailing directions, locations of navigational aids such as lights, buoys, etc., and similar up-to-date information required by the river pilot. For the Ohio, there are *Notices to Navigation Interests,* available from the Engineer Office at Pittsburgh.

Detailed information on rules and regulations applicable to the Mississippi may always be obtained from the Commander of the 2nd Coast Guard District at St. Louis.

One of the most helpful aids to the river pilot is the Light List, published by the U.S. Coast Guard. In it all lights, buoys and aids to navigation are tabulated, together with the river mileage (in statute miles to the nearest tenth) as reckoned from a zero point which may be at or near the mouth, as in the case of the Mississippi, or some other logical reference point, such as Pittsburgh on the Ohio. For the Lower Mississippi, a designation of Mile 104 AHP would be interpreted as 104 statute miles "Above the Head of Passes."

Aids to navigation along the river banks are conspicuously marked with mileages which correspond to the distances from the zero reference tabulated in the Light List. It is always an easy matter, therefore, to get a "fix." All you need do is read the mileage as posted on one of the light structures ashore, and compare with the mileage figures given on the chart. These lighted aids, of various shapes, are painted white and have names which appear on the charts and in the Light Lists as well. The mileage figures take the place of the odd and even numbers that are characteristic of buoys on coastal waters. They are a

*Portion of U.S. Lake Survey Chart No. 43 (Saint Claire River) scale 1:40,000, drawn on the polyconic projection, in which distortion is very small and relative sizes are correctly preserved. Depths are referred to the sloping surface of the river at specified lake levels above mean tide at New York. Note the International Boundary, in mid-stream, and separate channels around the flats for traffic upstream and downstream. River traffic here is heavy. Illustration is to the same scale as the chart itself.*

Ralph Smith, Omaha

*A light and mileage board, showing the river mile. Note the wake of the strong river current flowing past the piles of the dike. Currents are a factor to be reckoned with in river piloting.*

distinct convenience in computing boat speeds and figuring the total day's run from the log.

In the larger rivers, it is usually feasible to run close to shore to identify the aid from the Light List, then head for the next, picking it up with binoculars if necessary. In closer work on some narrower rivers, as previously cautioned, it may be wise to ease around bends to follow the channel trend as delineated by the buoys rather than running straight from aid to aid. With no aids to serve as guides, the safest practice usually is to favor the center, keeping at least one-quarter of the river's width off the bank.

Designation of the banks of a river may at first be confusing. Left and right banks are named relative to your course *downstream*. The left bank, in river terminology, is the left bank as you face downstream; the right bank to your right facing downstream. On the New York State Barge Canal, however, when regulations refer to the "starboard" side of the canal, they mean the right hand side entering from Waterford. Thus the starboard side of the Champlain Canal is the east side; but on the Erie Canal, the north side becomes the starboard side.

Most lights on the Mississippi River System show through 360°—visible, that is, all around the horizon. In some cases, however, directional aids project the light in one direction only. Some of these directional aids supplement the power of a 360° light by increasing the candlepower in one direction only. The arc through which the directional beam is visible varies with the navigational need of the locality. A concentrated beam may be used in a long narrow reach, but a wider spread in a more open area where conditions are less critical.

Generally speaking, lights on the Western Rivers are placed strategically at the upper and lower ends of crossings as marks to steer by, with additional lights between as required by conditions. Where there are no crossings, lights are used along the banks as passing lights. Reference to the chart will indicate how the light is to be used.

Daymarks on the Mississippi are usually white diamond shapes with number board at the top to designate the mileage. In the center, a red triangle is used for left bank aids (descending the river) and a vertical black rectangle for right (descending) bank aids. Daymarks have a reflector at each of the four corners, red on the left bank, white on the right bank. Daymarks among the trees on shore may take the form of two white boards crossed in the form of an X.

The coastal boatman will have no difficulty whatever with buoyage systems on the rivers. In the main, they will follow the same basic principle which puts black can-type buoys to port and red nun-type buoys to starboard when entering from seaward. Sometimes, as on the Mississippi, buoys will be topped with white for improved visibility, to show up against shore backgrounds.

Buoys on the Mississippi carry reflectors similar to those used on shore aids—red on the left bank, white on the right bank. Buoys marking wrecks show a quick flashing light, white or red on the left (descending) side of the channel, white or green on the right (descending) side. On buoys marking channel junctions or obstructions, the light characteristic is an interrupted quick flash (5 flashes 10 times a minute). Generally in mid-channel these lights will be white; red if toward the left side of the channel; and green if toward the right. As on the coast, the red-and-black horizontally banded buoy is used to mark junctions and obstructions. If found near the edge of a channel, it should be passed with caution, taking soundings to determine which is the proper side.

In all cases, buoys should be followed with reference to whatever charts or navigational maps may be available, as deviations from the conventional system of buoyage will be found in some rivers. On the New York State Barge Canal, for example, buoys are alike in shape on both sides of the channel. Entering from seaward, red buoys with red lights are on the starboard hand, but white buoys with white lights are found on the port hand. When craft are anchored at night along the side of the canal marked by red navigation lights, New York state authorities require the use of a red, rather than white, anchor light.

The chart, invariably, will prevent confusion and misunderstanding in following any system of buoyage. Symbols for can and nun buoys on Ohio River charts will seem particularly strange to coastal boatmen (See illustration, Part Two, from the legend.) In the Great Lakes Light List, Canadian buoys are specially identified by the letter C. Except for minor differences in design, the system of buoyage used in Canadian waters is in agreement with that adopted by the United States.

On some of the rivers, notably the Hudson and the Connecticut, where channels through flats in the river are stabilized and maintained by dredging, ranges on shore marked by conspicuous squares and diamonds are of great aid to the pilot in staying inside the limits of a narrow channel. Aligning the front and rear ranges, the pilot can hold his course in mid-channel, despite even heavy cross winds that might otherwise tend to set him off on the shoal to leeward.

### Special River Rules

If the coastal boatman cruises far inland, his course will inevitably lead him into waters where Pilot Rules for traffic afloat—the Rules of the Road—differ from those to which he is accustomed. Consequently he should study in detail the rules applicable to the particular waters he uses.

On the coast, vessels operate mainly under two sets of rules —the International Rules when outside the boundaries prescribed for the high seas (even though this be just outside the inlet or off the beach), and the Inland Rules for waters inside these boundaries, with certain exceptions. It is these exceptions which require attention. For example, on the Great Lakes and their connecting and tributary waters as far east as Montreal, and the St. Marys River, vessels are subject to the Great Lakes Rules. On the Mississippi River system, with its tributaries, between its source and the Huey P. Long Bridge, ten miles above New Orleans (including part of the Atchafalaya River), and the Red River of the North, they are subject to the Pilot Rules for Western Rivers.

Elsewhere, the specific differences in rules under the four jurisdictions have been treated at length (see "How Pilot Rules Differ," *Piloting, Seamanship and Small Boat Handling*, Chapter IV). It is outside the scope of this series to repeat them here. In broad principle, Western River Rules are largely in general agreement with International Rules. However, it is interesting to point up a few of the outstanding differences encountered on the rivers.

We have already called attention to one Western River rule for vessels meeting in narrow channels, which gives right of way to a vessel bound downstream. Here is an example of a

*A typical Mississippi river bank riprapped with cement to protect banks against erosion. Boatmen must use care near such banks due to risk of damage to the boat's bottom.*

special rule having particular significance to the river pilot. The ascending (burdened) vessel, bound upstream, must sound the first passing signal, but vessels pass on the side determined by the (privileged) descending vessel.

Ascending vessels, on the Western Rivers, stop if necessary below the entrance of narrow channels to allow descending vessels to pass through. At the confluence of two rivers, the vessel having the other to port gives the first signal.

Bends in rivers, insofar as floating traffic is concerned, may be compared with blind corners on the road. Western River Rules provide that when a vessel could not be seen at a distance of 600 yards, three distinct blasts are to be sounded on the whistle. This warning signal must be answered by any approaching vessel within hearing around the bend, and the vessels exchange the usual passing signals only when they come within sight of each other. (On waters other than Western Rivers, the warning signal at a bend is a long, or prolonged, blast.)

When a steam vessel leaves her dock or anchorage, she gives the same signal (three distinct blasts) as prescribed for steam vessels nearing a bend.

Commercial craft on Western Rivers use a special amber visual signal synchronized with their passing whistle signal blasts. Motorboats are exempt from this rule. On both the Western Rivers and Great Lakes passing whistle signals are given in all weathers, regardless of visibility.

The fog signal for power-driven vessels under way on the Rivers is 3 distinct blasts every minute (2 of equal length, followed by a longer one). Sailing vessels give the same fog signals as power-driven vessels, but use the fog horn.

When towing, power-driven vessels sound 3 distinct blasts of equal length, at intervals of not more than 1 minute. Steamers lying to during fog or thick weather, when another vessel is heard approaching, give 1 tap on the bell if lying at the right bank, 2 taps if lying at the left bank, at 1-minute intervals.

One other fundamental difference, peculiar to Western River rules, requires a privileged vessel to hold her course, but not her speed. When risk of collision exists, all power-driven vessels reduce speed or stop if necessary.

If in cruising the Great Lakes and northern rivers, you should cross the International Boundary into Canada, bear in mind that there are customs and immigration regulations to be observed.

For detailed information on rules of the road, right of way, whistle signals, fog signals, lights for all types of craft and other pertinent regulations, the boatman is referred to the Pilot Rules, available free from Coast Guard Marine Inspection Offices in principal ports, or the Commandant (CHS), U.S. Coast Guard, Washington, D.C.

## PUBLICATIONS OF INTEREST TO RIVER PILOTS

One of the best single sources of information concerning charts of inland waters and other publications on river piloting is the Mississippi River Commission, Corps of Engineers, U. S. Army, P.O. Box 80, Vicksburg, Miss. They publish a comprehensive mimeographed list of offices which issue charts of the various sections of the Mississippi, Missouri, Ohio and other tributaries, the Illinois Waterway, Great Lakes, etc. This list also includes mention of many publications of the Coast Guard and other government agencies. A Division Bulletin listing in detail all charts of the Ohio and its tributaries is prepared by the Division Engineer, Ohio River Division, P.O. Box 1159, Cincinnati 1, Ohio.

RIVER CHARTS, as well as the indispensable NAVIGATION BULLETINS and NOTICES TO NAVIGATION INTERESTS are distributed by the various offices of the Corps of Engineers, U. S. Army, in the areas over which they have jurisdiction. They are located at:

Memphis District—P.O. Box 97, Memphis 1, Tenn.
Vicksburg District—P.O. Box 60, Vicksburg, Miss.
New Orleans District—Foot of Prytania Street, New Orleans, La.
St. Louis District—420 Locust St., St. Louis 2, Mo.
Rock Island District—Clock Tower Building, Rock Island, Ill.
St. Paul District—U. S. Post Office & Customhouse, 180 E. Kellogg Blvd., St. Paul 1, Minn.
Missouri River Division—Farm Credit Bldg., 206 So. 19th St., Omaha 1, Neb.
Chicago District—475 Merchandise Mart, Merchandise Mart Plaza, Chicago 54, Ill.
North Central Division—536 So. Clark St., Chicago 5, Ill.
Ohio River Division—P.O. Box 1159, Cincinnati 1, Ohio.
Pittsburgh District—925 New Federal Bldg., Pittsburgh, Pa.
Huntington District—237 Fourth Ave., P.O. Box 2127, Huntington 18, W. Va.
Louisville District—830 West Broadway, P.O. Box 59, Louisville 1, Ky.
Nashville District—306 Federal Office Bldg., P.O. Box 1070, Nashville 1, Tenn.
Southwestern Division—1114 Commerce St., Dallas 2, Texas.
Galveston District—606 Santa Fe Bldg., Galveston, Texas.
Mobile District—2301 Grant St., Mobile 7, Ala.

CHARTS—Tennessee River—Available from the Tennessee Valley Authority, Maps and Engineering Records Section, 102A Union Building, Knoxville, Tennessee. Bound sets available from District Engineers at Cincinnati, Nashville and Louisville.

CHARTS—Great Lakes and connecting rivers, Lake Champlain, New York Canals and Minnesota-Ontario Border Lakes (including some Canadian waters). U. S. Lake Survey, Corps of Engineers, U. S. Army, 630 Federal Building, Detroit 26, Mich.

CHARTS—Canadian Waters. Hydrographic Chart Distribution, Canadian Hydrographic Service, Department of Mines and Technical Surveys, 615 Booth St., Ottawa, Canada.

CHARTS—Coastal Waters and Intracoastal Waterway, New York to Florida. Also Coast Pilots, Tide Tables and Current Tables, all for coastal waters. U. S. Coast & Geodetic Survey, Washington 25, D. C. (The Coast Pilot for the Gulf Coast contains much valuable data on the Mississippi River System.)

NOTICE TO MARINERS—Data for up-to-date corrections to coastal charts, Coast Pilots, etc. U. S. Oceanographic Office, Navy Department, Washington, D. C. (Local daily notices available from Commanders of the various Coast Guard Districts. For the Mississippi, from St. Louis and New Orleans offices.)

LIGHT LISTS—Separate volumes for Mississippi River System, Great Lakes, and coastal waters. Superintendent of Documents, Government Printing Office, Washington 25, D. C., and local Coast Guard offices at St. Louis and New Orleans.

GREAT LAKES PILOT—U. S. Lake Survey, Corps of Engineers, U. S. Army, 630 Federal Building, Detroit 26, Mich.

YACHTSMAN'S GUIDE TO THE GREAT LAKES—Seaport Publishing Co., 843 Delray Ave., S.E., Grand Rapids 6, Mich.

RULES OF THE ROAD—Separate volumes for Inland Waters of Atlantic and Pacific Coasts and Gulf of Mexico; Great Lakes; and Western Rivers. U. S. Coast Guard Headquarters, Washington 25, D. C. For Western Rivers, available also from local Coast Guard offices at St. Louis and New Orleans.

REGULATIONS to Govern the Use, Administration and Navigation of the Ohio River, Mississippi River above Cairo, Ill. and Their Tributaries—District Engineer, St. Louis, Mo. (Also available at any lock.)

RULES AND REGULATIONS to Govern the Operation of Drawbridges Crossing the Mississippi River and All Its Tributaries and Outlets—District Engineer, Chicago, Ill.

RULES AND REGULATIONS Governing Navigation and Use of the New York State Canal System—Superintendent of Operation and Maintenance, State Department of Public Works, Albany, N. Y.

NEW YORK STATE CANALS AND WATERWAYS—Official map, with condensed information on canal system, navigational aids, pleasure boat regulations, data on locks, etc. Superintendent of Operation and Maintenance, State Department of Public Works, Albany, N. Y.

CRUISING GUIDE BOOK for the New York State Barge Canal System and Connecting Navigable Canadian Lakes, Rivers and Waterways—Cruising Guidebook, 146 Sheridan Ave., Albany, N. Y.

MISSISSIPPI RIVER NAVIGATION—Division Engineer, Lower Mississippi Valley Division, Corps of Engineers, U. S. Army, P. O. Box 80, Vicksburg, Miss.

LOCKING THROUGH—Things you should know if you use navigation locks, District Engineer, St. Louis, Mo. Also available from other District Engineers.

OHIO RIVER HANDBOOK—Piloting information, statistics, lore and legend pertaining to the Ohio and its tributaries. Young & Klein, Inc., 1351 Spring Lawn Ave., Cincinnati 23, Ohio.

YOUR OHIO—Pamphlet of general interest. Corps of Engineers, Ohio Division.

RADIO AIDS TO NAVIGATION, GREAT LAKES—U. S. Coast Guard, 9th District, Main Post Office Building, Cleveland 13, Ohio.

INLAND WATERWAY GUIDE, Great Lakes Edition—Inland Waterway Guide, Inc., 101 North Andrews Ave., Fort Lauderdale, Fla.

RECREATION IN TVA LAKES—Tabulates boat docks and related services, with map. Information Office, Tennessee Valley Authority, Knoxville, Tenn.

BOATING AND FISHING GUIDE to the Great Lakes of the South—The Nashville Tennessean, Nashville, Tenn.

MAP, PRINCIPAL WATERWAYS OF THE UNITED STATES—Chief of Engineers, Department of the Army, Operations Division, Civil Works, Washington 25, D. C.

CHARTING THE GREAT LAKES—The story of the United States Lake Survey, United States Lake Survey, 630 Federal Bldg., Detroit 26, Mich.

CRUISING GUIDES AND CHARTS AND HARBOR BOOKLETS—Several of the large oil companies offer useful publications dealing with the inland waterways. Texaco Waterways Service, 135 E. 42nd St., New York 17, N. Y.; Gulf Tourgide Bureau, Box 8056, Philadelphia 1, Pa. (east of Mississippi); Mobil Touring Service, Mobil Oil Co., 150 E. 42nd St., New York, N. Y.; Esso Touring Service, 15 W. 51st St., New York 19, N. Y.

NAVIGATION LOCKS AND DAMS, MISSISSIPPI RIVER—District Engineer, St. Louis, Mo.

TIPS ON RIVER SAFETY—District Engineer, St. Louis, Mo.

MISSISSIPPI RIVER, CHAIN OF ROCKS CANAL AND LOCKS—District Engineer, St. Louis, Mo.

THE GULF INTRACOASTAL WATERWAY—District Engineer, Vicksburg, Miss. (Charts from same source.) More complete pamphlet available from Superintendent of Documents, Washington 25, D. C.

---

YOUR KEY TO THE LOCK—U. S. Army Engineer District, Corps of Engineers, Room 322, Federal Building, P. O. Box 991, Albany 1, N. Y. Pamphlet prepared for the guidance of yachtsmen passing through the Federal Lock at Troy, N. Y.

HOW THE LOCK WORKS

*From "Your Key to the Lock"*

Reproductions (reduced more than half) of two typical pages from the U. S. Lake Survey Recreational Chart Series No. 400 covering the Detroit River, Lake St. Clair and the St. Clair River. Charts of this kind are prepared for the express purpose of providing the boatman with a maximum of navigational information in convenient form. In these volumes, data are included which is not available on other chart series. In the original, Lake St. Clair (above) is shown on a scale of 1:60,000; Belle Isle and a portion of the Detroit River (below) 1:15,000. On the original, two tints of blue are used to define limits of the shoaler areas (up to one and two fathoms), thus emphasizing navigable deep-water channels which appear in white, with soundings in feet in black figures. Land areas are tinted light yellow.

# Outboard Seamanship

## CHAPTER XXIX

As in any workable partnership, it is essential that the components—in this case, boat and motor—can get along together. Within that boundary the boatman must determine 1) what he needs from 2) what is available within his budget.

For the new boatman especially, it is a deranging problem to sift the bag of brightly colored, boldly worded, attention-grabbing brochures, flyers, throw-aways; to disengage himself from the pouring of claims; to stand beyond the flood of "bigger and better," "mostest," and "fastest"; to de-

cide what he wants a boat for and, on the basis of competent knowledge, what he wants in a boat.

Now, if it is speed you want—and certainly the sensation of a planing hull streaking over the water is one of outboarding's pleasures—be sure to acquire the boat, motor and combina-

*Proper trim is important. In illustration above, boat lists heavily to port. Weight should be distributed to keep boat on even keel, as shown below.*

tion thereof that will give you maximum safe performance even at high speed ranges. Too heavy a motor—too heavy, that is, for the particular boat—will cause the boat to squat at the stern and keep the bow pointed acutely celestial. Too light a motor, conversely, will cause the boat to perform sluggishly.

Bear in mind when determining horsepower that a boat which makes 15 mph with a 7½-hp motor won't necessarily make 30 with a 15. The better boats are designed for certain speeds with certain power; exceed that plan and you will perhaps do no more than burn fuel and dangerously overload your craft's transom.

Apart from consulting with competent dealers and others with experience, you can obtain reliable advice from the Outboard Boating Club of America's (OBC) "capacity recommendation plate" affixed to the hulls of some outboard boats. It gives the maximum horsepower and load the boat is designed to take.

If your boat lacks such a plate, ask the dealer for recommendations, or request them directly from the builder. Following these limitations will help avoid two common causes of accidents: over-powering and overloading!

### TYPES OF BOATS

There is a wide array of boats from which to choose, from 4-hp car-top prams to buxom cruisers able to take two of the highest horsepower motors available. There are dinghies, skiffs, canoes, runabouts and utilities. There are special rigs like Sea Sleds, modified motor-catamarans and outboard-powered houseboats.

Your first question: What are you going to use your outboard boat for. Fishing? Family cruising? Skiing? Beach picnics? Skindiving? Photography? Speed? Combinations of any of these? Narrow your choice and you've practically decided on your type boat. A fisherman doesn't want to troll in a hydroplane designed to zoom at 50 mph!

Your second question: In what kind of water are you going to use the boat? Salt or fresh? Large, open bays and lakes, or shallow, sheltered rivers? The shoal-draft boat you drive on placid ponds may not stand you in good stead on open, rough waters.

Here is a brief rundown on the types of outboards available. Hulls break down into two basics: displacement and planing. Displacement boats cruise *through* the water, planing hulls lift and skim *over* the surface.

Often it is difficult to make a sharp distinction between "displacement" and "planing" types of hulls. Planing hulls receive a large part of their support at speed from the dynamic reaction of the water against the bottom, and part from buoyancy which diminishes with increased speed, but never quite disappears at any speed. Generally, planing begins when the water breaks cleanly away at the chines and transom. In these days of high horsepower, many cruisers are actually planing hulls. Practically all runabouts plane, of course.

Flat bottom (displacement type) hulls. Usually rowboats or skiffs 14' to 18'; used for fishing or utility purposes on shallow streams and small, protected lakes. They are not fast, are generally heavy and roomy. (Some light, flat bottom boats plane and are fast.)

Round bottom (displacement) hulls. Dinghies, tenders, car-top craft, occasionally runabouts 12' to 18'. These hulls at low speeds are often more easily driven and maneuvered than the flat-bottom craft. (Many fast, light, round bottom boats will also plane.)

Hydroplane (planing) hulls. Generally used for racing. Bottom, which is flat, may be "stepped," i.e., divided into two levels, about amidships. The resultant notch reduces wetted surface, increasing speed.

Vee-bottom hulls. Commonly used for runabouts, utilities and cruisers when speed is a factor. Forward undersection is usually deep "V" in shape. Bottom flattens toward amidships, until at the stern it becomes broad and flat.

A utility and a runabout, in effect, are practically interchangeable terms. Both craft function about the same, are

about the same size, take about the same horsepower, etc. The runabout, however, is generally considered to be a bit faster and more luxuriously equipped than a utility of comparable size.

Now, if you've made your choice, here are a couple of tips before actually buying. Take the boat and motor for a trial spin to see how they operate together and in various water conditions. Never buy a boat, especially a used boat, when it is in the water without first having her hauled. Check to see that bottom, frames, planking and fastenings are sound. If you are inexperienced, have a competent person examine the rig.

### UNDER THE LAW

Be sure you and your boat comply with federal, state and local boating laws. You will have to check the laws of your community yourself (OBC publishes a round-up of state laws; federal laws are obtainable from the Coast Guard).

Determine if your boat must be numbered. Under the Federal Boating Act of 1958, all boats regardless of length (but not documented) that carry an engine of *more* than 10 hp, and are used on navigable (federal) waters, must be numbered. Some states, enacting legislation under the federal act but varying from the hp specification, require that all boats carrying *any* propulsive machinery be numbered. Where states have not assumed the numbering function, the Coast Guard is doing the job, following the "more-than-10-hp" guide.

### FITTING HER OUT

Begin by installing the motor properly—manufacturer's diagrams will

*Heavy 22-foot runabout above can safely carry two large (60 hp here) motors. Even one of these would overpower small outboard below.*

*Remember, trailer always backs in direction opposite to that of car. Driver swings close to launching ramp (left), then cuts car away from ramp, placing trailer at angle to ramp and driveway, cuts wheels of car to left (center), backs slowly into ramp, as trailer moves to right. Driver straightens wheel after "jackknifing" car-and-trailer until both are in line, then backs slowly down ramp.*

help here. Generally the task is to seat the motor squarely on the center of the transom and to securely tighten the bracket screws (motor angle will be discussed later). Some motor makes provide special transom plates for mounting, and you may prefer using a transom pad beneath the clamps to reduce vibration and prevent the wood from being marred. A length of chain through the motor bracket and around a transom knee will prevent the motor from being lost overboard.

Next, let's buy our required equipment. The skipper has much leeway as to brand and type of equipment he'll carry in this category, provided it meets legal requirements. For life-saving devices, for example, he can purchase cushions or jackets or ring buoys—provided each is Coast Guard approved. He must, of course, have one such device for each person aboard. OBC strongly recommends life jackets for children and non-swimmers. and that these persons wear them at all times when aboard.

Make sure your passengers know where the life-saving devices are—keep them accessible!—and how they are used, before you get under way. A buoyant cushion, incidentally, is used by slipping the left arm through one of the loops and the right leg through the other (reverse this for left-handers). The wearer then holds the cushion against his chest with the bridled arm, keeping the other arm and both legs free for swimming.

If your hull is even partially enclosed, the law requires that you carry a fire extinguisher. Place it where it can be grabbed quickly! Extinguishers of the vaporizing liquid type, particularly carbon tetrachloride, can no longer be installed on boats. Those manufactured before December, 1958, however, and already installed and

serviceable, can be used until January 1962.

Even if you plan absolutely never to use your boat at night, you should install the lights prescribed for your class boat. Engine trouble, fuel problems or unexpectedly fine fishing may keep you out longer than you intended. Two lights are required (Inland Rules) for outboards up to 26': a combination red and green light on the bow, and a white stern light, visible all around the horizon (360°) for at least two miles.

Outboards between 16 and 26 feet must carry a horn, or a hand-, mouth- or power-whistle audible for at least ½ mile. This device can be used both for passing whistle signals and fog signals.

The equipment required by law does not cover all that is required by boating's exigencies. The law, for instance, says nothing about carrying an extra propeller, but if your motor should slam into some hefty debris, disabling the propeller, the situation would demand a spare. An anchor with enough line (at least ⅜" nylon or ½" manilla

for most outboards), a compass, enough fuel, a well-equipped tool box, a first-aid kit, flashlight, distress flares and smoke signals, are some of the items a prudent skipper will demand. The accompanying equipment list gives a complete rundown.

Don't pass over an oar, or paddle, on your list, even if it presents a stowage problem. An oar may turn out to be all you have for motive power at one time or another, and can be used to swing the bow around should you go aground. Not infrequently, an extended oar handle is used to help a person who has fallen overboard to get back to the boat.

**ON THE ROAD**

Trailers, like boats and motors, come in many varieties. They are produced variously equipped with electric winches, adjustable keel rollers, finger-tip controls for loading and launching, etc. Your problem, as before, is to get the right combination—this time the right trailer for your boat and motor.

You must have a trailer able to

*Although this runabout demonstrates great carrying capacity, she should never carry so many passengers. Overloading is dangerous practice in small craft. No one should be permitted on forward deck while under way.*

carry the weight of your motor(s), the boat, *and the gear stowed in the boat.* This last factor is too often overlooked in making calculations. That done, check the prospective trailer's load capacity, found usually on a plate affixed to the trailer. If the load to be carried (some builders underestimate the weight of their boats, so check carefully) is within 100 pounds of the trailer's listed weight capacity, buy the *next larger* model! Don't mislead yourself here, though, and purchase a huge trailer for a modest-size boat. The trailer must fit the hull!

Remember, a trailer, like any dry-land cradle, is an unnatural place for a boat, so you must baby the craft all you can. Make the trailer bed as comfortable as possible. See that it fits the contours of the hull (special trailers are made for the modified catamaran type of outboard). Plenty of padding and bracing may be needed. Treat the boat right on the trailer and you'll get sought-for results in the water. There must not be a "sag" in the hull or a "hook" (in the stern, from too short a trailer). Such things may change the shape of your boat permanently, affecting your speed in the water and handling of the boat.

One type of trailer—often referred to as the full-keel support type—rests the boat on a boom or series of adjustable rollers. Another kind supports the boat with cradles, usually one forward and one aft. A boat kept too long on such a cradle, though, as for winter storage, tends to sag.

If you trailer the boat with the motor clamped to the transom, be sure the clamps are tight and the lower unit is secured to the transom or to the trailer frame, this last step to prevent the motor from tilting forward during sudden stops.

Be sure, too, that your trailer is adequately supporting the weight of the motor. In some instances it may be necessary to relocate trailer wheels closer to the rear, thus providing more direct support and at the same time keeping the load weight heavier—by 50 to 60 pounds—at the trailer front.

With the center of gravity located somewhat forward, towing will be smoother. Also, when you disconnect the trailer from the car you will be able to walk away with it—even when the trailer's loaded!

A bumper hitch will serve if you are trailering a light rig. For the heavier jobs, though, use a hitch that

# EQUIPMENT CHECK LIST
## FOR SKIPPER, CREW AND BOAT

**POWER:**
Two outboard motors, one with generator
Set of engine controls
Two propellers
Tachometer with throw-switch
Two 12-volt batteries
Two battery boxes

**NAVIGATION:**
Charts • Light list • Log book
Pair of lucite parallel rules
Pair of dividers
Pair of 7 x 50 binoculars
Lead line
Coast Pilots
USPS textbook: Piloting, Seamanship and Small Boat Handling
Inland Waterway Guide
Oil company cruising charts
Compass
Plenty of paper, pens and pencils
Watch with second hand

**GROUND TACKLE:**
8-pound standard Danforth anchor
12-pound Hi-Tensile Danforth
Two 100-foot lengths of 3/8" nylon
Two 5-foot lengths of 1/4" galvanized chain
Four 1/4" galvanized shackles
Four 3/8" galvanized thimbles

**REQUIRED:**
Freon-type air horn with refill
2½-pound dry chemical fire extinguisher
Four approved life jackets
Four Coast Guard-approved buoyant cushions
Properly functioning running lights with spare bulbs, fuses
State registration certificate
State numbers properly mounted

**SAFETY EQUIPMENT:**
First-aid kit
Flares, day and night
Electric bilge pump
Manual bilge pump
12-foot oar • Boat hook
Portable radio
Two spare propellers
Cotter pins for propeller hubs
Hand flashlight

Hand lantern
Two extra spark plugs

**MOORING:**
Four 25-foot lengths of 3/8" nylon
One 50-foot length of 3/8" nylon
Three plastic-foam fenders
Six fender locks

**CLOTHING:**
Two pair of foul-weather suits
Two pair of boating shoes
Two ski parkas
Sun glasses • Towels • Warm socks
Chinos • Bathing suits • Underwear
Sweaters • Caps • Gloves
Shirts, warm and summery
Set of thermal underwear

**SLEEPING:**
Sheets • Pillows • Warm blankets
Alarm clock

**TOOLS:**
Fiberglass tool-tackle box
Several sharp pen knives
Set of regular screwdrivers
Set of Phillips screwdrivers
Interchangeable-headed hammer
Pliers, regular and long-nosed
Boat tape
Spark plug remover and gauge
Sandpaper and emery cloth
Various types of oil and graphite
Assortment of screws and bolts with nuts and washers
Wrenches, socket and open end
Wood filler
Waterproof sealer
Extra fuses
Extra "keys" for tanks

**GALLEY:**
Stainless steel ice pick
Alcohol
Cigarettes • Matches • Lighter fluid
Copper wool • Soap • Soap dish
Assorted pots and pans
Spice containers
Plastic plates and cups
Stainless-steel eating utensils
Aluminum foil
Can and bottle openers
Stainless steel cleaner

**HEAD:**
Toilet paper • Comb
Sun tan lotion • Insect repellent
Tooth brush • Tooth paste

**MISCELLANEOUS:**
Swab • Bucket • Sponges
Camera • Plastic wrap • Film
Bilge cleaner • Ash trays

ALL THE EQUIPMENT LISTED ABOVE IS CARRIED ABOARD ONE PARTICULAR BOAT, A 22-FOOT EXPRESS CRUISER POWERED BY TWO OUTBOARD MOTORS. BECAUSE THE BOAT IS REPRESENTATIVE OF A GREAT MANY CRAFT IN USE TODAY, THE LIST SERVES AS AN EXCELLENT REFERENCE FOR THOSE SEEKING AN EQUIPMENT GUIDE.

fits directly to the car's frame—a frame hitch. It's a good idea, too, to cover the motor while trailering to keep dust out. Remove the cover at journey's end so condensation does not cause damage.

Keep trailer tires correctly inflated.

Keep trailer lights and reflectors working properly.

Make sure your insurance covers your boat and motor while being trailered.

Know and comply with the trailer laws that obtain in the areas you use. Often, these laws vary from state to state.

For launching, you'll probably use one of the many hard-topped ramps available. Occasionally, you may launch from a natural site. In this case, choose an area with a gently sloping shore but with ground hard enough to give ample tire traction. You can increase traction by slightly deflating the tires—but remember this when you start homeward. Stop at the first place for air.

Maneuvering your trailered boat into the water takes practice: beginners often come to a stalemate when car and trailer are "V"-ed before the water. Have someone shout instructions while you back onto the launching ramp at a 90° angle to the water.

Remember that in backing if you want the trailer to go to the right, you turn the steering wheel to the left, and vice versa.

Don't back the trailer into the water immediately. When in position on the ramp, stop and 1) release any tie downs and 2) tilt the motor so it doesn't hit any obstacle. Now back the trailer slowly, making sure the water doesn't reach the car's hubcaps.

Unlock the bow winch and secure a line to the bow. Push the boat off the trailer into the water, always holding the bow line so the boat does not float away. Unlock the trailer winch cable and with the bow line ease the boat into position for boarding.

### GETTING ABOARD

If you are boarding from a beach, climb in over the bow when practical. When boarding from a float or low pier, step aboard as nearly amidships as possible. Bend so your weight is kept low, thus helping to keep the boat stable. Grasp the gunwale (the boat's side rails) for balance. In a small outboard, do not step on a gunwale or you'll flip the craft.

Do not carry bulky supplies while boarding. If you are alone, place the supplies where you can get at them from aboard. Or have someone hand them to you.

### FUELING

A half pint of gasoline has the destructive power of five sticks of dynamite. When you fuel, you deal with at least several gallons of gasoline. So take every precaution—take nothing for granted!

It is wise, for instance, to remove portable fuel tanks from the boat when possible and take them ashore to fill. Extinguish all flames and close all electrical circuits. Warn everyone aboard and everyone about that there'll be no smoking.

Make sure the gas pump hose nozzle is in contact with the rim of the fill tank opening to prevent generating a spark of static electricity, which might ignite the gas.

Watch your fuel mixture now, both as to gas-oil ratio and the physical mixing of the two. Both are important to the smooth operation of the motors. Afterwards, make sure the lid of the tank is on tight to prevent leakage.

If your outboard carries fuel tanks which would be impractical to remove for fueling—anything larger than a 6-gallon tank would probably be impractical to remove—or permanently installed fuel tanks, your fueling procedures closely follow those for inboards. Before taking on fuel, close all doors, hatches, windows, etc., to keep gasoline vapors from getting below. After fueling, open all doors, hatches, etc., and allow enough time for ventilation to clear these areas before starting the motors.

The mixing of gasoline and oil for large portable tanks and for permanently installed tanks can be done in several ways—all of which are time-consuming but, outboard motor engineers agree, extremely important, even more so than getting the exact gas-oil ratio.

One method is to use a metal (for grounding gas hose nozzle) funnel, preferably with a screen filter, which is inserted into the fill pipe or tank and into which can be poured the gas and oil at the same time, apportioning the oil at a slow rate and allowing the stream of gasoline to thoroughly blend with the oil.

A second method is to mix the gasoline and oil in a separate 5- or 6-gallon can (with pouring spout) and then pour from this into your fuel tanks.

Some gasoline companies are supplying their marinas with outboard pumps that serve up fuel already mixed. A dial regulates the ratio, according to your needs.

Do not, as should already be clear, pour the oil directly into the tank—it will not mix!

Check the fuel system now for leakage. Moreover, if you've spilled any gasoline, carefully wipe the area with a rag (which should then be disposed of) and hose down with fresh water, when possible.

Remember to thoroughly ventilate the boat before starting the motor. It is essential that you be alert for gasoline vapors. These vapors, heavier than air, crawl into the lower portions of the boat and wait, stubbornly and menacingly! A bilge blower, especially on an outboard cruiser, may be a prudent investment.

### MOTOR ANGLE

For best motor performance, the drive of the propeller should be in a line parallel to the keel of the boat and parallel to the flat surface of the water. This means you must set your motor at a 90° angle (or very close to it) to the water, straight up and down. If the propeller is tilted away from the stern—assuming a vertical transom—the bow of the boat tends to rise too high while the stern squats. If the propeller is tilted toward the stern, pushing it up, the bow tends to nose too deep, plowing its way unnecessarily.

### TRIM

The number of seats in a boat is no indication of the number of persons she can carry safely. Overloading, as has been pointed out, is a frequent cause of boating accidents. One of the best ways to avoid overloading is by planning how many people you will take—within the limits of your boat's capacity—and inviting *just so many*, no more!

Before discussing trim it would be well for readers to realize that the factors involved become more critical as boat size and weight decrease.

Have all weight evenly distributed (passengers seated toward the centerline of the boat and not hanging over the gunwales) so the boat will trim properly—slightly down by the stern; never down at the bow—and perform as she was designed to do. If the load is concentrated forward or aft, the boat will needlessly plow or drag, respectively, reducing your safety margin and increasing your fuel consumption.

Trim your boat as well as possible before getting under way. It is dangerous for passengers to change places or move around in a boat (except in a large outboard cruiser) that is scooting along briskly. If such movement becomes essential, stop or slow the craft first, remembering in rough weather to keep enough momentum to retain steerage control and to keep the boat headed into waves and wind. Have the person who must move keep low and near the boat's centerline.

*To this point we have dealt with such preliminary matters as choosing the outboard boat, motor and trailer, and fitting out the craft. Now we're ready to take the outboarder for a spin—the real test of the things he has bought and the things he should know.*

YOUR boat gets its directional "orders" from the stern. That outboard motor at the transom does more than provide propulsion: it acts as a rudder, pushing the transom in the direction of the drive and thus pointing the bow the opposite way. Remote control steering, however, that is, a steering wheel generally near the bow with cable installation aft to the motor, permits you to steer your boat in the manner of an automobile: turn the wheel to starboard (right) and your boat will head to starboard, turn to port and it will go to port. But let the boat-automobile simile end there. The pivoting action of a boat is not like the turning action of a car, and leaving or getting into a slip or float will quickly point up the distinctions.

Make a final check before getting under way. Do you have enough fuel? Are your passengers seated properly? Have you told them about the life-sav-ing devices, their location and their use? Is the way ahead or astern, as the case may be, clear?

Getting under way with an electric starting motor is as easy as pressing a button or turning a key. Once the motor is running, allow enough time for it to warm up before casting off. Listen carefully now, and from now on, to the running motor. Familiarity with that sound so that you detect even slight changes in it will enable you to pick up faults which may develop, such as worn plugs, improperly adjusted carburetor, wrong size propeller for the particular load or job, insufficient or contaminated fuel, and so on.

When the motor is running smoothly and the lines are free, ease the shift into gear and proceed slowly. Remember this about speed: the slower your boat is going the less room it needs to turn or stop, but your boat must be in gear—forward or reverse—for you to have steerage way. Guide your throttle accordingly.

### UNDER WAY

Exercise your knowledge of the Rules of the Road now, tempered by good sense, right of way or no! Small craft should stand off as far as possible from large yachts and commercial ships. Watch their wakes with vigilant care. Don't count on such ships to look out

---

### A BOAT HAS NO BRAKES

*Many persons who have not handled a boat have the misconception that one can be maneuvered and stopped as easily as an automobile. But a boat has no brakes. The new boat owner should practice landings and leaving of docks as often as possible. Work on steering too.*

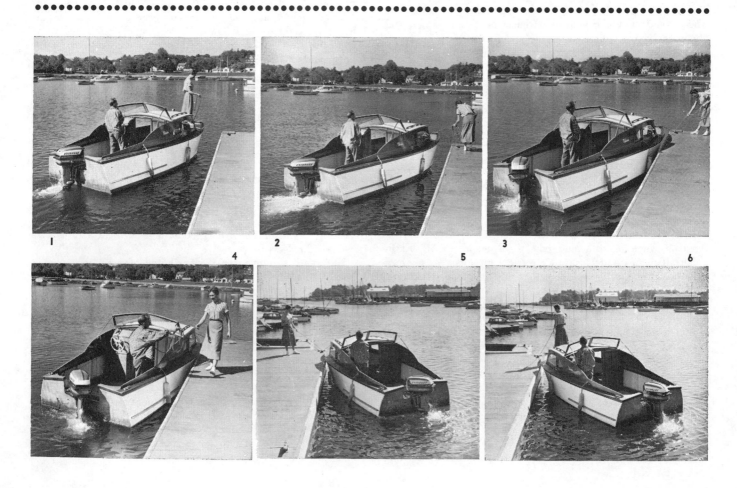

1    2    3

4    5    6

for you; they need more room to stop, are more difficult to turn, and sometimes have "blind spots"—areas which are obscure or entirely blocked to the helmsman. Never assume the pilot of a vessel sees you: stay clear.

It is courteous and incumbent, too, to tend to your own wake and wash so as not to cause damage to other craft. You are legally responsible for the damage caused by your wake or waves.

Should you come upon a tow in the bend of a river. or a tow maneuvering near shore, note whether the tow is swinging to port or starboard, and give it the room it needs.

You should not bring your boat near a moored vessel. If circumstances make it necessary to do so, be exceedingly wary. Strong river currents moving under a moored barge can pull a boat under. Moreover, cross currents, that is, a current that is running at about a right angle to your course, require great caution. When you get into such a situation, give any object, floating or made fast, an extra wide berth.

### WATCH THE WEATHER

Keep your mind on your course and boat handling but keep an eye on the weather. even if this morning's weathercast was for blue skies. Learn to recognize threatening cloud formations. Train yourself to be sensitive to shifts in wind direction; a shift in the wind often presages a change in the

weather. And know and observe official storm warnings.

### CARRY AN ANCHOR

In boating be prepared to do things you may not have planned to do. Anchoring, for instance. Always carry an anchor aboard, properly rigged with plenty of line and accessibly stowed.

In rough waters, anchoring will generally hold your bow into the wind or waves, a desirable effect to stay safest and driest, provided your boat is properly trimmed. A boat down at the bow while at anchor will not head into the wind. (We use "wind" here as a convenience. Actually, the direction and force of the current may have more effect on the position the boat will take at anchor than the wind alone. Experience along these lines is the best teacher.)

One auxiliary use of an anchor is to help get your boat clear should you run it aground. If a small boat is available or if the nearby water is sufficiently shallow so that you can wade, carry the anchor as far out as the line will permit—the farther the better—either from the bow or from the stern, wherever the deeper water is. A strong pull on the anchor line now will usually get the boat free.

Always check the water's depth, by chart, line or paddle, before letting go the anchor. Anchoring in relatively

Photograph from Lesnor-Maehr Marine Co. Inc.

*Important part of your job in deriving peak performance from boat is getting right propeller for job. Number of blades, diameter and pitch are factors to consider. Here outboarder uses dial device on variable pitch propeller to change pitch to one most suitable for boat's load and planned activity this time out. Check propeller frequently for nicks, dents and out-of-pitch blades. These should be corrected as speed, fuel consumption and smoothness of operation are affected by propeller's action.*

• • • • • • • • • • • • • • • • • • • • • • • • • • • • • • • • • • • • • • • • • • • • • • • • • • • • • • • • • • • • • • • • • •

## APPROACHING AND LEAVING A FLOAT WITH AN OUTBOARD

The outboard boat has true "power steering" in that the direction of thrust of the motor, and not a ruddder, guides the boat. As a result, outboard craft are exceptionally maneuverable. They handle easily in reverse because the boat follows the motor, making especially easy the maneuvers for approaching and leaving a float. With twin engines, one can be driven ahead and the other astern to provide an efficient means of turning in restricted waters. The technique of handling a single-screw outboard when approaching (Figures 1-4) and leaving (Figures 5-8) is illustrated here.

**1.** *Float is approached at an angle, with crew member ready to get bow line ashore. Fenders should be out.*

**2.** *Crewman takes line ashore and makes it fast to cleat on float.*

**3.** *Driver puts motor into reverse, turning his wheel to bring stern in.*

**4.** *Forward line will hold fast as motor brings it dockside. Stern line is then made fast to another cleat.*

**5.** *In leaving float when it is not practical to steer dead ahead, stern line is taken in while bow line is still fast to float. Motor is reversed and turned away from float.*

**6.** *Crewman releases bow line and steps aboard while taking in line.*

**7.** *As bow line is cast off, driver brings his wheel about to straighten boat, continuing in reverse until well clear.*

**8.** *With both lines in, driver switches gear to forward and pulls ahead, making certain stern is safe in case he should swing to port.*

7

8

Photographs from Evinrude Motors

deep water is inefficient; don't do it except in emergencies.

The type of anchor—or anchors, for a spare, heavier "hook" is worth springing for—you carry depends on the size of your boat, the kind of bottom in which you will generally anchor, and various other conditions. Coil the anchor rode (line) neatly for running, before you lower the anchor, and keep your feet out of the coils. Secure the bitter (inboard) end of the rode to a cleat, this apart from the hitch you make to stop the rode from running out (and check that the anchor is fast to the rode).

Don't throw the anchor overboard; lower it, and slowly so it doesn't arc into your hull. Don't lower it, however, until the boat's headway is stopped. Come up into the wind or current, whichever is strongest. Wait until the bow is over the spot where you want the anchor to lie. Then, when all headway is off and just before the boat makes sternway (drifts backwards), lower the anchor until the crown hits the bottom. You'll feel the gentle thud.

With the anchor on the bottom and the boat reversing slowly, let out the rode. As a general rule, pay out a scope of approximately six or seven times the depth of water. The longer the scope the better the anchor's holding power. Be sure, though, that you have room enough to swing around the amount of feet you've payed out.

You won't want to anchor too close to another craft. Privacy and safety are comforts skippers cherish.

In heavy weather you'll want to let out as much scope as possible. The length of the anchor rode is even more important in holding power than the weight of the anchor. A lightweight anchor with a long rode will hold in many cases where a heavy anchor with a short scope will drag.

### CAUSES OF ACCIDENTS

Various studies have shown the following to be major causes of accidents:

1) Overloading, overpowering and improper trim.

2) High speed turns, particularly in rough water.

3) Failure to keep a sharp lookout for obstructions.

4) Going out in bad weather.

5) Standing in a moving boat.

6) Having too much weight too high on the boat, as when someone sits on the deck of a small outboard.

7) Leaks in the fuel system.

8) Going too far off shore.

Photographs from Evinrude Boating Foundation

*Top: Boat at left is burdened vessel. She slows, yields right of way, and goes astern of privileged boat on right.*

*Center: Boatmen are cautioned against wearing cushions as life preservers, as shown. Straps are intended to be grasped. If arms are slipped through straps and cushion is held across chest, person will float face up.*

*Left: Like other boatmen, outboarders should have a working knowledge of piloting aids, buoyage systems, and navigational instruments. This will promote safety afloat and widen the range of boating activities.*

Each of these factors—and others not listed here—can and should be avoided. A carefully matched boat, motor, propeller, etc., operated in accordance with the law and with courtesy, will go a long way toward eliminating accidents and even distressing moments. But some possibility always remains. You should be prepared to act in an emergency.

One of the leading causes of death in boating accidents is drowning. Many of these fatalities result from people falling overboard. As the skipper of your boat you have a responsibility to *know how* to rescue such a person. You should practice the maneuvers involved in accomplishing this. A ring buoy with line attached can be used as a simulated victim. Practice enough so you'll be able to act almost instinctively should the need arise; the minutes saved can be a life saved.

The Outboard Boating Club of America suggests that you adopt the following rescue procedure:

As soon as someone falls overboard, maneuver the boat's stern away from him. Shift into neutral (cut the motor if you do not have a gearshift) and throw a ring buoy or buoyant cushion near him . . . *near* him, don't conk him with it. See that you are clear of the overboard person now before engaging the propeller.

Circle around quickly, selecting the course that will allow you to get to the person while the boat heads into the wind or waves. Approach him slowly, now, taking care to come alongside and not over the victim. Stop the motor before attempting to take him aboard.

When alongside, extend a paddle or boat hook to him, or toss him one end of a line. Lead him around to the stern, where freeboard is lowest, if there is enough space at the transom for him to get aboard without injuring himself on the motor. On many outboards the transom is cramped with motor, fuel tanks, junction boxes, etc., so that it would be necessary to help the victim aboard over the side, as far aft as possible. In either case, the use of a boarding ladder will help matters. To avoid capsize when he is boarding, passengers should help trim the boat by shifting their weight.

On very small outboards without remote controls, it may be practical to remove the motor and take the man-overboard in over the transom. When helping a person aboard, hold him under the armpits and lift.

If the person has sunk from sight, probe gently beneath the surface with a paddle. Dive for him only if you are an experienced swimmer, and then just as a last resort.

### OTHER EMERGENCIES

Stay with the boat if it capsizes! Almost invariably the temptation is to swim to shore, and almost invariably the shore is farther than it appears. Many outboard boats will float, even if filled with water. Aluminum and fiberglass boats usually have built-in flotation tanks. (Flotation tanks of wood or metal must be watertight, or they become a hazard. Sailboats with such tanks sometimes test them during the season by "sinking" the craft.) Some boats are fitted with materials like Styrofoam to give reserve buoyancy. And life jackets for persons in the water, of course, will provide much safety.

If your boat gets caught in a squall or in heavy seas, slow down immediately, maintaining only enough power to head the boat into or at a slight angle to the wind and waves. Have everyone don life preservers, yourself included. Don't try to smash your boat through the waves at high speed in an attempt to get home; you're inviting disaster. Rather, take the seas as gently as possible on the bow. The hull may pound, and the waves may toss up a lot of spray, but you'll have your best point of control over the boat. Should the craft get caught broadside in a trough, you run the risk of capsize.

If you find it difficult to keep the boat headed into the seas, or if the motor quits, some kind of drag, like a heavy anchor or a bucket, payed out with a long scope from the bow, may help in keeping the boat from falling into a trough. Some boats, though relatively few, carry sea anchors for this purpose, but opinions as to their effectiveness vary. As a rule, one would expect to use such a rig only in a storm at sea where there is plenty of sea room—not a situation the outboarder is likely to encounter. In heavy weather and where the motor can be idled, it is best to keep the motor going so it can be used instantly to keep the boat under control. Idling it will minimize fuel consumption.

Keep enough weight at the stern in stormy weather to hold the propeller in the water. Because the motor, as was pointed out earlier, serves as a rudder apart from providing propulsive power, you will have no helm control when the propeller leaves the water.

Whenever safely possible, of course, get to a protected harbor rather than attempt to ride out a storm. But don't let your haste disturb your judgment. Try to avoid taking large

waves on the stern; they can swamp the craft, though self-bailing wells aft reduce this potential. There's risk, too, of pitchpoling (turning end over end) in a heavy following sea, by being driven too fast before it. You may have to use reverse to check your speed.

If you must turn in a heavy sea watch for a lull in the wave formations in which to do it, so you won't get caught broadside in a trough by an approaching wave.

Always cross a large wave, or wake, at about a right angle. This lets you retain the best possible control over your boat.

Should your fuel supply run out—manually choking the motor will get the last few drops from the fuel tank—or should you be in need of other assistance, there are several distress signals that can be used. These include waving a white flag (a shirt or towel will serve), shooting smoke or flare signals, sending repeated blasts on a horn or whistle, lowering and raising both arms over your head and down to your sides, or flying an ensign upside down.

*As a starter your equipment should include at least these dozen items: 1) proper running lights; 2) 50 feet of extra line; 3) anchor and line; 4) bilge pump; 5) horn; 6) life jacket for each passenger aboard; 7) fire extinguisher; 8) compass; 9) hand lantern; 10) first-aid kit; 11) buoyant cushions, and 12) safety flares. You'll add to these later.*

### MOORING AND DOCKING

You've made a short, practice run now and are ready to return. When making a landing, proceed slowly. Your wake won't disturb other moored vessels; you'll be better able to gauge the effects of wind, wave or current upon your boat; you can easily avoid mooring buoys, frequently found in berthing areas; and, if your motor is of the gearshift type, the throttle will be closed enough for shifting gears.

If the water is shoal in your landing area, put the motor on "release" so it will kick up if anything is hit, or, lacking such a device, have someone stand by the motor, ready to tilt it up at your command.

In landing at natural areas, try to select a sandy beach with little surf breaking. What from the boat appears to be a gentle, undulating surf may from the beach be a boiling tempest breaking over an acute land slope.

Close the beach (bring the boat in) at a right angle. Tilt up the motor before it strikes bottom, and haul the boat up the beach as far as possible—allowing for tide—so it will not be battered nor broached by waves.

In bringing your boat alongside a pier or up to a mooring,

581

watch the wind. Do not land on the weather side of the pier unless necessary. A crowded gas dock, though, often makes it necessary. Bear in mind, in such a situation, that the wind will be nudging your craft into the pier, so maneuver and use your reverse gear as needed to keep your boat clear. Also, come into the pier at an angle that will permit you to lie alongside at least a boat length away, permitting the wind to move you next to the pier. See that your boat is properly fendered before you come up to the pier, and don't cut your motor(s) until you're safely secured.

When making a preferable landing, on the lee side of a pier, head your boat into the wind or current, thus retaining better control.

From whichever side you approach, turn the craft before it reaches the pier so that it comes parallel to the structure. If you have a gearshift, use reverse to stop headway, then shift to neutral and make the landing with the motor still running.

If you do not have a gearshift, throttle down to a low speed, pivot the motor 180° (which gives you the equivalent of reverse), and get a bow line to the pier. Using this as a spring, the stern can be brought in, if necessary, by going forward slowly with the propeller turned *away* from the pier. Once the boat is alongside, secure a stern line.

### MAKING FAST

An eye spliced into one end of each dock line makes it easy to quickly throw them over a bollard or around a cleat. In other situations, a couple of fast and handy knots to know and use are the clove hitch and bowline.

Generally you'll want to use at least a bow and stern line to make fast. Under certain conditions of wind and current, it may be desirable to tie with a bow line only, allowing your boat to float away from the pier; but if the boat's going to

be left untended, put out a stern anchor. A change in the wind or current may bring your boat bumping into the pier.

In tidal waters, allow enough line for rise and fall. You may otherwise return to find your boat lynched unceremoniously out of the water, if the cleats have not let go.

A block (pulley) and weight arrangement, a shackle and cable setup on pilings, etc., will allow the lines and thus the boat to ride the tide. Where such an arrangement is lacking, run the bow and stern lines several bollards (or equivalent) away from the boat so that the lines are at about 45° angles to the boat. This allows considerable flexibility for tidal variation.

### IN GENERAL

Keep your boat's speed under control at all times. Don't show off. Respect the rights, and comforts, of others afloat: slow down not only when your boat's in danger but when it's a matter of courtesy to others. When passing other craft in the same or opposite direction, give them a wide berth. Never attempt to "hose-down" those aboard another boat. When passing by or through an anchorage, throttle down to your lowest speed and keep an acutely alert lookout for moorings, swimmers, debris, etc.

If you are going off shore or for a relatively long cruise even on inland waters, make those at home familiar with your plans, in as much detail as possible. Should trouble develop, you'll find the Coast Guard most welcomely cooperative, ready to render assistance. The more they know about your plans and boat, the more help they can be.

Your actions on the water can do much to fight against the restricting legislation that inevitably will be proposed from time to time concerning boats and boatmen. And remember, your speed may be prima facie evidence of your guilt.

*Part of the job in becoming a boatman is learning the language inherent to the sport. Illustration above gives many of the commonly used terms you'll want to know and use.*

Above: For easy steering and proper trim, adjust the motor vertically on the transom with cavitation plate parallel to the water flow, as illustrated. In this position, propeller blades take an equal bite on the water on each side of the center line.

Below: If motor is tilted with lower unit toward transom, effective blade pitch on port side is practically zero, but increased on starboard side. Result easier steering to starboard and harder turning to port. With thrust not parallel to water line, stern will rise and bow will trim too low. Opposite effect results when motor is tilted aft.

*To insure safety, check your boat and motor against these curves and formulas, designed to prevent over-powering and overloading. A check list to use for trouble-shooting the motor; thoughts on propeller choice and additional miscellaneous equipment; safety suggestions; and a quiz to test your outboarding knowledge.*

*Twin-motor installation, increasingly popular on today's outboards, provides plenty of power and safety margin besides: if one motor quits the other will get boat in. Tachometer is helpful instrument to keep motors synchronized for most efficient operation.*

THIS series on outboarding, readers may recall, placed much emphasis on the matching of boat and motor. If the boat doesn't have an OBC (Outboard Boating Club of America) plate listing the hull's load and power limits, part one pointed out, it was suggested that you get sound advice on the matter. Here now is a way for you to determine those limits yourself.

For horsepower, simple multiplication and a look at the graph (right) will render the *maximum* horsepower that can be safely used on the boat in question. This horsepower can be derived from a single engine or as a total from a twin installation. Either way, it is an uppermost limit, a sort of safety belt that all boatmen are encouraged to use.

### THE HORSEPOWER CURVE

The first step, the simple arithmetic we talked about, is to multiply the hull's overall length by its maximum width *at the stern*. Length is measured from the stem to the transom on a straight line parallel to the keel. Don't include extensions like outboard brackets, fins, etc., in the measurement.

The second step is to take the product of the length-times-width problem (if fractions are involved use the nearest integer, or whole number) and find this figure along the vertical axis (left edge) of the graph. Enter here and follow the horizontal line to where it intersects the curve. Now follow down to the bottom. The figure you reach at the bottom scale is the maximum horsepower for that particular hull.

If the intersection falls between figures, the one at the right is taken as the maximum horsepower for the hull.

Example: The length-width product of a 14½-foot hull with a maximum transom width of 5 feet is 72.5. Enter the side of the graph at 73 and follow the horizontal line to its intersection with the curve. Reading this point of intersection along the bottom of the graph gives us a figure somewhere between 55 and 60. Because it is between ratings, we take the figure to the right of the intersection, so that 60 is our answer. The *maximum* power then that we can use on our 14½-footer is 60 horsepower, in the form of either a single 60-hp engine or two 30s.

**BOAT INTERIOR DIMENSIONS**

(A) QUARTER LENGTH FORWARD

(B) AMIDSHIPS

(C) QUARTER LENGTH AFT

(D) TRANSOM

HALF BREADTH PLAN

INDICATE SIGNIFICANT VARIATIONS FROM SAMPLE BOAT OUTLINE

DEGREES

TRANSOM

PROFILE

INDICATE SIGNIFICANT VARIATIONS FROM SAMPLE BOAT OUTLINE

KEEL LINE INSIDE PLANKING OR PLATING

BASE LINE

ANGLE

*Diagram 1 shows hypothetical hull in profile, plan, and section at four transverse stations: A, B, C and D. Horizontal breadths are noted a, b, c, d and e; H is symbol for height. Measurements taken inside hull should be expressed in feet, with fractions of a foot converted to three-place decimals (table is included in text).*

## A SAFE LOAD

Determining the load limit—that is, the *maximum* combined weight of passengers, engine and miscellaneous equipment a given hull can safely carry—is not quite so simple. The OBC, it is true, has provided us with a formula for the job, namely Maximum Weight Capacity = Cubic Capacity × 12.5 lbs. per cu. ft., but the equation contains *two* unknowns. We must find Cubic Capacity before we can solve for Maximum Weight Capacity. Follow the procedure carefully.

Diagram 1 shows a hypothetical hull in profile, plan, and section at four transverse stations. These are: A, ¼ length forward; B, amidships; C, ¼ length aft; and D, at the transom. Sections A, B and C divide the overall length, L, into four equal parts. Horizontal breadths are measured at top, a, and bottom, e, of height, H, and at three intermediate points: b, c and d. Measurements taken inside the hull should be expressed in feet, with fractions of a foot converted to three-place decimals (see Table A for conversions of fractions to decimals).

There are two steps now before working out the final equation. These are 1) computing areas of sections which will permit us to 2) compute cubic capacity.

### AREAS OF SECTIONS

Areas of Sections A, B and C are each found separately by using the formula:

$$Area = \frac{H}{12} (a+4b+2c+4d+e).$$

On the theory that excessive freeboard in proportion to beam does not necessarily contribute to a hull's safety, maximum values (see Table B) have been established for height, H.

### CUBIC CAPACITY

The formula to compute Cubic Capacity of the hull is based on the areas (found in step one) for Sections A, B and C in the formula:

Cubic Capacity of Hull =

$$\frac{L}{12} (4A+2B+4C).$$

Areas A, B and C are in square feet; the cubic capacity in cubic feet, to three places.

### MAXIMUM WEIGHT CAPACITY

This is the final step, and requires only the multiplication of the cubic capacity by the factor 12.5. The original

For full information on boat horsepower and weight capacities, flotation, standardized dimension of outboard boats and motors, ventilation, fuel systems, steering systems, lighting for small boats, safety equipment, trailer facts, fire protection standards and many other details of recommended practices for outboards, readers may consult the Engineering Manual published by the Outboard Industry Associations, 307 North Michigan Ave., Chicago 1, Illinois.

★ ★ ★

## TROUBLE SHOOTING THE OUTBOARD

**MOTOR WON'T START:**
*Fuel tank empty*
*Fuel line closed*
*Fuel tank air vent closed*
*Motor not primed or choked*
*Low speed carburetor needle valve needs adjusting*
*Spark plug improperly gapped, cracked, fouled or lose*
*Magneto points improperly gapped; coil or condenser weak*
*Improper fuel mixture*

**MOTOR MISSES:**
*Pinched or kinked fuel line*
*Fouled spark plugs*
*Carburetor needs adjustment and/ or cleaning*
*Fuel filter needs cleaning*
*Improper fuel mixture*
*Frayed lead wire insulation*

**MOTOR LOSES POWER:**
*Carburetor needs adjustment*
*Fuel line not clear*
*Wrong type spark plugs*
*Motor overheating, check cooling system*

**EXCESSIVE VIBRATION:**
*Carburetor needs adjustment*
*Propeller bent, broken or fouled*
*Spark plug not firing*
*Clamp screws or other device loose*

**MOTOR OVERHEATS:**
*Water pump defective*
*Water intake clogged*

★ ★ ★

equation, you'll perhaps remember, is:

Maximum Weight Capacity = Cubic Capacity × 12.5 lbs. per cu. ft. The result is an overall total in pounds, expressing to the nearest integer the safe maximum weight capacity of a given hull. But remember, a boat safely loaded and safely powered still has its limits, which is where seamanship and competent boat handling come into use.

## ADDED FLOTATION

Still another step can be taken to assure the safety of your passengers and your boating rig: built-in flotation. This can take the form of air chambers or of the addition of some buoyant material, in either case, of sufficient quantity to support the weight even if the boat is entirely submerged.

A note to the OBC, 307 North Michigan Ave., Chicago, Ill., will bring you information on how you can determine the amount of flotation you need for your craft. First, however, you might try writing directly to your boatbuilder; he may already have done the computation involved.

## WHAT PROP?

Your outboard motor, carefully selected under the foregoing considerations discussed in this series, may or may not come with a propeller. Either way, you want to be sure to turn the right wheel for the job your boat and motor must do.

Propeller manufacturers, and some outboard motor manufacturers, make a wide range of wheels for you to choose from. Ask their advice before buying. The choice, say, for a 16' to

### TABLE A
#### Conversion of Inches to Decimals in Feet

| Inches (or fractions) | Decimals in Feet | Inches (or fractions) | Decimals in Feet |
|---|---|---|---|
| 1/8" | .010' | 3" | .250' |
| 1/4" | .021' | 4" | .333' |
| 3/8" | .031' | 5" | .417' |
| 1/2" | .042' | 6" | .500' |
| 5/8" | .052' | 7" | .583' |
| 3/4" | .062' | 8" | .667' |
| 7/8" | .073' | 9" | .750' |
| 1" | .083' | 10" | .833' |
| 2" | .167' | 11" | .917' |

18' runabout might go from a 2-bladed propeller with a pitch ratio (pitch divided by diameter) of 1.3 for a high-speed, lightweight rig to a 3- or 4-bladed propeller with a pitch ratio of .8 for a heavily loaded, slow speed craft. Fuel economy and boat performance will be markedly affected by propeller selection.

## ELECTRONIC EQUIPMENT

Much of the electronic equipment previously held to be suitable only for yachts and their kin is now designed and produced for use in the smaller boat, including the outboard. Chief items in this equipment are the radiotelephone, depth finder and direction finder. Their price, bulk and weight have all been put into a range that will appeal to the outboarder, especially in the light of the equipments' various uses.

## MISCELLANEOUS EQUIPMENT

Many of the points to be made here, readers will observe, have been dealt with in preceding parts. They are repeated, briefly, because of their significance.

The fire extinguisher(s) you use aboard the boat must be of a Coast Guard-approved type. If there's any doubt as to the approval status of the particular extinguisher, check with your local Coast Guard Inspection Office.

Of the approved types now on the market you'd do well to buy a carbon dioxide, dry chemical or foam extinguisher. The vaporizing liquid type, both those that must be pumped and those with stored pressure, will not be accepted as approved after January 1, 1962.

Check your extinguisher regularly, and recharge or refill as needed.

Lifesaving devices too must be of an approved type. The choice ranges from preservers and cushions to ring buoys and vests. The buoyant materials used in these devices include kapok, cork, balsawood, and vinyl-covered fibrous glass.

Take care that you have enough of these devices (one for each person aboard) and that their location and use is common knowledge—*before* you get under way!

Fire prevention of course is the responsibility of everyone

aboard but it is the special province of the skipper. In that capacity you must insist upon certain rules—and see to it that they are followed. You must, for instance, see that all cigarettes are out when approaching a gas dock. And you must see that none of your passengers forgets the smoking moratorium during the fueling process.

Most outboards are equipped with portable tanks. If they are of six-gallons or less in capacity, remove them from the craft for fueling. And see that they are made secure when in the boat. Ventilation, leakage and spill, of course, are all things you'll have to watch vigilantly.

Outboards with permanent fuel tanks should conform with approved inboard practice, running fill pipes to decks outside the coaming and venting outside the hull. Fill pipes should extend almost to the bottom of the tank, and not terminate at the top of the tank.

Permanent or portable, ground the gas hose nozzle to the fill pipe when fueling. This prevents static electricity from generating a spark which, in turn, might ignite gasoline fumes and blast boat and passengers out of the running.

## IN CASE OF AN ACCIDENT

If you are involved in a boating accident on the navigable waters of the United States you are required by law to stop and give whatever help you can, without seriously endangering your boat or passengers. You must also identify yourself and your boat to any person injured or to the owner of any property damaged.

You must file a written accident report if there is 1) loss

### TABLE B
#### Maximum Allowable Height for a Transverse Section

| Beam of Section | Max. Height | Beam of Section | Max. Height |
|---|---|---|---|
| Up to 4.042' | 1.583' | 5.710' to 6.042' | 2.083' |
| 4.043' to 4.375' | 1.667' | 6.043' to 6.375' | 2.167' |
| 4.376' to 4.709' | 1.750' | 6.376' to 6.709' | 2.250' |
| 4.710' to 5.042' | 1.833' | 6.710' to 7.042' | 2.333' |
| 5.043' to 5.375' | 1.917' | 7.043' to 7.375' | 2.417' |
| 5.376' to 5.709' | 2.000' | 7.376' to 7.709' | 2.500' |

NOTE:—The maximum allowable height (H) is based on width (a) for that section on the Interior Dimensions. If the actual height of the section is **less** than the maximum allowable height, use the **actual height**. If the actual height of the section is **more** than the maximum allowable height, use the **maximum allowable height**.

of life, 2) injury causing a person to remain incapacitated for more than 72 hours, or 3) physical damage to property (including vessels) in excess of $100. If in doubt, report!

If you're in trouble while afloat, you'll find the Coast Guard, other boatmen and professional seamen ready to do what they can. To help the Guard assist you, the following steps are recommended:

1) Let somebody know your plans for the day including destination, intended stops en route, and estimated time of return. At the first opportunity notify those concerned of any change in plans.

2) Don't use MAYDAY in voice radio distress communications unless immediate assistance is required.

To get help when it's needed, of course, you'll want to know and carry some of the recognized distress signals. Apart from the radiotelephone, perhaps the most valuable distress aid available, there are a host of other devices. Flares, a continuous sounding with a whistle or horn, the raising and lowering of outstretched arms to each side, and so on, are some examples.

## YOUR RESPONSIBILITIES

When you are admonished to know the Rules of the Road you should be aware that there are four different sets of such rules in effect according to your boating locality. These are: 1) Inland, 2) Great Lakes, 3) Western Rivers and 4) International. Copies of the rules you're interested in can be secured from your local Coast Guard office.

Hints on understanding the Inland Rules appear in the CG booklet *Recreational Boating Guide*, for sale by the Superintendent of Documents, U.S. Government Printing Office, Washington 25, D.C., at 40 cents a copy. The section is worth quoting here:

"Note that in these rules, 'steam vessel' includes *any* vessel propelled by machinery.

"If you are equipped with both machinery and sail, the *only* time you are considered as a sailing vessel under the rules is when you are propelled by sail alone. (Note: If you carry an engine of more than 10 hp—or less where states have so specified—you are required to have a registration number.)

"Risk of collision can, when circumstances permit, be ascertained by carefully watching the compass bearing of an approaching vessel. If the bearing does not appreciably change, such risk should be deemed to exist.

"The law says that in obeying and construing these rules due regard shall be had to all dangers of navigation and collision and to any special circumstances which may render a departure from the rules necessary in order to avoid immediate danger.

"The rules of the road apply alike to the small pleasure craft and large commercial ships such as ocean liners or freighters. However, the large vessel with her great length and tremendous weight requires a great deal more room to maneuver; because her turning circle is large, her stopping distance is relatively great, and often her deep draft restricts her to little variance from channel courses. Common sense dictates that operating a small pleasure craft too close to the large oceangoing vessel or a tug with tow may be dangerous."

## QUIZ FOR OUTBOARD BOATMEN

1) Outboard boats on federal waterways are not required to follow the same Rules of the Road that apply to large commercial steamers.

2) A tacking sailboat always has right of way over an outboard boat.

3) Outboarders may disregard federal regulations that concern "steam vessels."

4) Outboard boats under way on federal waters must carry their registration certificates aboard.

5) Outboard boats powered by engines of 10 hp or less when used on federal waters are always required to be registered.

6) Money paid for boat registration fees is deductible from federal income taxes.

7) Sailboats with auxiliary outboard motors, used on federal waters, always must be registered.

8) Sailboats propelled by sail alone and used on federal waters are never required to be registered.

9) Outboard boats are required by law to have sufficient flotation to keep the boat afloat should it fill with water.

10) The proper propeller for a particular hull, motor and job helps achieve best boat performance.

11) Depth sounders are not suitable for use on outboard boats.

12) Life-saving equipment, like cushions, used on an outboard boat need not be Coast Guard-approved.

13) Liquid-type fire extinguishers have been CG-approved since January 1, 1962.

14) Fire extinguishers on an outboard boat should be kept in some remote place aboard, well out of the way of wind and water which may come aboard.

15) Portable fuel tanks should never be removed from the boat for filling.

16) You are not responsible for any damage caused by your boat's wake or waves.

17) In case of capsize, promptly swim as far from the boat as possible.

18) Only one set of Rules of the Road is in effect in the United States.

19) If your outboard boat is equipped with sail also, it is under the Rules considered a sailing vessel only when it is propelled by sail alone.

20) If you use both an outboard motor and a sail to propel your boat you are under the Rules considered a sailing vessel.

21) The Rules invariably require a large commercial vessel to keep clear of an outboard craft.

22) A boat propelled by oars must keep clear of an outboard boat.

23) You may anchor your outboard in a channel to fish, providing you keep clear of traffic.

24) A boating accident in which no one is killed need not be reported.

25) Any outboard hull is suited for the highest-powered stock outboard motor.

26) High-powered outboard motors on small, light hulls provide greatest speed and safety.

27) When under way at high speed give *all* your attention to your own safety.

28) Maintain your course and speed when passing another vessel close aboard.

29) Under all circumstances, maintain your course and speed when you have the right of way.

30) When an outboard boat turns, its stern swings in a direction opposite to the desired change in course.

31) Once your anchor is "holding bottom" the length of the anchor rode payed out is unimportant.

32) Wise practice to help assure proper anchor holding is to pay out anchor rode at least five times the depth of the water.

33) If you run aground you should attempt to get the anchor into deep water as far from the boat as possible.

34) The outboard motor(s) serves as a rudder on an outboard boat.

35) Maneuvering an outboard boat is relatively more difficult with two motors than with one.

36) The Coast Guard themselves can impose no penalty for the reckless operation of a boat on federal waters.

37) A bow line about 8 feet long and a stern line about 6 feet long, both made ready for landings, are always of sufficient size.

38) The bitter end of your anchor rode should be made fast when anchoring.

39) When anchoring, throw the anchor as far from the boat as possible.

40) Lower the anchor into the water, don't drop it.

41) Give the boat sternway after the anchor sets to test the anchor's holding power.

42) When attempting to get a person into the boat from the water, the boat's engine(s) should be kept running.

43) In a squall give the boat plenty of speed through the water.

44) When in a storm and heavy sea, stop your boat's engine(s) and drift.

45) Usually **try to cross a large wave** at about a right angle.

46) Because an unexpected delay might change your schedule, don't tell friends or relatives what your estimated time of arrival is, especially when making lengthy cruises or going off shore.

47) Don't equip your boat with running lights if you don't expect to run at night.

48) A compass is not required by federal law to be aboard an outboard boat.

49) Some states now issue boat registration numbers.

50) Some states now have jurisdiction over the federal waters within their state boundaries, concerning the equipment carried by and the inspection of boats operated upon those waters.

51) Boats exempted from their state's federally approved numbering provisions must apply to the Coast Guard for a number.

52) All violations of the Federal Motorboat Act of 1940 are punishable by a fine of not more than $2000.

53) Fog horns should not be used in place of a whistle.

54) The permanent seats in your new boat are an indication of how many persons that boat may safely carry.

55) It is preferable for safety's sake to have your outboard boat trim slightly by the stern rather than by the bow, when underway.

56) When adjusting trim underway by the relocation of passengers, never slow boat speed.

57) Your boat's freeboard is not a factor in determining the number of passengers you can safely carry.

58) The buoyancy of Coast Guard-approved kapok cushions remains unaffected when sat upon frequently.

59) It is desirable to paint the underbody of a boat moored in salt water with an anti-fouling paint, whether the boat is wood, fiberglass or metal.

60) At open throttle a 2-cycle outboard motor of 20 horsepower will consume less fuel than a 4-cycle inboard engine of 20 horsepower.

61) The improper mixing of oil and gasoline is apt to cause spark plug fouling on an outboard motor.

62) Gasoline spilled in a wet bilge, because it mixes with bilge water, loses its explosion potential.

63) Federal law requires U.S. pleasure boats underway to display the U.S. flag.

64) Speed limits posted on the water by the U.S. Corps of Army Engineers must be obeyed by boatmen.

65) A hull that makes 15 mph with a 7½-hp outboard motor will make 30 mph with a 15-hp outboard motor.

66) It is wise to carry a paddle or pair of oars of sufficient length (relative to the size of the boat) aboard an outboard boat.

67) Federal law requires all boat trailers to exhibit back-up lights.

68) Federal law specifies no minimum age for boat operators on federal waters.

69) A siren may be substituted for the whistle required by Pilot Rules for fog signals given by "steam vessels."

70) To insure sufficient ventilation when filling the permanent fuel tanks on your outboard boat, open all windows, hatches and doors.

---

### ANSWERS TO QUIZ QUESTIONS

*Compare your answers with these:*
Questions 4, 6, 10, 19, 30, 32, 33, 34, 38, 40, 41, 45, 48, 49, 53, 55, 59, 61, 64, 66, 68 and 69 are true. All others are false.

# CHAPTER 30

As with almost any form of modern-day human endeavor, there is a certain amount of "paperwork" involved with the ownership and operation of a boat. Although never really enjoyable, these necessary tasks and processes can be made less burdensome and more effective by an orderly and efficient approach.

A boat of almost any size larger than a dinghy or a sailboard is a relatively complex item that must be properly used and maintained for safety, efficient operation, maximum enjoyment, and the protection of one's investment in her. The use and maintenance of a craft might well be lumped together and termed "boat management"; the proper documents and records are a vital part of this function.

This chapter will offer broad guidance in connection with the paperwork of "boat management." It will remain the responsibility of each owner-skipper to work out the specific actions and records for his boat as every craft and its use are highly individualized matters. What is best for a cabin cruiser just won't be right for an outboard runabout or a sailboat—what is adequate for the weekend user of a Class 1 boat will fall short of meeting the needs of a cruising yachtsman. But in *all* cases, there is a requirement for a certain amount of

# "BOAT MANAGEMENT"

## Certificates and Documents

The term "ship's papers" has a long and honored history. Nearly all vessels, including the smallest of boats, have some official or legal papers relating to them. Even a dinghy too small in most states for registration and numbering will have a bill of sale or purchase receipt. Although the craft may now be used in a state where numbering is not required by reason of a 10 HP. lower limit, there is always the possibility of a change to one which registers all watercraft, and this paper will be needed to establish ownership.

Many items can be included in the term "ship's papers," among them the Certificate of Number or yacht document, radio licenses, insurance policies, personal certificates, etc.

### REQUIRED PAPERS

The owner of a boat registered by the Coast Guard, or by a state under a numbering plan approved in accordance with the Federal Boating Act of 1958, is issued a "Certificate of Number." This must be on board the boat whenever it is in use, and to facilitate this, the law prescribes that it shall be of "pocket size" and water resistant. If lost or destroyed, immediate action must be taken to obtain a duplicate.

In a number of states, a sticker or decal must be attached to the boat in a specified location. Broadly speaking, this small item can be considered a part of the ship's papers. It is visual evidence from a distance that the craft's registration is currently valid.

#### Documents

**Boats over a** specified minimum size *may* be "documented" by the Coast Guard in lieu of registration and numbering. Information on this procedure is given in Chapter 2.

Craft that are documented must carry this paper on board, and it must be renewed annually. These documents

are valid for one year from date of issue or renewal; there is no calendar or other fixed year.

A Certificate of Number or document must be produced for inspection by a law-enforcement official upon his request.

### Radio Licenses

A radio station aboard a boat must be licensed by the Federal Communications Commission. This includes "marine band" (2-3MHz) sets, VHF radiotelephones, and Citizen Band equipment, plus radar sets. No license is required for small "handitalkies" on CB frequencies provided that their power is not over 0.1 watt. No license is required for radio direction finders, loran receivers, electronic depth sounders, and other types of equipment that do not *transmit* radio signals.

For the operation of marine band and certain other radio transmitters, the individual must have an operator's license or permit. None is required for CB sets or radar equipment.

#### Posting of Licenses

The radio station license must be on board the boat, posted in a prominent location as near as practicable to the position from which the equipment is operated. A Restricted Radiotelephone Operator Permit may be carried on an individual's person; any higher class of license must be posted.

#### Copy of FCC Rules

Each radio station on a boat must have a copy of the current edition of Part 83 of the FCC Rules and Regulations. This *should* be on board and available for ready reference, but the regulations allow that it be kept in a "suitable place on shore."

A radio log, required by the Rules, must be maintained;

this will be covered later in this chapter.

Additional information on the "paperwork" related to marine radio stations will be found in Chapter 25.

## OPTIONAL BOAT PAPERS

Although not required by any law or regulation, an annual Courtesy Motorboat Examination by the Coast Guard Auxiliary is an excellent check on a craft's safety and "readiness for sea." If this examination is passed, a sticker will be awarded and the inspection form will be signed by the Auxiliarist and given to the Skipper. This signed form should be stowed safely away with the others of the ship's papers.

### Personal certificates

If a motorboat is not carrying "passengers for hire," there is no requirement for the operator to have a Coast Guard license—state requirements may differ and should be checked. (The term "non-commercial operation" is often used in this connection, but it is not strictly correct as a person commercially fishing, crabbing, lobstering, etc., does not need a USCG operator's license provided he has no passengers for hire on board.)

The circumstances of when a guest aboard is, or is not, a "passenger for hire" have been examined in some detail in Chapter 2. It has also been held that a salesman, broker, or owner demonstrating a boat to a prospective buyer must have an operator's license or else place the craft under the command of a licensed individual.

Many skippers, however, do get a USCG license in one or more of the categories in which they are issued, just for the sake of having one rather than from any regular need for it. If so, it should be posted where it can readily be seen. If nothing more, it may serve to reassure any nervous "landlubber" guests aboard for a cruise!

Likewise, the Skipper's membership certificate in the United States Power Squadrons, with its endorsements for qualifications in Advanced Grades and Elective Courses is often posted on his boat rather than at home ashore. The same, too, is frequently done with one's certificate of membership in the United States Coast Guard Auxiliary. As with a USCG operator license, these documents all attest to the owner's established qualifications and abilities —they should be proudly displayed.

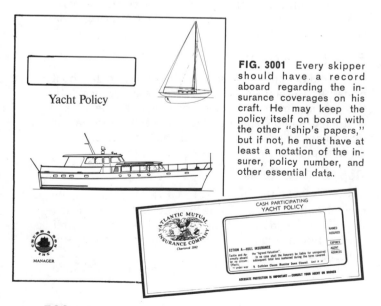

**FIG. 3001** Every skipper should have a record aboard regarding the insurance coverages on his craft. He may keep the policy itself on board with the other "ship's papers," but if not, he must have at least a notation of the insurer, policy number, and other essential data.

## Insurance Papers

Most boats are, or should be, covered by insurance policies; see page 64. The owner may either keep his policy on board, or ashore in a secure place such as a safe deposit box.

If the policy is not carried on board, there should at least be a memorandum of information in the ship's papers regarding it. It should list the insurance company, policy number, coverages, expiration date, and other pertinent information such as the agent's name, address, and telephone numbers, both office and residence.

# Logs and Log Keeping

An important part of the paperwork of "boat management" is the maintenance of the legally required or otherwise desirable logs. The plural form of "log" is used as it is often convenient to keep separate records of navigational, engine, and radio operations. These, however, can be within the same covers or binder if such is desired.

### Developing your log format

The first step in log-keeping is to have logs that fit your needs. It is useless to follow a format that provides space for recording many items of information that are not applicable to your style of boating—for example, the nature of the bottom as brought up by an "armed" lead, or true headings if you regularly use magnetic readings from the chart. Trying to use an unsuitable log format is a bad practice as it may lead to the neglect of making any entries at all. Many printed logs simply do not meet an individual's requirements—if they do, fine; but if they do not, then develop your own style for the data that you find necessary and useful at a later date. It is wasted effort to record information for which you have no future use.

A log should be kept in columnar form insofar as practicable, rather than in paragraph style, but columns should not be set up for data that are only occasionally entered as this would result in much wasted space.

Printed log books are available from *Motor Boating Books* and at most marine supply stores. These may be used as they are, or column headings may be modified. In general, the use of a loose-leaf notebook form of a log should be avoided as pages can get lost. Much more desirable is a bound, hard-cover book—often a "record" book, available from office supply stores, will do nicely for the boatman who rules his own columns. It is quite possible that *your* needs will be met by such a book ruled in just three columns—"Date," "Time," and "Remarks"—other entries may be many, but probably will not be so grouped as to make additional columns useful.

### Determining needs

It may take some time to determine just what is needed and what is not. Your requirements for log data may not even "jell" until after you have made a second cruise over some of the same areas months or more later; then you will learn just what information you should have recorded on your first visit there.

In considering which form to use, or in designing one of your own, be systematic. List the items that you wish to enter; consider their relative value. Sort possible entries

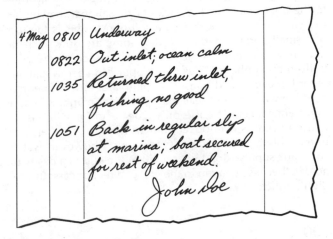

FIG. 3002 A log is a most important document for any craft. Its format and contents will vary with the boat, its use, and its skipper's way of doing things. Develop a log to fit your needs and desires—but do have one. Log-keeping can be a pleasure rather than a chore!

into two categories—frequent and occasional. The first group will guide you in establishing columns; the second category can be put in a general column headed "Remarks." Once you have worked out your needs, reduce your log-keeping to those items only, and buy or prepare a form most convenient to record them. Be careful, however, that you don't overlook data for which you may have only infrequent use, but which would be invaluable in case of accident, breakdown, tax or insurance inquiry, etc. —don't be too brief!

## DECK LOGS

A "deck log" is a record of navigational data—the time that you started a day's run and the time of reaching your destination, plus times of passing important navigational aids or landmarks and towns or cities. These latter items are particularly useful when cruising in inland waters where a constant speed cannot be maintained and you might later want to know the running time between such points. If your cruising takes you offshore, you will probably include your various headings and speeds, with the time of any change in either.

Other information that should be entered in the log are the names of any persons aboard other than the usual family "crew." Entries might be made of the weather—wind, visibility, sea conditions, etc.—at the start of the day's run and any significant changes. Entries should, of course, be made of any unusual events on board or seen; for example, engine trouble on your boat, or assistance rendered to another craft. These entries should be made in full detail so that reliance need not be placed on one's memory at a later date.

It is frequently useful to record in your log your operating expenses, such as fuel and dockage charges. Such records must, of course, be kept if you are able to take advantage of any business-related tax deductions. It is often of interest to record fuel prices at stops where no fuel is taken on, or dockage fees at brief daytime stops; this information may be of use in planning future cruises.

### A log for every boat

A deck, or navigational, log should be kept by every boatowner and used for all activities—local outings, fishing trips, water skiing runs, etc., as well as "cruises." It is ad-

visable that a boat's log account for *every* day, in port or underway. The former may easily be done by such a simple entry as "8-12 June. In regular slip; no one aboard." This may later prove to be a useful and valuable record.

### Validating the log

Regardless of format, certain essential elements should be entered. Each page should be numbered and the craft's name should appear somewhere on the page, usually at the top. Each day's entries, or a combined entry for several days in port, should be signed by the skipper as he completes them at the end of the day concerned. This authenticated record may be needed in connection with an insurance claim, a law suit, or other investigation. If a boat owner can state under oath that it is his practice to keep a daily log and then present a signed entry for the day involved, he has gone a long way toward legally establishing the situation as seen by him. Be sure that you *never* make erasures in a log—if you need to correct an item, rule out the old material without making it illegible, and then write in the correct entry if there is space, or make reference to where it will be found elsewhere in the log.

FIG. 3003 It is important that the log entries for each day's use, or period of time in port, be validated by the skipper with his signature. This may have important legal aspects if the log is ever needed to establish facts in a court of law.

Initial the correction and add the date if it is made on a later day.

## Why not an illustrated log?

With a bit of proper planning, log-keeping can be interesting and fun—and the log itself will be of interest and use long after a cruise is over. Why not consider an illustrated log? Use marginal sketches if you or your mate has the artistic ability; or put in photographs of scenes, events, and people.

## ENGINE LOGS

An engine log is kept in terms of hours of operation and is valuable in timing oil changes and other items of preventive maintenance. Record all routine maintenance and other significant events such as any troubles, repairs, etc. If a record is kept in the engine log of the addition of crankcase oil to maintain the proper level, any increase will soon become apparent and consumption can be accurately computed. Any increase in the use of oil may be a valuable warning of internal engine troubles. Likewise, fuel consumption can be periodically figured in terms of engine hours and any unusual change noted.

Hours can be estimated, or roughly figured from the deck log, but the easiest and by far the best way is by use of an engine-hour meter; see fig. 30. These instruments are not expensive, and a typical installation can be made in an hour or two by the average skipper. An engine log for the dinghy's outboard motor is not beyond reason, but here we confine ourselves to estimates of the running time if we remember to make an entry promptly after each use.

## RADIO LOG

If your craft is equipped with a radio transmitter, a certain amount of log-keeping is required by the FCC Rules and Regulations. In recent years, the number of entries that are required has been greatly reduced, but there is no excuse accepted for a lack of these if your station is inspected. Refer to your copy of Part 83 of the FCC Rules and keep at least the minimum log. You may want to add more to your radio log relating to contacts with the Coast Guard, other boats, or the marine operator.

## LOG-KEEPING TECHNIQUES

A most important feature of good log-keeping is the making of entries while the facts are fresh in your mind—the very best time is immediately after the occurrence of the event. On a small craft this may present problems—you may not be able to write neatly, or even legibly, due to the boat's motion; the cockpit of a sailboat may be far too wet for "paperwork." One solution to this is the use of a small portable tape recorder; some are now so small that they can easily be held in one hand, complete with built-in microphone. Thus the skipper can keep a running record of events and transcribe them later into the permanent log when he has reached a sheltered marina slip or a quiet anchorage. The use of a tape recorder will ensure that no event is overlooked, nor will the log be messy or unreadable at a later date. One caution however, watch your tape supply—don't get caught at the end of a day with no data because you ran to the end of a reel or cassette and didn't notice!

FIG. 3004 An excellent way to keep notes for logs —deck, engine, or radio, while underway is the use of a small hand-held tape recorder. Using this procedure, the actual log can be written up after the day's run and will be much more legible than one written at the helm while underway.

## Retention of logs

Since the maintenance of a deck or engine log is voluntary on a recreational boat, its retention is at the owner's discretion. In any case, it should be kept in a safe place until any possibility of litigation has passed. Many skippers keep their logs permanently and read them with fond memories years later. A radio log *must be retained* for the period specified by the current regulations.

## How about a "Fog"?

One further thought on log-keeping—the skipper's logs may well be supplemented by a "female's log," or "fog" for short. In this record, the skipper's wife records the names of boats seen, new friends made (and don't forget addresses), new recipes discovered, points of interest ashore, and any other bits of information that will aid her in planning for other cruises or will just bring back memories. If you are a "shutter-bug," here is the place to record enough information about your picture-taking so that months later you will not be wondering what in the world that particular photograph was intended to show.

# Instruction Books

It is most important that a boat owner have instruction manuals or data sheets for all equipment installed on his craft. Such papers are of great value in the performance of routine maintenance to keep the equipment working properly, or whenever repairs are necessary. These instruction books will normally include a "parts list" which will help greatly in obtaining the correct replacement components when needed.

The prudent skipper ensures that he has a *complete* set of instruction books. He starts with the main engines and goes straight through the inventory to the smallest motor, pump, horn, etc. There should be no item categorized as "too small," "too insignificant," or "too dependable" for inclusion in this check-up.

Rare, indeed, is the craft that has a complete set of manuals when it is purchased, either new or used. Those that are not on board must be obtained—sometimes from a local dealer, but more often directly from the manufacturer of that particular item of equipment. The boat owner can usually determine the manufacturer's address from the name plate on the equipment or from advertising in *Motor Boating* or other publications.

## Model and serial numbers

When making this check of equipment, it is wise to make a note of *both* model and serial numbers for all items. These can be recorded in a notebook set up for this purpose or in the back of a log book. The latter location is usually quite convenient, but it requires the transcribing of information when one volume of a log is filled and another is started.

When writing for an instruction book or a replacement part for any piece of equipment, be sure to include *both* model and serial numbers as often there are variations in design after a certain serial number without a change in model designation.

## Parts lists

Parts lists must include as a minimum the identification of those units which normally wear out with the passage of time and whose replacement is a matter of routine maintenance, especially those whose replacement is within the capability of the skipper or crew.

Much more desirable is to have the instruction manual or parts book so complete that it shows the identification of *all* parts and sub-assemblies. This will facilitate the ordering of proper replacements in the event of any sort of breakdown, and much time may be saved thereby.

## Names and addresses

Instruction manuals, parts lists, and the like should be annotated with the name, address, and telephone number of the nearest source of supply—the local dealer or his source, the area distributor. If service technicians must be obtained from a different firm, this, too, should be recorded with all necessary details.

## Sailboats

Sailboats should have complete information on each sail carried—manufacturer, date made, cloth type and weight, and all dimensions, including those relating to battens, if these are used. It is so much easier to take measurements under ideal conditions at one's convenience, and then look up the information in a notebook or log when needed, than it is to have to measure under adverse conditions, perhaps in an emergency.

### INFORMATION ON THE BOAT

Very few, if any, boats are delivered with what might be termed an instruction book on the craft itself. Such a document would typically include electrical wiring diagrams for each system of different voltage; a drawing of the fresh water system's pumps, lines, and valves; a diagram of the fuel lines and valves; information on the location of all seacocks and other through-hull fittings; and similar information regarding the boat and systems that are not a part of accessory equipment.

Unfortunately, some manufacturers consider that they have provided such a manual when they place on board each new boat a simple, generalized booklet of "safe boating tips," and nothing else.

If not found on board the boat when it is purchased, some or all of the above documents may possibly be obtained by writing to the manufacturer of the craft, being sure to include all available identification data including hull number. On a used boat, all such information, either coming with the boat or later obtained from the builder, should be verified as previous owners may have modified or added to one or more of the systems. In all probability, the owner will have to search out and record much of the information discussed above.

## Docking plan

For medium-size and larger craft, those over, say, 30 feet in length, there should be a "docking plan." This drawing shows where slings should be placed if the boat is to be lifted, or where shoring blocks must be placed if she is to be hauled on a marine railway. Close attention to this plan will prevent excessive stresses being placed on the hull when the craft is taken out of the water.

## Safe stowage of books

It is important that all instruction books, parts lists, and similar publications be on board, but kept safe from damage or loss. Usually, it will be most convenient to place them in a waterproof plastic envelope and then put that in a secure place. On larger craft, where water damage is less likely, a large heavy-paper case with lettered or numbered subdividers makes an excellent means of filing these documents for the easiest retrieval when needed.

# Check Lists

As the size of one's boat increases, its operation becomes more complex and there are more details to be remembered and executed at such times as getting underway or docking. While it should not be carried to extreme degrees that would complicate boat operation to the extent of decreasing enjoyment, the use of "check lists" can be valuable from a viewpoint of both safety and the avoidance of embarrassing situations. Their use can have real value in the prevention of expensive accidents and equipment damage.

## Applications

The situations for which check lists can be prepared, and their level of detail, will, of course, vary with the size, type, and use of the craft. They may well vary, too, with the personality of the skipper. Typically, for a cruising Class 2 or 3 boat there will be check lists for:

1. Getting underway
2. Approaching a pier or mooring
3. Securing after a day's operations
4. Departure from the boat for a day or more
5. Periodic routine preventive maintenance

## Importance for single-handed operation

Check lists are of particular importance and value for the person who is aboard by himself. Single-handed operation of a boat requires the maximum of thought and preplanning. Once underway, many tasks become much more difficult, if not impossible of accomplishment with safety, than if they had been performed before lines were cast off. A check list will minimize the reliance that must be placed on one's memory during the final minutes before casting off, and reduce the penalties for any forgetfulness.

## DEVELOPMENT OF CHECK LISTS

The contents of any check list will vary so much with the individual craft and her skipper that it will not be possible here to give more than sample items which may or may not be applicable to another person's situation.

Probably the most significant single characteristic of any check list is that it is a "living" document—it is never "completed" and final; it must always be considered as being under review each time that it is used.

### Getting underway

Before getting underway from a marina berth, many "disconnections" must be made—electric cords, water hose, possibly a telephone connection, and most certainly the lines which have held the craft fast to the pier or pilings. Forget just one of any of these and you're in trouble, but fast!

Even the most elementary "housekeeping" chores are candidates for a pre-departure check list. Trash and garbage should be put in proper containers ashore rather than being taken along for a day's cruise. Water tanks should be topped off, if appropriate, and certainly fuel tanks should be checked. Use of a check list helps prevent the omission of an item because each of two persons thought the other had done it.

Not too silly an item for family groups is a final head-count of all children and pets. Even if the individual is missed before the craft gets far away, it can mean another docking and undocking, an unnecessary waste of time.

For the single-hander, there are such matters as the proper setting of switches and valves, the raising or lowering of a radio antenna, or even the setting of the craft's colors. All of these are minor tasks, but they cannot be done underway without leaving the helm unattended.

### Coming into port

When approaching a pier or wharf, a much better landing will be achieved, and embarrassment often avoided, if the proper lines are laid out where needed and fenders are placed ready for use if required. Once made fast to the shore, there will be switches to be turned and valves to be opened or closed. Notations must be made for log entries while the information is still fresh in one's mind. Supplies of fuel and water should be checked so that refills can be arranged as needed.

**FIG. 3005** Larger craft should have on board diagrams of the electrical system—systems, if there is more than one voltage involved—and the network of tanks, valves, and lines of the fuel system. These will be of great value when troubles must be found and fixed.

FUEL SYSTEM, GASOLINE (SIMPLIFIED)

**FIG. 3006** A "docking plan" is a sketch indicating where a craft's keel ends and where shoring blocks must be placed if she is to be hauled on a railway or elevator platform. It shows where slings must be located if the boat is to be lifted out.

### Departure from the boat

This is a very important check list as items which are overlooked when leaving will often not be remembered until their execution is impracticable or even impossible. Primary choices for this list are items relating to the safety and security of the unattended craft—turning off fuel valves, the proper setting of electrical switches, pumping out the bilge and leaving the switch on automatic (if one trusts the switch) or making arrangements for such periodic pumping out as may be needed, and the physical security of ports, windows, hatches, and doors.

### Routine maintenance check lists

Routine maintenance check lists will include both items based on use of the craft (usually in terms of engine hours) and on calendar dates (weekly, monthly, etc., checks). Typical of the former are crankcase oil level checks and oil changes, and oil and fuel filter changes.

On a calendar basis are such matters as checking the water in storage battery cells, pressure gauges on dry-chemical fire extinguishers, and all navigation lights. The proper operation on and off of automatic bilge alarms or pump switches should be checked by deliberately running water into the boat. Seacocks should be periodically operated closed and open several times to ensure their free and easy operation if needed quickly in an emergency. Equipment and supplies carried on board for emergency use should be inspected for any signs of deterioration.

## CHECK LISTS MUST BE USED

The most important aspect of check lists is that they must be used *regularly*. They must be used if they are to be of any value to the skipper, and they must be used if they are to be kept up to date and increase in usefulness.

A pre-departure check list must be gone through *each* time the craft is gotten underway. A list prepared and filed away is of little value, and it may build up a false sense of security. For safety and to avoid any embarrassment, the boatman should train himself to automatically reach for the list when he is ready to start an operation for which a check list has been established. He should be like the aircraft pilot who goes through such a check list *every* time, no matter how many years experience he has or how many times he has taken off and landed that day.

The value of a check list lies in its use, not in its existence!

# CHAPTER 31

"What's that odd-looking flag on that boat over there?"

"What flag? Oh, you mean the one with blue and white vertical stripes?"

"Yes, that one—it has a red union for the anchor and stars, rather than the usual blue field."

"That's the Ensign of the United States Power Squadrons."

"The United States . . . what? What's that?"

"The United States Power Squadrons—a volunteer organization dedicated to making boating safer through education rather than legislation. I took their free Piloting Course—you should take it too."

"Perhaps I will; tell me more."

# The United States Power Squadrons

**FIG. 3101** The USPS Ensign is usually flown from the starboard spreader on a sailboat or a motorboat with a mast. On any craft, however, it can be displayed on a staff at the stern as shown above, and this is the normal procedure for smaller boats.

The United States Power Squadrons (USPS) is a non-profit, non-governmental organization of boatmen. Somewhat contrary to its name, which has more historical significance than current-day literal meaning, it is *not* limited to the owners of motorboats; many sailboat skippers belong, as well as quite a few individuals who do not own a boat at all.

## Purposes

The purposes of the USPS are best described by a direct quotation from its Constitution—

"The objects of the United States Power Squadrons shall be to establish a high standard of skill in the handling and navigation of yachts; to encourage the study of the science of navigation, piloting, seamanship, and small boat handling; to cooperate with agencies of the United States Government charged with the enforcement of the laws and regulations relating to navigation; and to stimulate interest in activities which will tend to the upbuilding of our Army, Navy, Coast Guard, and Merchant Marine."

## The USPS Ensign

The Ensign of the United States Power Squadrons may be flown on boats only when they are skippered by members of the organization. Rules for where and when it can be flown are given on pages BB and FF.

The USPS Ensign consists of *seven blue* and *six white vertical* stripes with a union in *red* on which is the same white fouled anchor and circle of stars as on the yacht ensign; see color illustration on page AA.

In the form of decals and stickers, automobile emblems, boating cap insignia, etc., the USPS design can be worn or displayed only by members in good standing.

THE ENSIGN is the name of the USPS monthly publication.

## HISTORICAL DEVELOPMENT

In 1912, the motorboat was just beginning to be a reliable type of craft, and was beginning to challenge the sailboat for a place in the field of recreational boating. A group in the Boston Yacht Club felt that there was a serious lack of knowledge on the part of some who were taking up this new form of boating, and decided to improve the situation by instituting special activities for motorboats and by conducting classes in their use. This program led to the formation of the "Power Squadron of the Boston Yacht Club," and set the educational basis for the USPS which remains its primary function.

### Formation of a national organization

In the next two years, similar situations arose in other yacht clubs along the Atlantic coast, and interest spread in the program that had been started in Boston. On 2 February 1914, a meeting was held at the New York Yacht Club which resulted in the formation of the "United States Power Squadrons."

The USPS had barely gotten underway when the approaching effects of World War I were felt. An extensive series of classes was organized as a part of the preparedness program. Over 5000 men who attended these courses entered the Armed Forces, with many of them receiving direct commissions on the basis of their boating experience and Power Squadron training.

### Changes in programs

The initial activities of the USPS, before World War I, had placed much stress on boat handling in the form of drills and maneuvers, together with signalling and other semi-naval procedures. With the end of the war, interest in such military aspects of boating was very low, and the programs of the USPS were reorganized into a format that emphasized instruction as a service to boatmen and boating in general. The old distinctions between "power" and "sail" faded, and the Squadrons began to have an appeal to all who used boats of any type. The word spread, and Squadrons were formed on the Great Lakes, in Florida, on the Pacific and Gulf Coasts, and on inland rivers and lakes.

## Growth after World War II

During World War II, the USPS again provided training to thousands of men before their entry into military service or the Merchant Marine. With the end of this war, boating boomed, and with it, the USPS. Squadrons were formed in many new areas, including Japan and Okinawa, as well as Hawaii, Alaska, Puerto Rico, and the Canal Zone.

## MEMBERSHIP

The USPS is a private organization and membership is by invitation. Members must be male U.S. citizens over 18 years of age who have met entrance qualifications set by the national organization and who have been elected by the local unit. As it is a volunteer organization depending upon its membership for support, an important aspect of a prospective member's qualifications is his willingness to "give" of his time and talents as well as "take" from the USPS of knowledge and improved skills.

There are also provisions for Apprentice status for male youths between 16 and 18½ years of age, and for a "Certificate Holder" status for women who have pased the qualifying examination. Individuals in both of these groups must be U.S. citizens.

## ORGANIZATION

The basic unit of the USPS is the local *Squadron.* These have names of geographic significance and may have as few as 20 to 30 members or as many as 1200 or more.

Squadrons are grouped into *Districts* which are numbered; this is the intermediate level between the local unit and the *National* organization.

FIG. 3102 The above organizational diagram is greatly simplified; there are 30 Districts and more than 380 squadrons. The number of Squadrons in a District varies from 5 to more than 30. Each echelon is led by elected officers.

## Officers

All levels of organization are led by elected officers. Squadrons and Districts have a *Commander,* plus several *Lieutenant Commanders* and *Lieutenants.* The USPS as a whole is directed by a *Chief Commander* and five department heads with the rank of *Vice Commander.* National Committee Chairmen and other staff officers hold the rank of *Rear Commander* or *Staff Commander.* All officers are unpaid volunteers; there is a small paid office staff at the National Headquarters at Montvale, N.J.

FIG. 3103 USPS members may wear any one of a series of blue and white uniforms as determined by the nature of the Squadron activity and the climate. A blazer is available for informal occasions. The purchase of a uniform is not required of all members.

## Uniforms, insignia, and flags

The USPS has a series of blue and white uniforms suitable for a wide variety of occasions and climates. The purchase of a uniform is optional for members, but is expected of officers. The various uniforms, plus insignia and flags of officers, are shown on pages BB and CC.

## The USPS today

In 1970, the United States Power Squadrons was comprised of more than 78,000 members. There were 384 Squadrons assigned to 30 Districts.

# Educational Programs

The educational programs of the USPS are its major activity. There are four major areas of educational effort. One of these is for the general public, some of whom will later be invited to membership. The other programs are for members only, and include two for further personal study and one for the internal training of the membership to improve their teaching abilities.

## THE PILOTING COURSE

Each local Squadron is required to give each year at least one public course in Piloting; many give the classes two or more times each year, varying the place and/or night of the week so as to reach the greatest number of boatmen and their families.

The Piloting Course is broader than its brief title would imply; it covers all basic areas of safety in small craft operation. Although the sequence and number of class sessions is determined by the local Squadron, each course includes the following topics—

Safety Afloat
Seamanship
Small Boat Handling
Equipment and Government Regulations
Rules of the Road Afloat
Mariner's Compass
Aids to Navigation
Charts and Chart Symbols
Chartwork
Manners and Customs; Radiotelephone Use
River Piloting (optional)

FIG. 3104 The principal activity of the Power Squadrons is the holding of "Piloting" classes for the general public. This free course covers all aspects of basic boating safety and is in furtherance of the aim of "safety through education, not legislation."

FIG. 3105 The USPS also has a progressive series of courses for its members. The initial courses are Seamanship and Advanced Piloting in which the basic material of the public course is studied in more detail and advanced aspects.

The course material is prepared and distributed on a national basis, as is the end-of-course examination. Instruction is by local USPS members, supplemented in some instances by outside experts and specialists. The course is given free of charge by the local Squadron, although students will usually find it desirable to purchase a textbook, notebook binder, plotting instruments, etc., if they do not already have them. In some areas, the course is presented as a part of the adult education program of a local school system and a small registration fee is charged by that organization; no part of this money goes to the USPS or any member.

Family groups are encouraged to take the Piloting Course together. The nominal minimum age limit is 16 years, but this may be lowered to 14 for the children of students in the class (or for those of a USPS member).

## THE ADVANCED GRADES PROGRAM

In keeping with its stated purpose of encouraging the study of the science of navigation, the USPS offers its members a progressive series of four courses.

The primary purpose of the *Seamanship Course* is to provide basic information about boating to people who have had little or no experience on the water. Knowledgeable boatmen, however, will find it quite valuable as a refresher course. The material covered in "S" applies to both motorboats and sailboats. The course includes instruction in "marlinespike seamanship" to develop a working knowledge of useful knots, bends, hitches, and splices.

The *Advanced Piloting Course* covers the basic principles and more important practices of pilotage, including modern electronic methods. The lessons will prove to be of great interest and practical value to the small boat skipper as much of the knowledge can be applied at once to the use of his own craft. This course includes a thorough study of the mariner's compass and its errors. The student is instructed in the use of government publications concerned with piloting. He learns how to determine the height of the tide or the strength of a tidal current at any specified time. Further instruction is given in the use of charts, in the laying of courses, and in the determination

FIG. 3106 The Advanced Grades program of USPS education culminates in the Junior Navigator and Navigator Courses covering celestial navigation. The final grade of "N" is highly esteemed by members.

of position by bearings, angles, and soundings.

The *Junior Navigator Course* teaches the "sailings"—the mathematical counterpart of plotting. The practical use of the marine sextant is covered, including the taking and reduction of sights on the sun, moon, planets, and stars. A main objective of this course is to provide instruction sufficiently complete in itself that the graduate could navigate out of sight of land and bring his craft safely back to port.

The *Navigator Course* deals with alternative methods, special situations, and more advanced techniques. It aims to develop greater skill in the taking if sights and higher precision in position finding. Throughout the course, orderly methods for carrying out the day's work of a navigator at sea are emphasized. The grade of "N" is the highest awarded by the USPS—its "PhD" in the field of boating study.

## THE ELECTIVE COURSES PROGRAM

The USPS also offers to its members, apprentices, and woman's certificate holders four "elective" courses in speciality subjects; these do not constitute a series and may be taken in any sequence.

*Engine Maintenance* familiarizes students with the general construction, operating principles, and simple

**FIG. 3107** At the Annual Meeting of the USPS there is a large exhibition of teaching aids developed by the local Squadrons. These are shown both for the recognition of achievement and for the mutual benefit gained from an exchange of ideas.

maintenance of marine gasoline and diesel engines, including outboard motors. As one of the major objectives of the course is to make the skipper a self-reliant and effective trouble-shooter, the diagnosis of all types of engine troubles is emphasized. EM is *not* intended to produce trained *mechanics,* only well-informed and resourceful *users* of marine engines.

*Marine Electronics* focuses on the legally proper and most effective *use* of marine radios and other electronic equipment that can be installed on boats for greater safety and convenience. This is *not* a technical course, and is well within the capabilities of the average USPS member. Students are prepared to take the FCC exam for a Third Class Radiotelephone Operator Permit.

The *Sail Course* is proof that the USPS is not just for the motorboat skipper! It covers sail terminology, types of rigs and hulls, the theory of sailing with emphasis on the balance of hull and sails, stability, and other related topics.

The *Weather Course* is concerned with what the weather is all about and how its many variations can be predicted.

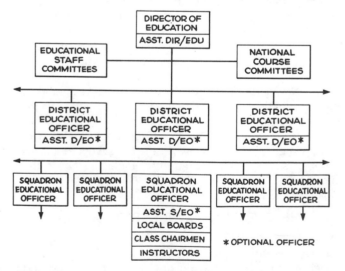

**FIG. 3108** The Educational Department is the largest sub-unit of the USPS. Many members holding other offices or engaging in other tasks also teach on the local level or serve on national and district committees of the Department. At any time, approximately 80% of the membership is active in educational work.

We may not be able to do anything about it, but we can boat more safely, and more comfortably, too, if we understand something about it. Throughout the course, the student is encouraged to make observations and predictions on his own, so that he may apply the principles learned in class to his activities on the water.

## THE INSTRUCTOR TRAINING PROGRAM

The USPS depends almost entirely upon its own membership as a source of instructors for all courses. For members who would like to teach, yet hesitate to do so for lack of experience, and for those now teaching who would like to increase their classroom effectiveness, the *Instructor Training Course* can be of great value.

**FIG. 3109** The USPS also engages in other programs oriented toward increased boating safety. Squadrons and individual members assist in the Cooperative Charting Program for the correction and improvement of nautical charts issued by the Coast & Geodetic Survey and the Lake Survey.

## Other Programs

The USPS participates in a *Cooperative Charting Program* with the Coast & Geodetic Survey and the Lake Survey. In this effort, the boating activities of thousands of USPS members are coordinated toward the reporting of errors, omissions, and changes for nautical charts and related publications. The limited field facilities of these federal agencies are thus much strengthened and expanded, and all boatmen are assured of more correct and accurate charts of the waters they use.

Many Squadrons also participate in events of a local nature such as boat shows and the annual observance of National Safe Boating Week.

### Social Activities

It's not "all work and no play" in the USPS. Squadrons hold a wide variety of social activities both afloat and ashore. Each District has a Fall and a Spring Conference. These are working sessions, but they are usually preceded or followed by evening social gatherings. The national-level Annual Meeting each January combines both intense official events with those of a much lighter nature.

## The Canadian Power Squadrons

In Canada, the Canadian Power Squadrons (CPS) is organized along lines generally similar to the USPS and conducts roughly equivalent education programs. There are close lines of communication and a well-developed sense of brotherhood between these two organizations.

# The U. S. Coast Guard and Coast Guard Auxiliary

# CHAPTER 32

**FIG. 3201** The United States Coast Guard is a military service although it is not normally under the Department of Defense. It is unique in its dual roles of public service in time of peace and naval operations in time of war. U.S. Coast Guard Photo

The never-ending work of the United States Coast Guard (USCG) touches upon the activities of the vast majority of U.S. boatmen. Even far from salt-water "coasts," far up the major rivers of this nation, the work of Coast Guardsmen assists and protects the boating public. In many of its functions, the Coast Guard is ably assisted by its civilian supporting organization, the Coast Guard Auxiliary (USCG Aux). (Note the correct abbreviation; it is *not* "USCGA," this stands for Coast Guard Academy.)

The principal activities of the Coast Guard relating to boating are in the areas of law enforcement and safety. These take many forms as will be discussed in this chapter. Auxiliarists do not have law-enforcement powers, but do engage in a wide variety of activities, afloat and ashore, that further the cause of safety on the water.

## The United States Coast Guard

The **U.S. Coast Guard** is a military service and a branch of the Armed Forces. It is *not,* however, normally a part of the Department of Defense. In peacetime, the USCG functions as an agency of the Department of Transportation. In time of war or national emergency, though, the Coast Guard, or units thereof, may be transferred to the Navy.

### The Coast Guard Ensign

The flag of the Coast Guard, its distinctive Ensign, is closely connected with its history. The red and white *vertical* stripes number *16,* the number of states in the Union when the flag was first authorized in 1799.

The Coast Guard Ensign is illustrated in color on plates Z and DD. It has the unusual feature that it is flown *day and night* on active USCG units afloat and ashore—a constant reminder that the Coast Guard is always on duty to render assistance.

Coast Guard cutters, ships, boats, aircraft, vehicles, etc., are easily identified by the distinctive red band with USCG emblem and blue stripe.

## FUNCTIONS RELATING TO BOATING

Boatmen come into contact with the Coast Guard in both of its major areas of law enforcement and safety. Many of the federal laws relating to boating are implemented by regulations issued by the Commandant of the USCG.

### Boating regulations

The Federal Boating Act of 1958 is the basis for the registration and numbering of motorboats. Although the Coast Guard performs this task itself in only three states and two other jurisdictions, the boat registration systems of those states that carry out this function for themselves must be approved by the Commandant. Coast Guard patrol vessels may check the registration papers of boats on all U.S. waters.

Boats of more than a specified minimum size may be "documented" rather than registered and numbered. In

**FIG. 3202** Coast Guard mobile boarding teams extend law enforcement and general boating safety activities to inland areas of navigable waters subject to federal jurisdiction. Such teams can also conduct limited rescue operations if an emergency arises.

FIG. 3203 Amphibious vehicles along the shore and helicopters in the air support the search and rescue operations of Coast Guard small craft and cutters. Every available means is used to save lives and property in times of emergency.

*all* states and territories, this function is performed by officials of the Coast Guard.

Coast Guard regulations also spell out the details of the safety equipment required by the Motorboat Act of 1940. USCG personnel are authorized to make inspections of boats to determine the adequacy of such equipment.

### Safety activities

Coast Guard craft make frequent patrols to keep a watchful eye for any reckless operation of boats and all hazards to navigation. They may make spot checks of boat registrations and required equipment. Races, regattas, and other marine events are patroled to ensure the safety of both participants and spectators.

Safe Boating Centers have been established in a number of major locations of small craft activity. At these, boatmen can get information, advice, and assistance on problems relating to safety on the water—the Coast Guard would much rather prevent an accident than to rescue one's victims!

### Aids to navigation

The Coast Guard is responsible for the operation of many thousands of aids to navigation, from unlighted buoys and daybeacons to very large lighthouses. The USCG also operates hundreds of radiobeacons and many of the stations of the world-wide Loran-A and Loran-C systems.

This is a quiet and unspectacular, but most necessary, service to all who travel on the water. The installation and maintenance of lighted and unlighted aids to navigation is a major function of the Coast Guard and one that affects most boatmen every time that they leave their moorings.

### Search and rescue

The rescue of mariners in distress is probably the most dramatic activity of the Coast Guard, the one that makes the headlines when a ship goes down at sea in a storm. Less publicized, but equally important, are the many instances when the USCG comes to the aid of the boatman who has lost his way at sea, gone aground, suffered dismasting or engine failure, or who has merely run out of fuel. Many boatmen, and especially their wives, venture out on the waters, offshore or inland, with a greater sense of security knowing that the Coast Guard is standing by to help, living up to its motto, "Semper Paratus"—"Always Ready."

Search and rescue units include amphibious vehicles, motorboats, and ships known as "cutters," a term with which historical reference for the Coast Guard. Fixed-wing aircraft and helicopters both extend the search capabilities of surface vessels and in many cases perform rescue mission themselves when wind and sea conditions permit.

## ORGANIZATION

The Commandant of the Coast Guard, an Admiral, and his staff are located at *USCG Headquarters* in Washington, D.C. Operational activities are geographically grouped into *Districts* each under its Commander, a Rear Admiral. Fig. 1502 shows the boundaries of the Districts of the contiguous 48 states; the 14th District is in Hawaii and the 17th District covers Alaskan waters. For better coordination of operational matters, primarily search and rescue, the Districts of the Atlantic/Gulf of Mexico and Pacific coasts have been placed under Eastern and Western *Area* commands, respectively.

The operating units of the Coast Guard, the individual bases, stations, cutters, boats, aircraft units, etc., may be under the direct control of a District, or these may be under an intermediate level, the *Group.*

### Officers and enlisted personnel

Personnel of the Coast Guard include commissioned officers, warrant officers, and enlisted men. Ranks are the same as in the Navy and uniforms are generally similar except for identifying USCG devices. A small shield is worn above an officer's stripes and on the lower right sleeve of an enlisted man's uniform shirt or jacket. There is a Coast Guard Reserve to support the regular establishment. Women serve in both commissioned and enlisted ranks in the Reserve.

## OTHER COAST GUARD FUNCTIONS

Functions of the Coast Guard not directly related to recreational boating include the Marine Inspection Service that establishes and enforces safety standards for both vessels and crews, and oceanographic research activities. Coast Guard icebreakers and cutters of reinforced construction often are busy keeping northern harbors open for commercial navigation in winter, and they also operate in the Arctic and Antarctic. In spring, cutters and aircraft with the International Ice Patrol keep track of the movement of icebergs into Atlantic shipping lanes.

A number of cutters are engaged as Ocean Station Vessels in the Atlantic and Pacific, providing meteorological information and communications and navigation support to air and surface traffic.

The final major function of the Coast Guard is to maintain at all times a high state of readiness to function as a specialized service in the Navy in time of war.

FIG. 3204 The Coast Guard Auxiliary includes both women and men as members. Many ladies have qualified in specialty subjects and participate actively in all aspects of Auxiliary work—education, examination, and operations.

FIG. 3205 Boats that are owned by members of the USCG Aux and have met the higher inspection standards of a "Facility" may fly the blue and white flag of the Auxiliary. If the owner is an officer, elected or appointed, he may also fly the pennant of his office.

FIG. 3206 Members of the Coast Guard Auxiliary make thousands of free voluntary courtesy checks each year on boats of all sizes and types. Deficiencies are brought to the attention of the owner, but are not reported to any law-enforcement officials.

# The Coast Guard Auxiliary

The **Coast Guard Auxiliary** is a *civilian* organization functioning under the direction of the Commandant of the Coast Guard. It is composed of persons interested in the Coast Guard and its principles, dedicated to the interests of their country, and concerned about the safety and welfare of their fellow men. Despite its uniforms and insignia, the Auxiliary is a non-military body.

The Auxiliary has a wide range of members. Eligibility extends to persons, male or female, who are over 17 years of age, U.S. citizens, and who own not less than a 25% interest in a boat, aircraft, or amateur radio station (or who have some other special qualification useful to the Auxiliary). An Auxiliarist is normally enrolled initially as a "conditional member" subject to further training and qualification to become a "regular member." In the language of the Auxiliary, the boat, aircraft, or radio station on which membership is based is termed a "Facility."

## The Auxiliary flag

A boat that has qualified as a facility may fly the Coast Guard Auxiliary flag—popularly known as the "Blue Ensign." This is a rectangular blue flag with a white diagonal slash on which is the USCG Aux emblem; see color illustration on page DD.

The Auxiliary flag shares with the regular USCG Ensign the distinction of being authorized to fly from boats *day and night.*

## PURPOSES

The U.S. Coast Guard Auxiliary has several fundamental purposes which are stated as follows in the Act of Congress that established the organization—

To promote safety and effect rescues on and over the high seas and on the navigable waters.

To promote efficiency in the operation of motorboats and yachts.

To foster a wider knowledge of, and better compliance with, the laws, rules, and regulations, governing the operation of motorboats and yachts.

To facilitate other operations of the Coast Guard.

## ACTIVITIES

In carrying out its stated purposes, the Auxiliary has three basic program areas—Education, Examinations, and Operations. All of these are focused on the objective of greater safety for those who go on the water in boats.

### Education

The Auxiliary offers several courses to the boating public, tailored to meet the needs of various types of boatmen and their families. Courses run from one lesson to eight or more; classes are held in the evenings or on weekends. Constant attention is given to the improvement of these courses and the development of new lessons or courses as required.

Members of the Auxiliary are actively encouraged to take "specialty" courses to improve their knowledge and increase their value to the organization. Typical subjects include vessel examination, communications, search and rescue, patrol procedures, administration, and others.

### Examinations

Many members of the Coast Guard Auxiliary are active in the "Vessel Examination" program. Boat owners are urged each year to request a "Courtesy Motorboat Examination." This purely voluntary action ensures that a thorough check is made of the craft and its equipment. Boats that pass are awarded the CME sticker for the current calendar year. Craft that do not pass are *not* reported to any authority—the owner is advised of the deficiencies and is encouraged to resubmit his boat for another check when they have been corrected.

Auxiliarists are also busy each year checking the craft of other members to determine their fitness for continued designation as "Facilities." Higher standards and equipment requirements are placed on such boats as they will be allowed to fly the Auxiliary flag. The highest standards are required for a craft that is designated an "Operational Facility" and will be used in operational programs under Coast Guard orders.

## Operational programs

Personnel and craft of the Auxiliary are used to perform missions in the fields of search and rescue, boarding, and regatta patrols where the resources of the regular Coast Guard are not sufficient to meet the demands placed upon them. This often occurs on weekends and during holiday periods. For such duties, orders are issued by a designated Coast Guard officer.

Auxiliary members have *no law enforcement powers*. In those cases where such is needed, a Coast Guard officer or petty officer will be embarked in the Auxiliary vessel and the craft will fly the regular Coast Guard Ensign.

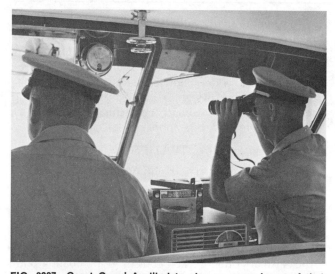

FIG. 3207 Coast Guard Auxiliarists give up many hours of their own family boating time to conduct search and rescue missions and safety patrols for the assistance and protection of their fellow boatmen. Such activities support and extend the efforts of regular Coast Guard units.

Auxiliary craft also conduct informal "Safety Patrols" without official orders. Other types of patrols include those to check on aids to navigation, or as a part of the Cooperative Charting Programs of the Coast & Geodetic Survey and Lake Survey for the reporting of errors and needed changes in charts.

Auxiliary operational facilities are often used to supplement regular Coast Guard units in search and rescue operations. Auxiliary aircraft aid in this work and are used

to make "twilight patrols" at the end of days of heavy boating activity to spot any craft that may need aid in reaching port safely.

Auxiliarists donate their time and abilities to the cause of safety on the water; there is no compensation for services rendered, except personal satisfaction, and only minor reimbursement of expenses, limited to activities under official orders.

### Fellowship Activities

Units of the Auxiliary work hard at their basic responsibilities, but not to the complete exclusion of social activities. Rendezvous, parties, dances, and other events which tend to promote goodwill and fellowship are held on appropriate occasions.

## ORGANIZATION

The basic unit of the Coast Guard Auxiliary is the *Flotilla*. This is a group of members and their facilities who work together in the various programs. Membership varies from the tens to the hundreds of individuals.

Flotillas are grouped geographically into *Divisions;* this is the normal intermediate level between the local flotilla and the District. In some cases, a District is divided into two or more Areas or Regions for better control.

## Officers

All units of the Auxiliary are headed by their own elected officers—Flotilla Commander, Division Captain, or District Commodore. These are assisted by other elected and appointed officers. The USCG Aux as a whole is headed by a National Commodore, with a Vice Commodore, Rear Commodore, and staff officers.

## UNIFORMS, INSIGNIA, AND FLAGS

Although the Auxiliary is *not* a military or naval organization, its members, other than those in a conditional status, are authorized a series of uniforms—blue, white, and khaki—quite similar to those worn by regular Coast Guard personnel. Uniforms are available for dress, ordinary service, and working situations. The purchase and maintenance of uniforms is optional for the individual, but are required for activities such as patrols and other duty under official orders.

## Officers' insignia

A series of "rank" insignia from single gold bars to two silver stars, each with the distinctive Auxiliary "A" superimposed, has been established for officers of the USCG Aux. These are shown on page EE.

The boats of officers of the Auxiliary are identified by pennants of special design for each office or level of office. These are illustrated on page DD. Past Officers may fly a burgee of generally similar design, but of different shape from the pennants of active officers.

## WHY NOT JOIN?

If you're an eligible boatman, or fit into one of the other categories, why not join the Auxiliary? You are sure to learn much for your boating safety and enjoyment, and there is nothing finer than the sense of satisfaction that comes from helping others. Ask any Coast Guard unit or Auxiliarist where *you* can "sign up."

# UNITED STATES COAST GUARD AUXILIARY
# FLAG CODE CONFIGURATIONS

**A** 2 STAFFS

**B** 2 STAFFS AND RADIO ANTENNA

**C** 2 STAFFS AND MAST EXTENSION

**D** SIGNAL MAST WITH YARDARM

**E** GAFF UNDERWAY—NO YARDARM

**F** NATIONAL ENSIGN ON SPEAKER'S RIGHT **ENSIGN ON PLATFORM**

**G** NATIONAL ENSIGN ON AUDIENCE'S RIGHT **LOCATED OTHER THAN ON PLATFORM**

The information on page 602 has been drafted to show in tabular form what the United States Coast Guard Auxiliary has approved as a flag code for power vessels. The problem would be simplified if there were no diversification of sizes and types of boats, thus providing a uniform number and arrangement of positions at which the flags might be displayed. To illustrate typical configurations on small craft for the display of the national ensign, Auxiliary ensign, USPS ensign, yacht club or Auxiliary officer's flag, and division or flotilla pennant, the chart above provides a key for the respective types, depending on what staffs, yardarms and halyards may be available. In addition to configurations shown for boats, figures F and G illustrate correct procedure when the national and Auxiliary ensigns are displayed at meetings ashore, the practice depending on whether or not the ensign is located on the platform.

# UNITED STATES COAST GUARD AUXILIARY FLAG CODE FOR POWER VESSELS

| FLAG | NATIONAL ENSIGN | COAST GUARD ENSIGN | AUX. ENSIGN | AUX. OFFICER PENNANT OR BURGEE | YACHT ENSIGN | USPS ENSIGN | USPS OFFICER FLAG | YACHT CLUB PENNANT OR UNIT | YACHT CLUB OFFICER FLAG | HOUSE FLAG | GAG FLAGS — MEAL, ETC. |
|---|---|---|---|---|---|---|---|---|---|---|---|
| FACILITY NORMAL CONDITION — FLOWN (STATUS 1) | STERN STAFF OR GAFF (Note #1) | NO | TRUCK — BOW STAFF (Note #2) (Note #14) | STB'D. YARD — BOW STAFF (Note #3) (Note #6) | (Note #4) | STB'D. YARD ONLY (Note #5) | (Note #6) | BOW STAFF (Note #10) | STB'D. YARD (Note #6) | NO (Note #7) | NO (Note #8) |
| UNDER ORDERS — FLOWN (STATUS 2) | STERN STAFF OR GAFF (Note #1) | NO | TRUCK — BOW STAFF (Note #2) (Note #14) | STBD. YARD — BOW STAFF (Note #3) (Note #15) | NO (Note #15) | NO (Note #15) | NO (Note #15) | NO (Note #15) | NO (Note #15) | NO (Note #7) | NO (Note #8) |
| UNDER ORDERS USCG OFFICER ABOARD — FLOWN (STATUS 3) | STERN STAFF OR GAFF (Note #1) | TRUCK (Note #16) | NO (Note #16) | NO (Note #16) | NO (Note #16) | NO (Note #16) | NO (Note #16) | NO (Note #16) | NO (Note #16) | NO (Note #7) | NO (Note #8) |
| HOURS FLOWN | 0800 TO SUNSET | DAY AND NIGHT UNDER ORDERS (Note #13) | DAY AND NIGHT (Note #9) | OFFICER ABOARD DAY AND NIGHT | 0800 TO SUNSET (Note #4) | 0800 TO SUNSET Note #5 | DAY AND NIGHT (Note #6) | 0800 TO SUNSET (Note #11) | DAY AND NIGHT (Note #12) | (Note #7) | NO |

NOTES

#1 **The National Ensign** shall be flown from the stern staff on a power boat except when the vessel is equipped with a gaff, in which case the ensign is flown from the stern staff at anchor, and the gaff when underway.

#2 **Auxiliary Ensign**
   (a) Shall be flown from the main truck when the vessel is equipped with a mast(s).
   (b) Without a mast, from the bow staff.

#3 **Auxiliary Officer**—Pennant or burgee shall be flown from the starboard yardarm when the vessel is equipped with a signal mast. If the vessel has no mast, it may be flown in lieu of the Auxiliary ensign from the bow staff. The pennant of a current officer shall take precedence over his own higher ranking past officer's burgee. However, as a matter of courtesy to a visiting officer, display the highest ranking officer flag (pennant or burgee).

#4 **The Yacht Ensign**
   (a) The flying of the yacht ensign on any yacht, numbered or documented, is neither mandatory nor forbidden.
   (b) A documented yacht operating under official orders, becomes a Government vessel, and Government vessels *may not* fly the "Yacht ensign."
   (c) All facilities *not documented* shall fly the U.S. ensign, whenever the Auxiliary ensign is flown.

#5 **USPS Ensign**—This is the only "service" organization recognized by this code. The USPS ensign may be flown only from the starboard yardarm of a signal mast, *never* from the stern staff or gaff. On facilities flying the Auxiliary ensign, this position of honor is *reserved* for the national ensign.

#6 **Officer Flags**—Auxiliary, USPS, yacht or boat club, either pennants or burgees, are flown from the starboard yardarm, except as noted in #3. Only *one* of these flags may be flown at a time.

#7 **House Flag**—The owner's private signal known as a house flag is correctly flown at the truck between morning and evening colors; therefore, it *cannot* be flown at the same time as the Auxiliary ensign.

#8 **Gag Flags**—Because of the quasi-official status of an Auxiliary facility, cocktail flags, ball-and-chain, or other humorous flags *shall not* be flown when the Auxiliary ensign is flown. Other flags, such as crew's pennant, owner's meal flag, guest flag, absent flag, also shall not be flown with the Auxiliary ensign.

#9 **The Auxiliary Ensign**—may be flown *day* and *night* on currently inspected facilities displaying decal, while in commission.

#10 **The Yacht Club Pennant**—can be flown from the bow staff.

#11 **The Yacht Club Pennant, Flotilla, or Division, Unit Flags**—shall be flown from 0800 to sunset.

#12 **Yacht Club Officer Flags**—shall be displayed day and night.

#13 **The Coast Guard Ensign**—shall be flown day and night while the facility is under orders with a Coast Guard officer aboard.

#14 **No Signal Mast**—When a boat is equipped with a bow and stern staff, and does not have a signal mast, but has a radio antenna, the Auxiliary ensign may be properly displayed by substituting the antenna for a signal mast. The height of the uppermost portion of the hoist of the Auxiliary ensign should be affixed at a point approximately ⅔ the height of the antenna. *No additional* antennas or outriggers may be utilized.

#15 **A Facility Under Official Orders** (STATUS 2) shall be permitted to fly the Auxiliary officer's pennant or burgee, in addition to the U.S. and Auxiliary ensigns. All other flags—yacht ensign, USPS ensign, yacht club pennants, officer flags, flotilla, division, etc. *shall not* be flown.

#16 **Coast Guard Officer Aboard Facilities Under Orders** (STATUS 3) the Coast Guard Ensign substitutes for the Auxiliary ensign; *all* other flags except the national ensign shall be taken down. This includes Auxiliary officer pennants or burgees, yacht ensign, unit flags, USPS ensign, yacht or boat club flags, etc.—only two flags shall be permitted—the national ensign and the Coast Guard ensign.

## SEE UNITED STATES COAST GUARD AUXILIARY FLAGS IN FULL COLOR, PAGE V

# RULES FOR SMALL PASSENGER VESSELS

Rules and regulations for small passenger vessels were prescribed under the Act of May 10, 1956, (Public Law 519) and their provisions made effective as of June 1, 1958. (Copies of the new rules and regulations (CG-323) may be purchased from U. S. Coast Guard Headquarters, Washington 25, D. C.)

Under this act a "passenger-carrying vessel" means any vessel which carries *more than six passengers* and which is:

(1) Propelled in whole or in part by steam or by any form of mechanical or electrical power and is of 15 gross tons or less; or

(2) Propelled in whole or in part by steam or by any form of mechanical or electrical power and is of more than 15 gross tons and less than 100 gross tons and not more than 65 feet in length measured from end to end over the deck excluding sheer; or

(3) Propelled by sail and is of 700 gross tons or less; or

(4) Non self-propelled and is of 100 gross tons or less.

A few exceptions are made, including: certain foreign vessels; vessels operating on non-navigable waters of the United States; vessels laid up and out of commission; public vessels; and lifeboats.

Vessels subject to the act must be inspected by the Officer in Charge, Marine Inspection, U. S. Coast Guard, from whom applications for inspection are obtained.

Certificates of inspection are valid for three years. They describe the area in which the vessel may operate; minimum crew required; maximum number of passengers; minimum lifesaving and firefighting equipment required, etc.

Effective June 1, 1959, no person holding only a "motorboat operator's license" is permitted to operate vessels subject to this law. The scope of licenses issued under the act varies according to the waters plied. For offshore waters, an "ocean operator's license" is issued. Within the coastline and on the Great Lakes, the license is an "operator's license" (illustrated herewith). Licenses are valid for 5 years; application is to be made on Coast Guard Form CG-866, to the nearest U. S. Coast Guard Officer in Charge, Marine Inspection.

Of particular interest to yachtsmen and boatmen who use their craft exclusively for pleasure is the definition, in the regulations, of a passenger. "A passenger is every person other than the master and the members of the crew or other persons employed or engaged in any capacity on board a vessel in the business of that vessel." (There are, however, certain exceptions, for example: aboard vessels on international voyages, children under one year of age; the owner or his representative; members of a paid crew; employees of the owner or charterer; and persons aboard tugs and towboats not over 50 gross tons who have not contributed for their carriage.) Most important exception, insofar as the yachtsman is concerned, is the following: *"any guest on board a vessel which is being used exclusively for pleasure purposes who has not contributed any consideration, directly or indirectly, for his carriage."*

The type of license now issued by the Coast Guard to operators of small passenger vessels (carrying more than six passengers) within the coastline and on the Great Lakes

---

## RADIO LICENSE FEES CHANGED
(See Pages 491-492)

The Federal Communications Commission has raised fees for radio station licenses, station licenses plus interim authorizations, station license renewals, and restricted operators' permits. At the time these fees were raised, the subject pages (491-492) were on the press for this edition.

The new fees are: station license, $20; station license plus interim authorization, $25; station license renewal, $20; and restricted operator permit, $8. The fee for a Third Class operator permit remains at $3. If an operator permit is lost, or becomes so mutilated it is illegible, a duplicate will be issued for the same fee as a new permit of the same grade.

# Bilge Ventilation

Gasoline in its liquid and vapor states is potentially dangerous, but this fact need *not* make recreational boating hazardous. All that is required is a respect for its potential, combined with safe boat construction and sensible operating procedures. To enjoy safe boating, one need only follow Coast Guard regulations and good common sense.

## WHEN REQUIRED

The "proper and efficient" ventilation of boat bilges was established as a requirement by the Motorboat Act of 1940 for all boats employing volatile fuels (gasoline) with certain limited exceptions. These are:

(1) Boats constructed before the effective date of the Act, 25 April 1940.

(2) Boats of "open" construction.

### Open construction defined

The Coast Guard has prepared a set of specifications to guide the boat owner as to whether his craft meets the definition of "open construction." To qualify for exemption from the bilge ventilation regulations, the boat must meet *all* of the following conditions.

(1) As a minimum, engine and fuel tank compartments must have 15 square inches of open area directly exposed to the atmosphere for each cubic foot of *net* compartment volume. (Net volume is found by determining total volume and then subtracting the volume occupied by the engine, tanks, other accessories, etc.)

(2) Fuel and engine compartments must have at least one square inch of open area per cubic foot within one inch of the compartment bilge level, or floor, so that vapors (which are heavier than air) can drain out into open areas.

(3) There must be no long or narrow unventilated spaces accessible from the engine or fuel tank compartments into which a fire could spread, unless the space meets requirements of item 4 below.

(4) Long, narrow compartments, such as side panels, if joining engine or fuel tank compartments and not serving as ducts, must have at least 15 square inches of open area per cubic foot through frequent openings along the compartment's full length.

### Be safe—be sure

If your craft does not meet one or more of the specifications above, or if there is *any* doubt, *play it safe and provide an adequate ventilation system.* To err on the safe side will not be costly; it may save a great deal, perhaps even a life.

### Diesel-powered boats

Diesel fuel does not come within the Coast Guard's definition of a "volatile" fuel, and thus bilge ventilation legal requirements are not applicable. It is, however, a sensible step to provide essentially the same ventilation system for your boat even if it is diesel-powered.

## VENTILATION FUNDAMENTALS

If a boat will entrap fumes, i.e., it is not an "open" boat, it is required to have at least two ventilator ducts fitted with cowls at their openings to the atmosphere.

The ventilators, ducts, and cowls must be installed so that they provide for efficient removal of explosive or flammable gases from bilges of *each* engine and fuel tank compartment. Intake ducting must be installed to extend from the cowls to at least midway to the bilge or at least below the level of the carburetor air intake. Exhaust ducting must be installed to extend from the lower portion of the bilge to the cowls in the open atmosphere. Ducts should not be installed so low in the bilge that they could become obstructed by a normal accumulation of bilge water.

Cowls attached to intake and exhaust ducts should be located and trimmed for maximum effectiveness, and so as to prevent recirculation of fumes through the bilges.

## ACTIONS OF 1966-67

The Coast Guard in 1966 and 1967 took action to implement much more stringently existing laws and regulations regarding "proper and efficient" bilge ventilation. The law did not change, only the interpretation and enforcement thereof. The tightened regulations are for the safety of the craft and those aboard—a wise skipper cheerfully complies and does more than meet minimum requirements.

## ACCEPTABLE VENTILATION SYSTEMS

No foolproof ventilation system has been developed. The efficiency of various shaped cowls and ducts, the size and location of components, the capacity of mechanical blowers, and the choice of materials are all related to safety. There is no such thing as a ventilation system "approved by the Coast Guard." There has been, however, a great deal of study and thought, some testing, and years of experience upon which to base requirements. These have led to the conclusion that, as a *minimum*, fresh air must be ducted into *each* engine and fuel tank compartment, and dangerous fumes ducted out of the craft.

To create a flow through the ducting system, at least when underway or when there is a wind, cowls (scoops) or other fittings of equal effectiveness are needed on all ducts. A wind-actuated rotary exhauster or mechanical blower is considered equivalent to a cowl on an exhaust duct.

### Ducts required

If it wasn't clear before, there's no mistaking it now: *ducts* are a necessary part of the ventilation system. A mere hole in the hull won't do; that's a vent, not a ventilator. "Vents," the Coast Guard explains, "are openings that permit venting, or escape of gasses due to pressure differential. Ventilators are openings that must be fitted with *cowls* to direct the flow of air and vapors in or out of *ducts* that channel movement of air for the actual displacement of fumes from the space being ventilated."

### Ducting materials

For safety and long life, ducts should be made of non-ferrous, galvanized ferrous, or sturdy high-temperature-resistant non-metallic materials. Ducts should be routed clear of, and protected from, contact with hot engine surfaces. Text continued on page 494(d)

STERN-DRIVE RUNABOUT—Note that all engine and fuel tank compartments need to be efficiently ventilated. Hence, not only the engine area aft should be ducted, but the fuel compartment forward also. As on all installations, an electric exhaust blower is recommended, to be installed externally if it is not of the sealed or arcless type.

STERN-DRIVE INSTALLATION—Be sure the cowls are arranged to prevent the exhaust being picked up by the intake. If you can't spread them sufficiently apart horizontally (4 feet), to achieve this you probably can work it out by arranging one higher than the other. Where a power-driven exhaust blower is used in a *separate* duct, its duct may terminate in a flush fitting without a cowl. If the blower is in a natural ventilation duct, a cowl must be used and located so as to be in a normal suction situation.

INSTALLATION WHERE TRANSOM FUEL TANK IS USED—The requirements remain the same: at least two cowl-fitted ventilators properly ducted and of sufficient capacity.

INSTALLATION WHERE AFT SEAT IS USED—Where the fuel tank is under a stern seat, ventilate as illustrated in the diagram. It's a good idea to be sure you can get to the tank quickly, if for nothing else, to inspect it. Hinge the seat if it is not already so constructed.

Wind Activated Rotary
Exhauster Head

Exhaust Duct

Fuel Tank

Intake Cowl

Intake Duct

INBOARD CRUISER INSTALLATION—A wind-activated rotary exhauster head may be substituted for a cowl. Note the good practice of locating the inlet and exhaust ducts on *opposite* sides of the boat to aid in preventing recirculation of vapors back into the bilges.

INBOARD CRUISER INSTALLATION—Note below the recommended practice for larger cruisers. Two intakes and two exhausts are shown, all cowled and ducted, with power exhaust outlet through the transom.

INTAKE COWL
AND DUCT

INTAKE COWL
AND DUCT

EXHAUST COWL
AND DUCT

EXHAUST COWL
AND DUCT

POWER EXHAUST
OUTLET

## Ventilation systems suitable for cruisers and larger boats

Intake Cowl

Wind Activated Rotary
Exhauster Head

Intake Duct

Exhaust Duct

Fuel Tank

AUXILIARY OR MOTOR SAILER INSTALLATION—Note that under any of the available industry standards the ducting should extend well down into the bilge; this is because gasoline vapors are heavier than air and so sink to the bottom of the hull. It is a good idea to always open the hatch to the engine compartment before starting the engine. This applies whether or not an exhaust blower is used.

### WHEN AUXILIARIES ARE RACING
The U.S. Coast Guard has ruled that "sailboats used for pleasure purposes need not be ventilated when under sail alone and may block off cowls and ducts leading to engine and fuel compartments when under sail alone."

Intake Cowl

Exhaust Cowl or
Blower Motor Outlet

Exhaust Duct

Intake Duct

Fuel Tank

AUXILIARY OR MOTOR SAILER INSTALLATION—Another possible ventilation arrangement is the midship installation instead of the fore and aft one as above.

## NATURAL VS. MECHANICAL VENTILATION

The systems described above provide for ventilation without mechanical assistance. The efficiency of a "natural" ventilation system is greatest when there is a breeze from forward of the beam. This will normally occur when underway or at anchor, and some of the time when in a slip. Although less efficient when the wind is abaft the beam, some scouring effect in bilges may be expected even then.

### Mechanical blowers

To provide a positive means of exhausting vapors when there is little or no movement of air, and especially before starting engines when risk of explosion is greatest, mechanical blowers are *recommended* for engine spaces. This is not, however, a legal requirement.

It is suggested that ducting separate from the natural ventilation system be installed for mechanical blowers. Exhaust blowers should be of the sealed or arcless type, and, if located within the compartment being ventilated, be positioned as high as possible. Blower fan blades or impellers should be non-sparking; if installed in the exhaust duct of the natural ventilation system, they should not interfere with functioning of the duct as a natural ventilator.

Exterior terminations of separate power exhaust ducts may be fitted with flush louvered fittings instead of cowls.

### Positioning of cowls

Normally, the intake cowl will face forward in an area of free airflow underway, and the exhaust cowl will face aft where a suction effect can be expected.

The two cowls, or sets of cowls, should be located with respect to each other, horizontally and/or vertically, so as to prevent return of fumes removed from any space to the same or any other space. Intake cowls should be positioned to avoid pick-up of vapors from fueling operations.

### Air for carburetors

Openings into the engine compartment for entry of air to the carburetor are in addition to requirements of the ventilation system.

### Size of ducts

Ventilation must be adequate for the size and design of the craft. There should be no constriction in the ducting system that is smaller than the minimum cross-sectional area required for reasonable efficiency. Where a stated size of duct is not available, the next *larger* size should be used.

**Small motorboats.** To determine the minimum crosssectional area of the cowls and ducts for motorboats having small engine and/or fuel tank compartments, see Table 10-1, which is based on *net* compartment volume (as previously defined).

**Cruisers and larger boats.** For most cruisers and other large motorboats, Table 10-2, which is based on the craft's beam, is a practical guide for determination of the minimum size of ducts and cowls.

## GENERAL SAFETY PRECAUTIONS

Ventilation systems are *not* designed to remove vapors in large quantities such as might be caused by breaks in fuel lines, leaking tanks, or dripping carburetors. If gas odors are detected, repairs are generally needed.

Before starting the engine, especially on calm days and on boats without a power ventilation system, the engine compartment should be opened to dissipate any vapors that may be present. The smaller the compartment, the quicker an explosive mixture of gasoline vapors can develop.

Regardless of the ventilation system installed, always open hatches and use your nose to detect any gasoline odors. Even the slightest trace should warn you to search for the cause and to ventilate the compartment thoroughly before pressing the starter switch.

## PASSENGER-CARRYING VESSELS

Vessels that carry more than six passengers *for hire* are subject to special regulations. Consult the nearest Coast Guard Marine Inspection Office for details.

| TABLE 10-1 | | | |
|---|---|---|---|
| | One *intake* and One Exhaust System | | Two *Intake and* Two Exhaust Systems |
| Net volume (cu. ft.) | Minimum inside diameter for each duct (inches) | Area sq. in. for cowl | Minimum inside diameter for each duct (inches) |
| Up to 8 | 2 | 3 | |
| 10 | 2¼ | 4 | |
| 12 | 2½ | 5 | |
| 14 | 3¾ | 6 | |
| 17 | 3 | 7 | |
| 20 | 3¼ | 8 | 2½ |
| 23 | 3½ | 10 | 2½ |
| 27 | 3¾ | 11 | 3 |
| 30 | 4 | 13 | 3 |
| 35 | 4¼ | 14 | 3 |
| 39 | 4½ | 16 | 3 |
| 43 | 4¾ | 19 | 3 |
| 48 | 5 | 20 | 3 |

| TABLE 10-2—*Two* Intake and *Two* Exhaust Systems | | |
|---|---|---|
| | Minimum inside | |
| Vessel beam (feet) | diameter for each duct (inches) | (Area square inches) |
| 7 | 3 | 7 |
| 8 | 3¼ | 8 |
| 9 | 3½ | 9 |
| 10 | 3½ | 10 |
| 11 | 3¾ | 11 |
| 12 | 4 | 12 |
| 13 | 4¼ | 13 |
| 14 | 4¼ | 14 |
| 15 | 4½ | 15 |
| 16 | 4½ | 16 |
| 17 | 4½ | 17 |
| 18 | 5 | 18 |
| 19 | 5 | 19 |

# Where To Obtain Charts, Cruising Information, And Other Publications

## CHARTS OF VARIOUS WATERWAYS

**Charts, U. S. Coastal Waters**—Charts of coastal waters such as the Atlantic, Pacific and Gulf Coasts, the Hudson River as far north as Troy, and the Atlantic and Gulf Intracoastal Waterways, are published by the United States Coast & Geodetic Survey, Washington Science Center, Rockville, Md., 20852, and are available from them, their distribution offices, or any of their sales agents, listed semi-annually in the Oceanographic Office Notice to Mariners.

**Charts, Great Lakes**—Charts of the Great Lakes and connecting rivers, Lake Champlain, New York State Canals, Lake of the Woods, and Rainy Lake are available from the U. S. Lake Survey, 630 Federal Bldg., Detroit, Mich. 48226. They also publish a catalog of charts issued by that office.

**Charts, New York State Canals**—A bound booklet of charts of the New York State canals (Champlain, Erie, Oswego, and Cayuga-Seneca), east of Lyons, is available from the U. S. Lake Survey, 630 Federal Bldg., Detroit, Mich. 48226.

**Charts, Mississippi River and Tributaries**—(*Middle & Upper Mississippi River; Cairo, Ill. to Minneapolis, Minn.*)
(*Middle Mississippi River; Cairo, Ill. to Grafton, Ill.*)
(*Mississippi River from Cairo, Ill. to Gulf of Mexico*)
(*Small Boat Navigation Chart; Alton, Ill. to Clarksville on the Mississippi River and Grafton, Ill., to LaGrange, Ill. on the Illinois River*)
(*Illinois Waterways; from Grafton, Ill. to Lake Michigan at Chicago and Calumet Harbors*)
U. S. Army Engineer District, 906 Olive Street, St. Louis, Missouri, 63101.

The offices listed below will supply exhaustive lists of available charts, detailing sources, prices, scales, and exact sections covered.
*Mississippi River and connecting waterways, north of Ohio River*—U. S. Army Engineer Division, North Central, 536 South Clark St., Chicago, Ill. 60605.
*Mississippi River and tributaries, below Ohio River*—Mississippi River Commission, P.O. Box 80, Vicksburg, Miss. 39181. This office also has a free booklet, "Mississippi River Navigation," discussing history, development and navigation of the river.
*Ohio River and tributaries; Pittsburgh, Pa., to the Mississippi River*—U. S. Army Engineer Division, P.O. Box 1159, Cincinnati, Ohio 45201.
*Tennessee and Cumberland Rivers*—U. S. Army Engineer District, P. O. Box 1070, Nashville, Tenn. 37202. Another general information source for the Tennessee is the Tennessee Valley Authority, Maps and Engineering Records Section, 102A Union Bldg., Knoxville, Tenn.
*Missouri River and tributaries*—U. S. Army Engineer District, 6012 U. S. Post Office and Court House, Omaha, Neb. 68102.

**Charts, Canadian Waters**—Charts of Canadian waters are available from Hydrographic Chart Distribution, Canadian Hydrographic Service, Department of Mines and Technical Surveys, 615 Booth St., Ottawa, Canada. These include charts of Canadian coastal waters; Canadian sections of the Great Lakes including Georgian Bay; the St. Lawrence River; Richelieu River; Ottawa River; The Rideau Waterway; and other Canadian lakes, canals, etc.
Prices and details are given in a Coastal and Inland Waters Catalog; indexes of charts for any area in Canada are available free from the address above.

**Charts, Foreign Waters**—These are published by the U. S. Naval Oceanographic Office, Washington, D. C. 20390, and are available through any of the sales agents listed twice a year in Notice to Mariners, published by the U. S. Naval Oceanographic Office. A general catalog and ten regional catalogs are available.

## NOTICE TO MARINERS

**Notice to Mariners**—This is a weekly pamphlet published by the U. S. Naval Oceanographic Office, Washington, D. C. 20390. Is is issued so mariners may keep nautical charts and Coast Pilots up to date. Twice a year the Notices contain lists of Branch Oceanographic offices; U. S. Coast Guard District offices; U. S. Coast & Geodetic Survey District offices; U. S. Engineer offices; agents for the sale of Oceanographic Office charts and publications; data on all publications of the Oceanographic Office; data on the various Coast Pilots, Tide Tables, Current Tables and Tidal Current Charts sold by the U. S. Coast & Geodetic Survey; data on U. S. Coast Guard Light Lists; and a list of agents for the sale of Coast and Geodetic Survey and Coast Guard publications.
Local Notices, of interest primarily within the limits of each of the Coast Guard Districts, are issued by Commanders of the respective districts, and are available from their district offices.

## COAST PILOTS

**Coast Pilots**—For coastal waters, and the Atlantic and Gulf Intracoastal Waterways, these are published by the U. S. Coast and Geodetic Survey, Washington Science Center, Rockville, Md. 20852, and are available from them, their distribution offices, or sales agents as listed semi-annually in Notice to Mariners. These volumes supplement the information given on charts, with detailed descriptions of routes, courses, distances, depths, harbors, sources of supplies, tides, currents, weather, list of yacht clubs, facilities for repairs, etc.
For the Great Lakes and other waters covered by U. S. Lake Survey charts, the publication corresponding to the Coast Pilot is called the Great Lakes Pilot. This is an annual publication, kept up-to-date during the navigation season by seven monthly supplements issued from May to November. It is obtained from the U. S. Lake Survey, 630 Federal Bldg., Detroit, Mich. 48226.
For Canadian waters—available from Hydrographic Chart Distribution, Canadian Hydrographic Office, Dept. of Mines and Technical Surveys, 615 Booth St., Ottawa, Canada. Details are given in the Coastal and Inland Waters Catalog available from Hydrographic Chart Distribution at the address given above. A descriptive list of Pilots and Sailing Directions is also available.

## LIGHT LISTS

**Light Lists**—These are published by the U. S. Coast Guard and are for sale by the Superintendent of Documents, Washington, D. C. 20402, or any of the Coast Guard sales agents listed semi-annually in the Oceanographic Office Notice to Mariners. They describe lighted aids, radio beacons, fog signals, unlighted buoys, and daymarks. Vol. I covers Atlantic Coast from St. Croix River, Me., to Little River, S. C. Vol. II, Atlantic and Gulf Coasts from Little River, S. C., to Rio Grande River, Tex., and the Antilles. Vol. III, Pacific Coast and Islands. Vol. IV, Great Lakes. Vol. V, Mississippi River.

## TIDE AND CURRENT TABLES

**Tide Tables, Current Tables and Tidal Current Charts**—These are also publications of the U. S. Coast & Geodetic Survey, Washington Science Center, Rockville, Md. 20852, and may be obtained from them, their distribution offices, or from any of their sales agents listed semi-annually in Notice to Mariners.

## RULES OF THE ROAD

**Rules of the Road**—Rules of the Road are published for three areas, namely: C.G. No. 169—Certain inland waters of the Atlantic and Pacific coasts and of the coast of the Gulf of Mexico; C.G. No. 172—The Great Lakes and their connecting and tributary waters and the St. Mary's River; and C.G. No. 184—The Western Rivers and the Red River of the North. They are published by the U. S. Coast Guard and copies may be obtained from Coast Guard Marine Inspection Offices in principal ports, or the Commandant (CHS), U. S. Coast Guard, Washington, D. C. 20226.

**Handbook of Boating Laws**—in four editions for Southern, Northeastern, North Central and Western states. Lists state requirements for registering, numbering, equipment and small boat operation; fuel tax laws; boat trailer laws; and applicable federal regulations. Available from Outboard Boating Club, 333 N. Michigan Ave., Chicago, Ill. 60601.

## NEW YORK STATE CANALS

**Rules and Regulations Covering Navigation and Use of the New York State Canal System**—A booklet by this title is published by and is available from New York State Dept. of Public Works, Division of Operation and Maintenance, Albany, N. Y. It contains a description of the New York Canal System, and regulations pertaining to use of the canal. Applications for free season permits to use the canals should be made to the same office.

**Canal Guide Book for the New York State Barge Canal System and Connecting Navigable Waterways**—A booklet of great value in cruising the Hudson River, Lake Champlain, New York State canals, and connecting Canadian waterways, including the St. Lawrence River and parts of Lake Erie and Lake Ontario. Lists sources of supplies such as fuel, oil, engine repairs, fresh water, provisions, anchorage and dockage. Available from Cruising Guide Book, 146 Sheridan Avenue, Albany, N. Y. 12210.

**The Northwest Passage**—Cruise kit and guide book, with charts, for Hudson River, Champlain Canal and Lake Champlain. Division of Motor Boats, New York Conservation Dept., Albany, N. Y. 12226.

**The Grand Canal**—Cruise kit and guide book, with charts, for Erie Canal, Oswego Canal, and the Cayuga Seneca Canals. Division of Motor Boats (address above).

## INTRACOASTAL WATERWAYS

**Waterway Guide**—A publication detailing for the yachtsman a vast amount of information concerning the inland waterways. The Northern Edition covers the coast from Maine to New York; the Middle Atlantic Edition from New York to Sea Island, Ga.; the Southern Edition from Sea Island, Ga., to Florida and Gulf Coast to New Orleans; the Great Lakes Edition from New York to the Great Lakes with connecting Canadian canals and rivers. Available from Waterway Guide, Inc., P. O. Box 2586, Jacksonville, Florida 32203.

**Intracoastal Waterway Booklets**—Comprehensive descriptions of the Intracoastal Waterway, with data on navigation, charts, distances, etc. Prepared by Corps of Engineers, U. S. Army, and sold by Superintendent of Documents, Washington, D. C. 20402. In two sections: (1) Atlantic Section, Boston to Key West, (2) Gulf Section, Key West to Brownsville, Tex.

**Intracoastal Waterway Bulletins**—Frequent bulletins giving latest information on the condition of the Intracoastal Waterway are published by the Corps of Engineers. These are available from the following District Offices of the Army Engineers: Foot of Front St., Norfolk, Va. 23510; P. O. Box 1890, Wilmington, N. C. 28402; P. O. Box 905, Charleston, S. C. 29402; P. O. Box 889, Savannah, Ga. 31402; P. O. Box 4970, Jacksonville, Fla. 32201; P. O. Box 1169, Mobile, Ala. 36601; P. O. Box 1229, Galveston, Tex. 77551.

## OTHER CRUISING PUBLICATIONS

**Cruising Charts, Guides and Booklets**—Some of the large oil companies provide free cruising services for yachtsmen. These companies will go to considerable length to provide such items as cruising charts from which the itinerary can be planned, harbor booklets showing the facilities available in all the principal ports, mimeographed outlines of various cruises containing a digest of up-to-date information on the waterways involved, etc. Sources for this kind of material include: Texaco Waterways Service, 135 E. 42nd St., New York 17, N. Y.; Gulf Tourgide Bureau, Box 8056, Philadelphia 1, Pa. (east of Mississippi); Mobil Touring Service, Mobil Oil Co., 150 E. 42nd St., New York 17, N. Y.; Esso Touring Service, 15 W. 51st St., New York 19, N. Y.

**The Yachtsman's Guide and Nautical Calendar**—A valuable handbook of boating and cruising information—tide and current tables, coast pilot data, charts, courses, distance tables, yacht club directory, buoyage, nautical terms, flag etiquette, knots and splices, piloting hints, etc. Published annually by Motor Boating, 959 Eighth Ave., New York, N. Y. 10019.

**Cruising Guide to the New England Coast**—Descriptions of harbors, anchorages, and waterways by Fessenden Blanchard. Includes Hudson River, Long Island Sound and the New Brunswick coast. Available from Sailing Book Service, 34 Oak Ave., Tuckahoe, N. Y. 10707.

**Cruising Guide to the Southern Coast**—Blanchard's guide to the Intracoastal Waterway—Norfolk to New Orleans, including other Florida waterways. Sailing Book Service (address above).

**Cruising Guide to the Chesapeake**—Another Blanchard guide, with a wealth of information on Chesapeake Bay. Sailing Book Service (address above).

**Yachtsman's Guide to Northern Harbors**—Harbors, boat basins and services around Long Island, and seacoast of New England. Seaport Publishing Co., 843 Delray Ave., S.E., Grand Rapids 6, Mich.

**Guide for Cruising Maryland Waters**—Prepared by Maryland Dept. of Tidewater Fisheries. Twenty full-color charts, with more than 200 courses and distances plotted. Maryland Board of Natural Resources, State Office Bldg., Annapolis, Md. Available from the same address is the booklet Maryland Marine Facilities.

**Chesapeake Bay Country**—With map in color of Chesapeake Bay country and tributaries, indexed marine facilities, and fishing grounds, Dept. of Tidewater Fisheries, Annapolis, Md. Boating Handbook for Maryland Waters also available.

**Boating Atlas of Tidewater Virginia**—An atlas of 53 charts in full color covering the ocean front, lower Chesapeake Bay, the James, York, Rappahannock and Potomac Rivers. Includes buoyage system, rules of the road, location of marine facilities, state and Coast Guard regulations, notes from the Coast Pilot, Tide Tables, safety suggestions, and a course protractor. Distributed by Paxton Co., 1019 Main St., Norfolk, Va.

**Florida Boating**—Pamphlet giving data on waterways, charts, Florida boat registration, and water safety regulations, fishing licenses, area maps and information, plus a directory of marine facilities throughout the state. Available from Florida Development Commission, Carlton Bldg., Tallahassee, Fla.

**Yachtsman's Guide to the Great Lakes**—Harbors, services, supplies on the Great Lakes, St. Lawrence, Richelieu and Hudson Rivers, Lake Champlain, and New York State Barge Canal. Seaport Publishing Co., 843 Delray Ave., S. E., Grand Rapids, Mich. 49506.

**Cruising the Georgian Bay**—Cruising information, with 23 pages of Ontario Government Aerial Survey Maps and tabulations of services and facilities at ports. Bellhaven House, 12 Dyas Road, Don Mills, Ontario.

**Cruising the North Channel**—Covers the waterway between Manitoulin Island and the north shore of Lake Huron. Bellhaven House, see address above.

**Cruising the Trent-Severn Waterway**—A cruising guide, including rules and regulations, supply points and services, mileages and general data. British Book Service, see address above.

**Trailer Boating Where the North Begins**—Written especially for the small boatman, and includes the Muskoka, Parry Sound, and Lake-of-Bays areas of Ontario. Bellhaven House, see address above.

**Harbor Guide to the Upper Mississippi River**—From Minneapolis to St. Louis, including St. Croix River. Covers harbors (services and location), cities and towns (population, transportation, shopping centers, tourist interest), locks and dams, mileage charts, source of navigation charts, history of river. Available from Mildred Quimby, 801 South Michigan, Prairie du Chien, Wisconsin.

**Yachtsman's Guide to the Bahamas**—A complete guide book for a cruise in the Bahamas. The data it contains is much like the information found in Coast Pilots. The Customs and Immigration information will be found especially valuable to those who have never cruised to foreign waters. Available from Tropic Isle Publishers, Inc., P. O. Box 613, Coral Gables, Fla. 33134.

**Yachtsman's Guide to the Caribbean**—Island, port and anchorage charts on courses from Florida through the Bahamas to the Greater Antilles and the Leeward and Windward Islands; lists of facilities, refueling places, customs and port formalities on all islands in the Caribbean. Seaport Publishing Co., 843 Delray Ave. S. E., Grand Rapids, Mich. 49506.

**The Alluring Antilles**—This cruising guide provides accurate, precise and ample information about every island in the West Indies. D. Van Nostrand Co., Inc., 120 Alexander St., Princeton, N. J. 08540.

**Virgin Islands**—Eggleston's descriptions of islands, harbors, people, history, passages, and facilities. Illustrated. Sailing Book Service, 34 Oak Avenue, Tuckahoe, N. Y. 10707.

## U. S. COAST GUARD PUBLICATIONS

**Recreational Boating Guide**—CG-340. 77 pp. Information on boat numbering; legal minimum equipment requirements; other equipment you should carry; responsibilities when operating; aids to navigation; hints on safety afloat; emergency procedures; and U. S. Coast Guard Auxiliary services. Contains copies of Federal Boating Act of 1958, and the Motorboat Act of April 25, 1940; sample of Application for Number form; Boating Accident Report; and Radio Distress Information Sheet. Superintendent of Documents, Government Printing Office, Washington, D. C. 20402.

**Pleasure Craft**—CG-290. Digest of boating laws and regulations. Numbering. Boating accidents. Sales to aliens. Law enforcement. Documentation. C. G. approved equipment. Equipment requirements. Suggestions for safety. U. S. Coast Guard offices.

**Aids to Marine Navigation of the United States**—U. S. Coast Guard publication CG-193. Illustrated. 32 pages. U. S. Coast Guard, Washington, D. C. 20226. Basic principles underlying the marking of coasts and waterways with lighthouses, lightships, fog signals, radiobeacons, loran, and buoys. Treats primarily of the manner in which the physical characteristics of various aids to navigation serve the mariner.

**Marine Radiobeacons**—U. S. Coast Guard. 16 pp. Obtainable from U. S. Coast Guard, Washington, D. C. 20226. Instructional pamphlet for the beginner studying navigation.

**Ocean Electronic Navigational Aids**—U. S. Coast Guard pamphlet CG 157-1. 73 pp. Loran, radiobeacon and radarbeacon systems; and loran, radio direction finder and radar ship equipment. Available from Superintendent of Documents, Washington, D. C. 20402.

**Rules and Regulations for Uninspected Vessels**—U. S. Coast Guard. 16 pages. Copies may be obtained from District Coast Guard Offices. Requirements for all vessels not subject to inspection, including those subject to the Motorboat Act of April 25, 1940. Every motorboat owner should obtain a copy. Refer to CG-258.

**Rules and Regulations for Numbering Undocumented Vessels**—U. S. Coast Guard publication CG-267. Available from District Coast Guard Offices or the Commandant (CHS), U. S. Coast Guard, Washington, D. C. 20226.

**Rules and Regulations for Small Passenger Vessels**—U. S. Coast Guard publication CG-323. Requirements for vessels carrying more than six passengers. Available from District Coast Guard Offices, or the Commandant, U. S. Coast Guard, Washington, D. C., 20226.

**Manual for Lifeboatmen and Able Seamen**—Illustrated. 63 pages. Obtainable from the U. S. Coast Guard, Washington, D. C. 20226. Lifeboats, life rafts, life floats, buoyant apparatus, davits, and releasing gear are described. Refer to C.G. 175.

## GASOLINE TAX REFUNDS

**Gasoline Tax Refunds**—Some states allow a refund, in whole or in part, of the gasoline tax when the fuel is used for boat purposes. However, the regulations differ greatly and it would be well for the yachtsman to become familiar with these regulations in advance.

## MISCELLANEOUS PUBLICATIONS
## OF THE OCEANOGRAPHIC OFFICE

The Oceanographic Office produces charts and Sailing Directions (Pilots) and lists of lights of all oceans and seas, and of foreign coasts and islands and harbors, but only general charts of the coasts of the United States.

### Information on Oceanographic Office Charts and Publications. H. O. Pub. 1-N. Catalog listing some of the more popular index charts, world charts, general nautical charts, magnetic charts, pilot charts, bathymetric charts, special charts, plotting charts, oceanographic and bottom sediment charts, aeronautical charts, loran charts, published by the U. S. Navy Oceanographic Office, with information on H. O. nautical, aeronautical and oceanographic publications. Free Introduction, Part I, is a general listing.

### Sailing Directions are books supplementing the nautical charts issued by the Oceanographic Office. They contain descriptions of coast lines, harbors, dangers, aids, port facilities, and other data which cannot be conveniently shown on charts.

### Notice to Mariners containing corrections to nautical charts and publications are issued weekly by the Oceanographic Office, Branch Oceanographic Offices, and United States Consulates.

### Daily Memorandum carries a synopsis of the latest information relating to dangers and aids to navigation, including reports of drifting buoys, wreckage, and other hazards together with advance items that will appear in the Notice to Mariners. The Daily Memorandum is issued locally by the Branch Oceanographic Offices and the most urgent of the reports are also broadcast by radio under the title, Government Hydro All Ships and Stations, and rebroadcast locally.

### Pilot Charts of the North Atlantic Ocean, North Pacific Ocean are issued monthly. These present information on average winds and currents, percentages of gales and calms, and other hydrographic data of a varied nature.

### H.O. Pilot Charts

#576 Atlas of Pilot Charts—South Atlantic Ocean and Central American Waters.
#577 Atlas of Pilot Charts—South Pacific, Indian Oceans.
#1400 Pilot Chart of the North Atlantic Ocean (Monthly).
#1401 Pilot Chart of the North Pacific Ocean (Monthly).

### H.O. Lists of Lights and Fog Signals

Light Lists published by the Oceanographic Office give detailed descriptions of navigational lights and fog signals, and mention signals of various kinds operated at lighthouses.
Vol. I covers the Coast of North and South America (only the seacoast lights of the United States), the West Indies, and the Hawaiian Islands.
Vol. II covers islands of the Pacific and Indian Oceans, Australia, Asia, and the East Coast of Africa.
Vol. III covers the West Coasts of Europe and Africa, the Mediterranean Sea, Black Sea, and the Sea of Azov.
Vol. IV covers the British Islands, English Channel, and North Sea.
Vol. V covers Norway, Iceland, and Arctic Ocean.
Vol. VI covers the Baltic Sea with Kattegat, Belts and Sound, and Gulf of Bothnia.
Volumes I, II, III, are revised and reissued annually and Volumes IV, V, VI at less frequent intervals. Volumes IV, V, VI are corrected by annual supplements containing changes that have taken place during the year or years since the books were published. These supplements are mailed free of charge to purchasers of the books. Weekly corrections to the Light Lists are published in the section, Corrections to H.O. Light Lists, at the end of the Notice to Mariners. This section includes minor corrections not appearing in the main body of the Notice.

### Other H. O. Publications of the Oceanographic Office

Chart #1—Nautical Chart Symbols and Abbreviations.
#9 American Practical Navigator. Originally by Nathaniel Bowditch, LL.D. etc. Revised (Including the Useful Tables.)
#234 Breakers and Surf; Principles in Forecasting.
#601 Wind, Sea, and Swell: Theory of Relations in Forecasting.

#602 Wind Waves at Sea, Breakers and Surf.
#102 International Code of Signals.
#117 Radio Navigational Aids. Marine Direction-Finding Stations, Radiobeacons, Time Signals, Navigational Warnings, Distress Signals, Medical Advice and Quarantine Stations, Loran, Consol, and Regulations Governing the Use of Radio in Territorial Waters.
#118 Radio Weather Aids. General weather information, broadcast schedules, international index numbers with locations of stations, key groups, and call signs.
#151 Tables of Distances Between Ports.
#2100 World Star Chart.
#2102D Star Finder and Identifier (AN Type).
#226 Handbook of Magnetic Compass Adjustment and Compensation.

### WEATHER

### Weather Forecasting—U. S. Department of Commerce, Weather Bureau. Illustrated. 40 pages. Generally accepted facts and theories of meteorology and some of the principles of weather forecasting, in popular style. Atmospheric Pressure, Circulation of the Atmosphere, Weather Forecasting, and An Atmospheric Survey, concerning the gathering of information by the Weather Bureau stations for weather maps. Superintendent of Documents, Washington, D. C. 20402.

### The Hurricane—United States Department of Commerce, Weather Bureau. Illustrated. 22 pages. An interesting paper dealing solely with the hurricane. The general information contained in this publication should be known by all who go to sea. Superintendent of Documents, Washington, D. C. 20402.

### Circular R. W. B. 1151 Preparation and Use of Weather Maps at Sea—U. S. Department of Commerce, Weather Bureau. Illustrated. 100 pages. The Ship's weather observation, Radio weather message and its uses, Radio weather bulletins, Preparation of weather maps, Weather types, Tropical storms. Drawing inferences from weather map.

### The Daily Weather Map—United States Department of Commerce, Weather Bureau. Five weather maps of the United States are included, data for which are prepared from observations taken daily at hundreds of stations throughout North America. A complete explanation of the maps, including all symbols and tables used in plotting the data appears on the reverse side of the Sunday map only. Superintendent of Documents, Washington, D. C. 20402.

### MISCELLANEOUS PUBLICATIONS

### Rules of the Nautical Road—U. S. Naval Institute, Annapolis, Md. Revised edition by Lt. Alfred Prunski, U.S.C.G., of the textbook by Captain Raymond F. Farwell, U.S.N.R., designed to show new changes in International Rules which took effect January 1, 1954. Gives comparison with up-to-date Inland Rules and Pilot Rules. Includes interpretations of rules by courts.

### The American Nautical Almanac—United States Naval Observatory. Copies purchased from the Superintendent of Documents. A compact publication containing all the ephemeris material essential to the solution of problems of navigational position. Contains a Star Chart which shows the position of the stars used in navigation. Instructions for its use are included. The Star Chart may be purchased separately. (Star Chart in larger form may be purchased from Oceanographic Office sales agents.)

### Tide and Current Investigations of the Coast and Geodetic Survey—U. S. Coast and Geodetic Survey, Washington, D. C. 20230. Illustrated. 50 pages. Types and forms of tides, earthquake waves, tidal currents, and wind currents.

### First Aid—Supt. of Documents, Washington, D. C. 20402. Illustrated. 160 pages. This is one of the best first aid manuals obtainable. Only first aid instruction is given.

### Miscellaneous Publication No. 9. The Ship's Medicine Chest and First Aid at Sea—United States Public Health Service. Illustrated. 498 pages. Prepared especially for seafaring people. An excellent treatise. Sections included give special instruction for emergency treatment, and First Aid by Radio. (Superintendent of Documents, Washington, D. C. 20402.)

### Magnetic Poles and the Compass—U. S. Coast and Geodetic Survey. Superintendent of Documents, Washington, D. C. 20402.

# TEXT OF THE MOTORBOAT ACT OF APRIL 25, 1940

As Amended to April 1970 (46 U.S.C. 526-526u)

*An act to amend laws for preventing collisions of vessels, to regulate equipment of certain motorboats on the navigable waters of the United States, and for other purposes*

**B**e it enacted by the Senate and House of Representatives of the United States of America in Congress assembled, That the word "motorboat" where used in this Act shall include every vessel propelled by machinery and not more than sixty-five feet in length except tugboats and towboats propelled by steam. The length* shall be measured from end to end over the deck, excluding sheer: *Provided,* That the engine, boiler, or other operating machinery shall be subject to inspection by the Coast Guard, and to its approval of the design thereof, on all said motorboats, which are more than forty feet in length, and which are propelled by machinery driven by steam. *(46 U.S.C. 526.)*

### Classes of Motorboats

*Sec. 2.* Motorboats subject to the provisions of this Act shall be divided into four classes as follows:

Class A. Less than sixteen feet in length.

Class 1. Sixteen feet or over and less than twenty-six feet in length.

Class 2. Twenty-six feet or over and less than forty feet in length.

Class 3. Forty feet or over and not more than sixty-five feet in length. *(46 U.S.C. 526a.)*

### Lights

*Sec. 3.* Every motorboat in all weathers from sunset to sunrise shall carry and exhibit the following lights when under way, and during such time no other lights which may be mistaken for those prescribed shall be exhibited:

(a) Every motorboat of classes A and 1 shall carry the following lights:

First. A bright white light aft to show all around the horizon.

Second. A combined lantern in the fore part of the vessel and lower than the white light aft, showing green to starboard and red to port, so fixed as to throw the light from right ahead to two points abaft the beam on their respective sides.

(b) Every motorboat of classes 2 and 3 shall carry the following lights:

First. A bright white light in the fore part of the vessel as near the stem as practicable, so constructed as to show an unbroken light over an arc of the horizon of twenty points of the compass, so fixed as to throw the light ten points on each side of the vessel; namely, from right ahead to two points abaft the beam on either side.

Second. A bright white light aft to show all around the horizon and higher than the white light forward.

Third. On the starboard side a green light so constructed as to show an unbroken light over an arc of the horizon of ten points of the compass, so fixed as to throw the light from right ahead to two points abaft the beam on the starboard side. On the port side a red light so constructed as to show an unbroken light over an arc of the horizon of ten points of the compass, so fixed as to throw the light from right ahead to two points abaft the beam on the port side. The said side lights shall be fitted with inboard screens of sufficient height so set as to prevent these lights from being seen across the bow.

(c) Motorboats of classes A and 1 when propelled by sail alone shall carry the combined lantern, but not the white light aft, prescribed by this section. Motorboats of classes 2 and 3, when so propelled, shall carry the colored side lights, suitably screened, but not the white lights, prescribed by this section. **Motorboats of all classes, when so propelled, shall carry, ready at hand, a lantern or flashlight showing a white light which shall be exhibited in sufficient time to avert collision.

(d) Every white light prescribed by this section shall be of such character as to be visible at a distance of at least two miles. Every colored light prescribed by this section shall be of such character as to be visible at a distance of at least one mile. The word "visible" in this Act, when applied to lights, shall mean visible on a dark night with clear atmosphere.

(e) When propelled by sail and machinery any motorboat shall carry the lights required by this section for a motorboat propelled by machinery only.

(f) Any motorboat may carry and exhibit the lights required by the Regulations for Preventing Collisions at Sea, 1948, Act of October 11, 1951 (65 Stat. 406-420; 33 U.S.C. 147-147d), as amended, in lieu of the lights required by this section. *(46 U.S.C. 526b.) (Amended by Act of June 4, 1956.)*

### Whistle, Bell and Life Preservers

*Sec. 4.* Every motorboat of class 1, 2, or 3, shall be provided with an efficient whistle or other sound-producing mechanical appliance. *(46 U.S.C. 526c.)*

*Sec. 5.* Every motorboat of class 2 or 3 shall be provided with an efficient bell. *(46 U.S.C. 526d.)*

*Sec. 6.* Every motorboat subject to any of the provisions of this Act and also all vessels propelled by machinery other than by steam more than sixty-five feet in length shall carry at least one life preserver, or life belt, or ring buoy, or other device of the sort prescribed by the regulations of the Commandant of the Coast Guard, for each person on board, so placed as to be readily accessible: *Provided,* That every such motorboat and every such vessel propelled by machinery other than by steam more than sixty-five feet in length carrying passengers for hire shall carry so placed as to be readily accessible at least one life preserver of the sort prescribed by the regulations of the Commandant of the Coast Guard, for each person on board. *(46 U.S.C. 526e.)*

### Licensed Operator

*Sec. 7.* No such motorboat, and no other vessel of fifteen gross tons or less propelled by machinery other than steam, while carrying passengers for hire, shall be operated or navigated except in charge of a person duly licensed for such service by the Secretary of the department in which the Coast Guard is operating. Whenever any person applies to be licensed as operator of any motorboat, or of any other vessel of fifteen gross tons or less propelled by machinery, carrying passengers for hire, the Secretary shall make diligent inquiry as to his character, and shall carefully examine the applicant orally as well as the proofs which he presents in support of his claim, and if the Secretary is satisfied that his capacity, experience, habits of living, and character are such to warrant the belief that he can safely be entrusted with the duties and responsibilities of the station for which he makes application, the Secretary shall grant him a license authorizing him to discharge such duties on any such motorboat, or on any other vessel of fifteen gross tons or less propelled by machinery, carrying passengers for hire, for the term of five years. Such license shall be subject to suspension or revocation on the same grounds and in the same manner with like procedure as is provided in the case of suspension or revocation of license of officers under the provisions of section 4450 of the Revised Statutes, as amended (U.S.C. 1952 edition, title 46, sec. 239): *Provided,* That motorboats and other vessels of fifteen gross tons or less propelled by machinery shall not be required to carry licensed officers except as required in this Act: *And provided further,* That licenses herein prescribed shall not be required of motorboats or of any other vessels of fifteen gross tons or less propelled by machinery engaged in fishing contests previously arranged and announced. *(46 U.S.C. 526f.) (Amended by Act of May 10, 1956.)*

### Fire Extinguishers

*Sec. 8.* Every motorboat and also every vessel propelled by machinery other than by steam more than sixty-five feet in length shall be provided with such number, size, and type of fire extinguishers, capable of promptly and effectually extinguishing burning gasoline, as may be prescribed by the regulations of the Commandant of the Coast Guard, which fire extinguishers shall be at all times kept in condition for immediate and effective use and shall be so placed as to be readily accessible. *(46 U.S.C. 526g.)*

### Racing Outboards Exempt

*Sec. 9.* The provisions of sections 4, 5, and 8 of this Act shall not apply to motorboats propelled by outboard motors while competing in any race previously arranged and announced or, if such boats be designed and intended solely for racing, while engaged in such navigation as is incidental to the tuning up of the boats and engines for the race. *(46 U.S.C. 526h.)*

### Flame Arresters

*Sec. 10.* Every motorboat and also every vessel propelled by machinery other than by steam more than sixty-five feet in length shall have the carburetor or carburetors of every engine therein (except outboard motors) using gasoline as fuel, equipped with such efficient flame arrester, backfire trap, or other similar device

* NOTE—The expression "length shall be measured from end to end over the deck excluding sheer" has been interpreted to mean a straight line measurement of the overall length from the foremost part of the vessel to the aftermost part of the vessel. Bowsprits, boomkins, rudders, outboard motor brackets, and similar fittings or attachments are not to be included in the measurement. Length shall be stated in feet and inches.

** Now carry 12-pt. white light aft.

as may be prescribed by the regulations of the Commandant of the Coast Guard: *Provided,* That this section shall apply only to such motorboats or vessls, the construction of which or the replacement of the engine or engines of which is commenced subsequent to the passage of this Act.

### Ventilation of Bilges

*Sec. 11.* Every such motorboat and every such vessel, except open boats, using as fuel any liquid of a volatile nature, shall be provided with such means as may be prescribed by regulations of the Commandant of the Coast Guard for properly and efficiently ventilating the bilges of the engine and fuel tank compartments so as to remove any explosive or inflammable gases: *Provided,* That this section shall apply only to such motorboats or vessels, the construction or decking over of which is commenced subsequent to the passage of this Act.

### Pilot Rules Not Required

*Sec. 12.* Motorboats shall not be required to carry on board copies of the pilot rules.

### Negligent Operation

*Sec. 13.* (a) No person shall operate any motorboat or any vessel in a reckless or negligent manner so as to endanger the life, limb, or property of any person. To "operate" means to navigate or otherwise use a motorboat or a vessel.

(b) In the case of collision, accident, or other casualty involving a motorboat or other vessel subject to this Act, it shall be the duty of the operator, if and so far as he can do so without serious danger to his own vessel, or persons aboard, to render such assistance as may be practicable and necessary to other persons affected by the collision, accident, or casualty in order to save them from danger caused by the collision, accident, or casualty. He shall also give his name, address, and identification of his vessel to any person injured and to the owner of any property damaged. The duties imposed by this subsection shall be in addition to any duties otherwise provided by law.

(c) In the case of collision, accident, or other casualty involving a motorboat or other vessel subject to this Act, the operator thereof, if the collision, accident, or other casualty results in death or injury to any person, or damage to property in excess of $100, shall file with the Secretary of the Department within which the Coast Guard is operating, unless such operator is required to file an accident report with the State under section 3 (c) (6) of the Federal Boating Act of 1958, a full description of the collision, accident, or other casualty, including such information as the Secretary may by regulation require.
*(46 U.S.C. 526l.) (Amended by Act of September 2, 1958.)*

### Penalty for Negligent Operation

*Sec. 14.* Any person who shall operate any motorboat or any vessel in a reckless or negligent manner so as to endanger the life, limb, or property of any person shall be deemed guilty of a misdemeanor and on conviction thereof by any court of competent jurisdiction shall be punished by a fine not exceeding $2,000, or by imprisonment for a term of not exceeding one year, or by both such fine and imprisonment, at the discretion of the court. *(46 U.S.C. 526m.)*

### Authority to Arrest

*Sec. 15.* Any officer of the United States authorized to enforce the navigation laws of the United States, shall have power and authority to swear out process and to arrest and take into custody, with or without process, any person who may commit any act or offense prohibited by section 13, or who may violate any provision of said section: *Provided,* That no person shall be arrested without process for any offense not committed in the presence of some one of the aforesaid officials: *Provided further,* That whenever an arrest is made under the provisions of this Act, the person so arrested shall be brought forthwith before a commissioner, judge, or court of the United States for examination of the offense alleged against him, and such commissioner, judge, or court shall proceed in respect thereto as authorized by law in cases of crimes against the United States. *(46 U.S.C. 526n.)*

### Penalties for Other Violations

*Sec. 16.* If any motorboat or vessel subject to any of the provisions of this Act is operated or navigated in violation of this Act or any regulation issued thereunder, the owner or operator, either one or both of them, shall, in addition to any other penalty prescribed by law be liable to a penalty of $100: *Provided,* That in the case of motorboats or vessels subject to the provisions of this Act carrying passengers for hire, a penalty of $200 shall be imposed on the owner or operator, either one or both of them, thereof for any violation of section 6, 7, or 8 of this Act or of any regulations pertaining thereto. For any penalty incurred under this section the motorboat or vessel shall be liable and may be proceeded against by way of libel in the district court of any district in which said motorboat or vessel may be found.
*(46 U.S.C. 526o.) (Amended by Act of September 2, 1958.)*

### Regulations and Enforcement

*Sec. 17.* The Commandant of the Coast Guard shall establish all necessary regulations required to carry out in the most effective manner all of the provisions of this Act, and such regulations shall have the force of law. The Commandant of the Coast Guard or any officer of the Coast Guard authorized by the Commandant may, upon application therefor, remit or mitigate any fine, penalty, or forfeiture incurred under this Act or any regulation thereunder relating to motorboats or vessels, except the penalties provided for in section 14 hereunder. The Commandant of the Coast Guard shall establish such regulations as may be necessary to secure the enforcement of the provisions of this Act by any officer of the United States authorized to enforce the navigation laws of the United States. *(46 U.S.C. 526p.)*

*Sec. 18.* The proviso contained in the last paragraph of section 2 of the Act of May 11, 1918 (40 Stat. 549; 46 U.S.C. 223), shall apply also with like force and effect to motorboats as defined in this Act.

Motorboats as defined in this Act are hereby exempted from the provisions of Revised Statutes 4399, as amended (48 Stat. 125; 46 U.S.C. 361). *(46 U.S.C. 526q.)*

### When Act Takes Effect

*Sec. 19.* This Act shall take effect upon its approval as to all of the sections hereof except sections 6, 7, and 8, which sections shall take effect one year from the date of said approval, and for a period of one year from the date of approval of this Act sections 5, 6, and 7 of the Motorboat Act of June 9, 1910 (Public, Numbered 201, Sixty-first Congress; 36 Stat. 462), shall continue in full force and effect, except that from and after the date of the approval of this Act the Secretary of Commerce shall have authority to remit or mitigate all fines or penalties heretofore or hereafter incurred or imposed under sections 5 and 6 of the Motorboat Act of June 9, 1910. Except as hereinabove expressly provided, the Motorboat Act of June 9, 1910, above referred to, is repealed upon the approval of this Act and as to sections 5, 6, and 7 of said Act hereinabove continued the said sections are hereby repealed effective one year from the date of approval of this Act. Nothing in this Act shall be deemed to alter or amend section 4417a of the Revised Statutes (U.S.C., 1934 edition, Supp. IV, title 46, sec. 391a), the Act of August 26, 1935 (U.S.C., 1934 edition, Supp. IV, ch. 7A, secs. 178 and 179), the Act of June 20, 1936 (U.S.C., 1934 edition, Supp. IV, title 46, sec. 367), or repeal Acts of Congress or treaties embodying or revising international rules for preventing collisions at sea. *(46 U.S.C. 526r.)*

*Sec. 20.* There are hereby authorized to be appropriated such sums as may be necessary to carry out the provisions of this Act. *(46 U.S.C. 526s.)*

### Application of Act

*Sec. 22.* (a) This Act shall apply to every motorboat or vessel on the navigable waters of the United States, Guam, the Virgin Islands, the Commonwealth of Puerto Rico, and the District of Columbia, and every motorboat or vessel owned in a State and using the high seas.

(b) As used in this Act—
The term "State" means a State of the United States, Guam, the Virgin Islands, the Commonwealth of Puerto Rico, and the District of Columbia.

(46 U.S.C. 526u.) (Added by Act of September 2, 1958.)
Approved: April 25, 1940 (as amended 1946 Reorganization Plan No. 3, July 16, 1946; 1950 Reorganization Plan No. 26, July 31, 1950; May 10, 1956, June 4, 1956 September 2, 1958, March 28, 1960).

# TEXT OF THE FEDERAL BOATING ACT OF 1958

Public Law 85-911 85th Congress, H. R. 11078
September 2, 1958

*An act to promote boating safety on the navigable waters of the United States, its Territories, and the District of Columbia; to provide coordination and cooperation with the States in the interest of uniformity of boating laws; and for other purposes.*

*Be it enacted by the Senate and House of Representatives of the United States of America in Congress assembled,* That this Act may be cited as the "Federal Boating Act of 1958".

## Definitions

SEC. 2. As used in sections 3 to 5, inclusive, and sections 7 to 13, inclusive, of this Act—

(1) The term "undocumented vessel" means any vessel which is not required to have, and does not have, a valid marine document issued by the Bureau of Customs.

(2) The word "vessel" includes every description of watercraft, other than a seaplane on the water, used or capable of being used as a means of transportation on water.

(3) The word "Secretary" means the Secretary of the Department in which the Coast Guard is operating.

(4) The word "owner" means the person who claims lawful possession of a vessel by virtue of legal title or equitable interest therein which entitles him to such possession.

(5) The term "State" means a State of the United States, a Territory of the United States, and the District of Columbia.

## Numbering of Vessels

SEC. 3. (a) Every undocumented vessel propelled by machinery of more than 10 horsepower, whether or not such machinery is the principal source of propulsion, using the navigable water of the United States, its Territories and the District of Columbia, and every such vessel owned in a State and using the high seas, shall be numbered in accordance with this Act, except—

(1) foreign vessels temporarily using the navigable waters of the United States, its Territories and the District of Columbia;

(2) public vessels of the United States;

(3) State and municipal vessels;

(4) ships' lifeboats; and

(5) vessels designated by the Secretary under section 7 (b) of this Act.

(b) The owner of an undocumented vessel required to be numbered under subsection (a) of this section shall secure a number for such vessel in the State in which it is principally used, in accordance with the State numbering system approved by the Secretary in accordance with subsection (c) of this section, or if no such numbering system has been approved by the Secretary for the State where such vessel is principally used, shall secure a number for such vessel in accordance with subsection (d) of this section.

(c) The Secretary shall establish an overall numbering system for the numbering of vessels required to be numbered under subsection (a) of this section. He shall approve any State system for numbering vessels which is submitted to him which meets the standards set forth below:

(1) The system of numbering shall be in accordance with the overall system of numbering established by the Secretary.

(2) The certificate of number and the number awarded shall be valid for a period not exceeding three years, unless canceled or surrendered, and may be renewed for additional periods.

(3) The number awarded shall be required to be painted on, or attached to, each side of the bow of the vessel for which it was issued, and shall be of such size, color, and type, as may be prescribed by the Secretary. No other number shall be permitted to be carried on the bow of such vessel.

(4) The certificate of number shall be pocket size and shall be required to be at all times available for inspection on the vessel for which issued, whenever such vessel is in use.

(5) The owner shall be required to furnish to a designated State official, notice of the transfer of all or any part of his interest in any numbered vessel, and of the destruction or abandonment of such vessel, within a reasonable time thereof. The owner shall be required to notify a designated State official of any change in his address within a reasonable time of such change.

(6) The State shall require that reports be made to it of accidents involving vessels numbered by it under its numbering system, and shall compile and transmit to the Secretary such statistics on such accidents.

(7) The State shall recognize the validity of a number awarded to any vessel by another State under a numbering system approved by the Secretary under this Act, or awarded a number by the Secretary, for a period of at least ninety days.

(8) In the case of a State having its numbering system approved after April 1, 1960, such State shall accept and recognize any valid certificate of number awarded under subsection (d) of this section for so long as such certificate would otherwise be valid under such subsection (d), except that where such a certificate would remain valid for more than one year after the date when such State's numbering system was approved, the State may accept and recognize the validity of such certificate for a lesser period, but such period shall not end sooner than one year from the date of approval of such system.

(9) The State may exempt any vessel or class of vessels from the numbering provisions of its system if such vessel or class of vessels has been made exempt from the numbering provisions of section 3 (d) by the Secretary under section 7 (b) of this Act.

(10) The States may charge fees in connection with the award of certificates of number and renewals thereof.

(11) The States may require that the operator of a vessel required to be numbered hereunder shall hold a valid safety certificate to be issued under such terms and conditions as may be provided by State law.

(d) The owner of an undocumented vessel required to be numbered under subsection (a) of this section who uses his vessel principally in a State which does not have a numbering system approved by the Secretary under subsection (c) of this section, shall make application to the Secretary, and upon payment of the fee established under section 5, such owner shall be granted a certificate of number containing the number awarded such vessel by the Secretary.

## Certificate Valid Three Years

(e) The certificate of number initially awarded to an owner under subsection (d) of this section shall be valid for three years from the date of the owner's birthday next occurring after the date the certificate of number is issued, unless surrendered or canceled pursuant to regulations of the Secretary. If at the end of such period such ownership has remained unchanged, such owner shall, upon application and payment of the fee established under section 5 of this Act, be granted a renewal of such certificate of number for an additional three-year period.

(f) The number awarded under subsection (c) or (d) of this section shall be painted on, or attached to, each side of the bow of the vessel for which it was issued, and shall be of such size, color, and type as may be prescribed by the Secretary. No other number shall be carried on the bow of such vessel.

(g) The certificate of number granted under subsection (c) or (d) of this section shall be pocket size and shall be required to be at all times available for inspection on the vessel for which issued whenever such vessel is in use, and shall constitute a document in lieu of a marine document that sets forth an official number issued by the Bureau of Customs.

(h) Whenever the Secretary determines that a State is not administering its approved system for numbering vessels in accordance with the standards set forth under subsection (c) of this section, he may withdraw such approval. The Secretary shall not withdraw his approval of a State system of numbering until he has given notice in writing to the State setting forth specifically wherein the State has failed to maintain such standards.

SEC. 4. The owner of any vessel numbered under section 3 (d) of this Act shall furnish to the Secretary notice of the transfer of all or any part of his interest in any numbered vessel, and of the destruction, or abandonment of such vessel, within a reasonable time thereof. The owner shall notify the Secretary of any change in his address within a reasonable time of such change.

Sec. 5. The Secretary may prescribe reasonable fees or charges for the numbering of a vessel, or renewal thereof, under subsections (d) and (e) of section 3 of this Act.

## Motorboat Act Amended

Sec. 6. (a) Section 13 of the Act entitled "An Act to amend laws for preventing collisions of vessels, to regulate equipment of certain motorboats on the navigable waters of the United States, and for other purposes", approved April 25, 1940 (46 U. S. C. 526l), is amended to read as follows:

"Sec. 13. (a) No person shall operate any motorboat or any vessel in a reckless or negligent manner so as to endanger the life, limb, or property of any person. To 'operate' means to navigate or otherwise use a motorboat or a vessel.

"(b) In the case of collision, accident, or other casualty involving a motorboat or other vessel subject to this Act, it shall be the duty of the operator, if and so far as he can do so without serious danger to his own vessel, or persons aboard, to render such assistance as may be practicable and necessary to other persons affected by the collision, accident, or casualty in order to save them from danger caused by the collision, accident, or casualty. He shall also give his name, address, and identification of his vessel to any person injured and to the owner of any property damaged. The duties imposed by this subsection shall be in addition to any duties otherwise provided by law.

"(c) In the case of collision, accident, or other casualty involving a motorboat or other vessel subject to this Act, the operator thereof, if the collision, accident, or other casualty results in death or injury to any person, or damage to property in excess of $100, shall file with the Secretary of the Department within which the Coast Guard is operating, unless such operator is required to file an accident report with the State under section 3 (c) (6) of the Federal Boating Act of 1958, a full description of the collision, accident, or other casualty, including such information as the Secretary may by regulation require."

(b) Section 16 of such Act of April 25, 1940 (46 U. S. C. 526o), is amended by striking out "than that contained in section 14 of this Act".

(c) Such Act of April 25, 1940 (46 U. S. C. 526–526t), is further amended by adding at the end thereof the following new section:

"Sec. 22. (a) This Act shall apply to every motorboat or vessel on the navigable waters of the United States, its Territories and the District of Columbia, and every motorboat or vessel owned in a State and using the high seas.

"(b) As used in this Act—

"The term 'State' means a State of the United States, a Territory of the United States, and the District of Columbia."

Sec. 7. (a) The Secretary shall make such rules and regulations as may be necessary to carry out the provisions of this Act: *Provided,* That such rules and regulations shall be submitted to the Speaker of the House and the President of the Senate when Congress is in session, and shall not become effective until sixty days thereafter.

(b) The Secretary may, from time to time, and for such periods as he may prescribe, exempt any vessel or class of vessels from the numbering provisions of subsection (d) of section 3 of this Act.

## Violations and Penalties

Sec. 8. (a) Whoever being the owner of a vessel required to be numbered under this Act, violates section 3 or 4 of this Act, or regulations established by the Secretary under section 7 of this Act, shall be liable to a penalty of $50 for each violation. Whoever operates a vessel in violation of section 3 of this Act, or regulations established by the Secretary under section 7 of this Act, shall be liable to a penalty of $50 for each violation.

(b) The Secretary may assess and collect any penalty incurred under this Act or any regulations prescribed pursuant to section 7 of this Act. The Secretary may, in his discretion, remit or mitigate any penalty imposed under this section, or discontinue prosecution therefor on such terms as he may deem proper.

(c) Commissioned, warrant, and petty officers of the Coast Guard may board any vessel required to be numbered under this Act at any time such vessel is found upon the navigable waters of the United States, its Territories and the District of Columbia, or on the high seas, address inquiries to those on board, require appropriate proof of identification therefrom, examine the certificate of number issued under this Act, or in the absence of such certificate require appropriate proof of identification of the owner of the vessel, and, in addition, examine such vessel for compliance with this Act, the Act of April 25, 1940, as amended, and the applicable rules of the road.

Sec. 9. It is hereby declared to be the policy of Congress to encourage uniformity of boating laws, rules, and regulations as among the several States and the Federal Government to the fullest extent practicable, subject to reasonable exceptions arising out of local conditions. In the interest of fostering the development, use, and enjoyment of all the waters of the United States it is further declared to be the policy of the Congress hereby to encourage the highest degree of reciprocity and comity among the several jurisdictions. The Secretary, acting under the authority of section 141 of title 14 of the United States Code, shall to the greatest possible extent enter into agreements and other arrangements with the States to insure that there shall be the fullest possible cooperation in the enforcement of both State and Federal statutes, rules, and regulations relating to recreational boating.

## Publication of Accident Reports

Sec. 10. The Secretary is authorized and directed to compile, analyze, and publish, either in summary or detailed form, the information obtained by him from the accident reports transmitted to him under section 3 (c) (6) of this Act, and under section 13 (c) of the Act entitled "An Act to amend laws for preventing collisions of vessels, to regulate equipment of certain motorboats on the navigable waters of the United States, and for other purposes", approved April 25, 1940 (46 U. S. C. 526l), together with such findings concerning the causes of such accidents and such recommendations for their prevention as he may deem necessary. Such information shall be made available for public inspection in such manner as the Secretary may deem practicable.

Sec. 11. (a) Except section 3 (d), this Act shall take effect on the date of its enactment.

(b) Section 3 (d) of this Act shall take effect April 1, 1960.

Sec. 12. The Act entitled "An Act to require numbering and recording of undocumented vessels", approved June 7, 1918, as amended (46 U. S. C. 288), and section 21 of the Act entitled "An Act to amend laws for preventing collisions of vessels, to regulate equipment of certain motorboats on the navigable waters of the United States, and for other purposes", approved April 25, 1940, as amended (46 U. S. C. 526t), shall not be applicable in any State having a numbering system approved by the Secretary under section 3 (c) of this Act. Such Act of June 7, 1918, and such section 21 of the Act of April 25, 1940, are repealed effective April 1, 1960.

## Law Enforcement

Sec. 13. The applicability and the jurisdiction for enforcement, upon the navigable waters of the United States, its Territories and the District of Columbia, of the laws of the United States and of any State which require the numbering and otherwise regulate the use of undocumented vessels, shall be as follows:

(1) Such laws of the United States shall be applicable and enforced on such waters by law enforcement officers of the United States.

(2) Such laws of any State in a State having a numbering system approved by the Secretary under section 3 (c) of this Act shall be applicable and enforced on such waters by law enforcement officers of the State or by law enforcement officers of the appropriate subdivisions of the State.

(3) Nothing herein shall preclude enforcement of State or Federal laws pursuant to agreements or other arrangements entered into between the Secretary and any State within the contemplation of section 9 of this Act.

(4) Nothing herein shall interfere with, abrogate or limit the jurisdiction of any State: *Provided, however,* That the Secretary shall not approve any State system for numbering which does not fully comply with the standards set forth in section 3 (c).

*Approved September 2, 1958.*

# UNITED STATES COAST GUARD REGULATIONS

## IMPLEMENTING THE FEDERAL BOATING ACT OF 1958

(Code of Federal Regulations, Title 46, Chapter 1, Sub-Chapter S—Numbering of Undocumented Vessels, Statistics on Numbering, and "Boating Accident Reports" and Accident Statistics)

### PART 170—GENERAL PROVISIONS
#### Authority and Purpose

§ 170.01–1 *Purpose of regulations.* The regulations in this subchapter provide:

(a) Standards for numbering under the Federal Boating Act of 1958.

(b) Requirements with respect to statistical information under the Federal Boating Act of 1958 and the Act of April 25, 1940, as amended.

(c) Requirements with respect to "Boating Accident Reports" and accident statistics.

§ 170.01–5 *Assignment of functions.* (a) The Department of Transportation Act (Public Law 89–670, 80 Stat. 931–950, 49 U.S.C. 1651–1659), transferred to and vested in the Secretary of Transportation "* * * all functions, powers, and duties, relating to the Coast Guard, of the Secretary of the Treasury and of other officers and offices of the Department of the Treasury" (subsection 6(b) (1), 49 U.S.C. 1655 (b)). This transfer is subject to certain conditions, modifications, and exceptions as set forth in such act. By a rule in 49 CFR 1.4(a) the Secretary of Transportation delegated to the Commandant, U.S. Coast Guard, authority to exercise certain functions, powers, and duties as set forth in subsections 6(a) (4), 6(b) (1), and 6(g) of such act (49 U.S.C. 1655), subject to conditions, exceptions and modifications as described in 49 CFR Part 1. By a rule in 49 CFR 1.9 the Secretary of Transportation continued in effect actions taken prior to April 1, 1967.

(b) The Commandant, U.S. Coast Guard, in a notice dated March 31, 1967, and effective April 1, 1967 (32 F.R. 5611), approved the continuation of orders, rules, regulations, policies, procedures, privileges, waivers, and other actions, which had been made, allowed, granted, or issued prior to April 1, 1967, and provided that they shall continue in effect according to their terms until modified, terminated, repealed, superseded, or set aside by appropriate authority.

#### Application

§ 170.05–1 *Scope.* The regulations in this subchapter are applicable in the United States, the Commonwealth of Puerto Rico, the Virgin Islands, Guam, and the District of Columbia.

§ 170.05–5 *Vessels subject to the requirements of this subchapter.* Except as specifically noted, this subchapter shall be applicable to undocumented vessels.

#### Definitions of Terms

§ 170.10–1 *Commandant.* This term means the Commandant of the U. S. Coast Guard.

§ 170.10–5 *Coast Guard District Commander.* This term means an officer of the Coast Guard designated as such by the Commandant to command all Coast Guard activities within his district.

§ 170.10–10 *Horsepower.* This term means the rated horsepower of the machine at maximum operating RPM.

§ 170.10–15 *Length.* As set forth in section 1 of the Act of April 25, 1940, as amended (46 U. S. C. 526), this term means the length of the vessel "measured from end to end over the deck excluding sheer."

§ 170.10–20 *Machinery.* This term includes inboard and outboard engines and all other types of motors or mechanical devices capable of propelling vessels.

§ 170.10–25 *Officer in Charge, Marine Inspection.* This term means any person from the civilian or military branch of the Coast Guard designated as such by the Commandant and who, under the superintendence and direction of the Coast Guard District Commander, is in charge of an inspection zone.

§ 170.10–30 *Operate.* As set forth in subsection 13 (a) of the Act of April 25, 1940, as amended (46 U. S. C. 526 *l*), this term "means to navigate or otherwise use a motorboat or a vessel."

§ 170.10–35 *Operator.* This term means the person who operates or who has charge of the navigation or use of a motorboat or a vessel.

§ 170.10–40 *Owner.* As set forth in subsection 2 (4) of the Federal Boating Act of 1958, this term "means the person who claims lawful possession of a vessel by virtue of legal title or equitable interest therein which entitles him to such possession."

§ 170.10–45 *Ships' lifeboats.* This term means lifeboats used solely for life-saving purposes and does not include dinghies, tenders, speedboats, or other types of craft carried aboard a vessel and used for other than lifesaving purposes.

§ 170.10–50 *State.* As set forth in subsection 2(5) of the Federal Boating Act of 1958, as amended .(46 U.S.C. 527 (5)), this term "means a State of the United States, the Commonwealth of Puerto Rico, the Virgin Islands, Guam, and the District of Columbia."

§ 170.10–55 *Ten horsepower.* As used in subsection 3 (a) of the Federal Boating Act of 1958, this term means the aggregate of all propellant machinery on a vessel.

§ 170.10–60 *Undocumented vessel.* As set forth in subsection 2 (1) of the Federal Boating Act of 1958, this term means "any vessel which is not required to have, and does not have, a valid marine document issued by the Bureau of Customs."

§ 170.10–65 *Vessel.* As set forth in subsection 2 (2) of the Federal Boating Act of 1958, this term "includes every description of water craft, other than a seaplane on the water, used or capable of being used as a means of transportation on water." This definition includes, but is not limited to, motorboats, sailboats, rowboats, canoes, ships, tugs, towboats, ferries, cargo vessels, passenger vessels, tank vessels, fishing vessels, charter boats, party boats, barges, scows, etc.

#### Appeals and Judicial Review

§ 170.15–1 *Judicial review or relief.* Nothing in this subchapter shall be so construed as to prevent any party from seeking a judiciaı review by, or relief in, an appropriate Court of law. This applies to any standard or regulation in this subchapter or to any decision or action taken pursuant thereto by the Coast Guard. If any provision of the regulations in this subchapter is held invalid, the validity of the remainder of this subchapter shall not be affected thereby.

§ 170.15–5 *Right of administrative appeal.* (a) Any person aggrieved by a decision or action taken by the Coast Guard under the regulations in this subchapter has a right to an administrative appeal therefrom. An appeal from a decision or action initially made or performed by an enforcing officer may be made to his commanding officer. Any decision or action of such commanding officer may be appealed to the Coast Guard District Commander of the district in which the action was taken or decision was made. A further appeal may be made to the Commandant, U. S. Coast Guard, from the decision of the District Commander.

(b) No special form is required, but such appeal shall set forth the decision or action appealed from and the reasons why it should be set aside or revised. Arrangements may be made for presenting an appeal in person.

§ 170.15–10 *Time limits.* (a) Any appeal to a Coast Guard District Commander shall be made in writing within 30 days after the decision or action appealed from shall have been rendered or taken.

(b) Any appeal to the Commandant shall be made in writing within 30 days after the decision or action appealed from shall have been rendered or taken.

§ 170.15–15 *Decision on appeal.* Pending the determination of an appeal, the decision or action appealed from shall remain in effect.

§ 170.15–20 *Initial decisions or actions of the Commandant.* Any person aggrieved by any decision or action initiated by the Commandant may request a review by writing to the Commandant within 30 days after the decision or action has been rendered or taken. Such a request shall set forth the decision or action desired to be reviewed and the reasons why it should be set aside or revised.

§ 170.15–25 *Reports and assessments of penalties for violations.* The reports of violations, assessments, collection, mitigation or remission of civil penalties shall be in accordance with § § 2.50–1 to 2.50–40 of Subchapter A (Procedures Applicable to the Public) of this chapter.

### PART 171—STANDARDS FOR NUMBERING
#### General

§ 171.01–1 *Vessels to be numbered.* (a) Certain undocumented vessels are required to be numbered by subsection 3 (a) of the Federal Boating Act of 1958, which reads as follows:

Every undocumented vessel propelled by machinery of more than 10 horsepower, whether or not such machinery is the principal source of propulsion, using the navigable waters of the United States, the Commonwealth of Puerto Rico, the Virgin Islands, Guam, and the District of Columbia, and every such vessel owned in a State and using the high seas, shall be numbered in accordance with this Act, except—

(1) Foreign vessels temporarily using the navigable waters of the United States, the Commonwealth of Puerto Rico, the Virgin Islands, Guam, and the District of Columbia;

(2) Public vessels of the United States;

(3) State and municipal vessels;

(4) Ships' lifeboats; and

(5) Vessels designated by the Secretary under section 7 (b) of this Act.

(b) Nothing in this section shall prohibit the numbering of any undocumented vessel, which may be propelled by machinery, upon request of the owner.

§ 171.01–5 *Exemptions.* Pursuant to subsections 3 (a) (5) and 7 (b) of the Federal Boating Act of 1958, the following are exempt from the requirement to be numbered:

(a) Undocumented vessels used exclusively for racing.

(b) Undocumented vessels operating under valid temporary certificates of number.

§ 171.01–10 *Determining horsepower of machinery.* (a) In general, for existing and new equipment, the manufacturer's rated horsepower at a stated maximum operating RPM as set forth on the nameplate attached to the engine, or as stamped on the engine, or as described in a "book of instructions" or other literature issued for such engine will be accepted as prima facie evidence of the horsepower of the machinery in question. In event the machinery does not have marked thereon or accompanying it any literature or tag setting forth the manufacturer's rated horsepower, or should the Coast Guard dispute the manufacturer's rated horsepower, then the Coast Guard's listing of horsepower will be accepted as prima facie evidence of the horsepower.

(b) In the event the owner or operator of a power propelled vessel disagrees with the findings of the Coast Guard as to horsepower, it shall be the responsibility of such owner or operator to prove to the satisfaction of the Coast Guard what is the actual horsepower of the propelling machinery.

**Vessel Identification**

§ 171.05–1 *Numbering pattern to be used.* (a) The numbers issued pursuant to the Federal Boating Act of 1958 shall be in accordance with the pattern described in this section.

(b) The number shall be divided into parts. The first part shall consist of the symbols identifying the State of principal use, followed by a combination of numerals and letters which furnish individual vessel identification. The group of digits appearing between letters shall be separated from those letters by hyphens or equivalent spaces. As examples: AL–001–AA, or AK 99 AZ.

(c) The first part of the number shall be an abbreviation in capital letters of the

State. The abbreviations of the States are as follows:

| | |
|---|---|
| Alabama—AL | North Dakota—ND |
| Alaska—AK | Nebraska—NB |
| Arizona—AZ | Nevada—NV |
| Arkansas—AR | New Hampshire—NH |
| California—CF | New Jersey—NJ |
| Colorado—CL | New Mexico—NM |
| Connecticut—CT | New York—NY |
| Delaware—DL | Ohio—OH |
| Florida—FL | Oklahoma—OK |
| Georgia—GA | Oregon—OR |
| Hawaii—HA | Pennsylvania—PA |
| Idaho—ID | Puerto Rico—PR |
| Illinois—IL | Rhode Island—RI |
| Indiana—IN | South Carolina—SC |
| Iowa—IA | South Dakota—SD |
| Kansas—KA | Tennessee—TN |
| Kentucky—KY | Texas—TX |
| Louisiana—LA | Utah—UT |
| Maine—ME | Virginia—VA |
| Massachusetts—MS | Virgin Islands—VI |
| Maryland—MD | Vermont—VT |
| Michigan—MC | Washington—WN |
| Minnesota—MN | West Virginia—WV |
| Mississippi—MI | Wyoming—WY |
| Missouri—MO | Wisconsin—WS |
| Montana—MT | District of Colum- |
| North Carolina—NC | bia—DC |

(d) The remainder of the boat number shall consist of not more than four arabic numerals and two capital letters or not more than three arabic numerals and three capital letters, in sequence, separated by a hyphen or equivalent space, in accordance with the serials, numerically and alphabetically.

(1) As examples of the first alternative:

| State designator | Maximum of 4 digits; numerical group | Maximum of 2 letters; alphabetical group |
|---|---|---|
| NY | 1 | A |
| NY | 83 | A B |
| NY | 345 | T R |
| NY | 9999 | Z Z |

(2) As example of the second alternative:

| State designator | Maximum of 3 digits; numerical group | Maximum of 3 letters; alphabetical group |
|---|---|---|
| NC | 1 | A |
| NC | 83 | A B |
| NC | 345 | P F |
| NC | 999 | Z Z Z |

(e) Since the letters "I", "O" and "Q" may be mistaken for arabic numerals, all letter sequences using "I", "O" and "Q" shall be omitted. Objectionable words formed by the use of two or three letters will not be used.

§ 171.05–2 *Arrangement of number placed on vessel.* (a) See § 171.05–1 for description of the number.

(b) In applying the identification number to the vessel there shall be a hyphen or space between the prefix letters (abbreviation of State) and the numerals, and a hyphen or space between the numerals and the suffix letters. The hyphen or space shall be equal to the width of any letter except "I" or any number except "1". As examples: PA–5678–EF, or NJ 1234 AB.

§ 171.05–5 *Display of number on vessel.* (a) Subsection 3 (f) of the Federal Boating Act of 1958 requires in part that "the number awarded * * * shall be painted on, or attached to, each side of the bow of the vessel for which it was issued * * * ".

(b) The numbers shall be placed on each side of the forward half of the vessel in such position as to provide clear legibility for identification. The numbers shall read from left to right and shall be in block characters of good proportion not less than 3 inches in height. The numbers shall be of a color which will contrast with the color of the background and so maintained as to be clearly visible and legible; i. e., dark numbers on a light background, or light numbers on a dark background.

(c) Subsection 3 (f) of the Federal Boating Act of 1958 also provides "no other number shall be carried on the bow of such vessel."

§ 171.05–6 *Definitions of terms used in § 171.05–5.* (a) As used in § 171.05–5(b) the phrase "forward half of the vessel" shall mean any portion of the vessel forward of a point equidistant from the stem and the stern of the vessel.

(b) As used in § 171.05–5(b) the phrase "in such position as to provide clear legibility for identification" shall mean on a section of the forward half of the hull or on the permanent superstructure located on the forward half of the hull (which is as nearly vertical as possible) where the number may be easily observed, or, when due to vessel configuration the above will not provide ready identification, on a bracket or fixture firmly attached on the forward half of the vessel. It is intended that the number shall not be placed on the obscured underside of a flared bow where the angle is such that the number cannot be easily seen from another vessel or ashore.

(c) In § 171.05–5(b) the phrase "block characters of good proportion" shall mean that the numerals and letters are vertical (not slanted) and of a plain style (not script or of varying thickness and preferably without border, trim, outlining or shading). Border, trim, outlining or shading of a character if used shall be disregarded in determining either style or color contrast.

(d) As used in § 171.05–5(b) the phrase "not less than 3 inches in height" shall mean that the numerals or letters used must measure not less than 3 full inches from top to bottom and they may be larger than 3 inches. The border, trim, outlining or shading of a character shall be disregarded in determining the height of a character.

(e) As used in § 171.05–5(b) the phrase "a color" shall mean one solid color exclusive of any colored border, trim, outlining, or shading.

(f) As used in § 171.05–5(b) the phrase "contrast with the color of the background" shall mean that the numerals and letters in the number will be of such a different color from that of the background so as to be distinctly visible and legible. Black numbers on a white background or white numbers on a black background will provide the best contrast for legibility. Pastel colored numbers may fail to meet these legibility requirements.

(g) As used in § 171.05–5(b) the word "background" shall mean that portion of the hull or superstructure or a specially provided backing plate upon which the numbers are placed. If a backing plate is used, such plate must be of sufficient size to provide good contrast and legibility for the number. The border, trim, outlining or shading on numerals and letters does not constitute a part of the number itself. By itself, the border, trim, outlining or shading fails to provide sufficient contrast for good legibility and does not constitute required background.

§ 171.05–10 *Numbering livery boats.* (a) The numbering requirement of this part shall apply to livery boats.

(b) The certificate of number of a livery boat shall be plainly marked, "livery boat."

(c) The description of the motor and type of fuel will be omitted from the certificate of number in any case where the motor is not rented with the boat.

§ 171.05–15 *Numbering of manufacturers' and dealers' boats.* (a) Numbering requirements of this part shall apply to boats operated by manufacturers and dealers.

(b) The description of the boat will be omitted from the certificate of number since the numbers and the certificates of number awarded may be transferred from one boat to another. In lieu of the description, the word "manufacturer" or "dealer," as appropriate, will be plainly marked on each certificate.

(c) The manufacturer or dealer may have the number awarded printed upon or attached to a removable sign or signs to be temporarily but firmly mounted upon or attached to the boat being demonstrated or tested so long as the display meets the requirements in § 171.05–5.

## Application for Number

§ 171.10–1 *Application submission.* (a) The owner of an undocumented vessel required to be numbered by Sub-part 171.01 who uses his vessel principally in a State that does not have an approved numbering system shall secure a number from the Coast Guard.

(1) Those jurisdictions in which applications shall be submitted directly to the Commandant (BBL), U. S. Coast Guard, Washington, D.C. 20591, are as follows:
Alaska
District of Columbia
New Hampshire
Washington

(2) Those jurisdictions in which applications shall be submitted directly to the local Officer in Charge, Marine Inspection, are as follows:
Guam

(b) An undocumented vessel principally used in a State which has an approved numbering system will not be numbered by the Coast Guard. The States which have approved numbering systems are as follows:

| | |
|---|---|
| Alabama | Nebraska |
| Arizona | Nevada |
| Arkansas | New Jersey |
| California | New Mexico |
| Colorado | New York |
| Connecticut | North Carolina |
| Delaware | North Dakota |
| Florida | Ohio |
| Georgia | Oklahoma |
| Hawaii | Oregon |
| Illinois | Pennsylvania |
| Indiana | Puerto Rico |
| Idaho | Rhode Island |
| Iowa | South Carolina |
| Kansas | South Dakota |
| Kentucky | Tennessee |
| Louisiana | Texas |
| Maine | Utah |
| Maryland | Vermont |
| Massachusetts | Virginia |
| Michigan | Virgin Islands |
| Minnesota | West Virginia |
| Mississippi | Wisconsin |
| Missouri | Wyoming |
| Montana | |

§ 171.10–2 *Procedures for making application to the Coast Guard.* (a) The application for an original number to be issued by the Coast Guard is a two-part form designated CG–3876 and CG–3876A. This form is available upon request at all First Class and Second Class Post Offices in States in which undocumented vessels must be numbered by the Coast Guard and at certain designated Third Class and Fourth Class Post Offices in those States; at Coast Guard Headquarters; at all Coast Guard District Offices and all Marine Inspection Offices; and at all Coast Guard units in those States where the Coast Guard is numbering such vessels. The instructions for filling in these forms are set forth on the back of the forms.

(b) The owner of any undocumented vessel required to be numbered by the Coast Guard shall complete the Application for Number (Form CG–3876) and the temporary certificate (Form CG–3876A) and submit them to the Commandant (BBL), U.S. Coast Guard, Washington, D.C. 20591, together with the fee prescribed by § 171.17–1 in the form of a personal check or money order made out to the "United States Coast Guard", or cash if presented in person in Washington, D.C.

§ 171.10–3 *Procedures for making application to the Coast Guard directly.* (a) The Coast Guard offices issuing applications for number in the States listed in § 171.10–1(a) (2) are as follows:
Guam: U.S. Coast Guard, Marine Inspection Office, Guam.

(b) The application for an original number to be issued by the Coast Guard is a two-part form designated CG–3876 and CG–3876A. The owner of any undocumented vessel required to be numbered by a Coast Guard office shall complete the application (Form CG–3876) and the temporary certificate (Form CG–3876A) in accordance with instructions set forth on the back of the forms and submit them to the appropriate Coast Guard office listed in paragraph (a) of this section together with the $3.00 numbering fee. No special fee stamp shall be affixed in the space provided on the back of the forms, but in its stead the Coast Guard office shall authenticate both forms (CG–3876 and CG–3876A) and indicate thereon the date upon which applications are made.

§ 171.10–5 *Application requirements.* The application for a number shall include the following:
(a) Name and address of owner.
(b) Date of birth of owner.
(c) Present citizenship of owner.
(d) State in which the vessel is principally used.
(e) Present bow number (if any).
(f) Hull material (wood, steel, aluminum, fiber-glass/plastic, other).
(g) Type of propulsion (outboard; inboard; outboard-inboard; sail only; auxiliary sail: Outboard, inboard; other).
(h) Type of fuel (gas, diesel, other).
(i) Length of vessel.
(j) Make and year built (if known).
(k) Hull serial number (if any).
(l) Statement as to use (pleasure, livery, dealer, manufacturer, commercial-passenger, commercial-fishing, commercial-other).
(m) Reason for application (original number, renewal of number, change of State of principal use, transfer of ownership (other than a lien holder), lien holder possession).
(n) A certification of ownership by the applicant.
(o) Signature of owner.

§ 171.10–15 *State in which vessel is principally used.* (a) For the purposes of numbering, the statement of the owner with respect to the State in which the vessel is to be principally used, as set forth in the application for number, will be accepted, prima facie, as true.

(b) If the vessel is to be principally used on the high seas, then it shall be assigned a number for the State in which the vessel is usually docked, moored, housed, or garaged.

§ 171.10–20 *Renewal of numbers.* (a) Numbers issued to owners of undocumented vessels pursuant to the regulations in this part shall be renewed not later than the expiration dates shown on the Certificates of Number. The number may be renewed at any time within the 90-day period preceding the expiration date on the Certificate of Number. However, the renewal application should be received by the Coast Guard 60 days prior to the expiration date shown on the Certificate of Number. The owner shall submit the renewal application to the Commandant (BBL), U.S. Coast Guard, Washington, D.C. 20591, together with the fee prescribed by § 171.17–1 in the form of a personal check or money order made out to the "United States Coast Guard," or cash if presented in person in Washington, D.C.

(b) Approximately 90 days prior to the expiration date as shown on the Certificate of Number the Coast Guard will forward to the owner of the vessel numbered a completed "Application for Number," Form CG–3876. The Application for Number shall contain information taken from Coast Guard numbering records, and instructions for submitting such application shall be forwarded. The failure by the Coast Guard to forward such an application and instructions, or the failure of the owner to receive them, does not excuse the owner from the requirement of renewing the number on or before the expiration date shown on the Certificate of Number as provided in paragraph (a) of this section.

(c) Should an owner of a vessel numbered pursuant to the regulations in this part fail to receive the "Application for Number" Form CG–3876, as described in paragraph (b) of this section, 60 days prior to the expiration date on his Certificate of Number, he shall obtain an "Application for Number" from one of the sources as described in § 171.10–2, and shall complete it in the manner described in the instructions set forth on the back of the form.

(d) Certificates of Number are void after the dates of expiration thereon. (See § 171.15–15 for period of validity of Certificates of Number.) A number not renewed as prescribed by paragraph (a) of this section may be renewed after the expiration date of the Certificate of Number: *Provided,* That the renewal application is received within one year from the date of expiration as shown on the Certificate of Number. Each renewal Certificate of Number shall be valid for a period ending three years from the date of expiration of the certificate renewed.

(e) A renewal application received more than a year after the date of expiration of the Certificate of Number shall be treated in the same manner as an application for an original number.

§ 171.10–25 *Lost or destroyed certificate of number for vessels numbered in States listed in § 171.10–1(a) (1).* (a) If a certificate of number is lost or destroyed, the owner within 15 days shall notify the Commandant (BBL) U.S. Coast Guard, Washington, D.C., 20591. The notification shall be in writing and shall describe the circumstances of the loss or destruction.

(b) If an application for a duplicate certificate of number (Form CG-3919) (see § 171.10-30) is submitted without delay, it may also provide the written notification required by paragraph (a) of this section.

§ 171.10-26 *Lost or destroyed certificate of number for vessels numbered by the Coast Guard in States listed in § 171.10-1(a) (2).* (a) If a certificate of number is lost or destroyed, the owner within 15 days shall notify the appropriate Coast Guard office listed in § 171.10-3(a). The notification shall be in writing and shall describe the circumstances of the loss or destruction.

(b) If an application for a duplicate certificate of number (Form CG-3919) (see § 171.10-31) is submitted without delay, it may also provide the written notification required by paragraph (a) of this section.

§171.10-30 *Duplicate certificate of number.* (a) The application for a duplicate certificate of number to be issued by the Coast Guard is a two-part form designated CG-3919 and CG-3919A. This form is available upon request at all First Class and Second Class Post Offices in States in which undocumented vessels must be numbered by the Coast Guard and at certain designated Third Class and Fourth Class Post Offices in those States; at Coast Guard Headquarters; at all Coast Guard District Offices and all Marine Inspection Offices; and, at all Coast Guard units in those States where the Coast Guard is numbering such vessels. The instructions for filling in these forms are set forth on the back of the forms. Space is provided on the application to describe the circumstances of the loss or destruction of the certificate of number so that, when submitted without delay, it may also provide the written notification required by § 171.10-25.

(b) The owner shall complete the application for a duplicate certificate of number (Form CG-3919) and the temporary duplicate certificate of number (Form CG-3919A), and submit them to the Commandant (BBL), U.S. Coast Guard, Washington, D.C. 20591, together with the fee prescribed by § 171.17-1 in the form of a personal check or money order made out to the "United States Coast Guard", or cash if presented in person in Washington, D.C.

(c) The duplicate certificate of number issued as a result of such application on Form CG-3919 will replace the certificate of number so lost or destroyed.

§ 171.10-31 *Duplicate certificate of number of vessels numbered by the Coast Guard in States listed in § 171.10-1(a) (2).* (a) The application for a duplicate certificate of number to be issued by the Coast Guard is a two-part form designated CG-3919 and CG-3919A. This form is available upon request at the appropriate Coast Guard office listed in § 171.10-3(a). The instructions for filling in these forms are set forth on the back of the forms. Space is provided on the application to describe the circumstances of the loss or destruction of the certificate of number so that, when submitted without delay, it may also provide the written notification required by § 171.10-26.

(b) The owner shall complete the application for a duplicate certificate of number (Form CG-3919) and the temporary duplicate certificate of number (Form CG-3919A) and submit them to the appropriate Coast Guard office listed in § 171.10-3(a), to-gether with the $1.00 fee. No special fee stamp shall be affixed in the space provided on the back of the forms, but in its stead the Coast Guard office shall authenticate both forms (CG-3919 and CG-3919A) and indicate thereon the date upon which applications are made.

## Ownership

§ 171.13-1 *Claim of ownership.* (a) The certified statement of ownership on the application for number shall be the minimum requirement for proof of ownership acceptable to the Coast Guard.

§ 171.13-5 *Liens.* Liens of all kinds, including reservations or transfers of title to secure debts or claims, will be disregarded in determining ownership under this subpart. A lienholder who acquires possession and title by virtue of default in the terms of the lien instrument, or any other person who acquires ownership through any such action of a lienholder, may apply for a number and shall attach to such application a signed statement explaining the fact in detail.

## Certificate of Number

§ 171.15-1 *Information required on certificates issued for vessels numbered in States listed in § 171.10-1(a) (1) and (2).* The certificate of Number shall include the following:

(a) Name and address of owner.

(b) Hull material (wood, steel, aluminum, fiber-glass/plastic, other).

(c) Type of propulsion (outboard; inboard; outboard-inboard; sail only; auxiliary sail: Outboard, inboard; other).

(d) Type of fuel (gas, diesel, other).

(e) Length of vessel.

(f) Make and year built (if known).

(g) Hull serial number (if any).

(h) Statement as to use (pleasure, livery, dealer, manufacturer, commercial-passenger, commercial-fishing, commerical-other).

(i) Number awarded to vessel.

(j) Expiration date of certificate.

(k) Notice to the owner that the operator shall:

(1) Always carry this certificate on vessel when in use.

(2) Report every accident involving injury or death to persons, or property damage over $100.

(3) Stop and render aid or assistance if involved in boating accident.

(l) Notice to the owner that he shall report within 15 days changes of ownership or address, and documentation, destruction or abandonment of vessel.

§ 171.15-5 *Size and characteristics of certificate.* The certificate of number shall be pocket size (approximately 2½" x 3½") and water resistant.

§ 171.15-10 (a) *Temporary certificate.* Pending the issuance of the original certificate of number, the owner of the vessel will be furnished a temporary certificate of number valid for 60 days from date of issue. This temporary certificate shall be carried on board when the vessel is being operated.

(b) For Form CG-3876A (temporary certificate of number) to be a valid temporary certificate, the Form CG-3876A shall be completely filled out by the applicant at the same time as he completes the attached application (Form CG-3876), and it shall bear an authentication stamp affixed by the Coast Guard indicating that the prescribed fee accompanied the application.

(c) For Form CG-3919A (temporary duplicate certificate of number) to be a valid temporary certificate, the Form CG-3919A shall be completely filled out by the applicant at the same time as he completes the attached application (Form CG-3919), and it shall bear an authentication stamp affixed by the Coast Guard indicating that the prescribed fee accompanied the application.

§ 171.15-11 *Temporary certificate and temporary duplicate certificate issued for vessels numbered by the Coast Guard in States listed in § 171.10-1(a) (2).* (a) Pending the issuance of the Certificate of Number, the owner of the vessel will be furnished a Temporary Certificate of Number valid for 90 days from date of issue. This temporary certificate shall be carried on board when the vessel is being operated.

(b) For Form CG-3876A (Temporary Certificate of Number) to be a valid temporary certificate, it shall be completely filled out by the applicant at the same time as he completes the attached application (Form CG-3876) and it shall bear an authentication identical to that on the application.

(c) For Form CG-3919A (Temporary Duplicate Certificate of Number) to be a valid temporary certificate, the form shall be completely filled out by the applicant at the same time as he completes the attached application (Form CG-3919) and it shall bear an authentication identical to that on the application.

§ 171.15-15 *Period of validity of certificate.* The original certificate of number initially awarded by the Coast Guard shall be valid for a period ending 3 years from the anniversary of the date of birth of the applicant next succeeding the issuance of the certificate. Each renewal shall be valid for a period ending 3 years from the date of expiration of the certificate so renewed. A certificate issued to other than an individual shall expire 3 years from date of issuance.

§ 171.15-20 *Notification of changes required by owners of vessels numbered in States listed in § 171.10- 1(a) (1).* (a) When the owner of a Coast Guard numbered vessel changes the State in which the vessel is principally used, he shall within 90 days surrender the certificate of number to the Coast Guard. The owner shall also apply for another original number to the office issuing numbers for that State.

(b) When the owner of a Coast Guard numbered vessel changes his address from that shown on his certificate, but does not change the State in which the vessel is principally used, he shall notify in writing the Commandant (BBL), U.S. Coast Guard, Washington, D.C. 20591, of his new address within a period not to exceed 15 days from such change. This written notification should be on Form CG-3920 (change of address notice), which is available upon request from any Post Office which handles applications for certificates of number (see § 171.10-2), or from any Coast Guard Marine Inspection Office.

(c) When a Coast Guard numbered vessel is lost, destroyed, abandoned, documented, or transferred to another person, the Certificate of Number issued for the vessel shall be surrendered to the Commandant (BBL), U.S. Coast Guard, Washington, D.C. 20591, within a period not to exceed 15 days after such event. When the numbered vessel is lost, destroyed, abandoned, documented, or transferred to another person, the owner shall within 15 days after such event notify in writing the Commandant (BBL), U.S. Coast Guard, Washington, D.C. 20591, of the change in the status of the vessel. This written notification should be on Form CG-3921 (Notification of change in status of vessel), which is available upon request from any Post Office which handles applications for Certificates or Number (see § 171.10–2), or from any Coast Guard Marine Inspection Office. If the Certificate of Number is lost or destroyed, a description of such circumstances shall be reported as required by § 171.10–25..

(d) The application for number by a new owner of a vessel shall, for purposes of fee, be regarded as an original application for number, but where the vessel will continue in use in the same State of principal use, the new number shall be identical with the previous one, except where a lienholder acquires title and lawful possession by virtue of his lien, in which case a new number shall be issued.

(e) A change of motor is not required to be reported to the Coast Guard.

§171.15–21 *Notification of changes required by owners of vessels numbered by the Coast Guard in States listed in § 171.10–1(a) (2).* (a) When the owner of a Coast Guard numbered vessel changes the State in which the vessel is principally used, he shall within 90 days surrender the certificate of number to the appropriate Coast Guard office listed in § 171.10–3(a). The owner shall also apply for another original number in accordance with the section of Subpart 171.10 which applies to the State in which the vessel is used.

(b) When the owner of a Coast Guard numbered vessel changes his address from that shown on his certificate, but does not change the State in which the vessel is principally used, he shall notify in writing the appropriate Coast Guard office listed in § 171.10–3(a). This written notification may be on Form CG-3920 (Change of Address Notice), which is available upon request from that office.

(c) When a Coast Guard numbered vessel is lost, destroyed, abandoned, documented, or transferred to another person, the certificate of number issued for the vessel shall be surrendered to the appropriate Coast Guard office listed in § 171.10–3(a) within 15 days after such event. When the numbered vessel is lost, destroyed, abandoned, documented, or transferred to another person, the owner shall within 15 days after such event notify that office in writing. This written notification may be on Form CG-3921 (Notification of change in status of vessel), which is available upon request from that office. If the Certificate of Number is lost or destroyed, a description of such circumstances shall be reported as required by § 171.10–26.

(d) The application for number by a new owner of a vessel shall, for purposes of fee, be regarded as an original application for number, but where the vessel will continue in use in the same State of principal use, the new number shall be identical with the previous one, except where a lienholder acquires title and lawful possession by virtue of his lien, in which case a new number shall be issued.

(e) A change of motor is not required to be reported to the Coast Guard.

§ 171.15–25 *One certificate for each vessel.* The intent of this subpart is that the owner of an undocumented vessel shall not have more than one valid number or valid certificate of number for any one vessel at any time. Therefore, the owner will violate the regulations if he retains more than one valid certificate of number for any one vessel.

§ 171.15–30 *Cancellation of certificate and voiding of number.* (a) Subsection 3 (e) of the Federal Boating Act of 1958 authorizes the cancellation of certificates of number, thereby voiding the numbers issued. This means that a certificate may be canceled and number voided by proper authority even though such action occurs before the expiration date on the certificate and such certificate is not surrendered to the issuing office.

(b) Certain causes for cancellation of certificates and voiding of numbers are:

(1) Surrender of certificate for cancellation.

(2) Issuance of a new number for the same vessel.

(3) Issuance of a marine document by the Coast Guard for the same vessel.

(4) False or fraudulent certification in an application for number.

(c) In the absence of an application for renewal as provided in §171.10–20 a number is automatically void on the date of expiration as shown on the certificate of number.

### Fees and Charges

§ 171.17–1 *Fees.* (a) The fees charged by the U. S. Coast Guard are based upon the estimated cost of the administration of the Coast Guard's numbering system.

(b) The fees are as follows:

(1) Original numbering—$3.00.

(2) Reissue of lost or destroyed certificate of number—$1.00.

(3) Renewal of number—$3.00.

§171.17–5 *Method of payment of fees in States listed in § 171.10–1(a) (1)* (a) The fee for original numbering shall be paid by personal check or money order made out to the "United States Coast Guard," which shall accompany the application for number (Form CG-3876) and the temporary certificate (Form CG-3876A), or cash if presented in person in Washington, D.C. (See §§ 171.10–2 and 171.17–1(b) (1) for procedures for submission of applications for number and fees.)

(b) The fees for reissue of lost or destroyed certificate of number (duplicate certificate of number) shall be paid by personal check or money order made out to the "United States Coast Guard," which shall accompany the application for duplicate certificate of number (Form CG-3919A), or cash if presented in person in Washington, D.C. (See §§ 171.10–30 and 171.17–1(b) (2) for procedures for submission of applications for duplicate certificates of number and fees.)

(c) The fee for renewal of number shall be paid by personal check or money order made out to the "United States Coast Guard" and shall accompany the renewal application or Form CG-3876 and CG-3876A, or cash if presented in person in Washington, D.C. (See §§ 171.10–20 and 171.17–1(b) (3) for procedures for submission of applications for renewal of number and fees.)

§ 171.17–6 *Method of payment of fee in States listed in § 171.10–1(a) (2).* (a) The fee for original numbering shall be paid by the owner in cash or by money

order at the appropriate Coast Guard office listed in § 171.10–3(a).

(b) The fee for reissue of lost or destroyed certificate of number (duplicate certificate of number) shall be paid in cash or by money order at the appropriate Coast Guard office listed in § 171.-10–3(a).

(c) No application for an original certificate of number or for a duplicate certificate of number will be processed without the prescribed authentication described in § 171.10–3(b).

### Availability of Records

§ 171.20–1 *Enforcement or assistance programs.* Upon request, information on ownership and identity of Coast Guard numbered vessels shall be available to Federal, State, and local officials, as needed, in any enforcement or assistance programs.

§ 171.20–5. *Disclosure of information.*

(a) The records pertaining to the numbering of undocumented vessels pursuant to this part are considered to be public records.

(b) Information based on such Coast Guard records may be released upon oral or written inquiry, subject only to reasonable restrictions necessary to carry on the business of the office. The Coast Guard may permit excerpts to be made or the copying or reproduction thereof by a private individual or concern authorized by the Coast Guard. The fees and charges for copying, certifying, or searching of records for information shall be assessed in accordance with 33 CFR 1.25.

## PART 172—INTERPRETIVE RULINGS— FEDERAL BOATING ACT AND ACT OF APRIL 25, 1940, AS AMENDED
### General Provisions

§ 172.01–1 *Scope.* (a) The regulations in this part are interpretive rulings of specific provisions of the Federal Boating Act of 1958 and the Act of April 25, 1940, as amended (46 U.S.C. 526 through 527h).

§ 172.01–10 *Penalties and violations.* (a) Failure to comply with any law as interpreted will be considered as a violation of such law and the penalty may be assessed as provided by law.

(b) The reports of violations, as well as the assessment, collection, mitigation or remission of civil penalties authorized by law, shall be in accordance with §§ 2.50–20 to 2.50–30 of Subchapter A (Procedures Applicable to the Public) of this chapter.

### Federal Boating Act

§ 172.05–1 *State of principal use.* (a) Subsection 3(b) of the Federal Boating Act (46 U.S.C. 527a(b)) states in part "The owner of an undocumented vessel * * * shall secure a number for such vessel in the State in which it is principally used, * * *." In determining the time a vessel may be in a State, the term "principally used" is interpreted as meaning the time when the vessel is "on" the navigable waters of the United States, which includes the time when the vessel is not in motion, as for instance when the vessel is moored or at anchor, equally with the time when the vessel is being navigated. Since the act would be only applicable to the vessel when it is on the navigable waters of the United States, those periods when the vessel is being transported by trailer or is stored on land are excluded from any computation of time in determining "the State in which it is principally used."

## PART 173—BOATING ACCIDENTS, REPORTS, AND STATISTICAL INFORMATION

### Boating Accidents

§ 173.01–1 *General.* (a) The provisions of this subpart shall apply (1) to all uninspected numbered vessels and (2) to all other uninspected vessels used for pleasure or recreational purposes. All other uninspected vessels shall be subject to the requirements contained in Part 136 of this chapter.

(b) The provisions in this subpart are applicable in the United States, the Commonwealth of Puerto Rico, the Virgin Islands, Guam, and the District of Columbia, as well as to every such vessel which is owned in a State, and using the high seas.

§ 173.01–5 *Reportable boating accidents.* (a) Subsection 13 (c) of the Act of April 25, 1940, as amended (46 U. S. C. 526*l*, reads as follows:

> In the case of collision, accident, or other casualty involving a motorboat or other vessel subject to this Act, the operator thereof, if the collision, accident, or other casualty results in death or injury to any person, or damage to property in excess of $100, shall file with the Secretary of the Department within which the Coast Guard is operating, unless such operator is required to file an accident report with the State under section 3 (c) (6) of the Federal Boating Act of 1958, a full description of the collision, accident, or other casualty, including such information as the Secretary may by regulation require.

(b) For the purpose of this subpart a "boating accident" means a collision, accident or other casualty involving (1) an uninspected numbered vessel or (2) any other uninspected vessel used for pleasure or recreational purposes.

(c) A vessel subject to this subpart is considered to be involved in a "boating accident" whenever the occurrence results in damage by or to the vessel or its equipment; in injury or loss of life to any person, or in the disappearance of any person from on board under circumstances which indicate the possibility of death or injury. A "boating accident" includes, but is not limited to. capsizing, collision, foundering, flooding, fire, explosion and the disappearance of a vessel other than by theft.

(d) A report is required whenever a vessel subject to this subpart is involved in a "boating accident" which results in any one or more of the following:

(1) Loss of life.

(2) Injury causing any person to remain incapacitated for a period in excess of 72 hours.

(3) Actual physical damage to property (including vessels) in excess of $100.

§ 173.01–10 *Written report required.* (a) Whenever death results from a boating accident, a written report shall be submitted within 48 hours. For every other reportable boating accident a written report shall be submitted within five (5) days after such accident.

(b) The operator(s) of the boat(s) shall prepare and submit the written report(s) to the Coast Guard Officer in Charge, Marine Inspection, nearest to the place where such accident occurred or nearest to the port of first arrival after such accident, unless such operator is required to file an accident report with a State under subsection 3 (c) (6) of the Federal Boating Act of 1958.

(c) Every written report shall contain the following information:

(1) The numbers and/or names of vessels involved.

(2) The locality where the accident occurred.

(3) The time and date when the accident occurred.

(4) Weather and sea conditions at time of accident.

(5) The name, address, age, and boat operating experience of the operator of the reporting vessel.

(6) The names and addresses of operators of other vessels involved.

(7) The names and addresses of the owners of vessels or property involved.

(8) The names and addresses of any person or persons injured or killed.

(9) The nature and extent of injury to any person or persons.

(10) A description of damage to property (including vessels) and estimated cost of repairs.

(11) A description of the accident (including opinions as to the causes).

(12) The length, propulsion, horsepower, fuel and construction of the reporting vessel.

(13) Names and addresses of known witnesses.

(d) The Coast Guard Form CG-3865 (Boating Accident Report) may be used for the written report required by this section.

### Statistics Required

§ 173.05–1 *Required reports.* The Coast Guard will obtain, compile, analyze, and publish periodic reports in a uniform manner with respect to vessels having currently valid certificates of number, and with respect to boating accidents.

§ 173.05–5 *Reports with respect to numbered vessels.* The Coast Guard will compile statistics on numbered vessels as of December 31 of each year. This informa-

tion includes as of the reporting date:

(a) The total number of all valid certificates of number outstanding.

(b) The total number of valid certificates of number held by vessels numbered under subsection 3 (a) of the Federal Boating Act of 1958.

(c) The total numbers of valid certificates of number held by vessels described by class, type, and construction.

§ 173.05–10 *Reports with respect to boating accidents.* The Coast Guard will compile statistics on boating accidents reported as of December 31 of each year. This information will include:

(a) The total number of boating accidents reported during each such period.

(b) The totals of boating accidents reported during each such period, grouped according to the cause, nature, and results and including the class, type, and construction of vessels involved.

(c) The totals of boating accidents reported during each such period by vessels required to be numbered under subsection 3 (a) of the Federal Boating Act of 1958 according to vessels described by class, type, and construction.

### Availability of Information

§ 173.10–1 *"Boating Accident Reports".* (a) The "Boating Accident Reports" are intended to furnish the information necessary for the Coast Guard to make findings of causes of accidents and recommendations for their prevention, and to compile information for use in making statistical reports.

(b) Except as provided in paragraph (c), individual "Boating Accident Reports," or copies of or excerpts therefrom, will not be released.

(c) "Boating Accident Reports" may be available for additional statistical studies, on the condition that information from individual reports shall not be disclosed, and subject to prior arrangements and reasonable restrictions necessary in the carrying on of the business of the office.

§ 173.10–5 *Statistical records and statistical reports.* After information has been released or published, the statistical records and statistical reports obtained and compiled by the Coast Guard, as distinguished from the individual "Boating Accident Reports" described in § 173.10–1, shall be made available for inspection and use by the public during normal office hours subject to reasonable restrictions necessary in the carrying on of the business of the office.

---

**Revisions as of July, 1970**
**Add:**

§ 171.15–12 *Indication of Currency of Coast Guard Certificate.* (a) With each certificate of number issued by the Coast Guard, two stickers also will be issued to provide ready identification of vessels with currently valid numbers.

(b) The stickers shall be approximately 3″ by 3″ and color coded to indicate the year of expiration of the assigned number. Each sticker will contain the date of expiration and the assigned number of the vessel. The sticker shall not be used on any other vessel.

(c) The stickers shall be displayed on each bow of the vessel at a location 3 inches beyond the last letter of the identification number and on a level therewith.

(d) If a sticker is destroyed a replacement may be ordered from the Commandant (BBL), U. S. Coast Guard, Washington, D.C. 20591. The order must contain an explanation as to why the replacement is necessary and the fee as provided by § 171.17–1 (b) (4).

(e) Stickers will be issued for original and renewal identification numbers issued on and after September 1. 1970.

**Change:** § **171.17–1 through (b) (3) to:**

§ 171.17–1 *Fees.* (a) The fees charged by the U. S. Coast Guard are based upon

the estimated cost of administering the numbering of undocumented vessels in accordance with the Federal Boating Act of 1958 (46 US.C. 527c).

(b) The fees are as follows:

(1) Original numbering, including stickers evidencing currency of certificate—$6.

(2) Reissue of lost or destroyed certificate of number—$1.

(3) Renewal of number, including stickers evidencing currency of certificate—$6.

(4) Replacement of lost or destroyed stickers evidencing currency of certificate—$0.25 each.

# WHERE TO APPLY FOR NUMBERING CERTIFICATES

The Federal Boating Act of 1958 called for the registration and numbering of all motorboats over a specified horsepower for identification, with a provision that the individual state should have jurisdiction in all cases where their state legislation would conform to the standard established by the federal act. Approval by the U. S. Coast Guard is required in each case.

By April, 1970, the Coast Guard had officially approved the numbering systems of all states except Alaska, New Hampshire, Washington, and Washington, D. C. In these jurisdictions application forms for Coast Guard registration numbers may be obtained through local post offices or any Coast Guard facility. In Guam, application should be made to the Officer in Charge, Marine Inspection, U. S. Coast Guard.

Boats principally used in states having an approved number-

ing law are numbered exclusively by the state; Coast Guard numbers are obsolete. In compliance with the Federal Act all of these state laws grant 90-day reciprocity to out-of-state boats awarded numbers pursuant to Federal law or a federally approved state numbering system.

The Outboard Boating Club of America (333 No. Michigan Ave., Chicago, Ill. 60601) has compiled all available information on state boating laws in handbooks for various regions of the country. These include not only the registration and numbering requirements, but also all related laws on equipment, operation, use of trailers, etc., which readers are urged to obtain.

Given below are extracts from OBC data, listing agencies responsible for boat numbering laws.

---

**ALABAMA** Department of Conservation, State Administrative Building, Montgomery, Alabama 36104.

**ALASKA** The State of Alaska does not have a boat registration and numbering law, but general information on boating can be obtained from Department of Natural Resources, Division of Lands, 344 6th Ave., Anchorage, Alaska 99501.

**ARIZONA** Game and Fish Department, 2211 W. Greenway Rd., Phoenix, Ariz. 85023.

**ARKANSAS** Revenue Department, State Revenue Building, Little Rock, Ark. 72201.

**CALIFORNIA** Department of Harbors and Watercraft, 1416-9th Street, Room 1336, Sacramento, California 95814.

**COLORADO** Game, Fish & Parks Department, 6060 Broadway, Denver, Colorado 80216.

**CONNECTICUT** Boating Commission, Department of Agriculture & Natural Resources, State Office Building, Hartford, Connecticut 06115.

**DELAWARE** Small Boat Safety Division, Commission of Shell Fisheries, P. O. Box 512, Lewes, Delaware 19958.

**FLORIDA** State Board of Conservation, 107 West Gaines Street, Tallahassee, Florida 32304.

**GEORGIA** State Game and Fish Commission, Room 715, Trinity-Washington Bldg., Atlanta, Ga. 30334.

**HAWAII** Harbors Division, Department of Transportation, Box 397, Honolulu, Hawaii 96809.

**IDAHO** Motor Vehicle Division, Department of Law Enforcement, P. O. Box 34, Boise, Idaho 83707.

**ILLINOIS** Conservation Department, 400 South Spring Street, Springfield, Illinois 62706.

**INDIANA** Department of Natural Resources, 605 State Office Building, Indianapolis, Indiana 46209.

**IOWA** State Conservation Commission, State Office Building, 300 4th Street, Des Moines, Iowa 50319.

**KANSAS** Forestry, Fish & Game Commission, P. O. Box 1028, Pratt, Kan. 67124.

**KENTUCKY** Division of Boating, Department of Public Safety, New State Office Bldg., Frankfort, Ky. 40601.

**LOUISIANA** Wild Life & Fisheries Commission, Wild Life & Fisheries Building, 400 Royal Street, New Orleans, Louisiana 70130.

**MAINE** Bureau of Watercraft Registration and Safety, State Office Building, Augusta, Maine 04330.

**MARYLAND** Department of Chesapeake Bay Affairs, State Office Building, Annapolis, Maryland 21404.

**MASSACHUSETTS** Division of Motorboats, 100 Nashua Street, Boston, Massachusetts 02114.

**MICHIGAN** Department of State, 2100 N. Larch Street, Lansing, Mich. 48906.

**MINNESOTA** Department of Conservation, 625 North Robert Street, St. Paul, Minnesota 55101.

**MISSISSIPPI** Boat and Water Safety Commission, 605 West Capitol Street, Jackson, Mississippi 39203.

**MISSOURI** Boat Commission, P. O. Box 603, Jefferson City, Missouri 65101.

**MONTANA** State Board of Equalization, Capitol Building, Helena, Montana 59601.

**NEBRASKA** State Game, Forestation & Parks Commission, Lincoln, Nebraska 68509.

**NEVADA** Fish and Game Commission, Box 10678, Reno, Nev. 89501.

**NEW HAMPSHIRE** Division of Motor Vehicles, Department of Safety, 85 Loudon Road, Concord, New Hampshire 03301. The State of New Hampshire registers powerboats operated on inland or nontidal waters. As this registration system does not com-

ply with the Federal Boating Act of 1958, the Coast Guard has retained the responsibility for registering and numbering undocumented vessels with more than 10 horsepower chiefly used on navigable waters of the United States within the territorial limits of New Hampshire.

**NEW JERSEY** Bureau of Navigation, Department of Conservation & Economic Development, Box 1889, Trenton, New Jersey 08625.

**NEW MEXICO** State Park and Recreation Commission, P. O. Box 1147, Santa Fe, New Mexico 87501.

**NEW YORK** Division of Motorboats, State Conservation Department, New York State Campus, 1220 Washington Avenue, Albany, New York 12226.

**NORTH CAROLINA** Wildlife Resources Commission, Box 2919, Raleigh, North Carolina 27602.

**NORTH DAKOTA** State Game & Fish Department, Bismarck, North Dakota 58501.

**OHIO** Watercraft Division, Department of Natural Resources, 802 Ohio Departments Building, Columbus, Ohio 43215.

**OKLAHOMA** State Tax Commission, 2101 N. Lincoln Blvd., Oklahoma City, Okla. 73105.

**OREGON** State Marine Board, State Agriculture Building, 635 Capitol Street, N.E., Salem, Oregon 97310.

**PENNSYLVANIA** Miscellaneous License Division, Pennsylvania Dept. of Revenue, Harrisburg, Pennsylvania 17127.

**RHODE ISLAND** Registry of Motor Vehicles, Executive Department, State Capitol Building, Providence, Rhode Island 02903.

**SOUTH CAROLINA** Wildlife Resources Department, P. O. Box 167, Columbia, South Carolina 29202.

**SOUTH DAKOTA** Department of Game, Fish & Parks, State Office Building, Pierre, South Dakota 57501.

**TENNESSEE** Game & Fish Commission, 706 Church Street, Doctors Building, Nashville, Tennessee 37203.

**TEXAS** Highway Department, Motor Vehicle Division, 40th & Jackson, Austin, Texas 78703.

**UTAH** Boating Division, Utah State Park & Recreation Commission, 132 South Second West, Salt Lake City, Utah 84101.

**VERMONT** Marine Division, Department of Public Safety, Montpelier, Vermont 05602.

**VIRGINIA** Game & Inland Fisheries Commission, P. O. Box 1642, Richmond, Virginia 23213.

**WASHINGTON** The State of Washington does not have a boat registration and numbering law, but the Washington State Parks and Recreation Commission, P. O. Box 1128, Olympia, Wash. 98501, can furnish general information on boating in the state.

**WEST VIRGINIA** Department of Natural Resources, State Office Building, Charleston, West Virginia 25305.

**WISCONSIN** Conservation Department, P. O. Box 450, Madison, Wisconsin 53701.

**WYOMING** Game & Fish Commission, P. O. Box 1589, Cheyenne, Wyoming 82001.

**DIST. OF COLUMBIA** The District of Columbia does not have a boat registration and numbering system; this is done by the Coast Guard. General information about boating regulations and restrictions can be obtained from the Harbor Precinct, Metropolitan Police Department, 550 Maine Avenue S.W., Washington, D.C. 20024.

**PUERTO RICO** Marine Operations Department, Ports Authority, San Juan, P.R.

**VIRGIN ISLANDS** Department of Commerce, Marine & Aviation Services, Charlotte Amalie, St. Thomas Island, Virgin Islands.

# USEFUL TABLES

## TABLE I—SPEED OVER A MEASURED MILE

| Sec. | 1 min. | 2 min. | 3 min. | 4 min. | 5 min. | 6 min. | 7 min. | 8 min. | 9 mid. | 10 min. | 11 min. | 12 min. |
|---|---|---|---|---|---|---|---|---|---|---|---|---|
| 0 | 60.000 | 30.000 | 20.000 | 15.000 | 12.000 | 10.000 | 8.571 | 7.500 | 6.667 | 6.000 | 5.455 | 5.000 |
| 1 | 59.016 | 29.752 | 19.890 | 14.938 | 11.960 | 9.972 | 8.551 | 7.484 | 6.654 | 5.990 | 5.446 | 4.993 |
| 2 | 58.064 | 29.508 | 19.780 | 14.876 | 11.921 | 9.945 | 8.531 | 7.469 | 6.642 | 5.980 | 5.438 | 4.986 |
| 3 | 57.143 | 29.268 | 19.672 | 14.815 | 11.881 | 9.917 | 8.511 | 7.453 | 6.630 | 5.970 | 5.430 | 4.979 |
| 4 | 56.250 | 29.032 | 19.565 | 14.754 | 11.842 | 9.890 | 8.491 | 7.438 | 6.618 | 5.960 | 5.422 | 4.972 |
| 5 | 55.384 | 28.800 | 19.459 | 14.694 | 11.803 | 9.863 | 8.471 | 7.423 | 6.606 | 5.950 | 5.414 | 4.965 |
| 6 | 54.545 | 28.571 | 19.355 | 14.634 | 11.765 | 9.836 | 8.451 | 7.407 | 6.593 | 5.941 | 5.405 | 4.959 |
| 7 | 53.731 | 28.346 | 19.251 | 14.575 | 11.726 | 9.809 | 8.431 | 7.392 | 6.581 | 5.931 | 5.397 | 4.952 |
| 8 | 52.941 | 28.125 | 19.149 | 14.516 | 11.688 | 9.783 | 8.411 | 7.377 | 6.569 | 5.921 | 5.389 | 4.945 |
| 9 | 52.174 | 27.907 | 19.048 | 14.458 | 11.650 | 9.756 | 8.392 | 7.362 | 6.557 | 5.911 | 5.381 | 4.938 |
| 10 | 51.428 | 27.692 | 18.947 | 14.400 | 11.613 | 9.730 | 8.372 | 7.347 | 6.545 | 5.902 | 5.373 | 4.931 |
| 11 | 50.704 | 27.481 | 18.848 | 14.343 | 11.576 | 9.704 | 8.363 | 7.332 | 6.534 | 5.892 | 5.365 | 4.925 |
| 12 | 50.000 | 27.273 | 18.750 | 14.286 | 11.538 | 9.677 | 8.333 | 7.317 | 6.522 | 5.882 | 5.357 | 4.918 |
| 13 | 49.315 | 27.068 | 18.653 | 14.229 | 11.502 | 9.651 | 8.314 | 7.302 | 6.510 | 5.873 | 5.349 | 4.911 |
| 14 | 48.648 | 26.866 | 18.557 | 14.173 | 11.465 | 9.626 | 8.295 | 7.287 | 6.498 | 5.863 | 5.341 | 4.905 |
| 15 | 48.000 | 26.667 | 18.461 | 14.118 | 11.429 | 9.600 | 8.276 | 7.273 | 6.486 | 5.854 | 5.333 | 4.898 |
| 16 | 47.368 | 26.471 | 18.367 | 14.062 | 11.392 | 9.574 | 8.257 | 7.258 | 6.475 | 5.844 | 5.325 | 4.891 |
| 17 | 46.753 | 26.277 | 18.274 | 14.008 | 11.356 | 9.549 | 8.238 | 7.243 | 6.463 | 5.835 | 5.318 | 4.885 |
| 18 | 46.154 | 26.087 | 18.182 | 13.953 | 11.321 | 9.524 | 8.219 | 7.229 | 6.452 | 5.825 | 5.310 | 4.878 |
| 19 | 45.570 | 25.899 | 18.090 | 13.900 | 11.285 | 9.499 | 8.200 | 7.214 | 6.440 | 5.816 | 5.302 | 4.871 |
| 20 | 45.000 | 25.714 | 18.000 | 13.846 | 11.250 | 9.474 | 8.182 | 7.200 | 6.429 | 5.806 | 5.294 | 4.865 |
| 21 | 44.444 | 25.532 | 17.910 | 13.793 | 11.215 | 9.449 | 8.163 | 7.186 | 6.417 | 5.797 | 5.286 | 4.858 |
| 22 | 43.902 | 25.352 | 17.822 | 13.740 | 11.180 | 9.424 | 8.145 | 7.171 | 6.406 | 5.788 | 5.278 | 4.852 |
| 23 | 43.373 | 25.175 | 17.734 | 13.688 | 11.146 | 9.399 | 8.126 | 7.157 | 6.394 | 5.778 | 5.270 | 4.845 |
| 24 | 42.857 | 25.000 | 17.647 | 13.636 | 11.111 | 9.375 | 8.108 | 7.143 | 6.383 | 5.769 | 5.263 | 4.839 |
| 25 | 42.353 | 24.828 | 17.561 | 13.585 | 11.077 | 9.351 | 8.090 | 7.129 | 6.372 | 5.760 | 5.255 | 4.832 |
| 26 | 41.860 | 24.658 | 17.476 | 13.534 | 11.043 | 9.326 | 8.072 | 7.115 | 6.360 | 5.751 | 5.248 | 4.826 |
| 27 | 41.379 | 24.490 | 17.391 | 13.483 | 11.009 | 9.302 | 8.054 | 7.101 | 6.349 | 5.742 | 5.240 | 4.819 |
| 28 | 40.909 | 24.324 | 17.308 | 13.433 | 10.976 | 9.278 | 8.036 | 7.087 | 6.338 | 5.732 | 5.233 | 4.813 |
| 29 | 40.450 | 24.161 | 17.225 | 13.383 | 10.942 | 9.254 | 8.018 | 7.073 | 6.327 | 5.723 | 5.225 | 4.806 |
| 30 | 40.000 | 24.000 | 17.143 | 13.333 | 10.909 | 9.231 | 8.000 | 7.059 | 6.316 | 5.714 | 5.217 | 4.800 |
| 31 | 39.561 | 23.841 | 17.062 | 13.284 | 10.876 | 9.207 | 7.982 | 7.045 | 6.305 | 5.705 | 5.210 | 4.794 |
| 32 | 39.130 | 23.684 | 16.981 | 13.235 | 10.843 | 9.184 | 7.965 | 7.031 | 6.294 | 5.696 | 5.202 | 4.787 |
| 33 | 38.710 | 23.529 | 16.901 | 13.187 | 10.811 | 9.160 | 7.947 | 7.018 | 6.283 | 5.687 | 5.195 | 4.781 |
| 34 | 38.298 | 23.377 | 16.822 | 13.139 | 10.778 | 9.137 | 7.930 | 7.004 | 6.272 | 5.678 | 5.187 | 4.774 |
| 35 | 37.895 | 23.226 | 16.744 | 13.091 | 10.746 | 9.114 | 7.912 | 6.990 | 6.261 | 5.669 | 5.180 | 4.768 |
| 36 | 37.500 | 23.077 | 16.667 | 13.043 | 10.714 | 9.091 | 7.895 | 6.977 | 6.250 | 5.660 | 5.172 | 4.762 |
| 37 | 37.113 | 22.930 | 16.590 | 12.996 | 10.682 | 9.068 | 7.877 | 6.963 | 6.239 | 5.651 | 5.165 | 4.756 |
| 38 | 36.735 | 22.785 | 16.514 | 12.950 | 10.651 | 9.045 | 7.860 | 6.950 | 6.228 | 5.643 | 5.158 | 4.749 |
| 39 | 36.364 | 22.642 | 16.438 | 12.903 | 10.619 | 9.023 | 7.843 | 6.936 | 6.218 | 5.634 | 5.150 | 4.743 |
| 40 | 36.000 | 22.500 | 16.364 | 12.857 | 10.588 | 9.000 | 7.826 | 6.923 | 6.207 | 5.625 | 5.143 | 4.737 |
| 41 | 35.644 | 22.360 | 16.290 | 12.811 | 10.557 | 8.978 | 7.809 | 6.910 | 6.196 | 5.616 | 5.136 | 4.731 |
| 42 | 35.294 | 22.222 | 16.216 | 12.766 | 10.526 | 8.955 | 7.792 | 6.897 | 6.186 | 5.607 | 5.128 | 4.724 |
| 43 | 34.951 | 22.086 | 16.143 | 12.721 | 10.496 | 8.933 | 7.775 | 6.883 | 6.175 | 5.599 | 5.121 | 4.718 |
| 44 | 34.615 | 21.951 | 16.071 | 12.676 | 10.465 | 8.911 | 7.759 | 6.870 | 6.164 | 5.590 | 5.114 | 4.712 |
| 45 | 34.286 | 21.818 | 16.000 | 12.632 | 10.435 | 8.889 | 7.742 | 6.857 | 6.154 | 5.581 | 5.106 | 4.706 |
| 46 | 33.962 | 21.687 | 15.929 | 12.587 | 10.405 | 8.867 | 7.725 | 6.844 | 6.143 | 5.573 | 5.099 | 4.700 |
| 47 | 33.644 | 21.557 | 15.859 | 12.544 | 10.375 | 8.845 | 7.709 | 6.831 | 6.133 | 5.564 | 5.092 | 4.693 |
| 48 | 33.333 | 21.429 | 15.789 | 12.500 | 10.345 | 8.824 | 7.692 | 6.818 | 6.122 | 5.556 | 5.085 | 4.687 |
| 49 | 33.028 | 21.302 | 15.721 | 12.457 | 10.315 | 8.802 | 7.676 | 6.805 | 6.112 | 5.547 | 5.078 | 4.681 |
| 50 | 32.727 | 21.176 | 15.652 | 12.414 | 10.286 | 8.780 | 7.660 | 6.792 | 6.102 | 5.538 | 5.070 | 4.675 |
| 51 | 32.432 | 21.053 | 15.584 | 12.371 | 10.256 | 8.759 | 7.643 | 6.780 | 6.091 | 5.530 | 5.063 | 4.669 |
| 52 | 32.143 | 20.930 | 15.517 | 12.329 | 10.227 | 8.738 | 7.627 | 6.767 | 6.081 | 5.531 | 5.056 | 4.663 |
| 53 | 31.858 | 20.809 | 15.451 | 12.287 | 10.198 | 8.717 | 7.611 | 6.754 | 6.071 | 5.513 | 5.049 | 4.657 |
| 54 | 31.579 | 20.690 | 15.385 | 12.245 | 10.169 | 8.696 | 7.595 | 6.742 | 6.061 | 5.505 | 5.042 | 4.651 |
| 55 | 31.304 | 20.571 | 15.319 | 12.203 | 10.141 | 8.675 | 7.579 | 6.729 | 6.050 | 5.496 | 5.035 | 4.645 |
| 56 | 31.034 | 20.455 | 15.254 | 12.162 | 10.112 | 8.654 | 7.563 | 6.716 | 6.040 | 5.488 | 5.028 | 4.639 |
| 57 | 30.769 | 20.339 | 15.190 | 12.121 | 10.084 | 8.633 | 7.547 | 6.704 | 6.030 | 5.479 | 5.021 | 4.633 |
| 58 | 30.508 | 20.225 | 15.126 | 12.081 | 10.056 | 8.612 | 7.531 | 6.691 | 6.020 | 5.471 | 5.014 | 4.627 |
| 59 | 30.202 | 20.112 | 15.063 | 12.040 | 10.028 | 8.592 | 7.516 | 6.679 | 6.010 | 5.463 | 5.007 | 4.621 |

Table I (right), boat speed over a measured 1-mile course can be picked out by inspection. For example, if it takes 4 minutes and 19 seconds to run a statute mile (5280-foot) course, the boat's speed is 13.9 statute miles per hour. If the course were a nautical mile (6080 feet), the speed is 13.9 knots (nautical miles per hour). (The international nautical mile, recently adopted by the Coast Guard, is taken to be 6076.1 feet.)

Table II (left) gives a scale for visibility of objects at sea, using numbers which can be recorded in the log.

Table III (right) indicates how the state of the sea can be recorded by numbers.

## TABLE II — SCALE OF VISIBILITY
### (Record number in log)

| Scale Number | Prominent Objects Not Visible At |
|---|---|
| 0 | 50 yards |
| 1 | 200 yards |
| 2 | 500 yards |
| 3 | ½ mile |
| 4 | 1 mile |
| 5 | 2 miles |
| 6 | 4 miles |
| 7 | 7 miles |
| 8 | 20 miles |
| 9 | More than 20 miles |

## TABLE III — STATE OF THE SEA
### (Using Numerals instead of letters. See Table B)

| Scale Number | Description Of Sea | Height Of Wave |
|---|---|---|
| 0 | Calm | 0 or less than 1 foot |
| 1 | Smooth | 1 to 2 feet |
| 2 | Slight | 2 to 3 feet |
| 3 | Moderate | 3 to 5 feet |
| 4 | Rough | 5 to 8 feet |
| 5 | Very rough | 8 to 12 feet |
| 6 | High | 12 to 20 feet |
| 7 | Very high | 20 to 40 feet |
| 8 | Precipitous | 40 feet or more |
| 9 | Confused | Record chief direction |

625

In a textbook such as **Piloting, Seamanship and Small Boat Handling,** its value to the student, and to all readers for reference purposes, is immeasurably enhanced by a comprehensive general index.

Where multiple listings make it desirable, the reader may turn to a basic head, such as compass, flags, lights, etc., and conveniently find the particular phase of the subject in question. Concerned with variation of the compass, for example, he may find it as a sub-head under the broad listing of "compass," or may turn directly to "variation" where various aspects of variation are, in turn, sub-headed. Generous use of cross-references has been made throughout.

Note: All color plates are designated by the letters A through Z, rather than by numbers, to provide greater flexibility in their placement in this and future editions, without changing numbers on text pages.

See also the Nautical Terminology Index beginning on the next page, and the Table of Contents, on page v.

# NAUTICAL TERMINOLOGY INDEX

Words and phrases listed here cover boating objects and actions described and/or defined in Chapter 1.

NEWARK BAY    NEW BEDFORD    NEW BRITAIN    NEW HAVEN    NEW LONDON    NEW ORLEANS    NEWPORT    NEW RIVER

NEW YORK    NIAGARA    NOBSCOT    NOR-MAC    NORTHEAST RIVER    NORTHERN NEW JERSEY    NORTHERN VIRGINIA    NORTH RIVER

NORWALK    NORWICH    OAKLAND    OAK ORCHARD    OAK RIDGE    OCALA    OKINAWA    OLD COLONY

OLD FIELD POINT    OLYMPIA    ORANGE    ORLANDO    OSHKOSH    PAINESVILLE    PALISADES    PALM BEACH

PASADENA    PATAPSCO RIVER    PATCHOGUE BAY    PATUXENT RIVER    PECONIC BAY    PEEKSKILL    PENOBSCOT BAY    PENSACOLA

PERALTA    PEQUOSSETTE    PHOENIX    PITTSBURGH    PLUM BEACH    POMPANO BEACH    PORT CLINTON    PORT HURON

PORTSMOUTH    POSSESSION SOUND    POTOMAC RIVER    POVERTY BAY    PYMATUNING    QUAD CITY    QUINCY    RACINE

RALEIGH    RARITAN BAY    RED JACKET    REDONDO BEACH    RICHMOND    RIO HONDO    ROCHESTER    ROCKFORD

ROME    ROWAYTON    SACANDAGA    SACRAMENTO    SADDLE RIVER    SAGINAW BAY    ST. ANDREW BAY    ST. JOSEPH

ST. LAWRENCE    ST. LOUIS    ST. PAUL    ST. PETERSBURG    SALISBURY    SALT CREEK    SAN ANTONIO    SAN CARLOS BAY

SAN DIEGO    SANDUSKY    SAN FERNANDO VALLEY    SAN FRANCISCO    SAN GABRIEL VALLEY    SAN JUAN    SAN LUIS REY    SANTA BARBARA

SANTA CLARA    SANTA MONICA BAY    SANTANA    SARASOTA    SAUGATUCK RIVER    SAVANNAH RIVER    SAYBROOK    SCHUYLKILL RIVER

SEATTLE    SENECA    SEQUOIA    SEWANHAKA    SHEBOYGAN    SHREVEPORT    SHREWSBURY    SINGING RIVER